AN EXPLORER'S GUIDE

Maine

Maine

Christina Tree & Nancy English

SPECIAL
25th
ANNIVERSARY
EDITION!

The Countryman Press * Woodstock, Vermont

THIRTEENTH EDITION

We welcome your comments and suggestions. Please contact Explorer's Guide Editor, The Countryman Press, P.O. Box 748, Woodstock, Vermont 05091, or e-mail countrymanpress@wwnorton.com.

Thirteenth Edition

ISBN-13 978-0-88150-718-8
ISBN-10 0-88150-718-0
ISSN 1533-6883

Maps by Mapping Specialists, © 2006 The Countryman Press
Book design by Bodenweber Design
Text composition by PerfecType, Nashville, TN
Cover photograph of Pemaquid Lighthouse © James Randklev/CORBIS
Interior photographs as noted

Published by The Countryman Press, P.O. Box 748, Woodstock, Vermont 05091

Distributed by W. W. Norton & Company, Inc., 500 Fifth Avenue, New York, NY 10110

Printed in the United States of America

10 9 8 7 6 5 4 3 2 1

DEDICATION

To Timothy and Yuko, married in Maine, and for their children Aki and Taiga
—C. T.

To Emma
—N. E.

EXPLORE WITH US!

We have been fine-tuning *Maine: An Explorer's Guide* for the past 25 years, a period in which lodging, dining, and shopping opportunities have more than quadrupled in the state. As we have expanded our guide, we have also been increasingly selective, making recommendations based on years of conscientious research and personal experience. We describe the state by locally defined regions, giving you Maine's communities, not simply her most popular destinations. With this guide you'll feel confident to venture beyond the tourist towns, along roads less traveled, to places of special hospitality and charm.

WHAT'S WHERE

In the beginning of the book you'll find an alphabetical listing of special highlights and important information that you may want to reference quickly. You'll find advice on everything from where to buy the best local lobster to where to write or call for camping reservations and park information.

LODGING

We've selected lodging places for mention in this book based on their merit alone; we do not charge innkeepers to be listed. This is the only travel guide whose writers try to check every bed & breakfast, farm, sporting lodge, and inn in Maine personally, and one of the few guides that do not charge for inclusion.

Prices. Please don't hold us or the respective innkeepers responsible for the rates listed as of press time in 2006. Some changes are inevitable. **The 7 percent state rooms and meals tax should be added to all prices unless we specifically state that it's included in a price.** We've tried to note when a gratuity is added, but it's always wise to check before booking.

Smoking. Maine B&Bs, inns, and restaurants are now generally smoke-free, but many lodging places still reserve some rooms for smokers and, depending on their license, some restaurants still offer a smoking area. If this is important to you, be sure to ask when making reservations.

RESTAURANTS

In most sections please note a distinction between *Dining Out* and *Eating Out*. By their nature, restaurants included in the *Eating Out* group are generally inexpensive.

KEY TO SYMBOLS

⚭ **Weddings**. The wedding-ring symbol appears next to lodging venues that specialize in weddings.

🎗 **Special value**. The blue-ribbon symbol appears next to selected lodging and restaurants that combine quality and moderate prices.

🐾 **Pets**. The dog-paw symbol appears next to venues that accept pets.

✎ **Child-friendly**. The crayon symbol appears next to lodging, restaurants, activities, and shops of special interest or appeal to youngsters.

♿ **Handicapped access**. The wheelchair symbol appears next to lodging, restaurants, and attractions that are partially or completely handicapped accessible.

We would appreciate any comments or corrections. Please write to:

Explorer's Guide Editor
The Countryman Press
P.O. Box 748
Woodstock, VT 05091

You can also e-mail
countrymanpress@wwnorton.com, or ctree@traveltree.net

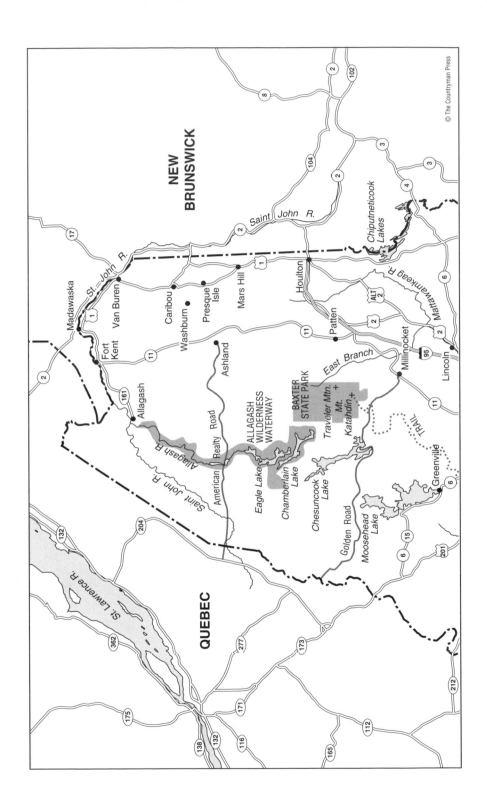

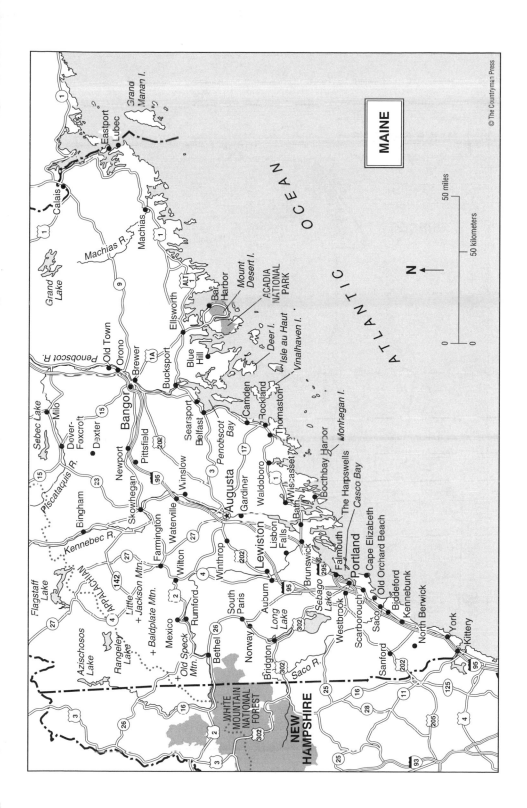

MAINE

© The Countryman Press

50 miles

50 kilometers

N

ATLANTIC OCEAN

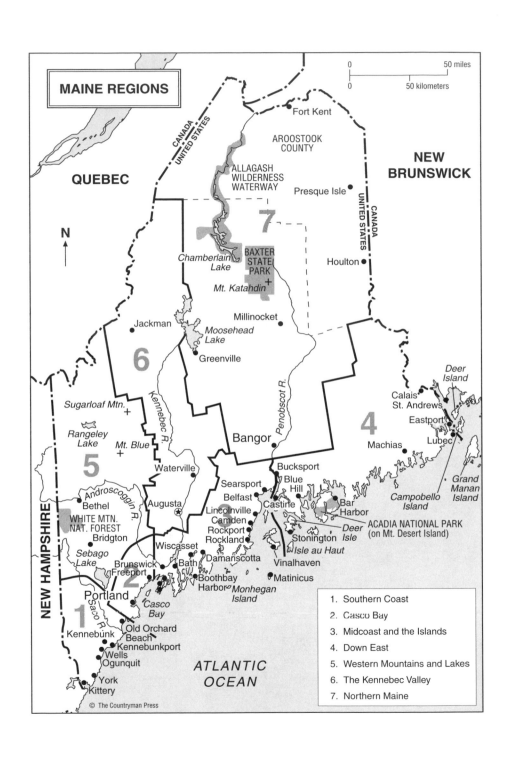

MAINE REGIONS

0 ——— 50 miles
0 ——— 50 kilometers

QUEBEC

N

NEW BRUNSWICK

CANADA
UNITED STATES

Fort Kent

AROOSTOOK COUNTY

ALLAGASH WILDERNESS WATERWAY

Presque Isle

Chamberlain Lake

BAXTER STATE PARK

Houlton

CANADA
UNITED STATES

Mt. Katahdin

Jackman

Moosehead Lake

Greenville

Millinocket

Penobscot R.

Deer Island

Calais
St. Andrews

Eastport

Sugarloaf Mtn.

Kennebec R.

Bangor

Machias

Lubec

Rangeley Lake

Mt. Blue

Waterville

Bucksport

Searsport

Blue Hill

Campobello Island

Grand Manan Island

5

Bethel

Androscoggin R.

Augusta

Belfast

Castine

Bar Harbor

ACADIA NATIONAL PARK
(on Mt. Desert Island)

WHITE MTN. NAT. FOREST

Lincolnville

Camden

Rockport

Rockland

Deer Isle

Stonington

Bridgton

Wiscasset

Sebago Lake

Brunswick

Freeport

Bath

Damariscotta

Isle au Haut

Vinalhaven

Portland

2

Boothbay Harbor

Matinicus

Casco Bay

Monhegan Island

Saco R.

Old Orchard Beach

1

Kennebunk

Kennebunkport

Wells

Ogunquit

ATLANTIC OCEAN

York

Kittery

NEW HAMPSHIRE

© The Countryman Press

1. Southern Coast
2. Casco Bay
3. Midcoast and the Islands
4. Down East
5. Western Mountains and Lakes
6. The Kennebec Valley
7. Northern Maine

CONTENTS

INTRODUCTION

He who rides and keeps the beaten track studies the fences chiefly.
—*Henry David Thoreau, The Maine Woods, 1853*

Over the past 25 years *Maine: An Explorer's Guide* has introduced hundreds of thousands of people to many Maines.

When this book first appeared, it was the first 20th-century guidebook to describe New England's largest state region by region rather than to focus only on the most touristed communities, listed alphabetically. From the start, we critiqued places to stay and to eat as well as everything to see and to do—based on merit rather than money (we don't charge anyone to be included).

The big news, however, isn't that *Maine: An Explorer's Guide* was first but that readers constantly tell us that it remains the best Maine guidebook—that despite current competition, this "Maine Bible" gets better with each edition.

And it should. With each new edition we build on what we know, still spending months on the road, checking every lodging we include, making sure it's a place we would personally like to stay.

Initially, back in 1981, this didn't seem like a tall order. Chris's three sons—ages 3, 6, and 8—helped her research reasonably priced rental cottages, ice cream stands, and beaches. The guide, however, quickly grew as inns, B&Bs, and other lodging options proliferated, along with things to do and see, dining venues, and shopping options. The book also soon included all the parts of Maine in which a visitor can find a campsite or commercial lodging, from Matinicus to Madawaska and from the White Mountains to the island of Monhegan, not to mention all of Rt. 1 from Kittery to Fort Kent.

After the first couple of editions it became obvious that no one person could explore this immense and richly textured state during one summer and fall.

We now describe more than 500 places to stay, ranging from campgrounds to grand old resorts and including farms as well as B&Bs and inns—in all corners of the state and in all price ranges. We have also checked out a similar number of places to dine and to eat (we make a distinction between dining and eating), and, since shopping is an important part of everyone's travels, we include special stores we encounter. We have opinions about everything we've found, and we don't hesitate to share them. In every category we record exactly what we see.

Chris was born in Hawaii and bred in Manhattan, came to New England to attend Mount Holyoke College, and has been living in Massachusetts since she came there to work for the *Boston Globe* in 1968. She is addicted to many Maines. As a toddler she learned to swim in the Ogunquit River and later watched her sons do the same in Monhegan's icy waters—and then learn to sail at summer camp in Raymond and paddle canoes on the Saco River and down the St. John. Her number two son was married on Little Cranberry Island off Mount Desert. For the *Globe*, she continues to write about a variety of things to do in Maine, from skiing at Sugarloaf and Sunday River and dogsledding into a North Woods sporting camp to llama trekking in Bethel to sea kayaking off points from Portland to Pembroke and windjamming on Penobscot Bay. Increasingly, too, she finds herself writing about Maine's art and artists (of which there are more per capita in Maine than in any other state). She values her vantage point from Boston, far enough away to give her the perspective on what it means to be a visitor, yet near enough to comfortably and continually explore Maine.

Born in New York City and raised in northeastern Vermont, Nancy has spent most of her adult life living in Portland, Maine. She heard the cry of a bobcat at night in Vermont and the calls of loons on lakes in Maine, along with the cries of geese migrating over Congress Street in the middle of Portland's downtown; nature and its wildlife have been an enduring interest through her writing career, spent most recently as the restaurant reviewer for the *Maine Sunday Telegram.* Her travel writing started in the 1970s while still an undergraduate at Vassar College, with articles in *Vermont Life* magazine; it includes work on a new edition of the *Coast of Maine Book* in 2000, and continues with that guide's latest version in 2005, when it was republished as *Chow Maine*, a guide to the best restaurants, cafés, lobsters shacks, and markets on the Maine coast. Working on this *Explorer's Guide* took her inland, to great restaurants far from the summer crowds, although some of them are the favorites of winter tourists, like Hugs in Carrabasset Valley just off the mountain road to Sugarloaf. Traveling in Maine is a pastime she shares with many other Mainers, who have their own seasonal traditions, from eating a lobster roll at Haraseeket Lunch every summer to fly-fishing in the North Maine Woods.

We are fascinated by Maine's history in general and her tourism history in particular. It seems ironic that back in the 1920s, "motor touring" was hailed as a big improvement over train and steamer travel because it meant you no longer had to go where everyone else did—over routes prescribed by railroad tracks and steamboat schedules. In Maine cars seem, however, to have had precisely the opposite effect. Now 90 percent of the state's visitors follow the coastal tourist route as faithfully as though their wheels were grooved to Rt. 1.

Worse still, it's as though many tourists are on a train making only express stops—at rush hour. At least half of those who follow Rt. 1 stop, stay, and eat in all the same places (such as Kennebunkport, Boothbay or Camden, and Bar Harbor)—in August.

Tourism has always been driven by images. In the 1840s Thomas Cole, Frederic Church (both of whom sketched and painted scenes of Mount Desert), and lesser-known artists began projecting Maine as a romantic, remote destination in the many papers, magazines, and children's books of the decade. While Henry

David Thoreau's *The Maine Woods* was not published until 1864, many of its chapters appeared as magazine articles years before (Thoreau first climbed Katahdin in 1846), and in 1853 *Atlantic Monthly* editor James Russell Lowell visited and wrote about Moosehead Lake.

After the Civil War, Maine tourism boomed. Via railroad and steamboat, residents of cities throughout the East and Midwest streamed into the Pine Tree State, most toting guidebooks, many published by rail and steamboat lines to boost business. Male "sports" in search of big game and big fish patronized "sporting camps" throughout the North Woods. Thanks to the rise in popularity of fly-fishing and easily maneuverable canoes, women were able to share in North Woods soft adventure. Splendid lakeside hotels were built on the Rangeley Lakes and Moosehead, and farms took in boarders throughout the Western Lakes region. Along the coast and on dozens of islands, hotels of every size were built, most by Maine natives. Blue-collar workers came by trolley to summer religious camp meetings, and the wealthy built themselves elaborate summer "cottages" on islands and around Bar Harbor, Camden, and Boothbay Harbor. Developments and sophisticated landscaping transformed much of the previously ignored sandy Southern Coast.

Although it's difficult to document, it's safe to say that Maine attracted the same number of visitors in the summer of 1900 that it did in 2000. This picture altered little for another decade. Then came World War I, coinciding with the proliferation of the Model A.

The 1922 founding of the Maine Publicity Bureau (the present Maine Tourism Association), we suspect, reflects the panic of hoteliers (founder Hiram Ricker himself owned three of the state's grandest hotels: the Mount Kineo House, the Poland Spring House, and the Samoset). Over the next few years these hotels went the way of passenger service, and "motorists" stuck to motor courts and motels along Rt. 1 and a limited number of inland routes.

By the late 1960s, when Chris began writing about Maine, much of the state had all but dropped off the tourist map; in the decades since, she has chronicled the reawakening of most of the old resort areas. Whale-watching and whitewater rafting, skiing and snowmobiling, windjamming and kayaking, outlet shopping, and the renewed popularity of country inns and B&Bs have all contributed to this reawakening. Maine is, after all, magnificent. It was just a matter of time.

Recently the extent of waterside (both coastal and inland) walks open to the public has dramatically increased. It's interesting to note that this phenomenon of preserving and maintaining outstanding landscapes—from Ogunquit's Marginal Way to the core of what's now Acadia National Park—was also an offshoot of Maine's first tourism boom. In this 13th edition we note the dramatic growth of coastal trails way Down East in Washington County and the ever-increasing ways of exploring the North Woods.

This edition of *Maine: An Explorer's Guide* also includes more web sites than ever as a way of amplifying our own descriptions. We assume you understand the difference between promotional images on the web and information based on the experience of personally seeing and choosing among what's out there. Given our unbiased selections and comments, we like to think of this book as the ultimate Maine search engine.

While the number of Maine guidebooks has proliferated, too, we remain proud of the depth and scope of this one. We strive not only to update details but also to simplify the format and to sharpen the word pictures that describe each area.

This book's introductory section, "What's Where in Maine," is a quick-reference directory to a vast variety of information about the state. The remainder of the book describes Maine region by region. The basic criterion for including an area is the availability of lodging.

Note that "off-season" prices are often substantially lower than those in July and August. September is dependably sparkling and frequently warm. Early October in Maine is just as spectacular as it is in New Hampshire and Vermont, with magnificent mountains rising from inland lakes as well as the golds and reds set against coastal blue and vast inland lakes. Be aware that the inland ski resorts of Sunday River near Bethel and the Sugarloaf area are "off-season" all summer as well as fall.

Maine is almost as big as the other five New England states combined, but her residents add up to less than half the population of greater Boston. That means there is plenty of room for all who look to her for renewal—both residents and out-of-staters.

It's our hope that, although this book should help visitors and Maine residents alike enjoy the state's resort towns, it will be particularly useful for those who explore off the beaten track.

We would like to thank Jennifer Thompson for her production help and Sarah Novak for her careful copyediting of this special edition. We would both also like to thank Nancy Marshall and Charlene Williams for unfailing response to all cries for help with gathering information whenever called for, and also Rose Whitehouse for her careful fact checking of "What's Where." Special thanks to Elizabeth Roundy Richards and to K. W. Oxnard for their contributions to *Maine: An Explorer's Guide* in previous editions.

Never has Chris owed thanks to so many people in Maine who helped with this edition. As always, thanks to Virginia Fieldman in Jonesboro, also to Robert Godfrey of Eastport, and to Linda Pagels and Vicki Farrell of Calais, Bill and Kathy Shamel of Grand Lake Stream, Mike McCabe of Whiting, Jean and Bill Conway of Cherryfield, Joyce Owen and Janice Meiners of Campobello, and Valery Kidney of New Brunswick Tourism. Moving down the coast, thanks to Nicole Purslow in Hancock, to the friendly staff of the Claremont, to Toby Strong of Southwest Harbor, and to Frances Jo Bartlett in Islesford. In the Blue Hill area heartfelt thanks are due Jim and Sally Littlefield of Brooksville, and Ann and Bob Hamilton of Brooklin. In the Rockland area, thank you to Shari Closter of the Rockland Chamber and to Captains Ken and Ellen Barnes, on Spruce Head to Neva Joseph, on Monhegan to John Murdock, and on North Haven to Hannah Pingree. In the Damariscotta area, thank you to Heather O'Bryan of the Damariscotta Chamber and to Bobby and Sherry Weare; in New Harbor to Lucy Finny and the Hardy Boat crew. In the Bath area, thank you to Nick Bayard, Ona Barnet, and Carolyn and Ann Church. In the Brunswick area, thank you to Steve and Mercie Norman. In York, thank you to Sue Antal and to Lou Hargan, and in South Berwick to Paul and Lee Fopeano.

Turning inland, first and foremost I owe thanks to East Vassalboro's Elizabeth Davidson, both as informant and as travel companion. For help with the Upper Kennebec Valley, thanks to Russell Walters and both Liz Caruso and Peter Dostie. In Rockwood thank you to John Willard and Bonnie Searles, in Greenville to Ruth MClaughlin and to Johnathan Pratt, in Millinocket to Brenda Wheaton, Jean Hoekwater of Baxter State Park, and Matt Polstein. Many, many thanks to Wende Gray for continuous help in organizing, editing, and carrying the sleeping bag I forgot to bring on our long ski treks into the North Woods.

Both of us would also like to thank all the people who have taken the time to write about their experiences in Maine. We can't tell you how much your input—or simply your reactions to how we have described things—means to us. We welcome your comments and appreciate all your thoughtful suggestions for the next edition of *Maine: An Explorer's Guide.* You can contact us directly by e-mail: ctree@traveltree.net.

Last but not least, wholehearted thanks are due the world's most helpful, talented, and long-suffering husband, former *Boston Globe* travel editor William A. Davis, who drove thousands of miles through Maine with me this past summer, doubling our efforts.

Nancy wishes to thank Ellen and Matt Libby, Kate and Kevin McCartney, and Gina Clark, who mapped out the great pleasures of a visit to Aroostook. Thanks go to John Marko and Sarah Faragher in Bangor, and for help in Rangeley to Nancy and Ed Ludwig, Nancy Birkett Vincent, Wes Connally and Joanne Koob, and the volunteers at the Rangeley Historical Society—as well as the volunteers everywhere, who answer so many questions on-duty. In western regions, Nancy thanks Julie Whelchel and Michael Myers, who took some time to assist a better understanding of the area. In Bethel, thanks go to Robin Zin, Adam and Alexandra LaNoue-Adler, and Wende Gray; and, at Sugarloaf, to Greg Sweetser. Along the coast the help has been generous. Thanks go to Helene Harton and Roy Kasindorf of Bar Harbor, Linda and Marv Snow of Ellsworth, Caroline Sulzer and David Walker of Surry, Nancy Barba and Cynthia Wheelock of Portland, Nancy-Linn Nellis of Searsport, and all the friendly people in Down East Maine who took time from their busy schedule to answer questions. Farther south Jane Hurd comes in tops on the list, with her long acquaintance with Boothbay Harbor and its businesses; many thanks are also due to Ed McDermott and Brian Lamb, Joseph Paolillo, Nancy Bosio-Pickett, and Karen Gosselin. The chambers of commerce of Maine are staffed with courteous and generous people who have also contributed many details to this book.

Thanks also are due to my daughter, who spent a lot of the summer and winter she turned 11 driving around Maine.

WHAT'S WHERE IN MAINE

AREA CODE The area code throughout Maine is **207**.

ABENAKI See *Wabanaki*.

ACADIANS Acadians trace their lineage to French settlers who came to in Nova Scotia in the early 1600s and who, in 1755, were forcibly deported by an English governor. This "Great Disturbance," dispersing a population of some 10,000 Acadians, brutally divided families. In a meadow overlooking the St. John River at Madawaska's **Tante Blanche Museum**, a large marble cross marks the spot on which several hundred displaced Acadians landed in 1787. **Village Acadien**, a dozen buildings forming a mini museum village just west of Van Buren, only begins to tell the story. While the sizable Franco-American communities in Biddeford, Lewiston, and Brunswick have a different history (their forebears were recruited from Quebec to work in 19th-century mills), they, too, have experienced a long repression of their culture and recent resurgence of pride in a shared French heritage. **La Kermesse**, held in late June in Biddeford, is a major Franco-American festival, as is the **Festival de Joie** in Lewiston. Con-

tact the **Maine Acadian Heritage Council** (207-728-6826) for more information.

AGRICULTURAL FAIRS The season opens in late June and runs through the first week of October, culminating with the large, colorful, immensely popular (traffic backs up for miles) **Fryeburg Fair**. Among the best traditional fairs are the **Union Fair** (late August) and the **Blue Hill Fair** (Labor Day weekend). **The Common Ground Country Fair** (third weekend in September, at the fairgrounds in Unity), sponsored by the Maine Organic Farmers and Gardeners Association (www.mofga.org), features wholesome food, folk dancing, and music and draws Maine's back-to-the-earth and organic gardeners from all corners of the state. Request a pamphlet listing all the fairs from the Maine Department of Agriculture (207-287-3491; getreal maine.com), 28 State House Station, Augusta 04333.

AIRPORTS AND AIRLINES Portland **International Jetport** (207-774-7301), with connections to most large American and Canadian cities, is served by several carriers: Continental

Airlines (1-800-525-0280), Delta Air Lines (1-800-221-1212), United Express (1-800-241-6522), U.S. Airways (1-800-428-4322), and American Airlines (1-800-433-7300). **Bangor International Airport** (207-947-0384; www.flybangor.com), serving northern and Down East Maine, also offers connections to all parts of the United States via U.S. Airways Express (1-800-428-4322), Delta Connection (1-800-221-1212), Northwest Airlink (1-800-225-2525), and American Eagle (1-800-433-7300). Colgan Air operates U.S. Airways flights (1-800-428-4322) to **Hancock County Regional Airport** (Trenton/Bar Harbor), **Augusta State Airport**, and **Knox County Regional Airport** (Rockland/Owls Head). **Northern Maine Regional Airport** (Presque Isle) is served by Business Express (1-800-433-7300) and U.S. Airways (1-800-428-4322).

AIR SERVICES Also called flying services, these are useful links with wilderness camps and coastal islands. Greenville, prime jumping-off point for the North Maine Woods, claims to be New England's largest seaplane base. In this book flying services are also listed under *Getting There* or *Getting Around* in "Rangeley Lakes Region," "Moosehead Lake Area," "Katahdin Region," and "Washington County." Check *Getting There* in "Rockland/Thomaston Area" for air taxis to several islands, including Vinalhaven, North Haven, and Matinicus.

AMTRAK Maine passenger service is not just back but working! Amtrak's **Downeaster** offers four round-trips per day between Boston's North Station and the Portland rail–bus station

just off I-95 (shuttles connect with the Old Port). It's less than 3 hours each way, with seven stops. Check out www.thedowncaster.com or www.amtrak.com, or phone 1-800-USA-RAIL. Also see www.exploremaine.org

AMUSEMENT PARKS
Funtown/Splashtown USA in Saco is Maine's biggest, with rides, waterslides, and pools. **Aquaboggan** (pools and slides) is also on Rt. 1 in Saco. **Palace Playland** in Old Orchard Beach is a classic, with a carousel, a Ferris wheel, rides, and a 60-foot water slide. **York's Wild Kingdom** at York Beach has a zoo and amusement area.

ANTIQUARIAN BOOKS Maine is well known among book buffs as a browsing mecca. **Maine Antiquarian Booksellers** publishes a printed directory of more than 80 members. Download it at mainebooksellers.org.

ANTIQUES A member directory listing more than 290 dealers is produced by the **Maine Antiques Dealers' Association, Inc.** The association maintains an active web site listing members as well as auctions: www.maineantiques.org. Other useful resources are the *Maine Fine Antiques Guide* (www.maineantiquesguide.com), the *Antique Dealer Directory*, the widely available monthly *Maine Antique Digest* (maineantiquedigest.com), and www.metiques.com. For a "Maine Antiquing Trail" with three loop tours, see www.visitmaine.com.

APPALACHIAN TRAIL
(www.appalachiantrail.org). The 267-mile Maine section of this 2,144-mile Georgia-to-Maine footpath enters the state in the Mahoosuc Range—

accessible there from Grafton Notch State Park (the Mahoosuc Notch section is extremely difficult)—and continues north into the Rangeley and Sugarloaf areas, on up through the Upper Kennebec Valley to Monson. West of Moosehead Lake it runs through Gulf Hagas and on around Nahmakanta Lake, through Abol Bridge to Baxter State Park, ending at the summit of 5,267-foot Mount Katahdin. Hikes along the trail are noted within specific chapters; lodging places catering to AT through-hikers include **Harrison's Pierce Pond Sporting Camps** in Bingham, **Northern Outdoors** in The Forks, and **Little Lyford Pond Camps** near Gulf Hagas. July, August, and September are the best months to hike this stretch. The Maine Appalachian Trail Club (www.matc.org) helps with maintenance and in other ways. For a list of publications, write to Appalachian Trail Conference, P.O. Box 807, Harpers Ferry, WV 25425-0807.

APPLES Fall brings plenty of pick-your-own opportunities across the state, and many orchards also sell apples and cider. For a map/guide to PYO orchards, see www.maineapples .org or the Department of Agriculture's web site: www.getrealmaine .com. And check out the Cornish Apple Festival and Apple Acres Bluegrass Festival, both held in Cornish in late September.

AQUARIUMS The **Marine Resources Aquarium** in Boothbay Harbor displays regional fish and sea creatures, many of them surprisingly colorful. The stars of the show are the sharks and skates in a large touch tank. The **Mount Desert Oceanarium** is a commercial attraction with several locations in the Bar Harbor area.

ART ASSOCIATIONS AND COUNCILS Recent years have seen a proliferation of regional associations and councils dedicated to promoting the arts within a specific area of Maine. Many of these organizations are producing detailed listings of arts-related organizations, individual artists, and businesses in the arts, in conjunction with the **Maine Arts Commission**. The commission has a searchable database on the web (www.mainearts.com) that can help you find area councils and listings.

ARTISTS AND ART GALLERIES Maine's dramatic coastal and island scenery, her lakes and mountains, have drawn major artists since the mid–19th century, and the experience of art as a major part of the Maine visitor's experience has increased in recent years. Within each chapter we describe a good percentage of the existing commercial galleries that have proliferated throughout the state but especially in Portland, Rockland, Northeast Harbor, Stonington, Blue Hill, and Eastport. Several recent art books are also popularizing the work of dozens of significant artists; a standout is *Art of the Maine Islands* by Carl Little and Arnold Skolnick (Down East Books). Artist-owned galleries, which have become destinations in their own right, are found in Sullivan and Stonington and on the islands of Monhegan, North Haven, Vinalhaven, and Little Cranberry. For weeklong summer arts workshops, see our *To Do—Special Learning Programs* listings in "Deer Isle, Stonington." **Rock Gardens Inn** (see "Bath Area") and **Oakland House** (see

"Blue Hill Area") also offer noteworthy arts workshops. The most prestigious summer arts workshop in Maine is the **Skowhegan School of Painting and Sculpture** (207-474-9345 or 212-529-0505; www.skowheganart.org).

ART MUSEUMS The **Portland Museum of Art** (PMA) is one of the country's finer smaller museums, with a strong collection of works by impressionist and postimpressionist masters as well as Winslow Homer. **The Farnsworth Art Museum** with its **Center for the Wyeth Family in Maine** in Rockland, moreover, has a stellar collection of Maine art, as well as frequent special exhibits that draw art lovers from around the country. The seasonal **Ogunquit Museum of American Art** and the **Colby College Museum of Art** in Waterville are also outstanding and described within their respective chapters. Seven of the state's museums have formed a partnership called the **Maine Art Museum Trail** and publish a brochure describing each of these museums. A copy can be requested at 1-800-782-6497, or peruse their web site: www.maineart museums.org.

BALLOONING Hot-air balloon rides are available across the state from **Balloons Over New England** (207-499-7575 or 1-800-788-5562) in Kennebunkport, **Hot Fun** (207-799-0193; www.hotfunballoons.com) in South Portland, and **Sails Aloft** (207-623-1136) in Augusta.

BEACHES Given the summer temperature of the Atlantic Ocean (from 59 degrees in Ogunquit to 54 degrees at Bar Harbor), swimming isn't the primary reason you come to the Maine coast. But Maine beaches (for instance at York, Wells, the Kennebunks, Portland, Popham, and Pemaquid) can be splendid walking, sunning, and kite-flying places. At **Ogunquit** and in **Reid State Park** in Georgetown, there are also warmer backwater areas in which small children can paddle. Other outstanding beaches include 7-mile-long **Old Orchard Beach** and, nearby, state-maintained **Crescent Beach** on Cape Elizabeth, **Scarborough Beach** in Scarborough, **Ferry Beach** in Saco, and **Sand Beach** in Acadia National Park. The state-maintained freshwater beaches are on **Lakes Damariscotta**, **St. George**, **Sebec**, **Rangeley**, **Sebago**, and **Moosehead**; also on **Pleasant Pond** in Richmond. All state beaches include changing facilities, restrooms, and showers; many have snack bars. The town of **Bridgton** has several fine little lakeside beaches.

BED & BREAKFASTS We have visited just about every B&B in Maine. They range from elegant town houses and country mansions to farms and fishermen's homes. Prices vary from $45 to more than $600 (on the coast in August) for a double and average $100–150 in high season on the coast. With few exceptions, they offer a friendly entrée to their communities. The *Maine Guide to Inns and Bed & Breakfasts and Camps & Cottages*, published by the Maine Tourism Association, is free and can be picked up at visitor centers or by request at 207-623-0363 or 1-888-624-6345; www.mainetourism.com.

BICYCLING **Mountain biking** is particularly popular on the carriage roads in **Acadia National Park**. Ski areas specializing in summer mountain biking with lift-assisted, high-altitude trails include **Shawnee Peak** in Bridgton; **Lost Valley** in Auburn also opens its trails to mountain bikers, and **Sugarloaf/USA** offers rentals and trail maps to trails on and off the mountain. Biking is popular on Swans Island off Acadia and on islands in Casco Bay. But Rt. 1 has too much traffic, and rural roads are generally narrow, curved, and have no shoulders, making them unsuitable for bicycling. Dedicated recreation paths are beginning to appear, notably in Portland and Brunswick/Bath. Bicycling also makes sense in heavily touristed resort areas in which a car can be a nuisance; rentals are available in Ogunquit, Kennebunkport, Camden, Southwest Harbor, Northeast Harbor, and Bar Harbor.

Check out the excellent Maine DOT site, **www.exploremaine.org/bike**, for a description of 21 tours ranging from 20 to 100 miles. The **Bicycle Coalition of Maine** (BCM; 207-623-4511; www.bikemaine.org) serves as a conduit for information about both off- and on-road bicycling throughout the state and maintains a calendar of bicycling events; request an information packet from BCM, P.O. Box 5275, Augusta 04332. Guided multiday tours are offered by **Summer Feet Cycling** (1-866-857-9544; www.summerfeet.net) and by **Bike Vermont** (1-800-257-2226; www.bikevermont.com).

BIRDING The Maine Audubon Society (207-781-2330; www.maine audubon.org), based at Gilsland Farm in Falmouth, maintains a number of birding sites and sponsors nature programs and field trips, which include cruises to Matinicus Rock and to

Joyce Morrell

Eagle Island. Note the special programming at Maine Audubon's Adirondack-style lodges on their 1,600-acre preserve at Borestone Mountain. **Laudholm Farm** in Wells, **Biddeford Pool**, **Scarborough Marsh**, **Merrymeeting Bay**, and **Mount Desert** are also popular birding sites. **Monhegan** is the island to visit in May and September. The **Moosehorn National Wildlife Refuge** (207-454-3521) in Washington County represents the northeastern terminus of the East Coast chain of wildlife refuges and is particularly rich in bird life. We recommend *Birder's Guide to Maine* by Elizabeth Cary Pierson, Jan Erik Pierson, and Peter D. Vickery (Down East Books). The annual **Downeast Birding Festival**, featuring guided hikes, cruises, and lectures, is held in the Cobscook Bay area Memorial Day weekend (www .downeastbirdfest.org). Also see *Puffin-Watching* and *Nature Preserves, Coastal* and *Inland*.)

BLUEBERRYING Maine grows 98 percent of America's lowbush blueberries. More than 65.5 million pounds are harvested annually from an estimated 25,000 acres. There are absolutely no human-planted wild blueberry fields. Few growers allow U-pick, at least not until the commercial harvest is over. (One exception is **Staples Homestead Blueberries** in Stockton Springs.) Then the public is invited to go "stumping" for leftovers. On the other hand, berrying along roads and hiking paths is a rite of summer. The **blueberry barrens**—thousands of blueberry-covered acres—spread across Cherryfield, Columbia, and Machias (site of the state's most colorful blueberry festival in August) in Washington County. For more about Maine's famous fruit, click on www.wildblueberries.com.

BOATBUILDING WoodenBoat School (207-359-4651 or 1-800-273-7447; www.woodenboat.com) in Brooklin (see "Blue Hill Area") offers a plethora of courses, including more than 24 on various aspects of boatbuilding. The **Maine Maritime Museum** (www.mainemaritimemuseum .org) in Bath offers an apprenticeship program; the **Landing School of Boatbuilding and Design** in Kennebunk offers summer courses in building sailboats; the **Apprenticeshop Boat Building School** (207-594-1800) in Rockland offers 2-year apprentice programs and 6-week (or longer) internships; and the **Washington County Community College Marine Trades Center** at Eastport attracts many out-of-staters.

BOAT EXCURSIONS You really won't know what Maine is about until you stand off at sea to appreciate the beauty of the cliffs and island-dotted bays. For the greatest concentrations of boat excursions, see "Boothbay Harbor Region," "Rockland/Thomaston Area," and "Bar Harbor and Ells-

worth"; there are also excursions from Ogunquit, Kennebunkport, Portland, Belfast, Camden, Castine, and Stonington. (Also see *Coastal Cruises; Ferries, in Maine* and *to Canada; Sailing;* and *Windjammers.* See "Sebago and Long Lakes Region" and "Moosehead Lake Area" for lake excursions.) A partial list of more than 50 cruises, ferries, and deep-sea-fishing options is published in the Maine Tourism Association's annual free magazine, *Maine Invites You* (see *Information*).

BOOKS Anyone who seriously sets out to explore Maine should read the following mix of Maine classics and guidebooks: *The Maine Woods* by Henry David Thoreau, first published posthumously in 1864, remains very readable and gives an excellent description of Maine's mountains (we recommend the Penguin edition). Our favorite relatively recent Maine author is Ruth Moore, who writes about Maine islands in *The Weir, Spoonhandle,* and *Speak to the Wind* (originally published in the 1940s and reissued by Blackberry Books, Nobleboro). Happily, the 1940s books by Louise Dickinson Rich, among which our favorites are *The Coast of Maine: An Informal History* and *We Took to the Woods,* are now published by Down East Books in Camden, along with Henry Beston's 1940s classic *Northern Farm: A Chronicle of Maine.* Sarah Orne Jewett's classic *The Country of the Pointed Firs and Other Stories* (W. W. Norton), first published in 1896, is still an excellent read, set on the coast around Tenants Harbor. The children's classics by Robert McCloskey, *Blueberries for Sal* (1948), *Time of Wonder* (1957), and *One Morning in Maine* (1952), are as fresh as the day they were written. For historical fiction, try any one of Pulitzer Prize–winner Kenneth Roberts's novels about Maine during the Revolutionary War. John Gould, an essayist who wrote a regular column for the *Christian Science Monitor* for more than 50 years, has published several books, including *Dispatches from Maine*, a collection of those columns, and *Maine Lingo* (with Lillian Ross), a humorous look at Maine phrases and expressions. E. B. White has some wonderful essay collections as well, along with his ever-popular children's novels, *Charlotte's Web* and *Stuart Little*.

Recent classics set in Maine include Carolyn Chute's *The Beans of Egypt, Maine* (1985), *Letourneau's Used Auto Parts* (1988), and *Merry Men* (1994); and Cathie Pelletier's *The Funeral Makers* (1987) and *The Weight of Winter* (1991). *Maine Speaks*, an anthology of Maine literature published by the Maine Writers and Publishers Alliance (www.maine writers.org), contains all the obvious poems and essays and many pleasant surprises. Linda Greenlaw's *The Lobster Chronicles* (2002) describes the island of Isle au Haut. It's a good read with insights into life on all Maine's surviving island communities.

Guides to exploring Maine include the indispensable *Maine Atlas and Gazetteer* (DeLorme) and, from Down East Books, *Birder's Guide to Maine* by Elizabeth Cary Pierson, Jan Erik Pierson, and Peter D. Vickery; *Walking the Maine Coast* by John Gibson; and *Islands in Time: A Natural and Cultural History of the Islands of the Gulf of Maine* by Philip W. Conkling. Serious hikers should secure the *AMC Maine Mountain Guide* (AMC Books); also *50 Hikes in the Maine Mountains* by Cloe Chunn and *50 Hikes in Coastal and Southern Maine* by John Gibson (both Countryman Press).

Also worth noting: *Maine*, by Charles C. Calhoun (Compass American Guides), complements this guide with its superb illustrations and well-written background text.

BUS SERVICE Concord Trailways (1-800-639-3317; www.concord trailways.com) serves Portland, Brunswick, Bath, Wiscasset, Damariscotta, Waldoboro, Rockland, Camden, Belfast, Searsport, Bangor, and the University of Maine at Orono (when school is in session). **Greyhound Bus Lines/Vermont Transit** (1-800-231-2222 or 1-800-451-3292; www .vermonttransit.com) serves Augusta, Lewiston, Waterville, Portland, Bangor, and (seasonally but crucially) Bar Harbor. See www.exploremaine.org for details about public transit buses.

CAMPING See "North Maine Woods" for details about camping within these vast fiefdoms, and also for camping in **Baxter State Park** (see "Katahdin Region") and along the **Allagash Wilderness Waterway** (see *To Do— Canoeing* in "Aroostook County"). For camping within **Acadia National Park**, see "Acadia National Park." For the same within the **White Mountain National Forest**, see "Bethel Area." For private campgrounds, the booklet ***Maine Camping Guide***, published by the Maine Campground Owners Association (207-782-5874; www.campmaine.com), lists most privately operated camping and tenting areas. Reservations are advised for the state's 13 parks that offer camping (see *Parks, State*). We have attempted to describe the state parks in detail wherever they appear in this book (see Damariscotta, Camden, Cobscook Bay, Sebago, Rangeley, and Greenville). Note that state campsites can accommodate average-sized campers and trailers, but there are no trailer hook-ups. **Warren Island** (just off Islesboro) and **Swan Island** (just off Richmond) offer organized camping, and primitive camping is permitted on a number of islands through the **Maine Island Trail Association** (MITA; see *Islands*). Within this book we occasionally describe outstanding campgrounds.

CAMPS, FOR ADULTS The **Appalachian Mountain Club** (617-523-0636; www.outdoors.org) maintains a number of summer lodges and campsites for adults and families seeking a hiking and/or canoeing vacation. Intended primarily for members, they are open to all who reserve space, available only after April 1. The full-service camps in Maine (offering three daily meals, organized hikes, evening programs) are at **Echo Lake** on Mount Desert and **Cold River Camp** in Evans Notch (near the New Hampshire border within the White Mountain National Forest). The Rockland-based **Hurricane Island Outward Bound School** offers a variety of adult-geared outdoor adventures on Hurricane Island (off Vinalhaven), in Newry (near Bethel), and in Greenville, as well as throughout the country. The **Maine Audubon Camp** on Hog Island off Bremen offers a series of weeklong courses (see "Damariscotta/Newcastle"). Photographers should check out the **Maine Photographic Workshops** in Rockport; also see *Boatbuilding* (**WoodenBoat** offers much more than boatbuilding) and check **Elder-**

hostel (617-426-7788; www.elder hostel.org), which offers a variety of programs throughout Maine for everyone over age 60. Also see the **Haystack Mountain School** under *Crafts* and arts workshops under *Artists and Art Galleries*.

CAMPS, FOR CHILDREN More than 200 summer camps are listed in the exceptional booklet published annually by the Maine Youth Camping Association (1-800-536-7712; www.maine camps.org).

CANOEING, GUIDED TRIPS Developed by the Wabanaki and still proudly manufactured in Old Town (see "Bangor Area"), the canoe remains the craft of choice on Maine rivers. Novices might begin with the slow-moving, shallow **Saco River**, which offers a number of well-maintained camping sites. Several outfitters in the Fryeburg area (see *To Do* in "Sebago and Long Lakes Region") offer rentals and shuttle service, and **Saco Bound**, just over the New Hampshire line, offers guided tours. The **Moose River** near Jackman (see *To Do* in "Upper Kennebec Valley") offers a similar camping/canoeing trip, and **Sunrise County Canoe Expeditions**, based on Cathance Lake (see *To Do* in "Calais and the St. Croix Valley" and "Washington County and the Quoddy Loop"), offers staging for trips down the Grand Lake chain of lakes and the St. Croix River. Within each chapter we describe canoe rentals and guided trips under *To Do*.

CANOEING THE ALLAGASH The ultimate canoe trip in Maine (and on the entire East Coast) is the 7- to 10-day expedition up the **Allagash Wilderness Waterway**, a 92-mile ribbon of lakes, ponds, rivers, and streams in the heart of northern Maine's vast commercial forests. We advise using a shuttle service. The general information numbers for the Allagash Wilderness Waterway are 207-941-4014 and 207-435-7963. A map pinpointing the 65 authorized campsites within the zone (and supplying other crucial information) is available free from the **Bureau of Parks and Lands** (207-287-3821), State House Station 22, Augusta 04333. A detailed map, backed with historical and a variety of other handy information, is DeLorme's *Map and Guide to the Allagash and St. John*. Be aware of blackflies in June and the "no-see-ums" when warm weather finally comes. For further information, see *Camping* and *Guide Services*, and check out www.maineoutdoors.com. Also see *To Do—Canoeing* in "Aroostook County."

CHILDREN, ESPECIALLY FOR
Throughout this book, restaurants, lodgings, and attractions that are of special interest to families with children are indicated by the crayon symbol ✎.

CHRISTMAS TREES AND WREATHS
Maine is a prime source of Christmas trees for the Northeast. The Maine Christmas Tree Association maintains a list of farms that welcome visitors to "tag'n'ship," and some permit tagging in summer with the understanding they will ship it to you in December. Call or e-mail the Maine Department of Agriculture (207-287-3491; getrealmaine@maine.gov).

CLAMMING Maine state law permits the harvesting of shellfish for personal use only, unless you have a commercial license. Individuals can take up to ½ bushel of shellfish or 3 bushels of hen or surf clams (the big ones out in the flats) in one day, unless municipal ordinances further limit "the taking of shellfish." Be sure to check locally at the town clerk's office (source of licenses) before you dig, and make sure there's no red tide. Some towns do prohibit clamming, and in certain places there is a temporary stay on harvesting while the beds are being seeded.

COASTAL CRUISES *Cruise* is a much-used (and -abused) term along the Maine coast, chiefly intended to mean a boat ride. *Maine Invites You* lists more than 60 cruises, ferries, and deep-sea-fishing choices, most of them described in the appropriate chapters of this book. Also check www.visitmaine.com. We have also tried to list the charter sailing yachts that will take passengers on multiday cruises and have described each of the windjammers that sail for 3 and 6 days at a time (see *Windjammers*).

COTTAGE RENTALS Cottage rentals are the only reasonably priced way to go for families who wish to stay in one Maine spot for a week or more (unless you camp). Request the booklet *Maine Guide to Inns and Bed & Breakfasts and Camps & Cottages* from the Maine Tourism Association (207-623-0363 or 1-888-MAINE-45; www.mainetourism.com). Many local chambers of commerce also keep a list of available rentals, and we list cottage rental web sites in most chapters.

COVERED BRIDGES Of the 120 covered bridges that once spanned Maine rivers, just 9 survive. The most famous, and certainly picturesque, is the **Artists' Covered Bridge** (1872) over the Sunday River in Newry, northwest of Bethel. The others are **Porter Bridge** (1876), over the Ossipee River, 0.5 mile south of Porter; **Babb's Bridge**, rebuilt after burning in 1973, over the Presumpscot River between Gorham and Windham; **Hemlock Bridge** (1857), 3 miles northwest of East Fryeburg; **Lovejoy Bridge** (1883), over the Ellis River in South Andover; **Bennett Bridge** (1901), over the Magalloway River, 1.5 miles south of the Wilson's Mills post office; **Robyville Bridge** (1876), Maine's only completely shingled covered bridge, in the town of Corinth; the **Watson Settlement Bridge** (1911), between Woodstock and Littleton; and **Low's Bridge**, carefully reconstructed in 1990 after a flood took the 1857 structure, across the Piscata-quis River between Guilford and Sangerville.

CRAFTS *Maine Guide to Crafts and Culture*, available free from the **Maine Crafts Association** (207-780-1807; www.mainecrafts.org), 15 Walton St., Portland 04104, is a geographic listing of studios, galleries, and museums throughout Maine. **United Maine Craftsmen, Inc.** (207-621-2818; www.unitedmaine craftsmen.com) also sponsors six large shows each year. **Haystack Mountain School of Crafts** (www.haystack -mtn.org; see "Deer Isle, Stonington") is a summer school nationally respected in a variety of crafts with 3-week courses mid-June through mid-September. The surrounding area (Blue Hill to Stonington) contains the largest concentration of Maine craftspeople, many of whom invite visitors into their studios.

DOGSLEDDING Although racing is a long-established winter spectator sport, the chance to actually ride on a dogsled is growing in popularity. **Telemark Inn** (www.telemarkinn .com) in West Bethel offers dogsledding. In the Moosehead Lake region, Stephen Medera's **Song in the Woods** (www.songinthewoods.com) and Ed Mathew's **Moose Country Safaris and Dogsled Trips** (www .maineguide.com/sportsmen/dogsled) offer a choice of trips. Don and Angel Hibbs have traveled more than 40,000 miles by dog team. Their **Nahma-kanta Lake Camps** (www.nahma kanta.com) in Rainbow Township serve as a base for driving teams (guests can ride or drive) on trails in a 27,000-acre preserve that's Maine's largest roadless preserve outside Katahdin—which is clearly visible from the trail system. Guests ski in 10 miles from the Golden Road.

EVENTS We have listed outstanding annual events within each chapter of this book; also see event listings on www.visitmaine.com and www.maine tourism.com. A listing of current community events is posted at www.maine publicradio.org.

FACTORY OUTLETS We note individual outlet stores in their respective chapters throughout; we also describe the state's two major outlet clusters: in Freeport (www.freeportusa.com) and Kittery (www.thekitteryoutlets.com). L. L. Bean (www.llbean.com), Freeport's anchor store, is open 24 hours and is the single most spectacular store in northern New England.

FALL FOLIAGE Autumn days tend to be clear, and the changing leaves against the blue sea and lakes can be spectacular. Off-season prices some-times prevail, in contrast with the rest of New England, at this time of year. Check the Maine Office of Tourism web site, www.visitmaine.com, for frequently updated foliage reports and suggested routes. Also see www .mainefoliage.com.

FARM B&BS The Maine Farm Vacation B&B Association describes its 17 members in its brochure and at www.mainefarm vacation.com. This is a promotional association, not an official approval and inspection group. Properties vary widely. Some offer plenty of space, animals, big breakfasts, and friendly informal atmosphere, but others are not working farms.

FARM STANDS, FARMS, AND FARMER'S MARKETS The **Maine Department of Agriculture** (207-287-3491; www.getrealmaine.com), 28 State House Station, Augusta 04333, publishes a handy 144-page guide listing more than 60 markets.

FERRIES, TO CANADA "The Cat," **Northumberland/Bay Ferries** (1-888-249-7245), will come to Portland in 2006, to ferry people and cars to Nova Scotia; see *Getting There* under

"Portland Area." It has operated its high-speed catamaran between Bar Harbor and Yarmouth (spring through fall) for several years. Mid-June through mid-September, **East Coast Ferries Ltd.** (506-747-2159), a small car ferry based on Deer Island (New Brunswick), serves Eastport (30 minutes) and Campobello (45 minutes), and the small provincial (free) **Deer Island–L'Etete Ferry** (506-453-2600) connects Deer Island with the New Brunswick mainland. The 65-car **Coastal Transport Ltd. Ferry** (506-662-3724) runs year-round from Blacks Harbour, not far east of L'Etete, to the island of Grand Manan.

FERRIES, IN MAINE Maine State Ferry Service (1-800-491-4883), Rockland 04841, operates year-round service from Rockland to Vinalhaven and North Haven, from Lincolnville to Islesboro, and from Bass Harbor to Swans Island and Frenchboro. They also run once a month (more in summer) from Rockland to Matinicus. For private ferry services to Monhegan, see "Boothbay Harbor Region" and "Midcoast Islands"; for the Casco Bay islands, see "Portland Area"; for Isle au Haut, see "East Penobscot Bay Region"; and for ferries from Mount Desert Island to the Cranberry Islands and Winter Harbor, see "Acadia Area" and "East Hancock County."

FILM Northeast Historic Film (1-800-639-1636; www.oldfilm.org) is based at "The Alamo," a vintage-1916 movie house in Bucksport. This admirable group has created a regional moving-image archive of films based on or made in New England that were shown in every small town during the first part of the 20th cen-

Nancy English

Kim Grant

tury. Request the catalog *Videos of Life in New England*. The **International Film & Television Workshops** in Rockport offers a variety of weeklong courses in various aspects of film. The **Maine International Film Festival** is a 10-day event, with more than 60 films shown at the Waterville Opera House and the Railroad Square Cinema. Portland also hosts the **Maine Jewish Film Festival** in mid-March. There are still three functioning **drive-ins** in Maine: at Bridgton, Skowhegan, and Westbrook.

FIRE PERMITS Maine law dictates that no person shall kindle or use outdoor fires without a permit, except at authorized campsites or picnic grounds. Fire permits in the organized townships are obtained from the local town warden; in the unorganized townships, from the nearest forest ranger. Portable stoves fueled by propane gas, gasoline, or Sterno are exempt from the rule.

FISHING Request the handy hunting and fishing map/guide available from the Maine Tourism Association (207-623-0363 or 1-888-MAINE-45;

www.mainetourism.com). Details about Maine sporting camps (www.mainesportingcamps.com) catering to fishermen can be found in "Western Mountains and Lakes Region," "North Maine Woods," and "Upper Kennebec Valley." The Maine Department of Marine Resources (207-624-6550) publishes *Maine: Saltwater Angler's Guide*, and the Maine Department of Inland Fisheries and Wildlife (207-287-8000) publishes a weekly fishing report at www.mefishwildlife.com. Registered Maine Guides (www.maineguides.org) know where and how to fish, and L. L. Bean Outdoor Discovery Schools (www.llbean.com/outdoors) offer frequent courses. One-day fishing licenses are available at general stores and from outfitters throughout the state and come with a regulations book. Also check out "FISHING" at www.visitmaine.com.

FORTS To be married to a fort freak is to realize that there are people in this world who will detour 50 miles to see an 18th-century earthworks. Maine's 20 forts are actually a fascinating lot, monuments to the state's unique and largely forgotten history. Examples described in their respective chapters include: **Fort Knox** (see "Bucksport") is the state's grandest fort and offers a lively seasonal schedule of events. **Fort William Henry** at Pemaquid (see "Damariscotta/Newcastle") is genuinely fascinating, while **Fort Edgecomb** off Rt. 1 in Edgecomb, just east of Wiscasset, is an easy hit. Also check out **Fort George** in Castine, **Fort McClary** in Kittery, **Fort Popham** near Bath, **Fort Pownall** at Stockton Springs, **Fort O'Brien** in Machiasport, and, at the northern end of Rt. 1, **Fort Kent** in Fort Kent.

GOLDEN ROAD This legendary 96-mile road is the privately owned high road of the North Maine Woods, linking Millinocket's paper mills on the east with commercial woodlands that extend to the Quebec border. Its name derives from its multimillion-dollar cost in 1975, but its value has proven great to visitors heading up from Moosehead Lake, as well as from Millinocket to Baxter State Park. It's also used by the whitewater rafting companies on the Penobscot River and the Allagash Wilderness Waterway, and for remote lakes like Chesuncook. Expect to pull to the side to permit lumber trucks to pass. Much of the road is now paved and well maintained, even (especially) in winter. Be sure to bring along your Maine atlas or another detailed map, however, as there are virtually no road markers. At this writing the Greenville Road—until recently a toll road linking Kokadjo and the Golden Road—is free but not well maintained.

GOLF *Maine Invites You*, published by the Maine Tourism Association (see *Information*), lists golf courses across the state. A slick Maine Golf Trail brochure detailing and picturing 41 courses is published by Golf Maine (1-877-533-4653; www.golfme.com). Also check out the Maine State Golf Association (www.mesga.org). Within the book we list golf courses within each chapter. The major resorts catering to golfers are the **Samoset** in Rockport, the **Bethel Inn** in Bethel, **Sebasco Harbor Resort** near Bath, the **Country Club Inn** in Rangeley, and **Sugarloaf/USA** in the Carrabassett Valley (where you should also inquire about **Moose Meadows**). Check out **Sunday River**'s course in Newry.

GORGES Maine has the lion's share of the Northeast's gorges. There are four biggies. The widest is the **Upper Sebois River Gorge** north of Patten, and the most dramatic, "Maine's Miniature Grand Canyon," is **Gulf Hagas** near the Katahdin Iron Works (see "Katahdin Region"). Both **Kennebec Gorge** and **Ripogenus Gorge** are now popular whitewater rafting routes.

GUIDE SERVICES In 1897 the Maine legislature passed a bill requiring hunting guides to register with the state; the first to do so was Cornelia Thurza Crosby (better known as "Fly Rod" Crosby), whose syndicated column appeared in New York, Boston, and Chicago newspapers at the turn of the 20th century. Becoming a Registered Maine Guide entails passing one of several specialized tests—in hunting, fishing, or one of a growing number of recreational categories, including whitewater rafting, canoeing, or kayaking—administered by the Maine Department of Inland Fisheries and Wildlife. There are currently some 3,000 **Registered Maine Guides**, but just a few hundred are full-time professional guides. The web site of the 500-member Maine Professional Guides Association is www.maineguides.org.

HANDICAPPED ACCESS Within this book, handicapped-accessible lodging, restaurants, and attractions are marked with a wheelchair symbol &. Maine, by the way, offers an outstanding handicapped skiing program, both cross-country and alpine; phone 1-800-639-7770 or click on www.skimhs.org.

HIKING For organized trips, contact the **Appalachian Mountain Club** (www.gwi.net/amcmaine). The AMC has recently acquired Little Lyford Camps just off the Appalachian Trail and a 37,000-acre adjacent parcel known as the Katahdin Iron Works (see "Moosehead Lake Area"). The AMC group's Boston office (617-523-0636; www.outdoors.org) is another good source of information. In addition to the *AMC Maine Mountain Guide* (available from AMC Books Division, Department B, 5 Joy St., Boston, MA 02108) and the AMC map/guide to trails on Mount Desert, we recommend investing in *50 Hikes in Coastal and Southern Maine* by John Gibson and *50 Hikes in the Maine Mountains* by Cloe Chunn (both from Backcountry Publications), which offer clear, inviting treks up hills of every size throughout the state. *The Maine Atlas and Gazetteer* (DeLorme) also outlines a number of rewarding hikes. While hiking is generally associated with inland Maine and with Acadia, an entirely new destination has been created within the past decade along the coast way Down East in Washington County. Thanks to the state-financed Land for Maine's Future and to conservation agencies, tens of thousands of acres of dramatic shore property is now preserved, much of it traversed by coastal trails detailed in the guidebook *Cobscook Trails*, available from the Quoddy Regional Land Trust (207-733-5509; www.qrlt.org). Within this book we list trails under *Hiking* or *Green Space* within each chapter. Also see *Appalachian Trail*; Baxter State Park in the "Katahdin Region" chapter; and "Acadia National Park."

HISTORY We tell Maine's rich history through the places that still recall or dramatize it. See *Wabanaki* in this section for sites that tell of the long precolonial history. For traces of early 17th-century settlement, see our descriptions of **Phippsburg**, **Pemaquid**, and **Augusta**. The French and Indian Wars (1675–1760), in which Maine was more involved than most of New England, are recalled in the reconstructed English Fort William Henry at Pemaquid and in historical markers scattered around **Castine** (Baron de Saint Castine, a young French nobleman married to a Penobscot Indian princess, controlled the coastal area we now call "Down East"). A striking house built in 1760 on **Kittery Point** (see "Kittery and the Yorks") evokes Sir William Pepperrell, credited with having captured the fortress at Louisburg from the French, and restored buildings in **York Village** (same chapter) suggest Maine's brief, peaceful colonial period.

In the Burnham Tavern at **Machias** you learn that townspeople captured a British man-of-war on June 1, 1775, the first naval engagement of the Revolution. Other reminders of the Revolution are less triumphant: At the Cathedral Pines in **Eustis** and spotted along Rt. 202 in the **Upper Kennebec Valley**, historical markers tell the poignant saga of Colonel Benedict Arnold's ill-fated 1775 attempt to capture Quebec. Worse: Markers at Fort George in Castine detail the ways in which a substantial patriot fleet utterly disgraced itself there. Maine's brush with the British didn't end with the Revolution: The Barracks Museum in **Eastport** tells of British occupation again in 1814.

Climb the six steep floors of the newly restored **Portland Observatory** (built in 1807) and hear how Portland ranked second among New England ports, its tonnage based on lumber, the resource that fueled fortunes like those evidenced by the amazingly opulent **Colonel Black Mansion** in Ellsworth and the elegant **Ruggles House** way Down East in Columbia Falls. In 1820 Maine finally became a state (the 23rd), but, as we note in our introduction to "The North Maine Woods," not without a price. The mother state, her coffers at their usual low, stipulated an even division of all previously undeeded wilderness, and some 10.5 million acres were quickly sold off, vast privately owned tracts that survive today as the unorganized townships.

Plagued in 1839 by boundary disputes that were ignored in Washington, the new, timber-rich state built its own northern forts (the **Fort Kent Blockhouse** survives). This "Aroostook War" was terminated by the Webster-Ashburton Treaty of 1842. In 1844 the state built massive **Fort Knox** at the mouth of the Penobscot River (see "Bucksport"), just in case. Never entirely completed, it makes an interesting state park. This era was, however, one of great prosperity and expansion within the new state.

As we note in the introduction to "Brunswick and the Harpswells," it can be argued that the Civil War began and ended there. Unfortunately the state suffered heavy losses: Some 18,000 young soldiers from Maine died, as Civil War monuments remind us. The end of the war, however, ushered in a boom decade. Outstanding displays in the **Vinalhaven Historical Society Museum** (see

"The Fox Islands") and in the **Deer Isle Granite Museum** in Stonington (see "Deer Isle, Stonington") present the ways that Maine granite fed the demand for monumental public buildings throughout the country, and both schooners and Down Easters (graceful square-rigged vessels) were in great demand (see the **Penobscot Marine Museum** in "Belfast, Searsport" and the **Maine Maritime Museum** in "Bath Area").

In the late 19th century many Maine industries boomed, tourism included. We describe Maine's tourism history in our introduction because it is so colorful, little recognized, and so much a part of what you see in Maine today.

Maine, the Pine Tree State from Prehistory to the Present by Richard Judd, Edwin Churchill, and Joel Eastman (University of Maine Press) is a good, recent, readable history (paperback).

HORSEBACK RIDING **Northern Maine Riding Adventures** (see "Moosehead Lake Area" and "Katahdin Region") offers entire days and overnights as well as shorter stints in the saddle, and special-needs riders are welcomed. We describe other riding options throughout the book.

HORSE RACING Harness racing can be found at **Scarborough Downs** (207-883-4331), Rt. 1 (exit 6 off the Maine Turnpike), April through November. The **Bangor Raceway** is open late May through late July. Many of the agricultural fairs also feature harness racing. Contact the Maine Harness Racing Commission (207-287-3221) for more information, or check the web site of the Maine

INFORMATION (OFFICIAL) ABOUT MAINE

The **Maine Office of Tourism** maintains a web site, www.visitmaine.com. Unfortunately, however, there's no staff person to answer specific questions. The 24-hour information line, 1-888-624-6345, connects (if you hold on long enough) with a fulfillment clerk who will send you the thick, helpful, four-season guide *Maine Invites You*, and— if you request them—the *Maine Hunting and Fishing Map* and *Maine Guide to Inns and Bed & Breakfasts and Camps & Cottages*. These are published by the **Maine Tourism Association** (MTA), which maintains its own helpful web site: www.mainetourism .com. You can contact them at 207-623-0363 or mtainfo@mainetourism.com. The MTA also operates unusually well-stocked and -staffed welcome centers at its southern gateway at Kittery (207-439-1319) on I-95 northbound (also accessible from Rt. 1); in Yarmouth just off Rt. 1 and I-95 (207-846-0833); in Hampden near Bangor on I-95 both northbound and southbound (207 862 6628 or 207-862-6638); in downtown Calais (207-454-2211); and in Houlton (207-532-6346). There's also an information center near the New Hampshire line on Rt. 302 in Fryeburg (207-935-3639). In each chapter we describe the local information sources under *Guidance*.

Christina Tree

Harness Racing Promotions Board at www.maineharnessracing.com for schedules.

HUNTING Hunters should obtain a summary of Maine hunting and trapping laws from the **Maine Depart ment of Inland Fisheries and Wildlife** (207-287-3371; www.me fishandwildlife.com), 284 State St., Augusta 04333. For leads on Registered Maine Guides who specialize in organized expeditions, contact the sources we list under *Fishing*; *Guide Services*; *Canoeing, Guided Trips*; and *Camping*. Within the book check out "Moosehead Lake Area," "Katahdin Region," "Upper Kennebec" and "Calais." The hunting and fishing map published annually by the Maine Tourism Association (207-623-0363; www.mainetourism.com) is worth having. Also see "HUNTING" at www .visitmaine.com.

ICE CREAM Here's the scoop on our favorite ice cream sources. The **Scoop Deck**, Rt. 1 in Wells (40 flavors for 20 years); **Round Top** ice cream, Business Rt. 1 in Damariscotta (in business 80 years); **Dorman's Dairy Dream** (closed Sunday; ginger is best), Rt. 1 in Thomaston; **Morton's Moo** in Ellsworth; and **Phil's Not-So-Famous Ice Cream** in Calais. Inland, check out **Shaner's Family Dining** in South Paris and **Smedberg's Crystal Spring Farm** in Oxford.

INNS Each edition of this book has become more selective as the number of places to stay increases. For each edition we personally inspect hundreds of inns and B&Bs. Our choices reflect both what we have seen and the feedback we receive from others;

they are not paid listings. We include web sites for individual lodging places. The **Maine Innkeepers Association** maintains a web site of their members at www.maineinns .com. The *Maine Guide to Inns and Bed & Breakfasts and Camps & Cottages* is also a useful resource (see the *Information (Official)* sidebar. Also check listings at www.visitmaine.com and www.mainetourism.com.

ISLANDS In all there are reportedly 3,250 offshore Maine islands, most uninhabited. We describe each of the islands that offer overnight lodging— **Chebeague**, **Great Diamond**, **Long**, and **Peaks Islands** in Casco Bay; **Monhegan**, **Vinalhaven**, **North Haven**, **Islesboro**, and **Matinicus** along the Midcoast; and **Isle au Haut**, **Islesford** (also known as **Little Cranberry**), **Swans Island**, and **Grand Manan** (New Brunswick) in the Down East section—in varying detail. In Casco Bay the ferry also serves **Cliff Island** (summer rentals are available); **Eagle Island**, former home of Admiral Peary, is served by daily excursion boats from Portland. For information on public and private islands on which low-impact visitors are welcome, contact the **Maine Island Trail Association** (207-596-6456; www.mita.org; P.O. Box C, Rockland 04841). MITA maintains 80 islands and charges $45 for membership, which brings with it a detailed guidebook and the right to land on these islands. **The Island Institute** (207-594-9209; www.islandinstitute .org), which began as one and the same as MITA, now serves as an umbrella organization for the island communities; with the $40 membership come its publications: *Island Journal* and *Working Waterfront*.

KAYAKING Outfitters offer guided half-day and full day trips, also overnight and multiday expeditions with camping on Maine islands. When paddling a kayak, you're so low that you can stare down a duck or a cormorant or study the surface of the water and its kaleidoscopic patterns. Maneuverable in as little as 6 inches of water, kayaks are ideal craft for "gunkholing" (poking in and out of coves). The leading outfitters are **Maine Island Kayak Company** (1-800-796-2373; www.maineisland kayak.com) on Peaks Island off Portland, and **Maine Sport Outfitters** (207-236-7120) in Rockport, both of which specialize in multiday camping trips and offer introductory lessons. Others that we have checked out include **H₂Outfitters** (207-833-5257) on Orrs Island near Brunswick, **Tidal Transit** (207-633-7140) in Boothbay Harbor, **Outward Bound School** (1-800-341-1744) in Rockland, **Granite Island Guide Service** (207-348-2668; www.granite islandguide.com) and **Old Quarry Ocean Adventures, Inc.** (207-367-8977; www .oldquarry.com) in Deer Isle, **Coastal Kayaking Tours** (207-288-9605) in Bar Harbor, **Sunrise County Canoe & Kayak** (207-454-7708 or 1-877-980-2300; www.sunrisecanoeand kayak.com), based at Cathance Lake but serving "the Bold Coast." **L. L. Bean Sea Kayak Symposium**, held in early July in Castine (by reservation only), is New England's oldest and still its biggest annual kayaking event (www.llbean.com). *Sea Kayaking Along the New England Coast* by Tamsin Venn (Appalachian Mountain Club) includes detailed guidance to kayaking routes from Portland to Cobscook Bay as well as an overall introduction to the sport. Dorcas Miller's comprehensive guidebook *Kayaking the Maine Coast: A Paddler's Guide to Day Trips from Kittery to Cobscook* (Countryman Press) is an excellent resource for kayak owners and competent kayakers.

LAKES Maine boasts some 6,000 lakes and ponds, and every natural body of water more than 10 acres is theoretically available to the public for "fishing and fowling." Access is, however, limited by the property owners. Because paper companies and other land management concerns permit public use (see *Camping*) there is ample opportunity to canoe or fish in solitary waters. Powerboat owners should note that most states have reciprocal license privileges with Maine; the big exception is New Hampshire. For more about the most popular resort lakes in the state, see the Bridgton, Rangeley, Moosehead, and Belgrade Lakes chapters. For state parks on lakes see **Aroostook** (camping, fishing, swimming; Rt. 1 south of Presque Isle), **Damariscotta Lake State Park** (Rt. 32, Jefferson), **Lake St. George State Park** (swimming, picnicking, fishing; Rt. 3 in Liberty), **Lily Bay State Park** (8 miles north of Greenville), **Peacock Beach State Park** (swimming, picnicking; Richmond), **Peaks-Kenny State Park** (Sebec Lake in Dover-Foxcroft), **Rangeley Lake State Park** (swimming, camping; Rangeley), **Range Pond State Park** (Poland), **Sebago Lake State Park** (swimming, picnicking, camping; near Bridgton), **Mount Blue State Park** (Weld), and **Swan Lake State Park** (Swanville). Families with small children should note the coastal area lakes surrounded by rental cottages (see *Cottage Rentals*).

LIGHTHOUSES Maine takes pride in its 65 lighthouses. The most popular to visit are **Portland Head Light** (completed in 1790, automated in 1990, now a delightful museum featuring the history of lighthouses) on Cape Elizabeth; **Cape Neddick Light** in York; **Marshall Point Light** at Port Clyde; **Fort Point Light** at Stockton Springs; **Pemaquid Point** (the lighthouse keeper's house is now a museum, there's an art gallery, and the rocks below are peerless for scrambling); **Bass Harbor Head Light** at Bass Harbor; and Lubec's **West Quoddy Head Light**, the start of a beautiful shore path. On **Monhegan** the lighthouse keeper's house is a seasonal museum, and at **Grindle Point** on Islesboro there is also an adjacent seasonal museum. True lighthouse buffs also make the pilgrimage to **Matinicus Rock**, the setting for several children's books. Lighthouse aficionados tell us that getting to **East Quoddy Head Lighthouse** on the island of Campobello, accessible at low tide, is the ultimate adventure; it is also a prime whale-watching post. Rockland's harbor is guarded by two distinctive and accessible lighthouses—**Owls Head** (1826) and the **Rockland Breakwater Light**—and the city's new **Gateway Visitor Center** features an evolving Maine Lighthouse Museum.

LITTER Littering in Maine is punishable by a $100 fine; this applies to dumping from boats as well as other vehicles. Most cans and bottles are redeemable.

LLAMA TREKKING The principle is appealingly simple: The llama carries your gear; you lead the llama. From the **Telemark Inn** (207-836-2703; www.telemarkinn.com), surrounded by semiwilderness west of Bethel, Steve Crone offers day and multiday treks. At **Pleasant Bay Bed & Breakfast** (207-483-4490; www.pleasantbay.com) in Addison guests can walk the property's waterside trails with the llamas. **Hidden Acres Llama Farm** (207-549-5575; www.farmvacation.com/hiddenacres) in Jefferson, near the northern tip of Damariscotta Lake, offers a one-bedroom apartment and the chance to participate in farm activities as well as to take llamas on treks over mountain trails.

LOBSTER-BOAT RACES The season's races (www.lobsterboatracing.com) represent one of the best spectator events along the Maine coast. Races begin mid-June in Boothbay Harbor, and the "World's Fastest Lobster Boat Races" are always held in Jonesport on the Fourth of July. Other venues are Stonington, Harpswell, Friendship, Winter Harbor, and Searsport. Participants accumulate points as they go along, and there's an awards ceremony and pig roast in Searsport in late September.

LOBSTER POUNDS In another era this term referred to the saltwater holding areas in which lobsters were literally impounded, but in tourist talk *lobster pound* now usually means a no-frills seaside restaurant that specializes in serving lobsters and clams steamed in seawater. The **Pemaquid Peninsula** (see "Damariscotta/Newcastle") is especially blessed: Check out **Shaw's** in New Harbor; the nearby **Harbor View Restaurant at the Pemaquid Fisherman's Co-op**; and, in Round Pond, **Muscongus Bay Lobster**. Not far from Rockland look for **Cod End** in Tenants Harbor.

Evie Douglas

Miller's Lobster Company is the local favorite on Spruce Head, and there is also **Waterman's Beach Lobsters** in South Thomaston. Other lobster-eating landmarks include **Robinson's Wharf** at Townsend Gut near Boothbay, the **Lobster Shack** in Cape Elizabeth near Portland, **Young's Lobster Pound** in East Belfast, the **Lobster Pound** in Lincolnville Beach, **Union River Lobster Pot** in Ellsworth, and **Trenton Bridge** on Rt. 3 at the entrance to Mount Desert Island; on Mount Desert Island **Beal's** is in Southwest Harbor, and **Thurston's**, which we prefer, is in Bernard. Minutes from Freeport's outlets, the **Harraseeket Lunch & Lobster Company** in South Freeport is a find. On the Southern Coast the **Ogunquit Lobster Pound** on Rt. 1 in Ogunquit is now a full-service restaurant, but waterside **Chauncey Creek** in Kittery is still no frills (BYO everything from salad to wine) and a good value. **Nunan's Lobster Hut** in Cape Porpoise and **Fisherman's Catch** in Wells Harbor are also the real thing.

MAINE GROWN Locally produced items include venison and beeswax as well as blueberries, Christmas wreaths, smoked seafood, teas, beer, wine, maple syrup, and lobster stew, to name just a few. The Maine Department of Agriculture, Food and Rural Resources (207-287-3491; www .getrealmaine.com) publishes several helpful guides.

MAINE MADE Maine craftspeople and entrepreneurs produce an ever-increasing variety of specialty foods, handcrafted furniture and furnishings, apparel, toys, and much more. Request a *Maine Made* catalog (1-800-541-5872, www.mainemade.com)

MAINE PUBLIC BROADCASTING Public broadcasting (www.mpbc.org) offers statewide television and radio. Maine Public Television stations are Channel 10 in Augusta, Channel 12 in Orono, Channel 13 in Calais, Channel 10 in Presque Isle, and Channel 26 in Biddeford. Local programming includes *Home: The Story of Maine*, *Made in Maine*, and *Maine Watch*, highlighting important issues in Maine each week. **Maine's seven public radio stations** can be found on the dial at 89.7 in Calais, 90.1 in Portland, 90.9 in Bangor, 91.3 in Waterville, 106.1 in Presque Isle, 90.5 in Camden, and 106.5 in Fort Kent. Local programming includes *Maine Watch*; *Maine Things Considered*, a news program highlighting state news; *The Humble Farmer*, a quirky jazz and talk show hosted by local celebrity Robert Skoglund; and *Maine Stage*, a classical music series. Check out www.mainepublicradio.org.

MAINE TURNPIKE For travel conditions and construction updates, phone 1-800-675-PIKE, or check www.maine turnpike.com. New exit numbers will throw you if your map predates 2004. Tolls are now a flat rate paid when getting on—and sometimes off—the turnpike. Heading north, the first booth is in York. If you remain on the turnpike all the way to Augusta, you will pass through two more booths requiring a toll (New Gloucester and Gardiner). Unless you need to exit at Gray or Lewiston/Auburn, it's cheaper and quicker to follow I-295 rather than the Maine Turnpike (I-95) north to Augusta.

MAPLE SUGARING Maine produces roughly 8,000 gallons of syrup a year, and the Maine Maple Producers Association (207-474-5262; www .mainemapleproducers.com) publishes a list of producers who welcome visitors on **Maine Maple Sunday** (also known as Sap Sunday) in late March.

MARITIME MUSEUMS The **Maine Maritime Museum** in Bath stands in a class by itself and should not be missed. The **Penobscot Marine Museum** in Searsport is smaller but still substantial, focusing on the merchant captains and their experiences in far corners of the world, featuring yearlong special exhibits. Request a copy of the *Maine Maritime Heritage Trail* brochure from 1-888-MAINE-45 (623-6345), ext. 45.

MOOSE-WATCHING Moose, Maine's state animals, have made a comeback from near extinction in the 1930s and now number more than 30,000 in the North Maine Woods alone. Moose are the largest animal found in the wilds of New England. They grow to be 10 feet tall and average 1,000 pounds. The largest member of the deer family, they have a large, protruding upper

lip and a distinctive "bell" or "dewlap" dangling from their muzzle.

"Bull" (male) moose have long been prized for their antlers, which grow to a span of up to 6 feet. They are shed in January and grow again. Female moose ("cows") do not grow antlers, and their heads are lighter in color than the bull. All moose, however, are darker in spring than summer, grayer in winter.

Front hooves are longer than the rear, as are the legs, the better to cope with deep snow and water. In summer they favor wetlands and can usually be found near ponds or watery bogs. They also like salt and so tend to create and frequent "wallows," wet areas handy to road salt (the attraction of paved roads).

Moose are vegetarians, daily consuming more than 50 pounds of leaves, grass, and other greenery when they can find it. In winter their diet consists largely of bark and twigs. Mating season is in mid-September until late October. Calves are born in early spring and weigh in at 30 pounds. They grow quickly but keep close to their mothers for an entire year. At best moose live 12 years.

Your chances of spotting one are greatest in early morning or at dusk on a wooded pond or lake or along logging roads. If you are driving through moose country at night, go slowly, because moose typically freeze rather than retreat from oncoming headlights. For details about commercial moose-watching expeditions, check "Rangeley Lakes Region," "Moosehead Lake Area," and the "Katahdin Region." The Moosehead Lake Region Chamber of Commerce sponsors **Moosemainea** mid-May through mid-June, with special events and a huge moose locator map. Suspicious that this promotion coincided with Moosehead's low tourist season, we queried the state's moose expert, who assures us that moose are indeed most visible in late spring. **Warning:** The state records hundreds of often deadly collisions between moose and cars or trucks. The common road sign and bumper sticker reading BRAKE FOR MOOSE means just that. Be extremely wary at dusk when vision is difficult and moose are active.

MUSEUMS Also see *Art Museums, Museum Villages, Maritime Museums*, and *Wabanaki*. Easily the most under visited museum in the state, the **Maine State Museum** in Augusta has outstanding displays on the varied Maine landscape and offers historical exhibits ranging from traces of the area's earliest people to rifles used by State of Mainers in Korea; it also includes exhibits on fishing, agriculture, lumbering, quarrying, and shipbuilding. The **Seashore Trolley Museum** in Kennebunkport and the **Owls Head Transportation Museum** near Rockland are family finds (inquire about special events at both). Our favorites also include the **Peary-MacMillan Arctic Museum** at Bowdoin College in Brunswick, the **Wilson Museum** in Castine, and the **L. C. Bates Museum** in Hinckley, probably the state's most old-time museum, filled with stuffed animals and Indian artifacts and surpassingly lively (see "Upper Kennebec Valley"). The **Lumberman's Museum** in "Katahdin Region" and the **Rangeley Lakes Region Logging Museum** are both glimpses of a recently vanished way of life in the North Maine Woods. The museum at the **Colonial Pemaquid Restoration** in Pemaquid, presenting archaeological finds

from the adjacent early 17th-century settlement, is also unexpectedly fascinating. The new **Downeast Heritage Center** in Calais dramatizes the 1604 settlement of nearby St. Croix Island and the culture of the local Passamaquoddy Nation. Click onto www .mainemuseums.org and/or request a free copy of *Maine Museums and Archives* (60 Community Dr., Augusta 04330; 207-287-5709 during business hours). Maine Office of Tourism has a fully staffed phone line at 1-888-624-6345, where a live human being will answer the phone 24/7 to provide information and guidance, including a brochure about the arts in Maine.

MUSEUM VILLAGES York Village, with its Old Gaol, school, tavern, church, and scattering of historic houses open to the public (www.old york.org), represents one of the country's earliest preservation efforts and adds up to a picture of 18th-century life in coastal Maine. **Willowbrook at Newfield** (www.willowbrookmuseum .org), by contrast, is a 19th-century village center consisting of buildings restored through the efforts of one man. Norlands (www.norlands.org), in Livermore, is a former estate with a neo-Gothic library, school, and farm buildings, all evoking rural life in the 1870s. Sabbathday Lake Shaker Community and Museum in New Gloucester is the country's last functioning Shaker religious community, but visitors are welcome to walk the grounds, visit the small museum/gift shop, and attend seasonal Sunday services in the meetinghouse.

MUSIC CONCERT SERIES Bowdoin International Music Festival (www .bowdoinfestival.org) in Brunswick is the state's most prestigious and varied chamber music series, and the **Kneisel Hall Chamber Music Festival** (207-374-2811) in Blue Hill is its oldest chamber music festival, also still outstanding. The **Mount Desert Festival of Chamber Music** (207-276-3988), the **Bar Harbor Festival** (207-288-5744), and the **Arcady Music Festival** (207-288-2141) are all highlights of the season on Mount Desert. The **Sebago/Long Lakes Region Chamber Music Festival** in North Bridgton is noteworthy, and **Bay Chamber Concerts**, presented in the **Rockport Opera House** (207-236-2823), are popular in the Camden/Rockport area. A series of outdoor picnic concerts are performed at the **Round Top Center for the Arts** (207-563-1507) in Damariscotta, while the **Machias Bay Chamber Concerts** in Machias (207-255-3889) are held in the town's Congregational church. There is, of course, the **Portland Symphony Orchestra** (207-842-0800), which also has a summertime pops series, and the **Bangor Symphony Orchestra** (207-942-5555 or 1-800-639-3221). Music lovers should also take note of the **Annual Rockport Folk Festival** in mid-July, the **Downeast Jazz Festival** in Rockland every August, the **Lincoln Arts Festival** of classical and choral music held throughout the Boothbay Harbor region in summer months, and the **Bluegrass Festival** at Thomas Point Beach in September. Click on www.mainemusic.org for daily updated musical events in Maine. **SummerKeys** (www.summerkeys.com) offers a series of summer Wednesday-evening concerts in Lubec, with water taxi service from Eastport.

MUSIC SCHOOLS Notable are the **Bowdoin International Festival** (see *Music Concert Series*); **Kneisel Hall** in Blue Hill (call 207-374-2811 only after June 24; prior inquiries should be addressed to Kneisel Hall, Blue Hill 04614); **Pierre Monteux Memorial School** in Hancock (207-442-6251); **Salzedo Summer Harp Colony** in Camden (207-236-2289); **New England Music Camp** in Oakland (207-465-3025); **Maine Summer Youth Music** at the University of Maine, Orono (207-581-1254); and **Maine Music Camp** at the University of Maine, Farmington. A popular recent addition is **SummerKeys** (207-733-2316; in winter, 973-316-6220; www.summerkeys.com) in Lubec, specializing in piano but welcoming students of all levels in a variety of instruments.

NATURE PRESERVES, COASTAL
From Kittery's **Brave Boat Harbor Trail** to the **Bold Coast Trail** way down in Washington County not far from West Quoddy Light, oceanside walking trails have multiplied in the last few years. Within each chapter we describe these under *Green Space* or *To Do—Hiking*. On the Southern Coast the **Wells National Estuarine Research Reserve** at Laudholm Farm includes two barrier beaches. On Casco Bay the Maine Audubon Society headquarters at **Gilsland Farm** in Falmouth includes 70 acres of nature trails; Maine Audubon also offers canoe tours and many summer programs at their **Scarborough Marsh Audubon Center** and maintains picnic and tenting sites at **Mast Landing Sanctuary** in Freeport. In Midcoast the **Boothbay Region Land Trust**, **Damariscotta River**

Association, and **Sheepscot River Watershed Association** now maintain a number of exceptional preserves, and **Camden Hills State Park** includes miles of little-used trails with magnificent views. Down East in the Blue Hill area, the 1,350-acre **Holbrook Island Sanctuary** in West Brooksville is a beauty, and in Ellsworth 40-acre **Birdsacre** includes nature trails and a museum honoring ornithologist Cordelia Stanwood. **Acadia National Park**, the state's busiest preserve, offers 120 miles of hiking paths on Mount Desert, also trails on Isle au Haut and at Schoodic Point. **Schoodic Mountain** north of Sullivan is one of the area's most spectacular hikes. Right across the line in Washington County, the 6,000-acre **Petit Manan National Wildlife Refuge**, based in Steuben, includes two coastal peninsulas and 24 offshore islands. Near Jonesport, **Great Wass Island** (accessible by land) is maintained by the Maine Chapter of The Nature Conservancy, a beautiful preserve with a 2-mile shore trail. **Western Head**, near Machias, is now maintained by Maine Coast Heritage Trust; Maine's Bureau of Parks and Lands maintains a 5.5-mile **Bold Coast Trail** along the high bluffs west of Cutler; **West Quoddy Light State Park** includes a splendid 2-mile shore trail. **Roosevelt Campobello International Park** also includes many miles of shore paths, and **Cobscook Bay State Park** (see "Eastport and Cobscook Bay") and **Moosehorn National Wildlife Refuge** (see "Calais and the St. Croix Valley") also offer hiking trails. Two islands that maintain magnificent hiking trails are **Monhegan** and **Vinalhaven**. The Maine Chapter of The Nature Conservancy (207-729-5181) has published *Maine Forever*, a guide to the state's Conservancy preserves. **The Maine Coast Heritage Trust** (207-729-7366) also makes available several useful brochures about its holdings.

NATURE PRESERVES, INLAND In the Rangeley area the **Rangeley Lakes Heritage Trust** has, in recent years, preserved more than 10,000 acres, including 20 miles of lake and river frontage and 10 islands; the **Stephen Phillips Memorial Preserve Trust** maintains a number of campsites on its land along Lake Mooselookmeguntic. In the Sugarloaf area the Maine Bureau of Parks and Lands now offers detailed maps to trails within the 35,000-acre **Bigelow Preserve**. Within each chapter we describe nature preserves along with state parks under *Green Space* or *To Do—Hiking*. Among our favorites are trails to the top of **Mount Kineo** overlooking Moosehead Lake (see "Moosehead Lake Area"), through **Gulf Hagas**, and in **Baxter State Park** (both in the "Katahdin Region"). The Bureau of Parks and Lands web site (www.parksandlands.com) is an excellent site for locating public lands scattered throughout the state, including the North Maine Woods.

PARKS AND FORESTS, NATIONAL **Acadia National Park** (207-288-3338; www.nps.gov/acad), which occupies roughly half of Mount Desert Island, plus scattered areas on Isle au Haut, Little Cranberry Island, Baker Island, Little Moose Island, and Schoodic Point, adds up to more than 40,000 acres offering hiking, ski touring, swimming, horseback riding, canoeing, and a variety of guided nature tours and programs, as well as a scenic 27-mile driving tour. Note that an entry fee is charged to drive the Park Loop Road. Camping is by reservation only at Blackwoods, and first come, first served at Seawall. See "Acadia National Park" for details. The **White Mountain National Forest** encompasses 41,943 acres in Maine, including five campgrounds under the jurisdiction of the Evans Notch Ranger District (207-824-2134), Bridge St., Bethel 04217. For details, see "Bethel Area."

PARKS, STATE The **Bureau of Parks and Lands** (207-287-3821; www .parksandlands.com), 22 State House Station, Augusta 04333, can send a packet of information describing each of the 32 parks and the 12 (plus the Allagash Wilderness Waterway) that offer camping facilities. We have described parks as they appear geographically. In 2005 day-use fees were were between $2 and $4.50 per adult, $1 for ages 5–11, and free for those under 5 and or over 65. The camping fee per site was $11–15 for residents, $14–20 for nonresidents. There is also a $2-per-night reservation fee for camping. Call the reservations hotline (within Maine, 1-800-332-1501; from outside the state, 207-287-3824) at least 7 days in advance to make a campground reservation, or use the online registration form. (Also see *Lakes*.)

PETS Throughout this book, lodgings and selected other places that accept pets are indicated with the dog-paw symbol 🐾. Please note that most lodgings require a reservation and a deposit or additional fee. Always call ahead when traveling with your pet.

PLOYE This traditional Acadian pancake/flat bread, as delicate as a crêpe, is a specialty throughout the St. John Valley. The **Bouchard Family Farm** produces a line of French Canadian food products: 1-800-239-3237.

POPULATION 1,274,923.

PUFFIN-WATCHING Atlantic puffins are smaller than you might expect. They lay just one egg a year and were heading for extinction around the turn of the 20th century, when the only surviving birds nested on either Matinicus Rock or Machias Seal Island. Since 1973 the Audubon Society has helped reintroduce nesting on Eastern Egg Rock in Muscongus Bay, 6 miles off Pemaquid Point, and since 1984 there has been a similar puffin-restoration project on Seal Island in outer Penobscot Bay, 6 miles from Matinicus Rock. The best times for viewing puffins are June and July or the first few days of August. The only place from which you are allowed to view the birds on land is at **Machias Seal Island**, where visitors are permitted in limited numbers. Contact **John Norton** (1-888-551-4895) in Jonesport and **Andrew Patterson**

Christina Tree

(207-259-4484) in Cutler. With the help of binoculars (a must), you can also view the birds from the water via tours with **Atlantic Expeditions** (207-372-8621) out to Matinicus Rock and Seal Island from Rockland, and around Eastern Egg Rock with **Cap'n Fish** (207-633-3244) from Boothbay Harbor and **Hardy Boat Cruises** (1-800-278-3346) from New Harbor. The **Audubon Camp** of the **Maine Audubon Society Ecology Camp** (see "Damariscotta/Newcastle") also offers programs at their facility near Eastern Egg Rock. Log onto www .mainebirding.com.

RAIL TRAVEL See *Amtrak* for passenger service from Boston to Portland. A seasonal train runs between Brunswick and Rockland; see *Railroad Excursion* in either town.

RAILROAD EXCURSIONS AND MUSEUMS **Boothbay Railway Village** (207-633-4727) delights small children and offers railroad exhibits in its depot. **The Maine Eastern Railroad** (1-866-637-2457; www.maine easternrailroad.com) offers 54-mile seasonal runs between Rockland and Brunswick, stopping in Bath and Wiscasset. It's a beautiful trip along the coast in plush 1940s and '50s coaches, a dining car, and (weekends only) a glass-domed observation car, behind a 1950s diesel electric engine. In 2005 there were round-trip runs Tuesday through Sunday, but check the web site for current information. In Portland the **Maine Narrow Gauge Railroad Company & Museum** combines displays and a 3-mile shoreside excursion. Inland, the **Sandy River & Rangeley Lakes Railroad** in Phillips in the Rangeley region operates short excursions one

Sunday per month in summer. A similar **Waterville & Farmington Railway Museum** (207-882-6897) at Sheepscot Station, Alna, preserves the history of another 2-foot narrow-gauge railroad and displays an 1891 2-footer locomotive, billed as the oldest in the United States. Rail buffs also find their way to **Maine Central Model Railroad** (207-497-2255) in Jonesport.

RATES Please do not regard any prices listed for *Lodging* as set in stone. Call ahead to confirm them. Rates are those in effect as we go to press. *MAP* stands for "Modified American Plan": breakfast and dinner included in rate. *AP* stands for "American Plan": three meals included in rate. *EP* stands for "European Plan": breakfast included in rate. *B&B* stands for "bed & breakfast": continental breakfast included in rate.

ROCKHOUNDING **Perham's of West Paris** at Trap Corner in West Paris displays Maine minerals and offers access to its four quarries. The store also offers information about other quarries and sells its own guidebooks to gem hunting in Oxford County and throughout the state. Open year-round 9–5 daily except Thanksgiving and Christmas. For other rockhounding meccas, check "Bethel Area." Thanks to the high price of gold, prospectors are back-panning Maine streambeds; a list of likely spots is available from the Maine Geological Survey (207-287-2801), Department of Conservation, 22 State House Station, Augusta 04333.

SAILING Windjammers and yacht charter brokers aside, there are a limited number of places that will rent small sailing craft, fewer that will offer lessons to adults and children alike. The **Mansell Boat Rental Company**, Southwest Harbor, rents sailboats by the day or longer. Learn-to-sail programs are offered by **WoodenBoat School** in Brooklin, and in Camden by both the **Camden Yacht Club** and **Bay Island Sailing School**. Sailboat rentals and daysails are listed throughout the book. (Also see *Windjammers*.)

SKIING, CROSS-COUNTRY

Carrabassett Valley Touring Center at Sugarloaf is the largest commercial Nordic network in the state. Bethel, with four trail networks (**Sunday River Inn**, **Bethel Inn**, **Carter's X-C Ski Center**, and **Telemark Inn**), offers varied terrain. The town of **Rangeley** also maintains an extensive trail network that enjoys dependable snow cover. For the most adventurous touring check the Katahdin/Moosehead area. The **Birches Resort** in Rockwood and **Little Lyford Pond Camps** near Brownville Junction offer guided wilderness tours. Stay tuned for progress reports on a 200-mile cross-country trail presently taking shape, complete with AMC-style huts, running from Bethel to Sugarloaf, up along the Dead River to The Forks, and on up to Rockwood.

SKIING, DOWNHILL Ski Maine Association

(207-761-3774; www.skimaine.com) lists information about mountains in Maine, snow conditions, and more on their web site. **Sugarloaf/USA** in the Carrabassett Valley and **Sunday River** in the Bethel area, both owned by the Bethel-based American Skiing Company, vie for the title of Maine's number one ski resort.

The two are very different and actually complement each other well. Sugarloaf is a high, relatively remote mountain with New England's only lift-serviced snowfields on its summit and a classy, self-contained condo village at its base. Sunday River, just an hour north of Portland, consists of eight adjoining (relatively low-altitude) mountains; snowmaking is a big point of pride, and facilities include a variety of slope-side condo lodgings. **Saddleback Mountain** (in the Rangeley area) is a big mountain undergoing development with an enthusiastic following. **Mount Abram** (also in the Bethel area) is a true family area with a strong ski school and some fine runs. **Shawnee Peak** in Bridgton is a medium-sized, family-geared area that offers night as well as day skiing. The **Camden Snow Bowl** in Camden is medium sized but satisfying.

SNOWMOBILING Maine has reciprocal

agreements with nearly all states and provinces; for licensing and rules, contact the Department of Inland Fisheries and Wildlife (207-287-2043), 41 State House Station, Augusta 04333. **The Maine Snowmobile Association** (MSA; 207-622-6983; www.mesnow.com), P.O. Box 80, Augusta 04333, represents more than 280 clubs and maintains some 12,500 miles of an ever-expanding cross-state trail network. Aroostook County, given its reliable snow conditions, is an increasingly popular destination. **Sled Maine** (1-877-2SLED-ME; www.sledme.com) is a visitor-geared group supplying information on destinations with lodging, rentals, and guided tours as well as trails. The Upper Kennebec Valley and Jackman as well as the entire Moosehead and Rangeley Lake areas are snowmobiling meccas. For maps and further information, write to the Snowmobile Program, Bureau of Parks and Lands, 22 State House Station, Augusta 04333; MSA maintains a trail-conditions hotline: 207-626-5717.

SPORTING CAMPS The Maine sporting camp is a distinctly Maine phenomenon that began appearing in the 1860s—a gathering of log cabins around a log lodge by a lake, frequently many miles from the nearest road. In the 19th century access was usually via Rangeley or Greenville, where "sports" urbanites arriving by train to hunt wild game—would be met by a guide and paddled up lakes and rivers to a camp. With the advent of floatplanes, many of these camps became more accessible (see *Air Services*), and the proliferation of private logging roads has put most within reach of sturdy vehicles. True sporting camps still cater primarily to anglers in spring and hunters in fall, but since August is neither a hunting season nor a prime fishing season, they are increasingly hosting families who just want to be in the woods by a lake in summer. True sporting camps (as opposed to "rental camps") include a central lodge in which guests are served all three meals; boats and guide service are available. The **Maine Sporting Camp Association** (www.mainesportingcamps.com), P.O. Box 119, Millinocket 04462, publishes a truly fabulous map/guide to its more than 50 members. Also see *Maine Sporting Camps: A Year-round Guide to Vacationing at Traditional Hunting and Fishing Camps* by Alice Arlen (Countryman Press).

THEATER, SUMMER **The Ogunquit Playhouse** (207-646-5511) is among

the oldest and most prestigious summer theaters in the country, and the **Arundel Barn Playhouse** (207-985 5552) in Kennebunk is the newest. The **Hackmatack Playhouse** in Berwick (207-698-1807) and **Biddeford City Theater** (207-282-0849) are other Southern Coast options. In Portland note the **Portland Stage Company** (207-774-0465), and in Brunswick the **Maine State Music Theater** and **Children's Theatre Program** on the Bowdoin campus (207-725-8769). Farther along the coast look for the **Camden Civic Theatre** based in the refurbished Opera House in Camden (207-236-2281), the **Belfast Maskers** in Belfast (207-338-4427), the **Surry Opera Company** in Surry (207-667-2629), the **Acadia Repertory Theatre** in Somesville (207-244-7260), and **Downriver Theater Productions** in Machias. Inland look for the **Theater at Monmouth** (207-933-2952), **Lakewood Theater** in Skowhegan (207-474-7176), **Deertrees Theatre** in Harrison (207-583-6747), and **Celebration Barn Theater** in South Paris (207-743-8452).

THEATER, YEAR-ROUND **Penobscot Theatre Company** in Bangor offers a variety of winter productions (207-942-3333). Other companies are the **Chocolate Church Arts Center** in Bath (207-442-8455) and the **Camden Civic Theatre** in Camden (207-236-2281). **Portland Stage Company** (207-774-0465) presents a series of productions at 25A Forest Ave., Portland. **The Portland Players** (207-799-7337) present a winter season of productions, as does the **Public Theatre** (207-782-3200) in Auburn. In Brunswick the **Theater Project**

(207-729-8584) performs year-round. Most universities and colleges also offer performances throughout the school year.

TRAFFIC AND HIGHWAY TRAVEL TIPS Maine coastal travel has its sticky wickets. By far the worst is the back-up at the tolls at the entrance to the Maine Turnpike as well as those not far south in New Hampshire. Get E-ZPass, an electronic toll system gadget for your car that works all over New England (www.ezpassmaine turnpike.com), or avoid passing through these tolls, if at all possible, at obvious peak travel times. We suggest ways around bottlenecks at Brunswick, Wiscasset, and Camden. Note that it takes no longer to reach a Down East than a Midcoast destination, thanks to the way the highways run. The quickest way to reach Rockland or Camden from points south is up I-295 to Brunswick and then coastal Rt. 1. Belfast and destinations east through the Blue Hill Peninsula, however, can be reached in roughly the same time by taking I-295 to Augusta and then Rt. 3 to coastal Rt. 1. You can reach Ellsworth (gateway to Mount Desert and points east) in equal time by traveling I-95 to the Maine Turnpike to Bangor and then down Rt. 1A.

WABANAKI *Wabanaki* means "people of the dawn." It's the name of Native Americans who have lived in Maine and eastern Canada for many thousands of years, judging from shell heaps and artifacts found in areas ranging from the coastal Damariscotta/Boothbay and Blue Hill areas to the Rangeley Lakes in western Maine. Ancient pictographs can be found on the Kennebec River and around Machias Bay. An excellent exhibit, *12,000 Years in Maine*, in the **Maine State Museum** in Augusta, depicts the distinct periods in this history and features the Red Paint People, so named for the red pigments found sprinkled in their burial sites. They flourished between 5,000 and 3,800 years ago and are said to have fished from large, sturdy boats. The **Abbe Museum** (www.abbemuseum .org) in Bar Harbor is dedicated to showcasing the cultures of Maine's Wabanaki, the 7,000 members of the Penobscot, Passamaquoddy, Micmac, and Maliseet tribes who live in the state. The permanent collection of 50,000 objects ranges from 10,000-year-old artifacts to exquisite basketry and craftswork from several centuries. The time line begins with the present and draws visitors back through 10,000 years and to its core, "the Circle of Four Directions." Two North Maine Woods sites are said to have been sacred: the **Katahdin Iron Works**, in Brownville Junction, source of the pigments found in their burial sites; and **Mount Kineo** on Moosehead Lake, source of the flint-like volcanic stone widely used for arrowheads. Early French missions at Mount Desert and Castine proved battlegrounds between the French and English, and by the end of the 17th century thousands of Wabanaki had retreated either to Canada or to the Penobscot community of **Old Town** and to **Norridgewock**, where Father Sebastian Rasle insisted that the Indian lands "were given them of God, to them and their children forever, according to the Christian oracles." The mission was obliterated (it's now a pleasant roadside rest area), and by the end of the French and Indian Wars only four tribes remained. Of these the Micmacs and Maliseets made the unlucky choice of siding with the Crown and were subsequently forced to flee (but communities remain near the Aroostook County–Canadian border in Presque Isle and Littleton, respectively). That left only the Penobscots and the Passamaquoddys.

In 1794 the Penobscots technically deeded most of Maine to Massachusetts in exchange for the 140 small islands in the Penobscot River, and in 1818 Massachusetts agreed to pay them an assortment of trinkets for the land. In 1820, when Maine became a state, a trust fund was set aside but ended up in the general treasury. The state's three reservations (two belonging to the Passamaquoddys and one to the Penobscots) were termed "enclaves of disfranchised citizens bereft of any special status." Indians loomed large in Maine lore and greeted 19th-century tourists as fishing and hunting guides in the woods and as snowshoe and canoe makers and guides, while Native American women sold their distinctive sweetgrass and ash-splint baskets and beadwork at the many coastal and inland summer hotels and boardinghouses.

In 1972 the Penobscots and Passamaquoddys sued to reclaim 1.5 million acres of land allegedly illegally appropriated by the state, and in 1980 they received an $80.6 million settlement, which they have since invested in a variety of enterprises. The Indian Island Reservation in Old Town is presently home to 500 of the tribe's 2,000 members, and the **Penobscot Nation Museum** there, while small, is open regularly and well worth checking. The Passamaquoddy tribe today numbers 2,500 members, roughly divided between the reservations at Indian Township on Schoodic

Lake and at Pleasant Point, near Eastport, site of the **Waponahki Museum and Resource Center** and of **Indian Ceremonial Days**, held annually in mid-August to celebrate Passamaquoddy culture and climaxing in dances in full regalia.

The new **Downeast Heritage Center** in Calais features displays on Passamaquoddy history, language, and craftsmanship. The **Hudson Museum at the University of Maine**, Orono, has a small display on local tribes and hosts an annual early-December **Maine Indian Basketmakers Sale and Demonstration**, featuring the work of all four tribes. A similar sale is held in Bar Harbor in early July. The **L. C. Bates Museum** in Hinckley (see "Upper Kennebec Valley") displays ancient artifacts and 19th- and early 20th-century craftsmanship, and **Nowetah's American Indian Museum** in New Portland (see "Sugarloaf and the Carrabassett Valley") displays a large collection of authentic basketry. Contact the Maine Indian Basketmakers Alliance (P.O. Box 3253, Old Town 04468; 207-827-0391) for a copy of the *Wabanaki Cultural Resource Guide*.

WATERFALLS The following are all easily accessible to families with small children: **Snow Falls Gorge** off Rt. 26 in West Paris offers a beautiful cascade (ask for directions at Perham's Gem Store); **Small's Falls** on the Sandy River, off Rt. 4 between Rangeley and Phillips, has a picnic spot with a trail beside the falls; **Jewell Falls** is located in the Fore River Sanctuary in the heart of Portland; **Step Falls** is on Wight Brook in Newry off Rt. 26; and just up the road in Grafton Notch State Park is **Screw Auger Falls**, with its natural gorge. Another Screw

Auger Falls is in Gulf Hagas (see *Gorges*), off the Appalachian Trail near the Katahdin Iron Works Road, north of Brownville Junction. **Kezar Falls**, on the Kezar River, is best reached via Lovell Road from Rt. 35 at North Waterford. An extensive list of "scenic waterfalls" is detailed in the *Maine Atlas and Gazetteer* (DeLorme). Check out 90-foot **Moxie Falls** at The Forks.

WEDDINGS At this writing no one conduit exists for information about the ever-increasing number of services (photographers, musicians, carriage operators, caterers, and florists, as well as inns and venues) geared to helping couples wed near Maine water. Several chambers of commerce, notably York, Kennebunkport, Boothbay, and Camden, are particularly helpful. Within the book we note properties that specialize in weddings with our ring ∞ symbol. A Maine marriage license currently costs just $20.

WHALE-WATCHING Each spring humpback, finback, and minke whales migrate to New England waters, where they remain until fall, cavorting, it sometimes seems, for the pleasure of excursion boats. One prime gathering spot is **Jeffrey's Ledge**, about 20 miles off Kennebunkport, and another is the **Bay of Fundy**. For listings of whale-watch cruises, see "The Kennebunks," "Portland Area," "Bar Harbor," and "Washington County." The East Quoddy (Campobello) and West Quoddy (Lubec) Lighthouses are also prime viewing spots.

WHITEWATER RAFTING This Maine phenomenon (spring through fall) began only in 1976, coincidentally the year of the last log drive on the Kennebec River. Logs were still hurtling through Kennebec Gorge on that day in the spring of 1976 when fishing guide Wayne Hockmeyer (and eight bear hunters from New Jersey) plunged through it in a rubber raft. At the time Hockmeyer's rafting know-how stemmed solely from having seen *River of No Return*, in which Robert Mitchum steered Marilyn Monroe down the Salmon River.

Hockmeyer founded **Northern Outdoors** and there are now more than a dozen other major outfitters positioned around The Forks, near the confluence of the Kennebec and Dead Rivers, all skilled in negotiating the rapids through nearby 12-mile-long Kennebec Gorge. Numbers on the river are now strictly limited, and rafts line up to take their turns riding the releases—which gush up to 8,000 cubic feet of water per second—from the Harris Hydroelectric Station above the gorge. Several rafting companies—notably **Northern Outdoors, Crab Apple White Water, North American Whitewater Expeditions, Magic Falls Rafting Company**, and **Three Rivers White Water**—have fairly elaborate base facilities in and around The Forks. Several outfitters—including **Northern Outdoors, Wilderness Expeditions, New England Outdoor Center**, and **Three Rivers White Water** have established food and lodging facilities for patrons who want to raft the Penobscot near Baxter State Park. Some 80,000 rafters of all ages and abilities now raft in Maine each year. For information about most outfitters, contact **Raft Maine** (1-800-723-8633; www.raft maine.com).

Evie Douglas

WINDJAMMERS In 1935 artist Frank Swift outfitted a few former fishing and cargo schooners to carry passengers around the islands of Penobscot Bay. At the time these old vessels were moored in every harbor and cove, casualties of progress. Swift's **Maine Windjammer Cruise** grew to include more than a dozen vessels. Competitors also prospered throughout the 1950s, but the entire windjammer fleet appeared doomed by rigorous Coast Guard licensing requirements in the 1960s. The 1970s and 1980s saw the rise of a new breed of windjammer captain. Almost every one of those now sailing has built or restored the vessel he or she commands or acquired it from the captain who did. Members of the current Maine windjammer fleet range from the *Stephen Taber* and the *Lewis R. French*, both originally launched in 1871, to the *Heritage*, launched in 1983, to the *Kathryn B* (a luxury version of the others), launched in 1996.

Former *Taber* co-captain Ellen Barnes recalls her own discovery of windjammers: "No museums had gobbled up these vessels; no cities had purchased them to sit at piers as public relations gimmicks. These vessels were the real thing, plying their trade as they had in the past with one exception: The present-day cargo was people instead of pulpwood, bricks, coal, limestone, and granite."

Choosing which vessel to sail on is the most difficult part of a windjammer cruise. All have ship-to-shore radios and sophisticated radar, and some offer more in the way of creature comforts; some are known for their food. Windjammers accommodate between 12 and 44 passengers. Excessive drinking is discouraged on all the vessels, and guests are invited to bring their musical instruments. Children under 14 are permitted only on some vessels. In the "Rockland/ Thomaston Area" and "Camden/ Rockport Area" In relevant chapters we have described each vessel in the kind of detail we devote to individual inns. Questions you might like to ask in making your reservation: (1) What's the bunk arrangement? Double bunks and cabins for a family or group do exist. (2) What's the cabin ventilation? Some vessels offer cabins with portholes or windows that open. (3) What's the rule about children? Several schooners schedule special family cruises with activities geared to kids. (4) What's the extent of weatherproof common space? It varies widely. (5) Is smoking allowed? (6) Is there evening entertainment of any kind?

The Maine Windjammers Association (1-800-807-WIND; www .sailmainecoast.com) represents all the major windjammers, which claim to be "the largest fleet of merchant ships operating under sail in America."

Southern Coast 1

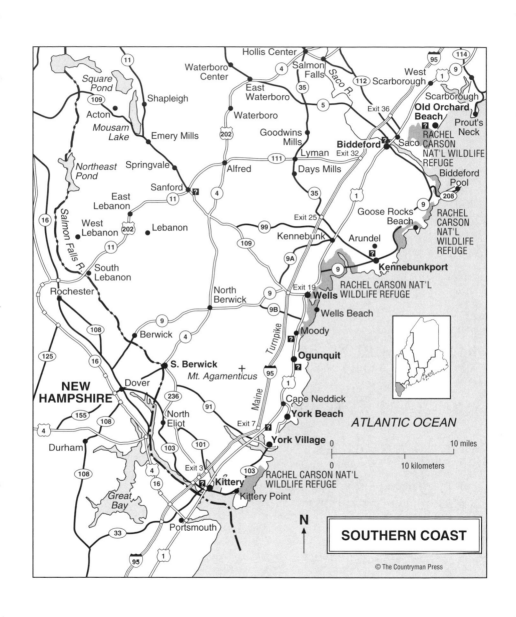

SOUTHERN COAST

N

ATLANTIC OCEAN

0   10 miles

0   10 kilometers

© The Countryman Press

SOUTHERN COAST

The smell of pine needles and salt air, the taste of lobster and saltwater taffy, the shook of cold green waves and, most of all, the promise of endless beach—this is the Maine that draws upward of half the state's visitors, those who never get beyond its Southern Coast. The southern Maine coast makes up just 35 miles of the state's 3,500 coastal miles but contains 90 percent of its sand.

Beyond their sand these resort towns—and the villages within them—differ deeply. York Village and Kittery are recognized as the oldest communities in Maine; Wells dates from the 1640s, and Kennebunkport was a shipbuilding center by the 1790s. All were transformed in the second half of the 19th century, an era when most Americans—not just the rich—began to take summer vacations, each in his or her own way.

Maine's Southern Coast was one of the country's first beach resort areas, and it catered then—as it does today—to the full spectrum of vacationers, from blue-collar workers to millionaires. Before the Civil War, Old Orchard Beach rivaled Newport, Rhode Island, as the place to be seen; when the Grand Trunk Railroad to Montreal opened in 1854, it became the first American resort to attract a sizable number of Canadians.

While ocean tides are most extreme way Down East, the ebb and flow of tourist tides wash most dramatically over this stretch of Maine. Nowhere are the 1930s-era motor courts thicker along Rt. 1, now sandwiched between elaborate condo-style complexes with indoor pools and elevators. Most of the big old summer hotels vanished by the 1950s, the era of the motor inns that now occupy their sites. But in the past few decades hundreds of former sea captains' homes and summer mansions have been transformed into small inns and bed & breakfasts, rounding out the lodging options. Luckily, the lay of the land—salt marsh, estuarine reserves, and other wetlands—largely limits commercial clutter.

GUIDANCE The **Coalition of Southern Maine Chambers of Commerce** maintains a toll-free number that connects with the major chambers: 1-800-639-2442, www.southernmainecoast.org.

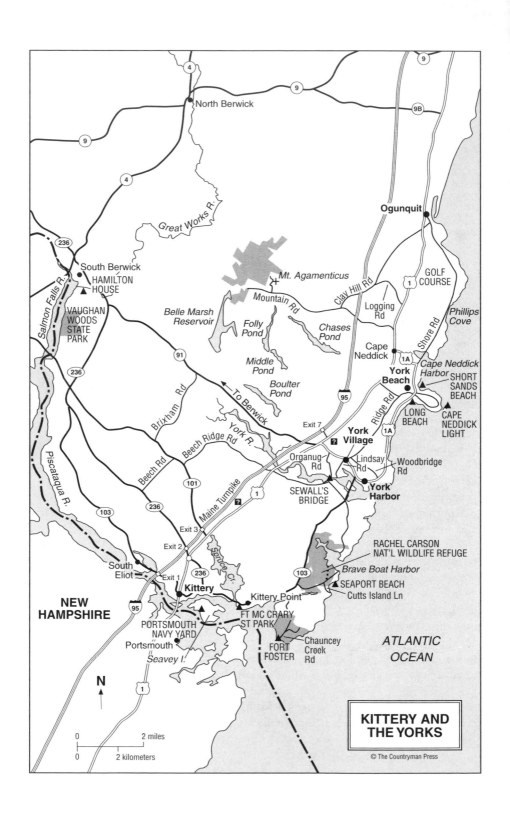

North Berwick

Ogunquit

Great Works R.

GOLF COURSE

South Berwick

HAMILTON HOUSE

Mt. Agamenticus

Clay Hill Rd

Logging Rd

Phillips Cove

VAUGHAN WOODS STATE PARK

Salmon Falls R.

Mountain Rd

Belle Marsh Reservoir

Chases Pond

Folly Pond

Cape Neddick

Cape Neddick Harbor

SHORT SANDS BEACH

Shore Rd

York Beach

Middle Pond

Boulter Pond

To Berwick

LONG BEACH

CAPE NEDDICK LIGHT

Brixham Rd

Ridge Rd

Exit 7

York Village

Beech Ridge Rd

York R.

Organug Rd

Lindsay Rd

Woodbridge Rd

Beech Rd

SEWALL'S BRIDGE

York Harbor

Piscataqua R.

Maine Turnpike

Spruce Cr.

Exit 3

RACHEL CARSON NAT'L WILDLIFE REFUGE

Exit 2

Brave Boat Harbor

South Eliot

Exit 1

Kittery

Kittery Point

SEAPORT BEACH Cutts Island Ln

NEW HAMPSHIRE

PORTSMOUTH NAVY YARD

FT MC CRARY ST PARK

ATLANTIC OCEAN

Portsmouth

Seavey I.

FORT FOSTER

Chauncey Creek Rd

N

0   2 miles

0   2 kilometers

KITTERY AND THE YORKS

© The Countryman Press

KITTERY, ELIOT, SOUTH BERWICK, AND THE YORKS

The moment you cross the Piscataqua River you know you are in Maine. You have to go a long way Down East to find any deeper coves and rockier ocean paths than those in Kittery and York.

Both towns claim to be Maine's oldest community. Technically Kittery wins, but York looks older . . . depending, of course, on which Kittery and which York you are talking about.

Kittery Point, an 18th-century settlement overlooking Portsmouth Harbor, boasts Maine's oldest church and some of the state's finest mansions. The village of Kittery itself, however, has been shattered by so many bridges and rotaries that it initially seems to exist only as a gateway, on the one hand for workers at the Portsmouth Naval Shipyard and on the other for patrons of the outlet malls on Rt. 1. Look more closely, however, and you will discover rewarding shopping around downtown Waterman Square, as well as strolling and swimming spots along coastal Rt. 103.

In the late 19th century artists and literati gathered at Kittery Point. Novelist and *Atlantic Monthly* editor William Dean Howells, who summered here, became keenly interested in preserving the area's colonial-era buildings. Novelist Sarah Orne Jewett, a native of nearby South Berwick and a contributor to the *Atlantic*, spearheaded restoration of Hamilton House, one of the area's most magnificent 18th-century mansions. Friend Sam Clemens (otherwise known as Mark Twain), who summered in York, was involved in the effort to buy up that town's splendid old school, church, burial ground, and abundance of 1740s homes, recognizing York as Maine's oldest surviving community.

In 1896 Howells suggested turning the "old gaol" in York Village into a museum. At the time you could count the country's historic house museums on your fingers. In the Old Gaol of today you learn about the village's bizarre history, including its origins as a Native American settlement called Agamenticus, one of many wiped out by a plague in 1616. In 1630 it was settled by English colonists, and in 1642 it became Gorgeana, America's first chartered city. It was then demoted to the town of York, part of Massachusetts, in 1670. Fierce Native American raids followed, but by the middle of the 18th century the present colonial village was established, a crucial way station between Portsmouth and points east.

York is divided into so many distinct villages that Clemens once observed, "It is difficult to throw a brick . . . in any one direction without danger of disabling a postmaster." Not counting Scotland and York Corners, York includes York Village, York Harbor, York Beach, and Cape Neddick—such varied communities that locals can't bring themselves to speak of them as one town; they refer instead to "the Yorks."

The rocky shore beyond York Village was Lower Town until the Marshall House was opened near the small gray sand beach in 1871 and its address was changed to York Harbor. Soon the hotel had 300 rooms, and other mammoth frame hotels appeared at intervals along the shore. Now all the old hotels are gone. All, that is, except the 162-room Cliff House, which, although physically in York, has long since changed its address and phone to Ogunquit, better known these days as a resort town.

Still, York Harbor remains a delightful, low-key retreat. The Marshall House has been replaced by the modern Stage Neck Inn, and several dignified old summer "cottages" are now inns and B&Bs. A narrow, mile-or-so path along the shore was first traced by fishermen and later smoothed and graced with small touches such as the Wiggly Bridge, a graceful little suspension bridge across the river and through Steedman Woods.

Landscaping and public spaces were among the consuming interests of the 19th-century summer residents, who around the turn of the century also became interested in zoning. In *Trending into Maine* (1935) Kenneth Roberts noted York Harbor's "determination to be free of billboards, tourist camps, dance halls and other cheapening manifestations of the herd instinct and Vacationland civilization."

A York Harbor corporation was formed to impose its own taxes and keep out unwanted development. The corporation's biggest fight, wrote Roberts, was against the Libby Camps, a tent-and-trailer campground on the eastern edge of York Harbor that "had spread with such funguslike rapidity that York Harbor was in danger of being almost completely swamped by young ladies in shorts, young men in soiled undershirts, and fat ladies in knickerbockers."

Libby's Oceanside Camp still sits on Roaring Rock Point, its trailers neatly angled along the shore. Across from it is matching Camp Eaton, established in 1923. No other village boundary within a New England town remains more clearly defined than this one between York Harbor and York Beach.

Beyond the campgrounds stretches 2-mile Long Sands Beach, lined with a simpler breed of summer cottage than anything in York Village or York Harbor. There is a real charm to the strip and to the village of York Beach, with its Victorian-style shops, boardwalk amusements, and the Goldenrod—known for its taffy Goldenrod Kisses. This restaurant is still owned by the same family that opened it in 1896, about the time the electric streetcar put York Beach within reach of the "working class."

During this "trolley era" half a dozen big hotels accommodated 3,000 summer visitors, and 2,000 more patronized boardinghouses in York Beach. Today's lodgings are a mix of motels, cottages, and B&Bs. There are beaches (with metered parking), Fun-O-Rama games and bowling, and York's Wild Kingdom, with exotic animals and carnival rides. York Beach, too, has now gained "historic" status,

and the Old York Historical Society, keeper of the half-dozen colonial-era buildings open to the public in York Village, now sponsors York Beach walking tours.

GUIDANCE **The Maine Tourism Association's Kittery Information Center**
(207-439-1319), Maine's gatehouse in a real sense, is on I-95 northbound in Kittery, with exhibits on Maine regions and products and a staffed information desk
good for local as well as statewide advice on lodging, dining, and attractions. You
can also check out regional web sites and lodging by computer. Open daily
except Christmas and Thanksgiving, 8–6 in summer months, otherwise 9–5
(bathrooms open 24 hours daily). The rest area also includes vending machines
and picnic tables under the pines.

Greater York Region Chamber of Commerce (207-363-4422; via the Southern Maine link, 1-800-639-2442; www.gatewaytomaine.org), 1 Stonewall Lane,
York 03909. On Rt. 1 just off exit 7 northbound (York), this handsome information center (with restrooms) modeled on a Victorian summer "cottage" is open
year-round, high season daily 9–5, off-season Mon.–Fri. 9–4, Sat. 10–4.

At Sohier Park, overlooking Nubble Light on York Beach, a seasonal information
center with restrooms is open May–mid-Oct., 10 AM–sunset.

GETTING THERE York is off I-95 exit 7, the last exit before the Maine Turnpike
tolls. The nearest bus service is to Portsmouth, New Hampshire, and the nearest
train stop is Wells, Maine. For air service, see "Portland Area." For Kittery, take
exits 1, 2, and 3.

GETTING AROUND **York Trolley Company** (207-748-3030; www.yorktrolley
.com). Late June–Labor Day, trolleys circle all day along the beaches and around
The Nubble. Inquire about special narrated tours and service to the Kittery Outlet Malls. $5 all-day pass, $3 for ages 10 and under.

WHEN TO COME With the exception of York Beach, which is highly seasonal,
this area can be an appealing seaside getaway June through December. It's
packed on July and August weekends. Thanks to the sizable year-round population, most restaurants remain open year-round. The Kittery outlets and
Stonewall Kitchen draw holiday shoppers.

✳ To See

In Kittery
Kittery Historical and Naval Museum (207-439-3080), Rt. 1, just north of the
Rt. 236 rotary. Open June–Columbus Day, Tue.–Sat. 10–4, then Wed. and Sat.
until Dec. Inquire about open house during Christmas shopping season. $3
adults, $1.50 ages 7–15. A fine little museum filled with ships' models and exhibits
about the early history of this stretch of the Southern Coast. Displays include
archaeological finds, early shipbuilding tools, navigational instruments, and
mariner folk art, including samples of work by Kittery master ship's carver John
Haley Bellamy (1836–1914). The lens from Boon Island Light is also displayed.

FORT MCCLARY

Kim Grant

Fort McClary, Rt. 103. A state park open seasonally (grounds accessible year-round). A hexagonal 1846 blockhouse on a granite base, it was the site of fortifications in 1715, 1776, and 1808. A good place to picnic, this site was first fortified in the early 18th century to protect Massachusetts's vessels from being taxed by the New Hampshire colony.

For **Fort Foster**, see *Green Space*.

In York

First Parish Church, York Village. An outstanding, mid-18th-century meetinghouse with a fine cemetery full of old stones with death's heads and Old English spelling.

Civil War Monument, middle of York Village. Contrary to the local legend that this was a Civil War memorial meant for a town in the South (the uniform suggests a Confederate rather than Union soldier), it's intended to honor all the town's "fallen heroes." Admittedly it's confusing: This particular soldier is wearing a Spanish-American War uniform, but the only years chiseled into its base are 1861–65.

In York Harbor and York Beach

Sayward-Wheeler House (603-436-3205), 79 Barrell Lane, York Harbor. Open June–Oct., first Sat. of the month, 11–4; tours on the hour. $5 adults, $3 ages 6–12. Maintained by Historic New England (207-384-2454; www.historicnew england.org). A fine, early-18th-century house built by Jonathan Sayward—merchant, shipowner, judge, and representative to the Massachusetts General Court—who earned the respect of the community despite his Tory leanings. It remained in the same family for 200 years and retains its Queen Anne and Chippendale furnishings, family portraits, and china brought back as booty from the expedition against the French at Louisburg in 1745. Accessible from York's Fisherman's Path, near the Wiggly Bridge.

YORK HARBOR

Christina Tree

Note: Historic New England also maintains the magnificent **Hamilton House** and the **Sarah Orne Jewett House** in South Berwick, described in *Scenic Drives*.

Nubble Light, York Beach. From Rt. 1A (Long Beach Ave.), take Nubble Rd. out through The Nubble (a cottage-covered peninsula) to Sohier Park at the tip of the peninsula. The 1879 Cape Neddick Lighthouse Station

OLD YORK HISTORICAL SOCIETY

(207-363-4974; www.oldyork.org). The nonprofit group maintains seven historic buildings, open to the public mid-June–mid-Oct., Mon.–Sat. 10–5; $10 adults, $9 seniors, $5 ages 6–16, $20 per family includes admission to all buildings; $5 per adult, $4 per senior, $3 per child, $15 per family for individual buildings. It's best to pay the umbrella price and spend several hours wandering through the seven 18th-century buildings scattered through the village, but if time is limited, pick the "Old Gaol" with its dank and dismal

OL York Historical Society

PORTRAIT IN THE ELIZABETH PERKINS HOUSE, OLD YORK HISTORICAL SOCIETY

cells and stories of luckless patrons, many of them women. Many were hanged at the gallows on Stage Neck (site of the present hotel by that name). The jail dates in part to 1719 and is said to be the oldest public building surviving from the English colonies. Begin with the orientation film in the vintage-1759 Jefferds Tavern visitor center, corner of Lindsay Rd. and York St. Exhibits change, and food is frequently cooking on the hearth at the tavern kitchen. The Old School House next door, an original, mid-18th-century York school, contains an exhibit on education of the period. In the Emerson-Wilcox House on York St., dating to 1742, period rooms and gallery space trace the development of local decorative arts, featuring a complete set of bed hangings embroidered by Mary Bulman before 1745. The Elizabeth Perkins House, South Side Rd. (at Sewall Bridge), is our favorite building, a 1730 house by the York River. It is filled with colonial-era antiques and with the spirit of Elizabeth Perkins, the real powerhouse behind the original Society for the Preservation of Historic Landmarks in York County. Nearby at 140 Lindsay Rd. are the 18th-century John Hancock Warehouse and Wharf and George Marshall Store (a former chandlery at which large schooners once docked), with changing exhibits on 18th-century life and industry on and around the York River. Frequent tours are offered of the Ramsdell House, a 1730s farm laborer's home, a work in progress. The society also sponsors walking tours and special events and offers a local historical research library (open year-round) and archives in its headquarters, a former bank building at 207 York St. in the middle of York Village.

Kim Grant

NUBBLE LIGHT

(better known as "Nubble Light") is perched on a small island of its own—but that's all the better for taking pictures from the park, which offers parking and a seasonal information center with restrooms and a small gift shop.

✍ ☟ **York's Wild Kingdom** (207-363-4911; www.yorkzoo.com), York Beach. Rides open daily Memorial Day weekend–late Sep. In July and Aug. the zoo is open daily 10–6 and the amusement area, noon–9:30; varying hours in shoulder seasons. This is a combination amusement area and zoo with paddleboats, midway rides, and more than 200 animals, including some real exotica. There are also mini golf and both pony and elephant rides. It's $16.25 adults, $12.75 ages 4–10, and $3.50 ages 3 and under for zoo/ride admission; less for zoo only.

SCENIC DRIVES **Kittery Point**, **Pepperrell Cove**, and **Gerrish Island**. From Rt. 1, find your way to Rt. 103 and follow its twists and turns along the harbor until you come to the white **First Congregational Church** and a small green across from a striking, privately owned Georgian-style house. An old graveyard overlooking the harbor completes the scene. Park at the church (built in 1730, Maine's oldest), notice the parsonage (1729), and walk across the road to the old **graveyard**. The neighboring magnificent house was built in 1760 for the widow of Sir William Pepperrell, the French and Indian Wars hero who captured the fortress at Louisburg from the French. Knighted for his feat, Pepperrell went on to become the richest man in New England. For a splendid view of the harbor, continue along Rt. 103 to Fort McClary. **Frisbee's Market**, in business since 1828, claims to be America's oldest family-run grocery store (also known for its handmade corned beef). Four large hotels once clustered in this corner of Kittery, but today it's one of the quietest along the Southern Coast. At the back of the parking lot across from Frisbee's, a seemingly forgotten tomb is inscribed with a plaque commemorating Colonel William Pepperrell, born in Devonshire in 1646, died in Kittery in 1734, and Sir William Pepperrell (1696–1759). Just beyond you can still see the foundations of one of the former summer hotels. Turn right beyond Pepperrell Cove and follow Gerrish Island Lane to a T; then take Pocahontas (the name of another vanished hotel) to World War I–era **Fort Foster**, now a park. Also check out **Chauncey Creek Lobster Pound** and **Seapoint Beach**. Rt. 103 winds on by the mouth of the York River and into York Harbor.

South Berwick. A short ride north of the Rt. 1 outlets transports you to a bend in the Salmon Falls River that is capped by a splendid 1780s Georgian mansion, restored through the efforts of local author Sarah Orne Jewett; a

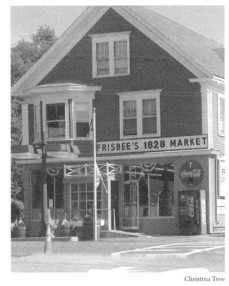

Christina Tree

FRISBEE'S 1828 MARKET

formal garden and riverside trails through the woods add to the unusual appeal of this place. From Kittery, take either Rt. 236 north from the I-95 Eliot exit or more rural Rt. 101 north from Rt. 1 at exit 3 (turn right at its junction with Rt. 236). From York, take Rt. 91 north. Hamilton House and **Vaughan Woods State Park** are the first left after the junction of Rts. 236 and 91 (Brattle St.); follow signs. **Hamilton House** is open June–Oct. 15, Wed.–Sun. 11–4, with tours on the hour ($8 adults, $7 seniors, $4 ages 5–12); grounds open every day dawn to dusk. Come at 4 PM on Sunday in July for picnic concerts in the restored flower gardens. The foursquare Georgian mansion built in 1785 on a promontory above the Salmon Falls River had fallen into disrepair by the time Sarah Orne Jewett (1849–1909) was growing up in nearby South Berwick; she used it as the setting for her novel *The Tory Lover* and persuaded wealthy Boston friends to restore it in 1898 (the same period that William Dean Howells was involved in restoring nearby York Village). Historic New England (207-384-2454; www.historicnewengland.org) also maintains the **Sarah Orne Jewett House** farther up Rt. 236, smack in the middle of the pleasant village of South Berwick at the junction with Rt. 4, open Fri.–Sun. 11–4, with tours on the hour. This is another fine 1774 Georgian house. Jewett, who is best known for her classic novel *The Country of the Pointed Firs*, actually grew up in the clapboard house next door, now the delightful town library. Here you learn that in the mid–19th

HAMILTON HOUSE

Christina Tree

century this picturesque village was home to extensive mills. A brick counting house by the Salmon Falls on Main St. (Rt. 4 at the bridge) houses the **Old Berwick Historical Society** (207-384-0000), open July 1–Oct. 1, weekends, sponsoring monthly lectures and events.

✳ To Do

BICYCLING **Mount Agamenticus** (see *Green Space*) is webbed with trails beloved by mountain bikers. **Berger's Bike Shop** (363-4070) in York Village rents mountain and hybrid bikes. Touring bikes—also motor scooters—can be rented from **Beached Wheels** (207-363-8021), 52 Main St. in York Beach. **Harbor Adventures** (207-363-8466), York Harbor, also offers mountain bike and coastal bike tours.

BOAT EXCURSIONS **Isles of Shoals Steamship Co.** (603-431-5500 or 1-800-441-4620; www.islesofshoals.com), Portsmouth, New Hampshire. Daily cruises in-season stop at Star Island, site of a vast old white summer hotel that's now a Unitarian conference center. Visitors are welcome to this barren but fascinating place, webbed with walking trails. The ride on the 90-foot replica of an old steamboat takes 1 hour each way.

FISHING Check with the Greater York Region Chamber of Commerce about the half-dozen deep-sea-fishing boats operating from York Harbor and Kittery. Surf casting is also popular along Long Sands and Short Sands Beaches and from Sohier Park in York. **Eldredge Bros. Fly Shop** (207-363-9269; www.eldredge flyshop.com), 1480 Rt. 1, Cape Neddick, is a full-service outfitter offering guided freshwater and saltwater trips.

FRIGHTS **Ghostly Tours** (207-363-0000; www.ghostlytours.com), 250 York St. (Rt. 1A), York Village. Late June–Halloween, Mon.–Sat. Candlelight tours through Old York Village guided by a hooded ghost-tale teller. $10 per person.

GOLF **The Ledges Golf Club** (207-351-3000; www.ledgesgolf.com), 1 Ledges Dr. (off Rt. 91), York. This is a destination course for much of southern Maine. Carts, pro shop, favored by local residents.

Cape Neddick Country Club (207-361-2011), Shore Rd., Cape Neddick. Designed in the early 1900s by Donald Ross, redesigned by Brian Silva in 1998, 18 holes, rolling fairways integrated with ledge outcroppings and wetlands. A pro shop and restaurant, **The Cape Neddick Grille** (207 361-2112).

The Links at Outlook (207-384-4653), Rt. 4, South Berwick. An 18-hole Scottish-style course and driving range.

HORSEBACK RIDING **Lightning C Ranch**, Bog Rd. (off Rt. 91), York. Open year-round for mellow trail rides, haunted hayrides in fall, country Christmas rides in December. Trails are through woods and meadows on private property.

SEA KAYAKING The tidal York River, stretches of the Piscataqua around and above Eliot, and the Salmon Falls River (accessible from Vaughan Woods State

Park in South Berwick) are particularly appealing to kayakers. **Harbor Adventures** (207-363-8466) in York Harbor and **Coastal Maine Excursions** (207-363-0181), based on Rt. 1, Cape Neddick, offer guided tours ranging from an hour to extended trips; Excursions and the **Eldredge Bros. Fly Shop** (see *Fishing*) both offer rentals.

SPAS The **Cliff House Resort & Spa** (207-361-1000, ext. SPA), Shore Rd., on the York–Ogunquit line. A variety of massage, face care, and body care services are offered and include use of the fully equipped fitness area as well as large indoor and outdoor pools. Exercise classes are also offered.

Portsmouth Harbor Inn & Spa (207-439-7060), 6 Water St., Kittery. Lacking the big pool and fitness room but otherwise a full-service spa housed in the attractive carriage house of this waterside inn.

SUMMER YOUTH PROGRAMS ♪ **York Parks & Recreation Department** (207-363-1040) offers summer baseball, basketball, mountain biking, and dance programs for younger children and teens. The office is in the Grant House, Goodrich Park, Rt. 1.

✳ Green Space
BEACHES

In Kittery
Seapoint Beach, Kittery, is long with silky soft sand. Parking is residents-only right at the sand, but there's limited public parking 0.5 mile back up Curtis Island Lane (off Rt. 103).

♪ **Fort Foster**, Gerrish Island, is shallow a long way out and also has low-tide tidal pools with crabs and snails.

In York
Long Sands is a 2-mile expanse of coarse gray sand stretching from York Harbor to The Nubble, backed by Rt. 1A and summer cottages, great for walking. Metered parking the length of the beach and a bathhouse midway. Lifeguard in high season.

♪ **Short Sands** is a shorter stretch of coarse gray sand with a bathhouse, parking lot (meters), and playground, just in front of the village of York Beach.

York Harbor Beach is small and pebbly, but pleasant. Very limited parking.

PARKS **Fort Foster Park**, Kittery. Beyond Pepperrell Cove, look for Gerrish Island Lane and turn right at the T onto Pocahontas Rd., which leads, eventually, to this 92-acre town park. The World War I fortifications are ugly, but there is a choice of small beaches with different exposures, one very popular with sailboarders; extensive walking trails and picnic facilities. Fee.

Piscataqua River Boat Basin (207-439-1813), Main St., Eliot. Open May–Oct. Boat launch, picnic area, beach, restrooms.

Mount Agamenticus (207-363-1040), York. Just 580 feet high but billed as the highest hill on the Atlantic seaboard between York and Florida. A defunct ski area now owned by the town of York, it can be reached by an access road from Mountain Rd. off Rt. 1 (turn at Flo's Hot Dogs). The summit is cluttered by satellite dishes and cell towers, but 8 miles of trails are set in pristine woods, with trail maps available at each trailhead. Spring and fall raptor migrations can be viewed from the summit.

Vaughan Woods State Park (207-384-5160), South Berwick. Seasonal. $2 ages 12 and above. Take Old Fields Rd. off Brattle St. A 250-acre preserve on the banks of the Salmon Falls River; picnic facilities and 3 miles of nature trails. The first cows in Maine are said to have been landed here at Cow Cove in 1634. See directions under South Berwick in *Scenic Drives*.

Sohier Park, Rt. 1A, York. See Nubble Light under *To See*. A popular picnic spot.

Goodrich Park, York. A good picnic spot on the banks of the York River, accessible from Rt. 1 south; look for the entrance just before the bridge.

Mason Park, Rt. 1A, York Harbor, adjoining Harbor Beach. Created in 1998 when several classic York Harbor cottages were destroyed in accordance with the wills of their former owners.

WALKS **Cliff Path** and **Fisherman's Walk**, York Harbor. For more than a mile, you can pick your way along the town's most pleasant piece of shorefront. Begin at the George Marshall Store and walk east along the river and through the shady Steedman Woods. Go across the Wiggly Bridge (a mini suspension bridge), then continue across Rt. 103, past the Sayward House, along the harbor, down the beach, and along the top of the rocks. Continue east from Mason Park above York Harbor Beach until the path ends at a private property line. This portion is a bit rough, and walkers are advised to keep to the path. Returning the way you've come is no hardship.

Brave Boat Harbor Trail, York. One of the few walkable segments in the 10-part Rachel Carson National Wildlife Refuge: A 2-mile trail begins at the pullout on Brave Boat Harbor Rd. off Rt. 103. It offers a little history and a lot of birds.

THE WIGGLY BRIDGE IN YORK

Kim Grant

✳ Lodging

Note: York Beach offers many **summer cottage rentals**, and rentals can also be found elsewhere in town. Check with the Greater York Chamber of Commerce for individual rentals as well as reliable Realtors. Also see www.seasiderentals.com.

INNS AND RESORTS *Note:* For details about the largest local resort, The Cliff House resort and spa, which sits on the Ogunquit–York line, see the "Ogunquit" chapter.

ω ✎ ⚬ **Dockside Guest Quarters** (207-363 2868 or 1-800-270-1977; www.docksidegq.com), P.O. Box 205, Harris Island Rd., York 03909. Open daily May–Oct., weekends the rest of the year. Situated on a peninsula in York Harbor, this family-run inn offers the best views of any lodging in town. The very best is from the porch of the gracious, 19th-century Maine House, which is the centerpiece of a 7-acre compound that includes four newer, multiunit cottages, plus the Dockside Restaurant (see *Dining Out*). In all there are 26 guest rooms—including several with gas fireplace and 6 apartment/suites with kitchenette—all with private deck and water views. Breakfast is served buffet-style in the Maine House, a morning gathering place for guests who check the blackboard weather forecast and plan their day. Guests can use the house fishing equipment, bicycles, rowing skiff, and Boston whaler. Two-night minimum stay during July and Aug. $155–215 in high season, $90–150 off-season; $180–249 for a suite with living room and kitchenette. Lunch and dinner are served in the Dockside Restaurant.

Stage Neck Inn (207-363-3850 or 1-800-222-3238), Stage Neck Rd., York Harbor 03911. Open year-round. An attractive 1970s complex of 58 rooms built on the site of the 19th-century Marshall House. Located on its own peninsula, the inn offers some water views, a formal dining room (see Harbor Porches in *Dining Out*), less formal **Sandpiper Grille**, tennis courts, an outdoor pool, a small indoor pool, and Jacuzzi; its grounds adjoin sandy Harbor Beach. $235–345 per room in-season, from $135 off-season, no meals included.

⚬ **York Harbor Inn** (207-363-5119 or 1-800-343-3869; www.yorkharbor inn.com), Box 573, York St., Rt. 1A, York Harbor 03911. Open year-round. The beamed lobby is said to have been built in 1637 on the Isles of Shoals. An exclusive men's club in the 19th century, this is now a popular dining spot (see *Dining Out*), and the Ship's Cellar Pub, with an elaborately carved bar, is a local gathering place. The 47 rooms all have a private bath and air-conditioning, several in the old house have a working fireplace, some in the Harbor Hill Inn have a Jacuzzi and sitting area, and most have water views. The neighboring **Harbor Cliffs Inn**, a former summer mansion, and 1730 **Harbor Crest** are now adjuncts to the inn proper with elegant common rooms and several suites. $139–349 double in high season, $99–329 off-season, continental breakfast included.

The Union Bluff (207-363-1333 or 1-800-833-0721; www.unionbluff .com), Beach St., P.O. Box 1860, York Beach 03910. Open year-round. First opened in 1868, this landmark has been recently renovated with rooms divided between the original and a 1980s wing. There's not much of a lobby, but the elevator accesses comfortable rooms with an ocean and beach view. All three meals are served, and there's a choice between the **Beach Street Grill** and an informal pub. $149–209 for ocean-view rooms mid-June–Labor Day, from $59 off-season; rates include golf privileges.

BED & BREAKFASTS

In York Harbor 03911
Inn at Tanglewood Hall (207-351-1075; www.tanglewoodhall.com), 611 York St., P.O. Box 490. Open

year-round. In this shingled 1880s summer mansion, onetime home of bandleader Tommy Dorsey, new owners Sue and Andy Wetzel now offer six nicely decorated and air-conditioned guest rooms, all with bed and private bath, three with gas fireplace or porch. We slept soundly in the ground-floor Billiard Room after lazing away a few hours on its private porch. Guests tend to mingle on the wraparound veranda, which overlooks the wooded garden. A full breakfast is served between 8 and 10 on the veranda or in the dining room, or brought to your room. Although the house has no water views, the most dramatic stretch of the Cliff Path is just down the road. $135-245; off-season rates available.

Edwards' Harborside Inn (207-363-3037; www.edwardsharborside.com), P.O. Box 866. Open year-round. Location! Location! Sited across from York Harbor Beach with a long wharf of its own, this solidly built summer mansion is owned by Jay Edwards, a third-generation innkeeper. Breakfast is served in one of the most pleasant rooms in the area: a sunporch with an unbeatable view of the harbor. Many of the 10 guest rooms (7 with private bath) also have water views, and all are air-conditioned and have TV and phone; the York Suite is a lulu, with water views on three sides and a Jacuzzi overlooking the water, too. Rooms are $180–200 and suites from $270 in July and Aug., $130–240 in shoulder months, $100–180 in winter. $50 per extra person.

& **Chapman Cottage** (207-363-2059 or 1-877-363-2059; www.chapman cottagebandb.com), 370 York St. Donna and Paul Archibald have transformed this three-story 1899 summer home into a luxurious B&B with seven guest rooms, complete with central air-conditioning and two suites with gas fireplace. There are gas fireplaces in the twin parlors and dining room, and a porch set high above the sloping lawn. The house commands distant water views, especially from our favorite third-floor rooms. Dinner is served by reservation offering a choice of entrées that usually includes an 8-ounce filet with béarnaise sauce and rack of lamb plus salad and dessert for $24.95. Full liquor license and respectable wine list. $125–250 per couple includes breakfast.

In York Beach 03910

☀ **The Katahdin Inn** (207-363-1824; in winter, 617-938-0335), 11 Ocean Ave. Extension. Open mid-May–Columbus Day weekend. "Bed and beach" is the way innkeeper Rae LeBlanc describes her pumpkin-colored 1890s guest house overlooking Short Sands Beach and the ocean. Eight of the 11 guest rooms have water views. Number 9 on the third floor is small and white with a window and skylight that seem to suspend it above the water. All rooms have a small fridge. From $85 (shared bath) to $105 for a large room, private bath; from $65 off-season. No breakfast, but morning tea and coffee are served.

Sand and Surf (207-363-2554 in-season; sand_and_surf@hotmail.com), 53 Ocean Ave. Extension. Open June–Labor Day, weekends from Memorial Day to Columbus Day weekends. The porch is what it's all about in this classic seaside lodging that's been welcoming guests for more than a century. There's a fireplace in the sitting room but no TV. The 11 rooms include a two-room suite; most have half baths. $60–142.

Candleshop Inn (207-363-4087; www.candleshopinn.com), 41 Freeman St., P.O. Box 1216. Open year-round. Barbara and Michael Sheff have transformed an old summer home into a tasteful, restful, and distinctive B&B. The 10 guest rooms offer a range of beds (from twin to king) and come with and without private bath; many have water views. Therapeutic massage and Reiki are offered; rates ($85–135 single, $95–145 double) include a full vegetarian breakfast. Children under age 5 stay free then $5 up until age 12, otherwise $15 per extra person. Inquire about off-season yoga and pampering weekends or creating your own group retreat.

In York 03909

The Apple Blossom Bed & Breakfast (207-351-1727; www.apple blossombandb.com), 25 Brixham Rd., is actually minutes away from High Meadows (see below) in a rural corner of York that was, until recently, all farms and orchards. Bob and Mary Lou Erickson's rambling white farmhouse dates in part to 1717 and is set on 11 pristine acres. The six guest rooms are divided between the second and third floors and offer a choice of queens and twins, all with private bath, cable TV, and air-conditioning, and nicely furnished with antiques. There's a swimming pool. $125–130 includes a full breakfast served in the dining room or on the screened porch.

In Kittery, Eliot, and South Berwick

The Portsmouth Harbor Inn and Spa (207-439-4040; www.innat portsmouth.com), 6 Water St., Kittery 03904. Open year-round. Nathaniel and Lynn Bowditch are the innkeepers at this 1890s brick village hide-

away just off the Kittery green, across the road from the Piscataqua River, within walking distance (across the bridge) of downtown Portsmouth, New Hampshire. Common rooms are cheerful and spacious, and the six guest rooms are smallish but carefully, imaginatively furnished; all have private bath (some with claw-foot tub), air-conditioning, ceiling fan, phone with dataport, and cable TV/VCR (there's an extensive video library). Nat, for many years one of Maine's top tourism officers, is your enthusiastic breakfast chef, while Lynn, a lawyer in a previous life, supervises staff in the full-service spa, housed in the carriage house. $145–210 in-season includes a full breakfast. From $110 off-season.

High Meadows Bed & Breakfast (207-439-0590; www.highmeadows bnb.com), Rt. 101, Eliot 03903. Technically in Eliot, this pleasant retreat is just a few miles off Rt. 1. Open Apr.–Oct. Elaine Michaud has been sharing her handsome 1736 house with guests for more than 20 years. There are four spacious, gracious guest rooms, some with queen, others with twin beds; all have exposed beams, original paneling, and private bath and are furnished in authentic antiques. There's a comfortable common room with a woodstove, a formal living room with a fireplace, and a wicker-furnished porch. Walking trails lead through the surrounding 30 acres. No children under 12. Rooms are $90, less off-season, full breakfast and afternoon snack included.

The Academy Street Inn (207-384-5633), 15 Academy St., South Berwick 03908. We highly recommend this 1903 mansion, just off the main drag in the attractive village that's home to Maine's oldest private school and to the several historic houses associated with the author Sarah Orne Jewett (1849–1909). Paul and Lee Fopeano have the right touch both in decorating and in helping orient guests. The twin parlors are richly paneled, with carved mantels and crystal chandeliers. There are five spacious guest rooms with private bath; a full breakfast is served at the dining room table or on the large porch. Early coffee is set out upstairs, within easy reach of guest rooms. $75–85.

In Cape Neddick 03902
Cape Neddick House (207-363-2500; www.capeneddickhouse.com), 1300 Rt. 1, P.O. Box 70. Open year-round. Although it's right on Rt. 1, Dianne Goodwin's Victorian house (in the Goodwin family for more than 100 years) offers an away-from-it-all feel and genuine hospitality. There are four guest rooms with private bath, plus one suite with a working fireplace, all furnished with antiques. Breakfast—maybe strawberry scones and ham with apple biscuits—is served on the back deck (overlooking garden and woods), in the dining room, or in the homey kitchen. A six-course dinner—from stuffed mushrooms to raspberry cheesecake, all cooked on the 80-year-old Glenwood woodstove—can be reserved in advance. Weekend cooking classes are also offered. $100–155 double, depending on room and season.

OTHER LODGING ♿ **View Point** (207-363-2661; www.viewpointhotel.com), 229 Nubble Rd., P.O. Box 1980, York Beach 03910. Office open daily in summer, selected days off-season. A nicely designed, oceanfront, condominium-style complex overlooking

The Nubble Lighthouse. All nine suites have a living room, kitchen, porch or patio, gas fireplace, phone, cable TV, CD stereo, VCR, washer-dryer. From $195 for one-bedroom to $500 for three-bedroom units. Weekly rates.

♪ ♿ **The Anchorage Inn** (207-363-5112; www.anchorageinn.com), Rt. 1A, Long Beach Ave., York Beach 03910. A total of 179 motel-style rooms, most with water views across from Long Sands Beach. For families, this is a good choice; facilities include indoor and outdoor pools, rooms that sleep four, TV, small fridge. In high season $159–360 (for a four-person spa suite) and in low season $61–282; inquire about packages.

🐾 ♥ **Country View Motel & Guesthouse** (207-363-7160 or 1-800-258-6598; www.countryviewmotel.com), 1521 Rt. 1, Cape Neddick 03902. Open year-round. True to its name, this complex faces one of the few remaining meadows on this stretch of Rt. 1, an anomaly like this big old house. Margaret Bowden offers six rooms with private bath ($98 in-season with continental breakfast) in the house itself and 16 units in the two-story motel (beyond the swimming pool), varying from standard units (with direct-dial phone, cable TV, and air-conditioning) to a two-story apartment ($89–215 in-season). Pets are $10 each per night with the proviso they not be left alone.

✳ Where to Eat

DINING OUT **Arrows** (207-361-1100; www.arrowsrestaurant.com), Berwick Rd., Cape Neddick. Dinner 6–9, late Apr.–Oct. Reservations recommended. Considered one of the best—and most expensive—restaurants in

Maine, with an emphasis on its own garden's ingredients. For a complete review, see "Ogunquit and Wells."

Clay Hill Farm (207-361-2272; www .clayhillfarm.com), 220 Clay Hill Rd., Cape Neddick. Open year-round for dinner but closed Mon. and Tue. in winter. Reservations suggested. A gracious old farmhouse set in landscaped gardens halfway up Mount Agamenticus, with valet parking and an elegant decor; geared to functions. The menu includes veal saltimbocca and roast half duckling. Entrées $18–26.

Dockside Restaurant (207-363-2722), Harris Island Rd. off Rt. 103, York Harbor. Open for lunch and dinner late May–Columbus Day (except Mon.). Reservations suggested for dinner. Docking as well as parking. The view of yacht-filled York Harbor from Phil and Anne Lusty's glass-walled dining room and screened porch is hard to beat. At lunch try the Maine crabcakes or chicken potpie; at dinner the specialties are seafood and roast stuffed duckling, but you can also get grilled eggplant. Children get a "Dockside Vacation" coloring book to use while waiting. Dinner entrées $15.95–26.95.

Cap'n Simeon's Galley (207-439-3655), Rt. 103, Pepperrell Cove, Kittery Point. Open year-round for lunch and dinner and Sunday brunch; closed Mon.–Wed. off-season. A special place with a water view. You enter through the original Frisbee's Store (the building is said to date back to 1680, the store to 1828). The dining area picture windows overlook the cove and beyond to Portsmouth Harbor. Seafood is the specialty and the chowder is good, but you can also just have a grilled cheese sandwich. All seafood is fried in 100 percent vegetable oil. The all-day menu ranges from burgers to $27.95 for a quart of fried oysters.

The York Harbor Inn (207-363-5119), Rt. 1A, York Harbor. Open year-round for dinner and Sunday brunch. Four pleasant dining rooms, most with views of water. The menu is large. The seafood chowder is studded with shrimp, scallops, crabmeat, and haddock ($6.95 a cup); fresh seafood is the specialty. Dinner entrées might include Yorkshire lobster supreme (lobster stuffed with a scallop-and-shrimp filling, $28.95) and lobster-stuffed breast of chicken ($26.95). The less formal downstairs **Ship's Cellar Pub** (open 4–11 PM) offers chowders, burgers, sandwiches, and salads but also New York sirloin and pan-roasted swordfish.

Harbor Porches (207-363-3850), Stage Neck Rd., York Harbor. Open year-round for breakfast, lunch, dinner, and Sunday brunch. The Gilded Era decor evokes the glory days of the Marshall House, a grand hotel that occupied this site for many decades, and the glass walls overlook the open ocean. The menu ranges from a vegetarian selection—maybe potato artichoke gratinée, grilled marinated vegetables, or tomato and fava bean ragout ($19)—to char-grilled sirloin ($27) and includes several seafood choices.

J. Ellen's Café & Wine Bar (207-363-3751), Meadowbrook Plaza, Rt. 1, York (north of the chamber of commerce). Open Tue.–Sat. for lunch and dinner in-season, less frequently off-season. The shopping mall location is a turn-off, but there's plenty of atmosphere inside. Lunch on shredded duck and mixed greens with goat cheese and dried cranberries, and dine on a vegetable sauté or organic filet mignon with peppercorns and roasted garlic ($15.50–27.50).

Mimmo's (207-363-3807), Rt. 1A, Long Sands, York Beach. Open nightly for dinner June–mid-Oct.; Wed.–Sun. off-season. Named for its colorful chef Mimmo Basileo, this trattoria is a hot spot in summer (reservations necessary). Tables are closely packed, the water view is limited, and the menu includes a variety of pastas as well as seafood. Entrées $17.95–19.95; BYOB.

Frankie & Johnny's Natural Foods (207-363-1909), 1594 Rt. 1, Cape Neddick. Open for dinner Wed.–Sun. in July and Aug., Thu.–Sun. in spring and fall. No credit cards. BYOB. This colorful place offers vegan and vegetarian dishes but also plenty of seafood and meat. It can hit the spot if you're in the mood for a blackened fish salad, toasted peppercorn-seared sushi-grade tuna on gingered vegetables, or homemade "harvest" pasta. Daily specials. Entrées $16.75–26.75.

Talpey's Tavern (207-351-1145), 1233 Rt. 1, Cape Neddick. Open for dinner from 4 PM (except Tue.). The specialty is quality, hand-cut steak, aged a minimum of 28 days. Limited options include a vegetarian hot plate and Maine lobster pie. Entrées $12.99–22.95.

LOBSTER **Cape Neddick Lobster Pound** (207-363-5471; www.cape neddick.com), Rt. 1A (Shore Rd.), Cape Neddick. Open Mar.–Nov. for lunch and dinner; come early in August or be prepared to wait. Sited by a tidal river, this attractive building with dining inside and on a deck is a local favorite. Besides lobster and clams, the menu offers a wide choice, from vegetable stir-fry, soups, and sal-

ads to filet mignon and bouillabaisse. Dinner entrées $11.95–23.95. Fully licensed.

Chauncey Creek Lobster Pound (207-439-1030), 16 Chauncey Creek Rd., Kittery Point. Open daily 11–8 in summer, weekends in Oct. Owned by the Spinney family since the 1950s, specializing in reasonably priced lobster dinners with steamers, served on picnic tables right on a pier on a tidal river walled by pine trees. Also available: lobster in rolls and in the rough, mussels, chowders, baked beans, a chicken dinner, pizza, and a raw bar. Coleslaw, corn, baked beans, and even popcorn shrimp and individual pizzas are also available. On summer weekends expect a wait. BYOB.

❧ **The Lobster Barn** (207-363-4721; www.thelobsterbarn.com), Rt. 1, York. Open year-round for lunch and dinner. A pubby, informal, popular dining room with wooden booths and a full menu. Try the scallop-and-shrimp pie. In summer lobster dinners (in the rough) are served under a tent out back. Entrées include a range of seafood and meat, all with an endless salad bar and fresh-made bread. Children's menu.

Warren's Lobster House (207-439-1630), 1 Water St., Kittery. Open year-round for lunch, dinner, and Sunday brunch; docking facilities. The rambling, knotty-pine dining room overlooks the Piscataqua River and Portsmouth, New Hampshire, beyond; a dining landmark with 1940s decor. The salad bar, with more than 50 selections, is a meal in itself. The specialty is "Lobster, Lobster, and More Lobster." The menu is, however, large and includes several beef dishes and plenty of seafood. Entrées $11.99–16.99.

Fox's Lobster House (207-363-2643), Nubble Point, York Beach. Open daily in-season 11:45–9. A large, tourist-geared place with a water view near The Nubble and a menu ranging from fried clam rolls to a full shore dinner: a 1.5-pound lobster, chowder, steamers, fries, and salad ($29.95).

Foster's Downeast Clambake (207-263-3255 or 1-800-552-0242; www .fostersclambake.com), P.O. Box 486, York Harbor 03991. This is all about lobster bakes for groups, at their place or yours, anywhere in the world (including the White House).

EATING OUT

Along Rt. 1 in Kittery and York (south to north)

Beach Pea Baking Co. (207-439-555), 59 State Rd. (Rt. 1 south), Kittery, south of the exit 2 Kittery traffic circle. Open Tue.–Sat., 7:30–6. Beloved by local residents for its artisan breads—from roasted garlic boules through country French and baguettes to focaccia—and for fabulous cakes, this is also a lunch find with standout sandwiches like marinated steak with Monterey Jack cheese on garlic bread. Many toppings and spreads; limited seating. The aromas alone are worth a stop.

Bob's Clam Hut (207-439-4233; www.bobsclamhut.com), Rt. 1 south, next to the Kittery Trading Post, Kittery. Open daily year-round, 11–9. Here since 1956 and definitely the best fried clams on the strip—some say the entire coast. The menu includes all the usual fried (using "cholesterol-free oil") seafood plus burgers and sandwiches. Order at the takeout and look for seating either inside or at the picnic tables around back.

Christina Tree

BOB'S CLAM HUT IN KITTERY

Stonewall Kitchen Café (207-351-2719), Rt. 1, just off I-95 exit 7 beside the chamber of commerce, York. Open daily for breakfast and lunch, also for Sunday brunch. At the Stonewall Kitchen flagship store (see *Selective Shopping*) you can order soup, salad, or sandwiches from the deli as takeout, or take your plate to a stand-up table or (weather permitting) outside café table. The "bistro dining menu" is, however, available only in the sit-down (inside) corner of the café. Try the pan-seared Maine crabcakes served with spicy corn sauce. Options might include a duck confit salad and a lobster BLT. Beer and wine served.

✍ **Wild Willy's Burgers** (207-363-9924), 765 Rt. 1, York. Daily (except Sun.) 11–7:30. This wildly popular family eatery features 100 percent certified Angus ground chuck hand shaped daily into burgers, topped with more combinations than you thought possible, and served with "country fair" fries.

Flo's Hot Dogs, Rt. 1 north, Cape Neddick. Open only 11–3 and not a minute later. The steamers are bargain priced, but that doesn't explain the long lines, and it's not Flo who draws the crowds because Flo has passed away. This is just a great place. It's even fun to stand in line here. Request the special sauce.

In York Village

🌸 **Carla's Bakery & Café** (207-363-4637), 241 York St. Open weekdays 6:30 AM–3 PM, Sat. 7 AM–noon. Even a write-up in *Gourmet* hasn't spoiled this genuine find: soups, salads, and sandwiches made with fresh ingredients from the local food co-op and suppliers. Launched by the popularity of her almond scones, Carla has honed her skills at culinary school. The breakfast menu includes eggs Benedict and Florentine as well as homemade corned beef hash and home fries. Luncheon options usually include delectable quiches and salads, sandwiches with roasted vegetables and homemade Boursin, as well as hand-cut chicken salad. Also try the daily-made coffee cakes and outrageous key lime squares as well as scones and muffins, and espresso, a choice of coffees, and (in summer) brewed iced teas.

CARLA'S BAKERY & CAFÉ

Christina Tree

🌸 🍴 **Fazio's** (207-363-7019; www .fazios.com), 38 Woodbridge Rd. Open daily for dinner from 4 PM. Locals give us mixed reviews. The decor is colorful and the menu, traditional, with pasta made daily; *bistecca* is the signature dish. Daily specials and children's menu. The La Stalla Pizzeria side of the place is a source of pizzas, subs, and salads, from 11 AM.

Rick's All Seasons Restaurant (207-363-5584), 240 R York St. Open daily from 4 AM for breakfast until 2 PM weekdays, closing earlier on weekends; for dinner only Wed. and Thu., until 8 PM. A reasonably priced local hangout; specialties include omelets, quiche, corned beef hash, and hot apple pie with cheese.

In York Harbor

🍴 **Lobster Cove** (207-351-1100), 756 York St. Open for breakfast through dinner. Just west of Long Sands Beach with an upstairs deck and water views. The Talpey family, owners of the Goldenrod, have created this moderately priced eatery. No surprises, but a good dinner bet for broiled haddock or baked stuffed shrimp. Burgers all day plus a children's menu.

In York Beach

York Beach Fish Market (207-363-2763), Railroad St. Billed as and generally agreed to be the best lobster rolls in York Beach. Eat in booths or walk to the beach to enjoy. Crab rolls, chowder, hot dogs, and more.

Sun n' Surf Restaurant (207-363-2961), Long Beach Ave. (Rt. 1A). Open for all three meals. Still owned by the family who opened a snack bar on this prime spot on Long Sands Beach in 1963, it's now a popular full-service restaurant.

🦞 🖋 **The Goldenrod** (207-363-2621; www.thegoldenrod.com), Rt. 1A. Open Memorial Day–Labor Day for breakfast, lunch, and dinner. Still owned by the Talpey family, who first opened for business here in 1896—just in time to serve the first electric trolleys rolling into York Beach from Portsmouth and Kittery. One of the best family restaurants in New England; same menu all day 8 AM–10:30 PM, but lunch and dinner specials are served up at time-polished, wooden tables in the big dining room with a fieldstone fireplace as well as at the old-style soda fountain. Their famous Goldenrod Kisses (saltwater taffy) are cooked and pulled in the windows. A wide selection of homemade ice creams and yogurts, good sandwiches. (Where else can you still get a cream cheese and olives or nuts sandwich? And for $3.55?)

Elsewhere
Crooked Lane Café (207-439-2244), 70 Wallingford Square, Kittery. Open daily (except Mon.), 6–5 Tue.–Wed., until 8 every other day except Sun., when it's 7–3. A brick-walled, storefront eatery in downtown Kittery. Good for "concoct-your-own" sandwiches, good salads, wine, and cheese.

🖋 **Fogarty's Restaurant and Bakery** (207-384-8361), South Berwick Village. Open daily 11–8:30, until 9 Sat. Big, casual, and friendly, a local institution with sandwiches, salads, and burgers served for dinner along with Yankee pot roast, tenderloin tips, and ham steak, all at amazingly digestible prices. Indian pudding and Aunt Pat's pies for dessert. Children's menu.

🖋 **Muddy River Marketplace** (207-748-3400; www.muddyriver.com), junction of Rts. 236 and 101, Eliot.

Open daily for lunch and dinner. While there's more on the menu, this is all about barbecue: pulled pork, baby backs, beef brisket, and smoked pulled chicken. An offshoot of the Portsmouth eatery with pleasant eat-in space as well as picnic tables. Children's menu.

SNACKS, TREATS, AND TAKE-HOME
Brown's Ice Cream (207-363-4077), Nubble Rd., 0.25 mile beyond the lighthouse, York Beach. Seasonal. All ice cream is made on the premises. Exotic flavors, generous portions.

Pie in the Sky Bakery (207-363-2656), Rt. 1, Cape Neddick. Open Thu.–Mon. except Jan.; hours vary off-season. The purple house at the corner of River Rd. is filled with delicious smells and irresistible muffins, pies, and scones baked here by John and Nancy Stern.

Cacao Chocolates (207-438-9001), 64 Government St. in downtown Kittery. Open noon–4, Sat. 10–4; closed Sun., Mon., and the month of Aug. Susan Tuveson and Greta Evans make amazing chocolates. Truffles and caramels are made by hand in small batches using fresh dairy cream, butter, and pure, natural flavorings, some of them surprising—like fine teas, chiles, and cheese. We were skeptical about a goat cheese and cognac truffle. Tasting was bliss.

Terra Cotta Pasta Company (207-375-3025), Rt. 1 north, below the Kittery traffic circle. Open Mon.–Sat. 9–6. Freshly made parsley and garlic linguine and wild mushroom lasagna are a sampling of what's offered, along with dozens of full-bodied sauces. It's also a good spot to pick up a sandwich for a picnic at nearby Fort McClary.

Food & Co. (207-363-0900; www .foodnco.com), 1 York St., York. Open Mon.–Sat. 8–6. A sleek gourmet market and café featuring artisan cheeses, small-producer wines, deli items, take-home dishes, and "handcrafted" sandwiches.

✳ Entertainment

Ogunquit Playhouse (see *To See* in "Ogunquit and Wells") is the nearest and most famous summer theater. Special children's presentations.

Hackmatack Playhouse (207-698-1807), in Berwick, presents summerstock performances most evenings; Thursday matinees.

Seacoast Repertory Theatre (603-433-4472 or 1-800-639-7650), 125 Bow St., Portsmouth, New Hampshire. Professional theater productions.

✳ Selective Shopping

ANTIQUES Half a dozen antiques dealers can be found along Rt. 1 between **Bell Farm Antiques** in York and **Columbary Antiques** (group shop) in Cape Neddick. Stop in one and pick up the leaflet guide to the couple of dozen member shops between York and Arundel.

TJ's (207-363-5673), 1287 Rt. 1, Cape Neddick. In a class of its own. All reproduction antiques, including fine arts and fabrics. Operated by interior designers Jerry Rippletoe and Tony Sienicki.

ART GALLERIES **York Art Association Gallery** (207-363-4049 or 207-363-2918), Rt. 1A, York Harbor. Annual July art show, films, and workshops.

George Marshall Store Gallery, 140 Lindsay Rd., York. Open mid-June–mid-Oct., Thu. 11–4, Sun. 1–4. Housed in an 18th-century store maintained by the Old York Historical Society. Exhibits feature regional contemporary art and fine crafts. Free.

Kittery Art Association (207-451-9384; www.kitteryart.org), Coleman Ave., Kittery Point. Open seasonally Thu. 3–6, Sat. noon–6, Sun. noon–5. Housed in a former firehouse marked (and just off) Rt. 103, changing shows by member artists.

CRAFTS **York River Place** (207-351-3266), 250 York St., York Village, features fine crafted pottery, prints, ceramics, jewelry, and clothing; also books, cards, and games.

Village Marketplace (207-363-7616), 211 York St. (Rt. 1A), York Village. Open mid-Apr.–Dec. 24, daily 9:30–5:30, Fri. until 8. Housed in the vintage 1834 "Olde Church" in the center of York Village: locally crafted toys, needlework, baskets, jellies, and much more.

SPECIAL STORES **Kittery Trading Post** (207-439-2700; www.kittery tradingpost.com), Rt. 1, Kittery. A local institution since 1926, the sprawling store completed a major expansion in 2004 and is always jammed with shoppers in search of quality sportswear, shoes, children's clothing, firearms, outdoor books, and fishing or camping gear. The summerend sales are legendary, and many items are routinely discounted, but this is not an outlet store.

In York

Stonewall Kitchen (207-352-2713 or 1-800-207-JAMS; www.stonewall kitchen.com), Stonewall Lane, Rt. 1, beside the chamber of commerce, York. Open May–Dec., 8–8; check in the off-season. What began as a display of offbeat vinegars at a local farmer's market in 1991 is now a mega specialty food business with a big wholesale and mail-order component. Owners Jonathan King and Jim Stott are quick to claim, however, that all their products—from roasted garlic and onion red pepper jelly or raspberry peach champagne jam through sun-dried tomato mustard to fresh lemon curd and dozens of vinegars, chutneys, and barbecue sauces— are still made with homemade care. You can sample them in the open-kitchen-style shop, and find kitchen and other home furnishings and a café (see *Eating Out*).

Old York Historical Society Museum Shop, 196 York St. (Rt. 1A), York Village. Open May–Dec., Mon.–Sat. 10–5. Some great gifts, cards, books.

Gravestone Artwear (1-800-564-4310), 250 York St., York Village. Open weekdays, 10:30–4. This departure point for Ghostly Tours is a trove of ghostly and graveyard-related products, from carvings to cards, T-shirts, and more.

Rocky Mountain Quilts (207-363-6800 or 1-800-762-5940), 130 York St. (Rt. 1A), York Village. Open May–Oct., daily 10–5; call off-season. Betsey Telford not only makes and restores quilts but also sells antique quilts (more than 300 in stock, "from doll to king"), blocks, and fabrics from the late 1700s to the 1940s; decorating accessories as well.

Knight's (207-361-2500; www.maine quiltshop.com), 1901 Rt. 1, Cape Neddick. A wide choice of bright fabric, quilt supplies, and small quilted gifts (but no quilts) are sold here. Inquire about quilting classes.

When Pigs Fly (207-363-0612; www .sendbread.com), 40 Brickyard Court, York. A bit difficult to find (1 mile south of the York exit off I-95; take a right and follow your nose), this is the visitor-friendly bakery for these widely distributed, all-natural breads.

Woods to Goods (207-363-6001; www.woodstogoods.com), 891 Rt. 1, York. Open daily 10–6; 10–5 off-season. Not all but many of the lamps, ships' models, and other decorative items in this roadside shop are made by inmates of Maine prisons. The "Prison Blues" T-shirts and sweatshirts with the catchy line MADE ON THE INSIDE TO BE WORN ON THE OUTSIDE are produced by Oregon inmates.

In Kittery

The antithesis of the mammoth Trading Post and outlet malls on Rt. 1 north of the I-95 exit 2 traffic circle, half a dozen distinctive owner-operated shops have recently opened south of the circle and in downtown Kittery. See Cacao Chocolates, Beach Pea Baking Co., Terra Cotta, and Crooked Lane Café under *Where to Eat*. **Papers, Ink!** (207-439-1955), 64 Wallingford Square, is part of this renaissance, selling cards, stationery, and fun things.

OUTLET MALLS **Kittery Outlets** (1-888-KITTERY; www.thekitteryoutlets .com). Open daily year-round, May–Jan. 1, Mon.–Sat. 9–8, Sun. 10–6; off-season Sun.–Thu. 10–6, weekends 10–8. Take I-95, exit 3. At this writing more than 100 discount stores within a 1.3-mile strip of Rt. 1 in Kittery represent a mix of clothing, household furnishings, gifts, and basics. All purport to offer savings of at least 20 percent on retail prices, many up to 70 percent.

✳ Special Events

Note: Be sure to pick up the area's unusually lively *Calendar of Events* at the Greater York Region Chamber of Commerce (see *Guidance*).

June: **Strawberry Festival**, South Berwick.

July: **Ellis Park Concerts** almost nightly, and **band concerts** Wednesday evening at Short Sands Pavilion, York Beach. **York Days Celebration** (*last days of the month*)—flower show, church supper, concerts, square dances, parade, and sand-castle contest.

Late August: **Seacoast Crafts Fair**.

Late September: **House Tours**. **Eliot Festival Days**.

October: **Harvestfest** (*the weekend after Columbus Day weekend, usually coinciding with peak foliage here*), York Village—an ox roast, oxcart races, hay- and horse rides, music, and live entertainment.

Sunday of Thanksgiving weekend: **Lighting of The Nubble**, Sohier Park, 5:45–7, with a shuttle bus from Ellis Park (207-363-1040). The famous lighthouse is illuminated in sparkling white lights for the Christmas season.

December: **Christmas Open House Tours**. **Kittery Christmas Parade and Tree Lighting** and **York Festival of Lights Parade** (*first weekend of the month*).

OGUNQUIT AND WELLS

O gunquit and Wells share many miles of uninterrupted sand, and the line between the two towns also blurs along Rt. 1, a stretch of restaurants, family attractions, and family-geared lodging places. The two beach resorts are, however, very different.

Named for the English cathedral town, Wells was incorporated in 1653 and remains a year-round community of 10,000 with seasonal cottages, condo complexes, and campgrounds strung along the beach and Rt. 1—parallel strips separated by a mile-wide swatch of salt marsh. Wells is a resort for families, the place to find a reasonably priced weekly rental.

Ogunquit was part of Wells until 1980 but seceded in spirit long before that, establishing itself as a summer resort in the 1880s and a magnet for artists in the 1890s through the 1940s. It remains a compact, walk-around resort village clustered between its magnificent beach and picturesque Perkins Cove; these two venues are connected by the mile-long Marginal Way, an exceptional shore path. The village offers a vintage movie house and the Ogunquit Playhouse, one of New England's most famous summer theaters. Most of Ogunquit's big old wooden hotels were razed during the 1960s and replaced by motor inns.

With the 1980s came condos, B&Bs, more restaurants, and boutiques. Luckily, the decade also brought trolleys-on-wheels to ease traffic at Perkins Cove and the beach. With a year-round population of 1,200 and 2,500 rooms for rent, Ogunquit regularly draws 35,000 on a summer weekend, 45,000 on holiday weekends year round. A reservation on summer weekends, or even on a weekday in August, is wise—but call the Ogunquit Chamber (listed below) for help if you are without one, and they can usually help. Our favorite time here is September and October.

GUIDANCE **Ogunquit Chamber of Commerce** (207-646-2939; www.ogunquit .org), P.O. Box 2289, Rt. 1, Ogunquit 03907 (beside the Ogunquit Playhouse). Open year-round, Mon.–Sat. 9–5; until 8 on Fri. and 6 on Sat. in July and Aug. Staff are helpful, and this large visitor center is well stocked with pamphlets and offers restrooms.

Wells Chamber of Commerce (207-646-2451 or 1-800-639-2442; www.wells chamber.org), 136 Post Rd. (Rt. 1, northbound side) in Moody. Open mid-May– Columbus Day, daily 9–5; weekdays and some Saturdays the rest of the year.

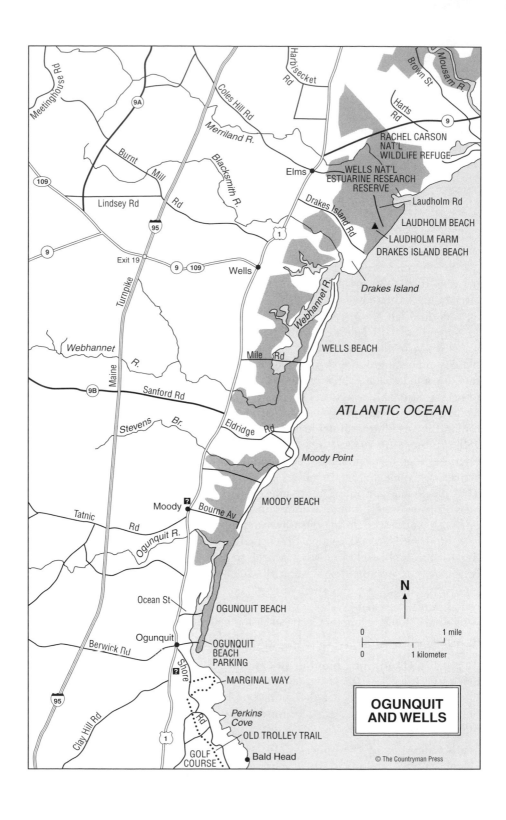

OGUNQUIT
AND WELLS

© The Countryman Press

GETTING THERE *By car:* Coming north on I-95, take exit 7 (York) and drive up Rt. 1 to the village of Ogunquit. Coming south on the Maine Turnpike/I-95, take turnpike exit 19 (Wells).

By train: The **Downeaster**, Amtrak's restored Boston–Portland service, makes five round-trips daily, year-round. The Wells Transportation Center stop is at 696 Sanford Rd. (Rt. 109) at the exit 2 tollbooth of the Maine Turnpike (I-95).

Brewster's Taxi (207-646-2141), billed as serving Ogunquit since 1898, offers local and long-distance service.

Front Line Taxi (207-646-7766 or 1-866-490-1214) is on call 24 hours, year-round.

GETTING AROUND Mid-May–Columbus Day **open-sided trolleys** circle through the village of Ogunquit, Perkins Cove, and out Rt. 1 in Wells, stopping at the main entrance to Ogunquit Beach and at Footbridge Beach. Fare is nominal. Trolley stops are mapped, and maps are available from the chambers of commerce.

PARKING Park and walk or take the trolley. In summer this is no place to drive. There are at least seven public lots; rates are $12–15 per day. There is also free parking (1-hour limit) on Rt. 1 across from the Leavitt Theatre just north of Ogunquit Square or adjacent to Cumberland Farms. Parking at the main entrance to Ogunquit Beach is $4 per hour ($12–15 per day at the other entrances). In Wells parking at the five public lots is $6 per day; monthly permits are available from the town office. Perkins Cove parking has a minimum charge of $3 for an hour, with a 2-hour maximum.

PUBLIC RESTROOMS *In Ogunquit:* At Footbridge Beach, Main Beach, Perkins Cove, Jacob's Lot, the Dunaway Center, and the information center.
In Wells: At the jetty, Wells Harbor Pier, Wells Beach, and Drakes Island parking areas.

WHEN TO COME Ogunquit shuts down in winter, with most of its restaurants closed and even the best operating on a shortened schedule. Wells, too, slows to a crawl. But since the height of summer is so busy in both places, visiting in September or June makes for a more leisurely experience.

✳ To See

Perkins Cove, Ogunquit. This is probably Maine's most painted fishing cove, with some 40 restaurants and shops now housed in weathered fish shacks. It is the departure point for the area's excursion and fishing boats, based beside the famous draw-footbridge. Parking is nearly impossible in summer, but public lots are nearby, and the trolley stops here regularly. The cove can also be reached on foot via the Marginal Way.

Ogunquit Museum of American Art (207-646-4909; www.ogunquitmuseum .org), Shore Rd., Ogunquit (0.4 mile west of Perkins Cove). Open July–Oct. 15,

Kim Grant

PERKINS COVE

daily 10:30–5; Sun. 2–5. Closed Labor Day. $5 adults, $4 seniors, $3 students, free under 12. Founded in 1952 and built superbly of local stone and wood, with enough glass to let in the beauty of the cove it faces, the museum displays select-ed paintings from its permanent collection, which includes the strong, bright oils of Henry Strater and other onetime locals such as Reginald Marsh; also Thomas Hart Benton, Marsden Hartley, Edward Hopper, Rockwell Kent, and William and Marguerite Zorach. Special exhibitions feature nationally recognized artists.

Historical Society of Wells & Ogunquit (207-646-4755), 936 Post Rd. (Rt. 1, opposite Wells Plaza). Open mid-May–mid-Oct., Tue.–Thu. 10–4 and Sat. 10–1; off-season, Wed.–Thu. 10–4. $2 donation per adult. Housed in a historic meetinghouse still used for weddings, concerts, and numerous special events; also a genealogy library, old photos, memorabilia, ships' models, and a gift shop.

OGUNQUIT MUSEUM OF AMERICAN ART

Christina Tree

🐾 ♿ **Wells Auto Museum** (207-646-9064), Wells. Open Memorial Day–Columbus Day, daily 10–5. More than 80 cars dating from 1900 to 1963, including a 1919 Stutz Bearcat and a 1941 Packard convertible, plus nick-elodeons, toys, and bicycles. Rides in antique cars are offered.

✻ To Do

BICYCLING Wheels & Waves (207-646-5774), 579 Post Rd. (Rt. 1), Wells. Rents as well as sells bikes; also a source of wetsuits and everything surf related.

BOAT EXCURSIONS

From Perkins Cove

Finestkind (207-646-5227) offers scenic cruises and "lobstering trips." Both the **Ugly Anne** (207-646-7202) and the **Bunny Clark** (207-646-2214) offer deep-sea-fishing trips. The excursion boat **Deborah Ann** (207-361-9501) offers 4½-hour whale-watching cruises out to Jeffrey's Ledge.

FISHING FROM SHORE Tackle and bait can be rented at Wells Harbor. The obvious fishing spots are the municipal dock and harbor jetties. There is surf casting near the mouth of the Mousam River. Also see "Kittery and the Yorks" and "The Kennebunks."

GOLF The area's major 18-hole golf courses are described in "Kittery and the Yorks."

Ogunquit Playhouse (207-646-5511; www.ogunquitplayhouse.org), Rt. 1 (just south of Ogunquit Village). Open mid-June–Labor Day. Billing itself as "America's Foremost Summer Theater," this grand old summer-stock theater opened for its first season in 1933 and is now owned by the Ogunquit Playhouse Foundation. It continues to feature top stars in productions staged Mon.–Fri. at 8 PM, Sat. at 8:30 PM; matinees are Wed. and Thu. at 2:30 PM, Sat. at noon for kids; Sun. concerts at 8 PM. Usually we describe summer stock under *Entertainment* near the end of a chapter; this is a must-see.

OGUNQUIT PLAYHOUSE

Kim Grant

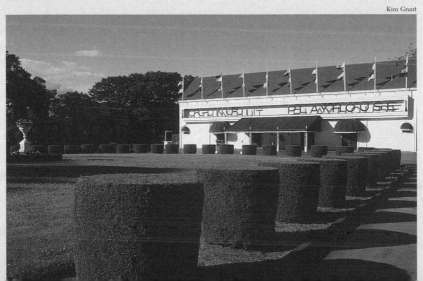

Merriland Farm (207-464-5008; www.merrilandfarm.com), 545 Coles Hill Rd. (off Rt. 1), Wells. Nine-hole, par-3 course on a working farm. Also a café serving Memorial Day weekend to early fall, 8–4.

Maplewood Farm Driving Range (207-641-8393), Laudholm Farm Rd., Wells. Putting green, sand traps, 20 tees and grass for wood or iron play.

MINI GOLF ✔ **Wells Beach Mini-Golf**, next to Big Daddy's Ice Cream, Rt. 1, Wells. Open daily in-season 10–10.

✔ **Wonder Mountain**, Rt. 1, Wells. A mini golf mountain, complete with waterfalls; adjoins Outdoor World.

✔ **Sea-Vu Mini Golf** (207-646-7732) is another Rt. 1 option in Wells.

SEA KAYAKING **World Within Sea Kayaking** (207-646-0455; www.world within.com), 746 Ocean Ave., Wells. Registered Maine Guide Andrew French offers guided estuary and ocean tours from the Norseman Resort, Ogunquit.

TENNIS Three public courts in Ogunquit. Inquire at **Dunaway Center** (207-646-9361). **Wells Recreation Area**, Rt. 9A, Wells, has four courts.

✳ Green Space

BEACHES Three-mile-long **Ogunquit Beach** offers surf, soft sand, and space for kite flying, as well as a sheltered strip along the mouth of the Ogunquit River for toddlers. It can be approached three ways: (1) The most popular way is from the foot of Beach St. There are boardwalk snacks, changing facilities, and toilets, and it is here that the beach forms a tongue between the ocean and the Ogunquit River (parking in the lot here is $4 per hour in-season). (2) The Footbridge Beach access (take Ocean St. off Rt. 1 north of the village) offers restrooms and is less crowded. $15 a day parking. (3) North Beach, Eldridge St., Wells. Be sure to park in the lot provided; $15 a day. Walk west onto Ogunquit Beach, not to Moody Beach, now private above the high-water mark.

Wells Beach. Limited free parking right in the middle of the village of Wells Beach; also parking at the east end by the jetty. Wooden casino and boardwalk, clam shacks, clean public toilets, a cluster of motels, concrete benches—a gathering point for older people who sit while enjoying the view of the wide, smooth beach.

Drakes Island, Wells. Take Drakes Island Rd. off Rt. 1. There are three small parking areas on this spit of land lined with private cottages.

NATURE PRESERVES AND PARKS **Wells National Estuarine Research Reserve at Laudholm Farm** (207-646-1555; www.wellsreserve.org), Laudholm Rd. (off Rt. 1, just south of its junction with Rt. 9, Wells; look for the sign between the Lighthouse Depot and the Maine Diner), managed by the Laudholm Trust. The reserve consists of 1,600 acres of estuarine habitat for the area's wildlife. *Estuarine*, by the way, describes an area formed where ocean tides meet freshwater currents (an estuary). The reserve is divided into two parts, each with its own access point. Grounds include meadows and two barrier beaches at the mouth of the Little River and Laudholm Farm, a former estate that began as a saltwater farm in the 1620s. Owned by the Lord family from 1881 until 1986 (George C. Lord was president of the Boston & Maine Railroad), it was farmed until the 1950s. This is a birder's mecca. The farm itself now includes a visitor center (open year-round, weekdays 10–4; also May–Oct., Sat. 10–4 and Sun. noon–4) with a slide show, exhibits, restrooms, and parking ($2 in July and Aug., as well as on weekends in June and Sep.). Seven miles of trails meander through fields, woods, and wetlands (bring a bathing suit if you want to swim at the beach). The Laudholm Trust grounds are open daily year-round (gates open daily at 8 and remain open until 8 in summer months; otherwise, until 5). Inquire about guided trail walks, artists' workshops, and programs for kids ages 6–9. The Laudholm Nature Crafts Festival is the weekend after Labor Day.

Rachel Carson National Wildlife Refuge (operated by the U.S. Fish and Wildlife Service), off Rt. 9 on the Wells–Kennebunk line. See the description in "The Kennebunks."

Dorothea Grant Common. Hidden away between Rt. 1 and the Dunaway Center, this quiet park surrounds the evolving Heritage Museum at Winn House.

WALKS **Marginal Way**. In 1923 Josiah Chase gave Ogunquit this windy path along the ocean. A farmer from the town of York, just south of here, Chase had driven his cattle around rocky Israel's Head each summer to pasture on the marsh grass in Wells, just to the north. Over the years he bought land here and there until, eventually, he owned the whole promontory. He then sold off sea view lots at a tidy profit and donated the actual ocean frontage to the town, thus preserving his own right-of-way. There is very limited parking at the mini lighthouse on Israel's Head.

 Wells Harbor. Here is a pleasant walk along a granite jetty and a good fishing spot. There is also a playground and gazebo where concerts are held.

Old Trolley Trail. An interesting nature walk and cross-country ski trail; begins on Pine Hill Rd. N., Ogunquit.

✷ Lodging

Note: Ogunquit's 2,500 "rooms" include many family-geared efficiencies, especially along Rt. 1, which we do not attempt to critique here but are listed on the Ogunquit Chamber of Commerce web site (www.ogunquit.org) and in its *Vacation Planner*.

All listings are in Ogunquit 03907, or have an Ogunquit mailing address, and are most convenient to Ogunquit, unless otherwise noted

RESORT ⊗ 🎯 ♿ **The Cliff House** (207-361-1000; www.cliffhousemaine.com), Shore Rd., P.O. Box 2274. Open late Mar.–Dec. Over the last few years, the Cliff House, opened in 1872 with a single building on the top of its spectacular location, has expanded with a monumental spa facility and 32 new, large rooms that feature gas fireplaces and of course ocean views. Guests in any of the 194 rooms in the entire resort can use the vanishing-edge" pool set out on the terrace, which gives swimmers the illusion of a sea dip without the low temperature of Maine ocean water. The spa gives guests the reality of luxurious massages and facials. Anyone in the area can take advantage of this spa.

Innkeeper Kathryn Weare is the great-granddaughter of the woman who opened this hotel, and hospitality remains the focus. Although the decor in the rooms in the main building is undistinguished (a problem also in the new building), every amenity you need is close to hand, from a dining room with that great view and good food (see *Dining Out*) to nearby golf courses, two indoor, heated pools, and an exercise room.

This place has risen from its own ashes after being run down under the temporary, exclusive use of the U.S. military for use as a lookout for Nazi submarines in World War II. Then innkeeper Charles Weare tried to sell it for $50,000 in 1946 with an ad in the *Wall Street Journal*, but received no offers.

High-season summer rates range $230–310 with no meals; a 3-day spa sampler package with breakfast and one dinner, and a $200 certificate for spa services, is $1,300 for a single in summer. All rates are lower off-season, and many packages are offered.

RESORT MOTOR INNS Our usual format places inns before motels, but in the 1960s some of Ogunquit's leading resorts replaced their old hotel buildings with luxury "motor inns."

✒ **Sparhawk** (207-646-5562), 85 Shore Rd., P.O. Box 936. Open mid-Apr.–late Oct. The 51 oceanfront motel units, each with a balcony, overlook the confluence of the Ogunquit

River and the Atlantic Ocean and the length of Ogunquit Beach. The 20 units in neighboring Ireland House (with balconies canted toward the water) are combination living room/bedroom suites. The Barbara Dean and Jacobs Houses, formerly village homes, add another 11 suites and 4 apartments, some with gas fireplace and Jacuzzi. The Little White House is a two-bedroom house overlooking the ocean. Guests register and gather in Sparhawk Hall. Recreation options include an outdoor pool, heated mid-June–mid-Sep., shuffleboard, croquet, tennis, and privileges at the local golf course and fitness center. One-week minimum stay July–mid-Aug.; $170–300 in high summer, $90–265 in spring and fall.

✒ **Aspinquid** (207-646-7072; www .aspinquid.com), Box 2408, Beach St. Open mid-Mar.–Oct. A picture of the old Aspinquid hangs outside the check-in counter of this condo-style complex just across the bridge from Ogunquit Beach. Built in 1971 by the owners of the old hotel, the two-story clusters still look modern. Rooms all have two double beds, phone, and TV; most have kitchenette. Sliding doors overlook the water, and you can hear the surf pounding on Ogunquit Beach. Facilities include a pool, a lighted tennis court, a sauna, a spa, and a fishpond with a waterfall ideal for peaceful reading and relaxation. Rates vary with the season: $135–300 in-season, $90–215 in spring and fall.

INNS AND HOTELS ✒ **Beachmere** (207-646-2021 or 1-800-336-3983; www.beachmereinn.com), 62 Beachmere Place. Open late Mar.–mid-Dec. Sited on the Marginal Way with water views, this complex consists of an expansive mansion and a two-story motel-style annex angled in such a way as not to detract from the main house and so that almost all units have water views; there are also rooms in Mayfair and Bullfrog Cottages 0.5 mile away on Israel's Head Rd. This has been owned by female members of the same family since 1937. All rooms have kitchenette and cable TV, and most have private balcony, deck, or terrace; many are large enough to accommodate families. In the mansion seven rooms have a working fireplace. The large inviting grounds overlook Ogunquit Beach, and smaller beaches are a few minutes' walk. High-season rates, $100–250, drop in the off-season and after Columbus Day to as low as $60–130.

The Grand Hotel (207-646-1231 or 1-800-806-1231; www.thegrandhotel .com), 276 Shore Dr. Open Apr.–Nov. An attractive three-floor, 28-suite hotel built as a condominium complex. All suites have two rooms, with wet bar, fridge, color cable TV, and private sundeck or balcony; fireplaces on the top floor. There's an elevator, an interior atrium, an indoor pool, and an outdoor hot tub. $180–240 in high season, $95–210 right after Labor Day, from $70 off-season.

BED & BREAKFASTS **The Trellis House** (207-646-7909 or 1-800-681-7909; www.trellishouse.com), 2 Beachmere Place, P.O. Box 2229. Open year-round. This is a find. Pat and Jerry Houlihan's shingled, turn-of-the-20th-century summer cottage offers appealing common areas, including a wraparound screened porch and comfortable seating around the hearth. Upstairs are three guest rooms, all with full private bath, one

with a water view. The most romantic room is a cottage in the garden. In the carriage house we prefer the upstairs to the downstairs rooms. This is one of those places where guests—whether they come alone or in couples—mingle without stiffness. The Houlihans are genuine hosts. $125–200 in-season, from $85 off-season, includes a breakfast (served anytime between 8:30 and 10) that might include apple-cinnamon French toast and sausage. The inn is handy both to the village and to Perkins Cove via the Marginal Way.

Marginal Way House and Motel (207-646-8801; in winter, 207-363-6566; www.marginalwayhouse.com), Box 697, Wharf Lane. Open late Apr.–Oct. Just a short walk from the beach and really in the middle of the village, this delightful complex is hidden down a waterside lane. There are old-fashioned guest rooms in the Main and Wharf Houses, all with private bath; Dockside houses six standard motel units. There are also seven one- and two-bedroom apartments. The landscaped grounds have an ocean view. High season $114–187, low $49–147; apartments are rented only by the week in high season.

Morning Dove (207-646-3891; www .morningdove.com), P.O. Box 1940, 13 Bourne Lane. Open year-round. On a quiet side street off Shore Rd., within walking distance of everything, this is a carefully restored 1860s farmhouse. We like the living room with its white marble fireplace, and the five nicely decorated guest rooms (two with a fireplace); the innkeepers are Jane and Fred Garland. $140–175 in-season, $100–145 off-season, full breakfast included.

🐚 **Ye Olde Perkins Place** (207-361-1119), 749 Shore Rd. (south of Perkins Cove), Cape Neddick 03902. Open late June–Labor Day. Overlooking the ocean, Prim and Dick Winkler's 1717 homestead has five guest rooms (four baths). Away from the village but within walking distance of Perkins Cove and right above a pebble beach in a pretty cove. $70–80 per room (2-night minimum); coffee, juice, and muffins included. No credit cards.

Above Tide Inn (207-646-7454; www.abovetideinn.com), 66 Beach St. Open May 15–Oct. 15. Location! Location! Sited right at the start of the Marginal Way and steps from the bridge leading over to Ogunquit Beach, also steps from village shops and jutting right out into the water. The nine rooms each have a sitting area and small fridge, TV, and shower or bath. All but one room have water views. Mid-July–Labor Day rates are $165–230; $100–140 off-season, continental breakfast included.

The Beauport Inn on Clay Hill (207-361-2400 or 1-800-646-8681; www.beauportinn.com), 339 Clay Hill Rd. Open year-round. Who says, "They don't build them like that anymore"? This stone manor, with vintage-1835 English oak floor-to-ceiling paneling in its great room, is brand new. George and Cathy Wilson created this luxuriously appointed retreat in a riverside field. Each of the guest rooms has a gas fireplace, cable TV, and VCR; there's also a two-room suite and a fully equipped apartment. A lap pool, steam room, and Jacuzzi are shared by all guests. $110–185 (depending on the season) includes a very full breakfast. The apartment is $1,100–1,350.

Beach Farm Inn (207-646-8493; www.beachfarminn.com), 97 Eldridge Rd., Wells 04090. Open year-round. This handsome old house has been taking in guests since the 19th century, when it still also served as a working salt-marsh farm. Now Nancy Swenson and Craig White have transformed the living room and dining room with Victorian upholstery by Nancy and furniture by Craig. A full breakfast featuring apple-baked French toast (or homemade pierogi in winter) is served on the bright sunporch. The guest pantry stocks Carpe Diem coffee, and the swimming pool beckons on the lawn. Eight attractive bedrooms lie upstairs, three with private bath; others can be rented with an unattached bath for private use. There are also two efficiency cottages. $90–135 per couple June–Sep. and holiday weekends, including breakfast, less off-season.

COTTAGES *Note:* We have noted just a few of the dozens of the area's summer rentals, especially plentiful in Wells. Contact the Wells Chamber of Commerce, which keeps track of rental cottages and condos.

Garnsey Bros. Rentals (207- 646-8301) specializes in Wells, and **Seaside Vacation Rentals** (207-646-7671) offers more than 500 rentals throughout the area.

✆ **The Dunes** (207-646-2612; www.dunesmotel.com), Box 917, 518 Main St. Open May–Oct. Owned by the Perkins family for more than 60 years, this is really a historic property, the best of the coast's surviving "cottage colonies," as well as a great family find. The 36 units include 19 old-style white cottages with green trim, many with fireplaces, scattered over well-

kept grounds fronting on the Ogunquit River, with direct access to
Ogunquit Beach by rowboat at high
tide and on foot at low tide. All rooms
have refrigerator and color TV. One-
and two-bedroom cottages are $180–
335 in-season (June 15–Labor Day),
$155–255 in the shoulder seasons,
and $130–220 in spring and fall. Min-
imum stay in July and Aug. in the
larger cottages. Rooms are $100–285
in-season, $80–190 in the shoulders,
and $75–150 off-season.

🦞 ⚓ **Cottage in the Lane Motor
Lodge** (207-646-7903; www.cottage
inthelane.com), 84 Drakes Island Rd.,
Wells 04090. There are 11 housekeeping cottages, all facing landscaped grounds under the pines (an
artistic play structure and a pool form
the centerpiece); salt marsh beyond.
It's a 0.75-mile walk or bike ride to
the beach. The quiet setting borders
the Rachel Carson Wildlife Refuge
and Laudholm Farm. $595–695 per
week for a three-room cottage accommodating four, and $755–795 for a
four-room cottage good for up to six
people; less in mid- and low season as
well as off-season.

⚓ **The Seagull Inn and Vacation
Cottages** (207-646-5164; www
.seagullvacations.com), 1413 Post Rd.
(Rt. 1), Wells 04090. Open late
Apr.–late Oct. Sixty-seven one- and
two-bedroom cottages, all with a
screened porch, fill what used to be
an open field; 60 of them were built
in 2004, after a Wells partnership
bought the place in 2003. The seven
old cottages that remain have been
updated with bathrooms and kitchens,
and all have views of the water. A
heated pool/hot tub is shared by
guests. Rentals by the week in summer (2-night minimum off-season),

$800–1,500 for the housekeeping cot-
tages.

MOTEL Riverside Motel (207-646-
2741; www.riversidemotel.com), P.O.
Box 2244, Shore Rd. Open late
Apr.–late Oct. Just across the draw-
footbridge and overlooking Perkins
Cove is this trim, friendly place with
42 units; also four rooms in the 1874
house. The property has been in
Michael Staples's family for more than
100 years. All rooms have color TV
and full bath, and all overlook the
cove; continental breakfast is included
and served in the lobby around the
fireplace or on the sundeck. $90–180,
depending on season and location of
room. Three-day minimum July
28–Aug. 17.

✳ Where to Eat

DINING OUT Technically in Cape
Neddick but just as handy to Ogun-
quit, **Clay Hill Farm** is described in
"Kittery and the Yorks."

∞ **Arrows** (207-361-1100; www
.arrowsrestaurant.com), Berwick Rd.,
Ogunquit. Open Tue.–Sun. in July and
Aug. at 6 PM, fewer days of the week
off-season, and closed Jan.–Mar. Voted
one of the country's top 50 restaurants
by *Gourmet*, this is one of the area's
destination restaurants, drawing
guests from all over the region. The
food is indeed very good, and sometimes extraordinary; lobster cannelloni
with ricotta, part of a multi-lobster
concoction entrée ($43.95), rang with
flavor. The big wine list is expensive,
as are the wines by the glass. A strict
dress code is enforced (no one in
shorts or jeans will be seated), and
24-hour notice is required for cancellations or a fee is charged on the
credit card required to make the

reservation. Despite the rules and the high expense, many judge this the best restaurant in Maine. Immaculate grounds surround the old house, and guests often tour the garden before dinner. Entrées $40–44 and up.

98 Provence (207-646-9898; www.98provence.com), 262 Shore Rd., Ogunquit. Open Apr.–Dec. 1, daily except Tue. for dinner (5:30–9:30) summer, less off-season. This classic French Provençal restaurant gets all the details right. The herb-crusted log of foie gras pâté, with buttered toast, creates happiness. Braised rabbit confit, beef fillet with black truffle butter, and salmon with caviar *beurre blanc* do, too. Entrées $26–37.50; a varying-price table d'hôte menu is offered, $48 the night of our visit. The wine list is dominated by France, and some lovelies are sold by the glass. Reservations advised.

Joshua's Restaurant (207-646-3355; www.joshuas.biz), 1637 Post Rd. (Route 1), Wells. Open for dinner daily in summer, closed Sunday off-season. The Mather family farm grows a lot of its restaurant's vegetables, and chef Joshua Mather puts them to spectacular use as sides with grilled rack of lamb, wood-oven roast-

THE CLIFF HOUSE RESORT AND SPA

Nancy English

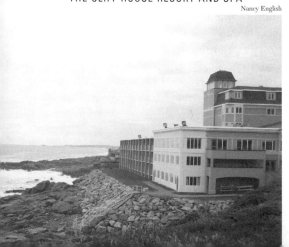

ed mushroom ravioli, and Maine crabcakes. Entrées $19–28.

The Cliff House (207-361-1000; www.cliffhousemaine.com), Shore Rd., Ogunquit. Open late Mar.–Dec. daily for dinner. Jackets required; no shorts, jeans, or sneakers allowed. The theme of the food here is complication, which doesn't always work. An appetizer of baked chèvre with tapenade and caramelized onion came to the table looking like a savory sundae, and proved delicious. But we can't say the same for the Cliff House blue berry halibut. Still, it's clear the kitchen is full of talent. The view is over the water from a high cliff. Entrées $23–30.

MC Perkins Cove (207-646-6263; www.mcperkinscove.com), Perkins Cove. Lunch and dinner daily in summer, closed some days of the week off-season. Owned by the inventive chefs of Arrows (see above), this is a casual place for fresh raw oysters, grilled steak, and seafood with all the splendid touches skill and imagination can devise. Entrées $19–29.

Five'O Shore Road (207-646-5001), 50 Shore Rd., Ogunquit Village. Open for dinner in-season nightly; light fare served until 11 PM, Thu.–Sun. in winter. This restaurant has gained a reputation for great service and good drinks, along with praise for the sophisticated food, like seared yellowfin tuna with a grilled ruby grapefruit, and filet mignon with wild mushroom demiglaze. Appetizers include mussels with garlic, Danish blue cheese, and cream. Entrées $20–29.

Joe Allen (207-646-4477; joeallenrestaurant.com), 215 Main St. A sophisticated restaurant with branches in New York, London, Paris, and

Miami, Joe Allen serves up lamb shank, roasted king salmon, grilled New York sirloin, and bluefin tuna. The meals are well made and the sides inventive. Entrées $18–26.

Gypsy Sweethearts (207-646-7021; www.gypsysweethearts.com), 30 Shore Rd., Ogunquit. Open Apr.–Oct. Dinner Tue.–Sun. from 5:30; weekends off-season. Meals with a Caribbean twist are served in a charming old house that all Ogunquit regulars hit at least once during their stay. Chef-owner Judie Clayton has made a Caesar-glazed sea bass, poblano rellenos, and shelled lobster with spinach tagliatelle. Award-winning wine list with 21 available by the glass. Entrées $17–27.

Jonathan's Restaurant (207-646-4777; www.jonathansrestaurant.com), 92 Bourne Lane, Ogunquit. Open year-round. There are two entirely distinct parts to this big place. The downstairs restaurant consists of a series of dimly lit, nicely decorated rooms (one with a 600-gallon tropical aquarium). Choices range from vegetarian pasta to caramelized salmon, marinated in a Grand Marnier vinaigrette and served with a lemon *beurre blanc*. Entrées $17–24. For more about what happens upstairs, see *Entertainment*.

Poor Richard's Tavern (207-646-4722; www.poorrichardstavern.com), 331 Shore Rd., Ogunquit. At this local dining landmark chef-owner Richard Perkins prides himself on his lobster stew and Infamous Lobster Pie, but he offers a large menu ranging from meat loaf to charbroiled fillet of salmon. Entrées $17–24.

Blue Water Inn (207-646-5559), Beach St., Ogunquit. The view of the Ogunquit River is hard to beat, and the specialty is fish—mackerel and haddock and the shore dinner. Entrées $13–18.

Old Village Inn (207-646-7088), 250 Main St., Ogunquit. Open all year but not all nights off-season. This village landmark includes various Victorian-style dining rooms (one in the rear with a fireplace) and an English pub-style bar with an equally varied menu, ranging from pastas and stir-fries to roast rack of lamb, filet mignon, and the lobster of the evening. Entrées $17–24. Early-bird specials.

LOBSTER *Note:* Maine's southernmost beach resorts are the first place many visitors sample real "Mane Lobstah" the way it should be eaten: messily, with bib, broth, butter, and a water view.

✦ **Barnacle Billy's, Etc.** (207-646-5575 or 1-800-866-5575; www.barnbilly.com), Perkins Cove. Open May–Oct. for lunch and dinner. What began as a no-frills lobster place (the one that's still next door) has expanded over 40 years to fill a luxurious dining space created for a more upscale waterside restaurant. Lobster and seafood dishes remain the specialty, and it's difficult to beat the view combined with comfort, which frequently includes the glow from two great stone fireplaces. Full bar; dinner entrées from $16.95 for grilled chicken to $26.95 for a lobster salad. You can also order lobster at the counter and wait for your number, dine on the outdoor deck, or order burgers.

🦞 ✦ ♿ **Lobster Shack** (207-646-2941), end of Perkins Cove. Open mid-Apr.–mid-Oct., 11–9 in-season. A family-owned, old-style, serious lobster-eating place since the 1940s (when it was known as Maxwell and Perkins); the tables are wide slabs of shellacked pine with plenty of room for lobster by the pound, steamer clams, good chowder, house coleslaw; also reasonably priced burgers, apple pie à la mode, wine, beer.

🖋 **Ogunquit Lobster Pound** (207-646-2516; www.ogunquitlobsterpound.com), Rt. 1 (north of Ogunquit Village). Open Mother's Day–Columbus Day weekend, and winter weekends for dinner. Expanded gradually over the years, this log landmark still retains its 1930s atmosphere and is still all about selecting your lobster and watching it (if you so choose) get steamed in the huge outdoor pots. "Steamers" (steamed clams) are the other specialty. The large menu, however, now ranges from angel-hair pasta to filet mignon with wild mushroom ravioli. Beer and wine are available. Entrées $10.95 for a grilled chicken breast to $16.95 for baked scallops.

🦞 🖋 **Fisherman's Catch** (207-646-8780), 134 Harbor Rd., Wells Harbor. Open May–Columbus Day, daily 11–9 in summer, closing earlier off-season. Set in a salt marsh, with rustic tables; a traditional seafood place with unbeatable prices. Good chowder and really good lobster stew, homemade crabcakes, lobster dinners, children's menu, beer on tap. Try the bread pudding with whiskey sauce.

Also see "Kittery and the Yorks."

EATING OUT **Amore Breakfast** (207-646-6661; www.amorebreakfast.com), 178 Shore Rd., Ogunquit. Open early spring–mid-Dec., in-season 7 AM– 1 PM, closed Wed. and Thu. Relaxed and pleasant, with the skill to get breakfast in front of you where it

belongs, this pine restaurant makes exuberant omelets and an eggs Benedict called "Be Still My Heart" that piles bacon, sausage, and melted cheese on top of a German potato pancake; $8.95. Also ingenious French toast, bagels with smoked salmon, and a place to park.

David's Restaurant, Shore Rd. in the middle of Ogunquit Village. Open Apr.–Oct. for lunch and dinner. Make a reservation for dinner. The outdoor tables, kept warm by terrace heaters on cold nights, are always full. A vegetarian lasagna with grilled seasonal vegetables fills one end of the spectrum, the Delmonico steak the other, with fresh fish in between, and great pies to finish up with. Entrées $12–24.

Lord's Harborside Restaurant (207-646-2651), Wells Harbor. Open end of Apr.–Oct. for lunch and dinner; closed Tue. A big, ungarnished dining room with a harbor view and a reputation for fresh fish and seafood. Lobster boiled and baked.

Jake's Seafood (207-646-6771), Rt. 1, Bourne Ave., Moody. Open for all three meals Apr.–Oct., breakfast and lunch Nov.–Mar. Specializes in good American cooking, fresh seafood, ice cream.

Congdon's Donuts Family Restaurant (207-646-4219), 1090 Post Rd. (Rt. 1), Wells. Open from 6 AM year-round. Fresh muffins, breads, pastries, and doughnuts; also ice cream made on the premises and a full menu for lunch and dinner. We've heard the doughnuts are fried in lard—the best way of all, for some of us.

🖋 **Billy's Chowder House** (207-646-7558; www.billyschowderhouse.com), Mile Rd., Wells. Open daily late Jan.–early Dec. Overlooking Wells

Harbor and salt marsh, a rambling old family favorite with a big menu, a famous chowder, and a selection of fried seafood, steamed shellfish, broiled scallops, and, of course, boiled lobster. There's also plenty of meat on the menu, including a hot dog and fries. Exotic drinks are a specialty. Billys2 up the road is a fast-food offshoot that makes pizza, but mainly serves fried fish.

Maine Diner (207-656-4441), 2265 Post Rd. (Rt. 1), Wells, near the junction of Rts. 1 and 9. Open year-round 7 AM–9 PM. This packed place can still boast about its seafood chowder, shrimp, scallops, lobster, and clams in a milky broth, but its stodgy chicken potpie has slid far downhill. We're begging them to go back to the old ways, which must have been good to win this plain building such a following.

☙ **Village Food Market** (207-646-2122), 230 Main St., Ogunquit. This landmark grocery store has gone with the times, adding daily baked goods, soups, salads, and a deli—even an upscale summer takeout called Fancy That, with an outdoor eating area. Call before 11 for a picnic takeout order to avoid the line.

SNACKS Bread & Roses Bakery (207-646-4227), 28 Main St., Ogunquit. Over the years Mary Breen's pleasant bakery has expanded into an attractive café serving muffins and coffee, and well known for delectable pastries. Some vegan and kosher items are made here.

Scoop Deck (207-646-5150), Eldridge Road (just off Rt. 1), Wells. Open Memorial Day–Columbus Day. Mocha almond fudge and Dinosaur Crunch (blue vanilla) are among the more than 40 flavors; the ice cream

is from Thibodeau Farms in Saco. Also yogurt, cookies, brownies, and hot dogs.

✳ Entertainment

THEATERS Hackmatack Playhouse (207-698-1807), 538 School St. (Rt. 9), Berwick, stages live performances throughout the season. Hope Hobbs Gazebo at Wells Harbor Park offers summer Saturday-night concerts.

☙ **Booth Theater** (207-646-8142; www.boothproductions.com), 13 Beach St., Ogunquit. A black-box theater (based in Worcester, Massachusetts, in winter) with productions Mon.–Sat., June–Aug. The theater seats 74, and the productions vary from musicals to dramas. Inquire about children's matinees, youth camp programs, and magic shows.

Leavitt Fine Arts Theatre (207-646-3123), 259 Main St., Ogunquit Village. Open early spring–fall. An old-time theater with new screen and sound; showing first-run films since 1923.

Ogunquit Playhouse. Such a must-see part of Ogunquit that we describe it under *To See*.

OTHERS Jonathan's Restaurant (207-646-4777), 92 Bourne Lane, Ogunquit. Memorial Day–Labor Day. You can check the current schedule on the web site, www.jonathans restaurant.com. Performers like Tom Rush appeared in 2005.

Ogunquit Performing Arts (207-646-6170) sponsors the Chamber Music Festival in June and the Capriccio annual arts festival at the beginning of September; also music, ballet, and theater year-round.

✳ Selective Shopping

ANTIQUARIAN BOOKS Boston book lovers drive to Wells to browse in this cluster of exceptional bookstores along Rt. 1. They include **Douglas N. Harding Rare Books** (207-646-8785), 2152 Post Rd., open year-round, which is huge and excellent with some 200,000 titles, including rare finds, maps, and prints. **The Book Barn** (207-646-4926), at South St. (Rt. 1), is a general bookshop with comic books, baseball cards, and collectors' supplies. **East Coast Books** (207-646-0416), Depot St. at Rt. 109 in Wells, has a large general collection, autographed copies, and art and historical books. **The Arringtons** (207-646-4124), 1908 Post Rd. (Rt. 1), specialize in military subjects as well as vintage paperbacks and postcards.

ANTIQUES SHOPS Rt. 1 from York through Wells and the Kennebunks is studded with antiques shops, among them: **MacDougall-Gionet** (207-646-3531), open Tue.–Sun. 10–5, a particularly rich trove of country furniture in a barn; 60 dealers are represented. **R. Jorgensen Antiques** (207-646-9444) has nine rooms filled with antique furniture, including fine formal pieces from a number of countries.

ART GALLERIES In addition to the Ogunquit Museum of Art there is the **Barn Gallery**, home of the **Ogunquit Art Association** (207-646-8400), Shore Rd. and Bourne Lane, Ogunquit. Open late May–early Oct., Mon.–Sat. 11–5 and Sun. 1–5. The Barn Gallery showcases work by members; also stages frequent workshops, lectures, films, and concerts. Ogunquit's galleries (all seasonal) also include, in Perkins Cove, the **George Carpenter Gallery** (207-646-5106). A longtime area resident, Carpenter paints outdoors in the tradition and style of New England's 1920s marine and landscape artists. **Shore Road Gallery** (207-646-5046), 112 Shore Rd., is open daily Memorial Day–Columbus Day weekend. Fine arts, jewelry, and fine crafts by nationally known artists.

SPECIAL SHOPS **Perkins Cove**, the cluster of former fish shacks by Ogunquit's famous draw-footbridge, harbors more than a dozen shops and galleries. Our favorites are the **Carpenter Gallery** (see above) and **Books Ink** (207-646-8393), a collection of toys, games, cards, wine, books, and other things owner Barbara Lee Chertok finds interesting or educational. Sit on the terrace and look over the cove.

Ogunquit Camera (207-646-2261), at the corner of Shore Rd. and Wharf Lane in Ogunquit Village. Open year-round, and featuring 1-hour film developing. A great little shop that's been here since 1952. It's also a trove of toys, towels, windsocks, beach supplies, and sunglasses.

Harbor Candy Shop, 26 Main St., Ogunquit. Seasonal. Chocolates and specialty candies are made on the spot; there's also a selection of imported candies.

Merriland Farm (207-646-5040; www.merrilandfarm.com), 545 Coles Hill Rd. (off Rt. 1), Wells. This 200-year-old farm offers a view of the Wells that was here for centuries before its sandy shore was developed. In addition to operating a café specializing in pies and berry shortcake and a nine-hole golf course, this is a place to pick cultivated highbush blueberries in July and August and to buy jams, raspberry vinegar, and gift baskets.

Lighthouse Depot (207-646-0608; www.lhdepot.com), Rt. 1 N., Wells. Look for the lighthouses outside (just before the turnoff for Laudholm Farm). Open daily year-round. Billed as "the largest selection of lighthouse gift items in the world," this is two floors filled with lawn lighthouses, lighthouse books, ornaments, jewelry, paintings, replicas, and much more. Inquire about the monthly *Lighthouse Digest*.

✳ Special Events

April: Big **Patriot's Day celebration** at Ogunquit Beach.

June: **Ogunquit Chamber Music Festival** (*first week*). **Laudholm Farm Day** (*midmonth*). **Wells Week** (*end of the month*)—a weeklong celebration centering on Harbor Park Day, with boat launchings, a chicken barbecue, a sand-sculpture contest, and a crafts fair.

July: **Fireworks** on July 4 and 3-day **Harbor Fest** in Wells.

August: **Sidewalk Art show** in Ogunquit.

September: **Open Homes Day**, sponsored by the Wells Historical Society. **Nature Crafts Festival** (*second weekend*) at Laudholm Farm. **Capriccio**, a celebration of the performing arts, and **Kite Day**, in Ogunquit. **Chili Festival**, Wells.

October: **Ogunquit Fest** (*third week*)—ghost tours and costume parade.

December: **Christmas parade** in Wells. **Christmas by the Sea** in Ogunquit.

THE KENNEBUNKS

The Kennebunks began as a fishing stage near Cape Porpoise as early as 1602, but the community was repeatedly destroyed by Native American raids. In 1719 the present "port" was incorporated as Arundel, a name that stuck through its lucrative shipbuilding and seafaring years until 1821, when it became Kennebunkport. Later, when the novel *Arundel* by Kenneth Roberts (born in Kennebunk) had run through 32 printings, residents gave the old name to North Kennebunkport.

That the Kennebunks prospered as a shipbuilding center is obvious from the quantity and quality of its sea captains' and shipbuilders' mansions, the presence of its brick customhouse (now the library), and the beauty of its churches.

In his 1891 guidebook, *The Pine-Tree Coast*, Samuel Adams Drake noted that "since the beginning of the century more than eight hundred vessels have been sent out from the shipyards of this river." He recalled: "When I first knew this place, both banks of the river were lined with shipyards . . . all alive with the labor of hundreds of workmen." But by the 1890s, Drake noted, shipbuilding was "moribund" and Kennebunkport had become "a well-established watering-place."

In 1872 this entire spectacular 5-mile stretch of coast—from Lords Point at the western end of Kennebunk Beach all the way to Cape Porpoise on the east—was acquired by one developer, the Sea Shore Company. Over the next couple of decades no fewer than 30 grand hotels and dozens of summer mansions evolved to accommodate the summer visitors that train service brought. The Kennebunks, however, shared the 1940s to 1960s decline suffered by all Maine coastal resorts, losing all but a scattering of old hotels.

According to the locals, the Kennebunks developed an almost countercultural feel in the 1960s and '70s. Then the tourist tide again turned, and over the past few decades the area has grown increasingly upscale: Surviving hotels have been condoed, inns have been rehabbed, and dozens of B&Bs and inns have opened. Still, if you look beyond the clichés, you'll discover the real Maine here, too. Dock Square's world-class shopping district now rivals those in Palm Beach (where many retail stores have sister shops) and other swanky spots, but a walk through the historic streets of Kennebunkport is free and quite idyllic. And a meal at one of the lobster shacks is as rustic, delicious, and affordable as any on the Maine coast.

You can bed down a few steps from Dock Square's lively shops and restaurants, 2 miles away in the quiet village of Cape Porpoise, or out at Goose Rocks, where the only sound is the lapping of waves on endless sand. Most B&Bs are, however, the former sea captains' homes grouped within a few stately streets of each other, many within walking distance of both Dock Square and the open ocean.

GUIDANCE **Kennebunk/Kennebunkport Chamber of Commerce** (207-967-0857 or 1-800-982-4421; www.visitthekennebunks.com), P.O. Box 740, Kennebunk 04043. Open Mon.–Sat. year-round, plus Sun. late May–late Oct. The information center, a yellow building on Rt. 9 just east of its junction with Rt. 35 (at the light in Lower Village), offers plenty of parking in the rear. Staff are unusually helpful, and the chamber publishes an excellent free guide. An office in the **Brick Store Museum** (see *Museums*) in Kennebunk is open Apr.–mid-Dec.

Kennebunkport Information and Hospitality Center (207-967-8600). Open May–mid-Dec. Restrooms and information at Dock Square.

GETTING THERE *By air:* You can fly your own plane into **Sanford Airport**; otherwise, **Portland International Jetport** (see "Portland Area") is served by various airlines and taxi services.

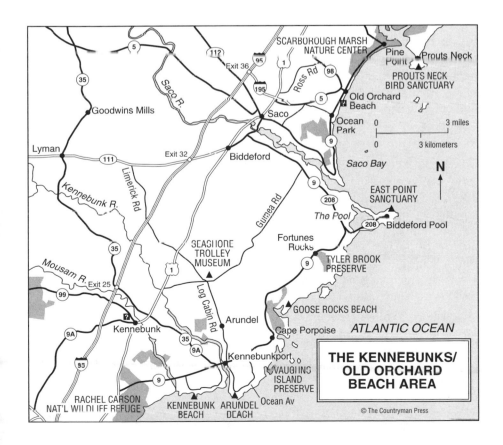

THE KENNEBUNKS/
OLD ORCHARD
BEACH AREA

© The Countryman Press

By car: Drive up I-95 to exit 25 and take Rt. 35 into Kennebunk, on to Kenne-bunkport and Kennebunk Beach. Coming up Rt. 1, take Rt. 9 east from Wells.

By train: See *Amtrak* in "What's Where." The new **Downeaster** service from Boston's North Station takes about 2 hours and stops in Wells.

GETTING AROUND Kennebunk is a busy commercial center straddling the strip of Rt. 1 between the Mousam and Kennebunk Rivers. A 10-minute ride down Summer St. (Rt. 35) brings you to Kennebunkport. Then there are Kennebunk Beach, Cape Porpoise, Goose Rocks Beach, Cape Arundel, and Kennebunk Lower Village. Luckily, free detailed maps are readily available.

Intown Trolley Co. (207-967-3686; www.intowntrolley.com), Kennebunkport, offers narrated sightseeing tours; $11 adults, $6 ages 14 and under, free for those 2 and under. The tickets are good for the day, so you can also use them to shuttle between Dock Square and Kennebunk Beach. Also available for private charter.

Bicycles work well here and are a good way to handle the mile between Dock Square and Kennebunk Beach.

PARKING A municipal paid parking lot is hidden behind the commercial block in Dock Square. You can find free parking at 30 North St., a short walk to Dock Square, and another paid parking lot near the bridge in Lower Village. Good luck!

WHEN TO COME One nice side effect of the Kennebunk tourist trade: This is the least seasonal resort town on the Southern Coast. Most inns and shops stay open through Christmas Prelude in early December, and many never close. Visit in fall, when crowds thin out and the colorful foliage makes the old mansions and crashing waves even more picturesque.

✳ To See

MUSEUMS **The Brick Store Museum and Archives** (207-985-4802; www .brickstoremuseum.org), 117 Main St., Kennebunk. Open year-round, Tue.–Fri. 10–4:30, Sat. 10–1. Admission is by donation. This block of early-19th-century commercial buildings, including William Lord's **Brick Store** (1825), hosts a per-manent exhibit documenting the region from the days of Native Americans, the arduous settlement years, and the subsequent colonial era through the period of shipbuilding glory. Changing exhibits focus on a wide variety of subjects. Visitors can do research on genealogy and local history in the archives. Architectural walking tours are offered May–Sep.

✑ **Seashore Trolley Museum** (207-967-2712; www.trolleymuseum.org), 195 Log Cabin Rd., located 3.2 miles up North St. from Kennebunkport or 2.8 miles north on Rt. 1 from Kennebunk, then right at the traffic light. Open daily, rain or shine, Father's Day–Columbus Day, weekends in May and through Oct.; call to check on special events. $7.50 adults, $5 ages 6–16, $5.50 seniors over 60, children under 6 free; discounted group rates available for groups of 12 or more. This nonprofit museum preserves the history of the trolley era, displaying more than 200 vehicles from all over the world. The impressive collection began in 1939, when the last open-sided Biddeford–Old Orchard Beach trolley was retired to an open field straddling the old Atlantic Shore Line. A 4-mile excursion on a trolley takes visitors through woods and fields along a stretch once traveled by summer guests en route to Old Orchard Beach. Interesting factoid: In recent years the U.S. Marines have used the museum for "urban training operations"—war games with paintball guns.

Kennebunkport Historical Society (207-967-2751; www.kporthistory.org) has three facilities. **Pasco Exhibit Center**, 125 North St., $3 adults, is open year-round, Tue.–Fri. 10–4; mid-June–mid-Oct., Sat. 10–1. The **Town House School**, at 135 North St., is used for research, $10, and is open year-round, Tue.–Fri. 10–1. Free on-site parking at both. The society also maintains the **Nott House**, 8 Maine St. (no parking), a Greek Revival mansion with Doric columns, original wallpapers, carpets, and furnishings. Open mid-June–Labor Day, Tue., Wed., and Fri. 1–4, Sat. 10–1, Thu. 10–4; Labor Day–Columbus Day, closed on Tue. Guided walking tours available. $5 adults.

HISTORIC SITES Wedding Cake House, Summer St. (Rt. 35), Kennebunk. This privately owned 1826 house is laced up and down with ornate white gingerbread. Legend has it that a local sea captain had to rush off to sea before a proper wedding cake could be baked, but he more than made up for it later.

South Congregational Church, Temple St., Kennebunkport. Just off Dock Square, built in 1824 with a Christopher Wren–style cupola and belfry; Doric columns added in 1912.

Louis T. Graves Memorial Library (207-967-2778), 18 Maine St., Kennebunkport. Built in 1813 as a bank, which went bust, it later served as a customhouse. It was subsequently donated to the library association by artist Abbott Graves, whose pictures alone make it worth a visit. You can still see the bank vault and the sign from the custom collector's office. At the Perkins House next door, the book saleroom is full of bargains.

First Parish Unitarian Church, Main St., Kennebunk. Built between 1772 and 1773 with an Asher Benjamin–style steeple added between 1803 and 1804, along with a Paul Revere bell. In 1838 the interior was divided in two levels, with the church proper elevated to the second floor. Popular legend holds that the pulpit was carved from a single log found floating in the Caribbean Sea and towed back to Maine.

Kennebunkport Maritime Museum & Shop (207-967-4195), Ocean Ave., Kennebunkport. Open May 15–Oct. 15, 10–4; closed Wed. Admission fee. This "museum" occupies the former boathouse in which Booth Tarkington wrote, and it highlights the last remnants of his schooner *Regina*, as well as a collection of early-19th-century scrimshaw and other nautical memorabilia. Check out the interesting museum shop.

SCENIC DRIVE Ocean Avenue, starting in Kennebunkport, follows the Kennebunk River for a mile to Cape Arundel and the open ocean, then winds past many magnificent summer homes. Stop along Parson's Way, located off Ocean Ave. on the right just after the Colony Hotel, and enjoy the park benches that take advantage of the magnificent view of the mouth of the Kennebunk River and Gooch's Beach. Continue north and east to Walker's Point, former president George H. W. Bush's summer estate (it fills a private 11-acre peninsula). Built by his grandfather in 1903, its position is uncannily ideal for use as a president's summer home, moated by water on three sides yet clearly visible from the pull-out places along the avenue. In July and August gawkers have lined up by the dozen in the hope of catching a glimpse of our 43rd president, George W. Continue along the ocean (you don't have to worry about driving too slowly, because everyone else is, too). Follow the road to Cape Porpoise, site of the area's original 1600s settlement. The cove is still a base for lobster and commercial fishing boats, and the village is a good place to lunch or dine. Continue along Rt. 9 to Clock Farm Corner (you'll know it when you see it) and turn right onto Dyke Rd. to Goose Rocks Beach; park and walk. Return to Rt. 9 and cross it, continuing via Goose Rocks Rd. to the Seashore Trolley Museum and then Log Cabin Rd. to Kennebunkport.

✳ To Do

BALLOONING **Balloons Over New England** (207-499-7575 or 1-800-788-5562; www.balloonsovernewengland.com), based in Kennebunk, offers champagne flights year-round.

Also see *To Do* in "Portland Area."

BICYCLING **Cape-Able Bike Shop** (207-967-4382; www.capeablebikes.com), 83 Arundel Rd. (off Log Cabin Rd.), Kennebunkport. Billed as Maine's biggest bike shop, Cape-Able rents a variety of bikes, including tandems and trail bikes; new owner Brandon Gillard is a good source of maps and advice. Open most of the year; in summer months, Mon.–Sat. 9–6, Sun. 8–3; closed Sun. off-season. The Kennebunks lend themselves well to exploration by bike, a far more satisfying way to go in summer than by car since you can stop and park wherever the view and urge hit you. Inquire about the **Bridle Path** (an old trolley-line route) and **Wonderbrook Park**. Guided on- and off-road tours offered.

BOATBUILDING SCHOOL **The Landing School of Boat Building and Design** (207-985-7976; www.landingschool.edu), 286 River Rd., Arundel, offers a Sep.–June program in building and designing sailing craft. Visitors welcome if you call ahead.

BOAT EXCURSIONS See *Fishing*, *Sailing*, and *Whale-Watching*, and check with the chamber of commerce.

CARRIAGE RIDES **Rockin' Horse Stables** (207-967-4288), 245 Arundel Rd., Kennebunkport. Tour Kennebunkport's historic district (25 minutes) in a spiffy white vis-à-vis carriage with burgundy-colored velvet seats and antique lanterns.

DAY CAMP ♂ **Kennebunk Beach Improvement Association (KBIA)**, 260 Beach Ave., Kennebunk Beach (207-967-2180; Sep.–May, 207-967-2181; www .kbia.net). Offers weekly sessions for 3- to 18-year-olds, featuring swimming, sailing, rowing, fishing, golf, tennis, arts and crafts, photography, and sand-castle building, June.

FISHING Deep-sea fishing is available on the charter boat *Lady J* (207-985-7304).

Stone Coast Anglers, Inc. (207-985-6005; www.stonecoastanglers.com), Kennebunk. They specialize in chartered boat trips along the coast for up to three guests as well as guided wading trips for saltwater and game fish.

GOLF Cape Arundel Golf Club (207-967-3494), Kennebunkport, 18 holes. The local links former president George H. W. Bush frequents are open to the public Apr.–Nov. except 11–2:30. **Webhannet Golf Club** (207-967-2061), off Sea Rd., Kennebunk Beach, 18 holes. Open to the public, but semiprivate, with limited tee times especially in July and Aug. **Dutch Elm Golf Course** (207-282-9850), Arundel, 18 holes; cart and club rentals, lessons, pro shop, snack bar, putting greens.

♂ **Hillcrest Golf** (207-967-4661), Kennebunk. Open daily 8 AM–dark; balls and clubs furnished.

Also see "Kittery and the Yorks."

KAYAKING Harbor Adventures (207-363-8466; www.harboradventures.com), Kennebunkport. Guided sea kayak tours for individuals and groups.

Kayak Adventures (207-967-8077), June–Sep. in Kennebunkport.

SAILING Bellatrix Sailing Trips (207-967-8685; www.sailingtrips.com), behind the Nonantum Resort Hotel, off Ocean Ave., Kennebunkport. Up to six passengers can experience the rugged southern Maine coastline from the comfortable cockpit of a 37-foot ocean racing yacht. Guests are even allowed to take the helm, and free sailing instruction is available if desired. $40 for a 2-hour sail.

Schooner *Eleanor* (207-967-8809; www.gwi.net/schoonersails). Two-hour sailing trips aboard a traditional, gaff-rigged, 55-foot schooner set sail from the docks at the Arundel Wharf Restaurant.

Several other schooners and yachts offer daysails; check with the chamber of commerce.

TROLLEY RIDE See **Seashore Trolley Museum** under *Museums.*

WHALE-WATCHING AND OCEAN TOURS This is a popular departure point for whale-watching on Jeffrey's Ledge, about 20 miles offshore. If you have any tendency toward seasickness, be sure to choose a calm day or take antinausea medication. Chances are you'll see more than a dozen whales. Frequently sighted species include finbacks, minkes, rights, and humpbacks. **Second Chance**

(207-967-5507 or 1-800-767-2628; www.firstchancewhalewatch.com), 4 Western Ave. in the Lower Village (at the bridge), also offers a scenic lobster cruise. **Atlantic Explorer** (207-967-4784; www.atlanticexposure.com) leaves from Nonantum Resort for tours of the water both above the waves and below. Using a remote-controlled vehicle that houses a camera, the operators of the cruise let you see what's underneath the vessel, mostly shellfish like lobsters.

✳ Winter Pastimes

CROSS-COUNTRY SKIING **Harris Farm** (207-499-2678; www.harrisfarm.com), 252 Buzzell Rd., Dayton. A 500-acre dairy farm with more than 20 miles of trails. Equipment rentals available, including snowshoes and ice skates. Located 1.5 miles from the Rt. 5 and Rt. 35 intersection.

SLEIGH RIDES **Rockin' Horse Stables** (207-967-4288), 245 Arundel Rd., Kennebunkport, offers 30- to 40-minute sleigh rides on a 100-acre farm.

✳ Green Space

BEACHES The Kennebunks discourage day-trippers by requiring a permit to park at major beaches. Day, week, and seasonal passes must be secured from the chamber of commerce, town hall, police department, or local lodging places. You can also park in one of the town lots and walk, bike, or take a trolley to the beach.

Goose Rocks Beach, a few miles north of Kennebunkport Village on Rt. 9, is the area's most beautiful beach: a magnificent wide, smooth stretch of silver-white sand backed by high dunes. Children here seem to mimic their less frenetic 19th-century counterparts, doing wonderfully old-fashioned things like flying kites, playing paddleball, and making sand castles.

Kennebunk and **Gooch's Beaches** in Kennebunk are both long, wide strips of firm sand backed by Beach Ave., divided by Oak's Neck. Beyond Gooch's Beach, take Great Hill Rd. along the water to **Strawberry Island**, a great place to walk and examine tidal pools. Please don't picnic. Keep going and you come to **Mother's Beach**, small and very sandy.

Arundel Beach, near the Colony Hotel at the mouth of the Kennebunk River, offers nice rocks for climbing and good beachcombing for shell and beach-glass enthusiasts.

NATURE PRESERVES ✐ ♿ **Rachel Carson National Wildlife Refuge** (207-646-9226; TDD/voice 1-800-437-1220). Headquarters for this almost 50-mile, 5,000-acre preserve are just south of the Kennebunkport line at 321 Port Rd. (Rt. 9) in Wells. Office open weekdays 8–4:30. The refuge is divided among 10 sites along Maine's Southern Coast. Pick up a leaflet guide to the mile-long, wheelchair-accessible nature trail here. Kayakers can enter the refuge traveling up the rivers, but no put-ins or takeouts allowed to avoid disturbing the wildlife. (Also see Laudholm Farm in "Ogunquit and Wells.")

Kennebunkport Conservation Trust (www.thekennebunkportconservation trust.org), P.O. Box 7028, Cape Porpoise 04014, maintains several properties.

These include the **Tyler Brook Preserve** near Goose Rocks, the 148-acre **Emmons Preserve** along the Batson River (access from unpaved Gravelly Rd., off Beachwood Rd.), the 740-acre **Kennebunkport Town Forest**, and the **Vaughns Island Preserve**, which offers nature trails on a wooded island separated from the mainland by two tidal creeks. Cellar holes of historic houses are accessible by foot from 3 hours after to 3 hours before high tide.

Kim Grant

GOOSE ROCKS BEACH

The Nature Conservancy (207-729-5181) maintains 14-acre **Butler Preserve** on the Kennebunk River, including Picnic Rock; owns 135 acres of the **Kennebunk Plains Preserve**; and assists in the management of 650 state-owned acres in West Kennebunk (take Rt. 99 toward Sanford) with nearly 4 miles of shoreline on the Mousam River in Kennebunk.

East Point Sanctuary, off Rt. 9 (east of Goose Rocks Beach) in Biddeford Pool. A 30-acre Maine Audubon Society preserve, well known to birders, who flock here during migrating seasons. Beautiful any time of year. From Rt. 9 turn right just beyond Goose Rocks Beach onto Fortune Rocks Beach Rd. to Lester B. Orcutt Blvd.; turn right, drive almost to the end, and look for a chain-link fence and AUDUBON sign. The trail continues along the golf course and sea.

WALKS Henry Parsons Park, Ocean Ave., is a path along the rocks leading to Spouting Rock and Blowing Cave, both sights to see at midtide. A great way to view the beautiful homes along Ocean Ave.

St. Anthony Monastery and Shrine (207-967-2011), Kennebunkport. Some 20 acres of peaceful riverside fields and forests on Beach Rd., now maintained by Lithuanian Franciscans as a shrine and retreat. Visitors are welcome; gift shop. (See St. Anthony's Franciscan Monastery and Guesthouse in *Other Lodging*.)

✳ Lodging

The Kennebunks represent one of the Maine coast's largest concentrations of inns and B&Bs, with more than 80 lodging places, or 1,400 rooms. We list a number of options in different price ranges, but still just a fraction of what's available. These places tend to stay open at least through the first two weekends in December, when the town celebrates Christmas Prelude, and many are open year-round.

All listings are in Kennebunkport 04046 unless otherwise noted

TOP-DOLLAR INNS AND B&BS **Captain Lord Mansion** (207-967-3141 or 1-800-522-3141; www.captainlord .com), P.O. Box 800. Open year-round at the corner of Pleasant and Green Sts. This three-story Federal home, built in 1812, is topped with a widow's walk from which guests can contemplate the town and sea beyond. All 16 rooms have a gas fireplace, antiques, and private bath, and some feature a four-poster or canopy bed. The Merchant Captain's Suite boasts what's probably the most elaborate bathroom in Maine. Some travelers may feel overwhelmed by the ornate, richly appointed rooms and attentive service, but others will appreciate the haute B&B experience. Phebe's Fantasy, a separate building with more low-key decor, has four rooms with fireplace. $149–499 per room in high season, $125–399 off-season, breakfast and tea included.

White Barn Inn (207-967-2321; www.whitebarninn.com), 37 Beach Ave., P.O. Box 560C, Beach St. Open year-round. The "barn" is now an elegant dining room (see *Dining Out*) attached to the inn. Built in the 1860s as a farmhouse, later enlarged as the Forest Hills House, this complex lies midway between Dock Square and Kennebunk Beach. Choose an antiques-furnished room in the original farmhouse; a suite in the carriage house with four-poster king bed, fireplace, and marble bath with whirlpool tub; a cottage suite with specially crafted furnishings, a double-sided fireplace, Jacuzzi, and steam shower. Guests breakfast in the inn's original, old-fashioned dining room; some rooms overlook the landscaped pool area. All 25 rooms have a plasma-screen TV. $280–725 per couple for rooms includes breakfast, afternoon tea, and use of touring bikes.

The Beach House (207-967-3850; www.beachhseinn.com), 211 Beach Ave. Open year-round. Laurie Bongiorno and his associates have spiffed up this formerly modest B&B across the street from Kennebunk Beach. The old sitting room and dining room remain comfortable but have obviously been decorated by a top designer. Breakfast is a bountiful continental spread, and afternoon tea is served.

RESORT HOTEL

🐾 ✏ ♿ **The Colony Hotel** (207-967-3331 or 1-800-552-2363; www.thecolony hotel.com), 140 Ocean Ave. and King's Hwy. Open May–Oct. With 124 rooms (all with private bath) in three buildings, this is among the last of New England's coastal resorts still maintained in the grand style. The Colony is also environmentally conscious, placing recycling bins in guest rooms, composting, and earning the accolade "Certified Wildlife Habitat" from the National Wildlife Federation. None of these practices, however, diminishes the luxuriousness of the hotel. Set on a rise overlooking the point at which the Kennebunk River meets the Atlantic, it's been owned by the Boughton family since 1948; many guests have been coming for generations. Amenities include a heated saltwater pool, a private beach, an 18-hole putting green, and a social and nature walk program. A 3-night minimum is required for weekend reservations for July and Aug. $125–430 single or double per day includes a full breakfast; $25 per extra person (children, too), plus $5-per-person service charge. Worth it. Pets are $25 per day.

The 34 rooms are $255–495 Apr.–Nov., $155–375 off-season, and in-room spa services are offered.

MODERATELY EXPENSIVE INNS AND B&BS

On the water

Cape Arundel Inn (207-967 2125; www.capearundelinn.com), 208 Ocean Ave., P.O. Box 530A. Open March–New Year's Eve. The most dramatic location in town, facing the open ocean with just the estate of former president George H. W. Bush interrupting the water view. Jack Nahil, former owner of the White Barn Inn and On the Marsh Tavern, has transformed this 19th-century mansion "cottage," an inn for some time, room by room. The inn features seven rooms in the main house and six in the adjacent motel, a 1950s addition with picture windows facing the water, parking in back, TVs. A carriage house water-view suite (up a flight of stairs) has a deck and sitting area. All rooms have a phone, and many have a fireplace. The living room is hung with interesting art, some of it Nahil's own. The dining room, which is open for dinner to the public (see *Dining Out*), is well loved. $275–345 in-season, from $150 off-season, includes a "creative continental" breakfast.

♪ **Tides Inn By-the-Sea** (207-967-3757; www.tidesinnbythesea.com), 252 Kings Hwy., Goose Rocks Beach. Open May–Oct. Marie Henriksen and her daughter Kristin Blomberg continue to make this very Victorian inn a delightful anachronism. No in-room phones or TVs, loads of charming chintz and lace—even a ghost who shakes one bed upstairs—mean a true Maine coast getaway. A few short miles from Dock Square, the inn

overlooks the area's long and silvery Goose Rocks Beach, full of families flying kites. Built by Maine's foremost shingle-style architect, John Calvin Stevens, in 1899, the Tides Inn has hosted Teddy Roosevelt and Sir Arthur Conan Doyle. The recently renovated Belvidere Club serves some of the area's best meals (see *Dining Out*), and rooms in the main building now feature new, bigger windows. We recommend the high-end rooms with the view, having been lulled to sleep in a front room listening to the waves. High-season rates range $195–325 for ocean-view (two guests) and family rooms (four guests); less in the off-season. Next door, **Tides Too** offers two-bedroom oceanfront suites.

♪ **The Ocean View** (207-967-2750; www.theoceanview.com), 171 Beach Ave., Kennebunk Beach 04043. Open Apr.–mid-Dec. Bob and Carole Arena's painted lady is right across from Kennebunk Beach. The main house has four bright oceanfront guest rooms and one suite, a comfortable TV room, a living room with fireplace, and a sunny breakfast room with a view of the ocean. A separate building houses four pretty water-view suites with sitting area, color TV,

CAPE ARUNDEL INN

Nancy English

and private terrace. All rooms offer lush bathrobes, a CD player, ceiling fan, mini fridge, and phone. Full gourmet breakfasts are consciously healthy, and breakfast in bed is served to guests in suites. High-season rates run $245–390; low, $160–280.

☀ ❀ Seaside Motor Inn & Cottages (207-967-4461; www.kennebunkbeach.com), P.O. Box 631, Gooch's Beach 04046. The motor inn is open year-round; cottages are rented May–Oct. An attractive complex formed by a 1720s homestead, a 1756 inn, a modern 22-room motor inn, and 10 housekeeping cottages—all set on 20 landscaped acres on a private beach next to one of Maine's best public strands. This property has been in the Gooch-Severance family for 13 generations. The homestead, which was built as a tavern (the tavern keeper operated the ferry across the mouth of the Kennebunk River here), is now rented as a cottage. The cheery breakfast room is a former boathouse for the 19th-century inn that stood here until the 1950s. Motor inn rooms feature two queen beds, a cable TV recessed in a highboy, private phone, and balcony or patio. Cottages, which vary in size and view, are per month in July and August, per week the rest of the season. One-week minimum in oceanfront rooms and 2-day minimum in terrace-side rooms in high season. Inn rooms are $229–239 per night, including buffet breakfast, less off-season; cottage rates range from $965 weekly to $9,180 monthly. Pets accepted in some cottages.

Bufflehead Cove Inn (207-967-3879; www.buffleheadcove.com), Box 499, off Rt. 35. Open Apr.–Nov. This hidden gem, sequestered on 6 acres at the end of a dirt road and overlooking an 8-foot-deep tidal cove, sits less than a mile from the village of Kennebunkport. Harriet Gott, a native of nearby Cape Porpoise, and her husband, Jim, offer four good-looking guest rooms, a suite, and a separate deluxe cottage. River View cottage lies off by itself, with a deck, kitchen, wood-burning fireplace, and whirlpool tub. The inn living room has a hearth and deep window seats; you'll also find an inviting veranda, and woods and orchard to explore. $155–350 includes a full breakfast on the white porch if the weather is fine, and afternoon wine and cheese.

The Inn at Harbor Head (207-967-5564; www.harborhead.com), 41 Pier Rd., Cape Porpoise 04046. Open May–Oct. We love this inn for so many reasons: its secluded location far from the madding crowd in Kennebunkport; the views over the beautiful working lobster harbor of Cape Porpoise; imaginative decor featuring sunken tubs, antique mahogany and brass beds, bath tiles hand painted with herons and terns, and chenille throws; and owners Dick and Eve Roesler's engaging presence. The inn offers three rooms and one suite with a fireplace in a rambling, shingled 1890 home. Guests share the dock, terrace, sitting rooms, hammock, and Adirondack chairs; there's an inviting fireplace in the library. Fresh baked goods top off large breakfasts; wine and cheese are served in the afternoon. Beach passes and towels provided for nearby Goose Rocks Beach. No smoking, no TV. $195–325 per room in-season, $150–275 in winter.

❀ ♿ Kennebunkport Inn (207-967-2621 or 1-800-248-2621; www.kennebunkportinn.com), 1 Dock Square, P.O. Box 111. Open year-round. Originally an 1890s mansion. Owners Debbie Lennon and Tom Nill have redecorated most of the 34 rooms, which, though a bit generic, attract guests in droves. Some offer river views; several have a gas fireplace. The inn has four sections—the main house; a 1980s Federal-style addition; a 1930s river house with smaller rooms; and the Wharfside, with 14 rooms including 2 family suites. In summer a small, enticing pool on the terrace offers respite from the Dock Square hubbub, and guests can dine in the **Port Tavern and Grill** year-round. The cocktail lounge is dark and friendly, with a huge old bar and evening piano music. High-season rates $159–299 per room, off-season $99–225.

&. **The Captain Fairfield Inn** (207-967-4454 or 1-800-322-1928; www.captainfairfield.com), P.O. Box 2690, corner of Pleasant and Green Sts. Open year-round. Owners Janet and Rick Wolf make this gray-clapboard inn utterly inviting. They have stocked the inn's Federal-style interior with everything from a cheerful colored-glass collection in the entryway and homemade lemonade on a summer afternoon to dataports in the guest rooms and homegrown herbs and rhubarb for the baked goods and breakfasts. Common spaces include a music room with a piano, a den with TV, and a lawn that stretches back across the width of the block into that of the neighboring Inn on South Street. The nine bedrooms all have a queen bed and private bath; six have gas fireplace, and The Library features a double whirlpool. The Wolfs offer a four-course breakfast that can go from fresh-baked croissants to Maine blueberry crêpes. $150–295 in

high season, $110–250 in low; $40 per extra person.

&. **The Breakwater Inn and Hotel** (207-967-5333; www.thebreakwater inn.com), 127 Ocean Ave., P.O. Box 560C, across from Mabel's Lobster Claw. A 19th-century riverside complex renovated in 2002 by Laurie Bongiorno. The 37 rooms are split between three buildings. Each room is equipped with a CD player, TV, phone, air-conditioning, and a granite-and-tile bath, varying in view and size. The inn, made up of two buildings, has rooms on four floors and no elevator; only the hotel has an elevator. Guests can dine at Stripers Fish Shack (see *Eating Out*). In-season rates range from as high as $329 at the inn and $349 for a suite in the hotel, and include continental breakfast and afternoon tea; $150–325 off-season and midweek. A 5.3 percent housekeeping fee is added. Request specific details about your room before booking.

Old Fort Inn (207-967-5353 or 1-800-828-FORT; www.oldfortinn.com), P.O. Box M. Open mid-Apr.–mid-Dec. Stepping into David and Sheila Aldrich's quiet respite is like falling into a plush wing chair after a long, hard day. The inn feels miles away from humming Dock Square, yet it's actually close enough for sightseeing on foot. The 16 guest rooms in the stone-and-brick carriage house boast carefully chosen Victorian furniture and memorabilia, color TV, phone, air-conditioning, and wet bar. The property includes a landscaped, heated pool, a tennis court, horseshoes, and shuffleboard. Two-night minimum during high season. $160–390; $99–250 off-season. Rates include a full buffet breakfast.

♥ 🐾 The Captain Jefferds Inn (207-967-2311 or 1-800-839-6844; www.captainjefferdsinn.com), 5 Pearl St., Box 691. This handsome Federal-era mansion is run expertly by the delightful Bartholomews (Dick, Pat, and their daughter Jane), who have named all 16 rooms for their favorite places. Assisi, a suite with a king-sized iron bed, features a gas fireplace, large Italian tiled shower, and indoor garden with a fountain ($305). We love California, which overlooks the inn's lush garden: pale green walls, a charming plaid daybed in the foyer, and a four-poster queen bed made of ornately carved wood. Guests enjoy the three-course breakfast by candlelight, and tea is served in the afternoon. Dick is a veterinarian who genuinely loves dogs, especially Kate, the inn's golden retriever. Guest dogs are accepted by reservation; $30 extra. $165–340 in-season, $110–285 the rest of the year.

🐾 Maine Stay Inn and Cottages (207-967-2117 or 1-800-950-2117; www.mainestayinn.com), Box 500A, 34 Maine St. Open year-round. A terrific place for families with children, the inn offers 6 guest rooms in the main house and 11 suites in 5 cottages nestled in nicely landscaped grounds—including a full swing set. The house was built in 1860 by Melville Walker and given to his wife as a Christmas present 5 years later. A wicker-filled wraparound porch, a spiral staircase, and several ornate fireplace mantels sustain the history. A full breakfast and afternoon tea are offered by owners Janice and George Yankowski, who moved here from Austin, Texas, because Janice summered in Maine as a child. $170–250 in-season, $105–175 off-season.

♿ The 1802 House (207-967-5632 or 1-800-932-5632; www.1802inn.com), P.O. Box 646-A, 15 Locke St. Open year-round. Marc and Susan Trottier offer six guest rooms furnished with antiques, plus a three-room suite with a fireplace, fridge, double shower, Roman garden room, and double whirlpool tub overlooking a private deck. Most rooms have a queen-sized four-poster and fireplace, and many have a whirlpool tub. The house has an out-in-the-country feel, shaded by large pines. Common rooms are airy and comfortable; cozy corners for winter. $188–375 in high season, $139–299 in low, includes full breakfast.

MODERATELY PRICED INNS AND B&BS 🦋 🐾 🐾 ♿ The Green Heron (207-967-3315; www.greenheroninn.com), P.O. Box 2578, 126 Ocean Ave. Open except for 2 weeks in January. This is truly a user-friendly little hotel with a casual atmosphere, now owned and run by Tony Kusuma and Dan Oswald. Within walking distance of both village and shore, the 10 rooms and coveside cottage are smallish but attractive, clean and bright, and equipped with private bath, air-conditioning, and color TV; some also have a refrigerator and a fireplace. Kids are welcome here, as are pets, whose owners receive rooms with separate entrances. On the west side of the inn a paved path overlooking the creek leads to a tiny gravel beach. There in the inlet you just might spot an egret, a cormorant, or one of the inn's namesake herons. In-season $150–255 for a double, off-season $110–180, including a full breakfast and afternoon refreshments.

Chetwynd House Inn (207-967-2235; www.chetwyndhouse.com), P.O.

Box 130, 4 Chestnut St. Open year-round. In 1972 Susan Chetwynd opened Kennebunkport's first B&B. Now owned by Robert Knowles, her son, it remains a gracious 1840s home near Dock Square. The four antiques-furnished guest rooms have private bath, TV, refrigerator, and air-conditioning; a top-floor junior suite has skylights and a river view. Generous breakfasts—with eggs cooked to order and a quarter melon with peaches, blueberries, and bananas or other fruit—are served family-style at the dining room table. $170–210 in-season; discounts come with off-season specials.

Harbor Inn (207-967-2074; www .harbor-inn.com), 90 Ocean Ave., P.O. Box 538A. Kathy and Bob Jones, longtime Port residents and owners of Cove House (see below), have acquired this fine old house and thoroughly brightened it, filling it with flowers and an airy, hospitable air. The five rooms and two-room suite (all with private bath) feature a mix of family antiques, paintings, and prints, and the long porch is lined with wicker. It's a short walk to the ocean, a longer but pleasant walk to Dock Square. $109–165 for rooms in-season, $75–150 off-season. Woodbine Cottage in the rear is $140–150.

🐚 **Cove House Bed & Breakfast** (207-967-3704; www.covehouse.com), 11 S. Maine St. Owner Barry Jones (son of the owners of Harbor Inn—see above) has decorated the inn with period antiques and gorgeous Oriental rugs, as well as playful touches like teddy bears and needlepoint samplers. The inn features architectural details such as a pretty side porch, original fireplace mantels, and richly burnished, foot-wide plank floors.

Barry doubles as a volunteer EMT and fireman, and his relaxed manner and Maine accent lend a refreshing authenticity to the place. Cove House is within walking distance of a beach and easy bicycling distance of Dock Square. Two of the four pleasant guest rooms have a private bath. Inn rooms are $125, $25 per extra person, and $750 per week for the cottage in July and Aug. (3-night minimum, when available, $135 a night), including breakfast.

The Waldo Emerson Inn (207-985-4250 or 1-800-248-2621; www.waldo emersoninn.com), 108 Summer St. (Rt. 35), Kennebunk 04043. This special house was built in 1784 by a shipbuilder who inherited the land and original 1753 cottage (the present kitchen) from Waldo Emerson, the great-uncle of the famous poet and essayist. The four cozy guest rooms all come with private bath and antiques. A quilt store is on the property, and the Wedding Cake House is next door. $95–140 per couple includes a full gourmet breakfast and afternoon refreshments.

OTHER LODGING St. Anthony's Franciscan Monastery and Guest House (207-967-4865; www.francis canguesthouse.com), 28 Beach Ave., Kennebunk. Open mid-May–Oct. With private bath, air-conditioning, and television, the 60 rooms here have the feeling of Maine the way it used to be. The rooms at this 1908 estate on the Kennebunk River were converted to a guest house in the 1960s; the monks live in the Tudor great house. The 66-acre garden is open to the public year-round during daylight hours (no pets), and walking the trails might take an hour and a half, past formal gardens and the stations of the cross, Our Lady of Lourdes, and other shrines and fountains. A modern abstract statue, with colored glass from the Vatican Pavilion at the 1964 World's Fair, stands in front of the monastery. Maps of the trees and shrubs planted under Frederick Law Olmsted's design, and of the shrines, are available. $80–135 in-season, $50–80 off-season, with breakfast made by the Lithuanian cook—a cross between a European and an American breakfast that includes homemade farmer's cheese, raisin bread, carrot bread, and potato bread.

🐾 ✿ ⚐ ♿ **Yachtsman Lodge and Marina** (207-967-2511; www .yachtsmanlodge.com), P.O. Box 560C, Ocean Ave. Open late Apr.–late Oct. This 30-room inn is great for the cruising crowd, who can sail right up the Kennebunk River to the lodge and take advantage of its 59-slip marina. Under the same ownership as the White Barn Inn, the Beach House, and others, the Yachtsman features rooms decorated to resemble the inside of a yacht, with private riverside patios. $159–314 includes continental breakfast in the marble-tiled breakfast room or under the pergola. Children and pets are okay and wheelchair access is easy. Bicycle and canoe rentals are free for guests at this or any hotel in the Bongiorno group.

🐾 🐾 ⚐ ♿ **Shorelands** (207-985-4460 or 1-800-99-BEACH; www.shore lands.com), P.O. Box 769, Rt. 9. Open May–Oct. A family-owned, family-geared motel and cottage complex of 4 guest rooms, 2 apartments, and 25 cottages within walking distance of the beach. Some units have a double whirlpool. Facilities include outdoor pool, covered outdoor hot tub, yard games, horseshoes, basketball, and grills. $69–175 in-season, $49–109 off-season, extra person $10. Weekly rates, off-season packages.

✳ Where to Eat

DINING OUT 🍴 ♿ **Kennebunk Inn** (207-985-3351; www.thekennebunk inn.com), 45 Main St. Kennebunk. Open Wed.–Sat. for dinner in the dining room; daily for dinner in the tavern and lunch on weekdays. Chef-owners Brian O'Hea and Shanna Horner O'Hea make meals here that draw repeat customers who spread the word—this is a place for quality at a moderate price. The dining room, with entrées $17–29, serves up game hen stuffed with biscuit, duck sausage, and apples, or swordfish with a roasted garlic butter sauce. The attached pub has a lower-priced menu (same desserts) with prices $4–15, for grilled flat-bread pizza, sandwiches, burgers, steak, and fish-and-chips.

Cape Arundel Inn (207-967-2125), Ocean Ave., Kennebunkport. Open mid-Apr.–Dec. for dinner (closed Mon. off-season). Jack Nahil, one of the area's most highly respected restaurateurs, has made this a superb dining room, matching its great location facing the ocean with skilled cooking that draws loyal customers from near and far. The à la carte menu lists a duck "Duo," with duck leg confit and a grilled duck breast, in a raspberry demiglaze that vies with the perfect lobster stew for top prize. Try the best profiterole with vanilla gelato and chocolate sauce that we've ever tasted. Entrées $24–34.

White Barn Inn (207-967-2321), 37 Beach Ave., Kennebunkport. Open for dinner year-round (except Jan.);

closed Sun. Reservations required. This award-winning restaurant is set in two restored 19th-century barns with a three-story glassed rear wall, exposed beams, and extravagant seasonal floral displays. Original art, hotel silver, and fine linens up the luxury ante, and the fare is contemporary and regional. The five-course prix fixe menu changes frequently, but you might begin with a salad of greens, roasted tomatoes, pesto goat cheese, and rosemary croutons, then continue to a grape and pinot noir sorbet to cleanse the palate, a corn-and-coconut soup, and an entrée of halibut and smoked scallop ravioli on beets with almond broccoli and champagne foam. A dress code requires jackets. $89 prix fixe plus tax, beverage, and gratuity.

On the Marsh Tavern (207-967-2299; www.onthemarsh.com), Rt. 9, Kennebunk Lower Village. Open daily for dinner May–Oct.; closed Mon. and Tue. off-season, closed in Jan. Continental dining with style overlooking a lovely salt marsh. Appetizers include lobster ravioli with leeks ($13) and crunchy tiger shrimp ($12), and among the entrées are lobster steak, two grilled lobster tails served over a risotto cake, and seared sea scallops with lobster risotto ($28). Entrées $18–29.

✔ **The Belvidere Club at the Tides Inn By-the-Sea** (207-967-3757), Goose Rocks Beach, 6 miles northeast of Dock Square. Open mid-May–mid-Oct. for dinner. In keeping with the Tides Inn's casual, family-oriented location on the beach, Kristin Blomberg and Marie Henriksen added a 19th-century mahogany bar, salvaged from the demolished Shawmut Inn in Kennebunkport (word has

it the presidential press corps used to swap stories around the antique brass rail), and an Eastlake molding around the back shelves. Now the room gives off the air of a friendly tavern. But the latest action is in the food on the plates. Jeff Savage arrived from 3 years at Fore Street and began serving up foie gras from Quebec. His lobster stew is made with the simplest ingredients, and a mushroom forager keeps him supplied with black trumpets for the great risotto. Kids' menu, too. Entrées $23–27.

Windows on the Water (207-967-3313), Chase Hill Rd., Kennebunkport. Open year-round for lunch and dinner. The dining room offers views of the port through arched windows; there's also a screened terrace for alfresco dining. A mixed seafood sampler, with coriander-encrusted ahi tuna carpaccio, poached shrimp, and crabcakes ($16), lobster-stuffed potato ($13), and grilled pizzas are popular at lunch. Dinner ranges from appetizers like lobster bisque and "colossal iced shrimp cocktail" to entrées such as pan-seared flank steak with sautéed peppers, onions, and mushrooms ($23). Dinner entrées $16–36; reservations for dinner a must.

✔ ✦ **The Colony Hotel** (207-967-3331), 140 Ocean Ave., Kennebunkport. The elegant dining room at this grand old resort overlooks the ocean and is open to the public for breakfast and dinner. Menu selections change each night and might include haddock baked and stuffed with crabmeat ($16.50), or a napoleon of lobster with layers of lobster and pastry in two different sauces, one with cognac and the other with white wine ($22.50). From July 4 through Labor Day the Colony offers a popular Friday-night

Mariner's Buffet ($30; reservations recommended). Children's menus also available. The poolside Marine Room Lounge serves cocktails and has weekend entertainment during summer months.

♂ ⅖ **Pier 77** (207-967-8500), Pier Rd., Cape Porpoise. Open for lunch 11:30–2:30, dinner at 5 daily in summer, off-season closing some days, closed Jan.–mid-Mar. This restaurant came under new ownership in 2004 and quickly gained a following for its range of dishes from spaghetti and meatballs in the downstairs bar called the Ramp to the chicken fettuccine with roasted mushrooms, red onion, spinach, goat cheese, and a "dash of cream" ($16), and seafood stew in saffron broth ($28), upstairs at dark wood tables with windows on the sea. Entrées $16–28.

🦞 ♂ **Mabel's Lobster Claw** (207-967-2562), Ocean Ave., Kennebunkport. Open Apr.–early Nov. daily for lunch and dinner. An informal favorite with locals, including former president Bush. Reservations recommended for dinner. Specialties include stuffed lobster Savannah, lobster stew, and shore dinner (clam chowder, lobster, and steamed clams). The lunch special is a lobster roll made with all fresh meat and served in a buttery, grilled hot-dog roll. Dinner entrées $12.95–29.95, but you can always get a hamburger ($6.95).

Grissini (207-967-2211), 27 Western Ave., Kennebunkport. Open year-round, except Jan., for dinner. A northern Italian trattoria created by the owner of the White Barn Inn, this is a 120-seat, informal, trendy restaurant with seasonal outdoor terrace dining and an à la carte menu. You might start with penne Bolognese,

then dine on grilled salmon or portobello mushrooms layered with fresh mozzarella and polenta. Large portions. Entrées $18.95–28.95.

LOBSTER AND CLAMS ♂ ⅖ **Nunan's Lobster Hut** (207-967-4362), Rt. 9, Cape Porpoise. Open for dinner May–mid-Oct. A long telescope of a building full of old benches, with buoys hanging from the rafters, Nunan's has been feeding lobster lovers since 1953 when Bertha Nunan started working here; she's still at it. The place can fill up by 5:15; people outside get a number and wait for a table. A 1.5-pound lobster comes with melted butter, potato chips, a roll, and pickles. Grilled cheese and a hamburger supply other tastes, and pie, brownies, and cheesecake are on the dessert list. Beer and wine. No credit cards.

♂ ⅖ **The Clam Shack** (207-967-3321 or 207-967-2560), Kennebunkport (at the bridge). Clams, lobsters, and fresh fish. A year-round seafood market and Mother's Day–Columbus Day takeout stand that's worth the wait. Other seafood markets include **Cape Porpoise Lobster Co.** (207-967-4268) in Cape Porpoise, where the locals get their fish and steamed lobster to go, and **Port Lobster** (207-967-2081), Ocean Ave., Kennebunkport, which offers live or cooked lobsters packed to travel or ship, and lobster, shrimp, and crab rolls to go (several obvious waterside picnic spots are within walking distance).

Also see **Mabel's Lobster Claw** under *Dining Out.*

EATING OUT 🦞 ♂ ⅖ **Cherie's** (207-985-1200), 7 High St., Kennebunk. Open for dinner 5:30–close, also

Sunday brunch 8–1. Originally a popular bakery, Cherie's grew into an attractive restaurant 4 years ago, and the dinner hour is when the most adventuresome dishes come out of the busy kitchen. Thai seafood soup with mussels, shrimp, scallops, and snow peas is served with lemongrass ginger broth over sticky rice; or try a pork on a skewer with black bean and hearts of palm salad. Entrées $14.75–17.25. Open 6–6 Mon.–Sat., until 1 PM Sun.

The Wayfarer (207-967-8961), 1 Pier Rd., Cape Porpoise. Open Tue.–Sat. for breakfast, lunch, and dinner, Sun. breakfast. Closed Mon. The chowder comes with high praise, and the lobster roll we enjoyed was the best of its kind, on a toasted hot-dog bun with lots of sweet fresh lobster meat and not too much mayonnaise ($10.95 for a regular, $13.95 for a large). Pies are homemade. Casual and well cared for, this is the place for a relaxing meal. BYOB from the general store across the road.

Stripers Fish Shack (207-967-3625), 131–133 Ocean Ave., Kennebunkport. Open in-season daily for lunch and dinner. This restaurant moved into the Breakwater Inn and went way upscale, with a long, thin aquarium harboring little blue fish that match pale blue slipcovered chairs with lime piping. Dinner entrées range from bouillabaisse and ale-battered fish-and-fries to a shelled, butter-poached lobster, at best fine examples of fried or grilled fish, but none of it got us excited. Entrées $20.50–46 (for a 2-pound lobster).

Alisson's (207-967-4841), 5 Dock Square, Kennebunkport. Open at 11 for lunch and 5 for dinner. A pub and grill "where the nicest people meet the nicest people," the true heart of Dock Square, with all the seafood you expect and a spectrum of burgers. Dinner entrées include seafood fettuccine, grilled salmon, steak, and steamers; vegetarians could go for the pizza. **The Market Pub** is Dock Square's meeting place. Entrées $13.95 22.95.

Federal Jack's Restaurant & Brew Pub (207-967-4322), 8 Western Ave., Kennebunk Lower Village. Open from 11:30 for lunch and dinner, offering a variety of handcrafted ales. This is the original Shipyard Ale brewery, squirreled away on the river, with parking right in the thick of things. The restaurant is upstairs, spacious, sleek, and sunny, with windows and seasonal terrace dining on the river. There are lobster rolls, burgers, seafood and pasta dishes, and seafood paella. Blue Fin stout might go with the Captain Jack's Feast—chowder, lobster, and mussels. Live acoustic music on weekends.

THE CLAM SHACK IN KENNEBUNKPORT

Kim Grant

🦞 🐚 ⚓ ♿ **Bartley's Dockside** (207-967-5050; www.bartleys-dockside.com), by the bridge, Kennebunkport. Lunch and dinner daily. Since 1977 this friendly, family-owned place has been a reliable bet for moderately priced meals—from lunchtime chowders and stews to a dinner bouillabaisse. What's gotten out of control recently is the demand for Mrs. B.'s wild Maine blueberry pie. People come in and reserve a piece of pie as soon as they sit down, because the place always runs out of pie sometime during the day. But it won't sell a whole pie. Thirty blueberry pies are enough to bake every day, and as it is they disappear too fast.

✳ Entertainment

🎭 **Arundel Barn Playhouse** (207-985-5552; www.arundelbarnplay house.com), 53 Old Post Rd. (just off Rt. 1 by the Blue Moon Diner), Arundel. Opened in 1998 in a totally revamped barn, this is a thoroughly professional, classic summer theater with performances every evening (with the exception of days between productions), June–late Aug., matinees Wed. and Fri.; tickets $19–24.

🎭 **Hackmatack Playhouse** (207-698-1807; www.hackmatack.org), 538 Rt. 9, Beaver Dam, Berwick. Local actors, rave reviews.

🎭 **Maritime Productions** (207-641-2313 or 1-877-SEA-SHOW; www .maritimeproductions.org), otherwise known as Kennebunk Theater Cruise, departing nightly June–Sep. from Kennebunkport Marina by the bridge in Dock Square. This 2-hour cruise features dramatic renditions of Seafaring Legends, Haunts, and Folklore; beer, wine, and light fare served.

🎭 **River Tree Center for the Arts** (207-967-9120; www.rivertreearts.org), 35 Western Ave., Kennebunkport. Encompassing the Chappell School of Music and the Irvine Gallery and School of Art, this multifaceted organization stages local concerts, productions, and happenings, as well as workshops in the visual and performing arts for all ages.

Thursday-night summer concerts are performed at 7 PM on the lawn of Kennebunkport's South Congregational Church in July and Aug. (rain location: Community House; 207-985-4343).

Also see **Federal Jack's** under *Eating Out*, and *Entertainment* in "Ogunquit and Wells."

✳ Selective Shopping

ANTIQUES SHOPS The Kennebunks are known as an antiques center, with half a dozen shops representing a number of dealers, most on Rt. 1.

ART GALLERIES You'll find some 50 galleries, most of them seasonal; **Mast Cove Galleries** (207-967-3453) on Maine St., Kennebunkport, is touted as the "largest group gallery in the area." Pick up a free copy of the annual *Guide to Fine Art, Studios, and Galleries*, published by the **Art Guild of the Kennebunks** (207-985-2959) and available at the chamber of commerce and most galleries.

FARMS 🌾 **Harris Farm** (207-499-2678; www.harrisfarm.com), Buzzell Rd., Dayton. July–Oct., visitors are welcome to tour the dairy barn; fresh milk, eggs, produce, and maple syrup sold. Pick-your-own pumpkins on the last Sunday in Sep. and the first two Sundays in Oct., with hayrides offered to the pumpkin patch. A short, pleasant ride up Rt. 35; call for directions.

SPECIAL SHOPS **Kennebunk Book Port** (207-967-3815), 10 Dock Square, Kennebunkport. Open year-round. The oldest commercial building in the Port (1775) is one of the most pleasant bookstores in New England. Climb an outside staircase into this inviting mecca, which is dedicated to reading as well as to buying. Helpful handwritten notes with recommendations from staff make browsing even easier. Books about Maine and the sea are specialties.

Tom's of Maine Natural Living Store (207-985-6331), in the Lafayette Center, Storer and Maine Sts., Kennebunk. Open daily year-round. This is the outlet for a variety of Tom's of Maine products made in town.

Port Canvas (207-985-9767 or 1-800-333-6788), Dock Square, Kennebunkport. Open Apr.–Christmas Prelude. Canvas totes, suitcases, and hats, all made in Kennebunkport.

The Good Earth (207-967-4160), Dock Square, Kennebunkport. Open daily May–Oct., varying hours afterward; closed Jan.–Mar. Stoneware in unusual designs—mugs, vases, and bowls. Great browsing in the loft showroom.

Clay Art (207-967-1177; www .moniquebousquet-clayart.com), 127 Ocean Ave., Kennebunkport. A studio-gallery featuring Monique Bousquet's hand-built porcelain.

KBC Coffee & Drygoods (207-967-1261), 8 Western Ave., Kennebunkport. Hidden away down on the river beneath Federal Jack's, this is a source of Kennebec Brewing Company ales and brew gear as well as souvenir clothing and gifts; also good for cappuccino, cookies, and muffins.

✳ Special Events

February: **Wedding Expo. Winter Carnival Weekend** (*first weekend*). Saturday **hay- and sleigh rides** all month. Weekend **"February Is for Lovers"** events (207-967-0857).

March: **County Home and Garden Show**.

April: **Presidential Road Race**.

June: **Summer Solstice Celebration**.

July: **Bed & Breakfast Inn and Garden Tour**. Old-fashioned **picnic, fireworks**, and **band concert**.

August: **Riverfest** (*first Saturday*).

September: **Old-Time Fiddlers Contest and Country Music Show** (*second Saturday*).

November: **Holiday Auction. Holiday Presents Weekend**.

December: **Christmas Prelude** (*first and second weekends*)—Dock Square is decked out for Yuletide, and there are champagne receptions, church suppers, concerts, and carols; holiday fairs and house tours.

OLD ORCHARD BEACH, SACO, AND BIDDEFORD

Old Orchard's name stems from an apple orchard, one of the first in Maine, planted in 1657 by pioneer settler Thomas Rogers. It was also one the first Maine towns to prosper by catering to tourists.

In 1837 a canny local farmer, Ebenezer C. Staples, recognized the region's potential as a summer playground. Initially taking in boarders on his farm for $1.50 a week, he later opened the first hotel, the still-operating Old Orchard Beach Inn. Staples's instincts proved right: The new railroads soon brought a wave of tourists from both the United States and Canada to frolic on Old Orchard's superb 7-mile-long white sand beach.

Thanks to the Grand Trunk Railroad, Old Orchard became the closest ocean beach resort to Montreal. The area, which has a large Franco-American population, is still a popular destination for French Canadian visitors, and in summer you are likely to hear Quebec-accented French spoken almost anywhere you go.

When the first pier at Old Orchard Beach was built in 1898, it stood 20 feet above and 1,800 feet out over the water and was constructed entirely of steel. The pavilions housed animals, a casino, and a restaurant. In the decades that followed, the original pier was rebuilt many times after being damaged by fire and storms, until a wider and shorter pier of wood was built in 1980.

An amusement area appeared in 1902 and grew after World War I. The 1920s brought big-name bands such as those led by Guy Lombardo and Duke Ellington to the Pier Casino, and thousands danced under a revolving crystal ball.

Fire, hard economic times, and the decline of the railroad and steamboat industries all took their toll on Old Orchard Beach over the years. In the early 1990s the citizens decided to reclaim their town. A major revitalization plan widened sidewalks, added benches and streetlights, and passed and enforced ordinances that prevent "cruising" (repeatedly driving the same stretch of road). The result is a cleaner, more appealing, yet still lively and fun vacation spot. For families, it can't be beat, with the beach, amusement park rides, mini golf just down the road, the kind of food kids love ("Mommy, I want a jumbo hot dog with everything!"), and reasonable lodging rates.

The area is also well known for the camp meetings that began in the mid-1800s, first by Methodists, then by Baptists and the Salvation Army. These meetings continue throughout the summer in the Ocean Park community today.

Biddeford and Saco, separated by the Saco River, are often called "the twin cities." No two Maine towns are more different yet more closely linked.

Saco is a classic Yankee town with white-clapboard mansions, a prestigious museum, and a long, dignified main street. However, it also has a rather garish strip of amusement and water parks along Rt. 1 that is a big draw in summer, particularly for families with young children.

Although it also includes the stately old seaside resort village of Biddeford Pool, the city of Biddeford is essentially a classic mill town with a strong French Canadian heritage and mammoth 19th-century brick textile mills that have largely stood idle since the 1950s.

Parts of Scarborough's 49 square miles belong more in Casco Bay descriptions, but Pine Point and its surrounding area is the easternmost tip of Old Orchard Beach and is often a less crowded, quieter spot to visit. A large saltwater marsh in Scarborough is also good for quiet relaxation and exploring by canoe.

GUIDANCE **Old Orchard Beach Chamber of Commerce** (207-934-2500; to get a free vacation planner by mail, 1-800-365-9386; www.oldorchardbeach maine.com), P.O. Box 600 (1st St.), Old Orchard Beach 04064, maintains a year-round walk-in information center (open 8:30–4:30 weekdays, also Sat. and Sun., June–Aug.) and offers help with reservations.

Biddeford-Saco Chamber of Commerce & Industry (207-282-1567, www .biddefordsacochamber.org), 110 Main St., Saco Island, Suite 1202, Saco 04072. Stocks many local brochures; helpful, friendly staff.

GETTING THERE *By air:* **Portland International Jetport** is 13 miles north, and rental cars are available at the airport. You can also fly your own plane into **Sanford Airport**.

By hired car: **D&P Associated Limousine Services** (207-878-6757 or 1-800-750-6757), 93 Hennesey Dr., Portland, provides service anywhere in New England, as does **David's Limousine** (207-829-3289; www.maine-limo.com), Lower Methodist Rd., Cumberland, which also goes to New York.

By car: Exits 36 and 42 off the Maine Turnpike (I-95) take you easily to Rt. 9 and the center of Old Orchard Beach. You can also find the town from Rt. 1.

By train: The **Downeaster** (1-800-USA-RAIL; www.thedowneaster.com), Amtrak's restored train service between Boston and Portland, makes four stops a day year-round at Saco and seasonally, May–Oct., at Old Orchard Beach.

GETTING AROUND From many accommodations in Old Orchard Beach, you are close enough to walk to the pier, the town's center of activity. **Shuttle Bus**, the local transportation service, connects the downtowns of Biddeford, Saco, Portland, and Old Orchard Beach. Call 207-282-5408 for schedules.

PARKING There are a number of privately owned lots in the center of Old Orchard Beach and one municipal lot. Most charge $5–15 for any length of time—10 minutes or all day. There are meters on the street if you don't mind circling a few times to catch an available one, but at 15 minutes for a quarter, you're better off in lots if you plan to stay long.

WHEN TO COME Biddeford is especially worth visiting during La Kermesse, the colorful 4-day Franco-American festival in late June. This festival—which features a colorful parade (some marching bands wear snowshoes), concerts, dances, fireworks, and public suppers with traditional stick-to-the-ribs French Canadian food—is one of the largest ethnic events in New England. Old Orchard Beach quiets way down after Columbus Day, but there are still many places to stay and four year-round restaurants for off-season visitors. The pier closes after Columbus Day weekend.

✳ Villages

Ocean Park is a historic community founded in 1881 by Free Will Baptists and well known for its outstanding religious, educational, and cultural programs. The Ocean Park Association (207-934-9068; www.oceanpark.org) sponsors lectures, concerts, movies, and other events throughout the summer in the cluster of old buildings known as Temple Square. Within the community there is also a recreation hall, shuffleboard and tennis courts, an old-fashioned ice cream parlor, and a smattering of gift shops. The entire community is a state game preserve, and you can find great walking trails through cathedral pines. A comprehensive guide to programs and recreation is put out by the association.

Pine Point. This quiet and less crowded end of the beach offers a selection of gift shops, restaurants, lobster pounds, and places to stay.

Camp Ellis. At the end of a peninsula where the Saco River blends with the ocean. Residents fight a constant battle with beach erosion, and some of the homes are frighteningly close to the shore. Fishing trips, whale-watching, a long breakwater great for walking, interesting shops, and a couple of restaurants.

Biddeford Pool. A small yachting port with lots of low-key charm where well-to-do families have been summering in the same big old shingled houses for generations. You'll find a few shops, a lobster pound, and a small restaurant, but not much else. Although politically part of blue-collar Biddeford, "the pool" is socially closer to fashionable nearby Kennebunkport.

✳ To See and Do

FOR FAMILIES The Rt. 1 strip in Saco and nearby Old Orchard Beach makes up Maine's biggest concentration of "family attractions." Kids go wild. Parents fear they may go broke.

✐ **Funtown/Splashtown USA** (207-284-5139), Rt. 1, Saco. Open daily (depending on the weather) mid-June–Labor Day, weekends in spring and fall. Water activities and a large amusement park. In addition to the 100-foot wooden roller

coaster "Excalibur," the park has bumper cars, New England's largest log flume,
plenty of carnival rides, a hydrofighter, kiddie rides, antique cars.

✒ **Aquaboggan Water Park** (207-282-3112), Rt. 1, Saco. Open June–Labor Day. Several waterslides, including a new high-thrills slide with mats or tubes, "Aquasaucer," swimming pool, bumper boats, mini golf, arcade, shuffleboard, toddler area, wave pool.

✒ **Pirate's Cove Adventure Golf** (207-934-5086), 70 1st St., Old Orchard Beach. Thirty-six up-and-down mini golf holes, waterfalls, ponds. Two separate courses available.

✒ **Palace Playland** (207-934-2001; www.palaceplayland.com), 1 Old Orchard St., Old Orchard Beach. Open daily June–Labor Day; arcade open through Columbus Day on weekends. For more than 60 years fun seekers have been wheeled, lifted, shaken, spun, and bumped in Palace Playland rides. There's a carousel (though it no longer contains the original 1906 horses), a Ferris wheel, a 60-foot-high (Maine's largest) waterslide, and a roller coaster. You can pay by the ride or buy an all-day pass.

GOLF **Dunegrass** (207-934-4513), 200 Wild Dunes Way, Old Orchard Beach, 27 holes (a 9-hole course and an 18-hole course are both available here).

Biddeford-Saco Country Club (207-282-5883), 101 Old Orchard Rd., Saco, 18 holes.

Dutch Elm Golf Course (207-282-9850), 5 Brimstone Rd., Arundel, 18 holes.

Deep Brook Golf Course (207-282-3500), 36 New County Rd., Rt. 5, Saco, nine holes.

Cascade Golf Center (207-282-3524), 955 Portland Rd., Saco, Driving range, lessons.

Willowdale Golf Club (207-883-9351), off Rt. 1, Scarborough, 18 holes.

Pleasant Hill Country Club (207-883-9340), Chamberlain Rd., Scarborough, nine holes.

MUSEUMS **Saco Museum** (207-283-3861), 371 Main St., Saco. Open Sun., Tue., Wed., and Fri. noon–4; Thu. noon–8. $4 adults, $3 seniors, $1 students. Free under 6. (Free to all 4–8 Thu.) Larger than it looks from the outside, and very well maintained and organized. Rotating exhibits, original paintings, furniture, decorative arts, tools, and natural history specimens. Inquire about frequent lectures, tours, and special exhibits. The institute's **Dyer Library** next door has an outstanding Maine history collection.

Harmon Historical Museum, (207-934-9319), 4 Portland Ave., Old Orchard Beach, is open June–Labor Day weekend, Tue.–Sat. 1–4, and by appointment. Home of the Old Orchard Beach Historical Society, the building is full of exhibits from the town's past. Each year, in addition to the regular school, fire, and aviation exhibits, there is a special exhibit on display. Pick up the time line of the area's history and the walking map of historic sites.

RACING **Scarborough Downs** (207-883-4331), off I-95, exit 6, in Scarborough. The largest harness-racing facility in New England. Live harness racing, as well as thoroughbred and harness racing via simulcast. **Downs Club Restaurant** (207-883-3022) is open for dinner and Sunday brunch.

Beech Ridge Motor Speedway (207-883-5227), Holmes Rd., Scarborough. Summer stock-car racing every Sat. night.

SAILING **Saco Bay Sailing** (207-283-1624). Offers sailing excursions from Camp Ellis.

SCENIC DRIVE From Saco there's a loop that heads out Rt. 112, past the **Way-Way General Store**. On the left a few miles out is the **Saco Heath Preserve**, worth a stop to explore. From there, continue on Rt. 112 until it intersects with Rt. 202. Turn left and stay on 202 until you see the intersection with Rt. 5. Turn left again and follow Rt. 5 along the river, back to the center of Saco.

TENNIS The **Ocean Park Association** (207-934-9068) maintains public tennis courts, open in July and Aug.

✳ Green Space

BEACHES Obviously, **Old Orchard Beach** is the big draw in this area, with 7 miles of sand and plenty of space for sunbathing, swimming, volleyball, and other recreation.

Ferry Beach State Park is marked from Rt. 9 between Old Orchard Beach and Camp Ellis, in Saco. The 100-plus-acre preserve includes 70 yards of sand, a boardwalk through the dunes, bike paths, nature trails, a picnic area with grills, lifeguards, changing rooms, and pit toilets. Even in the middle of summer it isn't terribly crowded here. $3 per person, $1 ages 5–11, free under 5 or over 65 with identification. Off-season the Iron Ranger (a green pole with a green can beside the booth) collects $1.50 adults, 50¢ for ages 5–11.

Bay View Beach, at the end of Bay View Rd. near Ferry Beach, is 200 yards of mostly sandy beach; lifeguards, free parking.

Camp Ellis Beach, Rt. 9, Saco. Some 2,000 feet of beach backed by cottages; also a long fishing pier. The commercial parking lots fill quickly on sunny days.

Pine Point, Rt. 9 (at the very end), Scarborough, is small and uncrowded, with a lobster pound and restaurant. The larger beach area just a bit closer to Old Orchard, with snack bar, changing room, and bathrooms, charges $10 a day in summer for parking in the adjacent lot.

HIKING **Saco Trails**, P.O. Box 852, Saco 04072, publishes a booklet called *Take a Hike in Saco*, which lists several trails that are maintained for hiking. Copies availabe at Biddeford-Saco Chamber of Commerce.

NATURE PRESERVES **Scarborough Marsh Audubon Center** (207-883-5100), Pine Point Rd. (Rt. 9), Scarborough. Open daily mid-June–Labor Day, 9:30–5:30.

The largest salt marsh (3,000 acres) in Maine, this is a great place for quiet canoe exploration. This Maine Audubon Nature Center offers canoe rentals, exhibits, a nature store, and guided walking and canoe tours throughout the summer.

Saco Heath Preserve, Rt. 112, Saco. Maybe this small Nature Conservancy preserve isn't crowded because nobody knows it's here, but it shouldn't be overlooked. The sign is hard to spot; look for it on the right-hand side a few miles out of Saco. A quiet, peaceful stroll through a peat bog on a wooden boardwalk.

East Point Sanctuary (207-781-2330), Lester B. Orcutt Blvd., Biddeford Pool. Open sunrise–sunset year-round. A 30-acre Maine Audubon Society preserve with trails, a view of Wood Island Light, and terrific birding in spring and fall.

✳ Lodging

INNS AND BED & BREAKFASTS **The Atlantic Birches Inn** (207-934-5295 or 1-888-934-5295; www.atlantic birches.com), 20 Portland Ave., Old Orchard Beach 04064. A Victorian, shingle-style home, built in the area's heyday. Five guest rooms in the main house are named for former grand hotels; they're cheerful, with a mix of old and new furnishings. The "cottage" next door offers three rooms and two kitchenette suites with separate entrances. The in-ground pool is perfect on a hot day. $89–135 in high season includes an enhanced continental breakfast.

🕏 🐾 **Crown 'n' Anchor Inn** (207-282-3829 or 1-800-561-8865; www.crownanchor.com), 121 North St., P.O. Box 228, Saco 04072. This is a find: a Greek Revival, pillared mansion built in 1827 as an enlargement of a smaller 18th-century home. Host John Barclay has restored the house from top to bottom, filling it with antiques, including the front room, which has been returned to its traditional role as a "receiving parlor." All guest rooms have a private bath. The Normandy Suite with its two working fireplaces and Jacuzzi is particularly nice. The inn is just up the street from the Saco Museum and a 10-minute drive from Saco's relatively uncrowded

sands. A full breakfast, always including a fruit and ice cream dish, is served by candlelight on fine china in the small (it can accommodate only two couples at a time) but formal dining room. Pets accepted. $90–140 in-season; $10 less off-season, $10 off for single travelers, and 4th night free if your stay is 3 nights or more.

Hobson House Celtic Inn (207-284-4113; www.hobsonhouse.com), 398 Main St., Saco 04072. A big yellow mansion in the heart of Saco's historic district, Hobson House was built in the 1820s by Jacob Hobson, Saco's first mayor. It wears its dignity lightly, however, and has a nice homey feel. There are three pleasant and comfortably furnished bedrooms, one with a private bath (the Alice May Hobson Suite, which also has a canopy bed, fireplace, and sitting area) and two sharing a bath. Common space includes a beautiful back garden with a large, free-form swimming pool. $95–105 with full breakfast.

✄ **Old Orchard Beach Inn** (207-934-5834 or 1-877-700-6624; www.oldorchardbeachinn.com), P.O. Box 720, 6 Portland Ave., Old Orchard Beach 04064. Ebenezer Staples's original hostelry, part of this inn dates from the 1730s, and the building is on the National Register of Historic Places as Maine's oldest continually operated inn. It was completely renovated a few years ago and now has traditional wide pine floorboards, antique furnishings, and a lot of period touches. All 18 rooms have air-conditioning, television, phone, and private bath. Room rates are $109–180 high season, $69–140 off-season, with a continental breakfast that includes homemade muffins and breads.

OTHER LODGING Old Orchard Beach offers an overwhelming number of motel, cottage, and condominium complexes both along the beach and on main roads. The chamber of commerce publishes a helpful *Old Orchard Beach Vacation Planner*.

Aquarius Motel (207-934-2626; www.aquariusmotel.com), 1 Brown St., Old Orchard Beach 04064. A small, family-owned and -operated 14-unit motel that's exceptionally clean, and right on the beach. The patio is a great place to relax after a day of sightseeing. Rates are $145 for a double with kitchenette in-season. Family-sized units also available. Many special rates in early spring and late fall. Three-night minimum on holiday weekends.

Ocean Walk Hotel (207-934-1716 or 1-800-992-3779; www.oceanwalk hotel.com), 197 E. Grand Ave., Old Orchard Beach 04064. Forty-four well-kept rooms, from studios to oceanfront suites. The top-floor rooms in one building have very high ceilings, giving them a light, airy, spacious feel. $150–240 in-season, $79–160 off-season.

& **Sea View** (207-934-4180 or 1-800-541-8439; www.seaviewgetaway.com), 65 W. Grand Ave., Old Orchard Beach

04064. Forty-nine rooms, some with oceanfront views. Pretty landscaping, with an outdoor pool and a beautiful fountain in front. Rooms are modern, bright, and clean. Two-bedroom suites with kitchenettes are also available. $80–230 in-season.

The Gull Motel & Inn (207-934-4321), 89 W. Grand Ave., Old Orchard Beach 04064. An attractive motel, immaculate and family oriented. The inn is right on the beach, with a great porch. Cottages also available by the week. Inn rates $70–150 per night; motel rates $65–150; cottages $1,100 per week.

✎ **Billowhouse** (207-934-2333 or 1-888-767-7776; www.billowhouse .com), 2 Temple Ave., Ocean Park 04063. This 1881 Victorian seaside guest house is Mary and Bill Kerrigan's retirement project, completely renovated yet with old-fashioned charm. There are three ground-level efficiency apartments and six more kitchenette units in the adjoining motel. The four B&B units include a large three-room suite with private deck, in-room Jacuzzi, and full kitchen; a two-room suite with private deck and outside hot tub; and two oceanfront rooms with private bath and sharing a deck overlooking the ocean. The beach is literally just steps away. $95–198 in-season, with discounts for extended stays, breakfast included for B&B guests only; $70–125 off-season.

The Nautilus by the Sea (207-934-2021 or 1-800-981-7018; www .nautilusbythesea.com), 2 Colby Ave., Ocean Park 04063. This 13-room B&B, built in 1890 as a private home, is smack up against the beach. A couple of rooms share baths, but all have beach or ocean views, with the most dramatic vista of all the one from the fourth-floor "penthouse suite," where you can lie in bed at night and watch the beam of Wood Island Light play across the water. Owners Dick and Patte Kessler have kept the decor simple and traditional, much as it would have been when the house was built. $70–160 in-season, $50–110 off-season, with continental breakfast.

CAMPGROUNDS Camping is a budget-minded family's best bet in this area. There are at least a dozen campgrounds here (more than 4,000 sites in the area), many geared to families and offering games, recreational activities, and trolley service to the beach in-season. Following are a few recommendations; check with the chamber for a full listing.

♂ ᵬ **Bayley's Camping Resort** (207-883-6043; www.bayleys-camping.com), 52 Ross Rd., Scarborough 04074. Just down the road from Pine Point are paddleboats, swimming pool, Jacuzzi, fishing, game room, special programs for children and adults—and a shuttle to take you to Pine Point Beach and Old Orchard's downtown. Four hundred sites and 50 rental trailers. $36–53 depending on hook-ups; lower rates in spring and fall.

♂ ᵬ **Powder Horn** (207-934-4733; www.mainecampgrounds.com), P.O. Box 366, Old Orchard Beach 04064. A 450-site campground with plenty of recreation options—playgrounds, shuffleboard, horseshoes, volleyball, rec hall and game room, activities program, mini golf, trolley service to the beach in-season. $40–55 per night in-season, $32–42 off-season. **Hidden Pines** is a sister campground next door for basic to full premium sites.

DINING OUT ♂ **Village Inn** (207-934-7370), 213 Saco Ave., Old Orchard Beach. Open for lunch and dinner, with a large and varied menu. Lunch specials include fried seafood, pastas, and chicken cordon bleu. At dinner choices range from seafood specialties and lobster to surf and turf or pasta. Children's menu. Entrées $8–19.

♂ **Lily Moon Café** (207-284-2233), 17 Pepperell Square, Saco. Open for breakfast and lunch Tue.–Sun., for dinner Wed.–Sat. This café was reborn after a 2003 Mother's Day fire, with the help of a community that loved it. Changing starters might be seafood bisque or tomato tortellini soup; entrées feature caramelized salmon or swordfish steak with watercress sauce, and blackened Jack Daniels rib-eye steak. Entrées $16.95–19.25. BYOB. Breakfast features eggs, pancakes, and cheese blintzes.

♂ ᵬ **Joseph's by the Sea** (207-934-5044; www.josephsbythesea.com), 55 W. Grand Ave., Old Orchard Beach. Open Apr.–Oct. Serving breakfast and dinner daily in-season; hours vary the rest of the year, so call ahead. The dining rooms overlook the water, or you can dine on the garden patio. Dinner entrées include seared scallops with pancetta crisps and pepper-crusted filet mignon. Entrées $17–29.

Traditions (207-282-6661), 162 Main St., Saco. A cozy trattoria-style restaurant specializing in pasta and traditional Italian meat and seafood dishes. Open for lunch and dinner. Entrées $7.95–15.95.

The Landmark (207-934-0156), 28 E. Grand Ave., Old Orchard Beach. Open at 5 for dinner Mar.–Dec.; daily

June–Columbus Day; otherwise, closed on Mon. Fine dining in a 1910 Victorian house. Menu specialties include roast duckling, lobster stew, and homemade desserts. $14.95–23.95.

EATING OUT ☙ **Chowderheads** (207-883-8333), Oak Hill Plaza, intersection of Rts. 1 and 114, Scarborough. Open for lunch and dinner daily. The award-winning seafood chowder is thick, hearty, and delicious. Specialties include swordfish and salmon steak dinners, and fried seafood dinners. Portions are quite generous.

Hattie's (207-282-3435), 109 Milestretch Rd., Biddeford Pool. The favorite local gathering spot for breakfast and lunch. The homemade muffins, cakes, and pies are deservedly famous.

Bufflehead's (207-284-6000; www .buffleheadsrestaurant.com), 122 Hills Beach Rd., Biddeford. Open year-round daily for lunch and dinner in summer; call for hours off-season. Offering indoor and outdoor seating with a great ocean view, this great family place makes quality food. Try the seafood crêpes with lobster, shrimp, and crab in a spicy cream ($8.95). Baked manicotti with a side of Italian sausage could do for someone ready to switch from seafood. Entrées $8.95–22.95.

Wormwoods (207-282-9679), 16 Bay Ave., Camp Ellis Beach, Saco. Open daily year-round for lunch and dinner. A large, friendly, old-fashioned place, with dark green booths, by the head of the breakwater. They go all-out decorating for the seasons—watch out for the screeching skull in October—and can be counted on for fried seafood ($12.95).

LOBSTER POUNDS **Bayley's Lobster Pound** (207-883-4571), Pine Point, Scarborough. A popular place for lobster and seafood.

Lobster Claw (207-282-0040), Rt. 5, Ocean Park Rd., Saco. Lobsters cooked outside in giant kettles, stews and chowders, cozy dining room, and takeout available. Twin lobster specials, also steamers, fried seafood. Lobster packed to travel.

TAKEOUT Near the pier and on the main drag of Old Orchard Beach are an abundance of takeout stands and informal restaurants serving pizza, burgers, hot dogs, fried seafood, fried dough, pier fries, ice cream, and more. Our favorites are **Bill's** for pizza, **Lisa's** for pier fries.

Rapid Ray's (207-282-1847), 179 Main St., Saco. A local icon for more than 40 years. Quick and friendly service from people who seem to know almost everyone who walks through the door. Burgers, hot dogs, lobster rolls, fries, onion rings, and the like at great prices. Open until around midnight.

DESSERTS **Milliken House** (207-283-9691; www.millikenhouse.com), 65 North St., Saco. Open Tue.–Fri. 5–9 PM in summer, Fri. and Sat. 2–10 PM from Labor Day till mid-Dec. This 1877 house, elaborately restored by owners Lisa and David Norburg, is the site of a full-blown historical fantasy during its hours of operation, with parlor maids in costume curtseying when you arrive, and occasional appearances by Mrs. Milliken herself in a Charles Worth–inspired gown. Cakes and sweets are served on old china, ornate silverware is ready to stir the tea, and occasional music entertains guests in the front parlors. Apple crumble pie, pecan chocolate brownie tart (both $3.95), tea and coffee, and more.

✳ Entertainment

City Theater (207-282-0849), Main St., Biddeford. This 500-seat, 1890s theater offers a series of live performances.

Saco Drive-In (207-284-1016), Rt. 1, Saco. Double features in spring, summer, and fall.

✳ Selective Shopping

Cascade Flea Market, Rt. 1, Saco. One of Maine's largest outdoor flea markets, open daily in summer.

Stone Soup Artisans (207-283-4715), 228 Main St., Saco. Quality crafts from more than 60 artisans.

✳ Special Events

January: **Annual Lobster Dip**—300 participants dip into the chilly Atlantic to benefit Special Olympics of Maine, in Old Orchard Beach.

Late June: **La Kermesse**, Biddeford—parade, public suppers, dancing, and entertainment highlighting Franco-American culture and traditions.

Early July: **Greek Heritage Festival**, St. Demetrius on Bradley St. in Saco.

Late July: **Saco Art Festival** and **Shriners Football Game** in Biddeford.

June–Labor Day: **Fireworks** near the Old Orchard Beach pier every Thursday at 9:30 PM.

August: **Ocean Park Festival of Lights** and **Salvation Army camp meetings** under the new pavilion in Ocean Park. **Beach Olympics**—3 days of competitions, music, displays, and presentations to benefit the Special Olympics of Maine. Annual **5K Race and Kids' Fun Run**, scholarship fund-raiser. **Saco Bay Wheels Festival**, a bicycle race.

September: Annual **Car Show**—with a car lineup and parade, Old Orchard Beach.

October: **Saco Pumpkin Fest**.

December: **Celebrate the Season by the Sea**—a tree-lighting ceremony with horse-drawn haywagon rides, refreshments, holiday bazaar, caroling, and a bonfire on the beach, in Old Orchard.

Casco Bay 2

PORTLAND AREA

FREEPORT

PORTLAND AREA

Lively, walkable, sophisticated, Maine's largest city is still surprisingly a working port. Greater Portland (230,000) accounts for one-quarter of Maine's total population, but Portland proper is a 3.5-mile-long peninsula (population 64,000) facing Casco Bay. Visitors head first for the Old Port, more than five square blocks built exuberantly during the city's peak shipping era and now laced with restaurants, cafés, shops, and galleries.

Portland's motto, *Resurgam* ("I shall rise again"), could not be more appropriate. The 17th-century settlement was expunged twice by Native Americans, then torched by the British. Finally it prospered as a lumbering port in the 1820s—as still evidenced by its many Federal-era mansions and commercial buildings like the granite-and-glass Mariner's Church in the Old Port, built in 1820 to be the largest building in the capital of a brand-new state. Then it happened again. On Independence Day in 1866 a firecracker flamed up in a Commercial Street boatyard and quickly destroyed most of the downtown. Again the city rose like the legendary phoenix, rebuilding quickly and beautifully, this time in sturdy brick, to create the core of northern New England's shipping, rail, and manufacturing businesses.

These very buildings, a century later, were "going for peanuts," in the words of a real estate agent who began buying them up in the late 1960s, when its handsome Grand Trunk Station was demolished. Down by the harbor artists and craftspeople were renting shop fronts for $50 per month. They formed the Old Port Association, hoping to entice people to stroll through the no-man's-land. That first winter they strung lights through upper floors to convey a sense of security, and they shoveled their own streets, a service the city had ceased to provide to that area. At the end of the winter they celebrated their survival by holding the first Old Port Festival, a street fair that is still held each June.

More recently it is Congress Street that has come back from the brink. Lining a ridge above the Old Port, this was the city's fashionable shopping and financial strip in the first half of the 20th century. The present Maine Bank & Trust Building was the tallest building in all New England when it was built in 1909. By the mid-1990s, however, the three department stores here had closed and foot traffic had shifted to the Maine Mall. Now some of it is back.

The glass-and-timber Portland Public Market, filled with dozens of vendors

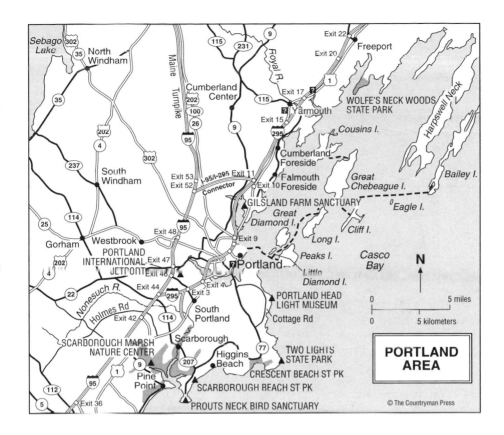

selling Maine produce and food products, is now just one block off Congress Street, near Monument Square. The Maine College of Art (MECA) has replaced Porteus Department Store in a five-story Beaux Arts building and maintains the street-level Institute of Contemporary Art. With a student body of more than 400 and a far larger continuing-education program, MECA has had a visual impact up and down Congress Street, which is now called the Arts District. Contemporary art galleries proliferate around the Portland Museum of Art. Scattered throughout the city are members of Portland's growing immigrant community, with families from Bosnia, Russia, Somalia, Congo, Vietnam, Puerto Rico, Mexico, making Portland the state's most diverse city.

Longfellow Square, in turn, abuts the gracious residential blocks of the West End. Spared by the fire that destroyed the Old Port, its leafy streets are lined with town houses and mansions in a range of graceful architectural styles (several are B&Bs).

The Portland Peninsula is English saddle shaped, with promontories at both ends. The Western Promenade was laid out as an overlook for the West End way back in 1836, as the Eastern Promenade was at the opposite end of the peninsula, along the verge of Munjoy Hill, overlooking Casco Bay. In 1879, the city gained Deering Oaks Park and was blessed by the design of city civil engineer

William Goodwin. In 1917, with turn-of-the-century plans by Frederick Law Olmsted, a dream of James Phinney Baxter, a mayor of Portland, came true when the Baxter Boulevard along Back Cove was opened to pedestrians.

Portland's Old Port is thriving and on its fringes new semi-high-rise, redbrick buildings blend with the old and link the Old Port with Congress Street. Condominiums now line a wharf or two, but Portland remains a real working port. In 2002 fish landings totaled 18 million pounds.

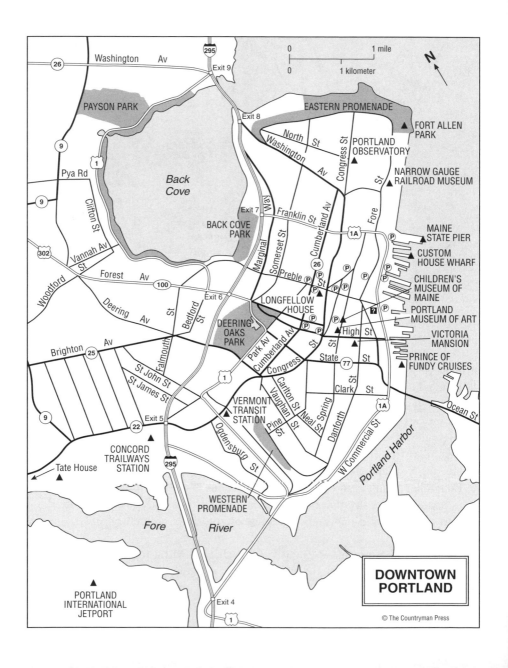

DOWNTOWN PORTLAND

© The Countryman Press

It's also a departure point for the ferry to Yarmouth (Nova Scotia) and for the fleet of Casco Bay liners that regularly transport people, mail, and supplies among Casco Bay's Calendar Islands. These range from nearby Peaks Island—offering rental bikes, guided sea kayaking, lodging, and dining—to Cliff Island, more than an hour's ride, with its remote, sandy roads. In summer these ferries bill their longer runs as Casco Bay Cruises and add a lazy circuit to Bailey Island. Excursion lines also service Eagle Island, preserved as a memorial to Arctic explorer Admiral Peary. The waterfront is, moreover, the departure point for deep-sea fishing, harbor cruises, whale-watching, and daysailing.

South Portland, connected to Portland proper by the soaring Casco Bay Bridge, is a city in its own right (Maine's fourth largest). While it is best known as home of the Maine Mall, its waterfront has become far more visitor-friendly in recent years, with the Spring Point Lighthouse, recently restored Bug Light, and Portland Harbor Museum as focal points along with a burgeoning number of restaurants and galleries.

Beyond South Portland lies Cape Elizabeth, home of the vintage-1791 Portland Head Light and its museum. Visitors come to see the lighthouse but stay to walk and swim at the beaches. Nearby Scarborough to the south and both Falmouth and Yarmouth, just north of the city, also offer surprisingly secluded seaside reserves for walking, boating, and birding.

GUIDANCE Convention and Visitors Bureau of Greater Portland (207-772-5800; www.visitportland.com), 245 Commercial St., Portland 04101, publishes *Greater Portland Visitors Guide*, listing restaurants, sights, museums, and accommodations, including cottages. Last-minute discount rates might be available here, lower than published rates because of cancellations or availability. The walk-in information center is open daily year-round. The CVB has a center (207-775-5809) at the Portland International Jetport.

Portland's Downtown District (207-772-6828; www.portlandmaine.com), 94 Free St., Portland 04101, offers information about performances, festivals, and special events. They publish a guide to services, attractions, dining, and lodging. For current entertainment, weather, and dining ratings, click onto one of several local newspaper web sites: the *Portland Phoenix*'s web page, **www.portland phoenix.com**, or **www.mainetoday .com**, maintained by the *Portland Press Herald*. The *Portland Forecaster*—a free weekly available in street vending boxes and at coffeehouses and shops—carries listings for galleries, music, and events.

The Maine Tourism Association (207-846-0833) staffs a major state information center on Rt. 1 in Yarmouth, just off I-95, exit 17.

Also see **Greater Portland Landmarks** under *To See*.

PORTLAND WATERFRONT

Kim Grant

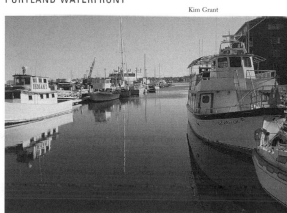

GETTING THERE *By air:* **Portland International Jetport** (207-774-7301) is served by Delta Air Lines (1-800-221-1212), Continental Airlines (1-800-525-0280), United Express (1-800-241-6522), U.S. Airways (1-800-428-4322), Northwest (1-800-225-2525), and American Airlines (1-800-433-7300). Car rentals at the airport include National, Avis, Hertz, Budget, and Alamo.

By bus: **Concord Trailways** (207-828-1151 or 1-800-639-3317) stops en route from Boston to Bangor and coastal points at a modern station just off I-95 (it's also the new train station—see *By train*); the buses offer movies, music, and a nonstop express to Boston and its Logan Airport. It's a $10 taxi ride from the bus station to downtown, or try the new Explorer bus (see *Getting Around*). **Vermont Transit** (207-772-6587 or 1-800-55-BUSES) offers frequent service among Portland, Boston, and Maine's coastal and inland points, using the Greyhound terminal, which unfortunately is dingy and offers little parking.

By ferry: **The Cat** (1-888-249-7245; www.catferry.com), a high-speed car ferry, will resume ferry service to Nova Scotia in the summer of 2006, after the *Scotia Prince* stopped running in 2005. Details were yet to be arranged by this edition's publication time, but should include three trips to Nova Scotia each week, departing in the early afternoon.

By car: From I-95, take I-295 to exit 44–Portland Waterfront and follow signs for the ferry. The **Convention and Visitors Bureau** information center (see *Guidance*) is at 245 Commercial St. between Becky's Diner and the ferry terminal; it's easy to miss.

By train: Amtrak service (1-800-USA-RAIL; www.amtrak.com). The **Downeaster** has finally arrived! It now runs five times daily between Boston's North Station and Portland's clean new rail–bus station on outer Congress St., and it takes about $2\frac{1}{2}$ hours.

GETTING AROUND Portland, like many interesting small cities, rewards the intrepid pedestrian with pleasures such as beautiful 18th- and 19th-century facades, engaging street musicians, creative window displays, and a sense of life slowed down to a more human pace. Do yourself a favor and find a good parking spot near your hotel or B&B, then hoof it as much as possible during your stay. You'll avoid the wrangle for parking on the peninsula, and you'll have that many more memories to take home.

Portland Explorer Express Bus Service (207-772-4457; www.vipcharter coaches.com) runs a 26-passenger, air-conditioned shuttle among the airport, the bus–rail station, the Maine Mall, and major downtown locations such as the Old Port and the Casco Bay lines ferry terminal 12:15–7 PM daily including most holidays. $2 one-way. Pay as you get on the bus.

The Metro (207-774-0351) bus transfer system serves Greater Portland. Metro city buses connect airport and city, as well as offer convenient routes around the city. $1.25 one-way, or $5 for a day pass; less for seniors over 65 and students.

PARKING Portland meters are 25¢ per half hour, but, as we have discovered the hard way, you get a $10 ticket after 2 hours, which climbs to $15 if you keep feeding the meter. The city urges visitors to use its many parking garages. The **Fore Street Garage** (439 Fore St.) puts you at one end of the Old Port, and the **Custom House Square Garage** (25 Pearl St.) at the other. The **Casco Bay Garage** (Maine State Pier) and **Free Street Parking** (130 Free St., just up from the art museum) are also handy. The **Gateway Garage** next to the East-land Park Hotel is large and convenient, as is the **Portland Public Market Garage** (Preble St.), which offers the first 2 hours free with a purchase in the market.

WHEN TO COME Portland makes a great destination any time of year, with its thriving restaurant and museum scene. The Victoria Mansion and the Tate House dress up in Christmas finery and offer holiday tours, though a whale-watching trip would have to be scheduled in the months of better weather. And the winter wind can blow bitterly cold on Portland streets—even when some of us are still out skating on Deering Oaks pond.

✳ To See

MUSEUMS

All listings are in Portland unless otherwise noted
Museum of African Culture (207-871-7188; www. tribalartmuseum.com), 122 Spring St., No. 1 (one block south of the Portland Museum of Art). This place is tiny but packed with more than 500 pieces representing more than 1,000 years of African history and art, including masks, bronzes, batiks, and wooden sculptures.

Center for Maine History (207-774-1822; www.mainehistory.org), 485 Congress St. Maintained by the Maine Historical Society, the center includes the **Wadsworth-Longfellow House, Maine History Gallery**, and **historical society library**, as well as the **Maine memory network** on the web site. The Wadsworth-Longfellow House is open June–Oct., daily 10–4 (closed July 4 and Labor Day); the gallery and library are open year-round, Tue.–Sat. 10–4. $7 adults for the house and gallery, $3 children under 18. Call for hours for a 45-minute guided tour of the house. Built in 1785 by the grandfather of Henry Wadsworth Longfellow, this was the first brick dwelling in town. Peleg Wadsworth was a Revolutionary War hero, and the entire clan of Wadsworths and Longfellows was prominent in the city for nearly two centuries.

The recently restored house is part of a 1-acre campus with changing exhibits and an interesting museum store. Visit the lovely small garden hidden behind the house, and another a couple of blocks down Congress beside the granite First Parish Church (No. 425), marking the site on which Maine's constitution was drafted in 1819.

🐾 ♿ **The Museum at Portland Head Light** (207-799-2661; www.portland headlight.com), 1000 Shore Rd. in Fort Williams Park, Cape Elizabeth. Open Memorial Day–Fri. after Columbus Day, 10–4, and off-season weekends 10–4. $2 adults, $1 ages 6–18. This is the oldest lighthouse in Maine, first illuminated in 1791 per order of George Washington. It is now automated, and the former keeper's house has been transformed into an exceptional lighthouse museum. Bring a picnic; there are tables with water views as well as the ruins of an old fort in the surrounding Fort Williams Park, just 4 miles from downtown Portland: Take State St. (Rt. 77) south across the bridge to South Portland, then turn left onto Broadway and right onto Cottage St., which turns into Shore Rd.

Institute of Contemporary Art/MECA (207-879-5742), 522 Congress St. Changing exhibits frequently worth checking; free. The ICA is a street-level

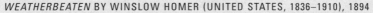

✎ ♿ **Portland Museum of Art** (207-775-6148; for a weekly schedule of events and information, 207-773-ARTS; www.portlandmuseum.org), 7 Congress Square. Open Tue., Wed., Thu., Sat., and Sun. 10–5, Fri. 10–9; Memorial Day–Columbus Day open Mon. 10–5; closed New Year's Day, Easter Sunday, July 4, Thanksgiving, and Christmas. $8 adults, $6 students and seniors (with ID), and $2 ages 6–17; under 6 free. Free admission Fri. 5–9 PM. Tours daily—inquire about times. Maine's largest art museum is a striking building designed by I. M. Pei's firm. Featured American artists include Winslow Homer, Edward Hopper, Rockwell Kent, Louise Nevelson, Andrew and N. C. Wyeth, John Singer Sargent, and Marguerite Zorach; the museum also has interesting European works by Renoir, Degas, Prendergast, Matisse, and Picasso. In 2002 the neighboring McLellan House, the lovely Federal-period home of the museum's original collection, was reopened, along with the Sweat Memorial Galleries, an impressive collection of 19th-century American paintings and decorative arts. The museum has plans to buy the Winslow Homer cottage on Prouts Neck, which may be opened to the public in the future.

WEATHERBEATEN BY WINSLOW HOMER (UNITED STATES, 1836–1910), 1894

gallery at the Maine College of Art (MECA) with 400 full-time students and many times that number enrolled in continuing-studies programs.

∅ **Maine Narrow Gauge Railroad Co. & Museum** (207-828-0814; www .mngrr.org), 58 Fore St. Open May 15–Oct. 15, daily 11–4, and weekends year-round except Jan. 2–Feb. 12. The museum and gift shop are free; excursion fares are $6 round-trip adults, $5 seniors, $4 ages 4–12. Hard to spot if you aren't looking for it: Drive through the complex of brick buildings and park on the waterside. The museum sells the tickets. From the 1870s to the 1940s five narrow-gauge lines carrying visitors linked rural Maine communities. A 3-mile round-trip excursion along Casco Bay is offered regularly May–Oct. It runs again during Dec., when the tracks are lined with lights in shapes ranging from a deer family to a North Pole castle.

∅ *&* **Children's Museum of Maine** (207-828-1234; www.childrensmuseumof me.org), 142 Free St. Open Memorial Day–Labor Day, Mon.–Sat. 10–5, Sun. noon–5; otherwise, closed Mon. $6 per person (under 1 free). Next door to the Portland Museum of Art, this fun museum features three levels of interactive, hands-on exhibits designed to help the young and old learn together. Permanent exhibits include *Our Town* (with ATM machine, farm, supermarket, bank, and fire department), a space shuttle, a news center, and a computer room. There's also a science center, a toddler area, and a black-box room that's a walk in camera obscura.

Portland Harbor Museum (207-799-6337; www.portlandharbormuseum.org), on Fort Rd., marked from Rt. 77 in South Portland. Open Memorial Day–Columbus Day, daily 10–4:30; mid-Apr.–May, and Columbus Day–Nov., Fri.–Sun. same hours. $4 adults, $2 ages 6–16. Sited in a brick repair shop that was part of Fort Preble and is now part of Southern Maine Technical College, this museum mounts changing exhibits on local maritime history and features pieces of the *Snow Squall*, an 1850s Portland clipper ship wrecked in the Falkland Islands, and artifacts of the ship's restoration. Spring Point Lighthouse, at the end of a breakwater, is another good vantage point on the harbor.

∅ *&* **Portland Fire Museum** (207-874 8400), 157 Spring St. (near the corner of State). Open June–Aug., Mon. evening 7–9 and by appointment. The only remaining firehouse in Portland with horse stalls, this wonderful old brick structure was built in 1837 and originally housed a girls' grammar school. The artifacts, photos, paintings, and fire equipment (including a 1938 pumper truck) chronicle the city's contentious relationship with fire, from the fire department's

∅ **Portland Observatory** (207-774-5561, ext. 104; www.portland landmarks.org/observatory), 138 Congress St. Open Memorial Day–Columbus Day, daily 10–5. $5 adults, $3 ages 6–16. Built in 1807, this imposing, octagonal, 86-foot-high shingled landmark atop Munjoy Hill is the last surviving 19th-century maritime signal station in the country. During a recent restoration, interpretive displays were added. Climb the 102 steps to the top and watch for ships entering Casco Bay

humble beginnings in 1768 and the city's destruction by fire at the hands of the British in 1775, to the Great Fire of 1866.

HISTORIC SITES

All listings are in Portland unless otherwise noted

🎗 **Victoria Mansion**, the Morse-Libby House (207-772-4841), 109 Danforth St. (at the corner of Park St.). Open for tours May–Oct., Tue.–Sat. 10–4, Sun. 1–5 (closed July 4 and Labor Day). Christmas hours: day after Thanksgiving–Dec. 29, Wed.–Sun. 11–5. $10 adults, senior discount, $3 students 6–17, under 6 free. Perhaps there are more elaborately gilded, frescoed, carved, and many-mirrored mansions in northern New England, but we haven't seen one. Ruggles Sylvester Morse, a Maine native who made his fortune as a New Orleans hotelier, built the mansion in 1859 as a summer home after relocating south just before the Civil War. The Italianate brownstone palazzo features a three-story grand hall with stained-glass windows, a stunning, recently restored skylight, and a flying staircase with 377 balusters hand carved from Santo Domingo mahogany. It was rescued from destruction and opened to the public in 1941, and its restoration since has been steady. The gift shop sells well-chosen Victoriana. In December the house is dressed to the hilt by professional decorators.

Tate House (207-774-6177; www.tatehouse.org), 1270 Westbrook St. Follow Congress St. (Rt. 22) west across the Fore River to Westbrook (it's just outside the Portland Jetport). Open June 15–Sep. 30, Tue.–Sat. 10–4, Sun. 1–4; open weekends through Oct. $7 adults, $5 seniors, $2 ages 6–12, under 6 free. George Tate, mast agent for the Royal Navy, built this Georgian house in 1755 to reflect his important position. Both the interior and exterior are unusual, distinguished by clerestory windows, a gambrel roof, wood paneling, and elegant furniture. An 18th-century herb garden is part of the historic landscape.

Neal Dow Memorial (207-773-7773; www.mewctu.org), 714 Congress St. Open year-round, Mon.–Fri. 11–4. Donation requested. Currently the headquarters of the Maine Women's Christian Temperance Union, this handsome Greek Revival mansion was built in 1829 by Neal Dow, the man responsible for an 1851 law that made Maine the first state to prohibit alcohol. He also championed women's rights and abolition.

TATE HOUSE

Nancy English

GUIDED TOURS **Greater Portland Landmarks** (207-774-5561; www.portlandlandmarks.org), 165 State St., Portland 04101. June 15–Columbus Day, this nonprofit organization offers downtown walking tours of the Old Port Mon.–Sat. beginning at 10:30 AM; $8 per adult; free under age 16. Tours depart from the Convention and Visitors Bureau at 245 Commercial St. Also note the organization's many excellent books and its *Discover His-*

toric Portland on Foot series of walking guides. GPL also runs the Portland Observatory.

135

PORTLAND AREA

◈ **Mainely Tours and Gifts, Inc.** (207-774-0808; www.mainelytours.com), 5½ Moulton St., Portland. Mid-May–Oct. This narrated, 90-minute trolley tour begins on Moulton St. in the Old Port, stops at the visitor center, and includes Portland Head Light. $14 adults, $13 seniors, $7 ages 6–12.

✳ Scenic Drives

Cape Elizabeth and Prouts Neck. From State St. in downtown Portland, head south on Rt. 77 across the Casco Bay Bridge to South Portland, then turn left onto Broadway and right onto Cottage St., which turns into Shore Rd. Enter 94-acre **Fort Williams Park** (4 miles from downtown) to see the **Museum at Portland Head Light**. There are also picnic tables with water views and a beach, as well as the ruins of the old fort. Many people like to come here early in the morning (the excellent and modestly priced **Cookie Jar Pastry Shop**, 554 Shore Rd., opens at 6 AM; try the sweet gingerbread). Follow Shore Rd. south to Rt. 77 and continue through Pond Cove, the main village in residential Cape Elizabeth, and on to **Two Lights State Park** with its views of Casco Bay and the open Atlantic, good for fishing and picnicking. **Crescent Beach State Park**, just beyond, is a mile of inviting sand, the area's premier beach.

Rt. 77 continues through **Higgins Beach**, a Victorian-era summer community of reasonable rentals and lodging with plenty of beach but limited parking. At the junction of Rts. 207 and 77 continue on Black Point Rd., past **Scarborough Beach State Park**, and on to exclusive **Prouts Neck**. Unless you are staying or eating at the **Black Point Inn**, parking in-season is all but impossible here. Park back at Scarborough Beach and walk or bike to the **Cliff Walk**, site of **Winslow Homer's studio**. Return by the same route (you are just 15 miles from downtown). A short and rewarding detour: At the junction of Cottage Rd. and Broadway, turn right onto Broadway to Southern Maine Technical College. A granite breakwater leads to the **Spring Point Light** overlooking Casco Bay. Look for signs for the **Spring Point Shoreway Path**, which follows the bay 3 miles to **Willard Beach**.

☀ **Falmouth Foreside**. From downtown Portland, take Rt. 1 north across the mouth of the Presumpscot River. Signs for the Governor Baxter School for the Deaf direct you down Andres Ave. and across a causeway to 100-acre **Mackworth Island**. Park and walk (dogs permitted) the 1.5-mile path that circles the island. Views are off across the bay, and a small beach invites strolling. Return to Rt. 1 and continue north, looking for signs for **Gilsland Farm Sanctuary**, headquarters for the Maine Audubon

THE LOBSTER SHACK AT TWO LIGHTS

Nancy English

Kim Grant

THE OLD PORT

Society. The blue sign comes up in less than 0.5 mile; follow the dirt road to the visitor center.

Yarmouth. From downtown Portland, take I-295 to exit 17. Commercial and tourist-geared businesses are relegated to Rt. 1, leaving the inner village lined with 18th- and 19th-century homes mixed with interesting stores and antiques shops. Note North Yarmouth Academy's original Greek Revival brick buildings, the 18th-century meetinghouse, and several fine old churches. The village green retains its round railroad station, and **Royal River Park** offers recreation (the Royal River is popular with sea kayakers) in all seasons. Also check out **Lower Falls Landing**, a former sardine cannery that now houses interesting shops. Don't miss the DeLorme Map Store on Rt. 1 with "Eartha," the world's largest rotating and revolving globe.

✳ Island Excursions

No one seems quite sure how many islands there are in Casco Bay. Printed descriptions range from 136 to 222. Seventeenth-century explorer John Smith dubbed them the Calendar Islands, saying there was one for every day of the year. Regardless of the actual number, there are plenty of offshore places for poking around. Regular year-round ferry service runs to six of the islands, five of which invite exploration.

For listings of summer cottages and other rentals in the Casco Bay Islands, contact **Port Island Realty** (207-766-5966; www.portisland.com) and **Ashmore Realty** (207-766-5702; www.ashmorerealty.com).

PEAKS ISLAND Just 3 miles from Portland (a 20-minute ferry ride), Peaks is the most accessible island. Ferry service runs regularly, even off-season, because many of the island's approximately 1,000 year-round residents commute to the mainland for work and school. In summer the population swells to between 5,000 and 6,000, and day-trippers are common. Check out the bulletin boards at the top of Welch St. and at **Hannigan's Market**. The 5-mile shore road around the island is great for walking or bicycling. Rent a pair of wheels at **Brad's ReCycled Bike Shop** (207-766-5631), 115 Island Ave., the most adorable bike rental place in the U.S. of A.; when Brad isn't there, folks fill out a form, place payment in the box, and return the bikes when they're through. The **Fifth Maine Regiment Center** (207-766-3330), Seashore Ave., is a striking building erected in 1888 to house Maine's largest collection of Civil War memorabilia (local history exhibits are on the second floor). Open June–Sep., weekends 11–4; July and Aug., Mon.–Fri. 1–4, weekends 11–4, or by appointment. **Maine Island Kayak Co.** (207-766-2373 or 1-800-796-2373; www.maineislandkayak .com) offers excellent, superbly guided half-day to multiday trips in Casco Bay, along the Maine coast, and elsewhere, along with renowned kayaking instruction. Food sources (some are open in summer only) include sandwiches at Hannigan's Market year-round. **Jones Landing** (207-766-3040), just off the ferry, serves lunch and dinner (burgers, sandwiches, fried seafood, steak, pasta) in-season and offers live entertainment often, as well as reggae music every Sunday. **Peaks Island House** (207-766-4400, 20 Island Ave.) serves all three meals in the summer season and has outside deck seating in nice weather. This place also provides overnight lodging (207-766-4406 for reservations). Four rooms, decorated in floral and sea motifs, with private bath and water views. $125–245 per night. You can also stay at the **Inn on Peaks Island** (207-766-5100; www.innonpeaks island.com), 33 Island Ave. This inn underwent another renovation by a new owner in the 2004–05 winter. All rooms previously had included king bed, TV/VCR, phone, dataport, ceiling fan, fireplace, Jacuzzi tub, and balcony. $199–259 for a double, room service available when restaurant is open, and continental breakfast included. The inn also features a restaurant. **DownFront** (207-766-5500), 50 Island Ave., at the top of the hill from the boat, sells great ice cream, candy, and souvenirs. **Peaks Café** (207-766-2479), Welch St., offers a complete range of coffee choices, as well as pastries, bagels, fruit, and juices, and is the locals' favorite place for breakfast.

GREAT CHEBEAGUE Great Chebeague is the largest island in Casco Bay: 4.5 miles long and 2 miles wide. Its population of 350 swells to eight times that in summer. A bike is the best way to explore the island. Jonathan Komlosy will be renting bikes at **Great Island Bike Rentals** (207-847-9317).

The **Sunset House** (207-846-6568; www.chebeague.com), 74 South Rd., is a comfortable B&B with four guest rooms (private bath); open year-round ($124–134). Full breakfast included, with fruit and vegetable frittatas and homemade muffins.

Chebeague Island Inn (207-846-5155; www.chebeagueinn.com). The dining room is open from the end of March to Thanksgiving, and the pleasures of the table here will make any visitor grateful. Rooms are available June–Columbus Day. The island's classic old summer hotel has 21 handsome rooms; all have private bath, a queen bed, and harbor or garden views. Features include a large

Nancy English

CHEBEAGUE ISLAND INN

open-beamed living room with massive stone fireplace, a long porch overlooking the water, and a nearby golf course. $185–315 double in-season, including breakfast. The dining room serves all three meals in summer, and dinner into spring and fall.

The Chebeague Orchard Inn (207-846-9488), 66 North Rd., open year-round, offers extensive flower and vegetable gardens, a common room with fireplace, and five antiques-furnished guest rooms, three with private bath, some with water views. Vickie and Neil Taliento are helpful hosts who keep bikes for guests and include a full breakfast (featuring their organic veggies). $110–160 in-season, less off-season.

You can pick up takeout at **Doughty's Island Market** (207-846-9997). To relax and enjoy the scenery, head to **Chandler's Cove**, a white sand beach, or the beach near **Coleman's Cove**. Golfers will want to try the **Great Chebeague Golf Club** (207-846-9478), a beautiful nine-hole course founded in 1920, where nonmembers can play anytime except Monday or Thursday morning. New facilities on the island include a recreation center with an Olympic-sized heated swimming pool, indoor gym, weight room, and outdoor tennis/basketball courts. The **Chebeague Island Historical Society** has restored the old District No. 9 Schoolhouse, open all day in summer with a visitor center and museum. Call 207-846-5237 for more details.

Casco Bay Lines ferries dock at the southern end of the island, and **Chebeague Transportation Company** (207-846-3700) offers faster, more frequent service from Cousins Island in Yarmouth to the dock at Chebeague Island Inn. Call for directions and parking details.

LONG ISLAND Three miles long and approximately a mile wide, Long Island, like the others, has a thriving summer population. **The Spar Restaurant** (207-766-3310) open in the summer to Columbus Day, serves lunch and dinner featuring fresh local seafood, lobster, steaks, and pasta. Full bar, moorings for boats, picnic lunches available. The **Chestnut Hill Inn** (207-766-5272; www.chestnut hillinn.com) is a seven-room (four with private bath) establishment open year-round. On weekdays continental breakfast is included, and on weekends a full breakfast is served. Dinner is available by reservation, both to guests and to others.

GREAT DIAMOND ISLAND A pleasant half-hour ferry ride from downtown, this 2-mile-long island is the site of Fort McKinley, built sturdily of brick in the 1890s, now restored as **Diamond Cove** (www.diamondcove.com), a resort-style development featuring 121 town houses (weekly summer rentals are few:

207-766-5804). **Diamond's Edge** (207-766-5850) is the big attraction here, a casually elegant restaurant open May 20–Oct. 11 for lunch and dinner, also for Sunday brunch in high season; a popular place for weddings. Guided tours aside, the resort grounds are private.

CLIFF ISLAND Cliff Island is a full 1½-hour ride down the bay. It is the most rustic of the islands, with 8 miles of dirt roads and no overnight accommodations, a peaceful feel, and sandy beaches. There's a seasonal sandwich shop on the wharf, and the general store sells sandwiches year-round. For **cottage rentals** check with the Greater Portland CVB.

❊ To Do

BALLOONING Hot Fun (207-799-0193; www.hotfunballoons.com), Box 2825, South Portland. Hot-air balloon rides for up to six passengers.

BICYCLING Hundreds of acres of undeveloped land offer some great bicycling. Call **Portland Trails** (207-775-2411; www.trails.org) for designated trails and a *Map and Trail Guide*. The **Bicycle Transportation Alliance of Portland** (BTAP, P.O. Box 4506, Portland 04112) publishes three maps that detail routes through historic Portland, the islands, and the lighthouse trail ($1 each). Rentals and service are available at several locations around the city. Local favorite **Back Bay Bicycle** (207-773-6906; www.backbaybicycle.com; 333 Forest Ave., Portland) and **Cycle Mania** (207-774-2933; www.cyclemania1.com; 59 Federal St., Portland) sponsor weekly group rides.

BOATING For ferry information to Chebeague Island, see also *Island Excursions*. **Casco Bay Lines** (207-774-7871; www.cascobaylines.com), Casco Bay Ferry Terminal, 56 Commercial St. at the foot of Franklin St., Portland. Founded in 1845, this business was said to be the oldest continuously operating ferry company in the country when it went bankrupt in 1980. The present, quasi-municipal Casco Bay Island Transit District looks and functions much the way the old line did, except that it now carries 800,000 passengers and 18,000 vehicles out to the bay's beautiful islands every year. The brightly painted ferries are still lifelines to six islands, carrying groceries and lumber as well as mail. The year-round, daily mail-boat run (3 hours) puts into all the islands in the morning and again in the afternoon. A variety of seasonal, special excursions includes a 5½-hour Bailey Island Cruise and a Moonlight Run at 9:15 PM. Also year-round, daily car ferry service to Peaks Island.

Coast Watch & Guiding Light Navigation Co. Inc. (207-774-6498; www.eagleislandtours.com), Long Wharf, Portland. Runs Memorial Day–Columbus Day. The Frappier family's two 49-passenger tour boats, the *Kristy K* and the *Fish Hawk*, take you out to Eagle Island, the former home of Admiral Peary, now maintained by the state as a historic site and nature preserve; they also run Lighthouse Lovers and sunset cruises. Group charters available. Ask about Captain William Frappier's book, *Steamboat Yesterdays on Casco Bay*.

Bay View Cruises (207-761-0496), Fisherman's Wharf, Portland. Mid-June– Sep., weekends from Apr. Six daily narrated harbor cruises aboard the *Bay View Lady*; harbor lunch cruise (bring your own sandwich or order from the snack bar) 12:10–12:50. Off-season mid-May–late Oct.

🐟 ***Lucky Catch* Lobstering** (207-233-2026; www.luckycatch.com), 170 Commercial St., Portland. Instead of just eating them, why not land one of those tasty crustaceans yourself? Captain Tom takes tourists and locals out to haul traps on the *Lucky Catch* five times daily Mon.–Sat., with side trips to Portland Head Light and White Head Passage. Each 80- to 90-minute cruise costs $20 per adult, $12 per child.

Olde Port Mariner Fleet (207-775-0727 or 1-800-437-3270; www.mariner fleet.com), Long Wharf, Portland. Whale-watches daily in summer, weekends in early June and after Labor Day. Also deep-sea fishing, harbor cruises, and a variety of other excursions.

Deep-sea fishing and sailing. Several deep-sea-fishing boats and sailing yachts are based in Portland every summer. Check with the Convention and Visitors Bureau (207-772-5800) for current listings.

BREWERY TOURS Like its namesake city in Oregon, Portland is famous for its microbreweries, and many feature restaurants alongside them. Most give tours, either on a regular basis or by appointment. For information, contact individual breweries: **Allagash Brewing** (207-878-5385 or 1-800-330-5385; www.allagash .com), 100 Industrial Way, Portland; **Casco Bay Brewing** (207-797-2020; www .cascobaybrewing.com), 57 Industrial Way, Portland; **D. L. Geary Brewing** (207-878-BEER), 38 Evergreen Dr., Portland; **Gritty McDuff's Brew Pub** (207-772-2739; www.grittys.com), 396 Fore St., Portland; **Shipyard Brewing** (207-761-0807; www.shipyard.com), 86 Newbury St., Portland; and **Sebago Brewing Company** (207-775-2337; www.sebagobrewing.com), 15 Philbrook Ave., South Portland.

FOR FAMILIES 🐟 **Southworth Planetarium** (207-780-4249; www.usm.maine .edu/~planet), University of Southern Maine, 96 Falmouth St., Portland. Astronomy and laser light shows throughout the year. Special shows for young children in summer and on holidays, including an astronomical exploration of the biblical Star of Bethlehem.

GOLF There are several popular 9- and 18-hole courses in the area, notably **Sable Oaks Golf Club** (207-775-6257), South Portland, considered among the most challenging and best courses in Maine (18 holes); **Riverside North** (18 holes, 207-797-3524) and **Riverside South** (9 holes, 207-797-5588), in Portland; **Val Halla** (18 holes, 207-829-2225), in Cumberland; and **Twin Falls** (9 holes, 207-854-5397), in Westbrook.

SAILING *Bagheera* (207-766-2500 or 1-87-SCHOONER; www.portland schooner.com), Long Wharf, Portland. Built in 1924 of long-leaf yellow pine, oak, and mahogany, this vintage Alden sailed all over the world before making

Casco Bay her home port in 2002. She can carry as many as 48 passengers on four cruises daily, Memorial Day–Columbus Day. $28 ($35 for sunset) adults, $12 children 12 and under.

SEA KAYAKING ♂ **Maine Island Kayak Co.** (207-766-2373 or 1-800-796-2373; www.maineislandkayak.com), 70 Luther St., Peaks Island. Late May–Oct. We love this company for many reasons: its exceptional guides, its state-of-the-art equipment, and its commitment to the leave-no-trace philosophy, crucial in heavily trafficked Casco Bay. MIKCO offers a limited schedule of trips, mostly private, but call for information.

✳ Green Space

BEACHES ♂ ♿ **Crescent Beach State Park** (8 miles from Portland on Rt. 77) is a mile of sand complete with changing facilities, a playground, picnic tables, and a snack bar. Fee charged for adults and ages 5–11. Good for young children, because it's protected from heavy surf.

Kettle Cove, just down the road from Crescent—follow the road behind the (excellent) ice cream shop on Rt. 77—is the rocky end of Crescent Beach. There is no admission fee, but parking is limited.

Higgins Beach, farther down Rt. 77 in Scarborough, is an extensive strand within walking distance of lodging—but there is no parking on the street. Private lots charge a fee. The swell can kick up quite a bit here, so beware the undertow.

Scarborough Beach State Park, Black Point Rd. (Rt. 207), 3 miles south of Rt. 1 on Prouts Neck. Open Memorial Day–Sep. ($3 admission), also for walking year-round. A 243-acre park with a superb beach, but only a 65-foot stretch is technically public. Get there early because parking is minimal, and facilities are limited to outhouses. For the scenic route from Portland, see *Scenic Drives*.

PARKS ♂ **Deering Oaks**, Portland's 51-acre city park designed by city civil engineer William Goodwin, has a pond, ducks and swans, fountains, a playground, a fine grove of oak trees, a multivariety rose garden, and a refurbished urban "ravine" complete with a wading pool and spray jets for summertime frolicking. A farmer's market is held here Wed. and Sat. mornings May–Nov. Ice skating on the pond in winter, with the newly renovated stone "Castle" to be open for refreshment and warming up. No admission fee.

Two Lights State Park, 66 Two Lights Rd., Cape Elizabeth, is open year-round. No swimming, but 40 acres of shore with stunning water views for picnicking and fishing.

Also see **Fort Williams Park** in *Scenic Drives* and **Fort Allen Park** under Eastern Promenade in *Walks*.

NATURE PRESERVES ♂ **Gilsland Farm Sanctuary** (207-781-2330; www.maine audubon.org), 20 Gilsland Farm Rd., Falmouth (3 miles east of Portland). Open Mon.–Sat. 9–5, Sun. noon–5 in warm weather, 2–5 in cold weather. Maine Audubon's headquarters are located at this 65-acre wildlife sanctuary of trails, rolling fields, river frontage, and salt marsh. The education center features exhibits throughout the year, a wildlife discovery room for children, and a Maine Audubon Nature Store selling binoculars and other optics. The education center hosts day and evening wildlife-related programs year-round and runs camps for children during summer and school breaks. The sanctuary is also open year-round for walking, sunrise to sunset.

Scarborough Marsh Audubon Center (207-883-5100), Pine Point Rd. (also marked as Rt. 9 west), Scarborough (10 miles south of downtown Portland). Visitors can walk the property any day of the year, dawn to dusk; the nature center is open May–June, Sat. and Memorial Day weekend; June–Labor Day, daily 9:30–5:30. The state's largest salt marsh can also be explored by canoe or kayak. The nature center houses an aquarium and mounted birds and mammals and sponsors walks, canoe tours, and rentals.

Fore River Sanctuary (207-781-2330; www.maineaudubon.org), near Maine Turnpike exit 8, off Brighton Ave., Portland. This 85-acre preserve owned by Maine Audubon is hidden behind a suburban neighborhood where explorers may not think to look. The 2.5 miles of hiking trails offer access to Portland's only waterfall, **Jewell Falls**. A set of railroad tracks (be careful—they are active) marks the beginning of a trail that leads you through woods and marshland.

Prouts Neck Cliff Walk and Wildlife Sanctuary. Winslow Homer painted many of his seascapes in the small studio attached to the summer home here, which was, and is, part of the exclusive community on Prouts Neck, beyond the Black Point Inn. It's not far from the Black Point Inn to Winslow Homer Rd., where the Cliff Path (unmarked) begins. It's a beautiful stroll along the rocks, around Eastern Point, and back almost to the inn; we've even seen a red fox here, chasing field mice toward one of the exclusive homes at dusk. You can also walk through the sanctuary between Winslow Homer Road (just east of St. James Episcopal Church) and Library Lane, donated by Winslow's brother Charles.

WALKS Portland Trails (207-775-2411; www.trails.org), 1 India St., Portland, an organization committed to developing hiking and biking trails in the city, sells a map describing several city parks and two dozen trails as well as bus routes to take you there. The Portland Trails Map costs $4.95 and can be bought from the web site or at the visitor information center.

✿ **The Eastern Promenade**. Follow Congress St. east to the Portland Observatory atop Munjoy Hill and then continue the extra block to the Eastern Promenade, a park-lined street high on this same bluff with sweeping views of Casco Bay. Follow it around, back toward the harbor, to 68-acre **Fort Allen Park**, which dates to 1814, set on a blustery point above the bay. Down along the bay itself the paved **Eastern Promenade Trail** runs along the base of Munjoy Hill, good for biking, walking, and in-line skating. (The railroad museum's excursion train runs alongside it.) You can also put in a canoe, kayak, or sailboat at the small marina here.

✿ ♿ **The Western Promenade**. It's ironic that Munjoy Hill (see above), the poorer section of town, has the million-dollar view (one reason why that varied ethnic neighborhood is now being gentrified) while the Western Promenade overlooks the airport and gas holding tanks. Still, this is Portland's poshest and most architecturally interesting residential neighborhood. Pick up a copy of the Portland Landmarks leaflet *Guide to the Western Promenade* ($1) from the visitors bureau.

☀ ✿ ♿ **Baxter Boulevard**. A popular 3.5-mile path around the tidal flats of Back Cove (unfortunately, just off I-295), also part of the original Olmsted Plan, connects with the Eastern Promenade Trail. It's a popular spot for dog walking, jogging, and biking. Fields also provide good kite flying and soccer, when they're not being used by local high schools.

Eastern Cemetery, Congress St. and Washington Ave. (near the Portland Observatory on Munjoy Hill). The oldest cemetery in Portland, its 9 acres hold more than 4,000 headstones dating from the mid–17th century to the early 19th; some are embellished with angels and death's heads.

✳ Lodging

HOTELS There are more than 2,000 hotel and motel rooms in and around Portland.

In downtown Portland 04101

✿ ♿ **Portland Regency** (207-774-4200 or 1-800-727-3436; www.the regency.com), 20 Milk St. We like the Regency for its quiet stateliness in the midst of the funky Old Port, even though some of the rooms don't have much in the way of windows. Stay in one of 95 rooms (including 8 suites) housed in a century-old armory. Rooms come with reproduction beds (a king or two doubles), floral chintz spreads and drapes, deluxe cable TV, phone with free local calls, dryer, iron, newspaper and coffee, individually controlled heat and air-conditioning, and honor bar; some suites feature a Jacuzzi tub. **Twenty Milk Street**, a steak house in the formal dining room, sells pricey but well-recommended meat and fish, and the **Armory Lounge** offers cocktails and lighter fare. A comprehensive downstairs gym and day spa, complimentary van service and valet parking. From $129–169 Jan.–Apr.; in-season (Memorial Day weekend–Oct.) $188–229.

☀ ✿ ♿ **Eastland Park Hotel** (207-775-5411 or 1-888-671-8008; www .eastlandparkhotel.com), 157 High St. This 1927 landmark's $2.5 million face-lift has refurbished everything from the gilt-and-marble lobby, ballroom, and 202 guest rooms and suites to the beloved **Top of the East** cocktail lounge, with stunning 360-degree views. All rooms have private bath, cable TV, new windows that open, air-conditioning, ironing board, and coffeemaker. Shuttle service from the Jetport is free, as is use of the in-hotel exercise room or nearby Bay Club Fitness. $129–219 in-season, $89–149 in winter. Pets allowed with a $25 one-time fee.

☀ ✿ ♿ **Portland Harbor Hotel** (207-775-9090 or 1-888-798-9090; www.theportlandharborhotel.com), 468 Fore St. This hotel garnered some controversy over its use of non-traditional building materials, including granite-look-alike rigid foam, but so far the exterior is holding up. An enviable location in the heart of the Old Port and an in-hotel restaurant and elevators make it a good bet for those more interested in comfort than character. Amenities include digital cable TV and radio, queen or king bed, cordless phone and dataport, wireless access for computers, marble bath, European-style glass shower, granite counters, nightly turn-down, and free pickup service from the Jetport or train station. Jacuzzi suites feature an oval spa tub, separate sitting area with sofa bed, and two TVs. **Eve's** serves fine dinners. $159–289, depending on view and season. Pets are allowed with a $35 fee per day.

✂ ⅋ **Holiday Inn by the Bay** (207-775-2311 or 1-800-HOLIDAY; www .innbythebay.com), 88 Spring St. Portlanders love to hate this ugly, 11-story, downtown high-rise, especially since it took over a beautiful neighborhood. But perhaps someday we'll regard its utilitarian architecture fondly, and the harbor and skyline views are great from the inside. Amenities include an indoor pool, small fitness center, full business services, cable TV with in-room movies and video-game hookups, free parking, laundry facility, and a restaurant and lounge. Two suites and 239 rooms range $142–183 in high season.

🐾 ✂ ⅋ **Hilton Garden Inn Portland Downtown Waterfront** (207-780-0780; www.hiltongardeninn portland.com.com), 65 Commercial St. Portland's newest corporate and leisure hotel rents 120 rooms, all with a bath, refrigerator and microwave, and high-speed Internet access. Two corner suites with views and a sitting area are also available. A small indoor pool and fitness center, and impressive views of the harbor from half of the rooms—the inn is located in the middle of the Old Port—make this a fun place to stay. Rates $259–279 in summer, as low as $159 in winter.

Note: Portland does host the major chains, but they are mainly located by I-95 at exit 8 in Westbrook or in South Portland.

Beyond Portland

✂ ⅋ **Black Point Inn Resort** (207-883-2500 or 1-800-258-0003; www .blackpointinn.com), 510 Blackpoint Rd., Prouts Neck 04074. Open year-round. This vintage-1878 summer hotel now has a summer activities coordinator, with kids' meals and family dining (in addition to their regular formal seating at dinner; see *Dining Out*). Everything else in this Prouts Neck institution blessedly remains the same; this includes the oldest elevator in the state of Maine, still hand operated by a polite staff member, and a wonderful widow's walk with 360-degree views of Scarborough, Old Orchard Beach, and the mighty Atlantic Ocean. Guests are permitted to use the Prouts Neck Country Club's 18-hole golf course and 14 tennis courts; they can also rent boats at the local yacht club; kayaks, canoes, and bikes are available at the inn. Facilities include two sandy beaches, indoor and outdoor heated pools, one children's pool, one Jacuzzi, a sauna, a room with exercise equipment, and a room for massages by appointment. There are 84 rooms, poolside lunch, afternoon tea with a pianist, evening cocktails, and seasonal dancing. In high season $400–680 for double MAP per night plus 15 percent gratuity (no hand tipping for meals or any other service); from $99 off-season with no meals.

🐾 ✂ ⅋ **Inn by the Sea** (207-799-3134; www.innbythesea.com), 40 Bowery Beach Rd., Cape Elizabeth 04107. A 15-minute drive from downtown Portland, this shingled complex maintains a high reputation for great hospitality, beautiful rooms, and delicious food (see Audubon Room in *Dining Out*). The 43 one- and two-bedroom condo-style suites all feature a combination living/dining area, full kitchen, porch or deck, and water view. Beach house units are generally larger, with a gas-burning fireplace and full water views. Facilities include an outdoor pool, tennis courts, and shuffleboard, plus walking and jogging trails, and golf privileges at nearby Purpoodock Club. Great bird-watching over the neighboring salt marsh. A boardwalk leads to the tip of Crescent Beach State Park. Summer prices range $359–699, winter $179–469.

✿ **Higgins Beach Inn** (207-883-6684; www.higginsbeachinn.com), 34 Ocean Ave., Scarborough 04074 (7 miles south of Portland). Open mid-May–mid-Oct. An 1890s three-story wooden summer hotel near sandy, gorgeous Higgins Beach. The dining room, **Garofalo's**, features seafood and pasta dishes from owner Diane's Sicilian family recipes (entrées $15–24). There is also a cocktail lounge, a homey TV room, and a sunporch. Upstairs, the 22 guest rooms are archetypal summer hotel rooms, simple, clean, and airy, 13 with private bath. Full breakfast available but not included in the room rates; $95–215 double, with a minimum 2-night stay most weekends.

INNS AND BED & BREAKFASTS ⅄

Pomegranate Inn (207-772-1006 or 1-800-356-0408; www.pomegranate inn.com), 49 Neal St., Portland 04102. Isabel Smiles, an interior designer and former antiques dealer, has turned this 1880s Western Promenade house into a work of art. Eight amazing rooms are furnished in a mix of antiques and modern design, most with bold, hand-painted walls. The walls of the wide entryway are a mottled tangerine. Room 4 glows with its pretty Oriental rug, hand-painted birds on the wall, and colored-tile fireplace; the upstairs suite has a huge tiled bathroom and a Greek Revival mantel. Guest rooms have phone, discreet TV, and private bath; five have a gas fireplace. Breakfast might be leek and goat cheese omelet with a side of prosciutto and focaccia. The fireplace surround and columns in the dining rooms are painted a green faux stone that might trick your early-morning eyes into thinking you're surrounded by green onyx. $175–285 per room in-season, $95–165 off-season, including breakfast.

⊗ ✿ **The Danforth** (207-879-8755 or 1-800-991-6557; www.danforth maine.com), 163 Danforth St., Portland 04102. Honeymooning couples, business travelers—even celebrities—make the Danforth their home away from home in Portland's historic West End. Barbara Hathaway's meticulously restored 1821 brick mansion appeals to anyone craving both luxurious pampering and downtown sophistication. Guests have access to a wood-paneled billiard room in the basement, a third-floor solarium, and a cupola with a star-studded ceiling, not to mention the gracious formal living room and sunny breakfast room. Guest rooms all have queen bed, sitting area, private bath, premier cable TV, air-conditioning, phone with voice mail, and dataport. Eight of the nine rooms have a working fireplace. Rates ($139–329 in-season) include concierge service most evenings, expanded continental breakfast. Some pets are welcome; check first.

🍷 ✎ **Wild Iris Inn** (207-775-0224 or 1-800-600-1557; www.wildirisinn .com), 273 State St., Portland 04101. This small Victorian on the hill into Portland's main street, Congress, is the favorite stop for business travelers and tourists who like a quiet place with all the basic comforts. Seven rooms, all but two with private bath, have been furnished by owner Diane Edwards with attractive quilts and furniture; all are air-conditioned. A Shaker-inspired dining room holds biscotti and tea at all hours, as well as a full breakfast in the morning. Downtown is a close walk, and a computer and printer are available for visitors. $85–175.

The Inn on Carleton Street (207-775-1910 or 1-800-639-1779; www .innoncarleton.com), Portland 04102. Sue and Phil Cox have lovingly restored this handsome 1860s town house, even the trompe l'oeil artwork in the entryway. They have furnished each of the six rooms with spectacularly heavy, high-Victorian bedroom sets, including one Egyptian Revivial headboard they found in Colorado. The breakfast table is another big antique. $179–229 in-season. Children 9 and older only. Two Maine coon cats in residence.

West End Inn (207-772-1377 or 1-800-338-1377; www.westendbb.com), 146 Pine St., Portland 04102. This 1870s brick town house combines natural elegance with a colorful decor, and is now owned by Dan and Michele Brown. The most popular of the six rooms is Cliff Island, with 12-foot ceilings, private deck, and white and blue accents. All come with private bath, cable TV, ceiling fan, and air-conditioning. Rates $159–209 in-season, including full breakfast. Children 10 and older welcome.

Inn at Park Spring (207-774-1059 or 1-800-437-8511; www.innatpark spring.com), 135 Spring St., Portland 04101. Nicely sited between the Arts District and the West End, the inn features one of the most convenient locations in town. New owners Nancy and John Gonsalves preside over six guest rooms, which become increasingly contemporary in decor as you climb to the third floor. All offer private bath and sitting area, fresh flowers, and amenities. A gourmet breakfast is served in the formal dining room, which, like the living room, has floor-to-ceiling windows. Late May–Oct. $125–180, otherwise $99–135.

🍷 🐾 ✎ ⓚ **Inn at St. John** (207-773-6481 or 1-800-636-9127; www.inn atstjohn.com), 939 Congress St., Portland 04102. A 40-room hotel built in 1897 to accommodate railroad passengers arriving at Union Station (unfortunately long gone), this place has undergone a renovation that brings many of its rooms into the modern age. Convenient for guests arriving by Vermont Transit, it's a hike to downtown, but the moderate rates and quality make up for the distance. Well-maintained, attractive rooms, and a lobby given a turn-of-the-20th-century feel by innkeeper Paul Hood. $60–200 (depending on season) includes continental breakfast, air-conditioning, cable TV with HBO, and coffeemaker.

🐾 **Andrews on Auburn** (207-797-9157; www.andrewsonauburn.com), 417 Auburn St., Portland 04103. A cozy little B&B in a 1780s home situated halfway between Portland and Falmouth. Five rooms, all with private bath, feature Shaker and colonial reproduction furniture. The Captain

Suite offers luxurious appointments such as cable TV, skylights, bidet, and Jacuzzi bath. Guests also have access to the gardens (tended by innkeeper Elizabeth Andrews), a library, solarium, formal living room, and guest kitchen. In-season rates run $105–185, including a full breakfast—perhaps banana-stuffed French toast.

✴ Where to Eat

The quality of the dining is exceptional in Portland, perhaps because many restaurants are locally owned by the chefs who cook the meals.

DINING OUT

In downtown Portland

Fore Street (207-775-2717), 288 Fore Street. Open for dinner nightly. Reservations a must, although it's sometimes possible to get a table at 5:30, when the dining room opens. Sam Hayward, whose fame has grown with his James Beard Award for Best Chef in New England in 2004, oversees the meals here, which are all full of his signature integrity. Before anyone knew about him, however, the word was out—this is the place for really good roast pork, turned on a spit in the open kitchen, or wood-fired oven-roasted fish, or roast quail, or just a few chicken livers sautéed quickly over the hot stove. Here's where the best steamed mussels have been served for years with garlic almond butter. And desserts like chocolate soufflé cake and peach tarte tatin have been making customers swoon as long as they've been on the menu. Entrées $18–35.

&. **Street & Company** (207-775-0887), 33 Wharf St. Open for dinner daily 5:30–9:30, Fri. and Sat. until 10,

year-round. Reservations recommended. The noisy, packed dining rooms here, and a comfortable bar with upholstered seats, do all the advertising this place has ever needed by feeding fans wonderful fish, inventive specials, and comfortable standards like lobster diavolo for two, mussels Provençal, and scallops in Pernod and cream. The raw bar serves up the best oysters in town. Bourbon pecan pie and peach crisp might be on the dessert menu. Entrées $21.95–28.95.

David's Creative Cuisine (207-773-4340), 22 Monument Square. Open for lunch Mon.–Fri., dinner daily 5–9, until 10 weekend nights. Starters like fried calamari salad with feta, olives, and tomato ($7) or clam chowder made with thyme, brown sugar, and bacon ($5.25) give a feel for the inventive place this is. Entrées run from a bacon-wrapped boneless pork chop to meat loaf with garlic mashed potatoes and exotic mushroom gravy. Two vegetarian pasta dishes are also on the menu. Entrées $14–24.

Cinque Terre (207-347-6154), 56 Wharf St. This restaurant makes delicious northern Italian food. The open-plan dining room has the tile floors, second-floor gallery, and engaging noise of a neighborhood trattoria. They get the portions right, keeping them small enough so you can enjoy two courses without remorse. The gnocchi, made here in fall and winter, are an important lesson in what these things taste like when they're made right—cheesy, buttery little soufflés. Any of the homemade stuffed pasta dishes will be wonderful, and the risottos are sublime. Entrées $17–25.

Five Fifty-five (207-761-0555), 555 Congress St. Good for brunch as well as fine dinners; even the hamburgers here are an unusual pleasure. Fine cheeses, steaks, fish, and vegetarian dishes made with imagination and skill, the entrées range from $20 to $27. Reservations advised.

DiMillo's Floating Restaurant (207-772-2216; www.dimillos.com), 25 Long Wharf. Open for lunch and dinner. Maine's only floating restaurant, this converted car ferry serves seafood, steaks, Italian cuisine, and, of course, lobsters, and caters to visitors. Entrées $14–44. Free parking at the heart of the waterfront is a definite plus.

Beyond downtown Portland

One Fifty Ate (207-799-8998), 158 Benjamin W. Pickett St., South Portland. Open for dinner Thu.–Sat. The dinner menu keeps it simple and without pretense, but the food soars. Opened first as a breakfast and lunch spot, this tiny restaurant serves entrées that vie with the best around. Scalloppine with pancetta and spinach cream ($12) and new potato and fresh herb pizzettes ($10) have been entrées on the five-course menu.

Joe's Boathouse (207-741-2780), Spring Point Marina (end of Broadway). Open daily for lunch and dinner, plus Sunday brunch. Joe Loring and Nate Chalaby have created a winning combination here with spectacular views of Casco Bay (there's a seasonal patio) and a creative menu. You might dine on filet mignon with port wine shallot sauce or lobster with fettuccine. Dinner entrées $15.95–25.95.

✑ **Black Point Inn** (207-883-4126), Prouts Neck. Dinner by reservation in a formal dining room with water views. The elegant room, piano music, good food, and great service make this one of the best places for dinner in the area—especially in summer, when a predinner cocktail or after-dinner brandy can be enjoyed on the porch overlooking Scarborough Beach. The inn now buys ingredients from Maine farms as much as possible. Swordfish and tuna are always on the menu, along with as many as 15 entrées like farm-raised venison saltimbocca. Family and adults-only seating. Entrées $18–32.

✑ **The Audubon Room** (207-767-0888), at the Inn by the Sea, 40 Bowery Beach Rd., Cape Elizabeth. Overlooking the beach and water, a dining room decorated with genuine Audubon prints and serving breakfast, lunch, and dinner to guests of the inn and the general public. Dinner is really wonderful, with attentive service, a soothing atmosphere, and great food. Entrées ($24–29) might include Black Angus tenderloin served with merlot bordelaise and a surprisingly good pilaf, or seared scallops on squid ink linguine with mango salsa.

✑ ✑ **Saltwater Grille** (207-799-5400; www.saltwatergrille.com), 231 Front St., South Portland. Open daily for lunch (11–3) and dinner (5–9). The food has steadied and improved here, and the location has always been fabulous. Entrées include scallops carbonara; scallops sautéed with bacon, mushrooms, and peas in a Parmesan cream sauce on bow-tie pasta ($18.95); and saffron seafood and gnocchi that adds sweet sausages for $21.95. Big servings.

EATING OUT *Note:* Most of the restaurants described under *Dining Out* also serve a reasonably priced lunch.

In and around the Old Port

✑ **PepperClub** (207-772-0531), 78 Middle St. Open for dinner Sun.–

Thu. 5–9, Fri. and Sat. 5–10. A funky, fun spot. Creative menu options change frequently and are written on two large blackboards (as well as smaller table versions). Choose from six or seven vegetarian, four fish, and three meat entrées every night, perhaps organic salmon with a varying sauce; two Indian curries with dal and chutney; Atlantic scallops with peanut-coconut sauce; or vegetarian lasagna and two curries with changing dal. Entrées $8.95–14.95. Free parking across the street.

Flatbread Pizza (207-772-8777), 72 Commercial St. One of a small chain of pizza joints (one in Portsmouth, New Hampshire, another in Sugarbush, Vermont), Flatbread bakes its unique pies in a clay, wood fired oven shaped like a low igloo—right in the middle of the restaurant. Kids are always sitting on a stone across from the oven's opening, mesmerized by the fire. Our favorite pizza features homemade, nitrate-free maple-fennel sausage, sun-dried tomatoes, caramelized onions, organic mushrooms, mozzarella and Parmesan cheese, and herbs ($16); but everything here is fresh and delicious, including the salads and desserts. In good weather you can sit on the deck next to the ferry terminal while the boats head out to the islands of Casco Bay.

Local 188 (207-761-7909), 188 State St. Open Tue.–Sat. for dinner, and Sunday brunch. A tapas bar and gallery run by a collective of artists and known for the quality of the art as well as the Spanish food, which comes in small, tasty mix-and-match portions. Spanish wines are a specialty. Try the gazpacho, and the garlic shrimp, and the browned scallops in red pepper mojo, and the chicken in

Romesco sauce. All so good. Entrées $15–18; tapas under $10.

&. **Mims Brasserie** (207-347-7478), 205 Commerical St. Open daily for breakfast, lunch, and dinner. This restaurant opened in 2004 with an à la carte menu for every part of the meal. We ate the eggs Benedict and thought it was the best we'd ever had— because it relied on Sunset Acres Farm for the tender ham and fresh eggs, and made up the purest example of hollandaise. The evening dinner of a brined pork chop from that same great farm was good, with a side of creamed spinach shared by two. The outdoor spaces are lovely. Entrées $7–15, for meat dishes only; vegetable sides extra.

Granny's Burritos (207-761-0751), 420 Fore St. Open daily for lunch and dinner. The best burrito east of the Mississippi. Vegan and vegetarian options, delicious quesadillas, rice and beans, and a kids' menu. Eat takeout-style at downstairs picnic tables, or be served by the wait staff in (relative) style on the second floor, where you can order beer and wine.

Black Tie Café (207-761-6665), 188 Middle St. (It's tricky to find: Walk through the alley between Abacus and Fibula on Exchange, and the café and tented patio are on the right.) Open Mon.–Fri. for lunch. Enjoy homey entrées like a pulled pork sandwich or Cobb salad wrap, along with more upscale items such as grilled chicken, shiitake mushrooms, and spinach sautéed in lemon oil ($8.95) or Maine crabcakes with rémoulade ($9.95). Children's menu. $7.95–12.95.

Gilbert's Chowder House (207-871-5636), 92 Commercial St. Open for lunch and dinner. As the name implies, Gilbert's serves delicious and filling chowders, but they also have a nice range of seafood appetizers and entrées, such as lovely steamed mussels with garlic butter. The decor is Early Dive, but you can sit outside on the wharf in-season.

☙ Federal Spice (207-774-6404), 225 Federal St. (across from the downtown post office). Open Mon.–Sat. from 11 AM. The soups du jour zing with flavor, as does the chili. Homemade falafel, yam fries, and sweet potato jalapeño corn bread round out the creative menu of hot and cold wraps and soft tacos.

Benkay (207-773-5555), 2 India St. Benkay is a hipster's dream: a happening sushi bar with Western- and Japanese-style tables (one in the shape of a dory), and Rock 'n' Roll Sushi Friday and Saturday nights.

Fuji (207-773-2900), 29 Exchange St. Open Tue.–Sun. for lunch and dinner. Another excellent Asian restaurant in the Old Port, Fuji makes fine sushi and Japanese dishes. Japanese steakhouse-style meals served on hibachis in the lower dining room; a reservation is a good idea for three or more.

☙ Tandoor (207-775-4259), 88 Exchange St. Open daily for lunch and dinner. We've tried them all, and we still think this is the best Indian place in town. Choose from classics like chicken and lamb cooked in the tandoor oven, or vegetarian favorites like dal (yellow lentils sautéed with cream and spices) and *sag paneer* (spinach with homemade cheese).

Beyond the Old Port
Blue Spoon (207-773-1116), 89 Congress St. Open for lunch and dinner Tue.–Sat., brunch on Sun. This small restaurant at the top of Munjoy Hill

made itself popular by serving classy meals for modest prices. The seafood stew, with a few clams, shrimp, and chunks of salmon and potato in a clear, savory broth, tasted pristinely fresh ($14). The delicious burger and large bowls of mussels with lemon and garlic are popular on the changing menu. Entrées $10–14.

☙ ♂ ♿ Becky's Diner (207-773-7070; www.beckys.com), 390 Commercial St. Open Tue.–Sat. 4 AM–9 PM, this is a genuine local favorite, known for soups and pies. Breakfast is the specialty here, with a killer fruit salad, granola-and-yogurt bowl, and delicious grilled, homemade corn and blueberry muffins. Also reasonably priced lunch and dinner specials, and good chowder.

☙ Norm's Bar & Grill (207-828-9944), 606 Congress St. Open daily for lunch and dinner. We have never had a bad meal here—in fact, we are continually wowed by the savory blackboard tapas and specials and the eclectic menu ranging from black bean soup (a staple) and steak salad with spinach or fried calamari to hot pastrami and grilled pork chops with BBQ sauce. Norm's is such a good value that even on weeknights it's advisable to slide into a booth by 5:30.

☙ ♂ Artemisia Café (207-761-0135), 61 Pleasant St. (just behind and to the east of Holiday Inn by the Bay). Lunch Mon.–Fri., brunch Sat. and Sun., dinner Thu.–Sat. Lunch covers a wide assortment of salads, wraps, and sandwiches, from lemon dill tuna salad wrap and salade Niçoise to grilled sweet potato sandwich with avocado spread. We loved the Tuscan grill with portobello mushrooms, pesto, and goat cheese ($6.50).

The Bayou Kitchen (207-774-4935), 543 Deering Ave. (across the street from Big Sky Bakery and an excellent art supply store). Serving breakfast and lunch Mon. and Wed.–Sat. 7–2, Sun. 8–2. For those of us with southern roots (or longings), this hole-in-the-wall off Forest Ave. offers the best grits and eggs in town, plus decent jambalaya, crawfish po'boys, and Cajun burgers.

Beyond Portland
Beale Street Barbeque and Grill (207-767-0130), 90 Waterman Dr., South Portland. This place serves authentic hickory-smoked chicken, beef, sausage, and pork, plus good corn bread, barbecued beans, and coleslaw.

✿ **The Lobster Shack** (207-799-1677; http://lobstershack-twolights .com), 225 Two Lights Rd., Cape Elizabeth (off Rt. 77 at the tip of the cape, near Two Lights State Park). Open Apr.–late Oct., 11–8. Dine inside or out at this local landmark built in the 1920s, set below the lighthouse and next to the foghorn. Herb and Martha Porch have gotten their line management down to a science. Lobsters, or, if you're lobstered out, dig into their delicious chowders and lobster stew, fried Maine shrimp, scallops, and clams, or the lobster and crabmeat rolls.

✿ ✿ **The Good Table** (207-799-4663), 526 Ocean House Rd. (Rt. 77), Cape Elizabeth. Open Tue.–Sun. for lunch and dinner 8 AM–9 PM in summer, from 11 AM in winter (with 3 PM closing Sun.). This place burned to the ground in 2002 but was completely rebuilt by the summer season. Beloved by its loyal regulars, the restaurant serves home-style entrées for lunch and dinner made with good ingredients and with skill; the weekend brunch menu might include eggs Benedict and a variety of interesting quiches.

✿ ✿ ✿ **Spurwink Country Kitchen** (207-799-1177), 150 Spurwink Rd. (near Scarborough Beach), Scarborough. Open mid-Apr.–mid-Oct., 11:30–8:30. Looking much the same and serving much the same food as when Hope Sargent opened it in 1955, with pine beadboard walls and gingham curtains. If you're in the mood for a down-home meal like fresh-roasted turkey with mashed potatoes and gravy, hamburgers, or chicken potpie, this is the place. Great homemade pies.

COFFEE BARS Portland, like its sister cities in the Pacific Northwest, is a coffee town. Maybe it's the long, cold, dark winters, or maybe it's the seafaring past that draws people to warm, fragrant cafés, but it seems you can find a spot for a cuppa joe on every other corner. At **Java Net** (207-773-2469 or 1-800-528-2638), 39 Exchange St., travelers can sip on a latte, cider, or chai while checking their e-mail or conducting business via the Internet. Bring your laptop or use their computers (hourly rates). **Coffee by Design** (207-772-5533), 620 Congress St., is the first in this friendly local chain (now also at 67 India St.), a cheerful spot with plenty of tables (sidewalk tables in summer), local art on display (and for sale), and all the usual coffee and espresso choices. **Arabica** (207-879-0792), 16 Free St. We like this place's baked goods, Victorian love seat, high ceilings, and cinnamon toast.

CASCO BAY

✳ Entertainment

All listings are in Portland unless otherwise noted

Cumberland County Civic Center (207-775-3458; www.theciviccenter .com), 1 Civic Center Square. An arena with close to 9,000 seats, the center hosts year-round concerts, ice-skating spectaculars, Portland Pirates hockey games, and more.

State Theatre (207-780-8265; www .liveatthestate.com), 609 Congress St. A funky art deco facility hosting a variety of performances, from rock to classical.

Center for Cultural Exchange (207-761-0591; www.centerforcultural exchange.org), 1 Longfellow Square. Multicultural events include annual Irish and Greek festivals, weekly Friday-night dance parties (Latin, African, Celtic), visiting artists such as Cambodian dancers, gospel groups, Puerto Rican plena bands, and many other offerings.

Top of the East (207-755-5411), Eastland Hotel, 157 High St. Open 4 PM–midnight daily, until 1 AM Thu.–Sat. Portland's only rooftop lounge, with a marble bar, leather banquettes, and floor-to-ceiling windows taking in views of Mount Washington and Casco Bay.

MUSIC **Portland Symphony Orchestra** (207-773-6128; www.portland symphony.com), Merrill Auditorium, 20 Myrtle St. (just off Congress St. behind city hall). The winter series runs Oct.–May; in summertime, outdoor pops concerts range from the shores of Casco Bay to Camden Harbor.

LARK Society for Chamber Music/Portland String Quartet (207-761-1522; www.portlandstring quartet.org). This distinguished chamber group performs in varied Portland locations and does educational outreach around the state.

Portland Opera Repertory Theatre (207-879-7678; www.portopera .org), Merrill Auditorium. This critically acclaimed company enters its twelfth season in 2006. Past productions include *The Barber of Seville* and *Faust*.

PCA Great Performances (207-773-3150; www.pcagreatperformances .com). A series of orchestra, jazz, and musical theater performances staged in fall and winter at Merrill Auditorium. Everything from *Stomp* and Dame Edna to Yo-Yo Ma.

PROFESSIONAL SPORTS The **Portland Pirates** (207-828-4665; www .portlandpirates.com), a professional minor-league hockey team, play their home games at the Cumberland County Civic Center. The **Portland Sea Dogs** (1-800-936-3647), a double-A baseball team, play in Hadlock Stadium on Park Ave. (next to the Expo).

THEATER **Portland Stage Company** (207-774-0465; www.portlandstage .com) is based in the city's old Odd Fellows Hall (25A Forest Ave.), now an elegant, intimate, 290-seat theater. This Equity group stages a variety of shows Oct.–Apr.

Portland Players (207-799-7338), Thaxter Theater, 420 Cottage Rd., South Portland. An excellent community theater, the Players put on productions Sep.–June.

Lyric Music Theater (207-799-6509), Cedric Thomas Playhouse, 176 Sawyer St., South Portland. Four musicals each winter.

St. Lawrence Arts & Community Center (207 775-5568, ext. 4), 76 Congress St. An umbrella performance space for several local professional theater companies, musicians, filmmakers, dance companies, and other artists. The schedule changes constantly, so call to see what's doing.

✳ Selective Shopping

All listings are in Portland unless otherwise noted

Angela Adams (207-774-3523; www.angelaadams.com), 273 Congress St. This store sells the gorgeous, swirling, colorful carpets and handbags designed by Angela Adams. Her work has won praise from all kinds of designers, and her rugs are now coveted items. The top-of-the-line pieces are expensive, but the store runs a handbag sale in September.

ANTIQUES There are a plethora of small shops, especially in the Old Port, along Congress St., and along Rt. 1 from south of town and north into Yarmouth. Here is a sampling:

Willmert-Newell Antiques and Decorative Objects (207-775-7414), 642 Congress St., Lafayette Square. Open Wed.–Sat. 10–5.

Flora Home (207-846-0565), Yarmouth; by appointment. Stephanie Pilk sells sophisticated flowers, plants, and some pottery.

Zinnia's (780-6622), 662 Congress St. Chock-full of interesting 19th- and 20th-century antiques, this place specializes in antique lighting and furniture.

ART GALLERIES Art Walks are held the first Friday of every month, when galleries citywide hold open house.

Greenhut Galleries (207-772-2693 or 1-888-772-2693; www.greenhutgalleries.com), 146 Middle St. Peggy Golden Greenhut represents many of Maine's top artists and sculptors. A destination gallery for collectors from around the country.

June Fitzpatrick Gallery (207-772-1961; www.fitzpatrickgallery.com), 112 High St. Well established and showcasing contemporary and fine art.

Aucocisco (207-874-2060; www.aucocisco.com), 615A Congress St. Andres Verzosa's small gallery is worth checking out, with its brilliant area artists.

Salt Gallery (207-761-0660; www.salt.edu), 110 Exchange St. The Salt Institute for Documentary Studies brings students from all over the United States and abroad to study photography, nonfiction writing, and documentary radio. You can view the fruits of their photographic work, usually about the state of Maine, in this 19th century Old Port building.

CRAFTS GALLERIES Edgecomb Potters Gallery (207-780-6727; www.edgecombpotters.com), 49 Exchange St. One of four in the state; a fine collection of reasonably priced, interesting pottery. Other merchandise includes glass designs, wind chimes, and jewelry.

Abacus (207-772-4880), 44 Exchange St. We love this store, one in a chain of four, which sells a seemingly endless and fascinating array of fine glass, ceramics, jewelry, textiles, and home furnishings.

Maine Potters Market (207-774-1633; www.mainepottersmarket.com), 376 Fore St. Work by 15 Maine potters.

BOOKSTORES Portland has become a mecca for book lovers. **Books Etc.** (207-774-0626; www.mainebooksetc.com), 38 Exchange St., fills two storefronts and features a terrific Maine books section. They also own a second store in Falmouth (207-781-3784), 240 Rt. 1 (the Shops at Falmouth Village). **Longfellow Books** (207-772-4045; www.longfellowbooks.com), 1 Monument Way, stocks a full range of titles and hosts frequent readings by local and national authors. **Casco Bay Books** (207-541-3842; www.cascobaybooks.com), 151 Middle St., carries maps as well as new and excellent used books; they have a nice café where you can sit and read for hours. **Borders Books and Music** (207-775-6110) in the Maine Mall parking lot (I-95, exit 7) has a huge selection and its own café.

Antiquarian-book lovers should check out **Carlson-Turner Books** (207-773-4200), 241 Congress St.; **Emerson Maps and Books** (207-874-2665), 18 Exchange St.; **Cunningham Books** (207-775-2246), 188 State St. on Longfellow Square, with a well-arranged selection of some 50,000 titles; and our favorite, Pat Murphy's famous **Yes Books** (207-775-3233), 589 Congress St., considered by some to be the best used-book store in Maine.

FOOD Portland Public Market (207-772-8140; www.portlandmarket.com). One block north of Congress between Preble and Elm Sts., open Mon.–Sat. 9–7, Sun. 10–5. Opened in 1997, the soaring, open-timbered market has had a hard time finding a customer base, but the interior is gorgeous, with lots of sun pouring in through the glass walls and an attractive stone fireplace in winter, and it features some interesting vendors. We like **Stone Soup**'s hot and cold potages, **Maine Beer & Beverage** (Maine beers, fine wines, and drinks ranging from Moxie to cider), **Horton's Smoked Seafood and Cheese**, with its array of fine Maine and domestic and imported cheeses, and the **Portland Spice Trading Company**, with every spice you can imagine or wish for. Park in the adjacent garage (2 free hours with a market receipt).

Standard Baking Co. (207-773-2112), 75 Commercial St. (below Fore Street restaurant). Open Mon.–Fri. 7–7, weekends 7–5. The best bread in Maine, period. Artisanal French and Italian breads are worth every penny, and the rolls, baguettes, brioches, and pastries make our mouths water. Specialties include small gingerbread cakes, brownies, cinnamon buns with or without nuts, croissants, and *pain au chocolat* made with exquisite dark chocolate.

Browne Trading Market (207-775-7560), 260 Commercial St. Open Mon.–Sat. 10–6. Formerly a fish wholesaler serving upscale restaurants throughout the United States, now selling their own smoked salmon, trout, shrimp, scallops, mussels, and salmon jerky as well as a variety of fresh seafood (some flown in daily from the Mediterranean) and caviar from Iran and Russia. Also offering a wide assortment of cheeses and one of the largest selections of wine north of Boston.

Portland Farmer's Market. May–Nov., Wed. 7–noon at Monument Square, and Sat. 7–noon in Deering Oaks Park. Produce, flowers, seeds, baked goods, and more, some organic and all grown and made in Maine. Visit the wading pool nearby in the park.

Harbor Fish Market (207-775-0251 or 1-800-370-1790, www.harborfish.com), 9 Custom House Wharf. Open Mon.–Sat. 8:30–5:30. The epicenter of fish, lobster, crabs, oysters, clams, eels, and squid, to name a few, able to ship anywhere you like.

MORE SPECIAL SHOPS

Clothing
Helene M (207-772-2564; www.helenem.com), 425 Fore St. Chic separates for women. Local shoppers wait for the sales, when the store hangs bargains on racks on the brick patio just outside.
Portmanteau (207-774-7276), 191 Middle St. Nancy Lawrence began by stitching canvas bags but has long since established a reputation for the distinctive tapestry handbags, totes, backpacks, luggage, and cloaks fabricated on her premises.

Other goods
Northern Sky Toyz (207-828-0911), 388 Fore St. An amazing kite shop, with a variety of other novelties and toys, including windsocks, banners, and games.
Leroux Kitchen (207-553-7665), 161 Commercial St. An amateur chef's dream: everything you could possibly need to make a gourmet meal, from marble mortar and pestles and Henckels knives to Viking cookware and extensive wines and prepared foods.
Fetch (207-773-5450), 195 Commercial St. Anyone owned by a dog or a cat must take a spin through this zany store full of pet paraphernalia. Fetch sells all-natural foods, supplements, and litters, as well as a smattering of chewtoys and shampoos. Owner Kathy and her pug Zip host a

Pug Night every Wednesday in summer. Pets, of course, are welcome.

Beyond Portland proper is the **Maine Mall** (exit 7 off I-95), whose immediate complex of more than 100 stores is supplemented by large shopping centers and chain stores that ring it for several miles.

✳ Special Events

First Sunday in June: **Old Port Festival**—a celebration that began in the 1970s with the revival of the Old Port; includes a parade, various performances, street vendors, and special sales.

Mid-July: **Yarmouth Clam Festival**—arts and crafts, plenty of clams, performances, more.

August: **Cumberland Crafts Fair**, Cumberland Fairgrounds. **Sidewalk Art Festival**, Congress St.

October: **Food Festival**—head to the Portland Public Market for a smorgasbord, with dozens of booths featuring cuisine from the menus of many of Portland's finest restaurants, plus microbrews and local charity auctions.

First weekend in November: **Maine Brewer's Festival**. Each year this event grows in size, due to the increasing number of Maine microbreweries.

Post-Thanksgiving—Christmas: **Victorian Holiday Portland**—with tree lighting, the arrival of Father Christmas, costumed carolers, special events through Christmas.

December 31: **Portland New Year's Celebration**—modeled after Boston's First Night, with alcohol-free performances and events throughout the city in the afternoon, catering to families.

FREEPORT

Think of Freeport, and you'll likely think of shopping. This is one coastal town that welcomes visitors every day of the year, even on Christmas morning, when the famous L. L. Bean store is open for business. A 24-hour, 365-day-a-year superstore, L. L. Bean has been a landmark since the famous boot was developed back in 1912. It grew in popularity in 1951 when the store opened around the clock. Beginning with the influx of seconds and factory stores in the early 1980s, the reputation of Freeport as a shopping mecca took hold.

Each year as many as 3.5 million visitors flock to the town, prowling both sides of Main Street (Rt. 1) in search of big deals in brand-name outlets. Freeport is definitely a bargain shopper's dream, but it has always featured upscale retailers as well, such as Cole-Haan, Burberry, and famous furniture makers like Thomas Moser.

Don't assume, however, that shopping is all Freeport has to offer. The retail facades belie a rich and varied history dating back more than 200 years. The first known residents of the area were several tribes of the Wabanaki. Attempts by colonists to settle in the area resulted in a series of wars throughout the 1600s and early 1700s. By 1715 epidemics of European diseases and the settlers' persistence ended the Native American hold on the area, and a peace treaty with the Penobscots was signed in 1725.

Originally a part of North Yarmouth, Freeport was granted a charter separating itself from the town in 1789. A longtime legend (somewhat controversial, because there is no documented evidence of the occurrence) holds that in 1820 the papers separating Maine from Massachusetts were signed in the historical Jameson Tavern.

Early citizens made a living through agriculture and timber. With the War of 1812, shipbuilding became an important industry, with one famous boat inspiring Whittier's poem "The Dead Ship of Harpswell." In the 1880s shoe factories sprouted up in Freeport, adding another industry to its economy.

Transportation advances also had their effect on Freeport's history. When an electric trolley was built to connect Portland and Yarmouth with Brunswick and Lewiston, it passed through Freeport. Just as many trolley companies built parks to encourage ridership, the developer built the Casco Castle Hotel to draw tourists to South Freeport. The hotel burned down, but a stone tower remains today (on private property) and can be best viewed from Winslow Memorial Park or from the harbor.

By 1980 the economy in Freeport was on a downward spiral. And then the outlets came to town. Despite the proliferation of shops, the village has retained the appearance of older days—even McDonald's has been confined to a gracious old house, with no golden arches in sight. The Freeport Historical Society operates a research library and museum in a historic house, in the midst of the retail sector. You can take a self-directed walking tour of Freeport historic sites.

Some come to the area simply to stroll wooded paths in Wolfe's Neck Woods State Park and the Maine Audubon's Mast Landing Sanctuary. Bradbury Mountain is just a short drive, and Pettengill Farm offers a look at 19th-century coastal life. The Desert of Maine is a quirky attraction as well. Canoeing, boat trips, golf, and summer concerts in the park outside L. L. Bean can round out the Freeport experience quite nicely.

GUIDANCE

The Freeport Merchants Association (207-865-1212 or 1-800-865-1994; www.freeportusa.com), P.O. Box 452, Freeport 04032, operates a visitor center in a replica of a historic hose tower on Depot St. Brochures, information, and restrooms can be found here, and the association's office is upstairs. They also gladly respond to telephone and mail requests for information. Among their materials is an excellent, free visitor walking map with a list of stores, restaurants, accommodations, attractions, and other services. Also ask for the fun brochure *101+ Things to Do within an Hour's Drive of Freeport.*

The Maine Tourism Association's welcome center in Kittery stocks some Freeport brochures, and there is another state information center on Rt. 1 just south of Freeport, in Yarmouth, at exit 17 off I-95.

GETTING THERE A number of **bus tour companies** also offer shopping trips to Freeport from Boston and beyond. Most people drive, which means there can be a shortage of parking spaces in peak season. One solution to this problem is to stay at one of the dozen or so inns or B&Bs within half a mile of L. L. Bean and leave your car there. The new Amtrak **Downeaster** from Boston to Portland, and the excellent bus service on **Concord Trailways** (see *Getting There* in "Portland Area") from Boston to Brunswick, however, provide a wonderful alternative: Leave the car at home, then take a taxi or car service to Freeport. Most of the local attractions are within walking or biking distance of Main Street.

WHEN TO COME The holiday shopping season is one of Freeport's busiest times, and a special "Sparkle" weekend celebrates it in December. For hiking and swimming, summer months are best.

✳ Villages

South Freeport has been a fishing center from its beginning, when it was known as Strout's Port. Between 1825 and 1830 up to 12,000 barrels of mackerel were packed and shipped from here each year. Later the area specialty became lobster packing. Offering a very different feel from the chaotic shopping frenzy of downtown Freeport, the harbor still bustles with activity and features great seafood. From here you can take a cruise to explore Eagle and Seguin Islands in summer.

Porter's Landing. Once the center of commercial activity, this now quiet residential neighborhood nestles amid rolling hills, woods, and streams. The village is part of the Harraseeket Historic District on the National Register of Historic Places.

✳ To See and Do

🦞 🐾 ♂ ♿ **Desert of Maine** (207-865-6962; www.desertofmaine.com), 95 Desert Rd., Freeport. Open daily, early May–mid-Oct., 9–5. Admission runs $7.75 adults, $5.25 ages 13–16, $4.25 ages 5–12. Narrated tram tours and self-guided walks through 40 acres of sand that was once the Tuttle Farm. Heavily farmed, then extensively logged to feed the railroad, the topsoil eventually gave way to the glacial sand deposit beneath it, which spread . . . and spread until entire trees sank below the surface. It is an unusual sand, rich in mineral deposits that make it unsuitable for commercial use but interesting to rock-hounds. Children love it, especially the gem hunt (stones have been scattered in a section of the desert for children to find). Overnight camping is available (see *Lodging*).

BOAT EXCURSIONS **Atlantic Seal** (207-865-6112), Town Wharf, South Freeport. Memorial Day–mid-Oct. Captain Thomas Ring (owner of the charming Atlantic Seal B&B) runs daily narrated trips into Casco Bay, including 3-hour cruises to Eagle Island, the former summer home of Admiral Robert E. Peary, the first person to reach the North Pole; Thu. 6-hour cruises to Seguin Island Lighthouse to see—and climb inside—the fascinating first-order Fresnel lens, and a visit to the museum run by the Friends of the Seguin Lighthouse Caretakers (with 50-foot humpback whale and porpoise sightings on the trip to the island); seal- and osprey-sighting trips; and fall foliage cruises mid-Sep. and Oct. Lobstering demonstrations usually included, except on Sunday, when lobstering is prohibited by Maine law.

CANOEING The **Harraseeket River** in Freeport is particularly nice for canoeing. Start at Mast Landing, the northeastern end of the waterway; there are also launching sites at Winslow Memorial Park on Staples Point Rd. and at South Freeport Harbor. Phone **Maine Audubon** headquarters in Falmouth (207-781-2330; www.maineaudubon.org) for details about periodic, scheduled guided trips through the area. Nearby lake canoeing can be found at **Run Around Pond** in North Pownal (the parking lot is off Lawrence Rd., 1 mile north of the intersection with Fickett Rd.).

CROSS-COUNTRY SKIING The areas listed under *Green Space* are good cross-country skiing spots; rent or purchase equipment from L. L. Bean, which also offers classes in cross-country skiing (see *Special Learning Programs*).

GOLF **Freeport Country Club** (207-865-4922), 2 Old County Rd., Freeport. Nine holes, golf clinics, pro shop, and snack bar.

JEWELRY MAKING ✐ **The Beadin' Path** (207-865-4785; www.beadinpath .com), 15 Main St., Freeport. Choose beads and findings from a wide variety (including vintage and contemporary Swarovski crystal), then sit at the table and create your own jewelry pieces. Prices are based on the beads you choose, so this can be a good, inexpensive rainy-day activity for kids (and adults).

MUSEUM ✐ **Harrington House** (207-865-3170), 45 Main St., Freeport. Open Tue., Thu., and Fri. 10–2:30, Wed. 10–7. Donations appreciated. Built of local brick and granite, this 1830 house and garden is maintained by the Freeport Historical Society as a museum, research library, and archive.

SPECIAL LEARNING PROGRAMS **L. L. Bean Outdoor Discovery Schools** (1-800-552-3261, www.llbean.com), Rt. 1, Freeport. An interesting series of lectures and lessons that cover everything from cross-country ski lessons (on weekends beginning in Jan.) to kayaking, wing-shooting, fly-fishing, and outdoor photography. Courses last from a couple of hours to weeklong trips. Call or visit the web site for a free program guide.

✳ Green Space

✐ **Winslow Memorial Park** (207-865-4198), Staples Point Rd., South Freeport. Open Memorial Day–Sep. A 90-acre municipal park with a sandy beach and large grassy picnicking area; also boating and 100-site oceanside campground ($18–20 per night). Facilities include restrooms with showers. Admission fee.

✐ **Mast Landing Sanctuary** (207-781-2330; www.maineaudubon.org), Upper Mast Landing Rd. (take Bow St. south), Freeport. Maintained by Maine Audubon, this 140-acre sanctuary offers trails through apple orchards, woods, and meadows, and along a millstream. Several paths radiate from a 1-mile loop trail. You might even get lucky and see mink, deer, or porcupines.

✐ **Bradbury Mountain State Park** (207-688-4712), Rt. 9, 528 Hallowell Rd., Pownal (6 miles from Freeport: From I-95, take exit 20 and follow signs). Open year-round. $3 adults, $1 ages 5–11, under 5 free. The summit, accessible by an easy (even for young children) 0.5-mile hike, yields a splendid view of Casco Bay and New Hampshire's White Mountains. Facilities in the 297-acre park include a small playground, a softball field, hiking trails, toilets, and a 41-site overnight camping area.

✐ ♿ **Wolfe's Neck Woods State Park** (207-865-4465; off-season, 207-865-6080), 425 Wolfe's Neck Rd. (take Bow St., across from L. L. Bean), Freeport. Open Apr.–Oct. Day-use fee. A 233-acre park with shoreline hiking along Casco Bay, the Harraseeket River, and salt marshes, as well as excellent birding with ospreys as the local stars. Guided nature walks, and scattered picnic tables and grills.

❧ ♪ **Pettengill Farm** (207-865-3170), Pettengill Rd., Freeport. Managed by the Freeport Historical Society and open for periodic guided tours. The public is invited to wander the grounds anytime from sunrise to sunset, and pets are very welcome here. A saltwater farm with 140 acres of open fields and woodland that overlook the Harraseeket Estuary, with a totally unmodernized vintage-1810 saltbox house. Come the weekend after Labor Day for the annual Pettengill Farm Days celebration.

✳ Lodging

All listings are in Freeport 04032 unless otherwise noted
INN ❧ ♪ ♿ **Harraseeket Inn** (207-865-9377 or 1-800-342-6423; www.stayfreeport.com), 162 Main St. The Gray family—Nancy, Paul, and their son and daughter Chip and Penelope (all former Maine Guides)—has a passion for Maine expressed in a meticulous yet warm innkeeping style. Just two blocks north of L. L. Bean, their luxury hotel is the largest in the area, with 84 rooms (including 5 suites) plus 9 town houses. The inn began as a five-room B&B in the 1800 Federal house next door, and it continues to offer the same elegant atmosphere. Many of the rooms feature antiques and reproductions, canopy bed, and Jacuzzi; 20 have fireplace. The inn has formal dining rooms (see *Dining Out*), conference spaces (one with outdoor terrace), and the casual and popular Broad Arrow Tavern (see *Eating Out*). Other public spaces include a drawing room, library, gym, ballroom, and a pretty, glassed-in pool overlooking the gardens. Rates in-season are $215–285, full buffet breakfast and afternoon high tea included. Two-night minimum stay required on some holiday weekends. Package plans available.

BED & BREAKFASTS ❧ ♪ **White Cedar Inn** (207-865-9099 or 1-800-853-1269; www.whitecedarinn.com), 178 Main St. Open year-round. In this restored Victorian former home of Arctic explorer Donald B. MacMillan, who went to the North Pole with Admiral Peary, seven bedrooms come with private bath, down comforters, and air-conditioning; some have a fireplace. A spiral staircase leads to the Bowdoin downstairs, which also has a private entrance, sitting area, and TV (pets are welcome here). Owners Rock Nadeau and Monica Kissane both left careers at IBM for a "whole new life." Full breakfast, included, is served at small tables in the sunroom, adjacent to the country kitchen. Doubles $129–175.

Captain Briggs House (207-865-1868 or 1-888-217-2477; www.captain briggs.com), 8 Maple Ave. Simple, pleasant rooms with private bath, all named for flowers. We like the Bayberry Room with its huge, sun-filled bay windows, pedestal sink, and decorative iron fireplace mantel. This place is quieter than some because it's set well off Rt. 1. The sitting room has cable TV, games, and books. $110–210 in-season includes full breakfast.

The James Place Inn (207-865-4486 or 1-800-964-9086; www.jamesplace inn.com), 11 Holbrook St. This place has everything we love in a B&B: charm, luxury, beautiful furnishings, and a relaxed atmosphere. Darcy and Bill James's impressive collection of landscapes and still-life paintings is alone worth a visit. The Pine Room in particular captured our fancy. It feels like a little cabin, with pine bead-board walls, queen bed with down comforter, blue braided rug, a TV/VCR, and a private porch. All seven rooms have air-conditioning and cable TV; two feature kitchenette and Jacuzzi. Enjoy the full breakfast at the café tables on the deck or in the pretty glassed-in breakfast room. $135–155 double in-season.

☙ **Applewood Inn** (207-865-9705 or 1-877-954-1358; www.applewoodusa .com), 8 Holbrook St. Jay and Jennifer Yilmaz have 11 rooms in two buildings for nightly rentals. The rooms are simply decorated and recently renovated. Two blocks north of L. L. Bean, the inn sits far enough off Rt. 1 to be very quiet, and each room has a private bath; some have a fireplace, skylights, Jacuzzi, and TV/VCR. Sit on the wide porch on an autumn afternoon and watch the leaves fall. Full breakfast included in the $140–170 in-season rates. Well-behaved pets welcome. The family also operates six AJ Dogs stands and two ice cream stands on Freeport's busy Main Street.

⚓ **Atlantic Seal B&B** (207-865-6112 or 1-877-ATL-SEAL), 25 Main St., Box 146, South Freeport 04078. Open year-round. Captain Tom Ring is the real deal: A fifth-generation Mainer with an authentic Maine accent, he still lives in his family's cozy 1850 Cape and skippers boat cruises to neighboring islands in high season. You can't beat this sweet little inn for water views or true Down East charm. Each room is named for a ship built in Freeport, and we're crazy about The Dash, with brass queen and double beds, a Jacuzzi tub, and a

fabulous private deck overlooking the tidal Harraseeket River. Ask Captain Tom about the trunk his grandfather brought on board when he sailed four-masted schooners along the Maine coast. Swimming off the private dock; a rowboat and two mountain bikes are available for guest use. There is a resident cat. Summer rates, including a "hearty sailor's breakfast"—like apple pancakes and pumpkin muffins in fall—start at $125 and go to $200. Guests also receive a discount on morning cruises.

Kendall Tavern (207-865-1338; www.kendalltavern.com), 213 Main St. This 200-year-old farmhouse, owned by Loree and Tim Rudolph, features seven rooms, all with private bath and air-conditioning. Pastel walls, quilts, and antiques like hand-painted armoires and four-poster beds make the rooms attractive; three are under the eaves on the top floor. Sit in one of two parlors with fireplaces, or hang out on the lovely front porch in summer; the shops are a 10 minute walk away. Rates range up to $165 in-season, and include a full breakfast. Children over 8 welcome.

☙ ⚓ ♿ **Royalsborough Inn at the Bagley House** (207-865-6566 or 1-800-765-1772; www.royalsborough inn.com), 1290 Royalsborough Rd., Durham 04222. A 10-minute drive from downtown Freeport in a serene country setting, this is the oldest house in town, built as a public house in 1772. The town's first worship services were held here, and it was the site of the first schoolhouse.Marianne and Jim Roberts have furnished the eight rooms with antiques and hand-sewn quilts. The Durham Suite has a four-poster queen with air-conditioning, cable TV, and gas fireplace. $125–175 double in-season includes full breakfast and afternoon refreshments.

Spar Cove Inn (207-865-3255), 14 Cooper Rd. (Turn off Rt. 1 at the Big Indian, then go right on South Freeport Rd. and right on Staples Rd.; take the first left onto Spar Cove Forest. Follow this road straight ahead to its end. Make a left onto Cooper Rd., and the Spar Cove Inn is on the right.) Open only May–Oct., this is just one suite, but it's quiet and so private. Owner Joanie Gogerty's suite features a queen brass bed covered with quilts, a sitting area, hardwood floors, a colorful private bath, a ceiling fan, and cable TV. Gogerty offers either a full breakfast with fresh-squeezed OJ or, for $20 less, a continental breakfast. Guests also have access to a living room with fireplace and cable TV. A dog and two cats are in residence. Rates range $125–145, depending on the season.

MOTELS **The Village Inn** (207-865-3236, reservations only 1-800-998-3649), 186 Main St., has rates starting at $85 and is within easy walking distance of all the shops. The very basic decor is perfectly clean, and the owners for over 20 years, Lewis and Jackie Corliss, are downhome Mainers who can tell you the history of their transformed town or help you get your disabled car fixed, as they did for us. Includes a breakfast of pancakes, French toast, or scrambled eggs. On Rt. 1, south of Freeport near the Yarmouth town line, there are a number of modern motels. Among these is the **Best Western Freeport Inn** (207-865-3106 or 1-800-99-VALUE; www .freeportinn.com), 31 Rt. 1. Set on 25 acres of lawns and nature trails, this place offers an upscale motel ambi-

ence at reasonable prices. All rooms have pretty designer bedspreads, carpeting, cable TV, air-conditioning, inroom phone, and wireless Internet access. Take a dip in the swimming pool, enjoy the playground, or take out a canoe on the Cousins River. Pets are allowed in 16 of the 80 rooms. Doubles are $119–160 inseason. The inn's restaurant and bakery, the Freeport Café, serves homestyle cooking all day. The **Casco Bay Inn** (207-865-4925 or 1-800-570-4970; www.cascobayinn.com) is family run, clean and comfortable, and completely refurbished in 2001, with budget rates ($90–115).

CAMPGROUNDS 🐾 ✍ ♿ **Cedar Haven Campground** (207-865-6254; reservations only, 1-800-454-3403; www.campmaine.com/cedarhaven), 39 Baker Rd. Fifty-eight mostly wooded sites, each with fireplace and picnic table. Water and electricity hook-ups, 12 with sewer as well. Cable TV at selected sites. Twelve tent sites. Store with wood, ice, and groceries; mini golf, playground, and swimming pond. Two miles from Rt. 1 and downtown Freeport. $19.50–32 per night.

🐾 ✍ ♿ **Desert Dunes of Maine Campground** (207-865-6962; www .desertofmaine.com), 95 Desert Rd. Located next to a kitschy attraction with a natural glacial sand deposit (see *To See and Do*), this campground offers 50 wooded and open sites with hook-ups, hot showers, laundry, convenience store, propane, fire rings, picnic tables, horseshoe pits, nature trails, and swimming pool. Campsites are $21–36 per night.

Also see **Winslow Memorial Park** under *Green Space*.

✳ Where to Eat

All listings are in Freeport unless otherwise noted

DINING OUT ⅃ **Harraseeket Inn Maine Dining Room** (207-865 9377 or 1-800-342-6423), 162 Main St. Open year-round for dinner and Sunday brunch 11:30–2. Continental cuisine and elegant service in three formal dining rooms. The chef uses fresh, in-season, and often organic ingredients from local gardeners and farmers to create mouthwatering entrées like roast quail with figs and mushrooms, and sirloin with ancho bordelaise. Entrées from $24 to $76 (for the rack of lamb for two). In addition to dinner the Harraseeket is known for its outstanding Sunday brunch, which often features such delicacies as caviar, oysters on the half shell, and even venison ($24.95).

Mediterranean Grill (207-865-1688; www.mediterranean grill.biz), 10 School St. Open Sun.–Thu. 11 AM to 9 PM, till 10 Fri. and Sat. A Turkish dinner awaits you here, from falafel and stuffed eggplant to kebabs, moussaka, and Adana, spiced grilled ground lamb. Choose from Turkish wines as well as the usual from California, and baklava or rice pudding to end. Don't miss this chance to taste something delicious. Entrées $14–23.

♪ ⅃ **Jameson Tavern** (207-865-4196), 115 Main St. Lunch 11:30–2:30 and dinner 5–closing. This place welcomes bus tours and, unfortunately, it looks like it. The 1779 building's interior needs a little TLC. It does, however, boast an interesting history: Locals claim that the papers separating Maine from Massachusetts were signed here in 1820. Dine on the outside patio in summer, or by one of several indoor fireplaces during cold

months. If there's a wait, you can order from the same menu in the neighboring Tap Room (see *Eating Out*). $12.95–22.95.

EATING OUT ♪ ⅃ **Crickets Restaurant** (207-865-4005), 175 Lower Main St. Open daily for lunch and dinner; opens for breakfast Sat. and Sun. at 7:30, plus weekend brunch specials. The almost overwhelming menu offers something for just about everyone, from lobster 10 ways and generous specialty sandwiches to fajitas, pasta dishes, steak, and seafood entrées. Reservations appreciated. The atmosphere is nothing to write home about—basically a multiroomed fern bar that would be at home in any mall—but this place packs 'em in. Entrées $5.95–15.95.

♪ ⅃ **The Broad Arrow Tavern** (207-865-9377), Harraseeket Inn, 162 Main St. Open for lunch 11:30–2. A ground-floor dining room overlooking the terrace, this place is constantly packed with locals, tourists, and inn guests, who come for the delicious food, unstuffy pub atmosphere, and interesting collection of stuffed animals on the wall (moose, fisher, deer). The open kitchen has a wood-fired oven and grill, and it serves up everything from brick-oven pizzas, sandwiches, and grilled steak to a Caesar we found a little overweighted by dressing. Rich desserts follow, like a double chocolate chip cookie, dished up hot out of the oven with double vanilla ice cream and chocolate sauce. Lunch entrées $9.95–34.95.

HARRASEEKET LUNCH & LOBSTER CO.

Conundrum (207-865-0303), 117 Rt. 1, South Freeport. This bistro, set right under the Big Indian, serves up good burgers and other bar basics in an intimate, dark blue room sporting 1920s liqueur ads and giant bottles of Perrier-Jouet champagne. We like the varieties of pâté and cheese (also sold in the owners' neighboring shop, Old World Gourmet; see *Snacks*), which you can order as entrées, and the wine selection, which won a *Wine Spectator* award in 2002 (also sold in the shop). You can get a taste of wine before deciding on a glass, or half glass, to drink. Entrées $8.50–15.

Tap Room (207-865-4196), Jameson Tavern, 115 Main St. This informal tavern to the rear of the building serves the full Jameson Tavern menu plus pub fare from 11:30 AM until late in the evening.

✿ ঐ **Gritty McDuff's** (207-865-4321), 187 Lower Main St. The only brewpub in Freeport, this branch of the popular Portland pub offers out-door dining, lobster, seafood, pizza, and pub food. Great ales and nachos, and we like the festive murals of maidens harvesting grains.

✿ ঐ **Muddy Rudder** (207-846-3082; www.muddyrudder.com), Rt. 1, Yarmouth. Operated by the nearby Freeport Inn, this popular restaurant overlooks the water and serves a wide selection of seafood dishes plus steaks, sandwiches, and salads; you can also have a full clambake on the deck. Renovated in 2001, the Rudder is still relaxed.

✿ **Harraseeket Lunch & Lobster Co.** (207-865-4888), foot of Main St., South Freeport (turn off Rt. 1 at the giant wooden Indian, then turn right at a stop sign a few miles down). Open May–Oct. A traditional lobster shack in the middle of the Harraseeket boatyard. Order lobsters and clams on one side, fried food on the other, and eat at picnic tables (of which there are never enough at peak hours) over-looking a boat-filled harbor. Lobsters

are fresh from the pound's boats; homemade desserts. There is also a small inside dining room. Worth seeking out, but be aware that it is a busy place; you may have to wait to eat.

🍴 **The Lobster Cooker** (207-865-4349), 39 Main St. Steamed lobster, excellent fresh-picked lobster and crabmeat rolls, sandwiches, and chowders; cafeteria-style dining on the outdoor patio. Beer and wine.

🍴 🍴 & **The Freeport Café** (207-865-3106), Rt. 1 (next to the Freeport Inn). Open daily 6 AM–8 PM. A bona fide local hangout, this small café makes up for its unappealing location right on Rt. 1 with good food at great prices. Extremely friendly service, great dinner specials, and a children's menu.

SNACKS Old World Gourmet (207-865-4477), Rt. 1 (next to the Big Indian). Every kind of foreign cheese, pâté, prepared food, and wine you could wish for, sold by the pound or bottle. You can also eat lunch here at one of the tables nestled next to the shop's shelves. Try one of their grilled panini, vegetarian sandwiches, composed salads, baked goods, Italian sodas, or lattes flavored with Torani syrup.

Royal River Natural Foods (207-865-0046; www.rrnf.com), 443 Rt. 1. A great place to buy vegetarian snacks for the road, such as organic fruits and vegetables, freshly made soups, pasta and green salads, sandwiches, and muffins. Also a full line of natural grocery items.

The Village Store (207-865-4230), 97 South Freeport Rd. (across the street from the South Freeport church). Locals rave about this place, which offers standard deli fare as well as a wonderful themed picnic menu. Choose from four options, including

the "Italian," $15 per person (antipasto platter, roast beef sandwich with fresh mozzarella and sun-dried tomatoes in a pesto wrap, pasta salad, melon, biscotti, and a bottle of pinot grigio wine). 24-hour notice required for picnic fare.

✳ Selective Shopping

FREEPORT FACTORY OUTLETS 🍴 As noted in the introduction to this chapter, Freeport's 125-plus factory outlets constitute what has probably become Maine's mightiest tourist magnet. *Boston Globe* writer Nathan Cobb described it well: "A shoppers' theme park spread out at the foot of L. L. Bean, the high church of country chic." Cobb quoted a local landlord: "The great American pastime now is shopping, not hiking."

Although hiking and hunting put L. L. Bean on the tourist map in the first place, tourists in Freeport have a lot to choose from these days. L. L. Bean has kept pace by selling fashionable, sporty clothing and an incredible range of sporting equipment, books, gourmet products, and gifts, as well as its golden boot.

L. L. Bean contends that it attracts at least 3.5 million customers annually—almost three times the population of Maine. In the early 1980s neighboring property owners began to claim a portion of this traffic. Instead of relegating the outlets to malls, they have deftly draped them in brick and clapboard, actually improving on the town's old looks (although longtime shopkeepers who were forced to move because of skyrocketing real estate prices might well disagree). Ample parking lots are sequestered behind the Main Street facade. In summer a festive atmosphere reigns, with hot-dog and ice cream vendors on key corners. But it's the quality of the shops that ensures a year-round crowd. Just about any well-known clothing, accessory, or home furnishing line has a factory store here. The following is a selected list of the more interesting outlets. Many stores claim 20 to 70 percent off suggested retail prices, and even L. L. Bean has a separate outlet, which you should check first for bargains before heading to the main store.

L. L. Bean Factory Store, Depot St. (across the street and down the block from the main store). Seconds, samples, and irregular merchandise of all kinds. You never know what you'll find, but it's always worth a look. Unlike the main store, the outlet is not open 24 hours a day.

Thomas Moser Cabinetmakers (207-865-4519, 1-800-708-9041; www .thomasmoser.com), 149 Main St. Open Mon.–Sat. 10–6, Sun. 11–5. Fine furniture inspired by Shaker, Arts and Crafts, Japanese, and art deco designs. This family business has been a Freeport institution for more than 25 years.

Dooney & Bourke (207-865-1366), 56 Main St. (in back). Stylish pocketbooks, shoulder bags, belts, wallets, and portfolios.

Burberry (207-865-4400), 42 Main St. Not just the raincoats lined with their famous tan tartan; you'll find chic women's, men's, and children's clothing, sweaters, hats, and accessories, too.

& **Cuddledown of Maine Factory Store** (207-865-1713), 475 Rt. 1. Comforters, pillows, gift items, all filled with goose down.

& **Maine Wreath & Flower Factory Outlet** (207-865-3019 or 1-800-973-4987; www.mainewreath.com), 13 Bow St. Quality Maine-dried flowers and wreaths at discount prices.

Cole-Haan Footwear and Accessories (207-865-6321), 66 Main St. Beautiful shoes, handbags, and socks. Pricey, but their quality is famous.

Buttons and Things Factory Outlet (207-865-4480), 24 Main St. A warren of rooms chock-full of buttons, beads, bead books, and collector thimbles.

& **Dansk Factory Outlet** (207-865-6125; www.dansk.com), 100 Main St., Suite 11. Scandinavian-designed tableware, cookware, and assorted kitchen gadgets.

SPECIAL SHOPS

All listings are in Freeport unless otherwise noted

Brown Goldsmiths (207-865-4126), 11 Mechanic St. Open Mon.–Sat. Original designs in rings, earrings, and bracelets.

Bridgham & Cook, Ltd. (207-865-1040 or 1-800-UK-BUYER), 6 Bow St. (behind Polo–Ralph Lauren). Packaged British and Irish foods, toiletries, teas, gifts—a must for the Anglophile.

Cold River Vodka (207-865-4828; www.coldrivervodka.com), 437 Rt. 1, south of Rt. 295 exit 20. Open Wed.–Sun. Using Maine potatoes grown on his farm in Fryeburg, Donnie Thibodeau teamed up with a professional brewer to open Maine's first vodka distillery in 2005. A gallery dramatizes the history of Maine potato farming. Tours are offered Wed.–Fri. noon–5, Sat. noon–7, Sun. noon–5.

L. L. Bean (1-800-809-7057 for orders or 1-800-341-4341 for customer service; www.llbean.com), 95 Main St. Open 24 hours a day, 365 days a year. With an outdoor Discovery Park, indoor trout pond, bookstore and café, and thousands of square feet of retail space, the building resembles a fancy shopping mall more than it does a single store. Its hunting and fishing store, with its own trout pond, adds to the impression. Back in 1912 Leon Leonwood Bean developed his boot, or Maine Hunting Shoe, a unique combination of rubber bottom and leather top. "You cannot expect success hunting deer or moose if your feet are not properly dressed," Bean wrote in his very first catalog. Ninety out of the first 100 boots he built literally fell apart at the seams, so Bean refunded the purchasers' money and began a company tradition of guaranteed customer satisfaction, including all-night hours for the outdoorsmen who passed through in the dead of night. Bean himself died in 1967, but Bean's grandson Leon Gorman, chairman of the board, and company president Christopher McCormick now oversee an empire of outdoor equipment. You can find a wide variety of clothing, luggage, and equipment as well as every conceivable gadget designed to keep you warm. Down the road behind corporate headquarters you can also try your hand at fly casting, archery, and clay shooting, or kayak from the company's private beach on a nearby cove. Inquire about Outdoor Discovery Schools and Walk-on Adventures.

L. L. BEAN

Kim Grant

✂ **DeLorme's Map Store** (207-865-4171), Rt. 1 (south of downtown Freeport). A good place to spend a couple of rainy hours watching the world turn—literally—and sifting through DeLorme's impressive store. Check out the publishing company's own maps, atlases, pamphlets, and guidebooks of the United States and the world as well as some interesting educational toys. A large bank of computers invites visitors to try out mapping software. Many people come just to see "Eartha," the world's largest rotating and revolving globe, which spins quietly in a glassed-in lobby.

Edgecomb Potters/Hand in Hand Gallery (207-865-1705 or 1-800-343-5529; www.edgecombpotters.com), 8 School St. Fine contemporary American crafts, including colorful porcelain made in Maine, jewelry, blown glass, and iron.

✂ ⚅ **Mangy Moose** (207-865-6414 or 1-800-606-6517; www.themangy moose.com), 112 Main St. Moose, moose, and more moose. A fun store filled with gifts, books, mounts— meaning stuffed moose, mountain lion, bobcat, caribou, and bear heads.

✂ ⚅ **Play and Learn** (207-865-6434 or 1-888-865-6434), 200 Lower Main St. A great source for educational toys and teaching resources.

20th Maine (207-865-4340; www .20thmaine.com), 49 West St. Devoted to the Civil War: books, art, music, and collectibles, plus a cute dog named (appropriately enough) Dixie. Call to ask about book signings and other events.

Sherman's Book & Stationery Store (207-869-9000; www.shermans .com), 128 Main St. Another branch of the Maine bookseller (also in Bar Harbor and Boothbay Harbor), featuring Maine books and gifts, cards, and toys.

✱ Special Events

Summer: Frequent musical and comedy performances in the **L. L. Bean Discovery Park**.

Labor Day weekend: **Sidewalk Sale**, with sales galore. **Fall in the Village** art exhibition.

Fall: **Pettengill Farm Days**—living history demonstrations, horse-drawn wagon rides, inside/outside house tours, children's days, fresh-pressed cider.

December: **Sparkle Weekend** (*first full weekend*)—caroling, horse-drawn wagons, Santa arriving in a Maine yacht, musical entertainment, holiday readings, storytelling, complimentary refreshment and hot-cocoa stops, open houses at local inns, a talking Christmas tree, and, of course, plenty of holiday shopping. **Christmas Open House Tours**.

Midcoast and the Islands

Kim Grant

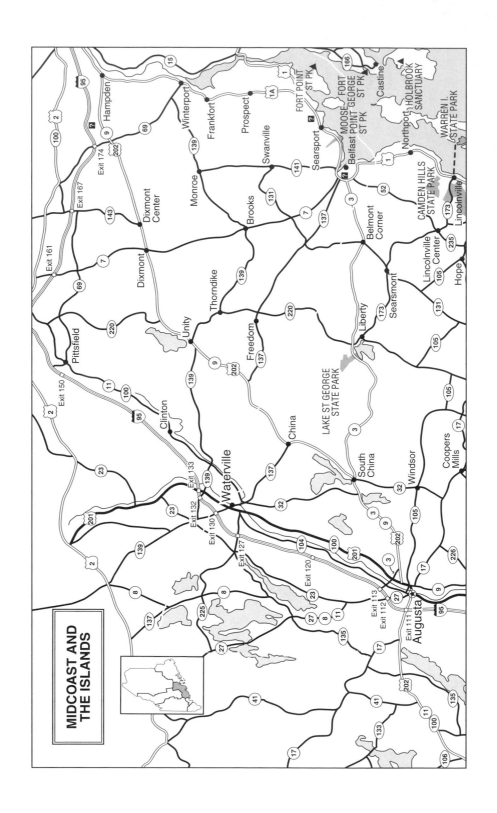

MIDCOAST AND
THE ISLANDS

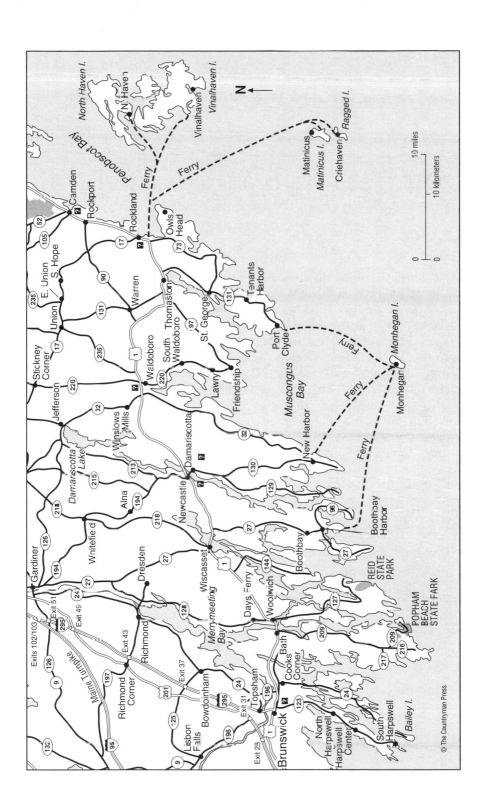

N

Penobscot Bay

North Haven I.

N. Haven

Vinalhaven

Vinalhaven I.

Matinicus

Matinicus I.

Criehaven

Ragged I.

10 miles

10 kilometers

Camden

Rockport

Rockland

Ferry

Ferry

Owls Head

Ferry

52

105

17

73

Union

E. Union / S. Hope

Stickney Corner

Jefferson

17

90

131

235

Warren

South Thomaston

Waldoboro

St. George

235

Tenants Harbor

Port Clyde

131

97

220

220

1

Winslows Mills

32

Lawry

Friendship

Muscongus Bay

Damariscotta Lake

Damariscotta

Monhegan I.

Ferry

Monhegan

213

215

218

194

32

130

Ferry

New Harbor

Alna

Newcastle

129

96

Ferry

Boothbay Harbor

Whitefield

Gardiner

126

218

27

Boothbay

27

27

194

Dresden

Wiscasset

144

Woolwich

REID STATE PARK

24

Exit 51

Exit 49

27

128

Merrymeeting Bay

Days Ferry

POPHAM BEACH STATE PARK

295

Maine Turnpike

Exits 102/103

9

126

197

Richmond Corner

Exit 43

Richmond

Exit 37

Bath

Cooks Corner

209

217

216

209

127

201

295

24

Bowdoinham

Topsham

24

123

9

132

95

125

196

196

1

Brunswick

North Harpswell

Harpswell Center

South Harpswell

Bailey I.

Lisbon Falls

Exit 31

Exit 23

© The Countryman Press

MIDCOAST AND THE ISLANDS

Beyond Casco Bay the shape of Maine's coast changes—it shreds. In contrast to the sandy arc of shoreline stretching from Kittery to Cape Elizabeth, the coast between Brunswick and Rockland is composed of a series of more than a dozen ragged peninsulas extending like so many fingers south from Rt. 1, creating myriad big and small harbors, coves, and bays. Scientists tell us that these peninsulas and the offshore islands are mountains drowned by the melting of the same glaciers that sculpted the many shallow lakes and tidal rivers in this area.

The 100 miles of Rt. 1 between Brunswick and Bucksport are generally equated with Maine's Midcoast, but its depth is actually far greater and more difficult to define. It extends south of Rt. 1 to the tips of every peninsula, from Potts Point in South Harpswell and Land's End on Bailey Island to Popham Beach on the Phippsburg Peninsula and Reid State Park in Georgetown and on through the Boothbays to Pemaquid Point, Friendship, Port Clyde, and Spruce Head. Along with Rockland, Camden, Belfast, Searsport, and the islands of Monhegan, Vinalhaven, North Haven, and Islesboro, these communities have all catered to summer visitors since steamboats began off-loading them in the mid–19th century. Each peninsula differs in character from the next, but all offer their share of places to stay and eat in settings you rarely find along Rt. 1.

North of Rt. 1, this midcoastal area also extends slightly inland. Above Bath, for instance, five rivers meld to form Merrymeeting Bay, and north of Newcastle the tidal Damariscotta River widens into 13-mile-long Damariscotta Lake. This gently rolling, river- and lake-laced backcountry harbors a number of picturesque villages and reasonably priced lodging places.

We would hope that no one who reads this book simply sticks to Rt. 1.

BRUNSWICK AND THE HARPSWELLS

The Civil War began and ended in Brunswick, or so say local historians. A case can be made. Harriet Beecher Stowe was attending a service in Brunswick's First Parish Church when she is said to have had a vision of the death of Uncle Tom and hurried home to begin penning the book that has been credited with starting the war. Joshua Chamberlain, a longtime parishioner in this same church, was, moreover, the Union general chosen for the honor of receiving the surrender of General John Gordon, commander of the Confederate infantry, at Appomattox.

Thanks largely to the Ken Burns PBS series *The Civil War*, Joshua Chamberlain has been rediscovered. Annual admissions to his house shot from 300 to more than 5,000 following the series and have since remained stable, fueling its restoration. A Brunswick restaurant is now "Joshua's," and the Pejepscot Histori cal Society dispenses maps that pinpoint sites ranging from Chamberlain's student dorm rooms to his gravestone.

This scholar-soldier-governor is, in fact, an entirely appropriate figurehead for a town that's home to Brunswick Naval Air Station as well as to Bowdoin College, over which Chamberlain presided as president after four terms as governor of Maine.

Brunswick began as an Indian village named Pejepscot, at the base of the Androscoggin River's Great Falls. In 1688 this site became a Massachusetts outpost named Fort Andros, and subsequently it has been occupied by a series of mills. Today, with a population of 21,170, this is Maine's largest town, a mix of Franco-Americans whose great-grandparents were recruited to work in mills, of military and retired military families, of Bowdoin and retired Bowdoin faculty and alumni, of old seafaring families, and of an increasing number of professionals who commute the half hour to work in Portland or Augusta (Brunswick is halfway between).

Brunswick's Maine Street is the state's widest, laid out in 1717 with a grassy "mall" (a long strip of greenery that's the scene of concerts and of farmer's markets) at the upper end, near the neo-Gothic First Parish Church and the Bowdoin College campus.

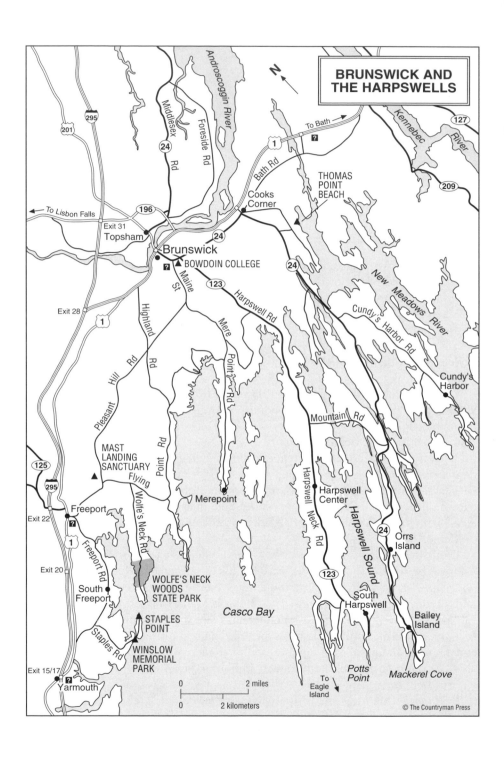

BRUNSWICK AND
THE HARPSWELLS

A small but prestigious college, chartered in 1794, Bowdoin is surprisingly welcoming to visitors, especially in July and August, when its buildings are filled with the practicing and the performing virtuoso musicians of the Bowdoin International Music Festival, and when Pickard Theater is the stage for the Maine State Music Theatre. The Bowdoin College Museum of Art and its Peary-MacMillan Arctic Museum are well worth a stop, as are the nearby Pejepscot Museum, Skolfield-Whittier House, and Chamberlain House.

Brunswick is, however, no tourist town. No kiosk proclaims the schedule of plays and concerts, because most patrons know enough to read about them in the Thursday edition of the *Times Record*. Maine Street's shops, galleries, and restaurants also cater to residents, and the Eveningstar Cinema screens art films for local consumption. Grand City is still a genuine five-and-dime with a lunch counter, a basement stocked with furniture and fabrics, and a summer supply of plastic sleds, found next to the boots and gloves that clammers also need. Freeport's 125-plus outlet stores are just miles yet light-years away.

South of Brunswick one peninsula and several bridge-linked islands stretch seaward, defining the eastern rim of Casco Bay. Collectively they form the town of Harpswell, better known as "the Harpswells" because it includes so many coves, points, and islands (notably Orrs and Bailey). Widely known for their seafood restaurants, these peninsulas are surprisingly sleepy, salted with crafts, galleries, and some great places to stay. They are Maine's most convenient peninsulas, yet they seem much farther Down East.

GUIDANCE Southern Midcoast Maine Chamber (207-725-8797; www .midcoastmaine.com), 59 Pleasant St., Brunswick 04011.

GETTING THERE *By bus:* Bus service to downtown Brunswick from Logan Airport and downtown Boston is unusually good: 2½ hours both via **Concord Trailways**, which stops on Rt. 1, and **Vermont Transit/Greyhound**, which stops in downtown Brunswick.

By car: The new I-295 (formerly I-95) exit for Brunswick and coastal points north is exit 28 to Rt. 1, or exit 31—which doglegs around Brunswick, bypassing it entirely. Instead, continue straight ahead up Pleasant St., which forms a T with Maine St. Turn right for the Bowdoin College campus and the Harpswells. For Topsham the new exits are 31 northbound and 31A southbound.

WHEN TO COME Brunswick is more than a college town and lively year-round community, but if you want to visit all its museums and take advantage of summer music and theater, come in July or August—and never on Monday.

☀ To See

Bowdoin College (207-725-3100; www.bowdoin.edu), Brunswick. Tours of the 200-acre campus with more than 60 buildings begin at the admissions office. Phone for current hours. Maine was part of Massachusetts when the college was founded in 1794, and the school is named for a Massachusetts governor. Nathaniel Hawthorne and Henry Wadsworth Longfellow were classmates here

Pejepscot Historical Society

JOSHUA LAWRENCE CHAMBERLAIN

JOSHUA LAWRENCE CHAMBERLAIN

Joshua Lawrence Chamberlain (1828–1914) was Maine's greatest Civil War hero, a college professor who became one of the most remarkable soldiers in American history.

An outstanding scholar—he had a graduate degree in theology and was teaching rhetoric and languages (he spoke or could read eight) at his alma mater, Bowdoin College, when the war began—Chamberlain proved to be an even better soldier. He fought in some of the bloodiest battles of the war, had horses shot out from under him five times, and was wounded six times, once so severely that he was given up for dead and his obituary appeared in Maine newspapers.

Of all his military achievements Chamberlain is best remembered for his valor and leadership on the second day of the battle of Gettysburg, July 2, 1863. A lieutenant colonel commanding an inexperienced and understrength regiment, the 20th Maine Volunteer Infantry, he defended Little Round Top, a key position on the extreme left of the Union line. Repeatedly attacked by a much larger Confederate force, he refused to retreat; when defeat seemed imminent—there was no more ammunition and most of his men were dead or wounded—he ordered an unorthodox bayonet charge that routed the Confederates.

Had the southerners taken Little Round Top they could have outflanked the Union army and won the battle—and with it, possibly, the war. Eventually, more than 30 years later, Chamberlain received the nation's highest military award, the Medal of Honor, for his "daring heroism and great tenacity" at Gettysburg.

He ended the war a major general and was chosen by General Ulysses S. Grant to accept the surrender of the Confederate Army of Northern Virginia following General Robert E. Lee's capitulation at Appomattox. As the Confederate regiments marched into the Union camp to lay down their arms, Chamberlain had his troops salute them, a gesture of respect that infuriated some northerners but helped reconcile many southerners to their defeat.

After the war Chamberlain served four one-year terms as governor of Maine. From 1871 to 1883 he was president of Bowdoin College, where he introduced science courses to modernize the curriculum and tried unsuccessfully to make military training compulsory. (Students rioted in protest.) He died in 1914, "of his wounds," it was said. Late in life he wrote *The Passing of the Armies*, an account of the final campaign of the Union's Army of the Potomac from the point of view of its Fifth Corps, which he commanded. Filled with vivid descriptive passages, the book is still in print.

A household name in his day, Chamberlain's memory eventually faded. That began changing in 1975 with the publication of Michael Shaara's best-selling and Pulitzer Prize–winning novel about the battle of Gettysburg, *Killer Angels*, in which Chamberlain was a major protagonist. In 1990 the story of his desperate defense of Little Round Top was a highlight of the acclaimed PBS television series *The Civil War*. A few years later actor Jeff Daniels convincingly portrayed Chamberlain, drooping handlebar mustache and all, in the epic film *Gettysburg* based on Shaara's novel. Daniels played Chamberlain again in a 2003 movie about the Civil War, *Gods and Generals*.

In 1983 the Pejepscot Historical Society acquired Chamberlain's old home at 226 Main Street, Brunswick, across from the Bowdoin campus, turning part of it into a museum. On display are Chamberlain's uniforms, medals, sword, bullet-dented boots, and the ornate chair he used as governor and college president. (After his death, the chair became the throne on which Bowdoin's homecoming queens were crowned.) The museum drew few visitors at first but now sees several thousand annually. In 2003 a statue depicting him as a major general was set in the small park beside the house. Seemingly as tenacious and enduring after death as he was in battle, Chamberlain appears to have now finally won from posterity the full recognition he deserves. The Chamberlain House is open May–June 14, Tue.–Fri. 1–5, Sat. 10–5, Sun. 1–5; June 14–Oct., Tue.–Sat. 10–5, Sun. 1–5. Last tour begins at 4. $5 adults, $2.50 children.

JOSHUA CHAMBERLAIN HOUSE AND MUSEUM

Christina Tree

in 1825; other notable graduates include Franklin Pierce and Robert Edwin Peary. Founded as a men's college, the school has been coed since the early 1970s and now has a student body of 1,677. Bowdoin ranks among the nation's top colleges both in status and in cost (the college provides substantial financial aid). It isn't necessary to take a tour to see the sights: June–mid-Aug., visitors can park in any designated parking area on campus unless otherwise noted.

Bowdoin College Museum of Art (207-725-3275), Walker Art Building, Bowdoin College, Brunswick. One of New England's outstanding art collections but, unfortunately, closed for renovations until early 2007. Parts of the collection are displayed in other college buildings.

✐ **Peary-MacMillan Arctic Museum** (207-725-3416), Hubbard Hall, Bowdoin College, Brunswick. Open year-round, Tue.–Sat. 10–5, Sun. 2–5; closed Mon. and holidays. Free. A well-displayed collection of clothing, trophy walruses and seals, polar bears and caribou, and other mementos from expeditions to the North Pole by two Bowdoin alumni. Robert Edwin Peary (class of 1877) was the first person to reach the North Pole, and Donald Baxter MacMillan (class of 1898), who was Peary's chief assistant, went on to dedicate his life to exploring Arctic waters and terrain. Displays include an interactive touch screen, photo blowups, and artifacts to tell the story.

Eagle Island State Historic Site (207-624-6080; www.pearyeagleisland.org). Open mid-June–Labor Day, 10–sunset. Accessible by boat (see *Boat Excursions*). Just 17 acres, this is the site of Admiral Robert E. Peary's shingled summer home where, on September 6, 1909, his wife received the news that her husband had become the first person to reach the North Pole. Peary positioned his house to face northeast on a rocky bluff that resembles the prow of a ship. He designed the three-sided living room hearth, made from island stones and Arctic quartz crystals, and stuffed many of the birds on the mantel. Bedrooms appear as though someone has just stepped out for a walk, and the dining room is strewn with photos of men and dogs battling ice and snow. A nature path circles the island, passing the pine trees filled with seagulls.

Pejepscot Historical Society Museums (207-729-6606). Founded in 1888 and named for an ancient Indian settlement (see the introduction to this chapter), this is one of Maine's oldest historical societies. It maintains three downtown Brunswick museums. For the first—the Joshua L. Chamberlain Museum—see the box. **The Pejepscot Museum**, 159 Park Row (Tue.–Fri. 9–5, until 8 Thu., Sat. 9–4; off-season, noon–4; free), is a massive, cupola'd mansion that displays changing exhibits on the history of Brunswick, Topsham, and Harpswell. The **Skolfield-Whittier House**, part of the same mid-19th-century Italianate double house (open May–Oct., Tue.–Sat. 10–2:30), is virtually unchanged since the 1925 death of Dr. Frank Whittier. Its high-Victorian drawing room is hung with crystal chandeliers and heavy velvet drapes, furnished in wicker and brocade, and filled with the photos, books, paintings, and clutter of three generations. A combination ticket for all three museums is $8 adults, $4 children. Inquire about walking tours.

The First Parish Church (UCC) (207-729-7331), Maine St. at Bath Rd., Brunswick. Open for noon summer organ concerts and tours July–mid-Aug.,

Tue. 12:10–12:50; for Sunday services; and by chance. This graceful neo-Gothic building was designed in the 1840s by Richard Upjohn, architect of New York City's Trinity Church. A dramatic departure from its Puritan predecessors, it's open beamed, is mildly cruciform in shape, and has deeply colored stained-glass windows. The large sanctuary window was donated by Joshua Chamberlain, one of the first people to be married here. The Hutchings-Plastid tracker organ was installed in 1883.

SCENIC DRIVE **A tour of the Harpswells, including Orrs and Bailey Islands**. Allow a day for this rewarding peninsula prowl. From Brunswick, follow Rt. 123 south past Bowdoin College 9 miles to the picturesque village of Harpswell Center. The white-clapboard **Elijah Kellogg Church** faces the matching **Harpswell Town Meeting House** built in 1757. The church is named for a former minister who was a prominent 19th-century children's-book author. Continue south through West Harpswell to **Potts Point**, where multicolored 19th-century summer cottages cluster on the rocks like a flock of exotic birds that have wandered in among the gulls. Stop by the first crafts studio you see here and pick up a map/guide to other members of the Harpswell Craft Guild.

Retrace your way up Rt. 123, and 2 miles north of the church turn right onto Mountain Rd., leading to busier Rt. 24 on Great (also known as Sebascodegan) Island. Drive south along **Orrs Island** across the only remaining **cribstone bridge** in the world, a National Historic Civil Engineering Landmark. (Its granite blocks are laid in honeycomb fashion without cement to allow tidal flows.) This bridge brings you to **Bailey Island**, with its restaurants, lodging places, picturesque Mackerel Cove, and rocky **Land's End** with a statue honoring all Maine fishermen. Return up Rt. 24 and take Cundy's Harbor Rd. 4.3 miles to another picturesque fishing harbor with a couple of good little restaurants.

✳ To Do

BICYCLING **The Androscoggin River Bicycle Path**, a 2.5-mile, 14-foot-wide paved bicycle/pedestrian trail, begins at Lower Water St. in Brunswick and runs along the river to Grover Lane in Cooks Corner. It connects with Topsham along the way via a bicycle lane on the new Merrymeeting Bridge.

CRIBSTONE BRIDGE

Kim Grant

BOAT EXCURSIONS From Bailey Island both **Capt. Jay McGowen Sportfishing** (207-833-6054) and **Sea Escape Charters** (207-833-5531) offer fishing trips, scenic cruises, and excursions in Casco Bay. Sea Escape specializes in tours to **Eagle Island**, as does **Atlantic Seal** (see "Freeport"). **Casco Bay Lines** (207-774-7871) offers a daily seasonal excursion from Cook's Lobster House on Bailey Island. It takes 1 hour and 45 minutes to circle around Eagle Island and through this northern end of Casco Bay. **Symbion II**, based at the Captain's Watch B&B, is Captain Ken Brigham's 38-foot Hunter sailboat, offering 3-hour daysails and overnight charters.

GOLF **Brunswick Golf Club** (207-725-8224), River Rd., Brunswick. Incorporated in 1888, an 18-hole course known for its beauty and challenging nature. Snack bar, lounge, and cart rentals.

RAILROAD EXCURSION **The Maine Eastern Railroad** (1-866-636-2457; www .maineeasternrailroad.com) offers 54-mile seasonal runs between Brunswick and Rockland, stopping in Bath and Wiscasset. Travel along the coast in plush 1940s and '50s coaches, a dining car, and (weekends only) a glass-domed observation car, behind a 1950s diesel electric engine. In 2005 round-trip runs were Tue.–Sun., but check the web site for current information.

SEA KAYAKING **H₂Outfitters** (207-833-5257 or 1-800-649-5257), P.O. Box 72, Orrs Island 04066. Located just north of the cribstone bridge on Orrs Island, this is one of Maine's oldest kayaking outfitters. No rentals. Lessons for all abilities, from beginners to instructor certification; guided day trips and overnight excursions are also offered.

✳ Green Space

BEACHES AND SWIMMING HOLES ✍ **White's Beach** (207-729-0415), Durham Rd., Brunswick. Open mid-May–mid-Oct. A pond in a former gravel pit (water no deeper than 9 feet). Facilities include a small slide for children. Sandy beach, lifeguards, picnic tables, grills, and a snack bar. Inquire about campsites.

✍ **Thomas Point Beach** (207-725-6009), off Thomas Point Rd., marked from Rt. 24, Cooks Corner. Open Memorial Day–Labor Day, 9 AM–sunset. The beach is part of an 85-acre private preserve on tidal water overlooking the New Meadows River and Thomas Bay. It includes groves for picnicking (more than 500 picnic tables plus a main lodge snack bar, playground, and arcade) and 75 tent and RV sites. It's the scene of a series of August events, including the Maine Highland Games and Bluegrass Festival. Admission fee.

✍ **Coffin Pond** (207-725-6656), River Rd., Brunswick. Open mid-June–Labor Day 10–7. Admission fee. A strip of sandy beach surrounding a circular pool. Facilities include a 55-foot-long waterslide, a playground, and changing rooms maintained by the town.

WALKS **Giant's Staircase**, Bailey Island. Turn off Rt. 24 at Washington Ave., park at the Episcopal church, and walk down to Ocean St.; follow the path along the water and follow the small sign to the well-named "stairs."

Brunswick-Topsham Land Trust (207-729-7694), 108 Maine St., Brunswick. The land trust has preserved some 700 acres in the area. Pick up map/guides to the nature loops at **Skolfield Nature Preserve**, Rt. 123, Brunswick (4 miles or so south of town), adjoining an ancient Indian portage between Middle Bay and Harpswell Cove, and to the **Bradley Pond Farm Preserve** in Topsham, a 2.5-mile trail system in a 162-acre preserve. **Crystal Spring Farm Trails**, a 2.5-mile trail on the 160-acre farm on Pleasant Hill Road in Brunswick.

❋ Lodging

🐾 ♿ **Brunswick Bed & Breakfast** (207-729-4914 or 1-800-299-4914; www.brunswickbnb.com), 165 Park Row, Brunswick 04011. Closed Jan. Architect Steve Normand and quilter Mercie Normand have restored this mid-1800s Greek Revival home on the town green, creating one of the most appealing places to stay in any Maine coastal town. There is an unusual amount of common space. The five guest rooms and three suites are furnished with antiques and a collection of both new and antique quilts; all have private bath and terry-cloth robes. At the back of the property the Carriage House includes six units (two handicapped accessible), with attractive common and meeting space. Beautifully served breakfasts are included in the rate: $100–225. A self-catering cottage right behind the house is $650 per week.

The Captain's Watch (207-725-0979), 926 Cundy's Harbor Rd. and Pinkham Point Rd., Harpswell 04079. Open year-round. Donna Dillman and Ken Brigham offer eight guest rooms that, at this writing, are divided between their longtime property, the Civil War–era former Union Hotel in Cundy's Harbor, and their new waterside home on Card Cove. Your choice is between spacious traditional rooms with fireplaces and antiques ($120–175, including a full breakfast) and two rooms in a modern house, facing directly on the water ($150 with breakfast). A large upstairs apartment is $1,000 per week.

Middle Bay Farm Bed & Breakfast (207-373-1375; www.middlebayfarm .com), 287 Pennellville Rd., Brunswick 04011. Open year-round. Sited on a quiet cove minutes from downtown Brunswick, this handsome clapboard house dates to the 1830s. In the early 1900s it was a summer boardinghouse (Helen Keller is said to have stayed here), but it had stood empty for 10 years when Clark and Phyllis Truesdell bought and renovated it. Common spaces include an elegant living room with a baby grand. The four spacious guest rooms (our favorite is Sea Shell) have private full bath, water views, sitting area, and cable TV/VCR hidden in an armoire. The 5 landscaped acres are on a rise above this tidal cove, with kayaks and canoes that guests can use. $150 in-season ($135 off-season) in the house, including a full breakfast; $170 in-season ($150 off-season) in the Sail Loft suites.

🐾 🐾 ❧ **Driftwood Inn and Cottages** (207-833-5461), P.O. Box 16, Bailey Island 04003. Open mid-May–Columbus Day weekend; the dining room (which is open to the public) is open July–Labor Day. Location, location! Sited on a rocky point within earshot of a foghorn and walking distance from the "Giant's Staircase" are these three gray-shingled, unheated (common rooms have a wood-burning fireplace), non-air-conditioned traditional Maine summerhouses. They contain a total of 16 doubles and 8 singles (9 with half bath); there are also 6 housekeeping cottages. We recommend Room 7 in Driftwood, pine walled with a firm queen bed and windows on the water. There is a small saltwater swimming pool set in the rocks. Your hosts are Charles and David Conrad, most recent in more than 75 years of ownership by one family. $80–120 per couple, $65 single (no minimum stay). Housekeeping cottages, available by the week, are $625–675; weekly room rates are $450 per person MAP. Children under 10 years are half price. On a per diem basis, breakfast is $6.50; dinner, $16.50–18.50. No credit cards. Pets are accepted in the cottages ($50 fee).

Harpswell Inn (207-833-5509 or 1-800-843-5509; www.harpswellinn .com), 108 Lookout Point Rd., Harpswell 04079. Built as the cookhouse for a boatyard, this three-story white-clapboard inn has taken in guests under a number of names but has never been as gracious. The 12 guest rooms vary widely and come with and without bath (only two share), hearth, and water views; there are also three suites with kitchens. We felt pampered in The Lookout with its cathedral ceiling, sitting area, deck, gas fireplace, and Jacuzzi. Children must be over 10. No smoking. In high season $89–150 for rooms, $165–230 for suites, includes a very full breakfast.

♂ & **Captain Daniel Stone Inn** (207-725-9898 or 1-877-573-5151; www .someplacesdifferent.com), 10 Water St., Brunswick 04011. Thirty-four modern rooms and four suites are annexed to a Federal mansion. All have TV, phone, VCR, and alarm clock–cassette player; some feature a whirlpool bath. Breakfast, lunch, dinner, and Sunday brunch are served in the **Narcissa Stone Restaurant**. Continental breakfast. From $130 off-season to $170–255 per room in-season.

The Log Cabin, An Island Inn (207-833-5546; www.logcabin-maine .com), Rt. 24, Bailey Island 04003. Open Apr.–Oct. Built decades ago as a lavish log summer home with a huge hearth (a moose head, of course, hangs above), this was for many years a popular restaurant, but the owners refitted it to offer nine rooms—four with kitchen, two with hot tub, all with private bath, fridge, coffee machine, and waterside deck and heated swimming pool. Breakfast is included for $99–299. Dinner is still served, but it's no longer open to the public (entrées $14.95–28.95).

The Black Lantern (207-725-4165 or 1-888-306-4165; www.blacklantern bandb.com), 6 Pleasant St., Topsham 04086. Open year-round. Tom and Judy Connelie don't know how the words YE CANA BE BOTH GRAND AND COMFORTABLE came to be carved above their living room hearth, but they suit this circa-1810 Federal-style house and the welcome guests receive here. One block from the Androscoggin in Topsham's historic district, an easy walk from downtown Brunswick, they offer three guest rooms with private bath. Quilters are particularly welcome (try your hand on the practice piece in the parlor), and guests can borrow a bike to test the riverside bike path (also good for joggers). $85–90 in-season, $80–85 off-season, includes a full breakfast.

COTTAGES **The Southern Midcoast Maine Chamber** (see *Guidance*) lists weekly cottage rentals on Orrs and Bailey Islands.

MOTELS **Little Island Motel** (207-833-2392; www.littleislandmotel.com), 44 Little Island Rd., Orrs Island

04066. Open mid-May–mid-Oct. An attractive motel with terrific views. Jo Atlass offers eight units, each with a small refrigerator and color TV. The motel is on its own mini island with a private beach, connected to other land by a narrow neck. $114–130 per couple includes continental breakfast and use of boats, bicycles, and the outdoor picnic area. $10 extra for each child under 12, $20 for anyone over.

✧ ⚅ **Bailey Island Motel** (207-833-2886), Rt. 24, Bailey Island 04003. Open early May–late Oct. Located just over the cribstone bridge. A pretty, gray-shingled building on the water's edge, offering ocean views and landscaped lawns with rocks and a dock to walk out on. The 11 rooms are clean and comfortable, with cable TV. No smoking. Morning coffee and muffins are included in $95–120. Guests are welcome to tie their boat up to the dock or a mooring.

✳ Where to Eat

DINING OUT

In Brunswick

Henry & Marty (207-721-9141), 61 Maine St. Open for dinner Tue.–Sat. Reservations a must. Recently expanded to fill a second warmly colored and decorated storefront. The food ranks among the best along Maine's Midcoast. Patrons share a smug sense of being savvy enough to be here, whether they're dining on thin-crust pizza, a halibut Niçoise salad, or the slow-roasted natural (local) beef brisket. Henry D'Alessandris and Marty Perry are former Manhattan performers. Entrées $14–26.

Back Street Bistro (207-725-4060), 11 Town Place. Just off Maine Street by the fire station, you can depend on

a good meal. A fish and shellfish gumbo varies nightly, but always comes with a deeply flavored broth. Bacon-wrapped pork chops or a pappardelle with mascarpone would keep anyone warm. Entrées $16–20.

⚑ **Star Fish Grill** (207-727-7828), 100 Pleasant St. (Rt. 1 southbound). Dinner Tue.–Sun. 5–9:30. Reservations are essential, along with directions. In the lineup of fast-food places and gas stations along Rt. 1 you don't expect to find one of Maine's best seafood restaurants, but here it is. Meals begin with a French baguette and dipping oil, and the reasonably priced wine by the glass is several cuts above the norm. Entrées range from $16 for veggies in a garlic white wine sauce tossed with pasta to $25 for a seafood cassoulet: grilled scallops, shrimp, halibut, and mussels with seasonal vegetables and lentils. Lobster paella for two ($45) is a specialty. Inquire about live jazz and blues on Sunday evening.

⚑ **The Great Impasta** (207-729-5858), 42 Maine St. Open daily (except Sun.) for lunch and dinner. A great stop even if you're simply traveling up or down Rt. 1, but arrive early to get a booth (plaques honor booth regulars). Specialties include pasta dishes like seafood lasagna; try the eggplant stuffed with smoked mozzarella, mushrooms, onions, and tomatoes and topped with roasted vegetables. Wine and beer served. Dinner entrées $11–15.

Richard's Restaurant (207-729-9673), 115 Maine St. Open for lunch and dinner Mon.–Sat. Continental fare like veal Oscar and grilled New York sirloin is featured, also satisfying dishes like *Gemischter salat*, Wiener schnitzel, and *Schlachtplatte*. Nightly

DOUG LAVALLEE AT SCARLETT BEGONIAS

specials include *Rinds-rouladen* (thinly sliced beef rolled with onions, bacon, mustard, and pickles). The beer list is impressive. Dinner entrées $8–18. Lighter fare and German beer are on tap in the Eidelweiss Lounge, also live piano music on weekends.

EATING OUT

In and near Brunswick

Scarlet Begonias (207-721-0403), 212 Maine St. Open Mon.–Thu. 11–8, Fri. 11–9, Sat. noon–9; closed Sun. In their attractive storefront "bistro," Doug and Colleen Lavallee serve some great sandwiches (we recommend the turkey spinach with mozzarella and basil mayo, grilled on sourdough bread) and chunky, fresh-herbed pastas like Rose Begonia.

Joshua's Restaurant & Tavern (207-725-7981), 121 Maine St. Open 11:30 AM–11 PM. Named for General Joshua Chamberlain, this is a pubby, pleasant place that's been revamped and slightly upscaled; seasonal tables on a porch overlook Maine St. We can recommend the Chamberlain burger, but it's a big menu—plenty of fried and broiled fish, soups, stews, and a wide choice of beers. Dinner entrées $13.95–18.95.

Sea Dog Brewing (207-725-0162), Great Mill Island, 1 Main St., Topsham. Open daily 11:30–1 AM. Music Thu.–Sat. Housed in a picturesque (former) paper mill, vintage 1868. A big, friendly brewpub with seasonal outdoor dining overlooking the churning Androscoggin. Specialties include sautéed scallops, grilled or teriyaki sirloin. The wide choice of beers includes more than half a dozen ales brewed here or in Bangor (there are three Maine Sea Dogs).

Old Munich Biergarten (207-729-1688), 6 1st St., Topsham. Open for lunch and dinner daily, except Mon. Within months of arriving from Germany in 1999, Hans and Barbara Haeussler had transformed an abandoned breakfast place into an appealing "restaurant, café and biergarten." Made-from-scratch wursts, on-tap German beers, and German tortes and cakes are the specialties.

Bangkok Garden Restaurant (207-725-9708), 14 Maine St. (Fort Andros). Open daily for lunch and dinner, Sun. 4–9. This attractive restaurant gets good reviews for classic dishes like green curry and pad Thai.

Wild Oats Bakery and Café (207-725-6287), Tontine Mall, 149 Maine St. Open Mon.–Sat. 7:30–5, Sun. 8–3. Set back from Maine St. with tables on the terrace and inside. A town meeting place serving coffees and teas, from-scratch pastries and breads, healthy sandwiches, and salads.

Fat Boy Drive-In (207-729-9431), Old Rt. 1. Open for lunch and dinner, late Mar.–mid-Oct. This is no 1950s reconstruct, just a real drive-in with carhops that's survived because it's so good and incredibly reasonably priced. If you own a pre-1970 car, you can come to the annual "sock hop."

Nancy English

MORSE'S LOBSTER SHACK

Morse's Lobster Shack (207-725-2886), 18 Bath Rd. (old Rt. 1 near Bowdoin College). Open mid-Apr.–mid-Nov., 11–8. An offshoot of the waterside lobster eatery in Harpswell. This handy in-town location, formerly Ernie's Drive-in, permits an expanded menu: lobster stew, chowders, and biscuits, plus hot dogs as well as lobster dinners. Waitresses will serve you in your car, but there's also inside seating.

The Humble Gourmet (207-721-8100), 103 Pleasant St. (Rt. 1 northbound), open 8–7 daily, except Sun. A road-food find with baked goods, great sandwiches on homemade bread, soups, and salads. A couple of doors up from the Miss Brunswick Diner (see below, easier to spot).

Miss Brunswick Diner (207-729-5948), 101 Pleasant St. (Rt. 1 northbound). Open daily 5 AM–9 PM. A convenient road-food stop, a remake of a diner that originally stood in Norway (Maine) but has now been here several decades; the neon lights, booths, and jukebox are all new, but the food is what it claims to be: "home cooking at a down-home good price."

Tess's Market (207-729-9531), 54 Pleasant St. Strictly takeout, but a

great source of sandwiches, pizza, and the area's best selection of wine.

In the Harpswells
Dolphin Chowder House (207-833-6000; www.dolphinchowderhouse.com), South Harpswell (marked from Rt. 123, it's 2.5 miles; also accessible by water). Open seasonally, 11–8 daily. The nicest kind of small Maine restaurant—owned by the Saxton family, overlooking a small but busy harbor. The dining room fills early for lunch and dinner. Chowder, lobster stew, and fried seafood are specialties. Our only complaint is the absence of anything besides blueberry muffins to accompany the chowder, stew, and steamers.

Block & Tackle (207-725-5690), Cundy's Harbor Rd. Open mid-May–mid-Oct., 11–8, breakfast from 7 AM on weekends. A family-run and -geared restaurant. Try shrimpster stew or real homemade clamcakes. The Friday special is corned hake.

LOBSTER **Morse's Lobster Shack** (207-833-2399), off Rt. 123 on Allens Point, Harpswell Neck. Open 11–7 daily, weather permitting, May–Sep. This is a great spot overlooking

DOLPHIN CHOWDER HOUSE
Nancy English

Harpswell Sound, a local favorite. Tables are topped with umbrellas and banked in flowers, with lobster available right off the boat in all the usual ways. Also first-rate crab rolls (a "small" is plenty).

Allen's Seafood (207-833-2828), Lookout Point Rd., Harpswell. Open Apr.–Oct, Tue.–Sun. 11–7. This longtime seafood wholesaler has added a takeout menu and picnic benches to take advantage of its glorious view. Steamed crabs as well as clams and lobsters plus a wide choice of fried dinners and baskets; also burgers and fried haddock, plus side orders like clam fritters and dough boys.

Middlebay Lobster (207-798-5868), 45 Ellen Way, Cundy's Harbor. The view is nonexistent, but the quality and price of fish and seafood are the best around. The menu includes a wide choice of sandwiches and "other stuff" as well as wine and beer. Try Mud Season for dessert.

Holbrook Wharf and Snack Bar (207-729-0848), Cundy's Harbor. Open Memorial Day–Labor Day. Members of the Saxton family (see the Dolphin Chowder Houset) now own this nicely sited, lobster-dining landmark. The chowder is great again, and the tartar sauce is homemade. BYOB.

Estes Lobster House (207-833-6340), Rt. 123, South Harpswell. Open mid-Apr.–mid-Oct., 11–9. Another old barn of a place with red-checked oilcloth tables. It's on a causeway with water views and the basics: steamed and fried clams and lobster every which way, broiled seafood baskets. Wine and beer, some waterside tables.

Cook's Lobster House (207-833-2818), Bailey Island. Open year-round, 11:30–10. A landmark barn of a place with knotty-pine walls, booths, and a classic Maine seafood menu right on the water (beyond the parking lots). Founded in 1955 and little changed since. No surprises. If there's a line and you don't mind settling for light fare, head for the deck where there's open seating. In July and August try to get here before noon, when the Casco Bay liner arrives with its load of day-trippers from Portland.

✳ Entertainment

MUSIC **Bowdoin International Music Festival** (box office, 207-725-3895; www.bowdoinfestival.org), Bowdoin College, Brunswick. Famed in classical music circles, this chamber music series brings together 200 talented young performers and 40 internationally acclaimed musicians, faculty members at the world's top music schools. It includes composers and choral artists as well as musicians performing original and classical pieces. The Friday-evening concerts (June–Aug.) are staged in the new Crooker Theater at Brunswick High School. Wednesday-evening "Upbeat" concerts, free Sunday and Tuesday student concerts, and the Gamper Festival of Contemporary Music series are all held in Bowdoin campus buildings.

Music on the Mall (207-729-4439). July–Aug., concerts at 7 PM Wed. on Brunswick's grassy downtown mall. Free.

Also see **First Parish Church** under *To See.*

THEATER ♪ **Maine State Music Theatre** (207-725-8769; www.msmt.org), Bowdoin College, Brunswick. Newly renovated (and air-conditioned)

Pickard Theater is housed in Memorial Hall, an 1873 memorial to the Bowdoin students who fought and died in the Civil War—ordered built, of course, by Joshua Chamberlain. This a fit stage for Maine's premier performing-arts group. This highly professional Equity company strives for a mix of classics and new scripts and frequently gets rave reviews. Summer performances at 8 PM, Tue.–Sat.; matinees Tue., Thu., and Fri. Special children's shows.

The Theater Project (207-729-8584), 14 School St., Brunswick. Serious drama presented year-round in a black-box theater, Wed.–Sun. at 8. Inquire about late-night cabarets and dinner theater.

FILM **Eveningstar Cinema** (207-729-6796 or 1-888-304-5486), Tontine Mall, 149 Maine St., Brunswick. The specialty is alternative film: foreign, art, biography, documentary, and educational. Also a monthly venue for folk, jazz, and other music performances.

✳ Selective Shopping

ANTIQUES **Cabot Mill Antiques** (207-725-2855), 14 Maine St. (at Rt. 1; Fort Andros), Brunswick. Open daily 10–5, a vast 140-dealer space with quality antiques; flea markets on summer weekends.

ART AND CRAFTS GALLERIES

In Brunswick
Galleries at the north end of Brunswick's Maine St. include **Bayview Gallery** (207-729-5500), 58 Maine St., showing traditional Maine, and the edgier, innovative **Icon Contemporary Art** (207-725-8157), around

the corner at 19 Mason St. Check out **Spindleworks** (207-725-8820), 7 Lincoln St., an artists' cooperative for people with disabilities that produces some striking handwoven fiber clothing and hangings, quilts, accessories, paintings, prints, and more. The **Window Tree Gallery and Frame Shop** (207-729-4366), 44 Maine St., is also worth checking. Inquire about **Second Friday Art Walks**.

In the Harpswells
Harpswell Art & Craft Guild is an association of studio-galleries along Rt. 123 on Harpswell Neck that regularly sponsors events. **The Gallery at Widgeon Cove** (207-833-6081; www .widgeoncove.com), open year-round, features the handmade papers and collages of Georgeann and the gold and silver jewelry of Condon Kuhl. **Ash Cove Pottery** (207-833-6004), farther down the road, displays a variety of hand-thrown and -glazed functional stoneware by Susan Horowitz and Gail Kass. On Rt. 24 (north of Mountain Rd.) the former Gunpoint Church now serves as a gallery for **Sebascodegan Artists** (named for the island on which it stands), a cooperative with 20 members. It's open July 4–Labor Day, Mon.–Sat. 10–5.

Hawke's Lobster (207-721-0472) in Cundy's Harbor is a seasonal source of not only seafood but also the work of local craftspeople.

BOOKSTORES **Gulf of Maine Books** (207-729-5083), 134 Maine St., Brunswick. A laid-back, full-service bookstore with a wide inventory, particularly rich in Maine titles, poetry, and "books that fall through the holes in bigger stores." Owners are photographer Beth Leonard and Gary Lawless, founder of Blackberry Press (note the full line here), which has reissued many out-of-print Maine classics. A true Renaissance man, Lawless is a well-known poet with an international following.

Brunswick Bookland & Cafe (207-725-2313), Cooks Corner Shopping Center. Open Mon.–Sat. 9 AM–10 PM, Sun. 9–6. A major full-service independent bookstore that includes the **Hardcover Café**, serving light meals, espresso, and desserts, good daily specials.

Old Books (207-725-4524), 136 Maine St., Brunswick. Upstairs from Gulf of Maine, Old Books features Clare Howell's floor-to-ceiling, well-arranged used books and a large stuffed couch, along with friendly nooks for reading.

SPECIAL STORES **Island Candy Company** (207-833-6639), Rt. 24, Orrs Island. Open year-round, 11–8. Melinda Harris Richter makes everything from lollipops to truffles. Try the almond cups.

Grand City V&S (207-725-8964), 128 Maine St., Brunswick. Open Mon.–Sat. 9–6, Sun. 10–4. See the chapter introduction. A must-stop for anyone who misses genuine five-and-dimes.

Wyler Crafts & Clothiers (207-729-1321), 150 Maine St., Brunswick, is a great mix of quality pottery, glassware, jewelry, and clothing; an offshoot Wyler Furniture and Home shop is at 100 Maine St.

✸ Special Events

⚓ *Mid-May–June:* **Fishway Viewing Room** (207-795-4290), Brunswick-Topsham Hydro Station, next to Fort Andros. Open during the spawning season, Wed.–Sun. 1–5. Watch salmon, smallmouth bass, and alewives climb the 40-foot-high fish ladder that leads to a holding tank beside the viewing room.

Throughout summer: **Farmer's market** (Tue. and Fri., May–Nov.) on the downtown Brunswick Mall (the town common), and Saturday mornings at Crystal Spring Farm, Pleasant Hill Road. Check the Thursday edition of Brunswick's *Times Record* for current happenings.

July: **Annual Lobster Luncheon**, Orrs Island United Methodist Church. **Bailey Island Fishing Tournament** (to register, phone Cook's Lobster House at 207-833-2818).

August: **Topsham Fair** (*first week*)—a traditional agricultural fair complete with ox pulls, crafts and food competitions, a carnival, and livestock; held at Topsham Fairgrounds, Rt. 24, Topsham. **A Weekend in Harpswell** (*late in the month*)—annual art show, garden club festival in historic homes, and beanhole supper. (A beanhole supper, for the uninitiated, features beans cooked all day in a cast-iron pot over a fire built in a hole in the ground.) **Maine Highland Games**, Thomas Point Beach—a daylong celebration of Scottish heritage, with piping, country dancing, sheepdog demonstrations, and Highland fling competitions. **Joshua Chamberlain Days**, observed in odd-numbered years—4 days of Chamberlain lectures and related events.

September: **Annual Bluegrass Festival** (*Labor Day weekend*), Thomas Point Beach. **Family Arts Festival** (*midmonth*)—music, dance, and storytelling on the downtown mall, Brunswick.

BATH AREA

Over the years some 5,000 vessels have been built in Bath. Think about it: In contrast to most communities—which retain what they build—here an entire city's worth of imposing structures have sailed away. Perhaps that's why, with a population of fewer than 9,300, Bath is a city rather than a town, and why the granite city hall, with its rounded, pillared facade and cupola (with a Paul Revere bell and a three-masted schooner for a weather vane), seems meant for a far larger city.

American shipbuilding began downriver from Bath in 1607 when the 30-ton pinnace *Virginia* was launched by Popham Colony settlers. It continues with naval vessels regularly constructed at the Bath Iron Works (BIW).

With around 7,000 workers, BIW employs fewer people than worked in Bath's shipyards in the 1850s. At its entrance a sign proclaims: THROUGH THESE GATES PASS THE WORLD'S BEST SHIPBUILDERS. This is no idle boast, for many current employees have inherited their skills from a long line of forebears.

Obviously, this is the place for a museum about ships and shipbuilding, and the Maine Maritime Museum has one of the country's foremost collections of ships' models, journals, logs, photographs, and other seafaring memorabilia. It even includes a 19th-century working shipyard. Both BIW and the Maine Maritime Museum are sited on a 4-mile-long reach of the Kennebec River where the banks slope at precisely the right gradient for laying keels. Offshore, a 35- to 150-foot-deep channel ensures safe launching. The open Atlantic is just 18 miles downriver.

In the 1850s Bath was the fourth largest port in the United States in registered tonnage, and throughout the 19th century it consistently ranked among America's eight largest seaports. Its past prosperity is reflected in the blend of Greek Revival, Italianate, and Georgian Revival styles in the brick storefronts along Front Street and in the imposing wooden churches and mansions in similar styles along Washington, High, and Middle Streets. Front Street, incidentally, once more offers a healthy mix of shops, several mansions that are now gracious B&Bs, and both parks and restaurants overlooking the river.

Today BIW dominates the city's economy as dramatically as its red-and-white, 400-foot-high construction crane—the biggest on the East Coast—does the city's waterfront. One of the largest civilian employers in Maine, the company actually

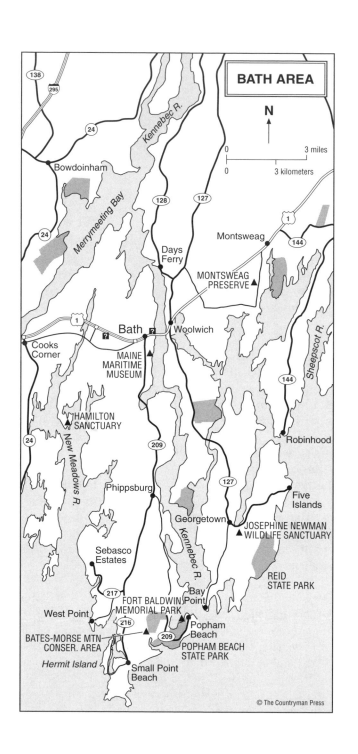

BATH AREA

N

0 _____ 3 miles
0 _____ 3 kilometers

138
295
24
Bowdoinham
Kennebec R.
24
Merrymeeting Bay
128
127
Days Ferry
Montsweag
1
144
MONTSWEAG PRESERVE ▲
1
Bath
Woolwich
Cooks Corner
MAINE MARITIME MUSEUM ▲
144
Sheepscot R.
HAMILTON SANCTUARY ▲
24
New Meadows R.
209
Robinhood
Phippsburg
127
Five Islands
Georgetown
JOSEPHINE NEWMAN ▲ WILDLIFE SANCTUARY
Sebasco Estates
Kennebec R.
REID STATE PARK
217
Bay Point
FORT BALDWIN MEMORIAL PARK
West Point
216
209
Popham Beach
BATES-MORSE MTN CONSER. AREA
POPHAM BEACH STATE PARK
Hermit Island
Small Point Beach

© The Countryman Press

produced more destroyers during World War II than did all of Japan, and it continues to keep to its pledge to deliver naval ships ahead of schedule and under budget. Note the 750-foot floating dry dock (visible from Washington Street) for launching and retrieval.

The story of BIW is one of many told in the Maine Maritime Museum—for which you should allow the better part of a day (lunch in its waterside café). Save another to explore the Phippsburg Peninsula south of Bath. Phippsburg's perimeter is notched with coves filled with fishing boats, and Popham Beach near its southern tip is a grand expanse of sand. Reid State Park on Georgetown Island, just across the Kennebec River, is the Midcoast's other major sandy strand. North of Bath, Merrymeeting Bay is a major flyway known to birders.

GUIDANCE **Southern Midcoast Maine Chamber** (207-725-8797; www .midcoastmaine.com), 59 Pleasant St., Bath 04011.

GETTING THERE *By car:* Rt. 1 passes above the city with exits from the elevated road accessing various points within the city. From points south take I-95 to 295 to exit 31 (Topsham) and the connector (Rt. 196) to Rt. 1.

By bus: **Concord Trailways** (1-800-639-3317), en route to and from Boston, stops in Bath at Coastal Plaza just off Rt. 1.

By air and limo: **Mid-Coast Limo** (207-236-2424 or 1-800-937-2424) makes runs by reservation from Portland International Jetport to Midcoast towns.

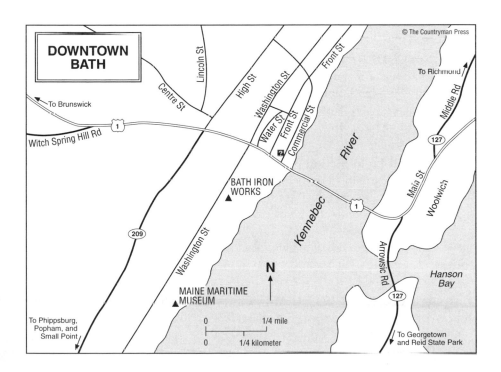

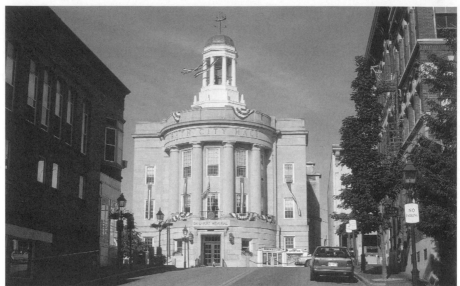

Kim Grant

BATH CITY HALL

GETTING AROUND Bath Trolley Company (207-443-9741) operates through-out the city, daily June–Sep.

WHEN TO COME Bath itself remains lively year-round, but both the Popham and Georgetown areas are June-through-Columbus-Day destinations. Note, however, that superb places to stay are open year-round on the Popham Peninsula—ideal for off-season beach walkers.

✳ To See

Bath Historic District. In the 18th and 19th centuries Bath's successful ship-building and seafaring families built impressive mansions on and around upper Washington St. **Sagadahoc Preservation, Inc.** (207-443-2174; www.sagadahoc preservation.org), 880 Washington St., offers periodic guided walks and produces an excellent brochure, *Architectural Tours—Self-Guided Walking and Driving Tours of the City of Bath*.

Seguin Island Light Station (www.seguinisland.org). Guarding the mouth of the Kennebec River, this 186-foot granite lighthouse stands on a bluff on a 64-acre island. Commissioned by George Washington in 1795, it's one of the oldest lighthouses in the country. It also boasts the highest elevation of any Maine light and the last continuously operational first-order lens north of Virginia. It's all maintained by the Friends of Seguin Island, Inc., and accessible on periodic trips offered by the Maine Maritime Museum, more frequently by **Atlantic Seal** (877-285-7325) and local charter boats and water taxis.

✐ **Woolwich Historical Society Museum** (207-443-483), Rt. 1 and Nequasset Rd., Woolwich. Open in-season Tue.–Sat. 10:30–2:30. Volunteer-run, this 19th-century rural life museum displays antique clothing, quilts, and seafaring memorabilia from local attics.

❧ **Maine Maritime Museum** (207-443-1316; www.mainemaritimemuseum .org), 243 Washington St., Bath. Watch for the turnoff from Rt. 1. Open year-round, daily 9:30–5; closed Thanksgiving, Christmas, and New Year's Day. Admission is $9.75 adults, $8.75 seniors, and $6.75 ages 7–17 (family admission is $28). Sited just south of BIW on the banks of the Kennebec River, this extensive complex includes the brick-and-glass Maritime History Building and the Percy & Small Shipyard, the country's only surviving wooden ship-building yard (its turn-of-the-20th-century belts for driving machinery have been restored). Its exhibits focus, understandably, on the era beginning after the Civil War when 80 percent of this country's full-rigged ships were built in Maine, almost half of these in Bath.

The pride of Bath, you learn, were the Down Easters, a compromise between the clipper ship and the old-style freighter that plied the globe from the 1870s through the 1890s, and the big multimasted schooners designed to ferry coal and local exports like ice, granite, and lime. The museum's permanent collection of artwork, artifacts, and documents is now said to include more than 20,000 pieces, and there is an extensive research library. Permanent exhibits range from displays on Maine's marine industries—fishing and canning as well as shipbuilding and fitting—to the story of BIW.

A seasonal café in Long Reach Hall serves coffee, pastries, and a full luncheon menu, with deck dining overlooking the river. Plan to take a narrated Kennebec River cruise; see *To Do*.

MAINE MARITIME MUSEUM

Maine Maritime Museum

SCENIC DRIVES The Phippsburg Peninsula. From the Maine Maritime Museum, drive south on Rt. 209 down the narrow peninsula that's the town of Phippsburg. Pause at the first causeway you cross. This is **Winnegance Creek**, an ancient shortcut between Casco Bay and the Kennebec River; look closely to your left and you'll see traces of the 10 tide mills that once operated here.

Continue south on Rt. 209 until you come to the **Phippsburg Center Store** on your right. Turn left on Parker Head Rd. into the tiny hamlet of **Phippsburg Center**. This is one of those magical places, far larger in memory than in fact—perhaps because it was once larger in fact, too. Notice the **giant linden tree** planted in 1774 between the white-clapboard Congregational church (1802) and its small cemetery. Another surviving linden was also planted in 1774, the year the striking Georgian mansion next door was built. Also look for the telltale stumps of piers on the river shore beyond, remnants of a major shipyard. Just off Rt. 209, note the **Phippsburg Historical Museum** (open in summer Mon.–Fri. 2–4, and by appointment: 207-442-7606).

Continue along the peninsula's east shore on the Parker Head Rd., past a former millpond where ice was once harvested. At the junction with Rt. 209, turn left. The road threads a salt marsh and the area at Hoss Ketch Point, from which all traces of the ill-fated **Popham Colony** have long since disappeared. Rt. 209 winds around Sabino Head and ends at the parking lot for **Fort Popham**, a granite Civil War–era fort (with picnic benches) at the mouth of the Kennebec River. A wooded road, for walking only, leads to World War I and II fortifications that constitute **Fort Baldwin Memorial Park**; a six-story tower yields views up the Kennebec and out to sea.

Along the shore at **Popham Beach**, note the pilings, in this case from vanished steamboat wharves. Around the turn of the 20th century, two big hotels served the passengers who transferred here from Boston to Kennebec River steamers, or who simply stayed a spell to enjoy the town's spectacular beach. Now **Popham Beach State Park**, this immense expanse of sand remains a popular destination for fishermen, beach walkers, sunbathers, and even a few hardy swimmers. From Popham Beach, return to Rt. 209 and follow it west to Rt. 217 and out to **Sebasco Harbor**, then back up to Phippsburg Center.

Arrowsic and Georgetown Islands. Just east of the Sagadahoc Bridge (at the Dairy Queen that's been there forever), turn south on Rt. 127. Cross a shorter bridge and you are on Arrowsic Island. Note **Robinhood Road** leading to two of the area's top restaurants (see *Dining Out*). Farther down Rt. 127 in **Georgetown Center** look for **Georgetown Pottery**;

PERCY & SMALL SHIPYARD

Maine Maritime Museum

the general store has a snack bar and is good for sandwiches to take to **Reid State Park** or out kayaking. The road ends at the **Five Islands** lobster pound; its competition is around the corner.

✳ To Do

BOAT EXCURSIONS **Long Reach Cruises** (1-888-538-6786; longreachcruises .com), 870 Washington St., Bath. June–Columbus Day, daily (weather permitting) cruises from the **Maine Maritime Museum** (excursions can also be booked though the museum; the price includes admission). These 1- to 3-hour narrated tours aboard the 64-passenger *Sagadahoc* ply the Kennebec River and Merrymeeting Bay, heading along the coast to Boothbay Harbor. Lighthouses are Captain Mike's passion, and cruises can include viewing up to six of them.

The M/V *Ruth*, based at Sebasco Estates (207-389-1161); the **M/V *Yankee*** (207-389-1788), based at Hermit Island Campground at Small Point; and **Kennebec Charters** (207-389-1883) at Popham Beach all offer coastal excursions. Also see Seguin Island under *To See*.

CANOE AND KAYAK RENTALS This area's many coves and quiet stretches of smaller tidal rivers lend themselves to kayaking, and outfitters have multiplied in recent years. **Taylor Rentals** (207-725-7400), 271 Bath Rd., Brunswick, rents canoes to explore Merrymeeting Bay. **Seaspray Kayaking** (207-443-3646), based at Sebasco Harbor Resort, offers daily guided tours and hourly rentals. **Up the Creek** (207-442-4845), 39 Main Rd. (Rt. 209), is sited beside a put-in not far south of Bath, renting Old Town canoes and kayaks.

FISHING **Kennebec Angler** (207-442-8239), 97 Commercial St., Bath, is fishing central for the area, a referral service for guides and charter boats. The shop is filled with tackle and gear and offers demo rods for full-day trials before purchasing. Surf fishing is popular at Popham Beach. Nearly 20 boats offer fishing on the river, while **Kayla D & Obsession Sportfishing Charters** (207-442-8581 or 207-443-3316) offers deep-sea-fishing charters.

GOLF **Bath Country Club** (207-442-8411), Whiskeag Rd., Bath, has 18 holes and a pro shop; lessons available. **Sebasco Harbor Resort Golf Club** (207-389-9060) is a recently renovated nine-hole course open to the public. Reservations advised.

SWIMMING 🐾 If you're traveling with a dog, it's important to know that they're allowed only in picnic areas, not on the beaches.

✧ **Popham Beach State Park** (207-389-1335), via Rt. 209 south from Bath to Phippsburg and beyond. One of the best state park beaches in Maine: 3 miles of sand at the mouth of the Kennebec River that never seem to be too crowded. Also a sandbar, tidal pools, and smooth rocks. It can be windy; extra layers are recommended. Day-use fees of $3 adults, $1 ages 5–11 (under 5 free), are charged mid-Apr.–mid-Oct.

☙ **Reid State Park** (207-371-2303), Rt. 127, Georgetown (14 miles south of Bath and Rt. 1). Open daily year-round. The bathhouse and snack bar overlook 2 miles of sand in three distinct beaches that seldom become overcrowded, although the limited parking area does fill by noon on summer weekends. You can choose surf or a slightly warmer sheltered backwater, especially good for children. Entrance fees of $3.50 adults and $1 ages 5–11 (under 5 free) are charged mid-Apr.–mid-Oct.

☙ **Charles Pond,** Rt. 27, Georgetown (about 0.5 mile past the turnoff for Reid State Park; 15 miles down the peninsula from the Carlton Bridge). Often considered the best all-around swimming hole in the area, this long and narrow pond has clear water and is surrounded by tall pines.

☙ **Pleasant Pond** (207-582-2813), Peacock Beach State Park, Richmond. Open Memorial Day–Labor Day. A sand-and-gravel beach with lifeguards on duty. Water depth drops off gradually to about 10 feet in a 30-by-50-foot swimming area removed from boating and enclosed by colored buoys. Picnic tables and barbecue grills. Nominal admission.

☙ **Sewall Pond**, Woolwich. Visible from Rt. 1, this popular swimming hole is just behind the Woolwich Historical Society Museum.

RAILROAD EXCURSION **The Maine Eastern Railroad** (866-636-2457; www .maineeasternrailroad.com) offers 54-mile seasonal runs between Brunswick and Rockland, stopping in Bath and Wiscasset. Travel along the coast in plush 1940s and '50s coaches, a dining car, and (weekends only) a glass-domed observation car, behind a 1950s diesel electric engine. In 2005 round-trip runs were Tue.–Sun., but check the web site for current information.

SPECIAL LEARNING PROGRAM **Shelter Institute** (207-442-7938; www .shelterinstitute.com), 873 Rt. 1, Woolwich. A year-round resource center for people who want to build or retrofit their own energy-efficient home, offering a wide variety of classes.

✳ Green Space

☙ **Fort Baldwin Memorial Park**, Phippsburg. An undeveloped area with a six-story tower to climb (steep stairs, but the railing is sturdy) for a beautiful view up the Kennebec and, downriver, out to sea. There are also remnants of fortifications from World Wars I and II. At the bottom of the hill is the site where members of the Popham Colony struggled to weather the winter of 1607–08, then built the pinnace *Virginia* and sailed away to Virginia.

☙ **Fort Popham Historic Site** (207-389-1335), Hunniwell's Point at Popham Beach. Open Memorial Day–Sep. Picnic sites are scattered around the ruins of this 1861 granite fort, built to guard the Kennebec during the Civil War. Beach and ocean fishing access.

Josephine Newman Wildlife Sanctuary, Georgetown. Bounded on two sides by salt marsh; 119 acres with 2 miles of walking trails. Look for the sign on Rt. 127, 9.1 miles south of Rt. 1.

Bates–Morse Mountain Conservation Area consists of some 600 acres extending from the Sprague to the Morse River and out to Seawall Beach. Allow 2 hours for the walk to and from this unspoiled private beach. Pack a picnic and towel, but please, no radios or beach paraphernalia: Seawall Beach is an important nesting area for piping plovers and least terns. There's a great view from the top of Morse Mountain, which is reached by an easy hike, just over a mile along a partially paved road and through river and marsh. Parking is very limited.

Hamilton Sanctuary, West Bath. Situated on a peninsula in the New Meadows River, offering a 1.5-mile trail system and great bird-watching. Take the New Meadows exit off Rt. 1 in West Bath; turn left on New Meadows Rd., which turns into Foster Point Rd.; follow it 4 miles to the sanctuary sign.

Montsweag Preserve, Montsweag Rd., Woolwich. A 1.5-mile trail takes visitors through woods, fields, and a salt marsh, and along the water. This 45-acre preserve is owned by The Nature Conservancy (207-729-5181). You will have to watch carefully for the turns (right onto Montsweag Rd. about 6.5 miles from Bath on Rt. 1, then 1.3 miles and a left into the preserve).

✳ Lodging

RESORTS ✐ ♿ **Sebasco Harbor Resort** (207-389-1161 or 1-800-225-3819; www.sebasco.com), P.O. Box 75, Sebasco Estates 04565. Open May–Oct. This 575-acre, 115-room family-geared waterside resort dates back to 1930, featuring a nine-hole golf course, tennis courts, a large swimming pool, kayaking, and full children's and adult activities programs. Sailing lessons and excursions, lobster cookouts, and live entertainment are also offered. Lodging is divided among the main lodge, a lighthouse-shaped annex, and 23 widely scattered and differing cottages, some with fireplace and kitchenette. Informal dining is at **The Ledges**, more formal at **The Pilot House** (entrées $14–23). High-season rates in the lodge are $209–275, in the waterside "Lighthouse," $275–315; cottages are $375–1,890 per night. All rates are based on two people, $15 per extra person. Add $35 per person MAP (breakfast and dinner), another $20 for golf. Less before July and after Labor Day. Children under 10 dine at no charge

when accompanied by an adult and ordering from the children's menu.

BED & BREAKFASTS

In Bath 04530
🦞 🐾 ✐ ♿ **The Inn at Bath** (207-443-4294 or 1-800-423-0964; www.innat bath.com), 969 Washington St. Open year-round. Elizabeth Knowlton, former owner of a Montana fly-fishing lodge but with many Maine connections, is the new keeper of Bath's leading inn. A restored 1810 mansion, the inn features deeply colored and richly decorated twin parlors with marble fireplaces, eight luxurious guest rooms with private bath, and a two-bedroom suite. Five rooms have a wood-burning fireplace; two of these also feature a Jacuzzi. Most also have a writing desk. All guest rooms have air-conditioning, phone, cable TV, VCR, and cassette-tape player with radio and alarm. Rooms are $125–175 for two, including a breakfast; $185–200 for suites. Children (over 4) and dogs are welcome.

✐ **Rock Gardens Inn** (207-389-1339; www.rockgardensinn.com), Sebasco Estates 04565. Open mid-June–late Sep. A hidden gem, sited on its own narrow peninsula between a cove and bay, within but beyond the Sebasco Harbor Resort grounds. Accommodating just 60 guests, it offers a more intimate atmosphere but access to all of Sebasco Harbor Resort's facilities as well as its own pool and dock with kayaks. Rock Gardens dates back more than 90 years. Ona Barnet has preserved an old-style atmosphere but constantly updates the 10 cottages (accommodating three to eight) and three inn rooms. August is family geared. In June, July, and September a series of Sebasco Art Workshops feature some surprisingly well-known teachers (Ona's father, Will Barnet, is a prominent artist). In high season, $110–200 per person MAP (but there are children's rates) includes a four-course dinner (BYOB) as well as breakfast; 5-night minimum in July and Aug., but check for cancellations; from $95 in June and Sep.; add 15 percent for service.

ROCK GARDENS INN

Christina Tree

Pryor House (207-443-1146; www.pryorhouse.com), 360 Front St. Don and Gwenda Pryor offer three crisp, attractive upstairs guest rooms with air-conditioning and private bath in this late-Federal-style home. The Captain's Room with its deep red wallpaper, white wicker, and tall four-poster is our favorite. Downstairs common space is inviting. Breakfast may feature tomato basil quiche or blueberry French toast. $90–120 in summer, from $85 off-season.

Fairhaven Inn (207-443-4391 or 1-888-443-4391; www.mainecoast.com/fairhaveninn), 118 North Bath Rd. Open year-round. Hidden away on the Kennebec River as it meanders down from Merrymeeting Bay, this 1790s house has eight pleasant, air-conditioned guest rooms, six with private bath. Dave and Susie Reed stayed here as guests some 20 times before buying the place. The inn's 16 acres of meadow invite walking in summer and cross-country skiing in winter. Two-night minimum stay on holidays and summer weekends. In-season rates, including a full breakfast, are $80–140. Inquire about the cottage.

On the Phippsburg Peninsula south of Bath

🍂 **The 1774 Inn at Phippsburg** (207-389-1774 or 1-888-244-1774; www.1774inn.com), 44 Parker Head Rd., Phippsburg 04562. Open year-round. Ranked among the most beautiful houses in Maine, this is an imposing cupola-topped, foursquare mansion, built in 1774 at the heart of picturesque Phippsburg Center. The home of Maine's first U.S. congressman, Mark L. Hill, and later owned by the area's premier shipbuilder, Charles V. Minot, this landmark has been restored by Debbie and Joe

Braun. Guests can choose from four splendid Federal-style guest rooms and three smaller bedrooms, all decorated in Willamsburg colors and fabrics, furnished with antiques, and all with private bath. $115–185.

🍂 **Popham Beach Bed & Breakfast** (207-389-2409; www.pophambeachbandb.com), 4 Riverview Ave., Popham Beach 04562. Open year-round. Peggy Johannessen has restored this former Coast Guard station, built in 1883 right on Popham Beach, to create a B&B with as much character as the building itself. The four guest rooms all have private bath and some of the most superb water views along the entire coast. The second-floor "Bunkroom," despite its name, may just be the most spectacular beachside room in New England. Breakfast is full and served at a common table, and the sitting room is large and beautifully furnished. From $175 in high season, with a 2-night minimum stay; from $160 off-season.

Stonehouse Manor (207-389-1141; www.stonehousemanor.com), 907 Popham Rd. (Rt. 209), Phippsburg 04563. Open year-round. Handy to Popham Beach but set off in its grounds beside a small spring-fed lake, this rambling old fieldstone-and-shingle house exudes the style of Maine's grand old cottages. Jane and Tim Dennis offer four large rooms, some with fireplace and Jacuzzi, each with a lake, bay, or garden view and private bath ($120–235). The Carriage House has a sitting area and kitchen (from $750 per week).

🐾 ♿ **Edgewater Farm Bed & Breakfast** (207-389-1322 or 1-877-389-1322; www.ewfbb.com), 71 Small Point Rd., Phippsburg 04562. Carol Emerson is a passionate gardener, and her restored circa-1800 farmhouse is set in 4 acres of gardens and fruit trees. Guests gather for breakfast in the Sun Room, a modern addition. Another addition houses an indoor pool with a large recreation room above it and an outdoor hot tub on a back deck. Of the six guest rooms, which include two suites (all with private bath), we like the lavender-and-blue room in the original house. $90–200. Dogs are $25 per stay.

🐾 ♪ **Small Point Bed & Breakfast** (207-389-1716), 312 Small Point Rd., Phippsburg 04562. David and Jan Tingle offer a nifty "Carriage House" unit with a loft and sitting area, a fridge and microwave, good for couples or up to a family of five. $120–150 including a full breakfast. No fee for dogs.

On the Georgetown Peninsula
🦞 **Coveside Bed and Breakfast** (207-371-2807 or 1-800-232-5490; www.covesidebandb.com), Georgetown (Five Islands) 04548. Open May–mid-Oct. Twelve miles down Rt. 127 from Rt. 1, beyond the turnoff for Reid State Park, Carolyn and Tom Church have created a rare retreat overlooking a quiet cove. This 100-year-old farmhouse holds seven guest rooms, all with private bath (one with a spa tub), divided between the main house and a neighboring guest cottage with three rooms, featuring a private deck and fireplace plus its own common space and screened porch. The style is an uncluttered, updated version of classic, turn-of-the-20th-century "Maine cottage." "It doesn't get better than this," we wrote in our notes from our many-windowed room in the main house. $115–175 includes a full breakfast, sometimes with crab-cakes.

⊗ **Grey Havens** (207-371-2616 or 1-800-431-2316; www.greyhavens .com), Seguinland Rd., P.O. Box 308, Georgetown 04548. Open May–Oct. The donor of the land for neighboring Reid State Park also built this turreted, gray-shingled summer hotel, opened in 1904, with a huge parlor window—said to have been Maine's first picture window. The 13 rooms, all with private bath (compared with 26 rooms and two baths in 1904), range from small doubles to large, rounded turret rooms; half have water views. Request a water view and call early, because it's frequently booked with weddings. $100–230 (for an ocean-front suite with balcony); 25 percent midweek discount through June 15. "Hearty continental" breakfast; 2-night minimum on weekends and holidays.

⊗ **The Mooring** (207-371-2790; www.themooringb-b.com), 132 Seguinland Rd., Georgetown 04548. Open May–Oct. In 2002 Paul and Penny Barabe, the great-granddaughter of Walter Reid—donor of the land for his namesake state park—opened their gracious home as a B&B. The five guest rooms all have private bath, and there are gracious common spaces and a great porch overlooking the lawns and water. Weddings are a specialty. $130–170 in high season includes a full breakfast.

OTHER LODGING 🦞 ♪ **Hermit Island Campground** (207-443-2101; www.hermitisland.com), 6 Hermit Island Rd., Phippsburg 04562; winter mailing address: 42 Front St., Bath 04530. This 255-acre almost-island at Small Point offers 271 nicely scattered camping sites, 51 on the water. Only tents, small to medium pop-ups, and small pickup campers are permitted. Owned since 1953 by the Sewall family, Hermit Island also has a central lodge with a recreation room and snack bar where kids can meet. Beyond the camping area are acres of private beach and hiking trails through unspoiled woods and meadows. $29–40 per night; less off-season. Repeats tend to mail in their reservations January 2, but it's always worth a try. No pets.

Cottage listings are available from the Southern Midcoast Maine Chamber (see *Guidance*) and in the Maine Tourism Association's *Maine Guide to Inns and Bed & Breakfasts and Camps & Cottages*. Also see *Cottage Rentals* in "What's Where."

✳ Where to Eat

DINING OUT Also see "Brunswick and the Harpswells."

The Robinhood Free Meetinghouse (207-371-2188; www.robinhood meetinghouse.com), Robinhood Rd. (off Rt. 127), Robinhood. Open nightly May–Oct., Thu.–Sat. off-season. Reservations advised. Michael Gagné, known regionally for his fresh, innovative dishes, has turned the vintage-1855 Robinhood Free Meetinghouse into an attractive dining space. The second-floor chapel, with a 16-foot ceiling and 10-foot windows, seems designed for wedding parties. The soup of the day might be cream of mushroom hazelnut ($6.50); as an entrée, you might select Szechuan beef tips with black bean sauce served with stir-fried vegetables over fettuccine, or pan seared lemon scallops with a lemon butter sauce, served with mixed greens. Entrées $24–28.

Mary Ellenz Italian Café (207-442-0960), 99 Commercial St., Bath. Summer hours are Tue.–Sat. for dinner. This intimate riverside restaurant deserves its good reviews. The menu ranges from linguine Alfredo to *zuppa di pesce* with lobster and might include haddock Provençal with roasted garlic, fresh herbs, and crispy polenta. Wine priced to sell, so drink and enjoy it. Entrées $11–24.

♪ ♿ **Mae's Cafe** (207-442-8577), corner of High and Center Sts., Bath. Closed on Mon. and 2 weeks in Jan. Open weekdays for all three meals, brunch and dinner on Sat., and brunch-only on Sun. Andy and Kate Winglass are the owners of this cheerful restaurant/café, the place to come for quiche, salads, and such specialty entrées as pan-seared crabcake and chicken pie with a cheddar cheese crust. You might dine on grilled duck breast topped with blueberry ginger chutney, or scallops sautéed in a ginger lime butter with toasted walnuts. Dinner entrées $14–18, including salad. A good selection of beers and wine, fully licensed.

Solo Bistro Bistro (207-443-3373), 128 Front St., Bath. Open for lunch and dinner. New in summer 2005, this cool spot makes popular lobster and crabcakes and seafood curry, as well as meat and vegetarian dishes. The menu changes monthly, with local produce featured when available. Entrées $20–28.

The Osprey (207-371-2530), at Robinhood Marina, Robinhood (just off Rt. 127, near Reid State Park). Open Memorial Day–Columbus Day for lunch and dinner. Sited in the Robinhood Marine Center, a full-service yacht yard with a waterfront park. The dining room overlooks water and, yes, an osprey nest on the day marker. Entrées include fried

MIDCOAST AND THE ISLANDS

seafood, grilled filet mignon, and oven-roasted lamb rack. $14.95–21.95.

J. R. Maxwell's (207-443-2014), 122 Front St., Bath. Open year-round for lunch and dinner daily. Located in the middle of the shopping district, in a renovated 1840s building that was originally a hotel. Burgers, salads, crêpes, and seafood sandwiches; also dinner steaks, prime rib, chicken, fresh seafood. Children's menu. Downstairs is the Boat Builder's Pub with pool tables and darts. Entrées $6.95–18.95.

Kennebec Tavern and Marina (207-442-9636), 119 Commercial St., Bath. Open for lunch and dinner daily; Sun. brunch 11–2. A casual, relaxing barn of a place with booths and tables overlooking the Kennebec River, and a seasonal terrace. The choice of seafood, chicken, steak, and combos is wide. It can hit the spot for us after a long day of driving. Dinner entrées $11.95–18.95.

EATING OUT

In Bath
Beale Street Barbeque and Grill (207-442-9514; www.maine bbq.com), 215 Water St. Open for lunch and dinner. No reservations.

STARLIGHT CAFE

Nancy English

Brothers Mark, Mike, and Patrick Quigg have built their slow-cooking pits and are delivering the real Tennessee (where Mark lived for 6 years) goods: pulled pork, ribs, sausage, a big Reuben; also nightly specials (frequently fish) to round out the menu.

Starlight Café (207-443-3005), 15 Lambard St. Open weekdays. This bright, funky place is a real find. Large, sandwiches (create your own by picking bread, meat, cheese, and veggies) and daily specials. Crowded at lunchtime, but worth a wait.

Note: If you are heading for the **Maine Maritime Museum** (see *To See*), plan on lunching at its café on the deck: good food and water views.

On the Popham Peninsula
Spinney's Restaurant and Guesthouse (207-389-1122), at the end of Rt. 209, Popham Beach. Open weekends in Apr. and daily May–Oct. for lunch and dinner. Our kind of beach restaurant: a pleasant atmosphere, basic chowder-and-a-sandwich menu, and (if you're lucky) a table on the glassed-in porch with water views. Glen and Diane Theal specialize in fresh fish and seafood, fried, steamed, and broiled; good lobster and crabmeat rolls. Fully licensed.

Water's Edge (207-389-1803), Black's Landing Rd., Sebasco Estates. Open daily 11–9. Located on a commercial fishing wharf, another classic place to eat steamed lobster, but the full menu also includes fettuccine Alfredo, New York sirloin, and dinner salads. Indoor as well as outdoor seating; beer and wine served.

*& **Lobster House** (207-389-1596), 395 Small Point Rd. (follow Rt. 1 to Rt. 209, then Rt. 209 to Rt. 216).

Open summer season only, Tue.–Sat. 5–9 PM, Sun. noon–8:30 PM. Reserve. Mrs. Pye's is a classic lobster place specializing in seafood dinners and homemade pastry; it's down near Small Point, surrounded by salt marsh. Beer and wine are served.

On the Georgetown Peninsula

🍴 **Mama D's** (207-371-2722), Moore's Turnpike Rd., Five Islands, marked from Rt. 127 at the Old Schoolhouse. Open daily 11:30–8 in summer, weekends from Memorial Day and again Labor Day–Columbus Day. The view, reasonably (less than the competition) priced lobster and steamers, great chowder, homemade onion rings, and pies are the big attractions, plus a sense of discovery. BYOB.

🍴 **Five Islands Lobster and Grill** (207-371-2990), Georgetown. Thirteen miles south of Rt. 1 at the end of Rt. 127 on Five Islands wharf. Open seasonally 11–8, specializing in steamed lobsters and clams, lobster rolls, fried clams, shrimp-fried seafood, and their "somewhat famous" crabcake sandwich. No credit cards.

✱ Entertainment

🍴 **Chocolate Church Arts Center** (207-442-8455), 804 Washington St., Bath. Year-round presentations include plays, concerts, and a wide variety of guest artists. Special children's plays and other entertainment are included on the schedule. There is also a very nice gallery in a separate building beside the Chocolate Church.

✱ Selective Shopping

ANTIQUES Along **Front Street** in Bath there are a number of interesting antiques shops. Of special note: **Brick Store Antiques** (207-443-

2790), 143 Front St., and **Front Street Antiques and Books** (207-443-8098), 190–192 Front St., a multiple-dealer shop.

ART AND ARTISANS **Midcoast REACH** (207-798-6964; www.baaca .org), 108 Maine St., Brunswick, is a good source of information on the arts in the Bath region.

Georgetown Pottery (207-371-2801; www.georgetownpottery.com), Rt. 127, Georgetown (some 9 miles south of Rt. 1). Open daily 8:30–5, later in summer. Jeff Peters produces an extensive selection of dishes, mugs, and other practical pottery pieces, including hummingbird feeders and soap dishes.

West Island Gallery (207-371-9090), 37 Bay Point Rd., Georgetown. Open May–Sep., Thu.–Sun. noon–6, plus weekends until Christmas. An outstanding gallery with a variety of well-chosen quality crafts as well as changing art exhibits.

Saltbox Pottery (207-443-5586; www.saltboxpottery.com), 4 Shaw Rd., Woolwich. Open daily year-round, 10–5:30. Traditional-style stoneware.

BOOKSTORE **Bath Book Shop** (207-443-9338), 96 Front St., Bath. Finally, a good independent bookstore located in Bath's downtown district.

FARMER'S MARKET **Waterfront Park**, Bath, May–Nov., Thu. and Sat. 8:30–12:30. Phone: 207-586-5067.

FLEA MARKET **Montsweag Flea Market** (207-443-2809), Rt. 1, Woolwich. A field filled with tables weighted down by every sort of collectible and curiosity you could imagine. Wednesday is Antique Day, and on weekends look for collectibles, crafts, and good junk.

SPECIAL SHOPS Bath's **Front Street** is lined with mid-19th-century redbrick buildings. Among the clothing and specialty shops, don't overlook **Reny's** (46 Front St.), one in a chain of Maine department stores that are good for genuine bargains. **Springer's Jewelers** (76 Front St.) is a vintage emporium with mosaic floors, chandeliers, and ornate glass sales cases.

Woodbutcher Tools (207-442-7938), 873 Rt. 1, Woolwich. The Shelter Institute (see *Special Learning Programs*) maintains this woodworker's discovery, specializing in hard-to-find woodworking tools.

North Creek Farm (207-389-1341), 24 Sebasco Rd. (junction of Rts. 217 and 209). Open year-round, 9–6:30. Suzy Verrier and Kai Jacob grow and sell flowers and herbs along with wine, baked goods, and gourmet and gift items; they also operate a small snack bar, encouraging patrons to picnic in their extensive perennial garden.

Five Islands Farm, Rt. 127, Five Islands. Heidi Klingelhofer's small, shingled emporium overflows with flowers and is a seasonal trove of Maine cheeses, wines, specialty foods, and lavender lemonade.

Native Arts (207-442-8399), Rt. 1, Woolwich. Open 10–6 daily, year-round. Native American art and craftwork from throughout the country.

✳ Special Events

June: **Bath House and Garden Tour**, sponsored by Sagadahoc Preservation, Inc. (207-443-2174; www.sagadahocpreservation.org).

❧ *Three days surrounding the Fourth of July:* **Bath Heritage Days**—a grand celebration with an old-time parade of antique cars, marching bands, clowns, guided tours of the historic district, crafts sales, art shows, musical entertainment in two parks, a triathlon, strawberry shortcake festival, carnival, train, and Fireman's Follies featuring bed races, bucket relays, and demonstrations of equipment and firefighting techniques. **Fireworks** over the Kennebec.

Second Saturday in July: **Popham Circle Fair** at the Popham Chapel features the sale of bird feeders (shaped like the chapel) that residents make all year; profits keep the chapel going.

July–August: Wednesday-evening concerts by the **Bath Municipal Band**, Library Park.

August: **Annual Antique Show and Sale**.

December: **Old-Fashioned Christmas** (*all month*), with competitions and special events.

WISCASSET AREA

Sea captains' mansions and mid-19th-century commercial buildings line Rt. 1 in this historic village—and on July and August weekends motorists have plenty of time to study them as they inch along. The wide new bridge across the Sheepscot River here was to have eased the traffic snarl, but Wiscasset is the first village through which cars heading up and down Rt. 1 must all file, stopping at pedestrian crossings.

It's an obvious place to stop. The places to eat are varied and good, antiques stores abound, and the historic buildings are worth visiting.

Still the shire town of Lincoln County, Wiscasset is only half as populous as it was in its shipping heyday—which, judging from the town's clapboard mansions, began after the Revolution and ended around the time of the Civil War. Lincoln County Courthouse, built in 1824 on the town common, is the oldest functioning courthouse in New England.

From Wiscasset, Rt. 27 runs northwest to meet the Kennebec River, Rt. 218 veers northeast paralleling the Sheepscot River, and Rt. 144 heads south down the spine of the quiet Westport Island to the Squire Tarbox Inn.

GUIDANCE Damariscotta Region Chamber of Commerce (207-563-8340; www.damariscottaregion.com) and **Southern Midcoast Maine Chamber** (207-725-8797) cover this area. See "Damariscotta" for details.

GETTING THERE *By bus:* **Concord Trailways** (1-800-639-3317; www.concord trailways.com) stops twice daily. For transfers from Portland's Jetport, see Mid-Coast Limo under "Bath Area."

By car: Note the shortcut around traffic northbound; turn right on Lee St., continue to Fore St. and Water St., and either park or continue north (right) on Rt. 1.

PARKING Parking is surprisingly easy. You can always find a slot in the parking lot or along Water St.

PUBLIC RESTROOMS Restrooms are in the **Waterfront Park**, corner of Water and Fore Sts. *Note:* This is also a great spot for a picnic.

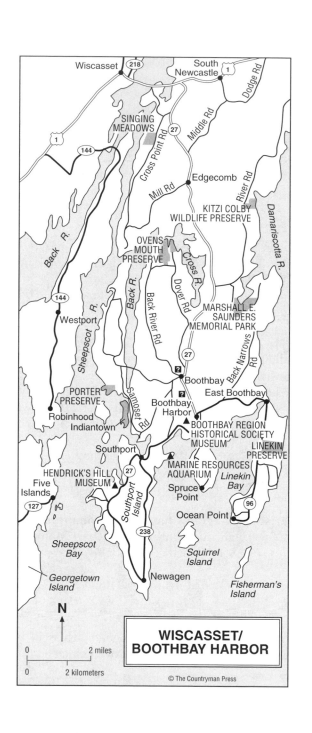

WISCASSET/
BOOTHBAY HARBOR

© The Countryman Press

In Wiscasset Village

Musical Wonder House (207-882-7163 or 1-800-336-3725; www.musical wonderhouse.com), 18 High St. Open daily Memorial Day–Labor Day, 10–5; through Oct., 1–3. Tours of exhibits throughout the ground floor are $15 per adult, $10 per child for a 1¼-hour tour; it's $8 per adult ($6 per child) for a half-hour tour; $30, three-hour tours of the entire house are by reservation only. No admission for the gift shop. A truly intriguing collection covering two centuries of musical history. Some 2,000 music boxes, reed organs, pump organs, Victrolas, and other musical machines displayed in a fine 1852 sea captain's mansion. An 1850s Swiss shadow box simulates Dutch windmills and sailboats; a bust of a Saint Bernard dog and entire symphonies seem contained in these works of art. Visitors are usually guided by Danilo Konvalinka, who has amassed this collection over almost 50 years.

Nickels-Sortwell House (207-882-6218), 121 Main St. (Rt. 1). Open June 1–Oct. 15, Fri.–Sun. 11–4. $5 adults, $4 seniors, $2.50 ages 12 and under. This classic Federal-era mansion in the middle of town was built by a shipowner and trader. After he lost his fortune, the house became a hotel for many years. In 1895 a Cambridge, Massachusetts, mayor purchased the property; some of the furnishings date to that time. It's now maintained by Historic New England.

Castle Tucker (603-436-3205), Lee and High Sts. Same hours, ownership, and prices as Nickels-Sortwell House. Castle Tucker was built in 1807 by Judge Silas Lee, who overextended his resources to present his wife with this romantic house. After his death it fell into the hands of his neighbors, to whom it had been heavily mortgaged, and passed through several owners until it was acquired in 1858 by Captain Richard Holbrook Tucker, whose descendants owned the house until 1997. Highlights include a freestanding elliptical staircase, Victorian furnishings, and original wallpapers.

Old Lincoln County Jail and Museum (207-882-6817, www .lincolncountyhistory.org), 133 Federal St. (Rt. 218). Open July and Aug., Tue.–Sat. 10–4. In June and Sep., open Sat. 10–4. $4 per adult, $2 per child. The museum consists of a chilling 1811 jail (in use until 1930) with damp, thick granite walls (some bearing interesting 19th-century graffiti), window bars, and heavy metal doors. The jailer's house (in use until 1953) displays tools and changing exhibits.

NICKELS-SORTWELL HOUSE

Kim Grant

In Dresden

Pownalborough Court House (207-882-6817), Rt. 128. Open July–Labor Day, Tue.–Sat. 10–4. In June and Sep., Sat. 10–4. $4 adults, $2 children. Worth the drive. Maine's only surviving pre–Revolutionary War courthouse, this striking three-story building, which includes living quarters upstairs for the judge, gives a sense of this countryside along the Kennebec in 1761, when it was built to serve as an outpost tavern as well as a courtroom. The courthouse is on the second floor, and the third floor is a museum of rural life. Bring a picnic (there are tables). Special events include a mustering of the militia and wreath-laying ceremonies on Memorial Day, and a cider pressing in October. From Wiscasset take Rt. 27 north for 8 miles to Dresden Mills, then Rt. 127 south for 3.7 miles to Rt. 197 and on to Rt. 128, where you head north for 1.3 miles.

In Edgecomb

Fort Edgecomb State Memorial (207-882-7777); the turnoff from Rt. 1 is just across the Sheepscot River. The fort is open May 30–Labor Day, daily 9–6. Nominal donation. This 27-foot, two-story octagonal blockhouse (built in 1808) overlooks a narrow passage of the Sheepscot River. For the same reasons that it was an ideal site for a fort, it is today an ideal picnic site, and tables are provided.

FOR FAMILIES *Morris Farm* (207-882-4080), Rt. 27, Wiscasset. A community working farm, open to the public during daylight hours for walking, hiking, and picnicking, with rolling pastures, forest trails, a pond, a waterfall, and streams. Also includes an education center offering a day camp for children, farm tours, various workshops throughout the year.

Sheepscot Village, **Head Tide Village**, and the **Wiscasset, Waterville, & Farmington Railway Museum** (207-882-4193; www.wwfry.org), Sheepscot Station, Alna. The museum is open Sat. 9–5 year-round, Sun. 10–5 from Memorial Day through the Columbus Day weekend. Trains run mid-Apr.–mid-Oct., every hour 10–4. Volunteers preserve the history of this 2-foot narrow-gauge railroad. The museum's pride is an 1891 2-footer locomotive, billed as the oldest in the United States. Volunteers have built replicas of the engine house/shop, original station, and freight shed, now housing the gift shop and museum. Half a mile of track has been laid. Trains are usually pulled by a diesel locomotive, but on special occasions a vintage-1904 steam engine is used. **Sheepscot Village** itself is a picturesque gathering of early-19th-century buildings. It's a few miles north of Wiscasset, just off Rt. 218. At the Alna Fire Station turn right and drive 1.2 miles to the parking lot for the 32-acre **Bass Falls Preserve**, with a mile-long trail down to the river. It's maintained by the Sheepscot Valley Conservation Associ-

POWNALBOROUGH COURT HOUSE
Christina Tree

another quiet cluster of old homes around the Old Head Tide Church (1858). Note the swimming hole beneath the milldam.

✳ To Do

Ledgewood Riding Stables (207-882-6346), Bradford Rd., Wiscasset. Trail rides by reservation. Minimum age 8, geared to riders with some experience, wooded trails.

Wiscasset Trading Post (207-882-9645), Rt. 1, south of Wiscasset Village, rents canoes and kayaks and stocks a large line of canoe and kayak equipment for sale.

✳ Green Space

Sunken Garden, Main St., Wiscasset. Down a few steps, easy to miss, but a wonderful little garden surrounded by a stone wall. Planted by the Sortwell family in the foundation of an old inn, the property was donated to the town in 1959. Quiet and peaceful, with the exception of passing Rt. 1 traffic sounds, this is a pretty place to take a break from browsing.

Sherman Lake Rest Area, Rt. 1 between Edgecomb and Newcastle. On a fine day consider picking up a picnic in Wiscasset and stopping at this region's most scenic Rt. 1 rest area.

✳ Lodging

INN Squire Tarbox Inn (207-882-7693 or 1-800-818-0026; www.squire tarboxinn.com), 1181 Main Rd. (Rt. 144; turn off Rt. 1 onto Rt. 144 just south of Wiscasset), Westport 04578. Open mid-May–late Oct. The inn, located more than 8 miles down a winding country road from Rt. 1, is one of the quietest country locations we have found on the coast. The handsome Federal-style farmhouse (begun in 1763, completed in 1825) holds 11 guest rooms and a common room for cribbage and music. The innkeepers, Swiss chef Mario De Pietro and his wife, Roni, perpetuate the inn's reputation for food and hospitality. Resident animals include goats and laying hens. Four large, formally furnished guest rooms are in the house, while seven more country-style rooms are in the 1820s convert-ed barn. All have a private bath. A five-course dinner (see *Dining Out*) is served. July–Oct., $125–190 per couple B&B; off-season doubles $95–167 per couple.

BED & BREAKFASTS ⑤ Marston House (207-882-6010 or 1-800-852-4137; www.marstonhouse.com), Main St., P.O. Box 517, Wiscasset 04578. Open May–Oct. The front of the house is an antiques shop specializing in textiles and painted furnishings. In the carriage house behind this build-ing—well away from the Rt. 1 traffic noise—are two exceptional rooms, each with private entrance, working fireplace, and private bath. Breakfast is served in the beautiful gardens or in your room and features fresh fruit, yogurt, home-baked muffins, and fresh orange juice. $90 double.

&. **Snow Squall** (207-882-6892 or 1-800-775-7245; www.maine.com/snowsquall), corner of Bradford Rd. and Rt. 1, Wiscasset 04578. Open May–Oct. and by special reservation off-season. Anne and Steve Kornacki offer elegant accommodations in this 1850s house named for a clipper ship. The four guest rooms in the main house, each named for a Maine clipper, have a private bath, king or queen bed, and phone. Each of the two suites in the Carriage House has two bedrooms (one and a half baths) and a private entrance. $100–150 for rooms and $140–220 for suites, depending on the number of guests. Full breakfast included. Less off-season.

Cod Cove Farm B&B (207-882-4299 or 1-800-293-7718; www.codcovefarm.com), 117 Boothbay Rd. (Rt. 27 south), P.O. Box 94, Edgecomb 04556. Open mid-Feb.–late Dec. Four themed rooms, two with private bath. Our favorite is Adirondack, with twig furniture and a bed made of birch. $95–140 includes a full breakfast.

✳ Where to Eat

DINING OUT **Squire Tarbox Inn** (207-882-7693 or 1-800-818-0626; www.squiretarboxinn.com), 1181 Main Rd. (Rt. 144; turn off Rt. 1 just south of Wiscasset), Westport (also see *Lodging*). Open mid-Apr.–Dec., dinner by reservation only, 6–8:30. Dinner is served in an 18th-century former summer kitchen with a large colonial fireplace and ceiling timbers that were once part of a ship. Goat cheese is set out at 5:30 in the common rooms. Swiss chef Mario De Pietro could start you off with Scandinavian dill-cured salmon, then serve entrées like rack of lamb roasted with rosemary served with Swiss-style

roesti potatoes, or salmon in a crust of tender pastry. Fresh strawberries (served with double cream) along with salad greens and many vegetables come from the inn's gardens. Prix fixe $29.50–39.50, depending on the entrée, includes soup and dessert. A 15 percent gratuity is added.

🍴 &. **Le Garage** (207-882-5409; www.legarageme.com), Water St., Wiscasset. Open daily in summer for lunch and dinner. Closed Jan. and Mon. off-season. A 1920s-era garage, now a good restaurant with a glassed-in porch overlooking the Sheepscot River (when you make reservations, request a table on the porch). The menu features plenty of seafood choices, steaks, and vegetarian meals. Specialties include traditional creamed finnan haddie, charbroiled native lamb, and chicken pie. Entrées are $9.95–25.45. "Light suppers" are also available from $9.50, giving you the option of smaller portions of many menu selections.

EATING OUT ✧ **Sarah's** (207-882-7504; www.sarahscafe.com), Main and Water Sts., Wiscasset. Open daily for lunch and dinner, with an outdoor deck for summer dining. Everything is prepared from scratch, and the extensive menu includes good pizza (try the Greek pizza with extra garlic), sandwiches in pita pockets or baked in dough, vegetarian dishes, Mexican fare, and lobster 12 different ways. Well known for their soup and bread bar.

The Sea Basket (207-882-6581 or 1-800-658-1883), Rt. 1, south of Wiscasset. Open 11–8; closed Tue. Call for hours. The Belanger family has owned and operated this cheerful diner for 20 years, keeping it shipshape and humming. "Famous" lobster stew is also sold frozen and shipped all over the country. Other seafood choices include lobster rolls and sea scallops. Bring your own beer or wine.

Treats (207-882-6192; www.treats ofmaine.com), 80 Main St., Wiscasset. Open daily year-round except major holidays. The most delicious prepared foods, and everything to go with them. Soups and salads, fine foods and baked goods, a wide selection of wines and of farmstead cheeses.

Sprague's Lobster (207-882-7814), Water St., Wiscasset. Open seasonally. Picnic tables on a pier beside the river are a great place to sample the fresh, bargain-priced lobsters with all the fixings, or crab rolls and road-food staples. A better bet for everything than Red's.

✔ **Red's Eats**, Water St., just before the bridge, Wiscasset. Open Apr.– Sep. until 2 AM on Fri. and Sat., until 11 weeknights, and noon–6 on Sun. Al Gagnon has operated this classic hot-dog stand since 1977. Tables on the sidewalk and behind, overlooking the river. Too many write-ups have, however, raised prices and reduced portions. No complaints about the hot dogs.

✳ Selective Shopping

ANTIQUES SHOPS Antiques are everywhere in Wiscasset. On and just off Water Street, in or attached to attractive old homes, are more than 20 shops by our count. Pick up a map (available in most shops) and browse the day away; many specialize in nautical pieces and country primitives.

Avalon Antiques Market (207-882-4029), Rt. 1, 2 miles south of Wiscasset Village, open daily 9–7, represents more than 100 dealers.

ART GALLERIES **Maine Art Gallery** (207-882-7511), Warren St. (in the old 1807 academy), Wiscasset. A historic schoolhouse with upper and lower galleries that house exhibits of Maine artists, including Andrew Wyeth, William Zorach, Dahlov Ipcar, and others.

Wiscasset Bay Gallery (207-882-7682; www.wiscassetbaygallery.com), Water St., Wiscasset. Changing exhibits in attractive, spacious exhibit rooms. Specializes in 19th- and 20th-century Maine and New England marine and landscape paintings.

OTHER **Sheepscot River Pottery** (pastel, floral designs), Rt. 1 just north of Wiscasset in Edgecomb, home base for one of Maine's major potteries.

Wiscasset Old General Store (207-882-6622), 49 Water St. Dating in part to 1797, a combination hardware and gift store, good browsing.

FARM **Winters Gone Farm** (207-882-9191 or 1-800-645-0188; winters gone.com), 145 Alna Rd. (Rt. 218), Wiscasset. An alpaca farm with nature trails and picnic areas, a store selling sweaters, scarves, jackets, teddy bears, toys, and more.

SPRAGUE'S LOBSTER

Nancy English

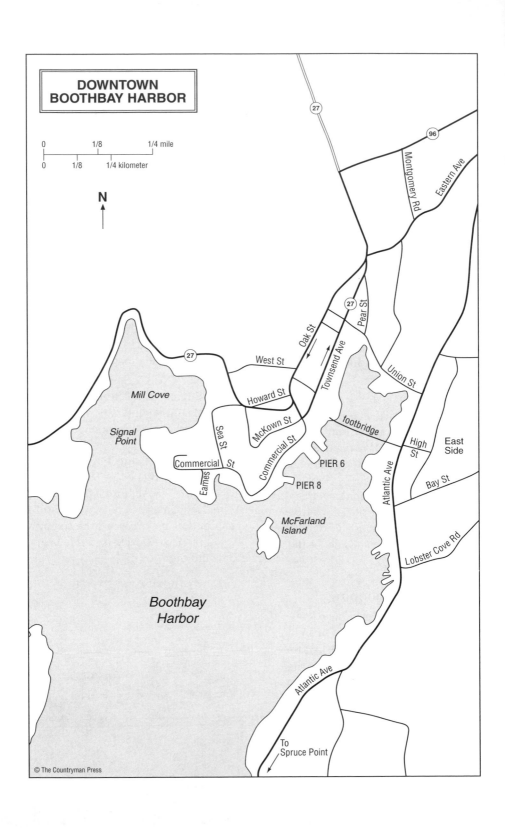

DOWNTOWN
BOOTHBAY HARBOR

0   1/8   1/4 mile
0   1/8   1/4 kilometer

N

27

96

Montgomery Rd

Eastern Ave

27

Pear St

Oak St

West St

Townsend Ave

Union St

Mill Cove

Howard St

Signal
Point

McKown St

Sea St

footbridge

High
St

East
Side

Commercial   St

Commercial St

PIER 6

Eames

PIER 8

Atlantic Ave

Bay St

McFarland
Island

Lobster Cove Rd

Boothbay
Harbor

Atlantic Ave

To
Spruce Point

© The Countryman Press

BOOTHBAY HARBOR REGION

The water surrounding the village of Boothbay Harbor brings with it more than just a view. You must cross it—via a footbridge—to get from one side of town to the other, and you can explore it on a wide choice of excursion boats and in sea kayaks. It is obvious from the very lay of this old fishing village that its people have always gotten around on foot or in boats. Though parking has increased in recent years, cars don't have room to pass each other, and still feel like an obvious intrusion. In the peninsula's other coastal villages, Southport and East Boothbay, roads are walled by pines, permitting only occasional glimpses of water, and offer little or no shoulder for pedestrians or cyclists.

Boats are what all three of the Boothbays have traditionally been about. Boats are built, repaired, and sold here, and sailing and fishing vessels fill the harbors. Excursions range from an hour-long sail around the outer harbor to a 90-minute crossing (each way) to Monhegan Island. Fishermen can pursue giant tuna, stripers, and blues, and nature lovers can cruise out to see seals, whales, and puffins.

In the middle of summer Boothbay Harbor itself is chockablock full of tourists licking ice cream cones, chewing freshly made taffy and fudge, browsing in shops, looking into art galleries, listening to band concerts on the library lawn, and, of course, eating lobster. You get the feeling it's been like this every summer since the 1870s.

Boothbay Harbor is just a dozen miles south of Rt. 1 as the road (Rt. 27) runs, down the middle of the peninsula. The coastline is, however, a different story, measuring 100 miles as it wanders down the Sheepscot, around Southport Island and up into Boothbay Harbor, out around Spruce Head, around Linekin Bay, out Ocean Point, and back up along the Damariscotta River.

Thanks to the fervor of developers from the 1870s on, this entire coastline is distinguished by the quantity of its summer cottages, many of which can be rented by the week for much less than you might think. Still, thanks to the Boothbay Region Land Trust, there are now also easily accessible waterside preserves with many miles of trail meandering through hundreds of acres of spruce and pine, down to smooth rocks and tidal pools. The area's roads may not allow strolling, but you can find plenty of places to indulge a walking habit in the Linekin Preserve and elsewhere.

It was precisely this landscape that inspired Rachel Carson, who first summered on the peninsula in 1946 and built a cottage on the Sheepscot River in 1953, to write much of *The Edge of the Sea* (1955) and then *Silent Spring* (1962), the book that changed global thinking about human beings' relation to basic laws of nature.

GUIDANCE **Boothbay Harbor Region Chamber of Commerce** (207-633-2353 or 1-800-266-8422; www.boothbayharbor.com), Rt. 27, P.O. Box 356, Boothbay Harbor 04538. Open year-round. A satellite information booth near the **Cod Cove Inn** (207-882-5539), junction of Rts. 1 and 27, is open mid-May–Oct., weekends in fringe times, daily in high season. This user-friendly, helpful chamber publishes an annual guide, maintains a Rt. 27 office stocked with brochures, keeps detailed books of cottage listings and photos, and tracks availability for cottages weekly and for lodgings daily. They also publish the walking map.

The Boothbay Information Center (207-633-4743), Rt. 27, Boothbay. Open daily Memorial Day–Columbus Day. An unusually friendly walk-in center that does its best to help people without reservations find places to stay. It keeps an illustrated scrapbook of options, also a cottage rental list.

Note: You can use the above numbers to find out who has current vacancies.

GETTING THERE *By air or bus:* Private planes can fly into the Wiscasset Airport. If you fly into the Portland International Jetport, several companies offer van service to the Boothbays: **Bath-Wiscasset Taxi** (207-443-4009; cell phone, 207-592-5008); and **Platinum Plus Taxi or Harbor Tour and Shuttle** (207-443-

BOOTHBAY HARBOR

Kim Grant

9166). These companies can also pick you up at the nearest Concord Trailways bus stop (in Wiscasset, 14 miles away). **D&P Associated Limousine Services** (207-878-6757 or 1-800-750-6757), 93 Hennesey Dr., Portland, provides service anywhere in New England, as does **David's Limousine** (207-829-3289; www .maine-limo.com), Lower Methodist Rd., Cumberland, who also goes to New York.

By car: Take I-95 from Portland, getting off at exit 28 (Brunswick) or exit 31 (Topsham). We prefer the Topsham exit, because you miss the commercial stretch of Rt. 1 that leads into Brunswick. Follow signs to Rt. 1 north through Bath and Wiscasset, turning onto Rt. 27 into Boothbay and Boothbay Harbor.

GETTING AROUND A trolley-on-wheels circulates among the Rocktide Inn on the east side of the harbor, the shops on the west, and the Aquarium on Southport Island. Runs every 30 minutes daily, 10–5, mid-June–Labor Day.

PARKING In-town parking has increased substantially in the past few years. We had a little trouble in August, when finding a spot in the center of Boothbay Harbor can mean circling the block a couple of times. Stop on your way into town at one of the information centers and pick up a detailed map to downtown. The biggest public lot is at the municipal building.

WHEN TO COME At least half of Boothbay's B&Bs are staying open year-round now, when the gas fireplaces are likely to be on high. Enjoying the area off-season gives you a glimpse of how the locals like it, along with uncrowded restaurants and a calm pace. But if it's bright warm days you're looking for, or a room by the sea in one of the older inns, summer can't be beat.

✴ To See
🐚 **Boothbay Region Historical Society Museum** (207-633-0820; www.booth bayhistorical.org), 72 Oak St., Boothbay Harbor. Summer hours Wed., Fri., and Sat. 10–4; winter Fri. 10–noon, Sat. 10–2, and by appointment (207-633-3462). This is a friendly museum filled with vintage lobster traps, Native American artifacts, ships' bells and wheels, and genealogical resources.

🐚 **Hendricks Hill Museum** (207-633-1102), 417 Hendricks Hill Rd., Rt. 27, Southport Island. Open July 1–Labor Day, Tue., Thu., and Sat. 11–3. The house looks much as it did in 1810, with a period kitchen, including a beehive oven, and pictures of Southport's grand hotels as well as other village memorabilia, wooden boats, and farm implements. Try to time your visit to coincide with the open hours at the Southport Memorial Library (Tue., Thu., and Sat. 1–4), which has an impressive butterfly collection. Southport lies in the narrow heart of the migratory route of the monarch butterfly.

FOR FAMILIES 🐚 ♿ **Boothbay Railway Village** (207-633-4727; www.railway village.org), Rt. 27 (about 3 miles north of Boothbay Harbor). Open daily 9:30–5, June–Oct. 12; a Ghost Train runs at the end of Oct. $8 adults, $4 ages 3–16. A 2-foot narrow-gauge railway wends its way through a miniature village made up of several restored buildings, including vintage railroad stations, the Boothbay Town Hall (1847), and the Spruce Point chapel (1923). Displays include a general store, a doll museum, and a 1920s-era home with an authentic 1929 GE refrigerator and period furniture. More than 50 antique autos (1907–49) are also on display. Many special events, including a weekend antique auto meet (more than 150 cars) in late July.

🦞 🖊 **Kenneth Stoddard Shell Museum** (207-633-4828), Hardwick Rd., Boothbay Harbor. Features one of the world's largest private collections of seashells, including lobster claws and sand dollars. Open daily May–mid-Sep.; by appointment the rest of the year. Admission free.

🦞 🖊 **Daffy Taffy and Fudge Factory,** the By-Way, Boothbay Harbor (see *Snacks*). If the weather is bad and the kids are restless, take them to watch the sweets being made by huge machines. No charge, unless they work up an appetite.

🦞 🖊 ♿ **Knickerbocker Lake**, Barter's Island Rd., Boothbay (near Knickerkane Island Park). Salt water too cold for the little ones? Head to this lovely freshwater lake for a dip.

🖊 **The By-Way**. Don't miss Boothbay Harbor's old-fashioned harborside boardwalk area. Walk from the By-Way down to the footbridge across the harbor.

✳ To Do

BICYCLING Tidal Transit Co. (207-633-7140), by the footbridge, Boothbay Harbor, rents mountain bikes in-season. Our favorite bike route begins at Boothbay Village and follows lightly trafficked Barter's Island Rd., past Knickerbocker Lake and Knickerkane Island Park to Hodgdon Island, and then on to Barter's Island and the Porter Preserve.

BOAT EXCURSIONS 🖊 **Balmy Days Cruises** (207-633-2284 or 1-800-298-2284; www.balmydayscruises.com), Pier 8, Boothbay Harbor. *Balmy Days II* offers sails to Monhegan every morning early June–early Oct. and weekends in shoulder seasons (see "Monhegan"). The crossing takes 90 minutes each way, and you have close to 4 hours on the island (a 30-minute boat ride around the island is also possible on the way back). Bring a picnic and hit the trail. Adults $30, chil-

🖊 **Marine Resources Aquarium** (207-633-9559), McKown Point Rd., West Boothbay Harbor. Open Memorial Day weekend–Sep. 30, daily 10–5. $5 adults, $3 ages 5–18 and over 60; 4 and under free. At this octagonal waterside aquarium, kids and adults alike can view tanks filled with sea creatures found in Maine waters such as striped bass, cod, alewives, and a 17-pound lobster named Louie. Dip your hands into the touch tank and feel the surprisingly smooth skin of a dogfish (a gentle species of shark) and skates. Presentations several times a day in summer, but get there early to ensure a good view.

dren $18. *Novelty* makes one-hour Boothbay Harbor tours all day. Balmy Days also offers mackerel fishing on the *Miss Boothbay* daily in-season, a great idea for families.

💠 **Boothbay Whale Watch** (207-633-3500 or 1-888-942-5363; www.whaleme .com), Fisherman's Wharf, Pier 6, Boothbay Harbor. This company offers guaranteed whale-watches: If you don't see a whale, your next trip is free. They also run Sunday reggae and Thursday classic oldies evening cruises with full bar and galley. In 2005 whale-watches were $32 adults, $20 ages 6–12; children 5 and under are free; call for changes.

💠 **Cap'n Fish Boat Cruises** (207-633-3244 or 1-800-636-3244; www.capnfish motel.com/boattrips), Pier 1 (red ticket booth), Boothbay Harbor. Operates mid-May–mid-Oct. daily. A variety of cruises: whale-watch, puffin, Pemaquid Point Lighthouse, seal-watch, Kennebec River–Bath, and a sunset sail. Coffee, snacks, soft drinks, beer, wine, and cocktails are available on board (don't bring your own). Children under 12 are half price.

Schooner ***Lazy Jack*** (207-633-3444) Pier 7, Boothbay Harbor. Captain Joe Tassi operates May–Oct., offering 2-hour trips, and can accommodate 13 passengers.

BOAT RENTALS **Midcoast Boat Rentals** (207-729-5248), Pier 8, Boothbay Harbor, rents powerboats for a minimum of 1 week.

Charger Charters (day, 207-380-4556; night, 207-882-9309), 80 Commercial St., Boothbay Harbor, and **Finest Kind Wooden Boats** (207-633-5636), West Boothbay, offer both power- and sailboat rentals.

BOWLING 💠 **Romar Bowling Lanes** (207-633-5721), at the By-Way, Boothbay Harbor. Open summer months only. In business since 1929, under the same ownership since 1946, this log-sided pleasure hall with its sandwich bar, pool tables, and video games is a genuine throwback. A great rainy-day haven.

FISHING Several deep-sea-fishing charters are based in Boothbay Harbor. Check with the chamber of commerce. Also see *Boat Rentals*.

The Tackle Shop at the White Anchor (207-633-3788), RR 1, Box 438 (Rt. 27), Boothbay, is one of the largest tackle shops on the Maine coast. Open daily year-round, 9–7. Rod and reel rentals, bait, plus a full line of fishing gear.

Charger Charters (207-882-9309; www.geocities.com/chargercharters/index .html), 80 Commercial St., Boothbay Harbor. The *Charger* runs three fishing trips daily for mackerel, stripers, and bluefish. Also half- and full-day private charter options for cod, cusk, pollack, and shark.

Blackjack Sportfishing & Charters (207-633-6445), Pier 7, next to Whale Park, Boothbay Harbor. Six-passenger 28-foot bass boat for sportfishing. Captain Dan Stevens offers charters for fishing, sightseeing, and transportation.

Redhook Charters (207-633-3807), P.O. Box 45, Boothbay. Leaves from Tugboat Inn Marina. Captain Mark Stover provides tackle for charters, sightseeing, and transportation.

Shark Five Sportsfishing (207-633-5929); Brown's Wharf Inn & Marina, 121 Atlantic Ave., Boothbay Harbor. Captain Barry Gibson has spent more than 36 years at striped bass fishing, tackle provided, in a 24-foot Boston whaler.

Sweet Action Charters (207-633-4741; sweetaction charters.com), Kaler's Crab and Lobster House, 48 Commercial St., Boothbay Harbor. Inshore fishing for mackerel, stripers, and bluefish on a 19-foot Seaway T-top, gear included.

GOLF AND MINI GOLF **Boothbay Region Country Club** (207-633-6085), Country Club Dr. (off Rt. 27), Boothbay. Open spring–Dec. Eighteen holes, restaurant and lounge, carts and clubs for rent, and a driving range.

✤ **Dolphin Mini-Golf** (207-633-4828), off Rt. 27 (turn at the lighthouse), Boothbay. Eighteen holes including lakes stocked with fish and a covered bridge.

HORSEBACK RIDING ✤ **Ledgewood Riding Stables** (207-882-6346), 432 Lowell Town Rd., Rt. 27, Wiscasset, has horses and trails for all levels of expertise. Hourly rates.

RECREATIONAL FACILITY ✤ **Boothbay Region YMCA** (207-633-2855; www.brymca.com), Townsend Ave., Rt. 27 (on your left as you come down the stretch that leads to town). An exceptional facility open to nonmembers (user fee charged) in July and Aug., with special swimming and other programs for children. Worth checking out if you're in the area for a week or more. A wide variety of programs for all ages: tennis, racquetball, gymnastics, aerobics, soccer, swimming in a heated six-lane indoor pool, saunas, and a fieldhouse with a three-lane track.

SAILING Several traditional sailing yachts offer to take passengers out for an hour or two, half a day, or a day. These include the *Tribute*, run by Windborne Cruises (207-882-1020), a classic Block Island 40 that sails from Smugglers Cove Inn in East Boothbay. *Bay Lady* (207-633-2284 or 1-800-298-2284; www.balmy dayscruises.com), Pier 8, Boothbay Harbor. A 13-passenger boat offers 30- and 60-minute excursions, and is part of Balmy Day cruises.

SEA KAYAKING ✤ **Tidal Transit Company** (207-633-7140; www.kayakbooth bay.com), Boothbay Harbor, in the "Chowder House" building by the footbridge, offers guided tours as well as hourly, half-day, and full-day rentals (basic instruction included). Offerings include a lighthouse tour with picnic lunch, 2- to 2½-hour wildlife tours, and sunset tours. They also rent bikes.

Additional kayak companies in the Boothbays are **Salty Kayaks** (207-633-4612; www.graysoceancamping.com) at Gray Homestead Oceanfront Camping on Southport Island (rentals only); and **East Boothbay Kayak Company** (207-633-7411 or 1-866-633-7411; www.eastboothbaykayaks.com) at Ocean Point Marina in East Boothbay.

TENNIS Public tennis courts are located across Rt. 27 from the YMCA, which also has indoor courts.

WALKING **Ocean Point**, at the tip of the East Boothbay peninsula, offers beautiful views of the ocean and several windswept islands, but parking can be tricky. Leave your car in the lot operated by the **Linekin Preserve** or in designated parking areas and walk the point by foot, being mindful of NO TRESPASSING signs.

✳ Green Space

BEACHES ✐ Beaches are all private, but visitors are permitted in a number of spots. Here are four: (1) Follow Rt. 27 toward Southport, across the Townsend Gut Bridge to a circle (white church on your left, monument in the center, general store on your right); turn right and follow Beach Rd. to the beach, which offers roadside parking and calm, shallow water. (2) Right across from the Boothbay Harbor Yacht Club (Rt. 27 south), just beyond the post office and at the far end of the parking lot, is a property owned by the yacht club, which puts out a float by July. There are ropes to swing from on the far side of the inlet, a grassy area in which to run, and a small sandy area beside the water, but the water is too deep for small children. (3) **Barrett Park**, Lobster Cove (turn at the Catholic church, east side of the harbor), is a place to picnic and get wet. (4) **Grimes Cove** has a little beach with rocks to climb at the very tip of Ocean Point, East Boothbay. (Also see **Knickerkane Island Park** under *Nature Preserves*.)

GARDEN **Coastal Maine Botanical Gardens** (207-633-4333), P.O. Box 234, Boothbay. Open dawn to dusk daily. Accessible from Barter's Island Rd. A relatively new public garden, it emphasizes more than 300 native species on 128 acres. The garden is being beautifully planted and improved. The popular Shore Walk includes Fern, Wetlands, and Shoreland Gardens; an Entrance Garden features a growing rhododendron collection; the Fern and Heath Trails focus on mosses, lichens, heaths, and ferns. Admission free until the visitor center opens, scheduled for 2006 as part of a huge expansion that will bring formal gardens and a garden of the five senses, among many other improvements.

NATURE PRESERVES **Boothbay Region Land Trust** (207-633-4818; www .bbrlt.org), 1 Oak St., P.O. Box 183, Boothbay Harbor. Open Mon.–Fri. 9–4. Pick up a brochure and map to the easily accessible properties, here or at the chamber of commerce, showing guided walks and 27 miles of trails. We walked down to the Sheepscot River in the Porter Preserve (19 wooded acres, including a beach) on Barter's Island, accessible by bridge. An osprey peered from its nest atop a marker along a ledge just offshore, and another ledge was so thick with seals that we assumed they were some kind of brown growth— until a dog barked and the entire ledge seemed to heave and rise, then flop and splash off in different directions. We also explored the Ovens

COASTAL MAINE BOTANICAL GARDENS
Nancy English

Mouth Preserve, a narrow passage between the Sheepscot and Back Rivers and a tidal basin. In the mid-1700s this area was settled by families from Dover, New Hampshire. They built ships and cleared pastures. Separating the two peninsulas that constitute this preserve is Ice House Cove, and across it are the remnants of the 1880s dam that once turned it into a freshwater pond. It's fascinating to think of schooners mooring just outside the dam and sailing for the Caribbean with their cargoes of ice. The former pond has reverted to salt marsh and teems with wildlife. The trust has numerous other properties; for a full listing, go to their web site.

Knickerkane Island Park, Barter's Island Rd., Boothbay. Paths lead from the parking lot onto a small island with picnic tables and swimming.

✳ Lodging

The chamber of commerce lists more than 100 lodging places in its region guide, from resorts to B&Bs to campgrounds and cottages. Families should explore the possibilities of the area's many rental cottages. Because the chamber of commerce is open year-round, it's possible to contact the people there in time to reserve well in advance. See *Guidance* for the numbers you can call to check current vacancies in the area.

RESORTS ✍ **Spruce Point Inn Resort & Spa** (207-633-4152 or 1-800-553-0289; www.sprucepointinn.com), 88 Grandview Ave., P.O. Box 237, Boothbay Harbor 04538. Open mid-May–late Oct.; spa open year-round. A full-service resort at the end of a 100-acre wooded peninsula jutting into Boothbay Harbor, the inn offers 9 guest rooms in the main building; 12 lodge rooms, some with cathedral ceilings and hardwood floors; 40 deluxe suites in condo-style structures featuring unusually large bedrooms and marble baths, TVs, woodstoves, and balconies with water views; and 7 cottages, 2 oceanfront, perfect for families. We loved swimming in the cold saltwater pool and warming back up again in the hot tub beside it, both on the edge of the sea. Large living room, TV room and study, recreation room (geared to kids), heated freshwater pool, clay tennis courts, lawn games, fitness center, full-service spa, and private pier. Organized children's programs in July and Aug., and room service is now available for breakfast and dinner. Good food (see *Dining Out*). $165–335 for guest rooms; cottages and condos $395–550. Many packages are available; children free under age 4. A service charge, 10 percent on rooms and 15 percent on cottages, is added for use of amenities.

⊙ ✍ ♿ **Newagen Seaside Inn** (207-633-5242 or 1-800-654-5242; www.newagenseasideinn.com), Rt. 27, Southport Island, Cape Newagen 04576. Open mid-May–mid-Oct. This resort reminds us of a Connecticut mansion in a 1940s Kate Hepburn movie. Clumps of dark green Adirondack chairs are set out on the lawn, with a playground set in sight and the stony coast filling the horizon. The 27 rooms and three suites in the main inn all have private bath; first-floor rooms have private deck. Take a chilly plunge in the bay off the dock, then hightail it to the heated freshwater pool and finish with a soak in the hot tub overlooking the little harbor. Also included in the rates: tennis courts, bicycles, lawn games, rowboats, and the Pine Room, which houses two funky 1940s-era candlepin bowling lanes, pool table, Ping-Pong, and big-screen TV with a large video library. Breakfast is included; boxed lunches and dinner available. Doubles are $130–275, depending on room and season. $25 for additional guests. The three cottages begin at $1,600 per week. Frequent visitors get 1 night free for every 5 they stay.

🐾 ♿ **Ocean Point Inn** (207-633-4200 or 1-800-552-5554; www.oceanpoint inn.com), P.O. Box 409, East Booth-bay 04544. Open Memorial Day–Columbus Day. Owner David Dudley has worked at Ocean Point since 1969, and he bought the inn in 1985—he even met his wife here! He takes obvious pride in the place, outfitting many of the 61 rooms, suites, cottages, and apartments with pretty wallpaper borders (scenes of ducks, early American houses, and the like), king and queen four-posters, and botanical prints. All rooms and cottages have private bath, air-conditioning, cable TV, mini refrigerator, and phone; many have a fireplace, ocean views, and porch. Guests can relax in the heated pool with a hot tub or the Adirondack chairs overlooking the ocean. The inn also offers an oceanfront dining room (see *Dining Out*). $101–203 in-season, breakfast $8.95 per person in-season, complimentary continental breakfast off-season.

INNS AND BED & BREAKFASTS **Five Gables Inn** (207-633-4551 or 1-800-451-5048; www.fivegablesinn.com), 107 Murray Hill Rd. (off Rt. 96), P.O. Box 335, East Boothbay 04544. Open mid-May–Oct. Five Gables combines incredible luxury with unstuffy relaxation, two desirable qualities that don't always go hand in hand. Fifteen of the 16 rooms offer gorgeous views of Linekin Bay; most have queen-sized beds (many with handmade quilts), and 5 have a working fireplace. De and Mike Kennedy have added details such as a mural of a seascape and driftwood and built-in beds and bookshelves crafted by Mike. Try one of the third-floor gable rooms, which are smaller but offer some of the best views of the water. In good weather take a dip off the public access dock across the street. An extensive buffet breakfast, prepared by Mike, a Culinary Institute of America graduate, is included in a $135–200 double. Afternoon tea comes with home-baked goodies and port.

🐾 🐾 ♿ **Topside Inn** (207-633-5404 or 1-877-486-7466; www.topsideinn .com), 60 McKown St., Boothbay Harbor 04538. Open mid-Apr.–Thanksgiving. Brian Lamb and Ed McDermott have redone this inn with a great location at the top of McKown Hill. Some of the 21 rooms

TOPSIDE INN

Nancy English

in the 1876 house and a pair of two-story motel-style annexes have views over the harbor, to the lighthouses and islands, and they all have private bath, TV, and telephone. Room 1 in the Main House has two double beds, handsome decor, and a Victorian love seat in a window alcove. Reasonable rates: $80–155, including a breakfast with fabulous house granola, yogurt, a bowl packed with all kinds of fruit, and a hot entrée as well as muffins, fruit, juice, and coffee.

Hodgdon Island Inn (207-633-7474; www.hodgdonislandinn.com), Barter's Island Rd., Boothbay (mailing address: Box 492, Boothbay 04571). Open year-round. Situated on a quiet road overlooking a cove (and the hand-cranked drawbridge featured in the film *In the Bedroom*), this lovely inn is great for those who want a Maine vacation away from the crowds. Steve and Sherri Matte have polished up these nine air-conditioned rooms with water views in a restored sea captain's house. All have private bath and ceiling fan, and two of the rooms share a porch. The heated swimming pool is set in a gorgeous landscaped garden. Guests can take the full breakfast on the front porch overlooking the Sheepscot River. $105–175 includes breakfast.

🐾 **Welch House** (207-633-3431 or 1-800-279-7313; www.welchhouse.com), 56 McKown St., Boothbay Harbor 04538. Open year-round. Susan Hodder and Michael Feldmann have put their heart and soul into making this place sing. All 14 rooms have private bath, air-conditioning, cable TV and VCR, and telephone, and some include whirlpool tub, fireplace, and a private deck. The Captain's Lady, with its king bed and gas fireplace, looks out on the harbor, as do other rooms. $75–195 includes a full breakfast that might feature lobster Benedict, served on the breathtaking second-floor deck.

🐾 ⚓ **Lawnmere Inn** (207-633-2544 or 1-800-633-7645; www.lawnmere inn.com), Box 505, West Boothbay Harbor 04575 (on Rt. 27 on Southport Island, 2 miles from downtown Boothbay Harbor). Open Memorial Day–mid-Oct. The location is difficult to beat, with broad lawns sloping to the water's edge, lupine and herb gardens, and seal's-eye views of lobster boats and the Sheepscot River. Most of the 11 rooms in the main inn and the 18 rooms (with decks) in the motel wing have water views; there's also a small cottage and the Pine View Guest House. The Lawnmere, built as a summer hotel in the 1890s, has a small, personal feel with lots of attractive common space. There is also a popular restaurant (see *Dining Out*). Small pets are accepted in a few of the motel wing rooms ($20 per night fee). $115–185 in summer; less off-season, includes a fine breakfast. Two-night minimum weekends in July and Aug.

Atlantic Ark Inn (1-800-579-0112; www.atlanticarkinn.com), 62 Atlantic Ave., Boothbay Harbor 04538. Open late May–Oct. Donna Piggot's clean, airy style permeates her pleasant inn, located at a remove from (but accessible by footbridge to) the bustle of the harbor. The five guest rooms and sweet cottage are all decorated with white walls, duvet covers, and drapes. All have private bath; some feature harbor views and private balcony. Our favorite: a third-floor room with a cathedral ceiling, oak floor, Jacuzzi, panoramic view of the harbor, and French doors opening onto a balcony.

Full breakfast is served on formal china, and a cheese plate with whole-grain breads is served in the afternoon on the wraparound porch. $105–185. Two-night stays on weekends.

Linekin Bay Bed & Breakfast (207-633-9900 or 1-800-596-7420; www.linekinbaybb.com), 531 Ocean Point Rd., East Boothbay 04544. Open year-round. A haven overlooking Linekin Bay, this secluded B&B has four charming rooms, all with water views, fireplace, and private bath. Owners Larry Brown, a retired police sergeant, and Marti Booth are friend-ly hosts. The Holbrook Suite, with its wonderful purple bedding, couch, and gas fireplace, looks like it could make a vacation. $130–180 includes a full breakfast, perhaps with cream-cheese-stuffed French toast. Brown also makes a great brownie, served among other sweets in the afternoon. Children 12 and over welcome.

1830 Admiral's Quarters Inn (207-633-2474; www.admiralsquarters inn.com), 71 Commercial St., Booth-bay Harbor 04538. Open year-round. Les and Deb Hallstrom have done a nice job renovating this big old sea captain's house, just steps from the heart of the busy harbor. The six tidy, bright rooms, most two-room suites, have a private bath, phone, cable TV, hair dryer, air-conditioning, fireplace, and deck, with a gull's-eye view of the waterfront. The sitting room is a solarium with that same great view. $165–195 in high season includes full breakfast with desserts like blueberry pie and bread pudding.

🐾 🐈 ✃ ♿ **Smuggler's Cove Inn** (207-633-2800 or 1-800-633-3008), Rt. 96, East Boothbay 04544. Four wood-shingled buildings that resem-ble rectangular ships tacking toward the same buoy. Every one of the 60 units has a view of Linekin Bay, and from a few you can even fish right off the balcony. The decor is simple and clean, second-floor rooms offer cathe-dral ceilings, and pets are allowed in certain rooms. Swim off the sandy beach or in the pool, row one of the inn-owned boats, take a cruise on the Windborne boat, or sail up in your own and use one of the Smuggler's Cove moorings. The 1820 House Restaurant offers breakfast, dinner, and Sunday brunch. $109–229 in-season, less off.

COTTAGES *Note:* Contact the cham-bers of commerce for lists of rental cottages; quality is traditionally high and prices are affordable in the Boothbays. In addition, the locally based **Cottage Connection of Maine** (207-663-6545 or 1-800-823-9501; www.cottageconnection.com) represents dozens of properties. **Boothbay Region Rental Proper-ties** (207-633-5471).

MOTELS 🐾 ✃ ♿ **Ship Ahoy Motel** (207-633-5222; www.shipahoymotel .com), Rt. 238, Southport Island (mailing address: Box 235, Boothbay Harbor 04538). Open late May–mid-Oct. No nonsense lodgings with great views at a sensational price. A family-owned motel with 54 tidy units, all with TV and air-conditioning, many with a private balcony right on the water, others tucked into the granite ledges and pines of the island. Guests who hanker for kitschy 1960s decor are in for a real treat. Amenities include a freshwater pool, coffee shop, and dock on 0.75 mile of waterfront. $79 per couple in high season; up to $49 off-season; breakfast extra.

🦞 🐾 🚣 ♿ **Hillside Acres Cabins and Motel** (207-633-3411; www .gwi.net/~hillside), Adams Pond Rd., P.O. Box 300, Boothbay 04537. Open year-round. Located off Rt. 27, this collection of seven old-fashioned cabins and motel rooms is also great for travelers with special needs: kayakers, guests traveling with children or pets, or anyone looking for great value. The very clean cabins include three efficiency units, and the motel building has four apartments and two B&B rooms. Electric heat, showers, color TVs, swimming pool. Muffins and coffee are served late June–Labor Day. Up to $80 in high season, $59 off-season, 10 percent weekly discount.

♿ **Flagship Inn** (207-633-5094 or 1-800-660-5094; www.boothbaylodging .com), 200 Townsend Ave. (Rte. 27), Boothbay Harbor. Open year-round.

HILLSIDE ACRES CABIN

Nancy English

Right next to the harbor and just redone, this affordable motel has air-conditioning, a swimming pool, and cable TV. $65–99, depending on the season.

Boothbay Harbor has a number of inviting motels, many of them expansive and on the water, but we defer to the Mobil and AAA guides.

CAMPING 🦞 🐾 🚣 ♿ **Gray Homestead Campground** (207-633-4612; www.graysoceancamping.com), 21 Homestead Rd., Southport Island 04576. Open May 1–Columbus Day. You can't beat the location—30 beautiful acres on the east coast of Southport Island. Forty sites for tents and RVs. Stephen Gray's family has been here since 1800. $26–32 per night for RVs, $24–26 for tents.

🐾 🚣 **Little Ponderosa** (207-633-2700; www.littleponderosa.com), 159 Wiscasset Road, Boothbay. Open May 15–Oct. 15. A big, family-oriented place, with 96 shaded sites, 36 on a tidal inlet. Many amenities and diversions. $22 per day for water-only sites in-season.

Shore Hills Campground (207-633-4782; www.shorehills.com), 553 Wiscasset Road, Boothbay. Open May 1–Columbus Day, with 150 sites, some on the waterfront. Amenities and recreation, and the motto "No rig too big." Tent sites $25, full-service RV sites $35 in summer.

✳ Where to Eat

DINING OUT **Lawnmere Inn** (207-633-2544 or 1-800-633-SMILE), Rt. 27, West Boothbay Harbor (just across the bridge). Open for breakfast and dinner daily in-season. Off-season hours vary; call ahead. Reservations appreciated. In a dining room paneled with knotty pine, overlooking a lawn sloping to the sea, we ate savory bruschetta with portobello mushrooms and chèvre. Old-fashioned rolls and banana bread were served with butter; the entrée of seared scallops in red pepper puree was perfect. And when we hankered for a bowl of berries for dessert, our helpful waitress said she'd make one up for us. Entrées $13–29.

🍴 **Andrews' Harborside Restaurant** (207-633-4074), 12 Bridge St., Boothbay Harbor (downtown, next to the municipal parking lot and footbridge). Open for breakfast, lunch, and dinner, daily May–Oct.; closed Sun. afternoon. The chef-owner specializes in creative seafood and traditional New England dishes. Wonderful cinnamon rolls at breakfast, the usual crab rolls ($9.95) and burgers at lunch, Round Top ice cream at the window, and seafood entrées at dinner.

🍴 **Lobsterman's Wharf** (207-633-3443), Rt. 96, East Boothbay (adjacent to a boatyard). Open mid-May–Columbus Day, serving 11:30–9, 10 on weekends. Just far enough off the beaten track to escape crowds, this place is popular with locals. The large menu includes all the usual seafood, lobster stew, and crabcakes, as well as spinach salad, pastas and pizzas, and decent house wine. Entrées from $5.75 for a burger to $23.95 for a fisherman's platter (lobster market price).

🍴 ♿ **Spruce Point Inn** (207-633-4152), east side of the outer harbor at Spruce Point. Open mid-May–late Oct.; reservations advised. Diners have two options: lobster roll or a steak in a relaxed setting at Bogie's Hideaway; or a more formal approach

and oceanfront views in the main dining room, 88 Grandview. Come here to watch the sun set over Boothbay Harbor as you dine on clam chowder and veal Oscar with lobster, asparagus, and béarnaise sauce. The atmosphere is elegant in the big formal room, informal in Bogie's Hideaway, but both are convivial. Entrées $19–29. Full breakfast available to the public.

⊙ 🍴 ♿ **Newagen Seaside Inn** (207-633-5242 or 1-800-654-5242), Rt. 27, Southport Island, Cape Newagen. Open for breakfast and dinner seasonally; occasionally closed for dinner to accommodate special events, closed Tue. at the end of the season. A pleasant, old-fashioned dining room with ocean and sunset views, and splendid grounds to walk off the meal. The Cape Harbor Grill, the name of the inn's dining room, features bourbon sea scallops over farfalle with mushrooms and scallions, and steak *au poivre*. Desserts are homemade, and wonderful. Entrées $18–32; simpler meals like sandwiches are available at dinner in the tavern.

🍴 ♿ **Ocean Point Inn Restaurant** (207-633-4200 or 1-800-552-5554), East Boothbay. Open mid-June–Columbus Day weekend. Serving full breakfast buffet in summer for $8.95, continental breakfast off season, and dinner nightly. Reservations suggested. More than 100 years of tradition in these three informal dining rooms with ocean views. Choices might include roast beef, fresh Maine salmon (prepared four ways), and Black Angus steaks. Children's menu and vegetarian options. $16–29.

Ports of Italy (207-633-1011), 47 Commercial St., Boothbay Harbor. Open for dinner daily, Apr.–mid-Oct. Christina Rossi and her husband,

David Rossi, from Milan, are cooking real Italian meals in this bright upstairs dining room. The seasons are followed respectfully, with strawberries or blueberries appearing in the fabulous zabaglione for dessert. The *risotto alla pescatore* arrived, with its lovely aroma, full of shrimp, scallops, and the best things from the sea ($14). Grilled fish and meat too. Entrées $20–28.

EATING OUT Blue Moon Café (207-633-2349), 54 Commercial St., Boothbay Harbor. Open Mon.–Sat. 7:30 AM–2:30 PM, Sun. 8–2. This little café with a seaside deck makes perfect crabcakes, and the side salad was filled with fresh greens. The chicken quesadilla with big pieces of chicken and melted Boursin and tomato made another great lunch. Order at the counter.

🦞 ✏ **Ebb Tide** (207-633-5692), Commercial St., Boothbay Harbor. Open year-round, 7 AM–9 PM; until 9:30 PM Fri. and Sat., 1 hour earlier off-season. Nothing fancy about this place, but they offer breakfast all day, plus lobster rolls, club sandwiches, fisherman's platters, and reasonably priced specials. Homemade desserts like peach shortcake and frappes are legendary. Old-fashioned, but with air-conditioning, and knotty-pine booths.

✏ ⟁ **Chowder House** (207-633-5761), Granary Way, Boothbay Harbor (beside the municipal parking lot and footbridge). Serving a light menu 11:30–9, mid-June–Labor Day. Situated off a waterfront deck, in an outdoor boat bar, a racing sloop under an awning with 30 bar stools and three tables. The menu includes chowders, crab rolls, Buffalo wings, grilled ribs, crab dip, with a full bar for daiquiris

and other specialty drinks. Desserts will be just two: Tollhouse Squares, a big chocolate chip cookie, and homemade blueberry pie.

89 Baker's Way (207-633-1119), 89 Townsend Ave., Boothbay Harbor. Open 5:30 AM–10 PM daily. Just the place for a doughnut or fried apple dumpling, you think, and then you smell lemongrass cooking and wonder where you are. There are two worlds here: a full bakery, very popular with locals, and a restaurant that serves traditional Vietnamese foods. Available 11 AM–closing, the Vietnamese menu includes appetizers like steamed buns with ground pork, onion, garlic, peas, eggs, and scallions ($2) and fresh spring rolls ($2.50). Try the fabulous stir-fried squid ($8.25), and dine in the back garden by the magnolia.

The Rocktide Inn (207-633-4455 or 1-800-762-8433), 35 Atlantic Ave., Boothbay Harbor. Open daily for breakfast 7:30–9:30 AM, dinner 5:30–9 PM, or drinks(4–11 PM; until 8:30 after Labor Day. Closed Columbus Day–mid-June. Come by boat or car for dinner (jackets required in the formal dining room) or a Rocktide martini in the **On the Rocks Bar**.

MacNab's Premium Teas & Tea Room (207-633-7222 or 1-800-884-7222), Back River Rd. (first driveway on your left), Boothbay. Open Tue.–Sat. 10–5 in July and Aug.; closes at 4 the rest of the year. A Scottish-style tearoom serving cock-a-leekie soup, scone sandwiches, salads, and Highland pie as well as tea and scones; afternoon tea and high tea by reservation, but we arrived without one and were seated without trouble. Great cookies and sweets, and wonderful tea. More than 100 varieties of teas and tisanes sold wholesale and retail.

✪ **Thai Cafe** (207-633-1005), 28 Union St. (on the way to the other side of the harbor), Boothbay Harbor. This Thai restaurant serves fresh Thai food in all its goodness, from spicy tom-yum soup to sautéed basil leaves, mushrooms, and onion in a chili garlic sauce combined with chicken, beef, pork, seafood, or tofu.

✪ **J. H. Hawk Ltd.** (207-633-5589), Boothbay Harbor (right on the dock in the middle of town, upstairs). Liberally decorated with nautical artifacts, with a large menu ranging from basic burgers to pastas and steaks, pan-blackened fish, and Louisiana Cajun–style meat dishes. Ask about live entertainment.

Dunton's Doghouse, Sea St., Boothbay Harbor. Open May–Sep., 11–8. Good, reasonably priced takeout food, including a tasty crabmeat roll.

LOBSTER POUNDS ✪ ♿ **Robinson's Wharf** (207-633-3830), Rt. 27, Southport Island (just across Townsend Gut from West Boothbay Harbor). Open mid-June–Columbus Day for lunch and dinner daily; children's menu. On a sunny day sit on the dock at picnic tables and watch the boats unload their catch. Lobsters and lobster rolls, fried shrimp, clams, scallops, fish chowder, lobster stew, sandwiches, and homemade desserts.

✪ **Boothbay Region Lobstermen's Co-op** (207-633-4900), Atlantic Ave. (east side of the harbor), Boothbay Harbor. Open mid-May–mid-Oct. from 11:30; closing time changes seasonally. Retail store open year-round. This is as inexpensive and authentic a place for lobster as you'll find anywhere along the Maine coast. Boiled lobsters and steamers can be eaten at picnic tables on a scenic outside deck

or indoors. Great crabmeat rolls, fried seafood dinners, hamburgers, and chicken, Samuel Adams beer on tap.

✪ **Clambake at Cabbage Island** (207-633-7200; www.cabbageisland clambakes.com). The *Argo* departs Pier 6 at Fisherman's Wharf daily in summer, twice on Sat. and Sun., carrying passengers to 6-acre Cabbage Island for a traditional clambake with lobsters, clams, corn, and potatoes steamed in seaweed then served on picnic tables. In bad weather a circa-1900 lodge seats up to 100 people by a huge fireplace. About $45 per person including boat ride and tax.

🦞 ✪ ♿ **The Lobster Dock** (207-633-7120; www.thelobsterdock.com), Boothbay Harbor, at the east end of the footbridge. Open 11:29–8:31 early June–early Oct. The lobster rolls are quite simply the best we've ever had, with two choices: hot and dressed with drawn butter, or cold with a dollop of mayo. Both are fantastic. Also lobster and shore dinners, steamed clams, mussels, steaks, and prime rib. Some people love the seafood fra diavolo: shrimp, scallops, mussels, an entire lobster, simmered in a zesty broth with herbs, garlic, bay leaf, tomato, red pepper flakes, and wine ($24.95).

SNACKS ✪ **East Boothbay General Store** (207-633-4503; ebgs@gwi.net), Ocean Point Rd. (Rt. 96), East Boothbay. At this wonderful throwback of a place, both customers and staff stand around talking about somebody's new dock and the recent property tax hike. Great prepared sandwiches and all the usual general-store stuff: sodas, candy, chips, clothing, and souvenirs.

✪ **Down East Ice Cream and Yogurt Factory** (207-633-3016), the By-Way, Boothbay Harbor. Homemade hard ice cream and yogurt, and a make-your-own sundae buffet; all sorts of toppings, including real hot fudge. Open 10:30–10:30 in the height of summer; hours vary off-season.

♪ **Daffy Taffy and Fudge Factory** (207-633-5178), the By-Way, Boothbay Harbor. No credit cards. Watch taffy being pulled, designed, and wrapped— then chew! The fudge is made with fresh cream and butter. Open 10–10 in the height of the season.

Cream teas are served at **MacNab's**; see *Eating Out*.

❋ Entertainment

🍴 ♪ ♿ **Carousel Music Theatre and Supper Club** (207-633-5297; www.carouseldinnertheatre.com), Rt. 27, Boothbay Harbor. Performances mid-May–mid-Sept. Doors open at 6 PM; show begins at 7. Closed Sun. and Mon. A full dinner menu, with entrées like chicken stuffed with sage and cranberry, and cocktails are served by the cast before an evening of Broadway tunes sung cabaret-style begins.

Thursday-evening concerts by the Hallowell Band on the library lawn, Boothbay Harbor. July 4–Labor Day, 8 PM.

Lincoln Arts Festival (207-633-4676). Concerts throughout the summer in varied locations.

❋ Selective Shopping

ART GALLERIES **Gold/Smith Gallery** (207-633-6252), 41 Commercial St., Boothbay Harbor. Shows upstairs have featured underwater photography by Bill Curtsinger and paintings by Italian artist Lorella Ciampelli.

Gleason Fine Art (207-633-6849), 31 Townsend Ave., Boothbay Harbor. Tue.–Sat. 10–5. Museum-quality paintings by Fairfield Porter and James Fitzgerald, as well as sculpture and paintings by some of Maine's best contemporary artists.

Mathias Fine Art (207-633-7404), on Barter's Island, 10 Mathias Dr. in Trevett. Featuring works by Culver, Bettinson, and others.

Ateliers Villard Studios (207-633-3507), 57 Campbell St., Boothbay Harbor. A studio and gallery featuring interesting woodblock prints, wood-carvings, and oil paintings by artists Kim and Philippe Villard.

Decker's Cove Art Studio (207-633-7992), 48 Plummer Rd., Southport. Open June–Sep. Check out Margaret Canepa's lush, colorful paintings of Genoa, Italy, and the Maine coast.

ARTISANS *The Lincoln County Cultural Guide*, available at the chamber, is a great starting point for searching out artisans in the area. Categorical listings make it simple to find what you're looking for.

Boothbay Harbor Artisans (207-633-1152), 11 Granary Way, Boothbay Harbor. A cooperative crafts market featuring a wide variety of gifts, including interesting stained glass, pottery, and gourmet food items.

Boothbay Region Art Foundation (207-633-2703), 7 Townsend Ave., Boothbay Harbor. Open May–late Oct. and also for fine crafts in Dec., Mon.–Sat. 10–5, Sun. 1–5. Three juried shows are held each season, with works selected from submissions by artists of the Boothbay region and Monhegan Island.

Andersen Studio (207-633-4397), Rt. 96 at Andersen Rd., East Boothbay. Acclaimed stoneware animal sculptures of museum quality made here for more than 50 years.

Hasenfus Glass Shop (207-633-6228), 62 Commercial St., Boothbay Harbor. It's called glassblowing, but it's really the heating and bending of glass tubes into all sorts of imaginative ornaments, from sailing ships to tiny animals.

A Silver Lining (207-633-4103), 17 Townsend Ave., Boothbay Harbor. Working metalsmiths. Original sculpture and jewelry in brass, sterling, and gold; an exceptional store.

Edgecomb Potters (207-882-9493 or 1-800-343-5529; www.edgecomb potters.com), Rt. 27, Edgecomb. Open year-round. Maine's largest, most famous pottery store (with branches in Portland and Freeport). A two-tiered gallery filled with deeply colored pots, vases, and table settings, lamps, bowls, cookware, and jewelry. There's also a sculpture garden and a small seconds corner.

Abacus Gallery (207-633-2166; www .abacusgallery.com), 12 McKown St., Boothbay Harbor. We love this shop (which has a sister store in Portland) full of eclectic items such as artsy silver jewelry, whimsical wooden pepper grinders, hand-painted furniture, and gifts.

Gold/Smith Gallery (207-633-6252), 41 Commercial St., Boothbay Harbor. An unusual selection of jewelry in gold and silver.

SPECIAL SHOPS **The Palabra Shop** (207-633-4225; www.palabrashop .com), 53 Commercial St., Boothbay Harbor. Open in summer, Mon.–Sat. 9–9, Sun. 9–7. A warren of 10 rooms offering everything from kitschy souvenirs to valuable antiques. Upstairs (open by appointment) is a Poland Spring Museum with an impressive collection of the Moses bottles this natural springwater used to come in.

Coast and Cottage (207-633-0671), 129 Commercial St. (at Sample's Shipyard), Boothbay Harbor. Home accessories with coastal elegance.

House of Logan (207-633-2293 or 1-800-414-5144), 20 Townsend Ave., Boothbay Harbor. Great men's and women's clothing, with a companion store, **The Village Store and Children's Shop**, selling gifts and furnishings, at 34 Townsend Ave.

Sherman's Book & Stationery Store (1-800-371-8128), 7 Commercial St., Boothbay Harbor. A two-story emporium filled with souvenirs, kitchenware, and games, as well as a full stock of books; specializing in nautical titles.

Rare Books at Vagabonds' House (207-633-7518), 5 Lincoln St., East Boothbay. Pam and Ron Riml stock rare and used books, plus nautical curios and glass art, in this small shop.

Calypso (207-633-3831), 80 Commercial St., Boothbay Harbor. Women's clothing. We love this place because the clothes are all so good looking.

✳ Special Events

April: **Fishermen's Festival**—contests for fishermen and lobstermen, cabaret ball, crowning of the Shrimp Princess, tall-tale contest, boat parade, and blessing of the fleet.

June: **Boothbay in Bloom** celebrates the season with summer merchandise, a fashion show, flower box competitions, special nature tours, pink lady's slipper count, pooches on parade, and more. **Windjammer Days**—parade of windjammers into the harbor, fireworks, band concert, parade of floats and bands up Main St., visiting U.S. Navy and Coast Guard vessels, live music on the waterfront, food, children's activities, and two crafts shows. The big event of summer.

July: **Antique Auto Days**, Boothbay Railway Village, Rt. 27. **Harbor Jazz Weekend**.

September: Held the weekend after Labor Day, the **Shipyard Cup**,

organized by East Boothbay's Hodgdon Yachts and the Boothbay Shipyard, brings some America's Cup boats here; all entrants are a minimum of 70 feet long, with many much longer.

October: **Fall Foliage Festival**— boat cruises to view foliage, as well as food booths, crafts sales, live entertainment, antique auto museum, steam train rides.

Early December: **Harbor Lights Festival**—parade, crafts, holiday shopping.

DAMARISCOTTA/NEWCASTLE AND PEMAQUID AREA

Damariscotta is a small region of large, quiet lakes, long tidal rivers, and almost 100 miles of meandering coastline, all within easy striking distance of Rt. 1. It encompasses the Pemaquid Peninsula communities of Bristol, Pemaquid, New Harbor, and Round Pond as well as communities around Lake Damariscotta, the exceptional twin villages of Damariscotta and Newcastle, and neighboring Waldoboro.

Damariscotta's musical name means "meeting place of the alewives," and in spring spawning alewives can indeed be seen climbing more than 40 feet up a fish ladder from Great Salt Bay to the fresh water in Damariscotta Lake.

The area's first residents must also have found an abundance of oysters here, judging from the shells they heaped over the course of 1,500 years, on opposite banks of the river just below Salt Bay. Native Americans also had a name for the peninsula jutting 10 miles seaward from this spot: *Pemaquid*, meaning "long finger."

Pemaquid loomed large on 16th- and 17th-century maps because its protected inner harbor was the nearest mainland haven for Monhegan, a busy fishing center for European fishermen. It was from these fishermen that the Pemaquid Native American Samoset learned the English with which he welcomed the Pilgrims at Plymouth in 1621. It was also from these fishermen that Plimoth Plantation, the following winter, secured supplies enough to see it through to spring. Pemaquid, however, lacked a Governor William Bradford. Although it is occasionally referred to as this country's first permanent settlement, its historical role remains murky.

The site of Maine's "Lost City" is a mini peninsula bordered by the Pemaquid River and Johns Bay (named for Captain John Smith, who explored here in 1614). At one tip stands a round stone fort. In recent years more than 40,000 artifacts have been unearthed in the adjacent meadow, many of them now on display in a small state-run museum. An old cemetery full of crooked slate headstones completes the scene.

Since the 19th-century steamboats began bringing guests, this region has supported summer inns and cottages. It is especially appealing to families

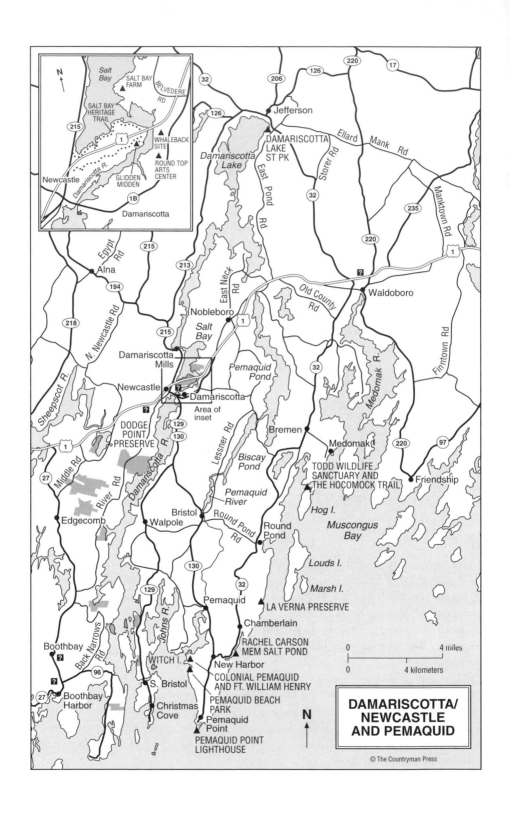

DAMARISCOTTA/ NEWCASTLE AND PEMAQUID

© The Countryman Press

Inset map labels:

Salt Bay
SALT BAY FARM
BELVEDERE RD
SALT BAY HERITAGE TRAIL
215
1
WHALEBACK SITE
ROUND TOP ARTS CENTER
Newcastle
GLIDDEN MIDDEN
1B
Damariscotta
N

Main map labels:

220
17
206
126
32
Jefferson
126
DAMARISCOTTA LAKE ST PK
Ellard
Mank Rd
Manktown Rd
Storer Rd
Damariscotta Lake
East Pond Rd
32
235
220
215
1
Egypt Rd
Alna
194
213
East Neck Rd
Old County Rd
?
Waldoboro
218
N. Newcastle Rd
215
Nobleboro
1
Salt Bay
Finntown Rd
Damariscotta Mills
Pemaquid Pond
32
Medomak R.
Newcastle
?
Damariscotta
Area of inset
?
129
130
DODGE POINT PRESERVE
Lessner Rd
Bremen
Medomak
220
97
Sheepscot R.
River Rd
Damariscotta R.
Biscay Pond
TODD WILDLIFE SANCTUARY AND THE HOCOMOCK TRAIL
Friendship
1
27
Middle Rd
Pemaquid River
Hog I.
Muscongus Bay
Edgecomb
Bristol
Walpole
Round Pond Rd
Round Pond
130
Louds I.
129
Marsh I.
Pemaquid
32
LA VERNA PRESERVE
Boothbay
?
Back Narrows Rd
Johns R.
Chamberlain
RACHEL CARSON MEM SALT POND
WITCH I.
New Harbor
96
?
S. Bristol
COLONIAL PEMAQUID AND FT. WILLIAM HENRY
PEMAQUID BEACH PARK
27
Boothbay Harbor
Christmas Cove
Pemaquid Point
PEMAQUID POINT LIGHTHOUSE
N

0   4 miles
0   4 kilometers

with young children since it offers warm-water lakes, including 15-mile-long Damariscotta, which has the kind of clarity and largely wooded shore that you expect to find much farther inland.

Pemaquid Light is pictured on Maine's new quarter as well as on countless calendars and books because it looks just like a lighthouse should and stands atop dramatic but clamber-friendly rocks. These are composed of varied seams of granite schist and softer volcanic rock, ridged in ways that invite climbing, and pocked with tidal pools that demand stopping.

While there is plenty to see and to do (and to eat), it's all scattered just widely enough to disperse tourist traffic. The villages are small. Damariscotta, with easy off/on access to Rt. 1, is just a few waterside streets built of mellow old local brick; it's the region's compact shopping, dining, and entertainment hub.

GUIDANCE **Damariscotta Region Chamber of Commerce** (207-563-8340; www.damariscottaregion.com), P.O. Box 13, Damariscotta 04543. The chamber office, open year-round, weekdays 8–4, fronts on the parking lot just off Main St. beside the Salt Bay Café. Inquire about cottage rentals.

The Damariscotta Region Information Bureau (207-563-3175), at the eastern end of Main St., junction of Rt. 1B and Vine St., is a walk-in center open seasonally Mon. and Sat. 10–1, Tue.–Fri. 10–4.

GETTING THERE *By bus:* **Concord Trailways** (1-800-639-8080) stops in Damariscotta and Waldoboro en route from Portland to Bangor.

By air: **Mid-Coast Limo** (within Maine, 1-800-834-5500; outside the state, 1-800-937-2424) runs to and from the **Portland International Jetport**. Most inns on the peninsula will pick up guests in Damariscotta, but basically this is the kind of place where you'll want to have a car—or a boat—to get around.

By car: The obvious way is up Rt. 1, but in high season many locals avoid traffic by taking I-295 to exit 43 and cutting cross-country through Richmond and Alna/Head Tide to Damariscotta Mills. Not a straight shot but a pretty ride.

PARKING Parking in Damariscotta is much better than it first looks. Large lots are sequestered behind buildings on both sides of Main Street.

✳ Villages

Damariscotta/Newcastle. The twin villages of Newcastle (population: 1,748, as of the 2000 census) and Damariscotta (2,041 residents) are connected by a bridge and form the commercial center of the region. Damariscotta's Main Street is flanked by fine brick commercial buildings built after the fire of 1845. It's studded with shops and restaurants, and more of the same are tucked down alleyways and around parking lots. Note the towns' two exceptional churches, and check the program of concerts and festivals at the Round Top Center for the Arts on Upper Main Street (see *Entertainment*). Damariscotta Mills, a short drive up Rt. 215 from Newcastle, has some elegant houses and a great picnic spot on Lake Damariscotta.

Waldoboro. An inscription in the cemetery of the Old German Church relates the deceptive way in which landholder General Samuel Waldo lured the town's first German settlers here. The church and much of the town overlook the tidal Medomak (pronounced with the emphasis on *med*) River. Bypassed by Rt. 1, this village includes some architecturally interesting buildings, one of the country's oldest continuously operating five-and-dimes, and a theater presenting films, concerts, and live performances. The Waldoborough Historical Society Museum, Rt. 220, just south of Rt. 1 (open daily 1–4:30 in summer months), includes a restored school, a barn and hall housing plenty of colorful local memorabilia, also a town pound. Free.

Round Pond. The name was obviously inspired by the village's almost circular harbor, said to have been a pirate base. It was once a major shipbuilding spot and then a quarrying center. It remains a working fishing harbor and a dining and shopping destination.

New Harbor. As picturesque a working harbor as any in Maine. Take South Side Road to Back Cove and walk out on the wooden pedestrian bridge for a great harbor view. Note the Samoset Memorial, honoring the Native American who greeted the Pilgrims at Plymouth and also sold land here, creating the first deed executed in New England. The village itself is far bigger than it looks at first. Hanna's Garage looks like a Mobil station but inside is a serious hardware and marine supply store with an upstairs (past the huge moose head) stocked with clothing ranging from T-shirts and Woolrich jackets to clamming gear. E. E. Reilly & Son (established 1828) offers far more than most supermarkets.

South Bristol. Chances are you will be stopped at "The Gut," the narrow channel spanned by the busiest swing bridge in Maine. This is the place to photograph lobster and fishing boats, always in view. Rt. 128 continues south to Christmas Cove, a long-established summer colony.

Jefferson, the village at the head of Damariscotta Lake, also at the junction of Rts. 126, 32, and 206. Old farmhouses, a general store, and summer homes along the river now form the core of the village, and Damariscotta Lake State Beach is on the fringe. Be sure to drive west a couple of miles on Rt. 213 to Bunker Hill, with its old church commanding a superb panorama down the lake.

SOUTH BRISTOL GUT

Christina Tree

＊ To See

HISTORIC SITES ✒ **Colonial Pemaquid State Historic Site** (207-677-2423), Pemaquid (off Rt. 130). Maintained by the state Bureau of Parks and Lands and open daily (with restrooms) Memorial Day–Labor Day, 9–5. Admission ($2 ages 12–64, otherwise free) also gains you entry to Fort William Henry and Old Fort House. In the early 19th century local farmers filled in the cellar holes of the 17th-century settlement that once stood here. Archaeologists have uncovered the foundations of early-17th-century homes, a customhouse, a tavern, and more. The museum displays dioramas of the original 1620s settlement and period tools and pottery, Spanish oil jars, and wampum—all found in the cellar holes just outside. Nearby, the old burial ground, dating to the early 1700s, overlooks the quiet inner harbor.

✍ **Fort William Henry**, off Rt. 130, Pemaquid Harbor. Open daily Memorial Day–Labor Day, 9–5. (For admission, see above.) This round, crenellated stone fort, built in 1907, is one of New England's very few reminders of the French and Indian Wars. It replicates 1692 Fort William Henry, the third fort on this spot, built to be "the most expensive and strongest fortification that has ever been built on American soil," but destroyed by the French a year later. Fort Frederick, built in 1729, was never attacked, but during the American Revolution locals tore it down lest it fall into the hands of the British. The present building contains exhibits on the early explorations of Maine and enshrines the "Rock of Pemaquid," obviously meant as a rival to Plymouth Rock, suggesting that settlers alighted on it long before the Pilgrims ever got to Plymouth. Both the proven and possible history of this place are fascinating: The stockade built on this spot in 1630 is said to have been sacked and burned by pirate Dixie Bull. In 1677 Governor Andros built a wooden redoubt fortified by 50 men, but this was captured by Baron Castine and his Native allies (see "Castine"). The distinctive square clapboard house, dating from the 1770s, contains a library, restored parlor, and changing exhibits. Picnic tables on the grounds command water views

✍ **Pemaquid Point Lighthouse** (207-677-2494 or 207-677-2726), Rt. 130 (at the end), Pemaquid Point. The tower is open 11–5 on weekdays and 10–5 on weekends, closed on rainy days. The point is owned by the town, which charges an entrance fee during summer. The lighthouse, built in 1824 and automated in 1934, is a beauty, looking even more impressive from the rocks below than from up in the parking lot. These rocks offer a wonderfully varied example of geologic upheaval, with tilted strata and igneous intrusions. The tidal pools are exceptional, but take care not to get too close to the dangerous waves. The rocks stretch for half a mile to Kresge Point. The **Fishermen's Museum** in the former lighthouse keeper's home(open Memorial Day–Columbus Day, Mon.–Sat. 10–5 and Sun. 11–5) contains photographs, ships' models, and other artifacts related to the Maine fishing industry and lighthouses. Voluntary donations. The complex also includes the Pemaquid Art Gallery, picnic tables, and public toilets.

PEMAQUID LIGHT

Christina Tree

Shell heaps. These ancient heaps of oyster shells, left by generations of Native Americans at their summer

encampments in what are now the villages of Newcastle and Damariscotta, have become incorporated into the hillsides along the riverbank. The heaps—or middens, as they are called—are accessible via the Great Salt Bay Preserve Heritage Trail (see *Green Space*).

Thompson Ice House (in summer, 207-644-8556), Rt. 129 in South Bristol, 12 miles south of Damariscotta. Open July and Aug., Wed., Fri., and Sat. 1–4. One of the few surviving commercial icehouses in New England, this 150-year-old family business uses traditional tools for cutting ice from an adjacent pond. In summer a slide and video presentation shows how the ice is harvested (in Feb.); tools are also on display.

✍ **Old Rock Schoolhouse**, Bristol (follow signs from Rt. 130 to Rt. 132). Open during summer months, Tue. and Fri. 2–4. Dank and haunting, this 1827 rural stone schoolhouse stands at a long-overgrown crossroads in the woods.

Chapman-Hall House, corner of Main and Church Sts., Damariscotta. Open July–Labor Day daily except Mon., 1–5; $2 adults. Built in 1754, this is the oldest homestead in the region. The house has been restored with its original kitchen, and an herb garden.

HISTORIC CHURCHES This particular part of the Maine coast possesses an unusual number of fine old meetinghouses and churches, all of which are open to the public.

Old German Church (207-832-5100), Rt. 32, Waldoboro. Open daily during July and Aug., 1–4. Built in 1772 with square-benched pews and a wineglass pulpit; note the inscription in the cemetery: "This town was settled in 1748 by Germans who immigrated to this place with the promise and expectation of finding a prosperous city, instead of which they found nothing but wilderness." Bostonian Samuel Waldo—owner of a large tract of land in this area—had not been straight with the 40 German families he brought to settle it. This was the first Lutheran church in Maine; it's maintained by the German Protestant Society. You may recognize this as the setting of one of Andrew Wyeth's most famous Helga paintings.

St. Patrick's Catholic Church (207-563-6038), Academy Rd., Newcastle (Rt. 215 north of Damariscotta Mills). Open year-round daily, to sunset. This is the oldest surviving Catholic church (1808) in New England. It's an unusual building: brick construction, very narrow, and graced with a Paul Revere bell. The pews and stained glass date to 1896, and there's an old graveyard out back. Mass is frequently said in Latin.

St. Andrew's Episcopal Church (207-563-3533), Glidden St., Newcastle. A charming half-timbered building on the bank of the Damariscotta River. Set among gardens and trees, it was the first commission in this country for Henry Vaughan, the English architect who went on to design the National Cathedral in Washington, DC.

Old Walpole Meeting House (207-563-5318), Rt. 129, South Bristol. Open during July and Aug., Sun. for 3 PM services, and by appointment. A 1772 meetinghouse with box pews and a pulpit with a sounding board.

Harrington Meeting House, Rt. 130, Pemaquid. Open during July and Aug., Mon., Wed., Fri., and Sat. 2–4:30. Donations accepted. The 1772 building has been restored and serves as a museum of Old Bristol. A nondenominational service is held here once a year, usually on the third Sunday in August.

OTHER Skidompha Library (207-563-5513; www.skidompha.org), 184 Main St., Damariscotta. Open except Sun. and Mon. from 9 AM; until 8 PM Thu. and noon on Sat., otherwise until 5 PM. This stunning library forms the heart of town. Note the children's wing, named for the late Barbara Cooncy (Damariscotta resident and noted children's-book illustrator and author) and the scene of many programs geared to visitors as well as regulars. There are also frequent authors' nights and an art auction in early August. Public computer available.

SCENIC DRIVES From Newcastle, Rt. 215 winds along **Damariscotta Lake** to Damariscotta Mills; continue along the lake and through farm country on Rt. 213 (note the scenic pullout across from the Bunker Hill Church, with a view down the lake) to Jefferson for a swim at **Damariscotta Lake State Park**.

The turn off Rt. 215 onto 194 above Damariscotta Mills brings you to the picturesque villages of **Alna** and **Head Tide** (see "Wiscasset Area"). Cross the bridge at Head Tide. Turn south on Rt. 218 to Wiscasset or follow it north through North Whitefield and east across Rt. 126 along Clary Lake to Jefferson.

Pemaquid Peninsula. Follow Rt. 129 south from Damariscotta, across the **South Bristol Bridge** to **Christmas Cove**. Backtrack and cross the peninsula via **Harrington Meeting House Road** to **Colonial Pemaquid** and **Pemaquid Beach** (this corner of the world is particularly beautiful at sunset). Turn south on Rt. 130 to **Pemaquid Point** and return via Rt. 32 and **Round Pond**; take Biscay Rd. back to Damariscotta or continue on Rt. 32 into Waldoboro.

DAMARISCOTTA LAKE

Christina Tree

✳ To Do

BIRDING ✐ **Audubon Camp**, Hog Island (0.25 mile offshore at the head of Muscongus Bay). June–Aug. One-week programs including family and adult camps and a 10-day Youth Camp (for 10- to 14-year-olds) focusing on the island's wildlife; also boat trips to see the puffins that were reintroduced to nearby Eastern Egg Rock by the Audubon-related Puffin Project. There are 5 miles of spruce trails, wildflower and herb gardens, mudflats surrounding rustic bungalows, and a dining room in a restored 19th-century farmhouse. For details, contact the Maine Audubon Society (207-781-2339; www.maineaudubon .org). For **puffin-watching and birding cruises**, see Hardy Boat Cruises (below). Also see *Green Space*.

BOAT EXCURSIONS ✐ **Hardy Boat Cruises** (Stacie and Captain Al Crocetti: 207-677-2026 or 1-800-278-3346; www.hardyboat.com), Shaw's Wharf, New Harbor. May–Oct., the 60-foot Maine-built *Hardy III* offers daily service to Monhegan (for a detailed description, see "Midcoast Islands"). Pick a calm day. It doesn't matter if it's foggy, but the passage is more than an hour and no fun if it's rough. A cruise also circles Eastern Egg Rock, one of only five Maine islands on which puffins breed; the tours are narrated by an Audubon naturalist. There are also sunset cruises to Pemaquid Point. Parking is free but roughly 0.25 mile back up the road (Gosnold Arms guests are just steps away). Crew members do everything they can to make the trip interesting, like a brief seal-watching detour on the way back from Monhegan.

Salt Water Charters (207-677-6229; www.saltwater-charters.com), based in Round Pond Harbor, offers island-hopping and coastal excursions on a 38-foot lobster boat for up to six people.

NEW HARBOR

Christina Tree

GUIDED KAYAK TOURS AND RENTALS **Sea Spirit Adventures** (207-529-4732; www.seaspirit adventures.com), Round Pond Village, offers sea kayak rentals and tours on Muscongus Bay and the Damariscotta River. **Wild Bill's Outfitting & Guide Service** (207-832-5197 in Friendship; 207-644-1535 in Christmas Cove) offers camping weekends as well as shorter guided tours.

BOAT RENTALS **Lake Pemaquid Camping** (207-563-5202), Egypt Rd., Damariscotta, rents canoes, kayaks, and paddle- and motorboats. Rentals on the northern end of Damariscotta Lake are from **Damariscotta Lake Farm Marina** (207-549-5252) in Jefferson.

FISHING Damariscotta Lake is a source of bass, landlocked salmon, and trout. See Mill Pond Inn under *Bed & Breakfasts*.

GOLF Wawenock Country Club (207-563-3938), Rt. 129 (7 miles south of Damariscotta), Walpole. Open May–Nov. A nine-hole course with 18 tee boxes and a full-service clubhouse.

Sheepscot Links (207-549-7060), 822 Townhouse Rd., Whitefield. A rural, nine-hole golf course, a former 50-acre dairy farm. Clubhouse, pull carts.

SWIMMING On the peninsula there is public swimming at **Biscay Pond**, off Rt. 32, and at **Bristol Dam** on Rt. 130, 5 miles south of Damariscotta (also see *Green Space*).

✳ Green Space

BEACHES Pemaquid Beach Park (207-677-2754), Rt. 130, Pemaquid. A town-owned area open Memorial Day–Labor Day, 9–5. Nominal admission. Bathhouse, restrooms, refreshment stand, and picnic tables. This is also a great place to walk and watch the sunset in the evening.

Damariscotta Lake State Park, Rt. 32, Jefferson. A fine sandy beach with changing facilities, picnic tables, and grills at the northern end of the lake. $3 per car.

Also see **Dodge Point Preserve** under *Nature Preserves*, below.

NATURE PRESERVES Rachel Carson Memorial Salt Pond, at the side of Rt. 32, just north of New Harbor. The pond is on the opposite side of the road from the parking lot. There's a beautiful view of the open ocean from here, and at low tide the tidal pools are filled with tiny sea creatures. Look for blue mussels, hermit crabs, starfish, and green sea urchins. Here Rachel Carson researched part of her book *The Edge of the Sea*. Inland from the pond, the preserve includes fields and forest.

Griggs Preserve, Newcastle, is maintained by the Sheepscot Valley Conservation Association (207-586-5616): A loop trail through 56 acres brings you to a view of the reversing falls at Sheepscot Village. Take Rt. 1 south to Cochran Rd. (turn right at Skip Cahill's Tires). After a mile turn left onto Trails End Rd. to the trailhead (on the left, before the bridge).

🐌 Todd Wildlife Sanctuary and the Hocomock Trail, Bremen (take Keene Neck Rd. off Rt. 32). A visitor center (207-529-5148) is open June–Aug., daily 1–4. The nature trail leads down to the beach. This is a great family picnic spot, accessible with short legs.

Damariscotta River Association (207-563-1393), based at 100-acre Heritage Center Farm (P.O. Box 333, Belvedere Rd., Damariscotta 04543), publishes a free map/guide to the properties that it maintains, frequently in conjunction with other landowners. These total more than 1,000 acres in over a dozen easily accessible places. They include **Great Salt Bay Preserve Heritage Trail**, which loops around Glidden Point, first hugging the shore of Great Salt Bay (look for horseshoe crabs, great blue herons, and eagles) and then tunnels right under Rt. 1 and leads down to the "Glidden Midden" of oyster shells that's now on the National Register and said to date back 2,400 years. The trail begins beside the Newcastle Post Office.

Dodge Point Preserve is a 506-acre property on Newcastle's River Rd. (2.6 miles south of Rt. 1). It includes a sand beach as well as a freshwater pond, a beaver bog, and trails.

Witch Island, South Bristol. An 18-acre wooded island lies 0.25 mile offshore at the east end of "the Gut," the narrow channel that serves as South Bristol's harbor. A trail around the island threads through oaks and pines, and there are two sheltered beaches.

✳ Lodging

INNS ⊙ **The Newcastle Inn** (207-563-5685 or 1-800-832-8669; www .newcastleinn.com), River Rd., Newcastle 04553. Open year-round. Laura and Peter Barclay offer 15 tasteful and comfortable rooms, all with private bath, some with water views, several with canopy bed, 9 with gas fireplace, and 2 with Jacuzzi. An inviting little bar with French doors opens onto a wide, awning-shaded deck with water views—the breakfast venue weather permitting. Dining is important here (see *Dining Out*). New innkeepers, the Barclays have enhanced the grounds, which slope to the river and overlook Damariscotta, with many plantings. Rates are $155–295 in high season, $125–225 in low, including a three-course breakfast. Inquire about special getaway weekends.

🦞 ✍ ♿ **Gosnold Arms** (207-677-3727; winter, 561-575-9549; www .gosnold.com), 146 Rt. 32, New Harbor 04554. Open mid-May–mid-Oct. Sited at the entrance to a picturesque working harbor, steps from the Hardy Boat cruises to Monhegan and around Egg Rock, this friendly family-owned and -run inn has been welcoming summer guests since 1925. Request one of the comfortable cottages with views of the water. There are also 11

guest rooms (with private bath) in the barn, above a large library with a stone fireplace. These can, however, be hot. The Hillside units squirreled away at the top of the property are good for families. Breakfast is served buffet-style on the enclosed porch overlooking the water. $95–117 double B&B in the inn, $95–208 for cottages (double occupancy).

♿ **Bradley Inn** (207-677-2105 or 1-800-942-5560; www.bradleyinn.com), 3063 Pemaquid Point, New Harbor 04554. Open year-round. Warren and Beth Busteed are energetic innkeepers who have established a culinary reputation for this turn-of-the-20th-century inn (see *Dining Out*). The 16 guest rooms are divided among the main house, the carriage house, and a cottage, all nicely furnished (and with private bath), all set in landscaped grounds. Old clunker bicycles are free, and the inn is less than a mile from Pemaquid Lighthouse and Kresge Point. From $155 off-season to $275 (for a carriage house suite) in-season; special birding weekends.

Coveside Inn (207-644-8282), Christmas Cove, South Bristol 04568. Motel units are open late May–mid-Oct.; the restaurant and inn rooms, early June–Labor Day. As many guests probably sail as drive to this holly-berry-red old summer hotel, recently spiffed up with new carpeting and wallpaper. It offers five old-fashioned guest rooms (with private bath, but some are across the hall), a big living room with a woodstove and plenty of books, shared with guests in the 10 shorefront motel units (private decks, pine paneling, and cathedral ceilings with skylights). The complex also includes a restaurant, serving all three meals, and a yacht brokerage. $85 for rooms in the inn and $85–105 for motel rooms, including continental breakfast.

♿ **The Hotel Pemaquid** (207-677-2312), Pemaquid 04554. Open mid-May–mid-Oct. A century old summer hotel just a short walk from Pemaquid Point but without water views. The 25 rooms are pleasant, divided among the main house and new annexes. The decor is "English country." Most rooms have private bath (four rooms in the inn itself share two baths). Coffee is set out 7–10 AM, and the nearby Sea Gull Shop (see *Eating Out*) overlooks the ocean. From $60 off-season with shared bath to $230 for a suite in Aug.; a four-bedroom housekeeping cottage is $775 per week.

BED & BREAKFASTS

In Newcastle/Damariscotta
The Flying Cloud (207-563-2484; www.theflyingcloud.com), River Rd., Newcastle 04553. Open most of the year. An 1840s sea captain's home expanding on a 1790s Cape with five spacious guest rooms, all with private bath, four with water views. All are named for ports of call made by the clipper ship *Flying Cloud.* Our favorite is third-floor Melbourne with

Christina Tree

MILL POND INN

its skylight and view of both the river and harbor. Karen and Dave Bragg make outstanding breakfasts. $90–185 per night double occupancy includes an outstanding breakfast, served in summer on the screened porch overlooking the garden.

⚉ ☯ **Mill Pond Inn** (207-563-8014; www.millpondinn.com), Rt. 215, Damariscotta Mills (mailing address: 50 Main St., Nobleboro 04555). Open year-round. Two-person hammocks swing under the willow trees, near a beach and (relatively) warm water. Enter the red door of Sherry and Bobby Whear's 1780 gray-clapboard house and you immediately feel at home. The seven rooms—including a two-bedroom suite with its own entrance—all have private bath and are so different from each other that you might want to ask for descriptions, but all cost $120 per couple. Breakfast might be an omelet with crabmeat and vegetables from the inn's garden. In winter pack a picnic lunch and skate across the lake to an island. In summer take a dip off the dock or ask for a ride in the 16-foot restored antique motorboat. Bobby

Whear, a Registered Maine Guide, is happy to arrange fishing trips.

The Harbor View Inn at Newcastle (207-563-2900; www.theharborview .com), P.O. Box 791, Newcastle 04553. Set above Main St. in Newcastle, this handsome 1840s house has a spacious, beamed, and many-windowed living room and second-floor reading room; there's also a deck overlooking the harbor. Joe McEntee offers just three guest rooms, all unusually large and luxurious. The two upstairs have a fireplace, river views, and private deck. Breakfast is special. $135–190.

&. **Oak Gables** (207-563-1476), P.O. Box 276, Pleasant St., Damariscotta 04543. Open year-round, high season June 15–Sep. 15. Set on its own 13 acres overlooking the Damariscotta River, with a heated swimming pool and boathouse, minutes from village shopping and dining, Martha Scudder's gracious house has four second-floor rooms that share a bath and a lavatory ($95 with breakfast). Also on the property: a riverside three-bedroom cottage ($1,200 per week, $185 per night off-season), a two-person studio ($875 per week, off-season $150 per night), an apartment in the guest wing ($875 per week, $150 per night off-season), and a riverview apartment above the garage ($980 a week; off-season $165 per night); off-season nightly rentals are all based on two people; $30 per extra person.

The Tipsy Butler (207-563-3394; www.thetipsybutler.com), P.O. Box 239, 11 High St., Newcastle 04553. Open year-round. The interior of this informal B&B belies its 1830s formal, pillared facade. The "tipsy butler" is a proudly displayed painting, and rooms

are variously named for the butler, maid, cook, and groundskeeper. We like the Maid's Room with its pencil-post king-sized bed and bath with bidet. $125–150 with discounts for 2 days or more; less off-season.

South of Damariscotta
The Inn at Round Pond (207-529-2004; www.theinnatroundpond.com), 1442 Rt. 31, Round Pond 04564. Sue and Bill Morton have brought new life to this 1830s Colonial with its mansard-roofed third floor, added around the turn of the last century, when it became the Harbor View Hotel. This remains the only place to stay in this picturesque waterside village with its crafts shops, galleries, and dining choices. Rooms have been reduced to three suites. Our favorite is the third-floor Monhegan Suite with a king-sized iron bed and a separate room with two twins. $130–190 Memorial Day–Columbus Day, otherwise $95–145, with breakfast.

&. *ᐧ* **Brannon-Bunker Inn** (207-563-5941 or 1-800-563-9225; brbnkinn @lincoln.midcoast.com), 349 Rt. 129, Walpole 04573. Open Mar.–Dec. This 1820s barn was a Prohibition-era dance hall before it became a B&B. The upstairs sitting area walls are hung with memorabilia from World War I, and there are plenty of antiques and collectibles around. Your hosts are the Hovance family, and children are welcome. There are five rooms in the main house; the neighboring Carriage House includes a suite with two bedrooms and two more rooms with private bath. $75–80 for two rooms that share a bath, $85–90 for those with private bath, and $100–150 for a suite with a kitchen, living room, and bathroom.

☙ **The Unique Yankee B&B** (1-866-644-1502), 53 Coveside Rd., P.O. Box 242, South Bristol 04568. Open year-round. From the outside this barnlike building is off-putting, but once you're inside its open common space and four spacious guest rooms are comfortable and airy. All are fitted with a gas fireplace, jetted tub, separate shower, queen beds, in-room coffee, fridge and microwave, and TV with VCR/DVD. Coveside has a distant water view and a deck to enjoy it from. Early coffee and sunset wine are set out in an observatory room atop the building. Richard and Cheryl Munson are seasoned innkeepers who also have a B&B in Fitzwilliam, New Hampshire. $120 includes a full breakfast.

Sunset Bed and Breakfast (207-644-8849; www.sunsetbnb.com), P.O. Box 91, 16 Sunset Loop, South Bristol 04568. Open May–Oct. Kay and Dick Miller have turned a vintage summer cottage into a surprisingly comfortable B&B with two second-floor rooms, one with twins and the other with a double bed, both with skylights and sharing a bath. $120 with private bath, $80 with shared, $60 single, including a full breakfast.

Tibbets Farm Bed and Breakfast (207-563-1619; www.tibbetsfarmbed andbreakfast.com), P.O. Box 275, 1242 Bristol Rd. (Rt. 130), Bristol 04539. A vintage-1772 farmhouse fronts on Rt. 130 but backs on the Pemaquid River, just below the Bristol Dam. Choose the Blue Room with its large queen-sized bed, or a suite with a double and twins, or just the double or twins; all have private bath. Nancy Zabriskie serves a full breakfast; $125–175.

In Waldoboro 04572

☙ **Blue Skye Farm** (207-832-0300; www.blueskyefarm.com), 1708 Friendship Rd. (Rt. 220). What a treasure! This is an exquisite house, dating back to 1775 but with an elegant Federal facade. It retains all its original woodwork and working fireplaces (in two of the five guest rooms as well as in common rooms); the stenciling in the front hall is thought to be by Moses Eaton. Brits Peter and Jan Davidson have restored all the original detailing. The two upstairs front rooms and one downstairs (the former North Parlor) are classically proportioned; a smaller downstairs room (the Library) overlooks the marshes. A full breakfast is served, but guests have access to the kitchen as well as outdoor grills for other meals. The owners share use of their outdoor pool. The 100-acre property includes gardens, hiking trails, and a skating pond. $110–135 in-season, from $95 off-season. Candlelit lobster dinners can be arranged when booking.

Broad Bay Inn & Gallery (207-832-6668 or 1-800-736-6769; www.broad bayinn.com), 1014 Main St. Closed Jan.–Mar. Within walking distance of performances at the Waldo Theatre, this is a pleasant 1830s home with Victorian furnishings. The five guest rooms share three baths. Our favorite is Sarah's Canopy Room, with its floor-to-ceiling windows and French armoire. The art gallery in the barn features host Libby Hopkins's watercolors of flowers and Maine scenes. Rates include a full breakfast: $75–110 double.

The Roaring Lion (207-832-4038; www.roaringlion.com), 995 Main St. Open year-round. Almost across from the Waldo Theatre, a 1905 home with tin ceilings, fireplaces, and a big screened porch. The kitchen can cater to special, vegetarian, and macrobiotic diets, and Bill Branigan is widely recognized for outstanding breakfasts. One room with private bath; three with shared bath. Request a room at the back of the house. $90–100 double, $65–75 single.

Also see "Rockland/Thomaston Area" for **Harbor Hill** and **Outsiders' Inn** in Friendship, just down the peninsula from Waldoboro.

In Jefferson 04348
❀ ✿ **Jefferson House** (207-549-5768; www.jeffersonhousebb.com), 95 Washington Rd. (Rt. 126). Jim and Barbara O'Halloron's comfortable 1835 farmhouse feels like home the moment you walk in. The large, bright kitchen with its big old cookstove is the center of the house, or you can breakfast on the deck overlooking the village and millpond. Guests can use the canoe on the river. The five rooms are homey and comfortable; shared bath. $60 double, $50 single; $75 for a room with a private bath. $10 additional for an extra person.

✿ ✿ **Hidden Acres Llama Farm** (207-549-5774), 84 Old County Rd. Sited near the northern tip of Damariscotta Lake, Philippa and Terry Beal's llama farm (21 llamas at last count) includes a fully equipped one-bedroom apartment. Guests are invited to take llamas along on treks over the farm's trails and welcome to participate in farm activities and to use the hot tub. In-season rates range from $250 for a weekend, $350 for 3 nights, and $400 for 4 nights to $650 for a full week. Ingredients are supplied for a hearty daily breakfast. From $100 per night off-season.

❀ ✿ **Blueberry Hill Farm** (207-549-7448; www.mainefarmvacation .com), 101 Old Madden Rd. This is another find: a secluded 125-acre farm with a 1774 farmhouse, tastefully restored and furnished with antiques and original art. There are three guest rooms in the house, one with a fireplace and one a small single (all shared bath); a studio room in the barn has a woodstove, sleeping loft, and outdoor shower. $50 for the single room, $65 per couple for the studio and doubles, $15 for additional guests, full breakfast included. $20 charge for a pet.

COTTAGES ❀ ✿ Many rental properties are listed with the Damariscotta area chamber; for cottages and apartments down on the peninsula, also request a copy of the current *Map & Guide* published by the Pemaquid Area Association (Chamberlain 04541). **Newcastle Square Vacation Rentals** (207-563-6500; www.maine coastcottages.com), 87 Main St., Damariscotta, handles more than 100 area cottages and houses.

❀ ✿ ✿ **The Thompson House and Cottages** (207-677-2317; www .thompsoncottages.net), New Harbor 04554. Open May–Nov. Merle and Karen Thompson are the third generation of a family that's been offering hospitality since they began taking guests in an 1874 house in 1920. There are still two sparkling clean rooms in the house, but the big attractions are the 21 equally tidy housekeeping cottages (maximum of five people), many with ocean views and facing New Harbor or Back Cove, all with fireplace (wood supplied). They run $950–1,500 a week, less off-season. Rooms (with private bath) in the house are $65 per night, $390 per week, and there are three apartments ($500 per week) on the property. No cats, but small dogs accepted.

Ye Olde Forte Cabins (207-677-2261), 18 Old Fort Rd., Pemaquid Beach 04554. Nostalgia buffs take note: These are classic 1922 cabins (sleeping one to four), stepped roof to roof along a wide central lawn sloping to a beach on John's Bay. There's a cookhouse equipped with everything you need to make meals, along with immaculate men's and women's shower houses. $410–595 per week, less if you bring your own linen.

MOTEL **The Oyster Shell Motel** (207-563-3747 or 1-800-874-3747), Business Rt. 1, Damariscotta (north of Damariscotta Village) 04543. A condo-style motel complex open all year. No view, but clean, comfortable, and air-conditioned; there's a heated pool. One-bedroom or two-bedroom suites with cooking facilities. Two-day minimum stay on July and Aug. weekends. From $89 for a one-bedroom off-season to $159 for a two-bedroom in-season.

CAMPING **Lake Pemaquid Camping** (207-563-5202), Box 967, Damariscotta 04543. Off Biscay Rd. Many tent and RV sites are right on 7-mile Lake Pemaquid, and canoe and boat rentals are available. Facilities also include tennis, a pool, swimming, a playground, a game room, laundry facilities, a sauna, and a store.

Where to Eat

DINING OUT

In Damariscotta/Newcastle

Lupines at the Newcastle Inn (207-563-5685 or 1-800 832-8669; www.newcastleinn.com), River Rd.,

YE OLDE FORTE CABINS

Christina Tree

Newcastle. Under new owners, the two intimate dining rooms look even more elegant, to match a four-course menu that might begin with foraged mushroom stew with an herb popover, followed by a salad and perhaps roast duck breast with plums and ginger, Swiss chard, and semolina gnocchi, concluding with German chocolate torte. $46 prix fixe plus 18 percent gratuity and tax.

🦞 ♪ **Damariscotta River Grill** (207-563-2992), 155 Main St. Open for lunch and dinner. A new brick-walled, two-floor, middle-of-Main-Street gem under the same ownership as the long and justly popular Anchor Inn in Round Pond. Begin either meal by splitting an order of Pemaquid oysters on the half shell with the house horseradish. At dinner feast on pan-seared scallops with roasted tomatoes and wilted spinach, drizzled with balsamic vinegar, or try the lobster cakes. Children's menu. Dinner entrées $13.83–15.84.

Backstreet Restaurant (207-563-5666), Elm St. Plaza, Damariscotta. Open daily year-round for lunch and dinner. In back of Main St., overlooking the Damariscotta River, this very pleasant, low-key restaurant and gathering place has good, dependable food. Lunch options include freshly made soups and a long sandwich board as well as quiche. Dinner entrées range from pastas and vegetarian dishes through local oysters to cider-brined pork loin chop. Dinner entrées $13–19.

On the Pemaquid Peninsula
🦞 ♪ **Anchor Inn** (207-529-5584), Round Pond. Open daily for lunch (11–2), dinner (from 5), and Sunday brunch (noon–3), mid-May–Labor Day, then open except Mon. and Tue.

until Columbus Day. Reserve for dinner. Jean and Rick Hirch's tiered dining room overlooking the harbor is a real standout. At either meal try the Italian seafood stew, loaded with fish, scallops, and mussels, served with garlic bread. Dinner options include pan-seared scallops with roasted red and yellow tomatoes, olives, capers, garlic, and fresh thyme. Children's menu. Dinner entrées $13.83–21.76.

Bradley Inn (207-677-2105 or 1-800-942-5560), Pemaquid Point Rd., New Harbor. Open by reservation for dinner year-round; nightly (except Wed.) in-season; Nov.–Mar., Thu.–Sun. Fine dining is what these two attractive dining rooms are about. The rooms are decorated in nautical antiques and soothing greens, and tables are well spaced and candlelit. The à la carte menu changes nightly but might feature grilled loin of lamb with barbecue sauce, pecan crust, and shoestring potatoes. Entrées $23–28.

Coveside Dory Bar and Shorefront Restaurant (207-644-8282), Christmas Cove, South Bristol. Open June–Labor Day, three meals daily. Not worth the drive all the way down to Christmas Cove but wonderful if you're already there or arrive by boat. This is a large, fully licensed waterside dining room. Dinner entrées range from roasted vegetable lasagna ($17.95) to rack of lamb ($25.95). Fully licensed.

EATING OUT

On or just off Rt. 1
♪ ♿ **Moody's Diner** (207-832-7785), Rt. 1, Waldoboro. Open Mon.–Fri. 4 AM–11:30 PM, Sat. 5 AM–11:30 PM, Sun. 6 AM–11:30 PM. A clean and warm, classic 1930s diner run by several generations of the Moody family

along with other employees who have been there so long, they've become part of the family. Renovated and expanded, it retains all the old atmosphere and specialties like cream pies and family-style food—corned beef hash, meat loaf, and stews—at digestible prices. You can now buy T-shirts and other Moody's paraphernalia, but you can also still get chicken croquettes at prices that haven't soared with fame.

✒ **King Eider's Pub** (207-563-6008), 2 Elm St., Damariscotta. Open year-round 11–11. A favorite among locals and visitors alike. The downstairs pub is the perfect foggy-evening spot for light grub and a boutique brew. The same moderately priced menu in the pleasant upstairs restaurant features local produce and seafood. Sandwiches and burgers are available at dinner, along with crabcakes, barbecued salmon, and fish-and-chips. $9.50–18.95.

✒ **Bullwinkle's Family Steakhouse** (207-832-6272), Rt. 1, Waldoboro. Locally loved and a good bet for road food. Steaks are the specialty, along with baby back ribs, seafood baskets, and subs.

✒ **Andrew's Pine View Restaurant** (207-563-2899), Rt. 1 north of the village, Damariscotta. Open daily for lunch and dinner, Sunday brunch 9–2:30. A good family-geared way stop.

Schooner Landing (207-563-7447), Schooner Wharf, Main St., Damariscotta. Open May–Sep. daily for lunch and dinner, just weekends in Apr. and Oct.; the pub remains open for live music on weekends through winter. A wharfside restaurant on the Damariscotta River; the view is the big draw here, along with the informal feel and draft brews.

Nancy English

MOODY'S DINER

Paco's Tacos (207-563-5355), off Main St. in the alley beside Sheepscot River Pottery, Damariscotta. Open weekdays 11–4. Better than average and handy to the public landing (parking and a picnic spot). Friday is enchilada day.

On the Pemaquid Peninsula: Rt. 130

Samoset Restaurant (207-677-2142), Rt. 10, New Harbor. Open daily year-round 11–9. No view, but great on a foggy or rainy day or evening. Geared to locals, with homemade specials, good chowder, and fresh seafood. Live entertainment on weekends and other selected nights.

Sea Gull Shop (207-677-2374), next to the Pemaquid Lighthouse at Pemaquid Point. Open daily in-season,

8–8, serving all three meals. The shop's Monhegan Room has water views. Standard menu. Entrées $5–20. BYOB.

On the Pemaquid Peninsula: Along Rt. 129 to Christmas Cove

Harborside (207-644-8751), South Bristol. Open year-round for breakfast, lunch, dinner. Heading south, on the left before the drawbridge at "the Gut," this is a general store that we passed many times before noticing all the pickups gathered at noon. It serves a standard road-food menu— fresh-dough pizza, omelets all day, sandwiches, and fried seafood—but the chowder was the best we found in an entire summer.

♪ **Osier's Wharf** (207-644-8101), Rt. 129 north of "the Gut" in South Bristol. Open seasonally for breakfast, lunch, and through the afternoon. Another classic spot from which to watch passing lobster boats. This is a general store and fish market, and the dining deck is upstairs overlooking the water; a place for a morning "clucker muffin," a crabmeat or lobster roll, steak and cheese at lunch, or fried seafood all day; also deli sandwiches.

Elsewhere

Country Farm (207-549-5985), corner of Rts. 126 and 218 in Whitefield. Open daily (except Mon.) for lunch and dinner. Very busy on Saturday night, popular with locals. The menu is large and varied. $20–35 for two.

ICE CREAM *♪* **Round Top Ice Cream** (207-563-5307), Business Rt. 1, Damariscotta. Open Memorial Day–Columbus Day. Restrooms.

LOBSTER POUNDS

Note: Muscongus Bay is a particularly prime lobster source, and genuine lobster pounds are plentiful around the harbors of the Pemaquid Peninsula.

♪ **Shaw's Wharf** (207-677-2200), Rt. 32, New Harbor. Open early May–mid-Oct., daily for lunch and supper. You can't get closer to a working harbor than this popular dockside spot. Pick your lobster out of the pool below and feed on it upstairs at picnic tables, either inside or out. Chowders and stews, a wide choice of sandwiches, dinner salads, sides, and fried and seafood dinners are also on the menu. Fully licensed.

Muscongus Bay Lobster Company (207-529-5528) offer no-frills (no toilets) facilities. The cook shed on the edge of the working Round Pond harbor has expanded in recent years with plenty of picnic tables on the deck. Probably the most reasonably priced place around; sample the area's oysters on the half shell, as well as the freshest of crabmeat, lobsters, corn, and fixings.

Harbor View Restaurant at the **Pemaquid Fisherman's Co-op** (207-677-2801; www.pemaquidlobsterco-op.com), off Pemaquid Harbor Road, Pemaquid Harbor. Open Memorial Day–Columbus Day, 11–8. Operated by Maine's oldest continuously run fishermen's cooperative: lobster, steamed clams and mussels, and shrimp, shore dinners and baskets, enjoyed at outdoor tables with a great view across John's Bay to Colonial Pemaquid.

You'll find delicious Round Top Ice Cream offered at restaurants throughout the region, but this is the original shop just up the road from the farm where it all began in 1924 (that property is now Round Top Center for the Arts). The ice cream comes in 36 flavors, including fresh blueberry.

SAUERKRAUT 🦞 **Morse's Sauerkraut** (207-832-5569), 3856 Washington Rd. (8 miles north of Rt. 1, on Rt. 220 in Waldoboro). Open year-round, daily 9–5 for the restaurant, till 6 for the store. Why this tiny, four-booth restaurant hasn't expanded is a mystery. On weekends the line stretches out the door for sausages and liverwurst, sauerbraten and Wiener schnitzel, plus German potato salad and the famous freshly made sauerkraut. You might want to buy ingredients for a German feast in the deli, featuring Schaller and Weber sausages as well as bread and jam

✳ Entertainment

Round Top Center for the Arts (207-563-1507; www.roundtoparts .org), Business Rt. 1, Damariscotta. On the grounds of the old Round Top Farm, this nonprofit organization offers an ambitious schedule of concerts, exhibitions, classes, and lectures. Summer concerts can be anything from the Portland Symphony Orchestra to rousing ethnic music by Mama Tongue. Bring a blanket and a picnic.

Lincoln Theater (207-563-3424; www.lcct.org), entrance off Main St., Damariscotta. The biggest hall east of Boston in 1875, later boasting the largest motion-picture screen in the state. Recently restored by the Lincoln County Community Theater, which stages its own productions here

in winter and spring. First-run films and special programs. A recently installed elevator eases access to the second-floor theater.

Waldo Theatre (207-832-6060; www .waldotheatre.org), Main St., Waldoboro. Mar.–Dec., a schedule of films, concerts, and live performances.

Thursday-night lectures at the University of Maine's Darling Marine Center (207-563-3146, ext. 252), 225 Clark's Cove Rd. (off Rt. 129) in Walpole. Topics in this July–Aug. series, sponsored by the Gulf of Maine Foundation, are marine related but of general interest.

Also check the lecture schedule at the Skidompha Library (see *To See*).

✳ Selective Shopping

ANTIQUES *Antiquing in the Midcoast Pemaquid Region*, a free pamphlet guide, lists more than two dozen dealers in this small area. Check local papers for auctions or call **Robert Foster** (207-563-8110), based at his auction gallery on Rt. 1, Newcastle.

ART AND CRAFTS GALLERIES AND STUDIOS **The Firehouse Gallery** (207-563-7299; www.thefirehouse gallery.com), corner of Main St. and Rt. 130, Damariscotta. Open Apr.–Dec., representing many of Maine's most prominent artists, also carrying fine crafts including distinctive jewelry.

Pine Tree Yarns (207-563-8909; www.pinetreeyarns.com), Main St., Damariscotta. A knitter's heaven, seemingly thousands of yarns in a riot of colors, many hand dyed by Elaine Eskesen on the premises. Elaine also designs patterns geared to current as well as classic tastes and holds out hope to those of us prone to dropping stitches: foolproof kits for making striking scarves.

Tin Fish Etc. (207-563-8204), above the Weatherbird Store, Northey Square, Damariscotta. Dana Moses fashions remarkable art pieces in all sizes made from recycled metal, mostly corrugated iron.

Damariscotta Pottery (207-563-8843), around back of the Weatherbird, Damariscotta. Open year-round except Sun. Majolica ware, decorated in floral designs. You won't see this advertised. It doesn't have to be. Watch it being shaped and painted.

Sheepscot River Pottery (207-882-9410 or 1-800-659-4794), Main St., Damariscotta. The big shop is on Rt. 1 in Edgecomb, but this stocks a range of distinctive hand-painted dinnerware, plates, and ovenware as well as lamps and tiles.

t. b. Pots (207-677-6515), 40 Harrington Rd., Walpole. Tracy and Eric Bradford make and sell their brightly glazed functional pottery here.

River Gallery (207-563-6330), Main St., Damariscotta. Open in-season Mon.–Sat. 10–3; features 19th- and early-20th-century landscapes.

Pemaquid Craft Co-Op (207-677-2077), Rt. 130, New Harbor. Open mid-May–mid-Oct., daily 10–6, then Fri.–Sun. until Dec. 24. Fifteen rooms filled with varied work by 50 Maine crafters.

Note: Artists and craftspeople clustered in and around the village of Round Pond publish their own map/guide, available at any of the galleries and studios. North of the village at 1794 Rt. 32, **Natural Expressions** (207-529-4411), a jewel-like gallery, displays the exquisite Maine tourma-

line and local pearl pieces designed and made on the premises. Just north of the village (1486 Rt. 32), look for the home of the **Village Weaver** (Phyllis Leck hand looms early-American-style textiles and cotton and wool blankets and rugs) and the **Scottish Lion Blacksmith** (Andre Leck forges shapes ranging from chandeliers and lamps to whimsical animals). In the village itself Sally DeLorme Pedrick's **Library Art Studio** (207-529-4210) features the artist's own interesting work, and the **Round Pond Art Gallery**, seemingly transplanted from the Rue Sisley, displays an interesting mix of "les beaux arts."

BOOKS ♂ **Maine Coast Book Shop** (207-563-3207), Main St., Damariscotta. One of Maine's best bookstores, with knowledgeable staff members who delight in making suggestions and helping customers shop for others. It now fills the entire first floor of the Lincoln Theater building and includes an inviting café with Internet access.

Jean Gillespie Books (207-529-5555), Rt. 32 south of the village of Round Pond. Open afternoons seasonally, or by appointment. An exceptional antiquarian bookstore, since 1961. Some 20,000 titles line shelves in a barnlike annex to the house. Specialties include the Civil War, cookbooks, and Maine. We recently found a 19th-century Maine guidebook that we had been hunting high and low for, reasonably priced.

SPECIAL SHOPS ✿ **Reny's** (207-563-3177; www.renys.com), Main St., Damariscotta. First opened in Camden in 1949, Reny's has since become a small-town Maine institution from Biddeford to Fort Kent. The stores sell quality items—ranging from TVs to sheets and towels and whatever "the boys" happen to have found to stock this week. The headquarters for the 15-store chain are in Damariscotta. On opposite sides of Main St., look for Reny's and **Reny's Underground**.

♪ **Weatherbird**, Northey Square, Damariscotta. Open Mon.–Sat. 8:30–5:30. A combination café and gift shop with mouthwatering pastries and specialty foods, wines, home accessories, clothing, gifts, toys, and cards.

♪ **Granite Hall Store** (207-529-5864), Rt. 32, Round Pond. Open Tue.–Sun. 10–5. There's penny candy up front, but this is no general store. It's filled with Scottish-, Irish-, and Maine-made woolens, among many things, and an ice cream takeout window.

Borealis Breads Store (207-832-0655; www.borealisbreads.com), 1860 Rt. 1 (across from Moody's Diner), Waldoboro. Open Mon.–Fri. 8:30–5:30, Sat. 9–4. Maine's most popular bread, widely distributed but baked here, more than a dozen kinds.

S. Fernald's Country Store (207-832-4624), 17 Friendship St., Waldoboro Village. Billed as the oldest five-and-dime in the country (established 1927), this friendly old establishment now offers an eclectic stock. "You never know what you will find here," says owner Sumner Richards, who serves deli-style sandwiches,

soups, and specials at the old-style soda fountain.

I'm Puzzled (207-563-5719), Nobleboro, marked from Rt. 1. Jigsaw puzzle buffs should follow the signs to Robert Havenstein's two-car garage, filled to overflowing with jigsaw puzzles, more than 850 different offerings ranging from $2 yard-sale rejects to antique wooden puzzles prized by collectors.

Fawcett's Antique Toy & Art Museum (207-832-7398), 3506 Rt. 1. Open Memorial Day–Columbus Day, Thu.–Mon. 10–4. Comic-book and antique-toy lovers alert: This is a major collection of original cartoon art, antique Disneyana, space toys, and the like ($3 admission). Antique toys also bought and sold.

✳ Special Events

July: **Annual July 4 fireworks**, Damariscotta and Wiscasset.

Early August: **Olde Bristol Days**, Old Fort Grounds, Pemaquid Beach—parade, fish fry, chicken barbecue, bands, bagpipers, concerts, pancake breakfast, road race, boat race, firemen's muster, crafts, and the annual Bristol Footlighters Show (which has been going on for more than 40 years).

Columbus Day weekend: **Round Pond Roundabout**, sponsored by local crafts studios and art galleries (207-529-4411).

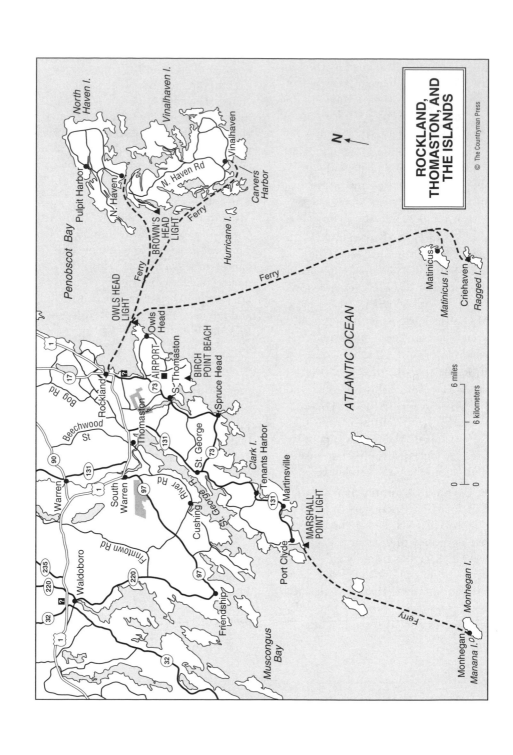

ROCKLAND, THOMASTON, AND THE ISLANDS

© The Countryman Press

ROCKLAND/THOMASTON AREA

The shire town of Knox County, Rockland (population: around 8,000) is the commercial center for a wide scattering of towns and islands. The departure point for ferries to the islands of Vinalhaven, North Haven, and Matinicus, it is also now home port for the majority of Maine's windjammers, as well as for several daysailers and an ever-increasing number of private yachts. Long billed as the "Lobster Capital of the World," it is now better known as home of the Farnsworth Museum, with its exceptional collection of Maine-based paintings, including works by three generations of Wyeths, housed in a middle-of-downtown, five-building campus.

Little more than a decade ago Rockland was far from the obvious Maine art venue. Camden-bound visitors avoided the place if they knew how to. Odors from the SeaPro fish-rendering plant were famous. A popular jingle ran: "Camden by Sea, Rockland by Smell." This gritty, sagging brick burg was not the Maine tourists came to see.

SeaPro has since gone the way of the city's two sardine-packing and other fish-processing plants, and the huge harbor, protected by a nearly mile-long granite—and walkable—breakwater, is now sparkling clean and equipped to accommodate pleasure boats. The wave of change is, moreover, washing down Main Street, bringing galleries, restaurants, and specialty shops. Along the waterfront, west of the already visitor-geared public landing, old industrial sheds have disappeared, replaced by office space. The harborside walking trail is lengthening.

Rockland, however, still prides itself on its grit. The city's industrial base still includes FMC Bio-Polymer (processing carrageenan from seaweed) and home-grown Fisher Snowplow, and the harbor, Maine's second largest after Portland, remains home to 700 vessels, including a sizable fishing and lobstering fleet, tugs, and U.S. Coast Guard and commercial vessels.

Rockland has remade itself several times over the centuries. Initially known for its shipbuilding, the city became synonymous in the late 19th century with the limestone it quarried, burned, and shipped off to be made into plaster. When wallboard replaced plaster, Rockland quickly switched to catching and processing fish. Now with fishing on the decline, city entrepreneurs are once more widening their base.

A century ago summer people heading for Bar Harbor as well as the islands took the train as far as Rockland, switching here to steamboats. Today a similar summer crowd rides the bus to the ferry terminal or flies into Knox County Regional Airport on Owls Head, just south of town, here transferring to rental cars, air taxis, or windjammers, to charter boats as well as ferries. The old train terminal is, moreover, still on Union Street, and passenger rail service from Boston to Rockland is again planned.

Southwest of Rockland, two peninsulas separate Muscongus Bay from Penobscot Bay. One is the fat arm of land on which the villages of Friendship and Cushing doze. The other is the skinnier St. George Peninsula with Port Clyde at its tip, the departure point for the year-round mail boat to Monhegan Island.

The peninsulas are divided by the 10-mile-long St. George River, on which past residents of Thomaston launched their share of wooden ships. Although its Main Street mansions stand today in white-clapboard testimony to the ship-builders' success, and Thomaston is a beautiful town, it was until recently best known as the site of the state prison—which has moved to neighboring Warren, but the popular prison shop remains.

GUIDANCE **Rockland-Thomaston Chamber of Commerce** (207-596-0376 or 1-800-562-2529; www.therealmaine.com), 1 Park Dr., Rockland (write P.O. Box 508, Rockland 04841). Open daily Memorial Day–Labor Day, Mon.–Sat. 9–5 and Sun. 10–4; then weekdays and 10–2 Sat. through the Columbus Day weekend. The chamber's spacious Gateway Visitor Center serves the entire Rockland area, which includes Owls Head, Thomaston, the peninsula villages, and the islands. It also lists cottage and vacation rentals.

GETTING THERE *By air:* **Knox County Regional Airport** (207-594-4131), at Owls Head, just south of Rockland. Daily service via **U.S. Airways Express** (operated by Colgan Air: 1-800-428-4322) to Boston, Bar Harbor, Augusta, and New York. Inquire about charter services to the islands. **Maine Atlantic Aviation** (207-596-5557 or 1-800-780-6071) and **Downeast Air** (207-594-2171 or 1-888-594-2171) offer charter service. Rental cars are available at the airport. Also see *By taxi* under *Getting Around;* all offer service to **Portland International Jetport** (see "Portland Area").

NORTHAVEN FERRY

Christina Tree

By bus: **Concord Trailways** (1-800-639-3317; www.concordtrailways.com) stops in Rockland at the Maine State Ferry Terminal.

By boat: The city has 20 moorings, and there are many more at commercial marinas. Contact the **harbormaster** (207-594-0312) and chamber of commerce.

By train: **The Maine Eastern Railroad** (1-866-637-2457; www.maine easternrailroad.com) offers seasonal

Thu.–Sun. service from Brunswick (where there's ample parking). Check their web-site for the current schedule and for shuttle service from Amtrak's **Downeaster** (Boston to Portland).

GETTING AROUND *By taxi:* **Schooner Bay Limo** (207-594-5000) and **Hit the Road Driver Service** (207-230-0095; beeper, 207-851-5506) will get you there. **All Aboard Trolley** (207-594-9300; www.aatrolley.com) offers seasonal daily, narrated, 9–5 service on a long loop around Rockland.

By ferry: Frequent service from the **Maine State Ferry Service Terminal** (207-596-2022 or 1-800-491-4883) to Vinalhaven, North Haven, and, less frequently, to Matinicus (see "Midcoast Islands"). **Monhegan Boat Line** (207-372-8848) serves Monhegan from Port Clyde.

Note: Rockland can be accessed and thoroughly enjoyed without a car.

WHEN TO COME Rockland stages a series of festivals that draw weekend crowds from mid-July through September. The biggest is the **Maine Lobster Festival**, first weekend in August. The Farnsworth Museum, major galleries, restaurants, and lodging all remain open year-round.

☀ Villages and Islands

Friendship. Best known as the birthplace of the classic Friendship sloop, first built by local lobstermen to haul their traps (originals and reproductions of this sturdy vessel hold races here every summer), Friendship remains a quiet fishing village. The **Friendship Museum** (207-832-4337), housed in a former brick schoolhouse at the junction of Rt. 220 and Martin's Point Rd., is open July–Labor Day, Mon.–Sat. 1–4 and Sun. 2–4. It features models and half hulls of Friendship sloops.

DOWNTOWN ROCKLAND

Christina Tree

Tenants Harbor has a good little library and, beyond, rock cliffs, tidal pools, old cemeteries, and the kind of countryside described by Sarah Orne Jewett in *The Country of the Pointed Firs*. Jewett lived just a few bends down Rt. 131 in Martinville while she wrote the book.

Port Clyde welcomes visitors at the tip of the St. George Peninsula (the end of Rt. 131) with a wharfside general store (sandwiches and outside tables), a small eatery, a hospitable inn, and good art gallery. **The Marshall Point Light** is well worth finding. Most importantly, this is the departure point for the year-round Monhegan–Thomaston Boat Line ferries to Monhegan Island.

Union is a short ride from the coast but surrounded by gentle hills and farm country (the Union Fair and the State of Maine Wild Blueberry Festival are big). This place is also a good spot to swim, eat, and explore the unusually interesting **Matthews Museum of Maine Heritage** at the fairgrounds (open July and Aug., daily except Mon., noon–5; 9:30–8 during Union Fair week).

Islands. An overnight or longer stay on an island is far preferable to a day trip. From Rockland you can take a Maine State (car) Ferry to **Vinalhaven** and **North Haven**. Together these form the Fox Islands, with just a narrow passage between them. Yet the islands are very different. On Vinalhaven summer homes are hidden away along the shore, and what visitors see is the old fishing village of Carver's Harbor. On North Haven shops and seasonal places to eat cluster by the ferry terminal. **Matinicus**, also accessible from Rockland, is the most remote Maine island and quietly beautiful. Tiny **Monhegan**, accessible from Port Clyde, offers the most dramatic cliff scenery and the most hospitable welcome to visitors. For details, see the descriptions of each island in the next chapter.

✳ To See

MUSEUMS AND HISTORIC HOMES ✐ **Montpelier General Knox Mansion** (207-354-8062), High St., Thomaston. Open June–early Oct., Tue.–Sat. 10–4. Admission $6 adults, $5 seniors, $3 ages 5–13 (family: $15). A 1926 re-creation of the grand mansion (financed by *Saturday Evening Post* publisher and Camden summer resident Cyrus Curtis) built (on another spot) in 1794 by General Henry Knox, the portly (5-foot-6-inch, 300-pound) Boston bookseller who became a Revolutionary War hero, then our first secretary of war. He married a granddaughter of Samuel Waldo, the Boston developer who owned all of this area (and for whom the county is named).

✐ **Owls Head Transportation Museum** (207-594-4418; www.ohtm.org), adjacent to the Knox County Regional Airport off Rt. 73, Owls Head (2 miles south of Rockland). Open daily year-round except Christmas, Thanksgiving, New Year's Day, and the first non-Easter Sunday in April. Apr.–Oct., 10–5; Nov.–Mar., 10–4. $7 adults, $6 seniors, $5 under 12, under 5 free. $18 for families. A dollar or two more on special-event days such as antique aeroplane air shows, or antique car and motorcycle auctions. One of the country's outstanding collections of antique planes and automobiles, and unique because everything works. On weekends there are special demonstrations of such magnificent machines as a 1901 Oldsmobile and a 1918 "Jenny" airplane; sometimes rides are offered in a spiffy

Model T. In the exhibition hall you can take a 100-year journey through the evolution of transportation, from horse-drawn carriages to World War I fighter planes; from a 16-cylinder Cadillac to a Rolls-Royce; from the Red Baron's Fokker triplane to a Ford trimotor.

Christina Tree

ROCKLAND BREAKWATER LIGHT

LIGHTHOUSES ✐ **Maine Lighthouse Museum** (207-594-0311; www.maine lighthousemuseum.com), Gateway Visitor Center, 1 Park Dr., Rockland. Open daily Memorial Day–Labor Day, Mon.–Sat. 9–5 and Sun. 10–4; then weekdays and 10–2 Sat. through Columbus Day weekend. Nominal entrance fee. Billed as the country's largest exhibit of lighthouse lenses and lifesaving artifacts, the display showcases more than a dozen Fresnel lenses. Working foghorns, flashing lights, search-and-rescue gear, buoys, bells, rescue boats, and half models round out rotating exhibits.

Maine has 65 lighthouses, and Penobscot Bay boasts the largest concentration. Three in the Rockland area are accessible by land. One is the **Rockland Breakwater Light** (www.rocklandlighthouse.com) at the end of the almost mile-long granite breakwater (turn off Rt. 1 onto Waldo Ave. just north of Rockland, then right onto Samoset Rd. to the end); the breakwater is a good spot for a picnic. The second lighthouse is the **Owls Head Light**, built in 1825 atop sheer cliffs, but with safe trails down one side to the rocks below—good for scrambling and picnicking. From Rockland or the Owls Head Transportation Museum, take Rt. 73 to North Shore Dr. After about 2 miles you come to a small post office at an intersection. Turn left onto Main St. and after 0.25 mile make a left onto Lighthouse Dr. Just north of the village of Port Clyde (turn off Rt. 131 onto Marshall Point Rd.) is the **Marshall Point Lighthouse Museum** (207-372-6450), open June–Sep., Sun.–Fri. 1–5 and Sat. 10–5; also weekends in May and Oct., 1–5. Built in 1885, deactivated in 1971, this is a small light on a scenic point; part of the former lighthouse keeper's home is now a lively museum dedicated to the history of the town of St. George in general and the light station (established in 1832) in particular. Even if the lighthouse isn't open, this is a great spot to sit, walk, and picnic.

OWL'S HEAD LIGHT

Christina Tree

THE MORRIS HOUSE BY N. C. WYETH

Farnsworth Art Museum and Wyeth Center (207-596-6457; www.farnsworth museum.org), 16 Museum St., Rockland. Open year-round, but days and hours vary: Memorial Day–Columbus Day, open daily 10–5 (call for evening hours); Columbus Day–May, Tue.–Sun. 10–4, plus holiday Mondays. Admission to the museum and Farnsworth Homestead (see below) is $10 adults, $8 senior citizens, $8 students over 18; no charge under 18. This exceptional art museum was established by Lucy Farnsworth, who amazed everyone when, on her death at age 97 in 1935, she had left $1.3 million to preserve her house and build a library and art gallery to honor the memory of her father. From the beginning the collection included paintings of Maine by Winslow Homer, George Bellows, and a (then) little-known local summer resident, Andrew Wyeth.

The museum's expansion, now housed in five buildings, has been steady and Maine focused. A permanent exhibit, *Maine in America: Two Hundred Years of American Art*, traces the evolution of Maine landscape paintings. The museum features Hudson River School artists like Thomas Cole, and 19th-century marine artist Fitz Hugh Lane; American impressionists Frank Benson, Willard Metcalf, Childe Hassam, and Maurice Prendergast; early-20th-century greats like Rockwell Kent and Charles Woodbury; and such "modernists" as John Marin and Marsden Hartley. Rockland-raised painter and sculptor Louise Nevelson is also well represented.

The Jamien Morehouse Wing, housing four new galleries, was added in 2000 and houses both the permanent collection and changing exhibitions. The Farnsworth's original Georgian Revival library houses an extensive collection and changing exhibits of reference materials and serves as the site for regularly scheduled lectures and concerts. Gardens connect the main

museum with the Wyeth Center. Note Robert Indiana's *Love* sculpture near
the museum entrance.

The MBNA Center for the Wyeth Family in Maine, a two-story exhibit
space in a former church, displays works by two members of America's
most prominent artistic dynasty: N. C. Wyeth (1882–1945) and Jamie Wyeth
(born 1946). Exhibits vary. (Andrew Wyeth's paintings are shown in the main
museum.)

Farnsworth Homestead (207-596-6457), Elm St., Rockland. Open Memorial Day–Columbus Day during main museum hours, and weekends in Dec.
(when it's decorated for Christmas and free). Included in museum admission.
The Farnsworth Homestead was built in 1850 by Miss Lucy's father, a tycoon
who was very successful in the lime industry and who also owned a fleet of
ships. Brimming with lavish, colorful Victorian furnishings (all original), it
remains—according to a stipulation in Miss Lucy's will—just as it was when
she died at the age of 97. Curious details of the decor include draperies so
long that they drag on the floor, to indicate that the family could afford to buy
more fabric than was required. Nevertheless, the walls are hung with inexpensive copies of oil paintings known as chromolithographs, a fireplace
mantel is glass painted to resemble marble, and doors are not made of fine
wood grains but, rather, have been painted to imitate them.

The Olson House (207-596-6457), Hawthorn Point Rd., Cushing. Open
Memorial Day–Columbus Day, daily 11–4. $4 over age 18; free under. Admin-
istered by the Farnsworth Art Museum, this house served as a backdrop for
many works by Andrew Wyeth, including *Christina's World*. It's been inten-
tionally left unfurnished except for interpretive materials. On Pleasant Point,
accessed by quiet back roads, this saltwater farm makes a good bicycle
destination. Built in the late 1700s, it was remodeled in 1872 but remained in
the same family, ultimately passing to Alvara and Christina (1892–1968)
Olson. It has been owned by the Farnsworth since 1991. The house, both
inside and out, evokes the familiar painting.

THE OLSON HOUSE

Farnsworth Art Museum

Island Institute (207-594-9209; www.islandinstitute.org), 386 Main St., Rockland. A nonprofit organization focusing on the human dimension of Maine's 14 surviving year-round island communities (a century ago there were 300). The idea initially was to get residents of different islands talking to each other. The monthly *Working Waterfront* newspaper as well as the glossy *Island Journal* focus on shared concerns ranging from fisheries to schools to mapping. Check out changing exhibits.

✳ To Do

BICYCLING **Bikesenjava** (207-596-1004; www.haybikesenjava.com), 143 Maverick St., Rockland, is the source of rental hybrid and mountain bikes, also tag-a-longs and 21-speed kid's mountain bikes and car racks, along with espresso, "designer" coffees, and chai tea.

Georges River Bikeways is the name of a free map/guide tracing routes along the river and in its watershed area from Thomaston north into Liberty. Check with the **Georges River Land Trust** (207-594-5166), 328 Main St., Rockland.

BOAT EXCURSIONS Check with the chamber of commerce for current excursions. Also see the **Maine State Ferry Service** under *Getting Around*. The ferry rides to both North Haven and Vinalhaven are reasonably priced and a good way to get out on the water. Both islands make good day trips, but a bike is very helpful on Vinalhaven. **Monhegan** is a justly famous day trip, and **Monhegan Boat Line** (207-372-8848) offers a variety of cruises as well as regular service from Port Clyde. All three islands are described in detail in the "Midcoast Islands" chapter.

Daysails and longer

Wendameen (207-594-1751; www.schooneryacht.com) is a classic 67-foot schooner, her wood and brass beautifully restored by owner-captain Neal Parker, who takes passengers on overnight cruises from Rockland. Board at 2 PM to sail and spend the night in a quiet cove. $180 per person includes dinner and breakfast. Fourteen passengers maximum.

Summertime **Cruises** (1-800-562-8290; www.schoonersummertime.com), 115 South St., Rockland, offers three- and six-day cruises on a 53-foot pinky schooner for up to six passengers throughout the summer. In spring and autumn Captain Bill Brown offers daysails.

∞ **Schooner** *Ellida* (888-807-6921; www.maineclassicschooners.com). Captain Paul and Kristina Williamson's vintage-1922 wooden yacht, designed by John Alden, offers a mix of cruises ranging from 1 to 5 days, accommodating just 10 passengers, also available for functions. Captain Paul performs nuptials.

Morning in Maine (207-691-7245; www.amorninginmaine.com), Rockland City Pier. A classic coastal ketch with an overall length of 55 feet, captained by marine biologist Bob Pratt, offers sails ranging from a few hours to overnights for up to 21 people.

Bugeye Schooner *Jenny Norman* (207-542-3695; www.sailmainebugeye.com). Captains Mike and Julie Rogers have restored this classic, 49-foot Chesapeake Bay vessel and offer daysails May–Oct. from Rockland. Inquire about sunset music and massage cruises.

BOAT RENTALS **Midcoast Yacht Sales and Rentals** (207-882-6445), Rockland, rents powerboats. **Bay Island Yacht Charters & Sailing School** (207-596-7550 or 1-800-421-2492), 117 Tilson Ave., Rockland, rents sailboats and motorboats. **Johanson Boatworks** (207-596-7060 or 1-877-456-4267), 11 Farwell Dr., Rockland, offers sailboat charters.

SEA KAYAKING **Breakwater Kayak** (207-596-6895; www.breakwaterkayak .com), behind Landings Restaurant on Commercial St., Rockland. Two-hour to multiday guided kayaking tours.

Port Clyde Kayaks (207-372-8128; www.portclydekayaks.com), 440 Glenmore Rd., Port Clyde. Guided tours take you across Port Clyde Harbor to Marshall Point Light and beyond. Also see **Maine Sport Outfitters** in the "Camden/Rockport Area" chapter and Vinalhaven-based **Sea Escape Kayak** in "Midcoast Islands."

FISHING AND HUNTING The **Rockland-Thomaston Chamber of Commerce** (see *Guidance*) offers information on fishing (both salt and fresh water) and registered duck hunting guides.

HORSEBACK RIDING **The Riding Center at Mount Pleasant Farm** (207-785-4628; www.mtpleasantfarm.org), Rt. 17, Union. Open May 12–Labor Day, Mon.–Sat. 9–5, weekends after Labor Day. Reservations required. Lessons, horsemanship day camp (7 years and older), and trail rides are offered on a 200-acre farm with 15 miles of trails. Home to Mountain Equine Rescue.

GOLF **Rockland Golf Club** (207-594-9322), 606 Old County Rd., Rockland. Open Apr.–Oct. This 18-hole public course gets high marks from pros; complete with a modern clubhouse serving meals from 7 AM.

For the local resort specializing in golf, see **Samoset Golf Course** in "Camden/Rockport Area."

RAILROAD EXCURSION **The Maine Eastern Railroad** (866-636-2457; www.maineeasternrailroad.com) offers 54-mile seasonal runs between Rockland and Brunswick, stopping in Bath and Wiscasset. It's a beautiful trip along the coast in plush 1940s and '50s coaches, a dining car, and (weekends only) a glass-domed observation car, behind a 1950s diesel electric engine. In 2005 there were round-trip runs Tue.–Sun., but check the web site for current information.

Gregg Cranna

SCHOONER *AMERICAN EAGLE*

WINDJAMMERS

Note: All these vessels are members of the **Maine Windjammer Association** (1-800-807-WIND; www.sailmainecoast.com). Also see *Windjammers* in "What's Where" and "Camden/Rockport Area." In 3 days aboard a windjammer you can explore islands and remote mainland harbors that would take hundreds of miles of driving and several ferries to reach. Three- and 6-day cruises are offered late May–mid-Oct. and run $395–915. All the vessels are inspected and certified each year by the Coast Guard.

American Eagle (207-594-8007 or 1-800-648-4544; www.schooner americaneagle.com), North End Shipyard, Rockland. One of the last classic Gloucester fishing schooners to be launched (in 1930), this 92-foot vessel continued to fish (minus her original stern and masts, plus a pilothouse) off Gloucester until 1983, when Captain John Foss brought her to Rockland's North End Shipyard and spent the next 2 years restoring and refitting her. The *Eagle* was built with an engine (so she still has one) as well as sails, and she offers some comfortable belowdecks spaces, well stocked with the captain's favorite books about Maine. The *Eagle* sails farther out to sea (to see whales and seabirds) than other windjammers and also offers a 10-day July cruise to New Brunswick and a Labor Day sail to Gloucester (Massachusetts) to participate in a race that she won in both 1997 and 1998. She offers 3- and 6-day cruises, accommodating 26 guests in 14 double cabins.

Heritage (207-594-8007 or 1-800-648-4544; www.schoonerheritage.com), North End Shipyard, Rockland. Captain Doug Lee likes to describe his graceful, 95-foot, 30-passenger vessel as "the next generation of coasting schooner rather than a replica." He notes that schooners were modified over the years to suit whatever cargo they carried. Here headroom in the cabins and the top of companionways was raised to accommodate upright cargo, and the main cabin is an unusually airy, bright space in which to gather. Captain Lee is a marine historian who, with his wife and co-captain, Linda, designed and built the *Heritage* in Rockland's North End Shipyard. Their two daughters, Clara and Rachel, have always summered aboard ship and now sometimes sail as crew. Both captains are unusually warm hosts.

J&E Riggin (207-594-1875 or 1-800-869-0604; www.mainewindjammer .com) was built in 1927 for the oyster-dredging trade. A speedy 90-footer, she was extensively rebuilt in the 1970s before joining the windjammer trade. Captains Jon Finger and Anne Mahle take 24 passengers in nine double and two triple cabins. Mahle, a graduate of the Culinary Institute of America, is an outstanding chef who has just published a cookbook, *At Home, At Sea*. The *J&E Riggin* welcomes families with children ages 6 and up on special family cruises.

Stephen Taber (207-594-0035 or 1-800-999-7352; www.stephentaber.com) was launched in 1871 and is the oldest documented U.S. sailing vessel in continuous use. She is 68 feet long and accommodates 22 passengers. Captain Noah Barnes is the first second-generation windjammer captain, taking over the helm from his parents (both licensed captains), who restored the vessel and sailed it for 25 years. The *Taber* continues to have an enthusiastic following. Inquire about special-interest cruises.

Victory Chimes (207-594-0755 or 1-800-745-5651; www.victorychimes .com). "There was nothing special about this boat in 1900 when she was built," Captain Kip Files is fond of telling his passengers at their first breakfast aboard. "But now she's the only three-masted American-built schooner left. And she's the largest commercial sailing vessel in the United States." The *Chimes* is 132 feet long, accommodating 40 passengers in a variety of cabins (4 singles, 2 quads, 1 triple, 12 doubles).

Nathaniel Bowditch (207-596-0401 or 1-800-288-4098; www.windjammer vacation.com) comes by her speed honestly: She was built in East Boothbay as a racing yacht in 1922. Eighty-two feet long, she took special honors in the 1923 Bermuda Race and served in the Coast Guard during World War II. She has since been rebuilt. Captain Owen Dorr's love of sailing runs deep in his family. His great-grandfather was mate aboard one of the last five-masted schooners to sail the East Coast. In the 1940s Owen's parents worked for

Continued on next page

Continued from previous page

Captain Frank Swift, the man credited with starting the Maine windjammer tradition. He and his wife, Cathie Dorr, met aboard a Maine schooner (she was a passenger, he, a crew member). According to Owen, windjamming is "like having people come to your house every week, except your backyard keeps changing!" The *Nathaniel Bowditch* accommodates 24 passengers in 11 double-bunked cabins and 2 single "Pullmans"; in-cabin sinks.

Isaac H. Evans (207-549-7956 or 1-877-238-1325; www.isaacevans.com). A trim 22-passenger schooner dating (in part) to 1886, built for oystering in Delaware Bay, now back in service with owner-captain Brenda G. Walker. There are 11 double berths, some side-by-side as well as upper–lower bunks. Three- and 4-day and weeklong cruises are offered. Specializes in family trips; children 6 and over welcome on shorter cruises.

WINDJAMMER *NATHANIEL BOWDITCH*

Maine Windjammer Assoc.

SPECIAL LEARNING PROGRAM **Hurricane Island Outward Bound School** (207-594-5548; www.hurricaneisland.org), 75 Mechanic St., Rockland 04841. Outward Bound challenges participants to do things they never thought they could—and then push themselves just a little farther. May–Oct., courses are offered in sailing, sea kayaking, and rock climbing in Wheeler Bay and Hurricane Island (near Vinalhaven).

✳ Green Space

BEACHES ✑ **Johnson Memorial Park**, Chickawaukee Lake, Rt. 17, 2 miles north of downtown Rockland. Restrooms, picnic area, a sand beach, and warm water add up to the area's best swimming, good for small children.

⚓ **Birch Point State Park**, also known as Lucia Beach, off Ash Point Rd. in Owls Head. Sandy, with smooth boulders for sunning, wooded walking trails, and picnic benches. Marked from Rt. 73.

Drift Inn Beach in Port Clyde, down Drift Inn Rd. by the Harpoon Restaurant, just off Rt. 31; a small beach in a great spot.

WALKING/PICNICKING Rockland waterfront. The area's most spectacular stretch of the **Rockland Harbor Trail** begins on the Samoset Hotel property just over the Rockport line and runs 1.7 miles out along the Rockland Breakwater to the lighthouse. There's always plenty of boat traffic. Another rewarding section of the trail runs from Harbor Park at the public landing, south along the water past **Sandy Beach Park** (picnic benches) to Mechanic St. and on to Snow **Marine Park**. Along Park Dr. **Gilbert and Adams Central Park** offers benches, flowers, a gazebo, and harbor views.

Owls Head Light State Park. This classic lighthouse is set into a beautiful point with walks and views on both the bay and harbor sides, picnic tables. See *Lighthouses* for directions.

Waldo Tyler Wildlife Sanctuary, Buttermilk Lane (off Rt. 73), South Thomaston, is a birding spot on the Weskeag River.

⚓ A Rt. 1 picnic area overlooks Glen Cove, between Rockland and Rockport.

The Georges River Land Trust (207-594-5166), 328 Main St., Studio 206, Rockland, publishes a map/guide to the Georges Highland Path, a foot trail through the hills of the Georges River watershed. Maps are available at the chamber of commerce.

FOXBORO THOROUGHFARE

Christina Tree

✳ Lodging

INNS AND BED & BREAKFASTS

In Rockland 04841

&. **The Captain Lindsey House**
(207-596-7950 or 1-800-523-2145;
www.lindseyhouse.com), 5 Lindsey St.
Built in 1837 as one of Rockland's first
inns, the current feel is that of a small
hotel. With richly paneled public
rooms and nine spacious guest rooms
(one handicapped accessible), it's a
gem, and the most convenient lodging
to the Farnsworth Museum and Main
Street shops. It's the creation of
schooner captains Ken and Ellen
Barnes, who also have restored and
operated the windjammer *Stephen
Taber* for more than 25 years. Each
guest room is different but all have
air-conditioning, phone, and TV as
well as private baths. Rates are $140–
190, from $85–110 off-season, includ-
ing an ample buffet breakfast, served
in the garden, weather permitting.

Berry Manor Inn (207-596-7696 or
1-800-774-5692; www.berrymanorinn
.com), 81 Talbot Ave., P.O. Box 1117.
This expansive 19th-century shingle-
style mansion is a sumptuous, romantic retreat. The 12 guest rooms,
divided among the second and third
floors of the mansion and the second
floor of the Carriage House, feature
queen- and king-sized beds, working
fireplaces, and luxurious baths with
soaking or whirlpool tubs. A two-room,
two-bath suite in the Carriage House
has a separate living room. All have
phone, dataport, and air-conditioning.
A tray with coffee and juice arrives (if
desired) at your door at 7 AM. $135–
235 for rooms, $320 for the suite mid-
June–mid-Oct., otherwise $95–215,
including a full breakfast.

∞ **LimeRock Inn** (207-594-2257 or
1-800-LIME-ROC; www.limerockinn
.com), 96 Limerock St. Pam Maus
continues to lighten and brighten this
1890s Queen Anne–style mansion on
a quiet residential street. The nine
guest rooms (all with private bath) are
furnished with antiques. Our favorite
by far is Island Cottage, with painted
cottage furniture and decorated in
Provençal blues and yellows, with a
private deck to the landscaped garden
beyond. $110–215 depending on sea-
son. Inquire about the reasonably
priced single. Rates include a full
breakfast.

❀ &. **Old Granite Inn** (207-594-9036
or 1-800-386-9036; www.oldgraniteinn
.com), 546 Main St. An 1840s mansion
built of local granite, attached to a
1790 house, set in a flower and sculpture garden, right across from the
Maine State Ferry Terminal (also the
Concord Trailways stop). The obvious
place to stay before boarding a ferry to
Vinalhaven, North Haven, or Matinicus. Innkeepers Ragan and John Cary
offer a living room and dining room
with rich woodwork, and the 12 guest
rooms (9 with private bath) are hung
with art and furnished with antiques.
Four rooms are on the ground floor
(all are wheelchair accessible), six are
on the second floor (the two with harbor views are the largest and most
expensive), and one third-floor room
has a queen bed, private bath, and
harbor views. $80–170 per night in
high season, less off season, includes
a full breakfast.

Lakeshore Inn (207-594-4209 or 1-
866-540-8800; www.lakeshorebb
.com), 184 Lakeview Dr. (Rt. 17). A
much-modified 1767 home set above
Rt. 17, overlooking Lake Chickawau-

kee (good swimming), 2 miles north of downtown Rockland. Innkeepers Jim and Pat Masson offer four air-conditioned rooms with private bath and phone and dataports; two overlook the lake. Amenities include an enclosed outdoor hot tub. Two-night, all-inclusive "Ladies Only Spa Weekends" ($579 per person) are a specialty. Two-night minimum in high season and on weekends. Breakfast is full. $145–155 double in-season.

On Spruce Head and on the St. George Peninsula

🐾 ⚓ **Craignair Inn** (207-594-7644 or 1-800-320-9997; www.craignair .com), Clark Island Rd., Spruce Head 04859. Open Apr.–Dec. Steve and Neva Joseph have breathed new life into this old inn. Sited on 4 shorefront acres, it offers 21 guest rooms, divided between the main house (5 with private bath; 8 share five baths) and more luxurious units (private baths) in the Vestry, a former chapel set in gardens in the rear. We like Room 8 in the house with twins, braided rug, rocker, oak dresser, and a view of Clark Island. The dining room overlooks the water and is open to the public for dinner. Walk across the causeway to the Clark Island shoreline. From $60 to $140 per couple, depending on season, including breakfast. Two-night minimum stay on holiday weekends. $10 extra for a pet.

🐾 ⚓ **Ocean House** (207-372-6691 or 1-800-269-6691; www.oceanhouse hotel.com), P.O. Box 66, Port Clyde 04855. Open May–Oct. Many patrons discover this friendly old village inn because it's the logical place to spend the night before or after boarding the morning ferry to Monhegan. Former islander Bud Murdock offers 10 pleasant upstairs guest rooms in this building (8 with private bath; 2 share), and several have water views (also available from the upstairs porch). This is a good place for a single traveler, thanks to the pleasant single rooms and rates and the ease with which you meet others. At this writing there's a Monday fish fry; breakfast is served to both guests and the public, 7–noon. Rooms are $75 (shared bath), $93 for a double with private bath, and $108 for a larger room. Add $5 for a 1-night stay.

⚓ **East Wind Inn** (207-372-6366 or 1-800-241-8439 www.eastwindinn .com), P.O. Box 149, Tenants Harbor 04860. Open Apr.–Nov. Under the longtime ownership of Tim Watts, this rather formal waterside inn has a large parlor with a piano, but the best seats in the house are on the wrap-around porch overlooking Tenants Harbor. Rooms vary from singles with shared baths ($129) and standard double with private bath ($159) to suites ($189) in the main house, waterside apartments in the Meeting House ($209), and luxurious units ($219–299) in Wheeler Cottage. All rates include a full breakfast and are less off-season. The dining room serves breakfast and dinner in-season (see *Dining Out*). A number of guests sail in. **The Chandlery** on the wharf offers light food as well as marine supplies and gifts.

⚓ **Weskeag Inn** (207-596-6676 or 1-800-596-5576; www.weskeag.com), Rt. 73, P.O. Box 213, South Thomaston 04858. Open year-round. Convenient to the Owls Head Transportation Museum and the Knox County Regional Airport (pickups provided, perhaps in an antique car). A hospitable

1830s home overlooking the Weskeag estuary, within walking distance of shops in South Thomaston, and handy to a public boat landing. Seven guest rooms have private bath; two share or are rented as a suite, some with water view. Guests are drawn down the lawn to the tidal Weskeag River. $100–150 in-season, from $85 off-season, includes a full breakfast.

Blue Lupin Bed & Breakfast (207-594-2673), 372 Waterman Beach Rd., South Thomaston 04858. In her delightfully old-fashioned home with its many books, Helen Mitchell offers three rooms and one suite, all with private bath, overlooking the Atlantic. Handy to the Waterman's Beach Lobster café (see *Lobster Pounds*) and to the beach at Birch Point State Park. All rooms have TV/VCR, and the library is well stocked with videos. $85–155 includes a full breakfast. Children 12 and older welcome.

In Friendship 04547

🐾 **Harbor Hill B&B** (207-832-6646), P.O. Box 35, 5 Harbor Hill Lane. Open May–Nov. 1, also winter weekends by arrangement. Liga and Len (Chip) Jahnke's 1800s farmhouse is set on a hillside sloping to the sea, with stunning views of the islands in Muscongus Bay. The large downstairs front suite is a beauty, furnished in antiques, well supplied with Maine books, and overlooking the harbor. All three suites have water views and private bath. Rates of $100–115 include a three-course Scandinavian-style breakfast that begins with fresh fruit and might include the best blueberry pancakes ever. A two-bedroom cottage is $575 per week or $125 daily (2-night minimum stay). Children welcome. Pets can stay in the cottage with prior arrangement.

🚣 **The Outsiders' Inn** (207-832-5197), corner of Rts. 97 and 220, 4 Main St. Open in summer months and by reservation off-season. Bill and Debbie Michaud have created a casually comfortable atmosphere in an 1830 house. Many guests take advantage of Bill Michaud's kayaking expertise; sea kayaks are available for rent and for guided expeditions in nearby Muscongus Bay. Pleasant doubles with private bath are $80; $65 with shared bath, $5 less for singles, breakfast included. A small cottage in the garden is $385 per week. Facilities include a sauna.

MOTEL **Navigator Motor Inn** (207-594-2131 or 1-800-545-8025; www .navigatorinn.com), 520 Main St., Rockland 04841. Open all year. Geared to families bound for the islands of Vinalhaven, North Haven, and Matinicus. The Maine State Ferry Terminal is across the street, so you can park your car in line for the early-morning ferry and walk back to your room. This is a five-story, 80-room motor inn with cable TV and a restaurant that serves from 6:30 AM. $79–115 in high season, more during festivals, less in winter.

COTTAGES AND EFFICIENCIES A list of cottages, primarily in the Owls Head and Spruce Head areas, is available from the **Rockland-Thomaston Chamber of Commerce** (see *Guidance*).

✳ Where to Eat

DINING OUT **Primo** (207-596-0770; www.primorestaurant.com), 2 S. Main St. (Rt. 73), Rockland. Open daily in summer, otherwise Wed.–Mon., 5:30–9:30 or less; call first. Reservations are a must. One of Maine's very special restaurants, it's also one of a handful in the entire country to grow so much of what it serves. "Primo" was chef and co-owner Melissa Kelly's grandfather and a butcher. Kelly raises her own pork and makes several kinds of sausages as well as preparing cuts of meats and overseeing the gardens and greenhouses on the property. Some water-view tables, but most patrons have their eyes on their roast striped sea bass Livornese, with caper berries, black olives, and tomatoes, or other great meals. Appetizers might include roast Pemaquid oyster with deviled crab and a salad of lettuce from outside the kitchen door. You might also dine on a great flat-bread pizza with tomato and house-made sausage. The house cannoli are crisp, rich, and excellent. A big wine list, and good mojitos and other special drinks. The menu is also available in the bar. Entrées $23–32.

Amalfi (207-596-0012; www.amalfi-tonight.com), 421 Main St., Rockland. Open year-round (except Mon.) for dinner. Chef David Cooke's downtown restaurant, larger than it looks from the street, deserves rave reviews for specialties drawn from all sides of the Mediterranean. You might want to begin with mussels steamed with garlic, shallots, and white wine, or grilled quail glazed with a Turkish mulberry sauce. Paella is the specialty, in the traditional mix of seafood, chorizo, and chicken, but also in all-seafood and vegetarian versions. Entrées $14–21.

Café Miranda (207-594-2034; www.cafemiranda.com), 15 Oak St., Rockland. Open year round 5:30–9:30. Be sure to reserve for dinner at chef Kerry Altiero's small, busy dining room. The open kitchen features a brick oven and seafood grill, and the large menu, "soulful ethnic and American" dishes that might range from Viet-style pork to duck confit (house-cured), fire roasted on spinach. Our pink-pottery platter of curried mussels and shrimp (both in the shell) was served on polenta with sweet peppers and onions, mopped up with flat bread and olive oil. Wine and beer are served. Entrées $13–21.

Grapes Restaurant (207-594-9050; www.grapesrestaurant.com), at the public landing, Rockland. Open daily for lunch and dinner. Location, location! A big barn of a place with great harbor views, plus a large steak and seafood menu. Sandwiches and salads all day. Dinner entrées $14.95–18.95.

Sul Mare (207-372-9995), 13 River Rd., Tenants Harbor. Open year-round 5–10 PM daily. In a building that now resembles a stuccoed and tile roofed Italian trattoria, chef-owner Kevin Kieley—"100 percent Irish but I went to school in Italy"—makes grilled steaks, roast prime rib, and grilled seafood. Grilled shrimp with Tuscan olive oil and cannelloni beans ($12) and grilled calamari with smoky chipotle mayonnaise ($12) are appetizers; risotto with lobster, artichokes, truffles, and Parmesan ($25) could be an entrée on the changing menu. The lobstermen who come here prefer to eat prime rib and drink Budweiser, Kieley says, but he has good Italian wine for the rest of us. Entrées $10–25.

Thomaston Café and Bakery (207-354-8589; www.thomastoncafe.com), 154 Main St., Thomaston. Open year-round for breakfast, lunch, and dinner, also Sunday brunch. Chef-owners Herbert Peters and Eleanor Masin-Peters have a strong local following.

Lunch on fresh-made soups, great sandwiches, specials like fish cakes with home fries, salads. The dinner menu ranges from wild mushroom hash to fresh fettuccine with brandied lobster meat. Lobster ravioli is a specialty. Dinner entrées $12–22.

Hannibal's Café (207-785-3663), 289 Common Rd., Union. Open year-round, from 11 AM Tue.–Fri., from 8 AM Sat., and for Sunday brunch 8–2. Dependably good for lunch and dinner with a wide choice of "classical, ethnic, and vegetarian cuisine," from tofu cutlet ranchero to maple-glazed pork loin, housed in an 1839 farmhouse with views of Seven Tree Pond. Entrées $8.95–17.

Craignair Inn (207-594-7644), Clark Island Rd., off Rt. 73, Spruce Head. Walk the shore before dining by a water-view window from a menu that might include fresh haddock, scallops, shrimp, and crabmeat broiled with lemon, white wine, and a light butter sauce. Lobster Newburg is a specialty. Entrées $16.95–22.95.

East Wind Inn (207-372-6366; www.eastwindinn.com), Tenants Harbor. Open for dinner daily Apr.–Nov. Reservations suggested. A dining room overlooking the working harbor with a porch on which cocktails are served in summer. Featuring local seafood and produce, dinners might include roast Atlantic salmon with horseradish and fresh herbs ($18.95) or rosemary boneless beef short ribs ($19.95).

EATING OUT

In Rockland
 Market on Main (207-594-0015), 315 Main St. Open daily for lunch, dinner, and Sunday brunch. An attractive and popular storefront café and

deli geared to the museum crowd; good for salads and sandwiches. Entrées, served all day, might include eggplant rollatini and lemon-pepper baked haddock. Serving wine, beer, and espresso.

 The Water Works (207-596-2753), 7 Lindsey St. Serving lunch and dinner daily, late light fare. The home of the Rocky Bay Brewing Company, a respectable microbrew, this informal pub is just far enough off Main St. to be an oasis on a day when Rockland's more obvious eateries are mobbed. Good burgers, steaks and salads, dine inside or out.

 The Brown Bag (207-596-6372), 606 Main St. (north of downtown). Open Mon.–Sat. 6:30 AM–4 PM. This expanded storefront restaurant is a local favorite, with an extensive breakfast and sandwich menu, soups, chowders, and daily specials. Make your selection at the counter and carry it to your table when it's ready.

 The Landings Restaurant & Marina (207-596-6563), 1 Commercial St. Open year-round. On the harbor with outside as well as inside seating; serves 11–9:30 from a menu that ranges from a hot dog to steak, lobster, and a full-scale clambake. Fried clams, fish-and-chips, and a good selection of sandwiches.

 Rockland Café (207-596-7556), 441 Main St. Open daily 6 AM–9 PM. This is a reliable family eatery, good for fish-and-chips, soups, salad, clam rolls, and daily specials. Warning: The crabcakes are more like crab pancakes. Look for the green-and-white-striped awning.

Kate's Seafood (207-594-2626), Rt. 1, south of Rockland. Apr.–Oct. A local favorite for fried, boiled, and steamed seafood, chowder, and lobster rolls. For dinner, try the seafood Primavera or seafood sauté with scallops, Maine shrimp, lobster, and mussels. Beer and wine served.

Salt Bay Café (207 563 3302), 277 Park St. Open year-round for lunch and dinner. A recent arrival in Rockland but bringing with it a strong reputation from Damariscotta, its original home. The large menu ranges from crabcakes, pastas, salads, and fried oysters to filet mignon. Best vegetarian menu in the area with more than a dozen choices at lunch, like veggie lasagna of the day. Dinner options might include crabcakes, pecan-crusted salmon, and a genuine choice of vegetarian dishes and pastas.

♂ **Wasses Wagon**, 2 N. Main St. A local institution for hot dogs.

In Thomaston
Harbor View Restaurant (207-354-8173), Thomas Harbor Point. Basically open year-round for lunch (11–2:30) and dinner (5–8). This harborside standby is good for daily soups, sandwiches, and salads at lunch; at dinner, seafood is the specialty. Dinner entrées range $10.95–19.95, but burgers are always available. Nightly specials. Full license. In-season there's dining on the deck.

Also see **Thomaston Café and Bakery** under *Dining Out.*

In the Port Clyde area
The Dip Net (207-372-6307), at the end of Rt. 131. Open seasonally 11–10. Seating inside is very limited, but on a pleasant evening this is a great spot for steamed clams and mussels, served at a waterside table right on the dock. The bouillabaisse gets raves. Soups, salads, sandwiches, and a veggie platter are also on Scott

Yokovenko's menu. The neighboring **Port Clyde General Store** makes great "chowda" and good sandwiches and has picnic benches on the same deck. The **Ocean House**, just up the road (see *Lodging*), serves breakfast, a real convenience if you've driven from a distance to catch the Monhegan ferry, which now requires you to be there an hour early.

♂ **Farmer's Restaurant** (207-372-6111), Rt. 131, Tenants Harbor. Open year-round for breakfast, lunch, and dinner. A dependable family restaurant with breakfast sides like corned beef hash and fish cakes, soups, sandwiches, and fried baskets for lunch; and moderately fried or broiled seafood dinners.

The Harpoon (207-372-6304), corner of Drift Inn and Marshall Point Rds., Port Clyde. Open May–mid-Oct. for dinner, Wed.–Sat. in shoulder months. This engaging seafood restaurant in the seaside village of Port Clyde (just off Rt. 131, around the corner from the harbor) specializes in the local catch. Try the blackened seafood, lazy lobster, fried combo plate, or prime rib. The bar is lively. Entrées $11.95–20.95.

LOBSTER POUNDS Miller's Lobster Company (207-594-7406), Wheeler's Bay, off Rt. 73, Spruce Head. Open 11–7, Memorial Day–Labor Day. This is our hands-down favorite: on a working harbor, old-fashioned, family owned and operated, with a loyal following. Tables are on the wharf; lobsters and clams are cooked in seawater, served with fixings, topped off with fresh-made pies. BYOB.

♂ **Cod End Cookhouse** (207-372-8981; www.codend.com), on the wharf, Tenants Harbor. Open Memorial Day

late Sep., daily 11–8:30. Hidden down a lane, a combination fish shop and informal wharfside eatery (tables inside and out) right on Tenants Harbor with a separate cookhouse: chowders and lobster rolls, lobster dinners and clams. Also burgers and sandwiches. Children's menu. Beer and wine served.

Waterman's Beach Lobsters (207-596-7419), off Rt. 73, South Thomaston. Open Thu.–Sun. 11–7 in summertime. Oceanfront feasting on the deck: lobster and clam dinners, seafood rolls, pies.

OTHER In Good Company (207-593-9110), 415 Main St., Rockland. Open from 3 PM nightly. A wine bar in a living-room-like setting, serving salads, cheeses, nibbles, and light meals such as cedar-planked salmon and cold sliced beef tenderloin.

Jess's Seafood Market (207-596-6068; www.jessmarket.com), 118 S. Main St., Rockland. Wholesale and retail lobsters, overnight shipping, also the city's prime seafood market, frequently augmented by fresh produce and takeout—which usually includes our best and most reasonably priced crabmeat rolls of the season. Wine and a wide selection of beers also sold.

✳ Entertainment

The Farnsworth Museum (207-596-6457; www.farnsworthmuseum.org) in Rockland stages a year-round series of Sunday concerts, free with museum admission; reservations advised.

The Strand Theatre (207-594-0070; www.rocklandstrand.com), 345 Main St., Rockland. Vintage 1923, a recently restored classic downtown theater offering films and live performances.

Down East Singers (207-549-0061; www.downeastsingers.com), Thomaston. The Midcoast's largest community chorus performs Sep.–June.

✳ Selective Shopping

Rockland's mile-long Main Street recalls 19th-century prosperity in florid brick. Since the opening of the **Farnsworth Museum Store** (corner of Main and Elm Sts.), boutique-style stores as well as galleries have proliferated around it. Note especially: **Archipelago** (No. 386), formerly Islands of Maine Gallery, now in expanded quarters at the new Island Institute quarters, representing roughly 100 craftspeople and artists on "hinged" as well as real islands. **Huston Tuttle & Gallery One** (No. 365) is a serious art store with a gallery upstairs; **The Store** (No. 435), featuring a wide selection of cooking supplies; **The Grasshopper Shop** (No. 400), a major link in a small Maine chain; **Meander** (No. 373), a mix of things you have never thought of needing; **G. F. MacGregor** (No. 338), a blend of tasteful furniture and furnishings obviously catering to museumgoers. More shops worth noting: **Sea Street Graphics Outlet Store** (No. 475), with silkscreened designs on T-shirts and clothing (made here, widely distributed); the **Black Parrot** (No. 328) specializes in its colorful fleece-lined reversible garments but carries a mix of clothing, toys, cards, and more; **Caravans** (No. 429) sells clothing with its own label, too, as well as much more; and we never pass up **Ravishing Recalls** (No. 389), a useful trove of secondhand clothing.

ART AND CRAFTS GALLERIES So many galleries have opened around the Farnsworth area that an *Arts District Walking Map* is available at most. They include the prestigious, recently expanded **Caldbeck Gallery** (12 Elm St., across from the museum, here since 1982; www.caldbeck.com); goldsmith Thomas O'Donovan's **Harbor Square Gallery** (www.harbor squaregallery.com), filling three floors of a former bank building (374 Main St.) with art but also featuring fine jewelry; **The Gallery at 357 Main** also shows top Maine artists. **Deborah Beckwith Winship**'s bright, primitive-style graphics are familiar to Maine visitors, and her studio at 53 Fulton St. is an excuse to explore Rockland's quickly changing South End. Wyeth fans should check out **OP Limited** (www.wyeth-archives .com) in Thomaston, an upstairs gallery at 157 Main St. selling out-of-print and limited-edition works on paper from the Wyeth Archive. At **Elan Fine Arts** (www.elanfinearts .com), 8 Elm St., Andrew and Ellen Eddy present fine art.

Along Rt. 131 to Port Clyde
Check out **St. George Pottery** (4.5 miles south of Rt. 1), George Pearlman's combination studio and contemporary ceramics gallery. **Noble Clay** in Tenants Harbor, open year-round, displays Trish and Steve Barnes's functional white-and-blue-glazed porcelain pottery with whimsical and botanical designs.

In South Thomaston
At Keag River Pottery (Westbrook St., marked from Rt. 73), Toni Oliveri shapes unusual but functional creations like the glazed vase we bought and love: Its inner ribbons of pottery make it easier to artistically display

flowers. **Old Post Office Gallery & Art of the Sea** on Rt. 73 displays nearly 100 museum-quality full-rigged ships' models; also half models and nautical paintings.

BOOKSTORES **The Reading Corner** (207-596-6651), 408 Main St., Rockland, is a full-service bookstore with an unusual interior filling two storefronts.

The Second Read (207-594-4123), 328 Main St., carries new and used books, and offers a place to drink fine coffee and eat one of the daily sandwich specials while you read.

✐ **The Personal Book Shop** (207-354-8058), 144 Main St., Thomaston. Open year-round 10–6. Marti Reed's shop is more like a book-lined living room than your ordinary bookstore:

HARBOR SQUARE GALLERY

Christina Tree

plenty of places to sit and read but also a large selection of titles; many Maine authors, including out-of-print John Gould and Elisabeth Ogilvie books, and a well-stocked children's room.

Dooryard Books (207-594-5080), 438 Main St., Rockland (open Memorial Day–Columbus Day). A good general stock of hardcover and paperback used books.

Lobster Lane Book Shop (207-594-7520), Spruce Head. Marked from the Off-Island Store. Open May weekends then June–Sep., Thu.–Sun. and weekends through Oct., 12:30–5. Vivian York's stock of 50,000 titles is well known in bookish circles. Specialties include fiction and Maine.

SPECIAL SHOPS **Maine State Prison Shop** (207-354-9237), Main St. (Rt. 1), Thomaston, at the south end of town. Open daily 9–5. A variety of wooden furniture—coffee tables, stools, lamps, and trays—and small souvenirs, all carved by inmates. The prison has moved to Warren but, happily, the shop is still here. Prices are reasonable, and profits go to the craftsmen.

✳ Special Events

June: **Warren Day**—a pancake breakfast, parade, art and quilt shows, chicken barbecue, and auction.

July: Thomaston **Fourth of July** festivities include a big parade, footraces, live entertainment, a crafts fair, barbecue, and fireworks. The **North Atlantic Blues Festival** (*mid-July*), Harbor Park, Rockland (www.north

atlanticbluesfestival.com), is huge. **Maine Windjammer Parade of Sail** (*midmonth*), Rockland Harbor. **Friendship Sloop Days** (*last weekend*) includes a regatta and festivities in Rockland and a parade, BBQ, and children's activities in Friendship.

August: **Maine Lobster Festival** (*first weekend, plus the preceding Wednesday and Thursday*) (www .mainelobsterfestival.com), Harbor Park, Rockland. This is probably the world's biggest lobster feed, prepared in the world's largest lobster boiler. Patrons queue up on the public landing to heap their plates with lobsters, clams, corn, and all the fixings. King Neptune and the Maine Sea Goddess reign over the event, which includes a parade down Main Street, concerts, an art exhibit, contests such as clam shucking and sardine packing, and a race across a string of lobster crates floating in the harbor. **Maine Boats & Harbor Show** (*midmonth*), Harbor Park, Rockland. The **Annual Transportation Spectacular and Aerobatic Show** (*midmonth*), Owls Head Transportation Museum. **Union Fair** and **State of Maine Wild Blueberry Festival** (*third week*) (www.union-fair.org)—a real agricultural fair with tractor- and ox-pulling contests, livestock and food shows, a midway, the crowning of the Blueberry Queen, and, on one day during the week, free mini blueberry pies for all comers.

September: **Rockland HarborFest Jazz and Art Festival.**

November–December: **Rockland Festival of Lights** begins on Thanksgiving—parade, Santa's Village, sleigh rides.

MIDCOAST ISLANDS
MONHEGAN; THE FOX ISLANDS: VINALHAVEN
AND NORTH HAVEN; MATINICUS

MONHEGAN

Eleven miles at sea and barely a mile square, Monhegan is a microcosm of Maine landscapes, everything from 150-foot sheer headlands to Cathedral Woods, from inland meadows to the smooth, low rocks along Lobster Cove. "Beached like a whale" is the way one mariner in 1590 described the island's shape: headlands sloping down to the small off-island of Manana, a blip on Monhegan's silhouette.

Monhegan is known for the quality (also quantity) of its artists and the grit of its fishermen—who lobster only from December through late May. The island's first recorded artist arrived in 1858, and by the 1870s a hotel and several boardinghouses were filled with summer guests, many of them artists. In 1903 Robert Henri, a founder of New York's Ashcan School and a well-known art teacher, discovered Monhegan and soon introduced it to his students, among them George Bellows and Rockwell Kent. Monhegan remains a genuine art colony. Jamie Wyeth owns a house built by Rockwell Kent. More than 20 artists open their studios to visitors (hours are posted on "The Rope Shed/Barn" and printed in handouts) during summer weeks.

The island continues to draw artists in good part because its beauty not only survives but also remains accessible to all. Prospect Hill, the only attempted development, foundered around 1900. It was Theodore Edison, son of the inventor, who amassed property enough to erase its traces and keep the island's cottages (which still number just 130) bunched along the sheltered harbor, the rest preserved as common space and laced with 17 miles of footpaths.

In 1954 Edison helped organize Monhegan Associates, a nonprofit corporation dedicated to preserving the "natural, wild beauty" of the island. Ironically, this is one of the country's few communities to shun electricity until relatively recently. A number of homes and one inn still use kerosene lamps. Vehicles are limited to a few trucks for those with businesses and golf carts for those with medical needs.

Petroglyphs on Manana Island (just offshore) are said to have been carved by Norsemen, but a plaque beside the schoolhouse states that the island was discovered by Captain John Smith in 1614. Native American artifacts on display in the Monhegan Museum may date back 8,000 years. The island's present settlement has been continuous since 1790; it's been a "plantation" since 1839. The year-round population of less than 70 swells to a little more than 600 (not counting day-trippers) in summer; visitors come to walk, to paint, and to reflect. An unusual number come alone.

Monhegan has three inns, several B&Bs, and a limited number of rental cottages. Fog and a frequently rough passage insulate it to some degree, but on summer days a high tide of day-trippers from Boothbay Harbor and New Harbor, as well as Port Clyde, washes over this small, fragile island. More worrisome still are skyrocketing real estate prices. Monhegan Island Sustainable Community Association (MISCA) is now dedicated to ensuring affordable housing for year-round residents.

GUIDANCE A booklet guide to the island is available, along with a confirmation of reservations from the Monhegan Boat Line (see below). Also check out **www .monhegan.com**, the site for Monhegan Commons, not your usual chamber of commerce (there isn't one). It's updated daily with fresh pictures and tracks social and political events.

GETTING THERE **Monhegan Boat Line** (207-372-8848; www.monheganboat .com) operates both the sleek *Elizabeth Ann* and the beloved old *Laura B* from Port Clyde; reservations a must. Service is three times daily in-season, less frequent in spring and fall, and only Mon., Wed., and Fri. in winter. It's a 50- or 70-minute trip, depending on which boat you catch. For details about the ***Balmy Days II*** (www.balmydaycruises.com), see "Boothbay Harbor Region," and for the **Hardy Boat Cruises** (www.hardyboat.com), see "Damariscotta/Newcastle."

MONHEGAN ISLAND

Christina Tree

Also note that the Ocean House in Port Clyde and the Gosnold Arms in New Harbor are within walking distance of two services, taking the sting out of making morning boats.

EQUIPMENT AND RULES Come properly shod for the precipitous paths. Hikers should wear long pants and socks against poison ivy and ticks; bring sweaters and windbreakers. Wading or swimming from any of the tempting coves on the back side of the island can be lethal. Kayaking is discouraged. Flashlights, heavy rubber boots, and rain gear are also good ideas. Public phones are few; cell phone reception has improved, thanks to an intrusive tower that now dwarfs the lighthouse, but is still undependable. Camping is prohibited. Do not bring bicycles or dogs (which must be leashed at all times). No smoking outside the village, and please don't pick the flowers. There is an ATM in the Barnacle (see *Selective Shopping*) at the ferry dock.

PUBLIC RESTROOMS The two public pay toilets are on a lane behind the Monhegan House.

GETTING AROUND Several trucks meet each boat as it arrives and provide baggage service. Otherwise visitors have no access to motorized transport; you need none, because distances are all walkable and there are no paved roads.

WHEN TO COME The spring migration season brings birds and birders. June can be rainy and foggy. July and August are prime time, but September is best for hiking; birds and birders return.

✳ To Do

BIRDING In May and again mid- through late September Monhegan is one of the best birding places on the East Coast. Your local Audubon Society may have a trip going.

HIKING Pick up a current Monhegan Associates Trail Map to the island's 17-mile network before setting out. Day-trippers should take the Burnt Head Trail and loop back to the village via the Whitehead Trail (No. 7), descending by the lighthouse. This way you get a sense of the high bluffs and the unusual rocks in Gull Cove. Day-trippers need to move right along to make their boat in the allocated four hours. Beyond this well-trod loop, trails are marked with few guideposts. It's easy to get turned around in Cathedral Woods (justly famed and known for its "fairy houses"), which, along with Pulpit Rock, should be reserved for an unhurried day. The path along the

COMING ASHORE ON MONHEGAN ISLAND
Christina Tree

southern outer tip of the island, from Burnt Head to Christmas Cove, is ledgy and unsuitable for children and shaky hikers. Note hiking advice under *Equipment and Rules*.

✳ Lodging

All listings are on Monhegan Island 04852

Note: Lodging may be limited, but it is remarkably varied.

INNS Island Inn (207-596-0371; fax, 207-594-5517; www.islandinn monhegan.com). Open Memorial Day–Columbus Day weekend. This is a shingled, cupola-topped, gabled, classic 1907 summer hotel, steps from the ferry dock and overlooking the boat-filled harbor and Manana Island. In recent years it has been steadily renovated, and its public rooms are a winning mix of old-fashioned and chic, with hand-painted murals preserved in a comfortable living room beside the newly lightened and brightened dining room, which serves three meals a day to the public as well as to overnight guests. Thirty-two rooms and suites are divided between the main inn and neighboring Pierce Cottage. Opt for a room with a view in the inn itself. Twenty-four units (including several suites) now have private bath; just eight share. In 2005 high season (late July–Labor Day), $145 per couple (shared bath, meadow view) to $315 for a suite with private bath and ocean view. Otherwise $115–290, depending on room and week. $4 gratuity added per day and $3 charge for 1-night stays. All rates include a full breakfast.

✐ **Monhegan House** (207-594-7983 or 1-800-599-7983; www.monhegan house.com), Box 345. Open Memorial Day–Columbus Day. Holden and Susan Nelson have revived Monhegan's oldest continuously operating summer hotel. Built in 1870s in the middle of the village, with 33 rooms on the second, third, and fourth floors. No closets, and the baths and

PLEIN AIR PAINTING

Christina Tree

Monhegan Island Light, built of granite in 1850 and automated in 1959, caps a hill that's well worth climbing for the view alone. The former keeper's cottage is now the **Monhegan Museum** (207-596-7003; open daily July–Aug., 11:30–3:30; in Sep., 12:30–2:30), $3 suggested donation. A spellbinding display of island art, artifacts, flora, fauna, some geology, lobstering, and an artistic history of the island, including documents dating back to the 16th century. A separate art museum preserves the invaluable paintings that have accrued to the museum and offers space for special exhibits. Inquire about viewing James Fitzgerald's work in the Kent-Fitzgerald-Hubert house. Built by Rockwell Kent, it later served as a home and studio for Fitzgerald. It was donated, along with the largest collection of works by Fitzgerald, to the museum by Ann Hubert, beloved, when she died in 2004 at age 95.

showers are all together in a wing off the middle of the second floor—but they are plentiful and immaculate. For couples and families we recommend the third floor; for singles the bargain-priced fourth-floor rooms have the best views (coveted by artists). The downstairs lobby is warmed by a gas fireplace; on sunny days guests opt for the porch, watching the comings and goings of everyone on the island. Children are welcome and free under age 3. A full breakfast is included in the rates (singles are $75, doubles $123–134, in high season; $65 and $99 in low); head for the dining room before 8 AM because it's open to the public and very popular. Dinner is also good (see *Where to Eat*).

✒ **The Trailing Yew** (207-596-0440). Open mid-May–mid-Oct. This quirky, affordable institution is New England's last genuine 19th-century-style "summer boardinghouse." The 35 rooms are divided among the main house and adjacent annexes and cottages on the grounds and up the road. Baths are shared but clean and equipped

with electricity. Guest rooms are comfortable, lit with kerosene lamps. Before meals guests gather around the flagpole outside the main building to pitch horseshoes. Dining is at shared tables, making this a great place for solo travelers. Food is not the reason you come here, but we understand that it's improved. Two rooms in Lower Seagull are geared to families. The Mooring Chain, a nearby annex, is geared to groups. $76 per person per day includes breakfast and dinner; sliding scale ages 2–11. No credit cards.

BED & BREAKFASTS **Shining Sails Guesthouse** (207-596-0041; fax, 207-596-7611; www.shiningsails.com), Box 346. Open year-round. John and Winnie Murdock offer rooms and housekeeping efficiency apartments in their charming water-view home, convenient to everything in the village. There are two rooms, one with views of the meadow and one of the ocean (our favorite guest room on the entire island); also five efficiencies accommodating up to four people. Three more units, two full apartments, and a studio apartment are also available in the middle of the village. All rooms are tastefully decorated. An ample continental breakfast is served May–Columbus Day. John Murdock is an island lobsterman, and the couple are helpful hosts. Rooms are $95–135 per night in-season, $625–885 per week; apartments are $110–185 per night, $650–1,195 per week.

Hitchcock House (207-594-8137; hhouse@midcoast.com), Horn's Hill. Open year-round. Hidden away on top of Horn's Hill with a pleasant garden and deck. Barbara Hitchcock offers several rooms and efficiencies with views of the meadows. The studio, a separate cabin, has a kitchen and bedroom. Two rooms sharing one bath are $80 per night, $520 per week; efficiencies are $120–130 per night, $760–840 per week in high season, less in June and after Labor Day.

Tribler Cottage (207-594-2445; www.monhegan.biz/tribler.html). Open mid-May–mid-Oct. On the edge of the Meadow, at the base of Lighthouse Hill, this remains in the same family that has been welcoming visitors here since the 1920s. Richard Farrell offers four housekeeping apartments and one housekeeping room. All have private bath; one apartment (Hillside) has a sundeck and living room with fireplace, while another (accommodating three) has a gas heater and is available off-season. $75–140 per night based on 2-night stay; $490–945 weekly.

COTTAGES AND EFFICIENCIES Cooking facilities come in handy here: You can buy lobster and good fresh and smoked fish (bring meat and staples) and a limited line of vegetables. **Shining Sails Cottage Rental** (207-596-

0041; fax, 207-596-7166; www.shining sails.com) manages two dozen or so rental cottages, available by the week. Demand is high, and it's wise to get in your bid in early January for the summer. $605–2,475 per week.

✳ Where to Eat

The Island Inn (mid-June–Sep.). Open to the public Memorial Day–Columbus Day for breakfast and dinner, lunch except for the very beginning and end of the season. This newly renovated dining room offers water views. Lunch, served 11:15–1:30, features chowders, sandwiches, and salad plates. You might begin with lobster-stuffed puff pastry with roasted red pepper cream sauce, and dine on vegetarian pasta, seafood paella, or rack of lamb. Entrées $13–34. BYOB.

Monhegan House offers an attractive, many-windowed dining room at the back of the inn, overlooking the village and meadow. Homemade breads and omelets for breakfast. At dinner you might begin with chowder or lobster spring rolls, and dine on scallops with beets and potato in a brown butter vinaigrette. The menu ranges from vegetarian to steak. Entrées $16–22. BYOB.

Fish & Maine, Monhegan Village, open seasonally for lunch and dinner. Christina Murdock serves up good chowders, crabmeat rolls, burgers, salads, and ice cream. Seating inside and out. BYOB.

The Trailing Yew (207-596-0440). Open to the public by reservation, mid-May–mid-Oct. The big attraction here is the conversation around communal tables. Strictly family-style with a set special that's the same each week: roast beef Monday, pork Tuesday, beans and hot dogs Saturday, et cetera. One seating at 5:45. BYOB. $24 per adult, $37 for lobster.

The Barnacle. Sited beside the ferry wharf and owned by the Island Inn, limited seating on the deck and inside, serving sandwiches, soups, and pastries, also espresso and prepared sandwiches. Wine and beer sold.

The Novelty, behind Monhegan House. Sue Jenkins has expanded her space and menu to include pizza, soups and sandwiches, salads and hot wraps. Her freshly made hermits and cookies are great hiking fuel as you set off up Horn's Hill. Hand-dipped ice cream and frozen yogurts hit the spot on the way down.

The Fish House Market, Fish Beach. Open daily 11:30–1:30 and 4–6:30. The source of all good seafood for anyone with cooking facilities, also of steamed clams and the island's best crab and lobster rolls. There are picnic tables steps away on Fish Beach.

North End Market (207-594-5546), open year-round 9–7. A general store and deli, wine and beer.

✳ Selective Shopping

ART GALLERIES **The Lupine Gallery** (207-594-8131; www.lupine gallery.com), 48 Main Street. Open early May–Columbus Day, 11–4:40. Bill Boynton and Jackie Bogel offer original works by close to 100 artists who paint regularly on the island. This is a very special gallery, showcasing the work of many professional artists within walking distance. Sited just uphill from the ferry dock, it's a good place to judge which studios you want to visit. Great cards, prints, and art books, also artists' supplies and framing.

Open studios: More than 20 resident artists welcome visitors to their studios; pick up a map/guide schedule, check "The Rope Shed/Barn," or look for shingles hung outside listing the hours they're open. **Don Stone** is the current dean of Monhegan painters, and his studio on the way to Burnt Head is open by chance or appointment. In the middle of the village, it's hard to miss (and you don't want to) the colorful seasonal studio featuring landscapes, sculpture, and portraits by **Ted Tihansky** and **Allison Hill**.

SPECIAL SHOPS **Carina**. Open in-season 6:30–6:30; off-season for residents only. The spiritual successor to the old Island Spa, the year-round island gathering place to linger in booths over coffee, tea, and fresh-baked goods. It's also a prime source of wines, produce, and canned, boxed, and paper goods plus daily newspapers.

Winterworks. Open daily Memorial Day–Labor Day, by the ferry dock. A former fish house is now the island co-op, filled with work produced by the island's 20 craftspeople: a surprising variety and quality of knitted goods, jewelry, Christmas decorations, and more.

Black Duck Emporium. Open Memorial Day–Columbus Day. This longtime island gift store has expanded to fill the former general store, offering cappuccino and pastries as well as a selection of imaginative T-shirts, books, kitchenware, pottery, jewelry, and more.

THE FOX ISLANDS: VINALHAVEN AND NORTH HAVEN

The Fox Islands Thoroughfare is a rowable stretch of yacht-filled water that separates Vinalhaven and North Haven, two islands roughly a dozen miles off Rockland. While you can get from one island to the other, no ferry stops at both.

Vinalhaven is heavily wooded and marked by granite quarries that include two public swimming holes. Life eddies around the village of Carver's Harbor, home to Maine's largest lobster fleet. In 1880, when granite was being cut on Vinalhaven to build New York's Customs House, 2,855 people were living here on the island, a number now reduced to about 1,200—a mix of descendants of 18th-century settlers and the stonecutters who came here from Sweden, Norway, Finland, and Scotland. In recent years the island has also attracted a number of artists, including Robert Indiana. Summer visitors now equal year-round residents, but there is no yacht club or golf course. This is Maine's largest offshore island with its largest year-round island community and claims the world's largest lobster fleet. It's not an island resort.

North Haven is half as big, with just 325 year-round residents and some 2,000 in summer. Founded well over a century ago by Boston yachtsmen, its summer colony now includes some of the country's wealthiest and most influential families. Over the years some members of these families have married islanders, while others have settled or retired here. The result is a creative mix. Its elementary school, one of the smallest in Maine, has produced a play (*Islands*) that has been performed on Broadway. The former general store by the ferry dock is now Waterman's Community Center, with a 140-seat state-of-the-art theater, the venue for summer lectures, concerts, and plays. Beyond the village a 10-mile loop beckons bicyclists through rolling, open fields, spotted with buttercups and idyllic farmhouses, most of them summer homes. There's also a public golf club and a private yacht club, the North Haven Casino, home to the island's distinctive dinghies.

It was British explorer Martin Pring who named the Fox Islands in 1603, ostensibly for the silver foxes he saw on both islands. A dozen miles out in Penobscot Bay, these islands are still understandably protective of

CARVER'S HARBOR

Christina Tree

their considerable beauty, especially in view of their unusual—by Maine island standards—accessibility by Maine State Ferry. Be it said that there is just one B&B on North Haven, and lodging is also limited on Vinalhaven.

For the kind of tourist who loves islands, especially less crowded islands with ample places to walk, Vinalhaven is a real find. And contrary to rumor, it's possible to cross the Thoroughfare (see *Getting Around*) to spend the day on North Haven, but you may have to wait a little while for transport. These islands dictate their own terms.

Vinalhaven makes sense as a day-trip destination only if it's a nice day and if you take the early boat. Pick up a map and don't be discouraged by the walk into Carver's Harbor, along the island's least attractive half mile. Don't miss the Historical Society Museum, and walk or bike out to Lane's Island. It really works better as a destination for a couple of days or more, and it's a great place to be on the Fourth of July. North Haven is better as a day trip. Lodging choices are very limited, but galleries, shops, food sources, and the new Waterman's Community Center all cluster beside the ferry terminal.

GUIDANCE Town offices on **North Haven** (207-867-4433) and **Vinalhaven** (207-863-4471 or 207-863-4393) field most questions. **The Vinalhaven Chamber**, P.O. Box 703, Vinalhaven 04863, also mails out a brochure and publishes a guide. Its helpful web site is www.vinalhaven.org. On-island pick up a free copy of *The Wind*, the island's weekly newsletter, for a sense of what's happening. For summer cottage listings and general information on that island, request a spring copy of the *North Haven News* (Box 363, North Haven 04853; nhaven@midcoast.com).

GETTING THERE **The Maine State Ferry Service** (in Rockland: 207-596-2202). The islands are serviced by different ferries, and neither ferry stops at both. From Rockland it's a 75-minute ride; service is frequent. Day-trippers never have a problem walking on; the bike fee is nominal. Each ferry takes a set number of cars, and only a handful of these spaces can be reserved; otherwise, cars are taken in order of their position in line. For the morning boats, it's wise to be in line the night before. During the summer season, getting off the island can be nerve racking. It doesn't make sense to bring a car unless you plan to stay awhile. *Note:* **Concord Trailways** stops daily at the **Rockland Ferry Terminal**.

Maine Atlantic Aviation (207-596-5557 or 1-800-780-6071) will fly you in from Portland or Boston as well as Rockland to either Vinalhaven or North Haven.

GETTING AROUND *By boat:* Shuttle service between North Haven and Vinalhaven is possible through **J. O. Brown & Sons Boatyard** (207-867-4621) in North Haven. Try calling from the phone on the boat landing on the Vinalhaven side of the Thoroughfare.

Note: **Day-trippers** to North Haven will find shopping and food within steps of the ferry dock, but on Vinalhaven the distances from the ferry to Carver's Harbor is 0.4 mile. It's another mile or so to the quarries and Lanes Island Nature Preserve.

ON VINALHAVEN

The Vinalhaven Historical Society Museum (207-863-4410; www.midcoast .com/~vhhissoc), top of High St. Open mid-June–Columbus Day, Wed.–Sun. 11–3 and by appointment. Sue Radley, director. One of Maine's most welcoming and extensive community museums, it's housed in the former town hall, which has also served as a theater and skating rink. It was built in 1838 in Rockland as a Universalist church, and floated over on a barge in 1878. Displays feature the island's granite industry, with photos of St. John the Divine's massive columns, for instance, quarried here.

The first order for Vinalhaven granite, you learn, was shipped to Boston in 1826 to build a jail, but production really skyrocketed after the Civil War, when granite was the preferred building material for the country's building boom. On an island map, 40 red pins mark the sites of major quarries, but there are also countless "motions," or backyard pits.

Museum displays also depict island life and other industries, like fishing (the Lane-Libby Fisheries Co. was once one of Maine's largest fish-processing companies) and lobstering (in the 1880s the Basin, a large saltwater inlet, was used as a giant holding tank, penning as many as 150,000 lobsters until prices peaked). Knitting horse nets (to keep off flies) in intricate designs was yet another island industry. Check out the nearby Carver Cemetery.

A Galamander, a huge wagon such as those used to carry stone from island quarries to schooners, stands in the small park at the top of the hill on the other side of town (junction of Main, Chestnut, Carver, and School Sts. and Atlantic Ave.).

The Victorian-style town of **Carver's Harbor** is picturesque and interesting, its downtown a single street straddling a causeway and narrow land strip between the harbor and Carver's Pond, its estuary. A boomtown dating from the 1880s when *Vinalhaven* was synonymous with *granite*, the village is built almost entirely of wood, the reason why many of the best of its golden-era buildings are missing. The strikingly Victorian Star of Hope Lodge, owned by artist Robert Indiana, is one of two surviving second-empire mansard buildings (there were once four) marking the center of town.

Brown's Head Lighthouse, now automated, commands the entrance to the Thoroughfare from the northern end of Vinalhaven, more than 8 miles from Carver's Harbor.

WHEN TO COME Only in July and August can you count on all visitor-geared facilities being open on both these islands. June and September, however, can be as beautiful.

✳ To See

On North Haven
North Haven Village. The village itself is charming with several shops, galleries, and a choice of places to eat. Pulpit Harbor, the island's second, much smaller community, several miles away, is the site of the general store and the **North Haven Historical Society Museum** (207-867-2248), open Tue. in July and Aug., 2–5.

✳ To Do

BICYCLING See *Getting There* and *Getting Around* on the logistics of bringing, renting, and riding bikes. The truth is that if you take care to keep to the roadside, both North Haven and Vinalhaven are suited to bicycling.

On North Haven we recommend the North Shore Rd.

On Vinalhaven we recommend the Granite Island Rd. out along the Basin or following Main St. the other direction out to Geary's Beach (see *Green Space*). The North Haven Rd. is an 8-mile slog up the middle of Vinalhaven, but the rewards are great: Browns Head Light, the Perry Creek Preserve, and views of North Haven.

GOLF North Haven Golf Club (207-867-2054), open June–Sep. A waterside course, nine holes.

SEA KAYAKING Sea Escape Kayak (207-863-9343; seaescapekayak@worldnet .att.net), Carver's Harbor, Vinalhaven. Burke Lynch has all the right credentials for guiding novices, from 2-hour harbor paddles to 2-day camping trips.

SWIMMING Lawson's Quarry. From the middle of Carver's Harbor, turn (uphill) at the Bank Building and continue up and up High St., past the historical society, and then turn right on the North Haven Rd. for 0.5 mile. For **Booth Quarry** continue east (uphill) on Main St. 1.5 miles past the Union Church. This is a town park and swimming hole.

✳ Green Space

On Vinalhaven
Lane's Island Preserve, on the southern side of Carver's Harbor (cross the Indian Creek Bridge and look for the sign on your left). It includes 45 acres of fields, marsh, moor, and beach. This is a great spot to picnic or to come in the evening. Stroll out along the beach and up into the meadows facing open ocean and filled with wild roses and beach peas.

Christina Tree

BOOTH QUARRY

Armbrust Hill is on the way to Lane's Island, hidden behind the medical center. The first place in which the island's granite was commercially quarried, it remained one of the most active sites on the island for many decades. Notice the many small pits ("motions") as well as four major quarries. The main path winds up the hill for a splendid view.

Grimes Park, just west of the ferry terminal, is a 2-acre point of rocky land with two small beaches. Note the rough granite watering trough once used by horses and oxen.

Geary's Beach. Turn right off Main St. a bit farther than the Booth Quarry, just after the Coke Statue of Liberty (you'll see), and bear left for this stony town-owned beach, its trails, and picnic table. The view is off to Isle au Haut, Brimstone, and Matinicus.

The Vinalhaven Land Trust (207-863-2543) maintains several of the preserves mapped on island handouts.

Note: This list is just a sampling.

✳ Lodging

On Vinalhaven 04863
🍴 **Tidewater Motel and Gathering Place** (207-863-4618; www.tidewater motel.com), Carver's Harbor. Open year-round. Phil and Elaine Crossman's waterside motel has evolved into a remarkable place to stay in the heart of both the harbor and the village. It spans a tidal stream connecting the harbor with Carver's Pond. The water swooshing under your room once powered a blacksmith shop and gristmill; now a turbine in it may be generating some of the motel's power. Many of the original 11 motel units have decks overhanging the water. The adjacent buildings house eight units—also over the water—including suites and efficiencies, one with a sleeping loft. Then there is the Harbor Master's Berth with its full kitchen, adjoining wood-paneled living room, and dining

room, fit for a large family or small conference. We've heard the sound of the water inspires amazing dreams. Note that the Crossmans also loan out bikes, rent or loan cars, meet the ferry, and help guests get around the island. Elaine Crossman is a noted artist, and Phil's fame as a writer is spreading (his book of essays, *Away Happens*, was published in 2005). $115–256 in high season, $70–172 off-season.

♪ Payne Homestead at the Moses Webster House (207-863-9963 or 1-888-863-9963; www.paynehomestead .com), Atlantic Ave. Open year-round. Lee and Donna Payne have young sons of their own and cater to families while offering some romantic rooms in this mansard-roofed, high-Victorian home. We prefer the upstairs rooms over those on the first floor. The five rooms (one with private bath) range $90–145 in high season, $50–85 in low, including a bountiful breakfast. Two-night minimum.

Libby House (207-863-4696; www .libbyhouse1869.com), Water St. Open June–Oct.; call for off-season availability (631-369-9172). Built in 1869, this handsome, rambling home is furnished with Victorian pieces, including heavily carved beds. Comfortable common spaces are often filled with music, from classical to the blues and jazz; innkeeper Philip Roberts is a music teacher. An enclosed porch with rockers available for relaxing. It's a short walk to Lane's Island Preserve. Breakfast is not included. $75–140.

On North Haven 04853
Our Place Inn and Cottages (207-867-4998; www.ourplaceinn.com), Crab Tree Point Rd. Open year-round. A guest house under many names

over the years. Marnelle and Gordon Bubar offers five rooms in the main house 2 miles from North Haven Village. $75–95 in high season with continental breakfast. There are also two efficiency cottages ($125 per night).

COTTAGE RENTALS Vinalhaven Rentals (207-863-2241) specializes in summer rentals. The **Island Group** (207-863-2554) offers both sales and rentals for both islands. For summer rentals on North Haven, see *Guidance*.

✳ Where to Eat

On Vinalhaven
The Haven Restaurant (207-863-4969), 49 Main St. Open Tue.–Sat. unless they're catering, with a 6 and 8:15 seating harborside, reservations required. On the street side you can eat from a lighter menu, pub style, and do not need a reservation. This island mainstay serves a variety of entrées that change almost nightly, always including fish, meat, with at least one steak, and pasta dishes.

Annabelle's (207-863-2789), 250 Main St. Open every day in summer 8 AM–9 PM; until 10 on weekend nights. Everything from Rock City coffee, Annabelle's ice cream, and home-baked goods to paninis, soups, and salads. Hole in the Wall bagels, Willow Bakeshop doughnuts, and a Tacchino—a turkey panini with pesto, roasted red peppers, and provolone ($5.95). Good burritos.

The Harbor Gawker (207-863-9365), Main St., middle of the village. Open daily 11–8; closed Sun. mid-Apr.–mid-Nov. Lobster rolls, crabmeat rolls, and baskets of just about anything. Homemade soups, chowders, and blueberry pies, along with ice cream and a dairy bar for dessert. Order at the counter and wait for a number to be called while you sit and enjoy the view of Carver's Pond.

Surfside (207-863-2767), Harbor Wharf, W. Main St. Donna Webster opens at 4 AM for the lobstermen and technically closes at 10:30 AM. A great harborside breakfast spot with tables on the deck, and specials like a crab-meat or lobster omelet, or a tomato herb cheese omelet with home fries.

✔ **The Pizza Pit** (207-863-4311) Main St., is open daily 4–9 PM, serving more than pizza. Kids love to come here.

On North Haven

Coal Wharf Restaurant (207-867-4739), hidden away in the J. O. Brown & Sons Boatyard, overlooking the Fox Island Thoroughfare. Open for lunch and dinner in July and Aug., specializing in local seafood and on-island organic produce. Dinner en-trées $15–25. Reservations advised.

The Landing. Open seasonally 11–3 for lunch, 5–8 for dinner, 11–8 for ice cream. This snack shop with seating inside and out is at the summer heart of the village. Good burgers, fried foods, and the like.

Waterman's Community Center, North Haven Village. Open daily 6:30–4 for coffee, tea, muffins, and bagels in an airy, comfortable living space with couches, tables, board games, table tennis, skittles, and newspapers.

✳ Selective Shopping

In Carver's Harbor on Vinal-haven

The Paper Store (207-863-4826) is the nerve center of the island, the place everyone drops by at least once a day. Carlene Michael is as generous about dispensing directions to visitors as she is news to residents. This is also the place to check for current hap-penings like plays and concerts, and to get a chart of the island.

CALDERWOOD HALL GALLERY, NORTH HAVEN

Christina Tree

New Era Gallery (207-863-9351), Main St. Artist Elaine Austin Crossman's gallery shows work by island coastal painters, sculptors, photographers, and fiber artists.

✎ **Go Fish** (207-863-4193), Main St. Open year-round, Tue.–Sat. 10–4:30. A cheerful kids-geared shop with books, games, and candy.

Second Hand Prose, Main St. Open Mon.–Sat. 9–4. Run by Friends of the Library and featuring secondhand books. Good selection of Maine and maritime titles. Coffee and muffins served.

Island Spirits (207-863-2192). Open Mon.–Sat. 11–6:30 in summer. Some of the "best cheeses you can ever hope for," great wines, beer and olives, and freshly ground coffee.

In North Haven Village
North Haven Gift Shop and Gallery (207-876-4444). Open Memorial Day–mid-Sep. (but closed Sun.), 9:30–5. Since 1954 June Hopkins (mother of Eric) has run this shop with rooms that meander on and on, filled with pottery, books, accessories, jewelry, and much more, including bags by the island's famous young designer, Angela Adams. Gallery exhibits change frequently. Hopkins keeps running accounts for summer families and knows the names of members of as many as six generations of a family when they walk in.

Calderwood Hall and North Island Fiber Shoppe (207-867-2265). Open Memorial Day–Columbus Day, Mon.–Sat. 9:30–5, Sun. until 4. Housed in a weathered building that has served as movie theater and dance hall, featuring paintings by owner Herbert Parsons; also offering an interesting mix of clothing and

gifts, many island made, and Mickey Bullock's lustrous yarns, hand spun from her sheep. Wine, beer, and water are also sold.

Eric Hopkins Gallery (207-867-2229; www.erichopkins.com). Open by chance or appointment. This gallery is the reason many people come to North Haven. One of Maine's best-known artists, Hopkins is the son of a North Haven fisherman and a graduate of prestigious art schools. The waterside gallery is hung with bold, distinctive paintings ranging from large canvases to small watercolors. Most Hopkins paintings are of clouds, deep blue water, and spiky green islands, all seemingly in motion.

❋ Special Events
Year-round: **North Haven Arts Enrichment Presentations** include exceptional plays, concerts, and lectures performed in Waterman's Community Center in North Haven Village at the ferry landing. For details, phone 207-867-2100; www.watermans.org.

Summer season: **Concerts**, primarily classical, chamber, and jazz, are staged through the summer on both islands, sponsored by **Fox Islands Concerts**.

July–August: **Saturday Farmer's Market** at the ball field, North Haven Village, features crafts as well as produce. **Saturday Flea Market**, 10 AM in the field next to the Galamander, Carver's Harbor, Vinalhaven. **Union Church Baked Bean Supper** (*every other Thursday*), Vinalhaven.

For details about other regular occurrences on both islands, consult *The Wind*, a weekly newsletter published on Vinalhaven.

MATINICUS

Home to fewer than than 60 hardy souls in winter, most of whom make their living lobstering, Matinicus's population grows to about 200 in summer. Maine's outermost island, it lies 22 miles at sea beyond the outer edge of Penobscot Bay. Quiet and unspoiled, it's a haven for birds and birders. Walking trails thread the meadows and shore, and there are two sand beaches—one at each end of the 750-acre island. Matinicus Rock is offshore, a protected nesting site for puffins, a lure for birders in June and July.

GUIDANCE For a brochure and general questions contact the **Matinicus Chamber of Commerce** (207-354-8354), 45 Thatcher St., Thomaston 04861.

GETTING THERE The flying time via **Penobscot Island Air** (207-596-7500) from Owls Head is 15 minutes, but flights may be canceled because of weather—and the fog can hang in there for days. That's when you contact **George Tarkleson** (207-691-9030), June 22–Oct. 20; it's a 70-minute ride. Inquire about puffin-, whale-, and seal-watching trips.

The Maine State Ferry (207-596-2022) takes 2¼ hours to ply between Matinicus and Rockland, four times a month May–Oct., and once a month the rest of the year.

✴ Lodging

🐾 ⚓ **Tuckanuck Lodge** (207-366-3830), Box 217, Shag Hollow Rd., Matinicus 04851. Open year-round. Well-behaved children and pets welcome. Nantucket native Bill Hoadley offers five rooms (two shared baths), some with a view of Old Cove and the ocean. $70–90 double, $50–60 single, including breakfast; half rate for children 12 and under; weekly rates available. Guests have kitchen privileges for lunch (bring your own fixings); the lodge offers supper with lobster (BYOB). Baked goods are available on-island, but there's no general store.

CAMDEN/ROCKPORT AREA
ISLESBORO

These opening lines from "Renascence" suggest the view from the top of Mount Battie. Millay's hometown—Camden—lies below the mountain on a narrow, curving shelf between the hills and bay.

Smack on Rt. 1, Camden is the most popular way station between Kennebunkport or Boothbay Harbor and Bar Harbor. Seemingly half its 19th-century captains' homes are now B&Bs. Shops and restaurants line a photogenic harbor filled with private sailing and motor yachts. It's also a poor man's yacht haven—open year-round—with a thriving fishing industry. The ski area would make a good winter vacation destination as well as a summer tour.

Here, in 1935, artist Frank Swift refitted a few former fishing and cargo schooners to carry passengers around the islands in Penobscot Bay. He called the boats windjammers. Half a dozen members of Maine's current windjammer fleet are still based here (the rest are in neighboring ports), and several schooners offer daysails. You can also get out on the water in an excursion boat or a sea kayak.

From the water you can see two aspects of Camden not apparent from land. The first is the size and extent of the Camden Hills. The second is the size and number of the palatial old waterside "cottages" along Beauchamp Point, the rocky promontory separating Camden from Rockport. Here, as in Bar Harbor, summer residents were wise and powerful enough to preserve the local mountains, seeding the creation of the present 6,500-acre Camden Hills State Park, one of Maine's more spectacular places to hike.

Camden's first resort era coincided with those colorful decades during which steam and sail overlapped. As a stop on the Boston–Bangor steamboat line, Camden acquired a couple of big (now vanished) hotels. In 1900, when Bean's boatyard launched the world's first six-masted schooner, onlookers crowded the neighboring ornate steamboat wharf to watch.

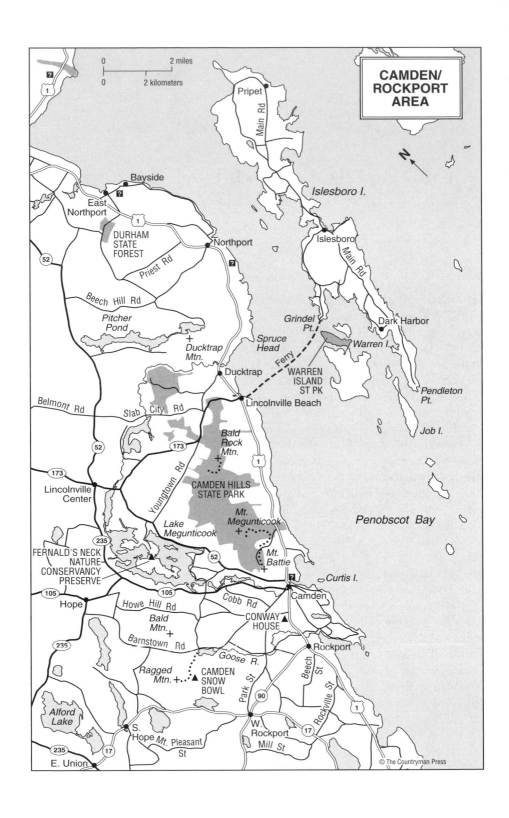

CAMDEN/
ROCKPORT
AREA

0   2 miles
0   2 kilometers

N

Pripet

Main Rd

Islesboro I.

Bayside

East
Northport

1

DURHAM
STATE
FOREST

52

Northport

Priest Rd

Beech Hill Rd

Pitcher
Pond

Islesboro

Main Rd

Dark Harbor

Ducktrap
Mtn.

Grindel
Pt.

Spruce
Head

Warren I.

Ferry

Ducktrap

WARREN
ISLAND
ST PK

Belmont Rd

Slab City Rd

Lincolnville Beach

Pendleton
Pt.

52

173

Bald
Rock
Mtn.

1

Job I.

173

Youngtown Rd

CAMDEN HILLS
STATE PARK

Lincolnville
Center

Lake
Megunticook

235

Mt.
Megunticook

Penobscot Bay

FERNALD'S NECK
NATURE
CONSERVANCY
PRESERVE

52

Mt.
Battie

105

Curtis I.

Hope

Cobb Rd

Camden

Howe Hill Rd

CONWAY
HOUSE

235

Bald
Mtn.

Barnstown Rd

Goose R.

Rockport

105

Ragged
Mtn.

CAMDEN
SNOW
BOWL

Park St

Beech St

Rockville St

Alford
Lake

S.
Hope

90

W.
Rockport

Mill St

17

1

235

17

Mt. Pleasant
St

E. Union

© The Countryman Press

In contrast with Boothbay and Bar Harbor, Camden has always been a year-round town that's never been overdependent on tourism. Camden's early business was, of course, building and sailing ships. By the mid-1800s half a dozen mills lined the series of falls on the Megunticook River, just a block or two from the waterfront. The vast wooden Knox Woolen Company—the "Harrington Mill" portrayed in the movie *Peyton Place*—made the felts used by Maine's paper mills to absorb water from paper stock. It operated until 1988, and the complex is now the New England headquarters for a major credit card company (and a small, MBNA-sponsored mill museum), the most recent among dozens of firms to locate in Camden.

Culturally enriched by its sophisticated populace—workaday residents, retired diplomats, military and intelligence officers, and summer people alike—Camden (along with Rockport) offers a bonanza of music, art, and theatrical productions surprising in quality. There are also world-renowned programs in filmmaking, computer science, woodworking, and photography.

Ironically, only a small fraction of the thousands of tourists who stream through Camden every summer take the time to discover the extent of its beauty. The tourist tide eddies around the harborside restaurants, shops, and galleries and continues to flow on up Rt. 1 toward Bar Harbor. Even in August you are likely to find yourself alone atop Mount Battie (accessible by car as well as on foot) or Mount Megunticook (highest point in the Camden Hills), or in the open-sided Vesper Hill Children's Chapel, with its flowers and sea view. Few visitors see, let alone swim in, Megunticook Lake or set foot on the nearby island of Islesboro.

A decade or two ago you could count on your fingers the number of places to stay here, but Camden has since become synonymous with B&Bs. A total of some 1,000 rooms can now be found in hotels, motels, inns, and cottages as well as the B&Bs between Camden and neighboring Lincolnville and Rockport.

GUIDANCE **Camden-Rockport-Lincolnville Chamber of Commerce** (207-236-4404 or 1-800-223-5459; www.visitcamden.com), P.O. Box 919, Public Landing (behind Cappy's), Camden 04843. Open year-round, Mon.–Fri. 9–5 and Sat. 10–5; also open Sun. noon–4, mid-May–mid-Oct. You'll find all sorts of helpful brochures here, plus maps of Camden, Rockport, and Lincolnville, along with knowledgeable people to send you in the right direction. The chamber keeps tabs on vacancies during the high season, as well as on what's open off-season and cottages available to rent (a list is ready for requests each year by Jan.). Be sure to secure their booklet *The Jewel of the Maine Coast*, as well as the Camden-Rockport Historical Society's *A Visitor's Tour*, which outlines tours of historic districts in Camden and Rockport.

GETTING THERE *By air:* **Knox County Regional Airport**, at Owls Head, about 10 miles from Camden, offers daily flights to and from Boston. **Bangor International Airport** and **Portland International Jetport** offer connections to all parts of the country.

By bus: **Concord Trailways** (1-800-639-3317) stops on Rt. 1 south of Camden en route from Bangor to Portland and Boston and vice versa.

Kim Grant

ROCKPORT HARBOR

By limo: **MidCoast Limo** (207-236-2424 or 1-800-937-2424; www.midcoastlimo .com) makes runs from Portland International Jetport by reservation. **Schooner Bay Limo** (207-594-5000; www.alldirections.net) goes to Portland and elsewhere.

By car: Our preferred route, to bypass Rt. 1 traffic, is to take I-95 to Gardiner, then follow signs to Rt. 226. When this road ends, take a right onto Rt. 17, which winds through pretty countryside to Rt. 90, and then intersects with Rt. 1 leading into Camden.

PARKING Parking is a problem in July and August. In-town parking has a stringently enforced 2-hour limit (just 15 minutes in a few spots, so be sure to read the signs). There are a few lots outside the center of town (try the Camden Marketplace and a lot on Mechanic St.). There's an advantage here to finding lodging within walking distance of the village. The chamber has a map that highlights all-day parking areas.

WHEN TO COME Camden and Rockport are open year-round with a thriving fishing industry; the ski area makes this area a good winter destination as well as a summer tour. But for sailing and swimming, summer is the time to come, and fall foliage makes a beautiful contrast with the blue water.

✳ Villages

Rockport's harbor is as picturesque as Camden's, and the small village is set high above it. Its quiet, subdued charm provides a nice respite from the hustle of Rt. 1. Steps (you have to look closely for them) lead down to Marine Park, a departure point in 1816 for 300 casks of lime shipped to Washington, DC, to help construct the Capitol building. In the small park you'll see the restored remains of a triple kiln, a saddleback steam locomotive, and a granite sculpture of André the Seal, the legendary performer who drew crowds every summer in the early and mid-1980s. The village (part of Camden until 1891) includes the restored Rockport Opera House, site of the Bay Chamber Concerts, the noted Center for Maine Contemporary Art, the Maine Photographic Workshops program, and a salting of restaurants and shops.

Lincolnville's landmarks—the Lobster Pound Restaurant and Maine State Ferry to Islesboro and the Whale's Tooth Pub, formerly a customhouse, with a big fireplace—serve as centerpieces for proliferating shops, restaurants, and B&Bs. The beach offers a nice swimming spot on hot days and good beachcombing when the temperature drops.

✳ To See

LIGHTHOUSE **Curtis Island Light**. A public park, the island is nevertheless accessible only by boat, and the lighthouse is not open to the public. The best views are from sightseeing cruises leaving Camden Harbor, but you can also walk down to where Bayview Street connects with Beacon to find a good lookout.

MUSEUMS ✑ ♿ **Old Conway Homestead and Cramer Museum** (207-236-2257), Conway Rd. (off Rt. 1 at the Camden–Rockport town line). Open July and Aug., Mon.–Thu. 10–4; admission $5 adults, $4 seniors 60-plus, $2 students 7–18, children 5 and under free; 10 percent AAA discount. Open June and Sep. by appointment. Administered by the Camden-Rockport Historical Society, this restored early-18th-century farmhouse features antiques from several periods. The barn holds collections of carriages, sleighs, and early farm tools; don't miss the Victorian privy, blacksmith shop, and 1820 maple sugar house where sugaring demonstrations are held each spring. **The Cramer Museum** displays local memorabilia and changing exhibits.

Schoolhouse Museum (207-789-5445), Rt. 173, Lincolnville Beach. June–Oct., open Mon., Wed., and Fri. 1–4; other times by appointment. Admission is free. A small museum detailing the history of Lincolnville, with exhibits that change often and include stereoptics and tintypes, early settlers' tools, and Native American artifacts. The museum also publishes *Ducktrap: Chronicles of a Maine Village*, an excellent book on local history.

SCENIC DRIVE Drive or, better yet, bicycle around **Beauchamp Point**. Begin on Chestnut St. in Camden and follow this peaceful road by the lily pond and on by the herd of **belted Galloway cows** (black on both ends and white in the middle). Take Calderwood Lane through the woods and by the **Vesper Hill Children's Chapel**, built on the site of a former hotel and banked with flowers, a great spot to get married or simply to sit. Continue along Beauchamp Ave. to Rockport Village to lunch or picnic by the harbor, and return via Union St. to Camden.

OTHER SITES **Cellardoor Winery** (207-763-4478; www.mainewine.com), 4150 Youngtown Rd., Lincolnville. A 5-acre vineyard with 18 varieties of grapes, the winery now makes Marechal Foch, DeChaunac, riesling, chardonnay, cabernet sauvignon, cayuga, pear, and apple wines. Open for wine tastings in the 18th-century barn 11–5 daily.

✳ To Do

BICYCLING ✍ **Camden Hills State Park**, Rt. 1, Camden, has a 10-mile (round-trip) ride through the woods on a snowmobile trail. Bikes are not allowed on hiking trails. The **Camden Snow Bowl** also offers a number of rides through woods and swamps, as well as riding on ski trails. It's a hearty ride, but the views from the top are terrific.

✍ **Georges River Bikeways**. The Georges River Land Trust (207-594-5166) puts out a pamphlet highlighting several good biking routes, with many scenic spots within the Georges River watershed.

✍ **Ragged Mountain Sports** (207-236-6664), 46 Elm St., Camden, rents a variety of mountain, road, and hybrid bikes, tandems, Kiddie Kart trailers, and accessories, then delivers them to inns and B&Bs in Camden and Rockport and to the Islesboro, Vinalhaven, and North Haven ferries. All rentals include helmet, lock, bottle cage, and maps. Ask about Wed. and Sun. group rides.

Maine Sport Outfitters (207-236-7120 or 1-800-722-0826; www.mainesport .com), Rt. 1, Rockport, rents Raleigh hybrids, as well as bike trailers and car racks for a day or extended periods. Rentals include helmet, lock, water bottles, and cable.

BOAT EXCURSIONS See also *Windjammers*.

Yacht charters are offered spring to autumn along the Maine coast. Most charters run for a week, although sometimes it's possible to charter a boat just for a long weekend, with or without crew. For more information, contact **Johanson Boatworks** (207-596-7060 or 1-877-4JOHANS), which rents everything from J-40 sloops to Ericson 38s. **Bay Island Yacht Charters** (1-800-421-2492; www .sailme.com) has yachts available for bareboat, skippered, or crewed charters out of Rockland as well as other ports the length of Maine's coast. They also run hiking, sightseeing, and kayak tours. **Rockport Charters** (207-691-1066) offers 20-passenger 3-hour wildlife charters to see puffins, eagles, ospreys, and more. Leaving from both Camden and Rockland, as well as Rockport, Captain Robert Iserbyt also provides transportation for workers out to North Haven.

It would be a shame to be in Camden and not spend some time on the water. **The 2-hour sailing excursions** are a wonderful way to get a taste of what the harbor has to offer if your time is limited. Remember to bring a jacket, because the air can get chilly once you're offshore, even on a sunny day. Wander down the wooden boardwalk and check the offerings, which include:

✍ **Schooner *Appledore II*** (207-236-8353 or 1-800-233-PIER; www.appledore2 .com), an 86-foot schooner (the largest of the daysailing fleet), has sailed around the world and now offers several trips daily, including sunset cruises.

Surprise (207-236-4687; www.camdenmainesailing.com), a traditional, historic, 57-foot schooner, offers entertaining, informative 2-hour sails. Captain Jack and wife Barbara Moore spent seven years cruising between Maine and the Caribbean, educating their four children on board in the process.

Olad (207-236-2323; www.maineschooners.com), a 55-foot schooner, offers 2-hour sails.

Schooner Yacht *Heron* (207-236-8605 or 1-800-599-8605; www.woodenboatco.com), runs full-day, half-day, and sunset sails (including lobster dinners) out of Rockport for a maximum of six passengers.

⚓ Betselma (207-236-4446; www.betselma.com), a motor launch, provides 1-hour coastal and 2-hour island trips (owner Les Bex was a longtime windjammer captain) around the harbor and nearby coast. Combine the two for a 3-hour journey.

⚓ Lively Lady Too (207-236-6672 or 418-839-7933; www3.sympatico.ca/lively.lady), a traditional lobster boat, takes passengers on 2-, 3-, and 4-hour cruises that can include watching lobster traps being hauled or an island lobster bake and sunset cruise.

Schooner *Lazy Jack II* (207-230-0602; www.schoonerlazyjack.com). Two-hour sails and private charters from Camden Harbor, with Captain Sean O'Connor.

&. Maine State Ferry from Lincoln-ville Beach to Islesboro (207-734-

Kim Grant

WINDJAMMERS IN CAMDEN HARBOR

6935). At $6 round-trip per passenger, $17.50 per vehicle, and $5.75 per bicycle, this is the bargain of the local boating scene. An extra $5 each way secures your reservation. (See *Getting There* under "Islesboro.")

BOWLING Oakland Park Bowling Lanes (207-594-5169), 714 Commercial St., Rockport. Susan and Joe Plaskas have updated this old-fashioned bowling alley.

GOLF Goose River Golf Club (207-236-8488), Simonton Road, Rockport. Nine holes, but you can play through twice using different starting tees. Cart rentals; clubhouse. Tee times recommended for weekends and holidays.

Golfers Crossing Miniature Golf (207-230-0090); water hazards and obstacles complete this mini golf experience on Route 1 in Rockport.

Samoset Resort Golf Course (clubhouse, 207-594-1431), Rockport, has an 18-hole, par-70 course with 7 oceanside holes and ocean views from 14 holes. A recent renovation includes a redesigned 18th hole featuring a stone seawall, a remodeled 185-yard, par-3 5th hole, and renovations to hole 4. The clubhouse has a pro shop, locker rooms, video golf simulator, and the **Clubhouse Grille**. Carts are available.

HIKING Bald Rock Mountain. This 1,100-foot mountain in Lincolnville once had a ski area at the top. Great views of Penobscot Bay and the Camden Hills. You'll find the trailhead 1.25 miles down a dirt road from the gate on Ski Lodge Rd. (off Youngtown Rd.). The climb is about 0.5 mile long and moderate. Ask about overnight camping at the Camden Hills State Park headquarters on Rt. 1 in Camden.

Georges Highland Path is a 25-mile trail network created and maintained by the Georges River Land Trust (207-594-5166; www.grlt.org). The most recent section travels through the Oyster River Bog, a magnificent semiwilderness area with a 7.2-mile trail that links the Thomaston Town Forest with the Ragged Mountain section. A map put out by the trust details distances and hiking times and shows where the trailheads are.

Riverdance Outfitters (see *Sea Kayaking*) and Bay Island Yacht Charters (see *Boat Excursions*) offer guided hiking tours.

Coastal Mountain Hiking (207-236-7731), Camden, offers guided hikes and packed lunches.

SEA KAYAKING Ducktrap Sea Kayak Tours (207-236-8608), Lincolnville Beach, offers 2-hour and half-day guided tours in Penobscot Bay. No experience is necessary; in fact, most patrons are first-time kayakers. Group and family tours, rentals, and lessons are also available.

Maine Sport Outfitters (207-236-8797 or 1-800-722-0826; www.mainesport .com), on Rt. 1 just south of Rockport, is a phenomenon rather than merely an outfitter. Be sure to stop. They offer courses in kayaking, guided excursions around Camden Harbor and out into Penobscot Bay, and island-based work- shops. They also rent kayaks and canoes. Contact them for their catalog of activi- ties (also see *Special Learning Programs*).

Riverdance Outfitters (207-763-3139 or 1-800-770-3139; www.riverdance outfitters.com), Camden. Joshua Perry, a Registered Maine Guide, offers half- day and 2-hour sunset canoeing and kayaking tours, as well as hiking and moun- tain biking trips.

THE CAMDEN HILLS

Far less recognized than Acadia National Park as a hiking haven, the Cam- den Hills offer ample challenge and some spectacular views for the average hiker. Mount Battie is accessible by a moderate and sometimes steep 0.5- mile trail just off Rt. 52 and is the only peak also accessible by car. The 1- mile Maiden Cliff Trail (park off Rt. 52, 2.9 miles from Rt. 1) is favored by locals for its views from the top of 800-foot sheer cliffs overlooking Lake Megunticook; it connects with the 2.5-mile Ridge Trail to the summit of Mount Megunticook (1,380 feet).

Maine Photographic Workshops (207-236-8581; www.theworkshops.com), Rockport. This nationally respected year-round school offers a choice of 200 programs that vary in length from 1 week to 3 months for every level of skill in photography, cinematography, television production, and related fields. The faculty includes established, recognized professionals from across the country; the students come from around the world. The school provides housing for most of its students and helps arrange accommodations for others. Also a gallery with changing exhibitions, open to the public.

SPECIAL LEARNING PROGRAMS ✍ **Camden Yacht Club Sailing Program** (207-236-4575; off-season 207-236-7033), Bayview St., Camden, provides sailing classes for children and adults, boat owners and non-boat-owners, during late June, July, and Aug.

Bay Island Sailing School (1-800-421-2492; www.sailme.com) is headquartered in Camden but based at Journeys End Marina in Rockland. This ASA-certified sailing school offers weeklong, weekend, and private sailing lessons for basic, intermediate, and advanced levels, plus offshore and navigation courses. Enroll online or in person at the school.

The Center for Maine Contemporary Art (207-236-2875; www.artsmaine.org; see *Entertainment* and *Selective Shopping*), 162 Russell Ave., Rockport (formerly Maine Coast Artists). Professional development for artists includes year-round weekend and long-term workshops and lectures for visual artists. Numerous gallery talks and art lectures open to the public. **Maine Sport Outfitters** (207-236-8797; www.mainesport.com), Rockport. This Rt. 1 complex is worth a stop whether you're up for adventure sports or not. The place has evolved over the years from a fly-fishing and canvas shop into a multi-tiered store that's a home base for adventure tours. Inquire about a wide variety of local kayaking tours and multiday kayaking workshops geared to all levels of ability, based at its facilities on Gay Island.

Center for Furniture Craftsmanship (207-594-5611; www.woodschool.com), 25 Mill St., Rockport. June–Oct. Hands-on 1- and 2-week workshops for novice, intermediate, and advanced woodworkers and cabinetmakers. Twelve-week intensive courses are also offered a couple of times a year.

SWIMMING ✍ Saltwater swimming from Camden's **Laite Memorial Park and Beach**, Upper Bayview St.; at **Lincolnville Beach**, Rt. 1 north of Camden; and in Rockport at **Walker Park**, across the road from Marine Park. Freshwater swimming at **Megunticook Lake**, Lincolnville (**Barret Cove Memorial Park and Beach**; turn left off Rt. 52 northwest of Camden), where you'll also find picnic grounds and a parking area; **Shirttail Beach**, Camden (Rt. 105); and at the **Willis Hodson Park** on the Megunticook River, Camden (Molyneaux Rd.). At the **Penobscot Bay YMCA** (207-236-3375), Union St., visitors can pay a day-use fee that entitles them to swim in the Olympic-sized pool (check hours for family swimming, lap swimming, and other programs), use the weight rooms, and play basketball in the gym.

TENNIS There are two public tennis courts at the **Camden Snow Bowl** on Hosmer Pond Rd. (first come, first served). In addition, **Samoset Resort** (207-594-2511), Rockport, has outdoor courts, as do the **Whitehall Inn** (207-236-3391) and the **Rockport Recreation Park** (207-236-9648).

WALKING TOUR The **Camden-Rockport Historical Society** (207-236-2257) has prepared a brochure (available at the chamber of commerce and the Kramer Museum) with a 2.5-mile walk past historic buildings. The brochure includes historical details and a sketch map. An expanded bicycle or car tour encompassing two towns is also included.

WINDJAMMERS ✍ Windjammer cruises are offered late May–mid-Oct. Fourteen traditional tall ships sail from Camden, Rockland, and Rockport on 3- to 6-day cruises throughout Penobscot Bay. For brochures and sailing schedules, contact the **Maine Windjammer Association** (1-800-807-WIND; www.sail mainecoast.com).

Angelique (207-785-3020 or 1-800-282-9989; www.sailangelique.com), Camden, is a 95-foot ketch that was built expressly for the windjammer trade in 1980. Patterned after 19th-century English fishing vessels, she offers 15 passenger cabins, a pleasant deck-level salon with piano, belowdecks showers, and rowboats for exploring the coast.

Timberwind (207-236-0801 or 1-800-759-9250; www.schoonertimberwind.com), Rockport. Built in Portland in 1931 as a pilot schooner, this pretty 74-foot vessel was converted to a passenger vessel in 1969. She has an enclosed handheld shower on deck and room for 20 passengers. The only windjammer sailing out of Rockport Harbor, the *Timberwind* welcomes families with children ages 5 and up on most cruises.

Lewis R. French (207-785-2883 or 1-800-469-4635; www.schoonerfrench.com), Camden, was launched on the Damariscotta River in 1871 and is the oldest documented vessel in the windjammer fleet. Before becoming a passenger vessel, the *French* carried cargo such as lumber, firewood, bricks, granite, lime—even Christmas trees—along the coast. She had three major rebuilds, the most recent in 1976 when she was brought into passenger service. Sixty-five feet long, the *French* accommodates 22 passengers in 13 private cabins with freshwater sinks and portholes that open. Hot, freshwater shower on board. Captain Garth Wells enjoys getting his guests actively involved in the experience of sailing an authentic 19th-century schooner.

Mary Day (1-800-992-2218; www.schoonermaryday.com), Camden, was the first schooner built specifically for carrying passengers. At 90 feet, she's among the swiftest; Captains Barry King and Jen Martin have extensive sailing experience. Features include a fireplace and parlor organ and hot, freshwater showers on the deck. The *Mary Day* accommodates up to 30 passengers, and meals include a New England boiled dinner, baked goods made in the galley's woodstove, and a lobster bake on 6-day cruises.

ℰ **Camden Snow Bowl** (207-236-3438; www.camdensnowbowl.com), Hosmer Pond Rd., Camden. The only place you can ski overlooking views of the Atlantic Ocean! With a 950-foot vertical drop, 10 trails for beginners through experts, and night skiing, this is a comfortably sized area where everyone seems to know everyone else. Facilities include a base lodge, rental and repair shop, ski school, and cafeteria, plus the Jack Williams Toboggan Chute ($1 ride) and tube sliding ($4 per hour). Come in early February, when the Snow Bowl hosts the hilarious annual U.S. National Toboggan Championship Races at the toboggan chute (right next to the ski area). Outlandishly costumed teams make mad runs down the chute at 40-plus miles an hour, bottoming out on the ice-covered Hosmer Pond.

Grace Bailey, **Mercantile, and** *Mistress* (207-236-2938 or 1-888-692-7245; www.mainewindjammercruises.com), Maine Windjammer Cruises, Camden. For years known as the *Mattie*, *Grace Bailey* took back her original name following a thorough restoration in 1990. Built in 1882 in New York, the 81-foot *Grace Bailey* once carried cargo along the Atlantic coast and to the West Indies. She has belowdecks showers. *Mercantile* was built in Maine in 1916 as a shallow-draft coasting schooner; 78 feet long, she has been in the windjammer trade since its beginning in 1942. There are belowdecks showers. *Mistress*, the smallest of the fleet at 46 feet, carries just six passengers. A topsail schooner built in 1967 along the lines of the old coasting schooners, she is also available for private charter. All three cabins have private head, but there is no shower on board.

CROSS-COUNTRY SKIING **Camden Hills State Park** (207-236-3109) marks and maintains some trails for cross-country skiing, and there's a ski hut on Mount Battie.

Tanglewood 4-H Camp (207-789-5868 or 1-877-944-2267), 1 Tanglewood Rd., off Rt. 1 near Lincolnville Beach. Ungroomed, scenic cross-country trails that wend through woodlands and along streams. Map and description of trails are available at the chamber.

✳ Green Space

ℰ ♿ **Camden Hills State Park** (207-236-3109; off-season, 207-236-0849), 280 Belfast Rd., Rt. 1, Camden. $3 adults, $1 ages 5–11; under 5, and 65 and older, free. In addition to Mount Battie, this 6,500-acre park includes Mount Megunticook, one of the highest points on the Atlantic seaboard, and a shoreside picnic site. You can drive to the top of Mount Battie on the road that starts at the park entrance, just north of town. At the entrance pick up a *Camden Hills State Park* brochure, which outlines 19 trails with distance and difficulty level. In winter many of the trails convert to cross-country ski runs, given snow. There are 107 campsites available May 15–Oct. 14.

Warren Island State Park, also administered by Camden Hills State Park, is just a stone's throw off the island of Islesboro. The park features picnic tables, trails, and tent sites. Accessibility is the problem: You can arrange to have a private boat carry you over from the mainland, rent your own boat in Camden, or paddle out in a sea kayak. Because of this, the island boasts a peace and quiet often hard to find on the mainland in high season.

Marine Park, off Russell Ave. (just after you cross the bridge), Rockport. A nicely landscaped waterside area with sheltered picnic tables. Restored lime kilns and a locomotive remind visitors of the era when the town's chief industry was processing and exporting lime. During a stroll you're likely to see several painters capturing the picturesque harbor on canvas.

Merryspring Horticultural Nature Park and Learning Center (207-236-2239; www.merryspring.org), Camden. Open year-round during daylight hours. A 66-acre private preserve with walking trails; herb, lily, demonstration, and rose gardens; raised beds; and an arboretum. The Goose River bisects the preserve, which is accessible via Conway Rd. from Rt. 1 in Camden. Wildlife abounds here, and if you're lucky you'll see white-tailed deer, ermine, otter, porcupine, raccoon, rabbit, even moose or bobcat. Weekly talks in summer; admission is free.

Fernald's Neck Nature Conservancy Preserve (207-729-5181). At the end of Fernald Neck Rd. off Rt. 52, just past the intersection with Youngtown Rd., Lincolnville and Camden. Open during daylight hours; no pets allowed. The preserve's 326 acres cover most of a heavily wooded peninsula that juts into Lake Megunticook. A brochure of walking trails is available at the registration box near the entrance. One trail leads to 60-foot cliffs. Trails can be boggy: Wear boots or old shoes.

Camden Amphitheatre (207-236-3440), Atlantic Ave., Camden. A magical setting for summertime plays and concerts, and a good place to sit, think, or read anytime. Tucked behind the library and across the street from the harbor park—a gentle, manicured slope down to the water.

Curtis Island, in the outer harbor. A small island with a lighthouse that marks the entrance to Camden. It's a public picnic spot and a popular sea kayaking destination.

✳ Lodging

All listings are in Camden 04843 unless otherwise noted
Note: Rates are for high season; most have off-season rates as well. If you choose one of the many B&Bs in historic houses on Elm, Main, or High St. (all are Rt. 1), you might want to ask what pains have been taken to muffle the sound of passing traffic.

Camden Accommodations (207-236-6090 or 1-800-344-4830; www.camdenac.com), 43 Elm St., is a reservations service representing cottages and weekly rentals in the Camden area.

Camden Bed & Breakfast Association (innkeeper@camdeninns.com), P.O. Box 553. The brochure lists 12 members with descriptions of each and contact information.

RESORT ♂ ᕦ **Samoset Resort** (207-594-2511 or 1-800-341-1650; www.samoset.com), 220 Warrenton St., Rockport 04856. The original Samoset lodge burned down in the 1980s, and the present resort has undergone ever-changing renovations and additions. Set on 230 oceanfront acres, Samoset offers a lot for families with young children and serious golfers. The 178 pleasant rooms include one- and two-bedroom suites, many with ocean views, all with balcony or patio, private bath, TV, air-conditioning, and heat. Time-share units and the two-bedroom Flume Cottage, perched on a rocky outcropping above the water, are also available (cottage weekly in-season). The Samoset has a world-class 18-hole golf course and golf center; outdoor tennis courts; Nautilus-equipped fitness club; racquetball courts; and indoor and outdoor pools. A children's program during summer months and other school holidays features games and arts and crafts. The dining room, Marcel's (see *Dining Out*), and the adjacent Breakwater Café have a large fireplace and floor-to-ceiling windows overlooking the water. Rooms are $269–529, off-season $129–369.

INNS **The Belmont** (207-236-8053 or 1-800-238-8053; www.thebelmont inn.com), 6 Belmont St. Open mid-May–Oct. The peaceful location a few blocks off Rt. 1 combined with Sherry and Bruce Cobb's hospitality make this a favorite inn. An 1890s Edwardian house with a wraparound veranda, the Belmont has six guest rooms, all with private bath and several with a gas fireplace. Full breakfast, afternoon tea, and dessert in the evening. $120–175 per night in-season.

🍴 ♿ **Whitehall Inn** (207-236-3391 or 1-800-789-6565; www.whitehall-inn .com), 52 High St. (Rt. 1). Open Memorial Day through the week after Columbus Day. There's an air of easy elegance and comfort to this rambling inn on Rt. 1, east of the village. The inn has been in operation for 100 years, with the Dewing family at the helm for over 30. The large, low-beamed lobby and adjoining parlors are fitted with Oriental rugs and sofas, games, and puzzles. The Millay Room, with its vintage-1904 Steinway, looks much the way it did on the summer evening in 1909 when a local girl, Edna St. Vincent Millay, read her poem "Renascence" to assembled guests. One of them was so impressed that she undertook to educate the young woman at Vassar. Forty guest rooms in the main inn, five more in the Maine House and the Wicker House across Rt. 1, are simpler than most found in neighboring B&Bs, but each has its appeal. Most have private bath, and all have the kind of heavy old hotel phone your children have never seen. Enjoy the tennis court and shuffleboard, and take a short walk to a "sneaker" beach (wear shoes because of the rocks) on Camden's outer harbor. Rooms $135–170; $85–125 off-season.

🐾 **The Blue Harbor House** (207-236-3196 or 1-800-248-3196; www .blueharborhouse.com), 67 Elm St. Open mid-May–Nov. This friendly 10-room inn serves dinner to guests (by reservation) as well as breakfast on the spacious sunporch. We haven't sampled the multicourse dinners ($40 per person), but guests rave about entrées like stuffed rack of lamb and the ever-popular Down East lobster dinner. Breakfast might include Dutch babies (custard-type pancakes with fresh fruit, Maine maple syrup, almonds, and powdered sugar) or blueberry pancakes. All rooms are pleasantly decorated with country antiques, stenciling, and handmade quilts; all have private bath, telephone, air-conditioning, and TV/VCR. Doubles $90–205.

Hartstone Inn (207-236-4259 or 1-800-788-4823; www.hartstoneinn .com), 41 Elm St. Open year-round. From the Quimper faience and luscious linens in the guest rooms to the world-class cuisine in the dining room and the collection of 400 live orchids in the common areas, Mary Jo and Michael Salmon get absolutely everything right. In fact, they have created one of the best—and most romantic—inns in town. The eight guest rooms and six suites (all with private bath) are tasteful and pretty, some offering a fireplace and canopy bed. Inn guests and the public alike may stay for dinner, an elegant, multicourse affair served by candlelight on the lovely porch (see *Dining Out*). $100–245 double with full breakfast and afternoon tea and cookies. Dinner is $45 prix fixe per person.

BED & BREAKFASTS **The Camden Maine Stay** (207-236-9636; www .camdenmainestay.com), 22 High St. (Rt. 1). Open year-round. Innkeepers Bob and Juanita Topper are friendly and engaging stewards of this Greek Revival house, one of the oldest and most famous in Camden's High Street Historic District. Stay in one of four standard rooms and four suites with names like the Common Ground Room, with a cathedral ceiling, skylight, and private deck over the garden. The lower-level carriage house room is especially appealing, with well-stocked, built-in bookshelves, a woodstove, and French doors opening onto a private patio with lawn and

woods beyond. The 2-acre property is embellished with gardens winding through the grounds and woods. You can have breakfast in the formal dining room or on the sunporch overlooking the gardens. Afternoon tea and sweets included in the $125–250 double room rate.

○○ **The Hawthorn** (207-236-8842; www.camdenhawthorn.com), 9 High St. (Rt. 1). Open Memorial Day–November 1. Owner Maryanne Shanahan has renovated each of the 10 guest rooms at this Victorian inn a short walk to Camden. The carriage house rooms each have a double Jacuzzi, TV and VCR, fireplace, and private deck. The innovative breakfast, served alfresco in good weather, may include homemade pecan Belgian waffles, and house hazelnut granola. $129–289 in high season. A newly landscaped garden can be the lovely site of a wedding. Children are welcome in rooms that accommodate more than two people. The inn's official greeter is a smooth fox terrier named Tori.

○○ **Norumbega** (207-236-4646 or 1-877-363-4646; www.norumbegainn .com), 63 High St. (Rt. 1). Open year-round. With one of the most imposing facades of any B&B anywhere, this turreted stone "castle" has long been a landmark just north of Camden. Inside, the ornate staircase with fireplace and love seat on the landing, formal parlor, and dining room make you feel as though you've stepped into a beautifully kept Victorian home. Eleven guest rooms and two suites named for European castles come with king or queen bed, private bath, antiques, as well as phone, TV, and dataport. Ask for the Library Suite, two rooms with a loft balcony full of books that formed the original castle library. Doubles are $160–475, including full breakfast and evening hors d'oeuvres. Two-night minimum on weekends. The inn welcomes children 7 and up, and offers murder mystery weekends, seminars, retreats, and weddings.

The Camden Windward House (207-236-9656 or 1-877-492-9656; www.windwardhouse.com), 6 High St. (Rt. 1). Open year-round. In 2003 Philip and Lee Brookes bought this handsome Greek Revival clapboard home. New paint and navy blue trim have brightened the exterior, and the breakfast now includes a full menu, with eggs any-way, orange yogurt pancakes, and other choices (soy milk and Egg Beaters also available). The five guest rooms and three suites all have private bath, air-conditioning, cable TV, clock-radio with CD player, and phone with dataport. The Chart Room Suite features a living room with fireplace, TV/VCR, library, sofa, Jacuzzi whirlpool tub, separate bedroom with queen canopy bed, and French doors that open onto a private deck overlooking the garden. $150–280 in high season, $109–199 in quiet season.

A Little Dream (207-236-8742; www.littledream.com), 60 High St. (Rt. 1). Open year-round except March. Raised up on a hill over busy Rt. 1, this place feels wonderfully secluded and intimate, while sustaining a high standard of elegance. Seven guest rooms include a carriage house suite called the Isle Watch. Overlooking the harbor and Curtis Island, it has a gas fireplace, king canopy bed, soaking tub, and covered porch complete with porch swing. If you stay here over July 4, you can view three separate fireworks displays right from

the inn. $159–295 double includes a multicourse breakfast in a lovely side porch or dining room. Two-night minimum on holiday weekends. Foreign guests are always welcome: Innkeeper JoAnna Ball speaks Italian, German, and French. Her husband, Bill Fontana, is a sculptor, and many guests are artists.

The Blackberry Inn (207-236-6060 or 1-800-388-6000; www.blackberry inn.com), 82 Elm St. Open year-round. We think the Blackberry offers the prettiest interiors in town (and it now owns The Elms next door as well, where rooms have been upgraded to Blackberry standards). Settees covered in silk damask, ornate Oriental rugs, decorative swords, pressed-tin ceilings set the style. Owners Cyndi and Jim Ostrowski provide rooms that vary from small and cozy to large and airy. Stay in the Bette Davis, where the movie star slept after the cast party for *Peyton Place*, with a queen brass bed and antique lighting fixture. The garden rooms are cozy, with fireplace and whirlpool bath. Children are welcome in the carriage house. Rates are $129–249 in-season, including a full breakfast served in the dining room or alfresco in the courtyard.

⅃ **Inn at Ocean's Edge** (207-236-0945; www.innatoceansedge.com), P.O. Box 258, Lincolnville 04849, accessible via a private drive off Rt. 1 a couple of miles north of the Camden line. Open year-round. This modern hotel features two separate buildings: the main inn with three common areas, a breakfast room, and 18 guest rooms; and the newer Hilltop building with 12 rooms nestled farther from the bay. Believe it or not, almost every single room features a water view, along with Jacuzzi, gas fireplace, TV, VCR, stereo, and more. Steps lead down to a private "shingle" beach, great for an evening stroll. The delicious breakfasts include eggs any-style as well as specials such as Grand Marnier French toast, and in the afternoon cookies are served. A new heated pool, spa with treatment rooms and sauna, and whirlpool are available to guests, and a fine-dining restaurant next door (see *Dining Out*). $159–295, depending on room and season, includes breakfast. Children 14 and up welcome.

The Inn at Sunrise Point (207-236-7716 or 1-800-435-6278; www.sunrise point.com), P.O. Box 1344, Lincolnville 04849. Open May–Oct. Set on a 4-acre waterfront estate just over the town line in Lincolnville, this small, luxurious B&B was acquired in 2002 by Irishman Stephen Tallon and his Australian-raised, American-born wife, Deanna. The location is a definite asset here. Five cottages named for Maine painters and writers—among them Edward Hopper, Winslow Homer, and Richard Russo—have large picture windows with an incredible view, fireplace, and Jacuzzi; the three rooms in the main house are named for Maine writers and feature a fireplace and water views. All accommodations offer queen or king bed, phone, and TV/VCR. Common rooms include a glass conservatory that lets the sun in, plus a snug, wood-paneled library with fireplace that's just right for cooler days. Rooms, suite, and the new Wyeth Loft are $225–405, cottages $265–495, with full breakfast included.

The Victorian by the Sea (207-236-3785 or 1-800-382-9817; www .victorianbythesea.com), Lincolnville Beach 04849. Open year-round.

Ginny and Greg Ciraldo own this quiet, romantic spot overlooking the water, away from the bustle of Rt. 1. As the name suggests, decor is Victorian. There are seven guest rooms, all with queen bed and private bath; most have a fireplace. We especially like the Victorian Suite, with a turret room, fireplace, and lovely water views in the off-season. The $155–235 rate includes full breakfast (crème brûlée French toast, peach strata, Ghirardelli chocolate Belgian waffles, and the like) and afternoon sweets. The Ciraldos also own the 13-unit motel at the top of the road and the house between the inn and the bay, and have created a nature path to the top of a 30-foot cliff overlooking Penobscot Bay, where guests have seen porpoises, seals, and bald eagles.

OTHER LODGING ❀ ☸ ❦ High Tide Inn (207-236-3724 or 1-800-778-7068; www.hightideinn.com), Rt. 1. Open May–Oct. Set far enough back from Rt. 1 to preclude traffic noise, this no-frills, easygoing complex appeals to singles and couples (who tend to choose one of the five rooms in the inn) and families (who opt for a cottage or motel unit, some with connecting sleeping rooms). Most of the 30 rooms have breathtaking views—especially for the price—and they're all extremely clean. The complex fills 7 quiet acres of landscaped grounds and meadow that slope to the water, where there's more than 250 feet of private ocean beach. Guests enjoy a generous continental breakfast, including just-baked popovers and muffins, on the glass-enclosed porch; the living room also has ample windows with views of the bay. Pets allowed in only three of the rooms. The porch, living room, and bar all have working fireplaces. $85–225 in-season. Two-night minimum weekends in July and Aug. and over holidays.

⚓ **Lord Camden Inn** (207-236-4325 or 1-800-336-4325; www.lordcamden inn.com), 24 Main St. Open year-round. This inn is named for the British nobleman who championed the American cause in the House of Lords during the Revolutionary War. Occupying a restored 1893 brick Masonic hall, the Lord Camden sits smack dab in the center of town and takes up several floors above a row of Main St. shops. Modern amenities include cable TV, private bath, telephone, air-conditioning, and elevator. Most rooms have two double beds and a balcony overlooking the town and harbor or the river and hills beyond; there are also three luxury suites on the first floor. Rates include a full breakfast. $89–269, depending on the view and season.

Cedarholm Garden Bay Inn (207-236-3886; www.cedarholm.com), Rt. 1, Lincolnville Beach 04849. Gorgeously landscaped grounds featuring mature trees and gardens lead you down to the four cottages set off by themselves. Named for birds found on the Maine coast (Osprey, Puffin, Tern, and Loon), these hidden gems overlook Penobscot Bay and abound with privacy and myriad features: fireplace, Jacuzzi, queen bed, Thomasville furniture, kitchenette, and private deck. Two recently renovated upper cottages, closer to Rt. 1, have a private bath and kitchenette. Continental breakfast includes muffins baked with berries grown here, and fresh fruit. All guests have access to a shared deck right on the beach. Upper units begin at $165 per night. Luxury cottages $195–340 per night.

CAMPING 🐾 ⚓ ♿ **Megunticook Campground by the Sea** (207-594-2428; www.campgroundbythesea .com), P.O. Box 375, Rockport 04856. Open May 15–Oct. 15. Wooded, oceanfront campground with 100 sites and 10 rustic camping cabins. Facilities include a store, recreation hall, fishing, heated pool, WiFi, and oceanfront picnic area and gardens for Saturday-night lobster bakes. $42 in-season. (**Camden Hills RV Resort** (207-236-2498), 30 Applewood Rd. in Rockport, is a sister park.)

⚜ Where to Eat

DINING OUT Francine Bistro (207-230-0083; www.francinebistro.com), 55 Chestnut St., Camden. Open Tue.–Sat. 5:30–10; reservations recommended. Small, intimate, and a little noisy because everyone is exclaiming about how good the food is. Chef-owner Brian Hill and his partner Lindsey Schechter took this place over after a year of working in it— and we are awarding them the coastal food word-of-mouth award for the most praised place in Maine. Chewy, dense bread, a rich soup of roasted corn and scallops with a wreath of basil oil started another chorus of pleasure, as did out six Pemaquid oysters with a slightly hot cucumber vinaigrette. Roast pork, served in a pool of apples and rimmed by parsley cream, made one great meal, criticized only for being too big; our own crisp redfish with green-colored potatoes and sautéed mushrooms and tomatoes was a culinary version of a gorgeous summer day. Entrées $22–25.

Natalie's at the Mill (207-236-7008), 43 Mechanic St., Camden. Open for dinner Tue.–Sat., also Sun. in summer.

Set looking out on the waterfall at Knox Mill, from the deck in summer and inside in winter, Natalie's offers a menu that changes more frequently than the seasons. French- and Asian-influenced fine dining amid sleek wood and a full bar with leather chairs. Entrées $26–34.

Bouchee Bistro (207-236-8998), 31 Elm St., Camden. Open for dinner till 9:30 weeknights, 10 weekends. A new restaurant that serves American cuisine with a French influence. Ami Moore, an owner, said the seared scallops over corn and lobster are a favorite. She favors small vineyards on her wine list, and extolled the crème brûlée, flecked with vanilla bean seeds. Entrées $18–25.

✆ ♿ **Marcel's** (207-593-1529), Rockport (at the Samoset Resort). Open daily for breakfast, dinner, and Sunday brunch. Like the Samoset itself, this place reminded us of a country club, with its rows of tablecloth-covered tables. But this is one of the last places that still offers tableside service, breaking an egg into your Caesar salad for two ($18) or carving grilled châteaubriand for two ($70). The uniformed waiters, well trained and warm, know their stuff. Jackets are suggested but not required for men at dinner; no T-shirts or jeans allowed. $17–35. Reservations suggested. The adjacent Breakwater Café offers entertainment.

Hartstone Inn (207-236-4259 or 1-800-788-4823; www.hartstoneinn .com), 41 Elm St., Camden. Open year-round. The five-course dinner, prix fixe $42.50, offers a limited but delectable choice here, with first courses like crab- and shrimp cakes and Thai pheasant spring rolls. The second course revolves around a salad, local greens when they're available, or gazpacho or other soups. In the middle is a palate cleanser like strawberry sorbet, to prepare your mouth for the potato-crusted filet mignon or rosemary-grilled salmon, and dessert, often a soufflé like chocolate cherry with a kirsch crème anglaise. Make reservations early— the popular Hartstone books up weeks in advance.

Atlantica (207-236-6011), 1 Bay View Landing, Camden. Open for dinner year-round, closed Tue. and Wed.; reservations suggested. Ken and Del Paquin serve interesting dishes such as tomatoes filled with crab and artichoke ($9); a salad of spinach, roast beets, feta, and bacon with port wine vinaigrette ($8); and rack of lamb with arugula pesto ($27). Customers have had to endure long waits recently, but service issues could be addressed by the time you visit and enjoy the porthole-level views of the fancy yachts in the harbor. Dinner $17–27.

✆ ♿ **Chez Michel** (207-789-5600), Lincolnville Beach (across the road from the beach). Open Apr.–mid-Nov., dinner Tue.–Sun., lunch and dinner on Sun. This pleasant restaurant serves French food that has won a spectrum of loyal customers. One local food lover advised ordering the mussels mariniere with small, wild mussels from Frenchman's Bay, garlic, onion, and white wine—$9.95 as an appetizer, $16.95 for dinner (with salad, potato, and French bread). Fisherman's chowder, with haddock, Maine shrimp, clams, and scallops, New England–style (with a milk and cream base), is $5.95 for a cup. Raspberry pie here is legendary, inspiring requests with reservations. Dinner entrées run $12–22.

The Gallery Café (207-230-0061; www.prismglassgallery.com), 297 Commercial St., Rockport. Open Wed.–Sat. 11–3 for lunch and 5–9 for dinner; Sunday brunch 10–3, dinner 5–9. The latest place sits within a gallery and studio for glassblowing along Rt. 1, and often watching some glass be blown is part of the visit. But even if the artist is absent, the food is so good you might not care. A mushroom tart with Parmesan custard and tarragon ($9) might start a meal that could go on to grilled striped bass over lemon thyme tapioca ($28) or a cassoulet of preserved duck ($20). Desserts are beautiful and delicious; we delighted in the key lime pie and the blueberry crisp with ice cream when we ate on the small patio. Entrées $16–28.

Peter Ott's (207-236-4032), 16 Bayview St., Camden. Open year-round for dinner, with a large, varied menu that features sirloin steak and fresh local fish. Entrées are served with the salad bar, unless you choose a lighter entrée. $16.95–25.95.

The Edge (207-236-4430), P.O. Box Stone Coast Road, Route 1, Lincolnville. Opened in the summer of 2006, and set to stay open year-round; call for nights open. You can sit on the oceanside outdoor patio or inside by the wood fire in one of the 66 seats at this new elegant restaurant. Entrées include cider-braised pork osso buco, a pork shank served with maple baked beans and mead-glazed carrots ($26); or crispy halibut with potato gnocchi, mushrooms, and bacon ($29). Salt-roasted lobster is cooked in the wood-burning oven ($29); desserts offer Guinness cheesecake and frozen nougat terrine with pistachio crème anglaise ($7–8), and Maine cheese plates.

In Camden

Camden Bagel Café (207-236-2661), 25 Mechanic St. Open Mon.–Sat. 6:30 AM–2 PM, Sun. 7:30–2. Bagels with substance are baked here, some in whole wheat. The plain interior makes a good refuge, and white shutters filter the sun as you enjoy a bagel with cream cheese or with an egg and bacon for breakfast. Soups and chili when things cool down.

Ephemere Pastry Shop and Café (207-236-4451), 51 Bay View St., Camden. Open for lunch 11:30–2:30, when salads, delicious soups, and other lunch specials have been drawing a pleased crowd. Also a source for fine pastry, tea and coffee, and a custom birthday cake.

Cappy's Chowder House (207-236-2254; www.cappyschowder.com), 1 Main St. Open year-round. Lunch and dinner daily in summer; closing one or two days in winter. They claim that "sooner or later, everyone shows up at Cappy's," and it's true. Good food from local ingredients with reasonable price tags: treats from the on-premises bakery for breakfast; croissant sandwiches, burgers, and full meals for lunch; seafood entrées, special pasta and meat dishes for dinner. Upstairs in the **Crow's Nest** (open in-season only) you'll find a quieter setting, a harbor view, and the same menu. A good bet if you just want chowder and a beer at the bar. Bakery, coffeehouse, and company store downstairs (open seasonally).

Cedar Crest Restaurant (207-236-7722), 115 Elm St. Open 7 AM–2 PM daily; dinner Fri. only at 5. This has become Camden's favorite breakfast spot, and the reasons are clear.

The big black coffee carafe stays at your table to empty as you wish, the homemade bread has some real flavor, and servers are responsive and quick to help you. The packaged, frozen home fries could be retired. Two eggs with toast is $3.50, and is served all day; but the wraps and quesadillas for lunch are good, too.

✔ **Quarterdeck Bar and Grill** (207-236-3272), 21 Bayview St. Open daily 11 AM–10 PM (pizza served until 11, and the bar stays open until 1 AM). Menu choices in this harborside setting include brick-oven pizzas, pasta, fresh seafood, and beef. Entrées $8–24.

✔ & **The Waterfront Restaurant** (207-236-3747), Bayview St. Open for lunch and dinner where you can watch the activity in the harbor. Popular and with a well-trained staff, this place fills up fast and doesn't take reservations, so be prepared to wait. Dinners include lobster entrées and a shore dinner (clam chowder, corn on the cob, steamers, mussels, and a lobster) for $24.95, and steaks.

✔ & **Village Restaurant** (207-236-3232), Main St. Open year-round for lunch and dinner, daily July–Oct.; closed Tue. the rest of the year. Family owned for more than 40 years, this is a longtime favorite with locals, but we found the breaded and fried fish too heavy. Try the broiled and sautéed seafood instead, and the home-baked desserts. Children's menu. The two dining rooms overlook Camden Harbor.

✔ & **Gilbert's Public House** (207-236-4320), Bayview St. Tucked underneath the shops along Bayview St. (you enter through a side door just off the road), this is a good place for a beer and a sandwich, burgers, chow-

der, snacks or light meals for the kids, pizza, or a simple supper before the evening's activities. Live music for dancing in the evening on weekends.

✔ **Boynton-McKay Food Co.** (207-236-2465), 30 Main St. (in the heart of downtown). Open daily year-round for breakfast, lunch, and takeout, closed Nov.–June on Mon. A fun, light-hearted place to have a yummy skillet breakfast, roast turkey wrap, fresh croissants, and *pain au chocolat.* Sit in one of the tall booths in this 1890s-era former apothecary designed by the owner to fit with the decor, and relax.

✔ & **Fitzpatrick's Café** (207-236-2041), Bayview Landing, Bayview St. Open for breakfast and lunch year-round, dinner in-season. Fitzy's is easy to miss as you walk to the public landing. But it's a find: a wide variety of sandwiches and salads plus daily specials. You order at the counter, and they call you by name when your food is ready. Popular with locals. Outside patio for summertime dining with views of the Camden Hills.

✔ & **Camden Deli** (207-236-8343; www.camdendeli.com), 37 Main St. All three meals served daily. More than 35 sandwich choices, combining all the regular deli meats and cheeses as well as some less expected choices, like chicken broccoli salad or hummus. Large selection of good homemade soups, salads, and desserts. The back dining room overlooks the waterfall in downtown Camden, and another dining room upstairs, with a deck open in summer, also overlooks the water.

In Rockport
✔ **The Helm** (207-236-4337), Rt. 1 (1.5 miles south of Camden). Open for lunch and dinner year-round, ex-

cept for 2 weeks in Nov. and in Apr. Breakfast is served as well Dec.–Apr. There's a French accent to the menu, but we cannot recommend the bouillabaisse, and sauce on the steak *au poivre* is too heavy. The chef's salad, however, one friend called the best in Maine. The menu offers about 50 entrées, and everybody leaves with containers of leftovers. Children's menu. At the takeout window you can order onion soup and delicious crabmeat rolls.

Rockport Corner Shop (207-236-8361), Central St., Rockport Village. Open daily year-round for breakfast and lunch in summer, closed in winter for two months. Regulars greet each other warmly at this spot in the heart of the village, but newcomers are made to feel welcome, too. An exceptional find with almost no decor but plenty of atmosphere. Fresh coffee cakes are baked each morning; all salads are made with garden-grown vegetables. Breakfast specialties include eggs Benedict and Swedish pancakes; lunch offers pocket sandwiches, crabmeat rolls, and daily specials. No liquor. Very reasonable prices.

LOBSTER POUND 🐾 ⴺ **Lobster Pound Restaurant** (207-789-5550), Rt. 1, Lincolnville Beach. Open every day for lunch and dinner from first Sun. in May–mid-Oct. This is a mecca for lobster lovers—some people plan their trips around a meal here. Features lobster, boiled or baked, also clams, other fresh seafood, roast turkey, ham, steaks, and chicken. A family-style restaurant that seats 246 inside and has an outside patio near a sandy beach. Takeout and picnic tables offered across the beach.

TAKEOUT **The Market Basket** (207-236-4371), Rts. 1 and 90, Rockport. Open Mon.–Fri. 7:30–6:30, Sat. 8–6. This specialty food store offers a wide variety of creative salads, delicious French bread, soups, entrées, sandwich specials for takeout, more than 500 wines from around the world, and over 75 varieties of cheese.

Scott's Place (207-236-8751), Elm St. (Reny's parking lot), Camden. Open 10–4. Since 1974 years this tiny building in the parking lot of a small shopping center has served thousands of toasted crabmeat and lobster rolls, chicken sandwiches, burgers, veggie burgers, hot dogs, and chips. Prices are among the best around: $1.39 for a hot dog, under $7.99 for a lobster roll. This is one of several small takeout buildings around town, but it's the only one open year-round.

Also see **The Helm** under *Eating Out*.

✳ Entertainment

Bay Chamber Concerts (207-236-2823; www.baychamberconcerts.org), Rockport Opera House (next to Mary Lea Park), Rockport. This renowned organization has presented outstanding concerts for more than 44 years. In July and August they sponsor Thursday- and Friday-evening chamber music concerts in the beautifully restored opera house with its gilded interior, with free preconcert lectures and postconcert receptions. Winter-season selections include classical and jazz music concerts and dance performances.

Camden Civic Theatre (207-236-2281; www.camdencivictheatre.com), Main St., Camden. A variety of theatrical performances are presented in

✎ ♿ **The Center for Maine Contemporary Art** (207-236-2875; www.arts maine.org), 162 Russell Ave., Rockport. Open year-round, Tue.–Sat. 10–5; also open Sun. 1–5. Call for details about special exhibits. $5 admission for nonmembers; members, children under 18, and Rockport residents free. Promoting contemporary Maine art and artists since 1952, through exhibitions and education. The building, which started out as a late-19th-century livery stable, then became a firehouse, then the town hall, now showcases contemporary Maine art. The gallery sponsors numerous shows each season, an art auction, a crafts show, gallery talks, a shop, and an evening lecture series. The shop features a mix of objects for gifts and home use. T-shirts that read FEAR NO ART go for $20.

the restored Camden Opera House, a second-floor theater with plum seats and cream-and-gold walls. Tickets are reasonably priced.

✳ Selective Shopping

Avena Botanicals (207-594-2403; www.avenabotanicals.org), 219 Mill St., Rockport. Open Mon.–Thu. 9–5. Customers can walk in the botanical garden when it's flourishing in summer, and watch employees inside making tinctures and other high-quality herbal remedies, creams, salves, and oils. You can also sign up for an herb class at the Avena Institute, in the same building.

ANTIQUES At the chamber of commerce, pick up the leaflet guide to antiques shops scattered among Camden, Rockport, and Lincolnville.

ART GALLERIES **Nan Mulford Gallery** (207-594-8481; www.nan mulfordgallery.com), 313 Main St., Rockland. Open Tue.–Sat. 10–5, Sun. noon–5. This little gallery, tucked up a narrow flight of stairs in a 19th-century building right in downtown Rockport, showcases resident and summer artists.

Check out their opening-night receptions, with food and wine and a chance to meet the artists.

Bay View Gallery (207-236-4534; www.bayviewgallery.com), 33 Bayview St., Camden. One of the largest galleries in the Midcoast area. Original paintings and sculptures by contemporary artists working in Maine. Expert custom framing, too.

A Small Wonder Gallery (207-236-6005), 1 Public Landing (across from the chamber of commerce), Camden. A small gallery with well-chosen limited-edition graphics, watercolors, hand-painted tiles, porcelain, and original sculpture.

The Northport Landing Gallery (see "Belfast, Searsport") is 10 minutes from Camden.

Prism Glass Gallery (207-230-0061; www.prismglassgallery.com), 297 Commercial St., Rockport. Open Wed.–Sat. 10 AM–9 PM, Sun. 10–3. Glassblower and gallery owner Patti Kissinger demonstrates her skills in the barn next door.

ARTISANS **Windsor Chairmakers** (207-789-5188; www.windsorchair .com), Rt. 1, Lincolnville Beach. Filling two floors of an old farmhouse, the inviting display encompasses not only Windsor chairs but also tables, highboys, and four-poster beds, all offered in a selection of finishes, including "distressed" (instant antique). A new gallery shows a line of Shaker-style furniture.

Maine Artisans (207-789-5376), Rt. 1, Lincolnville Beach. Open daily May–Oct., this charming store sells work by weavers, potters, and sock makers, among others.

The Foundry (207-236-3200; www .remsen.com), 531 Park St., West Rockport (next to the Baptist church). Custom metal castings in bronze and aluminum. Also handblown glass vases, bowls, and goblets, and giant sculptural fishing lures.

Phi Home Designs (207-230-0034; www.phihomedesigns.com), 270 Meadow St., Rockport. Furniture makers with a gallery that shows area artisans.

BOOKSTORES ABCD Books (207-236-3903), 23 Bayview St., Camden. Open June–Aug., Mon.–Sat. 10–9, Sun. 1–5; Sep.–May, 10–5, or later depending on business. Sun. by chance in winter. A Camden literary landmark: an unusually extensive and organized collection of rare and used books featuring maritime, art, New England, and history titles.

& **Down East** (207-594-9544), Rt. 1, Rockport. The headquarters for Down East Enterprises (publishers of *Down East*, *Fly Rod & Reel*, and *Shooting Sportsman* magazines, as well as a line of New England books) is a fine old mansion that includes a book and gift shop.

☏ **The Owl and Turtle Bookshop** (207-236-4769 or 1-800-876-4769), 32 Washington St. (one block north

of Rt. 1 on Rt. 105), Camden. One of Maine's best bookstores, now located in an old mill with old maple floors and dark wood bookcases, with a reading corner by a fireplace. The children's room has a little wishing well with a Plexiglas window on the Megunticook River. A marine room holds one of the best selections of marine books on the East Coast. Free parking on Mechanic St. and in a lot up the street. Maine history, travel and art. Great for browsing, and check out their frequent author book signings.

Sherman's Books (207-236-2223 or 1-800-803-5949; www.shermans.com), 8 Bay View St., Camden. Another in the fine chain of Sherman's bookstores on the Maine coast, Camden's Sherman's is filled with a wide variety of books and gifts.

SPECIAL SHOPS

All shops are in Camden and open year-round unless otherwise noted

Unique 1 (207-236-8717), 2 Bayview St. Woolen items made from Maine wool, designed and hand loomed locally. Also a full yarn shop for knitters and some pottery.

☏ **Once a Tree** (207-236-3995), 46 Bayview St. Wooden crafts, including beautiful clocks, kitchen utensils, desk sets; a large game and toy section.

☏ **The Smiling Cow** (207-236-3351; www.smilingcow.com), 41 Main St. Seasonal. Three generations ago a mother and five children converted this stable into a classic gift shop, one with unusual warmth and scope. We like the fun Maine-themed items like blueberry-print aprons and fragrant, locally made soaps.

🐚 **Heavenly Threads** (207-236-3203), 57 Elm St. (Rt. 1). Open Tue.–Fri. 10–4, Sat. 10–1. Wealthy summer folks and locals both donate to this extremely clean shop full of surprising finds. We found clothes by Ann Taylor, Calvin Klein, Head, and others for under $5 apiece, as well as books and housewares in excellent shape. Also men's and children's clothing, jewelry, gift items, and coffee-table books. Proceeds benefit Habitat for Humanity, Coastal Hospice, Rockland Soup Kitchen, and others.

Ducktrap Bay Trading Company (1-800-560-9568; www.ducktrapbay .com), 37 Bayview St. Many of these pieces—decoys, wildlife and marine art, scrimshaw, and paintings—have earned awards for their creators.

Danica Candleworks (207-236-3060), 569 West St., Rt. 90, West Rockport. In a striking building with a Scandinavian-inspired interior, you'll find a candle factory and shop that sells hand-dipped and scented candles as well as jewelry and candle accessories.

✳ Special Events

First weekend in February: **U.S. National Toboggan Championships**—teams from all over the country compete in two-, three-, and four-person races, often in costume (Camden Snow Bowl).

Mid-July: **Annual Open House and Garden Day**, sponsored by the Camden Garden Club. Very popular tour of homes and gardens in Camden and Rockport held every year for five decades. **Arts and Crafts Show** (*third Saturday and Sunday*), Camden Amphitheatre.

August: **The Center for Maine Contemporary Art's Annual Art Auction**—Maine's largest exhibit and auction of quality contemporary Maine art. **Merryspring's Annual Kitchen Tour**—see uniquely designed kitchens in Camden, Rockport, and Lincolnville, plus demonstrations and tastings from professional growers and chefs.

Late August: **Union Fair and Blueberry Festival,** Union Fairgrounds (see "Rockland/Thomaston Area").

Labor Day weekend: **Windjammer Weekend**, Camden Harbor. A celebration of the windjammer industry, featuring a parade of boats, music, nautical history, fireworks, and the Schooner Bum Talent Contest.

September: **Country Roads Artists and Artisans Tour** (207-763-4770; www.artisanstour.com), **Maine Fare** (www.mainefare.org), cooking demonstrations, fine food, wine pairings mostly at the Camden Snow Bowl.

First weekend in October: **Fall Festival of Arts and Crafts**, Camden Amphitheatre—75 artisans displaying work for sale.

First weekend in December: **Christmas by the Sea**—tree lighting, Santa's arrival, caroling, holiday house tour, refreshments in shops.

A 14-mile-long, string-bean-shaped island just 3 miles off Lincolnville Beach (a 20-minute ferry ride), Islesboro is a private kind of place.

There are three distinct communities on the island. The town of Islesboro with the necessary services (town office, post office, health center, and fire department) sits in the center between Dark Harbor and Pripet. Dark Harbor (described by Sidney Sheldon in his best seller *Master of the Game* as the "jealously guarded colony of the super-rich") has long been a summer resort village, where huge "cottages" peek from behind the trees along the road to Pendleton Point. Pripet is a thriving year-round neighborhood of boatbuilders and fishermen.

GETTING THERE The car-carrying **Maine State Ferry** (207-789-5611 or 207-734-6935; $6 round-trip per passenger, $17.50 per vehicle, and $5.75 per bicycle) from Lincolnville Beach lands mid-island at Grindle Point. The crossing is a 3-mile, 20-minute ride, the schedule depending on the season. If you go for a day trip only, pay close attention to when the last ferry leaves the island to avoid being stranded. At the landing you'll find a clean ferry terminal with public restrooms.

GUIDANCE The **Islesboro town office** (207-734-2253), 150 Main Rd., is a great source of information, with friendly service both on the phone and in person. When you board the Maine State Ferry, ask for a map and schedule. The detailed and informative island map shows a full view of the island as well as business locations, a ferry schedule, a brief description of the island, and a historical society events calendar.

WHEN TO COME Only in summer will visitors find a bookstore, two cafés, a gallery, and a few places with rooms to rent.

✴ To See and Do

The old lighthouse on **Grindle Point** (built in 1850, now automated) and keeper's cottage is now the seasonal **Sailors' Memorial Museum** (207-734-2253), open July–Labor Day, 9:30–4:30, closed Wed. and Sun. Look for summer musical and theatrical performances at the **Free Will Baptist Church**. Check out the **Up Island Church**, a fine old structure with beautiful wall stencils and fascinating old headstones in the adjacent graveyard.

The layout of the island makes at least a bicycle necessary to get a real feel for the place. The roads are narrow, winding, and have no shoulder. Bicyclists should use great caution. Even so, after both driving and biking the island, we prefer biking. A drive from one end of the island to the other is a nice way to spend a couple of hours, but on bicycles, it'll take you most of a day. In Dark Harbor you'll see huge "cottages" and impressive architecture. In summer you'll also find shops for browsing, including **Island Books** (207-734-6610), a great source for used books at good prices, and the **Dark Harbor Shop** (207-734-8878), with souvenirs, gifts, ice cream, and a deli. A picnic area and town beach at Pendleton Point have spectacular water views. The trip down the other side of the island will take you past the **Islesboro Historical Society** (207-734-6733) in the former town hall, which houses rotating exhibits on the first floor and a permanent collection upstairs.

✳ Lodging

The Islesboro town office (207-734-2253) is a welcoming source of information and can refer you to local real estate agents who handle cottage rentals.

Dark Harbor House (207-734-6669; www.darkharborhouse.com), Box 185, Jetty Rd., Dark Harbor, Islesboro 04848. Open mid-May–mid-Oct. Built on a hilltop at the turn of the 20th century as a summer cottage for the president of the First National Bank of Philadelphia, this imposing, yellow-clapboard inn offers elegance from a past era. Inside you'll find a summery living room with glass French doors opening onto a porch and a library with a fireplace, decorated with many mounted little antlers. All 11 guest rooms have private bath, some with a huge, deep old tub, and some feature a balcony. Children 12 and up welcome. We loved our dinner here, poached, rare wild salmon in a rim soup bowl filled with herbed broth, new green peas, and semolina gnocchi ($20), but barbecued duck breast with rice noodles and green curry sauce ($19) was slightly too sweet for our taste. The fresh salad came from an island farm, as did the strawberries served with vanilla ice cream for one dessert. Doubles $115–275, including a full breakfast. Dinner entrées $18–21.

Aunt Laura's B&B (207-734-8286; lbebb@aol.com), 812 Main Rd., Islesboro 04848. On the other side of the island, Louanne Bebb offers two guest rooms and a living room for guests in the wing attached to her 1855 Cape.

✳ Where to Eat

You can often pick up a snack (breakfast specials, burgers, lobster rolls, and such for lunch and dinner) at a takeout stand at the far end of the ferry terminal parking lot. The luncheonette in the **Dark Harbor Shop** is a local gathering place where you can get lunch and ice cream. **Durkee's General Store** (207-734-2201) and **The Island Market** (207-734-6672) both sell sandwiches, pizza, and provisions for picnics. The **Dark Harbor House** offers dinner by reservation upon availability.

✳ Selected Shopping

Seven Knots Gallery (207-734-8877; www.sevenknotsgallery.com), 300 Main Rd., Isleboro 04848. Exhibits and weekly workshops in the summer, open July and Aug., Tue.–Sun. 1–5. **Artisan's Books and Bindery** (207-734-6852; www.abebooks.com/home/artisan84), 113 Derby Rd., in the Dark Harbor Village. A nice little bookstore with coffee and muffins, where you can also find custom binding.

BELFAST, SEARSPORT, AND STOCKTON SPRINGS

Belfast's long, Victorian brick Main Street slopes steadily downward, away from Rt. 1, toward the confluence of the tidal Passagassawakeag River and Belfast Bay.

With just 7,100 residents and a small-town feel, Belfast is a city and the seat of Waldo County. Magnificent Greek Revival and Federal homes, proof of early prominence, line High and Church Streets. Lower blocks suggest a checkered commercial history that included a sarsaparilla company, a rum distillery, a city-owned railroad, and, most recently and memorably, poultry slaughtering and shipping.

An artist in one of Belfast's burgeoning galleries observes: "You have to want to come here. People who turn off Rt. 1 and take the downhill plunge are looking for something." What they find is a mix of boutiques and basic shops, trendy cafés, restaurants, and hometown eateries, a supermarket-sized health food store, a funky old movie house, and live theater, as well as B&Bs that could charge twice as much down the road in Camden. In Belfast the prime employer is now MBNA (credit cards).

High above downtown Belfast, Rt. 1 crosses the Passagassawakeag River into East Belfast, threading a string of shops, restaurants, and a mix of 1940s motor courts and motor inns with water views.

In Searsport Rt. 1 becomes, suddenly and briefly, a mid-19th-century brick-and-granite downtown. Stop at Mosman Park, with its picnic tables and playground right on Penobscot Bay (just down Water Street), for a sense of place. Then visit the Penobscot Marine Museum to learn that more than 3,000 different vessels have been built in and around Penobscot Bay since 1770. Searsport alone launched eight brigs and six schooners in one year (1845), and for many years boasted more sea captains than any other town its size, explaining the dozens of 19th-century mansions lining Rt. 1 in Searsport. What you don't see from the highway is Sears Island and its deepwater harbor, for which a series of projects has been planned in recent decades.

A number of these mansions are now B&Bs, which work not only as way stops but also as hubs from which to explore this part of Waldo County. If you have

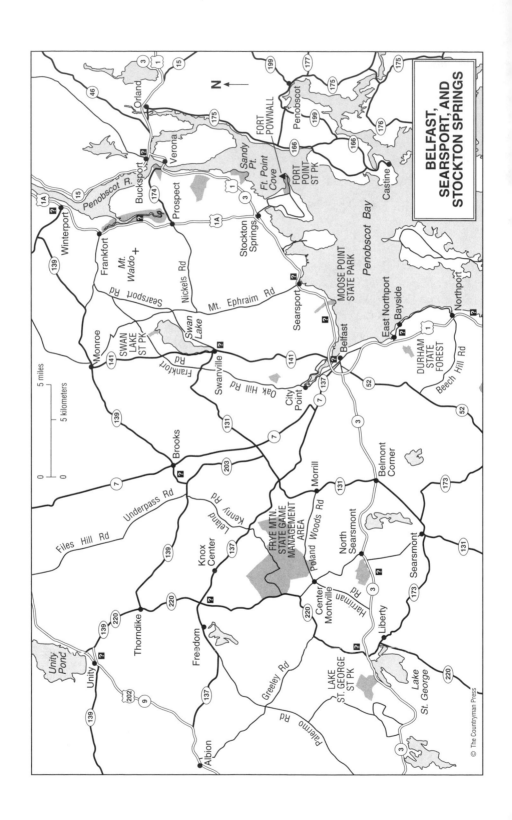

BELFAST,
SEARSPORT, AND
STOCKTON SPRINGS

© The Countryman Press

the time, take the scenic route to this region from Augusta, poking through the
communities of Unity, Thorndike, and Brooks, detouring to Liberty then down
to Belfast. Rt. 1 continues to shadow the shore as it narrows into what seems
more like a broad river.

GUIDANCE **The Greater Belfast Area Chamber of Commerce** (207-338-
5900; www.belfastmaine.org), P.O. Box 58, Belfast 04915, maintains an information booth on Main St. down near the waterfront; open May–Oct., 10–6.

Waldo County Marketing Association (1-800-870-9934; www.waldocounty
maine.com), P.O. Box 139, Searsport 04974. The web site is exceptional.

GETTING THERE *By air:* For commercial service, see "Rockland/Thomaston,"
"Bangor," and "Portland."

By car: The most direct route to this region from points south and west is via
I-95, exiting in Augusta and taking Rt. 3 to Belfast. An new I-95 exit (113) ac-
cesses a new connector to Rt. 3, offering motorists bound for the Midcoast a way
around Augusta. If you're coming up Rt. 1, take the first turnoff for downtown
Belfast. The approach is down Northport Ave. and Belfast City Park, then down
High St.

By bus: **Concord Trailways** (1-800-639-3317) stops in both Searsport and Belfast.

PUBLIC RESTROOMS At the public landing at the bottom of Main Street.

WHEN TO COME The town chugs along through winter, with most inns and
restaurants open throughout the year; still, the summer season gives the ocean a
friendlier look and fills the farm stands. Come to Belfast anytime to enjoy the
downtown, but wait for warm weather to sail, visit the wonderful museum, and
eat seafood along the shore.

✳ Villages

Brooks. In the center of this quiet county, surrounded by hills, this town has the
most scenic golf course around.

Liberty, straddling Rt. 3, is home to Lake St. George State Park and the **Liberty Tool Company** (207-589-4771; open June–mid-Oct., daily, fewer days off-
season, closed Jan. and Feb. and reopening the first Sat. in Mar. with a big sale)
on Main St. in Liberty Village, with its mix of antiques and items found in an
old-fashioned hardware store. The octagonal Liberty post office, also on Main
St., dates from 1867 and houses the Liberty Historical Society (207-589-4393),
open weekend afternoons in July and Aug.

Northport. A low-key community with yacht and golf clubs, as well as a mid-
19th-century former Methodist campground with hundreds of gingerbread cottages on the bay.

Unity. Home to the Belfast & Moosehead Lake Railroad, a rural college, a raceway, and the fairgrounds for the popular late September. Common Ground Fair,

Kim Grant

DOWNTOWN BELFAST

Stockton Springs. Rt. 1 now bypasses this former shipbuilding town. Follow East St. down to Fort Point.

✳ To See

MUSEUMS ✐ **Penobscot Marine Museum** (207-548-2529; www.penobscot marinemuseum.org), Rt. 1, Searsport. Open May–mid-Oct., Mon.–Sat. 10–5 and Sun. noon–5; year-round by appointment. $8 adults, $6 seniors; children 7–15 are $3. Family rate $18. (The library is open in summer and by appointment in winter.) The 13 buildings include 8 on the National Register of Historic Places. The museum shop is at the entrance to the complex, which lies west of Rt. 1 across two streets. Museum exhibits show off peapods, dories, canoes, and lobster boats, and the artifacts that exemplify the changing faces of Mainers over the centuries, from the first Wabanaki natives to the shipbuilders of the 1800s. Gorgeous nautical paintings convey the ship worship of a time when your fortune was made when your ship came in. The galleries in the **Captain Jeremiah Merithew House** have been refurbished and now hold a collection of paintings by father-and-son marine artists Thomas and James Buttersworth, whose depictions of ships in storm and calm are luminous and exciting. In 1889, 77 deep-sea captains lived in Searsport, 33 of whom piloted full-rigged Cape Horners. The museum displays the scrimshaw—carved whale teeth and bone—that the captains and crew brought home after perfecting their art at sea. Other exhibits focus on the working-class people who made their living here in the granite, lime, ice, fishing, and lobstering industries.

Belfast Historical Society and Museum (207-338-9229), 10 Market St., Belfast. Open early June–mid-Oct., Thu.–Mon. 11–4, and by appointment year-round. Local artifacts, paintings, newspaper clippings, and changing exhibits.

Harbor Church, Rt. 1, Searsport. Phone 207-548-6663 or pick up the key across the street and check out the fabulous stained-glass windows in this church, built in 1815. It's now maintained as a meditation space.

Bryant Museum (207-568-3665), Rich Rd. (junction of Rts. 220 and 129), Thorndike. Open year-round, Mon.–Sat. 8–4:30. What began as a stove shop has evolved into a fascinating museum. The front room is crammed with restored woodstoves. Walk through these to the doll circus, with its array of mechanical, musical dolls from Barbie to Disney characters and everything in between. The back room houses a collection of player pianos, nickelodeons, and vintage automobiles. Worth the drive.

SCENIC DRIVE **Rt. 3**, past Lake St. George and Sheepscot Pond, through the China Lakes region, is the most direct path between Belfast and Augusta, but take time to detour down Rt. 173 to **Liberty** to see the octagonal post office and the **Liberty Tool Company**. For a leisurely tour of the villages between Belfast and Augusta, head north from East Belfast on Rt. 141 to Monroe. Ask for directions to **Stone Soup Farm** to see their gardens, then check out **Monroe Falls**, just off Rt. 139, and maybe have a picnic. Head out on Rt. 139, through Brooks, and then on toward Thorndike, where you'll want to stop at the **Bryant Museum**. Continue on Rt. 139 to Unity, where you'll pass the new home of the Common Ground Fair and the pretty station for the **Belfast & Moosehead Lake Railroad**. Follow Rt. 139 into Kennebec County to Fairfield to meet up with I-95, or detour yet again onto Rt. 202, which will bring you through the China Lakes region to Augusta.

BAYSIDE IN NORTHPORT

Christina Tree

✳ To Do

BERRY PICKING Staples Homestead Blueberries (207-567-3393 or 207-567-3703), County Rd., Stockton Springs. Turn at the ball field on Rt. 1/3, then drive 3 miles to the T at County Rd.; turn right. Or ask directions in Stockton Springs Village. Open 8–5 daily while berries are in-season (mid-Aug.). Friendly owners Basil and Mary Staples will instruct you in the mysteries of blueberry raking then let you go to it, or you can pick by hand.

BOAT EXCURSIONS Belfast Bay Cruises (207-322-5530; www.belfastbaycruises .com), Thompson Wharf, Belfast. June–Oct., daily, the M/V *Good Return* cruises Penobscot Bay, offering a choice of itineraries. The 47-passenger wooden boat, built in 1966 in Southwest Harbor, is captained by Maine Maritime graduate Melissa Terry.

The *Kathryn B* (1-800-500-6077; www.kathrynb.com), Belfast. Sailing May–Oct. This 105-foot, three-masted steel-hulled schooner, a luxury version of the typical three-masted, 80-foot windjammer, was launched in 1996. She accommodates just 10 passengers in her five cabins; the staterooms have queen berths and private showers. Victorian detailing and furnishings, and working portholes, with a dining area for five-course meals topside. Three- to 6-day cruises $795–1,550.

GOLF Country View Golf Course (207-722-3161) in Brooks is the most scenic in the area: nine holes, par 36, cart and club rentals, lessons, clubhouse.

Northport Golf Club (207-338-1170), Northport. A fully irrigated nine-hole course, pro shop, snack bar, driving range, and rentals.

KAYAKING Water Walker Sea Kayaks (207-338-6424; www.touringkayaks .com), Belfast. Ray Wirth, a Registered Maine Guide and ACA-certified open-water instructor, offers tours ranging from several hours in Belfast Harbor or around Sears Island up to full-day trips out among offshore islands and from inn to inn.

BELFAST CO-OP

Nancy English

SWIMMING Lake St. George State Park (207-589-4255), Rt. 3, Liberty. Open May 15–Oct. 15. A great way station for travelers going to or from Down East. A deep, clear lake with a small beach, lifeguard, bathhouse, parking facilities, 31 campsites, and a boat launch. **Swan Lake State Park**, Rt. 141, Swanville (north of town; follow signs). This beach has picnicking facilities on Swan Lake. Belfast City Park, Rt. 1, Belfast (south of town). Swimming pool, tennis courts, picnicking facilities, and a gravel beach. **Sandy Point Beach**, off Rt. 1 north of Stockton Springs (it's posted HERSEY RETREAT; turn toward the water directly across from the Rocky Ridge Motel).

✳ Green Space

Also see Lake St. George State Park and Belfast City Park under *Swimming*.

Moose Point State Park, Rt. 1, south of Searsport. Open May 30–Oct. 15. A good spot for picnicking; cookout facilities are in an evergreen grove and an open field overlooking Penobscot Bay. Also check out **Mosman Park** in downtown Searsport with its playground and picnic benches by tidal pools and the public landing.

Fort Pownall and Fort Point State Park, Stockton Springs (marked from Rt. 1; accessible via a 3.5-mile access road). The 1759 fort built to defend the British claim to Maine (the Penobscot River was the actual boundary between the English and French territories) was burned twice to prevent its being taken; only earthworks remain. The adjacent park, on the tip of a peninsula jutting into Penobscot Bay, is a fine fishing and picnic spot.

Sears Island. After decades of debate about the future of this 940-acre island (it was slated to be a container port, nuclear power plant site, LNG port, and more), it's open to the public. Good for walking, biking, and fishing, it even has some sand beaches and views of the Camden Hills. It's connected to the mainland by a causeway. Off Rt. 1, take Sears Island Rd.

✳ Lodging

INNS AND BED & BREAKFASTS

In Belfast 04915
Harbor View House (207-338-3811 or 1-877-393-3811; www.harborview house.com), 213 High St. Open year-round. This vintage-1807 Federal mansion turned B&B seems to have it all: Federal-era grace, all the comforts, and a sweeping view of Penobscot Bay from its perch above downtown Belfast on Primrose Hill. All six rooms have a private bath with tub shower, working fireplace, and TV/VCR (there's a film library); five have water views. Our favorite is the second-floor Joshua Chamberlain Room ($145) with a queen bed and rocker by the fireplace. Rates (with off-season discounts) include a full breakfast served in the dining room, or in summer on the deck. On-site massage is available—$50 for an hour.

Your helpful hosts are Mary Ellen and her sister Trish Jakielski.

The Alden House (207-338-2151 or 1-877-337-8151; www.thealdenhouse .com), 63 Church St. Bruce and Sue Madara are your hosts in this gracious 1840 mansion, which has been totally renovated and includes wireless Internet access. Architectual details include Italian marble mantels and sinks and a circular staircase. There are seven guest rooms, one on the ground floor, five with private bath. In the Hiram Alden Room two antique chairs face a working fireplace, and fires also grace the library and South Parlor. The North Parlor features a grand player piano. $99–135 includes a full breakfast, served at separate tables.

The Jeweled Turret Inn (207-338-2304 or 1-800-696-2304; www .jeweledturret.com), 40 Pearl St.

Open year-round. A handsome gabled and turreted house built ornately inside and out in the 1890s. The fireplace in the den is said to be made of stones from every state in the Union at that time. Each of the seven guest rooms has a private bath, is decorated in shades reminiscent of the gem it's named for, and is furnished with antiques and plenty of knickknacks. The Opal Room features a marble bath with a whirlpool tub, and the popular Tourmaline Room has a working fireplace. Carl and Cathy Heffentrager are exceptional hosts, serving a full breakfast and afternoon sherry with cheese and crackers. Rates $105–155.

⊚ **The White House** (207-338-1901 or 1-888-290-1901; www.mainebb .com), 1 Church St. The pillared facade of this 1840 Greek Revival mansion with its octagonal cupola is strikingly handsome, set off by its triangular front lawn in the V between Church and High Sts. The eight guest rooms are elaborately decorated; all have phone, private bath, and a TV/ VCR. Weddings are a specialty, and one of the two innkeepers is licensed to officiate. Rates are $115–175 per couple, including a full breakfast.

In Searsport 04974
1794 Watchtide By the Sea (207-548-6575 or 1-800-698-6575; www .watchtide.com), Rt. 1. This is a bright house with a 60-foot-long, 19-windowed, wicker- and flower-filled sunporch with a periwinkle-blue floor. Nancy-Linn Nellis, a warm, welcoming host, also operates **Angels to Antiques**—a gift store for guests (specializing in angels) in the barn. The five guest rooms (private bath) are furnished with antiques. Eleanor Roosevelt slept here several times

when this was the College Club Inn (opened in 1917), and her namesake, ocean-view room has a two-person Jacuzzi and skylight. $85 (in library annex)–198 in high season, lower off-season, includes a breakfast that might begin with an egg roll with lobster and salsa. Nancy-Linn offers last-minute discounts—25 percent off high-season rates if a room is booked less than 15 hours before 4 PM check-in.

🐾 **Homeport Inn** (207-548-2259 or 1-800-742-5814; www.homeportbnb .com), 121 E. Main St. (Rt. 1). Open year-round. An 1861 captain's mansion complete with widow's walk overlooking the bay. Dr. and Mrs. George Johnson were the first Searsport B&B hosts. Rooms in front are old-fashioned—three of the four have shared bath—but the six downstairs rooms in the back are modern and elegantly decorated, with private bath and bay views. Also offered are three two-bedroom cottages, completely outfitted (pets accommodated here). The landscaped grounds slope to the water. $75 (single with shared bath) to $125 (double with private bath) with breakfast; lower rates Nov.–Apr. The cottages are $800–900 per week.

🐾 **Inn Britannia** (207-548-2007 or 1-866-548-2007; www.innbritannia .com), 132 W. Main St. (Rt. 1). Formerly the Captain Butman Homestead, this classic 1830s farmhouse has been thoroughly anglicized by two Missouri ladies. Caren Lorelle and Susan Pluff care for eight guest rooms, all with private bath and names like the Cotswolds, Brighton, and Nottingham. Windsor features a vaulted ceiling, gas stove, wet bar, TV, separate sitting room, and well-appointed bath. A full, English-style breakfast, awarded Best Breakfast by Arrington's, might include Cornish baked eggs—a savory meringue made with eggs from the house's own chickens—served on English china in a sunny breakfast room, and PG Tips tea. $100–220 in-season, less off-season.

🌺 **Fairwinds, The Captain Green Pendleton B&B** (207-542-9087 or 1-800-949-4403; www.fairwindsmaine .com), Rt. 1. Open year-round. Another fine old captain's home with 80 acres set well back from Rt. 1. The three bedrooms are comfortably furnished, and the spacious common rooms have a welcoming feel. All guest rooms have working fireplaces; there's a Franklin fireplace in the parlor. A path through the meadow and woods leads to a spring-fed trout pond. The Greiners are warm and helpful hosts. $85–120 per night includes a full breakfast.

Wildflower Inn (207-548-2112 or 1-888-546-2112; www.wildflowerinn me.com), 2 Black Rd. S. (corner of Rt. 1). Just off the main road, this attractive 1846 sea captain's home offers a double parlor and four guest rooms, two with king beds and one with a Jacuzzi. A queen room with a trundle bed and adjoining double room is a good suite for a family. The gardens fill half an acre with blooms, birdbaths, and water features. Rooms are $79-129, including breakfast; less off-season.

The Carriage House (207-548-2167 or 1-800-578-2167; www.carriage houseinmaine.com), 120 E. Main St. (Rt. 1). Three rooms with private bath are available in this 1874 Victorian home built by sea captain John McGilvery; it was later impressionist Waldo Peirce's place, and visited by Peirce's friend Ernest Hemingway, whose portrait he painted. Two of the

painter's works hang in the room named for him, which also has a view of the sea. There's a resident beagle, gardens, and a big collection of books on tape. Rates $85–115, less Nov.– mid-May, with full breakfast including muffins, fruit, and sometimes cognac French toast.

COTTAGES **Bayside Village**, built in the 1800s, has about 50 cottages on Penobscot Bay in Northport available for rent by the week by the Blair Agency (207-338-2257; www.bayside mainecottages.com), P.O. Box 368, Belfast 04915. Maureen and Blair Einstein run the agency, open year-round, renting the cottages out for between $650 and $1,500 a week over summer and early fall. Originally a Methodist campground, the cottages are ornately trimmed with Victorian gingerbread, some with stone fireplace. The village offers a main commons, a swim float and dock on the pebble beach, sailing lessons, and a little yacht club with children's activities in summer.

MOTELS 🐾 🍸 **Ocean's Edge Comfort Inn** (207-338-2090 or 1-800-303-5098), 159 Searsport Ave. (Rt. 1), Belfast 04915. Usually we don't include a Comfort Inn in our listings, but the location of this three-story facility is terrific. All 83 units (each with two double beds) have a balcony overlooking the bay; amenities include a full-service restaurant (see *Dining Out*), a guest laundry, an indoor pool with sauna and hot tub, free wireless Internet access, and a lobby computer. $89–329 in summer includes continental breakfast; less off-season. Try the 2-night special, $109.99 in winter midweek—the pool is heated to 86 degrees.

🐾 ✑ **Belfast Harbor Inn** (207-338-2740 or 1-800-545-8576; www.belfast harborinn.com), 91 Searsport Ave. (Rt. 1), Belfast 04915. Set back from Rt. 1 on 6 acres of lawn that stretch to the rim of the bay, this is an inviting, independently owned two-story motel with 61 units varying in price depending on their location—from poolside to ocean view. A generous continental breakfast is included in a top rate of $139 in high season, less late Sep.–late June.

✳ Where to Eat

DINING OUT Rhumb Line (207-548-2600), 200 E. Main St. (Rt. 1), Searsport. Open year-round, daily in summer and varying times off-season. Fine dining in a relaxed atmosphere. Owners Charles and Diana Evans ran a successful restaurant on Martha's Vineyard before coming to Searsport. Dinner guests mingle in the parlor for drinks before heading to tables. The menu changes daily but might include oven-poached, horseradish-crusted salmon or grilled rack of lamb with fig-infused mint vinegar ($28). Dessert choices may include French bread pudding or chocolate Grand Marnier mousse cake. Entrées $21–28.

The Twilight Café (207-338-0937), 70–72 Main St., Belfast. Mon.–Sat. 5:30–9 in summer, Thu.–Sat. in winter. This popular dining spot has become even more popular since moving off Rt. 1 into a great space, and the menu is the area's most upscale, ranging from portobello mushrooms stuffed with sausage, spinach, red peppers, and Reggiano to bouillabaisse and haddock with tapenade. Beer and wine are served.

✑ **The Ocean's Edge Restaurant** (207-338-2090), 159 Searsport Ave., Belfast. Open daily 4–9. Not just an amenity for the Comfort Inn to which it's attached, this spot is a local favorite given the view, the service, and the menu, which ranges from a Greek vegetarian sauté with kalamata olives, tomatoes, and onion flambéed with Sambuca, to surf and turf. Entrées $7.95–21.95. Children's menu.

Darby's Restaurant and Pub (207-338-2339), 155 High St., Belfast. Open daily for lunch and dinner. A storefront café with tin ceilings and local artwork. A reasonably priced dinner find: Entrées might include pecan haddock with mojito sauce, or a black bean enchilada "smothered in cheddar and Ranchero sauce" ($10.95). Soups, salads, and sandwiches are served all day. Entrées $7.95–18.95.

EATING OUT ✑ **Anglers** (207-548-2405), Rt. 1, Searsport. Open daily 11–8. Buddy Hall's Maine-style diner styles itself "Maine's Family Seafood Restaurant," and the seafood ranges from every kind of chowder and seafood stew through fried and broiled fish dinners, including lobster every which way. "Land Lovers" get a token chicken Parmesan and barbecued ribs, and the Minnow Menu is for "the smaller appetite" (you don't have to be small).

Abbraccci (207-548-2010), 225 W. Main St., Rt. 1, Searsport. A bakery, espresso bar, and lunch spot with pizza, calzone, and quiche. The Greek salad we enjoyed had watercress.

Chase's Daily (207-338-0555), 96 Main St., Belfast. Breakfast and lunch Tue.–Sat., dinner Fri. from 5:30. This storefront restaurant features produce from the owners' Chase Farm in Freedom, which is also sold from crates in the back of the space. A

Nancy English

PRODUCE FROM CHASE'S DAILY

vegetarian palace, a rarity in coastal Maine, it's good for shell bean and chicory salad, roasted artichoke and fennel on grilled sour wheat sandwich bread, green curry fried rice, a pepper pizza, or pasta of the day.

Bay Wrap (207-338-9757), 20 Beaver St. (off Main), Belfast. Open daily for lunch and dinner, except Sat. in winter. A small eatery with limited seating. On a foggy day we feasted on warm grilled eggplant with roasted red peppers, ricotta and feta cheese, mint, field greens, and salsa verde ($6.35).

Bell the Cat (207-338-2084), Reny's Plaza, Rt. 3, Belfast. Open 9–9, except Sun., when it's 9–5. Relocated from downtown to a spacious upfront corner of Mr. Paperback, this is the local, very casual favorite for designer sandwiches; suggested choices range from the PB&J ($2.95) to a fat Reuben. Also good for salads and soups. Coffees and teas.

Seng Thai (207-338-0010), 160 Searsport Ave. (Rt. 1), Belfast. Open daily (except Mon.) from 11:30. Not your ordinary Thai. Residents praise this inexpensive restaurant, and warn you not to try level-five spiciness. Our pad Thai and an eggplant special with shrimp, chicken, and peppers in black bean sauce ($7.95 for a lunch portion) were made with fresh ingredients, and delicious. Dinner entrées $8.85–13.95.

Three Tides (207-338-1707; www .3tides.com), 2 Pinchy Lane, Belfast. Open Tue.–Sat. from 3 PM, Sun. 1–8, later opening in winter. A fun spot with a serpentine concrete bar and an outdoor deck over the river, where you can drink special cocktails and eat pizzettes ($8.50) and salads and quesadillas and cream-free clam chowder.

Also see **Belfast Co-op** under *Selective Shopping.*

ICE CREAM Scoops (207-338-3350), 35 Lower Main St., Belfast. After a lot of walking, this is a comfortable place to rest and recoup with ice cream. The (homemade) chocolate chip cookie sundae with ice cream and hot fudge is $5.25, and a fruit-filled crêpe topped with honey ice cream is $5.85. Round Top Dairy makes the good ice cream.

LOBSTER POUND Young's Lobster Pound (207-338-1160), Mitchell Ave. (posted from Rt. 1 just across the bridge from downtown Belfast), East Belfast. Open in-season 7–6:30, and year-round (winter closing at 5:30) for live and cooked lobsters, crabs, clams, and mussels, or takeout. A pound with as many as 30,000 lobsters, and seating (indoor and outdoor) to accommodate 500. Order, and enjoy the view of Belfast across the Passagassawakeag River while you wait.

✳ Entertainment

In Belfast

✐ **The Belfast Maskers** (207-338-9668). A year-round community theater that puts on several shows each season at the Railroad Theater on the waterfront. Schedule available at the theater. They also offer acting workshops and classes for adults and children.

✐ **The Playhouse** (207-338-5777), Church St. A cozy 36-seat theater offering plays for adults as well as children's theater. Founder Mary Weaver teaches acting, directs, and performs.

The Colonial Theater (207-338-1930). The new home of the outsized carved elephants from a Belfast landmark, Perry's Nut House; three screens with nightly showings in a restored theater in downtown Belfast.

National Theater Workshop of the Handicapped (207-338-6894; www.ntwh.org), 96 Church St., Belfast. Theatrical productions are staged periodically, free and open to the public.

✳ Selective Shopping

ANTIQUES SHOPS Searsport claims to be the "Antiques Capital of Maine." **The Searsport Antique Mall**, 149 E. Main St., open more or less daily year-round, is a cooperative of more than 70 dealers, spread over two floors. **The Pumpkin Patch Antiques Center** (207-548-6047), 15 W. Main St., a 20-dealer shop, has been in business 29 years and is widely respected. New owner Cindy Gallant now runs **the Hobby Horse Flea Market** (207-548-2981, 379 E. Main St.), which fills a 4-acre complex with two retail stores. A flea market surrounds it every day but Tue., and it's open May–Columbus Day. Two other Searsport Flea Markets are held weekends in-season.

BOOKSTORES Left Bank Books (207-548-6400), 21 E. Main St. (Rt. 1), Searsport 04974. There is a cup of tea by the fireplace here, along with 5,000 select titles, from great mysteries to Arctic explorations. **Fertile**

COLONIAL THEATER

Nancy English

Mind Bookshop (207-338-2498), 105 Main St., Belfast. An outstanding browsing and buying place featuring Maine and regional books and guides, maps, and cards. **Victorian House/ Book Barn** (207-567-3351), E. Main St., Stockton Springs. Open every day of the year. A landmark collection of 20,000 antiquarian books, and a special find for mystery book buffs.

GALLERIES, ETC. Northport Landing Gallery and Espresso Bar (207-338-2210; www.northportlanding gallery.com), 1330 Atlantic Hwy. (Rt. 1, and 10 minutes from Camden), Northport. Joy Ambrust, owner, runs this handsome two-level gallery with a lot of charm—and also serves cappuccinos, chai, tea, and coffee. The gallery exhibits North American bronze artist Forest Hart, who is renowned for his wildlife sculptures. Two huge moose (and a flying pig by Barry Norling you can rock on) stand in the yard. Watercolors by Anne Kilham are also on permanent exhibit. Open Mon.–Sat. 9–5; closed Jan. and Feb.

A leaflet guide to all current Belfast galleries is available at any Belfast gallery. Don't miss **The Art Alliance**, 92 Main St., a cooperative gallery for seven very different and interesting artists; the **Parent Gallery**, 92 Main St., displaying fine black-and-white photographs by Neal Parent and daughter Joanne's vivid watercolors; **High Street Studio and Gallery**, 149 High St., featuring Susan Tobey White's many-peopled landscapes and amazing doll sculptures.

SPECIAL SHOPS

In Northport
Swan's Island Blankets (207-338-9691; www.swansislandblankets.com),

Christina Tree

ANTIQUES SHOPS IN BELFAST

231 Atlantic Hwy. (Rt. 1), Northport. The old looms are in use in the back room, visible through a window from the elegant showroom; and a few of the natural sources of dye stand in jars. But the real draw is the soft, beautiful, expensive blankets made from the owners' sheep, which may be grazing in the field near the store.

In Belfast
Belfast Co-op Store (207-338-2532), 123 High St. Open daily 7:30 AM– 8 PM. Everyone needs something in this store and café with its standout deli and lunches. **Coyote Moon** (207-338-5659), 54 Main St., is a nifty, reasonably priced women's clothing and gift store. **All About Games** (207-338-9984), 171 High St., is a great place to buy and play traditional

board games, as well as some more unusual nonautomated games. **Colburn Shoe Store** (207-338-1934), 79 Main St., bills itself as the oldest shoe store in America. **Reny's** (207-338-4588), Reny's Plaza, Rt. 3 just north of the junction with Rt. 1. One in Maine's chain of distinctive outlet stores. Always worth a stop (good for everything from TVs to socks).

North along Rt. 1
Perry's Nut House (207-338-1630), Rt. 1 just north of the Belfast Bridge. Reopened and working on being what it used to be. The nut collection is in the Smithsonian. The man-eating clam cannot be located. **Monroe Saltworks** (207-338-3460), Rt. 1, Belfast. This distinctive pottery, which originated in nearby Monroe, now has a wide following around the country. There are seconds and unusual pieces both here and in the Ellsworth outlets. **Mainely Pottery** (207-338-1108), 181 Searsport Ave. (Rt. 1), features the work of owner Jamie Oates and carries varied work by 24 other potters.

In Searsport and Stockton Springs
Silkweeds (207-548-6501), Rt. 1, Searsport. Specializes in "country gifts": tinware, cotton afghans, wreaths. **The Talisman** (207-548-6279), Navy St., Searsport. Open year-round except Sun. and Mon. Handcrafted gold and silver jewelry. **Birdworks of Maine** (207-567-

3030), School St. (just off Rt. 1), Stockton Springs. Open weekdays 9–5. Decorative pottery bird feeders, nesting roosts, suet keepers, and much more, all made on the premises. **Waldo County Co-op**, Rt. 1, Searsport Harbor. Open June–Oct., daily 9–5. A showcase for the local extension service. Dolls, needlework, wooden crafts, quilts, pillows, jams, and ceramics—and lots of them.

✳ Special Events
May–October: **Belfast Farmer's Market**—Tue., Fri., and Sat. at Reny's Plaza, junction of Rts. 1 and 3.

July 4: Parade, fairs, and fireworks in Searsport.

Mid-July: **Belfast Bay Festival**—a week of events, including a giant chicken barbecue, midway, races, and parade.

July–August: Free Thursday-night **street concerts** in downtown Belfast.

August: **Searsport Lobster Boat Races** and related events.

September: **Common Ground Fair** in Unity—organic farm products, demonstrations, children's activities, sheepdog roundup, crafts, entertainment.

Columbus Day weekend: **Fling to Fall celebration**—parade, bonfire, church suppers.

Second weekend in December: **Searsport Victorian Christmas**—open houses at museums, homes, and B&Bs.

Down East 4

Kim Grant

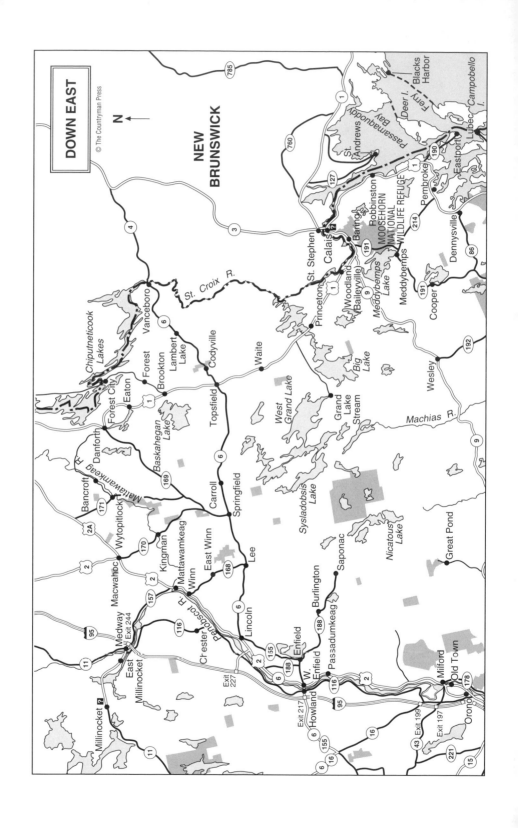

DOWN EAST

© The Countryman Press

N

NEW
BRUNSWICK

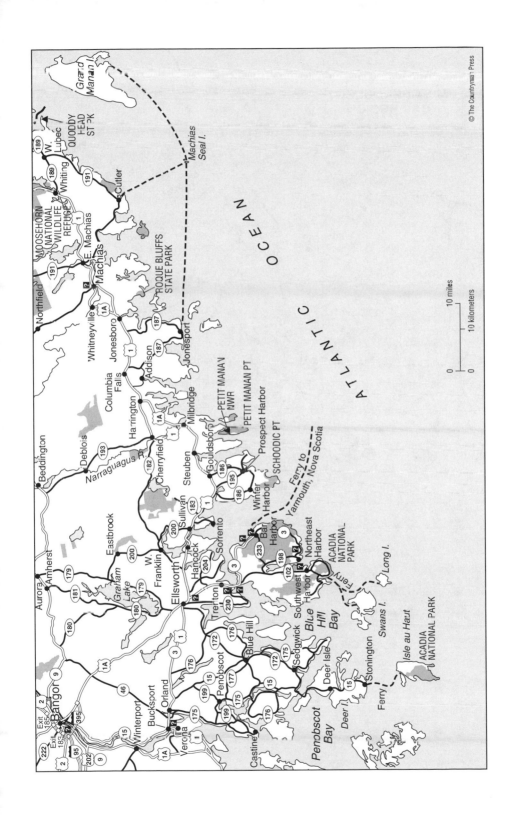

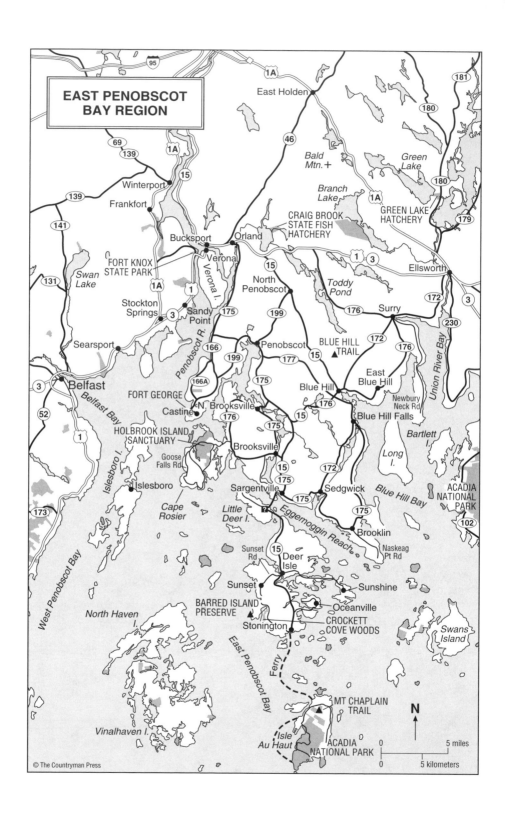

EAST PENOBSCOT
BAY REGION

95

1A

East Holden

181

180

69
139

1A

46

Bald
Mtn. +

Green
Lake

180

15

Winterport

Branch
Lake

1A

GREEN LAKE
HATCHERY

139

Frankfort

CRAIG BROOK
STATE FISH
HATCHERY

179

141

Bucksport

Orland

1   3

Ellsworth

FORT KNOX
STATE PARK

Verona

North
Penobscot

15

Toddy
Pond

172

3

Swan
Lake

131

1A

1

Stockton
Springs

3   Sandy
Point

175

199

176

Surry

172

230

Searsport

166

199

Penobscot

177

15

BLUE HILL
TRAIL ▲

172

176

3

Belfast

166A

175

East
Blue Hill

52

FORT GEORGE

N. Brooksville

Blue Hill

176

Newbury
Neck Rd

1

Castine

176

15

Blue Hill Falls

Bartlett
I.

HOLBROOK ISLAND
SANCTUARY

Brooksville

175

172

Long
I.

Goose
Falls Rd

15
175

Sargentville

Sedgwick

Blue Hill Bay

ACADIA
NATIONAL
PARK

Islesboro I.

Islesboro

Cape
Rosier

Little
Deer I.

175

Eggemoggin Reach

175

Brooklin

102

173

Naskeag
Pt Rd

15

Sunset
Rd

Deer
Isle

North Haven
I.

Sunset

Sunshine

Swans
Island

BARRED ISLAND
PRESERVE ▲

Oceanville

West Penobscot Bay

Stonington

CROCKETT
COVE WOODS

Ferry

East Penobscot Bay

MT CHAPLAIN
TRAIL ▲

N

Vinalhaven I.

Isle
Au Haut

ACADIA
NATIONAL PARK

0   5 miles

0   5 kilometers

© The Countryman Press

EAST PENOBSCOT BAY REGION

BUCKSPORT/ORLAND AREA; CASTINE; BLUE HILL AREA; DEER ISLE, STONINGTON, AND ISLE AU HAUT

BUCKSPORT/ORLAND AREA

The narrow, soaring, vintage-1931 suspension bridge above the confluence of the Penobscot River and Bay is scheduled to be replaced by the end of 2006. All the more reason to cross it now, while it still stands like a gateway, underscoring the sense of turning a corner in the coast. Beyond is Bucksport, a workaday river and paper mill town with a waterfront park, some shopping, restaurants, and a 1916 movie theater/museum showcasing New England films dating back to the turn of the 20th century.

Bucksport began as a major shipping port in 1764, the reason it was burned by the British in 1799 and was again occupied by the British during the War of 1812. In the 1820s it was the largest town in eastern Maine. Note the Jed Prouty Tavern in the middle of Main Street, now elderly housing but a dining stop for half a dozen presidents down through the years. Bucksport overlooks New England's biggest fort, a memorial to its smallest war.

East of Bucksport the town of Orland offers more than meets the eye along Rt. 1. The village itself overlooks the Narramissic River, and in East Orland, Alamoosook Lake is just north of the highway, accessible to the public from the Craig Brook National Fish (salmon) Hatchery with its visitor center, swimming, and hiking trails.

GUIDANCE **Bucksport Bay Area Chamber of Commerce** (207-469-6818; www.bucksportchamber.org), P.O. Box 1880, Bucksport 04416. The information office, next to the town offices on Main St., is open 24 hours for browsing; live assistance is normally available Mon., Tue., and Fri. 9:30–5.

✳ To See and Do

✎ **Fort Knox State Park** (207-469-7719 or 207-469-6553; www.fortknox.maine guide.com), Rt. 174 (off Rt. 1), Prospect (just across the Penobscot from Bucksport). Open daily May–Nov. 1, 8:30 AM–sunset. $3 adults, $1 ages 5–11; free for

Northeast Historic Film/The Alamo Theatre (207-469-0924; www.oldfilm.org), 85 Main St., Bucksport. This 125-seat, vintage-1916 restored theater is open year-round, featuring first-run movies, Dolby digital sound, low prices, and real buttered popcorn. It is also home to the 3-day midsummer Northeast Silent Film Festival and to concerts, theater, and other live performances. Call for showtimes. The theater was restored by nonprofit Northeast Historic Film, New England's only "moving-image" archive. Stock footage, technical services, and sales of *Videos of Life in New England* are available.

65 and over. The visitor center is open weekdays most of the year. Guided tours available Memorial Day–Labor Day, then weekends. Interpretative panels tell the story: Built in 1844 of granite cut from nearby Mount Waldo, it includes barracks, storehouses, a labyrinth of passageways, and even a granite spiral staircase. There are also picnic facilities. The fort was to be a defense against Canada during the boundary dispute, called the Aroostook War, with New Brunswick. The dispute was ignored in Washington, and so in 1839 the new, lumber-rich state took matters into its own hands by arming its northern forts. Daniel Webster represented Maine in the 1842 treaty that formally ended the war, but Maine built this fort two years later, just in case. It was never entirely completed and never saw battle. Troops were, however, stationed here during the Civil War and again during the Spanish-American War. Check out the interpretive center and gift shop.

Bucksport Historical Society Museum, Main St., Bucksport. Open July–Aug., Wed.–Fri. 1–4, and other announced times. Admission $1. Housed in the former Maine Central Railroad Station; local memorabilia.

At **Buck Cemetery**, near the Verona Bridge (across from the Shop 'n Save), a granite obelisk marks the **grave of Colonel Jonathan Buck**, founder of Bucksport. The outline of a leg on the stone has spurred many legends, the most popular being that a woman whom Judge Buck sentenced to death for witchcraft is carrying through a promise to dance on his grave.

Craig Brook National Fish Hatchery (207-469-2803), on Alamoosook Lake in East Orland (marked from Rt. 1). First opened in 1871, this is the country's oldest salmon hatchery. A large visitor center (open year-round, daily 8–3) offers films and interactive displays on Maine rivers, watersheds, and salmon. A small **Atlantic Salmon Museum** is open daily noon–3 in summer. The facility also includes a boat launch on Alamoosook Lake, a picnic area and swim beach on Craig Pond, and hiking/ski trails.

✳ Lodging

Orland House (207-469-1144; www .orlandhousebb.com), Box 306, 10 Narramissic Dr., Orland 04472. This imposing 1820 house stands above the Narramissic River. Alvion and Cynthia Kimball offer three guest rooms, all with private bath, and kayaks for use on the river. A "spa room," available to all guests, features a hot tub. $75–95 in season (otherwise $10 less) includes a full breakfast.

Jed Prouty Motor Inn (207-469-3113 or 1-800-528-1234), Main St., Bucksport 04416. Open year-round. Built as a modern annex to the old Jed Prouty Inn, now a Best Western offering 40 motel-style rooms with two double beds and great views of the mouth of the Penobscot River and Fort Knox. $79–149 per couple, depending on the season, includes continental breakfast.

Alamoosook Lakeside Inn (207-469-6393 or 1-866-459-6393; www.alamoosooklakcsidcinn.com), P.O. Box 16, Orland 04472. Open year-round. A log lodge built as a corporate retreat by a local paper company. The dining room, jutting out into Alamoosook Lake, is popular for functions. There are six guest rooms, all opening onto a sunporch. The lake offers freshwater swimming, canoeing, and fishing, also cleared for ice fishing and cross-country skiing in winter. $80–120 depending on season, breakfast included.

❧ Sign of the Amiable Pig (207-469-2561), P.O. Box 232, Orland 04472. Charlotte and Wes Piper offer three guest rooms in their handsome 17th-century home with its six working fireplaces. Two rooms ($60 each), one with a double and one with twins, both with working fireplace, share a bath, and there is a suite with private bath ($75). A carriage house set on the grounds (there are 4 acres) is a small jewel with a cathedral ceiling, crystal chandelier, Oriental rugs, antiques, and two baths, accommodating four at $550 per week. The name stems from the weather vane.

✳ Where to Eat

🍴 **MacLeods** (207-469-3963), Main St., Bucksport. Open nightly for dinner from 4:30. Dependable dining in a pubby atmosphere with booths. Entrées range from comfort food like baked meat loaf and barbecued ribs to specials like a baked scallop strudel. $10.95–15.95.

Riverview (207-469-7600), Main St., Bucksport. Open for all three meals. Adjacent to the public landing, overlooking the Penobscot and Fort Knox. Good road food; casual lounge.

✳ Selective Shopping

h.o.m.e. co-op (207-469-7961; www.homecoop.net), Rt. 1, Orland. Open daily 9–5. A remarkable complex that includes a crafts village (visitors can watch pottery making, weaving, leather work, woodworking); a museum of old handicrafts and farm implements; a large crafts shop featuring handmade coverlets, toys, and clothing; and a market stand with fresh vegetables, herbs, and other garden produce.

Mayari (207-469-0868; www.mayari.com), Rt. 1, Verona Island. Ariadne Donnell keeps a herd of rare San Clemente goats in the rear of her store, source of the goat's-milk lotions, soaps, and creams that she makes here and sells primarily by mail order.

Book Stacks (207-469-8992 or 1-888-295-0123), 71 Main St., Bucksport. Open Mon.–Sat. 9–8, Sun. 9–5. Not what you would expect to find on this brief Main Street: an inviting full-service bookstore.

The Old Bank (207-469-7080), 55 Main St., Bucksport. Stained-glass gallery, supplies, custom work, and gifts housed in a former brick bank building.

✳ Special Events

Late July: **Fort Knox Bay Festival**—encampments, parade, and a variety of events on the river; at the fort and along the Bucksport waterfront. Also check Fort Knox events, almost every weekend summer through Halloween.

July–August: **Bucksport Riverfront Market** every Sat. 9–3—art, crafts, baked goods, and produce.

August: **h.o.m.e's Annual Craft & Farm Fair and Benefit Auction** (207-469-7961; www.homecoop.net). A Saturday blueberry pancake breakfast, poetry readings, music, fish-fry supper, street dance, BBQ, children's games, crafts galore, and more.

CASTINE

Sited at a fingertip of the Blue Hill Peninsula, Castine is one of Maine's most photogenic coastal villages, the kind writers describe as "perfectly preserved." Even the trees that arch high above Main Street's clapboard homes and shops have managed to escape the blight that has felled elms elsewhere, and Castine's post office is said to be the oldest operating post office in the country.

Occupying a peninsula at the confluence of the Penobscot and Bagaduce Rivers, the town still looms larger on nautical charts than on road maps. Yacht clubs from Portland to New York visit annually. Castine has always had a sense of its own importance. According to the historical markers that pepper its tranquil streets, it has been claimed by four different countries since its early-17th-century founding as Fort Pentagoet. It was an early trading post for the Pilgrims but fell into the hands of Baron de Saint Castine, a young French nobleman who married a Penobscot Indian princess and reigned as a combination feudal lord and Indian chief over Maine's eastern coast for many decades.

Since no two accounts agree, we won't attempt to describe the outpost's constantly shifting fortunes—even the Dutch owned it briefly. Nobody denies that in 1779 residents (mostly Tories who fled here from Boston and Portland) welcomed the invading British. The commonwealth of Massachusetts retaliated by mounting a fleet of 18 armed vessels and 24 transports with 1,000 troops and 400 marines aboard. This small navy disgraced itself absurdly when it sailed into town in 1779. The British Fort George was barely in the making, fortified by 750 soldiers with the backup of two sloops, but the American privateers refused to attack and hung around in the bay long enough for several British men-of-war to come along and destroy them. The surviving patriots had to walk back to Boston, and many of their officers, Paul Revere included, were court-martialed for their part in the disgrace. The town was occupied by the British again in 1814.

Perhaps it was to spur young men on to avenge this affair that Castine was picked (150 years later) as the home of the Maine Maritime Academy, which occupies the actual site of the British barracks and keeps a training ship anchored at the town dock, incongruously huge beside the graceful, white-clapboard buildings of a very different maritime era.

In the mid–19th century, thanks to shipbuilding, Castine claimed to be the second wealthiest town per capita in the United States. Its genteel qualities were

recognized by summer visitors, who later came by steamboat to stay in the eight
hotels. Many built their own seasonal mansions.

Castine's current population hovers around 1,300, including the 700 Maine Maritime Academy students. Population roughly doubles in summer. Two of the hotels survive, and a couple of mansions are now inns. The town dock is unusually welcoming, complete with picnic tables, parking, and restrooms. It remains the heart of this walking town, where you can amble uphill past shops or down along Perkins Street to the Wilson Museum. While the remainder of the Blue Hill Peninsula has become notably more touristed in recent years, Castine seems to have become less so, another reason to spend a few days steeping in its beauty.

GUIDANCE **Castine Merchants Association** produces a helpful map/guide, available on request from the town office (207-326-4502) or around town. Also check the town web site: www.castine.me.us.

The obvious place to begin exploring is the **Castine Historical Society** on the common. Also see www.penobscotbay.com.

GETTING THERE *By air:* See *Getting There* in "Bar Harbor and Ellsworth" and "Portland Area" for air service. *By car:* The quickest route is I-95 to Rt. 295 to I-95 to Augusta, then Rt. 3 to Belfast, Rt. 1 to Orland, and 15 miles down Rt. 175.

WHEN TO COME Museums are highly seasonal, but the Maritime Academy contributes to the sense of a college town, a pleasant place to stay through October.

✳ To See

HISTORIC DISTRICT All of downtown Castine is on the National Register of Historic Places. Pick up the pamphlet *A Walking Tour of Castine*—it's free, available

MAIN STREET, CASTINE

Christina Tree

at shops and Dirigo House—and walk out along Perkins Street and up along Maine to Battle Avenue. Don't miss:

Castine Historical Society (207-326-4118), Abbott School Building, Castine town common. July–Labor Day, Tue.–Sat. 10–4; from 1 on Sun.; closed Mon. Note the stunning quilted mural stitched by more than 50 townspeople and the ornate chair, said to be carved from the wood of a sunken English warship.

Wilson Museum (207-326-8545), Perkins St., Castine. Open May 27–Sep. 30, Tue.–Sun. 2–5; free. Housed in a fine waterside building donated by anthropologist J. Howard Wilson, a summer resident who amassed many of the displayed Native American artifacts. There are also changing art exhibits, collections of minerals, old tools, and farm equipment, an 1805 kitchen, and a Victorian parlor. **Hearse House** and a blacksmith shop are open in July and Aug., Wed. and Sun. 2–5. The complex also includes the **John Perkins House**, open only during July and Aug., Wed. and Sun. 2–5 (admission): a pre–Revolutionary War home, restored and furnished in period style. Guided tours and crafts.

Fort George, Battle Ave. Open May 30–Labor Day, daylight hours. The sorry tale of its capture by the British during the American Revolution (see the chapter introduction) and again during the War of 1812, when redcoats occupied the town for 8 months, is told on panels at the fort—an earthworks complex of grassy walls (great to roll down) and a flat interior where you may find Maine Maritime Academy cadets being put through their paces.

State of Maine (207-326-4311), Castine town dock. The training vessel for Maine Maritime Academy cadets, a 498-foot former U.S. Navy hydrographic survey ship, is open to visitors daily from the second week in July–Aug.; 30-minute tours on the hour 10–6 are conducted by midshipmen (allow an hour), subject to security checks and alerts. Tours are also offered during the academic year 4–6, when classes are in session.

MAINE MARITIME TRAINING SHIP

Christina Tree

✒ **Corning School Maine Science Interpretive Information Center**. Housed in Dirigo House near the public landing, open seasonally, varying (posted) days and hours. Maintained by the Maine Maritime Academy and staffed by students: displays on local plants and sea creatures, with touch tanks.

✳ **To Do**

BICYCLING **Mountain Bike Rentals** (207-326-9045), available at Dennett's Wharf.

GOLF AND TENNIS Castine Golf Club (207-326-8844), Brattle Ave. Offers nine holes and four clay courts.

SEA KAYAKING Castine Kayak Adventures (207-326-9045; www.castinekayak .com). From Dennett's Wharf, full day and overnight tours, sales, and workshops.

✳ Green Space

Witherle Woods is an extensive wooded area webbed with paths at the western end of town. The ledges below **Dyce's Head Light**, also at the western end of town, are great for clambering. The **Castine Conservation Commission** sponsors nature walks occasionally in July and Aug.; check local bulletin boards.

✳ Lodging

In Castine 04421
ⅅ 🐾 **The Manor Inn** (207-326-4861; www.manor inn.com), P.O. Box 873, Battle Ave. Open except Christmas–Valentine's Day. An expansive 1890s stone-and-shingle summer mansion set above its lawns in 5 acres bordering conservation land. Innkeepers Tom Ehrman and Nancy Watson have renovated throughout, bringing new beds and new life to all 14 rooms, upgrading baths (all are private) and expanding the dining room while preserving private common space for guests. The price of guest rooms varies with size, ranging in high season from $110 for twin-bedded Dices Head to $210 for spacious Pine Tree with its king canopy bed, fireplace, and sitting porch, fit for a governor and his wife (who were checking in as we stopped by). Nancy Watson is a respected Iyengar yoga teacher, and guests are permitted to participate in scheduled classes (we slid into the back row and heartily recommend doing likewise). See *Dining Out* for the restaurant and pub. Rates include a full breakfast and drop to $95–165 in spring and fall, less in winter. Pets are $25 per stay.

🐾 **Pentagoet Inn** (207-326-8616 or 1-800-845-1701; www.pentagoet.com), P.O. Box 4, Main St. Open May–Oct. A very Victorian summer hotel with a turret, gables, a wraparound porch, even awnings. Jack Burke and Julie VandeGraaf have been restoring the 1894 building room by room. Guest rooms are unusually shaped and nicely furnished; one room at **Ten Perkins Street** (a neighboring 200-year-old home that's an annex) has a working fireplace. In all there are 16 guest rooms, each with private bath. Common space includes sitting rooms, the wicker-furnished and flowery veranda and back deck, the fine restaurant (see *Dining Out*) and the **Passports Pub**. $95–205 includes a full breakfast.

ⅅ **Castine Inn** (207-326-4365; www .castineinn.com), P.O. Box 41, Main St. Open May–Oct. Amy and Tom Gutow have put this 1890s summer hotel on the national culinary map. Rooms all have private bath and are simply furnished. Request a harbor view. Guests enter a wide, welcoming hallway and find a pleasant sitting room and a pub, both with frequently lit fireplaces. A mural of Castine by the previous innkeeper covers all four walls of the dining room—a delightful room with French doors leading out to a broad veranda overlooking the inn's terraced formal gardens. $90–215 (more for two-room suites if occupied by four) includes a full breakfast; less off-season. Minimum 2-day stay in July and Aug.

Rental cottages are available through **Jean de Raat Realty** (207-326-8448), **Castine Realty** (207-326-9392), and the **Endicott Agency** (207-326-8741).

✳ Where to Eat

All listings are in Castine
DINING OUT

Pentagoet Inn (207-326-8616), 26 Main St. Open for dinner in-season. Choose to sit in the airy, candlelit dining room with its well-spaced tables, on the porch, or in Passports Pub. You might begin with a big bowl of Blue Hill mussels with basil and lavender in white wine broth ($7.50), and dine on slow-roasted lamb shank with sage risotto, garlicky Swiss chard, and bitter orange compote. Entrées $20–23. Don't pass up dessert, the pride of innkeeper Julie VandeGraaf, former owner of a well-known Philadelphia pastry shop. Full bar.

The Manor Inn (207-326-4861), Battle Ave. Open for dinner Valentine's Day to Christmas, fewer nights of the week in off-season. A former enclosed porch has been expanded and transformed into the Commodore Room, an appealing dining room overlooking the sweeping front lawn and gardens. Co-owner Nancy Watson is the chef. The crabcakes are a family recipe, served as an entrée with mustard and aioli sauces. Other choices

on the daily-changing menu might include large shrimp in tomato cream curry sauce and rib-eye steak. Entrées $17–25. Full liquor license, and pub food in the **Pine Cone Pub**, entrées $8-15.

Also see Dennett's Wharf under *Eating Out*.

EATING OUT **Dennett's Wharf** (207-326-9045), Sea St. (off the town dock). Open daily May–Columbus Day, 11–9. An open-framed, harborside structure said to have been built as a bowling alley after the Civil War, the town's informal gathering place. It's a big menu with plenty of salads as well as seafood and BBQ back ribs at lunch, with expanded choices for dinner, a choice of steaks and entrées ranging from vegetable strudel to lobster pie. Entrées $13.95–28.95.

Bah's Bake House (207-326-9510), Water St. Open 7 AM–9 PM daily in-season; until 8 on Sun. A few tables and a great deli counter featuring sandwiches on baguette bread, daily-made soups, salads, and baked goods.

The Breeze (207-326-9034), town dock. Seasonal. When the summer sun shines, this is the best place in town to eat: fried clams, hot dogs, onion rings, and soft ice cream. The public facilities are next door and, with luck, you can dine at the picnic tables on the dock.

T&C Grocery (207-326-4818), 12 Water St. This well-stocked market has a first-rate deli, source of the best picnic fixings in town.

Castine Variety (326-8625), 1 Main St. Open 5 AM–7 PM year-round, until 10 in summer. The ultimate corner store with an ice cream counter dating back to its 1920 opening. Serving breakfast, light meals, pizza, and ice cream, as well as lobster and crab rolls in summer; they also sell newspapers, film, and a lot of other stuff.

Also see **Compass Rose Bookstore & Café** under *Selective Shopping*.

☀ Selective Shopping

In Castine
Leila Day Antiques (207-326-8786), Main St. An outstanding selection of early American furniture; also paintings, quilts, and Maine-made Shard Pottery. The shop is in the historic Parson Mason House, and the approach is through a formal garden.

McGrath-Dunham Gallery (207-326-9175), 9 Main St. Open May–mid-Oct., 10–5 except Sun. A long-established gallery featuring sculpture and pottery as well as paintings and original prints.

♂ **Compass Rose Bookstore & Café** (207-326-9366 or 1-800-698-9366), 3 Main St. Open Mon.–Sat. 10–6, Sun. 10–5, this local institution features children's titles, summer reading, nautical and regional books, as well as the pleasant **Linger Longer Café** serving coffee, tea, smoothies, snacks, and daily specials that make it a good bet for lunch.

Nancy English

CASTINE VARIETY

Four Flags (207-312-8526), 19 Water St. A long-established gift shop with an eclectic mix of Maine-made and exotic gifts.

Adam Gallery (207-326-8272), 140 Battle Ave. Open weekends in July and Aug., also most days by appointment. Susan Paris Adams's oils are worth a stop.

☀ Special Events

June: **Sky's the Limit**, Castine Art Association art and pottery exhibit.

July: **Sea Kayaking Symposium** sponsored by Castine Kayak Adventures.

In Maine, *Blue Hill* refers to a specific hill, a village, a town, a peninsula—and also to an unusual gathering of artists, musicians, and craftspeople. A shade off the beaten path, one peninsula west of Mount Desert, Blue Hill has its own following—especially among creative people.

Over the entrance of the Bagaduce (sheet music) Lending Library, a mural depicts the area as the center of concentric creative circles. Helen and Scott Nearing, searching for a new place to live "the Good Life" in the 1950s (when a ski area encroached on their seclusion in southern Vermont), swung a dowsing pendulum over a map of coastal Maine. It came to rest on Cape Rosier. For many decades the small town of Brooklin was a familiar byline in the *New Yorker* thanks to E. B. White, who also wrote *Charlotte's Web* and *Stuart Little* here at about the same time millions of children began to read about Blueberry Hill in Robert McCloskey's *Blueberries for Sal* and about Condon's Garage (still a South Brooksville family-owned landmark) in the 1940s classic *One Morning in Maine*.

Energy lines or not, this peninsula's intermingling of land and water—along lakes and tidal rivers as well as bays—creates a landscape that's exceptional, even in coastal Maine. Pause at the turnout on Caterpillar Hill, the height-of-land on Rt. 15/175 (just north of the Deer Isle Bridge), to appreciate the panorama. Then plunge down the hill to an improbably narrow, soaring suspension bridge.

Across the bridge lies Deer Isle, a chapter in its own right (see "Deer Isle, Stonington"), both physically and otherwise distinct from the Blue Hill Peninsula. Both areas are webbed with narrow roads threading numerous land fingers, leading to studios of local craftspeople and artists. What you remember afterward is the beauty of clouds over fields of wildflowers, quiet coves, some amazing things woven, painted, and blown, and conversations with the people who made them.

The 1939 bridge spans Eggemoggin Reach, a 10-mile-long passage dividing the Blue Hill Peninsula from Deer Isle but linking Penobscot and Jericho Bays. A century ago this was a busy thoroughfare, a shortcut from Rockland to points Down East for freight-carrying schooners and passenger steamboats. It remains a popular route for windjammers, yachts, and, increasingly, for sea kayakers. Rt. 175 winds along "the Reach" on its way through Sedgwick to Brooklin.

GUIDANCE **The Blue Hill Peninsula Chamber of Commerce** (207-374-3242; www.bluehillpeninsula.org), 28 Water St., P.O. Box 520, Blue Hill 04614, publishes a booklet guide and maintains a seasonal (June–Sep.) information center open Mon.–Fri. 9–4, Sat. 9–1, Sun. 11–3 (when volunteers are available).

The East Penobscot Bay Association publishes a map/guide covering the entire Blue Hill area, available locally and at **www.penobscotbay.com**. Also pick up the current free copies of the *Browser's Trail* and the *Gallery Guide*.

GETTING THERE *By car:* The obvious way is Rt. 1 to Rt. 15 to Blue Hill, but there are many shortcuts through the confusing web of roads on this peninsula; ask directions to your lodging place.

By air: The nearest airports are **Bangor International** (www.flybangor.com) and the **Hancock County & Bar Harbor Airport** in Trenton (between

Ellsworth and Bar Harbor) served by **Colgan Air** (www.colganair.com).

WHEN TO COME Blue Hill is somewhat seasonal, but several inns and restaurants remain open year-round for those who enjoy the slow pace of rural New England off-season.

✳ To See

Johnathan Fisher Memorial (207-374-2459), 0.5 mile south of Blue Hill Village on Rt. 15/176. Open June–mid-Oct., Mon.–Sat. 2–5. A house built in 1814 by Blue Hill's first pastor, a Harvard graduate who augmented his meager salary with a varied line of crafts and by teaching (he founded Blue Hill Academy), farming, and writing. His furniture, paintings, books, journals, and woodcuts are exhibited. Admission.

Holt House, Water St., Blue Hill. Open July–mid-Sep., Tue. and Fri. 1–4, Sat. 11–2. Open year-round on Thu. for research. Donation. The Blue Hill Historical Society collection is housed in this restored 1815 Federal mansion near the harbor and noted for its stenciled walls.

Blue Hill Library (207-374-5515), Main St., Blue Hill. Open daily except Sun. and Mon. A handsome WPA building with periodicals and ample reading space; changing art shows in summer.

Bagaduce Music Lending Library (207-374-5454; www.bagaducemusic.org), Rt. 15, Blue Hill. Open Mon.–Fri. 10–3. This Blue Hill phenomenon features roughly 100,000 titles of sheet music (instrumental, keyboard, and vocal), some more than a century old and most special for one reason or another—all available for borrowing. The collection includes 1,400 pieces about Maine, by Maine composers, or published in Maine. Stop by just to see the mural over the entrance.

✎ **MERI Marine Environmental Research Institute** (207-374-2135; www .meriresearch.org), 55 Main St., Blue Hill. Open year-round except Sun.; weekdays-only in the off-season. The focus of this nonprofit is on harbor seals. MERI offers a summer schedule of educational, guided cruises plus hands-on ocean science programs, some specially geared to youngsters ages 6–12 and others to older kids. The center is also the scene of lectures, videos, and children's story hours.

Sedgwick-Brooklin Historical Society & Museum (207-359-4447), Rt. 172, Sedgwick. Open July–Aug., Sun. 2–4. This complex includes the town's original parsonage, a restored schoolhouse, and an 1820s cattle pound. It is part of the Sedgwick Historic District and includes an 18th-century town house. Check out the large old **Rural Cemetery**.

Also see *Selective Shopping—Art Galleries*.

SCENIC DRIVES To come as far as Blue Hill Village and go no farther would be like walking up to a door and not opening it. The beauty of the peninsula lies beyond—via roads that wander west to **Brooksville** by taking Rt. 15 south to Rt. 176/175 north to Rt. 176 (yes, that's right) and across the **Bagaduce River** and south on Rt. 176 (never mind). Turn off at the sign for **Cape Rosier** to see **Holbrook Island Sanctuary** and **Forest Farm**. Return to Rt. 176 and continue

The Good Life Center (207-326-8211; www.goodlife.org), on the loop road, facing Orrs Cove (opposite side of the road), Harborside, on Cape Rosier. Open June–Sep., Thu.–Tue. 1–5; check off-season. Forest Farm with its stone home built in 1953 by Helen (deceased in '95) and Scott Nearing (deceased '83), coauthors of *Living the Good Life* and seven other books

THE GOOD LIFE CENTER

based on their simple, purposeful lifestyle, is now maintained by a nonprofit trust. Through a stewardship program a pair maintain the property year-round. Inquire about weekly programs in summer and periodic workshops. The grounds include an intensively cultivated organic garden, a greenhouse, and a yurt. A weekly series of evening talks are offered late June–mid-Sep.

Christina Tree

into the village of South Brooksville (don't miss **Buck's Harbor**). Rt. 176 rejoins Rt. 175 and then Rt. 15; turn south and follow Rt. 15 south over **Caterpillar Hill** (pull out, weather permitting, for one of the most spectacular panoramas from any coastal road) and then head down to **Eggemoggin Reach**. The alternate scenic route is Rt. 175 south across Blue Hill Falls and along Blue Hill Bay to **Brooklin** and back along the Reach through Sedgwick. These two routes meet at the **Little Deer Isle Bridge**. Be sure to cross the bridge (see "Deer Isle, Stonington").

✷ To Do

BOATING **Buck's Harbor Marine** (207-326-8839), South Brooksville, rents sail- and motorboats. Inquire about sailing lessons.

Perelandra (207-326-4279; www.windroseaway.com). Captain LeCain Smith offers daysails from Buck's Harbor in his 44-foot steel ketch.

Summertime (207-359-2067 or 1-800-562-8290; www.schoonersummertime .com). Bill Brown offers daysails in early summer and Sep. from Oakland House; longer, midsummer cruises on his 53-foot pinky schooner depart from Rockland.

SEA KAYAKING **Rocky Coast Outfitters** (207-374-8866), on Grindleville Rd. off Rt. 15 in Blue Hill, rents and offers free delivery of kayaks and canoes. The **Bagaduce River** north from Walker Pond is a favorite flatwater run for novices, with some popular whitewater at **Blue Hill Falls**, a reversing falls accessible off Rt. 175. Also see *To Do* in "Deer Isle, Stonington."

WoodenBoat School (207-359-4651 or 1-
800-273-7447; www.woodenboat.com), off Naskeag Point Rd., south of the village of Brooklin. A spinoff from *WoodenBoat* magazine, this seafaring institute
of national fame offers summer courses that range from building your own sailboat, canoe, or kayak to navigation and drawing and painting. For catalogs, write:
WoodenBoat School, Naskeag Road, P.O. Box 78, Brooklin 04616. Accommodations available. The recently expanded store is a shopping destination in its own
right; open weekdays 7:30–6, Sat. 9–5.

Also see **Haystack Mountain School of Crafts** in "Deer Isle, Stonington."

✳ Green Space

Blue Hill. Our friends at the Blue Hill Bookstore tell us that this was not the
setting for the children's classic *Blueberries for Sal*, by Robert McCloskey—a
longtime summer resident of the area. But we choose to disbelieve them. It
looks just like the hill in the book and has its share of in-season blueberries. The
big attraction, however, is the view of the Mount Desert mountains from the
934-foot summit. From Rt. 172 take Mountain Rd. to the parking area (on your
right). It's a mile to the top via the Hayes Trail through town conservation land,
and a little longer if you loop back down to the road via the Osgood Trail
through Blue Hill Heritage Trust land.

Blue Hill Heritage Trust (www.bluehillheritagetrust.org) is steadily increasing
the preservation of open space throughout the peninsula.

Blue Hill Town Park. Follow Water St. past the hospital to this pleasant park
with picnic tables and great rocks for kids.

CONSERVATION AREA
Holbrook Island Sanctuary (207-326-4012), 172 Indian Bar Rd. (off Rt. 176 in
West Brooksville on Cape Rosier), is a state wildlife sanctuary of 1,350
acres, including 2.3 miles of shore and 115-acre Holbrook Island. No camping is permitted, but a lovely picnic area adjoins a pebble beach. A network
of old roads, paths, and animal trails leads along the shore and through
marshes and forest. It's the creation as well as the gift of Anita Harris,
who died in 1985 at age 92, the sole resident of Holbrook Island. Her will
stipulated that her mansion and all the other buildings on the island be
demolished. She was also responsible for destroying all homes within
the sanctuary. Wildlife is plentiful and birding is exceptional, especially
during spring and fall migrations. Great blue herons nest around the pond
and the estuary. Bald eagles and peregrine falcons and an eagle's nest
may also be seen. Inquire about guided nature walks on Mon., Wed., and
Fri. in July and Aug.

✷ Lodging

RESORTS 🐾 🐾 ♂ Hiram Blake
Camp (207-326-4951; HBC@acadia
.net), Cape Rosier, Harborside 04642.
Open June–Sep. Well off the beaten
track, operated by the same family
since 1916, this is the kind of place
where you come to stay put. All cottages are within 200 feet of the shore,
with views of Penobscot Bay. Under
the able management of Deborah
Venno Ludlow, many have been renovated. There are five one-bedroom
cottages, six cottages with two bedrooms, and three with three bedrooms; each has a living room with a
wood-burning stove; some have a fireplace as well. Each has a kitchen, a
shower, and a porch. Guests with
housekeeping cottages cook for themselves in the shoulder months, but in
July and August everyone eats in the
dining room, which doubles as a
library because thousands of books
are ingeniously filed away by category
in the ceiling. There are rowboats at
the dock, a playground, and a recreation room with table tennis and
board games; also trails. From $500
per week MAP for the one-room
Acorn Cottage to $2,400 for a three-
bedroom cottage (up to five guests).
Additional guests are each $300 per
week. Rates drop during "housekeeping months" to $550–750 per week.

♂ **Eggemoggin Oceanfront Resort**
(207-359-5057 or 1-888-559-5057;
www.mainecoastexperience.com),
HC 64, Box 380, Brooklin 04616. This
place is about getting out on active
"adventures": excursions aboard a
lobster boat, sea kayaking, biking,
and whale-watching. Rooms are fairly
basic, but the central lodge (dining,
bar, and common space) is attractive,
overlooking Eggemoggin Reach. $180

per day includes breakfasts, with
"daily adventures" $30–55 each;
weekly packages with meals and activities are $1,950 per couple, $1,350
single, $500 per youth under 17. $120
per day B&B.

INNS AND BED & BREAKFASTS

In Blue Hill 04614

♿ **Blue Hill Inn** (207-374-2844 or
1-800-826-7415; www.bluehill.com),
Union St. (Rt. 177). Open mid-May–
Oct. A classic 1830s inn on a quiet,
elm-lined street in the village. Longtime owners Don and Mary Hartley
offer a dozen elegantly comfortable
guest rooms, some with sitting
room and/or working fireplace. The
handicapped-accessible Cape House
Suite, an adjoining cottage, has a full
kitchen and living room with fireplace,
good for families. In good weather
guests gather for cocktails in the garden. A full breakfast, afternoon tea,
and hors d'oeuvres are included in
$158–195 double (the inn is fully
licensed) high season, otherwise $138–
185. The Cape House Suite is $285,
open year-round; $245 Nov.–Apr.

🐾 **Blue Hill Farm** (207-374-5126;
www.bluehillfarminn.com), Box 437,
Rt. 15. Open year-round. Off by itself
between Rt. 1 and Blue Hill Village, a
former barn has been reworked as an
open-beamed combination breakfast/
dining/living room. Upstairs are seven
small guest rooms, each with a private
bath. The attached farmhouse offers
seven more guest rooms with shared
baths (including one appealing single)
and more common rooms, one with
a woodstove. In-season $85–99 dou-
ble, $75–85 single (less off-season),
including a generous continental
breakfast.

Elsewhere on the Blue Hill Peninsula

First Light Bed & Breakfast (207-374-5879; www.firstlightbandb.com), 821 E. Blue Hill Rd., Blue Hill 04614. A coveside home with a tower built in the 1970s to resemble a lighthouse. The dining room and living room have large windows overlooking the picturesque harbor and, on clear days, beyond to Mount Desert Island. Two bedrooms on the second floor share a bath, but the Lighthouse Suite is the real star: a round bedroom, with bird's-eye maple dressers built into the curve of the wall and rockers with views, plus a dressing room overlooking the cove (full bath). $110–200 in high season with a full breakfast and 2-night requirement; otherwise $100–170.

The Brooklin Inn (207-359-2777; www.brooklininn.com), P.O. Box 175, Rt. 175, Brooklin 04616. A casual, friendly inn in the middle of a minute village. Chip (a former tugboat captain) and Gail Angell are clearly the right innkeepers for this landmark that's well known for its restaurant (see *Dining Out*); below it is an inviting pub. Brooklin offers sheltered moorings to yachters. The five upstairs bedrooms share two baths. $95 per couple, $85 single, full breakfast included; a $145 winter special adds all you can eat for two.

⊗ ❦ **Brass Fox Bed and Breakfast** (207-326-0575; www.brassfox .com), Southern Bay Rd., Rt. 175, Penobscot 04476. Open year-round. This 19th-century farmhouse is filled with antiques. Common space includes two dining rooms (with original tin ceilings), a small library (with phone jack for Internet connection), and parlor. All the second-floor guest rooms (each with bath) share views off across fields and woods. A full breakfast includes freshly squeezed orange juice, an entrée, and homemade pastries; the Bagaduce Lunch (see *Eating Out*) is handy. Gerry and Dawn Freeman are helpful hosts. $90–110 ($5 less for 2 nights or more). Pets possible.

The Maples (207-359-8309), Box 222, Rt. 175, Brooklin 04616. Open year-round. We like the hospitable feel of this old-fashioned guest house with its resident cats. Dorothy Jordan offers upstairs rooms with shared baths and in summer two very pleasant downstairs rooms, also shared baths. $65–85 per room includes coffee but no breakfast.

COTTAGES AND MORE Peninsula Property Rentals (207-374-2428; www.peninsulapropertyrentals.com), Main St., Blue Hill. A range of area rentals. Also see **Maine Vacation Rentals** (207-374-2444; www.maine vacationrentalsonline.com), 105 Main St., Blue Hill.

SHORE OAKS

Sally Littlefield

OAKLAND HOUSE

Christina Tree

🐚 **Oakland House Seaside Resort** (207-359-8521 or 1-800-359-RELAX; www .oaklandhouse.com), 435 Herrick Rd., Brooksville 04617. Most cottages open May–Oct.; Lone Pine and Boathouse Cottages are open year-round. The picturesque old mansard-roofed hotel opened by Jim Littlefield's forebears in 1889 now houses only the dining rooms and serves as a centerpiece for this 50-acre property, with 0.5 mile of frontage on Eggemoggin Reach, and with lake as well as saltwater beaches. Scattered through the woods and along the shore are 15 cottages (each different; most with cooking facilities, living room, and fireplace), accommodating one to nine people. There are no TVs

✳ Where to Eat

DINING OUT Arborvine (207-374-2119), Main St., Blue Hill. Open 5:30–8 for dinner in-season, Wed.–Sun. off-season. Reservations a day or two in advance are a must during high season. Chef-owner John Hikade is widely respected in this area. Just south of the village on Rt. 172, housed in a 200-year-old building with several simple but elegant, open-beamed dining rooms with fireplaces. The mouthwatering entrées might include crispy roast duckling with amaretto glaze, or medallions of lamb with wild mushrooms and fresh basil. $19–26. Also see The Vinery under *Eating Out*.

Oakland House (207-359-8521), off Herrick Rd., Brooksville. Open mid-June–Sep. for dinner 6–8:30 and a Sunday brunch (9–11 in July and Aug.). On Thursday in July and August a lobster picnic is served, weather permitting, on the beach. Reservations requested. This delightfully old-fashioned dining room is a hidden gem: Chef Woody Clark uses local, seasonal ingredients featuring organic herbs and edible flowers from the resort's gardens to create a five-course menu that changes daily. Outside, guests can order à la carte from a choice of several entrées—perhaps seared pork tenderloin coated with whole-grain maple mustard sauce, red snapper dusted with southwestern seasonings, or a ratatouille of eggplant, zucchini, and yellow squash sautéed with garlic and blended with

(with the exception of Lone Pine), and firewood is free. Families feel particularly welcome. Facilities include a dock, rowboats, badminton, croquet, a recreation hall full of games, and hiking trails. Breakfast and dinner are served in the delightfully old-fashioned dining rooms, one reserved for families, the other adults-only. The current fare is on a par with the best around (see *Dining Out*). Thursday is lobster picnic night. In-season cottages rent by the week: $525–1,375 per adult MAP (children's rates slide) and in shoulder season $475–1,375 per week (housekeeping) per cottage, no meals.

A part of but apart from the larger resort is **Shore Oaks Seaside Inn**, one of the best-kept secrets of the region. Built as a private cottage in 1907, an era when Maine cottage signified something specific—namely, simplicity and a focus on surroundings—it has been sensitively restored by Sally Littlefield, a designer who recognized the quality of its Arts and Crafts–era architecture, detailing, and furnishings, all of which she has amplified. Shaded by huge old oaks and firs, this 10-room "cottage" features a long porch lined with rocking chairs and a gazebo right on the water, commanding sweeping views of Eggemoggin Reach, the Pumpkin Island Lighthouse, and Penobscot Bay beyond. Rooms have deep old tubs. Our favorites are Room 7, a corner room overlooking the water with no less than six windows and a working fireplace, Mission oak furniture, and a sense of space and comfort. We have also stayed on the third floor with shared bath, not a bad option. $99–395 per room MAP in-season; B&B rates less.

a home marinara, served atop polenta. Entrées $17–20. In spring and fall dinner is served in the smaller dining room at Shore Oaks Seaside Inn (see *Lodging*).

The Brooklin Inn (207-359-2777), Rt. 175, Brooklin Village. Reservations advised. Open 5:30–9 for dinner 6 nights in summer, 5 in winter. All meat is organic, fish is wild, and produce, whenever possible, is local. The seven entrées on a summer menu might range from half a small chicken on white bean stew with truffle oil to lobster, boiled, picked out of its shell, and sautéed with red chard, boiled potatoes, and a bourbon vanilla bean sauce. Entrées $18–34. The wine list and choice of beers are extensive. The

THE GAZEBO AT SHORE OAKS

Christina Tree

downstairs pub, with a menu featuring Guinness beef stew and chicken potpie ($10), is a favorite local gathering spot.

🍴 🎵 Blue Moose Restaurant (207-374-4374), 50 Main St., Blue Hill. Open mid-Apr.–mid-Oct. daily for lunch, dinner, and afternoon tea; buffet breakfast on weekends 8–11. "A fusion of foods" is the way chef Mike Menge describes what he serves. At lunch try a Santa Fe salad of grains and local greens with cumin tomato dressing; at dinner, perhaps Mongolian pork loin, marinated and grilled with braised red cabbage, Chinese mustard sauce, and mashed potatoes. All dinner entrées available in small portions. Dinner entrées $8.50–16.95 for large portions.

Bread and Water Café at the Buck's Harbor Market (207-326-8683), Corn Hill Rd., Brooksville Village. The attractive café is in the back of the store, open for dinner Thu.–Sun. most of the year (closed Sun. in winter). The menu usually lists half a dozen appetizers and entrées. You might begin with local mussels steamed in a Dijon cream broth, then dine on a vegetarian pasta, potato-

and horseradish-crusted halibut with mushrooms, or a burger from locally raised beef, ground here. Pizzas and salads are also a draw. Fully licensed. Entrées $12–25. Pizzas from $11.

Surry Inn (207-667-5091), Rt. 172, Contention Cove, Surry. Open nightly for dinner except Tue.; just Fri.–Sat. in winter. This pleasant dining room overlooking a cove is well known locally for reasonably priced fine dining, under the same ownership and management for some 25 years. The menu changes often but always includes interesting soups—maybe Hungarian mushroom or lentil vegetable—and a wide entrée selection that might include veal tarragon, steak *au poivre* bordelaise, spicy garlic frogs' legs, and scallops with almonds and mango. Entrées $14–21.

The Lookout Inn & Restaurant (207-359-2188), Flye Point, Brooklin. Open for dinner mid-June–mid-Oct. One of Maine's oldest family-owned summer hotels, set above gardens and a meadow that slope to the water. Entrées $18–26.

Also see *Dining Out* in "Deer Isle, Stonington."

EATING OUT 🍴 **Bagaduce Lunch**, Rt. 176, North Brooksville (at the reversing falls). Seasonal. Absolutely the best spot for seafood baskets and burgers. Try the fried salmon steaks or halibut sandwich. The salads are field greens, and the ice cream is Giffords. Picnic tables are scattered over a lawn that slopes to the Bagaduce River.

The Vinery (207-374-2441; www.arborvine.com), part of the Arborvine complex on the southern edge of Blue Hill Village, varying hours in-season, weekends after Columbus Day. Piano bar, wine by the glass, light bistro fare

BAGADUCE LUNCH

Nancy English

such as codcakes and sweet potato napoleon as well as pastas and classic pad Thai. $8.75–13.50.

🍴 **Marlintini's Grill** (207-374-2500), The Mines Rd. (Rt. 15/176) south of Blue Hill Village. Open for lunch and dinner. Expanded and relocated in 2004, this popular restaurant offers a sports bar and grilled and fried meat and seafood, salads, hot sandwiches, and nightly special.

🍴 **Morning Moon Café** (207-359-2373), Rt. 175, Brooklin. Open daily 7 AM–2 PM, except Mon.; also for takeout pizza 5–8 PM (days vary with the season). An oasis in the middle of Brooklin Village, our favorite kind of eatery with deep booths, good salads and sandwiches, pies and soups. The fresh-dough pizza is outstanding.

Pain de Famille (207-374-3839), Main St., Blue Hill Village. Open year-round, weekdays 8:30–7, Sat. 9–1. Closed Sun. Kathleen McCloskey's artisan breads are the best around. No preservatives, some vegan goodies, and standout sandwiches such as farm-fresh egg salad and falafel with lemon tahini spread. There's also a range of salads, a famous gazpacho, and Friday-night pizzas.

The Fish Net (207-374-5240), Blue Hill Village, Rt. 15, across from the turnoff (Rt. 176) to East Blue Hill. Open seasonally 11–8, until 9 on Fri.–Sat. Known for lobster rolls; also a convenient place to feast on lobster and steamers or buy a cooked lobster to take home, plus the usual fried seafood, burgers, and sandwiches.

Buck's Harbor Market (207-326-8683), Cornfield Hill Rd., Brooksville Village, Rt. 176. The market has a lunch counter, open year-round for breakfast and lunch. Baking is done

here, and the stuffed pockets and breads make great picnic fare).

Blue Hill Food Co-op Café (207-374-2165), Rt. 172 in Green's Hill Place, a small shopping center just north of the village. Open weekdays 8–7, Sat. 8–6, Sun. 10–5. This attractive café is part of a well-stocked market specializing in organic and local produce as well as wines, general health foods, and vitamins. Good organic coffees and teas and a selection of baked goods, soups, sandwiches, and specials. Also a source of premade sandwiches and quiche.

Also see *Eating Out* in "Deer Isle, Stonington."

PICNIC FIXINGS Don't waste a nice day by eating inside! For picnic sites, see *Green Space*. **Merrill & Hinckley** on Union St., middle of Blue Hill, an old-fashioned general store, makes good sandwiches fresh each morning and keeps them in a cooler way in back. Also see **Pain de Famille**, **Buck's Harbor Market**, and the **Blue Hill Food Co-op**, above.

✳ Entertainment

MUSIC 🎵 **Kneisel Hall Chamber Music School and Festival** (207-374-2811; www.kneisel.org), Pleasant St. (Rt. 15), Blue Hill. One of the oldest chamber music festivals in the country (dating back to 1924). Faculty present string and ensemble music in a series of Sunday-afternoon and Friday-evening concerts, June–Aug.; inquire about Young Artist Concerts.

WERU (207-469-6600; www.weru.org) is a major nonprofit community radio station based in East Orland (89.9 FM) known for folk and Celtic music, jazz, and reggae.

Bagaduce Chorale (207-374-5966), Blue Hill. A community chorus staging several concerts yearly, ranging from Bach to show tunes.

Flash in the Pans Community Steel Band (207-374-5247; www .peninsulapan.org), Brooksville. Monday-night "Street Dances" are 7:30–9 in varied locations around the area. Performances Mon. during summer months.

✳ Selective Shopping

ANTIQUES **Belcher's Antiques** (207-348-9938), 232 Ellsworth Rd. (Rt. 172), Blue Hill. Open daily May–Oct. A large farmhouse and barn are filled with country furniture, folk art, accessories, and more. Call off-season.

Sedgwick Antiques (207-359-8834), Rt. 172, Sedgwick. Tue.–Fri. 10–5, Sat. noon–5. A wide range with emphasis on formal styles. Jill Knowles and Bill Perry buy and sell year-round, but call off-season.

Steven J. Rowe Antiques & Mary Keeler Rowe Fine Arts (207-374-3811), 138 Main St., Blue Hill Village. Open in July and Aug., Tue.–Sat. 10–5; June and Sep. by chance or appointment.

Thomas Hinchcliffe Antiques (207-326-9411), Graytown Rd. (Rt. 176), West Sedgwick. Open 10–5 most days in-season.

Note: The Blue Hill Peninsula harbors a dozen dealers.

ART GALLERIES

In Blue Hill
Leighton Gallery (207-374-5001; www.leightongallery.com), Parker Point Rd. Open June–Columbus Day. One of Maine's most prominent con-temporary art galleries, with exhibits in the three-floor space changing every few weeks. Judith Leighton's own oils alone are worth a stop, as is the sculpture garden.

Jud Hartman Gallery and Sculpture Studio (207-374-917; www .judhartmangallery.com), Main St. Open mid-June–mid-Sep. daily. Now in newly expanded quarters with a water view, Hartman exhibits his realistic bronze sculptures of northeastern Native Americans.

Randy Eckard (207-374-2510), 4 Pleasant St. Open late June–Sep., Tue.–Sat. Limited-edition prints of the artist's precise, luminous landscapes.

Liros Gallery (207-374-5370; www .lirosgallery.com), Parker Point Rd., specializes in fine paintings, old prints, and Russian icons; appraisals, restoration.

Blue Hill Bay Gallery (207-274-5773; www.bluehillbaygallery.com), 11 Tenney Hill. Open 10–5 Memorial Day–Labor Day; weekends thereafter. Changing exhibits of 19th-century and contemporary art, featuring northern landscapes and the sea.

The Gallery at Caterpillar Hill (207-359-6577). Positioned right next to the scenic pullout (Rt. 15/17), it offers changing works featuring local landscapes.

Larson Studio and Gallery (207-326-8222), Rt. 175, South Penobscot. David Larson's powerful paintings depict human landscapes, a refreshing departure from seascapes.

Also see *Selective Shopping* in "Deer Isle, Stonington."

ARTISANS **Rowantrees Pottery** (207-374-5535), Union St., Blue Hill. Open year-round; June–Sep., Mon.–

Sat., otherwise weekdays. Find your way back behind the friendly white house into the large studio. A Blue Hill tradition since 1934 when, inspired by a conversation with Mahatma Gandhi in India, Adelaide Pearson conceived the idea of using glazes gathered from the town's abandoned copper mines, quarries, and bogs. Watch tableware being hand thrown and browse through the upstairs showroom filled with plates, cups, vases, and jam pots.

Rackliffe Pottery (207-374-2297; www.rackcliffepottery.com), Rt. 172, Blue Hill Village. Open Mon.–Sat. 8–5; also Sun. in July and Aug., noon–4. Since 1968 Phyllis and Phil Rackliffe have produced their distinctive pottery, featuring local glazes. Their emphasis is on individual small pieces rather than on sets. Visitors are welcome to watch.

Handworks Gallery (207-374-5613), Main St., Blue Hill. Open Memorial Day–late Dec., Mon.–Sat. 10–5. A middle-of-town space filled with stunning handwoven clothing, jewelry, furniture, rugs, and blown glass.

North Country Textiles (207-374-2715; www.northcountrytextiles.com), Levy House, Main St., Blue Hill. Carole Larson's woven overshot wall hangings, throws, spreads, and place mats are well worth a detour; the lovely napkins and place mats are six years old and going strong in our dining room.

BOOKSTORES **Blue Hill Books** (207-374-5632), 2 Pleasant St. (two doors up from the post office), Blue Hill. A long-established, full-service, family-run bookstore.

North Light Books (207-374-5422), Main St., Blue Hill. Bonnie Myers is a former schoolteacher, and her full-service, independent bookstore features a truly outstanding children's department; also art supplies and cards.

SPECIAL SHOPS **Blue Hill Wine Shop** (207-374-2161), Main St., Blue Hill. Open Mon.–Sat. 10–5:30. A long-established shop dedicated to the perfect cup of tea or coffee, a well-chosen wine, and the right blend of tobacco.

Blue Hill Yarn Shop (207-374-5631), Rt. 172 north of Blue Hill Village. Open Mon.–Sat. 10–4. A mecca for knitters in search of a variety of wools and needles. Lessons and original hand knits.

The Sow's Ear and Silk Purse (207-326-4649), junction of Rt. 176 and Herrick Rd. The winery is open Tue.–Sat. 10–5; the Silk Purse, 9–1. Also by chance or appointment. The winery here focuses on local, organically grown fruits; the specialty is dry, English-style cider and Wild Berry wine. **Gail Disney's weaving studio** is upstairs, featuring her unusual rag rugs.

Architectural Antiquities (207-326-4942; www.archantiquities.com), Harborside. Call for directions and to let them know what you're looking for. Specialties include brass lighting, hardware and fireplace items, Victorian plumbing fixtures, windows, doors, weather vanes, hand-hewn beams, and more.

✳ Special Events

Memorial Day–Labor Day: **Blue Hill Farmer's Market**, Blue Hill Fairgrounds, Rt. 15, Blue Hill, Beano Building. Sat., 9–11:30 AM. Crafts and baked goods as well as seasonal produce and flowers.

Last weekend in June: **Downeast Properties Flye Point Arts and Music Festival** at the Lookout Inn, Brooklin. Big names perform in a big meadow by the bay.

July: **Full Circle Fair** (*third weekend*), Blue Hill Fairgrounds—constant music ranging from traditional folk to hard rock, children's music, contra dancing, sponsored for more than 15 years by WERU. **Blue Hill Days** (*last weekend*)—arts and crafts fair, parade, farmer's market, antique-car rally, shore dinner, boat races.

August: **Academy Antiques Fair** (*first weekend*), George Stevens Academy, Blue Hill, is big. **Downeast Antiques Fairs** (*midmonth*).

Labor Day weekend: **Blue Hill Fair**, at the fairgrounds—harness racing, a midway, livestock competitions; one of the most colorful old-style fairs in New England.

December: A weekend of **Christmas celebrations**.

DEER ISLE, STONINGTON, AND ISLE AU HAUT

The narrow, half-mile-long suspension bridge across Eggemoggin Reach connects the Blue Hill Peninsula with Little Deer Isle, linked in turn by causeways and bridges to Deer Isle and its wandering land fingers. Loosely known as Deer Isle, this intermingling of land and water is characterized by the kind of coves and lupine-fringed inlets usually equated with "the real Maine." It's divided between the towns of Deer Isle and Stonington, and there are the villages of Sunset and Oceanville and of Sunshine, home of the nationally respected Haystack Mountain School of Crafts. Galleries display outstanding work by dozens of artists and craftspeople who live, or at least summer, in town.

Stonington, almost 40 miles south of Rt. 1, remains a working fishing harbor, but it, too, now has its share of galleries. Most buildings, which are scattered on smooth rocks around the harbor, date from the 1880s to the World War I boom years, during which Deer Isle's pink granite was shipped off to face buildings from Rockefeller Center to Boston's Museum of Fine Arts. At the height of the granite boom Stonington's population was 5,000, compared with 1,200 today.

In Stonington life still eddies around Billings Diesel and Marine, and the Commercial Pier, home base for one of Maine's largest fishing/lobstering fleets. But the tourist tide is obviously rising. Galleries and seasonal, visitor-geared shops are multiplying along Main Street; the restored Opera House is the scene of frequent films, live performances, and readings. According to the Stonington-based weekly, *Island Ad-Vantages*, 433 new lots were created by dividing existing lots on Deer Isle between 1980 and 2000—and property values have more than doubled in the past two decades.

Half of Isle au Haut, a mountainous island 7 miles off Stonington, is technically part of Acadia National Park. The mail boat makes seasonal stops at Duck

Harbor, near the island's southern tail, accessing a choice of hiking trails. The remaining half of the island, which supports less than 50 year-round residents and an old summer colony, is vividly depicted in *The Lobster Chronicles* by Linda Greenlaw.

GUIDANCE Deer Isle–Stonington Chamber of Commerce (207-348-6124; www.deerislemaine.com) maintains a visitor center (with restroom) on Rt. 15 at Little Deer Isle, south of the bridge. Open 10–4 mid-June–Labor Day, sporadically after that for a few weeks. Also check www.penobscotbay.com.

GETTING THERE Follow directions under *Getting There* in "Blue Hill Area"; continue down Rt. 15 to Deer Isle.

✳ To See

🖉 ♿ **Deer Isle Granite Museum** (207-367-6331), Main St., Stonington. Open Memorial Day–Labor Day, Mon.–Sat. 9–5, Sun. 1–4. Housed in the former pharmacy, this beautifully conceived and executed small museum features an 8-by-15-foot working model of quarrying operations on Crotch Island and the town of Stonington in 1900. Derricks move, and trains carry granite to waiting ships. Photo blowups and a video also dramatize the story of the quarryman's life during the height of the boom (see the chapter introduction).

The Salome Sellers House (207-348-2897), Rt. 15A, Sunset. Open late June–late Sep., Wed. and Fri. 1–4. Salome Sellers herself lived to be 108 years old in this snug 1803 red Cape, now the home of the Deer Isle–Stonington Historical Society, displaying ships' models, Native American artifacts, and old photos; interesting and friendly.

EGGEMOGGIN REACH BRIDGE

Christina Tree

Lighthouses. **Pumpkin Island Light**, 3 miles from the chamber booth, at the end of Eggemoggin Road, is now a private home. **Eagle Island Light** can be viewed from Sylvester Cove in Sunset or, better yet, from the Eagle Island mail boat, from which you can also see the **Heron Neck**, **Brown's Head**, and **Goose Rocks Lights**. From Goose Cove Lodge in Sunset you can see and hear the now automated **Mark Island Light** (its old bronze bell sits on the resort's lawn); the **Saddleback Ledge Light** is also visible on the horizon. (For details about reaching the **Isle au Haut Light**, see *Boat Excursions*.)

✳ To Do

BICYCLE RENTALS **Finest Kind Restaurant** and **Eggemoggin Landing** offer rental bikes; see *Sea Kayaking and Canoeing*.

BOAT EXCURSIONS ✸ ✿ **Isle-au-Haut Company** (207-367-5193; www.isleau haut.com) links Stonington with the island at least twice daily except Sun. year-round (one Sun. round-trip in summer). See *Green Space* for a description of the island. Note that the island's famous hiking trails cluster around Duck Harbor, a mail-boat run only between mid-June and Labor Day, daily except Sun.; a ranger usually meets the morning boat to orient passengers to the seven hiking trails, the picnic area, and drinking-water sources (otherwise, a pamphlet guide serves this purpose). The boat tends to fill up in July and Aug., so reserve with a credit card or aim for an early boat. The ferry takes kayaks and canoes for a fee (but not to Duck Harbor). $16 (reserved) adults, $8 children, $4 pets, $8 bicycle, $15 kayaks and canoes.

A **Penobscot Bay cruise** aboard the *Miss Lizzie* is also offered twice a day in-season by Isle-au-Haut Company (see above); 9 AM and 2 PM, with lobster hauling demonstrated on one or the other, at the end of Seabreeze Ave.

Eagle Island mail boat. Operated by the Sunset Bay Company (207-348-9316), the *Katherine* leaves Sylvester's Cove in Sunset mid-June–mid-Sep., Mon.–Sat., at 9 AM. Half a mile off Sunset, Eagle Island is roughly a mile long with rocky ledges, a sandy beach, and a working lighthouse. Inquire about island rentals. Kayaks are carried.

Old Quarry Ocean Adventures (207-367-8977), Oceanville Rd., offers charter fishing, sightseeing cruises, also sailing charters and lessons, accommodations.

Powerboat rentals are available from **Eggemoggin Landing** (207-348-6115), Little Deer Isle, just south of the bridge.

SEA KAYAKING AND CANOEING *Note:* The waters off Stonington, with their many islands—known as Merchant's Row—are among the most popular along the coast with kayakers, but it's imperative, especially for novices, to explore these waters with a guide.

Granite Island Guide Service (207-348-2668; www.graniteislandguide.com), Deer Isle. Dana Douglas, a Registered Maine Guide, a former whitewater canoe racer, and a Congregational minister who has biked around the world, and his wife, Anne, a veteran schoolteacher, offer guided kayaking and canoeing ranging from half a day to 3 days with overnight island camping. If you're not an ace kayaker familiar with local currents, it's far safer and more enjoyable to take a guided tour.

Old Quarry Ocean Adventures, Inc. (207-367-8977; www.oldquarry.com), Settlement Quarry Rd., marked from the Oceanville Rd. (off Rt. 15). Captain Bill Baker's campground is the departure point for half- and full-day guided kayak trips; rental kayaks and canoes are also offered, but boaters must prove competence. Tent sites and a camp store are geared to kayakers, and overnight guided kayaking trips are offered. A rental house is also available. Trails lead to the Settlement Quarry.

Kayak rentals are available from **Finest Kind Restaurant** (207-348-7714) at Joyce's Crossroad (off Rts. 15 and 15A); from **Eggemoggin Landing** (207-348-6115), Rt. 15, Little Deer Isle; and from **Old Quarry Charters** (207-367-8977) in Oceanville (see above).

GOLF AND MINI GOLF **Island Country Club** (207-348-2379), Deer Isle, welcomes guests mid-June–Labor Day; nine holes.

✒ **Finest Kind Restaurant** (207-348-7714), marked from Rt. 15 between Stonington and Deer Isle Village, operates an 18-hole mini golf course.

SPECIAL LEARNING PROGRAMS **Haystack Mountain School of Crafts** (207-348-2306; www.haystack-mtn.org), Deer Isle. Two- and 3-week sessions, June–Labor Day, attract some of the country's top artisans in clay, metals, wood, fibers, graphics, and glass. From its beginnings Haystack has been equated with cutting-edge design rather than traditional craft, and the architecture underscores the school's philosophy. It's intimate and self-contained, like the summer sessions

Haystack Mountain School of Crafts (207-348-2306; www.haystack-mtn.org), Deer Isle (south of Deer Isle Village; turn left off Rt. 15 at the Mobil station and follow signs 7 miles). This is one of the country's outstanding crafts schools, and the campus itself is a work of art: a series of spare, shingled buildings, studios with a central dining hall and sleeping quarters, all weathered the color of surrounding rocks and fitted between trees, connected by steps and terraced decks, floated above the fragile lichens and wildflowers on land sloping steeply toward Jericho Bay. Given the brevity and intensity of each session (see *Special Learning Programs*), visitors are permitted in the studios only on weekly tours (Wed. at 1 PM) and during the "walk-throughs" in which student and faculty work is displayed (4–6 on the second Thu. of each session, followed by a 7:30 PM auction). The public is also welcome in the Gateway Building auditorium for frequent 8 PM slide lectures, visiting artists' presentations, and occasional concerts. There are also biweekly auctions.

themselves, each limited to no more than 90 students. Workshop topics are determined by faculty members, and these, like the students, change every 2 or 3 weeks. Each group is carefully balanced to include young (minimum age 18) and old, neophytes as well as master craftsmen; repeaters are kept to a third.

The Stonington Painter's Workshop (207-367-2368; off-season, 617-776-3102). Nationally prominent artist and art teacher Jon Imber coordinates and teaches this July series of weeklong landscape workshops.

SWIMMING ♪ **Lily Pond**, off Rt. 15 north of Deer Isle Village. The island's freshwater swimming hole. Ask locally for directions.

Causeway Beach, Rt. 15. South of the information booth (with restroom; see *Guidance*), a roadside strand that at low tide can fill the bill on a hot day, especially if there are children in the car.

✳ Green Space

Island Heritage Trust (207-348-2455), P.O. Box 42, Deer Isle 04627. The trust publishes detailed maps of walking trails, which include Settlement Quarry and several offshore islands.

Ames Pond, east of town on Indian Point Rd., is full of pink-and-white water lilies in bloom June–early Sept.

Holt Mill Pond Preserve. A walk through unspoiled woodland and marsh. The entrance is on Stonington Cross Rd. (Airport Rd.)—look for a sign several hundred feet beyond the medical center. Park on the shoulder and walk the dirt road to the beginning of the trail, then follow the yellow signs.

Isle au Haut (pronounced *eye-la-ho*) is 6 miles long and 3 miles wide. More than half the island is part of Acadia National Park. Camping is forbidden every-

ISLE AU HAUT

Christina Tree

Christina Tree

STONINGTON

where except in the five Adirondack-style shelters at Duck Harbor (each accommodating six people), which are available by reservation only. For a reservation form, phone 207-288-3338 or write to Acadia National Park, P.O. Box 177, Bar Harbor 04609; the form must be sent on or as soon after April 1 as possible. Camping is permitted mid-May–mid-Oct., but in the shoulder season you have to walk 5 miles from the town landing to Duck Harbor. In summer months the mail boat arrives at Duck Harbor at 11 AM, allowing plenty of time to hike the island's dramatic Western Head and Cliff Trails before returning on the 6 PM boat. Trails are pine carpeted and shaded, with water views. For more about day trips to the island, see *Boat Excursions*.

Crockett Cove Woods Preserve (a Maine Nature Conservancy property) consists of 100 acres along the water, with a nature trail. Take Rt. 15 to Deer Isle, then Sunset Rd.; 2.5 miles beyond the post office, bear right onto Whitman Rd.; a right turn at the end of the road brings you to the entrance, marked by a small sign and registration box. From Stonington, take Sunset Rd. through the village of Burnt Cove and turn left onto Whitman Rd.

Settlement Quarry, Stonington. A 0.25-mile walk from the parking area follows an old road to the top of this former working quarry for a view off across Webb Cove and west to the Camden Hills. Side trails loop back through woods. It's on Oceanville Rd., 0.9 mile from Rt. 15 (just beyond the turn marked for Settlement Quarry Ocean Adventures); turn at Ron's Mobil.

Mariner's Memorial Park, Deer Isle. A picnic and bird-watching spot with views of Long Cove. Take Fire Rd. 501 off Sunshine Rd.

Edgar M. Tennis Preserve. Three miles of wooded and shore trails with shore views. Access is off Sunshine Rd., Fire Rd. 523.

Shore Acre Preserve. A 38-acre preserve with a loop trail to and along the shore with views of Oak Point and Goose Island. Take Sunshine Rd. 1.2 miles, bear left at the fork onto Greenlaw District Rd., and continue 0.9 mile to the parking area.

Barred Island Preserve is a 2-acre island owned by The Nature Conservancy, just off Stinson Point, accessible by a wide sandbar; request permission for access from Goose Cove Lodge (see *Lodging*).

✳ Lodging

RUSTIC RESORT ✍ & **Goose Cove Lodge** (207-348-2508; www.goose covelodge.com), Sunset 04683. Open mid-May–mid-Oct. On a secluded cove not far from Stonington, this is a many-windowed lodge with a library and dining room, common space and cabins. Joanne and Dom Parisi have retained the rustic feel but brightened the lodge, suites, and cottages (sleeping four to eight) with well-chosen art, quilts, hooked rugs, and attractive fabrics. The 21-acre preserve offers trails along the shore and low-tide passage to Barred Island, a Nature Conservancy property well known to birders. In-season, children dine early and enjoy an evening program in Toad Hall. Food is a point of pride (see *Dining Out*). Two suites are attached to the lodge; there are also annex rooms with shared sundecks and nearby "duplex

cabins." More widely scattered cabins are so secluded that you will need a flashlight to find them from the main lodge after dinner. Late June–Aug. a week's reservation is requested, but shorter stays are frequently available due to cancellations. $145–350 per couple B&B; inquire about children's rates, which include Kids Camp.

Also see **Oakland House** under "Blue Hill Area"; it's just across Eggemoggin Reach.

INNS AND BED & BREAKFASTS

In Deer Isle 04627
🐾 ✍ **Pilgrim's Inn** (207-348-6615 or 1-888-778-7505; www.pilgrimsinn .com). Open mid-May–mid-Oct. Built as a private home in 1793, this gracious, four-story, hip-roofed inn stands in the middle of Deer Isle Village yet both fronts and backs on water. A summer inn since 1899, it features big front parlors and guest rooms of varying sizes, all with private bath and water views. The rooms on the third floor have acquired private baths and skylights; three rooms have a gas log fireplace. There are also three two-bedroom cottages, also with water views, nicely decorated and fitted with a kitchen as well as dining and living rooms. Common space includes formal old parlors and less formal lounging space in front of an 8-foot-wide hearth on the garden level; a dining room is in the old barn, known for its popular fare (see *Dining Out*). Rates are stepped up and down several times depending on the season. Inn

DEER ISLE VILLAGE

Christina Tree

rooms $99–$269 depending on the season and the room, including breakfast. $50 charge for pets allowed in cottages.

☞ **The Inn at Ferry Landing** (207-348-7760; www.ferrylanding.com), Old Ferry Rd., RR 1, Box 163. Overlooking Eggemoggin Reach, Jean and Gerald Wheeler's 1840s seaside farmhouse offers magnificent water views, spacious rooms, patchwork quilts, and a great common room with huge windows and two grand pianos that Gerald plays and uses for summer recitals and spontaneous music sessions. The six guest rooms include a huge master suite with a woodstove and skylights. $110–120 for double rooms, $165 for the suite; less off-season. The Mooring, a two-story, two-bedroom, fully equipped housekeeping cottage, perfect for families, is $1,300 per week. Room rates include a full breakfast; minimum of 2 nights in high season.

In Stonington 04681

☜ **Pres du Port** (207-367-5007), Box 319, W. Main and Highland Ave. Open June–Oct. A find. This cheery, comfortable B&B has a common space that includes a light- and flower-filled sunporch overlooking the harbor and three imaginatively furnished guest rooms. One in back has a cathedral ceiling and loft, kitchenette, deck access, and private bath; the other two share two baths (each room also has its own sink) and have harbor views, plus there's an outdoor hot tub overlooking the water. Charlotte Casgrain is a warm, knowledgeable hostess who enjoys speaking French. The generous buffet breakfast—perhaps crustless crabmeat and Parmesan quiche—is served on the sunporch. $85–100 per couple, less per single, tax included.

The Inn on the Harbor (207-367-2420 or 1-800-942-2420; www.innon theharbor.com), P.O. Box 69. Open year-round. Innkeeper Christina Shipps has recently revamped all of the 14 comfortable rooms (private bath, phone, cable TV), each named for a different windjammer (the passenger schooners usually visit Stonington in the course of a summer week). While the inn is smack on Main Street, rooms face the ample deck and working harbor, one of Maine's most photographed views. Request this view, if possible, from a second-floor room like the Heritage (with a working hearth made of local granite). The Stephen Taber is a freestanding room retaining its tin walls and ceiling (it used to be a barbershop). $129–199 summer, $75–125 off-season, includes continental breakfast. Shipps also rents, from this inn, a housekeeping duplex in Patten called Mountain Glory Farm, mentioned in the Katahdin chapter.

On Isle au Haut 04645

The Keeper's House (207-335-2551; www.keepershouse.com), P.O. Box 26. Open mid-May–Oct. This turn-of-the-20th-century lighthouse keeper's house sits back in firs behind its small lighthouse on a point surrounded on three sides by water. Guests arrive on the mail boat from Stonington just in time for a glass of sparkling cider before dinner (BYOB for anything stronger), a five-course, candlelit event at which guests tend to sit together, four to a table. As the sky darkens, you can pick out pinpoints of light from other lighthouses and communities in Penobscot Bay. There are four guest rooms in the main house and a self-contained room in the tiny Oil House. Innkeeper Jeff Burk takes pride in the inn's off-the-grid alternative energy system. It's a hike to the island's most scenic trails in Duck Harbor. $300–375 per room includes breakfast, dinner, and a trail lunch. plus use of bikes; add round-trip fares for the ferry and parking fee.

The Inn at Isle au Haut (207-335-5141; innatisleauhaut.com), P.O. Box 78. This new addition is the only place in the book we haven't personally inspected, but its location on the ocean side of the island and its pictures (a square, steeply mansard-roofed Victorian-era cottage) seem appealing. Diana Santospago greets guests at the ferry. Bicycles are included in the $250–315 rates, along with three ambitious-sounding meals.

MOTELS 🐾 🛶 **Eggemoggin Landing** (207-348-6115), Little Deer Isle 04650. Open mid-May–mid-Oct. A nicely sited motel just beyond the Deer Isle suspension bridge, overlooking Eggemoggin Reach. The 20 rooms are clean. This is a great place for children, with plenty of room to run and a play area. $77–85 in-season, less in spring and fall.

🐾 🛶 **Boyce's Motel** (207-367-2421 or 1-800-224-2421; www.boycesmotel .com), P.O. Box 94, Stonington 04681. Right in the middle of Stonington, family run, clean, and comfortable, water views from decks. Eleven units have double or twin beds, and there are several efficiency units—one with two bedrooms, a living room, and kitchen. $60 per room, $65–115 per efficiency in high season, from $50 off-season; $10 per day per pet.

COTTAGES The best selection of rentals on Deer Isle and Isle au Haut is through **Island Vacation Rentals** (207-367-5095) in Stonington.

Also see **Old Quarry Ocean Adventures** under *Sea Kayaking and Canoeing.*

CAMPGROUND **Sunshine Campground** (207-348-2663 or 1-877-770-9804), RR 1, Box 521D, Deer Isle 04627. Open Memorial Day weekend–mid-Oct. Long established; wooded RV and tent sites. **Old Quarry Ocean Adventures** (see under *Sea Kayaking*) now owns this campground, as well as one in Oceanville Road, in Stonington. Kayaking, history lectures, lobstering lessons are all on offer; and visitors to the other campground can use facilities here.

✳ Where to Eat

DINING OUT **Whale's Rib Tavern** in Pilgrim's Inn (207-348-6615; www .pilgrimsinn.com), Main St., Deer Isle Village. Open year-round for dinner. Reservations highly recommended, but even with one there may be a wait. Most people don't mind, waiting for a table with a glass of something from the full bar. Comfort food—chicken potpies, meat loaf, and pot roast—start the menu, and bouillabaisse concludes it. "There are four generations of people on this island that have never stepped foot in that inn till this summer," said Deer Isle resident Ginger Lester; they all arrived for dinner in the summer of 2005. Owner Rob DeGennaro makes of point of keeping the range of meals wide, and the prices low, while his skilled chef makes it all good. Entrées $6–22.

Goose Cove Lodge (207-348-2508 or 1-800-728-1963), Goose Cove Rd., off Rt. 15A, Sunset. Open May–mid-Oct. for dinner by reservation. Water views and fine food are the draw here. The à la carte menu is less expensive than in years past. Entrées might include baby back ribs served with slow-cooked white beans, seafood tempura skewers served over stir-fried vegetables and fried rice, or a shore dinner; $16–25.

Maritime Café (207-367-2600; www .maritimecafe.com), 27 Main St., Stonington. Open daily May–Oct. for lunch and dinner. Reservations advised. This harborside restaurant got rave reviews during its initial season (2004). The view is unbeatable, and the menu is large and varied. For starters try the seafood stew, an Alsatian onion tart served with fresh greens, or Maritime Salad (watercress, spinach, and mesclun with oranges, toasted almonds, and dried cranberries tossed with a citrus chive vinaigrette; $7). Lobster is served several ways, including seafood crêpes (two crêpes filled with scallops as well as lobster, finished with a Pernod cream sauce). Entrées $14–23. BYOB.

Eaton's Lobster Pool Restaurant (207-348-2383), Deer Isle. Open 4:30–9 daily in summer, weekends between Mother's Day and mid-June, Labor Day till Columbus Day. New owners have upscaled this old dining landmark. A lobster salad is $19, crabmeat salad $14, lobster roll $11. You might also try steamed clams ($14), fried clams ($10), a clam or scallop dinner ($16), or twin lobsters ($30). The covered porch features a great view of a close island and distant hills beyond stretches of ocean. Fully licensed.

EATING OUT Lily's Café (207-397-5936), Rt. 15, Stonington. Open Mon., Tue., and Thu. for breakfast and lunch. This is a Rt. 15 house with

a series of attractive dining rooms upstairs and down. The table we like to lunch on is topped with a sheet of glass over a shell collection. Beloved by locals for such sandwiches as "Russel's Special" (hard salami, melted Havarti, artichoke hearts, lettuce, and the house vinaigrette on crusty French bread). Takeout.

🐦 ✏ **Harbor Café**, Stonington. Open year-round, Mon.–Sat. 6 AM–8 PM; in summer, open later on Fri. and Sat., plus Sun. 6–2. Spanking clean and friendly; dependable food. Soups and salads. Seafood rolls, sandwiches (including hot pastrami) and subs, fried and broiled seafood. Friday night it's a good idea to reserve for the all-you-can-eat seafood fries.

🐦 ✏ **The Cockatoo** (207-367-0900), Cottage Lane off Oceanville Rd. (just off Rt. 15; turn at Ron's Mobil). Open Memorial Day–Labor Day, noon–8. As different from the predictable coastal Maine takeout as a cockatoo is from a seagull. The Carter family's long-established waterside fish shop now offers not just takeout but also waterside tables to sit down and enjoy Suzen Carter's seafood creations. These include Portuguese specialties

THE COCKATOO

Nancy English

such as kale soup, distinctly Mediterranean fish soup, and mussels, plus "crabmeat snakes" (crabmeat baked in pastry). The decor is tropical, lit by tiki-style torches, and includes Peaches, the family's pet cockatoo—who seems to enjoy the hubbub he's inspired, especially on karaoke nights. BYOB.

🦞 ✎ The Fisherman's Friend Restaurant (207-367-2442), P.O. Box 781, 5 Atlantic Ave., Stonington. Open year- round. This restaurant just moved to waterfront next to the quarryman statue, and it now has more than 200 seats, a takeout window on the harbor, outdoor seating, a second floor with a great view, and a convenience store. Open in summer 11–9, closed Mon. and earlier off-season. A local favorite with a wide choice of fried and broiled fish, chowders and stews, burgers, and all the usual sandwiches, and great pies. Children's menu.

✎ Finest Kind (207-348-7714), marked from Rt. 15 between Stonington and Deer Isle Village. Open Apr.–Nov. for dinner 5–9. Neat as a pin, a log cabin with counter and booths. The mini golf course, part of this scene, makes this a favorite with families.

TEA AND JAM **✎ Nervous Nellie's Jams and Jellies and Mountainville Café** (207-348-6182; www .nervousnellies.com), 600 Sunshine Rd., Deer Isle. Open July and Aug., 10–5. Sculptor Peter Beerits displays his whimsical life-sized sculptures, sells his jams and jellies (wild blueberry preserves, blackberry peach conserve, hot tomato chutney), and serves tea, coffee, and scones. Children of all ages love the sculptures,

including a big red lobster playing checkers as a 7-foot alligator looks on. From Rt. 15, follow directions for Haystack (see *To See*).

✳ Entertainment

Stonington Opera House (207-367-2788; www.operahousearts.org), School St., Stonington. Open year-round. This shingled building with its skinny, four-story "fly tower" dates to 1912, when it replaced a larger, 1880s theater built during the town's boom era. Closed for a decade, it was restored and reopened in 2000 and now stages a full calendar of reasonably priced concerts and original theatrical productions. Movies Fri.–Sun. at 7 PM. Call for schedules of movies and live performances.

Community Performances, Inc. (207-367-2900), staged at the Deer Isle/Stonington Elementary School, North Deer Isle Rd. (Rt. 15), Stonington. A series of jazz, folk, and bluegrass concerts and other live performances.

✳ Selective Shopping

ART GALLERIES AND ARTISANS
Note: Studio crawling is a popular local pastime. Because local galleries feature work by local artists, it's frequently possible to trace a piece to its creator. Handout studio maps and postcards that picture individual artists' works are also readily available.

In and around Deer Isle Village
Deer Isle Artists Association (207-348-2330), 6 Dow Rd. Open June–late Sep. A 150-member cooperative gallery with exhibits changing every two weeks.

Turtle Gallery (207-348-9977; www .turtlegallery.com), Rt. 15, north of

Deer Isle Village. Open daily June–
Sep. Artist Elena Kubler's gallery
showcases exceptional jewelry as well
as biweekly changing shows featuring
fine art and contemporary crafts. It's
housed in the barn in which Haystack
faculty work was first displayed, back
when adjoining Centennial House
was home to Francis ("Fran") Sumner
Merritt, the school's founding director,
and his wife, Priscilla, a noted weaver.

The Blue Heron (207-348-6051),
22 Church St. (Rt. 15, near the center
of the village). Open daily June–
Columbus Day. An old barn attached
to Mary Nyburg's pottery studio is
filled with fine contemporary crafts
and features work by some 60 Haystack Mountain School faculty, past
and present.

Terrell S. Lester Photography
(207-348-2676), 4 Main St. Open
in-season Mon.–Sat. 10–5; also mid-
Oct. until Christmas, same days 1–5.
Maine landscapes in large format,
called lightscapes, catch this world at
moments of unusual beauty.

Green Head Forge (207-367-2632),
Old Quarry Rd., Stonington. The
studio displays Jack Hemenway's
sculptural metals and Harriet Rawle
Hemenway's metal jewelry and small
objects.

Hoy Gallery (207-367-2368), E.
Main St. Open daily July–Sep. A big
white barn set back from the street,
filled with Jill Hoy's bold, bright
Maine landscapes.

Watson Gallery (207-367-2900;
www.gwatsongallery.com), Main St.
Open May–Oct., Mon.–Sat. 10–5,
Sun. 1–5. This is a serious gallery
showing prominent contemporary
painting and sculpture, featuring New
England artists.

Kim Grant

TURTLE GALLERY

ELSEWHERE **Ronald Hayes Pearson Design Studio and Gallery**
(207-348-2535), Old Ferry Rd. (off
Rt. 15), Deer Isle. Creative designs in
gold and silver jewelry as well as delicately wrought tabletop sculpture in
other metals.

Greene-Ziner Gallery (207-348-
2601), 73 Reach Rd. (off Rt. 15).
Open July–Sep. In a barn surrounded
by meadows, iron sculptor Eric Ziner
displays his ornate and whimsical creations and potter Melissa Greene, her
thrown earthenware pots suggesting
Greek amphorae in shape but decorated with designs evoking tribal themes.

SPECIAL SHOPS

In Deer Isle
**Old Deer Isle Parish House
Antiques** (207-348-9964), Rt. 15.
Open daily June–Oct. A combination
antiques, crafts, and whatever shop
that's a phenomenon in its own right:
handmade quilts, used books, rag
rugs, whatever. Browser's heaven.

The Periwinkle, Deer Isle Village. Open June–mid-Oct., a tiny shop with a vintage-1910 cash register, crammed with books and carefully selected gifts.

In Stonington

Dockside Books and Gifts (207-367-2652), 62 W. Main St. Seasonal. Al Webber's waterside bookstore has an exceptional selection of Maine and marine books, also gifts, sweaters by local knitters, and a great harbor view from the balcony.

Stonington Sea Products (888-402-2729), Rt. 15. Open Memorial Day–mid-Sep., Mon.–Fri. 8–4. The quality of all fish and seafood is as good as it gets, as are the smoked salmon, scallops, and mussels—along with smoked salmon and haddock pâtés.

The Dry Dock (207-367-5528), Main St. Open daily mid-May–Oct., 9–5. Tempting clothing and craftwork; an outlet for Deer Isle granite products.

The Clown (207-367-6348), Main St. Ultimate proof of Stonington's resorti-fication: high-ticket European antiques, ceramics, fine wine, and art.

The Grasshopper Shop (207-367-5070), relocating on Main St. A Maine chain with a mix of clothing, gifts, and gadgets.

V&S Variety Stores (367-5570), Rt. 15A, Burnt Cove. The many boutiques and galleries have displaced the basic stuff of life—like groceries and everything a five-and-dime once carried. It's all moved out to Burnt Cove, where you'll also find the recycle shop, gas, and plenty of parking. Beside Burnt Cove Market (the supermarket) stands this huge, home-spun "variety store" stocking everything you forgot to bring with you, lost while you were on the road, or broke in the rental cottage.

Also see **Nervous Nellie's Jams and Jellies** under *Where to Eat*. The shop is open year-round, producing 15 flavors of jam, chutney, and marmalade.

✳ Special Events

May–October: Friday-morning (10–noon) **farmer's market** at the Island Community Center in Stonington.

May: **Memorial Day parade**.

June: **Lupine Festival**.

July: **Independence Day** parade, fish fry, and fireworks in Deer Isle Village. **Lobster-boat races** and **Stonington Fisherman's Festival**.

August: **Downeast Race Week** (www.downeastraceweek.com).

DEER ISLE FARMER'S MARKET

Nancy English

ACADIA AREA

MOUNT DESERT ISLAND; ACADIA NATIONAL PARK; BAR HARBOR AND ELLSWORTH; THE QUIET SIDE OF MOUNT DESERT; EAST HANCOCK COUNTY

MOUNT DESERT ISLAND

Mount Desert (pronounced *dessert*) is New England's second largest island, one conveniently linked to the mainland. Two-fifths of its 108 square miles are maintained as Acadia National Park, laced with roads ideally suited for touring by car, more than 50 miles of "carriage roads" specifically for biking and skiing, and 120 miles of hiking trails.

The beauty of "MDI" (as it is locally known) cannot be overstated. Twenty-six mountains rise abruptly from the sea and from the shores of four large lakes. Mount Cadillac, at 1,532 feet, is the highest point on the U.S. Atlantic seaboard; a road winds to its smooth, broad summit for a 360-degree view that's said to yield the first view of dawn (which usually attracts a crowd) in the United States. Sunset, however, attracts a far larger crowd. There are also countless ponds and streams, an unusual variety of flora, and more than 300 species of birds.

Native Americans populated the island for at least 6,000 years before 1604, when Samuel de Champlain sailed by and named it L'Isle de Monts Deserts. In 1613 two French Jesuits attempted to establish a mission on Fernald Point near present Southwest Harbor. They were welcomed by the local Wabanaki chief Asticou but massacred by an English ship, and for 150 years this part of Maine remained a war zone between French and English. Finally settled in the second half of the 18th century, this remained a peaceful, out-of-the-way island even after a bridge was built in 1836 connecting it to the mainland.

In the 1840s landscape painters Thomas Cole and Frederic Church began summering here, and their images of the rugged shore were widely circulated. Summer visitors began arriving by steamboat, and they were soon joined by travelers taking express trains from Philadelphia and New York to Hancock Point, bringing guests enough to fill more than a dozen huge hotels that mushroomed in Bar Harbor. By the 1880s many of these hotel patrons had already built their own mansion-sized "cottages" in and around Bar Harbor. These grandiose summer mansions numbered more than 200 by the time the stock market crashed. Many are now inns.

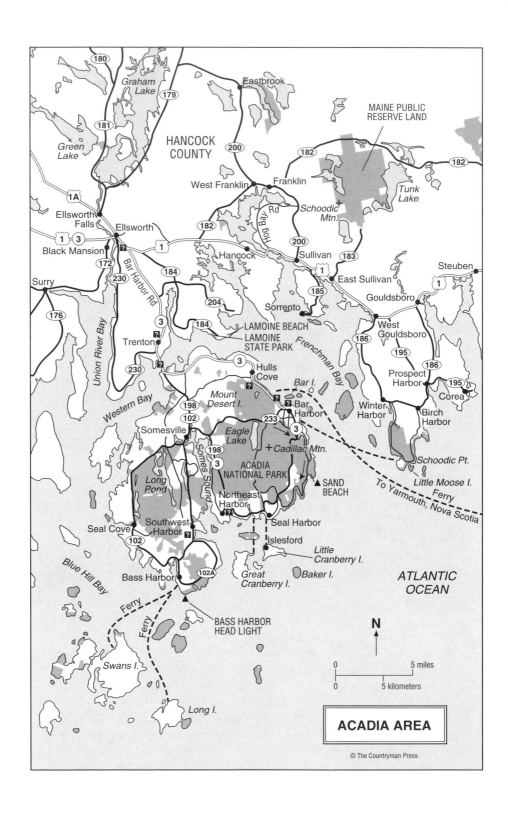

ACADIA AREA

© The Countryman Press

Mount Desert Island seems far larger than it is because it's almost bisected by Somes Sound, the only natural fjord on the East Coast, and because its communities vary so in atmosphere. Bar Harbor lost 67 of its 220 summer mansions and five hotels in the devastating fire of 1947, which also destroyed 17,000 acres of woodland, but both the forest and Bar Harbor have recouped, and then some, in recent decades.

Politically the island is divided into four townships: Bar Harbor, Mount Desert, Southwest Harbor, and Tremont. Northeast Harbor (a village in Mount Desert) and Southwest Harbor, the island's other two resort centers, also enjoy easy access to hiking, swimming, and boating within the park. Compared with Bar Harbor, however, they are relatively quiet, even in July and August, and the several accessible offshore islands are quieter still.

Mount Desert's mountains with "their gray coats and rounded backs look like a herd of elephants, marching majestically across the island," travel writer Samuel Adams Drake wrote in 1891, describing the first impression visitors then received of the island. They were, of course, arriving by steamboat instead of traveling down the unimpressive commercial strip that's Rt. 3. Today it's harder to get beyond the clutter and crowds—but not that hard. The memorable march of rounded mountains is still what you see from excursion boats and from Little Cranberry Island, as well as from the eastern shore of Frenchman Bay, the area described in this section as "East Hancock County."

ACADIA NATIONAL PARK

The legacy of Bar Harbor's wealthy "rusticators" is Acadia National Park. A cadre of influential citizens, who included Harvard University's President Charles W. Eliot, began to assemble parcels of land for public use in 1901, thus protecting the forests from the portable sawmill. Boston textile heir George Dorr devoted his fortune and energy to amassing a total of 11,000 acres and persuading the federal government to accept it. In 1919 Acadia became the first national park east of the Mississippi. It is now a more-than-47,000-acre preserve, with 30,300 acres and more than another 10,000 in easements encompassing almost half of Mount Desert Island.

Almost two-thirds of the park's three million annual visitors actually get out of their cars and hike the park's trails. Many now take the white and blue Island Explorer buses, for free. They usually begin by viewing the introductory film in the visitor center and then drive the 27-mile Park Loop Road, stopping to see the obvious sites and noting what they want to explore more fully (see below). The park has much more to offer, from simple hikes to rock climbing, horse-drawn carriage rides to swimming, bicycling, canoeing, and kayaking.

Within the park are more than 50 miles of carriage roads donated by John D. Rockefeller Jr. These incredible broken-stone roads take bikers, hikers, joggers, and cross-country skiers through woods, up mountains, past lakes and streams. The paths also lead over and under 17 spectacular stone bridges. In recent years volunteers have rallied to refurbish and improve this truly spectacular network. Isle au Haut (see "Deer Isle") and the Schoodic Peninsula (see "East Hancock County") are also part of Acadia National Park, but they are not located on Mount Desert Island and are much quieter, less traveled areas.

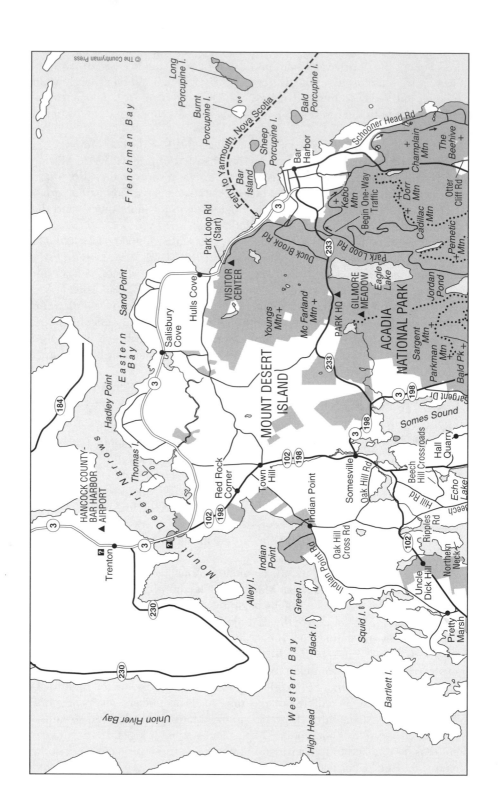

© The Countryman Press

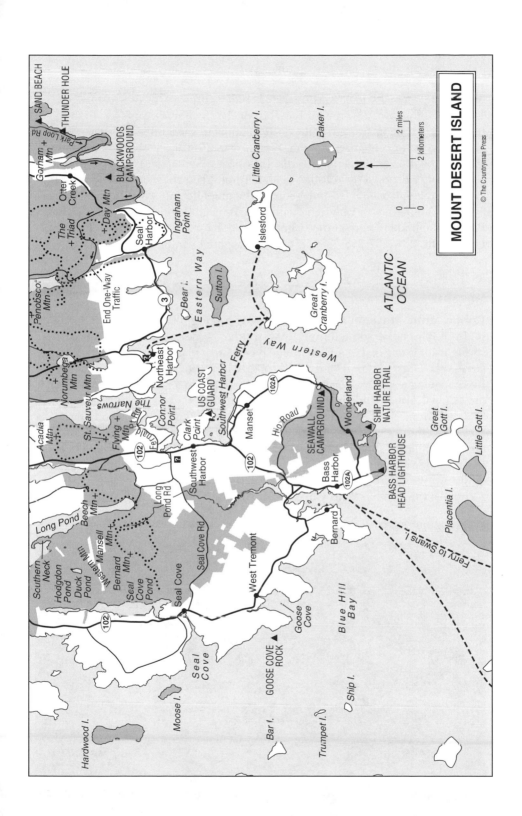

MOUNT DESERT ISLAND

© The Countryman Press

N

0   2 miles

0   2 kilometers

ATLANTIC OCEAN

SAND BEACH
THUNDER HOLE
Park Loop Rd
Gorham Mtn
Otter Creek
BLACKWOODS CAMPGROUND
The Triad
Day Mtn
Penobscot Mtn
Seal Harbor
End One-Way Traffic
Ingraham Point
3
Bear I.
Eastern Way
Sutton I.
Little Cranberry I.
Islesford
Baker I.
Norumbega Mtn
Northeast Harbor
The Narrows
St. Sauveur Mtn
Acadia Mtn
Flying Mtn
Clark Point
US COAST GUARD
Southwest Harbor
Ferry
Great Cranberry I.
Western Way
Fernald Pt Rd
Connor Point
102
Manset
102A
Hio Road
SEAWALL CAMPGROUND
Wonderland
SHIP HARBOR NATURE TRAIL
Great Gott I.
Little Gott I.
Long Pond
Beech Mtn
Western Mtn
Mansell Mtn
Bernard Mtn
Hodgdon Pond
Duck Pond
Seal Cove Pond
Southern Neck
Long Pond Rd
Seal Cove Rd
102
Southwest Harbor
102
West Tremont
Seal Cove
Bass Harbor
102A
BASS HARBOR HEAD LIGHTHOUSE
Bernard
Placentia I.
Ferry to Swans I.
Hardwood I.
Moose I.
Bar I.
Seal Cove
GOOSE COVE ROCK
Goose Cove
Trumpet I.
Ship I.
Blue Hill Bay

FEES The entrance fee for vehicles is $20 for a weekly pass. For individuals on foot or bicycle, the fee is $5 for a weekly pass.

GUIDANCE The park maintains its visitor center (207-288-3338; www.nps.gov/acad) at Hulls Cove, a section of Bar Harbor. It's open mid-Apr.–Oct. In mid-June–Aug. 31, hours are 8–6 daily; during shoulder seasons, 8–4:30. The glass-and-stone visitor center, set atop 50 steps, shows a 15-minute introductory film and sells books, guides, and postcards. Pick up a free map and a copy of the current *Acadia's Beaver Log* (a listing of all naturalist activities), and sign up for the various programs scheduled June–Sep. at the amphitheaters in Blackwoods and Seawall Campgrounds. Children of all ages are eligible to join the park's Junior Ranger Program; inquire at the visitor center. The park headquarters at Eagle Lake on Rt. 233 (207-288-3338) is open throughout winter, daily 8–4:30.

✳ To See

MUSEUM AND GARDENS

Robert Abbe Museum at Sieur de Monts Spring (207-288-3519), 2 miles south of Bar Harbor, posted from Rt. 3 (south of Jackson Laboratory). The spring itself is encased in a Florentine-style canopy placed there by park founder George B. Dorr, who purchased the property to prevent enterprising islanders from opening a springwater business here. It stands in a garden, and beyond is the original **Abbe Museum**, open mid-May–mid-Oct., daily 9–4. On exhibit at Sieur de Monts are Dr. Robert Abbe's original collections of stone and bone tools from the archaic periods. Admission to this octagonal, Mediterranean-style building, built by Abbe in 1928, is $2 adults, $1 ages 6–15, or free with a ticket from the downtown museum. The rest of Abbe's collection is exhibited in the downtown Bar Harbor Abbe Museum (see "Bar Harbor"). The park museum is accessible through the **Wild Gardens of Acadia**, a pleasant walk where more

OVERLOOKING FRENCHMAN'S BAY

Kim Grant

than 300 species of native plants are on display with labels. The **Park Nature Center** here (open mid-June–Sep., daily 9–5) has displays on park wildlife; children can record the animals they have seen in the center's logbook.

✳ To Do

BICYCLING The more than 50 miles of broken-stone carriage roads make for good mountain biking. Several outfitters in Bar Harbor (see "Bar Harbor") rent equipment and can help you find good trails.

Kim Grant

BICYCLING ON THE CARRIAGE ROADS

CAMPING The two campgrounds within the park are Blackwoods, 5 miles south of Bar Harbor, and Seawall, on the quiet side of the island, 4 miles south of Southwest Harbor. Both are in woods and close to ocean. One vehicle, up to six people, and two tents are allowed on each site. Neither campground has utility hook-ups. Facilities include comfort stations, cold running water, a dump station, picnic tables, and fire rings. Showers and a camping store are within 0.5 mile of each. There are also five group campsites at each campground, which must be reserved through the park. Call 207-288-3338 for details.

Blackwoods (207-288-3274), open all year. Reservations required May–Oct. through the National Park Reservation Service (1-800-365-2267). Cost of sites is $20 per night during the reservation period; fees vary during the off-season.

Seawall (207-244-3600), near Southwest Harbor, open late May–late Sep. Sites at Seawall are meted out on a first-come, first-served basis. Get there early because a line forms; as campers check out, others are checked in. Cost is $20 with a vehicle, $14 if you walk in.

HIKING The park is a mecca for hikers. Several detailed maps are sold at the visitor center, which is also the source of an information sheet that profiles two dozen trails within the park. These range in difficulty from the **Jordan Pond Loop Trail** (a 3.3-mile path around the pond) to the rugged **Precipice Trail** (1.5 miles, very steep, with iron rungs as ladders). There are 17 trails to mountain summits on Mount Desert. **Acadia Mountain** on the island's west side (2 miles round-trip) commands the best view of Somes Sound and the islands. The **Ship Harbor** on Rt. 102A (near Bass Harbor) offers a nature trail that winds along the shore and into the woods; it's also a great birding spot.

HORSE-DRAWN CARRIAGE TOURS
♿ **Carriages in the Park** (207-276-3622), Wildwood Stables, 2 miles south of the Jordan Pond House. One- and 2-hour horse-drawn tours in multiple-seat carriages are offered six times a day.

PARK LOOP ROAD

The 27-mile Loop Road is the prime tourist route within the park. There is a weekly fee of $20 per car on the road.

The Loop Road officially begins at the visitor center but may be entered at many points along the way. Most of the road is one-way, so be alert to how traffic is flowing. Places of interest along the Loop Road include Sieur de Monts Spring, a stop that could include the Wild Gardens of Acadia, the Abbe Museum, and Park Nature Center as well as the covered spring itself; Sand Beach, which is actually made up of ground shells and sand and is a great beach to walk down and from which to take a dip, if you don't mind 50-degree water (there are changing rooms and lifeguards); Thunder Hole, where the water rushes in and out of a small cave, which you can view from behind a railing; Jordan Pond House, popular for afternoon tea and pop-overs; and Cadillac Mountain. From Cadillac's smooth summit (accessible by car), you look north across Frenchman's Bay dotted with the Porcupine Islands, which look like giant stepping-stones, and way beyond Down East. To the west, Jericho and Blue Hill Bays are directly below, and beyond the Blue Hill Peninsula you see Penobscot Bay and the Camden Hills. Many visitors come at sunrise, but sunset can be far more spectacular, a sight not to be missed.

A VIEW FROM PARK LOOP ROAD

Christina Tree

RANGER PROGRAMS A wide variety of programs—from guided nature walks and hikes to birding talks, sea cruises, and evening lectures—are offered throughout the season. Ask at the visitor center for a current schedule.

ROCK CLIMBING Acadia National Park is the most popular place to climb in Maine; famous climbs include **the Precipice**, **Goat Head**, and **Otter Cliffs**. See "Bar Harbor" for guide services.

SWIMMING Within Acadia there is supervised swimming at **Sand Beach**, 4 miles south of Bar Harbor, and at **Echo Lake**, a warmer, quieter option, 11 miles west (see "The Quiet Side").

WINTER SPORTS More than 50 miles of carriage roads at Acadia National Park are maintained as ski touring and snowshoeing trails. Request the *Winter Activities* leaflet from the park headquarters (write to Superintendent, Acadia National Park, P.O. Box 177, Bar Harbor 04609).

BAR HARBOR AND ELLSWORTH

Bar Harbor is the island's resort town, one of New England's largest clusters of hotels, motels, inns, B&Bs, restaurants, and shops—all within easy reach of the park visitor center and main entrance on the one hand, and an array of water excursions and the ferries to Nova Scotia on the other.

Ellsworth is the shire town and shopping hub of Hancock County, a place with a split personality: the old brick downtown blocks along and around the Union River and its falls, and the strip of malls and outlets along the mile between the junction of Rts. 1A and 1 and Rts. 1 and 3. If you're coming down Rt. 1A from Bangor, you miss the old part of town entirely, and it's well worth backtracking. Downtown Ellsworth offers the restored art deco Grand Auditorium, several good restaurants, and rewarding shopping, as well a sense of the lumbering-boom era in which the Colonel Black Mansion, arguably the most elegant in Maine, was built.

The 6 miles of Rt. 3 between Ellsworth and Bar Harbor are lined with a mix of commercial attractions (some of which are vacation savers if you are here with children in fog or rain), 1920s motor courts and 1960s motels, newer motor inns and hotels.

In Bar Harbor itself shops and restaurants line Cottage, Mount Desert, West, and Main Streets, which slope to the Town Pier and to the Shore Path, a mile walk between mansions and the bay. On sunny days most visitors tend to be out in the park or on the water; half an hour before sunset (the time is announced each day in local publications), folks gather on and near the top of Cadillac Mountain for a show that can be truly spectacular. Dinner reservations are advisable because everyone then converges on restaurants at the same time, then walks around; most shops stay open until 9 PM.

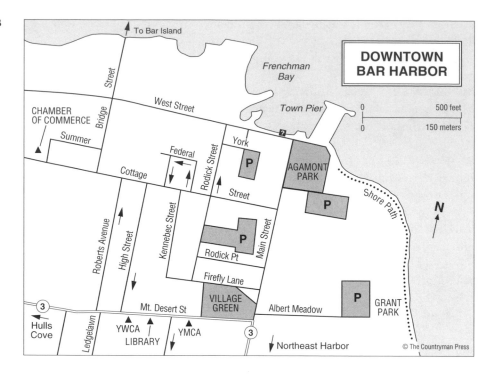

To Bar Island

Frenchman Bay

DOWNTOWN BAR HARBOR

Street

West Street

CHAMBER OF COMMERCE

Bridge

Summer

Town Pier

0   500 feet
0   150 meters

York

Cottage

Federal

Rodick Street

P

AGAMONT PARK

Shore Path

Street

P

N

Roberts Avenue

High Street

Kennebec Street

P

Main Street

Rodick Pt

Firefly Lane

VILLAGE GREEN

Albert Meadow

P

GRANT PARK

3

Mt. Desert St

Hulls Cove

Ledgelawn

YWCA

LIBRARY

YMCA

3

Northeast Harbor

© The Countryman Press

GUIDANCE Bar Harbor Chamber of Commerce (year-round 207-288-5103 or 1-888-540-9990; www.barharbormaine.com), P.O. Box 158, 93 Cottage St., Bar Harbor 04609, maintains year-round and seasonal information booths.

Mount Desert Island Information Center (207-288-3411) is open daily mid-May–mid-Oct. (9–8 during high season) on Thompson Island, just after Rt. 3 crosses the bridge. This is the island's most helpful walk-in center. It offers restrooms, national park information, and help with lodging reservations on all parts of the island, and keeps track of vacancies at Seawall Campground.

Ellsworth Chamber of Commerce (207-667-5584 or 207-667-2617; www .ellsworth.com), 163 High St., Ellsworth 04605, maintains an information center in the Ellsworth Shopping Center on the Rt. 1/3 strip; look for Burger King.

Also see "Acadia National Park."

GETTING THERE *By air:* **Colgan Air** (1-800-428-4322; www.colganair.com) has been absorbed by U.S. Airways but still serves the **Hancock County & Bar Harbor Airport** in Trenton (between Ellsworth and Bar Harbor) from Boston and Rockland. Rental cars are available at the airport. **Bangor International Airport** (207-947-0384; www.flybangor.com), 26 miles north of Ellsworth, offers connections with most American cities.

By boat: **"The Cat"** (207-288-3395 or 1-888-249-7245; www.catferry.com). With this high-speed ferry the trip to Nova Scotia now takes just 2½ hours (the old

Bluenose ferry took 6 hours), and the boat departs both Bar Harbor and Yarmouth twice daily, making a day trip feasible (though rather pricey).

By private boat: For details about moorings, contact the Bar Harbor harbormaster at 207-288-5571.

By bus: **Concord Trailways** (1-800-639-3317; www.concordtrailways.com) offers unbeatable year-round service from Boston's Logan Airport and South Station (5 hours) to Bangor. **Vermont Transit** (1-800-451-3292) runs one bus a day from Bangor at 5:25 PM, with a 6:45 arrival. It returns to Bangor at 6:30 AM. This service runs from the end of May through Oct.

By car: From Brunswick and points south (including Boston and New York), the shortest route is I-295 to I-95 in Augusta, to Bangor to I-395 to Rt. 1A south to Ellsworth. A slightly slower route that includes some coastal views is I-95 to Augusta, then Rt. 3 east to Belfast (stop for a swim at Lake St. George State Park), and north on Rt. 1 to Ellsworth.

GETTING AROUND Jump on the **Island Explorer** buses operated by Downeast Transportation (207-288-4573; www.exploreacadia.com). The buses travel eight routes around the island, are big and propane powered, carry bikes front and back, and are entirely free. They circulate through the park and the island's towns late June–Oct., and will stop on request wherever it's safe. Hikers take note: You can get off at one trailhead and be picked up at another. Bus schedules are timed to coincide with ferry departures to Nova Scotia, Swans Island, and the Cranberry Isles.

PARKING In high season, parking here is a pain. Note the lots on our Downtown Bar Harbor map. Much of the lodging is downtown (with parking), and the village is compact. Park and walk.

BEAR ISLAND

Nancy English

WHEN TO COME Since this is the most crowded summer place on the coast, everyone who lives nearby, from Portland north, prefers a visit in the off-seasons, preferably early fall. Although the Island Explorer bus's schedule is reduced and the nights are chilly, the scenery is spectacular and the museums are still open. Winter is quiet indeed.

✳ To See

In Bar Harbor

✎ **College of the Atlantic** (COA; 207-288-5015 or 207-288-5395; www.coa.edu), Rt. 3. Housed in the original Acadia National Park headquarters, the **George B. Dorr Museum of Natural History** is a worthwhile stop (open Mon.–Sat. 10–5 in summer, varying days and hours off-season). $3.50 adults, $2.50 seniors, $1.50 teens, $1 children ages 3 and older. Exhibits include the skeleton of a rare true-beaked whale and dioramas of plants and animals of coastal Maine. The **Ethel H. Blum Gallery** (same hours), with changing exhibits, is also worth checking. Founded in 1969, COA is a liberal-arts college specializing in ecological studies. Its waterside acreage, an amalgam of four large summer estates, is now a handsome campus for 230 students.

Bar Harbor Historical Society (207-288-0000; www.barharborhistorical.org), 33 Ledgelawn Ave. Open June–Oct., Mon.–Sat. 1–4. In winter, open by appointment. Free. Well worth finding. A fascinating collection of early photographs of local hotels, Gilded Era clothing, books by local authors and about Bar Harbor, and the story of the big fire of 1947.

In Ellsworth

Colonel Black Mansion (Woodlawn) (207-667-8461; www.woodlawnmuseum .com), W. Main St. (Rt. 172). Open May–Oct., Tue.–Sat. 10–4:30, Sun. 1–4. $7.50 adults, $3 children over 5. An outstanding Georgian mansion built as a wedding present in 1862 by John Black, who had just married the daughter of the local agent for a Philadelphia land developer, owner of this region. Supposedly the bricks were brought by sea from Philadelphia, and it took Boston workmen 3 years to complete the home. It is now open to the public, furnished just as it was when the Black family used it, with a carriage house full of old carriages and sleighs.

Birdsacre Wildlife Sanctuary (207-667-8460), Rt. 3. Old homestead and gift shop open May–Oct., daily 10–4; sanctuary open year-round. Token admission. Don't miss this exceptional place: a 160-acre nature preserve that is a memorial to Cordelia Stanwood (1865–1958), a pioneer ornithologist, nature photographer, and writer. The old homestead (1850) contains a collection of Stanwood's photos.

The Telephone Museum (207-667-9491; www.thetelephonemuseum.org), 166 Winkumpaugh Rd., marked from Rt. 1A north of Ellsworth. Open July–Sep., Thu.–Sun. 1–4. $4 adults, $2 children. The evolution of telephone service, from 1876 to 1983 (when the museum opened), is the subject of this quirky museum and its varied equipment.

FOR FAMILIES ✎ **Acadia National Park Junior Ranger Programs** (207-288-3338) are the best thing going here for youngsters: First complete the activities in the Junior Ranger booklet, then join a ranger-led program or walk to receive a Junior Ranger pin.

✔ **Family Nature Camp at College of the Atlantic** (see above) offers six 1-week programs in which families live in dorms, dine together, and spend days on field trips led by naturalists in Acadia National Park.

Rt. 3 attractions
You'll find waterslides, mini golf, and go-carts, as well as:

✔ **Mount Desert Oceanarium** (207-288-5005; www.theoceanarium.com). Open 9–5 daily, except Sun., late May late Oct. $9–12 adults, $5–7 ages 4–12, depending on what you want to see and do. Tour the lobster hatchery and the Thomas Bay Marsh Walk.

✔ **Acadia Zoological Park** (207-667-3244), Rt. 3, Trenton. Open spring–Christmas. $7.50 adults, $6 ages 3–12. Fifteen acres house native and exotic animals, as well as a rain forest display.

✔ **The Maine Lumberjack Show** (207-667-0067; www.mainelumberjack.com), Rt. 3, Trenton. Late June–Labor Day, nightly at 7. The show includes ax throwing, log rolling, speed climbing, and more.

✳ To Do

AIRPLANE RIDES Acadia Air (207-667-5534), Rt. 3, Hancock County Airport, Trenton. Flight instruction, aircraft rentals, and sightseeing flights.

Island Soaring Glider Rides (207-667-SOAR), also at the airport, offers motorless soaring flights.

BICYCLING The network of gravel carriage roads constructed by John D. Rockefeller Jr. in 1915 lends itself particularly well to mountain biking. In Bar Harbor, **Bar Harbor Bicycle Shop** (207-288-3886; www.barharborbike.com), 141 Cottage St., is the oldest bike outfitter in town and still rents only bikes: mountain, tandem, and everything that goes with them. **Acadia Bike & Canoe Company** (207 288 9605), 48 Cottage St., also rents every kind of bike and support item.

BIRDING Downeast Nature Tours (207-288-8128; www.mainebirding.net) offers guided bird tours daily. For special programs led by park naturalists, consult *Acadia's Beaver Log*, available at the park visitor center.

BOAT EXCURSIONS A number of cruises are available daily in summer. **Bar Harbor Ferry Co.** (207-288-2984; www.barharborferry.com) sails from the Bar Harbor Inn Pier, crossing Frenchman Bay to Winter Harbor several times a day; bring a bicycle, spend the day, and bike around Schoodic. **Lulu Lobster Boat Ride** (207-963-2341; www.lululobsterboat.com) offers sightseeing and storytelling (*le capitaine parle français*) on Frenchman Bay for a maximum of six passengers at a time. **Dive-in-Theater** (207-288-3483, www.divered.com) operates *The Seal*, an excursion boat from which passengers can watch Diver Ed (through an underwater camera) probe the depths of Frenchman Bay, and then get to touch what he fetches.

✐ ♿ **Abbe Museum** (207-288-3519; www.abbemuseum.org), 26 Mount Desert St. Open mid-May–mid-Oct. daily 9–5, off-season Thu.–Sun. 9–5, and closed in Jan. $6 per adult, $2 ages 6–15, under 6 free. Native Americans are free, too. The Abbe's new facility in the heart of Bar Harbor, facing the village green, is more than eight times the size of its original, seasonal facility. The museum is dedicated to showcasing the cultures of Maine's Wabanaki, the 7,000 members of the Penobscot, Passamaquoddy, Micmac, and Maliseet tribes who live in Maine. The permanent collection of 50,000 objects ranges from 10,000-year-old artifacts to exquisite basketry and crafts from several centuries. The orientation gallery and time line begin with the present and draw visitors back slowly and skillfully through 10,000 years to the core, a circular tower, the "Circle of Four Directions." Exhibits include a fabricated copy of the 1794 treaty between Massachusetts and the Wabanaki that deeded much of Maine to its Native people. Much of the museum space is devoted to major changing exhibits.

BREWERY TOURS Atlantic Brewing Company (207-288-BEER; www.atlantic brewing.com), in Town Hill (across from the Town Hill Market), has re-created an indoor–outdoor European brewery-pub. Daily tours and tastings at 2, 3, and 4.

Bar Harbor Brewing Co. and Sodaworks (207-288-4592; www.barharbor brewing.com), Otter Creek Rd., 1 mile north of Blackwoods Campground, also offers tours, from the end of June through August, between 3:30 and 5.

THE *MARGARET TODD* AND AN ERRATIC BOULDER

Nancy English

CANOEING AND SEA KAYAKING
Most ponds on Mount Desert offer easy access. **Long Pond**, the largest lake on the island, has three access points. Boats can be launched at **Echo Lake** from **Ike's Point**, just off Rt. 102. **Seal Cove Pond** is less used and accessible from fire roads north of Seal Cove. **Bass Harbor Marsh** is another possibility at high tide. Canoe rental sources offer suggestions and directions. **National Park Canoe Rentals** (207-244-5854) on Long Pond near Somesville offers tours as well as rentals, including kayaks. If you are not an experienced kayaker, be sure to take a guided tour. In Bar Harbor we can recommend **Coastal Kayaking Tours** (207-288-9605),

48 Cottage St.; put-in spots vary depending on the day's wind and weather. Bar Harbor outiftters include **Aquaterra Adventures** (207-288-0007), 1 West St., and **National Park Sea Kayak Tours** (207-288-0342), 38 Cottage St. **Loon Bay Kayak** (207-288-0099) in Trenton also offers tours, rents kayaks, and will deliver to your location for a minimal fee.

GOLF **Kebo Valley Club** (207-288-3000), Rt. 233, Bar Harbor. Open daily May–Oct. Eighteen holes. "Oldest golf grounds in America," since 1892. **Bar Harbor Golf Course** (207-667-7505), Rts. 3 and 204, Trenton. Eighteen holes.

FISHING Several charter boats offer deep-sea fishing. The **Bar Harbor Ferry Company** operates a party fishing boat (207-288-4584).

HIKING See "Acadia National Park."

HORSEBACK RIDING **Eochaidh Stables** (207-288-2519; www.northisle.com), Hulls Cove. Pronounced *yaw-KEE*. Joan Sullivan and David Andrews offer hour-long trail rides on 35 acres of meadows and woods bordering Acadia National Park; novices welcome.

HORSE-DRAWN CARRIAGE TOURS See "Acadia National Park."

ROCK CLIMBING **Acadia Mountain Guides** (207-288-8186; www.acadia mountainguides.com) and **Atlantic Climbing School** (207-288-2521) offer in-struction and guiding for beginner through advanced climbers. (Also see "Acadia National Park.")

"THE BUBBLES" AT JORDAN POND

Nancy English

SAILING The *Margaret Todd* (207-288-4585) sails from the Bar Harbor pier late June–early Oct. This new 151-foot four-masted schooner, designed and built by Captain Steve Pagels, cruises through Frenchman Bay several times a day in high season, less frequently in slower weeks.

SWIMMING ✿ **Lake Wood** near Hull's Cove is a pleasant freshwater beach, ideal for children. Also see "Acadia National Park."

WHALE-WATCHING The big operator is **Bar Harbor Whale Watch Co.** (207-288-2386; www.barharborwhales.com), 1 West St., Bar Harbor, which also offers seal-watching and lobstering tours. Bring a jacket, sunblock, binoculars, and a camera. Ask how long it takes to get out to the whales and about weather—and sea—conditions on the day you book.

✳ Lodging

Many of Bar Harbor's nearly 2,400 beds, ranging from 1920s motor courts to large chain hotels and motels, are strung along Rt. 3, north of the walk-around town—where a few dozen surviving summer mansions are now B&Bs commanding top dollar. Reservations are not as crucial as they used to be, with a surge in the number of rooms here, but still a good idea. We cannot claim to have inspected every room in town, but we have checked out the most appealing options.

DINING AT ULLIKANA B&B

Nancy English

WATER-VIEW BED & BREAKFASTS

In Bar Harbor 04609
Ullikana Bed & Breakfast (207-288-9552; www.ullikana.com), 16 The Field. Open May–Oct. This is our top pick in downtown Bar Harbor, steps from both Main Street and the Shore Path, yet with an away-from-it-all feel. Innkeeper Helene Harton combines a rare flair for decorating with a genuine warmth that sets guests at ease. Helene and her husband (and genial co-innkeeper), Roy Kasindorf, bought Ullikana, a vintage-1885 Tudor-style summer mansion, in 1990 and transformed it into such an attractive inn that the owners of the neighboring Yellow House, another classic Bar Harbor "cottage," actually asked if they would like to buy that, too. Breakfast (perhaps a berry-stuffed soufflé pancake, light and delicious) is served on the terrace overlooking the water or in Ullikana's attractive dining room. The 10 guest rooms—all with private bath, 3 with fireplace—in Ullikana itself are each decorated with imagination and taste (Audrey's Room simply sings), but we also like the crisp, airy old-style feel of the Yellow House. $160–295 in high season, varying with room size and view.

Balance Rock Inn (207-288-2610 or 1-800-753-0494; www.barharbor vacations.com), 21 Albert Meadow. The original mansion, built in 1903 for a Scottish railroad tycoon, is augmented by a heated pool and a matching new wing with a total of 14 individual rooms, most with ocean view, private balcony, whirlpool bath, and phone; some have a fireplace. The three suites have a kitchen, living room, and sauna in addition to the other basics. In high season a standard room with breakfast is $195–355; with ocean view it's $275–495; expect $495–625 for a suite. From $95 in early May, when suites begin at $195.

⚓ **The Shore Path Cottage** (207-288-0643; www.shorepathcottage .com), 24 Atlantic Ave. Open May–Oct. Roberta Chester has owned this delightful Bar Harbor "cottage" since 1973, and the feel is that of a family home rather than a formal B&B. The dining room, however, has a kind of authentic elegance that can't be imitated, with lovely china and decor. Guest rooms (all with private bath, a few with claw-foot tub) are named for the youngsters who grew up in them. Roberta is herself a writer, and the house is filled with books and art, along with a classic video library. Both kosher and vegetarian diets are honored here, and both solo travelers and children are particularly welcome. $120–250.

& **The Bass Cottage Inn** (207-288-1234; www.basscottage.com), 14 The Field. Open May to the beginning of Nov., this 10-room inn was completely redone before reopening in 2004, adding whirlpool tubs, gas fireplaces, and TVs with DVD players (which the innkeeper will remove if you ask). With a culinary degree to attest to

her skill, Teri Anderholm makes scrambled eggs with smoked trout for breakfast, served in a bright sunporch, and maki rolls for afternoon hors d'oeuvres. She and her husband, Jeff Anderholm, run things smoothly in the handsome and comfortable inn, where rates range $185–340 in-season, less before and after.

OTHER DOWNTOWN B&BS

In Bar Harbor 04609
Manor House Inn (207-288-3759 or 1-800-437-0088; www.barharbor manorhouse.com), 106 West St. Open mid-April–Oct. No real water views, but a short walk from Bar Island. There are nine comfortable rooms with private bath in the vintage-1887 "Manor" with its rich woodwork. The full acre of landscaped grounds also includes the Chauffeur's Cottage with guest room and two suites, and two cottages with gas fireplace. $125–250 (less off-season) includes full breakfast and afternoon tea.

Seacroft Inn (207-288-4669 or 1-800-824-9694; www.seacroftinn.com), 18 Albert Meadow. Open year-round. Beverly and Dave Brown's gracious, many-gabled old "cottage" is sequestered on a quiet street, steps from the Shore Path. Extended stays are the norm; all seven rooms have a fridge and a microwave. $99–129 in-season, substantially less off; a two-bedroom apartment, sleeping six, is $1,550 per week.

🐾 ⚓ **Primrose Inn** (207-288-4031 or 1-877-TIME-4-BH; www.primroseinn .com), 73 Mount Desert St. This is a spiffy 1878 stick-style "painted lady" Victorian summer cottage. The 10 guest rooms are bright with floral wallpaper and Victorian decor; several have gas fireplace, whirlpool tub, and private balcony. Children are welcome in the four one- and two-bedroom apartments with kitchenette and separate living/dining area. Rooms are $110–195 per couple including breakfast in high season; apartments are $650–1,100 per couple per week, plus $50 per extra guest. A dog is $75, and only in one apartment.

☃ ♂ Ledgelawn (207-288-4595 or 1-800-274-5335; www.barharbor vacations.com), 66 Mount Desert St. Open mid-May–Oct. A large, red-shingled classic turn-of-the-20th-century Bar Harbor "cottage" with 21 rooms filled with antique reproductions in the main house and 12 in the addition, which is designed to look like a Victorian carriage house. All rooms have a private bath, phone, and TV, and most have a fireplace. In July and Aug. guests have use of a swimming pool. Rates include a buffet breakfast made by the inn's Brazilian chef. $95–295 in high season, $75–195 before and after.

The Maples Inn (207-288-3443; www.maplesinn.com), 16 Roberts Ave. Open May–Oct. Innkeeper Tom Palumbo has a good reputation for the hospitality he offers in this pleasant 1903 house on a quiet side street within walking distance of shops and restaurants. The six rooms (all with private bath) are crisply decorated, furnished with a queen-sized bed, down comforter, and reading lamps, all looking spiffy. Red Oak, under the eaves, has its own small deck. Breakfasts are an event. $110–160 per couple; $70–110 off-season.

Canterbury Cottage (207-288-2112; www.canterburycottage.com), 12 Roberts Ave. Open year-round. Armando and Maria Ribeiro have pleasantly renovated this architectural-

ly interesting Victorian house (its original owner was the B&M stationmaster, and its architect specialized in railroad stations). Rooms are comfortably decorated, each with private bath. One has a small balcony. $100–125 double in-season includes breakfast served in the pretty dining room.

Cleftstone Manor (207-288-8086; www.cleftstone.com), 92 Eden St. Located a short drive from downtown, this 1880 mansion once owned by wealthy summer visitors has been an inn for 50 years. Lately it's been undergoing a renovation, but it still has (good) quirks and a wide range of rooms. Joseph Pulitzer summered here, and a few of the original antiques are still in place, like two crystal chandeliers in the dining room. Seventeen rooms with private bath, five with fireplace. In-season rates $100–225, less off-season.

Anne's White Columns Inn (207-288-5357 or 1-800-321-6379; www.anneswhitecolumns.com), 57 Mount Desert St. Built in the 1930s as a Christian Science church, hence the columns. The 10 rooms have private bath, air-conditioning, and cable TV. $100–150 July–Aug.; less before and after, including full breakfast and afternoon wine and cheese.

ᕫ Mira Monte Inn and Suites (207-288-4263 or 1-800-553-5109; www.miramonte.com), 69 Mount Desert St. Open May–mid-Oct. Bar Harbor native Marian Burns offers 13 comfortable guest rooms and two suites in her gracious 1864 mansion, many with a private balcony overlooking the deep, peaceful lawn in back or the gardens on the side. All rooms have private bath, phone, clock-radio, and TV; some have a gas fireplace. Rates include a full breakfast and afternoon refreshments. $165–285 for rooms and suites; $95–104 off-season.

HOTELS AND MOTELS

In Bar Harbor 04609

✒ ♿ **Bar Harbor Inn** (207-288-3351 or 1-800-248-3351; www.barharbor inn.com), Newport Dr. Open Mar.–Nov. With 153 units, this landmark hotel gets its share of groups, but its downtown waterside location is unbeatable. It's also a genuinely gracious hotel, with a 24-hour front desk, bellhops, a restaurant, and room service. The hotel-sized lobby with its formal check-in desk and seating near the fire is quite grand, the venue for complimentary lemonade and cookies in summer, hot cider in fall. The Reading Room Restaurant (see *Dining Out*), begun as an elite men's social club in 1887, offers fine dining with water views. The 51 guest rooms in the Main Inn were the first new hotel rooms available in town after the 1947 fire. Of these, 43 were completely rebuilt in 1998; balconies, jetted tubs, and fireplaces were added. The grounds also include a 64-unit Oceanfront Lodge with private balconies on the bay, and the Newport Building—38 equally comfortable rooms without views. All rooms have phone, cable TV, and access to the pool, Jacuzzi, fitness room, and 7 acres of manicured lawns on the water. Summer rates: $199–369, continental breakfast included.

Harborside Hotel & Marina (207-288-5033 or 1-800-328-5033; www .theharborsidehotel.com), 55 West St. Open May–Oct. Delightful views of the harbor and Porcupine Islands. Luxuriously furnished and accented with marble baths, many rooms and suites are equipped with full kitchens

Nancy English

BAR HARBOR INN

and some have fireplace in the master bedroom and Jacuzzi on the porch. On-site marina, waterfront dining at the **Pier** restaurant, outdoor heated pool, hot tub, exercise room, guest laundry, and business center. High season, standard rooms $175–325, suites $225–850; off-season $99–150, $175–$250.

✒ **Wonder View Inn** (207-288-3358 or 1-888-439-8439; www.wonder viewinn.com), P.O. Box 25, 50 Eden St. Open mid-May–mid-Oct. Children are welcome in the 79-unit motel built on 14 acres, the site of an estate once owned by Mary Roberts Rinehart, author of popular mystery stories. Near both the ferry terminal and downtown Bar Harbor, the motel overlooks Frenchman Bay and includes a swimming pool and the **Rinehart Dining Pavilion**, which serves breakfast and dinner. $99–219 in summer, less off-season. Most rooms have a balcony with an ocean view.

✒ **The Villager Motel** (207-288-3211 or 1-888-383-3211; www .acadia.net/villager), 207 Main St. This reasonably priced, middle-of-town, family-owned motel has done well and continues to provides immaculately clean and comfortable rooms. With a turquoise pool tucked into a back corner of the parking lot, and a friendly staff, this is the seasonal Bar Harbor stop for Vermont Transit. Summer rates $89–138, $59–79 off-season, $5 fee for children depending on season and age.

In Ellsworth 04605
🐾 ♪ **Twilite Motel** (207-667-8165 or 1-800-395-5097; www.twilitemotel .com) Rts. 1 and 3. Linda and Marv Snow keep things in perfect order at this motel, with flowers spilling out in between the 1950s-style but updated rooms, all with private bath and a little outdoor seating area. Coffee and baked goods are set out in the office in the morning. Rates $79–94, less off-season.

COTTAGES ♪ **Acadia Cottage Rentals** (207-288-3636; www.acadia .net/acadiarental) offers camps, cottages, private homes, and estates for a minimum of one week (Sat.–Sat.).

♪ **Emery's Cottages on the Shore** (207-288-3432 or 1-888-240-3432; www.emeryscottages.com), Sand Point Rd., Bar Harbor 04609. Open May–late Oct. In the family since 1961, these 22 cottages and an apartment on Frenchman Bay offer elec-

tric heat, shower, and cable TV; 14 have a kitchen. Linens, dishes, and cooking utensils provided. Private pebble beach. Telephone available for local calls. No pets. $550–1,025 per week late June–late Aug.; $425–750 late Aug.–Oct.; less in May and June.

PUBLIC CAMPGROUNDS **Lamoine State Park** (207-667-4778), Rt. 184, Lamoine. Open mid-May–mid-Oct. Minutes from busy Rt. 3 (between Ellsworth and Bar Harbor), this 55-acre waterside park offers a boat launch and 62 campsites (no hookups, but hot showers in a bathhouse), 2-night minimum, $20 per night for nonresidents in-season. Neighboring Lamoine Beach is great for skipping stones. *Note:* There are occasionally vacancies here in July and Aug. for when Acadia National Park campsites are full. (For reservations, phone 207-287-3824.)

Also see *To Do* in "Acadia National Park." There are more than a dozen commercial campgrounds in this area; check local listings.

✳ Where to Eat
DINING OUT All listings are in Bar Harbor unless otherwise noted

TWILITE MOTEL

Nancy English

The Burning Tree (207-288-9331), Rt. 3, Otter Creek. Open June– Columbus Day 5–10; closed Tue., also Mon. after Labor Day. Reservations a must. Admired for its fresh fish and organically grown produce, imaginatively prepared. Dine inside or on a lattice-enclosed porch on a wide choice of seafood, chicken, and vegetable entrées, no red meat. A favorite entrée is yellowfin tuna served rare with ginger tamari and wasabi-lime sauce ($25). Entrées from $18.50.

& **Café This Way** (207-288-4483), 14 Mount Desert St. Open seasonally for breakfast and dinner. Tucked back off the street, just off the village green, this is a winner. Start dinner with lobster, crab, and shrimp spring rolls ($10), or a fig and blue cheese pizza ($7), followed by grilled tuna, medium rare, served with sautéed apples, honey, and smoked shrimp ($19). Entrées $16–23. Full liquor license. Reservations a good idea. Breakfast is just as good.

George's Restaurant (207-288-4505; www.georgesbarharbor.com), 7 Stephen's Lane (just off Main St. behind the First National Bank). Open mid-June–late Oct. Dinner 5:30–10. Reservations, please. Creative, fresh, sporadically Greek cuisine in a summery house with organdy curtains. Extensive choice of appetizers, grazers, and entrées. The mustard shrimp are revered, as is the lobster strudel. Prix fixe for a three-course meal is $25–40, depending on choices.

Cleonice (207-664-7554; www.cleonice.com), 112 Main St., Ellsworth. Open year-round for dinner, lunch in summer Mon.–Sat. Chef Rich Hansen takes seafood into the Mediterranean here, with tapas like scungilli salad, made with Maine periwinkles, and

grilled sardines. Dinner could be baked cod with lobster roe, shallots, vodka, and cream sauce ($19.75), or a classic Turkish vegetarian kofte. Wines suggested. The dark wood bar adds to the illusion of being farther south and east.

♪ **Jordan Pond House** (207-276-3316), Park Loop Rd., Seal Harbor. Open mid-May–mid-Oct. for lunch and tea 11:30–6 in summer, ending earlier off-season, and for dinner 6–9. Reservations advised. First opened in the 1870s, this landmark was beautifully rebuilt after a 1979 fire, with dining rooms overlooking the pond and mountains. It's best known for popovers and outdoor tea (see *Afternoon Tea*) but is pleasant and least crowded at dinner (jackets suggested). Children's menu and half portions available. Dinner entrées $10.25–18.

& **Havana** (207-288-CUBA), 318 Main St. Open from 5:30 nightly; reservations suggested. The menu changes weekly, the accent ranges from the Caribbean to Africa, and people love it. Entrées ($18–27) have included Calle Ocho pork chops with a chipotle glaze, and yellowfin tuna with Thai pesto.

Galyn's (207-288-9706), 17 Main St. Lunch and dinner. Easy to miss among the shops near the bottom of Main St., this is bigger than it looks, with dining rooms upstairs and down, and one of the best bets in town. Try the crabcakes or Frenchman Bay stew. Entrées $17–19.

& **Café Bluefish** (207-288-3696), 122 Cottage St. Dark wood, books, cloth napkins patterned with varying designs, and mismatched antique china create a pleasant atmosphere. Chef-owner Bobbie Lynn Hutchins, a fourth-generation Bar Harbor native, specializes in chicken, vegetarian, and seafood entrées, plus dinner strudels. $16.95–26.95.

Maggie's Restaurant (207-288-9007), 6 Summer St., off Cottage (corner of Bridge). Open June–Oct., Mon.–Sat. 5–9:30. Maggie O'Neil worked on commercial draggers and sold fish to local restaurants before opening this place in 1987. Most vegetables and herbs are grown on Maggie's own farm, and the vegetarian dishes are a point of pride. Lobster crêpes inspire praise, and a Maine shrimp, cherrystone clam, mussel, and potato stew with chorizo and saffron keeps you warm. Entrées $17–25.

The Reading Room (207-288-3351), Bar Harbor Inn, Newport Dr. Opened in 1887 as an elite men's club, the horseshoe-shaped formal dining room commands a splendid harbor view; frequent piano music at dinner. Open for all three meals, specializing in daily lobster bakes on the outdoor terrace. Dinner entrées range from a Dijon-roasted rack of lamb to lobster pie (market price). $20–31. A Sunday brunch buffet is served 11:30–2:30 ($24 adults, $12 children).

124 Cottage Street (207-288-4383). Pleasant, flowery atmosphere with a garden right behind the dining room. Linguine with creamy pesto sauce and vegetables or smoked salmon is one entrée; another is seafood Veracruz, with shrimp and scallops ($21). Lobsters and a daily fish special. Entrées $17–25.

🍴 ♿ **Poor Boy's Gourmet** (207-288-4148), 300 Main St. Open for dinner from 4:30 nightly. Chef-owner Kathleen Field provides a decent dining experience at reasonable prices. Choices range from vegetarian entrées ($10.95) to a full lobster dinner—

including brownie à la mode—for $16.95. Early-bird specials. Wine and beer.

✈ **Testa's** (207-288-3327), 53 Main St. Open 8 AM–11 PM, June–Oct., when the family moves to its Palm Beach restaurant. In Bar Harbor since 1934. Extensive menu, including Italian and seafood specialties. Dinner entrées $14.95–26.95. Early-bird and children's menu.

LOBSTER POUNDS Lobster pounds are the best places to eat lobster. The easiest to find are the clutch around the Trenton Bridge on Rt. 3. The **Trenton Bridge Lobster Pound** (207-667-2977), open in-season 8–8, year-round 8–5, has been in George Gascon's family a long time, and the view is great.

♿ **Bar Harbor Lobster Bakes** (207-288-5031), Rt. 3, Hulls Cove, is a twist on the traditional lobster pound. Reservations are a must. Choices are lobster or steak. Watch the lobsters being steamed with your potatoes and corn in the large steel cookers. $27 per person includes tip and tax.

Also see **Union River Lobster Pot** under *Eating Out*, as well as *Lobster Pounds* in "The Quiet Side."

EATING OUT

In Bar Harbor

Miguel's Mexican Restaurant (207-288-5117), 51 Rodick St. Open 5–10 nightly. Fajitas, blue corn crabcakes with roasted red pepper sauce. A crab and avocado salad with Mexican beer hit the spot late one evening. Lively but pleasant; friendly to solo diners.

Lompoc Café & Brew Pub (207-288-9392), 36 Rodick St. Open daily 11:30–3 and 5–9:30. Billed as the original home of Bar Harbor Real Ale (the Atlantic Brewing Company itself has outgrown its birthplace), this is a congenial oasis with an open knotty-pine dining room, plus porch and terrace tables by a bocce court. Entrée choices include pizzas and salads; live music on weekends.

✔ **Rosalie's Pizza** (207-288-5666), 46 Cottage St. Locals head for a booth at Rosalie's when they want pizza. Calzones, salads, and baked subs are also served, and an eggplant dinner is just $6.75.

✔ **Epi Sub & Pizza** (207-288-5853), 8 Cottage St. Open 10–7. Tops for food and value but zero atmosphere. Cafeteria-style salads, freshly baked calzones, pizza, quiche, and pasta, and crabmeat rolls. Clean and friendly; game machines in back.

✔ **Island Chowder House** (207-288-4905), 38 Cottage St. Open 11–late. A toy train circles just below the ceiling, and the atmosphere is bright; good service, homemade soups, thick chowder, seafood, pasta, and chicken. Bar. Early-bird dinners (4–6): $8.99.

Café This Way (207-288-4483), 14½ Mount Desert St. Open for breakfast 7–11. The menu ranges from scrambled tofu to steak and includes omelets, eggs Benedict with smoked salmon, and corned beef hash with poached eggs, among many other things.

Jordan's Restaurant, 80 Cottage St. Open 5 AM–2 PM. Under David Paine's ownership (since 1976), this remains an old-style diner: breakfast all day, specializing in blueberry pancakes and muffins and a wide variety of three-egg omelets. The place to fuel up after watching the sunrise from Cadillac Mountain.

Nancy English

UNION RIVER LOBSTER POT

In Ellsworth

🌿 ✔ **Union River Lobster Pot** (207-667-5077), behind Rooster Brothers at the western edge of Ellsworth. Open daily June–mid-Sep., 11:30–8:30, dinner only in Sep. Brian Langley owns this pleasant riverside restaurant and serves a full menu, including St. Louis–style ribs, but the specialty is seafood cooked four ways. Leave room for pie. Beer and wine, and an eagle overhead.

Maidee's (207-667-6554), 156 Main St. Open Mon.–Sat. from 4 PM. At the core of this exotic restaurant and lounge is a 1932 Worcester Deluxe diner, but it's been expanded and transformed. The menu is an eclectic mix. Start with ginger wonton soup or clam chowder; entrées range from curry tofu stir-fry to chicken with passion fruit and mango. Wine and beer.

✔ **The Mex** (207-667-4494; www .themex.com), 185 Main St. Open daily for lunch and dinner. Changed little over the 25 years we've been coming, the Mex serves standard Mexican food—we always order too much. (The bean soup is a meal in itself.) Sangria, margaritas, and Mexican beer.

& **Riverside Café** (207-667-7220), 151 Main St. Open 6 AM–3 PM weekdays, 7–3 Sat., 7–2 Sun. for breakfast and lunch in expanded, bright, spacious quarters. Good food and coffees.

In Hulls Cove
Chart Room (207-288-9740), Rt. 3. Open for lunch and dinner. A dependable, family-geared waterside restaurant with seafood specialties.

AFTERNOON TEA **Jordan Pond House** (207-276-3316), Park Loop Rd., Seal Harbor. Tea on the lawn at the Jordan Pond House (served 11:30–6) has been de rigueur for island visitors since 1895. The tea comes with freshly baked popovers and homemade ice cream. Reservations suggested.

SNACKS **J. H. Butterfield Co.** (207-288-3386), 152 Main St., Bar Harbor. FANCY FOODS SINCE 1887, the sign says, and John Butterfield preserves the atmosphere of the grocery that once delivered to Bar Harbor's summer mansions. Now featuring Maine specialty foods. Carry sandwiches to a bench on the village green, or to Grant Park overlooking the water.

Rooster Brothers (207-667-8675), Rt. 1, Ellsworth. Just south of the bridge. Gourmet groceries, cheese, fresh-roasted coffee blends, takeout.

✳ Entertainment
MUSIC **Bar Harbor Music Festival** (207-288-5744), the Rodick Building, 59 Cottage St., Bar Harbor. Mid-July–

mid-Aug. For more than 30 years this annual series has brought top performers to the island. The 8:30 PM concerts are staged at a variety of sites around town.

Arcady Music Festival (207-288-2141). Late July–Aug. A relative newcomer (this is its 14th season) on the Mount Desert music scene. A series of concerts held at the College of the Atlantic.

Also see *Theater*, below, and *Entertainment* in "The Quiet Side."

FILM **Criterion Movie Theater** (207-288-3441), Cottage St., Bar Harbor. A vintage-1932, art deco, 891-seat theater, newly restored. You can see live music and performances as well as first-run and art films nightly. Rainy-day matinees. The Bar Harbor Jazz Festival is held here in August.

Reel Pizza Cinema (207-288-3828), 22 Kennebec Place, Bar Harbor. Pizza and art, foreign, and independent films in a funky setting (beanbag chairs and big sofas). Films at 6 and 8:30 nightly, year-round.

The Grand Auditorium (207-667-9500), Main St., Ellsworth. A classic old theater. Live performances; first-run and art films are shown.

Ellsworth Cinemas (207-667-3251), Maine Coast Mall, Rt. 1A, Ellsworth. First-run films.

THEATER

See **Acadia Repertory Theatre** in "The Quiet Side" and **Grand Auditorium** in Ellsworth under *Film*.

✳ Selective Shopping
ART AND FINE-CRAFTS GALLERIES
Eclipse Gallery (207-288-9048), 12 Mount Desert St., Bar Harbor. Sea-

sonal. A quality gallery specializing in contemporary handblown American glass, ceramics, and fine furniture; also showing metal sculpture, fine jewelry, and art photography.

Island Artisans (207-288-4214; www.islandartisans.com), 99 Main St., Bar Harbor. Open May–Dec. A cooperative featuring Maine artists and craftspeople: textiles, pottery, Native baskets. Glass, silver, and more.

Alone Moose Fine Crafts (207-288-4229), 78 West St., Bar Harbor. A long-established collection of "made in Maine" crafts, specializing in wildlife sculpture in bronze and wood.

Birdsnest Gallery (207-288-4054), 12 Mount Desert St., Bar Harbor. Open mid-May–Oct.: original oils, watercolors, and pastels.

Rocky Mann Studio Potter and Gallery (207-288-5478), Breakneck Rd., Hulls Cove. Turn off Rt. 3 at the Hulls Cove General Store. In summer open daily 10–5; off-season 11–4, closed Mon. After Christmas by appointment. Rocky Mann's ever-evolving work is worth a trip, as are paintings and cards by his wife, Carol Shutt.

BOOKSTORES **Sherman's Bookstore and Stationery** (207-288-3161; www.sherman.com), 56 Main St., Bar Harbor. Open 9 AM–10:30 PM. A great browsing emporium; really a combination five-and-dime, stationery store, gift shop, and well-stocked bookshop.

Big Chicken Barn Books and Antiques (207-667-7308), Rt. 1/3 south of Ellsworth. Open daily year-round; call for hours. Maine's largest used-book store fills the vast innards of a former chicken house. Annegret Cukierski has 120,000 books in stock:

hardbacks, paperbacks, magazines, and comics; also used furniture and collectibles.

Also see **Port in a Storm Bookstore** in "The Quiet Side."

✳ Special Events

Second Sunday in June: **Blessing of the Fleet**.

Throughout the summer: **Band concerts**, Bar Harbor village green (check current listings).

Late June: **Legacy of the Arts**, a week of art and culture with concerts, artists' events, and, at the week's end, **Bar Harbor Chamber of Commerce Art Show**, displaying original work on the Bar Harbor village green (207-288-5103).

July: **Bar Harbor Music Festival** (see *Entertainment*).

July 4 weekend: **Independence Day**—blueberry pancake breakfast, town parade, seafood festival focused on lobster, mussels, and strawberry shortcake. Live music, kids' games, and fireworks from the pier at night. **Native American Festival**—dances and a big sale by the Maine Indian Basketmakers at the College of the Atlantic (207-288-5744).

July–August: **Arcady Music Festival Summer Concert Series** (see *Entertainment*).

Late September: **Art in the Park** on the Bar Harbor village green throughout a weekend.

November: **Shopping in your PJs** downtown for extra discounts, with a parade and fashion show at 9 PM, prize for craziest sleepwear.

First weekend of December: **Island Arts Association Holiday Fair** at the YWCA (207-288-5008).

Tom Jones

ACADIA MOUNTAINS FROM ACROSS FRENCHMAN BAY

THE QUIET SIDE OF MOUNT DESERT

Bruce Carlson from the Mount Desert Chamber of Commerce claims to have coined the term *quiet side* for the longer, thinner arm of land that's divided by Somes Sound from the part of Mount Desert that's home to Bar Harbor and the Acadia National Park visitor center and Park Loop Road. The name generally also applies to Northeast Harbor.

"Northeast" is a yachting village, with a large marina geared to visiting yacht owners, summer residents, and ferries to the Cranberry Islands. Beyond a brief lineup of boutiques and art galleries, summer mansions trail off along Somes Sound. The village also offers splendid public gardens and a wide choice of ways onto the water. Try to get to Islesford (Little Cranberry Island), and be sure to follow Sargent Drive (rather than Rt. 3/198) along the Sound. The Mount Desert Historical Society in Somesville is well worth a stop. Some of Acadia's best hiking, as well as its best public swimming beach (at Echo Lake) and canoeing (on Long Pond), are found west of Somes Sound.

Southwest Harbor is a boatbuilding center, home of the Hinckley Company, the Rolls-Royce of yacht builders, one of many boatyards in this town that also ranks among Maine's top commercial fishing harbors. In the neighboring town of Tremont, Bass Harbor is a classic fishing village. It's also the departure point for Swans, a destination in its own right, and several other islands that were once far busier.

Ironically, back in the 1840s Mount Desert's first summer visitors—artists in search of solitude—headed for the Bar Harbor area precisely because it was then far less peopled than the villages on this western side of the island. Much as the Rt. 1 town of Ellsworth is today, Southwest Harbor back then marked the crossroads of Down East Maine, and several island harbors were as busy as any on the mainland today.

GUIDANCE **Mount Desert Chamber of Commerce** (207-276-5040), Sea St., Northeast Harbor. A walk-in cottage (with restrooms and showers), geared to visitors arriving by water, is open daily June Sep., 8–5, at the town dock. Pick up a copy of the current *Northeast Harbor Port Directory*.

Southwest Harbor/Tremont Chamber of Commerce (207-244-9264 or 1-800-423-9264; www.acadiachamber.com), 204 Main St., Southwest Harbor 04679. The visitor center is on Rt. 102, on the northern edge of the village. The walk-in info center is open weekdays 9–noon and 1–5; Sat. 9–3, Sun. 10–2.

GETTING THERE *By air and bus:* See *Getting There* in "Bar Harbor."

Note: **Airport & Harbor Car Service** (207-667-5995) meets planes, buses, and boats; serves the entire area.

By boat: Contact the harbormasters in **Northeast Harbor** (207-276-5737) and **Southwest Harbor** (207-244-7913) about transient moorings.

By car: From Ellsworth: Fork right off Rt. 3 as soon as it crosses the Mount Desert narrows; follow Rt. 102/198 to Somesville and Rt. 198 to Northeast Harbor, or Rt. 102 to Southwest Harbor.

GETTING AROUND This is one place in Maine where water transport is still as important as land. **MDI Water Taxi** (207-244 7312) supplements the services out of Northeast and Southwest Harbors listed under *Boat Excursions*, and the

ISLESFORD DOCK

Nancy English

Maine State Ferry Service (207-244-4353 or 1-800-491-4883) services Swans Island and Frenchboro.

Late June–Columbus Day, the free **Island Explorer Bus Service** (207-288-4573) stops frequently along the routes from Southwest Harbor to Bernard, up and down both sides of Somes Sound, and into the park and Bar Harbor, connecting with service from Northeast Harbor. Donations welcomed.

✳ To See

In Northeast Harbor

Asticou Terraces, **Thuya Garden**, and **Thuya Lodge** (207-276-5130). Parking for the Asticou Terraces (open July–Labor Day, 7–7; donation) is marked on Rt. 3, just east of the junction with Rt. 198. The exquisite 215-acre garden, begun by landscape artist Joseph Henry Curtis around 1900, features a system of paths and shelters on Asticou Hill. It's now open to the public along with his home, Thuya Lodge (open late June–Labor Day, 10–5). Thuya Garden behind the lodge was designed by the landscaper and artist Charles Savage. The gardens descend in terraces, then through wooded paths to the harbor's edge.

Asticou Azalea Gardens, Rt. 3 (near the junction of Rt. 198). Open Apr.–Oct. Also designed by Charles Savage. Stroll down winding paths and over ornamental bridges. Azaleas (in bloom mid-May until mid-June), rhododendrons, laurel, and Japanese-style plantings.

Great Harbor Maritime Museum (207-276-5262), 125 Main St. in the Old Firehouse. Open June–Columbus Day, Tue.–Sat. 10–5. $3 donation. A collection of model ships, small boats, and historical artifacts ranging from an early fire engine to a parlor room, clothing, sleighs, and a player piano; demonstrations and programs, changing exhibits.

ASTICOU AZALEA GARDENS

Kim Grant

Petite Plaisance (207-276-3940), South Shore Rd. Open mid-June–Aug., 9–4 by appointment petite plaisance@acadia.net). The former home of French author Marguerite Yourcenar has long been a pilgrimage destination for her fans. English translations of her books are available in local bookstores.

In Mount Desert

The tiny white wooden village of Someseville at the head of Somes Sound is a National Historic District; be sure to check out **Brookside Cemetery** and the **Somesville Museum** (207-244-5043; www.mdihistory.org), Rt. 102. Open mid-June into Sep., Tue.–Sat. 11–4 (donation), the

Mount Desert Historical Society maintains a lively museum: two tidy buildings, one dating back to 1780, connected by a moon bridge, house many artifacts and photographs of the island's vanished hotels and the shipyards for which this village was once widely known. Inquire about special programs. The society also maintains the 1892 **Sound School House Museum** (207-276-9323), Rt. 3/198 between Somesville and Northeast Harbor, open Memorial Day–Sep., Tue.–Sat. 10–4, housing changing exhibits, a children's program, library, and year-round activities relating to MDI history.

In Southwest Harbor
Wendell Gilley Museum (207-244-7555; www.wendellgilleymuseum.org), Rt. 102. Open May–Dec., 10–4 (10–5 in July and Aug.), daily except Mon.; Fri.–Sun. only in May, Nov., and Dec. $5 adults, $2 ages 5–12. Wendell Gilley was a local plumber who began hand carving birds as a hobby in the 1930s, over 50 years carving some 10,000 birds and acquiring a reputation as a master. With the help of friend and patron Steven Rockefeller, this handsome museum, housing more than 200 of his works, opened in 1981 and has evolved into a first-rate small museum, exhibiting changing art as well.

In Seal Cove
Seal Cove Auto Museum (207-244-9242), Pretty Marsh Rd. (off Rt. 102), between Bass Harbor and Somesville. Open June–mid-Sep., daily 10–5. Squirreled away in a little-trafficked corner of the island across from Cove Pond and Western Mountain, this collection is a real find: more than 100 gleaming antique cars and 35 motorcycles, including the country's largest assemblage of pre-1915 cars—the lifework of a private collector. $5 adults, $2 children.

ISLANDS **Swans Island 04685.** At the mouth of Blue Hill Bay, 6 miles out of Bass Harbor, with frequent car ferry service (see *Getting Around*), this is a large lobstering and fishing island with a year-round population of 350, a library, a general store (no alcohol), seasonal restaurants, **Quarry Pond** to swim in, and **Fine Sand Beach** to walk. With a bike it's a possible day trip, but be forewarned: The ferry dock is 4 hilly miles from Burnt Coat Harbor, the picturesque island center with Hockamock Light (built in 1872) at its entrance. Swans works better as an overnight, given its choice of places to stay and the beauty of local hiking trails (check out the new shore path at the light) and of kayaking options.

Swans Island recently gave up two of its three zip codes, but it maintains its historic geographic divisions into Atlantic (where the ferry docks), Minturn (site of the quarry pond and grocery store), and Swans Island Village, which has the Fine Sand Beach and the lighthouse. The island was named for James Swan, its original owner.

Maili Bailey coordinates seasonal property rentals, including cottages, houses, and apartments (**Swans Island Vacations**, 207-526-4350; off-season, 207-474-7370; www.swansislandvacations.info); rentals run $500–1,300 per week. **Harbor Watch Motel** (207-526-4563 or 1-800-532-7028; www.swansisland.com), open year-round at the head of Burnt Coat Harbor (next to the general store), offers four comfortable year-round units, two with a full kitchen, and Colleen will pick

THE CRANBERRY ISLES

(www.cranberryisles.com), 04646. Little Cranberry Island, also known as Islesford, is a 400-acre island 20 minutes offshore. It's exceptionally appealing, both naturally and in the ways visitors can interact with the people who live and summer here. The official "sight-to-see" is the incongruously brick and formal **Islesford Historical Museum** (207-244-9224; open daily mid-June–Sep., 10:45–4:30), built in 1928 with funds raised by Bangor-born, MIT-educated summer resident William Otis Sawtelle to house his fascinating local historical collection. Acadia National Park now maintains the museum, which means there are public restrooms. At the dock also check out **Winter's Work**, a small shop showcasing island-made crafts, and Marian Baker's **Islesford Pottery** (207-244-5686). It's an easy walk up the main road and following signs to Danny and Kate Furnald's **Islesford Artists Gallery** (207-244-3145), specializing in Maine's many excellent island artists.

Consider spending the night. Year-round, Franny Jo Bartlett offers three attractive guest rooms sharing a spanking-clean bath ($80) on the second floor of her vintage-1892 **Braided Rugs Inn** (207-244-5943). Rooms are hung with extraordinary turn-of-the-20th-century photos taken by Bartlett's grandfather Fred Morse. Common space includes the big old-fashioned, sunny kitchen in which Fanny Jo serves a full breakfast and dinner on request—and also permits guests to fix their own. Children are welcome, pets possible. At seasonal **Islesford House** (207-244-9309), Evelyn Boxley offers four guest rooms with shared bath; children welcome. $95 includes a full breakfast.

Islesford Market (207-244-7667) is the island's living room. Pizza and light lunches are served year-round, and island-bred postmistress Joy Sprague sells more stamps per year than any other post office in Maine,

you up at the ferry; $65–80. This is also the island's source of kayak and bicycle rentals. Not far from the ferry but off by itself with an ocean view, **Appletree House** (207-526-4438; www.appletreehouse.com) is a classic 1850s house with two upstairs guest rooms; it can be rented in its entirety or by the room ($80–100 with breakfast). Jeannie Joyce offers three rooms, shared bath (**Jeannie's Place**, 207-526-4116), open year-round at Burnt Coat Harbor ($55 double, $45 single). The **Island Bake Shoppe** (207-526-4578), a short walk from the ferry, serving breakfast and lunch, is known for its pastries. **Underwater Taxi, Inc.** (207-526-4202), 3 Quarry Rd. in Minturn, serves up fish and lobster, live and cooked, at picnic tables; the **Elegant Shack**, 257 Harbor Rd., serves ice cream and regulation fried food. **Iverstudio** (207-526-4350) offers weeklong workshops in woodblock printing. **Swans Island Educational Society** (207-526-4330), 326 Atlantic Rd., a historic complex that includes a store, school, old tools, and photographs, is less than a mile from the dock. **Swans Island Lobster & Marine**

despite the fact that Islesford has just 80 year-round and some 400 summer residents. Requests for Sprague's "Stamps by Mail" come from as far as Fiji, Iceland, and Istanbul—perhaps because with each order she encloses one of her fine island photos and a monthly newsletter (her address is USPO, Islesford 04646). Sprague also operates **Joy of Kayaking** (207-244-4309), renting one- and two-person kayaks.

Cynthia and Dan Lief's **Islesford Dock** restaurant (207-244-7494; www .islesford.com) is a big draw to Little Cranberry. Open mid-June–Labor Day except Mon., it serves lunch (11–3) and Sunday brunch (10–2), but it's really the place to watch the sun set behind the entire line of Mount Desert's mountains (dinner 5–9). On weekends, however, it's wise to check on whether the whole place has been reserved for a wedding. The Liefs grow their herbs and many vegetables, and secure most of their seafood and produce within a boat ride of their dock. Crabcakes are a big seller, and the menu always includes dock burgers and vegetarian dishes. Try the whole grilled fish with toasted red pepper, olive vinaigrette, summer vegetables, and mussels. We can vouch for this venue as magical for a wedding reception. Dinner entrées $14–17. Full bar.

Great Cranberry is less visitor geared, but the **Cranberry General Store** (207-244-5336) at the ferry landing is open in summer 7:30–3:30; shorter hours off-season. The evolving **Great Cranberry Historical Society Museum** (207-244-7358) is 0.7 mile from the dock in the building that also houses the town office, library (with Internet access), and school. Open most days mid-June–mid-Sep., it includes an eclectic mix of exhibits. Walk a short way farther to the **Whale's Rib** (207-244-5153), Polly Bunker's shop, carrying island-made Lisa Hall Jewelry as well as a selection of crafts and art; open daily Memorial Day–mid-Sep.

Museum (207-526-4423), open mid-June–mid-Sep., Wed., Thu., and Sun. 11–4, displays ships' models, fishing equipment, and photos. The **Swans Island Library** (207-526-4330) sponsors a summer speakers series. The big annual event is the **Sweet Chariot Festival**, usually the first week in August. Folksingers gather from throughout the East, and many members of the **Maine Windjammer Association** sail in to attend.

Frenchboro 04635. Eight miles out of Bass Harbor, with 50 year-round residents (up from 38 since 2000) with homes clustered around Lunts Harbor and two-thirds of the island (nearly 1,000 acres) preserved by the Maine Coast Heritage Trust. A network of hiking trails runs along the shoreline, and the birding is terrific. See *Boat Excursions* for access via the Maine State Ferry and **Island Cruises**. The **Dockside Deli** (207-334-2902) serves the basics, from veggie wraps to a lobster dinner; the fish chowder is good. The **Frenchboro Historical Society** (207-334-2932), open daily in-season 12.30–5.30, displays old tools, furniture, and local memorabilia, also sells crafted items. *Note:* One day a year (early in August) the island welcomes visitors with a lobster feed, plenty of chicken salad, and pies. Ferry service: 207-244-3254.

SCENIC DRIVES **Sargent Drive**, obviously built for carriages, runs from Northeast Harbor north half a dozen miles right along Somes Sound.

Rt. 102A loop. This isn't the quickest way between Southwest and Bass Harbors, but it's beautiful, following the shore at the **Sea Wall** with its oceanside picnic tables and the **Ship Harbor Nature Trail** down to gorgeous, flat pink rocks (see *Hiking* in "Acadia National Park"). Be sure to turn onto Lighthouse Road to see **Bass Harbor Light**, a photographer's delight. Continue on into Bass Harbor and Bernard.

✳ To Do

✎ **Acadia Ranger Programs**. Pick up a copy of *Acadia's Beaver Log* at Seawall Campground (Rt. 102A) if you can't find it in local chambers or shops. The free handout *Acadia Weekly* also lists programs ranging from guided walks and cruises to evening programs. Definitely worth doing.

BASS HARBOR LIGHT

Kim Grant

BICYCLING The 57-mile network of gravel carriage roads constructed by John D. Rockefeller Jr. in 1915 lends itself particularly well to mountain biking. The fire roads are also good for mountain biking, as is Swans Island. **Southwest Cycle** (207-244-5856 or 1-800-649-5856) in Southwest Harbor rents mountain and touring bicycles, children's bikes, baby seats, car racks, and jog strollers.

BIRDING For special programs led by park naturalists, consult *Acadia's Beaver Log*; also see the **Wendell Gilley Museum** under *To See* in this chapter and *To Do* in "Bar Harbor." Also see Island Cruises, below.

BOAT EXCURSIONS See Cranberry Isles, Swans Island, and Frenchboro under *To See*.

From Bass Harbor
Island Cruises (207-244-5785; www .harborcruises.com), Little Island Marine, Bass Harbor. Eric and Kim Strauss offer daily (weather-depend-

SWAN'S ISLAND

ent) lunch cruises to Frenchboro and around Placentia and Black Islands as well as Great and Little Gott Islands, all depicted in novels by Great Gott native Ruth Moore (1903–89). In *The Weir*, *Speak to the Winds*, and *Spoonhandle*, Moore describes the poignant ebb of life from these islands in the 1930s and 1940s. These are exceptional cruises, given the quality of the historical narration, scenery, and wildlife: a wide variety of birds, including several bald eagles and many harbor and gray seals.

The car-carrying **Maine State Ferry** (207-244-3254) makes the 40-minute run to Swans Island several times a day, twice weekly to Frenchboro.

From Northeast Harbor: **Beal & Bunker** (207-244-3575) offers year-round mail-boat and ferry service aboard *Island Queen* to the Cranberries and Sutton Island. The ***Delight*** (207-244-5724), an old-style launch, offers water taxi service. See the Cranberry Isles sidebar under *To See*.

From Southwest Harbor: **Cranberry Cove Boating** (207-244-5882) offers frequent service to the Cranberries from both Manset and Southwest. **Great Harbor Tours** (207-465-5200 or 207-244-9160), Clark Point Rd., operates the *Elizabeth T*. mid-May–mid-Oct. to Islesford Dock, two trips per day. **Downeast Friendship Sloop Charters** (207-266-5210; www.downeastfriendshipsloop .com) offers daysails and private charters.

BOAT RENTALS In Southwest Harbor both **Manset Yacht Service** (207-244-4040) and **Mansell Boat Rental Company** (207-244-5625), rent power- and sailboats and offer sail lesson cruises.

CANOEING AND KAYAKING **Long Pond**, the largest lake on any Maine island, has three access points. Boats can be launched at **Echo Lake** on Ike's Point, just off Rt. 102. **Seal Cove Pond** is less used and accessible from fire roads north of Seal Cove. **Bass Harbor Marsh** is another possibility at high tide. Canoe rental sources offer suggestions and directions. **National Park Canoe Rentals** (207-244-5854 or 1-877-378-6907; www.acadia.net/canoe), on Long Pond near Somesville, offers guided paddles and instruction. Guided half- and full-day paddles are offered by **Maine State Sea Kayak** (207-244-9500; www.mainestatekayak .com), 244 Main St., Southwest Harbor.

GOLF **Causeway Golf Club** (207-244-3780), Fernald Point Rd., Southwest Harbor. Nine-hole waterside course, clubhouse and pull carts, pro shop.

FISHING Deep-sea fishing is offered aboard the party boat *Masako Queen* (207-667-1912), departing Beal's Lobster Pier in Southwest Harbor June–Sep.

HIKING The highest mountains on the western side of Somes Sound are Bernard and Mansell, but both summits are wooded. The more popular hikes are up **Acadia Mountain** (3.5 miles round-trip, off Rt. 102) with an east–west summit trail commanding a spectacular view of the sound and islands. Admittedly we have only climbed **Flying Mountain**, a quick hit with a great view, too. The trail begins at the Fernald Cove parking area. Don't miss **Asticou Terraces** (see *To See*) and the **Indian Point Blagden Preserve** (see *Green Space*).

Ship Harbor Nature Trail. See *Hiking* in "Acadia National Park."

SAILING **Mansell Boat Rental Company** (207-244-5625), Rt. 102A, Manset (near Southwest Harbor), offers sailing lessons; also rents small sailboats. Also check **Hinckley Yacht Charters** (207-244-5008), Southwest Harbor, and **Manset Yacht Service** (207-244-4040) in Manset.

SWIMMING **Echo Lake** offers a beach with a lifeguard, restrooms, and parking; Rt. 102 between Somesville and Southwest Harbor. Another favorite spot is known as "the bluffs" or "the Ledges." Park in the Acadia Mountain parking area (about 3 miles south of Somesville on Rt. 102). A short path leads down to the lake.

✳ Green Space

Indian Point Blagden Preserve, a 110-acre Nature Conservancy preserve in the northwestern corner of the island, includes 1,000 feet of shorefront and paths that wander through the woods. It offers a view of Blue Hill Bay and is a tried-and-true seal-watching spot. From Rt. 198 north of Somesville, turn right on Indian Point Rd., bear right at the fork, and look for the entrance; sign in and pick up a map at the caretaker's house.

Seal Cove. An unpublicized waterside park with picnic tables, a beach at low tide, a kayaking put-in. From Rt. 102 turn at the red buoy onto the waterside extension of Seal Cove Rd.

Also see Asticou Terraces in *To See*.

✳ Lodging

GRAND OLD RESORTS ᯇ **Asticou Inn** (207-276-3344; www.asticou .com), Rt. 3, Northeast Harbor 04662. Mid-May–mid-Oct. The elegant Asticou, built at the head of Northeast Harbor in 1883, offers superb food, rooms with water views, luxurious public rooms with Oriental rugs and wing chairs by the hearth, and a vast porch overlooking formal gardens. In all there are 48 rooms and suites, all with private bath, divided among the main house and annexes, which include Cranberry Lodge across the road and the Topsider suites in modern water-view cottages. Try for Room 101. In recent years the mood has lightened here: Bellhops are now in shirtsleeves so as not to intimidate guests, and nonguests in shorts feel far more welcome at lunch, served on the deck overlooking the harbor; see *Dining Out*. Facilities include a cocktail lounge, tennis courts, and a heated swimming pool. In July and Aug., $225–325 EP; from $130 per couple EP off-season. This is a great place for a wedding.

INNS AND BED & BREAKFASTS

In Northeast Harbor 04662
🦞 ᗆ **Harbourside Inn** (207-276-3272; www.harboursideinn.com). Open June–Sep. An 1880s shingle-style inn set on 4 wooded acres, with 11 guest rooms and 3 suites (2 with kitchenette) on 3 floors, all with private bath; some kitchens. There are also working fireplaces in all the first- and second-floor rooms. This is a very special place, as only an inn with long term family management can be. Flowers from the garden brighten every guest room. Guests mingle over breakfast muffins served on the wick-

er-furnished sunporch. Most guests spend their days in adjacent Acadia National Park. The Asticou Azalea Gardens, shops, and the town landing with its water excursions are all within walking distance. $130–160 for a room; $195–250 for a three-room suite with kitchen. Inquire about the two-bedroom apartment with a large kitchen, dining area, and working fireplace, available by the week year-round.

🖉 ᗆ **The Maison Suisse Inn** (207-276-5223 or 1-800-624-7668; www .maisonsuisse.com), Main St. at Kimball Lane, P.O. Box 1090. Open late May–late Oct. A 19th-century Acadia summer mansion in the middle of Northeast Harbor's shops and restaurants, but set back behind its garden. Beth and David White offer a total of 16 rooms and suites divided between the main house and the Peregrine Lodge. All rooms have phone and TV. Three large common rooms are sparely, elegantly furnished, hung with Audubon prints, and warmed with fireplaces. High season $155–325, including breakfast at a café across the street.

Grey Rock Inn (207-276-9360; www .greyrockinn.com), Rt. 3/198. Open mid-May–Oct. An expansive 1910 summer mansion under longtime ownership with seven gracious rooms and a suite, some in-room fireplaces, and property bordering Acadia National Park. $185–375 in high season.

In Southwest Harbor 04679
🖉 ᗆ **Penury Hall** (207-244-7102; www.penuryhall.com), Box 68, Main St. Open year-round. An attractive village house with three guest rooms (private bath). This was the first B&B on the island. Toby and Gretchen Strong take their job as hosts seriously.

Christina Tree

THE PORCH OF THE CLAREMONT, OVERLOOKS THE HOTEL'S ANNUAL CROQUET CLASSIC.

✿ & **The Claremont** (207-244-5036 or 1-800-244-5036; www.theclaremonthotel .com), Claremont Rd., Southwest Harbor 04679. Open May–mid-Oct. Mount Desert's oldest hotel, first opened in 1884, has the grace and dignity but not the size of a grand hotel, along with the best views on the island. The Claremont has remained low-key and gracious but not stuffy with owners—just three over the years—who have preserved its appeal for families. The McCue family, current owners, have been summering on Mount Desert since 1871. "We didn't expect to make money, just to keep it going and to improve it" is the way the late Getrude McCue explained how she and her late husband, Allen, happened to buy the hotel in 1968. All 24 guest rooms have new plumbing, wiring, and phones, and each is carefully furnished in cottage furniture and wicker. Wood floors gleam around Oriental carpets in sitting

Breakfast includes a choice of eggs Benedict, blueberry pancakes, or a "penurious omelet." $110 May–Oct. also includes modest use of the fridge and laundry facilities, library and music, games (they play backgammon for blood); also a canoe and sauna. Guests receive a feline welcome from Widget.

✿ & **The Birches** (207-244-5182; www.acadia.net/birches), Fernald Point Rd., P.O. Box 178. Open year-round. A very special place. "Great-Grandma bought these 8 acres for $50

and for another $50 she could have had 20 more," Dick Homer quips. Dick and Rocky Homer's home, built in 1916, commands a water view from its spacious paneled living room and ample grounds (which include a croquet court). The three guest rooms are furnished in family antiques (private bath). $115–125, $90–100 off-season, includes a full breakfast.

The Inn at Southwest (207-244-3835; www.innatsouthwest.com), P.O. Box 593, Main St. Open May–Oct. Built in 1884 as a high-Victorian-style

rooms, the wraparound porch is lined with rockers, and every table in the dining room has a view. Visitors are welcome to dine (or to lunch) in The Boathouse (see *Eating Out*) and to attend Thursday-evening lectures (see *Entertainment*). There are large suites in Phillips, Clark, and Cole Cottages, as well as 14 individual cottages, each with living room and fireplace, all with kitchenette. Recreation options include tennis on clay courts, two croquet courts, badminton, and water sports; bicycles and rowboats are available. The Croquet Classic in August is the social high point of the season. A room in the hotel is $235–245 double MAP; rooms $120–170 B&B; cottages $195–265. Before July 15 and after Labor Day rates drop, and there are children's and weekly rates. A 10 percent gratuity is added in the cottages, 15 percent in hotel rooms.

Nancy English

annex to a now vanished hotel. Of the seven guest rooms, all with private bath and named for lighthouses, we particularly like Pemaquid Point, with its chapel-style window and a window seat. There are also a pair of two-room suites. Innkeepers Andrea Potapovs and Sandy Johnson obviously enjoy preparing breakfasts, such as eggs Florentine. $110–185 per couple in high season; from $75 in shoulder seasons.

Lindenwood Inn (207-244-5335 or 1-800-307-5335; www.lindenwood inn.com), 118 Clark Point Rd., Box

1328. This turn-of-the-20th-century sea captain's home set by the harbor among stately linden trees is open all year. Australian-born owner Jim King has a sure decorating touch in the nine rooms (all with private bath), many of which with water views, balcony, and fireplace. The heated pool and hot tub are appreciated after hiking or biking. A full breakfast is served in the paneled dining room, where the fire is lit most mornings. A full bar is also available. $105–279 double in-season, $95–225 in low. The high end is for the penthouse suite with its own hot tub and a great view; other choices include two housekeeping suites.

The Yellow Aster (207-244-4422 or 1-800-724-7228; www.yellowaster .com), 53 Clark Point Rd. Open year-round. The emphasis here is on health as much as serenity. The four guest rooms, all with private bath, are tastefully decorated, as are common rooms. Breakfast is full and both organic and vegetarian. Massage is available. $105 on weekends, high season. Your hosts are Peter, Bethany, and their young son.

♥ Harbour Cottage Inn and Pier One (207-244-5738 or 1-888-843-3022; www.harbourcottageinn.com), 9 Dirigo Rd., P.O. Box 258. Don Jalbert and Jauer Montesinos have revamped this old landmark to feature creature comforts and romance. The eight standard rooms are equipped not only with phone, computer port, and cable TV but also whirlpool bath or steam-sauna shower; of a pair of two-bedroom suites, one has a whirlpool tub. The Southwester (sleeping six) and Carriage House (sleeping four), both neighboring cottages, have full kitchens. Also weekly rentals in a delightful harborside compound, five skillfully furnished units with kitchens clustered near the bottom of Clark Point Rd. and collectively known as Pier One. $110–149 for standard rooms, $135–199 for suites, $135–250 for cottages. Rates include breakfast, snacks, and use of bicycles. Pier One weekly rentals run $1,260–1,570.

The Kingsleigh Inn (207-244-5302; www.kingsleighinn.com), 373 Main St. Open year-round. The check-in desk is the counter of a large, open kitchen, and the living room has a wood-burn-

ing fireplace; wicker chairs fill the wraparound porch. Dana and Greg Moos have brought new life to Room 5, with a balcony overlooking the harbor. A three-room suite on the third floor has a fireplace and a telescope, positioned in a turret window. In-season $130–160 for rooms, $260 for the suite, includes a very full breakfast.

The Moorings Inn (207-244-5523), P.O. Box 744. Partially open year-round. The big rambling white house on the edge of the Hinckley boatyard and at the entrance to Somes Sound has been owned and managed by the King family since the 1960s. There are 11 guest rooms in the main building, all with bath and phone, most with water views ($65–120). Also nine efficiency units ranging from free-standing cottages to units in Lookout Cottage and Lighthouse View Wing, some with fireplace, deck, two bedrooms, and amazing views, a find at $105–150, $10 per extra person. Rates include continental breakfast.

&. The Island House (207-244-5180; www.islandhousebandb.com). Ann and Charlie Bradford have sold their longtime B&B by this name and built a new single-story, ranch-style home, designed to accommodate guests in two rooms with private bath and shared, private common space. $110 in high season, less off-season, includes a full breakfast. An efficiency apartment is also available at $150.

In Bass Harbor 04653
(Go to the harbor between 2 and 4 and watch the lobster catch get unloaded.)

❦ Bass Harbor Inn (207-244-5157), P.O. Box 326. Open May–Oct. In an 1870 house with harbor views, within walking distance of village restaurants and the ferry to Swans Island, Barbara and Alan Graff offer seven rooms ranging from doubles with shared baths to a fabulous top-floor studio with kitchenette. One room with half bath has a fireplace, and several have decks. $70–120 in-season, $50–95 off-season, including breakfast.

Ann's Point Inn (207-244-9595, www .annspointinn), P.O. Box 398, Bass Harbor 04653. This contemporary waterfront home packs some unusual luxuries, like a hot tub, sauna and 32' x 12' indoor pool, and two double kayaks, which can be launched from the front lawn. Innkeepers Phil and Lesley DiVirgilio offer four rooms with plenty of space, light, and extras. We like the look of Eagle's Nest, previously an artist's studio. $150–295 depending on room and season, includes a full breakfast.

In Seal Cove 04674
& **West of Eden** (207-244-9695; www.acadia.net/westofeden), P.O. Box 65. Open all year. The only place to stay in the quietest corner of the "quiet side." This 1872 farmhouse on Rt. 102 is surrounded by gardens. The three upstairs rooms are light and airy; Room 3 is especially large and inviting, with a queen-sized bed, a private bath, a skylight, and a sleeping loft with futons—good for a family. Regina Ploucquet and George Urbanneck keep a vegetarian kitchen; breakfasts include homemade granola and sweet potato pancakes, pear pecan waffles, and lots of fresh fruit. $65–95 single, $80–110 double, $15 per extra person.

MOTELS Kimball Terrace Inn (207-276-3383 or 1-800-454-6225; www .kimballterraceinn.com), 10 Huntington Rd., P.O. Box 1030, Northeast Harbor 04662. Open Apr.–late Oct.

A motor inn replacing its predecessor hotel of the same name, this establishment occupies a prime site on the harbor, offering 70 large rooms, 52 with sliding doors opening onto private patios and balconies. Amenities include a full-service restaurant, outdoor pool, and tennis courts. $158–180 per room July–Labor Day, less before and after.

☜ ☜ ☜ Harbor View Motel & Cottages (207-244-5031 or 1-800-538-6463), P.O. Box 701, Southwest Harbor 04679. Open mid-May–mid-Oct. Lorraine and Joe Saunders have owned this pleasant 20-unit motel for 38 years. It's hidden down by the harbor. In July and Aug. the nine rooms with decks right on the water are $100–112, while others are $73–85; in Sep. rooms are $78–88 on the water, $57–67 otherwise, less for solo travelers and by the week. A third-floor apartment and seven cottages are available in high season by the week ($645–1,075, depending on the size and week). A continental breakfast is served in the cheerful lobby, and the landscaped grounds overlook the harbor.

Seawall Motel and Acadia Workshop Center (207-244-3020, 1-800-248-9250; www.seawallmotel.com), 566 Seawall Road, Southwest Harbor. Open year-round. Twenty rooms with private bath, cable TV. The ocean is right across the street, giving the clean, quiet motel rooms all a great view. Rehabed in 2000, this motel is next door to Acadia National Park. Rates up to $110 in summer. Nationally known artists teach workshops at the Acadia Workshop Center (www .acadiaworkshopcenter.com) in spring, summer and fall.

OTHER LODGING 🍃 **Appalachian Mountain Club's Echo Lake Camp** (207-244-3747), AMC/Echo Lake Camp, Mount Desert 04660. Open late June–Labor Day weekend. Accommodations are platform tents; family-style meals are served in a central hall. There is a rustic library and reading room, and an indoor game room, but more to the point are boats for use on the lake, daily hikes, and evening activities. Reservations should be made on April 1. Rates for the minimum 1-week stay (Sat.–Sat.) are inexpensive per person but add up for a family. All meals included. For a brochure, contact the AMC, 5 Joy St., Boston, MA 02108.

COTTAGES AND EFFICIENCIES Both chambers of commerce listed under *Guidance* keep and publish lists.

✳ Where to Eat

In the Southwest Harbor area
DINING OUT **Red Sky Restaurant** (207-244-0476), 14 Clark Point Rd., Southwest Harbor. Open nightly 5:30–10, Valentine's Day–New Year's Eve. The toast of this restaurant town, a comfortably low-key bistro with food to come back and back for: appetizers like leek and tomato tart with fresh basil and Gruyère cheese, main courses that might include lobster risotto with asparagus and sautéed porcini mushrooms. Ingredients are all as fresh and local as possible, owners Elizabeth and James Lindquist are very much your hosts, and the chef is Adam Bishop. Entrées $17–28.

The Claremont (207-244-5036; www.theclaremonthotel.com), Clark Point Rd., Southwest Harbor. Open for dinner late June–Columbus Day; lunch

at The Boathouse (see *Eating Out*) mid-July–Aug. Also the place for a drink before dinner, with a view that's as spectacular as any on the island, and an attractive bar off the dining room. Here most tables have some water view, and both food and service are traditional but the menu holds some pleasant surprises, such as a soy-seared darne of salmon served with a sun-dried tomato risotto cake, artichoke vinaigrette, and pesto oil; and seafood paella with lobster, scallops, mussels, squid, and shrimp with saffron rice cake. Plan to come on Thursday and stay for a lecture (see *Entertainment*). Entrées $19–23.

XYZ Restaurant & Gallery (207-244-5221), end of Bennett Lane off Seawall Rd. (Rt. 102A), Manset. Open high season nightly for dinner, varying hours shoulder seasons. Reservations suggested. Janet Strong and Robert Hoyt acquired an enthusiastic following for their "classical food from the Mexican interior" (X is for "Xalapa," Y for "Yucatán," and Z for "Zacatecas") at their previous location. In 2004 they built a new restaurant. The atmosphere remains intimate (just 30 seats) and colorful (decorated with Mexican folk art). Entrées change constantly but always include pork and chicken dishes, all $20, including salad. Fresh lime margaritas, Mexican beer, and wine are served.

Carlos Ristorante (207-244-5227), 386 Main St., Southwest Harbor. Open 5:30–9:30 (except Sun.) in-season, weekends off-season. A delightful newcomer serving "authentic Sicilian cuisine," with a menu that includes sweet-and-sour rabbit and a baked pasta pie in sautéed eggplant slices. Entrées $14.95–20. Full bar.

Café 2 (207-244-4344), 326 Main St., Southwest Harbor. Dinner served Tue.–Sun. 5–9 in-season. Reserve a booth. A vintage car dealership has been transformed into an informal, colorful café with a wide-ranging menu, from pasta to a brace of quail stuffed with lobster. The dinner salads are generous; signature dishes include a seafood pot au feu and sage-rubbed tenderloin of pork. Beer and wine served. Entrées $12.95–25.

In Northeast Harbor

La Matta Cena (207-276-3305), 5 Old Firehouse Lane. Open in-season daily for lunch and dinner. This Tuscan hideaway just off the main drag got rave reviews in its opening season. Lunch might be sweet grilled peaches wrapped in prosciutto, served with mixed greens. Dinner might be pappardelle ragout (handmade pasta noodles with braised meat) or salmon with caramelized red pearl onions, red currant jelly, and chile oil. Dinner entrées $18–27.

Asticou Inn (207-276-3344), Rt. 3. Open mid-May–mid-Oct. for breakfast, lunch, and dinner. The Thursday-night buffet and dance is an island tradition. Grand old hotel atmosphere with a formal waterside dining room (window seats, however, are reserved for longtime guests). Dinner entrées might include seared and oven-roasted halibut with white truffle vinaigrette and roasted vegetables, and fresh-herb-marinated lamb with bulgur, apricots, and pistachios ($19–32). Reservations required.

151 Main Street (207-276-9898). Open in-season, Tue.–Sun. from 5. A middle-of-the-village, casual bistro with a pleasant atmosphere and varied menu, from $15 for meat loaf or

vegetarian curry to $19 for hand-cut salmon. Pizza also served.

Also see **Islesford Dock** in our *Cranberry Isles* sidebar; it's accessible from both Northeast and Southwest Harbors.

LOBSTER POUNDS 🐑 🦞 **Thurston's Lobster Pound** (207-244-7600), Steamboat Wharf Rd., Bernard. Open Memorial Day–Columbus Day, daily 11–8:30, but closed Labor Day. Our favorite. Weatherproofed, on a working wharf overlooking Bass Harbor and just far enough off the beaten path not to be mobbed. Fresh and tender as lobster can be, plus corn and pie, also seafood stew, sandwiches, chowder, and blueberry cheesecake. Wine and beer.

🐑 **Beal's Lobster Pier** (207-244-7178 or 207-244-3202), Clark Point Rd., Southwest Harbor. Dock dining (also a weatherproofed area). Crabmeat rolls, chowder, fresh fish specialties, and lobster. Handy location. (Both pounds pack and ship.)

THURSTON'S LOBSTER POUND

Christina Tree

DOWN EAST

In Southwest Harbor

The Boathouse at the Claremont Hotel (207-244-3512), Clark Point Rd. Open July–Aug., serving lunch until 2 PM. This informal dockside facility on the grounds of the island's oldest hotel arguably offers the island's best view, east across the mouth of Somes Sound with Acadia's mountains rising beyond. Sandwiches, salads, and burgers; also good for drinks at sunset.

Little Notch Café (207-244-3357), 340 Main St. Open year-round at 9 for coffee and breads, 11–8 (except Sun. in Oct.) for light meals; closed weekends off-season. Arthur and Katherine Jacobs specialize in freshly made soups and sandwiches like grilled tuna salad with cheddar on wheat; also great pizza. Limited seating; takeout.

🐚 **DuMuro's Top of the Hill Restaurant** (207-244-0033), 1 Main St., Rt. 102 north of town. Open seasonally. We have had only good reports about this family-run and -geared place with a very reasonably priced menu ranging from fried chicken and salad plates to mussels marinara over linguine. Entrées $10–19; early-bird specials.

Eat-a-Pita (207-244-4344), 326 Main St. Open daily from 8 AM; at dinner this spot turns into Café 2 (see *Dining Out*). A lively, bright café with soups, salads, and pastas, specialty coffees, and pastries.

🐚 **Café Drydock** (244-5842), 357 Main St. Open daily 11–9:30, Sunday brunch 10–2. Convenient, pleasant, predictable, and dependable. Dinner specialties include chicken Boursin and baked stuffed haddock. Fully licensed. Dinner entrées $12.95–18.95.

🐚 **Westside Grill** (207-244-5959), Southwest Food Mart Plaza, Rt. 102 north of the village. Open daily for lunch and dinner. A family find. The perfect place for lunch or dinner while you're using the neighboring Laundromat, or even if you aren't. Burgers, including "little buckaroos," are a specialty, as are grilled "panini" sandwiches and the salad bar. Grilled fish to Angus steak. Dinner entrées $12.95–27; senior and children's menu.

In Northeast Harbor

🍴🐚 **Docksider** (207-276-3965), Sea St. Open 11–9. Bigger than it looks, with a no-frills, knotty-pine interior, amazingly efficient, friendly waitresses, passable chowder and Maine crabcakes; also salads, burgers, clam rolls, and a shore dinner. Wine and beer; lunch menu all day; early-bird specials 4:30–6.

🐚 **The Colonel's Restaurant** (207-276-5147), Main St. Open early Apr.–late Oct. Serving breakfast 6:30–11:30, lunch and dinner 11:30–9. A big, informal eatery with some outdoor tables, good for fresh-dough pizzas, burgers, also reasonably priced seafood dinners.

Pine Tree Market (207-276-3335), 121 Main St. Open daily 1–1, Sunday 8–6. Geared to boaters and summer residents, this classic old market prides itself on its meats, wines, and baked goods. Good picnic makings. There's a coin-operated laundry in the cellar.

In Bass Harbor

🐚 **Seafood Ketch** (207-244-7463), on Bass Harbor. Open mid-May–mid-Oct., daily 11–9. Longtime ownership by Lisa, Stuart, and Ed Branch has given this place a solid reputation for homemade breads and desserts, and fresh, fresh seafood. We were, however, disappointed in 2004 by tables too tightly packed, service slow, prices substantially up—and table wines over the top. We hope we just hit them on a bad night. Dinner entrées $16.95–28.95.

♂ **Freya's** (207-244-9404), Shore Rd. Open daily (except Mon.) 11–closing. An informal new wharf restaurant with an all-day menu of shellfish, soups, salads, seafood baskets, and platters as well as daily specials. BYOB.

✳ Entertainment

MUSIC Mount Desert Festival of Chamber Music (207-276-3988), Neighborhood House, Main St., Northeast Harbor. A series of six concerts presented for more than 37 seasons mid-July–mid-Aug.

See "Bar Harbor" for the Arcady and Bar Harbor Music Festivals.

THEATER Acadia Repertory Theatre (207-244-7260), Rt. 102, Somesville. Performances during July and Aug., Tue.–Sun. at 8:15 PM; matinees at 2 on the last Sun. of each run. A regional repertory theater group performs in the Somesville Masonic Hall, usually presenting half a dozen popular plays in the course of the season. Tickets are reasonably priced.

Deck House Restaurant and Cabaret Theatre (207-244-5044), Great Harbor Marina, Southwest Harbor. June–Sep. A dining/entertainment landmark since 1976. Sitting on and over the water with a stunning view of Great Harbor, this nightly cabaret theater by talented young people has a great reputation. Entertainment cover $8; $18–27 for entrées. Full bar.

The Claremont Hotel Thursday Evening Lecture Series (207-244-5036), Claremont Rd., Southwest Harbor. July and Aug. An impressive array of authorities speak on a variety of topics. One recent included a slide lecture on "American Artists at the Seaside" as well as talks on jazz, mountain climbing, and Mount Desert history. All lectures are at 8:30, the hour also of the **Tuesday Evening Music Series** (Aug. only).

✳ Selective Shopping

In Somesville
Port in a Storm Bookstore (207-244-4114 or 1-800-694-4114; www.portinastormbookstore.com), Rt. 102. Open year-round, Mon.–Sat. 9:30–5:30 and Sun. noon–6. A 19th-century general-store building with water views, two floors of carefully selected books. Specialties include Maine authors and Maine books, children's and young adult titles. An inviting second-floor space with water views is handy to books on writing, stationery, cards, poetry, and other inducements to actually writing. Jazz and classical music CDs and cassettes, soft music, reading nooks, coffee. An oasis for book lovers. Frequent readings and book signings.

Along Main St. in Northeast Harbor
The quality of the artwork showcased in this small yachting haven is amazing. **The Wingspread Gallery** (207-276-3910) has changing exhibits in the main gallery and a selection by well-established artists. **Redfield Artisans Gallery** (207-276-3609) offers a mix of high-end and affordable works. **Shaw Contemporary Jewelry** (207-276-5000; www.shawjewelry.com),

100 Main St., open year-round, is an outstanding gallery featuring Sam Shaw's own work. The village anchor stores are the **Kimball Shop** (207-276-3300), an upscale department store geared to summer residents' needs since 1935, **Sherman's Bookstore** (207-276-3205), a seasonal branch of the Bar Harbor store, and **Pine Tree Market** (see *Eating Out*).

In Southwest Harbor

Aylen & Son Fine Jewelry (207-244-7369), 320 Main St. Open year-round. Peter Aylen fashions gold, silver, pearl, and Maine gemstone jewelry with botanical themes, and Judy Aylen's hand-carved bead necklaces and work with a variety of stones are also distinctive.

Sandcastle (207-244-4118), 360 Main St. Open year-round, daily. Creations from and about the ocean and nature by more than 70 Maine artists and craftspeople: toys, educational kits, videos, music, chimes, and an assortment of lighthouses.

Rue Cottage Books (207-244-5542), 360, No. 3 Main St. (on the green). Nicols Fox proudly proclaims herself a Luddite. Her distinctive shop is a mix of old and new books about natural history, art, architecture, gardening, philophy. and much more, including antitechnology. It's named for a medicinal herb said to bring grace and renewal.

Carroll Drug Store (207-244-5588), just off Main St. at the north end of the village. A supermarket-sized store with a genuine general-store/five-and-dime feel.

In Bernard and Seal Cove

E. L. Higgins (207-244-3983; www.antiquewicker.com), Bernard Rd. (the way to Thurston's). Open mid-Apr.–mid-Oct., 10–5 or by appointment. An 1890s schoolhouse filled with Maine's largest stock of antique wicker (ask to see the coffin basket); also antique furniture and glassware.

Island Astronomy (207-244-9477; www.islandastro.com), Bernard Rd., Bernard. Housed in a lighthouse-shaped structure overlooking Bass Harbor, Peter and Linda Lord's shop is stocked with a wide selection of binoculars and telescopes. Serious astronomers who have built their own observatory nearby, the Lords host free Friday-evening astronomy lectures at the shop and astronomy workshops at the observatory.

Seal Cove Pottery and Gallery (207-244-3602), Kelly Town Rd., Seal Cove. Open Apr.–mid-Nov. Ed Davis is a fifth-generation (both sides) MDI native, and this shop with its handsome, functional pottery (glazes are made from scratch) is worth a special trip.

Also see the **Cranberry Isles** sidebar under *To See* for more galleries and studios.

✳ Special Events

July: **Independence Day fireworks** on Somes Sound. **Quietside Festival and Annual Pink Flamingo Canoe Race** at Seal Cove in Tremont (207-244-3713).

Early August: **Sweet Chariot Festival** on Swans Island. **Frenchboro Days** in Frenchboro. **Annual Art Show on the Green**, Southwest Harbor (1-800-423-9264).

Columbus Day weekend: **Octoberfest**—food, crafts, games at Smuggler's Den Campground, Southwest Harbor (1-800-423-9264).

Also see *Entertainment*.

At the junction of Rts. 3 and 1 in Ellsworth, it's Rt. 3 that continues straight ahead and Rt. 1 that angles off abruptly, obviously the road less taken. Within a few miles you notice the absence of commercial clutter. Nowhere in Maine does the coast change as abruptly as along this rim of Frenchman Bay.

On the western side is Mount Desert Island with busy Bar Harbor, magnet for everyone from everywhere. The northern and eastern shores are, however, a quiet, curving stretch of coves, tidal bays, and peninsulas, all with spectacular views of Acadia's high, rounded mountains. This is actually an old, now quiet resort area with high mountains, hidden lakes, fishing villages, fine inns, and rich cultural life.

In 1889 the Maine Central's Boston & Mount Desert Limited carried passengers in less than eight hours from Boston's North Station to Mount Desert Ferry, the name of the terminal in Hancock. Briefly billed as the fastest train in New England, it connected with ferries to several points on this far side of Frenchman Bay, as well as Bar Harbor. That era's huge old summer hotels are long gone, and only the surviving summer colonies in Sorrento, Grindstone Neck, and Hancock Point evoke the era of steamboats and railroads.

The 29 miles along Frenchman Bay that begin on Rt. 1 at the Hancock/Sullivan bridge and loop around the Schoodic Peninsula to Prospect Harbor are a National Scenic Byway. Beyond the bridge across the tidal Taunton River, Rt. 1 shadows the curve of Frenchman Bay, offering spectacular views. Be sure to stop at the scenic turnout (the site of a former inn) just before Dunbar's Store.

It's said that on a clear day you can see Katahdin as well as the Acadia peaks from the top of Schoodic Mountain, some 20 miles inland, back up between Sullivan and Franklin and handy to swimming at Donnell Pond. Most travelers who come this far are, however, bound for the Schoodic Point loop around the 2,100-acre headland that's part of Acadia National Park.

Schoodic is the name that has come to apply to the entire peninsula that forms the eastern side of Frenchman Bay. It's also known as the Gouldsboro Peninsula. In her 1958 book titled simply *The Peninsula*, Louise Dickinson Rich described the area as "thirty thousand acres of granite, heath and shallow topsoil."

At the entrance to the park, Winter Harbor serves the old summer colony on adjacent Grindstone Neck. Until recently it was also home to a secret U.S. naval base that sent and intercepted coded messages from ships and submarines. These buildings now house national park employees. Prospect Harbor, at the eastern end of the park, is more of a fishing village, the site of Maine's last sardine-processing plants (Stinson Seafood) and of red-flashing Prospect Harbor Light. Corea, beyond on Sand Cove, is another much-painted and -photographed fishing village set on pink granite rocks. The small village of Gouldsboro itself is just off Rt. 1.

Too many visitors simply day-trip to this area. Given the choice of attractive places to stay and to eat, to shop, and to hike—not to mention the kayaking and mountain biking and distinctive beauty of this area—East Hancock County should be viewed as a destination in its own right.

GUIDANCE Schoodic Peninsula Chamber of Commerce (207-963-7658; www.acadia-schoodic.org), P.O. Box 381, Winter Harbor 04693; request the helpful pamphlet guide.

GETTING THERE *By car:* For a shortcut to Hancock from Bar Harbor, take Rt. 3 north to Rt. 204, posted for Lamoine State Park. Turn left onto Rt. 184, immediately right at the town hall on Pinkham Road, and then left after a mile or so at the sign for Rt. 1 (Mud Creek Rd.).

From points south, see *Getting There* in "Bar Harbor."

By boat: The **Bar Harbor Ferry** (207-288-2984; www.barharborferry.com) offers frequent seasonal service across Frenchman Bay between Bar Harbor and Winter Harbor. There are six round-trips weekdays and five on weekends—but check. Bring a bike and ride the 12-mile loop from Winter Harbor around Schoodic Point. In summer months the Island Explorer (see below) meets the ferry.

GETTING AROUND **Island Explorer** (www.exploreacadia.com). This fabulous, free bus meets the **Bar Harbor Ferry** and makes an hourly circuit from Winter Harbor around Schoodic Point and through Birch and Winter Harbors.

✳ To See

SCENIC DRIVES **Acadia National Park**, Schoodic Peninsula. Allow 2 to 3 hours. The park's 7.2-mile one-way shore drive begins beyond Winter Harbor. **Frazer Point Picnic Area** (comfort station) is a good first stop, a place to unload bikes if you want to tour on two wheels. It's said to have been an Indian campsite for thousands of years.

A little more than 2.5 miles farther along, look for the unmarked, unpaved road on your left that leads up to **Schoodic Head**, where a short trail leads to a rocky summit, just 400 feet high but with long views.

The drive continues along Frenchman Bay and then bursts onto **Schoodic Point**, where the smooth rocks thrust into the Atlantic. On sunny days tidal pools invite clambering, but on stormy days surf and spray can shoot as high as 40 feet. It's a popular spectacle, but beware of the surf, which can be deadly.

Bear right along the drive to the **Blueberry Hill Parking Area** (about a mile beyond Schoodic Point) with its views of Moose and Schoodic Islands. Note the trail to the top of a 180-foot promontory, **The Anvil**. Continue along the drive 2 more miles to Rt. 186 in the village of Birch Harbor. The 29 miles or so of Rts. 1 and 186, beginning in West Sullivan and heading along the eastern rim of Frenchman Bay, are now the **West Sullivan–Schoodic Scenic Byway** (see the description in this chapter's introduction). Federal funding has improved signage and turnouts along this breathtakingly beautiful stretch of coast with views back across the bay to Acadia's mountains.

✳ To Do

BOAT EXCURSION Bar Harbor Ferry. See *Getting There.*

KAYAKING **Hancock Point Kayak Tours** (207-422-6854), 58 Point Rd., Hancock. Antonio Blasi offers guided paddling in Frenchman and Taunton Bays.

GOLF **Grindstone Neck Golf Course** (207-963-7760), Gerrishville. A nine-hole course dating to 1895 as part of this summer colony; open to the public June–Sep.

HIKING **Schoodic Mountain**, off Rt. 183 north of Sullivan, provides one of eastern Maine's most spectacular hikes, with 360-degree views. The Bureau of Parks and Lands (207-287-5936) has improved the parking area and trail system here. Take the first left (it's unpaved) after crossing the railroad tracks on Rt. 183; bear left at the Y and in 0.8 mile bear right to the parking lot. The hike to the top of Schoodic Mountain (1,069 feet) should take around 45 minutes; a marked trail from the summit leads down to sandy **Schoodic Beach** at the southern end of Donnell Pond (good swimming and half a dozen primitive campsites). Return to the parking lot on the old road that's now a footpath (0.5 mile). From the same parking lot, you can also follow a dirt path down to Donnell Pond or hike to the bluffs on Black Mountain, a mesmerizingly beautiful hike with summit views north to Tunk Lake and east across Washington County. Another trail descends to Schoodic Beach. This is now part of 14,000 acres known as **Donnell Pond Public Preserved Land**, which also includes Tunk and Spring River Lakes and primitive campsites.

SWIMMING See **Donnell Pond** just above, under *Hiking*. **Tunk Lake** offers a few access points off Rt. 183. Ask locally about **Molasses Pond** in Eastbrook.

✳ Lodging

☀ **Le Domaine** (207-422-3395 or 1-800-554-8498; www.ledomaine.com), 1513 Rt. 1, Hancock 04640. Best known for its dining room (see *Dining Out*), this elegant little Provençal-style inn offers three luxurious rooms and three exceptional suites. Chef-owner Nicole Purslow ran Maine's first genuine French restaurant, taking over from her mother, and continues to manage the business after selling it. The rooms, too, evoke Provence. Provençal antiques, fabrics, original paintings, and small niceties (like bowls of lavender) create real charm and a high comfort level. Bathrooms have a porcelain soaking tub and separate shower as well as a heated towel rack, lighted vanity mirror, and fluffy towels; the suites have a gas fireplace and cathedral ceilings, and all rooms have phone, bed light, and access to the balconies on which you can enjoy the flakiest of croissants with homemade honey and jam and French roast coffee. Pets are accepted for an additional charge. $200 per room, $285 per suite B&B. Add $85 per couple for a complete dinner.

♂ ♿ **Crocker House Country Inn** (207-422-6806 or 1-877-715-6017; www.crockerhouse.com), Hancock Point 04640. Open daily May–Oct., weekends Nov.–New Yea's Eve. The three-story, gray-shingled 1880s inn has 11 guest rooms, 9 in the inn itself and 2 on the second floor of the carriage house, including a big room that's good for families. All rooms have private bath and country antiques, quilts, and stenciling. Richard and Elizabeth Malaby have been the innkeepers since 1980, overseeing spacious common rooms, including the lounging space in the carriage barn near a hot tub. The second smallest post office in the United

States sits across the road next to the tennis courts; the octagonal library is a short walk. Breakfast and dinner are served in the dining room, which is open to the public (see *Dining Out*). $125–150 in Aug. includes a full breakfast; less in late June and July, still less before June 15 and after Oct. 15. Moorings are available, and a few touring bikes are kept for guests.

🐾 **Island View Inn** (207-422-3031; www.maineus.com/islandview), 12 Miramar Ave., Sullivan Harbor 04664. Open Memorial Day–mid-Oct. This is a spacious, gracious, 1880s summer "cottage" with a massive central hearth and airy sitting room set well back from Rt. 1 with splendid views of Frenchman Bay and the mountains on Mount Desert. Evelyn and Sarah Joost offer seven guest rooms, all with private bath and four with water views. All are nicely decorated, and there is a well-equipped guest pantry; a very full breakfast in the dining area overlooking the water is included. $135–195 in-season, $90–115 shoulder seasons; $20 per extra person. An 18-foot sailboat is available for guests to rent, and a canoe and rowboat are available at no charge.

⌒ **The Black Duck** (207-963-2689 or 1-877-963-2689; www.blackduck .com), P.O. Box 39, Corea 04624. Barry Canner and Robert Travers offer their fine old house overlooking one of Maine's most picturesque working harbors. Their four guest rooms and ample common areas are all comfortably, imaginatively furnished with antiques and contemporary art. The sunny dining room is a venue for morning feasts and good conversation. The working harbor is just across the road—unless you happen to be renting one of two house-keeping cottages that sit right on it. You can walk to sand beaches, but the nearby pond is more inviting for swimming. Two dogs will welcome you, so please leave your pets at home. One host can perform weddings. $125 for a pleasant upstairs room with a harbor view, or for a first-floor room with deck plus queen and twin beds; $145–190 for a two-bedroom suite; $160 for Harbor Studio (one bed and a kitchenette). Harbor Cottage is a weekly rental.

⌒ 🐾 ♿ **Oceanside Meadows Inn** (207-963-5557; www.oceaninn.com), P.O. Box 90, Prospect Harbor 04669. Open May–Oct., off-season by special arrangement. This 200-acre property/nature preserve includes an 1860s sea captain's home and neighboring 1820s farmhouse overlooking well-named Sand Cove. Sonja Sundaram and Ben Walter, passionate conservationists who met at an environmental research center in Bermuda, have renovated both houses, each with eight guest rooms, including several suites good for small families. All are within earshot of waves. The farmhouse in particular lends itself to rental as a whole, ideal for family reunions. The meadows and woods are webbed with trails leading to a salt marsh, good for spotting wildlife ranging from moose to eagles. A rehabbed open-timbered barn is the venue for a full schedule of concerts, lectures, and live performances and also works as a conference or wedding reception center. $128–168 for rooms, $178–198 for suites July–Columbus Day weekend, including Sandra's three- to four-course breakfasts. Less in May and June. See *Entertainment* for details about the Oceanside Meadows Institute for the Arts and Sciences.

☕ 🐾 ♿ Elsa's Inn on the Harbor
(207-963-7571; www.elsasinn.com),
179 Main St., Prospect Harbor 04669.
This gabled, mid-1800s house overlooks a working harbor, the last to
retain its sardine cannery. Cynthia and
Jeff (a sixth-generation lobster fisherman) Alley raised their children here,
and daughter Megan Moshier has
returned home, after stints in management at top hotels from Hawaii to
DC, to raise her son (with husband
Glenn). Together these personable
couples have totally renovated the old
homestead, creating six bright, spiffy
guest rooms with handmade quilts,
private baths, and water views, as well
as a comfortable living room, veranda,
and patio with water views. In all, 16
guests can bed down. $105–155 in
high season, from $75 off-season,
including a full breakfast that might
include crabmeat strata. Lobster bakes
ending with blueberry cobbler can be
arranged for in-house guests.

☕ 🐾 Mermaid's Purse Farm (207-
963-7344; www.mermaidspursefarm
.com), 50 Lighthouse Point Rd.,
Prospect Harbor 04669. Open year-
round. Penny Altman and Michael
Morton are artists, and their rambling
1840s farmhouse is a casual, comfortable haven with six guest rooms
fronting on a quarter mile of ocean
shore. While in the midst of an
unending renovation, the finished
rooms are really comfortable and
attractive. $85–145 (depending on the
season and room), breakfast, with the
likes of fresh fruit salad and a mozzarella omelet, included.

Bluff House Inn (207-963-7805;
www.bluffinn.com), Rt. 186, South
Gouldsboro 04607. This is a modern
lodge with a dining room featuring
floor-to-ceiling windows overlooking
the water and a comfortable sitting
area/lobby behind it. The eight guest
rooms line the upstairs hall; only the
two at the end have water views. It's
set off by itself above the pink granite
shore, from which you can launch a
kayak onto Frenchman Bay. $75–125
varying by the season. A two-bedroom
efficiency apartment is $165 per cou-
ple, $975 per week, in summer.

Bay View Farm (207-422-8228),
2543 Rt. 1, East Sullivan 04664. Charlie and Laurel Bartolomeo offer a
comfortable way stop in their 19th-
century house. Two cheery second-
floor guest rooms share a bath. You'll
find plenty of books, a TV, and a
DVD player in the living room. $65–
75 includes a full breakfast.

COTTAGES 🐾 **Albee's Shoreline
Cottages** (207-963-2336 or 1-800-
963-2336; www.theshorehouse.com),
Rt. 186, P.O. Box 70, Prospect Harbor
04669. Open Memorial Day–mid-Oct.
The 10 waterside cottages are classic
old Maine motor court vintage, but
each has been painstakingly rehabbed,
and all but 4 are right on the water;
all have gas heater, woodstove, or fireplace. Larry Caldwell and Richard
Rieth enjoy orienting guests to the
best of what's around. $69–107 per
night, $455–715 per week.

Sullivan Harbor Farm (207-422-
3735 or 1-800-422-4014; www
.sullivanharborfarm.com), Rt. 1, P.O.
Box 96, Sullivan 04664. Three particularly attractive cottages cluster on a
nicely sited property with a landscaped pool and resident hosts who
delight in turning guests on to local
hiking, kayaking, biking, and paddling
possibilities. Cupcake, a bright year-
round cottage with two working fireplaces, has water views and can sleep

MAMA'S BOY BISTRO, WINTER HARBOR

six ($1,350 per week; less off-season). Another cottage, Milo, sleeps four adults ($925 per week); Guzzle Cottage ($1,550) is a newly renovated three-bedroom, two-bath 1810 Cape with all conveniences and views across Frenchman Bay. A canoe is available. **Black Duck Properties** (207-963-7495; www.blackduck.com) in Corea handles local seasonal rentals. *Maine Guide to Inns and Bed & Breakfasts and Camps & Cottages*, free from the **Maine Tourism Association** (207-623-0363), lists rentals in this area.

CAMPGROUND **Ocean Woods Campground** (207-963-7194), P.O. Box 111, Birch Harbor 04613. Open early May–late Oct. Wooded, mostly oceanside campsites, some with hookups, some wilderness; hot showers.

✳ Where to Eat

DINING OUT **Le Domaine** (207-422-3395), Rt. 1, Hancock (9 miles east of Ellsworth). Open for dinner early June–Oct., Tue.–Sun. 6–9. Reservations recommended. Nicole Purslow, former *propriétaire et chef*, now manager, oversees highly rated French cuisine. Most summer residents on MDI know the shortcut to Le Domaine (see *Getting There*). Just 14 tables are nicely spaced in the softly lit dining rooms, decorated in Provençal prints with fresh flowers from the cutting garden and frequently a glowing fire, reflected in gleaming wood and copper. The meal might begin with the legendery *pâté de foie maison* or *cassoulets d'asperges* (paper-thin pastry filled with a blend of asparagus, mushrooms, and beans in a light broth cream sauce). The choice of entrées might include coquilles Saint-Jacques sauté (Maine scallops pan seared and garnished with fennel and white kidney beans), or thinly sliced veal sautéed and served with wild mushrooms in a rich cream sauce. The wine list numbers 5,000 bottles. The menu is à la carte with appetizers $11.50 and entrées $29.50. Also see *Lodging*.

Mama's Boy Bistro (207-963-2365), 10 Main St., Winter Harbor. Open for lunch and dinner in-season. Reservations recommended. Built by its first co-owner Lucas St. Clair, the son of Burt's Bees cofounder Roxanne Quimby, this restaurant is now owned by Michael Boland. Request a water view and begin with Sullivan Harbor Farm smoked salmon and a mix of local greens ($9), then dine on seafood cioppino with Darthia Farm's organic basil. Boland expects to add prime rib and lobster Newburgh, and a deck for outdoor dining and water views. Fully licensed with a long wine list. Entrées $14–24.

♪ **Bunkers Wharf** (207-963-2244), 260 East Schoodic Dr., Birch Harbor. Open year-round, in-season Mon.–Sat. for lunch and dinner; check off-season. Beautifully sited on a small harbor a mile from the park exit; a gem. Opened in 2004, this knotty-pine, glass-faced building, offering both patio and fireside tables, is an expanded version of the house owner Bill Osgood built himself in 1956. Lunch choices include all the seafood staples. The pan-blackened haddock sandwich with greens and roasted red pepper tartar sauce ($8.85) is a real standout. Entrées $17.75–25.95. A children's menu is available all day.

Crocker House Country Inn (207-422-6806), Hancock Point. Open nightly Apr.–Jan., weekends off-season for dinner, 5:30–9. A pleasant country-inn atmosphere and varied menu; the specialty is Crocker House scallops, sautéed with mushrooms, scallions, garlic, and tomatoes with lemon and wine sauce ($22.95). Entrées $21.95–29.50.

Chippers Restaurant (207-422-8238), 193 Main St. (Rt. 1), Hancock. Open year-round for dinner Tue.–Sat. 5–10, Sun. 4–8; Thu.–Sat. off-season. Not much from the road, but inside there's a serious dining atmosphere and menu. All meals begin with a very small bowl of rich haddock chowder. Entrée choices might include roasted salmon or breast of duck ($16.95) and Cajun seafood Alfredo ($20.95).

Fisherman's Inn Restaurant (207-963-5585), 7 Newman St., Winter Harbor. Open Apr.–Oct. for lunch 11:30–2:30; dinner is served year-round 4:30–9. Chef-owner Carl Johnson was voted Chef of the Year in 2004 by the Maine chapter of the American Culinary Association. His pleasant, dependably good restaurant offers a full menu ranging from baked stuffed portobello mushroom to char-grilled filet mignon. Still, seafood is the specialty: lobster several different ways, a Winter Harbor seafood casserole, finnan haddie, haddock stuffed with crabmeat, and crispy cooked salmon fillet with Thai spices. Dinner

entrées $13.95–26.95 (for the lobster bake).

Tidal Falls Lobster Restaurant (207-422-6457), 1.5 miles off Rt. 1 (take East Side Rd.), Hancock. Open for dinner late June–Labor Day, Mon.–Fri. 5–9, for lunch and dinner Sat. and Sun. 11:30–9. Sited by the reversing falls, home to seals, ospreys, blue herons, and bald eagles, it's now owned by the Frenchman Bay Conservancy. Feast on steamers, lobster, mussels, crabs, steak, and the view. Burgers, sandwiches and peppermint tea are also served. The Captain's Deck, a weatherproofed pavilion, can be reserved. BYOB.

EATING OUT Ruth & Wimpy's Kitchen (207-422-3723), Rt. 1, Hancock. Open year-round. Look for "Wilbur the Lobster." Wimpy Wilbur is a former long-haul truck driver, and this family-run mainstay is decorated with his collection of miniature trucks, license plates, beer bottles, and more. The menu includes burgers and steaks, overstuffed sandwiches, and seafood, including lobster with all the fixings.

Chase's Restaurant (207-963-7171), 193 Main St., Winter Harbor. Open all year for all three meals. A

RUTH & WIMPY'S

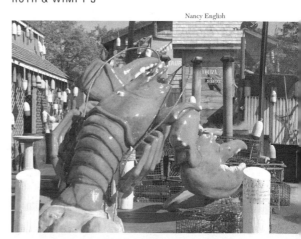

Nancy English

convenient, local hang-out on Rt. 186 near the entrance to the park. Booths, fried lobsters and clams, good chowder; will pack a picnic.

J. M. Gerrish Market & Café (207-963-2727), 352 Main St., Winter Harbor. Open Mon.–Sat. in high season 8–5, Sun. 9–5; lunch 11–3. Fewer days and shorter hours in May, June, and Sep. No longer the old-fashioned ice cream parlor beloved by generations of the summer community, this is now a slick coffee bar with big beer, wine, and specialty food sections; still some tables and sandwiches like smoked turkey, cheddar, and peach salsa.

Downeast Deli (207-963-2700), corner of Rts. 186 and 195, Prospect Harbor. Open Sun.–Thu. 10–8, weekends until 9. Boasting the biggest deli-style hoagies, sandwiches, and subs north of Boston along with standout pizza, Philly steaks, and garden salads. Inquire about picnic spots.

ELEGANT PICNIC FIXINGS AND TAKE-HOME Mano's Market, 1517 Rt. 1, Hancock Village. Open May–Dec., Tue.–Sat. 11–6. Owned by the previous owner-chef of next-door Le Domaine, this is the ultimate Down East gourmet takeout. Insulated wicker picnic baskets to go (and be returned) can be filled with spit-roasted chicken, salad Niçoise, and fresh French bread, among many other selections. Wine and cheese selections are large and well priced.

Sullivan Harbor Salmon (1-800-422-4014), Rt. 1, just east of Mano's, Hancock Village. The salmon is local, and visitors can see the smokehouse through windows in the expanded new retail area. Fish are cured in small batches, hand rubbed with a blend of salt and brown sugar, then rinsed in spring-fed water and slowly smoked over a smudge fire of hickory shavings in the traditional Scottish way. No preservatives or additives. Mustards, crackers, breads, and other gourmet items also sold.

Grindstone Neck of Maine (207-963-7347 or 1-800-831-8734; www.grindstoneneck.com), 311 Newman St. (Rt. 186), Winter Harbor. This impressive new smokehouse is a source of smoked mussels, oysters, scallops, and seafood spreads as well as salmon. Samples offered.

✳ Entertainment

🖔 **Schoodic Arts for All** (207-963-2569; www.schoodicarts.org), Hammond Hall, 427 Main St., Prospect Harbor. The concert series hosts a concert on the second Friday of every month, May–Oct.; the festival presents nightly concerts and more for the first two weeks of Aug. Hammond Hall has been renovated and is now heated and handicapped accessible; events are held into Dec.

Pierre Monteux Memorial Concert Hall (207-422-3931), Hancock, is the setting for a series of June and July Sunday symphony and Wednesday chamber music concerts, presented by faculty and students at the respected Pierre Monteux School for Conductors.

Oceanside Meadows Institute for the Arts and Sciences (207-963-5557; www.oceaninn.org/omias), staged in a renovated, open-beamed barn behind the Oceanside Meadows Inn, Rt. 195, Corea. May–Oct.: a Thursday-evening series of lectures and concerts and other performances, from classical music and light opera to jazz and chamber music.

☀ Selective Shopping
ART AND FINE CRAFTS GALLERIES

Listed geographically, more or less, heading east along Rt. 1
Gull Rock Pottery (207-422-3990), Eastside Rd. (1.5 miles off Rt. 1), Hancock. Open year-round, Mon.–Sat. 9–5. Torj and Kurt Wray wheel-throw functional blue-and-white stoneware with hand-brushed designs.

Raven Tree Art Gallery (207-422-8273), 536 Point Road, Hancock. Open Mon.–Sat. 9–5:30. Striking sculptures by Russell Wray and etchings, drypoints, and engravings; also jewelery and pottery by Akemi Wray.

Barter Family Gallery and Shop (207-422-3190; www.barterfamily gallery.com), Taunton Bay Rd., Sullivan. Open mid-May–mid-Oct., Mon.–Sat. 10–5, or by appointment or chance. Posted from Rt. 1 at Sullivan's common (it's 2.5 miles). "We never get busy here," Priscilla Barter will tell you. Never mind that her husband's paintings hang in museums and fetch big money in the best galleries. This gallery, attached to the small house that Philip Barter built and in which the couple raised seven children, is easily the most colorful in Maine, and still remote enough to keep browsers and buyers to a trickle. Here, added to dozens of distinctive Barter mountains, houses, and harbors, are off-the-wall pieces, wood sculptures, and Barter-made furniture. The gallery also features Priscilla's braided rugs.

On the way to the Barter Gallery
Art & Old Things (207-422-3551), 70 Taunton Dr., Sullivan. Open daily June–Oct. Joe Martell offers an irresistible mishmash of antiques and collectibles plus a first-rate upstairs gallery.

Angel Antics (207-422-2250; www .angelantics.net), 3 Garden Way, Sullivan. Just off Rt. 1, this shop sells a wide range of glasswork, from fused glass to small stained-glass pieces; everything but the marbles is made here.

Wildfire Run Quilt Boutique (207-422-3935), 0.7 mile down Taunton Dr. Peg McAloon's quilts, wall hangings, and clothing are well worth a stop.

Lunaform (207-422-0923), marked from Rt. 1 at the Sullivan common. Open year-round, Mon.–Fri. 9–5. Striking handmade, steel-reinforced concrete garden urns (some are huge) as well as pots and planters are made in this former granite quarry.

Also worth a detour
Hog Bay Pottery (207-565-2282; www.hogbay.com), 4 miles north of Rt. 1 on Rt. 200, Franklin. Open year-round. Susanne Grosjean's award-winning rugs and distinctive table- and ovenware by Charles Grosjean.

Spring Woods Gallery (207-442-3007), Rt. 200 (off Rt. 1), Sullivan. Open daily (except Sun.) 10–5. This gallery represents several members of the Breeden family. The adjoining gallery alone is worth a stop.

BARTER FAMILY GALLERY AND SHOP
Christina Tree

On the Schoodic Peninsula

Maine Kiln Works (207-963-5819), Rt. 186, West Gouldsboro (0.5 mile off Rt. 1). Over the years Dan and Elizabeth Weaver have come to specialize in distinctive stoneware sinks and towel bars, flameware platters and plates, as well as tableware.

U.S. Bells and Watering Cove Pottery (207-963-7184), Rt. 186, Prospect Harbor. Open daily in summer, by appointment off-season. Richard Fisher creates (designs and casts) bells that form musical sculptures, and Liza Fisher creates wood-fired stoneware and porcelain.

Lee Art Glass Studio (207-963-7004), 298 Main St., Winter Harbor. Open Memorial Day–Columbus Day, 10–4; closed Mon. It's difficult to describe this fused-glass tableware, which incorporates ground enamels and crocheted doilies or stencils. It works.

Stave Island Gallery (207-963-2040; www.properclay.com), 636 S. Gouldsboro Rd., (Rt. 186), Gouldsboro. Susan Dickson-Smith hand throws her pottery, from functional tableware to sculptural vases. The gallery also displays her weaving and works of other local craftspeople.

SPECIAL SHOPS **Bartlett Maine Estate Winery** (207-546-2408; www.bartlettwinery.com), just off Rt. 1, Gouldsboro. Open for tastings Memorial Day–Columbus Day, Mon.–Sat. 10–5; other times by appointment. Before Bob and Kathe Bartlett could open Maine's first winery back in 1982, they had to get the law changed. "Prohibition began in Maine," Bob Bartlett will remind you. An architect by training, he designed this low-slung winery sequestered in firs. The wines, which utilize Maine apples, blueberries, raspberries, and honey as well as regional pears and peaches, continue to win top honors in national and international competitions. Dry Oak Wild Blueberry is a personal favorite.

◊ **Hattie's Shed at Darthia Farm** (207-963-7771), 520 W. Bay Rd. (marked from Rt. 1), Gouldsboro. Open June–Sep. 8–5, Sat. until noon; closed Sun. A 133-acre organic farm with resident sheep, pigs, and turkeys. The farm stand is justly famed for its vinegars, jams, salsas, and cheeses; Hattie's Shed, a weaving shop also at the farm, features coats, jackets, scarves, and shawls.

Winter Harbor 5&10 (207-963-7927; www.winterharbor5and10.com), Main St., Winter Harbor. Open daily, year-round. Peter Drinkwater will tell you it isn't easy operating a genuine, old-style five-and-dime these days. While it sells some souvenirs, this is the genuine article; also the local stop for UPS, a copier, fax, and newspapers.

✱ Special Events

May: **Annual Trade Day and Benefit Auction**—peninsula-wide yard sales climaxed by an auction at the Winter Harbor Grammar School.

August: **Sullivan Daze** (*first Saturday*)—an art festival. **Schoodic Arts Festival** (*first 2 weeks*)—a major event with dozens of nominally priced workshops in a wide variety of arts and many performances at venues scattered throughout the Schoodic Peninsula (www.schoodicarts.org). **Winter Harbor Lobster Festival** (*second Saturday*), Winter Harbor—includes road race, lobster feed, and lobster-boat races.

WASHINGTON COUNTY AND THE QUODDY LOOP

THE ATLANTIC COAST: STEUBEN TO CAMPOBELLO ISLAND (NEW BRUNSWICK)

EASTPORT, COBSCOOK BAY, AND PASSAMAQUODDY BAY

CALAIS AND THE ST. CROIX VALLEY

ST. ANDREWS AND GRAND MANAN (NEW BRUNSWICK)

As Down East as you can get in this country, Washington County is a ruggedly beautiful and lonely land unto itself. Its 700-mile coast harbors some of the most dramatic cliffs and deepest coves—certainly the highest tides—on the eastern U.S. seaboard, but relatively few tourists. Lobster boats and trawlers still outnumber pleasure craft.

Created in 1789 by order of the General Court of Massachusetts, Washington County is as large as the states of Delaware and Rhode Island combined. Yet it's home to just 35,000 people, compared with 1.9 million in those states. Here they are widely scattered among fishing villages, logging outposts, Native American reservations, and saltwater farms. Many people (not just some) survive here by raking blueberries in August, making balsam wreaths in winter, and lobstering, clamming, digging sea worms, and diving for sea urchins the remainder of the year. Washington County is the world's largest source of wild blueberries.

Less than 10 percent of the visitors who get as far as Bar Harbor come this much farther. The only groups you see are scouting for American bald eagles or ospreys in the Moosehorn National Wildlife Refuge; for puffins, auks, and arctic terns on Machias Seal Island; or for whales in the Bay of Fundy. You may also see fishermen angling for landlocked salmon and smallmouth bass in the lakes.

Happily, word has begun to spread that you don't drop off the end of the world beyond Eastport or Campobello Island, even though—since the boundary was drawn across the face of Passamaquoddy Bay—New England maps have

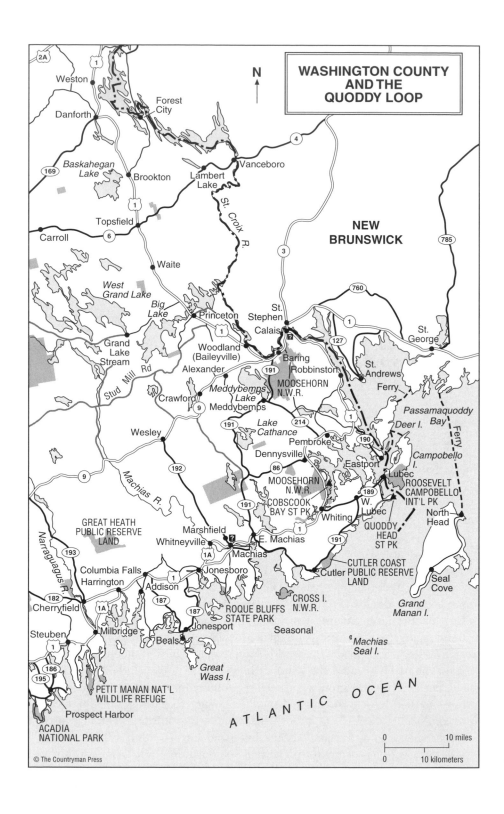

N

**WASHINGTON COUNTY
AND THE
QUODDY LOOP**

2A

1

Weston

Forest
City

Danforth

169

*Baskahegan
Lake*

Brookton

Lambert
Lake

Vanceboro

4

NEW
BRUNSWICK

785

1

Topsfield

St. Croix R.

Carroll

6

Waite

3

*West
Grand Lake*

760

*Big
Lake*

Princeton

St.
Stephen

1

St.
George

127

Calais

Grand
Lake
Stream

1

Woodland
(Baileyville)

Baring

St.
Andrews

Stud Mill Rd

Alexander

191

Robbinston

Ferry

*Passamaquoddy
Bay*

MOOSEHORN
N.W.R.

Crawford

*Meddybemps
Lake*

Deer I.

Ferry

9

Meddybemps

190

*Campobello
I.*

Wesley

191

*Lake
Cathance*

214

Pembroke

Eastport

9

Dennysville

Lubec

ROOSEVELT
CAMPOBELLO
INT'L PK

192

86

MOOSEHORN
N.W.R.

189

W.
Lubec

Machias R.

191

COBSCOOK
BAY ST PK

Whiting

North
Head

GREAT HEATH
PUBLIC RESERVE
LAND

1

QUODDY
HEAD
ST PK

191

Narraguagus R.

Marshfield

Whitneyville

E. Machias

Seal
Cove

193

1A

Machias

CUTLER COAST
PUBLIC RESERVE
LAND

*Grand
Manan I.*

Columbia Falls

1

Jonesboro

182

Harrington

Addison

Cutler

Cherryfield

1A

187

CROSS I.
N.W.R.

Steuben

Milbridge

187

Jonesport

ROQUE BLUFFS
STATE PARK

*Machias
Seal I.*

1

Beals

Seasonal

186

195

*Great
Wass I.*

PETIT MANAN NAT'L
WILDLIFE REFUGE

ATLANTIC OCEAN

Prospect Harbor

ACADIA
NATIONAL PARK

© The Countryman Press

0   10 miles

0   10 kilometers

included only the Maine shore and Campobello Island in New Brunswick, Canada (linked to Lubec, Maine, by a bridge), and Canadian maps have detailed only New Brunswick. In summer when the ferries are running, the crossing from either Eastport or Campobello to L'Etete, near the resort town of St. Andrews, New Brunswick, is among the most scenic in the East. This circuit, which is best done driving one way and taking ferries the other, has come to be known as the Quoddy Loop. The drive is up along the St. Croix River to Calais, and the ferry trip involves transferring from a small to a larger (free) Canadian ferry on Deer Island in the middle of Passamaquoddy Bay. Because St. Andrews itself probably offers a greater number and variety of "rooms" and dining than all Washington County combined, and because the exchange rate favors Americans, it is a logical place to spend the night. We also include the magnificent island of Grand Manan, which lies off Maine's Bold Coast but is also part of New Brunswick, accessible from Blacks Harbour not far from St. Andrews.

In recent decades tens of thousands of acres of shore property, some of the most spectacular in the county, have been acquired by the state and conservation groups; many miles of hiking trails now access remote cliffs and coves. For hikers, as writer Wayne Curtis has noted, a trip to Washington County is "like getting two destinations for the price of one." Curtis notes that here the North Woods comes down to the shore; "you can set off in search of moose and whales on the same hike." Kayaking outfitters, too, have appeared, accessing the beauty of the area's many sheltered tidal rivers and reaches.

For exploring purposes, Washington County is divided into three distinct regions: (1) the 60-mile stretch of Rt. 1 between Steuben and Lubec (with roughly 10 times as many miles of wandering coastline) and the island of Campobello, N.B., just across the bridge from Lubec; (2) Eastport and Cobscook Bay, the area of the highest tides and an end-of-the-world feel (by water, Lubec and Eastport—respectively the country's easternmost town and city—are less than 3 miles apart, but they're separated by 43 land miles); (3) Calais and the St. Croix Valley, including the lake-splotched backwoods and the fishermen's havens at Grand Lake Stream. In this chapter we also include St. Andrews and Grand Manan, New Brunswick, part of the Quoddy Loop and well worth exploring for anyone who has come this far.

Wherever you explore in Washington County—from the old sardine-canning towns of Eastport and Lubec to the coastal fishing villages of Jonesport and Cutler, and the even smaller villages on the immense inland lakes—you find a Maine you thought had disappeared decades ago. You are surprised by the beauty of old buildings such as the 18th-century Burnham Tavern in Machias and Ruggles House in Columbia Falls. You learn that the first naval battle of the Revolution was won by Machias men; that some local 18th-century women were buried in rum casks (because they were shipped home that way from the Caribbean); and that pirate Captain Richard Bellamy's loot is believed to be buried around Machias.

And if any proof were needed that this has always been one isolated piece of coast, there is Bailey's Mistake. Captain Bailey, it seems, wrecked his four-masted schooner one foggy night in a fine little bay 7 miles south of Lubec (where he should have put in). Considering the beauty of the spot and how far he was from the Boston shipowner, Bailey and his crew unpacked their cargo of lumber and settled right down on the shore. That was in 1830, and many of their descendants have had the sense to stay put.

GUIDANCE **Sunrise County Economic Council** (www.sunrisecounty.org) is good for natural and historical sights.

Maine's Washington County, a free 60-page-plus guide to the entire county, is available locally or by request from Jay Hinson, P.O. Box 38, Robbinston 04671. A *Quoddy Loop Tour Guide* at **www.quoddyloop.com** provides information about communities from Machias to Calais and a map of the area plus the New Brunswick communities.

No southern gateway info center for Washington County exists at this writing but at the New Brunswick border in Calais there are two: The **Maine Tourism Association** maintains a full-service center at 7 Union St., open daily year-round, while the **Downeast Heritage Center** (1-877-454-2500; www.down easteritage.org), 39 Union St., offers an overview of the region. Also note chambers listed under *Guidance* in the areas they promote within the county.

GETTING THERE *By air:* See "Bar Harbor" and "Bangor Area" for scheduled airline service. Charter service is also available to the following airports: **Eastport Municipal** (207-853-2951), **Machias Valley** (207-255-8709), **Lubec Municipal** (207-733-5532), and **Princeton Municipal** (207-796-2744).

By bus: **Concord Trailways** (1-800-639-3317) and **Vermont Transit** (1-800-451-3292) both serve Bangor year-round. **West's Coastal Connection** (207-546-2823 or 1-800-596-2823), based in Milbridge, runs a bus daily between Bangor Airport and Calais, with stops in Machias and Perry, flag-down stops (call ahead) in between.

By car: The fastest way is via I-95 and Rt. 295 to Bangor, Rt. 1A to Ellsworth, then Rt. 1. For coastal points east of Harrington, you save 9 miles by cutting inland on Rt. 182 from Hancock to Cherryfield. For northeastern Washington County, take I-95 to Bangor, then the Airline Highway (Rt. 9) for 100 miles straight through the blueberry barrens and woods to Calais. The state maintains camping and picnic sites at intervals along this stretch, and limited food and lodging can be found along the way.

GETTING AROUND **East Coast Ferries Ltd.** (506-747-2159 or 1-877-747-2159; www.eastcoastferries.nb.ca), based on Deer Island, serves both Campobello Island (30 minutes) and Eastport (20 minutes). Generally these run every hour from around 9 AM (Atlantic Time, or AT) to around 7 PM (AT), late June–early Sep., but call Stan Lord to check. In 2004 service was less frequent from Eastport. The Campobello ferry takes 12 cars, and the Eastport ferry takes 8 but gets fewer passengers. It's slightly more expensive from Campobello than from Eastport: $14 per car and driver compared with $11. Deer Island itself is more than a mere stepping-stone in the bay. Roughly 9 miles long and more than 3 miles wide, it's popular with bicyclists and bird-watchers. It boasts the world's three largest lobster pounds, the original Atlantic salmon aquaculture site, a lighthouse, and several B&Bs and an inn with upscale dining.

The free, larger, year-round **Deer Island–L'Etete (New Brunswick mainland) Ferry** (506-453-2600) crossing takes 20 minutes, departing Apr.–Sep. every hour, 7–7 (AT), but call to confirm. This ride across Passamaquoddy Bay is exceptional.

CROSSING THE BORDER Contrary to rumor, reentering the United States from Canada in Lubec, Calais, or Eastport is not that different from the way it was before September 11. You do want to bring a passport. It's not necessary, but definite proof of citizenship can now be required of anyone entering the U.S. Cars are checked more carefully than they were, but we are aware of no routinely long waits and encountered none. FYI: Do not bring a radar detector into Canada. They are illegal in the Maritime Provinces. Also, if you're driving a vehicle other than your own, you must have the owner's written permission, and if you're bringing in a dog or cat for more than a couple of days you must have proof of a rabies vaccination.

THE ATLANTIC COAST: STEUBEN TO CAMPOBELLO ISLAND (NEW BRUNSWICK)

GUIDANCE **The Machias Bay Area Chamber of Commerce** (207-255-4402; www.machiaschamber.org), P.O. Box 606, Machias 04654. A seasonal, weekday, walk-in information center on Rt. 1 is sequestered between Helen's Restaurant and the Irving station, in the rear of the Wall's Appliance building. It's well stocked with brochures and publishes a useful list of summer cottages. It serves the coastal and lake area extending from Jonesboro to Cutler and Whiting.

Cobscook Bay Area Chamber of Commerce (207-733-2201; P.O. Box 42, Whiting 04691; www.cobscookbay.com) is based at the Puffin Pines Country Gift Store, Rt. 1 in Whiting. Also look for the volunteer-run seasonal information center in the Lubec Historical Society, a former general store, as you enter town on Rt. 189.

The Campobello Island Tourist Information Center (506-752-7018 or 506-752-7043), just past Canadian Customs after crossing the bridge to the island, is open daily May–Columbus Day. New Brunswick tourist information is available from 1-800-561-0123; www.tourismnbcanada.com.

A Quoddy Loop Tour Guide (www.quoddyloop.com) has information and a map of the area from Machias to Calais as well as Campobello Island, Grand Manan, and other communities around Passamaquoddy Bay in Maine and New Brunswick.

✳ To See

Entries are listed geographically, heading east
Steuben, the first town in Washington County, is known as the site of the 6,000-acre **Petit Manan National Wildlife Refuge** (207-546-2124). The preserve includes two coastal peninsulas and 24 offshore islands.

Milbridge, a Rt. 1 town with a wandering coastline, is the administrative home of one of the oldest wild blueberry processors (Jasper Wyman and Sons). The town also supports a Christmas wreath factory and a great little movie theater. **McClellan Park**, overlooking Narraguagus (pronounced *nair-a-GWAY-gus*) Bay, offers picnic tables, fireplaces, campsites, restrooms, and drinking water. The **Milbridge Historical Museum** (207-546-7479) is open late May–Sep., Sat. and Sun. 1–4 and by appointment. This is a delightful window into this spirited community, with ambitious changing exhibits and displays on past shipyards, canneries, and 19th-century life. **Milbridge Days** in late July have attracted national coverage in recent years; the highlight is a codfish relay.

Cherryfield. A few miles up the Narraguagus River, Cherryfield boasts stately houses. The **Cherryfield-Narraguagus Historical Society** (207-546-7979), Main St. (just off Rt. 1), is open July and Aug., Wed. and Fri. 1–4. Stewart Park on Main St. and Forest Mill Dam Park on River Rd. are good places for a swim. Cherryfield (why isn't it called Berryfield?) bills itself Blueberry Capital of Maine; there are two processing plants in town.

Columbia Falls is an unusually picturesque village with one of Maine's most notable houses at its center. The **Ruggles House** (207-483-4637; www.ruggles house.com; 0.25 mile off Rt. 1; open June–mid-Oct., Mon.–Sat. 9:30–4:30, Sun. 11–4:30; nominal donation) is a Federal-style mansion built by wealthy lumber dealer Thomas Ruggles in 1818. It is a beauty, with a graceful flying staircase, a fine Palladian window, and superb woodwork. Legend has it that a woodcarver was imprisoned in the house for three years with a penknife. There is an unmistakably tragic feel to the place. Mr. Ruggles died soon after its completion. The house had fallen into disrepair by the 1920s, and major museums were eyeing its exquisite flying staircase when local pharmacist Mary Chandler, a Ruggles descendant, galvanized local and summer people to save and restore the old place.

Jonesport (population: 1,525) sits at the tip of a 12-mile-long peninsula facing Moosabec Reach, which is, in turn, spanned by a bridge leading to **Beals Island** (population: 667). Both communities are all about fishing. Together Jonesport and Beals are home to eastern Maine's largest lobstering fleet, and the bridge is a popular viewing stand for the **July 4 lobster-boat races**. Beals Island, populated largely by Alleys and Beals, is known for the distinctive design of its lobster

RUGGLES HOUSE

Kim Grant

boats, and it's not hard to find one under construction. It's connected, in turn, to **Great Wass Island**, a hiking destination with trails through a 1,579-acre tract maintained by The Nature Conservancy (there's good picnicking on the rocky shore, when you finally reach it). Also on Great Wass, the **Downeast Institute for Applied Marine Research and Education** (207-497-5769; open to the public year-round, daily 9–4) produces up to 10 million seed clams annually for distribution to local clam flats; old photos

JONESPORT

depict the history of local clamming. Lobsters are also grown. (Turn right, just before the conservancy parking lot.)

The village of Jonesport seems small the first time you drive through but grows in dimensions as you slow down. Look closely and you'll find a marina, food, antiques shops, B&Bs, chandleries, and more. Two out of three overnight visitors are here, however, to sail out with John Norton to Machias Seal Island to see **puffins**. Railroad buffs also come to see Buz and Helen Beal's **Maine Central Model Railroad** (call ahead: 207 497-2255), where 380 cars traverse 3,000 feet of tracks that wind through hand-built miniature replicas of local towns and scenery. The Tiffany-style stained-glass windows in the **Congregational church** are a point of local pride.

Jonesboro (population: 585) is represented on Rt. 1 by a general store (closed at present), a church, a post office, and (larger than any of these) the White House Restaurant. The beauty of this town, however, is in its shoreline, which wanders in and out of points and coves along the tidal Chandler River and Chandler Bay on the way to **Roque Bluffs State Park**, 6 miles south of Rt. 1. A public boat launch with picnic tables is 5 minutes south of Rt. 1; take the Roque Bluffs Rd. but turn right onto Evergreen Point Rd.

Machias (population: 1,773) is the county seat, an interesting old commercial center with the Machias River running through town and over the Bad Little Falls. **The Burnham Tavern** (207-255-4432), Main St. (up and around the corner from Rt. 1), is open early June–mid-Sep., Mon.–Fri. 9–5 and by appointment. A 1770s gambrel-roofed tavern, it's filled with period furnishings and tells the story of British man-of-war *Margaretta*, captured on June 12, 1775, by townspeople in the small sloop *Unity*. This was the first naval battle of the American Revolution. Unfortunately, the British retaliated by burning Portland. The **University of Maine at Machias** maintains an art gallery with changing exhibits. There is summer theater and music, including concerts in the graceful 1836 **Congregational church** (centerpiece of the annual **Wild Blueberry Festival**, the third weekend in August). Also note the picnic tables and suspension bridge at the falls and the many headstones worth pondering in the neighboring cemetery. Early in the 19th century Machias was second only to Bangor among Maine lumber ports. In 1912 the town boasted an opera house, two newspapers, three hotels, and a trotting park. Today Main Street Machias (Rt. 1) is pocked with empty storefronts and lots but still offers good places to shop and to eat.

Machiasport. Turn down Rt. 92 at Bad Little Falls Park in Machias. This picturesque village includes the **Gates and Cooper Houses** (207-255-8461, open mid-June–early Sep., Tue.–Sat. 12:30–4:30), Federal-style homes with maritime exhibits and period rooms. **Fort O'Brien** consists of earthen breastworks with cannons and includes the grass-covered remains of the ammunition powder magazine used during the American Revolution and the War of 1812. We recommend that you continue on down this road to the fishing village of Bucks Harbor and on to **Jasper Beach**, so named for the wave-tumbled and polished pebbles of jasper and rhyolite that give it its distinctive color. The road ends with great views and a beach to walk in **Starboard**.

Cutler. From East Machias, follow Rt. 191 south to this small fishing village that's happily shielded from a view of the Cutler navy communications station— one of the world's most powerful radio stations. Its 26 antenna towers (800 to 980 feet tall) light up red at night and can be seen from much of the county's coast. Cutler is the departure point for Captain Andy Patterson's excursions to see the **puffins** on Machias Seal Island. Beyond Cutler, Rt. 191 follows the shoreline through moorlike blueberry and cranberry country, with disappointingly few views. Much of this land is now publicly owned, and the high bluffs can be accessed via the **Bold Coast Trail**. If time permits, in South Trescott bear right onto the unmarked dirt road instead of continuing north on Rt. 191 and follow the coast through **Bailey's Mistake** (see the introduction to "Washington County") to West Quoddy Light. Otherwise continue to West Lubec and turn right on Rt. 189 into Lubec. Rt. 1 also runs from Machias to West Lubec.

Lubec. Visitors pass through this "easternmost town" on their way over the FDR Memorial Bridge to Campobello Island, New Brunswick. The **Lubec Historical Society Museum** (207-733-2274), open in summer Tue., Thu., and Sat. 9–3, fills the old Columbian Store on the edge of town and doubles as an information center. Once there were 20 sardine-canning plants in Lubec, an era evoked in the **Rier's Old Sardine Village Museum** (207-733-2822; not open in 2005, but may reopen in 2006). Barney and Becky Rier have spent many years assembling and interpreting this collection of sardine industry and related memorabilia. Check out the new full-service municipal **Lubec Marina** and the old town landing with its public boat launch, breakwater, and a view of **Mulholland Point Light** across the narrows on Campobello Island. The tide rushes in and out through these narrows, and frequently you can see seals playing and fishing in the water. Another light, Lubec Channel Light—known as **the Sparkplug**— can be viewed from the bridge and from Stockford Park, along the water south of the bridge. Lubec's **Water Sreet** is transitioning from sardine cannery row to an increasingly interesting lineup of shops, eateries, and galleries with a magnificent new library and the historic **McCurdy's Smokehouse** restoration at its center. Drawn in part by summerlong **SummerKeys** musical workshops and by the price of local real estate, new seasonal and year-round volunteer-minded "people from away" are fueling the revival of this colorful old community. Inquire about the free concerts presented Wednesday evenings during summer.

Quoddy Head State Park, S. Lubec Rd., Lubec (4.7 miles off Rt. 189). Open mid-Apr.–Oct., sunrise to sunset, with a **visitor center** open mid-May–Oct., 10–4. Displays tell the story of the lighthouse, which dates back to 1858, and of local industries; there's also a gallery with changing art exhibits. Despite its name, the red-and-white-striped **West Quoddy Head Lighthouse** marks the easternmost tip of the United States (the East Quoddy Head Lighthouse is on Campobello Island in Canada). The 532-acre Quoddy Head State Park, adjacent to the lighthouse, offers benches from which you are invited to be the first person in the U.S. to see the sunrise. There is also a fine view of Grand Manan Island, a pleasant picnic area, and the spectacular 2-mile **Coastal Trail** along the cliffs to Carrying Place Cove. Between the cove and the bay, roughly a mile back down the road from the light, is an unusual coastal, raised-plateau bog with dense sphagnum moss and heath.

Campobello Island is accessible from Lubec via the FDR Memorial Bridge. It's 9 miles long with some 3,000 year-round residents living primarily in the fishing villages of Wilson's Beach and Welshpool and above North Road. Granted to Captain William Owen in the 1760s, much of the island remained in the family until 1881, when a large part was sold to Boston developers who built three large (long-gone) hotels. Another major real estate development in the 1980s and '90s by the same Arkansas-based company that developed Whitewater (the Clintons were not involved in this one) failed. The land amassed for that venture is still being sold as house lots, while much of the undeveloped land is being logged. The International Park aside, Campobello offers whale-watching, golf, some good places to eat and sleep (priced in Canadian dollars), a (relatively) warm-water beach, and some very good hiking and birding.

♪ **Roosevelt Campobello International Park** (506-752-2922; www.fdr .net), Welshpool, Campobello Island, New Brunswick, Canada (for a brochure, write P.O. Box 129, Lubec 04652). Open Memorial Day weekend–mid-Oct., daily 9–5 eastern daylight time (10–6 Canadian Atlantic daylight time). Although technically in New Brunswick, this manicured 2,800-acre park with a visitor center and shingled "cottages" is the number one sight to see east of Bar Harbor. Follow Rt. 189 as it turns in Lubec, and there is the bridge (built in 1962) and U.S. and Canadian Customs.

The house in which Franklin Delano Roosevelt summered as a boy has disappeared, but the airy 34-room **Roosevelt Cottage**, a wedding gift to Franklin and Eleanor, is sensitively maintained just as the family left it, charged with the spirit of the dynamic

WEST QUODDY HEAD LIGHT

Christina Tree

man who contracted polio here on August 25, 1921. It's filled with many poignant objects, such as the toy boat FDR carved for his children. During his subsequent stints as governor of New York and then as president of the United States, FDR returned only three times. Neighboring Hubbard Cottage, with its oval picture window, gives another slant on this turn-of-the-20th-century resort. There's a visitor center here with an excellent historical exhibit and a 15-minute introductory film. Beyond stretch more than 8 miles of trails to the shore and then inland through woods to lakes and ponds. There are also 15.4 miles of park drives, modified from the network of carriage drives that the wealthy "cottagers" maintained on the island.

East Quoddy Head Lighthouse is beyond the park, accessible at low tide, a popular whale-watching station but a real adventure to get to (attempt only if you are physically fit).

✳ To Do

CANOEING AND KAYAKING **The Machias River**, fed by the five Machias Lakes, drops through the backwoods with technically demanding rapids and takes 3 to 6 days to run. The Narraguagus and East Machias Rivers are also good for trips of 2 to 4 days. For rentals and guided tours, see **Sunrise County Canoe and Kayak** (207-255-3375 or 1-877-980-2300; www.sunrisecanoeandkayak.com). Founded more than 30 years ago to offer canoeing on eastern Maine rivers, Sunrise now offers outfitting for the St. Croix and Machias Rivers as well as ambitious multiday kayaking expeditions along the Bold Coast, out to Grand Manan, and along the length of the Washington County coast. The operations base is Cathance Lake on Rt. 191, some 15 miles north of East Machias, but kayak and canoe rentals are also offered in Machias; shuttle service is a specialty.

On Campobello Island check out **Sea Kayak Journeys** (1-800-640-8944) at Head Harbour Wharf beyond Wilson's Beach.

Sunrise County Canoe and Kayak (207-255-3375 or 1-877-980-2300; www .sunrisecanoeandkayak.com), RR 1, Box 344A, Machias 04654. Mar.–Oct. Sea kayaking and canoe outfitter, with rental canoes and canoe outfitting, trip planning, and shuttle service for expeditions on the St. Croix River along the Maine–

CAMPOBELLO ISLAND

Joyce Morell

New Brunswick border and on the
Machias River to view petroglyphs.
Guided kayaking expeditions along
the Bold Coast. Also rents bicycles.

FISHING Atlantic salmon, long the
draw for fishermen to the Narraguagus and Machias Rivers, are currently
illegal to catch and will be until stocks
have been replenished. **Landlocked
salmon** are, however, still fair game
and can be found in **Schoodic Lake**
(8 miles north of Cherryfield), **Bog
Lake** in Northfield on Rt. 192 (10
miles north of Machias), **Gardner
Lake** in East Machias (look for the

Christina Tree

BEAL'S ISLAND

new boat ramp and parking area), and **Cathance Lake** on Rt. 191 (some 10
miles north of East Machias with a nice boat landing). Trolling lures, streamer
flies, or bait from a boat is the most popular way to catch landlocked salmon.

Brook trout can be caught in May and June in local rivers and streams, but in
warm weather they move to deeper water like **Six Mile Lake** in Marshfield (6
miles north of Machias on Rt. 192), Indian Lake along Rt. 1 in Whiting, and **Lily
Lake** in Trescott. **Brown trout** are found in **Simpson Pond** in Roque Bluffs
(park in Roque Bluffs State Park), as well as in the lakes listed above. **Gregg
Burr** (207-255-4210) is an experienced local fishing guide.

Saltwater and tidewater fishing is usually for striped bass or mackerel. For information about licenses, guides, and fish, check with the regional headquarters of
the **Inland Fisheries and Wildlife Department** in Jonesboro.

GOLF **Great Cove Golf Course** (207-434-2981), Jonesboro Rd., Roque Bluffs,
offers nine holes, water views, a clubhouse, rental clubs, and carts.

Barren View Golf Course (207-434-7651), Rt. 1, Jonesboro. This new course
offers nine holes with views of the blueberry barrens and boasts Maine's largest
sand trap. Facilities include a clubhouse plus rental carts and clubs.

Herring Cove Golf Course (506-752-2449), in the Herring Cove Provincial
Park (open mid-May mid-Nov.), has nine holes, a clubhouse restaurant, and
rentals.

HORSEBACK RIDING **Lucky Star Stables** (207-255-6124), Rim Rd., East
Machias. Kellie and Brenda Ramsdell offer ocean-view trail rides as well as lessons. See *Hiking* in "The Atlantic Coast."

PICNICKING **McClellan Park**, in Milbridge, 5 miles south of town at Baldwin's
Head, which overlooks the Atlantic and Narraguagus Bay (from Rt. 1, follow
Wyman Road to the park gates). A town park on 10.5 acres donated in 1926 by
George McClellan, a onetime mayor of New York City. There's no charge for
walking or picnicking.

PUFFIN-WATCHING AND OTHER BIRDING

Birders and naturalists should be aware that the area's many wildlife-rich offshore islands, such as Cross, Petit Manan, Bois Bubert, Seal, and Pond Islands, as well as Machias Seal Island, are the focus of the following excursions; inquire about exploring the islands themselves.

Machias Seal Island is a 15-acre, low-lying island that is one of the most remarkable bird-watching spots in America. It has been claimed by both the United States and Canada since the War of 1812 and is a prime nesting spot for puffins in June and July; it's also a place to see razor-billed auks and arctic terns in August and September. Visitors are strictly limited to formal groups and herded into blinds, which tend to be surrounded by birds. It's an unforgettable sight—and sound (a chorus of puffins sounds just like a chain saw). Although it's just 9 miles off Cutler, Canada maintains and staffs a lighthouse station as well as the wildlife refuge. **Norton of Jonesport** (207-497-5933; www.machiassealisland.com) pioneered bird-watching cruises to Machias Seal. The late Captain Barna B. Norton offered them in the 1940s and furthermore refused to concede the island to Canada. He insisted that it was not formally mentioned in the 1814 Treaty of Ghent that set the international boundaries in this area and was claimed by his grandfather (Tall Barney Beal) in 1865. His son, Captain John E. Norton, continues to offer birding trips to the island. The ride to the island takes one hour, 20 minutes in the Nortons' specially designed, 40-foot fiberglass boat.

Bold Coast Charter Company (207-259-4484; www.boldcoast.com) is based in Cutler, just 9 miles from Machias Seal Island, to which Captain Andrew Patterson offers daily 5-hour puffin-watching trips (weather permitting) May–Aug. Patterson also uses his partially enclosed 40-foot passenger vessel *Barbara Frost* to cruise the Bold Coast (as the stretch of high, rocky bluffs east of Cutler is known), to visit the Cross Island Wildlife Refuge (hiking trails thread a dense spruce forest, and there are many mosses, wild-

Roosevelt Campobello International Park's large natural area on Campobello Island, **Quoddy Head State Park** in Lubec, and **Roque Bluffs State Park** also all have picnic areas.

SPECIAL LEARNING PROGRAM (ADULT) **SummerKeys** (207-733-2316; in winter, 201-451-2338), 6 Bayview St., Lubec. Mid-June–Labor Day. New York piano teacher Bruce Potterton offers weeklong programs for a variety of instruments, especially piano for beginners to advanced students. Lodging is at local B&Bs.

SWIMMING ✍ **Roque Bluffs State Park**, Roque Bluffs (6 miles off Rt. 1). The pebble beach on the ocean is frequently windy, but a sheltered sand beach on a

MACHIAS SEAL ISLAND

flowers, and berries, as well as good birding) at the mouth of Machias Bay, and, on special request, to go all the way out to Grand Manan Island. Also see *To Do* in "St. Andrews and Grand Manan."

Captain Laura Fish (207-497-3064), Kelley Point Rd., Jonesport. Mid-June–mid-Aug. (weather permitting), the 23-foot *Aaron Thomas*, named for Jonesport's first settler—from whom the captain and first mate are descended—offers 3-hour cruises around the islands, lighthouses, beaches, and salmon farms; also a walk around **Mistake Island**, site of 72-foot-high Moosepeak (pronounced *MOOSE-a-peak*) Light.

East Coast Ferries Ltd. See *Getting Around*. Departing for Deer Island from Eastport and from Campobello Island every hour, this is the bargain cruise of the eastern seaboard: a small car ferry that sails out into Passamaquoddy Bay, past **Old Sow**—billed as the world's second largest whirlpool. Drive across Deer Island and take the free Canadian ferry from Lord's Cove to the **New Brunswick mainland**, or simply explore Deer Island and come back.

freshwater pond is good for children—though the water is cold. Tables, grills, changing areas with vault toilets, and a playground.

Sandy River Beach in Jonesport (off Rt. 187) is a rare white sand beach marked by a small sign, but the water is frigid. On Beals Island the **Backfield Area**, Alley's Bay, offers equally bracing saltwater swimming.

Gardner Lake, Chases Mills Rd., East Machias, offers freshwater swimming, a picnic area, and a boat launch. **Six Mile Lake**, Rt. 192, in Marshfield (north of Machias), is good for a dip.

Campobello Memorial Aquatic Park, Welshpool, Campobello Island. Changing rooms, toilets; this is landlocked saltwater swimming, so it's relatively warm.

Joyce Merrell

COMORANTS

HIKING

Within the past 10 years the number of coastal hiking options has increased dramatically. Entries are listed geographically, heading east, and are continued under *Green Space* in the next two subchapters.

Pigeon Hill, Steuben. The turnoff for the Petit Manan National Wildlife Area isn't marked on Rt. 1; look for Pigeon Hill Rd. After something more than 5 miles, look for a small graveyard on your left. Stop. The well-trod path up Pigeon Hill begins across the road. The climb is fairly steep in places. It's a pleasant 20-minute hike, and the view from the summit reveals the series of island-filled bays that stretch away to the east, as well as mountains inland.

Petit Manan Point, Steuben. Continue another mile or so (see above) down Pigeon Hill Rd. and past the sign announcing that you have entered a 2,166-acre preserve with more than 10 miles of shoreline, part of the 6,000-acre **Petit Manan National Wildlife Refuge**. There are two loop trails, and you can drive to the parking lot for the second. This is a varied area with pine stands, cedar swamps, blueberry barrens, marshes, and great birding (more than 250 species have been identified here). Maps are posted at the parking lots. A 0.5-mile shore path hugs the woods and coastline. For details about the entire refuge, contact Refuge Headquarters, Main St., Milbridge (207-546-2124).

Great Wass Island. The Maine Chapter of The Nature Conservancy owns this 1,579-acre tract at the southern tip of the Jonesport-Addison peninsula. Trail maps are posted at the parking lot (simply follow the main road to its logical end). The interior of the island supports one of Maine's largest stands of jack pine and is a quite beautiful mix of lichen-covered open ledge, wooded path, and coastal peatland. Roughly a third of the 5-mile loop is along the shore. Little Cape Point is a great picnic spot. Wear rubber-soled shoes.

Western Head, off Rt. 191, 11 miles south of East Machias, is maintained by the Maine Coast Heritage Trust, Brunswick (207-276-5156). Take the first right after the Baptist church onto Destiny Bay Rd. and follow it to the sign. The 3- to 4-mile loop trail is through mixed-growth woods and spruce to the shore, with views of the entrance to Cutler Harbor and high ledges with crashing surf, large expanses of open ocean, as well as the high, sheer ledges of Grand Manan to the northeast and Machias Seal Island to the southeast.

Bold Coast Trail. Look for the trailhead some 4 miles east of Cutler Harbor. Maine's Bureau of Parks and Lands (207-287-4920) has constructed inner and outer loop trails from Rt. 191 to the rugged cliffs and along the shore overlooking Grand Manan Channel. There are 5- and 10-mile loops. The Coastal Trail begins in deep spruce-fir forest, bridges a cedar swamp, and 1.5 miles from the parking lot climbs out of the woods and onto a promontory, continuing to rise and dip along the cliffs to Black Point Cove, a cobble beach. Note: The cliffs are high and sheer, not good for children or shaky adults. Bring a picnic and allow at least 5 hours. The trail continues from Black Point Cove to Fairy Head, site of three primitive campsites. The **Quoddy Regional Land Trust** (207-733-5509; P.O. Box 49, Whiting 04691; www.qrlt.org), with the help of the Maine Coast Heritage Trust, publishes a thick, ever-expanding booklet titled *Cobscook Trails: A Guide to Walking Opportunities Around Cobscook Bay and the Bold Coast*. It's widely available locally and from the trust. It also details hikes in 18 locations in Lubec to **Horan Head** (6 miles round-trip), to the **Boot Head Preserve** (less than 2 miles round-trip), along the South Lubec Sand Bar, and to **Commissary Point** in Trescott.

Quoddy Head State Park, Lubec (follow signs from Rt. 189). The lighthouse and visitor center are as far as most people come, but the 2-mile Coastal Trail along the cliffs here is one of the most dramatic in Maine, very similar to trails on the back side of Monhegan Island but fenced in most (though not all) precarious places. The views are back to the lighthouse, down the coast, and across to the sheer cliffs of Grand Manan 7 miles offshore. Bring a picnic.

Roosevelt Campobello International Park. At the tourist information center, pick up a trail map. We recommend the trail from Southern Head to the Duck Ponds. Seals frequently sun on the ledges off Lower Duck Pond, and loons are often seen off Liberty Point. Along this dramatic shoreline at the southern end of the island, also look for whales July–Sep.

Herring Cove Provincial Park on Campobello Island offers rewarding hiking trails.

East Quoddy Head Lighthouse, also officially known as Head Harbour Light Station, is sited at the far northern end of Campobello Island. Very photogenic, a prime whale-watching spot, but accessible only from the parking area at low tide, and a demanding hike.

WHALE-WATCHING The unusually high tides in the Bay of Fundy seem to foster ideal feeding grounds for right, minke, and humpback whales and for porpoises and dolphins. East Quoddy Head on Campobello and Quoddy Head State Park in Lubec are favored viewing spots. The commercial excursion boats, both based on Campobello Island, are **Captain Riddle's Sea Going Adventures** (1-877-346-2225) and **Island Cruise Whale Watching Tours** (506-752-2213 or 1-888-249-4400).

✳ Lodging

INNS AND BED & BREAKFASTS

Entries are listed geographically, heading east

✿ **Ricker House** (207-546-2780), 49 Parker St., Cherryfield 04622. Open May–Nov. A classic Federal house built in 1803 (it's on the National Register) with a double parlor and furnished comfortably with plenty of books, a big kitchen, and a truly big and inviting screened-in pine porch overlooking the river. Two guest rooms with river views, nicely furnished with antiques and old quilts, share a bath. Jean and Bill Conway are delighted to help guests explore the area, especially on foot, or by bicycle or canoe (both are available to guests). $70 per couple ($10 per extra person), $65 single, includes a full breakfast.

The Guagus River Inn (207-546-9737; www.guagusriverinn.com), 376 Kansas Rd., Milbridge 04658. Billy and Jackie Majors's contemporary house has a hot tub and small indoor lap pool and overlooks the Narragaugus River. Five of the six rooms are rented at any one time (there are five baths), and they are themed: Deer, Fish, Bear, et cetera. All are inviting, but the easy winner is Moose, with its big log bed and stained glass above the Jacuzzi. In-season rooms are $70–75, with the Moose Suite $150, with a 2-night minimum—but that, too, goes down to $120 off-season. Set in meadows, the B&B is 1.8 miles up a quiet road from Rt. 1A and the shore.

✿ ✐ **Pleasant Bay Bed & Breakfast** (207-483-4490; www.pleasantbay .com), P.O. Box 222, West Side Rd., Addison 04606. Open year-round. After raising six children and a number of llamas in New Hampshire, Leon and Joan Yeaton returned to Joan's girlhood turf, cleared this land, and built this gracious house with many windows and a deck and porch overlooking the Pleasant River. A living room is well stocked with puzzles and books for foggy days. This is a 110-acre working llama farm, and guests are invited to meander the wooded trails down to the bay with or without llamas. The four upstairs guest rooms with views include one family-sized room with private bath; there is also a two-room suite with a living room, kitchenette, and deck overlooking the water. There are moorings for guests arriving by water. $50–85 per couple ($10 per child) and $125 for the suite includes, if you're lucky, Joan's popover/pancake.

Harbor House on Sawyer Cove (207-497-5417; fax, 207-497-3211; www.harborhs.com), P.O. Box 468, 27 Sawyer Square, Jonesport 04649. Open year-round. Maureen and Gene Hart have transformed this handsome 1880s house, which at one time included a telegraph office, general store, ship's chandlery, and art gallery, into an antiques store downstairs and two large, attractive guest suites upstairs. One has a king-sized bed and windows overlooking the marina and harbor; both have a spacious sitting area, cable TV, and private bath. A full breakfast is served on the harborside porch overlooking the flower gardens and the harbor. $110 in-season, $85 off; weekly rates. Breakfast is included.

Jonesport by the Sea (207-497-2590 or 1-888-475-2590; www.jonesportbythesea.bigstep.com), P.O. Box 433, Jonesport 04049. Lobsterman Joe McDonald and his family offer this middle-of-the-village B&B geared to puffin patrons. There's a small sitting room and four guest rooms upstairs, one with two double beds and a private bath ($85 double), the others each with two doubles or a king but sharing a bath ($75). Rates include a full breakfast.

✎ **Moose-A-Bec Manor** (207-497-2121; www.mooseabecmanor.com), P.O. Box 557, Old House Point, Jonesport 04659. Open year-round for weekly rentals. Charlie and Abby Alley have renovated an 1875 waterside house that's been in Abby's family for generations, turning it into two large waterside apartments, each with two bedrooms plus a sleeper-sofa and full kitchen, including dishwasher, washer-dryer, and cable TV. Views are of Moosabec Reach. $100–125 per night includes linens.

🐾 **The Loft** (207-497-2139), 56 Kelley Point Rd., Jonesport 04659. This attractive efficiency unit above a garage by the water is tastefully furnished with cottage-style furniture, country quilts, and antiques. There's also a TV, gas fireplace, and kitchen

stocked with breakfast makings. The bed is a queen; a balcony overlooks the water, although the view is partially obscured by a house trailer. Pets are allowed with prior approval. $125 per night, $225 for 2 nights, $300 for 3, $600 per week.

Broadway Inn Bed and Breakfast (207-255-8551; www.lighthouselq.com), 14 Broadway St., Machias 04654. At this writing, a handsome downtown house that offers three themed guest rooms with private baths, writing desks, and access to a hot tub. $95–125.

The Blue Butterfly (207-255-0113), 9 Pleasant St., Machias 04654. Liz Flauver's informal, comfortable 1850s downtown house offers two rooms with shared bath. $85 per couple includes a full breakfast.

🐾 **Micmac Farm Guesthouses and Gardner House** (207-255-3008; www.micmacfarm.com), P.O. Box 336, Rt. 336, Machiasport 04655. Open Memorial Day weekend–Oct. This classic Cape, built by Ebenezer Gardner above the Machias River in 1776, is the oldest house in Machias and a real treasure. The house is home to Anthony Dunn, Bonnie, his wife, and their small daughter. In summer they occupy a separate wing and offer guests the large downstairs bedroom off the living room. Very private—with a deck overlooking the river and a bath with whirlpool tub—it's furnished in family antiques with a desk and a life's collection of books. Three comfortable, well-designed housekeeping cabins (we have boiled lobsters for five, and feasted on them, in one); each has two double beds and overlooks the river. $70–85 daily for either the guest room or cabin; $425–525 per week. Children are welcomed and pets accepted in the cabins. Ebenezer Gardner was born in Roxbury, Massachusetts, and moved to Nova Scotia in 1763, but because he sided with the Americans in the Revolution he moved back down the coast. He is buried in the family cemetery on the property.

Captain Cates (207-255-8812; www .captaincates.com), 307 Port Rd. (Rt. 92), Machiasport 04655. Open year-round. This 1820s sea captain's house overlooks the tidal river and offers guests six cheerful, antiques-furnished rooms on the second and third floors, sharing three baths. Downstairs there's a front parlor with a fireplace, dining rooms, and a back den with games, TV, and a great stained-glass window. From $60 for a small single to $110 for rooms with queens, full breakfast included.

🦐 **Riverside Inn** (207-255-4134 or 1-888-255-4344; www.riversideinn-maine.com), Rt. 1, East Machias 04630. Open year-round. The heart of this vintage 1805 house—actually the first thing guests see—is the kitchen. Innkeepers Ellen McLaughlin and Rocky Rakoczy will probably be there preparing for the evening meal (see *Dining Out*). We recommend one of the two suites (one with a living room, bedroom, and kitchen facilities; the other with two bedrooms) in the Coach House, nearer the river and with decks. There are also two nicely decorated upstairs guest rooms with private bath in the house, which was Victorianized in the 1890s; the clear glass in its fan lights was replaced with red and tin ceilings were added. $95–130 in high season, $85–115 in low, includes a full breakfast.

🦐 **Little River Lodge** (207-259-4437; www.cutlerlodge.com), P.O. Box 251, Cutler 04626. Open Memorial Day–Columbus Day. Built in 1845 to house workers in a lumber mill, this capacious, beautifully sited (across from Cutler Harbor) building became a summer hotel in 1870 when passenger steamers began stopping. Manager Jerusha Murray is a passionate birder and hiker, eager to steer guests to the nearby Boot Head Preserve, Western Head, and Hamilton Coves as well as to the Bold Coast trails. The inn is ideally sited for patrons of Captain Andy Patterson's puffin-watching trips. It offers five rooms, two with private bath, all simply, nicely decorated; three have harbor views; two smaller ones in the back ell. $70–90 includes a full breakfast. A brown-bag lunch of great-sounding sandwiches, something fresh baked, a granola bar, fruit, and water is $7.

Tide Run (207-259-3800; info@tide run.com), 212 Destiny Bay Rd., Cutler 04626. Open seasonally. Rich and Linda Houghton opened this attractive 1870s house as a combination restaurant and B&B in the summer of 2004. The three upstairs rooms are nicely furnished, all with queen-sized featherbed, satellite TV, and private bath. $125 per night. Also see *Dining Out*.

♿ **Whiting Bay Bed & Breakfast** (phone/fax 207-733-2463; www .whitingbay.com), Rt. 1, No. 7, Whiting 04651. A few miles from Cobscook Bay State Park and 11 miles from Lubec. Set back from Rt. 1 with nicely landscaped grounds bordering tidal water. Richard and Sandra Bradley offer two upstairs rooms (shared bath) in their house. Guests breakfast in the Carriage House, which also contains a ground-floor (handicapped-accessible) unit and one upstairs with a kitchenette and deck. $85–115 includes a buffet-style breakfast.

✦ **Peacock House** (207-733-2403; fax, 207-733-2403; www.peacock house.com), 27 Summer St., Lubec 04652. Open May–Oct. A gracious 1860s house on a quiet side street, home to four generations of the Peacock family, owners of the major local cannery. There are three carefully, comfortably furnished guest rooms and four suites, one handicapped accessible. The most luxurious suite, The Peacock, is especially spacious with a gas fireplace. Innkeepers Dennis and Sue Baker have the right touch. Rates, which include a full breakfast served at the dining room table (two sittings, 7:30 and 8:30), run $85 for the rooms, $95–105 for three of the suites, and $125 for The Peacock—good value.

Home Port Inn and Restaurant (207-733-2077 or 1-800-457-2077; www.homeportinn.com), 45 Main St., P.O. Box 50, Lubec 04652. Open May–mid-Oct. Happily, this long-established inn is flourishing under owners Dave and Suzannah Gale. The large, raspberry-colored living room is a great space to read or watch TV, and each of the seven guest rooms (private bath) has been tastefully decorated. We like Room 5, melon colored with a canopy bed. (Also see *Dining Out*.) $90–105 per couple; $10 for a rollaway.

✦ **BayViews** (207-733-2181; off-season, 718-788-2196), 6 Monument St., Lubec 04652. Open mid-May–Labor Day. An 1894 Victorian with not just bay views but also a porch, hammock, and lawn sloping to Johnson Bay. The house has been lovingly restored by Kathryn Rubeor, filled with period furniture, prints, books,

and collectibles, and fitted with two pianos, the better to serve participants in SummerKeys. There are five guest rooms (shared baths): a family suite with a double bed, twins, and a child's bed, with private bath; a room with its own piano and bath (twin beds); and three more rooms with double beds, sharing one bath. $50–80 includes a full breakfast.

✦ **Betsy Ross Lodging** (207-733-8942; www.atlantichouse.net), 61 Water St., Lubec 04652. Open most of the year. The style replicates that of the Betsy Ross House in Philadelphia, but this shingled building fits into the eclectic lineup on this funky old street. Bill and Dianna Meehan offer four pleasant rooms with private bath. $60–95 includes a credit for breakfast at the Atlantic House Coffee House and Deli across the street (see *Eating Out*). You may also be able to rent a unit in a former brick bank building down the street. It sleeps five, with one bedroom (with fireplace) in the old office and another in the vault, a spiffy open kitchen, and plenty of space: $800 per week.

BAYVIEWS B&B, LUBEC

Christina Tree

🍴 **The Owen House** (506-752-2977; www.owenhouse.ca), 11 Welshpool St., Welshpool, Campobello, New Brunswick, Canada E5E 1G3. Open late May–mid-Oct. This delightful inn is reason enough to come to Campobello. Built in 1835 by Admiral William Fitzwilliam Owen, son of the British captain to whom the island was granted in 1769, this is probably the most historic house on the island, and it's a beauty, set on a headland overlooking Passamaquoddy Bay. Joyce Morrell, a watercolor artist who maintains a gallery here, has furnished the nine guest rooms (seven with private bath) with friendly antiques, handmade quilts, and good art. Room 1 is really a suite with a single bed in the adjoining room; Room 2, the other front room, is our favorite. Guests gather around the formal dining room table for a full breakfast and around one of several fireplaces in the evening. Paths lead through the 10-acre property to the water, and the Deer Island ferry leaves from the adjoining beach. From $79.50 (U.S.) for the shared-bath third-floor rooms to $138 for the suite; $84.50–118 for a private room with bath, plus the 15 percent tax for which non-Canadians can get a refund.

🍴 **The Lupine Lodge** (506-752-2555; www.lupinelodge.com), 610 Rt. 774, Welshpool, Campobello, New Brunswick, Canada E5E 1A5. Open Memorial Day–Columbus Day. The log structure was built in 1915 for the Frederick Adams family, cousins of the Roosevelts. The big sitting room with its massive fireplace is now a restaurant (see *Eating Out*). Guest rooms, in two separate log buildings, vary from small and dark Room 7 to

Room 11 with two queen beds, a full bath, and a living room with fireplace ($65–125). A family could settle comfortably into Room 5 (a queen and a double sofa bed with a fireplace and water view), or Room 10, with a queen bed and two more twins in a loft. During the 1980s the rooms were decorated by Susan McDougal, who later went to prison rather than testify against Bill Clinton in the Whitewater scandal. The property is owned by the New Brunswick provincial government and located within the provincial park with its hiking trails, one leading to Herring Cove. $65–125.

Also, for a weekly rental, see **Columbia Falls Pottery** in *Selective Shopping*.

COTTAGES Check with the **Machias Bay Area** and **Cobscook Bay Chambers of Commerce** (see *Guidance*) and in the *Maine Guide to Inns and Bed & Breakfasts and Camps & Cottages*, available from the Maine Tourism Association (see *Information* in "What's Where"). Summer rentals in this area still begin at around $400 per week. Also see **Hearts of Maine Waterfront Rental Properties** (207-255-4210; www.boldcoast.com/maine-cottages).

MOTELS 🍴 **Blueberry Patch Motel and Cabins** (207-434-5411), Rt. 1, Jonesboro 04648. This spic-and-span 19-unit motel is next door to The White House restaurant. Each unit has a refrigerator, air-conditioning, a phone, TV, and coffee. There is a pool and sundeck surrounded by berries. The 1930s tourist cabins way in back are surprisingly roomy and comfortable (two double beds), and there are three efficiencies. $48–68 in-season.

🐾 🐾 Machias Motor Inn (207-255-4861; www.machiasmotorinn.com), Rt. 1 next to Helen's Restaurant, Machias 04654. Bob and Joan Carter maintain a two-story, 35-unit motel; most rooms are standard units, each with two double, extra-long beds, cable TV, and a phone. Rooms feature decks overlooking the Machias River. $65 double, $90 for efficiencies, less off-season. Pets (no cats) are extra.

🐾 🐾 Eastland Motel (207-733-5501), Rt. 189, Lubec 04652. Open year-round. A good bet if you're taking the kids to Campobello and want a clean, comfortable room with TV; $55–65 double mid-Apr.–mid-Oct., less off-season. Higher prices are for rooms in the newer section.

CAMPGROUNDS **McClellan Park**, marked from Rt. 1, Milbridge. Open Memorial Day–Columbus Day. See *To Do—Picnicking* for more on this dramatically sited, town-owned park. Free for day use plus a nominal charge for tenting and full campsites; 18 campsites and water are available, but no showers. For details, call the town hall at 207-546-2422.

Henry Point Campground (207-497-9633), Kelly Point Rd., Jonesport 04649. Open Apr.–Nov. Surrounded on three sides by water, this is another great town-owned campground that's usually got space (its crunch weekend is July 4). Neither showers nor water is available, but you can shower and use the coin-operated laundry at the Jonesport Shipyard across the cove. Good water is also available from an outside faucet at the town hall. This is a put-in place for sea kayaks. Turn off Rt. 187 at the purple house.

Herring Cove Provincial Park (506-752-2396), Campobello Island.

Adjoining the Roosevelt Campobello International Park is this campground offering 87 campsites; there's a beach, a golf course, and extensive hiking trails.

Also see **Cobscook Bay State Park** under *Lodging* in "Eastport and Cobscook Bay."

✳ Where to Eat

DINING OUT

Entries are listed geographically, heading east

Artist's Café (207-255-8900), 3 Hill St., Machias. Open late Apr.–Columbus Day, weekdays for lunch and Mon.–Sat. for dinner 5–8. Reservations accepted. Chef-artist Susan Ferro's delightful restaurant is tucked away off Rt. 1 south of the bridge, across from the university. Light, bright rooms are hung with local art, much of it by Ferro. Lunch on sandwiches with artistic names like The Impressionist (natural chicken breast sautéed and sliced on a French baguette with basil pesto mayonnaise). Dinner entrées might include stir-fried vegetables and tofu on brown rice, or rack of veal braised in white wine. Wine and beer. Dinner entrées $20.

🦞 Joyce's Lobster House (207-255-0719), Rt. 1, East Machias. Open June–Aug. for lunch and dinner. A gem. From the road this looks like another diner, but inside the walls are papered, and the sideboard is antique. Joyce O'Riley presided over the crisp dining room for years; now her daughter Debbi Farrar and partner Peter Russi are committed to preserving her commitment to "great food at fair prices." Try the sautéed scallops and shrimp with garlic and lemon-pepper on pasta, or veal parmigiana with homemade sauce. Entrées $8.95–14.50. BYOB. We picked up an inexpensive bottle of good pinot grigio at the "filling station" across the way.

Riverside Inn (207-255-4134; www .riversideinn-maine.com), Rt. 1, East Machias 04630. Open year-round. Open for dinner 6 nights a week in-season, 4 off-season. Innkeepers Ellen McLaughlin and Rocky Rakoczy have expanded the dining area in their winterized wraparound porch. Still, space is limited, and demand is large. Reservations are a must. Rocky is the chef, and the menu ranges from a choice of seafood dishes through dinner salads to steak, Jamaican baby back ribs, and New Zealand lamb chops. The house specialty appetizer is shrimp wrapped with fresh salmon and served with a turmeric-dill sauce. Entrées $16.95–22.95, including a salad and herbed bread. Dinner salads are $17.95. Full liquor license.

Tide Run (207-259-3800; www.tide run.com), 312 Destiny Rd., Cutler. Open seasonally. This new dining option on Destiny Bay is miles from anywhere, except some of the area's most dramatic hiking trails. We lunched on a passable quiche du jour with a fresh green salad. Dinner choices range from pork tenderloin with port wine sauce to vegetarian ravioli, local haddock with a crabmeat cream sauce, and coquilles Saint-Jacques. Entrées $16–20. Fully licensed.

Home Port Inn (207-733-2077; www .homeportinn.com), 45 Main St., Lubec. Open July to Labor Day for dinner 5–8. This is the fine-dining option in the Lubec area. Entrées range from a fresh lobster and artichoke salad to bouillabaisse, $15–24.

A house salad is $4. Wine and beer are served.

EATING OUT

Entries are listed geographically, heading east

Joshy's Place, Rt. 1, Milbridge. Good seasonal takeout. Having researched crab rolls up and down the coast, we think Joshy's rates an 8 on a scale of 1–10. Gifford's ice cream.

🦞 🕊 **The Red Barn** (207-546-7721), Main St. (junction of Rts. 1 and 1A), Milbridge. Open daily year-round, 7 AM–8 PM in summer. The main, pine-paneled dining room with its counter and booths is an old reliable, a welcoming dining landmark into which we have gratefully settled as our first stop after driving this far. The menu is large: pastas, burgers, steak, seafood, fried chicken, and an extensive salad bar. Fully licensed. Children's menu; great cream pies. Inquire about lodging in the attached motel.

Tall Barney's (207-497-2403), Main St., Jonesport, across from the Beals Island Bridge. Open daily 4 AM–8 PM. This legendary local gathering spot was the subject of an NPR radio story that inspired present owners John and Linda Lapinski to come and buy it; they have expanded the menu to include veggie burgers as well as a wide choice of seafood stews, fried fish, and self-consciously styled "Maine Meals" such as grilled franks and fried onions. This place is still particularly welcoming for breakfast on a foggy morning. The long "liar's table" down the middle of the front room is reserved for the local lobstermen, who drift in one by one. Many around here still claim descent from Tall Barney Beal (1835–99), who stood 6 foot 7 inches.

White House Restaurant (207-434-2782), Rt. 1, Jonesboro. Open 5 AM–8 PM. A classic roadhouse with genuine diner atmosphere and food.

🍴 **Helen's Restaurant** (207-255-6506), 32 Main St., Machias (north of town on the water). Open 6 AM–8 PM. The town's landmark restaurant, geared to bus groups at lunch. Generous servings and reasonable prices: a wide choice of seafood, as well as sandwiches, hot dogs, and burgers. Famed for "whipped" pies. Fully licensed. Children's plates.

🐦 🍴 **Blue Bird Ranch** (207-255-3351), Lower Main St. (Rt. 1), Machias. Open year-round for all three meals. Family owned with a diner atmosphere and food that's usually pretty good. Plenty of fried fish and steak choices, fresh-made chowders and seafood stews, burgers and sandwiches, pies and puddings. Fully licensed.

Murphy's Village Restaurant (207-733-4440), 126 Main St. (Rt. 189), Lubec. Open daily year-round, 6 AM–9 PM. Peter and Sue Murphy own this local gathering place serving "traditional downeast home-style cooking." It's breakfast all day long, fresh seafood, and homemade pies. Fully licensed.

Atlantic House Coffee House and Deli (207-733-0906), 52 Water St., Lubec. Open seasonally, daily 7–7. A welcome addition to this reawakening street: pastries, pizza, stromboli, calzones, and sandwiches. Dianna Meehan does it all. Note the back deck on the water.

Phil's Not-So-Famous Ice Cream, Washington St., right before the international bridge. Many flavors of ice cream, sorbet, crêpes, and more are made on the premises.

Lupine Lodge (506-752-2555), Campobello Island, New Brunswick. Open 8 AM–9 PM. This former log "cottage," built by cousins of the Roosevelts, features a great hearth with a chimney built from ship's ballast stones and has some charm. The dinner menu ranges from $18.95 (Canadian) for vegetarian pasta to $16.95 for a fried seafood platter (add 15 percent tax). Full liquor license.

Sweet Time Bakery and Coffee Shop (506-752-2428), Welshpool, Campobello Island, New Brunswick. Margo Malloch and Fae Anthony's bakery-turned-restaurant is a find, an island gathering place with "omelets of your choice" or fish cakes topped with fried eggs for breakfast, a wide choice of sandwiches on freshly baked bread for lunch, and superb pies. Inquire about dinner.

Family Fisheries (506-752-2470), Rt. 174, Wilson's Beach, Campobello Island, New Brunswick. Open from 11:30 through at least 8:30. This is a combination fish market, takeout (there's a screened eating area), and new sit-down dining room, a good bet for fish-and-chips, chowder, and lobster.

✳ Entertainment

🐦 🍴 **Milbridge Theater** (207-546-2038), Main St., Milbridge. Open nightly May–Nov., 7:30 showtime; Sat. and Sun. matinees for children's films; all seats $4.50. A very special theater: a refurbished movie house featuring first-run and art films at truly affordable prices. Fresh popcorn.

University of Maine, Machias (207-255-3313, ext. 284), offers both a winter and summer series of plays, performances, and concerts.

Downriver Theater Productions
(207-255-4997) stages plays June–
Aug. at University of Maine, Machias.
Community theater productions—a
mix of safe musicals and original plays.
We saw *Barefoot in the Park* and were
impressed. Tickets are very affordable.

Machias Bay Chamber Concerts
(207-255-3889), Center Street Con-
gregational Church, Machias. A
series of six chamber music concerts,
July–early Aug., Tue. at 7:30 PM.
Top groups such as the Kneisel Hall
Chamber Players and the Vermeer
Quartet are featured.

**Mary Potterton Memorial Piano
Concerts**, Sacred Heart Church
Parish Hall, Lubec. Wed. evenings
(7:30) all summer. Free. Featuring
SummerKeys faculty and guest artists.

✳ Selective Shopping

*Entries are listed geographically,
heading east*
Tunk River Gardens (207-546-2269),
Steuben Center. Open mid-May–mid-
Oct. by chance or appointment. Peter
and Jane Weil offer a first-rate gallery
and sculpture garden.

A&M Chain Saw Sculptures (207-
546-3462), Rogers Point Rd., Steuben. Arthur Smith's wooden animals
are truly amazing and exhibited in
widely respected galleries for many
times the price that he will sell them
to you from his roadside house-
gallery. Marie Smith is responsible
for painting the sculptures.

Sea-Witch (207-546-7495), Rt. 1,
Milbridge. Describing itself as "the
biggest little gift shop in Washington
County," this is a trove of trinkets and
treasures: collector dolls, spatterware,
and local specialty foods.

The Dusty Rose Antiques (207-
546-8997), Rt. 182, Cherryfield. Mary
Weston has a good mix of antiques
and interesting old stuff.

Columbia Falls Pottery (207-483-
4075 or 1-800-235-2512; www
.columbiafallspottery.com), 150 Main
St., Columbia Falls. Open year-round,
June–Dec. daily 9–5, otherwise
Thu.–Sat. 9–5. Striking, bright,
sophisticated creations by April
Adams featuring lupine, sunflower,
and iris designs; catalog.

Wild Blueberry Land (207-483-
BLUE), Rt. 1, Columbia Falls. The
blue geodesic dome suggests a
squashed blueberry and houses a wild
assortment of tourist stuff but also
local blueberries beyond the usual
season, and Jasper Wyman's locally
made 100 percent blueberry juice.

Jonesport Village has become an
antiques center. At **Jonesport Nautical Antiques** (207-497-5655 or 1-800-
996-5655; www.nauticalantiques
.com), Cogswell and Main Sts., nautical antiques and reproductions are the
specialty. **Moospecke Antiques** (207-
497-2457) on Sawyer Square, open
seasonally, Tue.–Fri. 10–noon and 1–4,
specializes in country furniture, fine
arts, and Americana. **Harbor House
on Sawyer Cove** (207-497-5417),
next door, is worth checking for art,
furnishings, and gifts.

Nelson Decoys Gallery and Gifts
(207-497-3488), Cranberry Lane,
Jonesport. Open May–Dec. Bob is the
carver and Charlene Nelson paints
the prizewinning decoys sold here.
Other local art and Maine-made gifts
also sold.

Machias Laundromat (207-255-
6639). Open in summer daily 8–8,
closing in winter at 6. Our favorite

Maine Laundromat, spanking clean and sited next to the river (just across the bridge as you come into town) so that you can dump your stuff, poke around, lunch, and come back. For a nominal fee they will also wash, dry, and fold for you.

The Sow's Ear (207-255-4066), 7 Water St., Machias. A mix of cards, jewelry, toys, clothing, and things "from away."

Machias Hardware Co. (207-255-6581), 26 Main St., Machias. An old-fashioned hardware store that's also

MAINE BLACKFLY BREEDER'S ASSOCIATION

You may have seen intriguing bumper stickers proclaiming SAVE THE BLACKFLY and T-shirts boasting WE BREED 'EM, YOU FEED 'EM. The entire state is abuzz with the puzzling message, which can be traced to Machias's Woodwind Gallery, where the standard greeting is "May the Swarm be with you." The nonprofit association traces its conception to the length and boredom level of Washington County winters. Proceeds from sale of all products—which include carved, finger-sized "fly-houses" in a variety of shapes, from trailers to condos—benefit Washington County charities. For $1 the association will send you a "certificate of membership" designed by artist Marilyn Dowling, featuring a blackfly striking an eaglelike pose. Dowling personally renders your name in flowing calligraphy. The source: **Woodwind Gallery** (207-255-3727), 62½ Dublin St. (Rt. 1 south of the bridge), Machias. Open in summer months year-round, Tue.–Sun. in July and Aug.; closed Sun. off-season. Holly Garner-Jackson's combination framery and gallery shows some 40 local artists and sculptors. Work includes glass, pottery, photography, paintings, and metal; art supplies, too.

an unexpected source of reasonably priced herbs and spices in 2-ounce and 1-pound packages. Also local products like those by A. M. Look's Canning (see below).

Whole Life Natural Market (207-255-8855), 80 Main St., Machias. Open year-round; summer hours Mon.–Sat. 9–6, Sun. 10–3. Finally, a first-class market featuring organic and local produce and environmentally safe products, beauty aids, and supplements. There's also a resource/lending library and sitting area.

Look's Gourmet Food Co. (207-259-3341 or 1-800-962-6258), Rt. 191 south of East Machias. Retail shop open year-round weekdays 8–4. Said to be the first company to successfully can crabmeat and the first to bottle clam juice (the product for which it's most famous) under the Atlantic label, Look's now produces a whole line of specialty products, from lobster spread to Indian pudding, under both the Atlantic and Bar Harbor labels.

Connie's Clay of Fundy (207-255-4574), Rt. 1, East Machias. Open year-round. Connie Harter-Bagley's combination studio-shop is filled with her distinctive glazed earthenware in deep colors. Bowls, pie plates, platters, lamps, and small essentials like garlic jars and ring boxes.

The Puffin Pines Country Gift Store (207-733-9782; www.puffin pines.com), Rt. 1, Whiting. Open year-round but closed Sun.; also Mon. in the off-season. This roadside stop is cram-full of every kind of Maine souvenir imaginable, as well as Passamaquoddy-made baskets. Owner Pat McCabe also coordinates the Cobscook Bay Chamber of Commerce, and a corner of the store is stocked with local visitor information.

Seaside Chocolates (207-733-4500), Lower Pleasant St., Lubec. **Bayside Chocolates** (207-733-8880), 72 Water St., Lubec.

Quoddy Mist Sea Salt (207-733-4847; www.quoddymist.com), 72 Water St., Lubec. Makes what one Lubecer called "the best sea salt in the world." Tested and equal in quality to famed Fleur de Sel, a French sea salt, Quoddy Mist is just starting to be distributed. If you call and arrange it ahead of time, you can tour and see how the brine from the boiled-down seawater crystallizes on tables, with high trace minerals, low sodium chloride levels, and a fine flavor.

Bold Coast Smokehouse (207-733-8912 or 1- 888-733-0807), 224 County Rd. (Rt. 189), Lubec. Open year-round. Vinny Gartmayer is the owner of this fine smokehouse. Stop at least to pick up some smoked salmon, halibut, or trout pâté.

Lubec Landmarks Gallery, Water St., Lubec. Open seasonally Tue.–Sun. noon–4. At this writing the Historic McCurdy Smokehouse buildings along Water St. are under restoration, but in the meantime a colorful gallery displays changing exhibits of local art.

Cottage Garden (207-733-2902), N. Lubec Rd., Lubec. Open in-season all week; 4.5 miles off Rt. 189 on N. Lubec Rd. Gretchen Mead welcomes visitors to her steadily expanding perennial gardens. A short trail through woods leads to a picnic meadow, and a deck behind the shop (herbs, flower wreaths, toys, Christmas ornaments, birdhouses) overlooks the garden and a small pond. There's also a new Shoreline Nature Center.

CHRISTMAS WREATHS More than half of Maine's Christmas wreaths are made in Washington County. The "tips" are arranged on poles and bundled, then sold to wreath makers ranging from big producers to individuals who decorate them in their homes. You can order in fall and take delivery of a freshly made wreath right before Christmas. Prices quoted include delivery. **The Wreath Shoppe** (207-483-4598), Box 358, Oak Point Rd., Harrington 04643 (wreaths decorated with cones, berries, and reindeer moss); and **Flo's Wreaths** (1-800-321-7136; floswreaths.net) are a couple among dozens of purveyors. Wreaths average $24 plus shipping.

✳ Special Events

Memorial Day weekend: **Downeast Birding Festival**—guided hikes, cruises, lectures (www.cobscookbay .com).

July 4: **Independence Day celebrations** in **Jonesport/Beals Island** (lobster-boat races, easily viewed from the bridge); **Cherryfield** (parade and fireworks); and **Steuben** (firemen's lobster picnic and parade); **Lubec** goes all-out with a grand parade, contests, and fireworks; **Cutler** and **Machias** also celebrate. **Campobello** celebrates Canada Day (July 1) in a big way.

Last weekend in July: **Milbridge Days** (207-546-2406) include a parade, a dance, a lobster dinner, and the famous codfish relay race.

August: **Wild Blueberry Festival and Machias Craft Festival** (*third weekend*) in downtown Machias, sponsored by Penobscot Valley Crafts and Center Street Congregational Church—concerts, food, a major crafts fair, and live entertainment.

EASTPORT, COBSCOOK BAY, AND PASSAMAQUODDY BAY

Eastport is just 3 miles north of Lubec by boat but 43 miles by land around Cobscook Bay. *Cobscook* is said to mean "boiling water" in the Passamaquoddy tongue, and tremendous tides—a tidal range of more than 25 feet—seemingly boil in through this passage and slosh up deep inlets divided by ragged land fingers along the north and south shores. One gap between the opposite shores is just 300 yards wide, and the tides funnel through it at 6 to 8 knots, alternately filling and draining the smaller bays beyond. For several hours the incoming tide actually roars through these "Cobscook Reversing Falls."

The force of the tides in Passamaquoddy Bay on Eastport's eastern and northern shores is so powerful that in the 1930s President Roosevelt backed a proposal by hydroelectric engineer Dexter Cooper to harness this power to electrify much of the Northeast Coast, including Boston.

The ecological considerations stacked against this "Quoddy Dam" project are, it turns out, huge. Thanks to the extreme tides and currents, marine life is more varied than in other places. Nutrients that elsewhere settle to the bottom, shoot here to the surface and nourish some forms of life that exist nowhere else. The fact that you can see only a short distance down into the water around Eastport is due not to pollution but to this rich nutrient life. It's no coincidence that

Christina Tree

FISHERMAN STATUE

Maine's first salmon farms were in Cobscook Bay, where this aquaculture industry continues today.

The sardine-canning process in Maine began in Eastport in 1875 and a boom era quickly followed, but today the population of this island "city" has dropped to below 1,700 compared with more than 5,000 in 1900. Still, Eastport—which once rivaled New York in shipping— remains a working deepwater port, the deepest on the U.S. East Coast. Large freighters regularly dock at the new shipping pier near Estes Head to take on woodland products, a reminder (as is the surviving Federal and Greek Revival architecture) that by the War of 1812 this was already an important enough port for the British to capture and occupy it.

Today there are many gaps in the old waterfront, now riprapped in pink granite to form a seawall. With its flat, haunting light, Eastport has an end-of-the-world feel and suggests an Edward Hopper painting. It's a landscape that draws many artists, and there are galleries along Water Street.

Eastport consists entirely of islands, principally Moose Island, which is connected to Rt. 1 by Rt. 190 via a series of causeways (actually, tidal dams built in the 1930s for the failed tidal power project), linking other islands. It's a departure point for the small car ferry and excursion boats that ply Passamaquoddy Bay. Old Sow, a whirlpool between Eastport and Deer Island said to be 230 feet in diameter, is reportedly the largest in the western hemisphere.

Rt. 190 runs through the center of Sipayik (pronounced *zeh-BAYH-igh*), the Pleasant Point Indian Reservation, home to some 700 members of the Passamaquoddy Indian tribe. The Waponahki Museum is dedicated to telling the story of the tribe, and finely crafted baskets are sold. The 3-day Indian Ceremonial Days in early August fully celebrate Passamaquoddy culture.

Unfortunately, the 20 miles of Rt. 1 between Whiting (turnoff for Lubec) and Perry (turnoff for Eastport) offer few glimpses of Cobscook Bay. Be sure to take the short detour into Cobscook Bay State Park and into the ghostlike village of Pembroke, with its empty commercial buildings—including a trapezoidal movie hall and general store, dating from the village's 1870s prime, when its ironworks and shipyards prospered. Today Pembroke is best known for Reversing Falls Park.

GUIDANCE **Eastport Chamber of Commerce** (207-853-4644; www.eastport .net), P.O. Box 254, Eastport 04631.

Cobscook Bay Area Chamber of Commerce (207-733-2201; www.cobscook-bay.com), P.O. Box 42, Whiting 04691. Information on the chamber and on the area between Lubec and Eastport can be found at the Puffin Pines on Rt. 1.

Island Tours (207-853-4831), 37 Washington St., Eastport. Jim Blankman offers lively, reasonably priced picnic tours of the Eastport area in a classic 1947 wood-paneled Dodge station wagon.

A complete map of Eastport, Maine, plus downtown Lubec and the Quoddy Loop—and an excellent map bridging the Canadian and Maine sides of Passamaquoddy Bay—is available from Old Sow Publishing (phone/fax 207-853-6036; www.quoddyloop.com), P.O. Box 222, Moose Island, Eastport 04631.

✳ To See

The Quoddy Maritime Museum (207-853-6630), 68–72 Water St. at the corner of Boynton St., Eastport, features a 14-by-16-foot concrete model of the Passamaquoddy Tidal Power Project (see the chapter introduction) and is open Memorial Day–Sep., daily except Sun. It triples as a museum, crafts cooperative, and **information center**.

The Tides Institute and Museum of Art (207-853-4047; www.tides institute.org), 43 Water St., Eastport. Several years ago the city's ornate, vintage-1887 bank building came up for sale and seemed in danger of demolition. It's presently under restoration as a cultural center archiving and exhibiting regional photography, also showing original works of art and serving as a media equipment and assistance resource and library.

Waponahki Museum and Resource Center (207-853-4001), Rt. 190, Pleasant Point. Theoretically open weekdays 8:30–4, but it's wise to call for an appointment. Easy to miss, a small red building adjacent to the large Youth Center and bingo hall. Passamaquoddy elder Joseph Nicholas has created an outstanding museum with photos, tools, baskets, and crafts that tell the story of the Passamaquoddy tribe.

Barracks Museum (207-853-6630), 74 Washington St., Eastport. Open mid-June–Labor Day, most afternoons 1–4. Originally part of Fort Sullivan and occupied by the British during the War of 1812, this house has been restored to its 1820s appearance as an officers' quarters and displays old photos and memorabilia about Eastport.

Reversing Falls Park. Turn off Rt. 1 at Rt. 214 into the village of Pembroke; follow the slight jog in the road then Leighton Neck for 3.4 miles, and turn right onto Clarkson Rd. (the sign may or may not be there) then left at the T. This last road degenerates before it ends at a parking area. A short trail leads to picnic tables and the water. Try to time your visit to coincide with the couple of hours before the height of the incoming tide, which funnels furiously through the gap between Mahar's Point and Falls Island. As the salt water flows along at 6 to 8 or more knots, it strikes a series of rocks, resulting in rapids. At low water this is a great place to hunt for fossils.

Old Sow. What's billed as the largest whirlpool in the western hemisphere, and one of five significant whirlpools in the world, is sited between the tips of Moose Island and Deer Island. It's said to be produced by 70 billion cubic feet of water rushing into Passamaquoddy Bay, much of which finds its way around the tip of Deer Island and an underwater mountain at this narrow point in the bay. The area's smaller whirlpools are called Piglets. See *Boat Excursions* for viewing. The Old Sow is visible from the ferry crossing. We once saw a small cruise ship heel over dramatically when it came too close to the vortex; small craft beware.

✳ To Do

BIRDING Birding is what Moosehorn National Wildlife Refuge is about. Vast tidal flats in Eastport are good places to watch migrating plovers, sandpipers, and other shorebirds. American bald eagles are frequently seen around Cobscook Bay; see *Green Space*. For details about the late-May Down East Spring Birding Festival, see www.downeastbirdfest.org, and for puffin-watching on Machias Seal Island check out *Birding* in the "Atlantic Coast" and "St. Andrews and Grand Manan" subchapters.

BOAT EXCURSIONS Harris Whale Watching/Eastport Windjammers (207-853-2500 or 207-853-4303; www.eastportwindjammers.com), out of Eastport, is a very special experience. Captain Butch Harris offers afternoon and sunset cruises on Passamaquoddy Bay aboard the two-masted, 84-foot schooner *Sylvina W. Beal*, a veteran of many years as a herring and mackerel seiner out of Lubec and Eastport. **Fishing trips** on Passamaquoddy Bay are also offered by the Harris family aboard the 35-passenger *Quoddy Dam*.

Ferry to Deer Island, New Brunswick, with connections to Campobello and the New Brunswick mainland. For details about **East Coast Ferries Ltd.** (506-747-2159; www.eastcoastferries.nb.ca.), see *Getting Around* in "Washington County." Late June–early Sep. the ferry departs every hour from the beach beside Eastport Lobster and Fish House. Be sure to take it at least to Deer Island. We strongly suggest you go the whole way around the Quoddy Loop (see the introduction to "Washington County").

MUSIC AT PEAVEY LIBRARY

Christina Tree

GOLF ⚑ **Downeast Adventure Golf** (207-853-9595), Rt. 1, Perry. An oversized putting course with 2 acres of terrain including a pond, splash fountains, arched bridges, and a batting cage.

SEA KAYAKING AND CANOEING Cobscook Hikes & Paddles (207-726-4776; off-season, 207-454-2130). Registered Maine Guides Stephen and Tessa Forek offer guided 2- and 3-hour kayaking paddles from Whiting to Calais.

The Quoddy Regional Land Trust (207-733-5509) publishes *Cobscook Trails*. See *Hiking* in "The Atlantic Coast."

WALKS **Shackford Head State Park** (posted from Rt. 190 near downtown Eastport) is a 90-acre peninsula with several trails including a roughly 0.7-mile path from the parking lot to a 173-foot-high headland overlooking Campobello Island and Lubec in one direction and Cobscook Bay in the other. Another 0.25-mile-long trail leads down the headland and permits access to the shore. Views are of the bay with its floating salmon pens. Look for fossils at low water.

Moosehorn National Wildlife Refuge, Unit 2, Edmunds (off Rt. 1 between Dennysville and Whiting). Some 7,200 acres bounded by Whiting and Dennys Bays and the mouth of the Dennys River. North Trail Rd. is 2.5 miles long and leads to a parking area from which canoes can be launched into Hobart Stream. South Trail Rd. covers 0.9 mile and leads to a parking area for a 10-mile unmaintained trail network. Trails in the Baring section (Unit 1) of the refuge are maintained.

Cobscook Bay State Park (207-726-4412), off Rt. 1 between Dennysville and Whiting, has 888 acres that include a 2-mile nature trail with water views and a 0.5-mile Shore Trail. Wildlife and birds are plentiful.

Gleason Point, Perry. Take Shore Rd. next to the Quoddy Wigwam Gift Shop on Rt. 1 and follow signs to the beach and boat landing.

✳ Lodging

INNS AND BED & BREAKFASTS 🔍

Weston House (207-853-2907 or 1-800-853-2907; westonhouse-maine.com), 26 Boynton St., Eastport 04631. Open year-round. An elegant Federal-style house built in 1810 with two large front guest rooms sharing a full bath. One of these has a working fireplace and a tall four-poster, views of the bay and gardens, and antiques, but it was in the other—equally spacious and gracious—room that John James Audubon slept on his way to Labrador in 1833. A small room, tucked into the back of the ell, is perfect for solo travelers. Jett and John Peterson continue to add "rooms"—a bricked terrace here and a rose garden with gazebo, the spot for a wedding. Rates are $70–85 double, including a sumptuous breakfast in the formal dining room: maybe Eastport salmon and eggs Benedict. Jett's four-course dinner or a picnic lunch can be arranged.

Kilby House Inn (207-853-0989 or 1-800-853-4557; www.kilbyhouseinn.com), 122 Water St., Eastport 04631. A stick Gothic Victorian house on the waterfront with an attractive double parlor that invites you to sit down and read. Innkeeper Gregg Noyes's passions include playing the organ and refinishing antiques. There are five pleasant upstairs guest rooms: the sunny master with its four-poster canopy bed and water view; two more antiques-furnished rooms with private bath. $50–80 includes a very full breakfast on weekends and during summer months when Gregg, who teaches down in Steuben, is on hand to prepare it.

🦞 🐾 🐕 ♿ **Todd House** (207-853-2328), 1 Capen Ave., Eastport 04631. Open year-round. A restored 1775 Cape, the oldest house in Eastport, with water views. In 1801 men met here to charter a Masonic order, and in 1861 the house became a temporary barracks. The four large double rooms (shared baths) vary in view, and access to baths. Our favorites are the ground-floor Cornerstone Room (but its bath is across from the common room) and the Masonic Room with a working fireplace ($65). In winter guests pay $5 less and get breakfast elsewhere. Innkeeper Ruth McInnis welcomes well-behaved children and pets; her own pets include a Maine coon cat, five cockatiels, and a pet seagull that keeps his eye on the goldfish in the ornamental pond.

The Milliken House (207-853-2955 or 1-888-507-9370; www.eastport-inn.com), 29 Washington St., Eastport 04631. Bill and Mary Williams are the owners of this 1840s house, which retains Victorian charm with a large double parlor, ornate detailing, and some original furniture. There are six guest rooms, all with private bath. $65–75 year-round includes a sumptuous breakfast.

MOTEL 🐾 🐕 ♿ **The Motel East** (207-853-4747), 23A Water St., Eastport 04631. This two-story motel has 14 units, some handicapped accessible, all with water views, some with balcony. Amenities include direct-dial phones, cable TV, eight kitchenettes. $90–110 per night, less off-season. Guest cottage next door.

COTTAGES AND MORE **Tide Mill Farm** (207-733-2110; www.tidemill farm.com), 40 Tide Mill Rd., Edmunds 04628. This 200-year-old working farm on Whiting Bay and Crane Mill Stream has been in the Bell family since 1765. It is set on 1,600 acres with 6 miles of shorefront. The century-old farmhouse has five bedrooms sharing one and a half baths. $1,200 per week in-season; off-season rates available. This is a lively family farm with draft horses, Hereford cattle, chickens, pigs, and organic dairy herd. The eighth generation raises organic produce and animals, with vegetables and eggs available in summer season.

🐕 **Yellow Birch Farm** (207-726-5807), 272 Young's Cove Rd., Pembroke 04666. June–Sep. Bunny Richards and Gretchen Gordon maintain a 200-year-old farm near the Reversing Falls and rent out a two-room cottage (sleeping four) with a fully equipped kitchen, outdoor hot shower, outhouse, woodstove, and small deck ($400 per week).

Note: Weekly **rental cottages** are also listed at www.eastport.net.

CAMPGROUND **Cobscook Bay State Park** (207-726-4412), S. Edmunds Rd. just off Rt. 1, between Dennysville and Whiting. Open mid-May–mid-Oct. Offers 150 camping sites, most of them for tents and many with water views. There are even showers (unusual in Maine state campgrounds). The 880-acre park also offers a boat-launch area, picnic benches, and a hiking and cross-country ski trail.

✳ Where to Eat

🐕 **The New Friendly Restaurant** (207-853-6610 or 1-800-953-6610), Rt. 1, Perry. Open daily 11–8. Good road food. A homey restaurant with booths and food that's known as the best around: fish stews and chowders, basics like liver and onions, not-so-basic meals like an elegant crab salad and the most lobster in a lobster sandwich. Desserts include Grape-Nut pudding as well as pies. Beer and wine served.

WaCo Diner (207-853-4046), Water St., Eastport. Open year-round, Mon.–Sat. 6 AM–8 PM. Begun as a pushcart in 1924, the WaCo has expanded to include a waterside Schooner Room and a deck dining room overlooking the bay that on a sunny day just could not be more pleasant. The old section with booths and a long shiny counter survives. You can get a full roast turkey dinner or lazy lobster; also beer, chowder, and great french fries.

☙ **Eastport Chowder House** (207-853-4700), 167 Water St., Eastport. Open seasonally, daily 11–9. A good location, on what's said to be the site of the country's first fish and sardine cannery. Sandwiches to fish stews and lobster. The downstairs pub on Cannery Wharf is informal, and it's possible to get takeout (thus park in line) for the ferry that departs from the adjacent beach.

La Sardina Loca (207-853-2739), 28 Water St., Eastport. Open daily 4–10 in-season, Thu.–Sun. off-season. "The crazy sardine" is so flashy, cheerful, and out of character with the rest of Water Street that you figure it's a mirage, or at best somebody's one-season stand. But it's been there for years with its Christmas lights, patio furniture, and posters, and a menu that's technically Mexican, including "la Sardina Loca" chili with hot chiles and sour cream. Where else can you get fresh crabmeat enchiladas? Fully licensed.

Rosie's Hot Dog Stand at the Breakwater in Eastport. Open seasonally for more than 25 years.

Crossroads Restaurant (207-726-5053), Rt. 1, "at the Waterfall," Pembroke. Open 4–9 daily, open 11 AM on weekends. Bigger than it looks, serving lobster rolls and deep-fried seafood pies; liquor served.

✳ Entertainment

Stage East (207-853-4747; www.stageeast.org), a 100-seat theater at the Eastport Arts Center in the 1887 Masonic hall at the corner of Water and Dana Sts., Eastport; summer-season performances Thu.–Sat. at 7, Sun. at 3.

SummerKeys via water taxi. See "Atlantic Coast" for details about this summer Wednesday-evening music series in Lubec. Concerts are at 7:30; the water taxi departs at 6:30, with a return at 9:30. For concert tickets and water taxi service to the concert from Eastport, stop by the *Sylvina Beal* office on Water St. (207-853-2500).

✳ Selective Shopping

Along Rt. 190 and in Eastport
Skicin Arts & Crafts (207-853-2840), on Rt. 190 at the Pleasant Point Reservation, is attached to the home of Passamaquoddy patriarch Joseph Nicholas and features Passamaquoddy-made baskets and handmade jewelry. This is the beautiful work that sells for many times the price in Bar Harbor stores.

Raye's Mustard Mill (207-853-4451 or 1-800-853-1903; www.rayesmustard.com), Rt. 190 (Washington St.), Eastport. Open daily 9–5 in summer; winter hours vary. In business since 1900, this company is billed as the country's last remaining stone-ground-mustard mill. This is the mustard in which Washington County's sardines were once packed, and it's sensational. Sample it in **The Pantry** gift store, which serves coffee (and on occasion espresso); tours in July and Aug.

The Commons (207-853-4123; www .thecommonseastport.com), 51 Water St., Eastport. Open year-round; in summer, Mon.–Sat. 9–6, Sun. 1–5, otherwise Mon.–Sat. 10–6. An outstanding gallery displaying the work of 40 local artists and artisans: botanical and wildlife paintings, hand-spun yarn, carved burl bowls, organic seeds, jewelry, felted garments, hand-knit sweaters, and more.

Jim Blankman Woodworker (207-853-4831), corner of Water and Sullivan Sts., Eastport. Jim Blankman is a consummate craftsman with wood. His colorful shop with its potbellied stove also features beautifully crafted skateboards and plain pine "woody-motif" coffins. Blankman prides himself on his vintage-1947 wood-paneled Dodge nine-passenger station wagon (see *Guidance*), for which he also makes teardrop-shaped made-to-order trailers.

THE COMMONS GALLERY, EASTPORT

Christina Tree

Earth Forms Pottery (207-853-2430; www.djsutherland.com), corner of Water and Dana Sts., Eastport. Open daily in-season. Nationally known potter Donald Sutherland specializes in large garden and patio pots, also in free-form sculptures and in smaller, functional but striking pieces like our fruit bowl.

The Eastport Gallery (207-853-4166; www.eastportgallery.com), 53 Water St., Eastport. Open daily in summer. A cooperative gallery representing more than 25 local artists.

Crow Tracks (207-853-2336; www .crowtracks.com), 11 Water St., Eastport. Open year-round. R. J. LaVallee carves a variety of birds, whales, and fantasy figures, from decoys to Christmas ornaments.

Quoddy Crafts. See *To See*. Sharing space with the Quoddy Maritime Museum and the town information center, this juried crafts outlet is well worth checking out.

S. L. Wadsworth & Sons (207-853-4343; www.slwadsworth.com), 42/44 Water St., Eastport. Billed as the country's oldest ship chandlery and Maine's oldest merchandiser (no one really noticed until the present generation took over), this marine-geared store has recently added "nautical gifts" to hardware. There's no question that it was founded in 1818 by Samuel Wadsworth, son of General Peleg Wadsworth and uncle of poet Henry Wadsworth Longfellow.

Along Rt. 1, heading north from Whiting

Cinqueterre Farm Bakery (207-726-4766), Ox Cove Rd. (off Rt. 1), Pembroke. Open May–Oct., Mon.–Sat. Les Prickett and Gloria Christie, both locally respected chefs, operate a bakery specializing in five-grain breads, pizza, and rolls; soups and eggs, honey, jams, and pickles are also available, along with a selection of wines.

Quoddy Wigwam Gift Shop (207-853-4812), Rt. 1, Perry. Open daily 9–6. This is a prime retail outlet for Passamaquoddy baskets, pottery, and quill jewelry, also for the high-quality Quoddy Trail Moccasins manufactured by Kevin and Kirsten Shorey next door (207-853-2488; www .quoddytrail.com). Hand sewn, these items have acquired a fine reputation.

Maine-ly Smoked Salmon Company (207-853-4794; www.mainely smokedsalmon.com), 144 South Meadow Rd., Perry. Hot and cold smoked salmon.

45th Parallel (207-854-9500; www .fortyfifthparallel.com), "halfway between the Equator and the North Pole" on Rt. 1, Perry (a red stone marks the spot). Open late May–Oct. Self-described as "an eclectic mix of new home furnishings, exotic antiques, architectural elements and accessories from around the Globe," this is not something you'd expect at the 45th parallel. Chicago designers Britani Holloway-Pascarella and Philip Pascarella have filled this space—from floor to 12-foot-high ceilings—with stained glass and antique beds, drawer pulls and lamps, jewelry and bird feeders.

Katie's on the Cove (207-454-8446; www.katieschocolates.com), Rt. 1, Mill Cove, Robbinston. All handmade and hand-dipped chocolates. Favorites, the luscious truffles aside, include Passamaquoddy Crunch, Maine Potato Candy, and Maine Black Bear Paws. A new line of mustard chocolates uses Raye's.

Wood on Water (207-853-9663; www.woodonwater.com), 75 Water St., Eastport. Open April–Dec. Features the wood-burning and hand-painting work of Amy Marcotte, who can custom-design seascapes and paint pet portraits on an assortment of objects. Also, a variety of gifts.

✳ Special Events

Memorial Day weekend: **Downeast Birding Festival**—guided hikes, boat tours, presentations (www.down eastbirdfest.org).

July: **Independence Day** is celebrated in Pembroke (parade, canoe races) and for a week in **Eastport**, with parades, a military flyover, and fireworks. Eastport's is the first flag in the United States to be raised on July 4 itself (at dawn).

Mid-August: **Annual Indian Ceremonial Days**, Pleasant Point Reservation—a celebration of Passamaquoddy culture climaxing with dances in full regalia. Annual **antiques show** sponsored by the Barracks museum. **Moose Island Antiques Show** (207-853-2208).

September: **Paint Eastport Day** (*Saturday after Labor Day*)—artists of all ages are invited to come paint their favorite scene of the island city. At the end of the day artists return to the gallery for a silent auction. **Eastport Salmon Festival** (*Sunday after Labor Day*)—a celebration of Eastport's salmon industry; salmon, trout, and Maine potatoes are grilled dockside, and tours of fish farms in the bay are offered, along with live entertainment, games, an art show, an antiques auction, and a fishing derby.

December: **Festival of Lights**, Eastport.

CALAIS AND THE ST. CROIX VALLEY

Calais (pronounced *CAL-us*), the largest city in Washington County, is the sixth busiest point of entry into the United States from Canada, just across the St. Croix River from St. Stephen, New Brunswick. The two communities are inextricably linked, celebrating a 9-day International Festival together in August.

The city's present population is 3,600, roughly 3,000 less than it was in the 1870s, the decade in which its fleet of sailing vessels numbered 176. The brick downtown was built soon after an 1870 fire had wiped out the previous city center. Happily, the city's wooden residential district seems largely to have escaped the fire and remains the best testament to the city's most prosperous era.

Down by the old waterfront the city shows signs of revival. The brick railroad station has been expanded and transformed into a Downeast Heritage Center, offering an overview of the region as well as exhibits on the Passamaquoddy Nation, local history, and the nature of surrounding land and water. It opened in 2004 to celebrate the 400th anniversary of the settling of nearby St. Croix Island (8 miles downstream in the middle of the river).

Rarely mentioned in American schoolbooks, St. Croix Island looms large in Canadian and French history. It was the first European settlement north of Florida and the beginning of the French presence in North America.

A French expedition was drawn here by the fur trade, and its leader, Pierre Dugua, Sieur de Monts, retained Samuel de Champlain as his mapmaker and chronicler. Probably the first European expedition to push up into Passamaquoddy Bay, they chose this 6.5-acre island for their settlement in June 1604 and set about building a storehouse and dwellings, despite the blackflies. The waters teemed with fish, and the Native inhabitants were friendly—but the first snow came in early October, the river froze, and 35 of the 79 settlers died. Finally, on June 15, supply vessels arrived, and Dugua sailed south in search of a better settlement site. He instead returned to Port Royal, Nova Scotia, seeding French culture in Canada.

DOWNTOWN CALAIS

Christina Tree

North of Calais the St. Croix Valley is as heavily forested and known for its fish-filled lakes as any spot in the North Maine Woods. Follow Rt. 1 north from Calais and your nose quickly reveals the area's big employer, the pulp and paper mill in nearby Woodland. Then the woods close in.

This area was first settled by Passamaquoddy Indians, who migrated up from the Bay of Fundy along the inland waterways. The small town of Princeton, flanked by Big Lake and Grand Falls Lake, is home to a number of fishing camps and to the Passamaquoddy community of Odeneg. The center of this Indian township reservation is, however, in Motahkomiqkuk at Peter Dana Point on Big Lake, a village with a moving Indian cemetery beside the old Catholic mission church of St. Anne's (Mass on Sunday at 11:15).

To visit Dana Point you have already turned off Rt. 1 on the road to Grand Lake Stream, a plantation that's a famous fishing outpost on West Grand Lake, with access to the vast Grand Lake chain. Grand Lake Stream claims to have been home to the world's biggest tannery, employing more than 500 people for some decades before it burned in the 1870s. The current lures are landlocked salmon, lake trout, smallmouth bass, pickerel, and white perch.

Despite the small population (125 year-rounders), this spirited and well-connected community has, in recent years, been successfully struggling to create a land trust to manage the surrounding woodland. Some outstanding fishing lodges and camps are clustered here, and there are many good and affordable lakeside rental camps, a find for families. Local innkeepers can get you into the historical museum, a trove of Native American artifacts, tannery-era photos, and canoe molding. Inquire about hiking and guided kayaking. The Grand Lake Stream Folk Festival in late July draws visitors from far and wide.

GUIDANCE **Maine Tourist Information Center** (207-454-2211), 15 Union St., Calais. Open year-round; July–Oct. 15, daily 8–6, otherwise 9–5:30. This center, operated by the Maine Tourism Association, is a source of brochures for all of Maine as well as the local area. The staff are friendly and eager to help, and there are public restrooms.

Downeast Heritage Museum (1-877-454-2500; www.downeastheritage.org), 39 Union St., Calais. Open daily 9–5 in summer, off-season Tue.–Sat. 11–3. No admission is charged to walk into the lobby area with its interactive map of the area. Push a button and a town and or activity lights up with detailed information. Also see *To See*.

St. Croix Valley Chamber of Commerce (207-454-2308 or 1-888-422-3112; www.visitcalais.com) is also helpful. Call or e-mail and they will send you information on the area before you visit.

Grand Lake Stream Chamber of Commerce (www.grandlakestream.com). It's all there on the web site: accommodations for the Grand Lake Stream, Princeton, and Woodland areas, also outfitters and fishing guides.

GETTING THERE *By car:* The direct route to Calais from Bangor and points west of Washington County is Rt. 9, the Airline Highway. From the Machias area, take Rt. 191.

WHEN TO COME Fly-fishers converge on Grand Lake Stream and the many lakes and ponds of the St. Croix Valley in May and June. The tourist season begins with July, and winter comes early (as Samuel de Champlain discovered) to this area. The area's two big events—the Grand Lake Stream Festival in late July and the Calais/St. Stephen International Festival in August—are as colorful as only big celebrations in small places can be.

✳ To See

✐ **St. Stephen Chocolate Museum** (506-466-7848; www.chocolatemuseum.ca), Rt. 1, St. Stephens, New Brunswick. Open Mar.–Nov. weekdays 9–5; June 15– Aug., Mon.–Sat. 9–6:30, Sun. 1–5. $5 adults, $4 seniors and students, $3 ages 6 and under, $15 family. An interesting museum that tells the story of the Ganong Bros. Ltd. Company. Displays of old candy boxes, hand-dipping demonstrations, videos, a game to test your packing speed, and free samples. Out front in the same building is the Ganong chocolatier, where you can purchase the tempting goodies.

Dr. Holmes Cottage/Museum (207-454-2604), 245 Main St. The oldest existing house in Calais, built in 1805 by Artemus Ward. Open July until the Friday before Labor Day, Mon.–Fri. 1–4:30. Restored to its 1850 look and maintained by the St. Croix Historical Society. Pick up a *Walking Tour Guide* to the Calais Residential Historic District, which includes several Gothic Revival gingerbread houses on S. Main St.

Whitlock Mills Lighthouse. The northeasternmost lighthouse in the country is best viewed from the Pike Woods Rest Area on Rt. 1, 3 miles south of Calais.

✳ To Do

BIRDING **Moosehorn National Wildlife Refuge** is a prime birding center with some 190 species recorded, as well as resident bald eagles. Also see *Green Space* and *Canoeing and Kayaking*.

BOAT EXCURSIONS ✐ **Up Close Tours** (207-454-2844), 261 Main St., Calais. Captain Louis Bernardini offers 2-hour, regularly scheduled lobster-boat tours downriver and around St. Croix Island. See ospreys and eagles, haul traps, circle St. Croix Island.

✐ **Lady H Cruises** (207-853-2500) offers regularly 2½-hour cruises, May–Oct., from the Calais waterfront down and around St. Croix Island, also hauling traps, searching for seals, eagles, and ospreys.

Note: To find out about scheduled river cruises, inquire at the Downeast Heritage Center.

CANOEING AND KAYAKING **Sunrise Canoe and Kayak** (207-255-3375, 1-877-980-2300; www.sunrisecanoeand kayak.com), RR1 Box 344A, Machias. Mar.–Oct. Sea kayak and canoe outfitter with rentals, trip planning, and shuttle service for expeditions on the St. Croix River along the Maine–New Brunswick border, and on the Machias River to view petroglyphs. Guided kayaking expeditions along the Bold Coast. also rents bicycles.

Grand Lake Outfitters (207-796-5561; stevelaura@aol.com), P.O. Box 24, Grand Lake Stream 04637. Anglers aren't the only ones who can enjoy these pristine waters. Steve and Laura Schaefer offer rentals and guided tours of West Grand Lake with an eye out for blue herons, eagles, ospreys, muskrats, and otters as well as moose and deer. Both Steve and Laura are longtime residents, and Steve is a Registered Maine Guide.

Downeast Heritage Museum (207-454-7878 or 1-877-454-2500; www.downeastheritage.org), 39 Union St., Calais. Open daily 9–5 in summer, off-season Tue.–Sat. 11–3. Adults $6, seniors $4, children $3, household $20. Inquire about the cruise down the river and around St. Croix Island. The saga of the 1604 settlement of St. Croix Island (see the chapter introduction) is dramatized in French and English. You discover that the settlement's houses and storehouses were half timbered, with brick chimneys, far more substantial than those the Pilgrims built two decades later at

DOWNEAST HERITAGE CENTER

Christina Tree

Plymouth. You also learn that the entire group would have perished were it not for help received from the region's Native American residents, the Passamaquoddy.

People of the Dawn, the center's second major exhibit, tells another long-overdue story—that of the Passamaquoddy tribe, whose members have managed, against all odds, to maintain their language, music, and crafts. Displays include replicas of local pictographs, some dating back 6,000 years; one depicts a 17th-century sailing vessel, probably Champlain's, which must have moored in Machias Bay, within view of the Native artist. The Passamaquoddy exhibit isn't large but attempts to be authentic. The mannequins' faces depict actual tribal members. The 18-foot-long oceangoing birch-bark canoe was built by David Moses Brieges exactly as his great-grandfather would have built it, and the centuries-old wampum belt belongs to Donald Soctomah, tribal preservation officer. According to Soctomah, the tribe presently numbers 3,300 widely scattered members, with 800 in Indian Township north of Calais and 250 on the Pleasant Point Reservation near Eastport. Another 500 to 600 live in surrounding Washington County.

St. Croix Island itself is flat, unprepossessing, and off-limits (due to ongoing excavations) to the general public. At St. Croix Island's **International Historic Site Overlook**, Rt. 1 in Red Beach (8 miles south of Calais), however, a path leads leads to a bronze replica of the settlement. Along the way you encounter half a dozen haunting, life-sized bronze statues, here elaborately dressed Frenchmen, there a young Passamaquoddy girl.

FISHING The St. Croix watershed is famed for its abundance of landlocked salmon, square-tailed trout, and some of the finest smallmouth bass fishing in Maine. Best May–mid-June. When ice is out in spring, trolling starts on West Grand Lake, Big Lake, and Pocumcus Lake. Grand Lake Stream itself, fast-flowing water linking West Grand and Big Lakes, is one of the country's premier fly-fishing spots for landlocked salmon. Fishing licenses, covering 3 days to a full season (also necessary for ice fishing), are available, along with lodging and supplies, in the woodland village of **Grand Lake Stream** (www.grandlakestream.com), the focal point of the region and base for the state's largest concentration of fishing guides: www.grandlakestreamguides.com. **Princeton**, on the way to Grand Lake Stream, is also worth noting for its waters, Big Lake and Grand Falls Lake. Both once ran freely into the St. Croix River but, thanks to a series of 19th-century industrial dams, are now known for their shallows and flowage, great for trout as well as moose-watching and canoeing.

Moosehorn National Wildlife Refuge (see *Green Space*). Several lakes and streams within the refuge are open for fishing.

GOLF St. Croix Country Club (207-454-8875), River Rd., Calais. A tricky nine-hole course on the banks of the St. Croix River.

SWIMMING Red Beach on the St. Croix River is named for the sand on these strands, which is deep red due to the red granite in the area. There is also swimming in dozens of crystal-clear lakes. **Round Pond** in Charlotte has a free beach and boat launch. North of Calais, follow the Charlotte Rd. 8 miles to the pond.

✳ Green Space

Moosehorn National Wildlife Refuge (207-454-7161), RR 1, Box 202, Suite 1, Baring 04964. This area is the northeast end of a chain of wildlife and migratory bird refuges extending from Florida to Maine and managed by the U.S. Fish and Wildlife Service. The 23,000-acre refuge is divided into two sections some 20 miles apart. The larger, 17,200-acre area is in Baring, 5 miles north of Calais on Rt. 1. Look for eagles, which nest each spring at the intersection of Charlotte Rd. and Rt. 1. The Edmunds division is found heading south on Rt. 1 from Calais, between Dennysville and Whiting (see "Eastport"). This 7,200-acre area lies on the border of the tidal waters of Cobscook Bay. Special programs—guided hikes, bike tours, and van tours, sometimes take you down roads you wouldn't be able to explore on your own—offered late June–Aug.

ST. CROIX INTERNATIONAL HISTORIC SITE OVERLOOK ON ROUTE 1, RED BEACH

Christina Tree

WALKS Calais Waterfront Walkway. A new 1.5-mile path follows a former railbed along the river, beginning at city landing parking lot. Formally a part of the East Coast Greenway, it's a good venue from which to appreciate the daily 25-foot tidal changes.

Devil's Head. A new trail leads to a promontory, said to be the highest point west of Cadillac Mountain; great views. Look for the sign on Rt. 1 south of Heslin's Motel.

✻ Lodging

In Robbinston 04671

⊙ ✸ **Brewer House** (207-454-2385; www.thebrewerhousebnb.com), 590 Rt. 1, P.O. Box 88. This columned, 1828 mansion has new owners: Norwegian concert violinist Trond Saeverud and artist Joan Siem. There are four rooms, all with private bath, three retaining massive carved beds from the previous owner. In the St. Andrews Room the headboard is a former altarpiece and the bath is large, with bay views. Captain John has an antique carved bed and a private bath (shower). Rates June 20–Oct. 15 are $95–155, including a full breakfast; otherwise $85–135. Pets are permitted in the two-bedroom Quoddy Cove Apartment ($94–125), with its own kitchenette and dining area. Chamber music is performed here throughout the summer.

Redclyffe Shore Motor Inn (207-454-3270), Rt. 1. Twelve miles south of Calais on Rt. 1, this one-story motel with 16 units is set high above the wide mouth of the St. Croix, many rooms (request one) with river views. The added plus is dinner, a few steps away (see *Dining Out*). $62–73 per couple.

In Calais 04619

✸ ♂ **Calais Motor Inn** (207-454-7111 or 1-800-439-5531; www.calaismotorinn.com), 293 Main St. A friendly, locally owned 70-unit motel with the bonuses of a new, indoor Olympic-sized swimming pool (with an aquatic lift), a hot tub and small fitness center, and a licensed restaurant (see *Dining Out*). $74–79 per couple in-season, $5 per extra person.

In Princeton 04668

🎗 ✸ ♂ **Lakeside Country Inn and Cabins** (207-796-2324 or 1-888-677-2874; thelakeside@hotmail.com), 14 Rolfe St. Open year-round; cabins May–Nov. A handsome inn built in 1854 with twin chimneys and seven guest rooms. There are also five basic housekeeping cabins on Lewy Lake (the outlet to Big Lake, also a source for the St. Croix River). Rooms in the inn are simple and nicely furnished; each has a sink, some share a bath. Hosts Gary and Jennifer seem right for this place, hospitable outdoorspeople who are gardeners and good cooks. Inn rooms are $38 per day for two; camps are $52–68 per night; meals are available at additional cost. They also offer guide service, boat rentals, and nonresident hunting/fishing licenses.

In Grand Lake Stream 04637

The Pines (207-557-7463; off-season, 207-825-4431; www.thepineslodge.com). Open May 15–Oct. 1. Twelve miles from Grand Lake Stream on Lake Sysladobsis, part of the Grand

Lake stream chain of lakes, The Pines is about 100 years away in atmosphere. It's the oldest sporting camp in the area; past guests include Andrew Carnegie and Calvin Coolidge. There are five cabins, also two housekeeping cottages on small islands. The oldest cabin dates to 1883 and the large, double-porched white-clapboard house, from 1884. The upright piano in the living room was ferried over on the *Manhattan*, the launch that served the camp until the 1950s, when the 12 miles of logging roads were built (the last mile or so is a narrow dirt track that peters out into a trail along the edge of the lake). Most guests fly in. The cabins are heated by woodstoves and have gas lights and a chemical toilet. The main house (which offers flush toilets) and bathhouse are electrified. Cabins are $80 per person per night with three meals, including a packed lunch, $60 for children 3–10. Housekeeping cottages are $550 per week for four or less, $125 per day, $137.50 for over four people. Steve and Nancy Norris have managed The Pines for the past 15 years.

✍ **Weatherby's** (207-796-5558; winter, 207-237-2911; www.weatherbys .com), P.O. Box 69. Open early May–Oct. Jeff McEvoy and Elizabeth Rankin are the new owners of this rambling white 1870s lodge set in roses and birches by Grand Lake Stream, the small river that connects West Grand Lake with Big Lake. It's restricted to fly-fishing—Weatherby's is now an Orvis-sponsored fly-fishing lodge. Each of the 16 cottages is different, but most are log-style with screened porches, a bath, and a Franklin stove or fireplace. Fishing is what this place is about, and it's a great spot for children. $120 per person double occupancy, $162 single; children under 14 are $55 (family rates available). Rates include all three meals, a trail lunch or cookout lunch as well as breakfast and dinner; motorboats are $50 per day, and a guide, $175; 15 percent gratuity added. Inquire about scheduled fly-fishing schools for novices and women as well as pros.

Leen's Lodge (207-796-2929 or 1-800-995-3367; www.leenslodge.com), P.O. Box 40. A peaceful cluster of cottages on the shore of West Grand Lake. This place has a 1950s feel. Ten cabins, scattered through the woods, range in size from one to eight bedrooms, each with a full bath, fireplace or Franklin stove (with gas heat as a backup), and fridge. The dining room overlooks the water. The Tannery, a pine-paneled gathering space with a picture window, is equipped with games, books, and a TV—a good spot to relax before dinner (BYOB). $100 per person per day double occupancy MAP, $125 per person single occupancy, includes breakfast and dinner. Family rates available in nonpeak periods; 15 percent gratuity; lunch, boat rentals, and guide service are extra.

✍ **Indian Rocks Camps** (207-796-2822 or 1-800-498-2821; indianrocks @nemaine.com). Open ice-out through October. The Canells offer five century-old log cabins and a central lodge, not quite on the lake but with docking facilities. It's a friendly compound that caters to families and fishermen. $78 per person double occupancy, $82 single, includes all meals; 5-day packages run $325 per person. Summer housekeeping cabin rentals are $425 per week. The dining room is open to the public by reservation.

☙ **Chet's Camps** (207-796-5557; www.chetscamps.com). Tidy, white lakeside cabins and a central lodge right on Big Lake serve as a base for fly-fishing workshops and canoe expeditions as well as laid-back family vacations. Cabins can accommodate from 4 to 10 people and can be booked on a housekeeping basis ($30–40) with meals available, or $110 per person ($85 per child) including all three meals. Inquire about the Grand Lake Stream Outdoor School.

☙ ✍ **Canal Side Cabins** (207-796-2796 or 1-888-796-2796; www.canalsidecabins.com), P.O. Box 77. Open year-round. These family-run, family-geared cabins sleep between four and eight with a living room and dining area, a furnace or fireplace, full kitchen, and screened porch. Daily rates $28–30 per person, minimum of two; family rates in July and Aug. run $450–525 per week.

✍ **Shoreline Camps** (207-796-5539), P.O. Box 127. Open ice-out until mid-Oct. An attractive set of camps on the banks of Big Lake. Peaceful and remote, offering hiking, swimming, boating, and fishing. Ten cabins range from one to three bedrooms, each with bath and private deck. Boat rental, guides, fishing licenses available. Facilities also include a coin-operated laundry. $37 per person per day with a $74 minimum for two-bedroom cottages. Children under 12 are $20 per night; under 3, free.

✳ Where to Eat

DINING OUT **The Chandler House** (207-454-7922), 20 Chandler St., Calais. Open 4–11 daily except Mon. Chef-owner William Condon specializes in seafood and is widely respected—with reason—in this corner of

Maine. On our last visit we began with sautéed mussels served with oyster sauce, fresh peppercorns, and green onions, and scallop chowder. Some two dozen seafood choices might include baked stuffed salmon; prime rib with Yorkshire pudding is a favorite. Entrées $12.95–25.95.

Bernardini's (207-454-2237), 89 Main St., Calais. Open year round (except Sun.) for lunch and dinner. Marilyn and Louis Bernardini's cheerful Italian trattoria glows with twinkly white lights and stained glass and wooden detailing from the demolished Immaculate Conception Church— and the food is good. Traditional Italian entrées, veal parmigiana, pasta specials, and desserts. Entrées ($12.95–14.50) come with salad and pasta or rice.

Redclyffe Shore Dining Room (207-454-3270), Rt. 1, Robbinston. Open 5–9 for dinner. The dining room overlooks the St. Croix River. The vast menu offers pasta, steaks, chicken, and seafood; specialties include baked haddock with lobster sauce, and "mariner's haul." Entrées $15.50–21.95. Reservations suggested.

Heslin's (207-454-3762), Rt. 1, Calais (south of the village). Open May–Oct., 5–9. A popular local dining room high above the river, specializing in steak ("the thickest cuts in town!") and seafood entrées; homemade desserts, fully licensed, $15.75 for salmon, $18.95 for lobster pie.

Calais Motor Inn Restaurant (207-454-7111), 293 Main St. (Rt. 1), Calais. Open for lunch and dinner. A large, comfortable dining room specializing in steak and seafood at dinner. Entrées $9–16.

EATING OUT **Wickachee** (207-454-3400), 282 Main St. (Rt. 1), Calais.

PINE TREE STORE, GRAND LAKE STREAM

Open year-round 6 AM–10 PM. Steak and seafood (with a big salad bar) are the dinner specialties; even dinner entrées start at just $7. Spacious, clean, and friendly, but the restrooms are tiny.

✳ Selective Shopping

J. B. Siem Gallery (207-454-0333), Rt. 1, Robbinston (12 miles south of Calais). Open Mon.–Sat. 10–5, Sun. noon–5, and by appointment. The gallery features haunting paintings by internationally respected artist Joan Burger Siem, along with guest exhibits.

Knock on Wood (1-800-336-7136), Rt. 1 west of Calais. Open daily 9–5. Larger than it looks from the outside, a gift shop with a wide variety of crafts, candles, and more.

Downeast Heritage Center (207-454-7878), 39 Union St., Calais. No museum admission necessary for the shop, which specializes in Passamaquoddy crafts and books and offers a quality selection of gifts.

Chimerto's (207-454-3300), 283 Main St., Calais. Open year-round, Mon.–Sat. in-season, otherwise Thu.–Sat. Native American baskets, dream catchers, Maine and children's books, jewelry, notecards, gifts.

The Urban Moose (207-454-8277), 80 Main St., Calais. Souvenirs galore.

Marden's (207-454-1421), 61 Main St. and Rt. 1, Calais. Two representatives of the chain of Maine discount centers, which has been doing business in the state since 1964. Big-time bargains can be found here, from furniture to fabrics, housewares to clothing.

Pine Tree Store (207-796-5027), Water St., Grand Lake Stream. Open daily year-round. Kurt and Kathy Cressey's outpost oasis offers one of the largest selections of fishing flies in Maine; also tackle, clothing, hunting and fishing licenses, groceries, and an astonishing selection of wines "with caps that don't screw" plus great sandwiches to take with you to countless waterside picnic spots.

✳ Special Events

Last weekend of July: **Grand Lake Stream Folk Art Festival**—bluegrass and folk music, woodsmen's skills demonstrations featuring canoe building, crafts, dinner cooked by Maine Guides.

August: **International Festival**, Calais and St. Stephen, New Brunswick—a week of events on both sides of the border, including pageants, a parade, entertainment, and more.

ST. ANDREWS AND GRAND MANAN (NEW BRUNSWICK)

Beyond Eastport and Calais, you don't drop off the end of the world. Instead you cross the Canadian border—either via Rt. 1 at Calais or via ferry across Passamaquoddy Bay—into coastal New Brunswick. Suddenly it's an hour later, distance is measured in kilometers, signs are in French as well as English, gas is priced by the liter, and—for Americans—everything is cheaper. Most tourists here are, of course, Canadian.

Historically and geographically, in this corner Maine and Canada are intrinsically linked. Both St. Andrews (New Brunswick's liveliest resort town) and the island of Grand Manan (a haven for whale-watchers, birders, and hikers) were settled by loyalists during the Revolution, and Grand Manan, which lies just 9 miles off West Quoddy Light, is geographically closer to Maine than to Canada.

GUIDANCE Complete lodging listings for both St. Andrews and Grand Manan are detailed in the **New Brunswick Touring Guide**, available by calling 1-800-561-0123 (toll-free in Canada and the United States); by visiting www.tourism nbcanada.com; or by writing to Economic Development & Tourism, P.O. Box 12345, Woodstock, New Brunswick, Canada E7M 5C3. A large **Provincial Tourist Information Centre** (506-466-7390), 5 King St., St. Stephen, is housed in a grand old railroad station a few blocks beyond the border crossing, surrounded by banks at which you can exchange American for Canadian dollars (there's also a currency exchange inside the center). The municipal visitor center in St. Andrews By-the-Sea (1-800-563-7397; stachamb@nbnet.nb.ca) can mail information that includes ferry schedules.

GETTING THERE In good weather the ride across Passamaquoddy Bay from Eastport or Campobello via Deer Island is a delight, certainly the way to go at least one way to St. Andrews (see "Washington County"). If you're heading directly to Grand Manan, however, it makes more sense to drive to Blacks Harbour to board that island's ferry. From the Calais–St. Stephens border, it's 19 miles to St. Andrews and 35 miles to Blacks Harbour. See "Grand Manan" for details about the ferry.

ST. ANDREWS

Christina Tree

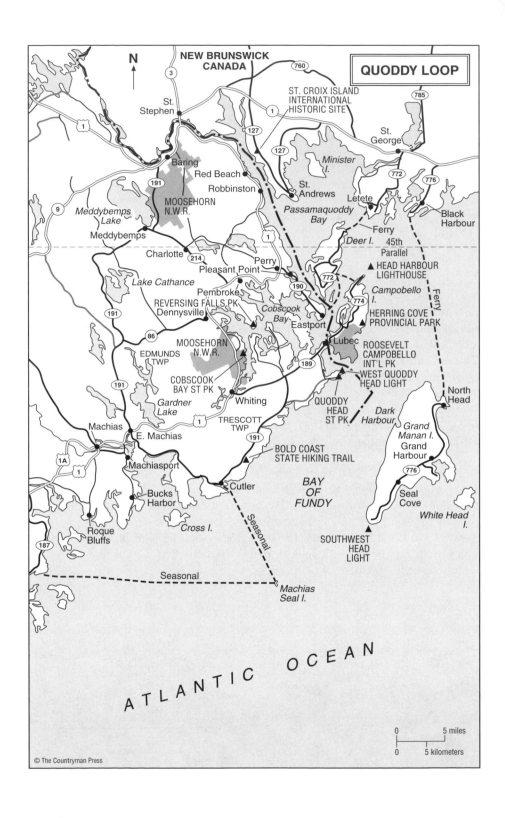

TIME Note that New Brunswick's Atlantic time is 1 hour ahead of Maine's eastern time (1 PM ET is thus 2 PM AT). Both Maine and New Brunswick observe Daylight Saving Time.

TAXES The Canadian Harmonized Sales Tax (HST) is 15 percent on food, lodging, and just about everything else in Canada. Visitors who spend more than $100 (Canadian) on goods and short-term accommodations will get most of the tax back by mailing in a Revenue Canada application and appending all receipts (forms are available at the provincial and municipal visitor centers).

ST. ANDREWS

St. Andrews retains a genteel 19th-century charm that has vanished in Bar Harbor. It's a pleasant resort town with shops lining well-named Water Street and plenty of choices for lodging, several restaurants, and a range of activities from historical tours to day adventures.

The big hotel is the Fairmont Algonquin, a 240-room, many-gabled, neo-Tudor resort dating from 1915. It sits enthroned like a queen mother above this tidy town with loyalist street names like Queen, King, and Princess Royal. St. Andrews was founded in 1783 by British Empire loyalists, American colonists who so strongly opposed breaking away from the mother country that they left the new United States after independence was won. Most came from what is now Castine, many of them unpegging their houses and bringing them along in the 1780s. Impressed by this display of loyalty, the British government made the founding of St. Andrews as painless as possible, granting the settlers a superb site. British army engineers dug wells, built a dock, constructed a fort, and laid out the town on its present grid. Each loyalist family was also given a house lot twice the usual size. The result is an unusually gracious, largely 19th-century town, hauntingly reminiscent of Castine. The focal point remains Market Wharf, where the first settlers stepped ashore—now the cluster point for outfitters offering whale-watching, sailing, and kayaking tours—and Water Street, lined with shops.

GUIDANCE St. Andrews Chamber of Commerce (506-529-3555; www.town .standrews.nb.ca), 46 Reed Ave., St. Andrews, New Brunswick, Canada E5B 1A1. The office is open year-round; the information center, May–Oct.

For New Brunswick tourist literature, including St. Andrews and Grand Manan, phone 1-800-563-7397 or e-mail stachamb@nbnet.nb.ca.

GETTING THERE *By car:* Rt. 1 via Calais. From the border crossing at Calais, it's just 19 miles to St. Andrews.

By car ferry: Late June–mid-Sep. only. See *Getting Around* and *Boat Excursions* in "Washington County." The ferry docks in L'Etete, and the road curves up the peninsula through the town of St. George, where you pick up Canadian Rt. 1, following it 13 unremarkable miles to the turnoff (Rt. 127) for St. Andrews.

WHEN TO COME The summer season is late June through September, but December is also big in St. Andrews, with many special events.

✳ To See

Ross Memorial Museum (506-520-5124), corner of King and Montague Sts., St. Andrews. Open Mon.–Sat. mid-June–Labor Day 10–4:30, then closed Mon. until mid-Oct. An 1824 mansion displaying the fine decorative art collection of the Reverend and Mrs. Henry Phipps Ross of Ohio, world travelers and collectors who fell in love with the area while on a picnic on Chamook Mountain. They purchased the 1824 house and donated it, along with their collections, to the town. Free.

Sheriff Andrews House Historic Site (506-529-5080), King St., St. Andrews. Open June–early Sep., Mon.–Sat. 9:30–4:30, Sun. 1–4:30. An 1820 house that belonged to Elisha Andrews, high sheriff of Charlotte County; fine detailing. Costumed guides offer tours and demonstrate open-hearth cooking techniques and traditional domestic handiwork, such as quilting.

Ministers Island Historic Site (506-529-5081), Chamcook. Open June–mid-Oct. One of the grandest estates, built around 1890 on an island connected by a "tidal road" (accessible only at low tide) to St. Andrews, **Covenhoven** is a 50-room mansion with 17 bedrooms, a vast drawing room, a bathhouse, and a gigantic and ornate livestock barn. The builder was Sir William Van Horne, the driving force in construction of the Canadian Pacific Railway. Preset 2-hour guided tours only. This is a real island, a short drive across the ocean floor (at low tide).

✐ **Huntsman Aquarium Museum Marine Science Centre** (506-529-1202; www.huntsmanmarine.ca), Brandy Cove Rd. (off Rt. 127), St. Andrews. Open Memorial Day–Columbus Day weekend, 10–6 in July and Aug., otherwise 10–4:30. $7.50 adult, $6.50 seniors, $5 children; ages 3 and under are free. A nonprofit aquaculture research center sponsoring educational programs and cruises. The aquarium museum features hundreds of living plants and animals found in the Quoddy region, including a family of resident harbor seals, providing a rare close-up view of these fascinating creatures—but we were appalled at the small and barren space allotted them. The touch pool is popular with kids.

✐ **Atlantic Salmon Interpretive Centre** (506-529-1384; www.asf.ca), Chamcook, 5 miles east of St. Andrews on Rt. 127. Open mid-May–mid-Oct., daily 9–5. $4 adults, $2.50–3.50 students, $10 per family of 4, and $2 per additional child. These undervisited post-and-beam buildings include the Atlantic Salmon International Hall of Fame—which resembles an old river lodge complete with great room. Exhibits examine the history, geography, and distressingly dwindling numbers of wild salmon. Chamcook Stream flows through the room, and salmon of all sizes can be seen in an aquarium.

Kingsbrae Horticultural Garden (506-529-3335), 220 King St., St. Andrews. $8.50 adults, $7 seniors and students. Twenty-seven acres of elaborately formal gardens with walking paths, a delightful café, an art gallery, and a gift shop. Built on the grounds of several long-gone estates, the garden uses mature cedar hedges, flower beds, and old-growth forest in the new design. Specialized areas include display gardens with rare and native plants, demonstration gardens, a woodland trail through the old-growth forest, a therapy garden, and bird and butterfly gardens. For more about the café, see *Eating Out*.

St. Andrews Blockhouse (506-529-4270), Centennial Park, St. Joe's Point Rd., St. Andrews. Open June–Aug., 9–8; until mid-Sep., 9–5. Erected during the War of 1812, partially restored but also partially original, this is one of the few such blockhouses that's survived in North America. Interpretive panels tell the story.

Green's Point Lighthouse Museum, L'Etete. After leaving the ferry landing, turn right and drive to the parking area near the keeper's garage. The official name of the light station is "L'Etete Passage Light."

✳ To Do

GOLF **Algonquin Signature Golf Course** (see *Lodging*). Open May–Oct. The resort's golf course, recently completely redesigned. Thomas McBroom, an award-winning architect, laid out the 18 holes. From oceanfront to forest holes, the natural flow of the course and the scenic views make this an unforgettable golfing experience. Clubhouse, pro shop.

SAILING **S/V Cory** (506-529-8116), St. Andrews Wharf, a 72-foot gaff- and square-rigged cutter built by her former captain in New Zealand, offers 3-hour sails in Passamaquoddy Bay and up the St. Croix River of the Bay of Fundy, where you can see whales, dolphins, and other wildlife. Passengers are welcome to take the helm or help hoist sails.

SEA KAYAKING AND CANOEING In St. Andrews, **Seascape** (506-529-4866; www.seascapekayatours.com) offers half- and full-day guided tours as well as longer expeditions. They teach several skills courses as well, including introductions to sea kayaking and sea kayak safety. **Eastern Outdoors** (1-800-56-KAYAK; www.easternoutdoors.com), 165 Water St., also offers guided half- and full-day tours; beginners welcome.

SWIMMING **Katy's Cove** (506-529-8823), Acadia Rd., St. Andrews, has (relatively) warm water, a sandy white beach, and a newly renovated clubhouse; nominal fee.

WHALE-WATCHING **Fundy Tide Runners** (506-529-4481; www.fundytide runners.com) and **Triton of the Bay** (506-529-4843; www.triton ofthebay.com) both feature fast, 24-foot, rigid-hulled Zodiac Hurricane boats, and clients wear flashy orange, full-length flotation suits; **Quoddy Link Marine** (506-529-2600; www.quoddylinkmarine.com) offers Whale Search and Island Cruises aboard two larger, slower vessels with enclosed, heated viewing areas as well as outdoor decks; **Island Quest Marine Adventures** (506-529-9885) offers a 3-hour tour on a custom-built 38-foot tour boat. **Surge Tours** (506-529-8185; www.whale-watch-east.com) features a 27-foot speedboat offering a 2 to 3 hour bay safari.

※ Lodging

RESORT ♂ ⚹ **The Fairmont Algonquin Hotel** (506-529-8823; in the U.S., 1-800-441-1414; www.fairmont .com), 184 Adolphus St., St. Andrews, New Brunswick, Canada E5B 1T7. Fully open mid-Apr.–mid-Nov., but some 50 rooms in the new wing remain open year-round. The last of the truly grand coastal resorts in northeastern America: a 240-room (including 13 suites), Tudor-style hotel with formal common and dining rooms, this hotel was built in 1889, with the castle facade, but only 80 rooms. Ownership began with the St. Andrews Land Company and passed to the Canadian Pacific Railway Company, then to the province of New Brunswick; this is now a Fairmont-managed property. The golf course has undergone extensive renovations in recent years, and there are five dining options, a spa and fitness center, fitness classes year-round, a heated outdoor pool, tennis courts, shuffleboard, and a daily activity program for children in July and August. Bellhops wear kilts. The rack rate averages $289–569 (Canadian) per couple, but there are many special packages.

INNS **Kingsbrae Arms Relais & Chateaux** (506-529-1897; www .relaischateaux.fr/kingsbrae), 219 King St., St. Andrews, New Brunswick, Canada E5B 1Y1. Canada's first five-star inn (as decreed by Canada Select) is this 1897 shingled mansion adjoining Kingsbrae Gardens. Innkeepers Harry Chancey Jr. and David Oxford treat guests as friends. The evening begins with cocktails in the library. The softly colored drawing room is elegant with its grand piano and gardens beyond. A five-course meal is served (see *Dining Out*). The five rooms and three suites have a king or queen bed, fireplace, telephone, marble bathroom with Jacuzzi, and water or garden views. $690–1,175 (U.S.), including a full breakfast and a four-course dinner. Minimum 3-night stay in July and Aug., 2 nights other times.

⚘ **Rossmount Inn** (506-529-3351; www.rossmountinn.com), 4599 Rt. 127, St. Andrews, New Brunswick, Canada E5B 2Z3. East of town, this boxy three-story hilltop mansion is a period piece—high Victorian with ornate chandeliers, woodwork, and appropriate furnishings. Built at the turn of the 20th century by the same Reverend and Mrs. Ross who endowed the Ross Museum in town, it has been recently revitalized by Chris and Graziella Aerni. A Swiss-born and trained chef, Chris quickly established the inn as a dining destination (see *Dining Out*). Most rooms are now charmingly furnished with antiques and a choice of double, twin, queen-, and king-sized beds. The extensive property includes a swimming pool and walking trails up Chamcook Mountain, the highest point on this side of Passamaquoddy Bay. $115–130 in high season, otherwise $69–89 (Canadian) plus 15 percent tax.

🐾 ♂ **The Windsor House of St. Andrews** (506-529-3330 or 1-888-890-9463; www.windsorhouseinn .com), 132 Water St., St. Andrews, New Brunswick, Canada E5B 1A8. This six-room hotel in the center of town is a gem, furnished in antiques and artwork from the private collection of American owners Jay Remer (who has worked at Sotheby's) and Greg Cohane. The building dates to 1798 but was substantially renovated in the 1880s and includes a (public) dining room (see *Dining Out*), a cozy bar, and a billiard room (the table is from a Newport mansion). Each of the four second-floor guest rooms has a fireplace and is deftly decorated. All have phone, Internet access, and concealed TV/VCR. $225–300 (Canadian) in high season, $125–200 off-season, includes a full breakfast.

BED & BREAKFASTS Check with the chamber of commerce for other reasonably priced B&Bs, many of which seem to change each season.

🐾 **Treadwell Inn** (506-529-1011 or 1-888-529-1011), 129 Water St., St. Andrews, New Brunswick, Canada E5B 1A7. Open May–Oct. A real find. Annette Lacey and Jerry Mercer offer six spacious rooms, imaginatively furnished in antiques; private baths. Two rooms have a balcony overlooking the water (35 feet away). Two third-floor efficiency suites have a sitting area and whirlpool bath with private waterside balcony. Originally built in 1820 by a ship's chandler, eventually serving as the town's customhouse. At $145–250 (Canadian)—$95–150 off-season—including breakfast, this is great value. Two-night minimum stay in waterfront rooms. Enjoy the street level a cozy bar with water-view seating.

It's the Cat's Meow (506-529-4717), 62 Water St., Box 206, St. Andrews, New Brunswick, Canada E5B IA4. Bonnie Nelson and her family offer four spacious rooms, decorated in style; private baths. There is always a rug-hooking project going—it's Bonnie's hobby. The cats live in the Nelsons' quarters but are brought out for visits upon request. $100–125 (Canadian; no tax) in high season includes a full breakfast served family-style in the dining room.

Inn on Frederick (506-529-2603 or 1-877-895-4400; www.innonfrederick .ca), 58 Frederick St., St. Andrews, New Brunswick, Canada E5B 1B7. Open year-round. This is one of the town's historic houses, dating to the early 1800s but since expanded with eight pleasant guest rooms and suites; private baths. $150–250 (Canadian) in high season, otherwise $150–112. Also see *Dining Out*.

OTHER 🐾 🐚 **St. Andrews Motor Inn** (506-529-4571), 111 Water St., St. Andrews, New Brunswick, Canada E5B 1A3. A three-story motel with 38 units and a heated indoor swimming pool. All rooms have two queen-sized beds and color TV, some have kitchenette, and all have private balcony overlooking Passamaquoddy Bay. $159–229 (Canadian) plus tax in high season includes coffee.

🐾 🐚 **Seaside Beach Resort** (506-529-3846 or 1-800-506-8677; www .seaside.nb.ca), 339 Water St., St. Andrews, New Brunswick, Canada E5B 2R2. Open early spring through autumn. We like the feel and the fabulous location of this complex: 24 one- and two-bedroom housekeeping units (towels changed daily) in a mix of old houses and cabins that's been evolving since the 1940s, fronting—with a big shared deck—on Passamaquoddy Bay. Either Beth Campbell or David Sullivan is in the office to meet, greet, and help. High season $90–110, off-season $75–95; $10 per extra person.

Also see **The Tin Fish** in *Selective Shopping*.

CAMPING **Passamaquoddy Park Campground** (506-529-3439), Indian Point Rd. Maintained by the Kiwanis Club of St. Andrews, this is a beautifully sited campground with full hook-ups as well as tent sites.

Island View Campground (529-3787), Rt. 127, with sites featuring full hook-ups and tent sites, pool, and beach access overlooking historic St. Croix Island.

✳ Where to Eat

All listings are in St. Andrews unless otherwise noted

DINING OUT **Rossmount Inn** (506-529-3351; www.rossmountinn.com), 4599 Rt. 127. East of town, this landmark inn (see *Lodging*) is once more a fabulous place to eat, thanks to Swiss-born and -trained chef-owner Chris Aerni. Reservations a must. The emphasis is on local ingredients—organic when possible—and all pastries are made here. The many-windowed yellow dining room is large and gracious, with crystal chandeliers, stained glass, and contemporary art. There's also a small, ornately comfortable bar. Entrées could include miso-marinated pork tenderloin with rice noodles, organic snow peas, shiitake mushrooms, and scallion tempura, and house-made haddock and shrimp sausage with lemon dill and spices. Somehow we also managed a vanilla bean panna cotta with chocolate sauce and berries. Entrées $15.50–22.50 (Canadian). Fully licensed.

Kingsbrae Arms (506-529-1897; www.kingsbrae.com), 219 King St. Open for dinner by reservation May–Oct. and during the Christmas season. A meal might begin with a petite maritime bouillabaisse and include nasturtium-wrapped turbot and a sugar snap berry basket with chocolate-pistachio mousse. $100 per person plus wine for the table d'hôte dinner.

Windsor House (506-529-4063 or 1-888-890-9463), 132 Water St. Originally built in 1798 as a private home by loyalist sea captain David Mowat and his wife, Mehetible. They raised 12 children here, and the house remained a private residence until the 1880s, when it was remodeled and opened as a Victorian hotel. Dinner choices include char-grilled free-range Alberta tenderloin stuffed with Stilton cheese, roasted baby new potatoes, and grilled asparagus; and quail wrapped in pancetta. Save room for the double chocolate soufflé with brandy crème anglaise. Entrées $24–38 (Canadian).

L'Europe (506-529-3818; www .leurope.ca), 48 King St. Open in-season for dinner daily (except Mon.). Established as a fine restaurant with a German accent in 1983, it continues on both counts under new owners master chef Markus Ritter and his wife, Simone, who moved to St. Andrews from Bavaria. Dine on pan-fried salmon in lemon butter with a vegetable bouquet and mashed potatoes, or on jaeger schnitzel—milk-fed veal scalloppine in a creamy mushroom sauce with vegetables and homemade spaetzle. Entrées $13.80–33.80 (Canadian). Fully licensed. Upstairs, air-conditioned rooms and suites are offered.

Niger Reef Tea House (506-529-8007), 1 Joes Point Rd. Open for dinner in July and Aug. Better known for lunch, brunch, and tea (see *Eating Out*), this delightful little restaurant with (weather permitting) outside dining by Centennial Park is known for superior food. The menu always features the fresh catch of the day—perhaps swordfish with fresh tarragon butter, halibut with mango salsa, or curried scallops with fresh ginger—and possibly satay pork tenderloin and chicken souvlaki with red lentil hummus. Entrées $16.95–25.95.

Inn on Frederick (506-529-2603), 58 Frederick St. Open for breakfast, dinner, and a Sunday buffet brunch. Chef-owner James Crouch worked for 25 years at Canadian Pacific hotels, for 10 at the Algonquin before opening his own inn. This is formal dining with entrées like salmon baked in phyllo pastry with cream cheese and scallops, and milk-fed veal quickly sautéed with artichoke hearts, onions, and mushrooms in a light cream sauce. Entrées $20.95–29.95 (Canadian).

The Passamaquoddy Dining Room at the Algonquin (506-529-8823), 184 Adolphus St. The dining room is huge, and its most pleasant corner is in the Veranda, with windows overlooking formal gardens. The menu is large, featuring local salmon and lobster. Entrées $17–28 (Canadian) plus tax. The hugely popular Sunday buffet is $29 (Canadian).

EATING OUT **The Niger Reef Tea House** (506-529-8007), 1 Joes Point Rd. Open May–Oct. for lunch and Sunday brunch (also see *Dining Out*). Built in 1926 as a summer cottage but serving for many years as a meetinghouse for the Daughters of the Empire (the Canadian version of the DAR), this delightful waterside cottage, with murals picturing Shanghai, was in danger of being destroyed when the St. Andrews Civic Trust stepped in and wisely asked Tim Currie and Lysa Huggins to run it. On a good day, with terrace dining, 50 people at a time can lunch on delicacies such as potato tart or a curried chick-

en sandwich with the soup of the day. Beer and wine are served, along with a great variety of teas, presented in fabulous pots. *Niger*, incidentally, was a ship that ran aground and sank not far offshore.

The Gables (506-529-3440), 143 Water St. Open 11–10. Reasonably priced, good food, and a tiered, shaded deck with a water view. Specialties include fresh fish ranging from fried haddock-and-chips to a seafood platter. We recommend the mussels. Fully licensed; wine by the glass and a wide selection of beers.

✑ **Lobster Bay Eatery** (605-529-4340), 113 Water St. Open daily in-season 11:30–10, Sun. 5–10. Famed for its bargain-priced lobster ($21.95 Canadian for a full dinner, $4.95 for a lobster roll), this waterside restaurant is generally a good bet for everything from grilled cheese and chowders to prime rib.

✑ **Kingsbrae Garden Café** (506-529-3335; www.kingsbraegarden .com), 220 King St. Open May–Oct. Housed in the original manor home on the grounds of this 27-acre formal

DINING AT THE GABLES

Christina Tree

garden, this delightful café is well worth knowing about before you get there, good for ample but ladylike luncheon salads and sandwiches served on a choice of freshly baked croissant, seven-grain roll, or wrap. Wine and beer. Afternoon tea with scones, finger sandwiches, and a deluxe chocolate brownie is served from 2:30.

Sweet Harvest Market (506-529-6249), 182 Water St. Open for breakfast and lunch, 7–5. Try the salmon mousse with dill, lemon, mayo, and cream.

✳ Selective Shopping

All listings are in St. Andrews
Cottage Craft Ltd. (1-800-355-9655; www.cottagecraftwoolens.com), 209 Water St. in Town Square. Open year-round, Mon.–Sat. Dating to 1915, Cottage Craft showcases yarns, tweeds, and finished jackets, sweaters, and skirts; also distinctive throws hand-woven in homes throughout Charlotte County. Upward of 250 knitters produce the sweaters, hats, scarves, and mittens, some wonderfully priced.

Seacoast Gallery (506-529-0005), 174 Water St. Lola Boyles showcases roughly 100 top artists and crafts-people from throughout New Bruns-wick. A landmark gallery not to be missed.

The Tin Fish (506-529-4496; www.tinfish.ca), 24 King St. This is a standout shop featuring Alanna Baird's amazing fish and other designs made from tin cans and scrap copper, also etchings and engravings and reduction lineoleum prints. Inquire about the equally zany, bright one-bedroom upstairs weekly summer rental with water views.

Cricket Cove (506-456-3897; cricket cove.com), 170 Water St. Fine hand knits and designer yards from throughout the world, including qivi-ut, alpaca, angora, cashmere, hand-spun, and hand-painted yarns.

The Crocker Hill Store (506-529-4303; www.crockerhill.com), 45 King St. A restored 1837 brick building houses this intriguing store devoted to gardening, birding, and art.

Mariner's Compass Quilt Shop (506-529-8351), 144 Water St. Open May–Dec. (except Sun.). A trove of things quilted: bed quilts, wall hang-ings, place mats, pillows, traditional and contemporary designs.

China Chest Ltd., 234 Water St. This store has been offering china and crystal since 1928. Also featuring can-dles, handcrafts, miniature tea sets, pewter miniatures, thimbles, and more.

Serendipin' Art (506-529-3327), 168 Water St. A large selection of hand-made New Brunswick crafts, includ-ing jewelry, handblown glass objects, pottery, hand-painted silks, and more.

Garden by the Sea (506-529-8905 or 1-888-788-SOAP; www.gardenbythe seasoap.com), 217 Water St. Rich, creamy aromatherapy soaps. Forty dif-ferent kinds are made by the owners, including impossible-to-resist "Saga-cious Sage" and "Spicy Spirit." Great soap dishes, great holiday presents.

✳ Special Events

December: **Winter Festival**—a full range of Christmas activities from a twinkling evening candlelight parade to the "garden of lights" dine-around experience (506-529-3555 or stach amb@nbnet.nb.ca, for a schedule of events and packages).

GRAND MANAN

Little more than 15 miles long and less than 7 miles wide, Grand Manan is Canada's southernmost island, far enough at sea to be very much its own place, a rugged outpost at the mouth of the Bay of Fundy.

Right whales are what draw many visitors. These are the largest, liveliest, and rarest of whales. Just 320 are known to exist worldwide, and they all seem to be here in summer months, feeding on krill and other nutrients in the tide-churned waters. Birds are another draw: 240 species frequent the island. Machias Seal Island, the prime viewing place for puffins, is as easily accessible from Grand Manan as from Maine. A 40-mile network of hiking trails is another plus, many miles hugging cliffs that vary from 100 to almost 400 feet.

Fishing boats line the wharves the way they used to in New England. While fish are fewer than they once were here, too, fishing is more profitable than ever. Connors Brothers sardine factory at Seal Cove was the island's largest employer until it closed in the spring of 2005, but salmon farming remains big, along with lobster and clams, periwinkles, and that Grand Manan delicacy: dulse. The hundreds of herring smokehouses for which the island was once known are, however, either gone or standing unused, with one preserved as an unusual museum.

Grand Manan's population has hovered around 2,700 since the late 19th century, clustered in the sheltered harbors and coves along its gentle Bay of Fundy shore, which is protected by many small islands. In contrast, the northern and southern "heads" of the island are soaring cliffs, as is almost the entire western shore. It's a mirror image of Maine's Bold Coast, with only well named Dark Harbour accessible by car. Trails and boats can make their way to Indian Beach, Money Cove, Bradfords Cove, and Little Dark Harbour.

In many ways Grand Manan remains as out-of-the-way and unspoiled as it was during the 20 summers (1922–42) that Willa Cather spent here, working on some of her most famous novels, including *Death Comes for the Archbishop*. Her cottage on Whale Cove is one among the island's many summer rentals.

GUIDANCE **Grand Manan Tourism Association**, 130 Rt. 776, Grand Manan, New Brunswick, Canada E5G 4K9. The seasonal **Visitor Information Center** (506-662-3442 or 1-888-525-1655; www.grandmanannb.com) is housed in the Business Center, the former North Head School (restrooms). Open mid-June–Sep. 1, daily 9–8; off-season, weekdays 1–4. The association publishes the inexpensive booklets *Grand Manan Trails* and *Grand Manan Guide*. The web site is by far the island's best source of information.

GETTING THERE *By car:* From Calais it's 19 miles to St. Andrews and 35 miles to Blacks Harbour.

By ferry: **Coastal Transport** (506-662-3724; www.coastaltransport.ca) operates ferries on the 20-mile, 90-minute sail between Blacks Harbour on the mainland (35 miles from the Calais–St. Stephen border) and North Head on the island. During high season (June 29–Labor Day), ferries run seven times a day, every 2 hours during summer months beginning at 7:30 AM. Service from the mainland is first come, first served. Things we wish we'd known: (1) The ferry terminal is a couple of miles beyond the village of Blacks Harbour, so you may want to stock up on food and drink before you get in line. (2) Call to check which ferry runs when. Avoid the M/V *Grand Manan*, the smaller seasonal ferry, which takes just around 20 cars or, as on our run, 15 cars (we were car 16) and a few big trucks; the M/S *Grand Manan V* is capable of swallowing many more vehicles. For the return trip limited reservations are available a day in advance. Food is available on both ferries. Pedestrians and bicyclists have no problem getting on. Parking is ample and free in Blacks Harbour, and whale-watching, sea kayaking tours, and rental bikes are also within walking distance of the ferry terminal on Grand Manan.

✳ To See

✎ ♿ **The Grand Manan Museum** (506-662-3524; www.grandmananmuseum .ca), 1141 Rt. 776, Grand Harbor, across from the school. Open May–Sep., Mon.–Sat. 9–5:30. The Allan Moses Bird Collection, an exhibit of more than 300 mounted birds, documents the island's bird life, and the history of the island's smoked herring industry is dramatized in paintings, photographs, and memorabilia. Novelist Willa Cather's typewriter and manuscript table are also here. Inquire about evening slide shows and rainy-day programs.

Dark Harbour. The only road across the width of the island ends abruptly at the harbor (it's a tight turnaround at high tide), the one nick in what is otherwise a wall of cliffs that run the length of the western shore. This is a prime dulse-harvesting spot, but there are no commercial enterprises, just seasonal cottages that are inaccessible except by boat.

SARDINE MUSEUM

Christina Tree

Southwest Head. Your first instinct is to drive the length of the island on the one north–south road, grandiosely numbered 776. It ends at Southwest Head Lighthouse, and a path leads along spectacular cliffs.

Hole in the Wall. The view of this much-photographed natural arch near the northern end of the island is most easily accessed via a fairly steep path, from a parking area that lies within Hole-in-the-Wall Park, a former airport that's now a commercial campground. Great viewing spots for whale-watching.

Sardine Museum and Herring Hall of Fame (506-662-9913), Seal Cove, Grand Manan. Open seasonally, most days. The island's herring smokehouses once numbered 300. Herring were hung on racks above smoldering fires until they turned the color of burnished gold, and lines of women gutted and deboned fish with the speed and skill of surgeons. This was the last smokehouse to close. A token rack of fish still hangs in one window, and the tables are there, thanks to New York architect Michael Zimmer and director Tony Nunziata. One building is now Zimmer's summer home, and the others house art installations, historic memorabilia, or both. An aluminum boat in the shape of a sardine can (the top is rolled back, complete with giant key) is moored to the wharf.

✴ To Do

HIKING Some 45 miles of marked hiking trails cover a variety of terrain along the shore. Pick up a copy of *Heritage Trails and Footpaths* (available in most island stores) and a picnic and you're set.

KAYAKING AND BIKE RENTALS **Adventure High** (506-662-3563 or 1-800-732-5492; www.adventurehigh.com), 83 Rt. 776. Guided tours range from a 2-hour moonlight trip to 6-hour explorations and include Seal Watch Tours and a Kayak Tour & Dinner on the Beach. Mountain and hybrid bikes are also rented. Inquire about the solar-heated rental cottage on a remote cove.

WHALE-WATCHING **Whales-n-Sails Adventures** (506-662-1999 or 1-888-994-4044; www.whales-n-sails.com), North Head, Fisherman's Wharf, offers two daily trips, weather permitting, June–mid-Sep. Sailing and whale-watching are a great combination. The 56-foot, 47-passenger ketch *Elsie Menota* supplements sail with power to reach the deeps in the Bay of Fundy (12 miles northeast of Grand Manan), where Atlantic right whales feed and play, but then it's quiet and pleasant to tack and jibe among these huge creatures. Owner Allan McDonald points out bird and sea life en route.

Sea Watch Tours (see *Birding*) also offers whale-watch cruises, and is the only boat that goes to Machias Seal Island, the home of the puffins.

✴ Lodging

Note: The choice of lodgings and cottages is large, and most are listed on www.grandmanannb.com. The following represent the best of the inns and B&Bs we checked.

✎ **The Inn at Whale Cove Cottages** (506-662-3181; www.holiday junction.com), 26 Whale Cove Cottage Rd., Grand Manan, New Brunswick, Canada 35G 2B5. The gray-shingled Main House dates from 1816, overlooking a quiet cove with a large fish weir, backed by rugged Fish Head. It was here in picturesque Orchardside cottage that Willa Cather

first came to write in 1922, eventually building a replica of it a way down the shore (also available for rent). The inn and cottages are owned and operated by Laura Buckley and her mother, Kathleen, who remembers waiting on Cather in the dining room three times a day. The Main House parlor has changed little since it began welcoming "rusticators" in 1910. The fireplace is large and usually glowing, and the walls are lined with books. Two-bedroom Cove View, with two decks and a full living room and library, is $800 per week. Coopershop features a huge fireplace and two upstairs bedrooms as well as a living room and kitchen/dining area ($700 per week). There are also the one-bedroom Bungalow ($105 per night) and three delightful rooms in the Main House ($105 per night). Rates are in Canadian dollars and include a very full breakfast. Dinner is also served (see *Dining Out*).

Compass Rose (506-662-8570; off-season, 613-692-1781; www.compass roseinn.com), 65 Rt. 776, North Head, Grand Manan, New Brunswick, Canada E5G 1A2. Open June–Oct. Within walking distance of the ferry terminal, water excursions, and bike rentals, this is a gem of an inn, overlooking the busy harbor of North Head. Owner Nora Parker has recently renovated the entire inn. Each of the seven guest rooms is furnished in antiques and has a private bathroom and harbor view, but they're also right on the road. The dining room, which is open to the public, is a must-stop for every visitor (see *Dining Out*). $89–129 (Canadian) per couple includes a full breakfast.

BIRDING AND NATURE

The island is visited annually by 240 species of birds and many, many more bird-watchers. Bird species are listed on the island web site (www.grand manannb.com). **Castalia Marsh**, accessible via a nature trail in Castalia Provincial Park, is a favorite spot at dawn and dusk. One of the first visitors was John James Audubon, who came in 1831 to check out the unlikely-but-true story that island seagulls nest in trees.

Sea Watch Tours (506-662-8332; www.seawatchtours.com) offers mid-June–early Aug. trips from Seal Cove Grand Manan to Machias Seal Island to see puffins, arctic terns, and razor-billed auks. Captain Peter Wilcox is a native of Grand Manan whose ancestors came here from New England during the Revolution. In 1969 his father began offering trips to Machias Seal, which is 10 miles south of the southern tip of in Grand Manan. We came aboard early one foggy July morning, ill prepared for the weather (most fellow passengers wore windbreakers and wind pants as well as hats and mittens). We clambered onto the island over seaweed-covered rocks and carefully walked a boardwalk, holding sticks above our heads to ward off the arctic terns defending their fledgling chicks. Our group divided into several bird blinds from which we could watch the puffins, which seem much larger than their 9- to 11-inch size and come within inches of the blinds, making an amazing racket resembling a chain saw. The numbers of visitors to the island are strictly controlled; this is the only Canadian-based operator. (For the two Maine-based excursions, see the "Atlantic Coast" section of "Washington County"). Machias Seal Island itself is a mile long and 300 feet wide, the largest nesting area for puffins accessible from New England and New Brunswick.

The Shorecrest Lodge (506-662-3216; www.shorecrestlodge.com), 100 Rt. 776, Grand Manan, New Brunswick, Canada E5G 1A1. Open May–Oct. Gunther Bogensperger and Evelyn Paine are steadily renovating this rambling old country inn on the edge of North Head Village. All rooms are nicely, unfussily comfortable and have a variety of bed arrangements and private baths. The food is good. We recommend Room 8. $75–119 (Canadian).

Marathon Inn (506-662-8488; www.angelfire.com/biz2/marathon), North Head, Grand Manan, New Brunswick, Canada E0G 2M0. Open year-round. This is a big white ark of a place on a hill overlooking the water in North Head. The rooms we saw (there are 24) were clean and cheerful, with tasteful prints and colorful quilts. We've been warned to avoid the annex. The large, sunny dining room, serving all three meals, is popular with birding groups and Elderhostel. $89–109 in-season, $49–89 off season.

McLaughlin's Wharf Inn (506-662-8760), 1863 Rt. 776, Grand Manan, New Brunswick, Canada E5G 3H1. Open July–Aug. Brenda McLaughlin converted the store in Seal Cove that had been in her family for generatons to a combination B&B and restaurant: six upstairs rooms with two shared baths, water views, TV lounge. $79 single to $89 double includes full breakfast. Dinner served.

Manan Island Inn (506-662-8624), 22 Rt. 776, Grand Manan, New Brunswick, Canada E5G 1A1. Open year-round. Conveniently sited in North Head across from the ferry terminal, an 1894 house with nine guest rooms, all with metal or wooden beds and private bath or shower. Guest refrigerator. $79–100 (Canadian) with continental breakfast (at this writing the inn is for sale).

Grand Manan Sea-Land Adventures (506-662-8997; www.sea-land adventures.com), 11 Bancroft Point Rd. Mid-June–Oct. Five unique, hand-built cottages lie in the woods here, overlooking a salt marsh. $65–130. Whale-watcher Captain James Bates can fill you in on the sea.

CAMPGROUNDS **The Anchorage** (506-662-7035 or 1-800-561-0123), 136 Anchorage Rd., Grand Manan, New Brunswick, Canada E5G-2H4. The 100 sites vary from wooded to waterside; 24 accommodate trailers.

Hole-in-the-Wall (506-662-3152 or 1-866-662-4489; www.grandmanan camping.com), 42 Old Airport Rd, Grand Manan, New Brunswick, Canada E5G 1A9. With 48 sites, there is a wide range in this sprawling property, from RV to wooded—some fairly spectacular.

Forest Edge Camping (506-662-3673; www.forestedgecamping.com). Thirty camper sites, 10 tent sites.

✳ Where to Eat

DINING OUT **The Inn at Whale Cove** (506-662-3181), 25 Whale Cove Cottage Rd., near North Head. Open nightly in-season, 6–8:30. Reservations required. The dining room in the early-19th-century cottage seats just 30 people. It's candlelit and decorated with vintage willowware. Chef-owner Laura Buckley uses local ingredients imaginatively. Saturday night features a five-course set meal. Fully licensed. Entrées $20–25 (Canadian).

Compass Rose (506-662-8570), North Head. Open June–Oct. for dinner (except Mon.). The harbor view is unbeatable, and even without it the dining room would strike you as unusually pleasant. Dinner might be seafood lasagna or pan-fried haddock; leave room for double chocolate cheesecake. Entrées $22.50–27 (Canadian).

ℰ **McLaughlin's Wharf Inn** (506-662-8760), 1863 Rt. 776, Seal Cove. Open July–Aug. for dinner. Begin with fresh mussels steamed in garlic butter or smoked salmon with lemon butter and homemade dill bread, then dine on sea scallops baked in garlic butter, served with vegetables, salad, and a fresh roll or lobster with tarragon cream on farfalle pasta. $11.95–19.95 (Canadian).

The Shorecrest Lodge (506-662-3216; www.shorecrestlodge.com), 100 Rt. 776. Open for dinner. Chef-owner Gunther Bogensperger is establishing a reputation for this attractive, old-fashioned hotel dining room. We feasted on scallops and salmon. Entrées $21–24 (Canadian).

EATING OUT *ℰ* **Gallaways Restaurant** (506-662-8871), Rt. 776, North Head. A sports bar with plenty of room to get away from the bar, the obvious place for a burger and beer, also salads, fried seafood, a kids' menu.

North Head Bakery (506-662-8862), Rt. 776 south of the village. Open 6–6. Seasonal. Using organic flours, no bleach, this is a both a first and last stop for patrons: first stop in the morning for croissants and doughnuts (coffee is served); last stop when leaving the island, taking baguettes and breads home with them.

The Lobster Deck, North Head at Fishermen's Wharf. Great fish chowder.

✳ Selective Shopping

Roland's Sea Vegetables (506-662-3866), 174 Hill Rd. (marked from the Dark Harbour Rd.), is a must-stop. Dulse and other seaweeds are hand harvested at Dark Harbour, then dried and packaged. We wish we had bought more bottles of dulse flakes.

Island Artisans (506-662-3625), North Head. Open seasonally. A mix of quality crafted items and art. Inquire about summer art workshops.

Grand Manan Historical Society Art Gallery, 21 Cedar St., Castalia.

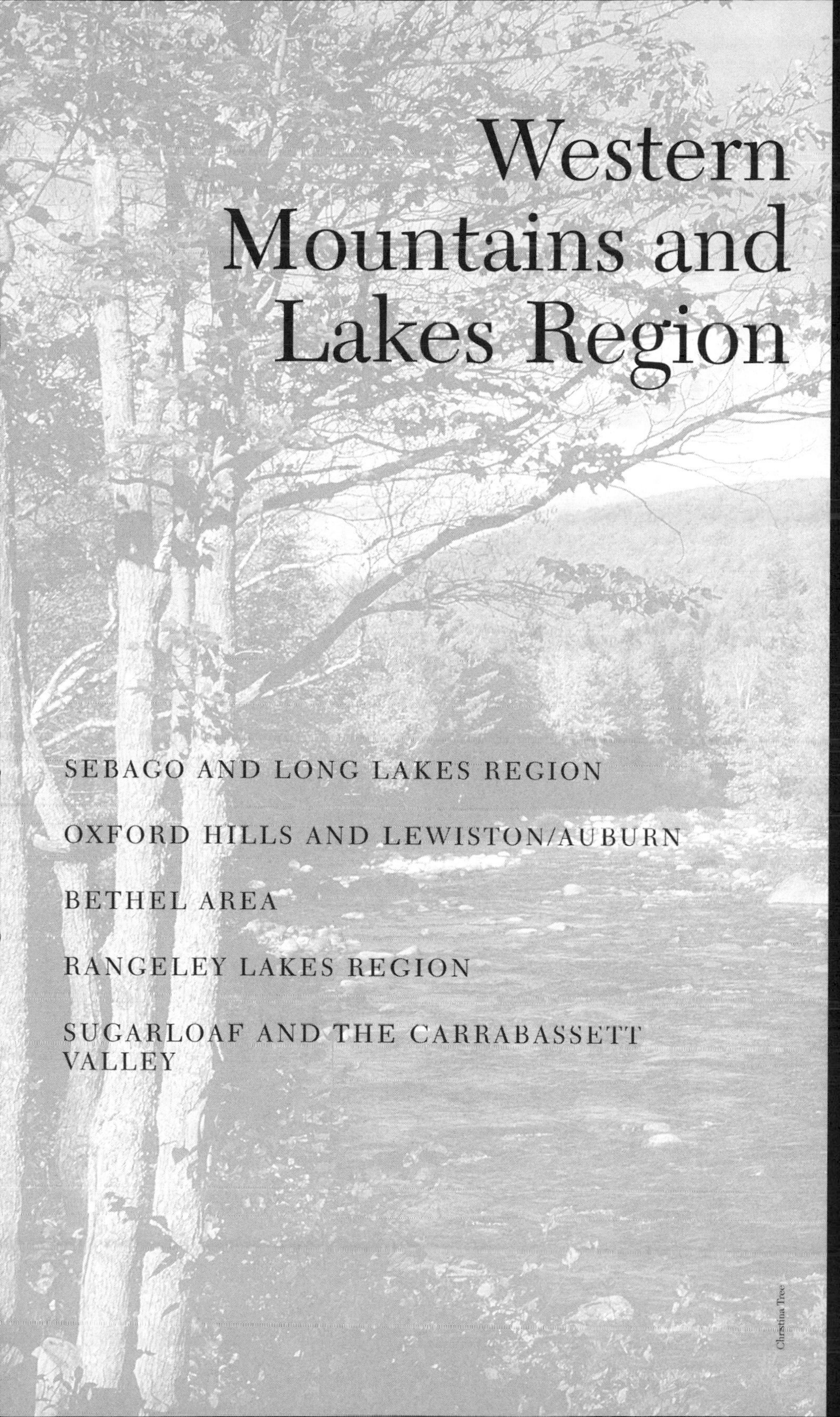

Christina Tree

5 Western Mountains and Lakes Region

SEBAGO AND LONG LAKES REGION

OXFORD HILLS AND LEWISTON/AUBURN

BETHEL AREA

RANGELEY LAKES REGION

SUGARLOAF AND THE CARRABASSETT VALLEY

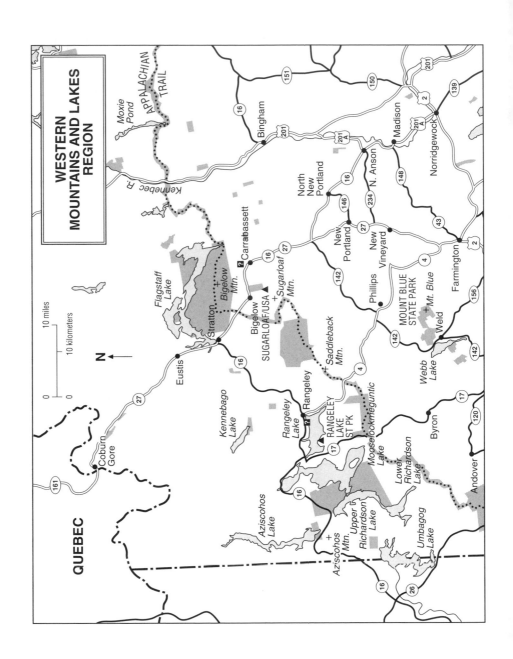

WESTERN
MOUNTAINS AND LAKES
REGION

QUEBEC

APPALACHIAN
TRAIL

Moxie
Pond

Kennebec R.

Bingham

151

150

201

Madison

Norridgewock

139

2

201
A

201

North
New
Portland

16

N. Anson

148

234

43

Carrabassett

New
Portland

27

New
Vineyard

2

Farmington

16

27

146

Flagstaff
Lake

Bigelow
Mtn.

Sugarloaf
Mtn.

142

4

156

Stratton

Bigelow
SUGARLOAF/USA

Phillips

MOUNT BLUE
STATE PARK

Mt. Blue

Eustis

16

Saddleback
Mtn.

142

Weld

142

N

10 miles

10 kilometers

27

Rangeley

4

Webb
Lake

Kennebago
Lake

Rangeley
Lake

RANGELEY
LAKE
ST PK

17

Mooselookmeguntic
Lake

Byron

17

Coburn
Gore

161

16

Lower
Richardson
Lake

120

Andover

Aziscohos
Lake

Aziscohos
Mtn.

Upper
Richardson
Lake

Umbagog
Lake

16

26

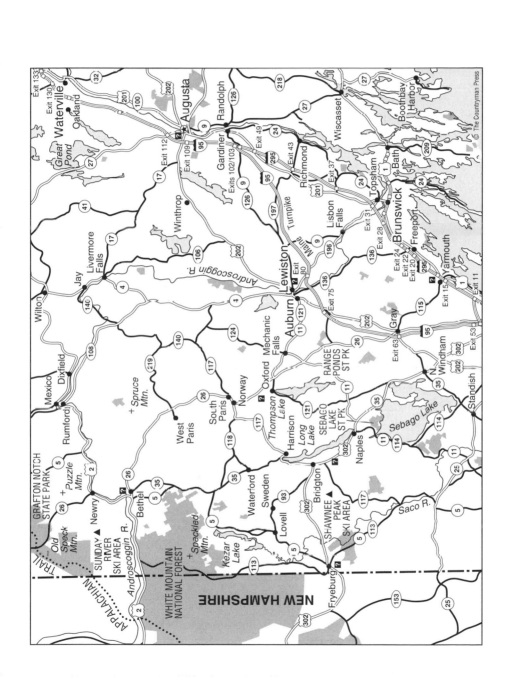

WESTERN MOUNTAINS AND LAKES REGION

Inland Maine is the most underrated, least explored piece of New England, frequently perceived as an uninterrupted flat carpet of firs.

Larger than Vermont and New Hampshire combined, it is actually composed of several distinct and unique regions and distinguished by a series of almost continuous mountain ranges, more extensive than New Hampshire's White Mountains and higher than Vermont's Green Mountains, but lacking a name (why aren't they the Blue Mountains?).

In contrast with the coast, inland Maine was actually more of a resort area a century ago than it is today. By the 1880s trains connected Philadelphia, New York, and Boston with large resort hotels in Rangeley and Greenville, and steamboats ferried "sports" to "sporting camps" in the far corners of lakes. Many of these historic resorts survive but today require far more time to reach, unless you fly in.

Today inland Maine seems even larger than it is because almost a third of it lies beyond the public highway system, a phenomenon for which we can blame Massachusetts and its insistence that Maine sell off the "unorganized townships" (and divide the profits) before it would be permitted to secede in 1820. In the interim most of this land has been owned and managed by lumber and paper companies. Debate currently rages about the future of these woodlands (somewhere between a third and almost half of inland Maine); many environmental organizations would like to see a Maine North Woods National Park, but locals remain adamantly against such an initiative. The reality of the way public roads run—and don't run—continues to physically divide Maine's mountainous interior into several distinct pieces.

One of these pieces is the Western Mountains and Lakes Region, extending from the rural farmland surrounding the lakes of southwestern Maine, up through the Oxford Hills and into the foothills of the White Mountains and the Mahoosuc Range around Bethel, then on into the wilderness (as high and remote as any to be found in the North Woods) around the Rangeley Lakes and the Sugarloaf area—east of which public roads cease, forcing traffic bound for the Moosehead Lake region to detour south into the farmland of the Lower Kennebec Valley.

The five distinct areas within the Western Mountains and Lakes Region are connected by some of Maine's most scenic roads, with farmhouses, lakes, mountains, and unexpected villages around each bend. Many of these views are not generally appreciated because the area is best known to skiers, accustomed to racing up to Sunday River and Sugarloaf (Maine's most popular ski resorts) by the shortest routes from the interstate. They don't know what they're missing. The roads around Rangeley offer views so spectacular, stretches of two of them (Rts. 4 and 17) are included in a newly designated National Scenic Byway.

In summer and fall we suggest following Rt. 113 through Evans Notch or heading north from Bridgton to Bethel by the series of roads that threads woods and skirts lakes, heading east along Rt. 2, continuing north to Rangeley via Rt. 17 through Coos Canyon and over the spectacular Height o' Land from which you can see all five Rangeley Lakes and the surrounding mountains. From Rangeley it's just another 19 scenic miles on Rt. 16 (better known as Moose Alley) to the Sugarloaf area. You can return to Rt. 2 by continuing along Rt. 16 to Kingfield, then taking Rt. 142 through Phillips and Weld.

SEBAGO AND LONG LAKES REGION

Fifty lakes can be seen from the summit of Pleasant Mountain, 10 within the town of Bridgton itself. These lakes are what draw summer visitors. They swim and fish, fish and swim. They cruise out in powerboats or paddle canoes and kayaks. On rainy days they browse through the area's abundant antiques and crafts stores. In winter visitors ski, downhill at Shawnee Peak (alias Pleasant Mountain) or cross-country almost anywhere.

Before the Civil War visitors could actually come by boat all the way to Bridgton from Boston. From Portland, they would ride 20 miles through 28 locks on the Cumberland & Oxford Canal, then across Sebago Lake, up the Songo River, Brandy Pond, and Long Lake to Bridgton. The first hotel atop Pleasant Mountain opened in 1850, and in 1882 the "2-footer" narrow gauge opened between Hiram and Bridgton, enabling summer visitors to come by train as well.

Today, as in the 1880s, most visitors waste little time getting onto or into water. The Naples Causeway is the base for water sports, and the departure point for cruises on Long Lake and through the only surviving canal lock. Sebago, Maine's second largest lake, is its most popular waterskiing area.

This southwestern corner of the state offers plenty on land, too: hiking, golf, tennis, mineral collecting, and such fascinating historic sights as Willowbrook in Newfield.

Fryeburg, just west of the lakes in the Saco River Valley, is the region's oldest community and the site of the state's largest agricultural fair. It is also headquarters for canoeing the Saco River. Sandy bottomed and clear, the Saco meanders for more than 40 miles through woods and fields, rarely passing a house. Too shallow for powerboats, it is perfect for canoes and kayaks. There is usually just enough current to nudge along the limpest paddler, and the ubiquitous sandbars serve as gentle bumpers. Tenting is permitted most places along the river, and there are public campgrounds. Outfitters rent canoes and provide shuttle service.

In summer most families come for a week to stay in lakeside cottages—of which there seem to be thousands. Motels, inns, and B&Bs still fill on weekends with parents visiting their children at camps—of which there seem to be hundreds. As more travelers discover the beauty and tranquility of the region, the

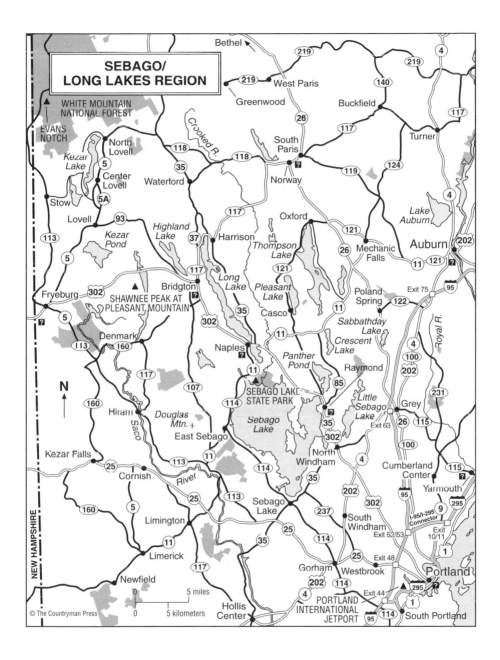

number of these types of lodgings, while nowhere near the glut of such establishments along the coast, is expanding every year.

GUIDANCE **Greater Bridgton Lakes Region Chamber of Commerce**
(207-647-3472; www.mainelakeschamber.com), 101 Portland Rd. (Rt. 302), Box 236, Bridgton 04009. The chamber maintains a walk-in information center

on Portland Rd. (Rt. 302). Request a copy of the *Greater Bridgton–Lakes Region Area Guide*. Year-round information is also available from the **Bridgton town office** (207-647-8786).

Sebago Lakes Region Chamber of Commerce (207-892-8265; www.sebago lakeschamber.com), P.O. Box 1015, Windham 04062, maintains a seasonal information booth at 911 Roosevelt Trail on Rt. 302 and a seasonal information bureau next to the Naples Historical Society Museum on Rt. 302. It also publishes a area tourism and information guide that covers the towns of Casco, Gray, Naples, Raymond, Standish, and Windham.

Cornish Association of Businesses (207-625-8083; www.cornish-maine.org), P.O. Box 573, Cornish 04020. Their web site is one of the best and most comprehensive in Maine, with maps, information about lodging and dining, shopping and events, and a brief history of the town.

Fryeburg Information Center (207-935-3639), Rt. 302, Fryeburg 04037. The Maine Tourism Association staffs this state-owned log cabin on the New Hampshire line. Pamphlets on the state in general, western Maine in particular.

GETTING THERE *By air:* The **Portland International Jetport**, served by several carriers, is 30- to 60-minute drive from most points in this area. Rental cars are available at the airport. (See "Portland.")

By bus and train: **Concord Trailways** (207-828-1151 or 1-800-639-3317) bus lines and **Amtrak's Downeaster** (1-800-USA-RAIL) serve the Portland area from the clean new rail–bus station on outer Congress St. in Portland.

By car: From New York and Boston, take I-95 to the Westbrook exit (exit 48), then Rt. 302, the high road of the lakes region. For Newfield and south of Sebago area, take Rt. 25 from I-95 at Westbrook (exit 48).

BIRCHES NEAR SUGARLOAF

Kim Grant

WHEN TO COME With some inns and B&Bs open year-round and good cross-country skiing available, this can be a place for a winter retreat. Ice fishing is another winter pastime some people love. Still, the big time here is summer.

✳ Villages

Bridgton has a plethora of antiques shops, including two country auction houses, making it a good way stop for browsers. Take time for a detour to the pretty campus of Bridgton Academy, a few miles from the center of town. Bridgton Hospital is Maine's first new major medical facility in 20 years.

Cornish. In recent years this pretty little town has been making efforts to attract more visitors. The colonial and Victorian homes lining Main and Maple Streets were moved here by teams of about 80 oxen in the 1850s after the arrival of a new stagecoach route. It's halfway between Portland and the Mount Washington Valley in New Hampshire. Pick up a copy of the local pamphlet, which includes a detailed map and business listings, at several area businesses.

Fryeburg is an interesting town that sees its share of traffic as travelers pass through en route to North Conway, New Hampshire, and the White Mountains. The traffic clog during the Fryeburg Fair (Maine's largest, most popular agricultural fair) can back up for more than an hour. The village itself is small and unassuming, with a smattering of historic homes (some now inns) and businesses. As noted in the chapter introduction, canoe trips down the Saco originate here as well.

✳ To See

MUSEUMS Willowbrook at Newfield (207-793-2784; www.willowbrook museum.org), off Rt. 11, Newfield. Open May 15–Sep. 30, daily 10–5. Admission charged. Although it's off the beaten track, the drive through the quiet countryside is well worth it. Devastated by fire in 1947, the village was almost a ghost town when Donald King began buying buildings in the 1960s. The complex now includes 37 buildings displaying more than 11,000 items: horse-drawn vehicles, tools, toys, a vintage-1894 carousel, and many other artifacts of late-19th-century life. Linger in the ballroom, ring the schoolhouse bell, or picnic in the area provided. A restaurant and ice cream parlor for light lunches, an old-time country store, and a Christmas gift shop open most of the year are located here as well.

Rufus Porter Museum (207-647-2828; www.rufusportermuseum.org), P.O. 544, 67 N. High St. (Rt. 302), Bridgton 04009. Open Memorial Day weekend to mid-Oct., Thu.–Sun. 1–4. Dedicated to Rufus Porter, a multi-talented man, this house contains his 1828 original murals, an icon of folk art. Porter founded the *Scientific American* magazine, and invented the Colt revolver; patented a churn, corn sheller, fire alarm, and cheese press among many other inventions; as well as painting murals in homes all over New England. Admission $5 adults, $4 students, 6 and under free.

HISTORIC BUILDINGS AND MUSEUMS Daniel Marrett House (207-642-3032), Rt. 25, Standish. Tours on the first Saturday of the month beginning at 11, June–Oct. Admission $5. Money from Portland banks was stored in this Georgian mansion for safekeeping during the War of 1812. Built in 1789, it remained in the Marrett family until 1944; architecture and furnishings reflect the changing styles over 150 years, and the formal perennial gardens bloom throughout summer, always open for a visit.

Parson Smith House, 89 River Rd., South Windham. Open mid-June–Labor Day, Tue., Thu., and Sun. noon–5; admission. A Georgian farmhouse with an exceptional stairway and hall; some original furnishings.

Narramissic, Ingalls Rd. (2 miles south of the junction of Rts. 107 and 117), Bridgton. Open July and Aug., most days; call for information. Admission fee. A Federal-period home and a Temperance Barn in a rural setting, this interesting site includes a working blacksmith shop and is the scene of frequent special events; check with the **Bridgton Historical Society Museum** (207-647-3699), Gibbs Ave., which also maintains a 1902 former fire station. The collection (open July and Aug., call for hours) includes slide images of the old narrow-gauge railroad.

Naples Historical Society Museum (207-693-4297), village green, Rt. 302, Naples. Open July and Aug., Fri. 10–2. The brick complex includes a rooftop brake coach, a diorama and great memorabilia on the Cumberland & Oxford Canal, photos of and information on the Sebago and Long Lake steamboats and the Songo Locks, and artifacts from vanished hotels, such as the Bay of Naples Hotel.

Hopalong Cassidy in the Fryeburg Public Library (207-935-2731), 98 Main St., Fryeburg. Open year-round, varying days. The library is housed in an 1832 stone schoolhouse and is decorated with many paintings by local artists. It also contains a collection of books, guns, and other memorabilia belonging to Clarence Mulford, creator of Hopalong Cassidy. The **Fryeburg Historical Society Museum** (207-935-4192), 511 Main St., is open Tue.–Thu. 10–2.

Harrison Historical Society and Museum (207-583-6225), 121 Haskell Hill Rd., Harrison. Open July and Aug., Wed. 1–4 and by appointment (call 207-583-2213); Apr.–Dec., open the first Wed. of the month (programs in the evening). The public is welcome at this small museum full of artifacts, cemetery records, town histories, and news clipping scrapbooks. The town's bicentennial was March 8, 2005; as we went to press, the society had plans to publish a book about Harrison's history.

OTHER HISTORIC SITES Songo Locks, Naples (2.5 miles off Rt. 302). Open May–Oct. Dating to 1830, the last of the 27 hand-operated locks that once allowed people to come by boat from Portland to Harrison still enable you to travel some 40 watery miles. Boat traffic is constant in summer.

✳ To Do

BOAT EXCURSIONS 𝒮 ♿ *Songo River Queen II* (207-693-6861), Naples Causeway. Operates daily July–Labor Day; reduced schedule in spring and fall. The *Queen* is a replica of a Mississippi River stern paddle wheeler, with accommodations for 300 passengers, a snack and cocktail bar, and restrooms. Take a 2½-hour Songo River ride across Brandy Pond and through the only surviving lock from the 1830 canal; the Songo River winds its way to the mouth of Sebago Lake, just 1.5 miles as the crow flies, but 6 miles as the Songo twists and turns. Also, 1-hour Long Lake cruises and moonlight charters available.

BOAT RENTALS Available regionwide. Inquire at local chambers. (Also see *Canoeing and Kayaking*.)

CANOEING AND KAYAKING Saco River Canoe and Kayak (207-935-2369 or 1-888-772-6573; www.sacorivercanoe.com), 1009 Main St. (Rt. 5), Fryeburg (across from the access at Swan's Falls). Fred Westerberg, a Registered Maine Guide, runs Saco River Canoe and Kayak with the help of his wife, Prudy, and daughters, Beth and Chris. They offer shuttle service and canoe and kayak rentals, which come with a map and careful instructions geared to the day's river conditions.

Saco Bound (603-447-2177), Rt. 302, Center Conway, New Hampshire (just over the state line, west of Fryeburg). The largest canoe outfitter around. Offers rentals, guided day trips and whitewater canoeing on the Androscoggin River in summer, a campground at Canal Bridge in Fryeburg, and a shuttle service. Its base is a big glass-faced store stocked with kayaks and canoes, trail food, and lip balm. Staff members are young and enthusiastic.

Sportshaus (207-647-3000), 103 Main St., Bridgton, rents canoes and kayaks by the day or week.

Canal Bridge Canoes (1-800-479-1929; www.canalbridgecanoes.com), 35 Bridgton Rd. (Rt. 302), Fryeburg Village. Pat and Carl Anderson offer canoe, kayak, and inner-tube rentals and a free shuttle service.

Woodland Acres (207-935-2529), Rt. 160, Brownfield. Full-facility camping, canoe rentals, and a shuttle service.

THE *SONGO RIVER QUEEN II*

Kim Grant

River Run (207-452-2500; www.riverruncanoe.com), P.O. Box 190, Brownfield. Canoe rentals, a shuttle, and parking Memorial Day–Labor Day weekends. They also have camping—see *Lodging*.

FISHING Fishing licenses are available at town offices and online at www.mefish wildlife.com; check marinas for information. Salmon, lake trout, pickerel, and bass abound.

GOLF AND TENNIS **Bridgton Highlands Country Club** (207-647-3491; www .bridgtonhighlands.com), Highland Rd., Bridgton, has an 18-hole course, snack bar, carts, a resident golf pro, and tennis courts. Also 18-hole **Lake Kezar Country Club** (207-925-2462), Rt. 5, Lovell; and 18-hole **Naples Golf and Country Club** (207-693-6424; www.naplesgolfcourse.com), Rt. 114, Naples.

HIKING **Douglas Mountain**, Sebago. A Nature Conservancy preserve with great views of Sebago and the White Mountains. The trail to the top is a 20-minute walk, and there's a 0.75-mile nature trail at the summit; also a stone tower with an observation platform. Take Rt. 107 south from the town of Sebago and turn right on Douglas Mountain Rd.; go to the end of the road to find limited parking.

Pleasant Mountain, Bridgton. Several summits and interconnecting trails, the most popular of which is the Firewarden's Trail to the main summit: a relatively easy 2.5-mile climb from base to peak through rocky woods.

✍ **Jockey Cap**, Rt. 302, Fryeburg. Watch for the Jockey Cap Motel beside a general store. The arch between them is the entrance to one of New England's shortest hikes to one of its biggest rewards. A 10-minute climb up the path (steep near the top) accesses a bald, garnet-studded summit with a sweeping view of the White Mountains to the west, lesser peaks and lakes to the east and south, all ingeniously identified on a circular bronze monument designed by Arctic explorer Admiral Peary.

HORSEBACK RIDING **Secret Acres Stables** (207-693-3441; www.secretacres stables.com), 185 Lambs Mill Rd. (1 mile off Rt. 302), Naples, offers trail rides and lessons.

✍ **Carousel Horse Farm** (207-627-4471; www.maine-horse-vacation.com), 69 Leach Hill Rd., Casco. Takes beginning through advanced riders on trail rides with views of lakes and the White Mountains. Ask about summer riding camps for kids, and riding vacations for adults.

MINI GOLF ✍ **Steamboat Landing** (207-693-6782; www.steamboatlandingmini golf.com), Rt. 114, Naples (0.25 mile off the causeway). Open daily Memorial Day weekend–Labor Day, 10–10. A lovely 18-hole course with a Maine theme in a wooded setting. Ice cream parlor with Gifford's ice cream, and game room for Wiffle ball, air hockey, and family-oriented video games.

✍ **Seacoast Fun Park** (207-892-5952; www.seacoastfunparks.com), Rt. 302, Windham. Open June–Oct. Elaborate mini golf, driving range, go-carts, bumper boats, arcade, waterslide, and trampoline: a ride that straps you into a bungee cord, hauls you high into the air, then lets you swing.

SAILING Sportshaus (207-647-3000), 61 Main St., Bridgton, rents Sunfish and Rhumbas by the week.

SWIMMING ✍ **Sebago Lake State Park** (Memorial Day–Labor Day, 207-693-6613; otherwise, 207-693-6231), off Rt. 302 (between Naples and South Casco). A great family beach with picnic tables, grills, boat ramp, lifeguards, and bathhouses. Day use only; there is a separate camping area (see *Lodging*). No pets.

The town of Bridgton maintains a tidy little beach on **Long Lake** just off Main St., another on **Woods Pond** (Rt. 117), and another on **Highland Lake**. The town of Fryeburg maintains a beach, with float, on the **Saco River**, and **Casco** maintains a small, inviting beach in its picturesque village.

✳ Winter Sports

CROSS-COUNTRY SKIING ✍ **Five Fields Farm X-C Ski Center** (207-647-2425; www.fivefieldsfarmx-cski.com), Rt. 107, 6 miles south of Bridgton. Open daily 9 AM–dusk. Pick your own apples in fall. Trails loop around the 70-acre working apple orchard and connect to logging roads. You can snowshoe to the top of Bald Pate Mountain for spectacular views. Full- and half-day rates, rentals, warming hut.

✍ **Harris Farm Cross Country Ski Center** (207-499-2678; www.harrisfarm .com), 280 Buzzell Rd., Dayton. Open daily 9 AM–dusk when there's snow. This 500-acre dairy and tree farm offers 40 km of groomed trails, from easy to difficult, over hills, by ponds and streams, and through the woods. Rentals available.

DOWNHILL SKIING ✍ **Shawnee Peak** (207-647-8444; www.shawneepeak.com), Rt. 302, Bridgton. An isolated 1,900-foot hump, 1 mile west of the center of town. Maine's oldest ski area has a vertical drop of 1,300 feet and offers 40 trails with 98 percent snowmaking capacity, a double, two triples, and a quad lift, plus a handle tow—and the only lit half-pipe in Maine. Open until 9 PM (until 10 Fri. and Sat.), night skiing is big here. Glades and free-style terrain park. Ski and snowboard instruction, rentals, childcare, and base lodge with pub. Rooms in a comfortable self-service guest house with private bath start at $79 per person weekdays, including lift ticket.

Sportshaus (207-647-3000), 61 Main St., Bridgton, rents skis, snowshoes, and snowboards by the day or week.

✳ Green Space

The **Lakes Environmental Association** (LEA; 207-647-8580; www.mainelakes .org), 102 Main St., Bridgton, has been working since 1970 to preserve the clear, unsullied lakes in western Maine from development, invasive species such as milfoil, and overuse. Trails and a boardwalk lead through the **Holt Pond Preserve**, an undeveloped watershed with a bog, a river, and other wetlands. The

Stevens Brook Trail follows the water body from Highland Lake to Long Lake. Tour the LEA's **Harry & Eunice Bradley Lake Center** in Bridgton to see the water-testing lab, buffer gardens, and educational displays.

Kezar Falls, reached from Lovell Rd. off Rt. 35, is a small, pretty waterfall on the Kezar River.

✳ Lodging

RUSTIC RESORTS The Western Lakes area offers unusual old resort complexes, each with cabin accommodations, dining, and relaxing space in a central, distinctively Maine lodge. In contrast to similar complexes found farther north, these are all geared to families or to those who vacation here for reasons other than hunting and fishing.

✧ ♿ **Migis Lodge** (207-655-4524; www.migis.com), P.O. Box 40, South Casco 04077 (off Rt. 302). Open early June–Columbus Day weekend. This classic Maine lakeside hotel takes excellent care of its guests, from beautiful quilts on the handcrafted beds and fully tiled baths to fresh flowers and paintings of Maine landscapes on the walls in all buildings. They even have a comforting fire going constantly in the main lodge, and we were charmed by the fences made of stacked firewood that frame the grounds. Deluxe accommodations include six rooms in the two-story main lodge, and 35 cottages with names like Skylark and Tamarack scattered throughout the pines on 97 acres. All cottages have a fireplace, and guests enjoy use of the private beach, tennis, lawn games, waterskiing, sailboats, canoes, boat excursions, and high-speed wireless Internet access throughout the property. Children 5 and under are not permitted in the dining room during high season (July–Labor Day), so the resort provides a family dining room as well as

supervised dining and playtime 6:30–8:30 PM; older children are also welcome to join in. $245–315 per adult per night (cottages) includes three meals; $235 per adult in lodge rooms, less in fall. Children's rates available; 15 percent service charge.

✧ **Quisisana** (207-925-3500; off-season 914-833-0293; www.quisisana resort.com), Lake Kezar, Center Lovell 04016. Mid-June–Aug. One-week minimum stay in high season. Guests and staff alike are passionate about this place, founded in 1917 as a place for music students and music lovers to relax in the pines by one of Maine's clearest lakes. Each evening climaxes with performances in the lakeside hall: musical theater, opera, and chamber music concerts performed by staff recruited from top music schools. The 75 guest rooms range from lodges to one- to three-room cottages (some with fireplace) scattered through the woods and around the soft beach. The lack of phones or TVs in the cabins means more time for waterskiing, boating, fishing, croquet, tennis, and swimming. The white-frame central lodge includes a big, homey sitting room and the kind of dining room you don't mind sitting in three times a day, especially given the quality of the food. $140–185 per person double occupancy includes three meals a day.

✧ **Aimhi Lodge** (207-892-6538; www.aimhilodge.com), Little Sebago Lake, North Windham 04062. Open late June–late Aug. For more than 80 years, this classic complex has operated in the same family. Little has changed, though the 23 cottages on Little Sebago Lake have been updated and modernized; they have one to three rooms, stone fireplace, Franklin stove, screened porch, and a dock. Down-home cooking: turkey every summer Sunday since the 1930s (at least), and Friday lobster bakes. Facilities include a game room (with a sitting area for adults and a billiard table), lawn games, a beach, sailboats, canoes, tennis, paddleboats, kayaks, supervised youth activities, and fishing. Adults $144–200 per person per day (children's rates are lower), including all three meals.

BED & BREAKFASTS ✐ **Noble House** (207-647-3733 or 1-888-237-4880; www.noblehousebb.com), 81 Highland Rd., Bridgton 04009. Open year-round. Rick and Julie Whelchel are the innkeepers at this former senator's manor. Nine guest rooms (all with private bath) are divided between the original house and newer doubles and suites in the former ell (five with whirlpool bath); all come with amenities such as alarm clocks and selections from the inn's book collection. The inn is across the street from a beach with a canoe and dock. $99–199 double includes a full breakfast and use of the canoe, along with access to the bottomless cookie jar.

✐ **Center Lovell Inn** (207-925-1575 or 1-800-777-2698; www.centerlovell inn.com), Rt. 5, Center Lovell 04016. Closed Nov.–mid-Dec. and Apr.–mid-May. Innkeeper Janice Sage runs this striking old inn with a cupola and an award-winning and busy restaurant (see *Dining Out*). The inn features four guest rooms on the second floor

(the two with shared bath can be a suite), nicely furnished with antiques and art. In the 1835 Harmon House there are five cozy rooms, three with private bath. $74–220 with no meals; breakfast and dinner additional.

✐ **Oxford House Inn** (207-935-3442 or 1-800-261-7206; www.oxfordhouse inn.com), 548 Main St., Fryeburg 04037. Open year-round. John and Phyllis Morris's gracious 1913 house in the middle of Fryeburg enjoys one of the most spectacular views in Maine: across bucolic fields and the placid Saco River to the White Mountains in New Hampshire. For the ultimate romantic weekend, come here in the off-season, putter around Fryeburg, dine in John's wonderful restaurant downstairs at sunset (see *Dining Out*) one night and the Center Lovell Inn (see below) the next. In summer this place makes a nice jumping-off point for hiking and boating on the Saco River, which guests can reach via a path. Four upstairs guest rooms, all large and decorated in Victoriana, come with private bath. $95–150 includes a full breakfast overlooking the mountains.

✐ **One Thirty Three Main Street** (207-935-7171; www.mainstbandb .com), Fryeburg 04037. Margaret Cugini has transformed this 1820 farmhouse in the heart of Fryeburg into a stunning and luxurious B&B, with the original woodwork, pumpkin pine floors in the hallway, and oak balustrade. The inn's five guest rooms, three with private bath and one with a 6-foot Jacuzzi, are furnished with antiques and lovely linens. Guests also have use of a sitting room with a TV/VCR. Full breakfast and afternoon tea, cocoa, and pastries included. $79–179.

Admiral Peary House (207-935-3365 or 1-800-237-8080; www.admiral pearyhouse.com), 27 Elm St., Fryeburg 04037. Named for Robert E. Peary, Maine's famed Arctic explorer, this homey B&B offers seven casual guest rooms named for Peary's partners, family members, and others; each has a private bath and air-conditioning, three have a gas fireplace, and one a whirlpool. Common space includes an outdoor hot tub overlooking 6.5 acres of lawn and woods. The top-floor North Pole Room, with king brass bed, features mountain views. $115–195 in-season includes a full breakfast; $95–145 off-season.

🐾 ✂ ♿ **Sebago Lake Lodge** (207-892-2698; www.sebagolakelodge .com), P.O. Box 110, White's Bridge Rd., North Windham 04062. A rambling old white inn on a narrows between Jordan Bay and the Basin, seemingly surrounded by water. Eight units have kitchen (one is a suite with an enclosed porch), and four standard rooms have kitchen privileges. There are also 12 moderately priced cottages. Facilities include an inviting beach, picnic tables, and grills; fishing-boat, rowboat, canoe, and motorboat rentals. Pets are allowed in cottages. $68 for a room in high season, $160–195 in the main lodge. Cottages by the week only, $800–1,295.

✂ **The Inn at Long Lake** (207-693-6226 or 1-800-437-0328; www.innat longlake.com), P.O. Box 806, Naples 04055. Buddy Marcum has renovated this wonderful place room by room, adding details like wicker and antique furniture bought at auction, gas stoves, and designer wallpaper and fabrics; the four-story clapboard building is just a block from the lake. Sixteen rooms include two suites,

most with queen beds. Each has private bath, TV, and air conditioner, and a few offer lake views. There is a dinner option for guests staying in the inn. $160–200 includes full breakfast.

✂ **Greenwood Manor Inn** (207-583-4445; www.greenwoodmanorinn .com), 52 Tolman Rd., Harrison 04040. Open year-round. A former carriage house on 108 hillside acres sloping down to Long Lake, the inn features seven guest rooms and two suites, some with a gas log fireplace, some with whirlpool tub, and all with private bath. The dining and living areas overlook a beautifully landscaped garden. Children under 2 stay free, but there are no cribs. $140 double, $120 single, includes a full breakfast; suites run $209. *Note:* Although this B&B is technically in Harrison, much of its property lies in the town of Bridgton, and it is thus much closer to the Sebago/Long Lakes area than to the Oxford Hills; as a result, we're listing it in both chapters.

Olde Saco Inn (207-925-3737; www .theoldesacoinn.com) Seven rooms and one suite will take care of the night here, and the billiard table and trails for snowshoeing, skiing, hiking trails on the 65-acre property could fill your days. Rates $85–179, depending on the season.

MOTELS 🅿 🐾 ✂ **Jockey Cap Motel, General Store and Cafe** (207-935-2306), 116 Bridgton Rd., Fryeburg 04037. Open year-round. Located at the trailhead for Jockey Cap Mountain, this simple place nevertheless offers all the important mod cons: one or two full-sized beds in each room, private bath with tub and shower, air-conditioning, cable TV, and continental breakfast included in rates:

$59–69 depending on the season. Small pets allowed.

COTTAGES The **Greater Bridgton Lakes Region Chamber of Commerce** (see *Guidance*) publishes a list of more than two dozen rental cottages, and many in this area are also listed in the *Maine Guide to Inns and Bed & Breakfasts and Camps & Cottages*, free from the Maine Tourism Association (see *Information* in "What's Where").

CAMPGROUNDS See *Canoeing and Kayaking* for information about camping along the Saco River. In addition to those mentioned, the Appalachian Mountain Club maintains a campground at Swan's Falls. The *Maine Camping Guide*, available from the **Maine Campground Owners Association** (207-782-5874), 655 Main St., Lewiston 04240, lists dozens of private campgrounds in the area.

🐾 ✍ **Sebago Lake State Park** (207-693-6613; before June 20 and after Labor Day, 207-693-6231), off Rt. 302 (between Naples and South Casco). Open through mid-Oct. Visitors return year after year to these 1,300 thickly wooded acres on the northern shore of the lake, so make your reservations early if you want a good site. The camping area (with 250 campsites, many on the water) comes with its own beach, hot showers, a program of evening presentations such as outdoor movies, and nature hikes. For information about reservations, call 1-800-332-1501, or 207-287-3824 from outside the state. No day use.

🐾 ✍ 🚲 **Point Sebago Resort**(207-655-3821 or 1-800-655-1232; www.pointsebago.com), 261 Point Sebago Rd., Casco 04015. Open May–Oct.

For those who want to camp on a Maine lake cheaply without roughing it, this complex offers a lot. One hundred sites for RV hook-ups on a 775-acre lakeside site, plus hundreds of small, manufactured "Park homes," for rent, some with linens and others empty, requiring you stock the basics. Everyone has access to the beach, marina, pavilion, children's activities, excursion boats, soccer and softball fields, horseshoe pitches, 18-hole championship golf course, 10 tennis courts, video-game arcade, general store, and combination restaurant/nightclub, with DJs, teen dances, and magic shows.

River Run (207-452-2500), P.O. Box 190, Brownfield 04010. Camp on more than 100 acres, with sites in the woods and along the Saco River. Amenities include public phone, group tenting area, swimming beaches, fire rings, picnic tables, and firewood for purchase.

✳ Where to Eat

DINING OUT Center Lovell Inn (207-925-1575), Rt. 5, Center Lovell. Open for dinner daily, except when the inn closes Nov.–mid-Dec. and Apr.–mid-May; call for reservations. This place is equally famous for its award-winning food in the antiques-filled dining rooms, and for its views over the White Mountains. Specialties include an appetizer of grilled venison sausage with a blueberry and balsamic sauce, and entrées like seafood Norfolk—shrimp, scallops, crabmeat, and lobster sautéed with garlic and brandy. Bison is served occasionally, and there is always a fish special. $18.95–27.95.

Olde Mill Tavern (207-583-9077; www.oldemilltavern.com), 56 Main St., Harrison. Open Mon.–Thu. 4–9,

Fri.–Sat. noon–10 PM, Sun. 10 AM–8 PM. From Cajun jambalaya to fish-and-chips, shrimp scampi, and chicken Parmesan, the bases are covered at this popular place. Entrées $13–18.

Black Horse Tavern (207-647-5300; www.sunnysidevillagemaine.com/blackhorsetavern), Rt. 302, Bridgton. Open daily for lunch and dinner, Sunday brunch from 10 AM. A large filet mignon, and salmon baked with orange and Dijon sauce, are likely to be found on the changing menu.

Venezia Ristorante (207-647-5333 or 207-647-5334), Bridgton Corners, Rts. 302 and 93, Bridgton. Open for dinner Tue.–Sun. 5–9 in summer, Thu.–Sun. in winter. Dependable, moderately priced Italian dishes.

Tom's Homestead (207-647-5726), Rt. 302, Bridgton. Lunch and dinner are served (closed Mon.) in this 1821 historic home. The menu includes scalloppine of veal Française, poached fresh haddock, and frogs' legs Provençal, as well as vegetarian entrées.

Oxford House Inn (207-935-3442 or 1-800-261-7206), 105 Main St., Fryeburg. Open for dinner every night in summer and fall, Thu.–Sun. in winter and spring. Reservations required. Our pick for the most romantic spot in western Maine, the dining room's back porch features sunset mountain views that will fill you with awe. Chef John Morris starts meals with appetizers like hot buttered Brie, and cooks entrées like blackened sirloin with red pepper sauce and scallops sautéed with shallots, Grand Marnier, orange juice, and crème fraîche.

EATING OUT Auntie M's (207-625-3889), Rt. 25, Cornish. Open for breakfast and lunch Mon.–Sat.; break-fast-only on Sun. Good, hearty home-cooked food. Their specialty is "the rhino burger": fresh vegetables (not soy or fillers) formed into a patty. Also homemade chili served with grilled bread and the requisite blueberry pancakes at breakfast.

Krista's (207-625-3600), 2 High Rd., Cornish. Open Wed.–Sat. 7–2 and 5–9; Sun. 7–1 and 5–9; Mon. 7–2. Breakfast is all homemade, with muffins and scones, and special spiced pumpkin waffles likely in fall. Dinner ranges from nachos to roast duck. Entrées $13.95–24.95.

Bray's Brew Pub (207-693-6806; www.braysbrewpub.com), Rts. 302 and 35, Naples. Open year-round for lunch and dinner daily. We loved our chili wrap and fine coleslaw on a quiet Monday; dinners in summer are a lot busier, and there can be a wait. Mike Bray and Michele Windsor brew excellent American ales using grains and malted barley, Oregon yeast, and Washington hops; a beer garden with horseshoe pits and a luxuriant hops vine is a pleasant place on warm nights. The Greek salad was a nice mix of mesclun, feta cheese, red onions, and Greek olives in a balsamic vinaigrette. Try the lobster stew, baby back ribs, and mussels with andouille steamed in beer. The dinner menu runs from grilled salmon to petit filet mignon; pub menu served till 9:30 PM.

Delicious Licks at the Lake (207-647-8216), Rt. 302, Bridgton. Generous portions.

Center Lovell Market (207-925-1051), Rt. 5, Center Lovell. This place combines the best of an old-fashioned general store (clothing, groceries, Maine-made items) with a deli and café. Pizza, salads, and more served to go or to eat in the pleasant dining area.

Route 160 Ice Cream and Hot Dog Stand, north of Kezar Falls on Rt. 160. Locals swear by the dogs here, as well as the hamburgers and ice cream. A good place to stop for lunch when traveling between Cornish and Fryeburg.

Beef and Ski (207-647-9555), 224 Portland Rd. (Rt. 302), Bridgton. Everything from hot sandwiches to seafood dinners. Onion rings are hand cut, fish is fresh, turkey and beef are roasted here for sandwiches and dinners. Takeout is the focus, but seating is available. Entrées $6–16. This is a franchise from a North Conway business.

Café DeCarlo, Internet Café and Espresso Bar (207-647-4596; www .cafedecarlo.com), 163 Main St., Bridgton 04009. Open 7 AM–7 PM, later in summer. Along with Carrabasset Coffee and wraps, salads, soups, breakfast sandwiches, and espresso brownies, you can get online here wherever you can set down your laptop; four computers are available for anyone without a machine. Dennis Lone and his wife, Carmen, started this WiFi hot spot in 2004.

* Entertainment

FILM **Windham Hill Mall Cinema** (207-892-7000), Rt. 302, North Windham, shows first-run movies. **Bridgton Drive-In** (207-647-8666), Rt. 302, shows first-run movies in summer.

MUSIC **Sebago–Long Lake Region Chamber Music Festival** (207-583-6747), Deertrees Rd., Deertrees The-

atre and Cultural Center, Harrison. A series of five world-class concerts held mid-July–mid-Aug.

The Saco River Festival Association (207-625-7116) holds a chamber music festival in Cornish in July and Aug. Call for a brochure detailing performances.

THEATER See **Deertrees Theatre and Cultural Center** in "Oxford Hills."

* Selective Shopping

ANTIQUES SHOPS Rt. 302 is chockablock full of antiques shops, so stop anyplace that looks interesting. Cornish has also grown into an antiques haven, and we relish the lack of crowds.

The Smith Co. (207-625-6030), 24 Main St., Cornish. Specializes in country-store fixtures and memorabilia—including old Coca-Cola collectibles and advertising signs.

BOOKSTORES **Bridgton Books** (207-647-2122), 140 Main St., Bridgton. More than 20,000 titles, new and used books, books on tape, cards and stationery, music.

CRAFTS SHOPS **Accessories Unlimited** (207-625-8421), 16 Old Pike Rd., Cornish. A combination of factory store (luggage and totes), antiques, and collectibles in a huge old building.

SPECIAL SHOPS **The Shops at South Casco** (207-655-5060), Rt. 302, South Casco. A three-building complex. **Cry of the Loon** encompasses unique pottery, glassware, and other handmade crafts. **The Nest** (207-655-5034) offers country furniture and

Kim Grant

BARGAIN HUNTING IN NAPLES

other items for your decor, including rugs. In **The Barn** (207-655-5066), you'll find cast-iron toys to wine racks. Downstairs from The Barn, at the **Blueberry Pantry**, there are free tastings of gourmet foods.

Shops at the Maine Difference (207-647-2706; www.angelsflight.biz), 82 Main St., Bridgton. Open Tue.– Sun. 10 AM–4 PM. Deb Snyder's **Angels Flight** offers spiritual readings and sells related material here, one of several businesses in one building on Main Street.

Sportshaus (207-647-3000), 61 Main St., Bridgton. Open daily. Known for its original Maine T-shirts; also a selection of casual clothes, canvas bags, tennis rackets, downhill and cross-country skis, athletic footwear, swimwear, and golf accessories. Canoe, kayak, sailboat, and waterski rentals in summer; ski shop in winter.

Craftworks (207-647-5436), 79 Main St., Upper Village, Bridgton. Open daily. Fills a former church and two neighboring buildings. Selective women's clothing, pottery, books, linens, handmade pillows, crafted jewelry, Stonewall Kitchen–prepared foods, and wines from all over the world.

The Sheep Shop (207-647-3584), 2056 High St., Bridgton. A sweet little shop just north of town featuring Bridgton Yarn, hand knits, spinning and knitting supplies, wool and sheepskin blankets, slippers, toys, "Babycare" lambskins, and other specialty items.

Blacksmiths Winery (207-655-3292; www.blacksmithswinery.com), 967 Quaker Ridge Rd., South Casco. Open May–Dec. 1, Mon.–Sat. 11–6, Sun. noon–5; Jan.–Apr., Thu.–Mon. 11–5, Sun. noon–5. Visitors can sample the surprisingly good cabernet sauvignon, chardonnay, blueberry, "Roughshod"—a port-style blueberry wine—and other wines here. (The grape juice comes from New York and Washington State.)

✳ Special Events

End of January/beginning of February: **Mushers' Bowl**, a dogsled race at the Fryeburg Fairgrounds with participants from all over the United States. Includes sleigh rides, crafts, dancing, stargazing, ice skating, snowshoeing, ice fishing, and more.

March: **March Maple Syrup Sunday**, with tapping and sugaring-off demonstrations around the area, including Pingree Maple Syrup, High Rd., Cornish; and Highland Farms Sugar Works, Towles Hill, Cornish.

April: **Sheepfest**, Denmark—demonstrations of spinning, carding, combing, knitting, dyeing, sheep shearing, hoof trimming, and more.

July: Independence Day is big in Bridgton and Naples, with fireworks, a parade, and the **4 on the Fourth Road Race**—a 5K walk/run/wheelchair race around Bridgton. Shawnee Peak hosts a **Portland Symphony Orchestra** concert that week on Pleasant Mountain. In **Naples** the fireworks over the lake are spectacular. Harrison and Casco also hold their **Old Home Days** this month, and check out the **Waterford World's Fair**. **Strawberry Festival**, Thompson Park, Cornish.

August: **Windham Old Home Days** (*beginning of the month*) parade, contests, and public feeds. In Lovell the **Annual Arts and Artisans Fair** (*midmonth*) is held at the new Suncook School—a juried crafts fair. The **Spinners and Weavers Show** at Narramissic has grown in popularity in recent years (see *To See*).

September: **Chili Cook-Off and Road Race**, Waterford. **Cornish Apple Festival**, including crafts booths, food vendors, quilt show, antique auto parade, apple pie contest, and the **Apple Acres Bluegrass Festival**. **Brewers' Festival** offers tastes from microbreweries, with crafts and children's activities; look at www.lakesbrewfest.com for details.

October: **Fryeburg Fair**, Maine's largest agricultural fair, is held for a week in early October, climaxing with the Columbus Day weekend. This is an old-fashioned agricultural happening—one of the most colorful in the country. **Haunted Happenings** with hundreds of pumpkins and refreshments at Mark's Lawn and Garden, Rt. 302, Bridgton; check www.marks lawnandgarden.com.

Early November: **Early-Bird Shopping**, featuring discounts at many local retail shops.

Late November–early December: **Christmas in Cornish**—open houses, concerts, Cornish Historical Society Walking Tour, horse-drawn carriage rides, children's story time, poinsettia display, and caroling. **Bridgton's Festival of Lights**— a parade with Santa Claus and tree lighting.

December: **Christmas Open House** and festivals in Harrison.

OXFORD HILLS AND
LEWISTON/AUBURN

Over the years many of Maine's small towns have banded together to form distinctive regional identities. One such area, a rolling gem- and lake-studded swatch of Oxford County, is known as the Oxford Hills. Technically made up of eight towns, the region seems to stretch to include many of the stops along Rt. 26, the region's traffic spine, as visitors pass through from Gray (an exit on the Maine Turnpike) to Bethel, an area with both summer attractions and winter ski resorts.

Its commercial center is the community composed of both Norway and South Paris, towns divided by the Little Androscoggin River but joined by Rt. 26. Off Rt. 26 is a quiet part of the Western Lakes and Mountains Region, with startlingly beautiful villages like Waterford and Paris Hill, and genuinely interesting places to see such as the country's last living Shaker community at Sabbathday Lake.

The Oxford Hills are best known for their mineral diversity. The area's bedrock is a granite composed of pegmatite studded with semiprecious gemstones, including tourmaline and rose quartz. Several local mines invite visitors to explore their "tailings," or rubble, and take what they find.

Otisfield is renowned for a unique summer camp devoted to healing the wounds of war, called Seeds of Peace Camp. It began with Palestinian and Israeli children campers, and now includes children from Afghanistan, India, Pakistan, Iraq, and Iran, who spend the summer getting to know children they might have encountered otherwise only as "enemies."

Lewiston and Auburn (Maine's "LA"), just east of the Oxford Hills, are the "cities of the Androscoggin" but for most visitors are seen as "the cities on the Turnpike," the exits accessing routes to the Rangeley and Sugarloaf areas. Both are worth a stop. By the 1850s mills on both sides of the river had harnessed the power of the Androscoggin's Great Falls, and the Bates Mill boomed with the Civil War, supplying fabric for most of the Union army's tents.

Today Lewiston is best known as the home of prestigious Bates College (founded in 1855), an attractive campus that's the summer site of the nationally recognized Bates Dance Festival. It's also the home of a growing number of Somali immigrants, who are bringing their own cultural flair to the region. The Bates Mill is now a visitor-friendly complex housing shops and restaurants, and

both Lewiston and Auburn offer interesting restaurants, shopping, and a number
of colorful festivals—some, like Festival de Joie, reflecting the rich diversity of
the residents.

GUIDANCE **Oxford Hills Chamber of Commerce** (207-743-2281; www.oxford
hillsmaine.com), 213 Main St., South Paris 04281, publishes a comprehensive
directory to the area.

Androscoggin County Chamber of Commerce (207-783-2249; www
.androscoggincounty.com), 179 Lisbon St., P.O. Box 59, Lewiston 04243.

GETTING THERE For the Sabbathday Lake–Poland Spring–Oxford area, take I-95
to Gray (exit 63) and Rt. 26 north. Auburn is exit 75 and Lewiston is exit 80 off
the Maine Turnpike.

WHEN TO COME This is lovely country in winter, but dinner choices can be limited to weekends in the countryside. We love the Lilac Festival at the McLaughlin Foundation Garden on Memorial Day weekend.

✳ Villages

Harrison. Once a booming lakeside resort town, Harrison is now a quiet village
resting between two lakes. Main Street has a popular restaurant and restored
clock tower. In the 1930s many of the country's most popular actors came to perform at the Deertrees Theatre, which is again offering theater, dance, music, and
children's shows to the area. Old Home Days and Christmas in Harrison festivities celebrate the town's cultural heritage.

Norway. Making up part of the commercial center of the region, the downtown
is quiet and quaint. L. M. Longley's hardware store has items from days gone by,
the town is home to Maine's oldest newspaper, and there are interesting art exhibits held by the Western Maine Art Group in the Matolcsy Art Center. The
Norway Sidewalk Arts Festival in July features close to 100 artists exhibiting
along Main Street.

Paris is a town divided into sections so different they don't feel like the same
town at all. Paris Hill has views of the White Mountains and a number of historic
houses and buildings, including the Hamlin Memorial Library. The buildings
in Market Square are brick, many with stamped-tin ceilings. Main Street, the
commercial center, is a row of the nondescript businesses found in many town
centers.

Oxford. Home of the Oxford Plains Speedway, which attracts stock-car-racing
fans throughout the season, and the Oxford County Fairgrounds (host to several
annual events). Oxford is also the largest manufacturing base in the area, including manufactured homes, information processing, textiles, and wood products.

✳ To See

The International Sign. At the junction of Rts. 5 and 35 in the village of
Lynchville, some 14 miles west of Norway, stands Maine's most photographed

roadside marker, pointing variously to Norway, Paris, Denmark, Naples, Sweden, Poland, Mexico, and Peru—all towns within 94 miles of the sign.

FOR FAMILIES ⚓ ♿ **Maine Wildlife Park** (207-657-4977), Rt. 26, Gray. Open Apr. 15–Nov. 11, daily 9:30–6 (no one admitted after 4 PM). $5 adults, $4 ages 61-plus, $3.25 ages 4–12, and free for those 3 and under. What started as a pheasant farm has evolved into a wonderful haven for injured animals. The park prepares animals to return to the wild, but while they're here it's a great opportunity to see species you might otherwise never glimpse. The park provides the most natural habitats possible, allowing visitors to observe animals as they live in the wild. Nature trails and picnic facilities round out the experience. Animals include moose, lynx, deer, black bears, red foxes, wild turkeys, eagles, and many more.

⚓ **Beech Hill Farm & Bison Ranch** (207-583-2515), 630 Valley Rd., Waterford. Paul and Marcia Hersey are raising a breeding herd of North American bison on their ranch. They offer tours, hayrides among the herd, and a trading post with bison meat and a variety of gifts. Worth a stop to see award-winning bison Chief Chadwick and Irish Warrior.

HISTORIC BUILDINGS **Preservation Park at Poland Spring** (207-998-7143; www.polandspring.com), 115 Preservation Way, Poland Spring. Open Tue.–Sun. 8–4. The original bottling plant and springhouse for the well-known bottled water, Poland Spring, is its own nonprofit branch set in its business park. The old spa had a renowned visitor list, and some are displayed in the gallery here, like Mae West and Babe Ruth. **Sadie's Place**, a café, serves breakfast and lunch and includes a gift shop. The museum and springhouse charge no admission.

State of Maine Building, Rt. 26, Poland Spring. Open July and Aug., daily 9–1; June and Sep., weekends 9–1. Admission charged. A very Victorian building that was brought back from the 1893 World's Columbian Exposition in Chicago to serve as a library and art gallery for the now vanished Poland Spring Resort (today the water is commercially bottled in an efficient, unromantic plant down the road). Peek into the **All Souls Chapel** next door for a look at its nine stained-glass windows and the 1921 Skinner pipe organ.

Hamlin Memorial Library and Museum (207-743-2980), Hannibal Hamlin Dr. off Rt. 26, Paris Hill, Paris. Open seasonally, varying from year to year. Call for hours. The old stone Oxford County Jail now houses the public library and museum. Worth a stop for the American primitive art; also local minerals and displays about Hannibal Hamlin (who lived next door), vice president during Abraham Lincoln's first term. This stop may not sound very exciting, but the setting is superb: a ridgetop of spectacular early-19th-century houses with views west to the White Mountains.

MUSEUMS **Sabbathday Lake Shaker Community and Museum** (207-926-4597; www.shaker.lib.me.us), 707 Shaker Rd. (Rt. 26), New Gloucester (8 miles north of Gray). Open Memorial Day–Columbus Day for six 2-hour tours daily (except Sun.), 10–4:30; $6.50 adults, $2 ages 6–12. Welcoming the "world's people" has been part of summer at Sabbathday Lake since the community's inception in 1794.

Founded by Englishwoman Ann Lee in 1775, Shakers numbered 6,000 Americans in 18 communities by the Civil War. Today, with only four Shaker Sisters and Brothers, this village is the only one that still functions as a religious community. These men and women continue to follow the injunction of Mother Ann Lee to "put your hands to work and your heart to God." Guided tours are offered of the 17 white-clapboard buildings; rooms are either furnished or filled with exhibits to illustrate periods or products of Shaker life. The **Shaker Store** sells Shaker-made goods, including oval boxes, knitted and sewn goods, homemade fudge, yarns, souvenirs, antiques, Shaker-style furniture, and Shaker herbs. During warm-weather months, services are held at 10 AM on Sunday in the 18th-century meetinghouse on Rt. 26. Sit in the World's People's benches and listen as the Shakers speak in response to the psalms and gospel readings. Each observation is affirmed with a Shaker song—of which there are said to be 10,000. This complex includes an extensive research library housing Shaker books, writings, and records.

Franco-American Heritage Collection, Lewiston-Auburn College/USM
(207-753-6545), 51 Westminster St., Lewiston. Open 8:30–5 Mon. and Wed., and 8–noon on Thu., this collection researches and promotes interest in the French roots of many of the region's inhabitants. Peruse documents, photographs, artifacts, and audiovisual materials.

SABBATHDAY LAKE SHAKER COMMUNITY AND MUSEUM

Kim Grant

Bates College Museum of Art, Olin Arts Center (207-786-6158; www.bates college.edu), 75 Russell St., Lewiston. Open Tue.–Sat. 10–5. Hosts a variety of performances, exhibitions, and special programs. The museum also houses fine artworks on paper, including the Marsden Hartley Memorial Collection. Lovers of the artist won't want to miss this small but excellent collection of bold, bright canvases by Hartley, a Lewiston native (call ahead to find out what's on display).

Finnish-American Heritage Society of Maine (207-674-3094; off-hours, 207-743-5677), 8 Maple St., West Paris. Open in July and Aug., Sun. 2–4. This organization features a museum, library, and gift shop focused on the Finnish settlers in this area. They sponsor a Finnish cultural gathering every third Sun., Sep.–June.

SCENIC DRIVES

Along Rt. 26

Patched with ugly as well as beautiful stretches, the 46 miles between Gray (Maine Turnpike exit 11) and West Paris don't constitute your ordinary "scenic drive," but this is the way most people head for Bethel and the White Mountains. The following sights are described in order of appearance, heading north:

Sabbathday Lake Shaker Community and Museum, New Gloucester (8 miles north of Gray), both sides of the road, a must-stop (see *Museums*).

State of Maine Building from the 1893 World's Columbian Exposition in Chicago (see *Historic Buildings*). An abrupt right, up through the pillars of the old Poland Spring Resort.

In Oxford two exceptional **farm stands** make ice cream from the milk of their own cows. Northbound, don't miss hilltop **Crestholm Farm Stand and Ice Cream** (on your right; 207-539-8832), which has a petting zoo (sheep, goats, pigs, ducks, and more) as well as cheeses, honey, and great ice cream; also a nice view. Southbound, it's **Smedberg's Crystal Spring Farm** (see *Where to Eat—Snacks*).

In South Paris highway hypnosis sets in big time after the light; it's easy to miss **Shaner's Family Dining** (see *Eating Out*).

Across from Ripley Ford, look for the **McLaughlin Foundation Garden & Horticultural Center** (see *Green Space*).

The **Oxford Hills Chamber of Commerce** (207-743-2281), 213 Main St., South Paris, is open year-round, and you can pick up the magazine guide to the area here.

Paris Hill is posted just beyond the second light in South Paris. The road climbs steadily up to Paris Hill common, a spacious green surrounded on three sides by early-19th-century mansions, with the fourth commanding a panoramic view of hills and valley and the White Mountains in the distance. Look for **Hamlin Memorial Library and Museum** (see *Historic Buildings*).

Christian Ridge Pottery (see *Special Shops*) is marked from Christian Ridge Rd., a way back to Rt. 26.

⌀ **Snow Falls Gorge**, 6 miles south of the center of West Paris on Rt. 26, left as you're heading north. A great picnic and walk-around spot, a rest area with tables and a trail by a waterfall that cascades into a 300-foot gorge carved by the Little Androscoggin. **The River Restaurant** (see *Dining Out*), just across the way, is recognized as one of the best "dining out" as well as "eating out" bets in the area.

⌀ **Trap Corner** in West Paris (junction Rt. 219) is rockhounding central (see *Rockhounding*).

Greenwood Shore Rest Area, Rt. 26 just north of Bryant Pond. A good waterside spot for a picnic.

STOCK-CAR RACING **Oxford Plains Speedway** (207-539-8865; www.oxford plains.com), Rt. 26, Oxford. Weekend stock-car racing, late Apr.–Oct.

✳ To Do

GOLF **Paris Hill Country Club** (207-743-2371), Paris Hill Rd., Paris, nine holes, founded in 1899, is the epitome of old-shoe; rental carts, snack bar. **Norway Country Club** (207-743-9840), off Rt. 118 on Norway Lake Rd., nine holes, long views. Nine holes as well at **Summit Golf Course** (207-998-4515), Summit Spring Rd., Poland Spring.

HIKING ⌀ **Streaked Mountain**. This is a relatively easy hike with a panoramic view, good for kids. From Rt. 26, take Rt. 117 to the right-hand turnoff for Streaked Mountain Rd. and look for the trailhead on your left. The trail follows a power line up to an old fire tower at just 800 feet. A round-trip hike takes about 1½ hours. Look for blueberries in-season.

Singlepole Mountain. Also off Rt. 117, nearer South Paris (see the *Maine Atlas and Gazetteer*, published by DeLorme), is a walk up a dirt road (bear left) through the woods to a summit with a view of Mount Washington and the Mahoosuc Mountains.

MOUNTAIN BIKING **Paris Hill Area Park**, near the common. You can bike the ridge roads radiating from here; inquire about routes in Hamlin Memorial Library and Museum.

Lost Valley Ski Area (207-784-1561; www.lostvalleyski.com), Lost Valley Rd., Auburn, opens its trails to bikers in biking season, early May–Nov., 9–6. Helmets and check-in and -out at ticket counter required. $2 for an all-day park access pass.

ROCKHOUNDING **Perham's of West Paris** (207-674-2341 or 1-800-371-GEMS), 194 Bethel Rd., West Paris. Open May–Dec., daily 9–5; closed Mon. Jan.–Apr., also winter holidays. Looking deceptively small in its yellow-clapboard, green-trim building (right side of Rt. 26, heading north), this business has been selling gemstones since 1919. Aside from displaying an array of locally mined amethyst, tourmaline, topaz, and many other minerals, as well as selling gem jewelry, Perham's offers maps to five local quarries in which treasure seekers are welcome to try their luck.

Rochester's Eclectic Emporium (207-539-4631), Rt. 26, Oxford. Nick Rochester displays a 54-carat amethyst that he found locally and steers visitors to local mines.

SWIMMING ♂ � **Range Pond State Park** (207-998-4104), Empire Rd., features a beach perfect for spreading out a picnic blanket. Lifeguards, snack bar, playground, ball field, changing rooms, bathrooms, swimming, and fishing, plus 2 miles of easy walking trails.

Pennesseewasee Lake in Norway is well off the road, but public and equipped with lifeguards.

In addition, most camps, cottages, and lodges have their own waterfront beaches and docks, and there are numerous local swimming holes.

✳ Winter Sports

CROSS-COUNTRY SKIING **Carter's X-C Ski Center** (207-539-4848; www
.cartersxcski.com/oxfordtrails.html), 420 Main St. (Rt. 26), Oxford. Extensive acreage used to grow summer vegetables is transformed into a ski center in winter. Equipment rentals, lessons, 40 km of groomed trails, some lighted trails for night skiing, and food.

Lost Valley Ski Area (207-784-1561), Lost Valley Rd., Auburn. Trails and rentals.

DOWNHILL SKIING **Lost Valley Ski Area** (207-784-1561; www.lostvalleyski
.com), Lost Valley Rd., Auburn. With 13 trails and two chairlifts, this small mountain is a favorite for schools and families.

SNOW TUBING ☃ ♂ **Mountain View Sports Park** (207-539-2454), Rt. 26, Oxford. A lighted 1,000-foot slope open Fri.–Sun., plus all school vacation days. Tubes, helmets, and a T-bar are the ingredients of this low-tech, low-cost sport. Snowmaking capability means you can enjoy the fun even during a mild winter.

✳ Green Space

The McLaughlin Foundation Garden & Horticultural Center (207-743-8820; www.mclaughlingarden.org), 97 Main St., South Paris. Garden open daily during growing season, 8–dusk. Free admission. In 1936 Bernard McLaughlin, who had no formal horticultural training, began planting. He welcomed visitors to his garden, set on his farmstead next to stone walls and a massive barn. The 2-acre floral oasis feels delightfully out of place in this commercial center. After his death in 1995, a nonprofit organization formed to preserve the home, barn, and garden. It's especially beautiful in lilac season (more than 100 varieties), when it holds an annual Lilac Festival with tours of the garden and lilac workshops and sales. The gift shop is open year-round, and a tearoom serving beverages and light lunches is open Memorial Day weekend–Labor Day, Wed.–Sat. 11–3.

✳ Lodging

INNS 🐾 🖋 **The Waterford Inne**
(207-583-4037; www.waterfordinne
.com), Box 149 (turn off Rt. 37 at the
shuttered Springer's General Store),
Waterford 04088. This striking mus-
tard-colored 1825 farmhouse with its
double porch is sequestered up a back
road, set on 25 quiet acres of fields
and woods. Mother and daughter
Rosalie and Barbara Vanderzanden
have welcomed guests since 1978, and
their unobtrusive style will appeal to
those who prefer more privacy. Eight
spacious rooms, six with private bath,
include the Chesapeake Room, with a
Franklin stove and a second-story
porch. A full breakfast is included in
$90–150 per room; dinner is available
(see *Dining Out*) at an additional cost.
Pets are accepted with a $15 pet fee.

Kedarburn Inn (207-583-6182 or 1-
866-583-6182; www.kedarburn.com),
Valley Rd. (Rt. 35), Waterford 04088.
Open year-round. London natives
Margaret and Derek Gibson offer
English hospitality in their seven guest
rooms, five with private bath; Margaret's specialty quilts throughout. We
particularly like the Balcony Room,
with a queen bed as well as a loft with
two twin beds. The quilt shop on the
ground floor is filled with Margaret's
creations. Quilting weekends and retreats Nov.–Apr. $85–130 double in-
season, including breakfast. English
afternoon tea is served by reservation.

Lake House (207-583-4182 or 1-800-
223-4182; www.lakehousemaine.com),
Rts. 35 and 37, Waterford 04088.
Open year-round. Michael and
Doreen Myers offer warm and genuine hospitality in this former stage
coach tavern. The first building in
Waterford when it was erected in the
1790s, the inn also used to be a sana-

torium for ladies and a private residence. The seven spacious guest
rooms, all with private bath, include
a two-room suite, five queen or king
country rooms, and the Grand Ballroom Suite, a 600-square-foot former
ballroom with a 10-foot vaulted ceiling and seven windows. Rooms have
phone, coffeemaker, hair dryer, and
bathrobes, among other amenities.
You don't have to leave the premises
to find great food at dinner (see *Dining Out*) during summer months and
Saturday in winter. $105–225 includes
breakfast.

King's Hill Inn (207-744-0204 or
1-877-391-5464; www.kingshillinn
.virtualave.net/inn.htm), 56 King Hill
Rd., South Paris. Two suites and three
rooms, all with private bath. Room 4
offers both a great view of the White
Mountains and a gas log fire. Enjoy
blueberry pancakes in the morning
before a tour of the perennial gardens
spreading out on the lawn under energetic owner Janice Davis. $95–160
per night for a double, depending
on season.

BED & BREAKFASTS ∞ **Bear
Mountain Inn** (207-583-4404; www
.bearmtninn.com), Rts. 35 and 37,
South Waterford 04081. Open year-
round. One of our favorite B&Bs in
Maine, this 150-year-old farmhouse is
set on 52 gorgeous acres next to Bear
Pond. Lorraine Blais takes a charming, bubbly, detail-oriented approach.
She decorates the 10 rooms, all with
private bath, with stuffed bears and
everything bear related, and somehow
it comes together as snug and welcoming without being cutesy. The
Sugar Bear Cottage has a fireplace,
kitchenette, claw-foot tub, and terrific
views over the lake from the private

patio. Common areas include a cozy, pine-paneled den with TV (plus a huge selection of tapes and DVDs) and fireplace, and wireless Internet access. Private beach with docks and canoes, kayaks and pedal boats. $120–295 per room includes a full breakfast; one fall morning, peach sour cream pancakes and herbed goat cheese soufflé were served. Canoe-and-kayak, golf, ski, and sailing packages.

♪ **Greenwood Manor Inn** (207-583-4445; www.greenwoodmanorinn .com), P.O. Box 551, Tolman Rd., Harrison 04040. Open year-round. A former carriage house on 108 hillside acres sloping down to Long Lake, the inn features seven guest rooms and two suites, some with a gas log fireplace, some with whirlpool tub, and all with private bath. Children under 2 stay free, but there are no cribs. $120 double, $100 single, includes a full breakfast. Guests also have access to snowshoes and trails on the property in winter, and canoes and bicycles in summer. *Note:* Although this B&B is technically in Harrison, much of its property lies in the town of Bridgton, and it is thus closer to the Sebago/ Long Lakes area than to the Oxford Hills; as a result, we're listing it in both chapters.

Wolf Cove Inn (207-998-4976; www .wolfcoveinn.com), 5 Jordan Shore Dr., Poland 04272. A romantic, quiet lakeside hideaway. Ten rooms, each named for a flower or herb, delicately decorated in simple, exquisite ways. Eight rooms have private bath. $110–250 in-season includes a full breakfast.

OTHER LODGING ♪ ♿ **Papoose Pond Resort and Campground** (207-583-4470; www.papoosepond resort.com), 700 Norway Rd., Rt. 118, Waterford 04088 (10 miles west of Norway). Family geared for 40 years, this facility is on 1,000 wooded acres with 0.5 mile of sandy beach on mile-long Papoose Pond. Cabins with or without bath, housekeeping cottages, bunkhouse trailers, tent sites (some with electricity, water, and sewage); rates in high season range from $26 per night for a tent site to $220 for a cottage. Amenities include a recreation hall, store, café, movie tent, canoes, rowboats, paddleboats, kayaks, fishing equipment, and a 1916 merry-go-round.

The Cape (207-539-4404; www .cape-cottages.com), 105 Cape Rd., Otisfield. Ten cottages are set in trees on the edge of Thompson Lake; the Garden House has three bedrooms and a woodstove, while number 7 is off by itself, with a screened porch over the water. $700–900 a week in-season, 15 percent less off-season.

✳ Where to Eat

DINING OUT **The Waterford Inne** (207-583-4037; www.waterford inne.com), Waterford (turn off Rt. 37 at the shuttered Springer's General Store). Open by reservation only. Come and enjoy a surprisingly sophisticated meal in this classic country inn. A four-course prix fixe dinner ($35) might include shrimp Pernod over angel-hair pasta, or crab and leek bisque and pork à la Normande with apples and Calvados. BYOB.

Lake House (207-583-4182 or 1-800-223-4182; www.lakehousemaine.com), Rts. 35 and 37, 686 Waterford Rd., Waterford. Open Tue.–Sun. for dinner from 5:30. Owner-chef Michael Myers is renowned for his elegant food served in two old-fashioned dining rooms with linen tablecloths and fresh flowers. Choose from entrées like roast duck with a triple berry sauce of blueberries, red raspberries, and blackberries ($22) or filet mignon (hand cut on the premises) with bourbon demiglaze ($30). This is a place to linger and enjoy, with wine recommendations to pair with the entrées from the extraordinary wine selection—like a Château de Clairfont Margaux with the filet mignon. For dessert, the profiteroles are lovely, or try the lemon soufflé cake with berries and lemon curd ($8). Dinner entrées $14–33.

Maurice Restaurant (207-743-2532; www.mauricerestaurant.com), 109 Main St., South Paris. Open for dinner daily from 4:30, lunch weekdays 11:30–2, Sunday brunch 11–2. Entrées also include coquilles Saint-Jacques ($14.95), scallops and mushrooms in a Mornay sauce, and rack of lamb ($19.95). Extensive wine list, $15 and up. Reservations recommended. $13.95–19.95.

& **The River Restaurant** (207-674-3800), nestled beside Snow Falls, Rt. 26 at West Paris. Open for lunch and dinner daily except Mon. Known for its creative fine dining at a reasonable price. All soups, dressings, and sauces are made in-house, and specialties include fettuccine Alfredo, crabcakes, and prime rib au jus. Entrées $11.95–18.95, including soup, salad, and vegetable side dishes.

Sedgley Place (207-946-5990; www.sedgleyplace.com), off Rt. 202, Greene. Reservations required. A Federal-style house with a well-known dining room. Five-course dinners with entrées that change weekly but always include prime rib, a fish, a poultry, and a fourth selection. Prix fixe $18.95–25.95 includes salad and dessert.

Korn Haus Keller (207-786-2379), 1472 Lisbon St., Lewiston. Lobster pie and lobster rolls are the most popular selections on a menu that also includes chicken cordon bleu, seafood, and beef. $9.95–18.95.

EATING OUT *&* **Olde Mill Tavern** (207-583-9077), Main St., Harrison. Open daily for dinner; also for lunch Sat. and Sun. Popular with local residents and families. Mexican enchiladas, fajitas, chicken Parmesan, chicken Marsala, penne Alfredo with chicken and broccoli, and burgers, among many other things on the varied menu. Entrées $8.50–22.

DaVinci's Eatery (207-782-2088), 35 Canal St., Bates Mill Complex, Lewiston. Open for lunch and dinner. Brick-oven pizza, classic Italian entrées.

Village Inn Restaurant and Lounge (207-782-7796), 165 High St., Auburn. Casual dining. Try their fried clams. $8.95–25.

& **Cole Farms** (207-657-4714; www.colefarms.com), 64 Lewiston Rd. (Rt. 100/202), Gray. Open Mon.–Thu. 5 AM–9 PM, Fri. and Sat. until 9:30, Sun. 6 AM–9 PM, till 9:30 every night in summer. No credit cards; checks accepted with ID. Maine cooking from family recipes, including fried seafood, hot chicken sandwiches, and daily specials like New England boiled dinner. Everything from soups, baked beans, and chowders to ice cream and pastries is made on the premises. No liquor. Kids can use a playground.

& **Trolley House Restaurant** (207-743-2211), 237 Main St., Norway. Open for lunch and dinner Mon.–Sat., Memorial Day–Labor Day; dinner Tue.–Sat. in fall and winter. Two attractive dining rooms decorat

ed with old photos portraying the building in its former incarnation, when it housed trolleys of the Norway & Paris Railway. Full bar, and seafood, chicken, steak, and pasta dishes, with daily specials. Dinner entrées $12.95–18.95.

✏ ⚹ **Val's Root Beer** (207-784-5592), 925 Sabattus St., Lewiston. Seasonal. Open daily 11–8 except Sun., when they open at noon. A 1950s-style drive-in with carhops and a *Happy Days* theme. Greasy burgers, great onion rings, hot dogs, and the like, and their specialty, homemade root beer. Popular summer hangout among locals.

Chickadee (207-225-3523), Rt. 4, Turner. A longtime local favorite, serving lunch and dinner daily. Specialties include seafood and beef. Entrées $3–20.

Shaner's Family Dining (207-743-6367), 193 Main St., South Paris. Open for breakfast, lunch, and dinner. A large, cheerful family restaurant with booths; specials like fried chicken, liver and onions, and chicken pie; creamy homemade ice cream in a big choice of flavors like Grape-Nut, buttercrunch, and ginger. Entrées $4–6.

SNACKS ✏ **Crestholm Farm Stand and Ice Cream** (207-539-2616), Rt. 26, Oxford. Farm stand, cheeses, honey, ice cream, and a petting zoo: sheep, goats, pigs, ducks, and more.

✏ **Smedberg's Crystal Spring Farm** (207-743-6723), Rt. 26, Oxford, sells its One Cow Ice Cream (there are actually a couple of dozen cows) in many flavors; also jams, honey, maple syrup, fruits and vegetables, cheese, berries, home-baked pies, and home-grown beef, pork, and lamb.

Springers General Store (207-583-2051), 1218 Waterford Rd., Waterford. This little country store makes pizza and soup to eat at one of the three picnic tables, and cinnamon buns and cookies.

✳ **Entertainment**

✏ **Celebration Barn Theater** (207-743-8452; www.celebrationbarn.com), 190 Stock Farm Rd. (off Rt. 117 north of South Paris). In 1972 theater and mime master Tony Montanaro founded a performance-arts school in this big old red racing-horse barn high on Christian Ridge. Summer workshops in acrobatics, mime, voice, clowning, and juggling by resident New Vaudeville artists from around the world, Fri. and Sat. in late June, July, and Aug.; tickets are reasonably priced.

Deertrees Theatre and Cultural Center (207-583-6747; www.deertreestheatre.org), Deertrees Rd., Harrison. A 300-seat historic theater, built as an opera house in 1936, saved from being used as an exercise for the local fire department in the 1980s, and restored to its original grandeur complete with perfect acoustics. The nonprofit performing arts center, run by the Deertrees Foundation, is host to the Sebago–Long Lake Music Festival concert series (see below), and the venue for dance, music, and theatrical productions through the summer, and children's shows. Also check out fine arts and sculpture in the **Backstage Gallery**, open an hour before showtime.

Sebago–Long Lake Region Chamber Music Festival (207-583-6747), Deertrees Rd., Deertrees Theatre and Cultural Center, Harrison. A series of five world-class concerts held Tue. mid-July–mid-Aug.

The Public Theatre (207-782-3200 or 1-800-639-9575), 2 Great Falls Plaza, Auburn. Professional Equity theater featuring high-quality productions of Broadway and off-Broadway shows.

L/A Arts (207-782-7228 or 1-800-639-2919; www.laarts.org), 221 Lisbon St., Lewiston. A local arts agency bringing exhibitions, community arts outreach, presentations, dance and musical performances, an international film series, and award-winning educational programs to the area.

The Maine Music Society (207-782-1403), 215 Lisbon St., Lewiston, is home to both the Maine Chamber Ensemble and the Androscoggin Chorale. A variety of performances throughout the year.

Bates Dance Festival (207-786-6381), Schaeffer Theater, Bates College, Lewiston. Mid-July–mid-Aug. Student, faculty, and professional performances.

✳ Selective Shopping

ANTIQUES **Mollyockett Marketplace Antique Center** (207-674-3939), 255 Bethel Rd., Rt. 26 at its junction with Rt. 219, West Paris. Call for hours. A two-story group shop; items priced to sell.

Orphan Annie's Antiques (207-782-0638), 96 Court St. Auburn. Open Mon.–Sat. 10–5, Sun. noon–5. If you're looking for art deco and art nouveau objects, this is the place. Tiffany, Steuben, Fiestaware, Depression glass, and much more. Three-floor warehouse sale every Mon. 10–1.

Antiques by Zaar (207-777-3800 or 1-866-868-9227), 301 Peacock Hill Rd., New Gloucester. Open by appointment only, Mon.–Fri. 8–3.

Interesting Asian furniture and home accessories, including 19th-century Chinese pieces.

BOOKSTORES ✐ **Books 'n' Things** (207-743-7197), 1570 Main St., No. 3, Oxford Plaza, Rt. 26, Oxford. Billing itself as "Western Maine's Complete Bookstore," a fully stocked shop with a good children's section.

Downtown Bookshop (207-743-7245), 200 Main St., Norway. Closed Sun. A source of general titles, stationery, cards, and magazines.

GEM SHOPS See *Rockhounding*.

SPECIAL SHOPS **United Society of Shakers** (207-926-4597), Rt. 26, New Gloucester. Open Mon.–Fri. 8:30–4:30, Memorial Day–Columbus Day. Sells Shaker herbs, teas, poultry seasoning, mulled cider mix, pumpkin pie spices, and handcrafted items.

Christian Ridge Pottery (207-743-8419; www.applebaker.com), 210 Stock Farm Rd., South Paris (marked from Rt. 26 and from Christian Ridge Rd.). Open Memorial Day weekend–Dec., daily 10–5, except Sun. noon–5. One of Maine's major potters, known for its functional, distinctive stippleware in ovenproof, microwave-safe designs: coffee- and teapots, bowls, and more; also specialty items like apple- and potato-baking dishes. Seconds are available.

Maine Discoveries (207-744-0444 or 1-877-776-2424), 356 Main St., Norway. Open Mon.–Sat. 8–4:30. The flagship store for a Maine chain that sells everything from gifts, housewares, and specialty foods to jewelry and furniture, all made in Maine.

Creaser Jewelers (207-744-0290 or 1-800-686-7633), 138 Main St., South

Paris. Open daily 10–6. Original designs using Maine tourmaline and amethyst.

Kedar Quilts (207-583-6182; www .kedarquilts.com), Rt. 35, P.O. Box 61, Waterford 04088. Margaret Gibson began making quilts as a child in England. Now she makes them for her Kedarburn Inn and for this quaint shop. The inn hosts quilting retreats Nov.–Apr.

OUTLETS **Bates Mill Store** (207-784-7626 or 1-800-552-2837; www.bates bedspreads.com), 49 Canal St., Lewiston. Open year-round; weekdays 9–4, Sat. 10–4. A genuine outlet for Bates bedspreads, towels, sheets, blankets.

Marden's Discount (207-786-0313), Northwood Park Shopping Center, Rt. 202, Lewiston. Like Reny's (see "Damariscotta/Newcastle") this is a Maine original, the first store in a Maine chain. The founder died in 2002, but the legend lives on. A mix of clothing, staples, furnishings— whatever happens to have been purchased cheaply, after a hurricane like Katrina, or, memorably, after 9/11, when designer clothes here were going at 90 percent off.

Oxford Mill-End Store (207-539-4451), 281 King St., Oxford. Open Mon.–Fri. 9–5, Sat. 9–1. Factory seconds and samples of wool coats, vests, hunting jackets, and blankets.

New Balance Factory Store (207-744-4242), 356 Main St., Norway. The running shoes you love at major discounts.

For more shops in this region, also see "Bethel."

※ Special Events

February: **Norway-Paris Fish and Game Ice Fishing Derby**, on Norway Lake.

May: **Maine State Parade** (*first Saturday*)—the state's biggest parade; theme varies annually. **Lilac Festival** at McLaughlin Foundation Gardens.

July: **The Oxford 250 NASCAR Race** draws entrants from throughout the world to the Oxford Plains Speedway; Harrison celebrates Old Home Days. **Founders Day** (*midmonth*) on Paris Hill. **Bean Hole Bean Festival** in Oxford draws thousands. **The Moxie Festival** (*second weekend*), downtown Lisbon, features live entertainment, plenty of food, and Moxie (Maine's own soft drink). The **Norway Sidewalk Arts Festival** has more than 100 exhibitors.

July–August: **Sebago–Long Lake Music Festival** at Deertrees Theatre, Harrison.

August: **Gray Old Home Days** (*beginning of the month*)—parade, contests, and public feeds. **Festival de Joie** (*first weekend*), Lewiston— music, dancing, and cultural and crafts displays. **Great Falls Balloon Festival** (*fourth weekend*), Lewiston—music, games, hot-air launches.

September: **Oxford County Agricultural Fair** (*usually second week*), West Paris—all the usual attractions: horse pulls, 4-H shows, fiddling contests, apple pie judging, and a midway.

November: **The Biggest Christmas Parade in Maine**, Thanksgiving Saturday in South Paris and Norway.

December: **Christmas open house and festivals** in Paris Hill.

BETHEL AREA

Bethel is a natural farming and trading site on the Androscoggin River. Its town common is the junction for routes west to the White Mountains, north to the Mahoosuc Mountains, east to the Oxford Hills, and south to the lakes.

When the trains from Portland to Montreal began stopping here in 1851, Bethel also became an obvious summer retreat for city people. But unlike many summer resorts of that era, it was nothing fancy. Families stayed the season in the big white farmhouses, of which there are still plenty. They feasted on home-grown and home-cooked food, then walked it off on nearby mountain trails.

Hiking remains a big lure for summer and fall visitors. The White Mountain National Forest comes within a few miles of town, and trails radiate from nearby Evans Notch. Just 12 miles northwest of Bethel, Grafton Notch State Park also offers short hikes to spectacles such as Screw Auger Falls and to a wealth of well equipped picnic sites. Blueberrying and rockhounding are local pastimes, and the hills are also good pickings for history buffs.

The hills were once far more peopled than they are today—entire villages have vanished. Hastings, for example, now just the name of a national forest campground, was once a thriving community complete with post office, stores, and a wood alcohol mill that shipped its product by rail to Portland, thence to England.

The Bethel Inn, born of the railroad era, is still going strong. Opened in 1913 by millionaire William Bingham II and dedicated to a prominent neurologist (who came to Bethel to recuperate from a breakdown), it originally featured a program of strenuous exercise—one admired by the locals (wealthy clients actually paid the doctor to chop down his trees) as well as by the medical profession. The inn is still known for at least two forms of exercise—golf and cross-country skiing.

Bethel is best known these days as a ski town. Sunday River Ski Resort, 6 miles to the north, claims to offer "the most dependable snow in New England." Powered by its snow guns (powered in turn by snowmaking ponds fed continuously by the Sunday River), the family-geared resort doubled and redoubled its trails, lifts, and lodging regularly between 1980 and 2002. Snowmaking capacity continues to expand. Mount Abram Family Resort, a few miles south of the village, remains an old-fashioned family ski area, with one of the largest snow tubing parks in Maine.

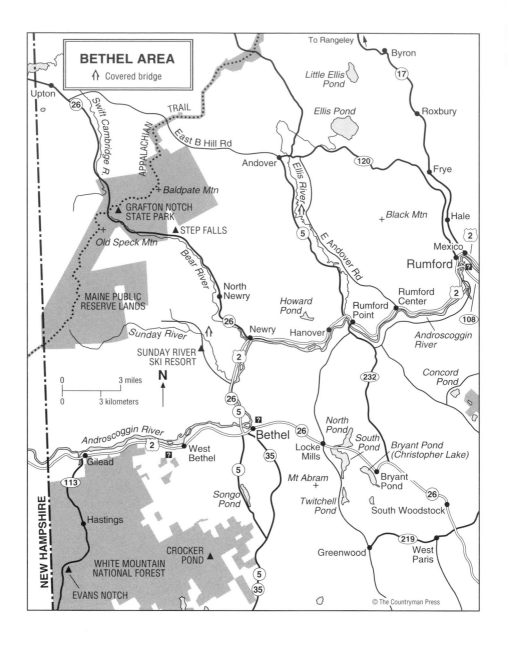

In summer, as it has been since settlement, Bethel is a natural way station—between the White Mountains and the coast, and between the lake resorts and children's camps to the south and Rangeley to the north.

Bethel is also home to Gould Academy, a coed prep school with a handsome campus, and is the summer home of the NTL Institute for Applied Behavioral Science, enrolling participants from all around the world. Hidden away in the

Newry woods, Outward Bound School also contributes to the mix that is Bethel: Several former instructors are now offering visitors outdoor-geared activities such as dogsledding, llama trekking, kayaking, and horseback riding.

For Bethel, tourism has remained the icing rather than the cake. Its lumber mills manufacture pine boards and furniture parts. Three dairy farms ship 7,000 gallons of milk per week. Brooks Bros. is still the name of the hardware store, not a men's clothier.

GUIDANCE **Bethel Area Chamber of Commerce** (207-824-2282 or 1-800-442-5826; www.bethelmaine.com), P.O. Box 1247, 8 Station Place, Bethel 04217, publishes an excellent area guide and maintains a large walk-in information center with restrooms in the depot-style Bethel Station, off Lower Main St. (Rt. 26). Open year-round, weekdays 9–5, varying hours on weekends. See *Lodging* for reservations services.

↗ **White Mountain National Forest Service** (207-824-2134) maintains an information center, with restrooms, on Rt. 2/5/26 merge, just south of the bridge over the Androscoggin River, next to Crossroads Diner and Rite Aid Pharmacy; open most days year-round, closed Sun. It offers detailed information about camping, hiking, and other outdoor activities in the national forest and other nearby natural areas. Pick up a pass for parking at trailheads within the White Mountain National Forest. Check out the natural habitat exhibit geared to kids.

GETTING THERE *By air.* The **Portland International Jetport**, served by several carriers, is 75 miles from Bethel. All major car rentals are available at the airport (see "Portland"). The **Bethel Airport** (207-824-2669), has a paved 3,818-foot runway, open year-round.

Northeast Charter & Tour (1-888-593-6328) is a 14-passenger van service that runs to the Portland International Jetport; Boston's Logan Airport; Manchester, New Hampshire; and all of New England.

By car: Bethel is a convenient way stop between New Hampshire's White Mountains (via Rt. 2) and the Maine coast. From Boston, take the Maine Turnpike to Gray, exit 63; Bethel is 52 miles north on Rt. 26.

GETTING AROUND **Mountain Explorer**. Thanksgiving to Christmas weekends and then daily through the first weekend in April, this free 28-passenger van connects Sunday River with Bethel shops and inns during ski season.

WHEN TO COME The ski season, especially Christmas and February vacations, is high season here; given Sunday River's famous snowmaking, snow is fairly dependable through March. April into June is very low season, and summer is quiet but beautiful, with golf, hiking, swimming, llama trekking, horseback riding, mountain and road biking, canoeing, and kayaking all readily available. Fall is even more beautiful, the best season for hiking. Late October through early December is, with reason, low season.

✳ To See

HISTORIC HOMES AND MUSEUMS **Bethel Historical Society's Regional History Center's O'Neil Robinson House** (207-824-2908; www.bethelhistorical.org), 14 Broad St., Bethel. Open year-round, Tue.–Fri. 10–noon and 1–4; also weekends (same hours) in July, Aug., and Dec. No charge for the changing (extensive) exhibits. Built in 1821, the O'Neil Robinson House was remodeled in the Italianate style in 1881 and also houses the museum shop. Next door is the **Dr. Moses Mason House** (open July and Aug., Tue.–Sun. 1–4), an exquisite Federal-style mansion built in 1813, proof of the town's early prosperity. Restored to its original grandeur, it has magnificent Rufus Porter murals in the front hall, fine furnishings in nine period rooms, and well-informed guides to tell you about the items you see throughout the house. Guided tours are $3 adults, $1.50 children. This complex has become a historical exhibit and research center for much of western Maine. Pick up a copy of the historical society's self-guiding walking tour of town.

COVERED BRIDGES **Artists' Covered Bridge**, Newry (across the Sunday River, 5 miles northwest of Bethel). A weathered town bridge built in 1872 and painted by numerous 19th-century landscape artists, notably John Enneking. A great spot to sun and swim. Other swimming holes can be found at intervals along the road above the bridge.

Lovejoy Covered Bridge, South Andover, roughly 0.25 mile east of Rt. 5. Built across the Ellis River in 1867, another local swimming hole (it's more than 7 miles north of Rt. 2).

SCENIC DRIVES **Evans Notch**. Follow Rt. 2 west to Gilead and turn south on Rt. 113, following the Wild and then the Cold River south through one of the most spectacular mountain passes in northern New England.

Grafton Notch State Park. A beautiful drive even if you don't hike. Continue on beyond Upton for views of Lake Umbagog; note the loop you can make back from Upton along the old road (East B Hill Road) to Andover (look for the vintage-1867 Lovejoy Covered Bridge across the Ellis River), then south on Rt. 5 to Rt. 2.

Patte Brook Multiple-Use Management Demonstration Area, a 4-mile, self-guided tour with stops at 11 areas along Patte Brook near the national forest's Crocker Pond campground in West Bethel. The tour begins on Forest Road No. 7 (Patte Brook Road), 5 miles south of Bethel on Rt. 5. A glacial bog, former orchards and homesites, and an old dam and pond are among the clearly marked sites.

Rangeley and Weld loops. See the introduction to "Western Mountains and Lakes Region" for a description of these rewarding drives. You can access both by following Rt. 2 north from Bethel along the Androscoggin River, but back-road buffs may prefer cutting up the narrow rural valleys threaded by Rumford Rd. or Rt. 232 from Locke Mills (Greenwood); both join Rt. 2 at Rumford Point.

OTHER SITES **Mount Zircon Bottle**. Walk down Bethel's Broad St. and you'll see this historic bottle-shaped lunch stand, built after the company's second bottling plant opened in 1922.

✳ To Do

BICYCLING/WALKING The **Bethel Pathway** offers a 1.2-mile round trip along the Androscoggin River beginning in the Davis Park picnic area and playground on the eastern edge of town off Rt. 26.

CAMPING In the **Evans Notch area** of the White Mountain National Forest there are five campgrounds: **Basin** (21 sites), **Cold River** (12 sites), **Crocker Pond** (7 sites), **Hastings** (24 sites), and **Wild River** (11 sites). All accept reservations for May 13–Oct. 11 through the National Recreation Reservation Service: 1-800-280-2267, Mon.–Fri. (Pacific time; from the East Coast, phone weekdays noon–9 PM or Sat. and Sun. 1–6 PM). For information, phone the **Evans Notch Ranger Station** (207-824-2134), West Bethel Rd. (Rt. 2), Bethel.

Also check with the **White Mountain National Forest Service** information center (see *Guidance*) about wilderness campsites, and see *Lodging* for commercial campgrounds.

CANOEING AND KAYAKING Popular local routes include the **Ellis River** in Andover (13 easy miles from the covered bridge in South Andover to Rumford Point); the **Androscoggin River** has become far more accessible in recent years with 10 put-in points mapped and shuttle service offered between Shelburne on the New Hampshire line and the Rumford boat landing; the **Sunday River** (beginning at the covered bridge) also offers great whitewater trips in spring. A chain of water connects **North**, **South**, and **Round Ponds** and offers a day of rewarding paddling, with swimming holes and picnic stops en route. You can learn details about these spots at Round Pond Corner Store, Rt. 26, Greenwood (and find canoe and kayak rentals).

Bethel Outdoor Adventure and Campground (207-824-4224 or 1-800-533-3607), Rt. 2, Bethel, offers shuttle service, canoe and kayak rentals, guided trips, and kayak clinics. **Sun Valley Sports** (207-824-7533 or 1-877-851-7533; www.sunvalleysports.com), 129 Sunday River Rd., Bethel, offers guided (and nonguided) kayak and canoe tours and rentals on the Androscoggin River and on local lakes and ponds. They also offer ATV tours. The **Telemark Inn** (207-836-2703) also offers guided canoeing.

Mahoosuc Guide Service (207-824-2073), 1513 Bear River Rd., Newry 04261. One- to 11-day trips, including a trip with Cree Indians in Quebec, and western trips too.

CHAIRLIFT RIDES **Sunday River Ski Resort** (207-824-3000) offers scenic chairlift rides, weather permitting, Memorial Day–Columbus Day weekend.

FISHING Temporary nonresident licenses are available at the Bethel, Newry, and Woodstock town offices; also at **Dave's Store** in Andover, **Round Pond Store** in Greenwood, **Bethel Outdoor Adventure** in Bethel, and **Sun Valley Sports** (207-824-7533 or 1-877-851-7533; www.sunvalleysports.com), 129 Sunday River Rd., Bethel. Fly-fishing is a growing sport here, especially along the Androscoggin, which is increasingly known for the size of its trout. **Sandy MacGregor** will take you fishing on the Androscoggin: www.mountainranger.com. For guiding and fly-fishing instruction also check with **Aldro French**, based at Middle Dam in Andover (www.rapidriverflyishing.com).

FOR FAMILIES 🐾 **The BIG Adventure Center** (207-824-0929), Rt. 2 and North Rd. (adjacent to the Norseman), Bethel. Summer hours, 11–11 daily; winter hours, Mon.–Fri. 2–10 PM, weekends 11–10. Indoor laser tag, indoor rock gym, two-lane waterslide, outdoor 18-hole miniature golf.

GOLF Bethel Inn Resort and Country Club (207-824-2175), Broad St., Bethel. An 18-hole championship-length course and driving range. Mid-May–Oct. the Guaranteed Performance School of Golf (PGA) offers 3- and 5-day sessions (classes limited to three students per PGA instructor); golf-cart rentals are available.

HIKING White Mountain National Forest, although primarily in New Hampshire, includes 41,943 acres in Maine. A number of the trails in the Evans Notch area are spectacular. Trail maps for the Baldface Circle Trail, Basin Trail, Bickford Brook Trail, and Caribou Trail are available from the **Evans Notch Ranger District** (207-824-2134), West Bethel Rd. (Rt. 2), Bethel; open Mon.–Fri. 8–4. Pick up detailed maps from the chamber of commerce.

Grafton Notch State Park, Rt. 26, between Newry and Upton. From Bethel, take Rt. 2 east to Rt. 26 north for 7.8 miles. Turn left at the Bear River Trading Post (Newry Corner) and drive toward New Hampshire for 8.7 miles. **Screw Auger Falls** is 1 mile farther—a spectacular area at the end of the Mahoosuc Range. Other sights include **Mother Walker Falls** and **Moose Cave**, a 0.5-mile nature walk. The big hike is up **Old Speck**, the third highest mountain in the state; up Old Speck Trail and back down the Firewarden's Trail is 5.5 miles.

Wight Brook Nature Preserve/Step Falls can be found just before the entrance to Grafton Notch State Park. From Newry Corner, drive 7.9 miles. On your right will be a white farmhouse, followed by a field just before a bridge. There is a road leading to the rear left of the field, where you may park. The well-marked trail is just behind the trees at the back. Please respect the private property adjoining the trail and falls. This scenic area on Wight's Brook, maintained by The Nature Conservancy, has been enjoyed by local families for generations.

In Shelburne there are hiking trails on **Mount Crag**, **Mount Cabot**, and **Ingalls Mountain**, and there are more trails in **Evans Notch**. For details, check the Appalachian Mountain Club's *White Mountain Guide* and John Gibson's *50 Hikes in Coastal and Southern Maine* (Backcountry Guides).

Mount Will Trail. Recently developed by the Bethel Conservation Commission, this 3.25-mile loop is a good family trip; many people choose to climb only to the

North Ledges (640 vertical feet in 0.75 mile), yielding a view of the Androscoggin Valley, which only gets better over the next 1.5 miles—climbing over ledges 1,450 feet and then descending the South Cliffs. The trailhead parking lot is opposite the recycling center on Rt. 2, just 1.9 miles east of the Riverside Rest Area (which is just beyond the turnoff for Sunday River).

HORSEBACK RIDING Sparrowhawk Mountain Ranch (207-836-2528; www .maineranch.com), 120 Fleming Rd., Bethel. Trail rides, lessons, riding packages with overnight accommodations.

LLAMA TREKKING ✎ **Telemark Inn** (207-836-2703), 10 miles west of Bethel. Treks offered Apr.–Oct. Primarily for guests of the Telemark Inn, but treks ranging from 1 to 4 days into the surrounding wilderness are available to nonguests as well. Steve Crone offered the first llama treks in New England, and we took one of the first that he offered. The llamas carry your gear, but you walk beside them.

MOUNTAIN BIKING Bethel Outdoor Adventure (207-824-4224), Rt. 2, Bethel, offers guided mountain bike maps as well as custom tours and rentals.

ROCKHOUNDING ✎ This corner of Oxford County is recognized as one of the world's richest sources of some minerals and semiprecious gems. More than a third of the world's mineral varieties can be found here. Gems include amethyst, aquamarine, tourmaline, and topaz. Mining has gone on around here since tourmaline was discovered at Mount Mica in 1821. Jim Mann's **Mt. Mann Jeweler** (207-824-3030) on Main St., Bethel, includes a mineral museum. In the cellar kids (of all ages) can explore "Crystal Cave": a dimly lit "mine" in which rockhounds can fill their cardboard buckets (for a nominal fee) and then identify the stones back in the museum. **Perham's of West Paris** (207-674-2341 or 1-800-371-GEMS), open 9–5 daily, offers maps to four local quarries. (Also see "Oxford Hills.") The **Annual Gem, Mineral, and Jewelry Show** (second weekend in July at Telstar High School) is a mega mineral event with guided field trips to local quarries.

SWIMMING There are numerous lakes and river swimming holes in the area. It's best to ask the chamber of commerce about where access is currently possible. Reliable spots include:

Angevine Park and Swim Pond (207-824-2669). The town of Bethel has created a new swimming spot open to all free of charge. It is located on North Rd., 2.2 miles from Rt. 2 (turn in at Big Adventure Center and the Norseman Inn & Motel). Open daily 10–7, summer only.

Artists' Covered Bridge. Follow SUNDAY RIVER SKI RESORT signs north from Bethel, but bear right at two Y-intersections instead of turning onto either of the ski-area access roads. Look for the covered bridge on your left. Space for parking, bushes for changing.

Wild River in Evans Notch, Gilead, offers some obvious access spots off Rt. 113, as does the **Bear River**, which follows Rt. 26 through Grafton Notch.

DOGSLEDDING **Mahoosuc Guide Service** (207-824-2073), 1513 Bear River Rd., Newry 04261. Polly Mahoney and Kevin Slater offer combination skiing and mushing trips. You can be as involved with the dogs as you want, for a day, or multiday, trips.

Winter Journeys (207-928-2026), based in Lovell. Day, multiday, and custom programs.

Skijoring. Skiing behind dogs is a specialty at the Telemark Inn (see *Lodging*).

CROSS-COUNTRY SKIING **Sunday River Inn and XC Ski Center** (207-824-2410), 23 Skiway Road, Newry. A total of 40 km of double-tracked trails loop through the woods, including a section to Artists' Covered Bridge. Thanks to the high elevation, careful trail prepping, and heavy-duty grooming equipment, snow tends to stick here when it's scarce in much of Maine. The center offers guided night skiing, rentals, instruction, and snacks.

Bethel Inn XC Ski Center and Snowshoe Center (207-824-2175), Bethel. Redesigned trails meander out over the golf course and through the woods, offering beautiful mountain views, solitude, and challenges suitable for all levels. Skating and classic trails, rental equipment, and lessons available.

Carter's X-Country Ski Center (207-539-4848), Intervale Rd. (off Rt. 26 south of the village), Bethel. Call to find out which days they're open. Dave Carter, a member of one of Bethel's oldest families and a longtime cross-country pro, maintains some 65 km of wooded trails on 1,000 acres, meandering from 600 up to 1,800 feet in elevation; an easy loop connects two lodges and runs along the Androscoggin River. Reasonably priced equipment rentals and lessons; additional center on Rt. 26 in Oxford.

Telemark Inn (207-836-2703), West Bethel. These 20 km of high-elevation wooded trails and unlimited backcountry skiing terrain frequently represent the best cross-country skiing in the area—but Steve Crone issues a limited number of passes a day, preserving the wilderness feel of his resort for Telemark Inn guests. So call before coming, and inquire about skijoring behind huskies!

Mahoosuc Mountain Sports (207-875-3786; www.teleskis.com), Rt. 26, Greenwood, rents and sells telemark skiing equipment.

See also **Mahoosuc Guide Service** in *Dogsledding*, and contact the **Bethel Ranger Station** (207-824-2134) for details about cross-country trails in the White Mountain National Forest.

DOWNHILL SKIING ✆ ♿ **Sunday River Ski Resort** (207-824-3000; resort reservations, 1-800-543-2SKI; www.sundayriver.com), Newry 04217. *Sunday River* has become synonymous with *snow*. Forty-eight miles of trails now lace eight interconnected mountain peaks, including the Jordan Bowl. Challenges include a 3-mile run from a summit and White Heat, considered one of the premier bump runs in the East. The trails are served by 18 lifts: 9 quad chairlifts (4 high-speed detachable), 4 triple chairlifts, 2 doubles, and 3 surface lifts. The vertical descent is 2,340 feet, and the top elevation is 3,140 feet. Snowmaking covers 92 percent

SUNDAY RIVER

of the skiing and riding terrain. You'll also find one quarter-pipe, one mini pipe, one half-pipe (one an in-ground competition superpipe), and four terrain parks, including the resort's signature Rocking Chair. Facilities include three base lodges and a Peak Lodge, ski shops, and several restaurants; a total of 6,000 slope-side beds (see *Lodging*). The Discovery Center ski school offers Guaranteed Learn-to-Ski in One Day and Perfect Turn clinics, Munchkins for ages 4–6, Mogul Meisters for ages 7–12, a Junior Racing Program, and a Maine Handicapped Skiing Program. A snowdeck park, two tubing runs, and an ice-skating rink are lit at night at the White Cap Base Lodge. This area is also the best spot for viewing fireworks Thu. and Sat. through most of the season. Lift tickets are $102 adults, $95 young adults (13–17), and $69 for juniors and seniors for 2 days on weekends; less midweek. Many lodging packages available.

✻ **Mount Abram Family Resort** (207-875-5000; www.skimtabram.com), Locke Mills (Greenwood). Open 9–4 Thu.–Sun., Maine school vacation weeks and holidays, and on Fri. and Sat. nights with night skiing. This remains a friendly family-owned and -geared ski area: 44 trails and slopes, with well-known learn-to-ski trails and also many black-diamond trails and a "cruiser" trail. The vertical drop is 1,150 feet. Facilities include 85 percent snowmaking; two double chairlifts and three surface lifts; and two base lodges that includes licensed daycare, cafeteria, retail shop, ski rentals, Loose Boots Lounge, a PSIA ski school, and special programs. Two of the longest runs in the state of Maine at the Flying Squirrel Tubing Park. $42 adults, $32 seniors and juniors on weekends and holidays; 6 and under free. Weekday specials. Two lift tickets for the price of one Thu. and Fri.

ICE SKATING In winter a portion of Bethel's common is flooded, and ice skates can be rented from the cross-country center at the Bethel Inn. Skate rentals are also available at the public skating rink at Sunday River's White Cap Base Lodge.

SLEIGH RIDES Bethel Inn Resort and Country Club (see *Lodging*) and **Meadowcreek Farm** (207-388-2044; www.meadow-creek-farm.com) offer sleigh rides.

SNOWMOBILING Local enthusiasts have developed a trail system in the area. Contact the Bethel Area Chamber of Commerce for information on where to get maps. Maine and New Hampshire also maintain 60 miles of trails in the Evans Notch District. **Sun Valley Sports & Guide Services** (207-824-7533 or 1-877-851-7533), 129 Sunday River Rd., Bethel, rents snowmobiles, offers guided snowmobile trips, and rents snowshoes. Also, **Fryeburg Snowmobile Rentals** (1-800-458-1838), 532 Main St., Fryeburg.

✳ Green Space

The Mahoosuc Land Trust (207-824-3806; www.megalink.net/~mlt), P.O. Box 981, Bethel 04217. Formed in 1988 to preserve land in the Mahoosuc Range and the Androscoggin Valley, the trust owns islands, shoreland, and floodplain land, along with easements on land in the eastern foothills and on the banks of a large pond.

✳ Lodging

All listings are in Bethel 04217 unless otherwise noted
The **Bethel Area Chamber of Commerce** maintains a lodging reservations service: 207-824-3585 or 1-800-442-5826; www.bethelmaine.com.

Sunday River Ski Resort maintains its own toll-free reservation number: 1-800-543-2SKI, good nationwide and in Canada; the service is geared toward winter and condo information but also serves local inns and B&Bs. Many other condos and rental homes are available in the Bethel area through **Maine Street Realty & Rentals** (207-824-2114 or 1-800-824-6024), **Connecting Rentals** (207-824-4829), and **Four Seasons Realty & Rentals** (207-875-2414). Also see **Lake House** and the **Kedarburn Inn** in "Oxford Hills."

INNS ∞ 🏕 ✐ ♿ **Bethel Inn Resort and Country Club** (207-824-2175 or 1-800-654-0125; www.bethelinn.com). This rambling, yellow wooden inn and its annexes frame a corner of the town common (for the history of this special resort, see the chapter introduction). In the past few years this vintage-1913 resort has undergone a major makeover with an eye to accommodating conferences and weddings. Some Main Inn rooms have gas fireplace. The lobby and parlor are large and formal, but inviting. The formal dining room is truly elegant (see *Dining Out*). The 61 rooms in the inn and guest houses vary widely in size and view (request a larger room in back, overlooking the mountains), all with phone, cable TV, and private bath, some with fireplace. Families should opt for one of the 48 one-, two-, and three-bedroom town houses on the golf course and on Mill Hill Rd. There's an indoor–outdoor pool (heated to 92 degrees in winter) that's great year-round; also two saunas, an exercise room, a game room, and a lounge. The 18-hole golf course, with 7 holes dating to 1915 and 11 more added by Geoffrey Cornish, is a big draw, with golf-school sessions offered throughout the season. Other facilities also include a Har-Tru tennis court, a boathouse with canoes, and a sandy beach on Songo Pond, as well as an extensive cross-country ski network. A day-camp program, free to inn guests, is offered for children in summer months. From $79 MAP per person in the inn; town houses, $199–699. Many packages are available, especially off-season. Children age 11 and under stay free in room with parent (plus $20 for the meal plan).

🐾 **Sudbury Inn** (207-824-2174; www.thesudburyinn.com), 151 Main St., P.O. Box 369. A nicely restored village inn built in 1873 to serve train travelers (the depot was just down the street). Innkeeper William White and his wife, Nancy, have made over this inn with good taste. They offer 11 guest rooms and 6 suites, all different shapes and decors. All have a private bath, television, and air-conditioning, and two suites have Jacuzzi tub. The dining room gets top reviews (see *Dining Out*). Suds Pub (see *Eating Out*) is a year-round evening gathering spot. Pets are accepted only in the Carriage House, an apartment available for rent. Apr.–Nov., $79–275; ski season, $79–350 double; includes breakfast.

🐾 **The Briar Lea Inn and Jolly Drayman Pub** (207-824-4717 or 1-877-311-1299; www.briarleainn.com), Rt. 2/26. Open year-round. One mile west of town, 5 miles east of Sunday River. Gary Brearley has turned this 150-year-old farmhouse into an attractive six-room inn, with private baths, cable TV, phones, and eclectic decor. The pub is open to the public (see *Dining Out*). The sitting area with a

fireplace, polished floors, and deep blue wallpaper is particularly attractive, as is the neighboring breakfast room. $89–129; pets $10 extra.

🐾 ✇ **L'Auberge** (207-824-2774 or 1-800-760-2774; www.laubergecountry inn.com), Mill Hill Rd. A former barn built in the 1850s for a long-vanished mansion. New innkeepers Sharon and Doron Haendel offer the same high-quality meals that have had people talking (see *Dining Out*), open to the public as well as guests. The property especially lends itself to groups because of its splendid living room, where you can enjoy a glass of wine by the fire, but it also hums along as a low-key inn. Hidden away just off the common, it's literally around the corner from village shops and restaurants. $89–249 per night for a double with breakfast.

🐾 ♿ **The Victoria** (207-824-8060 or 1-888-774-1235; www.thevictoria-inn .com), 32 Main St. Open year-round. The decor is high Victorian: lace, pillows, tasseled lamps. Each of the 12 rooms has a phone along with a TV and a wet bar hidden away in a massive armoire. A full breakfast is included. $89–229 for suites depending on season. See *Dining Out* for the restaurant.

✇ **Telemark Inn** (207-836-2703; www.telemarkinn.com), RFD 2, Box 800. It is a challenge to describe this unusual retreat, set among birch trees 10 miles from Bethel Village, 2.5 miles off the nearest back road and surrounded by national forest, with a herd of llamas, 60 huskies, four good riding horses, and a tame ox. Steve Crone is an avid naturalist who offers horseback riding (some experience required), as well as hiking, canoeing, and mountain biking; winter brings exceptional cross-country skiing and the opportunity to try "skijoring" (skiing behind huskies) and dogsledding. Meals are served family-style at the round cherrywood table supported by tree trunks. Six rooms share two baths and accommodate 12 to 17 guests. $95 per couple, $75 single with breakfast; $25 for each additional person, but really it's all about activity packages: $450 per adult, $300 per child for 3 days including trekking, hiking, canoeing, or whatever, plus meals and lodging.

☙ ♬ **Philbrook Farm Inn** (603-466-3831), 881 North Rd., Shelburne, New Hampshire 03581. Open year-round, except Nov.–day after Christmas, and Apr. Twenty miles west of Bethel, just over the New Hampshire line. The long, meandering farmhouse, owned by the same family since 1861, sits above a floodplain of the Androscoggin River with the Mahoosuc Range at its back. Each of the 19 guest rooms in the house is different, all wallpapered and most furnished with the kind of hand-me-downs that most innkeepers scour the hills for. Second-floor rooms have a private bath; third-floor rooms share. The family-style meals are as old-fashioned as the rest of the place (fish on Friday, ham and beans on Saturday night; BYOB). There are also four seasonal efficiency cottages (each different), plus two without kitchens. Pets are allowed in the summer cottages. Hiking is possible everywhere, and in winter there are miles of cross-country trails (untracked) as well as snowshoeing possiblities. $130–150 per couple MAP, plus a 15 percent service charge. B&B rates from $90.

BED & BREAKFASTS Black Bear B&B (207-824-0908 or 1-800-222-2160; www.bbearbandb.com), 829 Sunday River Rd., Newry 04261. Open year-round. Julie Bullard bought this B&B in 2004 after owning The Church Street B&B in San Francisco for 6 years. Now she's in charge of a large, attractive house with six guest rooms with private bath, less than 2.5 miles from Sunday River. Common areas include two TV/music rooms, both with fireplace. A big hot tub, snacks and hot beverages, Internet access and telephone use, a day cabin on the river, use of the outdoor pool and tennis court, and a full country or expanded continental breakfast, 6:30–11, are also included in the rates, which range $85–125 per night.

A Prodigal Inn & Gallery (207-824-8884 or 1-800-320-9201; www.prodigalinn.com), 162 Mayville Rd. (Rt. 2). Tom and Marcey White have taken over the old Douglass House, now completely renovated and remodeled, and turned it into a classy bed & breakfast, with a handsome common room with a fireplace, and elegant, deep-hued bedrooms. Six rooms with sitting areas, all with private bath, and some large bathrooms with Jacuzzi. Tom White's sculptures are scattered in the inn, and for sale; he works in a studio in the barn. $135–155 in winter, $120–140 in summer.

♬ **Chapman Inn** (207-824-2657 or 1-877-359-1498; www.chapmaninn.com), P.O. Box 1067. A find for both families and singles. Fred Nolte and Sandra Frye bring years in the hospitality business and new energy to this comfortable, rambling white wooden inn on the common. Six units now have a private bath, and four share;

there's cable TV and air-conditioning in some rooms, and a phone in all rooms. Common space includes, in the barn, a game room with a pool table and two saunas. Handy to cross-country trails at the Bethel Inn, also to village shops and restaurants. Summer: $49–99, $10 less for singles, $30 per person for the dorm, breakfast included. Winter: $59–129.

Holidae House (207-824-3400; www .travelbase.com/destinations/bethel/ holidae), P.O. Box 794. A gracious Main Street house (the first in Bethel to be electrified), built in the 1890s by a local lumber baron. Tom McGinniss offers nine units furnished in comfortable antiques, with cable TV, phone, and private bath, including a studio and a three-bedroom apartment. All have air-conditioning, and two have whirlpool bath. $40–150 double includes a continental-plus breakfast.

& **Crocker Pond House** (207-836-2027; www.bethelmaine.com/crocker pond), 917 New Bethel Rd. Off by itself on the Shelburne–Bethel Road (5 miles from downtown Bethel), facing south toward Evans Notch, this is a long, shingled, one-room-deep house designed and built by the architect-innkeeper Stuart Crocker. It's a beauty, filled with light and grace, and very quiet. Hiking and snowshoeing or just peace are what it offers, with in-room phones but no TVs. There is also a scenic farm pond. The four guest rooms all have private bath. $95 per couple ($25 per extra person) includes a full breakfast; less in summer.

♥ **The Perennial Inn** (207-369-0309; www.perennialinn.com), 141 Jed Martin Rd., Rumford Point 04279. An inviting Victorian farm-house set on 42 acres. Jordan and Darlene Ginsburg have recently renovated rooms and baths here, adding a new courtyard, screened porch, entrance, and billiard parlor. They offer five large guest rooms with pine floors and queen beds. Each has a sitting area; three have a private bath, while two share. There's also a two-room suite with shared bath, good for families. $85–195 for rooms for two, $195 for four-person suite, includes a full breakfast.

✐ & **The Norseman Inn and Motel** (207-824-2002; www.norsemaninn .com), P.O. Box 934, Rt. 2. An old farmstead with 9 light, pleasant guest rooms and 22 more units in the old barn. Guests can sit by the common room's fireplace made from local stones. The motel units are spacious; amenities include a laundry room and game room, a deck, and walking trails. $58–158 includes continental breakfast (seasonal).

SKI LODGES AND CONDOMINIUMS
✐ **Sunday River Ski Resort** (207-824-3000; resort reservations 1-800-543-2SKI), P.O. Box 450, now offers more than 6,000 "slope-side beds." There are condominium complexes ranging from studios to three-bedroom units. Each complex has access to an indoor pool, Jacuzzi, sauna, laundry, recreation room, and game room; **Cascades** and **Sunrise** offer large common rooms with fireplaces. **Merrill Brook Village Condominiums** have fireplaces, and many have a whirlpool tub. **South Ridge** also offers a fireplace in each unit, which range from studios to three-bedrooms. The 68-room **Snow Cap Inn** has an atrium with fieldstone fireplaces, an

exercise room, and an outdoor Jacuzzi; it also offers reasonably priced bunks. The 230-room **Grand Summit Hotel** has both standard and kitchen-equipped units and a health club with a pool, and conference facilities; it offers rooms and studios as well as one- and two-bedroom efficiency units. The 195-room **Jordan Grand Hotel** is off by itself but linked by ski trails as well as road, circled by the mountains of the Jordan Bowl; facilities include a health club, a swimming pool, and restaurants. Hotel prices range from $89.95 (includes a lift ticket) to $787. In winter, condo units are based on ski packages, from $59.95 per night or $299 per person for 5 days. All winter lodging rates include a lift ticket.

🖉 ♿ **Sunday River Inn** (207-824-2410 or 1-866-232-4354; www.sunday riverinn.com), 23 Skiway Rd., Newry 04261. Just down the road from the big ski resort but its antithesis: a homey, very personal place. Steve and Peggy Wight have been welcoming guests since 1971, catering to cross-country skiers and to small conferences in other seasons. A game room, sauna, and wood-heated hot tub just outside the back door are also available to guests. The 18 rooms (most with shared bath) range from dorms to private rooms in the inn or adjacent chalet. $55–95 per person includes two meals and cross-country ski passes; $25–65 per person B&B; children's rates.

CAMPGROUNDS 🐾 🖉 **Littlefield Beaches** (207-875-3290; www.little fieldbeaches.com), 13 Littlefield Lane, Greenwood 04255.Open mid-May–Sep. Arthur and Lisa Park run a clean, quiet family campground surrounded by three connecting lakes. Full hook-ups, a laundry room, miniature golf, a game room, swimming. $24–28 daily; seasonal rates available.

🐾 🖉 ♿ **Bethel Outdoor Adventure and Campground** (207-824-4224 or 1-800-533-3607; www.bethel outdoor adventure.com), Rt. 2. Jeff and Pattie Parsons have moved their base from West Bethel to their campground. RV and tent sites on the Androscoggin River (where you can swim), within walking distance of downtown shops and restaurants.

Pleasant River Campground (207-836-2000), Rt. 2, West Bethel Rd. Wooded sites, restrooms, pool, playground, and many recreational possibilities. Besides camping, Mike and Michelle Mador offer canoe and kayak rentals, Androscoggin River access, shuttle service available, and lobster boils, pig roasts, and barbecues.

Also see **Papoose Pond Resort and Campground** in "Oxford Hills." *To Do* lists noncommercial campgrounds in the White Mountain National Forest.

SPECIAL LODGING 🖉 ♿ **The Maine Houses** (1-800-646-8737; www.the mainehouses.com), Bryant Pond (reservations: P.O. Box 1138, Yarmouth 04096). Two of the three houses are located on or near Lake Christopher, the third just a short walk away. These unique, self-service guest houses are perfect for small groups or large reunions. The Maine House has nine bedrooms, seven and a half baths, a steam room, and a wraparound porch. In the Maine Farmhouse there are seven bedrooms, each with a private bath. The Maine Mountainview House features seven bedrooms, seven full baths, an indoor spa, and a fireplace. All three have fully equipped kitchen, access to the lake, canoes, and outdoor sports equipment, cable TV, VCR, and all bedding and towels. $20–50 per person per night.

✳ Where to Eat

DINING OUT ⅋ **Bethel Inn Resort and Country Club** (207-824-2175 or 1-800-654-0125), Bethel Common. Serves breakfast and dinner. An elegant formal dining room with a Steinway, a hearth, and large windows overlooking the golf course and hills, plus a year-round veranda. The menu offers a choice of a dozen entrées that might include veal scalloppine and lobster, roast duck breast, and roast rack of lamb; $16–24 including salad and vegetable.

Sudbury Inn (207-824-2174), Main St., Bethel. Dinner 5–9 seasonally. Open Tue.–Sun. year-round except Nov. and May, when it's Thu.–Sun. Attractive, traditional dining rooms and a sunporch in a 19th-century village inn. Widely respected chef Peter Bodwell is maintaining a fine reputation with a menu that ranges from chicken Sicilian, with mushrooms, tomatoes, artichokes, prosciutto, and spinach ($16), to grilled vegetables en croute, served on a bed of summer squash and carrot noodles ($14), to roast rack of lamb ($26).

L'Auberge Country Inn and Bistro (207-824-2774), Mill Hill Rd., Bethel. Open year-round, daily at 5:30 in winter. Reservations suggested. The new owners intend to find a source for fresh foie gras, to be served with a tawny port demiglaze, and continue to serve the well-loved dinners in L'Auberge's pleasant dining rooms. Entrées might include Cornish game hen with cassis and a pecan stuffing ($22), or steak, or crabcakes with a rémoulade. Entrées $18–50.

The Jolly Drayman at the Briar Lea Inn (207-824-4717), Rt. 2/26, Bethel. The inn's welcoming dining room serves dinner daily. Jenni Fredricks (who hails from England) and her husband, Richard, have transformed this restaurant into an English pub and restaurant. So, here in New England you'll find fish-and-chips and Indian-style curry, as well as other American favorites. This is a reliably good and reasonably priced place for dinner. Entrées $12–22.

The Victoria Restaurant (207-824-8060 or 1-888-774-1235; www.the victoria-inn.com), 32 Main St. Open year-round. Chef Christopher Hascall makes filet mignon and king salmon with braised rattlesnake beans, two of many dishes on his fine dining menu. Hand-painted murals adorn the walls. Entrées $22–28.

S. S. Milton (207-824-2589), 43 Main St., Bethel. Open Thu.–Mon. in winter for dinner 5–9, lunch in summer. Entrées ($16–23) might include scallops Nantucket with white wine, lemon, and cheddar cheese, topped with Ritz crackers ($16), and Boothbay fettuccine with Maine lobster, scallops, shrimp in a white cream wine sauce ($19). Children's menu.

Sunday River Resort operates several "fine-dining" restaurants: **Legends** (207-824-5858) at the Grand Summit Resort Hotel, and **Sliders** (207-824-5000) at the Jordan Grand.

Phoenix House & Well (207-824-2222; www.phoenixhouseandwell .com), Skiway Rd., just before South Ridge Base Lodge at Sunday River. With windows on a great view, pick from a list of pasta and sauces, or go for a steak, beef, or tuna. Live music in the Well in winter.

EATING OUT ✍ **Café di Cocoa** (207-824-5282; www.cafedicocoa.com), 125 Main St., Bethel. A market with breakfast and lunch items, and next door a restaurant for dinners on Fri. and Sat. in winter. Cathy DiCocco's cheerful eatery specializes in vegan and vegetarian dishes using local organic produce. In winter join them for an ethnic dinner party (by reservation only). Full bakery, juice and espresso bars, and wonderful hot chocolate. BYOB ($2-per-party corking fee).

✍ **Suds Pub** (207-824-6558, 1-800-395-7837), downstairs at the Sudbury Inn, 151 Main St., Bethel. Open year-round, from 4:30 PM daily. A friendly pub with the largest number of beers on tap west of Portland, and a reasonably priced pub menu with a wide choice of pizzas. Burgers, soups and salads, ribs and pasta. Kids' menu.

Crossroads Diner & Deli (207-824-3673), Rt. 2, Bethel. Breakfast, lunch, and dinner. This is the hangout for the loyal locals.

The Sunday River Brewing Co. (207-824-4ALE), junction of Sunday River Rd. and Rt. 2, North Bethel. Open from 11:30 daily for lunch and dinner. Dining areas surround brewing kettles and tanks. Patrons can choose from a variety of house brews to wash down soups and salads, burgers. Often has live-entertainment evenings.

Bethel's Best (207-824-3192), just west of Bethel on Rt. 2. Open from 7 AM for a full breakfast. Will deliver, and the pizza is good. Homemade clam "chowdah," chili, burgers, subs, salads, and "lobstah" rolls are also on the extensive menu.

Great Grizzly Bar and Steakhouse (207-824-8391) and **Matterhorn Wood-Fired Pizza and Fresh Pasta** (207-824-6271), both on Sunday River Rd., both ski-season only, are good options for casual dining in winter.

Cho Sun (207-824- 7370), 141 Main St., Bethel. Open Wed.–Sun., 5:30–9. Authentic Japanese and Korean cuisine, (owner Pok Sun Lee is Korean), sushi, teriyaki steaks, and seafood.

Kowloon Village Chinese Restaurant (207-824-3707), Lower Main St., Bethel. Simon and his wife are from Kowloon. Eat in or take out.

❋ **Entertainment**

Casablanca Cinema (207-824-8248), a four-screen cinema in the new Bethel Station development (Cross St.), shows first-run films.

The Mahoosuc Arts Council (207-824-3575) presents the Libbie Goodridge Kneeland Memorial Summer Series, Sunday-afternoon concerts on the Bethel common in memory of a longtime Bethel teacher. Bring a blanket; music begins at 4 PM.

Celebration Barn (207-743-8452; www.celebrationbarn.com), 190 Stock Farm Rd., off Rt. 117 north in South Paris. Programs year-round. In summer this restored barn, set on 10 acres, draws students from around the world for workshops in mime, voice, clowning, and other performing arts with public performances by students and faculty. Call for current productions.

Deertrees Theatre and Cultural Center (207-583-6747; www.deertrees theatre.org), Harrison. Late June–Aug., the stage of this restored summer theater is rarely dark. Call to check.

Also see the **Suds Pub** and **Sunday River Brewing Co.** in *Eating Out*, and *Entertainment* in "Oxford Hills."

✳ Selective Shopping

ANTIQUES **Playhouse Antiques** (207-824-3170), 46 Broad St., Bethel, specializes in antiques from Bethel-area homes. Open June–Oct.

ARTISANS **Bonnema Potters** (207-824-2821), Lower Main St., Bethel. Open daily 9:30–5:30, except Wed. Distinctive stoneware, noteworthy for both design and color: lamps, garden furniture, dinnerware, and the like produced and sold in Bonnema's big barn. Seconds are available.

GEM SHOPS This area is rich in semi-precious gems and minerals. Jim Mann at **Mt. Mann** (207-824-3030), Main St., Bethel, mines, cuts, and sets his own minerals and gems. **Mt. Mica Rarities** (207-875-3060), Rt. 26 in Locke Mills/Greenwood, is also a source of reasonably priced Maine gemstones. **Sunday River Gems** (207-824-3414), Sunday River Rd., Newry, offers handcrafted pieces with Maine gems, gemstone carvings, and more. Also see *Rockhounding* in "Oxford Hills."

SPECIAL SHOPS **Books 'n' Things** (207-824-0275 or 1-800-851-3219), 130 Main St., Bethel. A full-service bookstore in the Pok Sun Emporium.

Brooks Bros. Inc. Hardware Store (207-824-2158), 73 Main St., Bethel.

All kinds of old-fashioned hardware, along with up-to-date products and fine service.

Maine Line Products (207-824-2522), Main St., Bethel. Made-in-Maine products and souvenirs, among which the standout is the Maine Woodsman's Weatherstick. We have one tacked to our back porch, and it's consistently one step ahead of the weatherman—pointing up to predict fair weather and down for foul. A second store, an expanded version of this old landmark, is open in Locke Mills/Greenwood: even more pine furniture, toys, wind chimes, buckets, birdhouses.

Groan and McGurn's Tourist Trap and Craft Outlet (207-836-3645), Rt. 2, West Bethel. Begun as a greenhouse—to which the owners' specially silk-screened T-shirts were added. Now there is so much that an ever-changing catalog is available.

Mountain Side Country Crafts (207-824-2518), Sunday River Rd., Newry. Made-in-Maine gifts.

Philbrook Place, 162 Main St., Bethel, includes an interesting assortment of enterprises, among them **The Toy Shop** (207-824-8697); **Wild Rose** (207-824-3563), with eclectic clothing, gifts and cosmetics; **Deelz** (207-824-8697), discounted clothing; and **Brushfire Books** (207-824-2709), a new bookstore that offers Internet access.

Ruthie's Clothing (207-824-2989), Main St., Bethel. A really wonderful selection of women's clothing.

✳ Special Events

March: **Sunday River Langlauf Races** (*first Saturday*) at the Sunday River Ski Touring Center—for all ages and abilities. **Handicapped Skiing Skiathon** (*third weekend*).

April: **April Fool's Pole, Paddle and Paw Race** (*first Saturday*)—a combination ski-and-canoe event at the end of ski season.

June: **Androscoggin River Canoe/ Kayak Race. Annual Quilt Show. Biannual House Tours**.

July: **Bethel Historical Society Fourth of July Celebration. Bethel Annual Art Fair** (*first Saturday*). **Strawberry Festival**, Locke Mills Union Church (date depends on when strawberries are ready; announced in local papers). **Annual Art Fair. Annual Bike Rally**—family as well as competitive bicycle loops. The **Annual Gem, Mineral, and Jewelry Show** (*second weekend*) at Telstar High School in Bethel— exhibits, demonstrations, and guided field trips to local quarries. **Mollyockett Day** (*third Saturday*)—festivities include a road race, parade, bicycle obstacle course, fiddler contest, and fireworks, all to honor an 18th-century medicine woman who helped the first settlers. **Annual Maine State Triathlon Classic** (*last Sunday*), Bethel.

August: **Andover Old Home Days** (*first weekend*). **Sudbury Canada Days** (*second weekend*), Bethel— children's parade, historical exhibits, old-time crafts demonstrations, bean supper, and variety show.

September: **Bethel Harvest Fest** (*third weekend*).

Columbus Day weekend: **Bethel Antiques Show & Sale**.

November: **True Hometown Craft and Wares Fair** (*day after Thanksgiving*).

December: A series of Christmas fairs and festivals climaxes with a **Living Nativity** on the Bethel common the Sunday before Christmas. Free horse-drawn wagon rides on Saturdays. **New Year's Bethel**, various venues— music, storytelling, fireworks.

RANGELEY LAKES REGION

Rangeley Lake itself is only 9 miles long, but the "Rangeley Lakes Region" includes 112 lakes and ponds, among them vast sheets of water with names like Mooselookmeguntic, Cupsuptic, and Aziscohos.

The scenery is so magnificent that segments of the two roads leading into Rangeley, Rts. 4 and 17, have been designated National Scenic Byways. In summer be sure to approach the town of Rangeley via Rt. 17 and pull out at the Height o' Land. Below you, four of the six major Rangeley Lakes glisten blue-black, ringed by high mountains. Patterned only by sun and clouds, uninterrupted by any village or even a building, this green-blue sea of fir and hardwoods flows north and west to far horizons.

A spate of 1863 magazine and newspaper stories first publicized this area as "home of the largest brook trout in America," and two local women ensured its fishing fame through ensuing decades. In the 1880s Phillips native Cornelia "Fly Rod" Crosby pioneered the use of the light fly-rod and artificial lure and in 1897 became the first Registered Maine Guide; in 1924 Carrie Stevens, a local milliner, fashioned a streamer fly from gray feathers and caught a 6-pound, 13-ounce brook trout at Upper Dam. Stevens took second prize in *Field & Stream*'s annual competition, and the Gray Ghost remains one of the most popular fishing flies sold.

The Rangeley area is still reaping the rewards of these breakthroughs, which lured entire families, not just sports, to adopt the Rangeley Lakes as their second home. Hundreds of these families are still here, devoting energy and skill, as well as money, to community projects ranging from restoring the theater and expanding the library to preserving more than 144,000 wooded acres.

The Rangeley Lakes Historical Society is papered with photographs and filled with mementos of the 1880s through the 1930s, an era in which trainloads of fishermen and visitors arrived in Rangeley every day throughout the summer, to stay in dozens of wooden summer hotels and numerous sporting camps on islands and outlying lakes.

In the 1940s and 1950s hotels closed and burned, and in the 1980s many sporting camps were sold off as individual "condominiums," but the resort has continued to evolve as a magnificent, low-key destination.

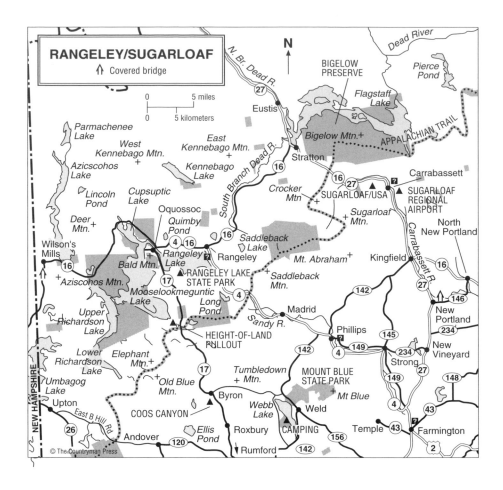

Landlocked salmon now augment trout in both local lakes and streams, and fly-fishing equipment and guides are easy to come by. Moose-watching, kayaking, and canoeing, as well as hiking and golf, are big draws. There are more shops and restaurants, events, and entertainment here than at any time since the 1930s. Still, stores and lodging places are all locally owned—no chains.

Rangeley is a town of 1,500 year-round residents, and "downtown" is a short string of single-story frame buildings along the lake. The village of Oquossoc, 7 miles west, is just a scattering of shops and restaurants on a peninsula between Rangeley and Mooselookmeguntic Lakes. The summer population zooms to 6,000, but both year-round homes and camps are hidden away by the water, and much of that water is itself sequestered in woodland.

Saddleback, Rangeley's 4,120-foot, 40-trail mountain, is New England's best-kept ski secret, averaging 500 skiers on weekends—and that's just half the number of snowmobilers in town to take advantage of one of Maine's most extensive and best-groomed trail networks. Because the area's snow is so dependable, a separate and well-groomed cross-country system has also evolved, and both ski and snowshoeing options in the backcountry abound.

The big news about this western neck of the Maine woods is that it's being preserved. Within the past dozen years hundreds of square miles have been protected through cooperative ventures involving state agencies, timberland owners, and the Rangeley Lakes Heritage Trust.

GUIDANCE **Rangeley Lakes Region Chamber of Commerce** (207-864-5364 or 1-800-MT-LAKES; www.rangeleymaine.com), P.O. Box 317, Rangeley 04970. Open year-round, Mon.–Sat. 9–5. The chamber maintains a walk-in information center in the village, publishes a handy *Accommodations and Services* guide and an indispensable map, keeps track of vacancies, and makes reservations.

GETTING THERE *By air:* **Lake Region Air Service** (207-864-5307). Inquire about services.

By car: From points south, take the Maine Turnpike to exit 75 (Auburn), then take Rt. 4 to Rangeley. In summer the slightly longer (roughly half an hour) but more scenic route is to turn off Rt. 4 onto Rt. 108 in Livermore, follow it to Rumford, and then take Rt. 17 to Oquossoc. From the Bethel area, take Rt. 17 to Rumford. From New Hampshire's White Mountains, take Rt. 16 east.

WHEN TO COME Rangeley's water is the focus of fishermen and -women in summer and fall, and its hills have good trails. Saddleback Mountain, undergoing an expansion, may make this a winter destination as well, as skiers discover the charms of a place still off the radar.

✷ To See

MUSEUMS **Rangeley Lakes Region Historical Society**, 2472 Main St., Rangeley. Open late June–Aug., Mon.–Sat. 10–noon, or when the flag is out. This is a great little museum occupying a former bank building in the middle of town. It features photographs and local memorabilia from Rangeley's grand old hotels, sporting camps, trains, and lake steamers. Note the basement jail cell and the bird's egg collection, coveted by the Smithsonian Museum.

✐ **Wilhelm Reich Museum** (207-864-3443), Dodge Pond Rd., off Rt. 4/16 between Rangeley and Oquossoc. Open July and Aug., Wed.–Sun. 1–5; in Sep. Sun. 1–5. $6 adults, 12 and under free. Guided hikes Wed. at 1. The 175-acre property, Orgonon, is worth a visit for the view alone. Wilhelm Reich (1897–1957) was a pioneer psychoanalyst with controversial theories about sexual energy. A short documentary video profiles the man and his work. The museum occupies a stone observatory that Reich helped design; it contains biographical exhibits, scientific equipment, paintings, and a library and study that remain as Reich left them. Inquire about special programs. The wooded trails on the property are open daily 9–5.

✐ **Rangeley Lakes Region Logging Museum** (207-864-3939 or 207-864-5595), Rt. 16, 1 mile east of Rangeley Village. Open July and Aug. weekends 11–4 or by appointment. Founded by woodsman and sculptor Rodney Richard, the museum features paintings about logging in the 1920s by local artist Alden

Grant; also traditional woodcarving and logging equipment. Inquire about Logging Museum Festival Days.

Phillips Historical Society (207-639-5013), Pleasant St., P.O. Box 216, Phillips 04966. Open June–Sep., first and third Sun. 1–3, and the third week in Aug. for Old Home Days; also by appointment. The library and historical society are both in an 1820 house in the middle of the village. Exhibits include a significant Portland Glass collection, as well as pictures of the town's own resort era (it had three hotels) and of the Sandy River Railroad.

Weld Historical Society (207-585-2586), Weld Village. Open July and Aug., Wed. and Sat. 2–4, and by appointment. The 1842 house is filled with period furniture, clothing, and photographs. The original Town House (1845) features farming, logging, and ice-cutting tools. Other buildings include Dr. Proctor's 1880s office (containing his equipment), a spruce gum shop that became a library around 1900, and a reconstructed garage/workshop filled with tools, artifacts, and school and post office equipment.

SCENIC DRIVES The roads in this area offer such great scenery that sections of Rts. 4 and 17 are included in a National Scenic Byway.

Phillips/Weld/Byron/Oquossoc/Rangeley loop

Rt. 4 to Phillips and Rt. 142 to Weld. Follow Rt. 4 from Rangeley 12 miles south to **Small's Falls** and on to Phillips, once the center of the Sandy River–Rangeley Lakes "2-footer" line, now a quiet residential area. Plan to come the first or third Sunday of the month, or on foliage weekends, to ride the rails behind the steam train. Stop at the **Phillips Historical Society** and ask directions to **Daggett Rock**, a massive 50-foot-high boulder that glaciers deposited several miles from town (off Rt. 142), having knocked it off Saddleback Mountain (the nearest place that matches it geologically). It's a pleasant mile's walk and has been the local sight-to-see in Phillips for more than a century. From Rt. 4 near Phillips, it's 12 miles on Rt. 142 to **Weld**, a quiet old lake village with several good hiking options, including **Tumbledown Mountain** and **Mount Blue**. You can also swim in **Lake Webb** at **Mount Blue State Park**.

Weld to Byron. From Weld, it's 12 miles to Byron. Drive 2 miles north on Rt. 142 to the STATE BEACH sign; turn left, go 0.5 mile, and turn right on the first gravel road. This is Byron Rd., well packed. Soon you follow the Swift River (stop and pan for gold) down into **Coos Canyon**; the picnic area and waterfalls are at the junction with Rt. 17. This is said to be the first place in America where gold was panned.

Rt. 17 to Oquossoc. From the picnic area, drive north on Rt. 17 for 10 miles to the **Height o' Land** (the pullout is on the other side of the road), from which the view is a spectacular spread of lakes and mountains; the view from the **Rangeley Lake Overlook** (northbound side of the road, a couple of miles farther) offers another panorama.

From Oquossoc, it's a beautiful drive west along the lakes on Rt. 16 to Errol. Roughly 20 miles west of Rangeley, be sure to detour 0.3 mile to see the

Bennett Covered Bridge (1898–99) spanning the Magalloway River in Wilson's Mills; follow signs to the Aziscohos Valley Camping Area.

Whether you are coming from Bethel or following the above loop, pick up Rt. 17 just beyond the **Mexico Chicken Coop Restaurant** (207-364-2710) on Rt. 2. Despite its exterior, this is a good way stop for Italian food, chicken, a huge salad bar, and fresh pastries.

✳ To Do

BOAT EXCURSIONS **Northern Expeditions** (207-864-3622), Rt. 17, Oquossoc, offers party-boat tours of Rangeley Lake daily in July and Aug. Ten-person limit per tour.

BOAT RENTALS Check with the chamber of commerce about the more than a dozen places in town that rent motorboats, canoes, sailboats, and kayaks. **River's Edge Sports** (207-864-5582), Rt. 4, Oquossoc, rents canoes and kayaks and offers shuttle service. **Oquossoc Cove Marina** (207-864-3463), Rt. 4, Oquossoc, offers the largest choice of motorboats. Be sure to get out on a lake one way or another.

CAMPING Wilderness camping is a part of what this area is about. The chamber of commerce lists more than a dozen sources of information about remote campsites. The **Stephen Phillips Preserve** (207-864-2003), Oquossoc, maintains 42 campsites with fireplaces, picnic tables, and toilet facilities; $16 per site per couple, $8 teenagers or extra person, $5 children. Also see **Rangeley Lake State Park** under *Green Space*. **Aziscohos Valley Camping Area** (207-486-3271) in Wilson's Mills offers easy boat access to Aziscohos Lake and the Magalloway River.

CANOEING AND KAYAKING

Rangeley is the departure point for an 8-mile paddle to Oquossoc. On Lake Mooselookmeguntic a 12-mile paddle south to Upper Dam is popular; many people portage around the dam and paddle another 8 miles down Upper Richardson Lake and through the Narrows to South Arm. Kayaks can be rented from **River's Edge Sports** (207-864-5582), Rt. 4 in Oquossoc.

A section of the 700 mile **Northern Forest Canoe Trail**, which follows the ancient water route of Native Americans traveling from New York to Fort Kent, comes through Umbagog Lake, the Richardson Lakes, and Mooselookmeguntic and Rangeley Lakes before hitting a long portage to the South Branch of the Dead River. This section takes 2 to 5 days to complete. A map, produced by **Native Trails Inc.** (P.O. Box 240, Waldoboro 04572), is available for $5.95 from the Rangeley Lakes Heritage Trust (207-864-7311) and from the Ecopelagicon Store in Rangeley.

FISHING As noted in the introduction to the "Rangeley Lakes Region," it's fishing that put Rangeley on the map. Both brook trout and landlocked salmon remain plentiful, and while early spring and September remain the big fishing seasons, summer months now also lure many anglers with fishfinders, downriggers, rods, and reels. Rangeley has, however, always been best known as a fly-fishing mecca, and both local sporting stores, **River's Edge Sports** (207-864-5582), Rt. 4 in Oquossoc, and the **Rangeley Region Sport Shop** (207-864-5615), Main St., Rangeley, specialize in fly-tying equipment; they are also sources of advice on where to fish and with whom (a list of local guides is posted). Request a list of members of the **Rangeley Region Guides & Sportsmen's Association**, P.O. Box 244, Rangeley 04970. The group traces its origins to 1896. The current chamber of commerce guide also lists local Registered Maine Guides as well as camps that specialize in boats, equipment, and guides. Guiding service averages $150 per half day, $250 for a full day. Nonresident fishing licenses, available from sporting stores, are $12 per day, $37 for 7 days.

COOS CANYON

Christina Tree

FEE-FISHING ✐ **Dunham's Pure Water Hatchery & Fee Fishing Pond** (207-639-2815), Mount Blue Rd. (off Rt. 4), Avon (between Phillips and Strong). Open year-round, daily in summer 9–6, off-season Tue.– Sun. 9–6. A great spot for kids and nonfishers to try their hand at catching rainbow or brook trout. You never miss. Equipment supplied. Fish are hatched in a hatchery on site. Dunham's also sells seafood and a variety of fish.

FITNESS CENTER Rangeley Region Health Center (207-864-2900), Dallas Hill Rd., Rangeley. This splendid new community facility offers short-term memberships for anyone wishing to use the equipment or join a variety of exercise classes.

GOLD PANNING Coos Canyon, on Rt. 17, 23 miles south of Oquossoc, is said to be the first place in America where gold was panned. The Swift River churns through a beautiful natural gorge, and there are picnic tables as well as gold-panning lessons and equipment—which can be rented or bought at the **Coos Canyon Rock & Gift Store** (207-364-4900).

GOLF Mingo Springs Golf Course (207-864-5021), Proctor Rd. (off Rt. 4), Rangeley. A historic (since 1925), par-70, 18-hole course with lake views; instruction, carts, and club rentals.

HIKING The Rangeley regional map published by the chamber of commerce outlines more than a dozen well-used hiking paths, including a portion of the Appalachian Trail that passes over **Saddleback Mountain**. The longest hike is up **Spotted Mountain** (4.5 miles to the top), and the most popular is the trail to the summit of **Bald Mountain** (3 miles round-trip); both yield sweeping views of lakes, woods, and more mountains. Other favorites are Bemis Stream Trail up **Elephant Mountain** (6 hours round-trip) and the mile walk in to **Angels Falls**—which is roughly 4 miles off Rt. 17; be sure to use a current trail guide.

In Weld the tried-and-true trails are **Mount Blue** (3.25 miles) and **Tumbledown Mountain** (a particularly varied climb with a high altitude).

MOOSE-WATCHING Rt. 16 north from Rangeley to Stratton is a good bet for seeing moose at dusk; your chances improve if you drive all the way to dinner at the **Porter House** in Eustis.

RAILROAD EXCURSION ✔ **Sandy River & Rangeley Lakes Railroad** (207-778-3621; www.srrl-rr.org), Phillips. Runs on the first and third Sunday of each month, June–Oct.; runs continuously through Phillips Old Home Days in late Aug. and Fall Foliage Days in late Sep. and early Oct., and on other special occasions. Check the web page. $4 adults, free under age 13. From 1873 until 1935 this narrow-gauge line spawned resort and lumbering communities along its 115-mile length. Begun as seven distinct lines, it was eventually acquired by the Maine Central, which built shops and a large roundhouse in Phillips. Since 1969 volunteers have been working to rebuild a part of the railroad, producing a replica of the old steam locomotive and the roundhouse, and laying 0.6 mile of track so that you can rattle along in an 1884 car just far enough to get a sense of getting around Franklin County "back when." Two original railroad buildings remain—Sanders Station and a freight shed. A depot houses railroad memorabilia, and rolling stock now includes five boxcars and two cabooses.

SUMMER PROGRAMS Rangeley Parks and Recreation Department Summer Programs (207-864-3326), open to everyone vacationing in town, include lessons in fly casting and -tying, golf, canoeing, swimming, tennis, and much more.

SWIMMING Rangeley Lake State Park offers a pleasant swimming area and scattered picnic sites. Day-use fee; free under age 12. There is also a town beach with lifeguards and a playground at **Lakeside Park** in the village of Rangeley. Almost all lodging places offer water access.

Mount Blue State Park also has a nice swimming area.

Coos Canyon, Rt. 17, Byron. It's terrifying to watch kids jump from the cliffs and bridge here, but there are several inviting pools among the smooth rocks and cascades.

Christina Tree

A PEACEFUL TREK THROUGH THE WOODS NEAR RANGELEY

✳ Winter Sports

CROSS-COUNTRY SKIING **Rangeley Lakes Trail Center at lower Saddle-back Mountain** (207-864-4309). Thirty-five kilometers of groomed trails with a skating lane and a track for classic skiing, 4 miles from downtown Rangeley. Plans to steadily increase the trails include year-round options of biking, birding, and snowshoeing. The winter of 2005–06 was the first in operation, with the company leasing land from Saddleback Mountain.

Mount Blue State Park (207-585-2347), off Rt. 156, Weld, offers extensive cross-country skiing trails.

DOWNHILL SKIING ✑ **Saddleback Mountain** (207-864-5671; snow phone, 207-864-3380; www.saddlebackmaine.com), off Dallas Hill Rd., Rangeley. This is a very big downhill ski area with a fiercely loyal following, on the verge of wider popularity under a new owner making a huge investment. Saddleback itself, 4,120 feet high and now webbed with 54 trails serviced by a quad chairlift, two double chairs, and two T-bars, forms the centerpiece in a semicircle of mountains rising above a small lake. Top-to-bottom snowmaking augments more than 200 inches of annual snowfall to keep the slopes open from December into April. Trails and slopes include glade skiing, a 2.5-mile beginner trail, and an above-tree-line snowfield in spring. The vertical drop is 2,000 feet. Intermediate runs such as Grey Ghost and Green Weaver are memorable cruising lanes. Experts will find plenty of challenge on Tightline, Wardens Worry, and the Nightmare Glades terrain; and there's an expanded a snowboard park, with a 200-foot half-pipe. Facilities include a new three-story lodge with cafeteria, lounge, ski school, shop, rentals, nursery, and mountain warming hut. Expansion here was blocked for 26 years by an impasse with the National Park Service over the segment of the Appalachian Trail that passes over Saddleback, but former president Clinton's 11th-hour moves to expand national park holdings cleared the way. The mountain's new owner has more trails under construction and a hotel in the future. $39 adults, $31 ages 13–18 and college students, $29 ages 7–12.

SNOWMOBILING Snowmobiling is huge in this region of the state. The **Rangeley Snowmobile Club** (www.rangeleysnowmobile.com), subsidized by the town, maintains 150 miles of well-marked trails connecting with systems throughout Maine and Canada. Snowmobile rentals are available from **Dockside Sports Center** (207-864-2424), and **River's Edge Sports** (207-864-5582).

SNOWSHOEING Marked trails abound on local conservation land, and rentals are available at the **Alpine Shop** (207-864-3741).

✳ Green Space

Lakeside Park, in the middle of the village of Rangeley, is a great spot with picnic tables, grills, a playground, portable toilets, and a boat launch.

✐ **Rangeley Lake State Park** (207-864-3858) covers more than 700 acres, including 117 acres on the shore. Open May 15–early Oct. There are 40 scattered picnic sites, a pleasant swimming area, a boat launch, and a children's play area; $3 adults, $1 ages 5–12.

Mount Blue State Park (207-585-2347), off Rt. 156, Weld. Open May 30–Oct. 15. This 6,000-acre park includes Mount Blue itself, towering 3,187 feet above the valley floor, and a beachside tenting area (136 sites) on Lake Webb. The lake is 3 miles wide, 6 miles long, and good for catching black bass, white perch, pickerel, trout, and salmon. There are boat rentals, and a recreation hall complete with fireplace. The view from the Center Hill area looks like the opening of a Paramount picture. Despite its beauty and the outstanding hiking, this is one of the few state camping facilities ($20 for nonresidents) that rarely fills up. Day-use fee $3 per person.

✐ **Small's Falls**, Rt. 4, 12 miles south of Rangeley. The Sandy River drops abruptly through a small gorge, which you can climb behind railings. A popular picnic spot. You can follow the trail to **Chandlers Mill Stream Falls**, equally spectacular.

Hunter Cove Wildlife Sanctuary, off Rt. 4/16, 2.5 miles west of Rangeley Village (across from Dodge Pond). A 95-acre Rangeley Lakes Heritage Trust preserve with color coded trails leading to the cove (boat launch). Bring insect repellent, waterproof footwear, and a picnic (tables are near the parking lot, and benches are scattered throughout).

Rangeley Lakes Heritage Trust (207-864-7311), Rt. 4/16, Oquossoc, open weekdays 9–4:30, Sun. 9–1. Since the trust's founding in 1991, more than 10,000 acres have been preserved, including 20 miles of lake and river frontage, 10 islands, and a

RANGELEY LAKE

Kim Grant

2,443-foot mountain. Request the map/guide and inquire about the guided hikes and nature-study programs offered.

Hatchery Brook Preserve is easily accessible, just 0.5 mile north of town on Rt. 4 (take a left on Manor Brook Rd. and look for the trailhead on your right in another 0.25 mile). We were lucky enough to hike this easy, rewarding loop in blueberry/raspberry season. Yum. There were also bunchberries and nice views of Rangeley Lake. This 50-acre Rangelely Lakes Heritage Trust was at one time slated for a 50-lot subdivision.

The Stephen Phillips Memorial Preserve Trust (207-864-2003) has preserved many miles of shore on Mooselookmeguntic and maintains a number of campsites (see *To Do*).

Also see *Lodging—Campgrounds*.

✳ Lodging

INNS AND LODGES 🐾 ♿ **Country Club Inn** (207-864-3831; www .countryclubinnrangeley.com), P.O. Box 680, Rangeley 04970. Open year-round except Apr. and Nov. This friendly retreat, set on a rise, offers the best views of Rangeley Lake of anyplace to stay in the region. The 20 simply but comfortably furnished old-fashioned rooms, all with private bath, all have picture windows framing water and mountains. Although set by the Mingo Springs Golf Course, only half its summer patrons even play golf; it was built by millionaire sportsmen as a private club in the late

COUNTRY CLUB INN

Christina Tree

1920s. Massive stone fireplaces face each other across a living room with knotty-pine walls, plenty of books, and puzzles. Owner-manager Margie Jamison is the second generation of her family to run the inn; her husband, Steve, is chef in the restaurant (see *Dining Out*). In winter you can cross-country ski from the door, and in summer there's an outdoor pool. $117 B&B for two; $173 MAP. Off-season rates available.

🐾 ♿ **Bald Mountain Camps** (207-864-3671 or 1-888-392-0072; www .baldmountaincamps.com), P.O. Box 332, Oquossoc 04964. Open mid-May–mid-Sep. This is a surviving American Plan (all three meals) fishing resort that dates to 1897, with scalloped oysters, or beef with bourbon BBQ sauce, for dinner. Nicely old-fashioned, with fireplaces in 15 cabins and a log-style dining room, a safe sand beach, tennis courts, and lawn games; guests have use of canoes, kayaks, and sailboats and can rent motorboats. Right on Mooselookmeguntic Lake, the camp exudes the kind of hospitality found only under long-term ownership. Stephen and Fernlyn Philbrick are your hosts. **Grey Ghost Outfitters** offers fly-fishing and hiking adventures from here as well. $130 adults, meals included, in Aug.; less for children and during May and June; 1-week minimum in July and Aug., but occasionally there are a few days open here and there. Some pets accepted. Friday nights feature a lobster cookout.

&. **Rangeley Inn and Motor Lodge** (207-864-3341 or 1-800-MOMENTS; www.rangeleyinn.com), Rangeley 04970. Open year-round. A blue-shingled, three-story landmark, on the site of a vanished grand hotel that stood across the road, overlooking the lake; the classic old hotel lobby dates from 1907. Charles and Dominique Goude are the new owners of this landmark, which is the physical and social heart of the village, and they have an upgrade in the works for the common rooms and landscaping. The 52 guest rooms are divided between the main building (12 with claw-foot tub, some with water views, all crisply decorated and comfortably furnished) and 15 nicely decorated motel units, some with kitchenette, whirlpool bath, and woodstove, overlooking Haley Pond. $84–140 double EP. All meals and special packages available.

BED & BREAKFASTS 🖉 &. **Kawanhee Inn** (207-585-2000; www.lakeinn.com), 12 Anne's Way, Weld 04285. Open Memorial Day–Columbus Day. A traditional Maine lodge set atop a slope overlooking Lake Webb with 10 rooms upstairs (6 private baths) and 8 cabins (one-, two-, and three-bedroom) down by the lake, with kitchenette. This is one of the most beautiful old lodges around, and its restaurant opened in 2004. Rooms $85–140 B&B; cabins $165–200 per night, $850–1,150 per week.

🦞 🖉 **Lake Webb House** (207-585-2479; www.lakewebbhouse.com), P.O. Box 127, Rt. 142, Weld 04285. A pleasant, welcoming 1870 farmhouse with a big porch, near the lake and village. Cheryl England makes the quilts that grace the beds in her three guest rooms (four in summer) and also sells them. The rooms share two bathrooms, but one has a private half bath as well. $70–80 double ($45 single) includes a full breakfast. Cheryl also operates the **Morning Glory Bake Shop** (behind the house), good for breads, moose cookies, whoopee pies, and lots more. Bakery open daily mid-June till Labor Day, weekends till Columbus Day.

Oquossoc's Own (207-864-5584), P.O. Box 27, Oquossoc 04964. Open daily year-round. For 24 years Joanne Koob has been sharing her comfy village home and its four guest rooms, making all the breads to go with a full breakfast, frequently served early enough for men to get out into the woods to work. Rooms share two baths. $75 double, $45 single, no charge for ages 12 and under.

SPORTING CAMPS Geared to serious fishermen in May, June, and September, and to families in July and August, these are true destination resorts, but don't expect organized activities.

🐾 🖉 **Bosebuck Mountain Camps** (207-446-2825; www.bosebuck.com), Wilson's Mills 03579. Open year-round. Accessible by boat or a 14-mile private gravel road, the camps are sited at the remote end of Aziscohos Lake. We have not visited since ownership changed in 1998. The lodge houses a dining room overlooking the water and a sitting room filled with books. The nine cabins have a woodstove, electric lights, flush toilet, and shower, powered by a generator that never shuts off. Three full meals are included in the rate, $129 per person per night; inquire about less expensive summer family packages; in mid-Aug., $95 per person per night.

🐾 🎣 Grant's Kennebago Lake Camps (1-800-633-4815; www.grants camps.com), P.O. Box 786, Rangeley 04970. Open after ice breaks up and through Oct. A serious fly-angler's haven located 9 miles up a private dirt road on Kennebago Lake. Large, excellent meals are served in the comfortable dining room with terrific lake views. Knotty-pine cabins are rustic, with a woodstove, screened-in front porch overlooking the water, and dock. Boat and canoe rentals available; also sailboat, sailboard, and mountain bikes available to guests at no charge. Floatplane rides and moose runs are offered. $145 per day for adults for 3 nights ($165 if you stay only 1 or 2 days) includes all meals. Children under 12, $58 per day. $15 pets.

🐾 🎣 Lakewood Camps (207-243-2959; www.lakewoodcamps.com), Middle Dam, Lower Richardson Lake, P.O. Box 1275, Rangeley 04970. Open after ice-out through Sep. Owners are Whit and Maureen Carter. Specialty is landlocked salmon and trout; fly-fishing in 5 miles of the Rapid River. Twelve truly remote cabins; meals feature fresh-baked breads, cakes, and pies. Access is by boat only, from Andover. This is very much the same place described in Louise Dickinson Rich's *We Took to the Woods*. $132 per person (2-day minimum), double occupancy, includes three full meals; $60 children under 12, $30 under age 5. $22 pets. Tax and gratuity not included. No credit cards; cash or check only.

COTTAGES AND CONDOS 🎣 Rangeley still has an unusual number of traditional family-geared "camps" and second homes available for rental year-round. Check with the chamber of commerce (see www.rangeley.com) for listings and local rental agents.

Clearwater Sporting Camps (207-864-5424; www.clearwatercamps maine.com), Bald Mountain Rd., Oquossoc 04964. Open from ice-out through Nov. Four cottages, all different, are scattered on private waterfront ledges along Mooselookmeguntic Lake; the fronts of two of the cottages open out almost completely onto the lake. This is a very private, beautiful spot. Michael and Tina Warren also offer boat rentals, a boat launch, swimming, and guide service, specializing in fly-fishing. $120 per day double; $750 per week. No pets.

Mooselookmeguntic House (207-864-2962; www.mooselookmeguntic house.com), Haines Landing, Oquossoc 04964. The grand old hotel by this name is gone, but the eight log cabins are well maintained and occupy a great site with a beach and marina. Many of the one- and two-bedroom cabins are on the water and have fireplace or woodstove. $575–725 per week.

North Camps (207-864-2247; www.northcamps.com), P.O. Box 341, Oquossoc 04964 (write to E. B. Gibson). Open spring through hunting season. Twelve cottages on Rangeley Lake among birches on a spacious lawn. Cottages have fireplace or woodstove, screened porch, and access to the beach, tennis, sailboats, fishing boats, and canoes. In July and Aug., weekly rentals only; nightly rates and rates that include all three

Kim Grant

MOOSELOOKMEGUNTIC LAKE

meals are available in spring and fall. $425–775 weekly.

Hunter Cove on Rangeley Lake (207-864-3383; www.huntercove .com), 334 Mingo Loop, Rangeley 04970. Open year-round. Chris and Ralph Egerhei offer eight nicely equipped one- and two-bedroom lakeside cabins with loft, full kitchen, some with hot tub. $140–200 per night; $850–1,100 per week.

Saddleback Ski and Summer Lake Preserve (207-864-5671; www.saddle backskiarea.com), Box 490, Rangeley 04970. There are two condo complexes at the ski resort, and most units are exceptionally luxurious, with views over the lake. Rock Pound guests have access to the clubhouse with its game room. $285–495 in winter, 2-night minimum, but inquire about 3-day ski/stay packages; lower, weekly rates available in summer.

CAMPGROUNDS For reservations in the following state parks, call 207-287-3821.

🐾 **Rangeley Lake State Park** (207-864-3858), between Rts. 17 and 4, at the southern rim of Rangeley Lake.

Some 50 campsites are well spaced among fir and spruce trees; facilities include a beach and boat launch, picnic sites, and a children's play area. $20 for nonresidents. Some private campgrounds and wilderness sites are accessible only by boat; inquire at the chamber of commerce.

Mount Blue State Park (207-585-2347), Weld. Campsites here ($20) tend to get filled up later than those in better-known parks.

Coos Canyon Campground (207-364-3880), on Rt. 17, 23 miles south of Oquossoc, is only about half an hour from Rangeley, but at these sites you feel as though you're in the middle of the woods. At $12.84 per night, tax included, the rates can't be beat, either. There's a small store and a shower house, but no flush toilets. Two fully equipped units in a log cabin are $70–80 per night.

✳ Where to Eat

DINING OUT Also see *Where to Eat* listings in "Sugarloaf and the Carrabassett Valley." **Porter House** in Eustis is a popular dining destination for Rangeley visitors.

The Gingerbread House (207-864-3602), Rt. 4/16, Oquossoc. Open for breakfast, lunch, and dinner in summer. An ice cream parlor since the turn of the 20th century, preserved and expanded by the Kfoury family. Lunch might be a barbecued pork sandwich and Black Angus burgers—or you can just come for ice cream (Annabel's). At dinnertime the tables are draped in linen, and the menu ranges from rib-eye Diane, with garlicky spinach and Dijon cognac cream ($29), to crabcakes with fresh horseradish sauce ($24). Ribs are served Friday and Saturday evenings. Dinner entrées $12–30.

Country Club Inn (207-864-3831), Rangeley. Open for breakfast daily and for dinner Wed.–Sun. in summer and fall; weekends in winter by reservation only. The inn sits on a rise above Rangeley Lake, the dining room windows maximize the view, and the food is good. Chef Steve Jamison's menu changes frequently but might include fresh swordfish broiled in wine with lemon-tarragon butter; roast duck with Bing cherry sauce is available every night. Entrées $13.95–22.95, including a salad.

Rangeley Inn (207-864-3341), Main St., Rangeley. Closed mid-Apr.–late May; otherwise, open for breakfast and dinner more or less daily. An attractive, old-fashioned hotel dining room with a high tin ceiling and a reputation for fine dining. Choices might range from chicken Marsala to filet mignon. All dinners include soup or salad. $9.95–24.95.

Bald Mountain Camps (207-864-3671), Bald Mountain Rd., Oquossoc. Mid-May–beginning of Oct. Dinner by reservation is available to non-guests in this classic sporting camp dining room by the lake at three seatings a night. The set menu varies with the night; Tuesday might be braised short ribs, Maryland fried chicken, fish cakes, or vegetarian stew. Entrées $18.95–29.95. BYOB.

EATING OUT Tavern Dining at the Rangeley Inn (207-864-3341), 51 Main St., Rangeley. Every town should have a pub like this, with reasonably priced pub grub such as steakburgers (with bacon and cheese), chicken potpie, and good chowder.

✔ **BMC Diner** (207-864-5844), Main St. and Richardson Ave., Rangeley. Open for breakfast and lunch; Sun. for breakfast only. The favorite place in town for breakfast (great omelets); friendly service.

Red Onion (207-864-5022), Main St., Rangeley. Open daily for lunch and dinner. A friendly Italian American dining place with a sunroom and biergarten; fresh-dough pizzas and daily specials.

Parkside & Main (207-864-3774), 76 Main St., Rangeley. Open 11–9 in summer; in winter open Sun.–Thu. 11:30–9, Fri. and Sat. until 10. An attractive dining room with plenty of windows and a deck overlooking the lake. Large menu with burgers, good homemade chowders, seafood, pastas, and daily specials.

The Four Seasons Café (207-864-2020), Rt. 4, Oquossoc. Open 11–9 in summer. Despite the bar that "carries on every night," a woodstove, tables with checked green cloths, and a big menu with Mexican dishes, salads, good soups, sandwiches, and vegetarian specials all make this a good place to eat. Fresh-dough pizzas are also a specialty, and Sunday brunch features omelet du jour with home fries.

Moosely Bagels (207-864-5955), 2588 Main St., Rangeley. Open for breakfast and lunch Mon.–Sat. 5:30–2:30, Sun. 5:30–noon. Great lakeside location and good bagels.

🖋 **Pine Tree Frosty** (207-864-5894), middle of Main St., Rangeley. Try the lobster roll packed full of meat. Gifford's ice cream, too.

Lakeside Convenience (207-864-5888), Main St., Rangeley. Great fried chicken, usually in at 9 AM and sold out by 2 PM.

✳ Entertainment

🖋 **Lakeside Youth Theater** (207-864-5000), Main St., Rangeley. A recently renovated landmark that offers first-run films, matinees on rainy days when the flag is hung out, art films on Thu. night. Live comedy shows in summer; off-season shows on weekends.

Rangeley Friends of the Performing Arts sponsors a July–Aug. series of performances by top entertainers and musicians at local churches, lodges, and the high school. For the current schedule, check with the chamber of commerce.

✳ Selective Shopping

Alpine Shop (207-864-3741), Main St., Rangeley. Open daily year-round. The town's premier clothing store, with name-brand sportswear and Maine gifts. (Check out its sale store down across Main Street a ways).

Books, Lines, and Thinkers (207-864-4355), Main St., Rangeley. Open year-round; hours vary depending on season. Wess Connally offers a good selection of art as well as books and music and sponsors a regular book discussion group.

🖋 **The Mad Whittler** (207-864-5595), Main St., Rangeley. Rodney Richard sculpts animals and folk characters using a chain saw and jackknife, and his son Rodney Richard Jr. executes his own whimsical creations with similar tools; chances are one or the other will be there working away. Look for the OPEN flag on the shop. Rodney Sr. lives in the neighboring house, so if no one is in the shop, "honk on the horn or bang on the door. Better yet, call ahead."

🖋 **Ecopelagicon, A Nature Store** (207-864-2771), 3 Pond St., Rangeley. In the middle of town but with windows on Haley Pond. Features ecological gifts, toys, music, and books; local history and maps.

Also see **River's Edge Sports** and **Rangeley Region Sport Shop** under *Fishing*.

✳ Special Events

All events are in Rangeley unless otherwise noted

January: **Rangeley Snodeo**—snowmobile rally and cross-country ski races. **Busch North Scene**, a snowmobile poker ride for charity.

July: **Independence Day** parade and fireworks, silent auction, cookout; **Old-Time Fiddlers Contest**; and **Logging Museum Festival Days**. **Heritage Day Fair** (*final Saturday*) in Weld Village.

August: **Sidewalk Art Show**; **Annual Blueberry Festival**; **Outdoor Sporting Heritage Days**; and **Phillips Old Home Days** (*third week*).

October: **Rangeley Lakes Logging Museum Apple Festival** (*first Saturday*).

December: **Walk to Bethlehem Pageant**, Main Street.

SUGARLOAF AND THE
CARRABASSETT VALLEY

The second highest mountain in the state, Sugarloaf/USA faces another 4,000-footer across the Carrabassett Valley—a narrow defile that accommodates a 17-mile-long town.

Carrabassett Valley is a most unusual town. In 1972, when it was created from Crockertown and Jerusalem townships, voters numbered 32. The school and post office are still down in Kingfield, south of the valley; the nearest drugstore, chain supermarket, and hospital are still in Farmington, 36 miles away. There are just 399 full-time residents, but there are now more than 5,000 "beds." Instead of "uptown" and "downtown," people say "on-mountain" and "off-mountain."

On-mountain, at the top of Sugarloaf's access road, stands one of New England's largest self-contained ski villages: a dozen shops and more than a dozen restaurants, a seven-story brick hotel, and a church. A chairlift hoists skiers up to the base lodge from lower parking lots and from hundreds of condominiums clustered around the Sugarloaf Inn. More condominiums are scattered farther down the slope, all served by a chairlift. From all places you can also ski down to the Carrabassett Valley Ski Touring Center, Maine's largest cross-country trail network.

More than 800 condominiums are scattered among firs and birches. To fill them in summer, Sugarloaf has built an outstanding 18-hole golf course; maintains one of the country's top-rated golf schools; fosters a lively special-events program; promotes rafting, mountain biking, and hiking; and even seriously attempts to eliminate blackflies.

Spring through fall the focus also shifts off-mountain to the backwoods hiking and fishing north of the valley. Just beyond the village of Stratton, Rt. 27 crosses a corner of Flagstaff Lake and continues through Cathedral Pines, an impressive sight and a good place to picnic. The 30,000-acre Bigelow Preserve, which embraces the lake and great swatches of this area, offers swimming, fishing, and camping. Eustis, a small outpost on the lake, caters to sportsmen and serves as a P.O. box for sporting camps squirreled away in the surrounding woodland.

Kingfield, at the southern entrance to the Carrabassett Valley, was founded in 1816. This stately town has long been a woodworking center and produced the first bobbins for America's first knitting mill; for some time it also supplied most of the country's yo-yo blanks. It is, however, best known as the onetime home of the Stanley twins, inventors of the steamer automobile and the dry-plate coating machine for modern photography. The Stanley Museum includes fascinating photos of rural Maine in the 1890s by Chansonetta, sister of the two inventors. Kingfield continues to produce wood products and also offers outstanding lodging and dining.

The Carrabassett River doesn't stop at Kingfield. Follow it south as it wanders west off Rt. 27 at New Portland, then a short way along Rt. 146, to see the striking vintage-1841 Wire Bridge. Continue on Rt. 146 and then west on Rt. 16 if you're heading for The Forks and the North Woods; to reach the coast, take Rt. 27 south through Farmington, a gracious old college town with several good restaurants and an unusual opera museum.

GUIDANCE **Sugarloaf Area Chamber of Commerce Kiosk** (www.sugarloaf areachamber.org), on Rt. 27 just south of Sugarloaf/USA. The kiosk is stocked with brochures on the area as well as statewide information. **Sugarloaf/USA's** toll-free reservations and information number for the eastern seaboard is 1-800-THE-LOAF; you can also call 207-237-2000, or log onto www.sugarloaf.com. Pick up a copy of *Maine's Western Mountains and Lakes Region*, an area guide available locally.

GETTING THERE *By air:* **Portland International Jetport** (207-779-7301), 2½ hours away, offers connections to all points. **Rental cars** are available at the airport.

By car: From Boston it theoretically takes 4 hours to reach the Carrabassett Valley. Take the Maine Turnpike to exit 75 (Auburn), then Rt. 4 to Rt. 2, to Rt. 27; or take I-95 to Augusta, then Rt. 27 the rest of the way. (We swear by the latter route, but others swear by the former.)

GETTING AROUND In ski season the **Valley Ski Shuttle Bus** runs from the base lodge to the Carrabassett Valley Ski Touring Center and Rt. 27 lodges.

WHEN TO COME Summer hikes and winter skiing trips work in this area, with its year-round accommodations and restaurants. Sporting camps run from spring ice-out to late fall. Whitewater rafting is at its prime in spring.

✳ To See

MUSEUMS ✒ **Stanley Museum** (207-265-2729; www.stanleymuseum.org), 40 School St., Kingfield. Open year-round, Tue.–Sun. 1–4 (closed weekends Nov.–May). $4 adults, $2 ages 12 and under. Free for seniors over 65. Housed in a stately wooden school donated by the Stanley family in 1903, this is a varied collection of inventions by the Stanley twins, F. O. and F. E. (it was their invention of the airbrush in the 1870s that made their fortune). Exhibits range from violins to the steam car for which the Stanleys are best known. Three Stanley Steamers (made between 1905 and 1916) are on exhibit.

Nordica Homestead Museum (207-778-2042), 116 Nordica Lane on Holley Rd. (off Rt. 4/27), north of Farmington. Open June–Labor Day, Tue.–Sat. 10–noon and 1–5, Sun. 1–5. Appointment-only till Oct. 15. Adults $2, children $1. This 19th-century farmhouse is the unlikely repository for the costumes, jewelry, personal mementos, and exotic gifts given to the opera star Lillian Norton, who was born here (she later changed her name to Nordica).

Nowetah's American Indian Museum (207-628-4981; www.mainemuseums .org, click on "AMERICAN INDIAN"), Rt. 27, New Portland. Open daily 10–5; no admission charge. Nowetah Timmerman, a member of the Susquehanna and Cherokee tribes, displays Native American artifacts from the United States, Canada, and South America, with a focus on the Wabanaki of Maine. A special room holds more than 300 Maine baskets and bark containers. Almost all the items in the gift shop are made by the Native Americans who run this museum.

Red School House Museum (207-778-4215), Rt. 2/4, Farmington. Open Tue.–Fri. 9–4. A schoolhouse built in 1852 and used as a school until 1958. Old desks, books, and memorabilia; also houses the Farmington/Wilton Chamber of Commerce.

Wilton Farm & Home Museum (207-645-2091), Canal St., Wilton. Open by appointment. A Civil War–era building housing displays of items owned by the Bass family, Bass shoes, period costumes, display on Sylvia Hardy ("The Maine Giantess"), and a large collection of Maine bottles, among other things.

HISTORIC SITES **Kingfield Historical House** (207-265-4032), High St., Kingfield. Open during Kingfield Days in July or by appointment. Built in 1890, this high-Victorian house museum is operated by the Kingfield Historical Society and full of period furnishings. Personal possessions and information about Maine's first governor, William King (also where Kingfield got its name). There's a country store in the barn with artifacts from the turn of the 20th century.

Dead River Historical Society (207-246-6901 or 207-246-2271), Rts. 16 and 27, Stratton. Open weekends in summer 11–3. A memorial to the "lost" towns of Flagstaff and Dead River, flooded in 1950 to create the present 22,000-acre, 24-mile Flagstaff Lake. Artifacts include carpentry and logging tools, china and glass. When the water is low you can still see foundations and cellar holes, including that of a round barn in the Dead River.

THE WIRE BRIDGE IN NEW PORTLAND

Kim Grant

Wire Bridge, on Wire Bridge Rd., off Rt. 146 (not far) off Rt. 27 in New Portland. Nowhere near anywhere, this amazing-looking suspension bridge across the Carrabassett River has two massive shingled stanchions. The bridge is one of Maine's 19th-century engineering feats (it was built in 1841). There's a good swimming hole just downstream and a place to picnic across the bridge; take a right through the ball field and go 0.5 mile on the dirt road. Note the parking area and path to the river.

FOR FAMILIES *Sugarloaf Outdoor Adventure Camp* (207-237-6909), Riverside Park, Rt. 27, Carrabassett Valley. Runs weekdays mid-July–Aug. Begun as a town program and now operated by Sugarloaf. Open to visitors (reservations required); designed for ages 4–13: archery, swimming, biking, golf, climbing, camping, fly-fishing, and arts and crafts.

Sugarloaf Dorsets Sheep Farm (207-582-8539; www.sugarloafdorsets.com), 259 Birmingham Rd., Chelsea (300 feet from the Kingfield town line on Rt. 27 headed north). On the site of a turn-of-the-20th-century sheep farm. Come see lambs being born or just stop to pet the animals.

SCENIC DRIVES **Rt. 142 from Kingfield to Phillips** (11 miles) runs through farmland backed by Mount Abraham. Stop at the **Phillips Historical Society** and **Daggett Rock** and continue to **Mount Blue State Park**; return to Kingfield via New Vineyard and New Portland, stopping to see the **Wire Bridge**.

Rt. 16 though North New Portland and Embden is the most scenic as well as the most direct route from Kingfield to the Upper Kennebec Valley and Moosehead Lake.

✳ To Do

BOATING See *Fishing* for rental canoes, kayaks, and motorboats.

CANOEING AND KAYAKING The **Carrabassett River** above East New Portland is a good spring paddling spot, with Class II and III whitewater. The north branch of the **Dead River** from the dam in Eustis to the landing after the Stratton bridge is another good paddle, as is the upper branch of the **Kennebago River**.

FISHING Through **Guide Adventures at Sugarloaf USA**, guests can take spring and summer fly-fishing lessons (207-237-6718). The village of Stratton, north of Sugarloaf/USA, serves as the gateway to serious fishing country. **Northland Cash Supply** (207-246-2376) rents canoes and is a genuine backwoods general store that also carries plenty of fishing gear. "We've got everything, clothing, souvenirs, wine, the Lottery." The **White Wolf Inn** (207-246-2922) rents canoes and kayaks. In Eustis both **Tim Pond Wilderness Camps** and **King & Bartlett Fish and Game Club** are traditional fishing enclaves. In Farmington **Aardvark Outfitters** (207-778-3330) offers a wide selection of fly-fishing gear. Inquire about fly-fishing schools at Sugarloaf.

GOLF **Sugarloaf/USA Golf Club** (207-237-2000), Sugarloaf/USA. This spectacular, 18-hole, par-72 course, designed by Robert Trent Jones Jr., is ranked among the nation's best, as is its golf school (now affiliated with Mount Snow's long-established Original Golf School). Inquire about weekend and midweek golf programs and packages.

🎣 **Junior Golf Camp** (207-237-2000), Sugarloaf/USA (5 midweek days), designed for ages 12–18, is offered several times between mid-June and mid-August.

HIKING There are a number of 4,000-footers in the vicinity, and rewarding trails up **Mount Abraham** and **Bigelow Mountain**. The APPALACHIAN TRAIL signs are easy to spot on Rt. 27 just south of Stratton; popular treks include the 2 hours to **Cranberry Pond** or 4-plus hours (one-way) to **Cranberry Peak**. The chamber of commerce usually stocks copies of the Maine Bureau of Parks and Lands' detailed map to trails in the 35,000-acre **Bigelow Preserve**, encompassing the several above-tree-line trails in the Bigelow Range (the trails are far older than the preserve, which dates to 1976 when a proposal to turn these mountains into "the Aspen of the East" was defeated by a public referendum).

🎣 **West Mountain Falls** on the Sugarloaf Golf Course is an easy hike to a swimming and picnic spot on the South Branch of the Carrabassett River. Begin at the Sugarloaf Clubhouse.

Poplar Stream Falls is a 51-foot cascade with a swimming hole below. Turn off Rt. 27 at the Valley Crossing and follow this road to the abandoned road marked by a snowmobile sign. Follow this road 1.5 miles.

Check in at the Sugarloaf/USA Outdoor Center, then head up **Burnt Mountain Trail**, a 3-mile hike to the 3,600-foot summit. At the top you'll have a 360-degree view of mountains, Sugarloaf's Snowfields, and Carrabassett Valley towns. The trail follows a streambed through soft- and hardwoods.

MOOSE-WATCHING Moose Cruises (207-237-6830) depart from the Sugarloaf/USA Outdoor Center, Wed. and Sat. evenings in early summer: View a video while sipping complimentary champagne, and ride the "Moose Express" van to likely moose-watching spots.

MOUNTAIN BIKING Sugarloaf/USA offers 50 miles of marked trails ranging from flat to vertical. Pick up maps, rentals, and information at the Bike Shop in the hotel (207-237-2000) at the Village Center. A popular ride begins here at the bottom of the lifts and is a steady downhill all the way down the access road and along the old narrow-gauge railway bed to the Carrabassett Valley Town Park. Fri.–Sun. you even avoid the schlep back up by hopping the **Bike Shuttle**. The **Sugarloaf/USA Outdoor Center** (207-237-2000), Rt. 17, is also a source of maps, info, and rentals and is the hub of a trail system designed for cross-country skiers that also serves bikers well. More adventurous bikers can, of course, hit any number of abandoned logging roads. Inquire about guided tours.

A 19.5-mile loop begins at Tufulio's Restaurant (see *Eating Out*). Park there, cross the Carriage Rd. bridge, and turn left onto Houston Brook Rd. This will lead you into the **Bigelow Preserve** on double-track logging roads. When the road forks, heading uphill with a hard right, stay instead to the left on the single-track trail. You'll go past Stratton Brook Pond and the Appalachian Trailhead. When you reach Rt. 27, head south to Bigelow Station. Follow the Narrow Gauge Trail back to Tufulio's. This is a good trip for intermediate-level bikers.

SWIMMING ✧ **Cathedral Pines**, Rt. 27, Stratton. Just north of town, turn right into the campground and follow signs to the public beach on Flagstaff Lake; changing rooms, playground. Free.

✧ **Riverside Park**, Rt. 27, 0.5 mile south of Ayotte's Country Store, is among the Carrabassett River's popular swimming holes. It features a natural waterslide and a very small beach, ideal for small children. Look for a deeper swimming hole off Rt. 27, 0.5 mile south of Riverside Park on the corner of the entrance to Spring Farm.

Also see **Wire Bridge** under *Historic Sites*.

TENNIS **Riverside Park**, Rt. 27, Carrabassett Valley. This municipal park along the Carrabassett River also features volleyball, basketball, a playground, and bathroom facilities.

WHITEWATER RAFTING See the outfitters listed in "Upper Kennebec Valley" and reserve a ride: phone 1-800-RAFT-MEE.

Sugarloaf/USA (1-800-765-RAFT) has entered into a partnership with Northern Outdoors, providing rafting trips and packages.

✳ Winter Sports

CROSS-COUNTRY SKIING **Sugarloaf/USA Outdoor Center** (207-237-6830), Rt. 27, Carrabassett Valley. Open in season 9 AM–dusk. This is Maine's largest touring network, with 100 km of trail loops, including race loops (with snowmaking) for timed runs. Rentals and instruction are available. The center itself includes the **Klister Kitchen**, which serves soups and sandwiches; space to relax in front of the fire with a view of Sugarloaf; and a rental area.

Titcomb Mountain Ski Touring Center (207-778-9031), Morrison Hill Rd. (off Rt. 2/4), West Farmington. A varied network of 19 km of groomed trails and unlimited ungroomed trails, plus a lodge with snack bar and fireplace and ski rentals. $9 adults, $7 ages 6–12, under 6 free.

DOWNHILL SKIING/SNOWBOARDING ✧ **Sugarloaf/USA** (general information, 207-237-2000; snow report, ext. 6808; on-mountain reservations, 1-800-THE-LOAF; www.sugarloaf.com). Sugarloaf Mountain Corporation was formed in the early 1950s by local skiers, and growth was steady but slow into the 1970s. Then a boom decade produced one of New England's largest self-contained resorts, including a base village complete with a seven-story brick hotel and a forest of condominiums. Sugarloaf has been expanding and improving snowmaking and services ever since. Snowmaking now even covers much of its alpine cap.

Trails number 133, and glades add up to 54 miles. The vertical drop is a whopping 2,821 feet. The 15 lifts include a gondola, a detachable quad, a triple chair, 8 double chairs, a T-bar, and a surface lift. Facilities include a Perfect Turn Development Center, a Perfect Kids school, a ski shop, rentals, a base lodge, a cafeteria, a nursery (day and night), a game room, and a total of 22 bars and restaurants.

The nursery is first-rate; there are children's programs for 3-year-olds to teens; also mini mountain tickets for beginners. In 2005–06, 1-day lift rates were $61 adults, $55 young adults 13–18, $40 juniors 6–12 and seniors. Also multiday, early- and late-season, and packaged rates. Under age 5, lifts are free.

ICE SKATING **Sugarloaf/USA Outdoor Center** (207-237-6830) maintains a lighted rink and rents skates.

SNOWMOBILING Snowmobile trails are outlined on many maps available locally; a favorite destination is **Flagstaff Lodge** (maintained as a warming hut) in the Bigelow Preserve. **Flagstaff Rentals** (207-246-4276) and **T&L Enterprises** (207-246-2922), both in Stratton, rent snowmobiles. Inquire about guided tours.

TUBING **Sugarloaf/USA** offers a Turbo Tubing Park with a surface lift on a special run, to the left as you face the mountain. Tubers fly down the mountain in a huge inner tube, channeled through bumpers of snow and sliding up a ramp to stop. It's fun but can be scary for little ones—and some adults, too.

✳ Lodging

On-mountain

✐ ♿ **Sugarloaf/USA Inn and Condominiums** (207-237-2000 or 1-800-THE-LOAF; www.sugarloaf.com), Carrabassett Valley 04947. More than 250 ski-in, ski-out condominiums are in the rental pool. Built gradually over more than 20 years (they include the first condos in Maine), they represent a range of styles and sites; when making a reservation, you might want to ask about convenience to the base complex, the **Sugarloaf/USA Sports and Fitness Club** (to which all condo guests have access), or the golf club. The 42-room **Sugarloaf Inn** offers attractive standard rooms and fourth-floor family spaces with lofts; there's a comfortable living room with fireplace and a solarium restaurant (see The Seasons under *Dining Out*). The front desk is staffed around the clock, and the inn is handy to the health club as well as to the mountain. Packages $59–299 per person in winter, from $89 in golf season.

✐ ♿ **Grand Summit Resort Hotel & Conference Center** (1-800-527-9879), RR 1, Box 2299, Carrabassett Valley 04947. So close to the base complex that it dwarfs the base lodge, this is a massive, seven-story, 120-room brick condominium hotel with a gabled roof and central tower. We like the large rooms, which, though outfitted with uninspired furnishings, feature a small refrigerator and microwave. Request a view of the mountain or you might get stuck overlooking the less attractive back of the hotel. A pair of two-bedroom suites come with a living room and kitchen. If you're ready to splurge, try one of the two palatial tower penthouses, each with three bedrooms, three baths, and a hot tub. There's a library and a health club with a large hot tub (opens at 2 PM) and plunge pool, sauna and steam room. Midwinter $109–159 per night for a one- or two-bedroom, $224–650 for suites; less in summer; multiday discounts.

Off-mountain

INNS AND BED & BREAKFASTS ✿

The Herbert Grand Hotel (207-265-2000 or 1-888-656-9922; www.herbertgrandhotel.com), P.O. Box 67, Kingfield 04947. Open year-round. This three-story Beaux Arts–style hotel was billed as a "palace in the wilderness" when it opened in 1918 in the center of Kingfield. The "fumed oak" walls of the lobby gleam. Soak up the warmth from richly uphol-stered chairs and enjoy music from the grand piano. The attractive dining room is frequently filled, and the fare is exceptional (see *Dining Out*). Look for the sink on the dining room wall, where stagecoach customers used to clean up before dining. The 26 rooms (including 4 suites) are furnished with antiques and cable TV, and many bathrooms feature a Jacuzzi. $85–175 includes continental breakfast, tax, and gratuities.

Three Stanley Avenue (207-265-5541; www.stanleyavenue.com), Kingfield 04947. Designed by a younger brother of the Stanley twins, now an attractive B&B with six Victorian-inspired rooms (three with private bath) next to the ornate restaurant One Stanley Avenue, also owned by Dan Davis (see *Dining Out*). Although there's no common room, guests are welcome to use the elegant sitting room with flocked wallpaper and a grandfather clock next door at One Stanley Avenue. In summer the lawns and woods are good for walking. Break-fast is included in the rates, $60–70.

MOTEL ✿ ✿ **Spillover Motel** (207-246-6571), P.O. Box 427, Stratton 04982. An attractive, two-story, 20-unit (14 nonsmoking) motel just south of Stratton Village. Spanking clean, with two double beds to a unit, cable TV, and phone. $85 per unit includes continental breakfast; $5 pets.

SPORTING CAMPS ✿ **Tim Pond Wilderness Camps** (207-243-2947; in winter, 207-897-4056; www.timpondcamps.com), Eustis 04936. Open from ice-out through Nov. Located on a pond where there are no other camps, and down a road with gated access, here are 11 cabins, each with a fieldstone fireplace or woodstove. Mountain biking, moose-watching, deer and moose hunting, swimming, canoeing, fishing, and boating on this clear, remote lake sur-rounded by 4,450 acres of woodland; also good for hiking. $135 single per night (plus 15 percent gratuity) includes three meals served in the lodge; family rates in Aug.

✿ ✿ **King & Bartlett Fish and Game Club** (207-243-2956; www.kingandbartlett.com), P.O. Box 4, Eustis 04936. A century-old sporting camp catering to fishermen, families, and hunters, set on its own 34,000 acres—including 18 ponds and lakes and four streams, for canoeing, kayak-ing, and moose tours. Each of the 11 log cabins can sleep two to six people; all have lake views, full bath, and daily maid service. $215 per person per night May–Oct., includes all meals, use of boats, motors and gas, canoes and safety equipment. Inquire about family rates, drastically reduced sum-mer rates, and Registered Maine Guide service.

COTTAGES AND CONDOS For a list of rental units ranging from classic old A-frames to classy condos, contact the **Sugarloaf Area Chamber of Com-merce** (see *Guidance*).

CAMPGROUNDS 🐾 ✐ **Cathedral Pines Campground** (207-246-3491; www.eustismaine.com/pines), Rt. 27, Eustis 04936. Open mid-May–Sep. Three hundred town-owned acres on Flagstaff Lake, with 115 wooded tent and RV sites set amid towering red pines. Recreation hall, beach, and canoe and paddleboat rentals.

🐾 ✐ **Deer Farm Camps & Campground** (207-265-4599 or 207-265-2241; www.deerfarmcamps.com; deerfarm@aol.com), Tufts Pond Rd., Kingfield 04947. Open May–mid-Oct. Fifty wooded tent and RV sites near Tufts Pond (good swimming); facilities include a store, playground, and hot showers. $15 tent sites, $16.50 with water and electric; hook-ups available. $225 per week for cabins.

✳ Where to Eat

DINING OUT ✐ ♿ **Porter House** (207-246-7932), Rt. 27, Eustis. Open year-round, closed Wed.. A country farmhouse located 12 miles north of Sugarloaf, drawing patrons from Rangeley, Kingfield, and beyond. Entrées around $14 range from a half duck to cedar-planked salmon and seared venison on baked pumpkin with barley risotto, under the eyes of chef Brian Anderson and partner Connie Jones. The Blue Heron Pub has a pub menu.

♿ **One Stanley Avenue** (207-265-5541), Kingfield. Closed Apr.–Dec.; otherwise, open after 5 PM except Mon. Reservations are a must. Small, but generally considered one of the best restaurants in western Maine. Guests gather for a drink in the Victorian parlor, then proceed to one of three intimate dining rooms. Entrées include roast duck with rhubarb sauce, and beef and chestnut pie including local produce like fiddlehead ferns. Owner-chef Dan Davis describes his methods as classic, the results as distinctly regional. $16.75–30.50 includes fresh bread, salad, vegetables, starch, coffee, and tea, but it's difficult to pass on the wines and desserts.

✐ **The Herbert** (207-265-2000), 246 Main St., Kingfield. Appetizers include bacon-wrapped scallops, with entrées from steak to fish and pasta. This elegant old hotel dining room gleams with cut glass; friendly service in a casual atmosphere, with surroundings that make you feel both privileged and comfortable. Marcie Herrick, the owner of the hotel, makes the raspberry pudding with butter sauce ($5).

Hugs (207-237-2392), 3001 Town Line Rd. (Rt. 27). Open mid-July–mid-Dec. Wed.–Sun. for dinner; open every night for dinner in winter. The green metal roof and board-and-batten siding keep this restaurant looking modest—but inside you'll find some great food. Past the shrine to pasta, among festoons of grapevines, you can enjoy wild mushroom ravioli with Gorgonzola, fresh tomato and spinach sauce, accompanied by great pesto bread—or chicken, veal, and seafood. All entrées can be altered, our good waiter told us.

The Double Diamond Restaurant (207-237-2222, ext. 4220), Grand Summit Hotel, Carrabassett Valley. Lounge 7–10, dinner 4–9:30. This is the most ambitious restaurant in the Sugarloaf complex, with some hits and a few misses. The menu ranges from lobster (served nightly from a tank on premises) to prime rib on Thursday. Entrées begin at $12.95.

Bullwinkle's (1-800-THE-LOAF), at the top of Bucksaw run. On Saturday night (and possibly another night) this place converts from a daytime ski cafeteria into a charming on-mountain bistro. Reserve early, because it fills up quickly in high season. We were lucky enough to ride up in the Sno-Cat during a lovely snowstorm, then we luxuriated in the warmth of the wine, the fun-loving staff, and the elegant food. Soups like lobster and corn bisque were spectacular, and the venison and lobster filled us up nicely after a day on the slopes. Two sittings per night mean you can have a drink in the **Widowmaker Lounge** at the base of the mountain before or after, watching the powder collect on the runs you'll ski the next morning.

EATING OUT The Orange Cat Café (207-265-2860), The Brick Castle, 329 Main St., Kingfield. Open 7–5. Run alongside a flower shop, this place is pretty from the door. Good coffee and homemade pecan pie are served under a map of the world; you can also get great lunch dishes, like a jalapeño chicken salad sandwich ($5.95) or bacon and cheese quiche ($3.75, or $6.75 with the soup du jour). Best hot chocolate in the valley.

Longfellows Restaurant & Riverside Lounge (207-265-4394), Main St., Kingfield. Open year-round for lunch (11–3) and dinner (from 5 PM). An attractive, informal dining place in a 19th-century building decorated with photos of 19th-century Kingfield. A find for budget-conscious families at dinner. Chicken fingers, hot dogs, and PB&J for the kids.

Mainely Yours (207-246-2999), 9 Main St., Stratton Village. Open year-round for breakfast, lunch, and dinner. Reservations suggested for dinner. Theresa Stauss used vintage photographs of Stratton to decorate. Specials include best-selling prime rib, summertime lobsters. Breakfast features bottomless cups of coffee, while Tuesday night has two-for-one dinners. Reese's pie tastes just like a Reese's Peanut Butter Cup.

Tufulio's Restaurant & Bar (207-235-2010), Rt. 27, Carrabassett (6 miles south of Sugarloaf). Open for dinner 5–9 daily; happy hour begins at 4. A pleasant dining room with large oak booths, specializing in a wide selection of pastas, seafood, steaks, and microbrews. Children's menu and game room.

The Woodsman, Rt. 27, Kingfield (north end of town). Open Mon.–Sat. for breakfast and lunch; Sun. for breakfast only. Pine paneled, decorated with logging tools and pictures, this is a friendly barn of a place. Good for stacks of pancakes, great omelets, homemade soups and subs, and local gossip.

Theo's Microbrewery & Pub (207-237-2211), Sugarloaf Access Rd., Carrabassett. Home of the Sugarloaf Brewing Company's pale ale, plus a killer root beer. Burgers, steaks, salads, and pastas also served. Monday is two-for-one pizza night. If you come for a late-Sunday après-ski meal, you might actually meet some locals.

In Farmington
Soup for You! (207-779-0799), 222 Broadway. This small restaurant offers homemade soups, salads, and sandwiches that bear the names of *Seinfeld* characters and other whimsical monikers like Don Quixote and Barking Spider. Juice bar; cappuccino and espresso, too.

The Granary Brewpub (207-779-0710; www.thegranarybrewpub.com),

147 Pleasant St. Open daily 11–10. Home of the Narrow Gauge Brewing Company, obviously popular with local college students and faculty, and featuring a large menu of soups, sandwiches, and moderately priced entrées like veggie burgers, popcorn shrimp, and French dip, a roast beef sandwich with onion soup.

The Homestead Bakery Restaurant (207-778-6162), 186 Broadway (Rt. 43). Open 7 AM–9 PM for all three meals, except Sun. and Mon. closing at 2. Dinner includes steaks, seafood, and chicken. The best place in town for breakfast and lunch, and a good dinner stop en route to Sugarloaf.

🍴 **Gifford's Famous Ice Cream** (207-778-3617), 293 Main St. (Rt. 4/27). Open seasonally from noon. Nearby Skowhegan is home base for this exceptional ice cream that comes in 40 flavors. Foot-long hot dogs also served.

✳ Selective Shopping

Grand Central Station (207-265-2893; www.grandcentralstation.com), 244 Main St., Kingfield. Selling items made by Kingfield Wood Products (www.kingfieldwood.com) and others. Open Mon.–Sat. 10–6, Sun. 11–3. A trove of wooden furniture, housewares, and needlepoint supplies.

🍴 **Devaney, Doak & Garret Booksellers** (207-778-3454), 193 Broadway, Farmington. Open daily. A bookstore worthy of a college town, and one with a good children's section. Music and comfortable seating invite lingering.

Sugarwood Gallery (207-778-9105), 248 Broadway, Farmington. A cooperative gallery showing the work of local artists, mostly woodworkers, with stained glass, pottery, and fabric as well.

Mainestone Jewelry (207-778-6560), 179 Broadway, Farmington. Ron and Cindy Gelinas craft much of the jewelry here—made from Maine-mined gems—and carry the work of other local craftspeople. Local artists' work is exhibited, too.

✳ Special Events

January: **White White World Winter Carnival**—Great Whatever Bodyslide, snow sculpture contest, Annual Dummy Jump, and discounts at Sugarloaf/USA.

March: **St. Patrick's Day Leprechaun Loppet**—a 15 km citizens' cross-country race at Sugarloaf/USA Outdoor Center.

April: **Easter Festival at Sugarloaf**—costume parade, Easter egg hunt on the slopes, and sunrise service on the summit. **Reggae Fest weekend**.

June: **Family Fun Days**, Stratton—games and children's events, live entertainment, fireworks.

Late July: **Kingfield Days Celebration**—4 days with parade, art exhibits, potluck supper.

August: **Old Home Days** in Stratton, Eustis, and Flagstaff. **Weekend jazz series**, Sugarloaf/USA.

September: **Franklin County Fair**, Farmington.

October: **Skiers' Homecoming Weekend**, Sugarloaf Mountain.

December: **Blues Festival** at Sugarloaf. **Yellow-Nosed Vole Day**, Sugarloaf Mountain. **Chester Greenwood Day**, Farmington—honors the local inventor of the earmuff with a parade and variety show in Farmington.

The Kennebec Valley

AUGUSTA AND MID-MAINE, INCLUDING
THE BELGRADE LAKES REGION

THE UPPER KENNEBEC VALLEY AND
MOOSE RIVER VALLEY, INCLUDING
THE FORKS AND JACKMAN

Kim Grant

AUGUSTA AND MID-MAINE
INCLUDING THE BELGRADE LAKES REGION

Augusta is elusive. Your approach from the interstate is up a commercial strip. The capitol dome is clearly visible, just a couple of blocks away. Then comes a confusing roundabout, and before you know it you're high above the Kennebec, looking back at this small city, rising in tiers above the river. What you've just missed is one the best state museums in New England, for starters.

If time permits, approach Augusta via the Kennebec instead of the highway. Follow Rt. 201, the old river road, at least for 6 miles from Gardiner up through Hallowell's mid-19th-century Water Street, lined with antiques and specialty shops and restaurants. However you come, find the Maine State Museum, which does an excellent job of showcasing Maine's natural history and traditional industries, as well as tracing human habitation back 12,000 years.

Augusta and neighboring Hallowell both mark the site of Native American villages. In 1625 the Pilgrims came here to trade "seven hundred pounds of good beaver and some other furs" with the Wabanaki for a "shallop's load of corn." They procured a grant for a strip of land 15 miles wide on either side of the Kennebec, built a storehouse, and with the proceeds of their beaver trade were soon able to pay off their London creditors.

With the decline of the fur trade and rising hostilities with the Wabanaki, the tract of land was sold to four Boston merchants and it wasn't until 1754, when the British constructed Fort Western (now reconstructed), that serious settlement began. Augusta was selected as the nascent state's capital in 1827, for the same reasons that so many Maine visitors and residents tend to pass through it whether they're headed up or down the coast as well as into or out of Maine's interior. It's a pivotal crossroads.

The statehouse, originally designed by Charles Bulfinch and built of granite from neighboring Hallowell, was completed in 1832 (it's been expanded and largely rebuilt since). During the mid–19th century, this area boomed: Some 500 boats were built along the river between Winslow and Gardiner, and river traffic between Augusta and Boston thrived.

This Lower Kennebec Valley remains rolling, open farmland with breathtaking views from its ridge roads, spotted with surprisingly large spring-fed lakes. It's

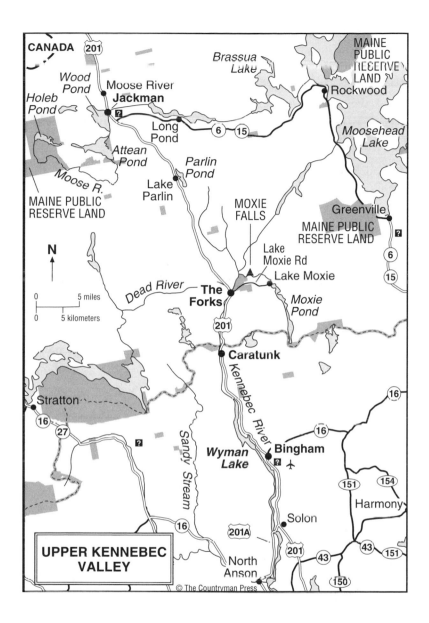

UPPER KENNEBEC VALLEY

© The Countryman Press

the site of numerous (now vanished) 19th-century summer hotels and boarding-houses and still-thriving kids' summer camps. The Belgrade Lakes Region, just north of Augusta, remains a low-key *On Golden Pond* kind of resort with old-style family-geared "sporting camps," summer rental cottages, and widely scattered B&Bs. East of the city, the China Lakes is another old low-profile summer haven. Golf courses (former farms) are proliferating, and summer theater can be found in Monmouth, west of Augusta, upriver in Waterville, and farther upriver in Skowhegan.

GUIDANCE Kennebec Valley Chamber of Commerce (207-623-4559; www .augustamaine.com or www.kennebecvalley.org), with a pamphlet-stocked office in the civic center complex just off I-95 (Rt. 27 exit), publishes the *Kennebec Valley Guidebook*.

Belgrade Lakes Region Business Group, Inc. (207-4952744; www.belgrade lakesmaine.com). The most visitor-oriented local chamber with an excellent web site and annual guide; also a seasonal information booth on Rt. 27 south of Belgrade.

Mid-Maine Chamber of Commerce (207-873-3315; www.midmainechamber .com) publishes a Waterville area guide.

GETTING THERE *By air:* **The Augusta State Airport** is served by U.S. Airways Express, which is operated by **Colgan Air** (207-623-7527).

By bus: **Vermont Transit** (1-800-451-3292) serves Augusta and Waterville.

By car: You don't have to take the Maine Turnpike to reach the Augusta area; from points south, Rt. 295 is both quicker and cheaper (I-95 and the Maine Turnpike merge just south of Augusta). Note the new bridge, completed in 2004, facilitating access to Rt. 3 east.

SUGGESTED READING *A Midwife's Tale*, a Pulitzer Prize winner by Laurel Thatcher Ulrich, vividly describes life in this area 1785–1812. *Empire Falls*, a Pulitzer Prize novel by Richard Russo, describes current life in a town resembling Waterville.

STREET SCENE, HALLOWELL

Christina Tree

✳ Villages

Richmond (population: 3,400). I-295 exit 43 is a popular exit, because many residents of the Damariscotta area use it as a scenic shortcut rather than battling coastal traffic. Onion-domed churches suggest a Russian population, now dwindling from its high of 500 in the 1960s. No trace remains of 18th-century Fort Richmond, which was attacked in 1750; 13 captives were taken. It was rebuilt and in 1753 served as site of a peace conference with the Wabanaki of eastern Maine. The present village is clustered compactly between the railroad tracks and the river. Near the town landing you can rent a kayak to circle Swan Island just offshore, but to land on it requires a reservation. Cross the bridge and visit the **Pownalborough Court**

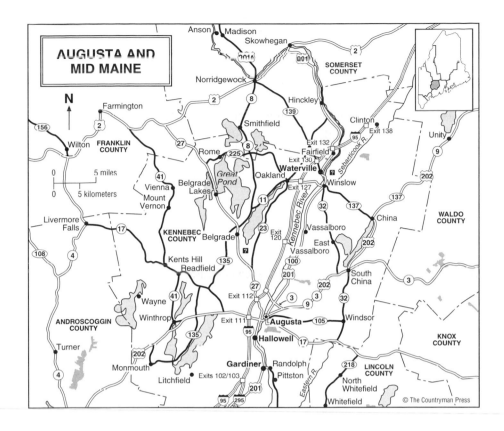

House, which we have described in "Wiscasset Area," a remarkable museum conveying a sense of this area in the 18th century. It's just upriver on Rt. 128.

Hallowell (www.hallowell.org). Two miles south of Augusta, this "city" (population: 2,467), with its line of brick two- and three-story buildings along the Kennebec River, looks much the way it did at the time this, not Augusta, was the region's commercial center. Shipbuilding and granite quarrying were the big industries here, along with ice. Residential streets, stepped into the slope above the shops, are worth driving to see fine houses and churches dating to every decade in the 19th century. The city's revival dates from the 1970s. A road-widening proposal threatened to level most of Water Street, but residents rallied; the anniversary of their protest, the last weekend in July, is now observed as Old Hallowell Day. Walk in Vaughan Woods, part of the city's most historic estate, dating to the 18th century. Water Street, now all a National Historic District, is lined with two- and three-story mid-19th-century buildings, housing quality, individually owned shops (no chain stores) and the best restaurants around.

Gardiner (population: 6,198). Sited at the confluence of the Kennebec River and Cobbosseecontee Stream, this old industrial (shoe, textile, and paper) town has been hovering on the verge of renaissance for more than a decade. The **Al Diner** is a draw for travelers and locals alike, as are performances at the **Johnson Hall Performing Arts Center** and the increasingly varied shopping along Maine Street.

Waterville. Twenty-five miles north of Augusta on the Kennebec River, Waterville (population: 17,200) is an old mill town with an interesting ethnic mix, restaurants and shopping worth finding in the downtown beyond the commercial strip, and home to prestigious Colby College (better posted than the downtown) with its small but distinguished art museum. Waterville is the thinly disguised subject of Richard Russo's best-selling novel *Empire Falls*. Check out the **Waterville-Winslow Two Cent Bridge**, Front St.—one of the only known remaining toll footbridges in the country. The toll taker's house is on Waterville side. Free. The **Redington Museum and Apothecary** (207-872-9439), 64 Silver St. (open mid-May–Sep., Tue.–Sat. 10–2) houses the local historical collection: furniture, Civil War and Native American relics, a children's room, period rooms, and a 19th-century apothecary. **Colby College** (207-872-3000; www .colby.edu) is the pride of the city. Founded in 1813, it enrolls 1,821 students at its 714-acre campus, with brick ivy-covered buildings and a 128-acre arboretum and bird sanctuary with nature trails and a picnic area and the 274-seat Strider Theater, offering performances throughout the year. For a self-guided tour, stop by admissions. Also see the **Colby College Museum of Art** under *To See*.

Belgrade Lakes. At the heart of the seven Belgrade Lakes is Belgrade Village, and at the heart of Belgrade Lakes Village is **Day's Store** (207-495-2205). Open year-round, recently expanded to serve as general store; state liquor store; fishing license, gear, boot, and gift source; and rainy-day mecca. The Belgrade chain of lakes consists of East, North, Great, Long, McGrath, and Salmon Ponds and Messalonskee Lake.

Winthrop (population: 6,232). A proud town with 12 lakes and many summer cottages within its boundaries, Winthrop seems to be thriving despite closure of the woolen mill. Shops and restaurants here are worth checking. The downtown air is frequently filled with the aroma of roasting Cobbesee Coffee.

✳ To See

In Waterville
&. **Colby College Museum of Art** (207-872-3228), Colby College. Open Mon.–Sat. 10–4:30, Sun. noon–4:30. Free. Founded in 1959, this wonderful museum has a permanent collection of 18th-, 19th-, and 20th-century art that is displayed in spacious, appealing galleries. An 11-gallery addition houses some 150 works from the permanent collection, which had previously remained in storage. Three exhibit 18th-century work, two house 19th-century paintings and sculpture, another is for impressionist paintings, two are for primitive 19th-century work, and two galleries are devoted to 54 works by John Marin, who spent most of his summers in Maine; much of his work in oils and watercolors reflects Maine subjects, from Mount Katahdin to seascapes. The Paul J. Schupf Wing rotates more than 400 paintings and sculptures by artist Alex Katz. The museum also offers

IN AUGUSTA

✦ ♿ **Maine State Museum** (207-287-2301; www.mainestatemuseum.org), State House Complex, marked from Sewall St., also accessible from State St. (Rt. 201/27). Open Tue.–Fri. 9–5, Sat. 10–4. $2 adults, $1 ages 6–18, $1 seniors. Maine's best-kept secret, this is a superb and fairly large museum, just a few blocks off the interstate but badly posted. It's well worth finding, especially if there are children along.

The *Back to Nature* exhibit features animals such as the lynx and snowshoe rabbit, deer, moose, beaver, and birds in their convincingly detailed habitats (the trout are real) with plenty of sound effects. The *Maine Bounty* exhibits depict the way the state's natural resources have been developed through fishing, agriculture, granite quarrying, ice harvesting, shipbuilding, and lumbering. Exhibits include a gigantic wagon used to haul stone from quarries and the equally huge Lombard Hauler and 1846 narrow-gauge locomotive Lion, used to transport lumber. Archival films such as *From Stump to Ship* (narrated by Tim Sample) bring the era to life. *Made in Maine* depicts more than a dozen 19th-century industrial scenes: textile mills and shops producing shoes, guns, fishing rods, and more, again with sound effects. Our favorite exhibit, *12,000 Years in Maine*, traces the story of human habitation in the state from the Paleo Indians down through the "ceramic period" (3,000 BC–AD 500) with reproductions of petroglyphs and genuine artifacts. This fascinating exhibit also dramatizes early European explorations and displays 19th-century Penobscot and Passamaquoddy craftsmanship, from beaded moccasins and highly decorative bent birch boxes to birch-bark canoes.

From I-95 exit 109 follow Eastern Ave. (Rt. 17/202) and turn right at the light across from the armory (posted for the capitol complex). Follow signs for the capitol until you see the museum posted (a right turn onto Sewall St.) and turn into the parking lot. The museum is in the low-slung modern building that also houses the state library and archives. If you miss the first turn, continue around the rotary, take Rt. 27/201 south, then make your first right after passing the capitol. This takes you to the other side of the same parking lot.

Tours of the State House (open by reservation 9–1) and of the governor's mansion, Blaine House (open Tue.–Thu. for half-hour guided tours by reservation at 2, 2:30, and 3), are arranged by calling the museum.

Colby College

COLBY COLLEGE MUSEUM OF ART

special exhibits, gallery talks, a museum shop, lectures, and receptions throughout the year.

In Winslow

Fort Halifax, Rt. 201 (1 mile south of the Waterville-Winslow Bridge at the junction of the Kennebec and Sebasticook Rivers). Just a blockhouse remains, but it's original, built in 1754—the oldest blockhouse in the United States. There's also a park with picnic tables here.

Also see **L. C. Bates Museum** in Hinckley, described in "Upper Kennebec."

FOR FAMILIES ✔ **Old Fort Western** (207-626-2385; www.oldfortwestern.org), City Center Plaza, 16 Cony St., Augusta. Open Memorial Day–July 3, daily 1–4; July 4–Labor Day, weekdays 10–4, weekends 1–4; Labor Day–Columbus Day, 1–4 weekends only; Nov.–May, first Sun. of every month, 1–3. $5 per adult, $4 seniors, $3 ages 6–16. The original 16-room garrison house has been restored to reflect its use as a fort, trading post, and lodge from 1754 to 1810. The blockhouse and stockade are reproductions, but the main house (barracks and store) are original. The fort is a designated National Historic Landmark and the oldest surviving wooden fort in New England. Costumed characters answer questions and demonstrate 18th-century domestic activities. Many special events.

✔ **Children's Discovery Museum** (207-622-2209), 265 Water St., Augusta. Open Tue.–Thu. 9–4, Fri. 9–8, Sat. 10–4, and Sun. 1–4; extended hours during school vacations and summer. $4 per person (under age 1, free). An excellent hands-on museum, with a stage for kids to videotape a performance and then watch themselves on TV; post office, diner, and supermarket play areas; a construction site complete with real equipment; and a weather station and communications center with computers and a ham radio.

✔ **Norlands Living History Center** (207-897-4366; www.norlands.org), 290 Norlands Rd., Livermore. From Rt. 4 take Rt. 108 east for 1.2 miles, then travel

1.6 miles up Norlands Rd. Call or check the web page for frequently changing hours and pricing. Norlands tries to keep its doors open daily 9–4 year-round, but staff may not always be available for tours. This 455-acre complex includes a restored Victorian mansion, large barn, farmer's cottage, church, granite library, and a one-room schoolhouse. These buildings and grounds provide the backdrop for rural late-19th-century living history experiences ranging from tours to day-long and overnight programs. Become a scholar in the one-room schoolhouse, hear the story of the Washburn family and their 11 sons and daughters, or take part in the daily chores of the 1870s. Special events are held throughout the year.

✳ To Do

BALLOONING **Sails Aloft** (207-623-1136; www.sailsaloft.com), Augusta, offers sightseeing flights in central and Midcoast Maine.

BICYCLING The **Kennebec River Rail Trail** (www.krrt.org) theoretically runs along the river from Augusta to Gardiner, but at this writing just the initial 2 miles from Augusta (most easily accessed from Capitol Park) to Hallowell are complete. It's also possible to begin in Gardiner at the Hannaford parking lot and bike or walk a mile north along the river. The 6.5-mile trail is due for completion in 2006.

BOAT EXCURSIONS **Great Pond Marina** (207-495-2213), Belgrade Lakes Village, operates the **Mail Boat on Great Pond** (the inspiration for the book and movie *On Golden Pond*). Also moorings, boat rentals (canoes, sailboards, sailboats, fishing boats), and service.

✐ **D.E.W. Animal Kingdom** (207-293-2837), 918 Pond Rd. (Rt. 41), West Mount Vernon. Open mid-June–Labor Day, daily (except Mon.) 10–5; weekends in shoulder seasons and by appointment. $8 per person. Julie and Bob Miner stress that this is a "farm," not a "zoo." But what began as a traditional farm with pigs and cows has evolved into the most exotic menagerie in New England: some 190 animals contained within chain-link pens on 41 wooded acres. What's striking is the way the animals relate to Julie and Bob, who have raised most from birth. Cougars and lions nuzzle them. A female lynx offers her tail to be pulled. The tigers lumber up to be hugged. Eddie the Camel offers slurpy kisses to visitors as well. It's certainly a magic place. A wallaby baby peaks from its mother's pouch. Mallard and eider ducks follow you around. You can feed the several kinds of goats, but this isn't a petting farm—just a place to marvel at animals that are native (deer and black bear) or fairly familiar (ostrich and llamas), and also those you may have only read about—from badgers to black leopards to some so exotic you couldn't have imagined them.

CAMPING Steve Powell Wildlife Management Area (Swan Island), in Merrymeeting Bay off Richmond. State-owned Swan Island is managed as a wildlife preservation area in Merrymeeting Bay, a vast tidal bay that's well known among birders. Limited camping in primitive Adirondack shelters is available, along with a motorboat shuttle from Richmond, through the Department of Inland Fisheries and Wildlife (207-547-5322).

Lake St. George State Park (207-589-4255), Rt. 3, Liberty, offers 38 campsites and a boat launch ($20 for nonresidents). Also see *Swimming*.

FISHING The Belgrade Lakes are a big lure for anglers. The seven ponds and lakes harbor smallmouth bass, brook, pickerel, and landlocked salmon, among many other species. The sporting camps listed under *Lodging* all offer rental boats and cater to fishermen, especially in May, June, and September. **Day's Store** (207-495-2205) in Belgrade Lakes Village is a source of fishing licenses and devotes an entire floor to fishing gear. Boat rentals are available. **Great Pond Marina** (207-495-2213), Belgrade Lakes Village, rents boats.

GOLF AND TENNIS Belgrade Lakes Golf Club (207-495-GOLF), Belgrade, is a new 18-hole golf course, designed by renowned English golf architect Clive Clark. Just off Rt. 27 with views of both Great and Long Ponds, it's rated among the best golf courses in the country. Fees vary with season; call for current fees and tee times.

Natanis Golf Club (207-622-3561), Webber Pond off Rt. 201, Vassalboro, offers a 36-hole course; tennis courts. **Waterville Country Club** (207-465-9861), Waterville (off I-95). Eighteen holes, clubhouse with restaurant, carts, and caddies.

KAYAKING AND CANOEING Kennebec Tidewater Bike and Boat Rentals (207-737-4695; www.kennebectidewater.com), on the waterfront, Richmond, offers seasonal kayak and canoe, also bike rentals. This is a particularly rewarding place to get out on the Kennebec and paddle around Swan Island.

Belgrade Canoe and Kayak (207-495-2005 or 1-888-CANOE-11), Belgrade Village. Rentals and tours.

Maine Wilderness Tours (207-465-4333; www.mainewildernesstours.com), guided canoe and kayak trips on the Belgrade Lakes and down the Kennebec as well as fishing, moose-watching, and rafting farther afield.

Belgrade Boat Rentals & Storage (207-495-3415), a variety of rental boats, free delivery and pickup.

SPA The Senator Inn & Spa (207-622-3138), 284 Western Ave., Augusta. The three-story spa wing contains a fitness center, saltwater lap pool, aerobics and yoga studio, hot tub and steam room, and outdoor pool. A full menu of spa services is offered: hairstyling, manicure and pedicure, coloring, and a long list of skin care, massage, and other treatments for both men and women. All treatments include full use of the facilities.

✍ **Peacock Beach State Park**, Richmond (just off Rt. 201, 10 miles south of Augusta). A small, beautiful sand beach on Pleasant Pond; lifeguards and picnic facilities. $1.50 adults, free under age 12.

Sunset Camps Beach (207-362-2611) on North Pond in Smithfield, and **Willow Beach** (207-968-2421) in China. Although public access is limited at the Belgrade and China Lakes, every cottage cluster and most rental "camps" there are on the water.

Lake St. George State Park (207-589-4255), Rt. 3, Liberty. A pleasant, clean, clear lake with a sandy beach and changing facilities; a perfect break if you are en route from Augusta and points south to the coast. $3 day-use fee.

✳ Green Space

Capitol Park, across from the State House Complex, is a good place for a picnic. Also located here is the Maine Vietnam Veteran's Memorial, three triangular structures with a cutout section in the shape of soldiers that visitors can walk through.

Pine Tree State Arboretum (207-621-0031), 153 Hospital St., Augusta. (At Cony Circle—the big rotary across the bridge from downtown Augusta—turn south along the river; it's a short way down on the left, across from the Augusta Mental Health Institute.) Open daily dawn to dusk. Visitor center open 8–4 weekdays. There are 224 acres, with trails through woods and fields. More than 600 trees and shrubs (including rhododendrons and lilacs), as well as hostas and a rock garden. Cross-country ski trails, too.

Vaughan Woods, Hallowell. In 1791 Charles Vaughan settled in the town named for his grandfather Benjamin Hallowell; in 1797 his brother Benjamin arrived and built himself a fine house here, transforming the property into an agricultural showplace. A substantial portion of this property remains in the family seven generations later, and 152 acres have been granted as a conservation easement to the Kennebec Land Trust. Vaughan Woods represents the largest acreage open to the public, and it's beautiful: webbed with footpaths through mixed forest and open fields. The best entrance is from Litchfield Rd. at the end of Middle St. Park at the stone wall and look for the path.

Swan Island (207-547-5322 Mon.–Fri., 7:30–11 AM). Open by reservation only May–Labor Day and on a limited basis until the end of Sep. No pets allowed. Managed by the Maine Department of Inland Fisheries and Wildlife. Day use and overnight camping, but only 60 visitors at a time are allowed; $4 adult day-use fee per visit. The landing is in Richmond Village, and transport is provided. Tours are available in an open slat-sided truck; plenty of area for walking. At the head of Merrymeeting Bay, the island is 4 miles long and less than a mile wide, a haven for wood ducks, mergansers, white-tailed deer, bald eagles, wild turkeys, and more. It was the site of an ancient Indian village, and in 1614 Captain John Smith visited. Several early houses survive; Aaron Burr slept in one.

Jamies Pond Wildlife Management Area, Meadow Hill Rd., Hallowell. These 800 acres of woodlands, managed by the Maine Department of Inland Fisheries and Wildlife, include 6 miles of trails good for walking and cross-country skiing, and a 107-acre pond. There is a small parking lot and a launch ramp.

✳ Lodging

INNS AND BED & BREAKFASTS

⊙ ✐ ㅴ **Maple Hill Farm** (207-622-2708 or 1-800-622-2708; www.mapleBB.com), 11 Inn Rd. (off the Outlet Rd.), Hallowell 04347. This pleasant old house, not far from the turnpike and downtown Augusta, sits on 130 acres of fields and woods with trails, a spring-fed swimming hole, and a small abandoned quarry adjoining a 800-acre wildlife reservation. Scott Cowger and Vincent Hannan offer eight rooms tastefully furnished, with phone, television, VCR, clock-radio, high-speed wireless Internet access, air-conditioning, and private bath. Some have a whirlpool tub, private deck, and/or fireplace. As you meander up the driveway, watch for chickens (which provide the morning eggs). Four goats, nine llamas, four cows (one a dwarf), a pony, and a cat are also in residence. This is, however, more of a grown-up's than family retreat (children are welcome). The carriage house is perfect for wedding receptions (the inn is fully licensed), and the Gathering Place seating up to 125 people hosts functions. In winter trails are maintained for cross-country skiing. A choice of a full breakfast included in rates of $85–190 per couple in high season; off-season rates.

✐ **Home-Nest Farm** (207-897-4125; www.mainefarmvacation.com/homenest), 76 Baldwin Hill Rd., Fayette 04349. Open year-round. The main house, built in 1784, offers a panoramic view of the White Mountains. Lilac Cottage (1800) and the Red Schoolhouse (1830) are available for rent as separate units. The property has been in host Arn Sturtevant's family for seven generations. Arn can relate some interesting family tales while showing you Civil War memorabilia. $60 for one room, $100–120 for one- to three-bedroom units with kitchens, including breakfast. Two-night minimum stay July–Oct.

ㅴ **A Rise and Shine Bed and Breakfast** (207-933-9876; www.riseandshinebb.com), 19 Moose Run Dr. (Rt. 135), Monmouth 04259. Ten miles west of Augusta, with a distant view of Lake Cobbosseecontee, this rambling house with its even larger stables was for many years a racehorse farm, part of a 2,000-acre spread belonging to the Woolworth family. Local Tom Crocker and Lorette Comeau have replaced 76 windows, used up some 300 gallons of paint, as well as installing gas- and pellet-fired hearths in many of the eight guest rooms. Lorette has also painted murals on many walls. Our favorite is the Sunshine Room, the former master bedroom with a king-sized bed, hearth, and steam shower. $100–180, $300 for the housekeeping cottage, including a full breakfast. Horses are welcome, and there's lake access.

Maple Tree Inn B&B (207-377-5787), 34 High St., Winthrop 04364. Open May–Nov. Lloyd and Ann Lindholm have created an attractive suite with its own parlor, kitchen, bedroom, and bath on the second floor of their early-1900s house on a shady dead-end street. $55–85 includes a full breakfast served on a garden-side porch, weather permitting, otherwise in the dining room.

In the Belgrade Lakes region
Wings Hill Inn (207-495-2400 or 1-866-495-2400; www.wingshillinn.com), Rt. 27 and Dry Point Dr., Belgrade Lakes 04918. Open year-round.

This 200-year-old white-clapboard farmhouse rambles across a knoll, above its lawns just north of the village of Belgrade Lakes, overlooking Long Pond. The name recalls a one-time owner, U.S. Air Force general Edmund "Wings" Hill. Current innkeepers Christopher and Tracey Anderson met in culinary school, and the inn is known for fine dining (see *Dining Out*). The seven guest rooms, all with private bath (one with a Jacuzzi), have been individually decorated with an eye for romance. A full breakfast is served, along with afternoon tea. $120–175 May–Oct. includes a three-course breakfast and afternoon tea; less off-season.

The Pressey House Lakeside Bed & Breakfast (207-465-3500 or 1-877 773-7738; www.presseyhouse.com), 32 Belgrade Rd., Oakland 04963. Open year-round. Lorie and Lorne McMillan have divided an 1850s octagonal house on Messalonskee Lake into five guest units, each with its own bedroom, bath, living room with TV, and kitchen. A large common room with a fireplace overlooks the water. Guests can use a canoe, paddleboat, and small motorboat and swim off the dock. All just 2.5 miles off I-95. Open mid-May–mid-Oct. and major weekends. $100–150 including breakfast; less off-season.

Yeaton Farm Inn Bed & Breakfast (207-495-7766; www.yeatonfarm inn.com), 298 West Rd., Belgrade 04917. This is a classic 1829 Federal-style house on a quiet road. Because it survived in the same family for so long, it retains its original windows and big kitchen hearth as well as detailing. A mother and daughter, both named Connie Parker, are the enthusiastic hosts, offering three bedrooms with private bath. There's also a front parlor with a hearth and upright piano. The Belgrade Lake Golf Course is just up the road. $135 weekends includes a full breakfast.

Among the Lakes Bed & Breakfast (207-465-4900; www.amongthe lakes.com), 58 Smithfield Rd., Belgrade 04917. Open year-round. This is a handsome old house with five bright, comfortable guest rooms, offering a choice of king, queen, or single beds, private or shared baths, and air-conditioning. There's lake access. Polly Beatie and Sandy Famous actually live across the road. Breakfast is included in $90–100 per night.

In Richmond 04357

Richmond Bed and Breakfast and Sauna (207-737-4752 or 1-800-400-5751; www.richmondsauna.com), 81 Dingley Rd. (off Rt. 197), Richmond 04357. Open year-round. A handsome Federal home built in 1831 set on 70 wooded acres. Five guest rooms share two baths, and a two-room apartment has a private bath. Kitchen privileges, Finnish-style saunas (closed Mon.), hot tub, and pool. Innkeeper Richard Jarvi rents the six authentic Finnish-style saunas (private rooms) on the premises by the hour. Visitors should be aware that clothing is optional here. In fact, daytime nude sunbathing and swimming are available for $5 per person, and evening use of the hot tub, sauna, and pool is $20 per person. Open 6–10 PM (5–9 in winter). Use of all facilities is included for overnight guests. $75 double, $60 single, includes continental breakfast. The entire house is frequently rented for workshops or retreats. Alcohol is discouraged.

In the Belgrade Lakes region

🐾 ♿ **Bear Spring Camps** (207-397-2341; www.bearspringcamps.com), 60 Jamaica Point Rd., Rome 04957. Open mid-May–Sep. Ron and Peg Churchill run a very special family resort and fishing spot, set on 400 acres of woods and fields and in the family since 1910. Serious anglers come in early May for trout and pike, and in July there's still bass. The 32 cabins are strung along the shore of Great Pond, each with a bathroom, hot and cold water, a shower, heat, an open fireplace, and its own dock and motorboat. There's a tennis court, a golf driving range, and a variety of lawn games. The swimming is great (the bottom is sandy). Meals are served in the big white farmhouse set a way back across open lawns from the lake. Weekly rates from $725-800 per couple include all meals; special children's and group rates.

🐾 **Castle Island Camps** (207-495-3312; in winter, 207-293-2266; www.castleislandcamps.com), P.O. Box 251, Belgrade Lakes 04918. Open May–Sep. John and Rhonda Rice are the owners of this great old family compound: a dozen comfortable cottages clustered on a small island (connected by bridges) in 12-mile Long Pond. Geared to fishing (the pond is stocked; rental boats are available). Three daily meals are served in the cozy central lodge, where guests also gather around an open fireplace, and in a recreation room with pool tables, table tennis, and darts. $75 per person double, $511 per week includes all meals; children's rates. No pets.

🐾 🐾 **Alden Camps** (207-465-7703; www.aldencamps.com), 3 Alden Camps Cove, Box 1140, Oakland

CASTLE ISLAND CAMPS

Christina Tree

04963. Founded by A. Fred Alden in 1910 with just one rental unit, it's still in the family with 18 one- to three-bedroom log cabins with screened porch and woodstove or Franklin fireplace, scattered among the pines on the shores of East Lake. Meals are served in a wonderfully rambling old clapboard house with a big dining room and sitting area and a long porch. Activities include fishing, golf nearby, swimming, waterskiing, boating, tennis, hiking, and several playing fields. Children are welcome, and pets can be accommodated for an extra fee. $75–150 per person per day, and $450–900 per person per week, includes all three meals.

COTTAGES **Lake & Country Real Estate** (207-495-2525; www.belgrade lakeandcountry.com), Rt. 27, P.O. Box 276, Belgrade Lakes 04918. The largest rental agency in the Belgrade Lakes region; rates $250–1,500 per week.

MOTEL ☀ ♿ **Best Western Senator Inn and Spa** (207-622-5804 or 1-877-772-2224; www.senatorinn.com), 284 Western Ave., Augusta 04330. A longtime gathering spot for Maine politicians, this property, with 125 guest rooms and suites, extends far back from the road and offers some amenities rarely found in motor inns—namely one of the area's best restaurants and a full-service spa featuring a glass-walled, Grecian-columned saltwater lap pool, hot tub, and fitness center (see *Dining Out* and *To Do*). Sited right off I-95 and minutes from the Maine State Museum and downtown Augusta, this is a surprisingly quiet, friendly, and relaxing place to stay. There are some genuinely attractive suites with fireplace,

a writing area, jetted tub, and fridge. The property includes walking/cross-country skiing trails. You'll also find a guest laundry, and an inviting little bar. $89–259, depending on room and season, includes breakfast. $9 per pet.

✳ Where to Eat

DINING OUT **Wings Hill Inn** (207-495-2400), Rt. 27, Belgrade Lakes Village. Open for dinner Thu.–Sun. year-round. Seatings at 6 and 8. Reservations requested. Chef-owner Christopher Anderson and his wife, Tracey (who makes the desserts), trained at the Culinary Institute of America. Together they orchestrate seasonal five-course menus served to a maximum of 16 diners seated in adjoining rooms. An evening's feast might begin with a walnut and feta pâté in a phyllo crust, moving on to curried chicken soup or gazpacho, a salad of greens or a small Caesar, and a choice of four entrées, among them excellent sea bass with chanterelles and leeks, a fantastic eggplant Parmesan, and rack of lamb. To finish, there is frozen Grand Marnier mousse or brown sugar crème brûlée. The menu changes every week. Service is friendly and fast, and tables are set off by themselves in different rooms. Diners bring their own wine, served by the staff at the table (no corking fee); an 18 percent service fee is added to the bill. $40 prix fixe; a three-course, $30 prix fixe meal is also offered.

Slate's (207-622-9575), 167 Water St., Hallowell. Breakfast, lunch, and dinner Tue.–Fri., brunch and dinner Sat., brunch-only on Sun. Colorful coffeehouse atmosphere in three adjoining storefronts with brick walls, tin ceilings, changing art, a great bar, and a patio in back. The brunch menu is huge and popular. The dinner menu changes daily but might include mussels steamed in dry vermouth with garlic herb butter to begin with, and a choice of entrée salads and salmon grilled with tamarind and toasted pepper sauce. Live music Fri. and Sat. nights, and during Sun. brunch. Always a big blackboard menu of daily specials. Dinner entrées $10.95–21.95.

✍ **Senator Inn Restaurant** (207-622-5804), 284 Western Ave., Augusta. Open daily 6:30 AM–10 PM. Generally regarded as one of the best places to eat in the Augusta area, this facility is in the midst of a makeover, trading its old-fashioned look for a trendier bistro decor. The Maine crabcake, served at both lunch and dinner, is unusually light and tasty, and lobster is served up many ways (we can recommend the lobster quesadilla). Dinner options include pasta, "light" fare, and dinner salads as well as steaks and a mouthwatering seafood medley. Beware: Portions are large, and most entrées include the salad bar. Dinner entrées $16–24, with the shore dinner priced daily. Children's menu. The elaborate Sunday brunch buffet (11–2) is $14.95, less for seniors and children.

Freedom Café (207-859-8742; www.freedomcafefood.com), 18 Silver St., Waterville. Open for dinner Thu.–Sat. 5–9. One of central Maine's most unlikely and most popular restaurants. James Swinton usually greets guests at the bottom of the steps, and Janice Swinton can be seen in the open kitchen, cooking. Entrées change weekly, sometimes daily, but all have roots as southern as their owners, like crawfish-stuffed peppers, crabcakes with shrimp sauce, sweet and tangy boneless barbecued ribs. Desserts

range from white chocolate bread pudding to lemon icebox pie. The basement-level dining rooms are nicely lit and decorated. No reservations for groups smaller than six. $15.95–19.95 includes entrée, beverage, and dessert. Children 6–10 are $6.95; under 5 eat free. Wine is served. No credit cards, just cash or checks.

The Bread Box Café (207-873-4090), 137 Main St., Waterville. Open Tue.–Sat. 11–9. Brick walled and dimly lit, this is a welcome new option, good for luncheon sandwiches like hot turkey, Havarti, artichoke, roasted red pepper, and pesto on pumpernickel; grilled eggplant with chèvre, sweet red pepper, and pesto on a roll; or butternut squash ravioli with mascarpone cream. There's also a wide choice of salads. Dinner features salads and entrées such as chargrilled duck breast with apricot ginger glaze, or pan scallops and artichoke hearts tossed with white wine cream and angel-hair pasta. $15–21.

The Last Unicorn (207-873-6378), 8 Silver St., Waterville. Open daily 11–9, until 10 Fri. and Sat.; Sunday brunch until 2:30. Colorful and conveniently sited right off the central parking lot. There are usually 15 different dinner specials; soups, desserts, and most dressings and spreads are made here. The menu ranges from tortellini with mushrooms and cream sauce laced with sherry ($7.95 at lunch, $13.95 at dinner) to grilled beef tenderloin ($21.95).

Village Inn (207-495-3553), Rt. 27, Belgrade Lakes. Open Memorial Day–mid-Oct., Mon.–Sat. 5–9 and Sun. 11:30–8; weekends off-season. The summer of 2005 brought only good reviews for this rambling old dining landmark with a lake view. The specialty is duckling, roasted for up to 12 hours and served with a choice of sauces. Entrées $15.95–29.95.

Lakewood Inn Restaurant (207-474-7176; www.lakewoodtheater.org), Rt. 201, Skowhegan. Open Memorial Day–mid-Oct., Tue.–Sat. for dinner plus a Sunday buffet brunch (10:30–2). This old inn once served the likes of Humphrey Bogart and Vincent Price. It was on the verge of being razed when it was restored and reopened as an elegant restaurant—in time to celebrate the centennial year of the adjoining summer theater (see *Entertainment*). The inn itself dates to 1925 and features three fieldstone fireplaces. The à la carte menu ranges from vegetarian fettuccine Alfredo to rack of lamb and prime rib. Entrées $14–19.

EATING OUT

In Augusta
Beale Street Barbeque & Grill (207-622-8899), 300 Water St. Open daily for lunch and dinner. An offshoot of the famous Bath restaurant, and considered by some the best: smoked chicken quesadilla, hickory-smoked ribs, daily-made soups with corn bread, chili, bayou pilaf, and more.

Java Joe's (207-622-1110), 287 Water St. Open weekdays 7–2. A cozy place with baked goods, an interesting lunch menu, and the usual coffee and espresso drinks.

Also see **Senator Inn Restaurant** under *Dining Out*. It makes a surprisingly reasonably priced bet for breakfast and lunch; also brick-oven pizza.

In Hallowell
Hattie's Chowder House (207-621-4114; www.hattieslobsterstew.com), 103 Water St. Open daily 11–9, Fri.

and Sat. until 10. A small space with a big menu. Both chowder and fish are available to take home—and just about everyone around here does. Pick up chowder, a salad, or a sandwich and head for Vaughan Woods or to the bench by the river across the street.

Liberal Cup (207-623-2739), 115 Water St. Open for lunch and dinner, Fri. and Sat. until 10. Mid-Maine's only brewpub, noisy on the bar side, less so in the dining room. Half a dozen good brews (crafted here) on tap. Live music Thu.–Sat. evenings. Most menu items, including sandwiches, are served all day, along with shepherd's pie, fish-and-chips, and drunken pot roast.

Café de Bangkok (207-622-2638), 232 Water St. Just south of the village with river views, this is a highly respected local dining option. The menu includes the usual Tom Yum and miso soups, a soft-shell crispy crab salad with hot chili lime sauce on lettuce, "pad" and fried rice dishes. The chef's specials include crispy fried red snapper with ginger sauce and vegetables, and half a crispy roast duck with peanut sauce and steamed vegetables. Entrées $8.95–16.95. Lunch specials include a sushi combo.

Also see **Slate's** under *Dining Out*. The menu is reasonably priced, and this remains your best bet for both lunch and dinner. **Slate's Bakery** (207-622-4104), a couple of doors down, is a good source of ready-made takeout sandwiches.

In Gardiner
The A1 Diner (207-582-4804; www.a1diner.com), 3 Bridge St. Open Mon.–Sat. for all three meals, brunch-only on Sun. (8–1). A vintage 1946

Worcester diner with plenty of Formica; blue vinyl booths; blue and black tile; a 14-stool, marble-topped counter; and a neon-blue-and-pink clock with the slogan TIME TO EAT. You won't find typical diner fare here, however. The breakfast menu includes banana almond French toast and a wide variety of omelets, as well as eggs and hash; there are always specials, superb soups (this time around we lunched on Tuscan minestrone), and chili. Dinner is less exciting. Beverages range from herbal tea to imported beers and wines. You can always get tapioca pudding, and the route to the restroom is still outside and in through the kitchen door.

A1 To Go Community Market and Café (207-582-5586), 347 Water St. Open Mon.–Sat. 7–7. Next door to their famous diner, longtime owners Niel Andersen and Michael Giberson have added its antithesis, a trendy café with an espresso bar and featuring smoothies, panini, and wraps (try the crab, avocado, and scallions with pickled ginger, nori, and wasabi mayo!); also grilled wraps, soups, and salads. Dinners-to-go are a specialty, just the thing if you're heading for a cottage and don't want to cook when you get there. Wine, beer, and assorted gourmet items are also stocked.

In Waterville/Winslow
The Lobster Trap and Steakhouse (207-872-0529), 25 Bay St., Winslow. Open for lunch and dinner. The view of the river and the fresh fish at reasonable prices are what recommend this locally popular place. Fully licensed.

Also see **The Bread Box** and **The Last Unicorn** in *Dining Out*, good lunch options.

In Belgrade Lakes
& **The Sunset Grille** (207-495-2439), 4 West Rd., Belgrade Lakes Village. Open year-round, 7–7. Hopping in the summer, casual, family fare, waterside. Saturday-evening karaoke.

THE A1 DINER

Kim Grant

In Richmond

🍴 **Railway Café** (207-737-2277), 64 Main St. Open Mon.–Sat. 6:30 AM–8 PM, until 9 Fri. and Sat.; Sun. 7–4. Minutes off I-95, this pleasant restaurant makes a good food stop: There's a wide choice of morning omelets and lunchtime sandwiches, burgers, salads, and pizzas, and a huge, reasonably priced dinner menu, including "Just for Kids." Allow a few minutes to walk around this historic Kennebec River town.

In South China

Dog Days Gourmet Bakery and Café (207-445-4745), 241 Rt. 3. Open Mon.–Fri. 6:30–6:30, Sat. 7:30–2. Exactly where you need it, this oasis appears like a mirage not far off Augusta en route to the coast. The café features one or more daily soups made from scratch, plus salads and sandwiches such as "rustic rufus" (roast beef, Havarti, sprouts, fresh greens, and sun-dried tomato spread on multigrain bread). Need we mention the latte, cappuccino, and fresh-baked scones?

In Winthrop

🍴 **Sully's** (207-377-5663), Main St. Open Mon.–Sat. for lunch and dinner, Sun. dinner noon–7. Set back from Main St. with plenty of parking to accommodate its local following. Salads as well as burgers and sandwiches for lunch, seafood dishes, like a seafood medley that includes lobster and salad; liver and onions and an old-fashioned roast turkey dinner ($9.99).

COFFEEHOUSES **Jorgensen's Café** (207-872-8711), 103 Main St., Waterville. An inviting café with at least a dozen flavored coffees, as well as tea and espresso choices. The deli serves quiche, soups, salads, and sandwiches. Coffee and tea supplies.

ICE CREAM **The Daily Scoop** (207-623-3113), 136C Water St., Hallowell. It's Gifford's ice cream where you can enjoy it, in the middle of this shopping street but with benches to sit and a view of both street traffic and the Kennebec River.

❋ Entertainment

LIVE PERFORMANCES 🍴 **Theater at Monmouth** (207-933-2952; www .theateratmonmouth.org), Main St., Monmouth. May to beginning of Oct. season, Thu.–Sun. in shoulder season, Wed.–Sun. in July, Tue.–Sun. in Aug. Housed in Cumston Hall, a striking turn-of-the-20th-century building designed as a combination theater, library, and town hall. A resident company specializes in Shakespeare but also presents contemporary shows throughout the season.

Waterville Opera House (207-873-7000; www.operahouse.org), 93 Main St., Waterville, presents a number of shows throughout the year, including music performances and theater productions. It's also the site of several shows during the Maine International Film Festival (see *Film* in "What's Where").

Gaslight Theater (207-626-3698; www.gaslighttheater.org), City Hall Auditorium, Hallowell. This community theater stages productions throughout the year.

Johnson Hall Performing Arts Center (207-582-7144; www.johnson hall.org), 280 Water St., Gardiner. A restored historic space where workshops, dances, and other performances occur frequently.

⌀ **Lakewood Theater** (207-474-7176; www.lakewoodtheater.org), RFD 1, Box 1780, Rt. 201, Skowhegan. Late May–mid-Sep. A resident company (Curtain Up) performs in Maine's century-old summer theater. Check out the Lakewood Jesters matinee performances for children.

FILM Railroad Square Cinema (207-873-4021; www.railroadsquarecinema.com), Main St., Waterville. From I-95 exit 130 head toward downtown; turn left between Burger King and the railroad tracks. Art and foreign films, and mid-July home of the Maine International Film Festival.

Skowhegan Drive-in (207-474-9277), Rt. 201 south. A genuine 1950s drive-in with nightly double features "under the stars" in July and Aug.; weekends in June.

The Skowhegan Cinema (207-474-3451), 7 Court St., is another period piece, dating to the 1920s; films nightly.

✳ Selective Shopping

ANTIQUES SHOPS A dozen antiques stores cluster in Hallowell, each with a different specialty. **JCM Designs** (207-622-5527), 122 Water St., antiques, gifts, and home decor. **Brass and Friends** (207-626-3287), 154 Water St. (look for the gargoyles atop the building) is a large trove of antique lighting fixtures. **Josiah Smith Antiques** (207-622-4188), 101 2nd St., specializes in Asian and British ceramics and early glass. **Johnson-Marsano Antiques** (207-623-6263), 172 Water St., sells Victorian, art deco, and estate jewelry.

ART GALLERIES Kennebec Valley Art Association/Harlow Gallery (207-622-3813), 160 Water St., Hallowell. A cooperative, good-quality gallery.

The Loft Gallery (207-873-1733; www.artisansofmaine.com), 76 Main St., 3rd floor, Waterville. Work by local artists is featured. **Hallowell Clay Works** (207-626-7687), 100 Water St., Hallowell. The gallery shows local potters.

BOOKSTORES Barnes & Noble Booksellers (207-621-0038), the Marketplace at Augusta, directly across from the Augusta Civic Center. A full-service bookstore with music and computer software sections, as well as a café.

Apple Valley Books (207-377-3967; www.applevalleybooks.com), 121 Main St., Winthrop. Rita Moran and Eric Robbins run a welcoming full-service bookstore, stocking used as well as new titles.

⌀ **Children's Book Cellar** (207-872-4543), 52 Main St., Waterville.

Merrill's Bookshop (207-623-2055), 134 Water St., 2nd floor, Hallowell. This is an antiquarian bookshop among antiquarian bookshops. Some 30,000 titles include many odd and unusual titles.

SPECIAL STORES Brahms/Mount Textiles (207-623-5277; www.brahmsmount.com), 19 Central St., Hallowell. Open weekdays 9–5. Inquire about special sales. The former Bodwell Granite Works holds the antique looms that weave the textiles here, and the showroom displaying exceptional linen and "personal blankets" designed and woven by Claudia Brahms and Noel Mount. Nationally respected through catalog and wholesale distribution, the shop usually has seconds and specials.

Cobbossee Coffee Company, 134 Main St., Winthrop (207 377 2208), Named for a 9-mile-long local lake (said to be the third largest in Maine), this company roasts its coffee in Winthrop and sells it in the retail shop.

Maine Made & More (207-872-7378; www.mainemadeshop.com), 93 Main St., Waterville, and seasonally in Belgrade Lakes Village (207-495-2274). George and Paula Gordon began with the small shop in Belgrade Lakes and now operate a far larger store in downtown Waterville, and others in Norway, Oakland, and Augusta. Plenty of souvenirs; also some good clothing and other buys.

Reny's (207-582-4012), 185 Water St., Gardiner. Open daily, weekdays 9–5:30, Fri. until 8, Sat. 9–5, Sun. 10–4. Recently expanded, one of the largest representatives of this amazing Maine discount chain, good for clothing, peanut butter, art supplies, and an amazing range of everything in between.

The Potter's House (207-582-3632; www.thepottershouse.com), 335 Water St., Gardiner, and 664 Rt. 133, Winthrop. Mary K. and Jeff Spencer's pottery works are standouts, and the Gardiner Store (steps from the A1) also displays work of other Maine potters.

The Green Spot (207-465-7242), Kennedy Dr., Oakland. Open May–Columbus Day, daily 9–7; closed Tue. A quarter mile or so west of I-95 look for a small yellow store on the left. Locally loved as a source of amazing daily fresh breads, organic produce, fine wines, and terrific deli items, Tanya and Brenda Athanus's small store on the way from Waterville to Oakland is well worth seeking out.

Johnny's Selected Seeds (207-861-3900; www.johnnyseeds.com), 955 Benton Ave., Winslow. Open Mon.–Sat. in-season, selective days off-season. A catalog seed company with more than 2,000 varieties.

✳ Special Events

June–July: During its 9-week sessions the prestigious **Skowhegan School of Painting and Sculpture** (207-474-9345) sponsors a lecture series on weekday evenings that's free and open to the public.

July: The **Whatever Family Festival** (*week preceding the Fourth of July*), Capitol Park—children's performances, soapbox derby, Learn the River Day, entertainment, carnival, and more. **Maine International Film Festival** (*midmonth*) in Waterville. **China Connection**—public supper, pageant, road race, pie-eating and greased-pig contests in China. **Old Hallowell Day** (*third weekend*)— parade and fireworks, crafts and games. **Richmond Days** in Richmond; **Pittston Fair**, Pittston.

August: **Windsor Fair**, Windsor; **Monmouth Fair**, Monmouth; **Readfield Heritage Days**, Readfield. **Skowhegan State Fair**, one of the oldest and biggest fairs in New England—harness racing, a midway, agricultural exhibits, big-name entertainment, tractor and oxen pulls.

September: **Oosoola Fun Day**, Norridgewock, includes the state's oldest frog-jumping contest (up to 300 contestants) around a frog-topped totem pole; also canoe races, crafts fair, flower and pet contests, live music, barbecue. **Litchfield Fair**, Litchfield. **Common Ground Fair**, Unity (see *What's Where*).

THE UPPER KENNEBEC VALLEY AND MOOSE RIVER VALLEY
INCLUDING THE FORKS AND JACKMAN

B y right this upper stretch of the Kennebec Valley and certainly the Moose River Valley belong in the "Northern Maine" section of this book, but the Kennebec is a classic north–south corridor, inextricably linking northern woodland with Mid-Maine mills and farms.

For more than 140 years beginning in 1835, logs were floated downriver from the woods to the mills. Then in 1976 fishing guide Wayne Hockmeyer discovered the rush of riding the whitewater through dramatic 12-mile-long Kennebec Gorge. On his first ride through the gorge, Hockmeyer had to contend with logs hurtling all around him, but, as luck would have it, 1976 also marked the year in which environmentalists managed to outlaw log drives on the Kennebec.

Rafting companies now vie for space to take advantage of up to 8,000 cubic feet of water per second released every morning from late spring through mid-October from the Harris Hydroelectric Station. No more than 1,000 rafters, however, are allowed on the river at a time. In order to compete, outfitters based in and around The Forks have added their own lodging; roughly half of these operations have evolved into year-round sports-based resorts, thanks to the popularity of snowmobiling and the recent availability of rental machines. This booming sport, combined with hunting, fishing, and rafting seasons, has created a boomlet in and around The Forks in recent years.

Sited at the confluence of the Dead and Kennebec Rivers, The Forks is technically a "plantation" (an unorganized township). In reality the village includes The West Forks, north of the Rt. 201 bridge. The only obvious landmarks remain the old Marshall Hotel with its electrified yellow COCKTAILS sign, and Berry's General Store with its stuffed wildlife. Look more closely, however, and you will see Crab Apple's vast lodge and restaurant-lounge tucked up behind the Marshall Hotel, and Berry's (which has added an ATM) is now within walking distance of shops, restaurants, and several B&Bs. One by one century-old cabins around here are being renovated, and new luxurious log structures appear with each season. This season several major outfitters have merged, and the resort area continues to evolve.

Empty as it seemed when rafting began, this stretch of the Upper Kennebec had been a 19th-century resort area. A now vanished 100-room, four-story Forks Hotel was built in the middle of The Forks in 1860, and the 120-room Lake Parlin Lodge soon followed on nearby Lake Parlin. Caratunk, The Forks, and Jackman were all railroad stops, and "rusticators" came to fish, hike, and view natural wonders like 90-foot Moxie Falls. During Prohibition the area was also known for its steady flow of liquor. Half a dozen remote sportsmen's camps on fishing ponds date to this period.

The entire 78-mile stretch of Rt. 201 north from Solon to the Canadian border is now officially The Old Canada Road Scenic Byway. Solon, with its Greek Revival meetinghouse, old hotel, and general store, still seems a part of the long-settled valley, but Bingham (just 8 miles north) has the feel of the woodland hub it is. A couple of miles north of Bingham is the 155-foot-high hydro dam built in the 1930s by Central Maine Power, which walls back the river, raising it more than 120 feet and creating wide, shimmering Wyman Lake. The lake gradually narrows as Rt. 201 follows it north and is best viewed from the rest area at its northern end. Drive slowly and carefully along this twisty road. It's frequented by both lumber trucks and lumbering moose.

North of The Forks, Rt. 201 traverses lonely but beautiful woodland. Wildlife abounds: More than 100 species of birds have been seen in the region, and this section of the Kennebec supports five types of game fish. The route is known as the Arnold Trail because Benedict Arnold came this way in 1775 to Quebec City, which is little more than 100 miles north of Jackman.

Jackman and Moose River form a community (divided by a brief bridge) on Big Wood Lake. In warm weather you notice that something is missing here and don't realize what it is unless you revisit in winter (November through April): It's snow, which softens the gaps of this shrunken old border community with its outsized French Canadian Catholic church, some good restaurants, motels, and reasonably priced camps.

Jackman is named for the man who built the Canada Road from the border down to The Forks. The town boomed after the Canadian Pacific Railroad arrived in 1888, setting the lumbering industry into high gear. While most of the mills have since disappeared, this former rail junction is now a major hub of Maine's snowmobiling network and 400 miles of ATV trails. It's also a base for exceptional canoeing and kayaking. From Rt. 201, we urge you to branch off on Rt. 15/6, the lonely 31-mile road that follows the Moose River east to Moosehead Lake.

Most American (as opposed to Canadian) visitors approach this area from I-95 and follow Rt. 201 north through Hinckley over the dam and past the giant wooden statue of an Indian in Skowhegan. Those who would rather shadow the Kennebec north can follow its curve through the gracious old town of Norridgewock and on up Rt. 201A through Anson and Embden (just across a bridge from Solon), where petroglyphs evoke a culture that dates back several thousand years.

GUIDANCE **Kennebec Valley Tourism Council** (www.kennebecvalley.org) publishes a helpful annual guide, *Kennebec Valley Guidebook*. **Skowhegan Chamber of Commerce** (207-474-3621; www.skowheganchamber.com)

maintains a year-round information center on Russell St. (Rt. 201) that should stock the Kennebec Valley guide; no more restrooms.

Upper Kennebec Valley Chamber of Commerce (207-672-4100) maintains an information center at 356 Main St. (Rt. 201) in Bingham Village. Open year-round, weekdays 9–3 and on weekends when volunteers are available. Displays evoke local history.

Forks Area Chamber of Commerce (www.forksarea.com) publishes a snowmobile map to the area.

Jackman Region Chamber of Commerce (207-668-4171 or 1-888-633-5225; www.jackmanmaine.org) maintains a seasonal information center near the Lakeside Town Park.

GETTING THERE *By car:* The obvious route from points south and west is I-95 to exit 133, then Rt. 201 north all the way to The Forks. The approach from the Rangeley and Sugarloaf areas, Rt. 16, is also a beautiful drive.

✳ To See

NATURAL BEAUTY SPOTS Moxie Falls (90 feet high) is said to be the highest falls in New England. The view is striking—well worth the detour from The Forks (see *To Do—Hiking*).

Attean View. Heading north toward Jackman from The Forks, only one rest area is clearly marked. Stop. The view is splendid: Attean Lake and the whole string of other ponds are linked by the Moose River, with the western mountains as a backdrop. There are picnic tables.

MOXIE FALLS

Kim Grant

MUSEUMS AND HISTORIC SITES

Entries are listed geographically, south to north

🖉 **L. C. Bates Museum** (207-238-4250; www.gwh.org), Rt. 201, Hinckley. Open Wed.–Sat. 10–4:30, Sun. 1–4:30, but look for the OPEN flag; it's frequently staffed on "closed" days. $2 adults, $1 children 17 and under. Across the road from the Kennebec River, one in a lineup of brick buildings that are part of the campus of the Good-Will Hinckley School (founded in 1889 for "disadvantaged chidden"), this ponderous Romanesque building houses a large and wonderfully old-fashioned collection, with stuffed wildlife, dioramas by noted American impressionist Charles D. Hubbard, and some significant Wabanaki craftsmanship, with examples ranging from several thousand years old to early-20th-century items. Allow at least an hour. The annual summer art exhibit, usually incorporating work by faculty and/or students at the nearby Skowhegan School of Painting, is a bonus. The 2,540-acre campus includes many miles of walking and biking trails, an arboretum, and a picnic area.

Margaret Chase Smith Library Center (207-474-7133; www.mcslibrary.org), 54 Norridgewock Ave., Skowhegan. Open year-round Mon.–Fri. 10–4. Turn left at the first traffic light heading north out of town. Set above the Kennebec, an expanded version of Senator Smith's home, this research and conference center houses records and scrapbooks dealing with "the lady from Maine"—as Margaret Chase Smith (1897–1995) was known during her years as a congresswoman (1940–49) and senator (1949–73). Displays include tape recordings, memorabilia, and a video.

WABANAKI CULTURAL LANDMARKS

Wabanaki heritage is particularly strong along this stretch of the Kennebec River. Your clue might be the 62-foot-high Skowhegan Indian, billed as "the world's largest sculptured wooden Indian." He stands in the downtown parking lot, visible (and accessible) from Rt. 201. Finding genuine evidence of longtime Indian habitation, however, requires some sleuthing. There are two sites, one commemorating an early-18th-century Indian mission village and the second consisting of genuine Indian petroglyphs. To find the first from Skowhegan, follow Rt. 201A along the Kennebec for just a few miles to Norridgewock. If you are interested only in the petroglyphs, you can remain on Rt. 201 into Solon.

French Jesuit Sebastian Rasle established the mission in Norridgewock, insisting that Native American lands "were given them of God, to them and their children forever." Rasle and his mission were wiped out by the English in 1724. Norridgewock Oosoola Park features a totem pole topped by a frog (this is a good picnic spot and boat-launch site). The site of the village itself is marked by a pleasant riverside picnic area in a pine grove.

Continue on Rt. 201A toward Madison across the bridge and up a steep hill. Turn left at the top of the hill onto the Father Rasle Monument Rd. (also known as Ward Hill Rd.); continue 3 miles.

The petroglyphs (pictured in the Maine State Museum) are in Embden on an arrowhead-shaped rock that juts into the Kennebec. From Rt. 201 in Solon, turn at the sign for the Evergreens Campground. Cross the Kennebec and turn south on Rt. 201A. The trail to the river is just down the road; it's not marked, but it's easy to see. If you are coming from the mission village site, continue straight ahead; the road hugs the river all the way to Solon. Also see the L. C. Bates Museum, on page 584.

South Solon Meeting House, off Rt. 210, Solon. Open year-round. An 1842 Greek Revival building with murals and frescoes by WPA and Skowhegan School artists.

✳ To Do

AIR TOURS **Jackman Air Tours** (207-668-4461), 7 Attean Rd., Jackman. Jim Schoenmann offers scenic air tours of the entire area.

ATV This is a mecca for people who love to ride their all-terrain vehicles, with 400 new miles of trails.

BIKING AND MOUNTAIN BIKING Local terrain varies from old logging roads to tote paths. Rentals are available from many rafting outfitters (see below). A 7-mile multiuse (ATV/walking/biking) trail now follows the old railbed along the Kennebec from Solon to Bingham. Check out www.jackmanmaine.org for descriptions. Jackman claims to have one of the most extensive mountain bike trail systems in Maine.

CANOEING AND KAYAKING **The Moose River Bow Trip** is a Maine classic: A series of pristine ponds forms a 34-mile meandering route that winds back to the point of origin, eliminating the need for a shuttle. The fishing is fine, 21 remote campsites are scattered along the way, and the put-in is accessible. One major portage is required. Canoe rentals are available from a variety of local sources. Several rafting companies rent canoes and offer guided trips, but the kayaking specialists here are Registered Maine Guides Amy and Leslie McKendry at **Cry of the Loon Outdoor Adventures** (207-668-7808; www.cryoftheloon.net) in Jackman. Canoe rentals are also plentiful in Jackman.

FISHING Fishing is what the sporting camps (see *Lodging*) are all about. The catch is landlocked salmon, trout, and togue. Rental boats and canoes are readily available. Camps also supply guides, and a number of them are listed on the Jackman chamber's web site.

GOLF **Moose River Golf Course** (207-668-5331), Rt. 201, Moose River (just north of Jackman). Mid-May–mid-Oct.; club rental, putting green, nine holes.

HIKING **Moxie Falls** in The Forks is a 90-foot waterfall considered the highest in New England, set in a dramatic gorge. It's an easy 0.7-mile walk from the trailhead (it can be very muddy and wet). Turn off Rt. 201 onto Moxie Rd. on the south side of the bridge across the Kennebec in The Forks. Park off the road at the trailhead sign on your left.

Pleasant Pond Mountain in Caratunk. With an open ledge peak at 2,477 feet, the view is 360 degrees. It's a 1½-hour hike. Turn east off Rt. 201 at the Maine Forest Service Station in Caratunk and head toward Pleasant Pond on the road across from the post office and general store. At the fork (with Pleasant Pond in view), bear left. The pavement ends, the road narrows, and at 5 miles from the post office take Fire Lane 13 on the right. The trail begins on the left just beyond the AT lean-to.

Owls Head, Jackman. A 10-minute hike (0.75 mile) begins at the Attean Lookout on Rt. 201 (see *To See*) south of Jackman Village. This is one of Maine's most amazing easily accessible panoramas, stretching all the way to the Canadian border and encompassing Big Wood Lake, Slide Down Mountain, and Spencer Valley. The trail begins at the north end of the picnic area.

MOOSE-WATCHING The best time to see a moose is dawn or dusk. Favorite local moose crossings include Moxie Rd. from The Forks to Moxie Pond; the Central Maine Power Company road from Moxie Pond to Indian Pond; the 25 miles north from The Forks to Jackman on Rt. 201; and the 30 miles from Jackman to Rockwood on Rt. 6/15. Drive these stretches carefully; residents all know someone who has died in a car–moose collision.

SCENIC DRIVE **Old Canada Road National Scenic Byway** (207-672-3971). Now that it has a name and official status as one of America's most beautiful highways, the 78 miles of Rt. 201 between Solon and the Canadian border has acquired interpretive historical panels at its rest areas in Bingham, Moscow, The Forks, Parlin Pond, and the Attean Pond Overlook south of Jackman. Also note the Upper Kennebec Valley Chamber of Commerce information center with its displays in Bingham. Local advocates hope that the road's new status will ultimately mean more passing lanes, more pull-outs, and enforcement of speed limits for the through truck traffic, which currently includes many oversized loads. Two prefab homes recently collided in the middle of Bingham. For a description of Rt. 201, see the chapter introduction.

WHITEWATER RAFTING See the introduction to this chapter. Wimps like us have no reason to fear the 12-mile run down the **Kennebec River** from Harris Dam. There are 4 miles of Class II and IV rapids—notably Magic Falls, though this comes early in the trip—and after that it's all fun. We have also tried the slightly more challenging run on the **Dead River**, available less often (releases are less frequent) but offered by most outfitters. The safety records for all outfitters are excellent, or they wouldn't be in this rigorously monitored business. Note that many outfitters in the Forks area also offer trips on the Penobscot River (see "Katahdin Region"). Apr.–Oct. all offer the basics: a river ride with a hearty cookout and a chance to view (and buy) slides of the day's adventures. Variables include the morning put-in time, whether you eat along the river or back at camp afterward, the comfort level of the lodging, and the size and nature of the group you will be rafting with. The minimum suggested age is 10 on the Upper Kennebec and 8 on the lower section, compared with 15 on the Dead River. Note that some outfitters are on lakes or ponds, good for kayaking and canoeing. River trips begin between 7 and 9 and end between 3 and 4. Obviously it makes sense to spend the night before you raft at your outfitter's base camp, hence our attempt to describe the variety of what's available. Children, seniors, and others who want to experience smaller rapids can join the trip later in the day. Most rafts carry between 6 and 10 people. Most offer hot tubs. Rates run $80–186. Most outfitters package lodging and rafting. **Raft Maine** (1-800-723-8633; www.raftmaine.com) is the group to which all major outfitters belong. Most outfitters based in The Forks also offer rafting trips on the Penobscot.

✎ *Note:* Although whitewater rafting began as a big singles sport, it's becoming more and more popular with families, who frequently combine it with a visit to Quebec City. Minimum age requirements vary, but weight is also a consideration (usually no less than 90 pounds). We identify the outfitters who cater to kids and/ or offer Lower Kennebec trips geared to children as young as 6 with our ✎ sign.

✎ **Northern Outdoors, Inc.** (207-663-4466 or 1-800-765-7238; www.northern outdoors.com), P.O. Box 100, The Forks 04985. Open year-round. The first and still its biggest outfitter on the Kennebec, now with two distinct bases, its **Forks Resort Center** and **Lakeside Resort Center** offer a total of 350 beds year-round plus 100 campsites in summer. The Forks is its original, attractive open-timbered lodge with high ceilings, a huge hearth, comfortable seating, a cheerful dining room (see *Dining Out*), a major brewpub, a pool, a private pond, platform tennis, volleyball and basketball, a sauna, and a giant hot tub. Here accommodations run from riverside camping to lakeside cabins, from lodge rooms to "logdo-miniums" (condo-style units with lofts and a kitchen/dining area). Northern Outdoors recently recently purchased 30 acres of land adjacent to Wyman Lake, just 3.5 miles south of The Forks Resort Center. This Lakeside Resort Center includes six guest houses (sleeping up to 10 people) with a full kitchen, plus four new luxury rental houses (leather furniture, queen-sized beds, decks). Amenities include an outdoor Jacuzzi, sand volleyball, a dining pavilion, and kayak rentals. The Base Lodge houses a common area with free Internet access for guests, a retail area, changing rooms, and showers. All accommodations have lake views, and there's direct access to Wyman Lake for boating, fishing, and kayaking. In addition to rafting, they offer float trips, fishing trips, rock climbing, a ropes

RAFTING THE KENNEBEC

Raft Maine

course, and lake kayak touring. Inquire about "family camps" where children as young as 8 are welcome. In winter the lodge caters to snowmobilers with snowmobile rentals and guided tours. $49–169 for a 1-day raft trip.

New England Outdoor Center (207-723-5438 or 1-800-766-7238; www.neoc.com). Matt Polstein's is also one of the oldest, largest, and classiest rafting operations in The Forks, but in the past year he's shifted his focus to the Millinocket area, selling his former base camp to Northern Outdoors (see above). He retains the 17-room **Sterling Inn** in Caratunk, a 19th-century stage stop that dates to 1816 and offers attractive country-inn-style guest rooms and delightful common rooms. NEOC also continues to lodge their rafters in the Lakeside Resort Center.

Crab Apple White Water (207-663-4491 or 1-800-553-7238; www.crabappleinc.com), The Forks 04985. A family-owned and geared outfitter with a base camp that offers eight "luxury suites" (with wet bar, fridge, Jacuzzi, and deck); also four cottages accommodating four to eight people in bunk-style rooms, six motel units, and a large lodge with a restaurant right in The Forks. "Funyaks" (inflatable kayaks) and half-day "float trips" are also offered. Rafting/lodging packages are $123–186 per person. Inquire about winter snowmobile rentals and packages.

North American Outdoor Adventure (1-800-727-4379; www.nawhitewater.com), P.O. Box 64, Rt. 201, West Forks 04985. The co-owners, river guides Liz Caruso and Peter Dostie, have been in business since 1984, offering rafting in Connecticut's Housatonic and the Kennebec, Dead, and Penosbscot in Maine. Lodging is in two attractive B&Bs that can accommodate 36 right in The West Forks, and one new snowmobilers' and year-round lodge for six on the Dead River. Request a room in the **River House** with its luxurious Great Room with sliding glass doors overlooking the river. Peter can't seem to stop building on to this complex, which also now includes the Hawk's Nest restaurant-pub with an indoor climbing wall as well as the Dead River Outfitters Shop. ATV tours, hiking, kayaking, hunting and fishing tours, snowmobile rentals, snowshoeing, and cross-country are also offered. From $25 per person, $120 per room to $300 (one to three people) with breakfast.

Magic Falls Rafting (207-663-2220 or 1-800-207-7238; www.magicfalls.com), P.O. Box 9, West Forks 04985, has a riverside base camp that includes a pleasant B&B (four rooms), cabin tents, and campsites on the banks of the Dead River in The Forks. Magic also owns the old **Marshall Inn** in the middle of the village and **Dead River Lodge**, a new facility at the base camp with king and queen rooms, half baths, decks, and a living room with big-screen TV. In addition to rafting they offer "funyaks" (an inflatable cross between a canoe and a kayak) and rock climbing. Rafting $69–99; rafting/lodging packages $97–154 per person.

Moxie Outdoor Adventures (1-800-866-6943; www.moxierafting.com), HC 63, Box 60, The Forks 04985. This long-established outfitter is based in a set of traditional cabins on Lake Moxie, offering camping, platform tents, and cabin lodging, specializing in 2- and 3-day canoe trips as well as rafting. Two nights with rafting and four meals is $185 per person in a cabin, substantially less if camping

Three Rivers Whitewater (1-800-786-6878; www.threeriversfun.com), P.O. Box 10, West Forks 04985. Just 8 years old but with an excellent safety record, some new riverfront log cabins, a focus on "having fun," and its **Boatman's Bar & Grill**, the happening place on the rivers. Open in winter with lodging and sled rentals. Three Rivers has recently absorbed Unicorn Rafting, a very different kind of outfitter (family oriented), and is emerging as one of the area's major year-round players, with a base in Millinocket for Penobscot trips and an ever-expanding Forks base with its lodge and cabins.

Windfall Rafting (207-668-4818 or 1-800-683-2009; www.raftwindfall.com), Rt. 201, P.O. Box 505, Jackman 04945. Based in a classic 1890s schoolhouse in Moose River (just north of downtown Jackman), Windfall has been in business one way or another since 1982. Tim Blake books you into the gamut of what's available in Jackman; he also offers inflatable-kayak trips on the Kennebec's East Outlet.

✇ **Adventure Bound** (1-888-606-7238; www.adv-bound.com), The Forks 04985. An offshoot of Northern Outdoors, this is an entirely separate family- and kids-geared outfitter. Facilities include an outdoor pool, indoor climbing wall, and ice cream bar. It has its own base lodge and cabin-tent village.

Professional River Runners (1-800-325-3911; www.proriverrunners.com), P.O. Box 92, West Forks 04985. The specialty is overnight trips, beginning with a run down the East Outlet and camping out the night before you run the Kennebec. We were lucky enough to see a spectacular display of the northern lights on our trip, and the food (campfire-grilled steak shish kebabs, fresh blueberry pancakes, and more) was outstanding. Accommodations are at the **Grand View B&B**, also in one- and two-bedroom condos and a cottage.

Inn by the River Outdoor Adventures (1-866-663-2181; www.innbytheriver .com), based at the Inn by the River (see *Lodging*). Innkeepers, owners, and staff are all longtime river guides. Last year they began offering small-rafting trips, canoe trips, and other outdoor adventures. On the fall weekday we visited theirs was the only trip going out. Snowmobiling tours also offered. Inquire about camping with breakfast, many specials.

North Country Rivers/Maine Whitewater (1-800-348-8871; www.north countryrivers.com), P.O. Box 633, Bingham 04920. The former Maine Whitewater base in Bingham: 60 acres with camping and RV sites, platform tents and new log cabins, also a restaurant and private airport on the riverside grounds. $144–174 per person for rafting/lodging in-season.

✳ Winter Sports

SNOWMOBILING Snowmobiling is huge in this region, with The Forks serving as a hub for more than 150 miles of the Interconnecting Trail System (ITS) trails over mountains, rivers, and lakes and through woods with connections to the Rangeley and Moosehead areas, and to Canada (for which trail passes must be purchased). Rentals and guided trips are available from most major rafting companies. Also check with the **Jackman Region Chamber of Commerce** (see *Guidance*) and **Sled Maine** (1-877-2SLED-ME; www.sledme.com). Sled rental prices run around $150 per day single, $175 double, plus insurance.

✳ Lodging

SPORTING CAMPS While these camps were originally geared exclusively to fishermen, they now also welcome families and hikers.

Harrison's Pierce Pond Sporting Camps (radiophone, 207-672-3625; Thanksgiving–May 15, call 603-524-0560), Box 315, Bingham 04920. Open mid-May–Columbus Day. Sited on the Appalachian Trail, 20 miles from Bingham; 15 of those miles are along a dirt road. Fran and Tim Harrison have brought new life to this classic 1930s log sporting camp. Nine mile-long Pierce Pond is a short walk across the stream and through the woods. Five of the nine log cabins have a half bath, and there are three full-facility bathhouses on the premises. Fly-fishing is the heart of this sporting camp. Rates include three abundant meals per day (lunch is generally packed). Word has gotten out about Fran's cooking, and some people actually drive the bumpy road for Sunday turkey or Friday lobster (with a reservation). $79–85 per person per day in high season, less off-season and per week, includes all meals (based on double occupancy and a 2-night minimum); half price for children; 3-night minimum in high season; lower rates July 7–Aug. 6; also group rates. Guides and boat rentals available.

✒ **Cobb's Pierce Pond Camps** (in summer, 207-628-2819; in winter, 207-628-3612), North New Portland 04961. Open from ice-out to Oct. 1. Twelve guest cabins accommodate from two to eight people; each has a screened porch, woodstove, bathroom, and electricity. Home cooked meals and between-meal snacks are served in the main lodge. This traditional sporting camp dates to 1902,

and the Cobb family has been running it for more than four decades; 90 percent of the guests are repeats. It's the kind of place that doesn't advertise. It has a loyal following among serious anglers; sand beaches nearby. Guiding services available. $97 per person per day includes three meals; children's rates.

✒ **Attean Lake Lodge** (207-668-3792; www.atteanlodge.com), Jackman 04945. Open Memorial Day weekend–Sep. Sited on Birch Island in Attean Lake, surrounded by mountains. The resort is easily accessible from Jackman; you phone from the shore, and a boat fetches you. It has been in the Holden family since 1900; 15 log cabins, luxurious by sports lodge standards, with full bath, Franklin fireplace, kerosene lamps, and maid service daily. There is a relatively new central lodge (the old one burned) with a dining room overlooking the lake. Fishing boats, kayaks, and canoes are available. $240–280 per couple includes meals; children's rates and weekly rates available; 13 percent service charge.

OTHER LODGING **Inn by the River** (207-663-2181 or 1-866-663-2181; www.innbytheriver.com), 2777 Rt. 201, The Forks Plantation 04985. Open year-round. Bill and Cori Cost, longtime teachers and rafting guides, have built—from scratch when it proved impossible to save the old building—a traditional inn on a bluff above the Kennebec. It's well done. The Great Room with its fireplace and piano opens onto a porch and gardens. Guest rooms have a private bath and are all nicely furnished. Trails out the back door lead up into the woods and in winter connect with much of Maine via snowmobile that can be rented here (ITS 86, 87, 89). You might want to reserve dinner (see *Dining Out*). As **Inn by the River Outdoor Adventures** (see *Whitewater Rafting*), Bill and Cori now also offer their own rafting and kayaking trips. There's also a pub for guests. $75–200 includes breakfast.

Also see **River House**, owned by North American Outdoor Adventure, under *Whitewater Rafting*. Most lodging described for the outfitters under *Whitewater Rafting* is available to nonrafters.

Kennebec Riverside Cabins (1-866-787-7433; www.krcabins.com), Rt. 201, P.O. Box 123, The Forks 04985. Melissa Howes, a Registered Maine Guide when she's not working as an airport controller at Bangor International, has rehabbed the four, century-old, literally riverside one- and two-bedroom housekeeping cabins across from the Marshall Inn in the middle of The Forks. $120–160 for up to four people, $35 per extra person (they sleep 6 to 10).

🐾 **Sally Mountain Cabins** (207-668-5621 or 1-800-644-5621; www.sally mtcabins.com), 9 Elm St., Jackman 04945. Open year-round. Sited at the end of a quiet street, right on Big Moose Lake, basic but cheerful housekeeping cabins with cable TV, accommodating 2 to 5 people, up to 10 in larger condo-style units back across the street. Rental canoes and ice-fishing shacks. $26 per person per night, $155 per person per week. Pets welcome at no charge.

🐾 ♿ **Cedar Ridge Outfitters** (207-668-4169; www.cedarridgeoutfitters .com), P.O. Box 744, 3 Cedar Ridge Dr., Jackman 04945. Registered guides Sal and Debbie Blood have

been steadily expanding this operation. Sited on a quiet road are seven two- and three-bedroom housekeeping cabins with TV, VCR, and phone. Amenities include hot tubs and a heated swimming pool; "adventure packages" include fishing, guided snowmobiling, and whitewater rafting. Basic cabin rentals are $38 per person per night, half price for children, minimum 2-night stay.

Bishop's Country Inn Motel (207-668-3231 or 1-888-991-7669; www .bishopsmotel.com), 461 Main St., Jackman 04945. This two-story motel in the middle of Jackman Village offers clean and spacious rooms and all the bells and whistles it takes for AAA to give it three diamonds. $84.95 per couple in winter (high season), $79.95 per couple in rafting season.

✳ Where to Eat

Note: In this little-populated area the line between "eating" and "dining" out blurs—and if you're between rafting and snowmobiling seasons, it comes down to what's open. Listings are in geographic order along Rt. 201, south to north.

Moose Point Tavern (207-668-4012), on Big Wood Lake, Jackman. Open year-round for dinner. This is by far the most popular and attractive dining room in the area. Meals are cooked to order. Fully licensed. Entrées might include chicken cordon bleu and haddock stuffed with shrimp.

Old Mill Pub (207-474-6627), 41-R Water St., Skowhegan. Open daily for lunch and dinner. While this is technically in the "Lower" rather than the "Upper" Kennebec Valley, it's just where you may want to stop en route: a picturesque old mill building set back from the main drag with a seasonal deck overlooking the Kennebec. A friendly bar and scattered tables; sandwiches (a good Reuben), quiche, and specials for lunch; spinach lasagna or stir-fried shrimp for dinner; music on Fri. and Sat.

Valley View Market (207-672-3322), Rt. 201, Bingham. Source of pizza and good takeout sandwiches if you're running late or want to eat by the lake.

Northern Outdoors (207-663-4466 or 1-800-765-RAFT), Rt. 201, The Forks. The pine-sided dining room in the lodge is open daily year-round for all three meals. Informal, with great photos of The Forks in its big-time logging and old resort days adorning the walls. This is also a brewpub, and both food and beer are fine. A good steak and salad is $15.95.

Inn by the River (207-663-2181), 2777 Rt. 201, The Forks Plantation. Reservations recommended. The country-inn atmosphere is more intimate than at other local options. Entrées from $9.95 (for chicken of the day) to $16.95 for pork tenderloin, grilled with a southwestern sauce. Fully licensed.

✎ **Crab Apple** (1-800-553-7238), Crab Apple Acres, just off Rt. 201, The Forks. Open daily for dinner Memorial Day–Labor Day; otherwise, Wed.–Sun. The large new base lodge includes both a pub and a more formal restaurant. Dinner options range from vegetable pasta Alfredo to prime rib and Yorkshire pudding ($21.95). Children's menu.

The Marshall Inn (207-663-4455), The Forks. Open for dinner most nights; live bands on weekends. A genuine old hotel with rooms still upstairs, but a better place to eat than to sleep.

Appleton's (207-663-2114), Rt. 201, The Forks. Open 6:30 AM–9 PM year-round. Sit-down dining, and pizzas, subs, and "breakfast burgers"; Gifford's ice cream.

Hawk's Nest (207-663-4430), Rt. 201, West Forks. Open for lunch and dinner year-round. Peter Dostie spent more than a year building this lodge with 100- and 200-year-old logs that had been petrified, making them lighter to carry and place by hand. The elaborate animal carvings on the deck and large totem inside are the work of longtime guide and well-known carver Jeff Samudosky. There's a bar, game room, and indoor climbing wall (no alcohol allowed before climbing); the dining room offers homemade soups in bread bowls and burgers at lunch. Sandwiches are served at dinner, but you can also get seafood, steaks, or pasta dishes. Entrées $11–22.

Mama Bear's Den (207-668-4222), Rt. 201, Jackman Village. Open 4 AM–8 PM, from 6 AM on weekends. Of the three restaurants within steps of each other, this was most highly recommended—and we had no complaints with a soup-and-sandwich

3 BEARS, HAWK'S NEST, WEST FORKS

Christina Tree

BERRY'S IN THE FORKS

lunch. The menu ranges from poutine to surf and turf with Vidalia onions. Fully licensed.

Four Seasons Restaurant (207-668-7778), Jackman. Open 5 AM–9 PM. One big room, booths, good road food, blackboard specials.

✳ Selective Shopping

General stores in Solon and on up through Jackman are generally the only stores, ergo community centers. Our favorite is **Berry's in The Forks** (open 6 AM–9 PM), source of fishing/hunting licenses and liquor, lunch, flannel jackets, rubber boots, and groceries as well as gas. Stuffed birds and other wildlife are scattered throughout the store, most of it shot by Gordon Berry, who has been behind the counter for 36 years. Until the rafting/snowmobiling boom hit, Berry notes, he and his parents could manage the place alone; now it takes a staff of up to 10.

Dead River Outfitter Shop (1-800-727-4379), Rt. 201, West Forks. A Quonset hut has been refaced in logs and filled with about every kind of clothing and equipment that might come in handy for rafting, snowmobiling, cross-country skiing, and hiking. In winter, snowmobile rentals and service as well as guided tours are offered; also ATV rentals and tours.

Jackman Trading Post (207-666-2761; www.moosealley.com), 281 Main St. (Rt. 201 south of the village). Open May–Thanksgiving, 8–6. A peerless selection of Far North T-shirts and souvenirs.

✳ Special Events

March: **Gadabout Gaddis ice-fishing derby**, Bingham. **Northeast Sled Dog Races**, Jackman.

Late September: **Fly-In**, Gadabout Gaddis Airport, Bingham (207-672-4100). **Annual Fall Festival**, Jackman (207-668-4171).

November: **Annual Hunter's Supper**, Jackman.

December: **Sled dog races**.

Northern Maine

Nancy English

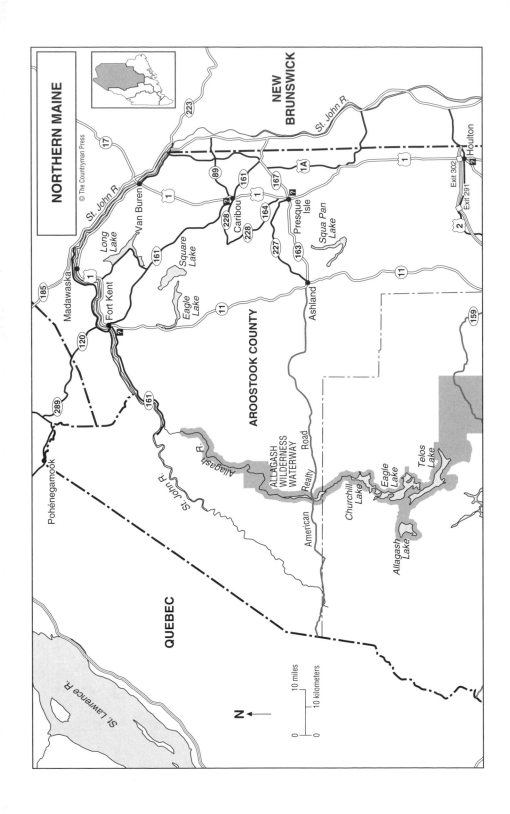

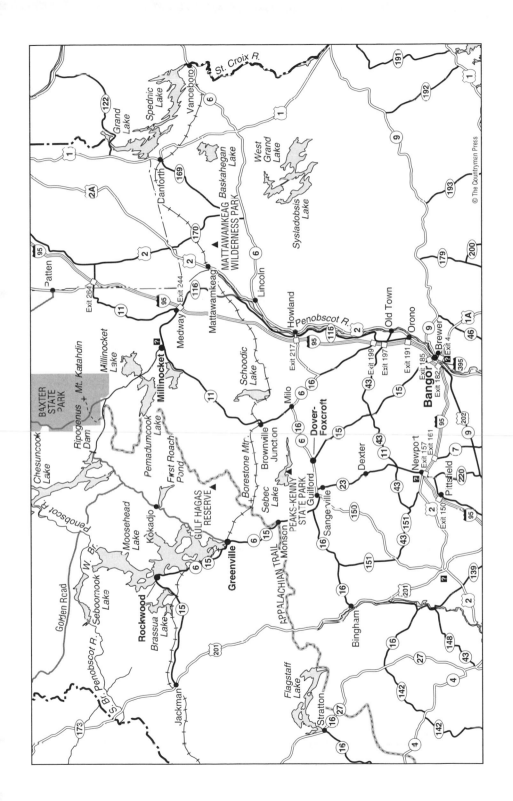

© The Countryman Press

BANGOR AREA

Bangor is both the natural gateway to much of northern and eastern Maine and the largest city in the region. It makes a good layover spot for those venturing into either the Baxter State Park region or the vast expanse of Aroostook County. With Brewer on the other side of the Penobscot River, and Orono, home of the main campus of the University of Maine, the Bangor metropolitan area is a vibrant commercial and cultural hub. The Bangor Mall on the north side of the city is the largest in northern Maine, and Bangor International Airport (referred to locally as BIA) is a departure point for flights to every corner of the globe.

Once the home of the National Folk Festival, Bangor began to host its own Folk Festival starting in 2005—celebrating the richness and variety of American culture through music, dance, traditional storytelling, and food. It also saw the opening of Maine's first slot machine gambling site, called Hollywood Slots. Another larger and permanent facility is scheduled to open in 2007; gambling revenues are intended to benefit the state's harness-racing tracks, trainers, and breeders.

Despite all this activity, residents will tell you wistfully that the city's real glory days were in the mid–19th century, when the pine tree was arboreal gold and Bangor was the most important lumber port in the world. Back then the city was a brawling, boisterous boomtown where fortunes were quickly made and lost in timber deals and land speculation. Local lumber barons built grandiose hilltop mansions, sparing no expense. After a long winter's work in the woods, the loggers who labored for them spent their hard-earned money, roistering in the bars and brothels of the city's notorious red light district, known as "the Devil's Half Acre."

The Bangor of today is a quieter, less colorful place. A fire in 1911 wiped out much of the old business district, and an urban renewal project later bulldozed away what was left of the Devil's Half Acre.

Two neighborhoods still hint at the city's past grandeur. One is the West Market Square Historic District, a mid-19th-century block of downtown shops. The other is the Broadway area, lined with the Federal-style homes of early

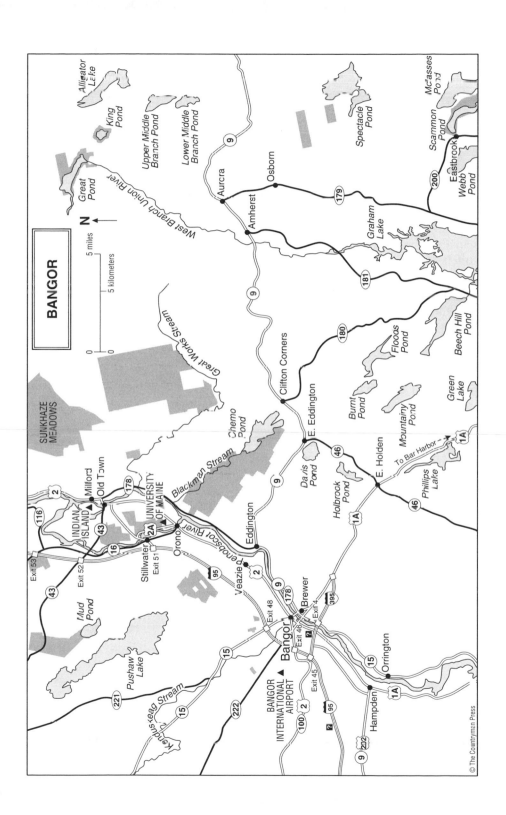

BANGOR

prominent citizens and later lumber barons' mansions. Across town, West Broadway holds a number of even more ornate homes, including the turreted and thoroughly spooky-looking Victorian home of author Stephen King, with its one-of-a-kind bat-and-cobweb wrought-iron fence.

The outsized symbol of Bangor's romantic timber boom era is native son Paul Bunyan. The mythical lumberjack superhero was conceived in tall-tale-swapping sessions in the logging camps of northern Maine and the saloons of the Devil's Half Acre. When most of the tall stands of virgin pine in Maine's North Woods had been cut down, ending the boom, lumberjacks began moving west, taking Paul with them—and making him bigger and his feats more incredible with every subsequent move. Scattered across the forested northern tier of the United States, all the way to the Pacific Northwest, are villages and small towns named Bangor settled by nostalgic Maine loggers who all had a Paul Bunyan tale to tell.

His legend may have moved west, but Paul Bunyan is still very much a presence in Bangor: A 31-foot-high fiberglass statue of the great logger, depicted wearing a red-and-black-checked shirt and carrying a huge ax, stands in a city park named for him—and casts a very long shadow.

GUIDANCE Bangor Region Chamber of Commerce (207-947-0307; www .bangorregion.com), 519 Main St., P.O. Box 1443, Bangor 04402 (just off I-395 exit 3B, which is off I-95 exit 182A, across from the Holiday Inn), maintains a seasonal visitor information office in Paul Bunyan Park—you can't miss the giant lumberjack statue—on lower Main St. (Rt. 1A).

Bangor Convention and Visitors Bureau (207-947-5205; www.bangorcvb .org) operates staffed, year-round information centers at One Cumberland Plaza, Suite 300, and at Bangor International Airport.

Maine Tourism Association maintains two rest areas/information centers on I-95 in Hamden between exits 174 and 180: northbound (207-862-6628) and southbound (207-862-6638).

GETTING THERE *By air:* **Bangor International Airport** (207-942-0384; www .flybangor.com) is served by Delta Air Lines, Northwest Airlink, and U.S. Airways Express. **Rental cars** are available at the airport.

By bus: **Greyhound** (207-942-1700) offers daily service to the downtown terminal. **Concord Trailways** (207-945-5000 or 1-800-639-5150) has express trips, complete with movies and music, daily from Portland and Boston. **Cyr Bus Line** (207-827-2335) provides daily scheduled service all the way to Caribou, with stops in between.

By car: I-95 from Augusta.

WHEN TO COME The Folk Festival draws a lot of folks at the end of August, but other reasons to explore—from the Penobscot Nation Museum in Old Town to Bookseller's Row in downtown Bangor—can be enjoyed any time of year. If you visit in midwinter, you'll be able to imagine how the lumberjacks managed in the deep woods.

Hampden. Adjacent to Bangor, but offering a more rural setting. The academically excellent Hampden Academy is found here.

Orono. A college town, housing the University of Maine, but still a small town where almost everyone knows everyone else. Downtown there are some nice shops and local dining landmarks, and on campus look for a wide variety of cultural activities.

Old Town. Definitely a mill town, but also the home of the famous Old Town Canoe factory. There's a great little museum worth visiting.

Winterport. An old river town, once home of many sea captains and now a quiet little area with a historic district. Walking-tour brochure available from area businesses.

✳ To See and Do

MUSEUMS **Cole Land Transportation Museum** (207-990-3600), 405 Perry Rd. (junction of I-95 and I-395), Bangor. Open May 1–Nov. 11, daily 9–5. $6 adults, $4 seniors, under 19 free. A collection of 200 antique Maine vehicles going back to the 19th century: snowplows, wagons, trucks, sleds, rail equipment, and more.

PAUL BUNYAN

Kim Grant

Hose 5 Fire Museum (207-945-3229), 247 State St., Bangor. Open by appointment. A working fire station until 1993, now a museum with firefighting artifacts from the area. Three fully restored fire engines, wooden water mains, and plenty of historical pictures. Free, but donations gladly accepted.

University of Maine Museums, Rt. 2A, Orono. **Hudson Museum** (207-581-1901), in the **Maine Center for the Arts** (open Tue.–Fri. 9–4, Sat. 11–4), is an exceptional anthropological collection including a special section on Maine Native Americans and Maine history. Tour programs are offered by prior arrangement. **University of Maine Museum of Art** (207-561-3350), 40 Harlow St., Bangor, shows a fraction of its 4,500-work collection, which includes an extensive selection of 19th- and 20th-century European and American prints by Goya, Picasso, Homer, and Whistler

INDIAN ISLAND

In 1786 the Penobscot tribe deeded most of Maine to Massachusetts in exchange for 140 small islands in the Penobscot River; they continue to live on Indian Island, which is connected by a bridge to Old Town. The 1970s discovery of an 18th-century agreement that details the land belonging to the tribe (much of it now valuable) brought the island a new school and a large community center, which attracts crowds to play high-stakes bingo (call 1-800-255-1293 for the schedule). The Indian Island Reservation, the Penobscot homeland for more than 5,000 years, is presently occupied by about 500 tribal members. At 5 Center St. the **Penobscot Nation Museum** (207-827-4153; www.penobscotnation.org/museum) is open spring and summer, Mon.–Thu. noon–5 and Sat. and Sun. 10–2; fall and winter hours are Mon.–Thu. 10–3. The museum now occupies the former Indian agent's office, the fifth building on the right after crossing the bridge, but there are plans to build a larger facility. Curator James Neptune greets visitors, explaining that the birch table is by the legendary Passamaquoddy craftsman Tomah Joseph (who taught Franklin Roosevelt to paddle a canoe) and that the beaded deerskin dress belonged to Indian Island's Molly Spotted Elk, a dancer, actress, and writer known around the world in the late 1930s. Most items in this authentic and informal collection—which includes a 150-year-old birch-bark canoe and some exquisite beaded work, war bonnets, war clubs, and basketry—have a human story. The island is accessible from Rt. 2, marked from I-95, exit 197.

and modern American paintings by George Inness, John Marin, Andrew Wyeth, and others. Tours are available by prior arrangement, and tours on tape are also available. **Page Farm Home Museum** (open May 15–Sep. 15, daily 9–4; closed Sun. and Mon. off-season). Free. Historical farm implements and household items from 1865 to 1940.

Old Town Museum (207-827-7256), N. 4th St. Extension, Old Town. Open early June–end of Aug., Wed.–Sun. 1–5. A former waterworks building houses a great little museum with exhibits on the Penobscot tribe and on local logging. You'll also find early area photos, an original birch-bark canoe, and well-informed guides.

Old Town Marine Museum, 240 Main St., No. 2, Old Town, displays vintage canoes, boats, and outboard motors. Admission is free.

Maine Forest and Logging Museum (207-581-2871), Leonard's Mills, off Rt. 178 in Bradley (take Rt. 9 north from Brewer; turn left onto 178 and watch for signs). Open during daylight hours. "Living History Days" on two weekends, one in mid-July and another in October, features people in period attire yarding logs with horses or oxen and performing various duties using 18th-century tools. Located on the site of a 1790s logging and milling community, it includes a covered bridge, water-powered sawmill, millpond, saw pit, barn, and trapper's line camp. Special events include Children's Day and Woodsmen's Day.

HISTORIC HOMES AND SITES Bangor Museum and Center for History (207-942-1900), 6 State St., Bangor. Open Tue.–Fri. 10–4, Sat. noon–4. The center operates this local history museum on the ground floor of a former bank building, put-

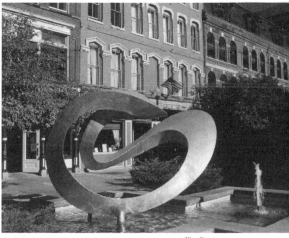
SCULPTURE IN MARKET SQUARE

ting up exhibits with its large collections. On our visit mourning jewelry made with human hair, and photos of the great Bangor fire, kept us fascinated. Admission is free.

Thomas A. Hill House (207-942-5766); 159 Union St. (at High St.), Bangor. Tours are by appointment only. $5 adults, children and members free. The downstairs of the Hill House has been restored to its 19th-century grandeur with Victorian furnishings and an elegant double parlor.

Mount Hope Cemetery in Bangor is one of the nation's oldest garden cemeteries, designed by noted Maine architect Charles G. Bryant. Abraham Lincoln's first vice president, Hannibal Hamlin, is buried here.

FOR FAMILIES ✔ **Maine Discovery Museum** (207-262-7200), 74 Main St., Bangor. The largest children's museum in Maine, with three floors of kid-oriented displays and activities. Exhibits include an indoor river, world cultures area, book town, and more. There is also a gift shop; special events are held throughout the year. $6 per person, 12 months or older.

GAMBLING Hollywood Slots at Bangor (207-262-6146; www.pngaming.com/main/bangor), 427 Main St., Bangor. 10 AM–2 AM daily, Sunday noon–2 AM. This temporary facility has 475 slot machines and two small restaurants. You must be 21 to enter and use the slot machines. A permanent facility is planned at the site of two hotels across the street from Bass Park on Main St., scheduled to open in late 2007.

GOLF Bangor Municipal Golf Course (207-945-9226), Webster Ave., Bangor; 27 holes. **Penobscot Valley Country Club** (207-866-2423), Bangor Rd., Orono; 18 holes. **Hermon Meadow Golf Club** (207-848-3741), Newberg Rd., Hermon; nine holes.

SWIMMING ✐ **Jenkins' Beach**. Popular beach on Green Lake for families with children. Store and snack bar.

Violette's Public Beach and Boat Landing (207-843-6876), East Holden (between Ellsworth and Bangor). $2 admission. Also on Green Lake, a popular spot for college students and young adults. Swim float with slide, boat launch, and picnic tables.

Beth Pancoe Aquatic Center (207-992-4490), run by the Bangor Parks and Recreation Department. An outdoor Olympic-sized pool with a waterslide and a couple of fountains, this new facility has a slow slope into the water, easy on the old and young, and was built with a gift from Stephen King, Bangor's best-selling novelist. Open end of June–Aug. $1 children, $2 adults for residents; $2 children, $4 adults from away.

DOWNHILL AND CROSS-COUNTRY SKIING **Mt. Hermon Ski Area** (207-848-5192), Newburg Rd., Hermon (3 miles off I-95 from exit 43, Carmel; or off Rt. 2 from Bangor). Popular local downhill skiing area, with a chairlift and a T-bar and 20 runs (the longest is 3,500 feet); rentals available; base lodge, night skiing, snowboarding. A tubing park, with a lift, runs day and night, too.

Hermon Meadow Ski Touring Center (207-848-3471), Newburg Rd., Hermon. Approximately 6 miles of groomed cross-country skiing trails on a golf course.

See also **Sunkhaze Meadows** under *Green Space*, below.

✳ Green Space

Sunkhaze Meadows (207-827-6138), Milford. Just north of Bangor, this 9,337-acre refuge includes nearly 5 miles of Sunkhaze Stream and 12 miles of tributary streams. Recreation activities include canoeing, walking logging trails, and hunting and fishing in accordance with Maine laws. Also excellent bird-watching and cross-country skiing opportunities. The refuge office is on Rt. 2 in Old Town and is open 7:30–4 weekdays.

A brochure titled ***Trails in the Bangor Region*** is available at the chamber visitor center and lists close to a dozen trails for biking, walking, picnicking, running, hiking, cross-country skiing, and other outdoor activities.

✳ Lodging

&. **The Charles Inn** (207-992-2820; www.thecharlesinn.com), 20 Broad St., Bangor 04401. A historic inn on W. Market Square, a vest-pocket park in the heart of downtown Bangor, a perfect location for getting to know the city. Connie Boivin bought this hotel in 2005; 35 rooms are pleasant, each decorated simply but differently and with mahogany or cherrywood beds. All have antique brass water faucets, private bath, air-conditioning, and TV. There are two suites and an extended-residency apartment. Continental kosher breakfast is served in the café. $89 in-season, $119 for the suites.

🐾 **Best Inn** (207-942-1234), 570 Main St., Bangor 04401. A 51-room motel that is clean, comfortable, and convenient. We loved relaxing here, with all the basic conveniences, and videos for rent at the desk. **Geaghan's**, the on-site restaurant, serves decent food, with Irish specials. Rates are $64–85, including continental breakfast. Children under 18 stay free.

Country Inn at the Mall (207-941-0200 or 1-800-244-3961), 936 Stillwater Ave., Bangor 04401. Despite the name, this is essentially a 96-room motel—but brighter and more cozily decorated than most. There's no restaurant, newsstand, or gift shop, but with the Bangor Mall (largest in northern Maine) right next door that's not an inconvenience. $45–74.95 with continental breakfast.

The Lucerne Inn (207-843-5123 or 1-800-325-5123; www.lucerne inn.com), RR 3, Box 540, Holden 04429. A 19th-century mansion on Rt. 1A, overlooking Phillips Lake in East Holden. Best known as a restaurant (see *Dining Out*), it also has 31 rooms with private bath, working fireplace, heated towel bars, whirlpool bath, phone, and TV. $99–199 in-season includes continental breakfast. Lower rates off-season.

Note: Bangor also has many hotels and motels, mainly located by the mall and near the airport.

✷ Where to Eat

DINING OUT

The Lucerne Inn (207-843-5123 or 1-800-325-5123), Rt. 1A, East Holden (11 miles out of Bangor, heading toward Ellsworth). Open for dinner daily, as well as a popular Sunday brunch. A grand old mansion with a view of Phillips Lake. Brunch specialties include Belgian waffles and chicken cordon bleu. Entrées $18–more than $30 for a steamed lobster and filet mignon.

Chocolate Grille (207-827-8971), 301 N. Main St., Old Town. The glass-walled dining room looks out on the Penobscot River, and diners often get glimpses of a family of eagles that nest nearby and swoop up and down the river. Entrées may include bacon-wrapped filet mignon with Gorgonzola demiglaze ($17.95) and grilled salmon en croute ($14.95). There are 20 desserts on the menu—most of them, unsurprisingly, involving chocolate. Open daily for lunch and dinner.

Captain Nick's (207-942-6444), 1165 Union St., Bangor. Open daily for lunch and dinner. A large, locally popular place with good seafood and steaks.

✤ **Governor's** (207-947-7704), 643 Broadway in Bangor; and Stillwater Ave. in Old Town (207-827-7630). Open from early breakfast to late dinner. The Stillwater restaurant is the original in a statewide chain. Popular at all meals, large breakfast menu, hamburgers to steaks; specials like shepherd's pie, fresh strawberry pie, ice cream.

Momma Baldacci's (207-945-5813), 12 Alden St., Bangor. A longtime family-owned and -operated restaurant open for lunch and dinner, and serving Italian specialties at reasonable prices. The restaurant is run by the brother of Maine's governor.

EATING OUT **Momma B's Kitchen** (207-942-6325), 96 Hammond St., Bangor. An offshoot of Momma Baldacci's, also run by the Baldacci

family, and with a different menu and more contempory decor. Delicious lunch salads and entrées. Open for lunch and dinner.

Café Nouveau (207-942-3336), 84 Hammond St., Bangor. An attractive bistro-style restaurant with an interesting international menu. Open Tue.–Sat. 11–3 and 5–9. Small portions with high quality are devised to accompany the wines. Full bar.

New Moon Café (207-990-2233), Park St., Bangor. Spacious and open with a tile floor and interesting art on the walls. Open Tue.–Sat. for dinner, with late hours for the bar.

🍲 **Dysart's** (207-942-4878), Coldbrook Rd., Hermon (I-95, exit 180). Open 24 hours. Billed as "the biggest truck stop in Maine," but it isn't just truckers who eat here. At breakfast you'll see drivers, families, and businesspeople among the patrons. Known for great road food and reasonable prices. Homemade bread and seafood are specialties.

Pat's Pizza (207-866-2111), Mill St., Orono. A local landmark, especially popular with high school and univ-ersity students and families. Now franchised throughout the state, but this is the original with booths and a jukebox, back dining room, and downstairs taproom, plus Pat's son Bruce and his family still running the place. Pizza, sandwiches, Italian dinners.

Margarita's Mexican Restaurant (207-866-4863), 15 Mill St., Orono. A moderately priced, cheerfully decorated eatery that's popular with students from the nearby University of Maine campus.

Java Joe's Café (207-990-0500), 98 Central St., Bangor. Breakfast and

lunch, and the all-important morning latte. Open Mon.–Fri. 7:30–3, with bagels, eggs, sandwiches, salads and wraps, and a friendly, helpful staff.

Sea Dog Brewing Company (207-947-8004; www.seadogbrewing.com), 26 Front St., serves its own microbrews and a long menu of seafood, burgers, and steaks, and a band on most Fri. and Sat. nights.

COFFEEHOUSES AND SNACKS

🍽 **The Store & Ampersand** (207-866-4110), 22 Mill St., Orono. A combination health food store, coffee bar, and gift shop. Great for snacks (try the big cookies) and specialty items. Kids love to browse the gift shop.

Friar's Bakehouse (207-947-3770), 21 Central St., Bangor. Open Wed.–Fri. 7–3, Sat. 8–2. This bakery run by the Franciscan Brothers of Hungary, an Episcopal order from Brewer, makes and sells muffins, chocolate chip cookies, whoopee pies and lots of bread. You can pray here in a chapel up the stairs, always open for prayer and meditation.

✳ Entertainment

🍽 **Maine Center for the Arts** (207-581-1805; www.mainecenterforthearts .org), at the University of Maine in Orono, has become the cultural center for the area. It hosts a wide variety of concerts and events, from classical to country-and-western, children's theater, and dance. Many performances are held in Hutchins Concert Hall, Maine's first concert hall. To get tickets, call 207-581-1755 for the box office.

🍽 **Penobscot Theatre Company** (207-947-6618), 131 Main St., Bangor. This company has been putting on quality shows for more than 30 years. Performing in the Bangor Opera House, the company performs *A Christmas Carol* every year, plus a variety of plays during the season; *The Crucible* was a recent production. In summer the company sponsors the Creative Arts Program for young people.

Maine Masque Theater (207-581-1792), Hauck Auditorium, University of Maine, Orono. Classic and contemporary plays presented Oct.–May by University of Maine theater students.

Bass Park (207-942-9000), 100 Dutton St., Bangor. The complex includes **Bangor Auditorium**, **Civic Center**, **State Fair**, and **Raceway** (featuring harness racing Thu.–Sun., May–July, with plans to install slot machines for Maine's first Racino). Band concerts in the park by the Paul Bunyan statue on Tuesday in summer.

Bangor Symphony Orchestra (207-942-5555). The symphony began in 1895 and is still going strong, with performances at the Bangor Opera House Oct.–May.

✳ Selective Shopping
BOOKSTORES

In Bangor

Bangor has what some like to call a Bookseller's Row right downtown. The first listings below all cluster together and sell a wonderful range of books, from children's classics to historical works and the latest mysteries. With Java Joe's coffee and the Friar Bakehouse's homemade muffins in the same block, this stretch of downtown makes a kind of introvert's paradise.

Sarah's Books (207-992-2080), 32 Central St., second floor. Open year-round Mon.–Fri. 11–5:30, and most Saturdays, same hours. This is our favorite bookstore, beautifully organized, with clean secondhand editions of great books. Emphasis on Maine, history, travel, and literature.

BookMarcs (207-942-3206; www.bookmarcs.com), 78 Harlow St. A first-rate, full-service downtown bookstore with new, used, and discounted books. Particular specialties are books about Maine and by Maine authors. Java Joe's Café is connected to the store.

W. J. Lippincott Books (207-942-4398), 36 Central St. A large street-level bookstore with some 30,000 used and rare titles. Specialties include books on the North Maine Woods, logging, and Indians of the northeastern United States. Also carries detective and science fiction.

✐ **The Briar Patch** (207-941-0255), 27 Central St. A large and exceptional children's-book store, with creative toys, puzzles, and games.

Elsewhere

Betts' Bookstore (207-947-7052; www.bettsbooks.com), 584 Hammond St., Bangor. A small bookstore specializing in the works of local author Stephen King, who has used Bangor and surroundings as the setting of several novels. New editions but also used and hard-to-find copies. Also stocks books on aviation and automobiles.

Mr. Paperback. Bangor is home base for this eastern Maine chain, which has a store at the Airport Mall (207-942-9191) with a good selection of Maine books.

Borders Books and Music (207-990-3300), 116 Bangor Mall Blvd. at

Bangor Mall. Part of a nationwide chain, but a good place to both find a book and sip an espresso.

CAMPING AND HIKING The Map Store (207-827-4511; www.themap store.biz), 240 Main St., No. 5, Old Town. An independent store stocking a large selection of Maine topographic maps and nautical charts along with U.S. and worldwide maps and aerial photos.

CANOES Old Town Canoe & Kayak Factory Outlet Store (207-827-1530), 139 Main St., Old Town. Varieties sold include fiberglass, wood, Kevlar, Crosslink, and Royalex. Factory-tour video shows how canoes are made.

SPECIAL SHOPS Winterport Boot Shop (207-989-6492), 264 State St., Twin City Plaza, Brewer. Largest selection of Red Wing work boots in the Northeast. Proper fit for sizes 4–16, all widths.

Antique Marketplace & Café (207-941-2111; www.antiquemarketplace cafe.com), 65 Main St., Bangor. Booths display antique carpets, china, and more, and a café sells tea, coffee, and pie.

✿ **The Grasshopper Shop** (207-945-3132), 1 W. Market Square, Bangor. Trendy women's and kids' clothing, toys, jewelry, gifts, and housewares. Also a children's store across the street as well as a branch at Bangor International Airport.

The Bangor Mall, Hogan Rd. (just west off the I-95, exit 187, interchange). The centerpiece of a whole range of satellite malls and stores. Since this is precisely the kind of

commercial strip many visitors come to Maine to escape, we won't elaborate, but it certainly has its uses.

Wabanaki Arts Center Gallery (207-827-0391), P.O. Box 3253, 137 N. Main St., Old Town 04468. Operated by the Maine Indian Basketmakers Alliance, a nonprofit arts service organization, this is a lovely small gallery shop staffed by Native American crafters from the Penobscot, Passamaquoddy, Maliseet, and Micmac tribes and selling beautifully made baskets, carvings, and jewelry. There are also displays of antique baskets and carvings, including some rare and unusual war clubs. Open Mon.–Fri. 10–5, Sat. 10–4.

Penobscot Indian Art (207-827-4725), 276 Main St., Old Town. An established store selling locally made handicrafts and a wide variety of Indian-themed objects and souvenirs. Owners S. C. and Cheryl Francis are members of the Penobscot tribe.

✳ Special Events

April: **Kenduskeag Stream Canoe Race**.

July: **Bangor State Fair**, Bass Park—agricultural fair with harness racing.

August: **WLBZ Sidewalk Art Festival**, downtown Bangor. **American Folk Festival** (*last weekend*), Bangor—a celebration of American culture through song, dance, storytelling, and food. Free.

September: **Paul Bunyan Festival Days**, at Paul Bunyan Park—crafts, food, entertainment.

Mid-December: **Native American basketmaker's market**, Hudson Museum, University of Maine at Orono.

THE NORTH MAINE WOODS

Like "Down East," the "North Maine Woods" may seem a bit of a mirage, always over the next hill. In fact, 15 of Maine's 22 million acres are privately owned woodland. Much of this land lies within the area already described in this book as the "Western Mountains and Lakes Region." However, the one particular tract of forest that tends to be equated with "the Maine Woods" is the section bordered on the north and west by Canada, the one that on highway maps shows no roads. This is the largest stretch of unpeopled woodland in the East, but wilderness it's not.

Private ownership of this sector, technically part of Maine's 10.5 million acres known as the unorganized townships, dates from the 1820s when Maine was securing independence from Massachusetts. The mother state, her coffers at their usual low, stipulated that an even division of all previously undeeded wilderness be part of the separation agreement. The woods were quickly sold by the legislature for $12\frac{1}{2}$ ¢ to 38¢ per acre.

Pine was king, and men had already been working this woodland for decades. They lived together in remote lumber camps such as the one Thoreau visited in 1846 at Chesuncook. They worked in subzero temperatures, harvesting and hauling logs on sleds to frozen rivers. They rode those logs through the roaring spring runoffs, driving them across vast lakes and sometimes hundreds of miles downstream to mills. These were lumberjacks, the stuff of children's stories and adult songs, articles, and books. They were the cowboys of the East, larger than ordinary men.

What's largely forgotten is that by the second half of the 19th century, the North Maine Woods were more accessible to and popular with visitors than they are today. By 1853 *Atlantic Monthly* editor James Russell Lowell could chug toward Moosehead on a cinder-spraying train; by 1900 Bostonians could ride comfortably to Greenville in a day, while Manhattanites could bed down in a Pullman and sleep their way to the foot of Moosehead Lake. The Bangor & Aroostook Railroad published annual glossy illustrated guidebooks to Moosehead and its environs, and detailed maps were circulated.

By 1882 the Kineo House, with 500 guest rooms and half a mile of verandas overlooking Moosehead Lake, was said to be the largest hotel in America. In Greenville Sanders & Sons, the era's L. L. Bean, outfitted city "sports" with the clothing, firearms, and fishing gear with which to meet their guides and board steamers bound for far corners of the lake, frequently continuing on by foot and canoe to dozens of backwoods "sporting camps."

With the advent of World War I, the Depression, and the switch from rails to roads, the North Woods dimmed as a travel destination. In the 1920s the steamboat *Katahdin*, once the pride of the Moosehead fleet, was sold to a logging company as a towboat, and the Maine state legislature refused to protect woodland around Mount Katahdin, the state's highest mountain. Governor Percival Baxter then bought the core of current Baxter State Park with his own money. In 1938 the Kineo House burned to the ground.

In ensuing decades the wisdom of Governor Baxter's puchase became increasingly apparent. Mount Katahdin, as the terminus of the 2,144-mile Appalachian Trail from Georgia, attracted recognition and serious hikers from throughout the world. Hunters and fishermen continued to make spring and fall trips to their fathers' haunts, and families to find their way to reasonably priced lake camps. In 1966 a 92-mile ribbon of lakes, ponds, rivers, and streams running northwest from Baxter State Park was designated the Allagash Wilderness Waterway, triggering interest among canoeists—though only a very narrow corridor was actually preserved because the state owns only 400 to 800 feet from the high-water mark. Still, it can control activities up to a mile on each side of the river.

Meanwhile the timber industry was transforming. This woodland was harvested initially for tall timber, but in the late 19th century the value of less desirable softwood increased when the process of making paper from wood fibers was rediscovered. (It seems that the method first used in AD 105 had been forgotten, and New England mills had been using rags to make paper.) By the turn of the 20th century many pulp and paper mills had moved to their softwood source. The city of Millinocket boomed into existence (the population skyrocketed from two families to 2,000 people between 1888 and 1900, and to 5,000 in 1912) around mammoth mills built by Great Northern, which also maintained far-flung farms to support more widely scattered lumber camps.

In 1900 it's said that some 30,000 men worked seasonally in the Maine woods. By 1970, however, just 6,500 loggers were working year-round; by 1988 this number fell to 3,660 men. On the other hand, the total wood harvest in Maine doubled between 1940 and 1970, and again by the mid-1980s. These numbers mirror technological changes, from axes to chain saws, skidders, and ultimately mammoth machines unselectively cutting thousands of trees per day, creating clear-cuts as large as 8 miles square. Today the Maine Forest Practices Act does not allow clear-cuts larger than 75 acres.

Changes in North Woods ownership have in recent years been equally dramatic. Through most of the 20th century large timber companies assumed much of the management responsibility and taxes as well as the cost of building hundreds of miles of roads (log drives ended in the 1970s) in this area. They also accommodated limited recreation, maintaining campsites and honoring long-term leases for both commercial and private camps. Over the past three decades, however, mergers and sales have fragmented ownership, and much of this "working forest" has been bought by both out-of-state and foreign firms, not just by timber companies but also by investment businesses. It's said that more than 5.5 million acres have changed hands in the last seven years. With this unprecedented level of land sales came increased clear-cut timber harvesting in the '70s and '80s—and unprecedented development. During the 1990s, 3,000 seasonal camps were built within the state's unorganized territories (not all of them in this particular area). Now there are about 900 camp leases in the NMW area.

North Woods ownership continues to shift and splinter. On the one hand, the organization Restore: The North Woods advocates creation of a North Woods National Park. On the other, its many opponents argue that a national park would destroy the traditional economy and lifestyle in the region. Maine's Bureau of Parks and Lands has quietly acquired large tracts, and major nonprofit groups such as The Nature Conservancy, The New England Forestry Foundation, and the Appalachian Mountain Club have secured millions of acres outright and in easements permitting timber management. Grassroots coalition groups like the Northern Forest Alliance work quietly to maintain the balance between economic and recreational needs.

These "recreation needs" have also significantly altered in recent decades, notably with the popularity of snowmobiling and whitewater rafting. The area's reliable December-through-March snow cover makes equally reliable whitewater releases, permitting rafting April to October on the West Branch of the Penobscot River. But the crowds once attracted have started to diminish. Still, the resurgence and popularity of moose and moose tours—not to mention adventure and ecotravel, the resurgence of fly-fishing, kayaking, dogsledding, and cross-country skiing—all contribute to the rediscovery of the beauty of these magnificent woods, a phenomenon not to be confused with second-home development.

To date the effect of increased visitation has been limited. Whitewater rafting companies have established bases in and around Millinocket and Baxter State Park, a lake-studded area in which year-round lodging is increasing, along with

OLD-TIME LUMBERJACKS

Maine Highlands

guiding and dining options, to meet the demand. On Moosehead Lake, The Birches resort now holds 11,000 acres of woodland, while Greenville now offers several upscale inns.

Two dozen major woodlands owners have worked cooperatively through North Maine Woods, a nonprofit organization the landowners formed 35 years ago, to maintain some 500 campsites and operate 14 staffed checkpoints at entry points of industrial logging roads (visitors pay a day-use and camping fee). These roads have themselves altered the look and nature of the North Maine Woods. Many remote sporting camps, for a century accessible only by water, and more recently by air, are now a bumpy ride from the nearest town. However, many of the sporting camps themselves haven't changed since the turn of the 20th century. They represent Maine's inland windjammers, holdovers from another era.

There are four major approaches to this North Maine Woods. The longest, most scenic route is up the Kennebec River, stopping to raft in The Forks, and along the Moose River to the village of Rockwood at the dramatic narrows of Moosehead Lake, then down along the lake to Greenville, New England's largest seaplane base.

From Greenville you can hop a floatplane to a sporting camp or set off up the eastern shore of Moosehead to the woodland outpost of Kokadjo and on up to the Golden Road, a 96-mile private logging road running east from Quebec through uninterrupted forest to Millinocket. As Thoreau did in the 1850s, you can canoe up magnificent Chesuncook Lake, camping or staying in the outpost of Chesuncook Village. With increased interest in rafting down the West Branch of the Penobscot River through Ripogenus Gorge and the Cribworks, this stretch of the Golden Road has become known as the West Branch Region.

The second and third routes, leading respectively to Greenville and Millinocket, both begin at the I-95 exit in Newport and head up through southern Piscataquis County, itself an area of small villages, large lakes, and stretches of woodland that here includes Gulf Hagas, Maine's most magnificent gorge.

For those who come this distance primarily to climb Mount Katahdin and camp in Baxter State Park, or to raft the West Branch of the Penobscot, the quickest route is up I-95 to Medway and in through Millinocket; it's 18 miles to the Togue Pond Gatehouse and Baxter State Park.

While Interstate 95 has replaced the Penobscot River as the highway into the North Maine Woods, it has not displaced Bangor, sited on both the river and I-95 (25 miles east of Newport and 60 miles south of Medway) as the commercial hub and gateway of this entire area. A recent effort seeks to promote the two counties—Penobscot and Piscataquis, which include Moosehead Lake, Baxter State Park, Bangor, and a good portion of the North Maine Woods—as a distinct region named "the Maine Highlands."

Contrary to its potato-fields image, Aroostook County to the north is also largely wooded and includes a major portion of the Allagash Wilderness Waterway. Northern reaches of Baxter State Park and the lakes nearby are best accessed from the park's northern entrance via Patten in "The County." Both Ashland and Portage are also points of entry, and Shin Pond serves as the seaplane base for this northernmost reach of the North Maine Woods.

GUIDANCE **North Maine Woods** (207-435-6213; www.northmainewoods.org), P.O. Box 425, Ashland 04732, publishes map/guides that show logging roads with current checkpoints, user fees and campsites, and a list of outfitters and camps licensed and insured to operate on the property. The web site is excellent. The map/guides are currently available for $3 plus $2 mailing.

Maine Bureau of Parks and Lands (207-287-3821; www.parksandlands.com), 22 State House Station, Augusta 04333. The bureau publishes a map/guide identifying holdings, but what's golden here is the web site. It details specific areas such as Nahmakanta Public Reserved Land—43,000 acres of backcountry hiking trails and remote campsites.

Maine Sporting Camp Association (www.mainesportingcamps.com), P.O. Box 89, Jay 04239, publishes a booklet guide to its members.

Maine Forest Products Council (www.maineforest.org) offers links to local resources. Also check the New England Forestry Foundation (www.newengland forestry.org), the Northern Forest Alliance (www.northernforestalliance.org), and The Nature Conservancy (www.nature.org).

SUGGESTED READING *Northeastern Wilds: Journeys of Discovery in the Northern Forest*, photography and text by Stephen Gorman (Appalachian Mountain Club Books, 2002). *The Maine Woods*, by Henry David Thoreau (Penguin Nature Library). *The Maine Atlas and Gazetteer*, DeLorme (2005), essential for navigating this region.

MOOSEHEAD LAKE AREA

As Rt. 15 crests Indian Hill, you see for a moment what Henry David Thoreau described so well from this spot in 1858: "A suitably wild looking sheet of water, sprinkled with low islands . . . covered with shaggy spruce and other wild wood." After a sunset by the shore of Moosehead Lake you also see what he meant by: "A lake is the Earth's eye, looking into which the beholder measures the depth of his own nature."

Moosehead is Maine's largest lake—40 miles long, up to 20 miles wide, with some 400 miles of shoreline—and its surface is spotted with more than 50 islands. Greenville at its toe is the sole "organized" town (population: 1,623 in winter, around 10,000 in summer). Rockwood, with fewer than 300 residents, is halfway up the western shore.

Moosehead's shoreline remains predominantly green, but the massive real estate developments predicted for this magnificent shore are beginning to take shape under the direction of Plum Creek Timber Company, starting with 975 house lots. You can no longer board a Pullman car in New York City and ride straight through to Greenville the way you could around the turn of the 20th century; but some of the new summer residents would like to fly here in a private jet.

Greenville began as a farm town but soon discovered its best crops to be winter lumbering and summer tourists—a group that, since train service and grand hotels have vanished, now consists largely of anglers, canoeists, whitewater rafters in spring and summer, and hunters in late fall. Thanks to snowmobilers, augmented by skiers, cross-country skiers, and ice fishermen, winter is now almost equally as popular. In late September and early fall when the foliage is most brilliant and mirrored in the lake, leaf-peepers are, however, still surprisingly few.

Unlike 1890s "sports" (the game hunters and trophy fishermen who put Moosehead Lake on the world's resort map), many current outdoors enthusiasts want to watch—not kill—wildlife and to experience "wilderness" completely but quickly; that is, by plunging through whitewater in a rubber raft, pedaling a mountain bike over woods trails, or paddling an hour or two in Thoreau's trail or in search of a moose.

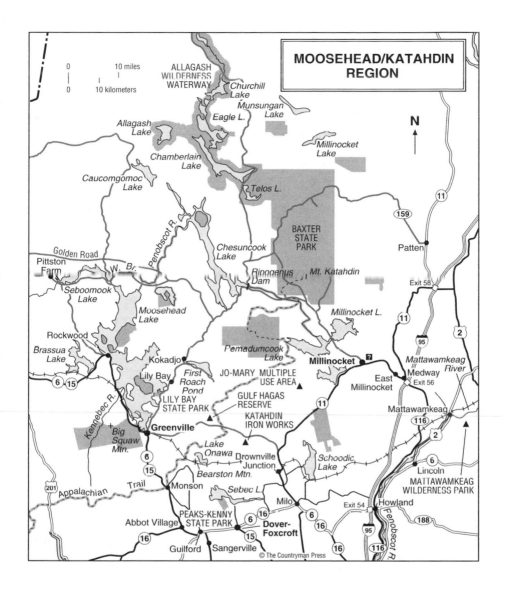

MOOSEHEAD/KATAHDIN REGION

Moosehead has become Maine's moose mecca. Experts debate whether the name of the lake stems from its shape or from the number of moose you can see there. During "Moosemainea," a mid-May through mid-June festival that courts Moosemaniacs with a series of special events, moose sightings average 3,500.

Immense and flanked by mountains, the lake possesses unusual beauty and offers a family a wide choice of rustic, old-fashioned "camps" at reasonable prices as well as an increasing number of upscale inns and B&Bs. Greenville remains a lumbermen's depot with a salting of souvenir and offbeat shops. It's also still a major seaplane base, with flying services competing to ferry visitors to remote camps and campsites in the working woodland to the north and east.

The community of Rockwood, half an hour's drive north of Greenville on the lake's west shore, is even more of an outpost: a cluster of sporting camps and stores between the lake and the Moose River. Hidden away here on the lake, overlooking Kineo, The Birches is a genuine North Woods resort with traditional lakeside cottages and 11,000 acres stretching back to Brassua Lake.

Rockwood sits at the lake's narrows, across from its most dramatic landmark: the sheer cliff face of Mount Kineo, a place revered by Native Americans. According to local legend, the mountain is the petrified remains of a monster moose sent to earth by the Great Spirit as a punishment for sins. It was also the Native Americans' source of a flintlike stone used for arrowheads. The Mount Kineo House once stood at the foot of this outcropping. First opened as a tavern in 1847, it evolved into one of the largest hotels in America, maintaining its own farm as well as a golf course, yacht club, and stables. It's all but vanished, leaving just a ghostly staff building, a huge elm tree, and a row of shingled Victorian-style summer homes, some available as private rentals. Most of Kineo, an island-like peninsula, is now owned by the state, and the climb to the abrupt summit is one of the most rewarding hikes in Maine.

Most Greenville visitors explore Moosehead's eastern shore at least as far as Lily Bay State Park, and many continue to the outpost village of Kokadjo, prime moose-watching country. It's another 40 miles northeast over private roads to Chesuncook Lake and to Ripogenus Dam, from which logging roads lead north into the Allagash and east to Baxter State Park and Millinocket.

Come December this vast area is dependably snow covered and stays that way well into March, a phenomenon appreciated by snowmobilers—who have become the mainstay of the winter economy, enabling area lodging, including remote camps, to remain open all winter. Reasonably priced Big Squaw draws its share of skiers, and two formal trail systems, along with several sporting camps,

GULF HAGAS

Timothy Ellis, Jr.

cater to cross-country skiers. Snowshoeing and dogsledding are also popular ways of traversing this backcountry in all its frozen magnificence.

GUIDANCE Moosehead Lake Region Chamber of Commerce (207-695-2702 or 1-888-876-2778; www.mooseheadlake.org), P.O. Box 581, Greenville 04441. A four-season resource. The walk-in information center up on Indian Hill (Rt. 15 south of town) is open daily in summer, five days a week Oct.–May.

Rockwood Information Station (207-534-7300; www.rockwoodonmoosehead .org), P.O. Box VG, Rockwood 04478, is a source of year-round information about the Rockwood area. The Maine Frame Gallery, Rt. 15, doubles as an information center May–Columbus Day.

GETTING THERE *By car:* Greenville is 54 miles north of I-95, exit 157, at Newport. Follow Rt. 7 to Dexter, Rt. 23 to Sangerville (Guilford), and Rt. 15 to Greenville. The longer, more scenic route is up Rt. 201 (I-95, exit 133) through The Forks (see "Upper Kennebec Valley" for suggestions about whitewater rafting). From Rt. 201 in Jackman, take Rt. 5/15 east to Rockwood.

GETTING AROUND *By air:* **Currier's Flying Service** (207-695-2778; www .curriersflyingservice.com), Greenville Junction, offers day trips; scenic flights, including Mount Katahdin, Mount Kineo, and others; and service to camps. They will book camps and guides. **Jack's Air Service** (207-695-3020), May–Oct.1, caters to Allagash canoe trips, fly-ins to housekeeping cottages, and sightseeing flights. **Folsom's Air Service** (207-695-2821), Greenville, founded by Dick Folsom in 1946, now headed by his son Max, specializes in scenic flights ranging from 15-minute flights to hour-long moose-watches.

By boat: **Kineo Shuttle** is being run now by the Mt. Kineo Golf Course; call 207-534-9012 for a schedule.

By car: If you plan to venture out on the area's network of private roads, be fore-warned that gate fees at "20 mile" gate on the Pittston Farm and Golden Roads are currently $8 for nonresidents ($5, residents) and you need a car with high clearance, preferably four-wheel drive.

WHEN TO COME Greenville's seasons begin with spring fishing, which overlaps in April with "Moosemainea." June can be uncomfortably buggy (blackflies), but they are gone by July; high season here lasts through the second weekend in September, the annual "fly-in" of floatplanes from throughout the country and Canada. Fall is beautiful but low-key until deer season begins in mid-November. With snow comes snowmobile season, which seems bigger every year.

✳ To See

✦ **The S/S** *Katahdin* **and Moosehead Marine Museum** (207-695-2716, www .katahdincruises.com), Greenville. Home for the S/S *Katahdin*, a restored vintage-1914 steamboat that cruises Moosehead Lake from Memorial Day through Columbus Day but on a fairly complicated schedule. Three- and 5-hour cruises

Christina Tree

S/S *KATAHDIN*

offered. Private charters available. One of 50 steamboats on the lake at its height as a resort destination, the *Katahdin* was the last to survive, converted to diesel in 1922 and in the 1930s modified to haul booms of logs, something we can remember her doing in 1976, the year of the nation's last log drive. This graceful 115-foot, 225-passenger boat was restored through volunteer effort and re-launched in 1985. The Louis Oakes Map Room displays regional, historical maps, and displays depict the lake's resort history from 1836.

The Panorama from Big Squaw. The state has changed the mountain's name to Moose Mountain, but the resort here retains its old name. Turn at the sign on Rt. 15, drive up the ski area access road to the base area, and park at the lodge for the area's most superlative panorama: Moosehead Lake spread below you, and beyond it woodlands stretching to Mount Katahdin.

Eveleth-Crafts-Sheridan House (207-695-2909; www.mooseheadhistory.org), 444 Pritham Ave., Greenville. Guided hour-long tours offered June–early Sep., Wed.–Fri. 1–4. $4 adults, $2 children under 12. Home of the Moosehead Historical Society, this is a genuinely interesting 19th-century home with displays on the region's history, including postcards and photos picturing early hotels and steamboats, and changing exhibits on the "sunporch." The carriage house has been renovated as a lumberman's museum.

MOOSE Don't leave the area without seeing at least one. See *Moose-Watching* under *To Do*.

SCENIC DRIVES

Along the western shore
Follow **Rt. 6/15** north through Greenville Junction. If **Squaw Mountain's** chairlifts are running, the ride is well worth taking for the views. Continue to **Rockwood** and take the shuttle to **Mount Kineo**; allow the better part of a day for exploring this dramatic spot. From Rockwood, you can continue north for 20 miles to the North Maine Woods checkpoint (gate fee for out-of-staters). **Pittston Farm**, a short distance beyond, was once the hub of Great Northern's operations for this entire western swath of North Woods. It's now a backwoods lodge. Note that from Rockwood you can also continue on to Quebec City (via Jackman).

Along the eastern shore
Lily Bay State Park (207-695-2700), 8 miles north of Greenville, offers a sandy beach, a grassy picnicking area, and camping. It's a superlatively beautiful spot.

Kokadjo, 18 miles north of Greenville, is a 100-acre parcel of independently owned land on First Roach Pond, in the center of lumber-company-owned forest. Most of the buildings here were once part of a lumbering station and are now camps attached to the **Kokadjo Trading Post**; **Northern Pride Lodge** rents canoes and boats. Continuing north, the road turns to dirt and is fairly bumpy for the first few miles. The road surface improves when you pass the (now unstaffed) gate entering paper company land and is fairly smooth (but you must now pull over to let lumber trucks pass); it improves even more in a dozen miles when you hit the **Golden Road**, where you turn right (east).

Cushing's Landing, at the foot of **Chesuncook Lake**, is worth a stop. The woodsman's memorial here was created from a post in the doorway of a Bangor tavern; it's decorated with tools of the trade and an iron bean pot. This is also the logical boat launch for visiting **Chesuncook Village**, one of the few surviving examples of a 19th-century North Maine Woods lumbermen's village, now on the National Register of Historic Places. In summer access is by charter aircraft from Greenville or by boat from **Chesuncook Dam**. In winter you can come by snowmobile. Writing about the village in 1853, Henry David Thoreau noted, "Here immigration is a tide which may ebb when it has swept away the pines." Today a church, a graveyard (relocated from the shore to a hollow in the woods when Great Northern raised the level of the lake a few years ago), an inn, and a huddle of houses are all that remain of the village.

Ripogenus Dam, just east of Chesuncook Lake, is the departure point for a number of whitewater rafting expeditions. This is one of the two major centers for whitewater rafting in Maine—the other is The Forks. Beginning at the dam, the West Branch of the Penobscot drops more than 70 feet per mile—seething and roiling through Ripogenus Gorge—and continues another 12 miles, with stretches of relatively calm water punctuated by steep drops. You can get a view of the gorge by driving across the dam. **Pray's Store** (207-723-8880), a short distance from the dam, is open year-round with a snack bar and staples.

The Telos Road leads to the **Allagash Wilderness Waterway**, a 92-mile-long chain of lakes, ponds, rivers, and streams that snakes through the heart of the North Woods. The traditional canoe trip through the Allagash takes 10 days, but 2- and 3-day trips can be worked out. Brook trout, togue, and lake whitefish are plentiful. For details, see *Canoeing the Allagash* in "What's Where" and *Canoe and Kayak Rentals* and *Trips*, below.

LILLY BAY STATE PARK

Christina Tree

✳ To Do

AIRPLANE RIDES See descriptions of scenic flights offered by flying services under *Getting Around*.

BOAT EXCURSIONS See *S/S Katahdin* under *To See.*

The Birches Resort offers pontoon-boat cruises. Check with the chamber of commerce for current options.

Also see *Canoe and Kayak Rentals* and *Trips* for guided excursions, and *Fishing* for guided fishing trips.

CANOE AND KAYAK RENTALS are available in Greenville from **Northwoods Outfitters** (207-695-3288; www.maineoutfitter.com) and **Indian Hill Trading Post** (207-695-2104) and in Rockwood from The Birches Resort as well as **Moose River Landing** (207-534-2897), which also rents a pontoon boat.

Note: Most sporting camps also rent canoes or kayaks, and all the flying services will ferry canoes into remote backcountry.

CANOE AND KAYAK TRIPS *𝒮* **Allagash Canoe Trips** (207-237-3077; www .allagashcanoetrips.com), based in Greenville, May–Oct. A family business since 1953, this is the oldest continuously running guided canoe trips service in Maine. It's now operated by third-generation guide Chip Cochrane and offers weeklong expeditions into the Allagash Wilderness Waterway, on the West Branch of the Penobscot, and on the St. John River. Also special teen trips. Sep.–May, Chip (a former member of the U.S. ski team) coaches at Carrabassett Valley Academy at Sugarloaf.

Northwoods Outfitters (see *Canoe and Kayak Rentals*) offers 5- to 7-day Allagash and 2- to 7-day Penobscot wilderness canoe trips as well as overnight camping on Moosehead; also 1-day excursions on Moosehead.

Wilderness Expeditions (207-534-2242; 207-534-7305; or 1-800-825-WILD), P.O. Box 41, Rockwood 04478. Based at The Birches Resort, offering a variety of guided kayak trips, including a 3-day/2-night tour up Moosehead Lake that retraces Thoreau's exact canoe route north from Greenville to Northeast Carry (35 miles).

Back to Basics (207-534-7725; www.comebacktobasics.com), P.O. Box 127, based at Rockwood Cottages in Rockwood 04478. Robert Dumont, a Registered Maine Guide and naturalist with a love of local history, and his bride, Jennifer Dumont, a wilderness instructor who has hiked the AT among many other adventures, offer guided canoeing adventures ranging from gentle to whitewater. Also canoe rentals, shuttle service, and moose safaris with BBQ meals included.

Also see *Moose-Watching.*

FISHING Troll for landlocked salmon, togue, and brook trout in Moosehead Lake, and fly-fish in the many rivers and ponds—rental boats and boat launches are so plentiful that they defy listing.

There are two prime sources of fishing information: the **Inland Fisheries and Wildlife** office (207-695-3756), Greenville, and the **Maine Guide Fly Shop and Guide Service** (207-695-2266), Main St., Greenville. At the Fly Shop, Dan Legere sells 314 different flies and a wide assortment of gear; he also works with local guides to outfit you with a boat and guide or to set up a river float trip or a fly-in expedition. The resurgence of fly-fishing as a popular sport is reflected in the variety of gear and guides available in this shop. Deep lake trolling is, however, also popular. For a list of local boat rentals as well as a list of local guides, check with the **Moosehead Lake Region Chamber of Commerce** (see *Guidance*). Also see the listings under *Rustic Resorts*, all of which are on water and cater to fishermen.

Ice fishing usually begins in January and ends with March. Icehouse rentals are available locally. Inquire at the chamber.

GOLF **Mount Kineo Golf Course** (207-534-8812). A spectacularly sited nine-hole course at Kineo, accessible by frequent boat service from Rockwood; carts and club rentals.

Squaw Mountain Village (207-695-3609), Rt. 15, Greenville, offers 9 holes; $15 for 9 holes, $22 for 18.

HIKING There are two stellar, not-to-be-missed hikes in this area.

Mount Kineo, an islandlike peninsula, has trails to the back side of the famous cliff that rises 763 feet above the water and the apron of land once occupied by the Kineo House resort. Most of the island (8,000 acres) is now state owned, and trails along its circumference and up the back of the cliff are maintained. Take the **Indian Trail**, which heads straight up over ledges that are a distinct green: This is one of the world's largest masses of rhyolite, a flintlike volcanic rock. This trail is shaded by red pines, oaks, and a surprising variety of hardwoods. The view down the lake from the fire tower is spectacular. The **Bridle Trail** is easier for the descent, and a good option on the way up for small children. A carriage trail also circles the island, which is accessible from Rockwood by frequent water shuttle (see *Getting Around*). Bring a picnic and lunch at the Kineo House site.

Gulf Hagas, billed as the "Grand Canyon of Maine," is just 15 miles east of Greenville via the airport road (see *Green Space* under "Katahdin Region" for details). In winter this is the far more accessible approach and a fabulous adventure (see Little Lyford Pond Camps under *Rustic Resorts*).

OTHER GOOD HIKES INCLUDE *✐* **Borestone Mountain Audubon Sanctuary**, 10 miles out Elliotsville Rd. from Rt. 6/15 at Monson. A good hike for families. The trail begins at the gate (elevation 800 feet) on a 1.3-mile road to the visitor center maintained by Maine Audubon (207-631-4050; www.maineaudubon.org) at Sunrise Pond. A footpath continues another mile up to Borestone's rocky West Peak; a blazed trail continues another 0.5 mile to the East Peak (elevation 2,000 feet) for a 360-degree view.

Check local sources for details about hiking **Little and Big Spencer Mountains** and **Elephant Mountain**, and walking into **Little Wilson Falls**, a majestic 57-foot cascade in a forested setting. The Moosehead Lake Region Chamber of Commerce publishes a detailed, free *Hiking Guide*.

HORSEBACK RIDING AND WAGON RIDES See Northern Maine Riding Adventures in "Katahdin Region."

Rockies Golden Acres (207-695-3229), Greenville, offers 1½- to 2-hour trail rides through the woods to Sawyer Pond; mountain views. Call after 7 PM, or leave a message.

MARINAS **Big Lake Equipment Marina** (207-695-4487) in downtown Greenville offers slips, fuel, and supplies.

Beaver Cove Marina (207-395-3526; www.beavercovemarina.com), 8 miles north of Greenville on the eastern side of the lake, offers slips and a selection of rental boats, parts and service, fuel and clothing.

MOOSE-WATCHING **"Moosemainea,"** sponsored by the Moosehead Lake Chamber of Commerce mid-May–mid-June, is the largest, most colorful moose-watching event in New England. Still, chances are you can spot the lake's mascot any dawn or dusk, especially if you go on a guided moose-watching tour.

Greenville's three flying services offer moose-watching both strictly from the air and by flying in to prime spots. See *Getting Around.*

Moose Cruises aboard pontoon boats are offered mornings and evenings by **The Birches Resort** (207-534-7305).

Moose Country Safaris (207-876-4907; www.moosecountrysafaris.com) offers early-morning and evening moose cruises in the Kokadjo area using canoes and vehicles. **Northwoods Outfitters** (207-695-3288) also offers moose-watching excursions by kayak or canoe.

✍ **Northern Pride Lodge** (207-695-2890; www.northernpridelodge.com), 3405 Lily Bay Rd., Frenchtown Township.

✍ **Back to Basics** (see *Canoe and Kayak Rentals*) and the **Maine Guide Fly Shop** (see *Fishing*) also specialize in moose canoe cruises.

MOUNTAIN BIKING **Northwoods Outfitters** (207-695-3288), Main St., Greenville, rents bikes and has trail information available.

The Birches Resort (207-534-7305 or 1-800-825-WILD), Rockwood, offers mountain bike rentals for use on its extensive cross-country ski network.

RECREATIONAL FACILITY ✍ **Greenville Athletic Complex**, Greenville. Facilities include an outdoor rink for skateboarding/roller hockey in summer and ice hockey in winter, as well as a 0.25-mile, 8-foot-wide paved in-line skating track. You'll also find a sand volleyball court, a 0.25-mile running track, outdoor tennis courts, a basketball court, and a playground.

SWIMMING See **Lily Bay State Park** under *Scenic Drives.*

Red Cross swimming beach, halfway between Greenville Village and the Junction, is a good beach on the lake, with lifeguards.

WHITEWATER RAFTING AND KAYAKING **Moosehead Lake** is equidistant from Maine's two most popular rafting routes—Kennebec Gorge and Ripogenus Gorge. **Wilderness Expeditions** (207-534-2242 or 1-800-825-WILD), based at

The Birches Resort in Rockwood, is a family-run business specializing in half-day whitewater rafting trips on the Kennebec at East Outlet (minimum age is 7); also longer expeditions on the Kennebec and on the Penobscot from a base near Baxter State Park. Also see the "Upper Kennebec" and "Katahdin Region" chapters.

✳ Winter Sports

Northwoods Outfitters (207-695-3288), Main St., Greenville, is a full-service retail shop, selling and renting cross-country and downhill skis, snowboards, snowshoes; it offers a list of trails good for exploring.

CROSS-COUNTRY SKIING Formal touring centers aside, this region's vast network of snowmobile trails and frozen lakes constitutes splendid opportunities for backcountry skiing.

Birches Ski Touring Center (207-534-7305), Rockwood. The Birches Resort maintains an extensive network of trails, taking advantage of an 11,000-acre forested spread across the neck between Brassua and Moosehead Lakes; you can spend the night in yurts spaced along the trail. You can also ski to Tomhegan, 10 miles up the lake, or out past the ice-fishing shanties to Kineo. Rentals and instruction; snowshoes, too.

Little Lyford Pond Camps offers a network of groomed trails connecting with backcountry trails, including the Appalachian Trail and leading into Gulf Hagas.

🎣 **A Fierce Chase** (207-997-3971), Elliotsville Rd., posted from Rt. 15 (it's 1 mile) in Monson. Open when there's snow, 8 AM–sunset. John and Susan Chase groom 14 km of cross-country ski trails for both classical and skate skiing. Ski and snowshoe sales, rentals, and lessons available. Trail fees $10 adults, $7 students (9–18); ages 8 and under free.

Chesuncook Lake House and **Medawisla** (see *Lodging*) also cater to cross-country skiers.

DOGSLEDDING **Moose Country Safaris and Dogsled Trips** (207-876-4907; www.moosecountrysafaris.com), 191 North Dexter Rd., Sangerville. Ed Mathew offers 1- and 2-hour trips in the Moosehead Lake region, with heated warming huts along the way.

Also see **Maine Dogsledding Adventures** (207-731-8888; www.mainedog sledding.com) in the "Katahdin" chapter. Based at Nahmakanta Lake Camps in Rainbow Township, halfway between Greenville and Millinocket, this is the most extensive dogsledding program in the area.

Song in the Woods (207-876-4736; www.songinthewoods.com), Abbot. Stephen Medera and his team of huskies offer not only sled rides but also full-day adventures featuring snowshoeing.

DOWNHILL SKIING 🎣 **Big Squaw Mountain Resort** (207-695-1000; www.big squawmountain.com), Rt. 15, Greenville. Though the state has changed the mountain's name to Moose Mountain, the resort has elected to keep the name it has had since 1963, when it opened with one of New England's first base area hotels. Owned by Scott Paper, it then languished under ownership by the state and has further deteriorated under present private, absentee ownership. Even in summer you are struck by the small number of trails streaking such a big mountain: just 33 trails, but with a 1,750-foot drop. A double chair is reputed to be under repair, and may be reopened after a year's shutdown. Lifts are limited to the triple chair and a T-bar. Other facilities include a base lodge and cafeteria, ski school, ski shop, and lodging in 52 rooms. Weekend lift tickets cost just $19 adults. On-mountain motel-style rooms begin at $69 per couple.

SNOWMOBILING **Snowmobiling** is huge in this area, with 500 well-maintained miles of snowmobile trails. **Moosehead Riders Snowmobile Club** offers a 24-hour trail-condition report (207-695-4561). Its clubhouse is open Sat. and Sun. in winter. The club also sponsors guided tours. Interconnecting Trail System (ITS) Rts. 85, 86, and 87 run directly through the area, and there are many locally groomed trails as well. The 100-mile Moosehead Trail circles the lake. Rt. 66 runs east–west from Mount Kineo to Kokadjo. Snowmobile rentals are available from **Northwoods Outfitters** (207-695-3288) and **Big Lake Equipment** (207-695-4487) in Greenville; from **The Birches Resort** (1-800-825-9453) and **Moosehead Sled** (207-534-2261; www.mooseheadsledrentals.com) in Rockwood; and from **Kokadjo Trading Post** (207-695-3993), among others. Inquire about guided tours.

✳ Lodging

INNS **The Blair Hill Inn** (207-695-0224; www.blairhill.com), Lily Bay Rd., P.O. Box 1288, Greenville 04441. Set high above Moosehead Lake at the top of Blair Hill overlooking the lake, this is one of the most exquisite

BLAIR HILL INN

Christina Tree

inns, serving some of the best food, in all of Maine. A Victorian mansion, built in 1891 as the centerpiece of a 2,000-acre gentleman's farm, it's been restored to original grandeur by Dan and Ruth McLaughlin. The upstairs guest rooms have all been deftly decorated and offer sitting areas, a featherbed, fine linens, a writing desk, and CD player. Seven rooms overlook the lake (four have a wood-burning fireplace), and there are two genuine two-room suites with second rooms, good for families (children must be 10 or older). All baths are private and fitted with hand-cut soaps and terrycloth robes, but there are no Jacuzzis. Our favorite is Room 1, the original master bedroom with a hearth and a king-sized four-poster. A hot tub on the 90-foot veranda also has magnificent views. From spring through fall the inn is filled with fresh flowers from its garden. $250–425 includes a multicourse breakfast. Dinner is served Fri. and Sat. (see *Dining Out*). Summer Thursday-evening concerts are presented on the lawn.

& **The Lodge at Moosehead Lake** (207-695-4400 or 1-800-825-6977; www.lodgeatmooseheadlake.com), Box 1175, Lily Bay Rd., Greenville 04441. Open year-round. Sonda and Bruce Hamilton offer five guest rooms in the main house (four with lake views), each designed with immense care around a theme. Carved four-poster beds depict each theme (moose, bear, loon, totem). All rooms have cable TV, gas fireplace, air-conditioning, and bath with Jacuzzi tub. A carriage house holds three luxurious suites with double Jacuzzi and private deck. A full breakfast is served in the glass-walled dining room, and dinner is also available to guests some evenings (ask when you book). $275–475 double occupancy includes a full breakfast.

& **Greenville Inn** (207-695-2206 or 1-888-695-6000; www.greenvilleinn .com), Norris St., Box 1194, Greenville 04441. Open all year (B&B Nov.–May). A lumber baron's mansion set atop a hill with a view of Moosehead Lake. Rich wood paneling, embossed walls, working fireplaces, and leaded glass all contribute to the sense of elegance. A master suite with a fireplace has a lake view; there are four more second-floor rooms, a suite in the carriage house that's good for families, and six cottages. New owners Terry and Jeffrey Johannemann have added a plush Valentine-red tower suite with an in-room, two-person Jacuzzi. Rooms $175–210, suites $200–350, cottages $185–210, buffet breakfast included., off-season rates available. Also see *Dining Out*.

✒ **Northern Pride Lodge** (207-695-2890; www.northernpridelodge.com), 3405 Lily Bay Rd., Frenchtown Township 04441. Open year-round. Built as a hunting lodge for lumber baron Sir Harry Oaks, now a friendly lodge with five guest rooms, each with enough beds for a family or group; four shared, one private bath. The living room has a hearth, stained-glass windows, and a sense of opulence; the dining room, on a glassed-in porch overlooking First Roach Pond, is open to the public by reservation (see *Dining Out*). There are also 24 campsites, rental canoes, motorboats, and moose-watching trips. Owners Barbara and Wayne Plummer are both Registered Maine Guides and offer hunting and fishing. In winter the lodge caters to snowmobilers and cross-country skiers. $90 per couple, $59 single, $125 for the room with private bath (includes breakfast). Another $45 covers all three meals. The lodge is surrounded by its campground but the pond is just beyond; rental canoes and kayaks are offered along with pontoon rides and paddles guaranteed to spot a moose.

BED & BREAKFASTS **Pleasant Street Inn** (207-695-3400; www .pleasantstreetinn.com), 26 Pleasant St. (P.O. Box 1261), Greenville 04441. An 1890s house, built proudly with a square tower and tiger oak woodwork on a quiet side street by the owner of the region's big outfitter. The six guest rooms vary in size, and each is artfully decorated differently. Paintings throughout the house are striking, and the fourth-floor Tower Room, accessible to all, commands a view of the lake. Common space includes an upstairs sitting room, a well-stocked butler's pantry, and a dining room

Christina Tree

THE BIRCHES

🐾 ✐ THE BIRCHES RESORT

(207-534-7305 or 1-800-825-WILD; www.birches.com), P.O. Box 41, Rockwood 04478. Open year-round. The Willard family has transformed this 1930s sporting camp into a genuine all-season, many-faceted North Woods resort. Its 15 rustic cabins are spaced among birch trees along Moosehead Lake,

with a fireplace, the setting for full breakfasts and for dinner by reservation ($35–40). $110–175; suites to $260. Your hosts are Timothy Shelep, Daniel Turek, and John Cusick.

The Evergreen Lodge at Moosehead (207-695-3241 or 1-888-624-3993; www.evergreenlodgemoosehead.com), 182 Greenville Rd. (Rt. 15), Greenville 04441. South of Greenville, this contemporary house is set back in its gardens, surrounded by 30 acres of birch and evergreen. Hank and Janice Dyer offer two sitting rooms with TV and fireplace, and six guest rooms, all brightly, comfortably furnished, all with private bath, two with log fireplace. $110–150 includes a full breakfast.

EASILY ACCESSIBLE RUSTIC RESORT (traditional sporting camp)

🍴 🐾 **Maynard's in Maine** (207-534-7703; www.maynardsinmaine.com), just off Rt. 6/15 over the bridge in Rockwood 04478. Open May–hunting season. "The only thing we change around here is the linen," says Gail Maynard, who helps run the sportsmen's camp founded by her husband's grandfather in 1919. Overlooking the Moose River, a short walk from Moosehead Lake, Maynard's includes 13 tidy moss-green frame buildings with dark Edwardian furniture, much of it from the grand old Mount Kineo Hotel. The lodge is filled with mounted fish, birds, and other trophies. Two meals a day are served, plus one

overlooking Mount Kineo. They range from one to four bedrooms and from traditional hand-hewn log "camps" to a luxurious new cabin with four bedrooms,
four baths, and a hot tub. Each has at least a porch and a Franklin stove or fireplace in a sitting room, and all have a kitchen (some don't have an oven), but
three meals are offered at the lodge. Several new "lakeside homes" are also
available for rent, along with units in the Riverview Lodge on the Moose River.
The main lodge features a cheerful open-timbered dining room (see *Dining Out*),
an inviting lobby with a trout pool, and a living room with a hearth and a corner
bar with tree stump stools. Upstairs are four guest rooms with decks overlooking the lake (shared bath); there are also "cabin tents" near the lodge and several yurts scattered along wooded cross-country ski/biking trails. Facilities
include an outside hot tub and sauna near the lodge and a fitness center out by
the marina. Moose Cruises and guided kayak, hiking, backwoods jeep and biking tours are offered, along with scenic floatplane rides with innkeeper John
Willard. Sailboards, sailboats, kayaks, canoes, fishing boats, and mountain
bikes are available. In winter this is a major cross-country ski center, but snowmobiles are also rented and there's ice fishing within walking distance of the
cabins. Rates: $70–80 double in the lodge, $110–175 per night and $750–1,150
per week for one- and two-bedroom "rustic" cabins, $225 per night ($1,200–
1,300 per week) for the luxury four-bedroom cabin sleeping six. Cabin tents
begin at $25 single per day, and yurts at $30 per person. Inquire about rafting,
canoeing, and other packages. Pets are $10 extra.

"packed." Per person $60 with three meals, $30 in a housekeeping cabin (no meals), $325 per week in Nov. (meals and lodging). $20 per pet (for duration of the stay).

REMOTE SPORTING CAMPS (requiring a four wheel-drive or high-clear-
ance vehicle, and in winter possibly
either snowmobile or nonmotorized
access)

☙ ✍ **Little Lyford Pond Camps**
(603-466-2727; www.outdoors.org/
lodging/lyford), Box 310, Greenville
04441. Open Dec. 15–Mar. 31 and
May 10–Oct. 31. Reservations are
required. Sited in a sheltered alpine
valley, these camps were built in the
1870s as a logging company station on
a "tote road," a road designed to move
people and supplies during any kind of
construction. The seven shake-roofed
log cabins (without plumbing or electricity) sleep from one to four. Each
has a private outhouse. In 2003 Little
Lyford and 37,000 surrounding acres
were acquired by the Boston-based
Appalachian Mountain Club, the
country's oldest outdoor recreation/
preservation group. Former Little
Lyford owner Bob LeRoy remains
as manager at a new lodge with comfortable gathering and dining areas.
Amenities include a hot shower in
summer and cedar sauna (no shower)
in winter. Gulf Hagas is a 7-mile
round-trip hike or ski. In winter you
can ski, sled, or dogsled to the camps

or hitch a snowmobile shuttle, along with your luggage. The camps are 3.5 miles off the Appalachian Trail and 12 miles via a gated logging road from Greenville. We last came in March and enjoyed exceptional cross-country skiing into Gulf Hagas and around the camps. $92 per person in summer, $120 per person in winter (less for children and AMC members), includes all meals (with an emphasis on vegetarian). There's a charge for the snowmobile shuttle and gear shuttle.

∞ **Chesuncook Lake House** (207-745-5330; www.chesuncooklakehouse.com), Box 656, Rt. 76, Greenville 04441. Open year-round. At a homey, 1864 farmhouse, David and Luisa Surprenant are carrying on a long-standing tradition of hospitality with four guest rooms (shared bath) and nearby cabins. For an additional charge guests can be shuttled in by boat or snowmobile; they can also hike, fly, ski, or canoe in. With braided rugs, patterned tin walls and ceilings, comfortable furnishings, and woodstoves, not to mention running water, beds with sheets and blankets, and the enticing aromas emanating from the big Vulcan stove in the kitchen, this is a peaceful, magical spot. When we last visited it was winter and our car was parked 14 miles down a snow-covered tote road. $125 person per night includes three meals; $35 per person in the housekeeping cabins. Small weddings can be arranged, using Chesuncook Village Church.

🐾 ∂ **Nugent's Chamberlain Lake and McNally's Camps** (207-944-5991; www.nugent-mcnallycamps.com), HCR 76, Box 632, Greenville 04441. Open year-round. John Richardson and Regina Webster acquired the original 1930s Nugent's Camps from Patty Nugent in 1987, adding a couple of new cabins but retaining the old-fashioned feel. This is sited on the Allagash Wilderness Waterway, 50 miles north of Millinocket between Baxter State Park and Allagash Mountain. It's best reached via floatplane; otherwise, it's a 4-mile boat or snowmobile ride up Chamberlain Lake. The seven housekeeping cabins have the traditional front overhang and outhouses; they sleep 2 to 16. Boats are available. AP, MAP, or housekeeping plans available. $30–100 per person. John and Regina now also own the even more remote **McNally's Ross Stream Camps**: five classic log structures accommodating two to four people, equipped with flush toilet, sink, and shower in warm-weather months. $100 per person includes all meals.

∂ **Medawisla** (radiophone year-round, 207-695-2690; www.medawisla.com), HCR 76, Box 592, Greenville 04441. Open year-round. The LeRoys offer six fully equipped cabins with woodstove, flush toilet, hot shower, and gas stove. Each can sleep 2 to 10 people. These camps cater to a quiet clientele. We love the "reading room," a spot outside overlooking a dam that was once the only road in. Meals available Oct.–Mar. On our last visit Shannon LeRoy demonstrated her skills as an herbalist, brewing a tea that actually cured sniffles. Boats and canoes are available. The loons on the soundtrack from the movie *On Golden Pond* were taped here. $90–120 per couple per day; weekly rates are available. Meal plans are offered in fall and winter. This is a cross-country ski haven with close to 30 miles of trails; cross-country skiing and dogsledding trips are offered.

🐾 ✒ ♿ **West Branch Pond Camps** (207-695-2561; www.westbranch pondcamps.com), P.O. Box 1153, Greenville 04441. A 10-mile drive from the main road at Kokadjo. Open after ice-out through Oct., and Feb. 1–Mar. 24. First opened as a moose-hunting lodge in the 1880s, across the pond from the majestic bulk of Whitecap Mountain. The camps are rustic; some of the furnishings are a bit worn, but that all adds to the authentic feel. All cabins have wood stoves, electricity, and bath. Eric Stirling is the fourth generation of his family to operate the camps. Motor-boats and canoes are available. Food is hearty New England fare with a set menu—prime rib on Thursday and turkey dinner on Sunday—with fresh vegetables and greens from the organic garden June–Sep. and vegetarian fare on request. It's no secret that First West Branch Pond is the area's prime moose-viewing spot. In winter the camps cater to cross-country skiers and snowshoers with 15 km of trails. $80–90 per person per day includes three meals and use of a canoe; children 5–11 $45–55.

CAMPS (no regular food service in a central lodge)

Tomhegan Wilderness Resort (207-534-7712; www.tomhegan.com), P.O. Box 308, Rockwood 04478. Open year-round. A 10-mile ride up a dirt road from Rockwood Village; 1.5 miles of frontage on Moosehead Lake. Hand-hewn two-bedroom cottages—plus one with four bedrooms—along a wooden boardwalk have a kitchen and living room, rock-ing chairs on the porch, full bath, woodstove, and gas grill; four efficiency apartments are available in the vintage-1910 lodge, which can be rented in its entirety. Boats and canoes are available; cross-country skiing and snowmobiling in winter. Cabins range $625–1,295 per week; lodge apartments begin at $98 per night.

🦆 🐾 ✒ **Rockwood Cottages** (207-534-7725; www.mooseheadlake lodging.com), Box 176, Rockwood 04478. Open May–Nov. Ron and Bonnie Searles maintain eight clean, comfortable housekeeping cottages with screened-in porches overlooking the lake and Mount Kineo just across the narrows. All but one of these have two bedrooms. Canoe and motorboat rentals, and hunting and fishing licenses are available, and guests have free docking. There's also a sauna, a barbecue area, and an impressive view of Moosehead. $85 per couple, $20 per additional person; $510 per couple per week, $100 per additional person. $5 per day per dog. Note that this also serves as base for **Back to Basics** (207-534-7725; www.comebackto basics.com), offering moose tours and guided canoeing and kayaking.

🐾 ✒ **Beaver Cove Camps** (207-695-3717 or 1-800-577-3717; www.beaver covecamps.com), P.O. Box 1233, Greenville 04441. Open year-round. Eight miles north of Greenville on the eastern shore of Moosehead Lake are six fully equipped housekeeping cabins (four waterfront) dating to 1905, each with full kitchen and bath. Owners Dave and Marilyn Goodwin offer launching and docking facilities. $90 per couple per night plus $20 for each additional person; $5 per pet per night. Weekly rates available.

MOUNT KINEO FROM ROCKWOOD COTTAGES

🦌 ♿ **Spencer Pond Camps** (207-843-5456; www.spencerpondcamps .com), 806 Spencer Pond Rd., East Middlesex Township 04441. Open May–mid-Nov. Bob Croce and Jill Martel maintain the traditions of this long-established cluster of six house-keeping camps (sleeping 2 to 10) in an unusually beautiful spot, accessible by logging road from Lily Bay Rd. Guests are welcome to fresh vegetables from the garden. Along with gas and kerosene lights and hand-pumped water, each cottage is stocked with cooking utensils and dishes and has a private shower room (Sunshower) and outhouse. Canoe, kayak, and mountain bike rentals available. From $60 per couple; family rates available.

🐾 **Wilson Pond Camps** (207-695-2860, 1-877-695-2860; www.wilson pondcamps.com), P.O. Box 1354, Greenville 04441. Open year-round.

Bob and Martine Young are the owners of five modern, waterfront cottages (most with woodstoves) and two cottages overlooking Lower Wilson Pond, 3.5 miles from Greenville. A remote cottage called Top Secret Lodge, on Upper Wilson Pond, accepts pets. The housekeeping cottages offer one to three bedrooms, fully equipped kitchens, and screened-in porches. Boats and motors, kayak and canoe rentals are available. From $110 a day for two off-season to $650 a week for three; 2-day minimum in July and August.

LODGE 🦌 ♨ **Big Squaw Mountain Resort** (207-695-1000), P.O. Box 430, Greenville 04441. Open year-round. A 1960s lodge built as part of the ski area, this facility sits high on the side of Moose (alias "Big Squaw") Mountain with sweeping views of the lake; the 52 units have been recently renovated and are nicely furnished. From $69 double, $89 for four people; dorm rooms from $83 per couple plus $5 per additional person. Inquire about packages including morning coffee and tea in-season. In winter the ski-area restaurant is open, but in summer guests have a ways to go for food and drink.

RENTALS Private camp rentals are listed with the chamber of commerce and handled by **Century 21 Muzzy Real Estate** (207-695-4741) and **Vacation Rentals, Inc.** (207-534-9703; www.connectmaine.com/vacation).

CAMPGROUNDS & **Lily Bay State Park** (207-695-2700). Open May–Oct. 15. Nine miles north of Greenville on the east shore of Moosehead Lake. Ninety well-spaced sites, many along the shore, two wheelchair accessible; facilities include a shower house, boat launch, and beach. $19 for non-residents, $14 for Maine residents.

Seboomook Wilderness Campground (207-280-0555; www .seboomookwildernesscampground .com), HC 85, Box 560, Rockwood 04478. Open May–Dec. 8. Accessed by dirt road (some 32 miles from Rockwood), in the northwest corner of the lake. Sites for RVs and for campers and tents ($18–30); Adirondack shelters ($30) on the water. Photos in the camp store (where there's a lunch counter) document this as the site of a World War II POW camp. $50–100 for cabins depending on season. Canoe and kayak rentals and boat rentals.

Maine State Bureau of Forestry (207-695-3721) maintains free (first-come, first-served) "authorized sites"

(no fire permit required) and "permit sites" (permit required) scattered on both public and private land along Moosehead Lake and on several of its islands.

✳ Where to Eat

DINING OUT **Blair Hill** (207-695-0224; www.blairhill.com), Lily Bay Rd., Greenville. Open to the public late June–mid-Oct., Fri. and Sat., also serving inn guests on Sat. evening in winter. Culinary Institute of America–trained chef Jack Neal prepares a four-course menu with a choice of three entrées, served in the dining room or on the porch with lake views. You might begin with crab-stuffed tempura shiitake caps, move on to butternut squash soup, then pine-roasted rack of lamb with garlic mashed Yukon gold potatoes, finishing with a pecan tartlet with dark chocolate ganache atop sauce anglaise. $50 prix fixe. The wine list is large and varied. Blair Hill is the region's outstanding inn, see *Lodging*.

✐ **Rod'n'Reel Café** (207-695-0388), downtown Greenville, across from the lake. Open year-round, 11 AM–closing. Greenville on Sunday night tends to shut down tight by 8 PM, the hour we knocked on the window of this cozy-looking restaurant, which had just closed down its kitchen. Karen LeClair, however, is not about to let anyone go hungry, and she fed us, at the bar, one of the best baked haddocks ($11.95) in memory. The day-long menu runs from a hot dog or burger to prime rib (Fri. and Sat. only). Fully licensed. Dinner entrées $10–21. Tadpoles menu.

The Birches Resort (207-534-2242), Rockwood. Open year-round: daily in summer, closed sporadically, please check. This popular resort (see *Lodging*) has one of the area's most attractive dining rooms—log sided with a massive stone hearth, a war canoe turned upside down in the open rafters, and hurricane lamps on the highly polished tables. The menu offers grilled or baked options; specialties include baby rack ribs, prime rib roast, and "Sicilian haddock" (baked with Parmesan, black olives, and parsley in red wine and garlic). Entrées $14–18. Reservations suggested. There's also an inviting pub.

Northern Pride Lodge (207-695-2890), Kokadjo. Open year-round. The dining room in this classic lumber baron's hunting lodge (see *Lodging*) is a heated sunporch, overlooking First Roach Pond. Dinner is served lto the public by reservation, and it's known as one of the best places to eat in the Moosehead area. The choice of entrées might include roast duckling with crispy skin and tender meat, served with a homemade orange sauce, and baked salmon with the house raspberry maple glaze. Entrées $18–21.

Maynard's Dining Room (207-534-7703), off Rt. 6/15, Rockwood. Open Mother's Day–Columbus Day. Dine (6–8) much as your grandparents would have in the traditional old lodge dining room overlooking the Moose River. Choices vary with the night; $16.95 includes juice or soup, salad, choice of potato or veggie, bread, dessert, and beverage. BYOB. This is known as a first-rate place to dine.

Greenville Inn (207-695-2206 or 1-888-695-6000), Norris St., Greenville. Dinner served in-season June–mid-Oct., Mon.–Sat., weekends in May and June. Reservations requested. With a chef's entrée and catch of the day; $11 for crab spring roll appetizer, $19 for linguine puttanesca, and New Zealand lamb $27. The menu reads: "An 18 percent to 20 percent gratuity is customary in fine dining for first-class service." Patrons are told that an hour-and-a-half wait for dinner is "customary with fine dining."

EATING OUT

In Greenville

Stress Free Moose Pub & Café (695-3100), 65 Pritham Ave., Greenville. Lunch–10 PM weekdays, till 11 Fri.–Sat. Dining on the back deck with a lake view in summer, otherwise inside around the bar and with limited seating by the deli; coffeehouse atmosphere upstairs. The signature sandwich is chicken salad with cranberry and walnuts, served on fresh homemade oat bread and topped with lettuce and tomato. Regulars also swear by the chili.

✿ **Auntie M's Family Restaurant** (207-695-2238), Lily Bay Road, Greenville. Open 5 AM–closing; great breakfast, homemade soups, and specials. We love this place. Everything always tastes good.

Flatlander's Pub (207-695-3373), Pritham Ave., Greenville. Open daily (except in winter when closed on Wed.) from 11 AM "til close." Hamburgers, broasted chicken, seafood; homemade desserts. Nice atmosphere, in the middle of town.

The Black Frog (207-695-1100; www.theblackfrog.com), Pritham Ave., Greenville. Open daily for lunch and dinner. Leigh Turner was a founder of The Road Kill Café in Greenville Junction not that many years ago. Ask and he will recount his brush with Wall Street, a brief period during which Road Kill Cafés prolif-erated around New England but then went bust. The Black Frog offers waterside dining with a menu featur-ing the likes of "the chicken that did-n't make it across the road," "the moose is loose," and "oops-soups."

Beyond Greenville
Kokadjo Trading Post (207-695-3993), Kokadjo. Open 7 AM–9 PM; open earlier during hunting season. Fred and Marie Candeloro offer a cozy dining room with a large field-stone fireplace and a view of First Roach Pond.

Rockwood Trading Post (207-534-7453; www.rockwoodtradingpost .com), Rockwood Village. Jim and Lynne Fisk have expanded the lake-view dining area in the back of this capacious store. Breakfast bagels, "pizza of the day" (available by the slice), as well as a variety of burgers, subs, and roll-ups are offered.

Historic Pittston Farm (207-280-0000; www.pittstonfarm.com), HC 85, Box 525, Rockwood 04478. Open year-round 7 AM–7 PM. *Authentic* only begins to describe this classic outpost, a wilderness farm on the National Historic Register built around 1910 as a major hub of Great Northern's log-ging operations. Jenn and Bob Mills are the new owners, surrounded by 329,000 acres of logging history. Buf-fet all-you-can-eat dinner, 5–7 every night. BYOB. Lodging too.

Spring Creek Bar-B-Q (207-997-7025), Rt. 15, Monson. Open Thu.–Sun. 10–8. Closed Dec. and Apr. Ribs are the big specialty here, but you might want to reserve (you can call days ahead) because they run out toward the end of the day. Also good for standard road food.

✳ Selective Shopping
Indian Hill Trading Post (207-695-3376), Greenville. Open daily year-round, Fri. until 10 PM. Huge—a combination sports store, supermar-ket, and general store, stocking every-thing you might need for a week or two in the woods.

Moosehead Traders (207-695-3806), Moosehead Center Mall, Rt. 15 in downtown Greenville. The most upscale shop in the North Maine Woods: furs, moose antlers and moose antler furnishings (like chandeliers), camp furnishings, antiques, books, and many tempting gifts. The moose is not for sale.

🖋 **Breakneck Ridge Farm** (207-997-3922; www.breakneckridgefarm .com), 160 Mountain Rd., Blanchard. Some 200 head of fallow deer and a small herd of buffalo are raised on this farm, which is visitor geared with a shop (tours and shop July and Aug., Wed., Thu., and Sat. noon–4) selling sandwiches, some made from venison and bison. Hayride tours of the farm are offered July and Aug., Wed., Thu., and Sat. at 10; $6 adults, $6 seniors, $5 children, 3 and under free.

MOOSEHEAD TRADERS

Christina Tree

Christina Tree

CHAIN SAW SIGN CARVER

Joe Bolf, Woodcarver (207-695-3002; www.joebolf.com), 11 Minden St., across from the firehouse, Greenville. Bolf is the area's outstanding carver of signs (WELCOME TO GREENVILLE is a sample); also chain saw sculpture, totem poles, figures, and camp furniture.

Great Eastern Clothing Company (207-695-0770), a trendy emporium, has replaced the old landmark Indian Store in the Shaw Block.

Northwoods Outfitters (207-695-3288), selling sporting gear and wear, now occupies the space vacated by Greenville's other old commercial landmark, Sanders Store.

Maine Mountain Soap and Candle Co. (207-695-3926), Rt. 15, downtown Greenville. The real thing. Good soap.

The Corner Shop (207-695-2142), corner of Main and Pritham (across from Great Eastern Clothing), Greenville; gifts, books, magazines.

Moosin' Around Maine (207-695-3939), Pritham Ave., downtown Greenville. Pottery, jewelry, blown glass from Maine and beyond.

See also **Maine Guide Fly Shop** under *Fishing*.

※ Special Events

February: **Winter Festival**, Greenville—snowmobile events and poker runs.

Late May–mid-June: **Moosemainea** month, sponsored by the chamber of commerce, takes place throughout the area. It's big; see "What's Where."

July: The **Fourth of July** is big in Greenville, with a crafts fair, food booths, music, parade, fireworks, and street dance.

July–August: **Blair Hill Concert series**, Thursdays on the lawn at Blair Hill Inn (207-695-0224)—jazz, bluegrass, and chamber music concerts. $20 per ticket, with a percentage of all concerts benefiting Greenville High School.

August: **Forest Heritage Days**, Greenville—crafts fair and many forestry-related events.

September: **International Seaplane Fly-In Weekend** (*second weekend*), Greenville.

Columbus Day weekend: **Moose on the Run**, a 5K race.

KATAHDIN REGION
INCLUDING LOWER PISCATAQUIS AND LINCOLN LAKES

M ile-high Mount Katahdin is the centerpiece not only for Baxter State Park but also for a surprisingly large area from which it is clearly visible. Like a huge ocean liner in a relatively flat sea of woodland, the massive mountain looms above the open countryside to the east, the direction from which it's most easily accessible.

Maine's highest mountain and its surrounding 204,733-acre park are unquestionably the prime draw, but the Katahdin Region offers its share of wooded lake country and represents one of the most reasonably priced destinations in Maine for families who want to get away together to hike, fish, and swim.

The quest to reach the top of Maine's highest peak makes this the most popular hike in the region, but those seeking a milder experience will find that the many lower peaks within the park are far less trafficked. Whitewater rafting on the West Branch of the Penobscot River is another big attraction, and rafting companies have built base camps near the Togue Pond Gatehouse to Baxter State Park and in nearby Millinocket. Local facilities have also expanded to meet the ever-growing winter demand from snowmobilers.

There are beds nearer to Baxter State Park but the nearest community is Millinocket (5,200 people), a lumbering outpost built by the Great Northern Paper Company around the turn of the 20th century at major drops in the Penobscot River—110 feet in Millinocket itself, and 25 and 50 feet in East Millinocket. In recent years the mills here have changed repeatedly; layoffs have been severe. At this writing both the Millinocket and East Millinocket mills are running, but recognition of the area as a resort destination is steadily growing. Admittedly, the commercial strip along Rt. 157 between East Millinocket and Millinocket is a turnoff (Baxter State Park Headquarters sits beside McDonald's). Still, the whitewater rafting base camps and most of the other lodging we list are located either on one of the area's many lakes or on a part of the Penobscot.

Southwest of Millinocket, lower Piscataquis County is largely woodland framed by (east–west) Rt. 16/6 on the south and traversed by (north–south) Rt. 11, the old road to Millinocket before the advent of I-95. This is a slice of "the real Maine," with Dover-Foxcroft (population: circa 4,300) as its big town. The very real and relatively little-known treasures here are 13-mile-long Sebec Lake, site of Peaks-Kenny State Park, and Gulf Hagas, billed as "Maine's Grand Canyon." Southeast of Millinocket, the Lincoln Lakes region offers some 15 lakes as well as the Penobscot and Mattawamkeag Rivers.

GUIDANCE **Katahdin Area Chamber of Commerce** (207-723-4443; www .katahdinmaine.com), 1029 Central St., Millinocket 04462. The chamber maintains a seasonal information center on Rt. 11/157 east of Millinocket; it serves as a year-round source of information about lodging and dining. An unstaffed information kiosk, open 24 hours, is sited on Rt. 157 in Medway, just off exit 244, I-95.

The Baxter State Park Headquarters (207-723-5140; www.baxterstate parkauthority.com), 64 Balsam Dr., Millinocket 04462, is open Memorial Day– Columbus Day, daily 8–4; otherwise weekdays. It offers picnic tables, restrooms, and a selection of guides to the park. It's 1 mile east of Millinocket on Rt. 11/157. A visitor information center located just before Togue Pond Gate (open 5 to 7 days a week, Memorial Day–Labor Day) offers trip advice, up-to-date weather and trail information, and map/guides for sale.

Southern Piscataquis County Chamber of Commerce (207-564-7533; www .spccc.org), 1033 South St. (Rt. 7), Dover-Foxcroft 04426. Open weekdays 9–5; in summer, daily 9–noon. A log-cabin-style information booth serves the gateway area to both the Moosehead Lake and Katahdin regions, including Brownville Junction, Dexter, Dover-Foxcroft, Guilford, Milo, Monson, and Sangerville. The web site lists many rental camps and other lodging options.

The Maine Highlands (www.themainehighlands.com) is an umbrella promotional group for the area that includes the Katahdin, southern Piscataquis, Lincoln Lakes, Bangor, and Moosehead Lake regions. The web site offers a good overview but few useful details.

GETTING THERE The most direct route is I-95 to exit 244 in Medway (73 miles northeast of Bangor), and 12 miles into Millinocket. From here, it's about 10 miles to Millinocket Lake, and from there another 8 miles to the Togue Pond entrance to Baxter State Park.

DOGSLEDDING ACROSS RAINBOW LAKE FROM NAHMAKANTA
Christina Tree

From the Moosehead Lake area: Millinocket is 70 miles northeast of Greenville—but getting there is an adventure in itself. The 18 miles to Kokadjo are paved (see the previous chapter for Kokadjo facilities), but the next stretch, "the Greenville Road," is badly marked and maintained (the North Maine Woods Gate is unmanned). Once you hit the **Golden Road** (turn right), however, the surface improves. This legendary 96-mile logging road, owned by private companies, runs from Millinocket to Quebec. It's mostly paved along the West Branch of the Penobscot; you can cross over onto the newly paved Baxter State Park Rd. at Ambajejus Lake. This is definitely the scenic, adventurous way to come. Be aware, however, that logging trucks have the right-of-way; slow down and pull to the side to permit them to pass. Your odds of spotting a moose here are high. For a detailed description of sights along this road, see "Moosehead Lake Area."

GETTING AROUND **Katahdin Air Service Inc.** (207-723-8378; www.katahdin air.com), Millinocket. Available May–Nov. to fly in to remote camps and shuttle in canoes and campers; will drop hikers at points along the Appalachian Trail. **Scotty's Flying Service** (207-528-2626) at Shin Pond also serves wilderness camps, as does **West Branch Aviation** (207-723-4375) in Millinocket.

WHEN TO COME Spring draws fishermen; June brings moose-watching and blackflies, July and August are great for swimming, canoeing, and rafting; September and early October are best for hiking and foliage. Snowfall is dependable December through March, but January brings subzero temperatures. February is warmer and snowier and March can be magnificent, bringing the brightest days of the year with intense blue skies above dazzling white lakes and mountains.

✳ To See

The Katahdin Iron Works. Open mid-Apr.–Nov. Turn at the small sign on Rt. 11, 5 miles north of Brownville Junction, and go another 6 miles up the gravel road. The spot was a sacred place for Native Americans, who found yellow ocher paint here. From the 1840s until 1890, an ironworks prospered in this remote spot, spawning a village to house its 200 workers and producing 2,000 tons of raw iron annually. Guests of the Silver Lake Hotel (1880s–1913) here came on the same narrow-gauge railroad that carried away the iron. All that remains is a big old blast furnace and an iron kiln. Tours, books on the ironworks, and videos are offered by local author and backwoods guide Bill Sawtell (207-965-3971; rtell@kynd.net) in Brownville. The site may not be worth your effort unless you plan to continue on down the gravel road to hike in **Gulf Hagas** or to camp.

Patten Lumbermen's Museum (207-528-2650; www.lumbermensmuseum .org), Shin Pond Rd. (Rt. 159), Patten. Open Memorial Day–Columbus Day, Tue.–Sun. 10–4 in summer, Fri.–Sun. 10–4 spring and fall. Nominal admission. The museum, which encompasses more than 4,000 displays housed in nine buildings, was founded in 1962 by bacteriologist Lore Rogers and log driver Caleb Scribner. Exhibits range from giant log haulers to "gum books," the lumberman's scrimshaw: intricately carved boxes in which to keep spruce gum, a popular gift for a sweetheart. There are replicas of logging camps from different periods, dioramas, machinery, and photos. This road leads to the Matagamon Gate, the northern, less trafficked corner of Baxter State Park.

A. J. Allee Scenic Overlook, some 15 miles beyond the Medway exit off I-95. Mount Katahdin rises massively from woods and water.

The Ambajejus Boom House (www.moreairphotos.com/boomhouse), Ambajejus Lake. Open year-round, $2 donation. Accessible via boat or snowmobile, or even by walking if you don't mind getting your feet wet. River man Chuck Harris has single-handedly restored this old boom house, former quarters for log drivers, as a museum about life during the river drives. Exhibits include tools, paintings, and photographs among the artifacts of the river-driving years.

✳ To Do

AIR RIDE Katahdin Air Service, Inc. (207-723-8378), offers several scenic flights daily, ranging from a 15-minute flight along the base of Mount Katahdin to a day exploring Henderson Pond and Debsconeag Lake. Inquire about fly-and-dine packages.

BOAT CRUISE Katahdin Scenic Cruises (207-723-2020; www.katahdinscenic cruises.com): wildlife cruises on Millinocket Lake daily June–Oct.

CANOEING AND KAYAKING This area is often used as a starting point for trips on the Allagash Wilderness Waterway (see "Aroostook County") and St. John River. Good canoeing on the East and West (not for beginners) Branches of the Penobscot River as well and on the area's many lakes.

New England Outdoor Center (207-723-5438 or 1-800-766-7238; www.neoc .com), Rt. 157, Millinocket, offers a canoe and kayak school, guided tours, and rentals.

Katahdin Outfitters (207-723-5700 or 1-800-862-2663; www.katahdinoutfitters .com), in Millinocket, offers rentals, planning, transport, and shuttle for trips on the Allagash, St. John, and Penobscot Rivers.

Maine Quest Adventures (207-746-9615; www.mainequestadventures.com), on the East Branch of the Penobscot River, Medway. Canoe, kayak, and fishing-boat rentals and shuttles. Paddling instruction.

Peaks-Kenny State Park (see *Green Space*) rents canoes to use on Sebec Lake.

FISHING Dolby Flowage is good for bass fishing, and the **West Branch of the Penobscot River** offers good salmon and trout fishing. **New England Outdoor Center** (207-723-5438; see *Whitewater Rafting*) offers guided fishing trips. Licenses are available at the **Millinocket municipal office** on Penobscot Avenue, and many of the stores in the area, including **Lennie's Superette** in Medway, the **Katahdin General Store** in Millinocket, and **North Woods Trading Post** on Millinocket Lake. For a more complete list of guide services, contact the **North Maine Woods** office (207-435-6213; www.northmaine woods.org) in Ashland, and the **Katahdin Area Chamber of Commerce** (207-723-4443; www.katahdinmaine.com) in Millinocket.

GOLF JaTo Highlands Golf Course (207-794-2433), Town Farm Rd., Lincoln; 18 holes with full-service clubhouse, rental carts, and clubs.

Green Valley Golf Course (207-732-3006), Rt. 2, West Enfield. Eight holes.

Hillcrest Golf Course (207-723-8410), 59 Grove St., Millinocket. Nine holes with full-service clubhouse, rental carts and clubs.

HIKING See the **Baxter State Park** box and **Gulf Hagas** under *Green Space.*

HORSEBACK RIDING AND WAGON RIDES ↭ **Northern Maine Riding Adventures** (207-564-3451; www.mainetrailrides.com), Dover-Foxcroft. Judy Cross-Strehlke and Bob Flury-Strehlke, Registered Maine Guides and skilled equestrians, offer half-day and full-day rides from their four-season facility and into Drew Valley near Borestone Mountain; also overnight treks based at their camp in the backwoods around Katahdin Ironworks. Special-needs riders are welcome. Judy is a nationally recognized specialist in centered riding.

MOOSE-WATCHING Mainely Photos Moose/Photo Tours (207-723-5465), 353 Penobscot Ave., Millinocket. Dale Stevens offers frequent van tours into the woods to see moose. Reservations only. Inquire about lodging. May–Oct.

SWIMMING Peaks-Kenny State Park in Dover-Foxcroft is a great family beach, with lawns, playground equipment, and a roped-in swimming area. Hiking trails and camping. $3 per vehicle day-use fee.

Mattawamkeag Wilderness Park (207-736-4881 or 1-888-724-2465), off Rt. 2 in Mattawamkeag (11 miles southeast of I-95's Medway exit), offers a sand beach on the river, also picnic tables, hot showers, a recreation hall, and a playground. Nominal day-use fee.

Note: Swimming opportunities abound in Baxter State Park and the many lakes around Millinocket.

Medway Recreation Complex in Medway has a family beach area, picnic area, volleyball net area, playground equipment, and a roped-in swimming area on the East Branch of the Penobscot River.

Ambajejus Lake has a public boat landing and also offers a small public beach area.

WHITEWATER RAFTING The West Branch of the Penobscot is deemed the ultimate challenge in Maine rafting, best for experienced rafters (to run the whole river you must be at least 15). Rafters are bused from their base camps to the put-in below McKay Station. The 14-mile trip begins with a 2-mile descent through Ripogenus Gorge. Rapids are rated Class II through V (the latter include the legendary Exterminator, Nesowadnehunk Falls, and the Cribworks). Trips run late Apr.–mid-Oct., but we suggest midsummer through early foliage season. Rates are $70–90 during the week, $90–125 on weekends.

New England Outdoor Center (207-723-5438 or 1-800-766-7238; rafting@ neoc.com) offers the largest range of lodging options to rafters. **Rice Farm** (off Rt. 157 east of Millinocket) includes River Drivers, a popular restaurant (see *Dining Out*), along with a wraparound deck with water views, hot tub, changing room and showers, and complete outfitters shop. A campground offers tent and cabin-tent sites, fire rings, and a shower house. Nearby **Twin Pine Camps** on

PERCIVAL BAXTER AND KATAHDIN

BAXTER STATE PARK

Like Acadia National Park, Baxter State Park's acreage was amassed privately and given to the public as a gift. In this case it was the gift of one individual: Percival Baxter (1876–1969). In 1921, at age 44, Baxter became one of the state's youngest governors; he was then reelected for another term. He was unsuccessful, however, in convincing the Maine legislature to protect Katahdin and surrounding lands. Instead, in 1930 he himself paid $25,000 to buy 6,000 acres that included Maine's highest mountain. For the remainder of his life he continued to negotiate with paper companies and other landowners to increase the size of the park. Thanks to his legacy, it continued to grow even after his death and presently encompasses 204,733 acres.

While nominally a state park, it receives no state funds, and the Baxter State Park Authority operates under its own unique and complicated rules, dedicated to ensure that this preserve "Shall forever be kept and remain in the Natural Wild State." Camping and even day-use admissions to the park are strictly limited.

There are only two entry points: **Togue Pond Gate** 18 miles east of Millinocket, by far the most popular, is open 6 AM–9 PM (5 AM during busy summer months and some fall weekends; please call the park to verify), May 15–Oct. 15. **Matagamon Gate**, in the northeast corner of the park, is also open

6 AM–9 PM mid-May–Oct. 15. Vehicles with Maine plates are admitted free, but others pay a $12 day-use fee at the gate. Day-trippers should be aware that the number of vehicles allowed in the park at restricted trailheads, notably Katahdin, is limited; arrive early to avoid being turned away.

The list of rules governing the park is long and detailed. No motorcycles, motorized trail bikes, ATVs, or pets are allowed in. Bicycles can be used on maintained roads only. Snowmobiles are allowed only on the ungroomed perimeter road of the park. The list goes on and on; be sure to pick up a copy at park headquarters and read it through before heading in.

The park is open daily, but note the restricted camping periods and the special-use permits required Dec.–Mar. Vehicular access is not guaranteed once snow blocks the roads, usually after Oct. 15, the end of the camping season. Also note that a park prohibition on the collection of any park plants, animals, or artifacts is strictly enforced unless you have applied at least 6 months in advance and have been approved by the director. Rental canoes are available at several locations in the park.

Ever since the 1860s—when Henry David Thoreau's account of his 1846 ascent of "Ktaadn" began to circulate—the demanding trails to Maine's highest summit (5,267 feet) have been among the most popular in the state. Climbing Katahdin itself is considered a rite of passage in Maine and much of the rest of New England. The result is a steady stream of humanity up and down the Katahdin trails, while other peaks, such as 3,488-foot Doubletop, offer excellent, little-trafficked hiking trails and views of Katahdin to boot.

Day-use access to specific parking lots cuts off when they fill. Eighty percent of day-trippers head for lots in the southern end of the park, with access to the most popular trails—but with 42 miles of road, 46 mountain peaks, and 205 miles of trails, there's plenty of room for everyone.

Still, if you are determined to access the parking area for the **Knife's Edge Trail** (the legendary narrow link between Baxter and Pamola Peaks), arrive early, really early. Our writer Elizabeth Roundy arrived at the Togue Pond Gate at 5 AM and was the 47th car in line. Instead she climbed the **Abol Trail**, up the face of an old rockslide. It was steep and slow going, and she had to watch every step for loose rocks. She cautions to bring plenty of water—rest stops were frequent. This last mile wasn't as steep and featured a well-beaten path to the peak. The top of the mountain is anything but peaceful; for some, it's the end of the long trek from Georgia on the Appalachian Trail. There's often a line of hikers waiting to take pictures by the sign marking the top. Her descent was on the **Hunt Trail**, part of the AT. One of the park's most heavily hiked trails, it took longer than the climb up Abol Trail. Again, make sure you bring plenty of water—you'll need just as

Continued on next page

much on the way down. The round-trip climb of close to 10 miles took 10 hours, moving at a fairly steady pace.

A recommended alternative hike is **Sentinel Mountain** from the Kidney Pond Trailhead. The trail goes through moderate wooded terrain until the very end, when it abruptly ascends to a series of excellent vantage points in several directions. A flat alternative is the Daicey Pond Nature Trail, 1.7 miles around Daicey Pond. **Doubletop Mountain** offers a full day hike with several mileage options: 9.6 miles round-trip hiking up and down from Kidney Pond Trailhead, 6.6 miles round-trip from the Nesowadnehunk Trailhead, and 7.9 miles hiking from Kidney to Nesowadnehunk Trailhead or vice versa. **South Turner Mountain Trail** from Roaring Brook via Sandy Stream Pond (4 miles round-trip) is a good wildlife-watching trail. In all, there are 46 mountain peaks and about 205 miles of well-marked trails in Baxter. Many hikers base themselves at Chimney Pond Campground and tackle Katahdin from there on one of several trails. A wide selection of retail maps and trail guidebooks is available at park headquarters. *Katahdin, A Guide to Baxter State Park and Katahdin* by Stephen Clark and *50 Hikes in the Maine Mountains* by Cloe Chunn (Backcountry Guides) detail many of Baxter's trails.

CAMPING RESERVATIONS

Camping is permitted May 15–Oct. 15 and Dec.–Apr. 1. As a rule, campsites are booked solid before the season begins (see details below); don't come without a reservation. The 10 campgrounds are widely scattered; there are no electric, water, or sewer hook-ups, and you carry out what you carry in. Daicey Pond and Kidney Pond both offer traditional cabins with beds, gas lanterns, fire-

Millinocket Lake is a traditional sporting camp set in the woods, with an indoor pool and hot tub among the facilities (see *Lodging*).

Northern Outdoors (1-800-765-7238; northernoutdoors.com) and **Wilderness Expeditions** (1-800-825-9453; www.birches.com) share the **Penobscot Outdoor Center** (www.penobscotoutdoorcenter.com) on Pockwockamus Pond. Facilities include log cabin rentals as well as **The Katahdin Bar & Grill**, hot tub, game room, sauna, canoes, and kayaks; lodging is at campsites and in cabin tents. This is the closest commercial campground to Baxter State Park, 2 miles from the entrance.

Three Rivers Whitewater (1-800-786-6878; www.threeriverswhitewater.com) maintains a 26-acre Penobscot Outpost facility in Millinocket.

Magic Falls Rafting (www.magicfalls.com) and **North Country Rivers** (www .ncrivers.com) are based at the **Big Moose Inn, Cabins & Campground** (see *Lodging*).

wood, and tables and chairs (summer fees $22 per person per night minimum; $39 minimum for a two-bed cabin, $52 minimum for three-bed cabins, and $65 minimum for a four-bed cabin; ages 1–6 are free, 7–16 are $13 each). Six more campgrounds, accessible by road, offer a mix of bunkhouses, lean-tos, and tent sites (in summer bunkhouses cost $9 per person per night; lean-tos and tenting space are also $9, with a minimum of $16 for both). The two backcountry, hike-in campgrounds, Chimney Pond and Russell Pond, are among the most popular. Several backcountry sites are available by reservation for backpackers. Check restrictions before planning your trip. Ideally, allow 3 to 5 days at a campground like Trout Brook Farm Campground in the northern wilderness area of the park, or base yourself at Russell Pond (a 7- or 9-mile hike in from the road, depending on where you begin) and hike to the Grand Falls and Lookout Ledges.

Due to high demand, Baxter State Park has recently implemented a rolling reservation system for the summer season (May 15–Oct. 15). Reservations can be made in person or by mail 4 months or fewer before the start date of your desired stay using credit cards, check, or cash. Reservations can be made by phone 10 days or fewer before your desired start date (credit card only, and usually only to fill last-minute cancellations). Payment in the form of cash, check, or credit card must accompany the reservation request. The mailing address is Baxter State Park, 64 Balsam Dr., Millinocket, ME 04462. Please send a stamped, self-addressed envelope if you want to receive a confirmation. July through mid-August. weekends tend to fill up quickly, but tent sites midweek and earlier or later in the season are possible. For compete details on the rolling reservation system for summer camping, please contact the park directly (see *Guidance*) or visit its excellent web site (www.baxterstateparkauthority.com).

✳ Winter Sports

CROSS-COUNTRY SKIING ANDSNOWSHOEING **Millinocket Municipal X-C Ski Area** is the name of the community's free, 40 km-plus network of groomed cross-country ski trails (20 km novice, 10 km intermediate, and 10 km expert terrain). These are divided between two distinct areas, linked by a 5-mile wooded trail. The **Bait Hole Area** is well marked 2.7 miles south of town on Rt. 11; the **Northern Timber Cruisers Clubhouse** (see *Snowmobiling*) on the Baxter State Park Road is the departure point for the second network. Many skiers also continue on the Baxter State Park Road and ski Periphery or Telos Rd. Within Baxter State Park, the road to the **Hidden Springs campground** is maintained for skiers. To check daily conditions during winter months, phone 207-723-4329. Trail maps are available at the area information kiosk on Rt. 244 in Medway, just off I-95. Local skiers take pride in the fact that they can usually ski 100 days of the year.

Christina Tree

CROSS COUNTRY SKIING

Note: **Nahmakanta Lake Camps** and **Katahdin Lake Wilderness Camps** cater to cross-country skiers, offering spectacular backcountry trails, accessible only by skis. See *Lodging*.

DOGSLED TOURS **Maine Dogsledding Adventures** (207-731-8888; www.mainedogsledding.com), Nahmakanta Lake Camps, Rainbow Township. Don and Angel Hibbs have traveled 40,000 miles by dog team, finishing in the top 10 of the 1995 Yukon Quest—a 1,000-mile race in Alaska—and first in the Labrador 400 (mile) event in Canada. They offer long dogsled runs down wooded trails and across frozen lakes with no need to slow for human traffic. Guests are permitted to drive the teams; inquire about lodging packages ranging from a half day to 3 days. Winter access is by dogsled or skis; see *Lodging*.

SNOWMOBILING This region offers more than 350 miles of groomed trails, and more than 10 snowmobile clubs in the area to consult. A snowmobile map is available at the Katahdin Area Chamber of Commerce, showing the Interconnecting Trail System (ITS) trails. The **Northern Timber Cruisers Antique Snowmobile Museum** (207-723-6203), on the Baxter State Park Rd. next to the Northern Timber Cruisers Clubhouse, traces the history of snowmobiling in the region. It's open winter weekends.

New England Outdoor Center (207-723-5438 or 1-800-766-7238; www.neoc .com) has the area's largest rental fleet and clothing at Twin Pines (see *Lodging*). They offer half-day, full-day, and overnight guided snowmobile excursions, overnight and multiday packages, and a complete shop.

✴ Green Space

Note: **Baxter State Park**, the big "Green Space" in this area, is described separately in the box.

Gulf Hagas Reserve is most easily accessed (3.1 miles) from the Katahdin Iron Works. Billed as the Grand Canyon of Maine, this 2.5-mile-long canyon with walls up to 40 feet high was carved by the West Branch of the Pleasant River. At the beginning of the trail you will need to cross the river in ankle- to calf-high water. Bring water shoes for the crossing, or be prepared to take off your shoes and wade barefoot (be aware that the rocks are very slippery; find a good walking stick to help with balance). The trail threads a 35-acre stand of virgin white pines, some more than 130 feet tall, a landmark in its own right known as The Hermitage and preserved by The Nature Conservancy of Maine. The trail then follows the river, along the Appalachian Trail for a way, but turns off along the rim of the canyon toward dramatic **Screw Auger Falls** and on through The Jaws to **Buttermilk Falls**, **Stair Falls**, and **Billings Falls**. We started early in the day and found ourselves alone for most of the hike. The trail winds through the woods, almost always moving either up or down, with a series of small side paths. Turnouts offer great views of the falls and the gorge. The hike back is flatter, and logs cover mud in some spots. The Gulf Hagas trails are much less traveled than those at Katahdin; many visitors come only as far as the first waterfall for a swim and a picnic. Allow 6 to 8 hours for the hike, and plan to camp at one of the waterside campsites within the **Jo-Mary Lake Campground**. In winter we have also skied into Gulf Hagas from Little Lyford Pond Camps—a magnificent experience.

Mattawamkeag Wilderness Park (207-736-4881 or 1-888-724-2465), Rt. 2, Mattawamkeag. This town-owned preserve offers 15 miles of hiking trails, campsites, also canoeing and swimming along the Mattawamkeag River 11 miles south of the I-95 Medway exit.

Peaks-Kenny State Park (207-564-2003), Sebec Lake Rd., Dover-Foxcroft. The centerpiece of this park is Sebec Lake (13 miles long, 3 miles wide) with its popular beach, but there are also 9 miles of hiking trails and campsites.

Also see **KI Jo-Mary Multiple Use Forest** under *Campgrounds* and **Borestone Mountain Sanctuary** in "Moosehead Lake Area."

✳ Lodging

Note: For details about a choice of motels handy to I-95, check with the **Katahdin Area Chamber of Commerce** (see *Guidance*).

In and around Millinocket 04462
For a Patten housekeeping duplex at Mountain Glory Farm, rented weekly, call Inn on the Harbor (207-367-2420, 1-800-942-2420), Stonington.

Big Moose Inn, Cabins & Campground (207-723-8391; www.big moosecabins.com), Millinocket Lake. Open June–Oct., and Jan.–mid-Mar. for snowmobiling. This classic 1830s white-clapboard inn has been a family-run business since 1977, offering 11 guest rooms with double or twin beds (shared baths), 11 log cabins, including 2 large enough for groups,

and 40 campsites. Four new suites with a private bath and lake view are planned for 2006. Beautifully sited on the water with lake swimming; 8 miles from the Togue Pond entrance to Baxter State Park and 8 miles from Millinocket. Two rafting companies (North Country Rivers and Magic Falls) use the premises for the rafting trips on the West Branch of the Penobscot. The dining room is open to the public (see *Dining Out*). $45–49 per person for inn rooms, $42–45 per person for cabins, $10 per person per campsite, $13 for lean-tos. Canoe rentals available.

Twin Pine Camps (1-800-766-7238; www.neoc.com), P.O. Box 669, Medway Rd. Sited on Millinocket Lake with a superb view of Katahdin, these 10 housekeeping camps are spaced along the shore under the pines. Now owned by New England Outdoor Center (www.neoc.com), they offer alternative lodging for the whitewater rafting company's Rice Farm Campground 14 miles to the east in Millinocket and are just a bit more than 8 miles from the Togue Pond entrance to Baxter State Park. Canoes are available for guests; kayaks and motorboats are rented. In winter managers Shorey and Jim Ewing offer Ski-Doo rental sleds, with groomed trails on the ITS 86. $37–75 per person, depending on cabin and season.

& **5 Lakes Lodge** (207-723-5045; www.5lakeslodge.com), HC 74, Box 544, South Twin Lake. Open year-round. Rick LaVasseur has created a luxury lodge on the footprint of a dramatically sited marina on a narrow point of land, surrounded by water, with a superb view of Katahdin. Windows maximize lake and Katahdin views. Five guest rooms are luxurious with a gas fireplace, cathedral ceiling, and double Jacuzzi. $250 in-season includes a full breakfast.

Katahdin B&B (207-723-5220), 96 Oxford St. Open year-round. Marylou and Rodney Corriveau offer five clean, comfortable rooms with a private bath and cable TV on a quiet street. There's also a two-bedroom suite (sleeps five) with private bath and sitting area. Washer-dryer and kitchen available for guest use; off-street parking. $50–70 includes a full breakfast. Rodney is a Maine Guide.

Pray's Cottages and Country Store at Ripogenus (207-723-3582; www.campsorent.com/prays.htm), T3R11, 101 Moran Lane. Sited just off the Golden Road at the Ripogenus Dam,

Nancy Pray offers four three-bedroom, ranch-style cottages with living room and three bedrooms (up to nine beds) as well as four efficiencies with a double and either a bunk bed or two singles. The store is an oasis in the seeming middle of nowhere, serving breakfast and lunch, offering fishing and camping supplies. In spring and summer $55 per person per night.

In southern Piscataquis County
& **Brewster Inn** (207-924-3130; www.brewsterinn.com), 37 Zion's Hill, Dexter 04930. Open year-round. Dexter is a proud old Maine town, and this is its proudest house—fit for the governor who built it. Michael and Ivy Brooks have furnished the 10 guest rooms (including 2 suites) with antiques and bright fabrics. $79–119 per couple includes breakfast.

❦ **The Guilford Bed & Breakfast** (207-876-3477; www.guilfordbandb.com), P.O. Box 88, Elm St., Guilford 04443. Harry and Lynn Anderson offer warm hospitality in their gracious 1905 mansion built by the family of the local woolen mill owner. A great stop on the way to the Moosehead or Katahdin region. Four second-floor rooms are unusually attractive, with private bath; two third-floor guest rooms, one with a stained-glass window, share a bath. $70–105 includes a full breakfast.

REMOTE SPORTING CAMPS
& **Bradford Camps** (207-746-7777; www.bradfordcamps.com), P.O. Box 729, Ashland 04732. Open following ice-out through Nov. Sited at the Aroostook River's headwaters, Munsungan Lake. Virtually inaccessible by land (unless you want to weather 47 miles on logging roads), this unusually tidy lodge has well-tended lawns and

eight hand-hewn log cabins on the waterfront, all with full private bath. $124 per person per night includes meals, but boat and motor are extra. Family rates in July and Aug.

☙ **Shin Pond Village** (207-528-2900; www.shinpond.com), 1489 Shin Pond Rd., Mount Chase 04765. Ten miles down Rt. 159 from Patten. Open year-round. Craig and Terry Hill run this recreational facility, which offers 30 campsites, 7 housekeeping cottages, and 3 guest suites. The north entrance to Baxter State Park isn't far. Cottages accommodate three to eight people and have full bath, linens, towels, and cookware. Canoe rentals in summer; snowmobile rentals in winter. Camping is $16.99 per night; cottages are $82 and up, depending on the number of people.

☙ ☙ **Frost Pond Camps** (radiophone, 207-695-2821; www.frostpond camps.com), Box 620, Star Rt. 76, Greenville 04441. Open year-round. Off the Golden Road (35 miles from Millinocket, 45 miles from Greenville) across Ripogenus Dam and 3 miles up along Chesuncook Lake and then down to Frost Pond. Gene Thompson and Maureen Raynes are the owners of these 7 traditional North Maine Woods housekeeping cottages (5 on the waterfront) and 10 campsites on the shore of Frost Pond. Cabins have gas lights, refrigerator, and stove and are heated by woodstove in spring, fall, and winter. One has plumbing; each of the others has a clean pit toilet. A great base for exploring the wilderness. $44–51 per person per night for cabins, $21 per night for campsites. Rental boats, canoes, and kayaks available.

Nahmakanta Lake Camps (207-731-8888; www.nahmakanta.com),

P.O. Box 544, Millinocket 04462. Open year-round. Founded in 1872, this is a remote set of eight lakefront cabins (accommodating two to eight people) with picture windows, screened porch, woodstove, gas lights and fridge, and three common shower houses with hot water and flush toilets as well as clean privies to go with each cabin. Guests can choose from housekeeping at $85 per person per day MAP (breakfast and dinner), or $110 per person with all meals (packed lunch); special children's rates. Boat rentals, guide service, and dogsled tours in winter are the house specialties. Nahmakanta is within walking distance of the Appalachian Trail. In summer access is via road, but in winter you need to ski in— which, may the record reflect, we have done (10 miles).

Katahdin Lake Wilderness Camps (207-723-9867 or 207-723-4050; www .katahdinlakecamps.com), Box 398,

NAHMAKANTA CAMPS

Christina Tree

Millinocket 04462. At the end of a private 3.5-mile tote trail from Roaring Brook Rd. in Baxter State Park; it's an hour's walk or a short flight from Millinocket Lake (Katahdin Air Service: 207-723-8378). Dec.–Mar. the camps are open to welcome those hardy souls who ski the 16 miles in from the Abol Bridge Store. Ten log cabins (one to eight people per cabin) and a main lodge built on a bluff overlooking the lake, running since 1885; firewood, linens, kerosene lamps, and shower houses; several also have a gas stove for housekeeping. The view of Mount Katahdin continues to lure artists as it did Frederic Church and Marsden Hartley. Fishing in the 717-acre lake May–Sep. yields native brook trout. $125 per day includes all three meals—same rate simce 2001. No access for snowmobilers.

CAMPGROUNDS 🐾 ♂ **Katahdin Shadows Campground** (207-746-9349 or 1-800-794-5267; www .katahdinshadows.com), Rt. 157, Medway 04460. David and Theresa

TWIN PINE CAMPS ON MILLINOCKET LAKE
Kim Grant

Violette own this full-service, family-geared four-season campground with a central lodge, swimming pool, dock, weekend hayrides, a big playground, athletic fields, a "community kitchen," tent and hook-up sites, hutniks, and well-designed cabins with kitchen facilities. Pets are welcome. Tent sites $20–25, cabins $40–85.

KI Jo-Mary Multiple Use Forest (207-965-8135). Open May–Oct., a 200,000-plus-acre tract of commercial forest stretching almost from Greenville on the west to the Katahdin Iron Works on the east, and north to Millinocket. There are 150 miles of privately maintained roads (lumber trucks have right-of-way). Seasonal checkpoints are open 6 AM–8 PM (Thu.–Sat, until 10 PM in May, June, and Aug.; 10:30 PM in July). Good fishing, hunting, and plenty of solitude. The **Jo-Mary Lake Campground** (207-723-8117) is located within the forest near Gulf Hagas but offers modern facilities with flush toilets, hot showers. Open mid-May–Oct. 1. It also offers more than 60 authorized campsites, some on rivers and lakes.

Peaks-Kenny State Park (207-564-2003), Rt. 153, 6 miles from Dover-Foxcroft. Open mid-May–Sep. with 56 campsites on Sebec Lake; $15 per site for Maine residents, $20 for visitors. Reservations are a must.

Mattawamkeag Wilderness Park (207-746-4881; www.mwpark.com), Mattawamkeag (off Rt. 2; half an hour's drive from the I-95 Medway exit) 04459. Fifty campsites, 11 Adirondack shelters, bathrooms, hot showers, small store, recreation building, picnic facilities, 15 miles of hiking trails, 60 miles of canoeing on the Mattawamkeag River with patches of whitewater, and bass, salmon, and trout fishing.

Scraggly Lake Public Lands Management Unit (contact the Bureau of Public Lands, Presque Isle; 207-764-2033). A 10,014-acre forested preserve laced with ponds and brooks. It has 12 "authorized" campsites (no fire permit needed). Scraggly Lake is good for salmon and brook trout; a 0.5-mile hiking trail loops up Owls Head.

Also see the **Baxter State Park** box and both the **Penobscot Outdoor Center** (www.penobscotoutdoor center) and the **Rice Farm Campground** (www.neoc.com) described under *Whitewater Rafting.*

✳ Where to Eat

DINING OUT ✼ **Fredericka's at Big Moose Inn** (207-723-8391), Millinocket Lake, 8 miles west of Millinocket on Baxter State Park Rd. Open for dinner Wed.–Sat., June–early Oct.; also Sun. in July–Aug. A hot breakfast is also served Sat.–Sun. in-season. Reservations required. A pleasant Maine woods atmosphere. You might begin with a mushroom- and lobster-stuffed phyllo, then enjoy warm orange and fennel salad with smoked salmon. The entrée might be burgundy-marinated roast quail with autumn root vegetable puree, caramelized shallots, and fresh figs. Music on Saturday nights. Fully licensed. Entrées $15–20.

✼ **River Drivers' Restaurant** (207-723-8475), at the New England Outdoor Center's Rice Farm (off Rt. 157 east of Millinocket). Open for dinner year-round; closed Sun. off-season.

Sleek, contemporary decor is the setting for memorable dining. Known for excellent bread and soups and a dessert tray that usually includes its signature flourless chocolate cake. Rosemary rack of lamb with mustard butter sauce and salmon with roasted pineapple salsa are two of the $17–34 entrées. Fully licensed with a separate bar.

EATING OUT **Appalachian Trail Café** (207-723-6720), 210 Penobscot Ave., Millinocket. Open for all three meals year-round. Good home cooking; reasonable prices.

✐ **Scootic Inn** (207-723-4566), 70 Penobscot Ave., Millinocket. Open for lunch and dinner. George and Bea Simon are third-generation owners. Menu choices include fresh-dough pizza, calzones, seafood, and prime rib. Children's menu.

The Restaurant (207-943-7432), Milo. Open for all three meals. Great road food, homemade sandwich bread, wooden booths, blue frilly curtains, dinner specials ranging from liver and onions to salmon steak.

✳ Special Events

February: **Winterfest**—snowmobile parade, antique snowmobile display, bonfire, cross-country ski events, and poker run.

July: **Independence Day celebration** in Millinocket features a weekend full of activities and a fireworks display.

August: **Katahdin Area Wooden Canoe Festival** in Medway showcases the wooden canoe with demonstrations, a canoe race, and more.

AROOSTOOK COUNTY

Aroostook is Maine's least populated county but the largest in area, almost as large as all of Massachusetts. Within the state it's usually referred to simply as The County. The name *Aroostook* comes from a Native American word meaning "bright," and that's the best way we can think to describe it. The luminosity of its sky—broader seeming than elsewhere in New England—is The County's most striking characteristic. Bounded by Canada on two sides and the North Maine Woods on the third, Aroostook is so far off traditional tourist routes—it actually gets more visitors in winter than it does in summer—that many New England maps omit it entirely. Maine pundits are fond of noting that Portland is as far from Fort Kent, the northern terminus of Rt. 1, as it is from New York City.

But a summer trip through this beautiful countryside can be a rewarding, peaceful, and lovely experience. Although admittedly rural, Aroostook has long suffered from the popular misconception that all it has to offer are views of potato fields. In fact, The County is rich in cultural traditions, friendly faces, and has an interesting ethnic heritage that includes a Swedish colony and a string of French-speaking Acadian settlements. Small but fascinating historical museums are scattered from the southern part of The County to its northern tip at the top of the state, treasure troves of information on the areas and the people who first settled here.

Acadians trace their lineage to French settlers who came to farm and fish in what is now Nova Scotia in the early 1600s and who, in 1755, were forcibly deported by an English governor. This "Grand Dérangement," dispersing a population of some 10,000 Acadians, brutally divided families (a tale told by Longfellow in "Evangeline"). Many were returned to France, only to make their way back to a warmer New World in Louisiana, and many were resettled in New Brunswick, from which they were once more dislodged after the American Revolution when the British government gave their land to loyalists from the former colonies.

In a meadow overlooking the St. John River behind Madawaska's Tante Blanche Museum (named for an 18th-century local Acadian folk heroine), a large marble cross and an outsized wooden sculpture of a voyageur in his canoe mark the spot on which several hundred of these displaced Acadians landed in 1785. They settled both sides of the St. John River, an area known as Mattawaska

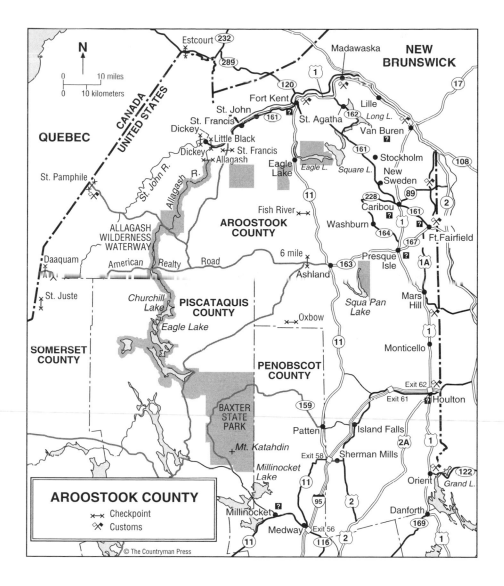

AROOSTOOK COUNTY

✕—✕ Checkpoint

⚒ Customs

("land of the porcupine"). Not until 1842 did the St. John River—still Rivière St-Jean to Acadians—become the formal boundary dividing Canada and Maine.

The 1842 Webster-Ashburton Treaty settled the Aroostook War, a footnote in American history recalled in the 1830s wooden blockhouses at Fort Kent and Fort Fairfield. Until relatively recently this bloodless conflict between the United States and Canada was the area's chief historic claim, but the valley's distinctive Acadian heritage is gaining increasing recognition.

In 1976 Acadian Village, a seasonal living history museum, was created in Van Buren. Now consisting of 16 buildings, many historic and most moved to the

Rt. 1 site from around the St. John Valley, it's an interesting place and the scene of many special events. But the Acadian heritage is also visible in the very shape of St. John Valley towns, where wooden houses are strung out along roads that stretch like arms from the cathedral-sized Catholic churches always at their heart.

Despite intense pressure to assimilate from both civil and ecclesiastical authorities—at one time children could be punished for speaking French anywhere on public school grounds, and parochial schools also discouraged the language—Acadians have stubbornly preserved their traditions and distinctive "Valley French," a blend of old Acadian and Quebec dialects. Today bilingual signage is common in the valley, schools offer French immersion programs, Catholic churches have Masses in both French and English, and there is a bicultural studies program at the Fort Kent campus of the University of Maine, which also has an extensive collection of Acadian historical materials.

Swedes, who settled in and around New Sweden after the Civil War, are a far smaller and more assimilated community than the Acadians but have preserved some colorful Old World traditions. Best known of these is a midsummer festival that attracts Swedish Americans and other visitors from around the country. The Swedes also made an enduring recreational contribution to The County: They are credited with introducing cross-country skiing.

The County cannot be easily categorized topographically. Within the boundaries there are three distinct regions, each with a unique feel and appearance. The Upper St. John Valley, at the top of The County, is a broad ribbon of river land backed by woodland to the west and by a high, open plateau to the east; it has its own distinctly Acadian look, language, and cuisine. Central Aroostook— the rolling farmland around Fort Fairfield, Presque Isle, and Caribou—is generally equated with the entire county. It, too, has its appeal, especially around Washburn and New Sweden, sites of two of New England's more interesting museums. Houlton, the northern terminus of I-95 and the county seat, is in southern Aroostook, a mix of farmland, lonely woods, and lakes.

Four million of Aroostook's 5 million acres are wooded, forestland that includes most of the Allagash Wilderness Waterway and more than 1,000 lakes. Many visitors actually enter The County in canoes, paddling up the Allagash River, which flows north and empties into the St. John River at Allagash, a minuscule hamlet that's become widely known as Mattagash to readers of novels (*The Funeral Makers, Once Upon a Time on the Banks*, and *The Weight of Winter*) by Allagash native Cathie Pelletier. Local residents will tell you that the names of Pelletier's characters have been changed only as slightly as that of her town, and that the interplay between Catholics and Protestants (descendants of Acadian and Scottish settlers, respectively) chronicled in her books remains very real.

Aroostook County still produces about 1.5 million tons of potatoes a year, but the family farms—once the staple of The County's landscape and social fabric— are fading, replaced by consolidated spreads that grow other crops, notably broccoli, barley, and sugar beets. The family potato farm is already the stuff of museum exhibits. Our favorites are in the New Sweden Museum, which commemorates not only family farms but also one of the most interesting immigration stories in American history.

The tourist experience in The County is far different from that along the coast. There are often many miles between attractions, interesting shops, and sights, and the largest part of the experience is driving the peaceful country roads. Rt. 1 looks different in this region, passing through small downtown centers with long stretches of rolling farmland in between. Ask locally for directions to the best places to walk, ski, and fish; feast on fiddleheads, ployes (buckwheat crêpes), and poutine (fries with cheese and gravy). B&Bs are small (often just two or three rooms), with a more personal feel than most downstate. The hospitality we've encountered here is overwhelmingly warm, and hosts are genuinely excited about sharing what The County has to offer.

Winter brings predictable snowfall and is the big draw. Most visitors come in this season to snowmobile (The County has 2,200 miles of maintained snowmobile trails), snowshoe, or dogsled. (Dogsled races are held annually.) The Maine Winter Sports Center, a nonprofit organization that encourages traditional snow sports, recently opened state-of-the-art facilities in Fort Kent and Presque Isle for biathlon and cross-country training, both with free groomed public trail systems.

Winter driving is considered less daunting here than elsewhere in Maine because, thanks to the region's consistently low temperatures, the snow is drier and less icy. Summer temperatures also tend to be cooler, and in early July the potato fields are a spread of pink and white blossoms. Fall colors, which usually peak in the last weeks of September at the end of potato harvest, include reddening barley fields as well as maples.

The conventional loop tour around The County is I-95 to its terminus at Houlton, then Rt. 1 north to Fort Kent and back down Rt. 11. We suggest doing it in reverse—the views from the highway are more scenic going clockwise.

Canada's proximity means that residents of The County are as likely to travel across the border to dine or shop as to venture into other parts of the state. An international bridge over the St. John River links the downtowns of Madawaska and Edmundston, New Brunswick, for instance, making them in effect one mini metropolis. So we also include a few Canadian recommendations within this chapter.

GUIDANCE As noted in the chapter introduction, The County is divided into three distinct regions. For details about northern Aroostook (the Upper St. John Valley), contact the **Greater Fort Kent Area Chamber of Commerce** (207-834-5354; www.fortkentchamber.com), P.O. Box 430, Fort Kent 04743; and the **Greater Madawaska Area Chamber of Commerce** (207-728-7000; www.townofmadawaska.com), 363 Main St., Madawaska 04756. A walk-in information center at the Fort Kent Blockhouse, staffed by Boy Scouts, is open seasonally. For central Aroostook, contact the **Presque Isle Area Chamber of Commerce** (207-764-6561 or 1-800-764-7420; www.pichamber.org), P.O. Box 672, Presque Isle 04769; and **Caribou Chamber of Commerce** (1-800-722-7648; www.cariboumaine.net), 24 Sweden St., Caribou 04736. For southern Aroostook, see the **Greater Houlton Chamber of Commerce** (207-532-4216; www.greaterhoulton.com), 109-B Main St., Houlton 04730. The County has recently been trying to market itself as a tourist destination, with color brochures inviting people to "discover the other Maine." This campaign is headed by the **Northern Maine Development Commission** (1-800-427-8736), which will send you fact sheets that list lodging, dining, and recreational options for all three regions.

The big walk-in information center in The County is maintained by the Maine Tourism Association, just off I-95 at the intersection of Rt. 1 in Houlton (207-532-6346).

Note: The North Maine Woods information office on Rt. 1 in Ashland is described under *Guidance* in "The North Maine Woods."

GETTING THERE *By car:* Our preferred route is to take I-95 to Benedicta or Sherman Mills, then Rt. 11 up through Patten, Ashland, and Eagle Lake to Fort Kent, from which you can explore west to Allagash and east along the Upper St. John Valley to St. Agatha and/or Van Buren. Stop at the New Sweden Museum, for a meal in Caribou, and for a final overnight in the Houlton area. An alternate route through The County, especially if you are beginning Down East, is to follow Rt. 1 through rolling hills and past scenic lakes (Grand Lake is breathtaking from the top of one hill), through tiny town centers, to Houlton. From here, continue through Presque Isle and Caribou to Van Buren, then follow Rt. 1 along the St. John River to Fort Kent. Return on Rt. 11 to Sherman Mills, where you can pick up I-95 south.

By plane: Regularly scheduled service to **Presque Isle/Northern Maine Regional Airport** is limited to **U.S. Airways Express** (1-800-428-4322). **Scotty's Flying Service** (207-528-2626), Shin Pond, is a commercial floatplane operation geared to shuttling canoeists, hunters, and anglers to remote lakes and put-in places along the St. John, Allagash, and Aroostook Rivers.

By bus: **Cyr Bus Line** (207-827-2335 or 1-800-244-2335) operates daily between Caribou and Bangor.

WHEN TO COME Snowmobilers and cross-country skiers flock here in the deep of winter to pursue their sports, but the long summer appeals to many more of us. The roads stretch out for miles, inviting the bicycle trips that are a natural for the area, and the lakes and museums along the Acadian region's northern stretch are open and ready for visitors when the weather warms up, when the sporting camps do much of their business. Hunters will want to arrange a visit in fall.

✳ To See

MUSEUMS A brochure detailing The County's historical museums and attractions is available from most area chambers of commerce. Following are those we found of particular interest (in order of suggested routing). Because most of these museums are entirely run by volunteers, and there are many miles between them, always call before visiting to be sure they are open.

See "Katahdin Region" for details about the **Lumbermen's Museum** in Patten.

Fort Kent Historical Society Museum (207-834-5121), Main and Market Sts., Fort Kent. Open mid-May–Labor Day, Tue.–Fri. 1–4. The former Bangor &

Aroostook Railroad depot is filled with local memorabilia and exhibits on the economic and social history of the area, focusing on lumbering and agriculture.

Nancy English

MUSEÉ CULTUREL DU MONT CARMEL

Fort Kent Blockhouse Museum, off Rt. 1, Fort Kent. Open Memorial Day–Labor Day, usually 9–dusk, and maintained by the town and the local Boy Scout troop. This symbol of the northern terminus of Rt. 1 is a convincingly ancient, if much-restored, two-story 1830s blockhouse with documents and mementos from the Aroostook War. Be sure to wander down to the Fish River behind the blockhouse, a pleasant walk to picnic and tenting sites.

Madawaska Historic Center and Acadian Cross Shrine (207-728-4518), Rt. 1, Madawaska. Open early June–end of Aug., weekdays 10:30–12:30 and 1:30–3:30, Sun. 1:30–3:30. The complex includes the **Tante Blanche Museum** (local memorabilia) and, if you follow the dirt road behind the museum to the river, the 18th-century **Albert Homestead**, plus the *Voyageur* statue and stone cross described in the introduction to this chapter.

Acadian Village & Levasseur-Dube Art Museum (207-868-5042), Rt. 1, Van Buren. Open mid-June–mid-Sep., daily noon–5. The 16 buildings include a school and store, a barbershop, a train station, old homesteads with period furnishings, a gallery, and a reconstructed 18th-century log church. $3.50 adults, $1.50 children.

Ste. Agathe Historical Society Museum (207-543-6911), 433 Main St. in St. Agatha. Open late June–early Sep., Tue.–Sun. 1–4. The oldest house in this unusually pleasant village on Long Lake, the Pelletier-Marquis home dates just to 1854; it's filled with a sense of the town's unusually rich ethnic and social history.

❧ **New Sweden Historical Society Museum** (207-896-5843), just east of Rt. 161, New Sweden. Open late May–mid-Oct., Tue.–Fri. noon–4, weekends 1–5. Entering the community's reconstructed Kapitoleum (meetinghouse), you are faced with the imposing bust of William Widgery Thomas, the Portland man sent by President Lincoln to Sweden in 1863 to halt the sale of iron to the Confederacy. Thomas quickly learned Swedish, married two countesses (the second after her sister, Thomas's first wife, died), and eventually devoted his sizable energies to establishing a colony of Swedish farmers in Maine. In 1870 the House of Representatives authorized the project, granting 100 acres of woodland to each Swedish family. A pink granite memorial in a pine grove behind the museum complex commemorates the arrival and hardships of those who settled here between 1870 and 1875. Despite the severe climate and thin soil (Thomas had been struck by the similarities between Sweden and northern Maine), New Sweden prospered, with 1,400 immigrants in 1895 and 689 buildings, including 3 churches, 7 general stores, and 2 railroad stations. New Sweden's annual festivals draw thousands of local descendants. The museum remains a cultural touchstone for Swedes living throughout the Northeast, and the town continues to attract visitors from Sweden, even an occasional immigrant. Also check out nearby Thomas Park, with a picnic area, the monument and cemetery behind the museum, and the other historic buildings in New Sweden, including the Larsson Ostlund Log Home, Lars Noak Blacksmith and Woodworking Shop, and the one-room Schoolhouse.

The Salmon Brook Historical Society (207-455-4339), Rt. 164, Washburn. Open July 4–Labor Day, Sun. 1–4, Wed. 8–11, and by appointment. The pleasant 1852 **Benjamin C. Wilder Farmstead** (13 rooms of 1850–1900 period furnishings) and the **Aroostook Agricultural Museum** (potato-harvesting tools and trivia housed in the neighboring barn) offer a sense of life and potato farming in the late 19th century. Washburn's Taterstate Frozen Foods claims to have invented the frozen french fry.

✧ **Nylander Museum** (207-493-4209), 393 Main St., Caribou. Open June–Sep., Tue.–Sun. 12:30–4:30; off-season by appointment. A small but intriguing museum displaying permanent collections of fossils, minerals and rocks, shells and other marine life, butterflies and moths, birds, and early human artifacts, most collected by Swedish-born Olof Nylander; also a medicinal herb garden in the back with more than 80 specimens.

Caribou Historical Center (207-498-2556), Rt. 1, Caribou. Open June–Aug., Wed.–Sun. 11–5. A log building filled with local memorabilia from the mid–19th century to the 1930s, including antiques, historical papers, photographs, home furnishings, and tools. Also a replica of an 1860s one-room school with a bell in the cupola.

Northern Maine Museum of Science (207-768-9482), Folsom Hall, University of Maine at Presque Isle. Open during university hours. Interesting exhibits, including an herbarium (library of plant species), a coral-reef environment, an extensive display of plant and shell specimens collected by Leroy Norton (a well-known local amateur naturalist), topographic maps, and Aroostook potato varieties, among much more.

The Presque Isle Air Museum (207-764-2542), 650 Airport Dr., Presque Isle. Open during normal airport hours. The Presque Isle Historical Society has created this museum as a testament to the rich history of air travel in Presque Isle. During World War II, Presque Isle became the departure point for planes and equipment going overseas. An army airfield was created, and more planes left PIAAF bound for Europe than from any other U.S. base. In the early 1960s the missile wing was deactivated and the base was closed.

Aroostook County Historical and Art Museum (207-532-6687), 109 Main St., Houlton. Open Memorial Day–Columbus Day, Tue.–Sat. 1–4 and by appointment. Same building as the Houlton Area Chamber of Commerce. A large, well-organized collection of local memorabilia.

Oakfield Railroad Museum (207-757-8575), Station St., Oakfield. Open Sat. noon–4, Sun. 1–4. This 1910 Bangor & Aroostook Railroad station is one of three remaining wood-framed railroad stations between Searsport and Fort Kent. Exhibits include photographs from the early days of the railroad, vintage signs and advertising pieces, maps, newspapers, a rail motor car, and a C-66 caboose.

Webb Museum of Vintage Fashion (207-862-3797 or 207-463-2404), Rt. 2, Island Falls. Open June– early Oct., Mon.–Thu. 10–4. Fourteen of the 17 rooms in this Victorian-era house are filled with some 6,000 articles of clothing amassed by Frances Stratton—hats, jewelry, combs, and mannequins dressed to represent the people to whom their outfits once belonged. It's a spooky, fascinating place, chronicling life in a small town as well as what its inhabitants wore from the 1890s to the 1950s. *Note:* This museum can be accessed either from Rt. 11 (it's 9 miles east of Patten) or from I-95.

CHURCHES As noted in the introduction to this chapter, tall, elaborate, French Canadian–style Catholic churches form the heart of most Upper St. John Valley villages: **St. Thomas Aquinas** in Madawaska, **St. Louis** in Fort Kent (with distinctive open filigree steeples and a fine carillon), **St. David's** in the village of St. David, and **St. Luce** in Frenchville. When the twin-spired wooden church dominating the village of Lille was condemned, it was purchased by local resident Don Cyr (207-895-3339), who converted it into **Musée culturel du Mont-Carmel**, an Acadian cultural center and a setting for concerts and workshops. On Labor Day weekend the center sponsors the **Lille Classical Impressionist Music Festival**.

OTHER ATTRACTIONS ✍ ⅊ **A. E. Howell Wildlife Conservation Center and Spruce Acres Refuge** (207-532-6880; http://spruceacresrcfuge.tripod.com), 101 Lycette Rd. (off Rt. 1), Amity (14 miles south of Houlton). Open mid-May–Oct., Tue.–Sat. 10–4; $5 adults, $2 seniors; children 16 and under free. Art Howell Jr., one of the best-known and -respected of Maine's more than 90 wild animal rehabilitators, specializes in rehabilitating black bears, moose, deer, and bald eagles that have been wounded, to return them to the wild if possible. The center has 64 acres of woods with a picnic area and a pond stocked with fish for members; also a camping area. No dogs are allowed. Handicapped accessible.

SCENIC DRIVES **Flat Mountain**. The single most memorable landscape that we found in all Aroostook is easily accessible if you know where to turn. The high plateau is well named Flat Mountain and is just above but invisible from Rt. 1 east of Fort Kent. Ask locally about the road through the back settlements from Frenchville to St. Agatha, a lake resort with several good restaurants.

Watson Settlement Covered Bridge. Follow Main St. through Houlton's Market Square Historic District (a *Walking Tour Guide* to this area is available from the chamber of commerce) until it turns into Military St. (dating to the Aroostook War). Turn north on Foxcroft Rd.; in 2 miles note your first view of Mars Hill Mountain (the area's only mountain, at 1,660 feet). The mountain's ownership was disputed in the Aroostook War; it is now a ski area. At roughly 3.5 miles, note the road on your left descending to a small iron bridge across the Meduxnekeag River; the covered bridge, built in 1902, is midway down this hill. The road rejoins Rt. 1 10 minutes north of Houlton.

Driving Rt. 1 from Presque Isle to Houlton, you will see **a scale model of the solar system**. The community project is headed by Kevin McCartney, a professor at the University of Maine at Presque Isle and director of the Northern Maine Museum of Science. The solar system is a scale model, both in diameter of planets and in distance between planets, of 1:93,000,000. Jupiter, the largest planet, is 5 feet in diameter. Pluto, just an inch in diameter, is located at the Maine Tourism Association's Information Center in Houlton. An informational brochure details where the planets are and facts about the planets and moons.

✳ To Do

BIKING The Ski Shop (207-868-2737), 31 Main St., Van Buren, will rent bicycles if used bikes are in stock. Biking on these long slow hills and plains is one of the best ways to tour Aroostook. **Aroostook Bicycle** (207-764-0206), 96 State St., Presque Isle, **The Bike Shop** (207-834-7000), Fort Kent Mills, and **Daigle Sport Center** (207-728-3881), 356 Main St., Madawaska, all rent bikes and can provide a brochure with recommended bike routes.

CANOEING Allagash Wilderness Waterway. This is considered *the* canoe trip in Maine, and after a 3-day expedition we have to agree. The whole trip, 92 miles of lake and river canoeing, takes far longer than 3 days. We put in at Round Pond and paddled the shorter 32-mile trip to Allagash Village. Though it's possible to shuttle your own vehicles, leaving one at the beginning and one at the end, we recommend using a transportation service, which will bring you, your gear, and your canoes into your put-in spot and retrieve you at takeout. This simplifies the parking issue; also, you won't have to go back into the woods to retrieve your car at the end of the trip, and the transportation companies are experienced in negotiating the bumpy dirt roads that can lead to blown tires and rocks thrown at the windshield. **Norman L'Italien** (207-398-3187), P.O. Box 67, St. Francis 04774, was well informed, helpful, and friendly. After we checked in at the gate (road-use fee of $8 per person for non-Maine-residents per day, $5 for residents; overnight camping fee $5 per person per night for non-Maine-

AROOSTOOK ROAD

Nancy English

residents, $4 for residents), his driver dropped us off at the bridge just above Round Pond and told us to call when we were off the river. Norman also operates **Pelletier's Campground** in St. Francis, a good spot to stay the night before your departure. Keep in mind that the trip to the area from Sherman Mills, where you leave I-95, is at least 3 hours; head up the night before your trip. Plan to arrive in daylight if you need to set up tents. The **Maine Bureau of Parks and Lands** (207-941-4014) manages the wilderness waterway and is a source of general information as well as a map and a list of outfitters.

Paddling and floating with the current, sunlight twinkling off the water, you'll feel you're truly in a wilderness paradise. Even when the sun hid behind the clouds, the river wasn't the least bit gloomy or less beautiful. We were there on Labor Day weekend, and the weather and bugs cooperated quite nicely—but come prepared for both rain and pests. Blackflies, mosquitoes, and no-see-ums can be brutal, so bring plenty of bug repellent, maybe even protective netting. On our trip, however, bugs were not a problem, and we slept out underneath the stars 2 of the 3 nights. Remember that there are no stores around the next corner; if you leave it at home, you do without. Pack light, but bring enough spare clothing so that if some gets wet, you'll still be comfortable. Pack in waterproof backpacks, or seal items in plastic bags to prevent soaking should your canoe tip. Bring extra garbage bags to wrap around sleeping bags and pillows. Don't forget a camera and extra film. **Allagash Falls** is particularly nice, and the portage around the waterfall is an easy 0.5-mile hike. The trail and picnic area are well maintained. This is actually a good place to cook a solid meal, using up your heaviest supplies before carrying your stuff around the falls. The trip after the falls to Allagash is just one more overnight, and if you plan remaining meals accordingly, you can lighten your load around the portage.

Campsites on the waterway are clean and comfortable, with plenty of space for a group to spread out. Sites are available on a first-come, first-served basis, so the earlier in the day you begin paddling, the better choice you have. During our visit the river was far from crowded, even on a holiday weekend. We saw fewer than 15 people outside our group on our 3-day journey. The rangers keep track of who is on the river, so there's no need to be nervous that you will be too isolated should something happen. If you're not an experienced canoeist, don't worry: A 3-day trip is easily manageable without putting too much strain on infrequently used muscles. Paddling the whole waterway takes 7 to 10 days, though it's best to be flexible in case wind or rain delays your trip.

If you aren't comfortable venturing out on your own, several area guides can take you down the river. Following are a few suggestions. Contact **North Maine Woods** (see *Guidance* in "The North Maine Woods") for other options.

Allagash Guide Service (207-398-3418; www.allagshguideservice.com), 928 Allagash Rd., Allagash. Kelley and Sean Lizotte rent paddles and canoes and also offer transport and car pickup.

Allagash Canoe Trips (207-237-3077; see "Moosehead Lake Area"). This outfitting company was founded in 1953. Chip Cochrane and other guides continue to lead trips, providing all equipment and meals. Trips vary in length.

Nancy English

AROOSTOOK LUMBER

Maine Canoe Adventures/Cross Rock Inn (207-398-3191; www.mainecanoe adventures.com), Rt. 162, Allagash. Gorman Chamberlain offers 5- to 7-day trips on the St. John and Allagash Rivers; also guided trips into the nearby Debouille area, departing from his lodge. There are three guest rooms, a tenting area, and canoe rentals.

FARM TOUR ✿ **Knot-II-Bragg Farm** (207-455-8386), Box 150, Wade 04786. Open June–Oct., Tue.–Sat. 9:30–6. $6.50 adults, $5 children; family rates available. Natalia Bragg gives a fantastic tour of the farm, including the herb gardens and flower gardens. Natalia will describe such things as making butter, soap, and maple syrup, as well as giving detailed explanations of the uses for the oils she makes from her herbs. Fee-fishing is available in Copper Penny Pond, by appointment only—or join the club and take your maximum of 15. The gift shop sells items made on the farm, from soaps and oils to cedar "twig" handcrafted furniture. Natalia is warm, friendly, and fascinating. Ask for a copy of the tourist guide to Washburn that she put together, detailing all businesses in the northern Maine community.

FISHING The catch here is so rich and varied that it's recognized throughout the country. Salmon grow to unusual size, and trout are also large and numerous. The 80-mile Fish River chain of rivers and lakes (Eagle, Long, and Square Lakes) is legendary in fishing circles. Fish strike longer in the season than they do farther south, and fall fishing begins earlier. Contact the Maine Department of Inland Fisheries and Wildlife in Ashland (207-435-3231; in-state, 1-800-353-6334).

GOLF The County's topography lends itself to golf, and the sport is so popular that most towns maintain at least a nine-hole course. The most famous course, with 18 holes, is **Aroostook Valley Country Club**, Fort Fairfield (207-476-8083); its tees are split between Canada and Maine. The 18-hole **Va-Jo-Wa Golf**

Course (207-463-2128) in Island Falls and the **Presque Isle Country Club** (207-764-0439) are also considered above par. **Houlton Community Golf Club** (207-532-2662) is on offer in the south.

HIKING See the **Debouille Management Unit** and **Aroostook State Park** under *Green Space*.

Fish River Falls. Ask locally for directions to the trail that leads from the former Fort Kent airport down along the river, an unusually beautiful footway through pines. Note the swimming holes below the falls. **The Dyke in Fort Kent** is also worth finding: a 0.5-mile walk along the Fish River. The trail up **Mount Carmel** (views up and down the river valley) begins on Rt. 1 at the state rest area near the Madawaska–Grand Isle town line.

✳ Winter Sports

CROSS-COUNTRY SKIING The same reliable snow that serves out-of-state snowmobilers allows residents to take advantage of hundreds of miles of trails maintained exclusively for cross-country skiing by local towns and clubs. Any town office or chamber of commerce will steer you to local trails.

Maine Winter Sports Center (207-328-0991; www.mainewsc.org). The organization, funded by the Libra Foundation, has developed a network of community trails for use by schoolchildren and local residents. It also has built two Nordic events facilities, used for training high school skiers and Winter Olympics hopefuls. **10th Mountain Division Center** (207-834-6203) in Fort Kent includes a biathlon range, links to recreational ski trails, and a handsome lodge. A similar facility, the **Nordic Heritage Center** (207-328-0991) in Presque Isle, focuses on cross-country skiing.

Kate McCartney at the Old Iron Inn in Caribou (207-492-4766) has compiled a brochure of northern Maine cross-country trails, which lists nine centers dedicated to the sport, including phone numbers, rates, and locations.

DOWNHILL SKIING Big Rock (207-425-6711, 1-866-529-2695; www.bigrock maine.com), Mars Hill. A downhill and cross-country facility owned by Maine Winter Sports Center, this place focuses on getting everyone involved, with adult weekday tickets at $20, weekend at $25, seniors and juniors $15 and $18.

SNOWMOBILING Snowmobiling is the single biggest reason that visitors come to The County. It's the easiest way to see some of the more remote sporting camps and wilderness areas, since riding over well-maintained trails is often smoother than bumping down logging roads in summer. Trails lead from one end of The County to the other and are far too numerous for us to detail here. Call any Aroostook County chamber of commerce for a *Trail Map to Northern Maine* detailing 2,200 miles of trails maintained by The County's 40-plus snowmobile clubs and including locations of clubhouses, warming huts, and service areas. On the back of the map are ads for several companies that cater to snowmobilers, from rentals and service to lodging and dining.

✳ Green Space

Debouille Management Unit, including Debouille Mountain and several ponds, is a 23,461-acre preserve managed jointly by the state and North Maine Woods (charging gate and camping fees; see *Guidance* in "North Maine Woods"), accessible by gated logging roads from St. Francis and Portage. Campsites are clustered around ponds (good for trout) and near hiking trails leading to the distinctive summit of Debouille Mountain. For details, contact the Bureau of Public Lands in Presque Isle (207-764-2033).

Aroostook State Park (207-768-8341), marked from Rt. 1, 4 miles south of Presque Isle. Open May 15–Oct. 15. A 600-acre park with swimming and picnicking at Echo Lake; also 30 campsites (June 15–Labor Day only) at 1,213-foot Quaggy Joe Mountain—which offers hiking trails with views from the north peak across a sea of woodland to Mount Katahdin. Note the monument in the small **Maxie Anderson Memorial Park** next door; a tin replica of the *Double Eagle II* commemorates the 1978 liftoff of the first hot-air balloon to successfully cross the Atlantic.

Aroostook Valley Trail and **Bangor and Aroostook Trail** (207-493-4224). A 7.5-mile recreational trail system connecting Caribou, Woodland, New Sweden, Washburn, Perham, Stockholm, and Van Buren. Many bogs, marshes, wetlands, and streams lie along these trails, which are owned by the Maine Bureau of Parks and Lands. There are several parking lots and rest areas on the trails as well. Good for biking, walking, cross-country skiing, and snowmobiling.

Also see **Fish River Falls** under *Hiking* and the **Allagash Wilderness Waterway** under *Canoeing*.

✳ Lodging

HOTELS **The Northeastland Hotel** (207-768-5321 or 1-800-244-5321; www.mainerec.com/eastland.html), 436 Main St., Presque Isle 04769. Built in 1934 in the heart of downtown, this 51-room, two-story hotel remains a favorite with business and pleasure travelers alike. Guest rooms are unusually large, sparely but nicely furnished, and spotless, equipped with a full, mirrored closet, phone, coffeemaker, iron, and blow dryer. The hotel's **Sidewalk Café** serves all three meals and has a liquor license. Double rooms (two queen beds) are $76 year-round, no charge for children; single $70.

🐾 **Caribou Inn and Convention Center** (207-498-3733 or 1-800-235-0466; www.caribouinn.com), junction of Rts. 1 and 164, Caribou 04736. This is a sprawling 73-room motor inn with an indoor pool, hot tub and fitness center, and the full-service **Greenhouse Restaurant**. Rooms are large, suites have kitchenettes, and it fills a need. Quiet in summer and fall but noisy on winter weekends—this is snowmobiler central, and the guests mostly male. $94–104; children stay free, and pets are welcome.

🐾 **Presque Isle Inn and Convention Center** (207-764-3321 or 1-800-533-3971; www.presqueisleinn.com), 116 Main St. (Rt. 1), Presque Isle 04769. With 151 guest rooms and suites as well as meeting and banquet space, this is the largest facility of its kind in The County. Amenities include an Italian restaurant, bar and lounge, heated indoor pool, and full fitness center. Like its sister property in Caribou, it's very popular with snowmobilers in winter, when rates are higher. Pets welcome. Standard double room $78.

Northern Door Inn ("La Porte du Nord") (207-834-3133; www.northern doorinn.com), 356 Main St., Fort Kent 04743. A pleasant and comfortable 43-unit property located directly across from the international bridge to Canada and drawing guests (including many snowmobilers in winter) from both sides of the border. $55–71 includes continental breakfast.

BED & BREAKFASTS River Watch (207-728-7109; jcayer@nci1.net), 520 Riverview St., Madawaska 04756. A small place in the heart of the St. John Valley, offering three guest rooms with shared baths. A full breakfast is served, which might be Belgian waffles or double-decker French toast. $50–65.

The Yellow House on Clark's Hill, a bed, breakfast and catering company (207-757-8797; www.yellow housebedandbreakfast.com), 270 Ridge Rd., Oakfield 04763. Located 1.5 miles off I-95 (exit 286) between Island Falls and Houlton, this vintage-1862 homestead has been in the Clark family since it was built. Gina Iacoponi Clark enjoys helping guests explore The County, and lavishes guests with slippers and terry-cloth robes, refreshments, and videos to watch on the room TV. A multicourse breakfast is served in the travel library or in a glass atrium. There is a hot tub on their outdoor deck. Alcohol , smoking , and pet-free. $100–135 with private bath.

🍴 **Old Iron Inn** (207-492-4766; www.oldironinn.com), 155 High St., Caribou 04736. Kate and Kevin

GOUGHAN'S BERRY FARM

Nancy English

McCartney offer four rooms (two with private bath, the other two sharing a bath and a half) furnished with antiques and decorated old irons, from tiny little irons for pressing ruffles to big ones it's hard to conceive were ever used. The hosts are up to date on everything going on in The County; Kate put together a brochure on cross-country ski places. On the third Friday of the month the McCartneys host a music night, free and open to all (see *Entertainment*). $45–69 includes a good breakfast. A furnished two-bedroom guest cottage is available by the week or month.

✾ **Rum Rapids Inn** (207-455-8096; www.rumrapidsinn.com), Rt. 164, Crouseville 04738 (not far from Presque Isle). One of the oldest houses in The County (vintage 1839), this eclectically but elegantly decorated small inn is set on 15 acres on the Aroostook River. Clifton and Judy Boudman offer candlelight dinners by special arrangement as well as two rooms with private bath and two solar cottages without bathrooms. Guest amenities include robes, a sauna, and nearly 5,000 movie videos. Multi-course dinners are open to the public by reservation. Entrées might include tuna steaks with wasabi and green onion mayonnaise. Several courses are $38–48. Room rates start at $89 double, including a full breakfast. Wireless Internet connection.

SPORTING CAMPS Gardner's Sporting Camps (207-398-3168), Box 127, Allagash 04774. Open May–Dec. Five tidy camps along a ridge overlooking the confluence of the St. John and Allagash Rivers across the road from Roy and Maude Gardner's welcoming old farmhouse. B&B and hiking, hunt-

ing, camping, and fishing guide service also offered. $30 per person per night; $150 per week.

🐾 ♿ **Moose Point Camps** (207-435-6156; www.moosepointcamps.com), Portage 04768. Open May 10–early Dec. Ten hewn-log camps on the east shore of Fish Lake (5 miles long and connecting with other lakes linked by the Fish River). The central lodge features a library, a large stone fireplace, and a dining room overlooking the lake where meals are served (BYOB). The camps are 17 miles from Portage, up a paper company road. $395 per person per week or $85 per person per day May–Aug., $495 per week per person Sep.–early Dec. Rates include three meals a day and housekeeping service; children's rates. Boats and canoes available.

✾ **Libby Sporting Camps** (207-435-8274; www.libbycamps.com), P.O. Box 810, Ashland 04732. Open ice-out through Nov. One of the area's original sporting camps, which has been Libby owned and operated for more than 110 years. The peeled spruce cabins overlook 6-mile-long northern Millinocket Lake and are lighted with propane, with handmade quilts on the beds. In the day guides can take you to 40 lakes and ponds for fishing, orchid hunting, a night at one of 10 outpost cabins, or just exploring. In between, Ellen Libby and daughter-in-law Jess make great meals served in the lodge, with homemade bread. Matt Libby can tell you where the taxidermied bobcat, lynx, and a golden eagle, to name a few in the lodge, arrived from. There is a seaplane based at the camps, available at a fee for day and overnight trips. $145 per person ($165 single) per night includes all meals, boats, motor, kayaks, sailboat, and canoes. Pets are accepted, with an additional fee.

Eagle Lake Sporting Camps (207-444-5108; www.eaglelakesporting camps.com), 105 Old Main St., Eagle Lake 04739. In business for more than 130 years, Eagle Lake Camps consists of 13 lakeside log cabins accommodating 4 to 10 people each. Previous owners Ben and Betty Ricciardi owned the camp for 40 years, and took over again in 2005. $75 per person per night, $450 per week, double occupancy. All three meals are available. Queen of the Water, which sleeps up to four people, is available as a housekeeping cabin: $100 a night, off-season $75 a night, for up to four guests.

Fish River Junction (207-834-4699; www.fishriverjunction.com), 19 Levesque Lane, Fort Kent 04743. Although just a short ride from downtown Fort Kent, this camp, on a locally famous fishing river and open year-round with access to major snowmobile trails, has a country feel to it. Two log cabins with toilets and loft sleeping areas and two frame cabins have bunk beds; shower facilities are in a separate building. Weekly rates are $320 per cabin, double occupancy; daily rates are $55 a night. Limited morning and evening meals can be delivered to cabins for an extra charge.

MOTEL **Long Lake Motor Inn** (207-543-5006), Rt. 162, St. Agatha 04772. Ken and Arlene Lerman pride themselves on the cleanliness and friendliness of this motel overlooking Long Lake. There is a lounge, and continental breakfast is included in $54 for standard room, double occupancy ($48 single); $71 for the suite, which has a Jacuzzi.

Nancy English
A CABIN AT LIBBY SPORTING CAMPS

🐌 🐾 ✿ **Brookside Motel** (207-757-8456), 2277 Rt. 2, Smyrna Mills 04780. Just north of exit 291 off I-95, this is a plain place with nine units; the basics are all here, including air-conditioning and impeccable housekeeping. You'll also be next door to a wonderful, inexpensive restaurant, the Brookside, that does all the home cooking everybody else used to do (see *Dining Out*). Rates $50 single, $55 double.

✳ Where to Eat

DINING OUT ✿ **River House** (207-834-5266), 315 W. Main St., Fort Kent. The Roy family operates this hospitable, homey restaurant. Choices range from chicken to seafood, steaks, and Italian specialties. Salad bar and a decent wine selection. Dinner entrées $8–20.

🦞 🍴 **Brookside Restaurant** (207-757-8456), 2277 Rt. 2, Smyrna Mills (at exit 291 off I-95). Make this a lunch stop on your way north, and you won't regret it. Old-fashioned the right way, with homemade, fabulous pies—the raspberry was wonderful—great meat loaf, perfect lobster rolls, and a side of turnips. The fried clams are rated high, too, but when you're in a place that makes good food, it's all good. And so reasonable. On the Tuesday of our visit it was customer appreciation day, with free chocolate cake. Carmel and Carl Watson do it right.

♿ **Long Lake Sporting Club** (207-543-7584 or 1-800-431-7584), Rt. 162, Sinclair. Open daily year-round. Sit down in the lounge with a drink, order, and then go to your table when your meal is ready. Specialties include appetizer platters (wings, mozzarella sticks, ribs, and shrimp), steaks, seafood, jumbo lobsters (3.5-pound hardshells), and barbecued ribs. Huge portions. Right on Long Lake, with terrific views. 8.95–16.95.

♿ **Lakeview Restaurant** (207-543-6331), Lakeview Dr., St. Agatha. Open daily for breakfast, lunch, and dinner. Set on a hilltop with a view across the lake and valley. Steak, seafood, and barbecued baby back ribs are the specialties. Most entrées are around $10.

Daniel's (207-868-5591), 52 Main St., Van Buren. A large restaurant and lounge open for lunch and dinner. At lunch choose from sandwiches and light entrées like chicken stir-fry. The dinner menu includes linguine with white clam sauce, filet mignon, and pressure-fried chicken dinners (party boxes available to go). Dinner entrées $8.75–13.95.

Eureka Hall (207-896-3196), Stockholm. Open for dinner on weekends; reservations recommended. A new gourmet dining spot, with steak, seafood, local organic produce, and homemade breads and desserts. You can start your dinner with delicious corn fritters and maple syrup.

York's (506-273-2847), Perth Andover, New Brunswick, Canada. Open seasonally (spring–early fall) for lunch and dinner. A large, popular dining room overlooking the St. John River. Home cooking, from steak to lobster and duck. Huge portions.

EATING OUT **Mary's Place** (207-365-4402), intersection of Rt. 11 and I-95, Sherman. A takeout stand with a cozy, pine-paneled dining area in the rear. Good burgers, pizza, and ice cream. Open daily 11–8.

Cindy's Sub Shop (207-498-6021), 264 Sweden St., Caribou. Open daily 7 AM–9 PM, till 8 on Sun. Turkey and bacon sub, $3.50 for small, great lobster rolls, homemade soups like chicken stew and fish chowder. Homemade pies, "Swirl Delight" squares, and whoopee pies, too.

Rock's Family Diner (207-843-2888), 378 W. Main St., Fort Kent. A local institution for nearly 60 years. Standard diner fare, but a particularly good place to get a stick-to-the-ribs breakfast.

Doris's Café (207-834-6262), Fort Kent Mills, open for breakfast and lunch; everything prepared from scratch.

Dickey Trading (207-398-3157), St. Francis. Open 5 AM–7 PM. A combination general store (with stuffed bobcat and lynx), sporting goods shop, and Formica-topped coffee shop.

Frederick's Southside Restaurant
(207-498-3464), 217 S. Main St., Caribou. Good home-style cooking, generous portions, reasonable prices.
Closed Mon.

Winnie's (207-769-4971), 79 Parsons St., Presque Isle. A small, local favorite for more than 50 years. Their lobster stew has made a name for itself and is now sold frozen as Hancock's Gourmet Lobster Stew. Burgers, seafood rolls, sandwiches, and a huge variety of ice cream.

The Courtyard Café (207-532-0787), 59 Main St., Houlton. Continental breakfast, lunch, and dinner. A great little place that has a more cosmopolitan feel than you might expect in Houlton. Great sandwiches, daily specials, coffee, and sweets. The "Forget-Me-Not" is a roast beef sandwich made with herb and garlic cream cheese ($6.50).

Elm Tree Diner (207-532-3181), Bangor Rd., Houlton. Open early and late but just in summer, an outstanding classic diner for more than 50 years. Everything is made from scratch; daily specials.

✳ Entertainment

Monthly music nights are put on at the **Old Iron Inn** (see *Bed & Breakfasts*), and everyone is welcome. A different style of music each month.

✳ Selective Shopping

Main Street Emporium, Main St., Houlton. A nicely renovated old building with several small gift shops and a nice little café (see the Courtyard Café under *Eating Out*).

Bradbury Barrel Co. (207-429-8188 or 1-800-332-6021), P.O. Box A, 100 Main St., Bridgewater 04735. Show-room of white cedar barrels of all sizes as well as other wood products. Mail-order catalog. Tours of the company are available by prior arrangement.

Fish River Brand Tackle (207-834-3951), Fort Kent. Call for directions. Tackle made by Don Baker—one of his big metal flashers secured the $10,000 grand prize in the Lake Champlain Fishing Derby in 1994. Makes 2,000 tip-ups a year; also a fishing guide.

Bouchard Family Farm (207-834-3237), Rt. 161, Fort Kent. Stop by the family kitchen and buy a bag of *ploye* mix. *Ployes* are crêpelike pancakes made with buckwheat flour (no eggs, no milk, no sugar, no oil, no cholesterol, no fat—*c'est magnifique*).

✍ **Goughan Farms** (207-496-1731), Rt. 161, Fort Fairfield. Open weekdays 10–5, Sun. noon–5. Pick-your-own strawberries; also a farm stand and animal barn.

BOOKSTORES Volumes Book Store (207-532-7727), 8 Water St., Houlton. Housed in a onetime parochial school, Volumes boasts the largest selection of used books in The County, some 50,000 of them, but also carries new books along with Maine souvenirs and gifts. If you can't find what you're looking for in the maze of shelves, proprietor Gerry Berthelette can lay his hands on it almost instantly.

✳ Special Events

February: **Mardi Gras** in Fort Kent—the 5 days before Ash Wednesday bring a parade, ice sculptures, kids' day, Franco-American music, and exhibitions. **International Snowmobile Festival** (*usually second weekend*) in Madawaska—a 3-day event that attracts both Canadian and American sledders.

Early March: The **Can Am Sled Dog Race**—Triple Crown 60- and 250-mile races, starting and ending at Fort Kent.

June: **Acadian Festival** in Madawaska—parade, traditional Acadian supper, and talent revue. **"Midsommar"** (*weekend nearest June 21*) is celebrated at Thomas Park in New Sweden and at the New Sweden Historical Society Museum with Swedish music, dancing, and food.

July: **Maine Potato Blossom Festival**, Fort Fairfield—a week of activities including mashed-potato wrestling, Potato Blossom Queen pageant, parade, entertainment, dancing, industry dinner, and fireworks. **Ployes Festival** (*last weekend of the month*), Fort Kent—a celebration of the beloved buckwheat crêpe and other traditional Acadian dishes.

End of July/beginning of August: **Historical Pavilion**, Caribou. For 3 days, 20 or more historical societies come together and put on a show, with individual displays, like the history of butter in 2004, and spinners and weavers featured as living history.

August: **Northern Maine Fair**, Presque Isle. **Potato Feast Days** in Houlton—arts and crafts, potato-barrel-rolling contest, potato games, carnival, and more.

First Saturday in December: **Holiday Light Parade**, Presque Isle—94 lighted floats in 2003.

INDEX